BRITISH HIT SINGLES

Jonathan Rice   Paul Gambaccini   Tim Rice

8TH EDITION

Editorial Assistant: Tony Brown

GUINNESS PUBLISHING

ACKNOWLEDGEMENTS

The three authors would like to thank Alan Jones, Graham Walker and Scott Whittock for their contributions to this edition.

Special thanks, too, to Eileen Heinink and Jan Rice. We also want to thank *New Musical Express* and *CIN* for their charts, and the many record company press offices for their patient help.

© **GRR Publications Ltd 1991**
First edition 1977. Second edition 1979. Third edition 1981. Fourth edition 1983. Fifth edition 1985. Sixth edition 1987. Seventh edition 1989.

Published in Great Britain by Guinness Publishing Ltd., 33 London Road, Enfield, Middlesex.

Distributed in the United States by Billboard Books, an imprint of Watson-Guptill Publications, a division of BPI Communications, Inc., 1515 Broadway, New York, NY 10036.

Printed and bound in Great Britain by The Bath Press.

'Guinness' is a registered trade mark of Guinness Publishing Ltd.

The right of Paul Gambaccini, Tim Rice and Jonathan Rice to be identified as Authors of this Work has been asserted in accordance with the Copyright, Designs & Patents Act 1989.

Editor:
David Roberts

Deputy Editors:
Paola Simoneschi and John English

Picture Editor:
Alex Goldberg

Page make-up:
Alex Reid, Stewart Newport, Sallie Collins, Amanda Ward and CXT Creative

Illustrations:
Carol Wright

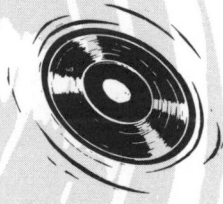

A catalogue record for this book is available from The British Library.

ISBN 0-85112-941-2

CONTENTS

All statistics and information cover the period 14 November 1952 to 29 December 1990, and are as follows:

2

PART 2 Alphabetically by Title:

15,048 hits listed alphabetically by title, with artists' names and year of initial chart entry. Different versions of the same song and different songs with the same title are indicated.

1

PART 1 Alphabetically by Artist:

4,021 chart acts listed alphabetically with chronological title list showing date disc first hit the chart, title, label, catalogue number, highest position reached and number of weeks on chart. Top Ten placings and number ones are highlighted.

3

PART 3 Facts and Feats:

All you need to know and more about the record charts record breakers including
- Most Weeks On Chart
- Most Top Ten Hits
- Longest Gap Between Chart Hits
- Top Twenty Acts Of All Time
- Christmas Hits
- Oldest Chart Toppers
- Least Successful Chart Act
- The Number One Hits

To paraphrase the Buffalo Bob voice track famously sampled by Coldcut, 'What year is it, kids?' Popular music fans of several generations could have found something to delight them in the charts of late 1990: re-issues from the Sixties, revivals from the Seventies and even a top three re-entry of an Eighties number one. Not only in styles, but in years of origin, the charts are music's great melting pot.

Pundits tried to find evidence for their own arguments in these developments. A famed DJ on one of the successful Gold stations clucked: "I like to play this new stuff, like 'Blue Velvet' and 'Unchained Melody'." Doomsayers tolled the bell for pop music, saying that the ringing success of the Righteous Brothers indicated there was nothing new of value being made anymore. Mediawatchers gloated that the men and women who shaped popular taste were more skilled than ever in its manipulation. Give them a biker and 'The Joker' and they'll buy jeans and the Steve Miller Band. Hit them with a David Lynch movie and a commercial for beauty cream and everyone from the weird to the wired will buy Bobby Vinton. Make 'em weep in the most successful movie of 1990, *Ghost*, and the first stop out of the cinema will be not home but rather the record store to stock up on the Righteous Brothers. Use a film song in a car commercial and prove that a ballad like 'Take My Breath Away' can sell everything from aeroplanes to automobiles.

There is a serious flaw in the argument that current record buyers actively prefer old records. Most of them don't realize these tunes are timewarped. How could they? 'Blue Velvet', an American number one in 1963, never charted here, nor did 'The Joker', a 1974 US list leader. People wanted these records because of their suitability in their lives and on the airwaves today.

What they are actually looking for is a song. The biggest selling hits of 1990 outside 'Unchained Melody' were 'Nothing Compares 2 U' and 'Sacrifice'. Both classic ballads were written by established songwriters, Prince and the Elton John/Bernie Taupin team respectively. The charts contained an extraordinary amount of dance material in the past two years, but in the end most of the very greatest favourites were songs, suggesting a gap in the market waiting to be filled by new writers. The only problem here is that the successful artists of the past couple of years don't write songs in what Charles Aznavour might call the old-fashioned way. Technological advances have led artists to concentrate on making interesting sounding records rather than constructing songs. Indeed, the catchiest parts of rap hits like 'Ice Ice Baby' and 'U Can't Touch This' are samples of old records.

The most perceptive, if disgruntled, commentaries on popular music taste in recent years have come from *The Sunday New York Times*. The newspaper expanded its coverage of popular music in the post-Beatle period to reflect mainstream acceptance of popular music as one of the lively arts. It then found itself with a large amount of room to fill with fewer records to cover that reflected the tastes of its highly literate readership. The result has been a series of fascinating trend pieces that have all but sounded the death knell of popular music as we know it and accepted that modern pop is inferior to that of the past. Among the themes covered in notable articles are the death of melody (even hummable songs seem to repeat a hook rather than sustain an entire chorus), the triumph of rhythm over composition, declining standards of musical and lyrical literacy, and the increased importance of the visual image and promotional video in selling a song. The tendency for major artists

to mime part or all of their live show so they can concentrate on the acrobatics of choreography has also been noticed.

As Pete Townshend of the Who noted sagaciously years ago, it is always the young generation that shapes the music market, since each new era has an emotional investment in its own music that its predecessors, who already have their own, cannot. The current generation will spend more time listening to and more money consuming its sound than any group that went before. These older folk tend to have formed opinions as to what good popular music is and will buy as much of the old stuff as they will of the new. Try telling a regular patron of acid house parties, or of late night raves, that the music that is the soundtrack of their life is without merit, and expect to receive a hostile reception. Adamski or Technotronic are as important to one section of the population as big band music once was to another.

What is missing now is the transcendent artist who makes a personal difference not only to members of his or her immediate age group but to a wider public, not only for the ten weeks a record is in the chart but for decades. This century stars like Frank Sinatra, Elvis Presley and the Beatles come to mind. Whole movements of Sixties music, such as Tamla Motown, fit this category. Beginning around 1972, when Don McLean's 'American Pie' mourned 'the day the music died', popular music has tended to diverge into various streams rather than flow as a mighty river.

The chart used to offer different expressions of a common ethos. Now it celebrates the champions of musical sects which are often intolerant of each other. It has become a major problem for popular music radio to decide what to programme since many singles in the chart are now considered 'tune out' records. Bluntly put, this means that even if, for a friendly example, Iron Maiden fans succeed in putting them in at number three in the first week of release, a sizeable portion of the listening audience will figuratively run to the hills if the record comes on the radio. The result is their song will receive far less airplay than would once have been considered automatic for a number three single, and a 'safe' record suitable for passive listening will be played instead.

Notice the cover of this edition. We have depicted 7-inch and 12-inch vinyl, cassette and CD configurations. These are the four leading forms of delivery in the United Kingdom at the present time. Cassette and CD have come into their own in the singles market only during the past two years. Record companies finally realized they had

to pay attention to how people listened to music. Car stereos, headsets and boom boxes all required cassettes. Vinyl was useless to anyone driving, jogging, walking or listening through personal headphones. Offering the public singles on cassettes swelled sales. Giving them superior sound reproduction on CD appealed to the quality-conscious end of the market. In the period surveyed by this edition, 1989 and 1990, 7-inch vinyl sales decreased from 67.0 per cent of the market to 48.8 per cent, while 12-inch sales increased from 29.4 per cent to 30.9 per cent, CD singles from 3.4 per cent to 9.9 per cent and cassette singles from 0.2 per cent to 10.4 per cent.

Now that forms of singles have increased and sales have recovered, we hold our collective breath, feeling certain that some transcendent artist or style is approaching.

The social and political changes that have swept the world in the past two years seem to be ushering in an era of new concerns. There is an opportunity for artists to become part of, and perhaps embody, these movements, and become as important to the general public as artists of earlier eras were. As we welcome you to our eighth edition, we look forward to the continued evolution of the single, both in musical and technical terms. We expect artists of global significance for the more integrated international community of the 1990s, and we will be as surprised as we will be disappointed if they do not appear. Enter, somewhere, the young.

Paul Gambaccini ▪ Tim Rice ▪ Jonathan Rice

THE CHARTS

We have used the charts published by the *New Musical Express* from the date of the very first chart published in the UK, 14 November 1952, until the appearance of the first UK Top 50 in what was then *Record Retailer*, on 10 March 1960.

Occasionally a week went by with no chart being compiled (this often happened at Christmas). In these cases, the previous week's chart has been used again. If ever a chart was compiled but not published, this chart has been found and used.

1

NEW MUSICAL EXPRESS

14 Nov 52 First ever chart, a Top 12 only. **1 Oct 54** Chart becomes a Top 20. **30 Dec 55** Top 25 published, for this week only. **13 April 56** Chart becomes a Top 30. **26 Feb 60** Last *NME* Top 30 used by *British Hit Singles*.

2

RECORD RETAILER/MUSIC WEEK

10 March 60 Top 50 inaugurated. This is a publication date, the chart date being 5 March, which is why the 4 March *NME* chart is not used. **3 Jan 63** Top 50 now independently audited. **13 Feb 69** Top 50 now compiled for *RR* and BBC by British Market Research Bureau. **6 Feb 71** Top 40 only for 7 weeks (postal strikes limited the collection of chart sales information). **27 March 71** Top 50 resumes. **6 Jan 73** Top 30 only, for 1 week. **22 Dec 73** Top 30 only, for 1 week. **6 May 78** Top 75 begins. **8 Jan 83** Chart compilation taken over by Gallup, now described as 'The British Record Industry Charts © Social Surveys (Gallup Poll) Ltd'.

1989

In a year when record producers employed featured vocalists and numerous samples it was impossible to say who the singer was on any given copy of the best-selling single. The Italian outfit Black Box outsold all rivals with 'Ride On Time', and in so doing ran the first six-week marathon at number one for five years. Initial pressings featured hacked-up vocals from Loleatta Holloway's old dance smash 'Love Sensation'. When Ms Holloway discovered the unauthorized use of her work she raised the disco roof, and a new shouter impersonated her for further copies. Radio stations continued to play their original promotional discs and no attempt was made to separate sales on the two versions.

The two greatest chart feats of the year also featured a variety of vocalists. Jive Bunny and the Mastermixers scored three number ones with their first three releases, the first act to achieve this most difficult of deeds since Frankie Goes To Hollywood and only the third overall (Gerry and the Pacemakers were first). Jive Bunny records sampled classic rock 'n' roll tracks, some at great length, and recreated with uncredited artists those that could not be licensed. The most prominent voice was that of Chubby Checker; having been heavily sampled on the first two number ones he performed original material on the third, continuing the unorthodox comeback he had begun with the Fat Boys a few years earlier.

The production trio of Stock Aitken Waterman achieved its apotheosis in 1989. Mike, Matt and Pete scored seven number ones, the most by a producer since George Martin supervised seven in 1963. The partners were also involved in parts of the process in which Martin wasn't, writing four of the fan favourites and issuing six on their own PWL label.

Two of the Stock Aitken Waterman list leaders were charity records by aggregations of stars. 'Ferry 'Cross the Mersey' aimed to assuage the effects of the Hillsborough football disaster, while the remake of 'Do They Know It's Christmas', like the 1984 original, raised funds for famine relief. Stock

Stock Aitken Waterman

Aitken Waterman chirpers Bananarama became the one act to appear on both Band Aid outings, joining Gerry Marsden ('You'll Never Walk Alone') and Cliff Richard ('Living Doll') as the only artists to appear on two different number one versions of the same song. Marsden's featured vocals on charity number ones in both 1985 ('You'll Never Walk Alone') and 1989 ('Ferry 'Cross the Mersey') made him the first man to get to the top with two re-recordings of his own old hits. Cliff became the first artist to appear on two consecutive Christmas number ones since the Beatles managed the seasonal stunt in the mid-Sixties.

Stock Aitken Waterman's biggest stars in 1989 were the Australian soap opera stars Kylie Minogue and Jason Donovan. They began the year at number one with their duet 'Especially For You'. Jason went on to achieve two solo chart toppers and Kylie one. Miss Minogue ended a string of six top two hits in her first half-dozen tries, the best chart start ever by a solo artist.

The 'featured vocalist' phenomenon was further exemplified by 'Back to Life (However Do You Want Me)' by Soul II Soul featuring Caron Wheeler and

'Something's Gotten Hold of My Heart' by Marc Almond featuring Gene Pitney. The Rockville (Connecticut) Rocket had enjoyed the original hit of the latter tune in 1967. By joining the list of number one stars he ended 15 years in the chart wilderness.

Bobby Brown was the only artist to average one chart appearance each week, accumulating 52 weeks on chart during 1989. In this category Gloria Estefan was the leading lady with 42 and the London Boys the greatest group with 38. The Boston-bred Brown, who had performed on the 1983 New Edition number one 'Candy Girl', managed the frustrating feat of three Top Ten hits without breaking into the top three.

The relative dearth of original material and star artists was a disturbing feature of the year, but Madonna went some way towards compensating for some of her underachieving contemporaries. She extended her string of consecutive Top Ten hits to 21 of which all but one were top five smashes. In most other respects she was already the leading female solo star in chart history.

1990

This year's charts gave fresh significance to the clichéd expression 'something old, something new, something borrowed, something blue'. There was some new material, but there was also a lot of old, either reissued, remixed or covered.

The 'something borrowed' was the number one hit of the year, 'Unchained Melody' by the Righteous Brothers. The song got its title because it came from the 1955 film *Unchained*. It was literally the melody from the movie --- the 'Unchained Melody'. This is a unique way of naming a song. No mentions are made of either chains or melodies in the lyric. Thirty-five years later, the song was borrowed in the form of the Righteous Brothers' 1965 version for another film, *Ghost*. Just as that was the number one box office hit of the year, 'Unchained Melody' wound up Britain's top selling single of 1990.

The 'something blue' was Bobby Vinton's 'Blue Velvet', an American number one from 1963 reissued after its use in the David Lynch film of the same name and, more immediately, a skin cream commercial. By peaking at number two it just missed establishing the new record for the longest gap between number one placings on the two sides of the Atlantic. The mark had just been set by the Steve Miller Band, whose 'The Joker' had been a 1974 American number one and repeated the feat in Britain 16 years later after acting as the soundtrack for a jeans advertisement.

The second best-selling single of the year, 'Nothing Compares 2 U' by Sinead O'Connor, was a cover version of a song penned by Prince and performed by his protégés the Family. The third biggest blast was provided by Elton John, who achieved the solo number one which had previously and famously eluded him. 'Sacrifice'/ 'Healing Hands' was a coupling of American hits which had fallen short of the UK Top Forty in 1989. The success of the same songs so shortly afterwards may have been curious, but it was highly profitable to the handful of AIDS charities to which Elton donated all his royalties.

Sinead O'Connor

Number four in the year's hit parade was 'Ice Ice Baby' by Vanilla Ice, a powerful example of how recycling was affecting the chart. The artist brazenly sampled the instrumental hook of Queen and David Bowie's 'Under Pressure' to provide a catchy base on which to rap. Only months earlier MC Hammer had done the same with Rick James' 'Super Freak' for his 'U Can't Touch This'.

Other vintage vibes in the top 20 of the year came from Bombalurina, who rearticulated Brian Hyland's 1960 fashion statement 'Itsy Bitsy Teeny Weeny Yellow Polka Dot Bikini', Beats International Featuring Lindy Layton, whose 'Dub Be Good to Me' eclipsed the S.O.S. Band's 1984 original 'Just Be Good To Me', and Luciano Pavarotti, whose aria 'Nessun Dorma' from *Turandot* was the year's biggest selling single that did not get to number one. It had been used as the theme music for BBC television coverage of the 1990 World Cup. The official team tune of the competition, 'World In Motion' by Englandneworder, did become a number one.

The Puccini/Pavarotti piece was, even more than 'Blue Velvet', a classic case of the power of television to sell a single. TV focuses the attention of a large segment of the population on the same subject at the same time, and if millions of people learn

simultaneously of the hitherto secret virtues of a song, whether it be 'Nessun Dorma' or 'The Joker', thousands of them are likely to buy it in the same week. The actual records themselves do not in any way constitute a musical trend. They merely show that television can affect the charts outrageously, as when 'Take My Breath Away' by Berlin, a 1986 number one, returned to the top three after its use in a car commercial.

Few, indeed, were the standout singles that did not have some sort of media tie-in. In addition to 'Unchained Melody', three more of the year's top 15 sellers came from films: Maria McKee's 'Show Me Heaven' (*Days of Thunder*), 'Turtle Power' by Partners in Kryme (*Teenage Mutant Ninja Turtles*), and 'It Must Have Been Love', the ballad by Roxette (*Pretty Woman*).

Completely original hits which succeeded solely on musical appeal were led by former acid house hero Adamski's 'Killer'. Snap rapped to the top with 'The Power' and Madonna notched up her seventh number one with 'Vogue'. This moved her into sole possession of seventh place on the all-time chart-toppers' table. She extended her streak of consecutive Top Ten releases to 23, equalling Elvis Presley, and lying short of only the Beatles (24) and Cliff Richard (26).

Whether he was the Peter Pan of Pop or the Methuselah of Music, it didn't matter: Cliff was still setting standards. With two new Top Ten hits he passed Elvis in that career category, and in scoring the Christmas number one, 'Saviour's Day', he managed to be on the big holiday hit three years running, twice on his own and once with Band Aid II. The Beatles were the only other act to achieve a similar triple, scoring with their own hits in Decembers 1963-65.

In contrast to the ageless Cliff, it was New Kids On The Block who were the year's top act, both in terms of weeks on chart and singles sold. It was therefore somewhat surprising that they did not have any of the year's 20 biggest hits. Snap and Stone Roses tied for second most weeks on chart, Snap doing better on the sales side, while Adamski was the top male soloist and Madonna the top female. For Ms Ciccone it was the first time she had led the women's weeks on chart category since her triple triumph of 1985-87. It was a sign of her domination of the field that she was the only artist with three new top three hits.

1

BRITISH HIT SINGLES

ALPHABETICALLY BY ARTIST

The information given in this part of the book is as follows: date disc first hit the chart, title, label and catalogue number, highest position the disc reached on the chart, the number of weeks spent on the chart. It should be noted that the date given for entry of a disc into the chart is the week ending date, which is the way the charts have historically been dated. In other words, Abba's 'Waterloo' entered the chart in the week ending 20 April 1974, which means that their first day of chart action was actually 14 April 1974.

Number one records are highlighted with a star, other Top Ten records by a dot. A dagger indicates hits still on the chart at 29 December 1990, as follows:

★ NUMBER ONE SINGLE
● TOP TEN SINGLE
† SINGLE STILL ON CHART AT 29 DECEMBER 1990

For the purposes of this book, a record is considered a re-issue if it hits the chart for a second time with a new catalogue number. Otherwise, the reappearance of any record is considered a mere re-entry.

Describing a recording act in one sentence is often fraught with danger, but we have attempted to do so above each act's list of hits. Although we are aware that many of the 'vocalists' thus described also play an instrument, we have only mentioned this fact where the artist's instrumental skills were an important factor in their chart success.

Once more we have calculated the total weeks spent on the chart by every single

act, and this total appears at the top right of each act's entry. Alert readers will note that some acts (e.g. Elvis Presley and Cliff Richard) have a weeks on chart grand total that is slightly less than the figure obtained by adding up the weeks totals of each of their hit titles. This is because in the early days of the charts (the *NME* charts of 1952 to 1960) both sides of the same record were sometimes listed simultaneously in different positions (e.g. Elvis Presley's 'Party' and 'Got A Lot O' Livin' To Do'). In these instances the two sides score only one week towards the act's total, not two.

Catalogue numbers are generally those of the 7-inch version of the single, but where there is a good reason for using an alternative (if, for example, the record was not issued on a 7-inch single), then the best selling alternative format catalogue number is used.

NEW KIDS ON THE BLOCK
The best selling act of 1990

ABBA Sweden/Norway, male/female vocal/instrumental group   247 wks

20 Apr 74	★ WATERLOO Epic EPC 2240	1	9 wks
13 Jul 74	RING RING Epic EPC 2452	32	5 wks
12 Jul 75	I DO I DO I DO I DO I DO Epic EPC 3229	38	6 wks
20 Sep 75	● S. O. S. Epic EPC 3576	6	10 wks
13 Dec 75	★ MAMMA MIA Epic EPC 3790	1	14 wks
27 Mar 76	★ FERNANDO Epic EPC 4036	1	15 wks
21 Aug 76	★ DANCING QUEEN Epic EPC 4499	1	15 wks
20 Nov 76	● MONEY MONEY MONEY Epic EPC 4713	3	12 wks
26 Feb 77	★ KNOWING ME KNOWING YOU Epic EPC 4955	1	13 wks
22 Oct 77	★ THE NAME OF THE GAME Epic EPC 5750	1	12 wks
4 Feb 78	★ TAKE A CHANCE ON ME Epic EPC 5950	1	10 wks
16 Sep 78	● SUMMER NIGHT CITY Epic EPC 6595	5	9 wks
3 Feb 79	● CHIQUITITA Epic EPC 7030	2	9 wks
5 May 79	● DOES YOUR MOTHER KNOW Epic EPC 7316	4	9 wks
14 Jul 79	● ANGELEYES/ VOULEZ-VOUS Epic EPC 7499	3	11 wks
20 Oct 79	● GIMME GIMME GIMME (A MAN AFTER MIDNIGHT) Epic EPC 7914	3	12 wks
15 Dec 79	● I HAVE A DREAM Epic EPC 8088	2	10 wks
2 Aug 80	★ THE WINNER TAKES IT ALL Epic EPC 8835	1	10 wks
15 Nov 80	★ SUPER TROUPER Epic EPC 9089	1	12 wks
18 Jul 81	● LAY ALL YOUR LOVE ON ME Epic EPC A 1314	7	7 wks
12 Dec 81	● ONE OF US Epic EPC A 1740	3	10 wks
20 Feb 82	HEAD OVER HEELS Epic EPC A 2037	25	7 wks
23 Oct 82	THE DAY BEFORE YOU CAME Epic EPC A 2847	32	6 wks
11 Dec 82	UNDER ATTACK Epic EPC A 2971	26	8 wks
12 Nov 83	THANK YOU FOR THE MUSIC CBS A 3894	33	6 wks

Russ ABBOT UK, male vocalist   22 wks

6 Feb 82	A DAY IN THE LIFE OF VINCE PRINCE EMI 5249	61	1 wk
20 Feb 82	A DAY IN THE LIFE OF VINCE PRINCE (re-entry) EMI 5249	75	1 wk
29 Dec 84	● ATMOSPHERE Spirit FIRE 4	7	13 wks
13 Jul 85	ALL NIGHT HOLIDAY Spirit FIRE 6	20	7 wks

Gregory ABBOTT US, male vocalist   13 wks

22 Nov 86	● SHAKE YOU DOWN CBS A 7326	6	13 wks

ABC UK, male vocal/instrumental duo   87 wks

31 Oct 81	TEARS ARE NOT ENOUGH Neutron NT 101	19	8 wks
20 Feb 82	● POISON ARROW Neutron NT 102	6	11 wks
15 May 82	● THE LOOK OF LOVE Neutron NT 103	4	11 wks
4 Sep 82	● ALL OF MY HEART Neutron NT 104	5	8 wks
15 Jan 83	THE LOOK OF LOVE (re-entry) Neutron NT 103	71	1 wk
5 Nov 83	THAT WAS THEN BUT THIS IS NOW Neutron NT 105	18	4 wks
21 Jan 84	S.O.S. Neutron NT 106	39	5 wks
10 Nov 84	HOW TO BE A MILLIONAIRE Neutron NT 107	49	4 wks
6 Apr 85	BE NEAR ME Neutron NT 108	26	4 wks
15 Jun 85	VANITY KILLS Neutron NT 109	70	1 wk
18 Jan 86	OCEAN BLUE Neutron NT 110	51	3 wks
6 Jun 87	WHEN SMOKEY SINGS Neutron NT 111	11	10 wks
5 Sep 87	THE NIGHT YOU MURDERED LOVE Neutron NT 112	31	8 wks
28 Nov 87	KING WITHOUT A CROWN Neutron NT 113	44	3 wks
27 May 89	ONE BETTER WORLD Neutron NT 114	32	4 wks
23 Sep 89	THE REAL THING Neutron NT 115	68	1 wk
14 Apr 90	THE LOOK OF LOVE (re-mix) Neutron NT 116	68	1 wk

The act were a UK, male vocal/instrumental group for first six hits, and a UK/US, male/female vocal/instrumental group for the next four.

Paula ABDUL US, female vocalist   44 wks

4 Mar 89	● STRAIGHT UP Siren SRN 111	3	13 wks
3 Jun 89	FOREVER YOUR GIRL Siren SRN 112	24	6 wks
19 Aug 89	KNOCKED OUT Siren SRN 92	45	3 wks
2 Dec 89	(IT'S JUST) THE WAY THAT YOU LOVE ME Siren SRN 101	74	1 wk
7 Apr 90	● OPPOSITES ATTRACT Siren SRN 124	2	13 wks
21 Jul 90	KNOCKED OUT (re-mix) Virgin America VUS 23	21	5 wks
29 Sep 90	COLD HEARTED Virgin America VUS 27	46	3 wks

Opposites Attract credits the Wild Pair - US, male vocalist.

Father ABRAHAM and the SMURFS   36 wks
Holland, male vocalist as himself and Smurfs

3 Jun 78	● THE SMURF SONG Decca F 13759	2	17 wks
30 Dec 78	DIPPETY DAY Decca F 13798	13	12 wks
2 Dec 78	CHRISTMAS IN SMURFLAND Decca F 13819	19	7 wks

Colonel ABRAMS US, male vocalist   35 wks

17 Aug 85	● TRAPPED MCA MCA 997	3	23 wks
7 Dec 85	THE TRUTH MCA MCA 1022	53	3 wks
8 Feb 86	I'M NOT GONNA LET YOU (GET THE BEST OF ME) MCA MCA 1031	24	7 wks
15 Aug 87	HOW SOON WE FORGET MCA MCA 1179	75	2 wks

Father ABRAPHART and the SMURPS   4 wks
UK, male vocal group (Jonathan King under an assumed name)

16 Dec 78	LICK A SMURP FOR CHRISTMAS (ALL FALL DOWN) Petrol GAS 1	58	4 wks

Hit transferred to Magnet MAG 139 after first week on chart. See also Jonathan King.

AC/ DC Australia/UK, male vocal/instrumental group   111 wks

10 Jun 78	ROCK 'N' ROLL DAMNATION Atlantic K 11142	24	9 wks
1 Sep 79	HIGHWAY TO HELL Atlantic K 11321	56	4 wks
2 Feb 80	TOUCH TOO MUCH Atlantic K 11435	29	9 wks
28 Jun 80	DIRTY DEEDS DONE DIRT CHEAP Atlantic HM 2	47	3 wks
28 Jun 80	HIGH VOLTAGE (LIVE VERSION) Atlantic HM 1	48	3 wks
28 Jun 80	IT'S A LONG WAY TO THE TOP (IF YOU WANNA ROCK 'N'ROLL) Atlantic HM 3	55	3 wks
28 Jun 80	WHOLE LOTTA ROSIE Atlantic HM 4	36	8 wks
13 Sep 80	YOU SHOOK ME ALL NIGHT LONG Atlantic K 11600	38	6 wks
29 Nov 80	ROCK 'N' ROLL AIN'T NOISE POLLUTION Atlantic K 11630	15	8 wks
6 Feb 82	LET'S GET IT UP Atlantic K 11706	13	6 wks
3 Jul 82	FOR THOSE ABOUT TO ROCK (WE SALUTE YOU) Atlantic K 11721	15	6 wks
29 Oct 83	GUNS FOR HIRE Atlantic A 9774	37	4 wks
4 Aug 84	NERVOUS SHAKEDOWN Atlantic A 9651	35	5 wks
6 Jul 85	DANGER Atlantic A 9532	48	4 wks
18 Jan 86	SHAKE YOUR FOUNDATIONS Atlantic A 9474	24	5 wks
24 May 86	WHO MADE WHO Atlantic A 9425	16	5 wks
30 Aug 86	YOU SHOOK ME ALL NIGHT LONG (re-issue) Atlantic A 9377	46	4 wks
16 Jan 88	HEATSEEKER Atlantic A 9136	12	6 wks
2 Apr 88	THAT'S THE WAY I WANNA ROCK 'N' ROLL Atlantic A 9098	22	5 wks
22 Sep 90	THUNDERSTRUCK Atco B 8907	13	5 wks
24 Nov 90	MONEYTALKS Atco B 8886	36	3 wks

ACE UK, male vocal/instrumental group   10 wks

9 Nov 74	HOW LONG Anchor ANC 1002	20	10 wks

ᴀᴄᴇ Jamaica, male vocalist — 2 wks

2 Dec 78	**STAYIN' ALIVE** *Blue Inc. INC 2*	66	2 wks

ACES – See Desmond DEKKER and the ACES

ACT UK/Germany, male/female vocal/instrumental group — 2 wks

23 May 87	**SNOBBERY AND DECAY** *ZZT ZTAS 28*	60	2 wks

ACT ONE US, male/female vocal/instrumental group — 6 wks

18 May 74	**TOM THE PEEPER** *Mercury 6008 005*	40	6 wks

Arthur ADAMS US, male vocalist — 5 wks

24 Oct 81	**YOU GOT THE FLOOR** *RCA 146*	38	5 wks

Bryan ADAMS Canada, male vocalist/instrumentalist – guitar — 50 wks

12 Jan 85	**RUN TO YOU** *A & M AM 224*	11	12 wks
16 Mar 85	**SOMEBODY** *A & M AM 236*	35	7 wks
25 May 85	**HEAVEN** *A & M AM 256*	38	5 wks
10 Aug 85	**SUMMER OF '69** *A & M AM 267*	42	7 wks
21 Dec 85	**CHRISTMAS TIME** *A & M AM 297*	55	2 wks
22 Feb 86	**THIS TIME** *A & M AM 295*	41	7 wks
12 Jul 86	**STRAIGHT FROM THE HEART** *A & M AM 322*	51	3 wks
28 Mar 87	**HEAT OF THE NIGHT** *A & M ADAM 2*	50	2 wks
20 Jun 87	**HEARTS ON FIRE** *A & M ADAM 3*	57	3 wks
17 Oct 87	**VICTIM OF LOVE** *A & M AM 407*	68	2 wks

See also Bryan Adams and Tina Turner.

Bryan ADAMS and Tina TURNER — 6 wks
Canada/US, male/female vocal duo

2 Nov 85	**IT'S ONLY LOVE** *A & M AM 285*	29	6 wks

See also Bryan Adams; Tina Turner.

Cliff ADAMS UK, orchestra — 2 wks

28 Apr 60	**LONELY MAN THEME** *Pye International 7N 25056*	39	2 wks

Gayle ADAMS US, female vocalist — 1 wk

26 Jul 80	**STRETCHIN' OUT** *Epic EPC 8791*	64	1 wk

Marie ADAMS – See Johnny OTIS SHOW

Oleta Adams US, female vocalist — 5 wks

24 Mar 90	**RHYTHM OF LIFE** *Fontana OLETA 1*	52	2 wks
3 Nov 90	**RHYTHM OF LIFE (re-entry)** *Fontana OLETA 1*	56	3 wks

See also Tears For Fears.

ADAMSKI UK, male instrumentalist/producer — 34 wks

20 Jan 90	**N-R-G** *MCA MCA 1386*	12	6 wks
7 Apr 90 ★	**KILLER** *MCA MCA 1400*	1	18 wks
8 Sep 90 ●	**THE SPACE JUNGLE** *MCA MCA 1435*	7	8 wks
17 Nov 90	**FLASHBACK JACK** *MCA MCA 1459*	46	2 wks

Featured vocalist on Killer was Seal. See also Seal.

ADDRISI BROTHERS US, male vocal duo — 3 wks

6 Oct 79	**GHOST DANCER** *Scotti Brothers K 11361*	57	3 wks

ADEVA US, female vocalist — 31 wks

14 Jan 89	**RESPECT** *Cooltempo Cool 179*	17	9 wks
12 Aug 89	**WARNING** *Cooltempo Cool 185*	17	8 wks
21 Oct 89	**I THANK YOU** *Cooltempo Cool 192*	17	7 wks
16 Dec 89	**BEAUTIFUL LOVE** *Cooltempo Cool 195*	57	5 wks
28 Apr 90	**TREAT ME RIGHT** *Cooltempo Cool 200*	62	2 wks

See also Paul Simpson featuring Adeva.

ADICTS UK, male vocal/instrumental group — 1 wk

14 May 83	**BAD BOY** *Razor RZS 104*	75	1 wk

ADONIS featuring 2 PUERTO RICANS, A BLACK MAN AND A DOMINICAN — 4 wks
US, male vocal/instrumental group

13 Jun 87	**DO IT PROPERLY ('NO WAY BACK')/ NO WAY BACK** *London LON 136*	47	4 wks

ADRENALIN M.O.D. US, male vocal/instrumental group — 5 wks

8 Oct 88	**O-O-O** *MCA RAGAT 2*	49	5 wks

ADULT NET UK/US, male/female vocal/instumental group — 2 wks

10 Jun 89	**WHERE WERE YOU** *Fontana BRX 2*	66	2 wks

ADVENTURES UK, male vocal/instrumental group — 23 wks

15 Sep 84	**ANOTHER SILENT DAY** *Chrysalis CHS 2000*	71	2 wks
1 Dec 84	**SEND MY HEART** *Chrysalis CHS 2001*	62	4 wks
13 Jul 85	**FEEL THE RAINDROPS** *Chrysalis AD 1*	58	3 wks
9 Apr 88	**BROKEN LAND** *Elektra EKR 69*	20	10 wks
2 Jul 88	**DROWNING IN THE SEA OF LOVE** *Elektra EKR 76*	44	4 wks

ADVENTURES OF STEVIE V US, male producer — 18 wks

21 Apr 90 ●	**DIRTY CASH** *Mercury MER 311*	2	13 wks
27 Sep 90	**BODY LANGUAGE** *Mercury MER 331*	29	5 wks

ADVERTS UK, male/female vocal/instrumental group — 11 wks

27 Aug 77	**GARY GILMORE'S EYES** *Anchor ANC 1043*	18	7 wks
4 Feb 78	**NO TIME TO BE 21** *Bright BRI*	38	4 wks

AEROSMITH US, male vocal/instrumental group — 26 wks

17 Oct 87	**DUDE (LOOKS LIKE A LADY)** *Geffen GEF 29*	45	5 wks
16 Apr 88	**ANGEL** *Geffen GEF 34*	69	2 wks
9 Sep 89	**LOVE IN AN ELEVATOR** *Geffen GEF 63*	13	8 wks
24 Feb 90	**DUDE (LOOKS LIKE A LADY) (re-issue)** *Geffen GEF 72*	20	5 wks
14 Apr 90	**RAG DOLL** *Geffen GEF 76*	42	4 wks
1 Sep 90	**THE OTHER SIDE** *Geffen GEF 79*	46	2 wks

AFRICAN BUSINESS Italy, male vocal/instrumental group — 1 wk

17 Nov 90	**IN ZAIRE** *Urban URB 64*	73	1 wk

11

AFTER 7 US, male vocal group — 3 wks

3 Nov 90	**CAN'T STOP** *Virgin America VUS 31*	54	3 wks

AFTER THE FIRE UK, male vocal/instrumental group — 12 wks

9 Jun 79	**ONE RULE FOR YOU** *CBS 7025*	40	6 wks
8 Sep 79	**LASER LOVE** *CBS 7769*	62	2 wks
9 Apr 83	**DER KOMMISSAR** *CBS A 2399*	47	4 wks

AFTERNOON BOYS – *See Steve WRIGHT*

AGE OF CHANCE — 13 wks
UK, male/female vocal/instrumental group

17 Jan 87	**KISS** *Fon AGE 5*	50	6 wks
30 May 87	**WHO'S AFRAID OF THE BIG BAD NOISE!** *Fon VS 962*	65	2 wks
20 Jan 90	**HIGHER THAN HEAVEN** *Virgin VS 1228*	53	5 wks

A-HA Norway, male vocal/instrumental group — 117 wks

28 Sep 85	● **TAKE ON ME** *Warner Bros. W 9006*	2	19 wks
28 Dec 85	★ **THE SUN ALWAYS SHINES ON TV** *Warner Bros. W 8846*	1	12 wks
5 Apr 86	● **TRAIN OF THOUGHT** *Warner Bros. W 8736*	8	8 wks
14 Jun 86	● **HUNTING HIGH AND LOW** *Warner Bros. W 6663*	5	10 wks
4 Oct 86	● **I'VE BEEN LOSING YOU** *Warner Bros. W 8594*	8	7 wks
6 Dec 86	● **CRY WOLF** *Warner Bros. W 8500*	5	9 wks
28 Feb 87	**MANHATTAN SKYLINE** *Warner Bros. W 8405*	13	6 wks
4 Jul 87	● **THE LIVING DAYLIGHTS** *Warner Bros. W 8305*	5	9 wks
26 Mar 88	● **STAY ON THESE ROADS** *Warner Bros. W 7936*	5	6 wks
18 Jun 88	**THE BLOOD THAT MOVES THE BODY** *Warner Bros. W 7840*	25	4 wks
27 Aug 88	**TOUCHY!** *Warner Bros. W 7749*	11	7 wks
8 Dec 88	**YOU ARE THE ONE** *Warner Bros W 7636*	13	10 wks
13 Oct 90	**CRYING IN THE RAIN** *Warner Bros. W 9547*	13	7 wks
15 Dec 90	**I CALL YOUR NAME** *Warner Bros. W 9462*	44†	3 wks

AIR SUPPLY UK/Australia, male vocal/instrumental group — 15 wks

27 Sep 80	**ALL OUT OF LOVE** *Arista ARIST 362*	11	11 wks
2 Oct 82	**EVEN THE NIGHTS ARE BETTER** *Arista ARIST 474*	44	4 wks

Laurel AITKEN and the UNITONE — 3 wks
Jamaica/Cuba, male vocal/instrumental group

17 May 80	**RUDI GOT MARRIED** *I-Spy SEE 6*	60	3 wks

Jewel AKENS US, male/vocalist — 8 wks

25 Mar 65	**THE BIRDS AND THE BEES** *London HLN 9954*	29	8 wks

ALARM UK, male vocal/instrumental group — 62 wks

24 Sep 83	**68 GUNS** *IRS PFP 1023*	17	7 wks
21 Jan 84	**WHERE WERE YOU HIDING WHEN THE STORM BROKE** *IRS IRS 101*	22	6 wks
31 Mar 84	**THE DECEIVER** *IRS IRS 103*	51	4 wks
3 Nov 84	**THE CHANT HAS JUST BEGUN** *IRS IRS 104*	48	4 wks
2 Mar 85	**ABSOLUTE REALITY** *IRS ALARM 1*	35	6 wks
28 Sep 85	**STRENGTH** *IRS IRM 104*	40	4 wks
18 Jan 86	**SPIRIT OF '76** *IRS IRM 109*	22	5 wks
26 Apr 86	**KNIFE EDGE** *IRS IRM 112*	43	3 wks
17 Oct 87	**RAIN IN THE SUMMERTIME** *IRS IRM 144*	18	5 wks
12 Dec 87	**RESCUE ME** *IRS IRM 150*	48	2 wks
20 Feb 88	**PRESENCE OF LOVE (LAUGHERNE)** *IRS IRM 155*	44	3 wks

16 Sep 89	**SOLD ME DOWN THE RIVER** *IRS EIRS 12..*		
4 Nov 89	**A NEW SOUTH WALES/ THE ROCK** *IRS EIRS 129...*		
3 Feb 90	**LOVE DON'T COME EASY** *IRS EIRS 134*	48	3.
27 Oct 90	**UNSAFE BUILDING 1990** *IRS ALARME 2*	54	2 wks

A New South Wales features Morriston Orpheus Male Voice Choir.

Morris ALBERT Brazil, male vocalist — 10 wks

27 Sep 75	● **FEELINGS** *Decca F 13591*	4	10 wks

ALBERTO Y LOST TRIOS PARANOIAS — 5 wks
UK, male vocal/instrumental group

23 Sep 78	**HEADS DOWN NO NONSENSE MINDLESS BOOGIE** *Logo GO 323*	47	5 wks

ALESSI US, male vocal duo — 11 wks

11 Jun 77	● **OH LORI** *A & M AMS 7289*	8	11 wks

ALFI and HARRY — 5 wks
US, male vocalist, David Seville under two false names

23 Mar 56	**THE TROUBLE WITH HARRY** *London HLU 8242*	15	5 wks

See also David Seville.

ALISHA US, female vocalist — 2 wks

25 Jan 86	**BABY TALK** *Total Control TOCO 6*	67	2 wks

ALL ABOUT EVE — 37 wks
UK, female/male vocal/instrumental group

31 Oct 87	**IN THE CLOUDS** *Mercury EVEN 5*	47	5 wks
23 Jan 88	**WILD HEARTED WOMAN** *Mercury EVEN 6*	33	4 wks
9 Apr 88	**EVERY ANGEL** *Mercury EVEN 7*	30	5 wks
30 Jul 88	● **MARTHA'S HARBOUR** *Mercury EVEN 8*	10	8 wks
12 Nov 88	**WHAT KIND OF FOOL** *Mercury EVEN 9*	29	4 wks
30 Sep 89	**ROAD TO YOUR SOUL** *Mercury EVEN 10*	37	4 wks
16 Dec 89	**DECEMBER** *Mercury EVEN 11*	34	5 wks
28 Apr 90	**SCARLET** *Mercury EVEN 12*	34	2 wks

ALL STARS – *See Louis ARMSTRONG*

ALL-STARS – *See Junior WALKER and the ALL-STARS*

ALL SYSTEMS GO UK, male vocal/instrumental group — 2 wks

18 Jun 88	**POP MUZIK** *Un1que NIQ 03*	63	2 wks

Richard ALLAN UK, male vocalist — 1 wk

24 Mar 60	**AS TIME GOES BY** *Parlophone R 4634*	44	1 wk

Steve ALLAN UK, male vocalist — 2 wks

27 Jan 79	**TOGETHER WE ARE BEAUTIFUL** *Creole CR 164*	67	1 wk
10 Feb 79	**TOGETHER WE ARE BEAUTIFUL (re-entry)** *Creole CR 164*	70	1 wk

Far Right: PAULA ABDUL embraces LL Cool J at the 1989 American Music Awards.

Right: ADAMSKI (Adam Tinley) was the leading disc jockey of acid house.

Right: ABC are shown during the period they made money giving lessons in earning.

Below Right: ATLANTIC STARR starred best with their ballads.

Those who saw *The Beat of the Brass* TV special were introduced to HERB ALPERT singing 'This Guy's In Love With You', included as a change of pace from his instrumentals with the Tijuana Brass.

Donna ALLEN US, female vocalist — 22 wks

18 Apr 87	●	SERIOUS *Portrait PRT 650744 7*	8	12 wks
3 Jun 89	●	JOY AND PAIN *BCM BCM 257*	10	10 wks

ALLISONS UK, male vocal duo — 27 wks

23 Feb 61	●	ARE YOU SURE *Fontana H 294*	2	16 wks
18 May 61		WORDS *Fontana H 304*	34	5 wks
15 Feb 62		LESSONS IN LOVE *Fontana H 362*	30	6 wks

ALLNIGHT BAND UK, male instrumental group — 3 wks

3 Feb 79	THE JOKER (THE WIGAN JOKER) *Casino Classics CC 6.*	50	3 wks

ALMIGHTY UK, male vocal/instrumental group — 2 wks

30 Jun 90	WILD AND WONDERFUL *Polydor PO 75*	50	2 wks

Marc ALMOND UK, male vocalist — 58 wks

2 Jun 84		THE BOY WHO CAME BACK *Some Bizzare BZS 23*	52	5 wks
1 Sep 84		YOU HAVE *Some Bizzare BZS 24*	57	3 wks
24 Aug 85		STORIES OF JOHNNY *Some Bizzare BONK 1*	23	5 wks
26 Oct 85		LOVE LETTER *Some Bizzare BONK 2*	68	3 wks
4 Jan 86		THE HOUSE IS HAUNTED (BY THE ECHO OF YOUR LAST GOODBYE) *Some Bizzare GLOW 1*	55	5 wks
7 Jun 86		A WOMAN'S STORY *Some Bizzare GLOW 2*	41	5 wks
18 Oct 86		RUBY RED *Some Bizzare GLOW 3*	47	3 wks
14 Feb 87		MELANCHOLY ROSE *Some Bizzare GLOW 4*	71	1 wk
3 Sep 88		TEARS RUN RINGS *Parlophone R 6186*	26	7 wks
5 Nov 88		BITTER SWEET *Some Bizzare R 6194*	40	3 wks
14 Jan 89	★	SOMETHING'S GOTTEN HOLD OF MY HEART *Parlophone R 6201*	1	12 wks
8 Apr 89		ONLY THE MOMENT *Parlophone R 6210*	45	2 wks
3 Mar 90		A LOVER SPURNED *Some Bizzare R 6229*	29	4 wks
19 May 90		THE DESPERATE HOURS *Some Bizzare R 6252*	45	2 wks

The label for Some Bizzare GLOW 2 credits the Willing Sinners - UK, male/female vocal/instrumental group. See also Marc and the Mambas; Bronski Beat and Marc Almond. Something's Gotten Hold Of My Heart features Gene Pitney. See also Gene Pitney.

Herb ALPERT US, male instrumentalist - trumpet — 106 wks

3 Jan 63		THE LONELY BULL *Stateside SS 138*	22	9 wks
9 Dec 65	●	SPANISH FLEA *Pye International 7 N 25335*	3	20 wks
24 Mar 66		TIJUANA TAXI *Pye International 7 N 25352*	37	4 wks
27 Apr 67		CASINO ROYALE *A & M AMS 700*	27	14 wks
3 Jul 68	●	THIS GUY'S IN LOVE WITH YOU *A & M AMS 727*	3	16 wks
26 Mar 69		THIS GUY'S IN LOVE WITH YOU (re-entry) *A & M AMS 727*	47	1 wk
9 Apr 69		THIS GUY'S IN LOVE WITH YOU (2nd re-entry) *A & M AMS 727*	49	1 wk
7 May 69		THIS GUY'S IN LOVE WITH YOU (3rd re-entry) *A & M AMS 727*	50	1 wk
18 Jun 69		WITHOUT HER *A & M AMS 755*	36	5 wks
12 Dec 70		JERUSALEM *A & M AMS 810*	47	1 wk
2 Jan 71		JERUSALEM (re-entry) *A & M AMS 810*	42	2 wks
13 Oct 79		RISE *A & M AMS 7465*	13	13 wks
19 Jan 80		ROTATION *A & M AMS 7500*	46	3 wks
21 Mar 87		KEEP YOUR EYE ON ME *Breakout USA 602*	19	9 wks
6 Jun 87		DIAMONDS *Breakout USA 605*	27	7 wks

Spanish Flea, Tijuana Taxi, Casino Royale, Without Her and Jerusalem credit Herb Alpert and The Tijuana Brass. The Lonely Bull credits only The Tijuana Brass. Alpert vocalises on This Guy's In Love With You and Without Her. Janet Jackson provides vocals on Diamonds. See also Janet Jackson.

ALPHABETA – See Izhar COHEN and ALPHABETA

ALPHAVILLE Germany, male vocal/instrumental group — 13 wks

18 Aug 84	●	BIG IN JAPAN *WEA Int. X9505*	8	13 wks

Gerald ALSTON US, male vocalist — 1 wk

15 Apr 89	ACTIVATED *RCA ZB 42681*	73	1 wk

ALTERED IMAGES — 60 wks

UK, male/female vocal/instrumental group

28 Mar 81		DEAD POP STARS *Epic EPC A 1023*	67	2 wks
26 Sep 81	●	HAPPY BIRTHDAY *Epic EPC A 1522*	2	17 wks
12 Dec 81	●	I COULD BE HAPPY *Epic EPC A 1834*	7	12 wks
27 Mar 82		SEE THOSE EYES *Epic EPC A 2198*	11	7 wks
22 May 82		PINKY BLUE *Epic EPC A 2426*	35	6 wks
19 Mar 83	●	DON'T TALK TO ME ABOUT LOVE *Epic EPC A 3083*	7	7 wks
28 May 83		BRING ME CLOSER *Epic EPC A 3398*	29	6 wks
16 Jul 83		LOVE TO STAY *Epic EPC A 3582*	46	3 wks

ALTHIA and DONNA Jamaica, female vocal duo — 11 wks

24 Dec 77	★	UP TOWN TOP RANKING *Lightning LIG 506*	1	11 wks

AMAZULU UK, female/male vocal/instrumental group — 57 wks

6 Jul 85		EXCITABLE *Island IS 201*	12	13 wks
23 Nov 85		DON'T YOU JUST KNOW IT *Island IS 233*	17	11 wks
15 Mar 86		THE THINGS THE LONELY DO *Island IS 267*	43	6 wks
31 May 86	●	TOO GOOD TO BE FORGOTTEN *Island IS 284*	5	13 wks
13 Sep 86		MONTEGO BAY *Island IS 293*	16	9 wks
10 Oct 87		MONY MONY *EMI EM 32*	38	5 wks

AMEN CORNER UK, male vocal/instrumental group — 67 wks

26 Jul 67		GIN HOUSE BLUES *Deram DM 136*	12	10 wks
11 Oct 67		WORLD OF BROKEN HEARTS *Deram DM 151*	26	6 wks
17 Jan 68	●	BEND ME SHAPE ME *Deram DM 172*	3	12 wks
31 Jul 68	●	HIGH IN THE SKY *Deram DM 197*	6	13 wks
29 Jan 69	★	(IF PARADISE IS) HALF AS NICE *Immediate IM 073*	1	11 wks
25 Jun 69	●	HELLO SUZIE *Immediate IM 081*	4	10 wks
14 Feb 76		(IF PARADISE IS) HALF AS NICE (re-issue) *Immediate IMS 103*	34	5 wks

AMERICA US, male vocal/instrumental group — 20 wks

18 Dec 71		HORSE WITH NO NAME *Warner Bros. K 16128*	49	2 wks
8 Jan 72	●	HORSE WITH NO NAME (re-entry) *Warner Bros. K 16128.*	3	11 wks
25 Nov 72		VENTURA HIGHWAY *Warner Bros. K 16219*	43	4 wks
6 Nov 82		YOU CAN DO MAGIC *Capitol CL 264*	59	3 wks

AMERICAN BREED US, male vocal/instrumental group — 6 wks

7 Feb 68	BEND ME SHAPE ME *Stateside SS 2078*	24	6 wks

AMES BROTHERS US, male vocal group — 6 wks

4 Feb 55	●	NAUGHTY LADY OF SHADY LANE *HMV B 10800*	6	6 wks

AND WHY NOT? UK, male vocal/instrumental group — 18 wks

14 Oct 89		RESTLESS DAYS (SHE CRIES OUT LOUD) *Island IS 426*	38	7 wks
13 Jan 90		THE FACE *Island IS 444*	13	8 wks

| 21 Apr 90 | SOMETHING YOU GOT *Island IS 452* | 39 | 3 wks |

Angry ANDERSON *Australia, male vocalist*   **13 wks**

| 7 Jan 89 | ● SUDDENLY *Food For Thought YUM 113* | 3 | 13 wks |

John ANDERSON BIG BAND *UK, big band*   **5 wks**

| 21 Dec 85 | GLENN MILLER MEDLEY *Modern GLEN 1* | 63 | 2 wks |
| 11 Jan 86 | GLENN MILLER MEDLEY (re-entry) *Modern GLEN 1* | 61 | 3 wks |

Glenn Miller Medley includes the following tracks: In The Mood/American Patrol/Little Brown Jug/Pennsylvania 65000.

ANDERSON BRUFORD WAKEMAN HOWE *UK, male vocal/instrumental group*   **2 wks**

| 24 Jan 89 | BROTHER OF MINE *Arista 112379* | 63 | 2 wks |

Carl ANDERSON *US, male vocalist*   **4 wks**

| 8 Jun 85 | BUTTERCUP *Streetwave KHAN 45* | 49 | 4 wks |

Laurie ANDERSON *US, female vocalist/multi-instrumentalist*   **6 wks**

| 17 Oct 81 | ● O SUPERMAN *Warner Bros. K 17870* | 2 | 6 wks |

Leroy ANDERSON *US, orchestra*   **4 wks**

28 Jun 57	FORGOTTEN DREAMS *Brunswick 05485*	28	1 wk
12 Jul 57	FORGOTTEN DREAMS (re-entry) *Brunswick 05485*	30	1 wk
6 Sep 57	FORGOTTEN DREAMS (2nd re-entry) *Brunswick 05485*	24	2 wks

Lynn ANDERSON *US, female vocalist*   **20 wks**

| 20 Feb 71 | ● ROSE GARDEN *CBS 5360* | 3 | 20 wks |

Moira ANDERSON *UK, female vocalist*   **2 wks**

| 27 Dec 69 | HOLY CITY *Decca F 12989* | 43 | 2 wks |

Chris ANDREWS *UK, male vocalist*   **36 wks**

7 Oct 65	● YESTERDAY MAN *Decca F 12236*	3	15 wks
2 Dec 65	TO WHOM IT CONCERNS *Decca F 22285*	13	10 wks
14 Apr 66	SOMETHING ON MY MIND *Decca F 22365*	45	1 wk
28 Apr 66	SOMETHING ON MY MIND (re-entry) *Decca F 22365*	41	2 wks
2 Jun 66	WHATCHA GONNA DO NOW *Decca F 22404*	40	4 wks
25 Aug 66	STOP THAT GIRL *Decca F 22472*	36	4 wks

Eamonn ANDREWS *Ireland, male vocalist*   **3 wks**

| 20 Jan 56 | SHIFTING WHISPERING SANDS (PARTS 1 & 2) *Parlophone R 4106* | 18 | 3 wks |

ANEKA *UK, female vocalist*   **16 wks**

| 8 Aug 81 | ★ JAPANESE BOY *Hansa HANSA 5* | 1 | 12 wks |
| 7 Nov 81 | LITTLE LADY *Hansa HANSA 8* | 50 | 4 wks |

ANGELETTES *UK, female vocal group*   **5 wks**

| 13 May 72 | DON'T LET HIM TOUCH YOU *Decca F 13284* | 35 | 5 wks |

ANGELIC UPSTARTS   **30 wks**
UK, male vocal/instrumental group

21 Apr 79	I'M AN UPSTART *Warner Bros. K 17354*	31	8 wks
11 Aug 79	TEENAGE WARNING *Warner Bros. K 17426*	29	6 wks
3 Nov 79	NEVER 'AD NOTHIN' *Warner Bros. K 17476*	52	4 wks
9 Feb 80	OUT OF CONTROL *Warner Bros. K 17558*	58	3 wks
22 Mar 80	WE GOTTA GET OUT OF THIS PLACE *Warner Bros. K 17576*	65	2 wks
2 Aug 80	LAST NIGHT ANOTHER SOLDIER *Angelic Upstarts Z 7*	51	4 wks
7 Feb 81	KIDS ON THE STREET *Angelic Upstarts Z 16*	57	3 wks

Bobby ANGELO and the TUXEDOS   **6 wks**
UK, male vocal/instrumental group

| 10 Aug 61 | BABY SITTIN' *HMV POP 892* | 30 | 6 wks |

ANGELS *US, female vocal group*   **1 wk**

| 3 Oct 63 | MY BOYFRIEND'S BACK *Mercury AMT 1211* | 50 | 1 wk |

ANGELWITCH *UK, male vocal/instrumental group*   **1 wk**

| 7 Jun 80 | SWEET DANGER *EMI 5064* | 75 | 1 wk |

ANIMAL NIGHTLIFE   **22 wks**
UK, male/female vocal/instrumental group

13 Aug 83	NATIVE BOY (UPTOWN) *Innervision A3584*	60	3 wks
18 Aug 84	MR. SOLITAIRE *Island IS 193*	25	12 wks
6 Jul 85	LOVE IS JUST THE GREAT PRETENDER *Island IS 200*	28	6 wks
5 Oct 85	PREACHER, PREACHER *Island IS 245*	67	1 wk

ANIMALS *UK, male vocal/instrumental group*   **105 wks**

16 Apr 64	BABY LET ME TAKE YOU HOME *Columbia DB 7247*	21	8 wks
25 Jun 64	★ HOUSE OF THE RISING SUN *Columbia DB 7301*	1	12 wks
17 Sep 64	● I'M CRYING *Columbia DB 7354*	8	10 wks
4 Feb 65	● DON'T LET ME BE MISUNDERSTOOD *Columbia DB 7445*	3	9 wks
8 Apr 65	● BRING IT ON HOME TO ME *Columbia DB 7539*	7	11 wks
15 Jul 65	● WE GOTTA GET OUT OF THIS PLACE *Columbia DB 7639*	2	12 wks
28 Oct 65	● IT'S MY LIFE *Columbia DB 7741*	7	11 wks
17 Feb 66	INSIDE - LOOKING OUT *Decca F 12332*	12	8 wks
2 Jun 66	● DON'T BRING ME DOWN *Decca F 12407*	6	8 wks
7 Oct 72	HOUSE OF THE RISING SUN (re-issue) *RAK RR 1*	25	6 wks
18 Sep 82	HOUSE OF THE RISING SUN (re-entry of re-issue) *RAK RR 1*	11	10 wks

See also Eric Burdon.

ANIMOTION *US/UK, male/female vocal/instrumental group*   **12 wks**

| 11 May 85 | ● OBSESSION *Mercury PH 34* | 5 | 12 wks |

Paul ANKA *Canada, male vocalist*   **134 wks**

| 9 Aug 57 | ★ DIANA *Columbia DB 3980* | 1 | 25 wks |
| 8 Nov 57 | ● I LOVE YOU BABY *Columbia DB 4022* | 3 | 15 wks |

8 Nov 57		TELL ME THAT YOU LOVE ME *Columbia DB 4022*	25	2 wks
31 Jan 58	●	YOU ARE MY DESTINY *Columbia DB 4063*	6	13 wks
30 May 58		CRAZY LOVE *Columbia DB 4110*	26	1 wk
26 Sep 58		MIDNIGHT *Columbia DB 4172*	26	1 wk
30 Jan 59	●	(ALL OF A SUDDEN) MY HEART SINGS *Columbia DB 4241*	10	13 wks
10 Jul 59	●	LONELY BOY *Columbia DB 4324*	3	17 wks
30 Oct 59	●	PUT YOUR HEAD ON MY SHOULDER *Columbia DB 4355*	7	12 wks
26 Feb 60		IT'S TIME TO CRY *Columbia DB 4390*	28	1 wk
31 Mar 60		PUPPY LOVE *Columbia DB 4434*	33	4 wks
14 Apr 60		IT'S TIME TO CRY (re-entry) *Columbia DB 4390*	47	1 wk
5 May 60		PUPPY LOVE (re-entry) *Columbia DB 4434*	37	3 wks
15 Sep 60		HELLO YOUNG LOVERS *Columbia DB 4504*	44	1 wk
15 Mar 62		LOVE ME WARM AND TENDER *RCA 1276*	19	11 wks
26 Jul 62		A STEEL GUITAR AND A GLASS OF WINE *RCA 1292*	41	4 wks
28 Sep 74	●	(YOU'RE) HAVING MY BABY *United Artists UP 35713*	6	10 wks

UP 35713 featured Odia Coates - US, female vocalist.

ANKLEBITERS – *See Fogwell FLAX and the ANKLEBITERS from FREEHOLD JUNIOR SCHOOL*

ANNETTE *UK, female vocalist*   **2 wks**

20 Jan 90	DREAM 17 *deConsruction PT 43372*	64	2 wks

Dream 17 was one track from The Further Adventures Of North EP. The other tracks were Carino 90 by T-Coy, The Way I Feel by Frequency 9 and Stop This Thing by Dynasty Of Two featuring Rowetta. See also T-Coy, Frequency 9; Dynasty Of Two featuring Rowetta.

ANOUCHKA – *See Terry HALL*

Adam ANT *UK, male vocalist*   **188 wks**

2 Aug 80		KINGS OF THE WILD FRONTIER *CBS 8877*	48	5 wks
11 Oct 80	●	DOG EAT DOG *CBS 9039*	4	16 wks
6 Dec 80	●	ANTMUSIC *CBS 9352*	2	18 wks
27 Dec 80	●	YOUNG PARISIANS *Decca F13803*	9	7 wks
24 Jan 81		CARTROUBLE *Do It DUN 10*	33	9 wks
24 Jan 81		ZEROX *Do It DUN 8*	45	9 wks
21 Feb 81	●	KINGS OF THE WILD FRONTIER (re-entry) *CBS 8877*	2	13 wks
9 May 81	★	STAND AND DELIVER *CBS A 1065*	1	15 wks
12 Sep 81	★	PRINCE CHARMING *CBS A 1408*	1	12 wks
12 Dec 81	●	ANT RAP *CBS A 1738*	3	10 wks
27 Feb 82		DEUTSCHER GIRLS *Ego 5*	13	6 wks
13 Mar 82		THE ANTMUSIC EP (THE B-SIDES) *Do It DUN 20*	46	4 wks
22 May 82	★	GOODY TWO SHOES *CBS A 2367*	1	11 wks
18 Sep 82	●	FRIEND OR FOE *CBS A 2736*	9	8 wks
27 Nov 82		DESPERATE BUT NOT SERIOUS *CBS A 2892*	33	7 wks
29 Oct 83	●	PUSS 'N BOOTS *CBS A 3614*	5	11 wks
10 Dec 83		STRIP *CBS A 3589*	41	6 wks
22 Sep 84		APOLLO 9 *CBS A 4719*	13	8 wks
13 Jul 85		VIVE LE ROCK *CBS A 6367*	50	4 wks
17 Feb 90		ROOM AT THE TOP *MCA MCA 1387*	13	7 wks
28 Apr 90		CAN'T SET RULES ABOUT LOVE *MCA MCA 1404*	47	2 wks

Tracks on The Antmusic EP (The B-Sides): Friends/Kick/Physical. First 11 hits credited to Adam and the Ants - UK, male vocal/instrumental group.

Billie ANTHONY *UK, female vocalist*   **16 wks**

15 Oct 54	●	THIS OLE HOUSE *Columbia DB 3519*	4	16 wks

Miki ANTHONY *UK, male vocalist*   **7 wks**

3 Feb 73	IF IT WASN'T FOR THE REASON THAT I LOVE YOU *Bell 1275*	27	7 wks

Ray ANTHONY *US, orchestra*   **2 wks**

4 Dec 53	●	DRAGNET *Capitol CL 13983*	7	1 wk
8 Jan 54		DRAGNET (re-entry) *Capitol CL 13983*	11	1 wk

Richard ANTHONY *France, male vocalist*   **15 wks**

12 Dec 63	WALKING ALONE *Columbia DB 7133*	37	5 wks
2 Apr 64	IF I LOVED YOU *Columbia DB 7235*	48	1 wk
23 Apr 64	IF I LOVED YOU (re-entry) *Columbia DB 7235*	18	9 wks

ANTHRAX *US, male vocal/instrumental group*   **23 wks**

28 Feb 87	I AM THE LAW *Island IS LAW 1*	32	5 wks
27 Jun 87	INDIANS *Island IS 325*	44	4 wks
5 Dec 87	I'M THE MAN *Island IS 338*	20	6 wks
10 Sep 88	MAKE ME LAUGH *Island IS 379*	26	3 wks
18 Mar 89	ANTI-SOCIAL *Island IS 409*	44	3 wks
1 Sep 90	IN MY WORLD *Island IS 470*	29	2 wks

ANTI-NOWHERE LEAGUE   **10 wks**
UK, male vocal/instrumental group

23 Jan 82	STREETS OF LONDON *WXYZ ABCD 1*	48	5 wks
20 Mar 82	I HATE ... PEOPLE *WXYZ ABCD 2*	46	3 wks
3 Jul 82	WOMAN *WXYZ ABCD 4*	72	2 wks

ANTI-PASTI – *See EXPLOITED and ANTI-PASTI*

ANTONIA – *See BOMB THE BASS*

ANTS – *See Adam ANT*

APHRODITE'S CHILD   **7 wks**
Greece, male vocal/instrumental group

6 Nov 68	RAIN AND TEARS *Mercury MF 1039*	30	7 wks

Kim APPLEBY *UK, female vocalist*   **9 wks**

3 Nov 90	●	DON'T WORRY *Parlophone R 6272*	2†	9 wks

See also Mel and Kim.

APPLEJACKS *UK, male/female vocal/instrumental group*   **29 wks**

5 Mar 64	●	TELL ME WHEN *Decca F 11833*	7	13 wks
11 Jun 64		LIKE DREAMERS DO *Decca F 11916*	20	11 wks
15 Oct 64		THREE LITTLE WORDS *Decca F 11981*	23	5 wks

Charlie APPLEWHITE *US, male vocalist*   **1 wk**

23 Sep 55	BLUE STAR (THE MEDIC THEME) *Brunswick 05416*	20	1 wk

Helen APRIL – *See John DUMMER and Helen APRIL*

APRIL WINE *Canada, male vocal/instrumental group*   **9 wks**

15 Mar 80	I LIKE TO ROCK *Capitol CL 16121*	41	5 wks
11 Apr 81	JUST BETWEEN YOU AND ME *Capitol CL 16184*	52	4 wks

AQUA MARINA – *See FAB*

AQUARIAN DREAM
1 wk
US, male/female vocal/instrumental group

24 Feb 79	YOU'RE A STAR *Elektra LV 7*	67	1 wk

ARCADIA *UK, male vocal/instrumental group*
13 wks

26 Oct 85 ●	ELECTION DAY *Odeon NSR 1*	7	7 wks
25 Jan 86	THE PROMISE *Odeon NSR 2*	37	4 wks
26 Jul 86	THE FLAME *Odeon NSR 3*	58	2 wks

ARCHIES *US, male/female vocal group*
26 wks

11 Oct 69 ★	SUGAR SUGAR *RCA 1872*	1	26 wks

ARGENT *UK, male vocal/instrumental group*
27 wks

4 Mar 72 ●	HOLD YOUR HEAD UP *Epic EPC 7786*	5	12 wks
10 Jun 72	TRAGEDY *Epic EPC 8115*	34	7 wks
24 Mar 73	GOD GAVE ROCK AND ROLL TO YOU *Epic EPC 1243*	18	8 wks

Ship's Company and Royal Marine Band of H.M.S. ARK ROYAL *UK, male choir and Marine band*
6 wks

23 Dec 78	THE LAST FAREWELL *BBC RESL 61*	46	6 wks

Joan ARMATRADING *UK, female vocalist*
51 wks

16 Oct 76 ●	LOVE AND AFFECTION *A & M AMS 7249*	10	9 wks
23 Feb 80	ROSIE *A & M AMS 7506*	49	5 wks
14 Jun 80	ME MYSELF I *A & M AMS 7527*	21	11 wks
6 Sep 80	ALL THE WAY FROM AMERICA *A & M AMS 7552*	54	3 wks
12 Sep 81	I'M LUCKY *A & M AMS 8163*	46	4 wks
16 Jan 82	NO LOVE *A & M AMS 8179*	50	5 wks
19 Feb 83	DROP THE PILOT *A & M AMS 8306*	11	10 wks
16 Mar 85	TEMPTATION *A & M AMS 238*	65	2 wks
26 May 90	MORE THAN ONE KIND OF LOVE *A & M AM 561*	75	1 wk

ARMOURY SHOW *UK, male vocal/instrumental group*
6 wks

25 Aug 84	CASTLES IN SPAIN *Parlophone R 6079*	69	2 wks
26 Jan 85	WE CAN BE BRAVE AGAIN *Parlophone R 6087*	66	1 wk
17 Jan 87	LOVE IN ANGER *Parlophone R 6149*	63	3 wks

Louis ARMSTRONG
80 wks
US, male jazz band leader, vocalist/instrumentalist - trumpet

19 Dec 52 ●	TAKES TWO TO TANGO *Brunswick 04995*	6	10 wks
13 Apr 56 ●	THEME FROM THE THREEPENNY OPERA *Philips PB 574*	8	11 wks
15 Jun 56	TAKE IT SATCH (EP) *Philips BBE 12035*	29	1 wk
13 Jul 56	THE FAITHFUL HUSSAR *Philips PB 604*	27	2 wks
6 Nov 59	MACK THE KNIFE *Philips PB 967*	24	1 wk
4 Jun 64 ●	HELLO DOLLY *London HLR 9878*	4	14 wks
7 Feb 68 ★	WHAT A WONDERFUL WORLD/ CABARET *HMV POP 1615*	1	29 wks
26 Jun 68	SUNSHINE OF LOVE *Stateside SS 2116*	41	7 wks
16 Apr 88	WHAT A WONDERFUL WORLD (re-issue) *A & M AM 435*	53	5 wks

Take It Satch *tracks:* Tiger Rag/Mack The Knife/The Faithful Hussar/Back O'Town Blues. Mack The Knife *is a re-issue of* Theme From Threepenny Opera *under a different title.* Cabaret *was not listed with* What A Wonderful World *until 14 Feb 68. The four hits on Philips are all credited to Louis Armstrong with his All Stars.*

ARNIE'S LOVE *US, male/female vocal/instrumental group*
3 wks

26 Nov 83	I'M OUT OF YOUR LIFE *Streetwave WAVE 9*	67	3 wks

Eddy ARNOLD *US, male vocalist*
21 wks

17 Feb 66 ●	MAKE THE WORLD GO AWAY *RCA 1496*	8	17 wks
26 May 66	I WANT TO GO WITH YOU *RCA 1519*	49	1 wk
9 Jun 66	I WANT TO GO WITH YOU (re-entry) *RCA 1519*	46	2 wks
28 Jul 66	IF YOU WERE MINE MARY *RCA 1529*	49	1 wk

P. P. ARNOLD *US, female vocalist*
27 wks

4 May 67	FIRST CUT IS THE DEEPEST *Immediate IM 047*	18	10 wks
2 Aug 67	THE TIME HAS COME *Immediate IM 055*	47	2 wks
24 Jan 68	(IF YOU THINK) YOU'RE GROOVY *Immediate IM 061*	41	4 wks
10 Jul 68	ANGEL OF THE MORNING *Immediate IM 067*	29	11 wks

See also Beatmasters.

ARPEGGIO *US, male/female vocal group*
3 wks

31 Mar 79	LOVE AND DESIRE (PART 1) *Polydor POSP 40*	63	3 wks

Steve ARRINGTON *US, male vocalist*
19 wks

27 Apr 85 ●	FEEL SO REAL *Atlantic A 9576*	5	10 wks
6 Jul 85	DANCIN' IN THE KEY OF LIFE *Atlantic A 9534*	21	8 wks
7 Sep 85	DANCIN' IN THE KEY OF LIFE (re-entry) *Atlantic A 9534*	75	1 wk

ARRIVAL *UK, male/female vocal/instrumental group*
20 wks

10 Jan 70 ●	FRIENDS *Decca F 12986*	8	9 wks
6 Jun 70	I WILL SURVIVE *Decca F 13026*	16	11 wks

ARROW *Montserrat, male vocalist*
12 wks

28 Jul 84	HOT HOT HOT *Cooltempo ARROW 1*	59	5 wks
13 Jul 85	LONG TIME *London LON 70*	30	7 wks

ARROWS *US/UK, male vocal/instrumental group*
16 wks

25 May 74 ●	A TOUCH TOO MUCH *RAK 171*	8	9 wks
1 Feb 75	MY LAST NIGHT WITH YOU *RAK 189*	25	7 wks

ARSENAL F.C. FIRST TEAM SQUAD
7 wks
UK, male football team vocalists

8 May 71	GOOD OLD ARSENAL *Pye 7N 45067*	16	7 wks

ART COMPANY *Holland, male vocal/instrumental group*
11 wks

26 May 84	SUSANNA *Epic A 4174*	12	11 wks

ART OF NOISE *UK, male/female studio group*
57 wks

24 Nov 84 ●	CLOSE (TO THE EDIT) *ZTT ZTPS 01*	8	19 wks
13 Apr 85	MOMENTS IN LOVE/ BEAT BOX *ZTT ZTPS 02*	51	6 wks
9 Nov 85	LEGS *China WOK 5*	69	1 wk
22 Mar 86 ●	PETER GUNN *China WOK 6*	8	9 wks
21 Jun 86	PARANOIMIA *China WOK 9*	12	9 wks
18 Jul 87	DRAGNET *China WOK 14*	60	4 wks
29 Oct 88 ●	KISS *China CHINA 11*	5	7 wks

THE BEASTIE BOYS look like they won their right to party.

Far Left: WINIFRED ATWELL is the only solo female instrumentalist to reach number one.

JOAN ARMATRADING seems surprised she did not have more than one hit in 1990.

| 12 Aug 89 | | YEBO *China CHINA 18* | 63 | 3 wks |
| 16 Jun 90 | | ART OF LOVE *China CHINA 23* | 67 | 1 wk |

WOK 6 features Duane Eddy. WOK 9 features Max Headroom, UK, computer generated male voice.
China 11 features Tom Jones. Yebo features Mahlathini and the Mahotella Queens - South Africa,
male/female vocal group. See also Duane Eddy; Tom Jones.

ARTISTS UNITED AGAINST APARTHEID   8 wks
Multi-national, male/female vocal/instrumental charity assembly

| 23 Nov 85 | | SUN CITY *Manhattan MT 7* | 21 | 8 wks |

ASAP *UK, male vocal/instrumental group*   4 wks

| 14 Oct 89 | | SILVER AND GOLD *EMI EM 107* | 60 | 2 wks |
| 3 Feb 90 | | DOWN THE WIRE *EMI EM 131* | 67 | 2 wks |

ASHAYE *UK, male vocalist*   3 wks

| 15 Oct 83 | | MICHAEL JACKSON MEDLEY *Record Shack SOHO 10* | 45 | 3 wks |

Tracks on medley: Don't Stop Til You Get Enough/Wanna Be Startin' Something/Shake Your Body
Down To The Ground/Blame It On The Boogie.

John ASHER *UK, male vocalist*   6 wks

| 15 Nov 75 | | LET'S TWIST AGAIN *Creole CR 112* | 14 | 6 wks |

ASHFORD and SIMPSON *US, male/female vocal duo*   22 wks

18 Nov 78		IT SEEMS TO HANG ON *Warner Bros. K 17237*	48	4 wks
5 Jan 85	●	SOLID *Capitol CL 345*	3	15 wks
20 Apr 85		BABIES *Capitol CL 355*	56	3 wks

ASHTON, GARDNER AND DYKE
UK, male vocal/instrumental group   14 wks

| 16 Jan 71 | ● | RESURRECTION SHUFFLE *Capitol CL 15665* | 3 | 14 wks |

ASIA *UK, male vocal/instrumental group*   13 wks

3 Jul 82		HEAT OF THE MOMENT *Geffen GEF A2494*	46	5 wks
18 Sep 82		ONLY TIME WILL TELL *Geffen GEF A2228*	54	3 wks
13 Aug 83		DON'T CRY *Geffen A 3580*	33	5 wks

ASSEMBLY *UK, male vocal/instrumental group*   10 wks

| 12 Nov 83 | ● | NEVER NEVER *Mute TINY 1* | 4 | 10 wks |

ASSOCIATES *UK, male vocal/instrumental group*   47 wks

20 Feb 82	●	PARTY FEARS TWO *Associates ASC 1*	9	10 wks
8 May 82		CLUB COUNTRY *Associates ASC 2*	13	10 wks
7 Aug 82		18 CARAT LOVE AFFAIR/ LOVE HANGOVER *Associates ASC 3*	21	8 wks
16 Jun 84		THOSE FIRST IMPRESSIONS *WEA YZ 6*	43	6 wks
1 Sep 84		WAITING FOR THE LOVEBOAT *WEA YZ 16*	53	4 wks
19 Jan 85		BREAKFAST *WEA YZ 28*	49	6 wks
17 Sep 88		HEART OF GLASS *WEA YZ 310*	56	3 wks

18 Carat Love Affair listed until 28 Aug only. Act was duo on 1982 hits.

ASSOCIATION *US, male vocal/instrumental group*   8 wks

| 22 May 68 | | TIME FOR LIVING *Warner Bros. WB 7195* | 23 | 8 wks |

Rick ASTLEY *UK, male vocalist*   77 wks

8 Aug 87	★	NEVER GONNA GIVE YOU UP *RCA PB 41447*	1	18 wks
31 Oct 87	●	WHENEVER YOU NEED SOMEBODY *RCA PB 41567*	3	12 wks
12 Dec 87	●	WHEN I FALL IN LOVE/ MY ARMS KEEP MISSING YOU *RCA PB 41683*	2	10 wks
27 Feb 88	●	TOGETHER FOREVER *RCA PB 41817*	2	9 wks
24 Sep 88	●	SHE WANTS TO DANCE WITH ME *RCA PB 42189*	6	10 wks
26 Nov 88	●	TAKE ME TO YOUR HEART *RCA PB 42573*	8	10 wks
11 Feb 89	●	HOLD ME IN YOUR ARMS *RCA PB 42615*	10	8 wks

Before 9 Jan 88 When I Fall In Love was listed by itself. After that date My Arms Keep Missing
You was the side listed.

ASWAD *UK, male vocal/instrumental group*   50 wks

3 Mar 84		CHASING FOR THE BREEZE *Island IS 160*	51	3 wks
6 Oct 84		54-46 (WAS MY NUMBER) *Island IS 170*	70	3 wks
27 Feb 88	★	DON'T TURN AROUND *Mango IS 341*	1	12 wks
21 May 88		GIVE A LITTLE LOVE *Mango IS 358*	11	8 wks
24 Sep 88		SET THEM FREE *Mango IS 383*	70	2 wks
1 Apr 89		BEAUTY'S ONLY SKIN DEEP *Mango MNG 105*	31	6 wks
22 Jul 89		ON AND ON *Mango MNG 708*	25	8 wks
18 Aug 90		NEXT TO YOU *Mango MNG 753*	24	6 wks
17 Nov 90		SMILE *Mango MNG 767*	53	2 wks

Gali ATARI – *See MILK AND HONEY*

Chet ATKINS *US, male instrumentalist - guitar*   2 wks

| 17 Mar 60 | | TEENSVILLE *RCA 1174* | 46 | 1 wk |
| 5 May 60 | | TEENSVILLE (re-entry) *RCA 1174* | 49 | 1 wk |

ATLANTA RHYTHM SECTION   4 wks
US, male vocal/instrumental group

| 27 Oct 79 | | SPOOKY *Polydor POSP 74* | 48 | 4 wks |

ATLANTIC STARR   46 wks
US, male/female vocal/instrumental group

9 Sep 78		GIMME YOUR LOVIN' *A & M AMS 7380*	66	3 wks
29 Jun 85		SILVER SHADOW *A & M AM 260*	41	6 wks
7 Sep 85		ONE LOVE *A & M AM 273*	58	4 wks
15 Mar 86	●	SECRET LOVERS *A & M AM 307*	10	12 wks
24 May 86		IF YOUR HEART ISN'T IN IT *A & M AM 319*	48	4 wks
13 Jun 87	●	ALWAYS *Warner Bros. W 8455*	3	14 wks
12 Sep 87		ONE LOVER AT A TIME *Warner Bros. W 8327*	57	3 wks

ATMOSFEAR *UK, male vocal/instrumental group*   7 wks

| 17 Nov 79 | | DANCING IN OUTER SPACE *MCA 543* | 46 | 7 wks |

ATOMIC ROOSTER *UK, male vocal/instrumental group*   25 wks

| 6 Feb 71 | | TOMORROW NIGHT *B & C CB 131* | 11 | 12 wks |
| 10 Jul 71 | ● | THE DEVIL'S ANSWER *B & C CB 157* | 4 | 13 wks |

ATTRACTIONS – *See Elvis COSTELLO and the ATTRACTIONS*

Winifred ATWELL *UK, female instrumentalist - piano*   117 wks

12 Dec 52		BRITANNIA RAG *Decca F 10015*	11	1 wk
9 Jan 53	●	BRITANNIA RAG (re-entry) *Decca F 10015*	5	5 wks
15 May 53		CORONATION RAG *Decca F 10110*	12	1 wk
29 May 53	●	CORONATION RAG (re-entry) *Decca F 10110*	5	5 wks
25 Sep 53		FLIRTATION WALTZ *Decca F 10161*	12	1 wk

9 Oct 53	● FLIRTATION WALTZ (re-entry) Decca F 10161	10	1 wk
6 Nov 53	● FLIRTATION WALTZ (2nd re-entry) Decca F10161	12	1 wk
4 Dec 53	● LET'S HAVE A PARTY Philips PB 213	2	9 wks
23 Jul 54	● RACHMANINOFF'S 18TH VARIATION ON A THEME BY PAGANINI Philips PB 234	9	7 wks
1 Oct 54	RACHMANINOFF'S 18TH VARIATION ON A THEME BY PAGANINI (re-entry) Philips PB 234	19	2 wks
26 Nov 54	★ LET'S HAVE ANOTHER PARTY Philips PB 268	1	8 wks
26 Nov 54	LET'S HAVE A PARTY (re-entry) Philips PB 213	14	6 wks
4 Nov 55	● LET'S HAVE A DING DONG Decca F 10634	3	10 wks
16 Mar 56	★ POOR PEOPLE OF PARIS Decca F 10681	1	16 wks
18 May 56	PORT AU PRINCE Decca F 10727	18	6 wks
20 Jul 56	LEFT BANK Decca F 10762	14	7 wks
26 Oct 56	● MAKE IT A PARTY Decca F 10796	7	12 wks
22 Feb 57	LET'S ROCK 'N ROLL Decca F 10852	28	2 wks
15 Mar 57	LET'S ROCK 'N ROLL (re-entry) Decca F 10852	24	2 wks
6 Dec 57	● LET'S HAVE A BALL Decca F 10956	4	6 wks
7 Aug 59	SUMMER OF THE SEVENTEENTH DOLL Decca F 11143	24	2 wks
27 Nov 59	● PIANO PARTY Decca F 11183	10	7 wks

Various hits listed above were medleys as follows: Let's Have a Party: Boomps A Daisy/Daisy Bell/If You Knew Suzie/Knees Up Mother Brown/The More We Are Together/She Was One Of The Early Birds/That's My Weakness Now/Three O'Clock In The Morning. Let's Have Another Party: Another Little Drink/Broken Doll/Bye Bye Blackbird/Honeysuckle And The Bee/I Wonder Where My Baby Is Tonight/Lily of Laguna/Nellie Dean/Sheik of Araby/Somebody Stole My Gal/When The Red Red Robin. Let's Have a Ding Dong: Happy Days Are Here Again/Oh Johnny Oh Johnny Oh/Oh You Beautiful Doll/Ain't She Sweet/Yes We Have No Bananas/I'm Forever Blowing Bubbles/I'll Be Your Sweetheart/If These Lips Could Only Speak/Who's Taking You Home Tonight. Make It a Party: Who Were You With Last Night/Hello Hello Who's Your Lady Friend/Yes Sir That's My Baby/Don't Dilly Dally On The Way/Beer Barrel Polka/After The Ball/Peggy O'Neil/Meet Me Tonight In Dreamland/I Belong To Glasgow/Down At The Old Bull And Bush. Let's Rock 'n Roll: Singin' The Blues/Green Door/See You Later Alligator/Shake Rattle and Roll/Rock Around The Clock/Razzle Dazzle. Let's Have a Ball: Music Music Music/This Ole House/Heartbreaker/Woody Woodpecker/Last Train To San Fernando/Bring A Little Water Sylvie/Puttin' On The Style/Don't You Rock Me Daddy-O. Piano Party: Baby Face/Comin' Thru' The Rye/Annie Laurie/Little Brown Jug/Let Him Go Let Him Tarry/Put Your Arms Around Me Honey/I'll Be With You In Apple Blossom Time/Shine On Harvest Moon/Blue Skies/I'll Never Say Never Again/I'll See You In My Dreams. See also Various Artists - All Star Hit Parade.

Brian AUGER – *See Julie DRISCOLL, Brian AUGER and the TRINITY*

AURRA *US, male/female vocal duo*   **18 wks**

4 May 85	LIKE I LIKE IT 10 TEN 45	51	5 wks
19 Apr 86	YOU AND ME TONIGHT 10 TEN 71	12	8 wks
21 Jun 86	LIKE I LIKE IT (re-issue) 10 TEN 126	43	5 wks

David AUSTIN *UK, male vocalist*   **3 wks**

21 Jul 84	TURN TO GOLD Parlophone R 6068	68	3 wks

Patti AUSTIN and James INGRAM   **10 wks**
US, female/male vocal duo

12 Feb 83	BABY, COME TO ME Qwest K 15005	11	10 wks

See also James Ingram with Michael McDonald; Quincy Jones.

AUTUMN *UK, male vocal/instrumental group*   **6 wks**

16 Oct 71	MY LITTLE GIRL Pye 7N 45090	37	6 wks

Peter AUTY and the SINFONIA OF LONDON *UK, male vocalist with UK orchestra*   **9 wks**

14 Dec 85	WALKING IN THE AIR Stiff LAD 1	42	5 wks
19 Dec 87	WALKING IN THE AIR (re-issue) CBS GA 3950	37	4 wks

Label credits the Snowman featuring Peter Auty.

AVALON BOYS – *See LAUREL and HARDY with the AVALON BOYS*

Frankie AVALON *US, male vocalist*   **15 wks**

10 Oct 58	GINGERBREAD HMV POP 517	30	1 wk
24 Apr 59	VENUS HMV POP 603	16	6 wks
22 Jan 60	WHY HMV POP 688	20	4 wks
28 Apr 60	DON'T THROW AWAY ALL THOSE TEARDROPS HMV POP 727	37	4 wks

AVERAGE WHITE BAND   **45 wks**
UK, male vocal/instrumental vocal group

22 Feb 75	● PICK UP THE PIECES Atlantic K 10489	6	9 wks
26 Apr 75	CUT THE CAKE Atlantic K 10605	31	4 wks
9 Oct 76	QUEEN OF MY SOUL Atlantic K 10825	23	7 wks
28 Apr 79	WALK ON BY RCA XC 1087	46	5 wks
25 Aug 79	WHEN WILL YOU BE MINE RCA XB 1096	49	5 wks
26 Apr 80	LET'S GO ROUND AGAIN PT.1 RCA AWB 1	12	11 wks
26 Jul 80	FOR YOU FOR LOVE RCA AWB 2	46	4 wks

AVONS *UK, male/female vocal group*   **22 wks**

13 Nov 59	● SEVEN LITTLE GIRLS SITTING IN THE BACK SEAT Columbia DB 4363	3	13 wks
7 Jul 60	WE'RE ONLY YOUNG ONCE Columbia DB 4461	49	1 wk
21 Jul 60	WE'RE ONLY YOUNG ONCE (re-entry) Columbia DB 4461	45	1 wk
27 Oct 60	FOUR LITTLE HEELS Columbia DB 4522	45	2 wks
1 Dec 60	FOUR LITTLE HEELS (re-entry) Columbia DB 4522	49	1 wk
26 Jan 61	RUBBER BALL Columbia DB 4569	30	4 wks

AWESOME 3 *UK, male vocal/instrumental duo*   **3 wks**

8 Sep 90	HARD UP A & M AM 591	55	3 wks

Hoyt AXTON *US, male vocalist*   **4 wks**

7 Jun 80	DELLA AND THE DEALER Young Blood YB 82	48	4 wks

Roy AYERS *US, male vocalist/instrumentalist - vibraphone*   **7 wks**

21 Oct 78	GET ON UP, GET ON DOWN Polydor AYERS 7	41	4 wks
2 Feb 80	DON'T STOP THE FEELING Polydor STEP 6	56	3 wks

See also Roy Ayers and Wayne Henderson.

Roy AYERS and Wayne HENDERSON   **5 wks**
US, male duo, Ayers vocalist/instrumentalist - vibraphones, Henderson instrumentalist

13 Jan 79	HEAT OF THE BEAT Polydor POSP 16	43	5 wks

See also Roy Ayers.

Charles AZNAVOUR *France, male vocalist*   **29 wks**

22 Sep 73	THE OLD FASHIONED WAY Barclay BAR 20	38	15 wks
22 Jun 74	★ SHE Barclay BAR 26	1	14 wks

AZTEC CAMERA *UK, male vocal/instrumental group*   **61 wks**

19 Feb 83	OBLIVIOUS Rough Trade RT 122	47	6 wks
4 Jun 83	WALK OUT TO WINTER Rough Trade RT 132	64	4 wks
5 Nov 83	OBLIVIOUS (re-issue) WEA AZTEC 1	18	11 wks
1 Sep 84	ALL I NEED IS EVERYTHING WEA AC 1	34	6 wks
13 Feb 88	HOW MEN ARE WEA YZ 168	25	9 wks
23 Apr 88	● SOMEWHERE IN MY HEART WEA YZ 181	3	14 wks
6 Aug 88	WORKING IN A GOLDMINE WEA YZ 199	31	5 wks

8 Oct 88	DEEP AND WIDE AND TALL *WEA YZ 154*	55	3 wks
7 Jul 90	THE CRYING SCENE *WEA YZ 492*	70	3 wks

See also Aztec Camera and Mick Jones.

AZTEC CAMERA and Mick JONES   8 wks
UK, male vocal/instrumental group and male vocalist.

6 Oct 90	GOOD MORNING BRITAIN *WEA YZ 52*	19	8 wks

See also Aztec Camera.

AZYMUTH *Brazil, male instrumental group*   8 wks

12 Jan 80	JAZZ CARNIVAL *Milestone MRC 101*	19	8 wks

Bob AZZAM *Egypt, singing orchestra*   14 wks

26 May 60	MUSTAPHA *Decca F 21235*	23	14 wks

B

Derek B *UK, male rapper*   15 wks

27 Feb 88	GOODGROOVE *Music Of Life 7NOTE 12*	16	6 wks
7 May 88	BAD YOUNG BROTHER *Tuff Audio DRKB 1*	16	6 wks
2 Jul 88	WE'VE GOT THE JUICE *Tuff Audio DRKB 2*	56	3 wks

Eric B. and RAKIM *US, male vocal/instrumental duo*   20 wks

7 Nov 87	PAID IN FULL *Fourth & Broadway BRW 78*	15	6 wks
20 Feb 88	MOVE THE CROWD *Fourth & Broadway BRW 88*	53	2 wks
12 Mar 88	I KNOW YOU GOT SOUL *Cooltempo COOL 146*	13	6 wks
2 Jul 88	FOLLOW THE LEADER *MCA MCA 1256*	21	5 wks
19 Nov 88	THE MICROPHONE FIEND *MCA MCA 1300*	74	1 wk

See also Jody Watley.

JAZZIE B – *See Maxi PRIEST; SOUL II SOUL*

Tairrie B *US, female rapper*   2 wks

1 Dec 90	MURDER SHE WROTE *MCA MCA 1455*	71	2 wks

B B and Q BAND *US, male vocal/instrumental group*   15 wks

18 Jul 81	ON THE BEAT *Capitol CL 202*	41	5 wks
6 Jul 85	GENIE *Cooltempo COOL 110*	40	4 wks
20 Sep 86	(I'M A) DREAMER *Cooltempo COOL 132*	35	5 wks
17 Oct 87	RICCOCHET *Cooltempo COOL 154*	71	1 wk

Full title of act on second single was Brooklyn Bronx and Queens.

Alice BABS *Sweden, female vocalist*   1 wk

15 Aug 63	AFTER YOU'VE GONE *Fontana TF 409*	43	1 wk

BABY O *US, male/female vocal/instrumental group*   5 wks

26 Jul 80	IN THE FOREST *Calibre CAB 505*	46	5 wks

BABYS *US/UK, male vocal/instrumental group*   3 wks

21 Jan 78	ISN'T IT TIME *Chrysalis CHS 2173*	45	3 wks

BACCARA *Spain, female vocal duo*   25 wks

17 Sep 77	★ YES SIR I CAN BOOGIE *RCA PB 5526*	1	16 wks
14 Jan 78	● SORRY I'M A LADY *RCA PB 5555*	8	9 wks

Burt BACHARACH *US, orchestra and chorus*   11 wks

20 May 65	● TRAINS AND BOATS AND PLANES *London HL 9968*	4	11 wks

BACHELORS *Ireland, male vocal group*   187 wks

24 Jan 63	● CHARMAINE *Decca F 11559*	6	19 wks
4 Jul 63	FARAWAY PLACES *Decca F 11666*	36	3 wks
29 Aug 63	WHISPERING *Decca F 11712*	18	10 wks
23 Jan 64	★ DIANE *Decca F 11799*	1	19 wks
19 Mar 64	● I BELIEVE *Decca F 11857*	2	17 wks
4 Jun 64	● RAMONA *Decca F 11910*	4	13 wks
13 Aug 64	● I WOULDN'T TRADE YOU FOR THE WORLD *Decca F 11949*	4	16 wks
3 Dec 64	● NO ARMS CAN EVER HOLD YOU *Decca F 12034*	7	12 wks
1 Apr 65	TRUE LOVE FOR EVER MORE *Decca F 12108*	34	6 wks
20 May 65	● MARIE *Decca F 12156*	9	12 wks
28 Oct 65	IN THE CHAPEL IN THE MOONLIGHT *Decca F 12256*	27	10 wks
6 Jan 66	HELLO DOLLY *Decca F 12309*	38	4 wks
17 Mar 66	● THE SOUND OF SILENCE *Decca F 12351*	3	13 wks
7 Jul 66	CAN I TRUST YOU *Decca F 12417*	26	7 wks
1 Dec 66	WALK WITH FAITH IN YOUR HEART *Decca F 22523*	22	9 wks
6 Apr 67	OH HOW I MISS YOU *Decca F 22592*	30	8 wks
5 Jul 67	MARTA *Decca F 22634*	20	9 wks

BACHMAN-TURNER OVERDRIVE   18 wks
Canada, male vocal/instrumental group

16 Nov 74	● YOU AIN'T SEEN NOTHIN' YET *Mercury 6167 025*	2	12 wks
1 Feb 75	ROLL ON DOWN THE HIGHWAY *Mercury 6167 071*	22	6 wks

BACKBEAT DISCIPLES – *See Arthur BAKER*

BAD COMPANY *UK, male vocal/instrumental group*   23 wks

1 Jun 74	CAN'T GET ENOUGH *Island WIP 6191*	15	8 wks
22 Mar 75	GOOD LOVIN' GONE BAD *Island WIP 6223*	31	6 wks
30 Aug 75	FEEL LIKE MAKIN' LOVE *Island WIP 6242*	20	9 wks

BAD ENGLISH *UK/US, male vocal/instrumental group*   3 wks

25 Nov 89	WHEN I SEE YOU SMILE *Epic 655347 1*	61	3 wks

BAD MANNERS *UK, male vocal/instrumental group*   111 wks

1 Mar 80	NE-NE NA-NA NA-NA NU-NU *Magnet MAG 164*	28	14 wks
14 Jun 80	LIP UP FATTY *Magnet MAG 175*	15	14 wks
27 Sep 80	● SPECIAL BREW *Magnet MAG 180*	3	13 wks
6 Dec 80	LORRAINE *Magnet MAG 181*	21	12 wks
28 Mar 81	JUST A FEELING *Magnet MAG 187*	13	9 wks
27 Jun 81	● CAN CAN *Magnet MAG 190*	3	13 wks
26 Sep 81	● WALKING IN THE SUNSHINE *Magnet MAG 197*	10	9 wks
21 Nov 81	BUONA SERA *Magnet MAG 211*	34	9 wks
1 May 82	GOT NO BRAINS *Magnet MAG 216*	44	5 wks
31 Jul 82	● MY GIRL LOLLIPOP (MY BOY LOLLIPOP) *Magnet MAG 232*	9	7 wks
30 Oct 82	SAMSON AND DELILAH *Magnet MAG 236*	58	3 wks

| 14 May 83 | THAT'LL DO NICELY *Magnet MAG 243* | 49 | 3 wks |

BAD NEWS *UK, male vocal group*   **5 wks**

| 12 Sep 87 | BOHEMIAN RHAPSODY *EMI EM 24* | 44 | 5 wks |

Bad News are most the Young Ones under another name. See also Cliff Richard and the Young Ones.

Wally BADAROU *France, male instrumentalist - keyboards*   **6 wks**

| 19 Oct 85 | CHIEF INSPECTOR *Fourth & Broadway BRW 37* | 46 | 6 wks |

Karen BADDINGTON and Mark WILLIAMS   **1 wk**
Australia, female/male vocal duo

| 2 Sep 89 | HOME AND AWAY *First Night SCORE 19* | 73 | 1 wk |

BADFINGER *UK, male vocal/instrumental group*   **34 wks**

10 Jan 70	● COME AND GET IT *Apple 20*	4	11 wks
9 Jan 71	● NO MATTER WHAT *Apple 31*	5	12 wks
29 Jan 72	● DAY AFTER DAY *Apple 40*	10	11 wks

Joan BAEZ *US, female vocalist*   **47 wks**

6 May 65	WE SHALL OVERCOME *Fontana TF 564*	26	10 wks
8 Jul 65	● THERE BUT FOR FORTUNE *Fontana TF 587*	8	12 wks
2 Sep 65	IT'S ALL OVER NOW BABY BLUE *Fontana TF 604*	22	8 wks
23 Dec 65	FAREWELL ANGELINA *Fontana TF 639*	35	3 wks
20 Jan 66	FAREWELL ANGELINA (re-entry) *Fontana TF 639*	49	1 wk
28 Jul 66	PACK UP YOUR SORROWS *Fontana TF 727*	50	1 wk
9 Oct 71	● THE NIGHT THEY DROVE OLD DIXIE DOWN *Vanguard VS 35138*	6	12 wks

Philip BAILEY *US, male vocalist*   **20 wks**

| 9 Mar 85 | ★ EASY LOVER *CBS A 4915* | 1 | 12 wks |
| 18 May 85 | WALKING ON THE CHINESE WALL *CBS A 6202* | 34 | 8 wks |

First entry was a duet with Phil Collins. See also Phil Collins.

Adrian BAKER *UK, male vocalist*   **8 wks**

| 19 Jul 75 | ● SHERRY *Magnet MAG 34* | 10 | 8 wks |

Anita BAKER *US, female vocalist*   **20 wks**

15 Nov 86	SWEET LOVE *Elektra EKR 44*	13	10 wks
31 Jan 87	CAUGHT UP IN THE RAPTURE *Elektra EKR 49*	51	5 wks
8 Oct 88	GIVING YOU THE BEST THAT I GOT *Elektra EKR 79*	55	3 wks
30 Jun 90	TALK TO ME *Elektra EKR 111*	68	2 wks

Arthur BAKER *US, male producer/multi-instrumentalist*   **7 wks**

| 20 May 89 | IT'S YOUR TIME *Breakout USA 654* | 64 | 2 wks |
| 21 Oct 89 | THE MESSAGE IS LOVE *Breakout USA 668* | 38 | 5 wks |

It's Your Time features Shirley Lewis - US, female vocalist; The Message Is Love credits the Backbeat Disciples and features Al Green. See also Al Green; Criminal Element Orchestra; Wally Jump Jr. and the Criminal Element.

Hylda BAKER and Arthur MULLARD   **6 wks**
UK, female/male vocal duo

| 9 Sep 78 | YOU'RE THE ONE THAT I WANT *Pye 7N 46121* | 22 | 6 wks |

George BAKER SELECTION   **10 wks**
Holland, male/female vocal/instrumental group

| 6 Sep 75 | ● PALOMA BLANCA *Warner Bros. K 16541* | 10 | 10 wks |

BALAAM AND THE ANGEL   **2 wks**
UK, male vocal/instrumental group

| 29 Mar 86 | SHE KNOWS *Virgin VS 842* | 70 | 2 wks |

Long John BALDRY *UK, male vocalist*   **36 wks**

8 Nov 67	★ LET THE HEARTACHES BEGIN *Pye 7N 17385*	1	13 wks
28 Aug 68	WHEN THE SUN COMES SHININ' THRU *Pye 7N 17593*	29	7 wks
23 Oct 68	MEXICO *Pye 7N 17563*	15	8 wks
29 Jan 69	IT'S TOO LATE NOW *Pye 7N 17664*	21	8 wks

Kenny BALL and his JAZZMEN   **136 wks**
UK, male jazz band, Kenny Ball vocals and trumpet

23 Feb 61	SAMANTHA *Pye Jazz Today 7NJ 2040*	13	15 wks
11 May 61	I STILL LOVE YOU ALL *Pye Jazz 7NJ 2042*	24	6 wks
31 May 61	SOMEDAY *Pye Jazz 7NJ 2047*	28	6 wks
9 Nov 61	● MIDNIGHT IN MOSCOW *Pye Jazz 7NJ 2049*	2	21 wks
15 Feb 62	● MARCH OF THE SIAMESE CHILDREN *Pye Jazz 7NJ 2051*	4	13 wks
17 May 62	● THE GREEN LEAVES OF SUMMER *Pye Jazz 7NJ 2054*	7	14 wks
23 Aug 62	SO DO I *Pye Jazz 7NJ 2056*	14	8 wks
18 Oct 62	THE PAY OFF *Pye Jazz 7NJ 2061*	23	6 wks
17 Jan 63	● SUKIYAKI *Pye Jazz 7NJ 2062*	10	13 wks
25 Apr 63	CASABLANCA *Pye Jazz 7NJ 2064*	21	11 wks
13 Jun 63	RONDO *Pye Jazz 7NJ 2065*	24	8 wks
22 Aug 63	ACAPULCO 1922 *Pye Jazz 7NJ 2067*	27	6 wks
11 Jun 64	HELLO DOLLY *Pye Jazz 7NJ 2071*	30	7 wks
19 Jul 67	WHEN I'M 64 *Pye 7N 17348*	43	2 wks

Michael BALL *UK, male vocalist*   **14 wks**

| 28 Jan 89 | ● LOVE CHANGES EVERYTHING *Really Useful RUR 3* | 2 | 14 wks |

See also Michael Ball and Diana Morrison.

Michael BALL and Diana MORRISON   **2 wks**
UK, male/female vocal duo

| 28 Oct 89 | THE FIRST MAN YOU REMEMBER *Really Useful RUR 6* | 68 | 2 wks |

See also Michael Ball.

BALTIMORA *Ireland, male vocalist*   **12 wks**

| 10 Aug 85 | ● TARZAN BOY *Columbia DB 9102* | 3 | 12 wks |

BAM BAM *US, male vocalist/multi-instrumentalist*   **2 wks**

| 19 Mar 88 | GIVE IT TO ME *Serious 7OUS 10* | 65 | 2 wks |

Afrika BAMBAATAA and James BROWN   **5 wks**
US, male vocal duo

1 Sep 84	UNITY (PART 1 - THE THIRD COMING) *Tommy Boy AFR 2*	49	5 wks

See also Afrika Bambaataa and the Soul Sonic Force; Time Zone; Afrika Bambaataa with UB40 and Family; James Brown.

Afrika BAMBAATAA and the SOUL SONIC FORCE   **7 wks**
US, male vocalist and male vocal/instrumental backing group

28 Aug 82	PLANET ROCK *Polydor POSP 497*	53	3 wks
10 Mar 84	RENEGADES OF FUNK *Tommy Boy AFR 1*	30	4 wks

Afrika BAMBAATAA with UB40 and FAMILY   **8 wks**
US, male vocalist with UK, male vocal/instrumental group and US, instrumental group

27 Feb 88	RECKLESS *EMI EM 41*	17	8 wks

See also UB40.

BANANARAMA *UK, female vocal group*   **161 wks**

10 Apr 82	● REALLY SAYING SOMETHING *Deram NANA 1*	5	10 wks
3 Jul 82	● SHY BOY *London NANA 2*	4	11 wks
4 Dec 82	CHEERS THEN *London NANA 3*	45	7 wks
26 Feb 83	NA NA HEY HEY KISS HIM GOODBYE *London NANA 4*	5	10 wks
9 Jul 83	● CRUEL SUMMER *London NANA 5*	8	10 wks
3 Mar 84	● ROBERT DE NIRO'S WAITING *London NANA 6*	3	11 wks
26 May 84	ROUGH JUSTICE *London NANA 7*	23	7 wks
24 Nov 84	HOTLINE TO HEAVEN *London NANA 8*	58	2 wks
24 Aug 85	DO NOT DISTURB *London NANA 9*	31	6 wks
31 May 86	● VENUS *London NANA 10*	8	13 wks
16 Aug 86	MORE THAN PHYSICAL *London NANA 11*	41	5 wks
14 Feb 87	TRICK OF THE NIGHT *London NANA 12*	32	5 wks
11 Jul 87	I HEARD A RUMOUR *London NANA 13*	14	9 wks
10 Oct 87	● LOVE IN THE FIRST DEGREE *London NANA 14*	3	12 wks
9 Jan 88	I CAN'T HELP IT *London NANA 15*	20	6 wks
9 Apr 88	● I WANT YOU BACK *London NANA 16*	5	10 wks
24 Sep 88	LOVE, TRUTH AND HONESTY *London NANA 17*	23	8 wks
19 Nov 88	NATHAN JONES *London NANA 18*	15	9 wks
10 Jun 89	CRUEL SUMMER (re-mix) *London NANA 19*	19	6 wks
28 Jul 90	ONLY YOUR LOVE *London NANA 21*	27	4 wks

Really Saying Something credited to Bananarama with Funboy Three. The listed flip side of Love In The First Degree was Mr Sleaze by Stock Aitken Waterman. See also Stock Aitken Waterman; Funboy Three; Funboy Three and Bananarama; Bananarama/La Na Nee Nee Noo Noo.

BANANARAMA/ LA NA NEE NEE NOO NOO *UK, female vocal groups*   **9 wks**

25 Feb 89	● HELP *London LON 222*	3	9 wks

See also Bananarama.

BAND *Canada, male vocal/instrumental group*   **18 wks**

18 Sep 68	THE WEIGHT *Capitol CL 15559*	21	9 wks
4 Apr 70	RAG MAMA RAG *Capitol CL 15629*	16	9 wks

BAND AID *International, male/female vocal/instrumental group*   **26 wks**

15 Dec 84	★ DO THEY KNOW IT'S CHRISTMAS? *Mercury FEED 1*	1	13 wks
7 Dec 85	● DO THEY KNOW IT'S CHRISTMAS? (re-entry) *Mercury FEED 1*	3	7 wks
23 Dec 89	★ DO THEY KNOW IT'S CHRISTMAS? *PWL/Polydor FEED 2*	1	6 wks

FEED 2 credited to Band Aid II.

BAND AKA *US, male vocal/instrumental group*   **12 wks**

15 May 82	GRACE *Epic EPC A 2376*	41	5 wks
5 Mar 83	JOY *Epic EPC A 3145*	24	7 wks

BAND OF GOLD   **11 wks**
Holland, male/female vocal/instrumental group

14 Jul 84	LOVE SONGS ARE BACK AGAIN (MEDLEY) *RCA 428*	24	11 wks

BANDWAGON – *See Johnny JOHNSON and the BANDWAGON*

Honey BANE *UK, female vocalist*   **8 wks**

24 Jan 81	TURN ME ON TURN ME OFF *Zonophone Z 15*	37	5 wks
18 Apr 81	BABY LOVE *Zonophone Z 19*	58	3 wks

BANG *UK, male vocal duo*   **2 wks**

6 May 89	YOU'RE THE ONE *RCA PB 42715*	74	2 wks

BANGLES *US, female vocal/instrumental group*   **94 wks**

15 Feb 86	● MANIC MONDAY *CBS A 6796*	2	12 wks
26 Apr 86	IF SHE KNEW WHAT SHE WANTS *CBS A 7062*	31	7 wks
5 Jul 86	GOING DOWN TO LIVERPOOL *CBS A 7255*	56	3 wks
13 Sep 86	● WALK LIKE AN EGYPTIAN *CBS 650071 7*	3	19 wks
10 Jan 87	WALKING DOWN YOUR STREET *CBS BANGS 1*	16	6 wks
18 Apr 87	FOLLOWING *CBS BANGS 2*	55	3 wks
6 Feb 88	HAZY SHADE OF WINTER *Def Jam BANGS 3*	11	10 wks
5 Nov 88	IN YOUR ROOM *CBS BANGS 4*	35	6 wks
18 Feb 89	★ ETERNAL FLAME *CBS BANGS 5*	1	18 wks
10 Jun 89	BE WITH YOU *CBS BANGS 6*	23	8 wks
14 Oct 89	I'LL SET YOU FREE *CBS BANGS 7*	74	1 wk
9 Jun 90	WALK LIKE AN EGYPTIAN (re-issue) *CBS BANGS 8*	73	1 wk

BANNED *UK, male vocal/instrumental group*   **6 wks**

17 Dec 77	LITTLE GIRL *Harvest HAR 5145*	36	6 wks

BANSHEES – *See SIOUXSIE and the BANSHEES*

BAR-KAYS *US, male vocal/instrumental group*   **15 wks**

23 Aug 67	SOUL FINGER *Stax 601 014*	33	7 wks
22 Jan 77	SHAKE YOUR RUMP TO THE FUNK *Mercury 6167 417*	41	4 wks
12 Jan 85	SEXOMATIC *Club JAB 10*	51	4 wks

Chris BARBER'S JAZZ BAND   **30 wks**
UK, male jazz band, Chris Barber trombone

13 Feb 59	● PETITE FLEUR *Pye Nixa NJ 2026*	3	22 wks
31 Jul 59	PETITE FLEUR (re-entry) *Pye Nixa NJ 2026*	22	2 wks

9 Oct 59	LONESOME Columbia DB 4333	27	2 wks
4 Jan 62	REVIVAL Columbia SCD 2166	50	2 wks
1 Feb 62	REVIVAL (re-entry) Columbia SCD 2166	43	2 wks

BARBRA and NEIL US, female/male vocal duo   12 wks

25 Nov 78	● YOU DON'T BRING ME FLOWERS CBS 6803	5	12 wks

Barbra and Neil are Barbra Streisand and Neil Diamond. See also Barbra Streisand; Neil Diamond.

BARCLAY JAMES HARVEST   9 wks
UK, male vocal/instrumental group

2 Apr 77	LIVE (EP) Polydor 2229 198	49	1 wk
16 Apr 77	LIVE (EP) (re-entry) Polydor 2229 198	49	1 wk
26 Jan 80	LOVE ON THE LINE Polydor POSP 97	63	2 wks
22 Nov 80	LIFE IS FOR LIVING Polydor POSP 195	61	3 wks
21 May 83	JUST A DAY AWAY Polydor POSP 585	68	2 wks

Tracks on Live EP: Rock'n'Roll Star/Medicine Man (Parts 1 & 2).

BARDO UK, male/female vocal duo   8 wks

10 Apr 82	● ONE STEP FURTHER Epic EPC A2265	2	8 wks

BARNBRACK UK, male vocal/instrumental group   7 wks

16 Mar 85	BELFAST Homespun HS 092	45	7 wks

Richard BARNES UK, male vocalist   10 wks

23 May 70	TAKE TO THE MOUNTAINS Philips BF 1840	35	6 wks
24 Oct 70	GO NORTH Philips 6006 039	49	1 wk
7 Nov 70	GO NORTH (re-entry) Philips 6006 039	38	3 wks

BARRACUDAS UK/US, male vocal/instrumental group   6 wks

16 Aug 80	SUMMER FUN EMI-Wipe Out Z 5	37	6 wks

Wild Willy BARRETT – *See John OTWAY and Wild Willy BARRETT*

J. J. BARRIE Canada, male vocalist   11 wks

24 Apr 76	★ NO CHARGE Power Exchange PX 209	1	11 wks

Ken BARRIE UK, male vocalist   15 wks

10 Jul 82	POSTMAN PAT Post Music PP 001	44	8 wks
25 Dec 82	POSTMAN PAT (re-entry) Post Music PP 001	54	3 wks
24 Dec 83	POSTMAN PAT (2nd re-entry) Post Music PP 001	59	4 wks

BARRON KNIGHTS UK, male vocal/instrumental group   94 wks

9 Jul 64	● CALL UP THE GROUPS Columbia DB 7317	3	13 wks
22 Oct 64	COME TO THE DANCE Columbia DB 7375	42	2 wks
25 Mar 65	● POP GO THE WORKERS Columbia DB 7525	5	13 wks
16 Dec 65	● MERRY GENTLE POPS Columbia DB 7780	9	7 wks
1 Dec 66	UNDER NEW MANAGEMENT Columbia DB 8071	15	9 wks
23 Oct 68	AN OLYMPIC RECORD Columbia DB 8485	35	4 wks
29 Oct 77	● LIVE IN TROUBLE Epic EPC 5752	7	10 wks
2 Dec 78	● A TASTE OF AGGRO Epic EPC 6829	3	10 wks
8 Dec 79	FOOD FOR THOUGHT Epic EPC 8011	46	6 wks
4 Oct 80	THE SIT SONG Epic EPC 8994	44	4 wks
6 Dec 80	NEVER MIND THE PRESENTS Epic EPC 9070	17	8 wks
5 Dec 81	BLACKBOARD JUMBLE CBS A 1795	52	5 wks
19 Mar 83	BUFFALO BILL'S LAST SCRATCH Epic EPC A 3208	49	3 wks

Joe BARRY US, male vocalist   1 wk

24 Aug 61	I'M A FOOL TO CARE Mercury AMT 1149	49	1 wk

John BARRY UK, male instrumental group/orchestra   78 wks

10 Mar 60	● HIT AND MISS Columbia DB 4414	10	12 wks
28 Apr 60	BEAT FOR BEATNIKS Columbia DB 4446	40	2 wks
9 Jun 60	HIT AND MISS (re-entry) Columbia DB 4414	45	1 wk
14 Jul 60	NEVER LET GO Columbia DB 4480	49	1 wk
18 Aug 60	BLUEBERRY HILL Columbia DB 4480	34	3 wks
8 Sep 60	WALK DON'T RUN Columbia DB 4505	49	1 wk
22 Sep 60	WALK DON'T RUN (re-entry) Columbia DB 4505	11	13 wks
8 Dec 60	BLACK STOCKINGS Columbia DB 4554	27	9 wks
2 Mar 61	THE MAGNIFICENT SEVEN Columbia DB 4598	48	1 wk
16 Mar 61	THE MAGNIFICENT SEVEN (re-entry) Columbia DB 4598	45	2 wks
6 Apr 61	THE MAGNIFICENT SEVEN (2nd re-entry) Columbia DB 4598	50	1 wk
8 Jun 61	THE MAGNIFICENT SEVEN (3rd re-entry) Columbia DB 4598	47	1 wk
26 Apr 62	CUTTY SARK Columbia DB 4806	35	2 wks
1 Nov 62	JAMES BOND THEME Columbia DB 4898	13	11 wks
21 Nov 63	FROM RUSSIA WITH LOVE Ember S 181	44	1 wk
19 Dec 63	FROM RUSSIA WITH LOVE (re-entry) Ember S 181	39	2 wks
11 Dec 71	THE PERSUADERS CBS 7469	13	15 wks

Billed as the John Barry Seven on Hit and Miss, Walk Don't Run, Black Stockings, The Magnificent Seven and Cutty Sark. Others John Barry Orchestra.

Len BARRY US, male vocalist   24 wks

4 Nov 65	● 1-2-3 Brunswick 05942	3	14 wks
13 Jan 66	● LIKE A BABY Brunswick 05949	10	10 wks

Lionel BART UK, male vocalist   3 wks

25 Nov 89	HAPPY ENDINGS (GIVE YOURSELF A PINCH) EMI EM 121	68	1 wk
23 Dec 89	HAPPY ENDINGS (GIVE YOUSELF A PINCH) (re-entry) EMI EM 121	71	2 wks

BAS NOIR US, female vocal duo   1 wk

11 Feb 89	MY LOVE IS MAGIC 10 TEN 257	73	1 wk

Rob BASE and D.J. E-Z ROCK US, male vocal duo   19 wks

16 Apr 88	IT TAKES TWO Citybeat CBE 724	24	6 wks
14 Jan 89	GET ON THE DANCE FLOOR Supreme SUPE 139	14	7 wks
4 Mar 89	IT TAKES TWO (re-entry) Citybeat CBE7 24	49	3 wks
22 Apr 89	JOY AND PAIN Supreme SUPE 143	47	3 wks

BASIA Poland, female vocalist   7 wks

23 Jan 88	PROMISES Epic BASH 4	48	4 wks
28 May 88	TIME AND TIDE Epic BASH 5	61	3 wks

See also Matt Bianco.

Count BASIE – *See Frank SINATRA*

Toni BASIL US, female vocalist   16 wks

6 Feb 82	● MICKEY Radialchoice TIC 4	2	12 wks
1 May 82	NOBODY Radialchoice TIC 2	52	4 wks

Alfie BASS – *See Michael MEDWIN, Bernard BRESSLAW, Alfie BASS and Leslie FYSON*

Fontella BASS US, female vocalist   **15 wks**

| 2 Dec 65 | | RESCUE ME Chess CRS 8023 | 11 | 10 wks |
| 20 Jan 66 | | RECOVERY Chess CRS 8027 | 32 | 5 wks |

BASS-O-MATIC UK, male multi-instrumentalist   **16 wks**

12 May 90		IN THE REALM OF THE SENSES Virgin VS 1265	66	3 wks
1 Sep 90	●	FASCINATING RHYTHM Virgin VS 1274	9	11 wks
22 Dec 90		EASE ON BY Virgin VS 1295	61†	2 wks

Shirley BASSEY UK, female vocalist   **313 wks**

15 Feb 57	●	BANANA BOAT SONG Philips PB 668	8	10 wks
23 Aug 57		FIRE DOWN BELOW Philips PB 723	30	1 wk
6 Sep 57		YOU YOU ROMEO Philips PB 723	29	2 wks
19 Dec 58		AS I LOVE YOU Philips PB 845	27	2 wks
26 Dec 58	●	KISS ME HONEY HONEY KISS ME Philips PB 860	3	17 wks
9 Jan 59	★	AS I LOVE YOU (re-entry) Philips PB 845	1	17 wks
31 Mar 60		WITH THESE HANDS Columbia DB 4421	38	2 wks
21 Apr 60		WITH THESE HANDS (re-entry) Columbia DB 4421	31	2 wks
12 May 60		WITH THESE HANDS (2nd re-entry) Columbia DB 4421	41	2 wks
4 Aug 60	●	AS LONG AS HE NEEDS ME Columbia DB 4490	2	30 wks
11 May 61	●	YOU'LL NEVER KNOW Columbia DB 4643	6	17 wks
27 Jul 61	★	REACH FOR THE STARS/ CLIMB EV'RY MOUNTAIN Columbia DB 4685	1	16 wks
23 Nov 61	●	I'LL GET BY Columbia DB 4737	10	8 wks
23 Nov 61		REACH FOR THE STARS/ CLIMB EV'RY MOUNTAIN (re-entry) Columbia DB 4685	40	2 wks
15 Feb 62		TONIGHT Columbia DB 4777	21	8 wks
26 Apr 62		AVE MARIA Columbia DB 4816	34	4 wks
31 May 62		FAR AWAY Columbia DB 4836	24	13 wks
30 Aug 62	●	WHAT NOW MY LOVE Columbia DB 4882	5	17 wks
28 Feb 63		WHAT KIND OF FOOL AM I? Columbia DB 4974	47	2 wks
26 Sep 63	●	I (WHO HAVE NOTHING) Columbia DB 7113	6	20 wks
23 Jan 64		MY SPECIAL DREAM Columbia DB 7185	32	7 wks
9 Apr 64		GONE Columbia DB 7248	36	5 wks
15 Oct 64		GOLDFINGER Columbia DB 7360	21	9 wks
20 May 65		NO REGRETS Columbia DB 7535	39	4 wks
11 Oct 67		BIG SPENDER United Artists UP 1192	21	15 wks
20 Jun 70	●	SOMETHING United Artists UP 35125	4	21 wks
2 Jan 71		THE FOOL ON THE HILL United Artists UP 35156	48	1 wk
23 Jan 71		SOMETHING (re-entry) United Artists UP 35125	50	1 wk
27 Mar 71		(WHERE DO I BEGIN) LOVE STORY United Artists UP 35194	34	9 wks
7 Aug 71		FOR ALL WE KNOW United Artists UP 35267	46	1 wk
21 Aug 71	●	FOR ALL WE KNOW (re-entry) United Artists UP 35267	6	23 wks
15 Jan 72		DIAMONDS ARE FOREVER United Artists UP 35293	38	6 wks
3 Mar 73	●	NEVER NEVER NEVER United Artists UP 35490	8	18 wks
14 Jul 73		NEVER NEVER NEVER (re-entry) United Artists UP 35490	48	1 wk

See also Yello.

Mike BATT UK, male vocalist   **8 wks**

| 16 Aug 75 | ● | SUMMERTIME CITY Epic EPC 3460 | 4 | 8 wks |

Mike Batt is, among other things, the voice behind the Wombles - see Wombles. On this hit, billed as Mike Batt (with the New Edition).

BAUHAUS UK, male vocal/instrumental group   **35 wks**

18 Apr 81		KICK IN THE EYE Beggars Banquet BEG 54	59	3 wks
4 Jul 81		THE PASSIONS OF LOVERS Beggars Banquet BEG 59	56	2 wks
6 Mar 82		KICK IN THE EYE (EP) Beggars Banquet BEG 74	45	4 wks
19 Jun 82		SPIRIT Beggars Banquet BEG 79	42	5 wks
9 Oct 82		ZIGGY STARDUST Beggars Banquet BEG 83	15	7 wks
22 Jan 83		LAGARTIJA NICK Beggars Banquet BEG 88	44	4 wks
9 Apr 83		SHE'S IN PARTIES Beggars Banquet BEG 91	26	6 wks

| 29 Oct 83 | | THE SINGLES 1981-83 Beggars Banquet BEG 100E | 52 | 4 wks |

Tracks on Kick In The Eye EP: Kick In The Eye (Searching For Satori)/Harry/Earwax.

Les BAXTER US, orchestra and chorus   **9 wks**

| 13 May 55 | ● | UNCHAINED MELODY Capitol CL 14257 | 10 | 9 wks |

BAY CITY ROLLERS UK, male vocal/instrumental group   **113 wks**

18 Sep 71	●	KEEP ON DANCING Bell 1164	9	13 wks
9 Feb 74	●	REMEMBER (SHA-LA-LA) Bell 1338	6	12 wks
27 Apr 74	●	SHANG-A-LANG Bell 1355	2	10 wks
27 Jul 74	●	SUMMERLOVE SENSATION Bell 1369	3	10 wks
12 Oct 74	●	ALL OF ME LOVES ALL OF YOU Bell 1382	4	10 wks
8 Mar 75	★	BYE BYE BABY Bell 1409	1	16 wks
12 Jul 75	★	GIVE A LITTLE LOVE Bell 1425	1	9 wks
22 Nov 75	●	MONEY HONEY Bell 1461	3	9 wks
10 Apr 76	●	LOVE ME LIKE I LOVE YOU Bell 1477	4	6 wks
11 Sep 76	●	I ONLY WANNA BE WITH YOU Bell 1493	4	9 wks
7 May 77		IT'S A GAME Arista 108	16	6 wks
30 Jul 77		YOU MADE ME BELIEVE IN MAGIC Arista 127	34	3 wks

BBG UK, male vocal/instrumental group   **7 wks**

| 28 Apr 90 | | SNAPPINESS Urban URB 54 | 28 | 5 wks |
| 11 Aug 90 | | SOME KIND OF HEAVEN Urban URB 59 | 65 | 2 wks |

BE BOP DELUXE UK, male vocal/instrumental group   **13 wks**

| 21 Feb 76 | | SHIPS IN THE NIGHT Harvest HAR 5104 | 23 | 8 wks |
| 13 Nov 76 | | HOT VALVES (EP) Harvest HAR 5117 | 36 | 5 wks |

Hot Valves EP contains the following tracks: Maid In Heaven/Blazing Apostles/Jet Silver And The Dolls Of Venus/Bring Back The Spark.

BEACH BOYS US, male vocal/instrumental group   **263 wks**

1 Aug 63		SURFIN' USA Capitol CL 15305	34	7 wks
9 Jul 64	●	I GET AROUND Capitol CL 15350	7	13 wks
29 Oct 64		WHEN I GROW UP (TO BE A MAN) Capitol CL 15361	44	2 wks
19 Nov 64		WHEN I GROW UP (TO BE A MAN) (re-entry) Capitol CL 15361	27	5 wks
21 Jan 65		DANCE DANCE DANCE Capitol CL 15370	24	6 wks
3 Jun 65		HELP ME RHONDA Capitol CL 15392	27	10 wks
2 Sep 65		CALIFORNIA GIRLS Capitol CL 15409	26	8 wks
17 Feb 66	●	BARBARA ANN Capitol CL 15432	3	10 wks
21 Apr 66	●	SLOOP JOHN B Capitol CL 15441	2	15 wks
28 Jul 66	●	GOD ONLY KNOWS Capitol CL 15459	2	14 wks
3 Nov 66	★	GOOD VIBRATIONS Capitol CL 15475	1	13 wks
4 May 67	●	THEN I KISSED HER Capitol CL 15502	4	11 wks
23 Aug 67		HEROES AND VILLAINS Capitol CL 15510	8	9 wks
22 Nov 67		WILD HONEY Capitol CL 15521	29	6 wks
17 Jan 68		DARLIN' Capitol CL 15527	11	14 wks
8 May 68		FRIENDS Capitol CL 15545	25	7 wks
24 Jul 68	★	DO IT AGAIN Capitol CL 15554	1	14 wks
25 Dec 68		BLUEBIRDS OVER THE MOUNTAIN Capitol CL 15572	33	5 wks
26 Feb 69	●	I CAN HEAR MUSIC Capitol CL 15584	10	13 wks
11 Jun 69		BREAK AWAY Capitol CL 15598	6	11 wks
16 May 70	●	COTTONFIELDS Capitol CL 15640	5	17 wks
3 Mar 73		CALIFORNIA SAGA - CALIFORNIA Reprise K 14232	37	5 wks
3 Jul 76		GOOD VIBRATIONS (re-issue) Capitol CL 15875	18	7 wks
10 Jul 76		ROCK AND ROLL MUSIC Reprise K 14440	36	4 wks
31 Mar 79		HERE COMES THE NIGHT Caribou CRB 7204	37	8 wks
16 Jun 79	●	LADY LYNDA Caribou CRB 7427	6	11 wks
29 Sep 79		SUMAHAMA Caribou CRB 7846	45	4 wks
29 Aug 81		BEACH BOYS MEDLEY Capitol CL 213	47	4 wks
19 Nov 88		KOKOMO Elektra EKR 85	25	9 wks
2 Jun 90		WOULDN'T IT BE NICE Capitol CL 579	58	1 wk

See also Fat Boys.

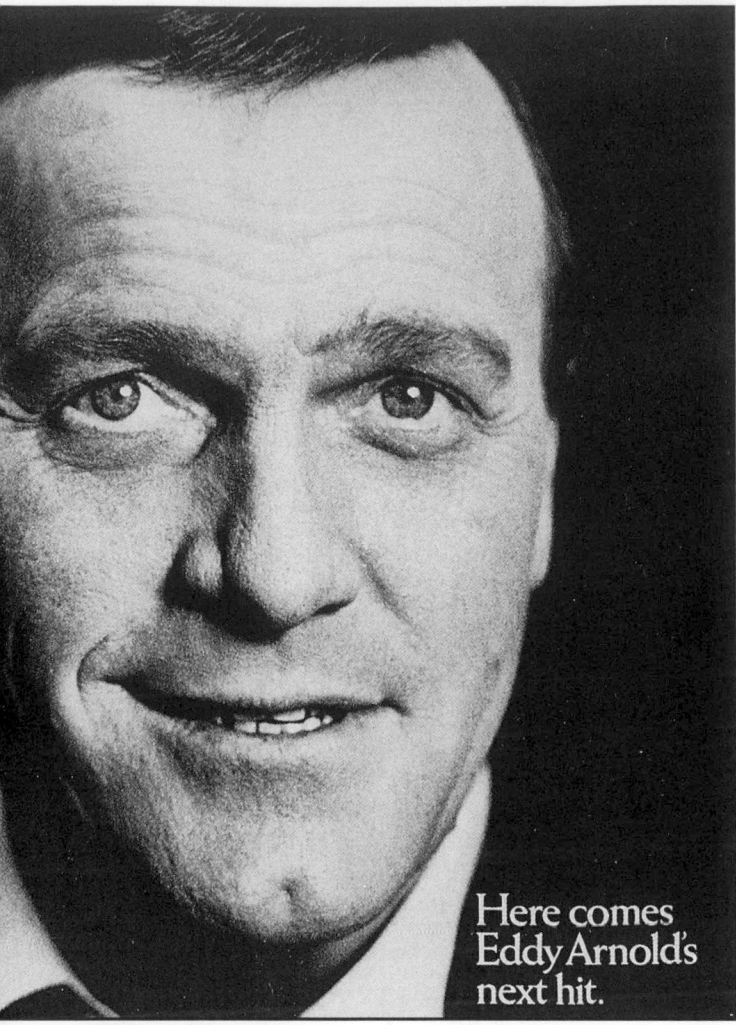

Here comes
Eddy Arnold's
next hit.

HELLO GOODBYE

Far Left: The world has been waiting for the next hit by country giant EDDY ARNOLD since 1966.

THE BEATLES were at their psychedelic peak in advertising their Christmas 1967 number one.

The original version of the number one by BEATS INTERNATIONAL had been the biggest hit for the S. O. S. Band.

BEAKY – *See Dave DEE, DOZY, BEAKY, MICK and TICH*

Walter BEASLEY *US, male vocalist* **3 wks**

23 Jan 88	I'M SO HAPPY *Urban URB 14*	70	3 wks

BEASTIE BOYS *US, male rap group* **30 wks**

28 Feb 87	(YOU GOTTA) FIGHT FOR YOUR RIGHT (TO PARTY) *Def Jam 650418 7*	11	11 wks
30 May 87	NO SLEEP TILL BROOKLYN *Def Jam BEAST 1*	14	7 wks
18 Jul 87	● SHE'S ON IT *Def Jam BEAST 2*	10	8 wks
3 Oct 87	GIRLS / SHE'S CRAFTY *Def Jam BEAST 3*	34	4 wks

BEAT *UK, male vocal/instrumental group* **90 wks**

8 Dec 79	● TEARS OF A CLOWN/ RANKING FULL STOP *2 Tone CHS TT 6*	6	11 wks
23 Feb 80	● HANDS OFF - SHE'S MINE *Go Feet FEET 1*	9	9 wks
3 May 80	● MIRROR IN THE BATHROOM *Go Feet FEET 2*	4	9 wks
16 Aug 80	BEST FRIEND/ STAND DOWN MARGARET (DUB) *Go Feet FEET 3*	22	9 wks
13 Dec 80	● TOO NICE TO TALK TO *Go Feet FEET 4*	7	11 wks
18 Apr 81	DROWNING/ ALL OUT TO GET YOU *Go Feet FEET 6*	22	8 wks
20 Jun 81	DOORS OF YOUR HEART *Go Feet FEET 9*	33	6 wks
5 Dec 81	HIT IT *Go Feet FEET 11*	70	2 wks
17 Apr 82	SAVE IT FOR LATER *Go Feet FEET 333*	47	4 wks
18 Sep 82	JEANETTE *Go Feet FEET 15*	45	3 wks
4 Dec 82	I CONFESS *Go Feet FEET 16*	54	3 wks
30 Apr 83	● CAN'T GET USED TO LOSING YOU *Go Feet FEET 17*	3	11 wks
2 Jul 83	ACKEE 1-2-3 *Go Feet FEET 18*	54	4 wks

BEAT SYSTEM *UK, male vocal/instrumental group* **2 wks**

3 Mar 90	WALK ON THE WILD SIDE *Fourth & Broadway BRW 163*	63	2 wks

BEATLES *UK, male vocal/instrumental group* **432 wks**

11 Oct 62	LOVE ME DO *Parlophone R 4949*	17	18 wks
17 Jan 63	● PLEASE PLEASE ME *Parlophone R 4983*	2	18 wks
18 Apr 63	★ FROM ME TO YOU *Parlophone R 5015*	1	21 wks
29 Aug 63	★ SHE LOVES YOU *Parlophone R 5055*	1	31 wks
5 Dec 63	★ I WANT TO HOLD YOUR HAND *Parlophone R 5084*	1	21 wks
26 Mar 64	★ CAN'T BUY ME LOVE *Parlophone R 5114*	1	14 wks
9 Apr 64	SHE LOVES YOU (re-entry) *Parlophone R 5055*	42	2 wks
14 May 64	I WANT TO HOLD YOUR HAND (re-entry) *Parlophone R 5084*	48	1 wk
11 Jun 64	AIN'T SHE SWEET *Polydor 52 317*	29	6 wks
9 Jul 64	CAN'T BUY ME LOVE (re-entry) *Parlophone R 5114*	47	1 wk
16 Jul 64	★ A HARD DAY'S NIGHT *Parlophone R 5160*	1	13 wks
3 Dec 64	★ I FEEL FINE *Parlophone R 5200*	1	13 wks
15 Apr 65	★ TICKET TO RIDE *Parlophone R 5265*	1	12 wks
29 Jul 65	★ HELP! *Parlophone R 5305*	1	14 wks
9 Dec 65	★ DAY TRIPPER/ WE CAN WORK IT OUT *Parlophone R 5389*	1	12 wks
16 Jun 66	★ PAPERBACK WRITER *Parlophone R 5452*	1	11 wks
11 Aug 66	★ YELLOW SUBMARINE/ ELEANOR RIGBY *Parlophone R 5493*	1	13 wks
23 Feb 67	● PENNY LANE/ STRAWBERRY FIELDS FOREVER *Parlophone R 5570*	2	11 wks
12 Jul 67	★ ALL YOU NEED IS LOVE *Parlophone R 5620*	1	13 wks
29 Nov 67	★ HELLO GOODBYE *Parlophone R 5655*	1	12 wks
13 Dec 67	● MAGICAL MYSTERY TOUR (DOUBLE EP) *Parlophone SMMT/MMT 1*	2	12 wks
20 Mar 68	★ LADY MADONNA *Parlophone R 5675*	1	8 wks
4 Sep 68	★ HEY JUDE *Apple R 5722*	1	16 wks
23 Apr 69	★ GET BACK *Apple R 5777*	1	17 wks
4 Jun 69	★ BALLAD OF JOHN AND YOKO *Apple R 5786*	1	14 wks
8 Nov 69	● SOMETHING / COME TOGETHER *Apple R 5814*	4	12 wks
14 Mar 70	● LET IT BE *Apple R 5833*	2	9 wks
24 Oct 70	LET IT BE (re-entry) *Apple R 5833*	43	1 wk
13 Mar 76	● YESTERDAY *Apple R 6013*	8	7 wks
27 Mar 76	HEY JUDE (re-entry) *Apple R 5722*	12	7 wks
27 Mar 76	PAPERBACK WRITER (re-entry) *Parlophone R 5452*	23	5 wks
3 Apr 76	GET BACK (re-entry) *Apple R 5777*	28	5 wks
3 Apr 76	STRAWBERRY FIELDS FOREVER (re-entry) *Parlophone R 5570*	32	3 wks
10 Apr 76	HELP! (re-entry) *Parlophone R 5305*	37	3 wks
10 Jul 76	BACK IN THE U.S.S.R. *Parlophone R 6016*	19	6 wks
7 Oct 78	SGT. PEPPER'S LONELY HEARTS CLUB BAND - WITH A LITTLE HELP FROM MY FRIENDS *Parlophone R 6022*	63	3 wks
5 Jun 82	● BEATLES MOVIE MEDLEY *Parlophone R 6055*	10	9 wks
16 Oct 82	● LOVE ME DO (re-entry) *Parlophone R 4949*	4	7 wks
22 Jan 83	PLEASE PLEASE ME (re-entry) *Parlophone R 4983*	29	4 wks
23 Apr 83	FROM ME TO YOU (re-entry) *Parlophone R 5015*	40	4 wks
3 Sep 83	SHE LOVES YOU (2nd re-entry) *Parlophone R 5055*	45	3 wks
26 Nov 83	I WANT TO HOLD YOUR HAND (2nd re-entry) *Parlophone R 5084*	62	2 wks
31 Mar 84	CAN'T BUY ME LOVE (2nd re-entry) *Parlophone R 5114*	53	2 wks
21 Jul 84	A HARD DAY'S NIGHT (re-entry) *Parlophone R 5160*	52	2 wks
8 Dec 84	I FEEL FINE (re-entry) *Parlophone R 5200*	65	1 wk
20 Apr 85	TICKET TO RIDE (re-entry) *Parlophone R 5265*	70	2 wks
30 Aug 86	ELEANOR RIGBY/ YELLOW SUBMARINE (re-entry) *Parlophone R 5493*	63	1 wk
28 Feb 87	PENNY LANE/ STRAWBERRY FIELDS FOREVER (2nd re-entry) *Parlophone R 5570*	65	2 wks
18 Jul 87	ALL YOU NEED IS LOVE (re-entry) *Parlophone R 5620*	47	3 wks
5 Dec 87	HELLO GOODBYE (re-entry) *Parlophone R 5655*	63	1 wk
26 Mar 88	LADY MADONNA (re-entry) *Parlophone R 5675*	67	1 wk
10 Sep 88	HEY JUDE (2nd re-entry) *Apple 5722*	52	2 wks
22 Apr 89	GET BACK (2nd re-entry) *Apple R 5777*	74	1 wk

Get Back is with Billy Preston. Tracks on Magical Mystery Tour EP: Magical Mystery Tour/Your Mother Should Know/I Am The Walrus/Fool On The Hill/Flying/Blue Jay Way. See also Billy Preston; Tony Sheridan and the Beatles.

BEATMASTERS *UK, male/female instrumental group* **43 wks**

9 Jan 88	● ROK DA HOUSE *Rhythm King LEFT 11*	5	11 wks
24 Sep 88	BURN IT UP *Rhythm King LEFT 27*	14	10 wks
22 Apr 89	● WHO'S IN THE HOUSE *Rhythm King LEFT 31*	8	9 wks
12 Aug 89	● HEY DJ I CAN'T DANCE TO THAT MUSIC YOU'RE PLAYING/ SKA TRAIN *Rhythm King LEFT 34*	7	11 wks
2 Dec 89	WARM LOVE *Rhythm King LEFT 37*	51	2 wks

Rok Da House features the Cookie Crew. Burn It Up is with P.P. Arnold. Who's In The House features Merlin - UK, male rapper. Hey D.J...features Betty Boo and Warm Love, Claudia Fontaine -UK, female vocalist. See also Cookie Crew; P.P.Arnold; Betty Boo; Various Artists - The Brits.

BEATS INTERNATIONAL **23 wks**
UK, male/female vocal/instrumental group

10 Feb 90	★ DUB BE GOOD TO ME *Go Beat GOD 39*	1	13 wks
12 May 90	● WON'T TALK ABOUT IT *Go Beat GOD 43*	9	7 wks
15 Sep 90	BURUNDI BLUES *Go Beat GOD 45*	51	3 wks

First hit features Lindy Layton. See also Lindy Layton featuring Janet Kay.

BEAUTIFUL SOUTH **44 wks**
UK, male/female vocal/instrumental group

3 Jun 89	● SONG FOR WHOEVER *Go! Discs GOD 32*	2	11 wks
23 Sep 89	● YOU KEEP IT ALL IN *Go! Discs GOD 35*	8	8 wks
2 Dec 89	I'LL SAIL THIS SHIP ALONE *Go! Discs GOD 38*	31	8 wks
6 Oct 90	● A LITTLE TIME *Go! Discs GOD 47*	1†	13 wks
8 Dec 90	MY BOOK *Go! Discs GOD 48*	43†	4 wks

Gilbert BECAUD *France, male vocalist* **12 wks**

29 Mar 75	● A LITTLE LOVE AND UNDERSTANDING *Decca F 13537*	10	12 wks

Jeff BECK *UK, male vocalist/instrumentalist - guitar* **39 wks**

23 Mar 67	HI-HO SILVER LINING *Columbia DB 8151*...............	14	14 wks
2 Aug 67	TALLYMAN *Columbia DB 8227*	30	3 wks
28 Feb 68	LOVE IS BLUE *Columbia DB 8359*......................	23	7 wks
4 Nov 72	HI-HO SILVER LINING (re-issue) *RAK RR 3*	17	11 wks
9 Oct 82	HI-HO SILVER LINING (re-entry of re-issue) *RAK RR 3*	62	4 wks

See also Jeff Beck and Rod Stewart; Donovan with the Jeff Beck Group.

Jeff BECK and Rod STEWART **6 wks**
UK, male vocal/instrumental duo

5 May 73	I'VE BEEN DRINKING *RAK RR 4*	27	6 wks

See also Jeff Beck; Rod Stewart.

Robin BECK *US, female vocalist* **13 wks**

22 Oct 88	★ FIRST TIME *Mercury MER 270*	1	13 wks

Peter BECKETT – *See Barry GRAY ORCHESTRA*

BEDROCKS *UK, male vocal/instrumental group* **7 wks**

18 Dec 68	OB-LA-DI OB-LA-DA *Columbia DB 8516*.....................	20	7 wks

Celi BEE and the BUZZY BUNCH **1 wk**
US, male/female vocal/instrumental group

17 Jun 78	HOLD YOUR HORSES BABE *TK TKR 6032*	72	1 wk

BEE GEES *UK, male vocal/instrumental group* **288 wks**

27 Apr 67	NEW YORK MINING DISASTER 1941 *Polydor 56 161*.......	12	10 wks
12 Jul 67	TO LOVE SOMEBODY *Polydor 56 178*	50	1 wk
26 Jul 67	TO LOVE SOMEBODY (re-entry) *Polydor 56 178*	41	4 wks
20 Sep 67	★ MASSACHUSETTS *Polydor 56 192*......................	1	17 wks
22 Nov 67	● WORLD *Polydor 56 220*	9	16 wks
31 Jan 68	● WORDS *Polydor 56 229*	8	10 wks
27 Mar 68	JUMBO/ THE SINGER SANG HIS SONG *Polydor 56 242*...........................	25	7 wks
7 Aug 68	★ I'VE GOTTA GET A MESSAGE TO YOU *Polydor 56 273*	1	15 wks
19 Feb 69	● FIRST OF MAY *Polydor 56 304*......................	6	11 wks
4 Jun 69	TOMORROW TOMORROW *Polydor 56 331*	23	8 wks
16 Aug 69	● DON'T FORGET TO REMEMBER *Polydor 56 343*..	2	15 wks
28 Mar 70	I.O.I.O. *Polydor 56 377*	49	1 wk
5 Dec 70	LONELY DAYS *Polydor 2001 104*	33	9 wks
29 Jan 72	MY WORLD *Polydor 2058 185*...................	16	9 wks
22 Jul 72	● RUN TO ME *Polydor 2058 255*...................	9	10 wks
28 Jun 75	● JIVE TALKIN' *RSO 2090 160*...................	5	11 wks
31 Jul 76	● YOU SHOULD BE DANCING *RSO 2090 195* ...	5	10 wks
13 Nov 76	LOVE SO RIGHT *RSO 2090 207*..................	41	4 wks
29 Oct 77	● HOW DEEP IS YOUR LOVE *RSO 2090 259*...	3	15 wks
4 Feb 78	● STAYIN' ALIVE *RSO 2090 267*...................	4	12 wks
15 Apr 78	★ NIGHT FEVER *RSO 002*	1	20 wks
13 May 78	STAYIN' ALIVE (re-entry) *RSO 2090 267*........	63	6 wks
25 Nov 78	● TOO MUCH HEAVEN *RSO 25*..................	3	13 wks
17 Feb 79	★ TRAGEDY *RSO 27*............................	1	10 wks
14 Apr 79	LOVE YOU INSIDE OUT *RSO 31*..............	13	9 wks
5 Jan 80	SPIRITS (HAVING FLOWN) *RSO 52*	16	7 wks
17 Sep 83	SOMEONE BELONGING TO SOMEONE *RSO 96*	49	4 wks
26 Sep 87	★ YOU WIN AGAIN *Warner Bros. W 8351*	1	15 wks
12 Dec 87	E.S.P. *Warner Bros. W 8139*....................	51	5 wks
15 Apr 89	ORDINARY LIVES *Warner Bros. W 7523*	54	3 wks
24 Jun 89	ONE *Warner Bros. W 2916*.....................	71	1 wk

Act was UK/Australia up to and including Tomorrow Tomorrow.

BEGGAR and CO *UK, male vocal/instrumental group* **15 wks**

7 Feb 81	(SOMEBODY) HELP ME OUT *Ensign ENY 201*	15	10 wks
12 Sep 81	MULE (CHANT NO.2) *RCA 130*.	37	5 wks

BEGINNING OF THE END **6 wks**
US, male vocal/instrumental group

23 Feb 74	FUNKY NASSAU *Atlantic K 10021*.........................	31	6 wks

Harry BELAFONTE *US, male vocalist* **79 wks**

1 Mar 57	● BANANA BOAT SONG *HMV POP 308*	2	18 wks
14 Jun 57	● ISLAND IN THE SUN *RCA 1007*	3	25 wks
6 Sep 57	SCARLET RIBBONS *HMV POP 360*......................	18	6 wks
1 Nov 57	★ MARY'S BOY CHILD *RCA 1022*	1	12 wks
22 Aug 58	LITTLE BERNADETTE *RCA 1072*	16	7 wks
28 Nov 58	● MARY'S BOY CHILD (re-entry) *RCA 1022*	10	6 wks
12 Dec 58	SON OF MARY *RCA 1084*	18	4 wks
11 Dec 59	MARY'S BOY CHILD (2nd re-entry) *RCA 1022*	30	1 wk

See also Harry Belafonte and Odetta.

Harry BELAFONTE and ODETTA **8 wks**
US, male/female vocal duo

21 Sep 61	HOLE IN THE BUCKET *RCA 1247*.....................	32	2 wks
12 Oct 61	HOLE IN THE BUCKET (re-entry) *RCA 1247*	34	6 wks

See also Harry Belafonte.

Archie BELL and the DRELLS **33 wks**
US, male vocal/instrumental group

7 Oct 72	HERE I GO AGAIN *Atlantic K 10210*	11	10 wks
27 Jan 73	THERE'S GONNA BE A SHOWDOWN *Atlantic K 10263* ..	36	5 wks
8 May 76	SOUL CITY WALK *Philadelphia International PIR 4250*	13	10 wks
11 Jun 77	EVERYBODY HAVE A GOOD TIME *Philadelphia International PIR 5179*	43	4 wks
28 Jun 86	DON'T LET LOVE GET YOU DOWN *Portrait A 7254*.......	49	4 wks

See also Philadelphia International All-Stars.

Freddie BELL and the BELLBOYS **10 wks**
US, male vocal/instrumental group

28 Sep 56	● GIDDY-UP-A-DING-DONG *Mercury MT 122*.................	4	10 wks

Maggie BELL *UK, female vocalist* **4 wks**

15 Apr 78	HAZELL *Swan Song SSK 19412*........................	37	3 wks
13 May 78	HAZELL (re-entry) *Swan Song SSK 19412*..................	74	1 wk

See also B.A. Robertson and Maggie Bell.

William BELL *US, male vocalist* **8 wks**

29 May 68	TRIBUTE TO A KING *Stax 601 038*........................	31	7 wks
26 Apr 86	HEADLINE NEWS *Absolute LUTE 1*........................	70	1 wk

See also Judy Clay and William Bell.

BELL and JAMES *US, male vocal duo* **3 wks**

31 Mar 79	LIVIN' IT UP (FRIDAY NIGHT) *A &M AMS 7424*..........	68	1 wk
14 Apr 79	LIVIN' IT UP (FRIDAY NIGHT) (re-entry) *A &M AMS 7424*..................................	59	2 wks

BELL BIV DEVOE US, male vocal group   **14 wks**

| 30 Jun 90 | **POISON** MCA MCA 1414 .... | **19** | 11 wks |
| 22 Sep 90 | **DO ME** MCA MCA 1440 .... | **56** | 3 wks |

BELLAMY BROTHERS US, male vocal duo   **29 wks**

17 Apr 76	● **LET YOUR LOVE FLOW** Warner Bros. K 16690	**7**	12 wks
21 Aug 76	**SATIN SHEETS** Warner Bros. K 16775	**43**	3 wks
11 Aug 79	● **IF I SAID YOU HAVE A BEAUTIFUL BODY WOULD YOU HOLD IT AGAINST ME** Warner Bros. K 17405	**3**	14 wks

BELLBOYS – See Freddie BELL and the BELLBOYS

Regina BELLE US, female vocalist   **1 wk**

| 21 Oct 89 | **GOOD LOVIN'** CBS 655230 .... | **73** | 1 wk |

BELLE and the DEVOTIONS UK, female vocal group   **8 wks**

| 21 Apr 84 | **LOVE GAMES** CBS A 4332 .... | **11** | 8 wks |

La BELLE EPOQUE France, female vocal duo   **14 wks**

| 27 Aug 77 | **BLACK IS BLACK** Harvest HAR 5133 .... | **48** | 1 wk |
| 10 Sep 77 | ● **BLACK IS BLACK (re-entry)** Harvest HAR 5133 .... | **2** | 13 wks |

BELLE STARS UK, female vocal/instrumental group   **42 wks**

5 Jun 82	**IKO IKO** Stiff BUY 150	**35**	6 wks
17 Jul 82	**THE CLAPPING SONG** Stiff BUY 155	**11**	9 wks
16 Oct 82	**MOCKINGBIRD** Stiff BUY 159	**51**	3 wks
15 Jan 83	● **SIGN OF THE TIMES** Stiff BUY 167	**3**	11 wks
16 Apr 83	**SWEET MEMORY** Stiff BUY 174	**22**	9 wks
13 Aug 83	**INDIAN SUMMER** Stiff BUY 185	**52**	3 wks
14 Jul 84	**80'S ROMANCE** Stiff BUY 200	**71**	1 wk

BELMONTS – See DION and the BELMONTS

BELOVED UK, male vocal/instrumental duo   **24 wks**

21 Oct 89	**THE SUN RISING** WEA YZ 414	**26**	7 wks
27 Jan 90	**HELLO** WEA YZ 426	**19**	7 wks
24 Mar 90	**YOUR LOVE TAKES ME HIGHER** East West YZ 463	**39**	3 wks
9 Jun 90	**TIME AFTER TIME** East West YZ 482	**46**	4 wks
10 Nov 90	**IT'S ALRIGHT NOW** East West YZ 541	**48**	3 wks

Pat BENATAR US, female vocalist   **52 wks**

21 Jan 84	**LOVE IS A BATTLEFIELD** Chrysalis CHS 2747...............	**49**	5 wks
12 Jan 85	**WE BELONG** Chrysalis CHS 2821	**22**	9 wks
23 Mar 85	**LOVE IS A BATTLEFIELD (re-issue)** Chrysalis PAT 1	**17**	10 wks
15 Jun 85	**SHADOWS OF THE NIGHT** Chrysalis PAT 2	**50**	4 wks
19 Oct 85	**INVINCIBLE (THEME FROM THE LEGEND OF BILLIE JEAN)** Chrysalis PAT 3	**53**	3 wks
15 Feb 86	**SEX AS A WEAPON** Chrysalis PAT 4	**67**	3 wks
2 Jul 88	**ALL FIRED UP** Chrysalis PAT 5	**19**	10 wks
1 Oct 88	**DON'T WALK AWAY** Chrysalis PAT 6	**42**	5 wks
14 Jan 89	**ONE LOVE** Chrysalis PAT 7	**59**	3 wks

David BENDETH   **5 wks**
UK, male vocalist and multi-instrumentalist

| 8 Sep 79 | **FEEL THE REAL** Sidewalk SID 113 .... | **44** | 5 wks |

BENELUX and Nancy DEE Belgium/Holland/   **4 wks**
Luxembourg, female vocal group

| 25 Aug 79 | **SWITCH** Scope SC 4.. | **52** | 4 wks |

Nigel BENN – See PACK featuring Nigel BENN

Boyd BENNETT US, male vocalist   **2 wks**

| 23 Dec 55 | **SEVENTEEN** Parlophone R 4063 .... | **16** | 2 wks |

Chris BENNETT – See MUNICH MACHINE

Cliff BENNETT and the REBEL ROUSERS   **23 wks**
UK, male vocal/instrumental group

1 Oct 64	● **ONE WAY LOVE** Parlophone R 5173	**9**	9 wks
4 Feb 65	**I'LL TAKE YOU HOME** Parlophone R 5229	**42**	3 wks
11 Aug 66	● **GOT TO GET YOU INTO MY LIFE** Parlophone R 5489	**6**	11 wks

Peter E. BENNETT UK, male vocalist   **1 wk**

| 7 Nov 70 | **THE SEAGULL'S NAME WAS NELSON** RCA 1991 .... | **45** | 1 wk |

Tony BENNETT US, male vocalist   **61 wks**

15 Apr 55	★ **STRANGER IN PARADISE** Philips PB 420	**1**	16 wks
16 Sep 55	**CLOSE YOUR EYES** Philips PB 445	**18**	1 wk
13 Apr 56	**COME NEXT SPRING** Philips PB 537.......................	**29**	1 wk
5 Jan 61	**TILL** Philips PB 1079	**35**	2 wks
18 Jul 63	**THE GOOD LIFE** CBS AAG 153	**27**	13 wks
6 May 65	**IF I RULED THE WORLD** CBS 201735	**40**	5 wks
27 May 65	**I LEFT MY HEART IN SAN FRANCISCO** CBS 201730	**46**	2 wks
30 Sep 65	**I LEFT MY HEART IN SAN FRANCISCO (re-entry)** CBS 201730	**40**	5 wks
9 Dec 65	**I LEFT MY HEART IN SAN FRANCISCO (2nd re-entry)** CBS 201730	**25**	7 wks
23 Dec 65	**THE VERY THOUGHT OF YOU** CBS 202021	**21**	9 wks

Gary BENSON UK, male vocalist   **8 wks**

| 9 Aug 75 | **DON'T THROW IT ALL AWAY** State STAT 10 .... | **20** | 8 wks |

George BENSON US, male vocalist/instrumentalist - guitar   **136 wks**

25 Oct 75	**SUPERSHIP** CTI CTSP 002.....................................	**30**	6 wks
4 Jun 77	**NATURE BOY** Warner Bros. K 16921	**26**	6 wks
24 Sep 77	**THE GREATEST LOVE OF ALL** Arista 133	**27**	7 wks
31 Mar 79	**LOVE BALLAD** Warner Bros. K 17333	**29**	9 wks
26 Jul 80	● **GIVE ME THE NIGHT** Warner Bros. K 17673	**7**	10 wks
4 Oct 80	● **LOVE X LOVE** Warner Bros. K 17699	**10**	8 wks
7 Feb 81	**WHAT'S ON YOUR MIND** Warner Bros. K 17748	**45**	5 wks
14 Nov 81	**TURN YOUR LOVE AROUND** Warner Bros. K 17877	**29**	11 wks
23 Jan 82	**NEVER GIVE UP ON A GOOD THING** Warner Bros. K 17902	**14**	10 wks
21 May 83	**LADY LOVE ME (ONE MORE TIME)** Warner Bros. W 9614	**11**	10 wks
16 Jul 83	**FEEL LIKE MAKIN' LOVE** Warner Bros. W 9551	**28**	7 wks
24 Sep 83	● **IN YOUR EYES** Warner Bros. W 9487	**7**	10 wks
17 Dec 83	**INSIDE LOVE (SO PERSONAL)** WEA Int. W 9427	**57**	5 wks
19 Jan 85	**20/ 20** Warner Bros. W 9120	**29**	9 wks
20 Apr 85	**BEYOND THE SEA (LA MER)** Warner Bros. W 60	**60**	9 wks
16 Aug 86	**KISSES IN THE MOONLIGHT** Warner Bros. W 8640	**60**	4 wks
29 Nov 86	**SHIVER** Warner Bros. W 8523	**19**	9 wks
14 Feb 87	**TEASER** Warner Bros. W 8437	**45**	4 wks
27 Aug 88	**LET'S DO IT AGAIN** Warner Bros. W 7780	**56**	3 wks

Billed as George 'Bad' Benson on first hit. See also Aretha Franklin and George Benson.

Brook BENTON US, male vocalist   18 wks

10 Jul 59		ENDLESSLY Mercury AMT 1043	28	2 wks
6 Oct 60		KIDDIO Mercury AMT 1109	42	3 wks
3 Nov 60		KIDDIO (re-entry) Mercury AMT 1109	41	3 wks
16 Feb 61		FOOLS RUSH IN Mercury AMT 1121	50	1 wk
13 Jul 61		BOLL WEEVIL SONG Mercury AMT 1148	30	9 wks

Ingrid BERGMAN – See Dooley WILSON

BERLIN US, male/female vocal/instrumental group   39 wks

25 Oct 86	★	TAKE MY BREATH AWAY (LOVE THEME FROM 'TOP GUN') CBS A 7320	1	15 wks
17 Jan 87		YOU DON'T KNOW Mercury MER 237	39	6 wks
14 Mar 87		LIKE FLAMES Mercury MER 240	47	3 wks
20 Feb 88		TAKE MY BREATH AWAY (LOVE THEME FROM 'TOP GUN') (re-entry) CBS A 7320	52	3 wks
13 Oct 90	●	TAKE MY BREATH AWAY (re-issue) CBS 656361 7	3	12 wks

Elmer BERNSTEIN US, orchestra   11 wks

| 18 Dec 59 | ● | STACCATO'S THEME Capitol CL 15101 | 4 | 10 wks |
| 10 Mar 60 | | STACCATO'S THEME (re-entry) Capitol CL 15101 | 40 | 1 wk |

Chuck BERRY US, male vocalist/instrumentalist - guitar   91 wks

21 Jun 57		SCHOOL DAY Columbia DB 3951	24	2 wks
12 Jul 57		SCHOOL DAY (re-entry) Columbia DB 3951	24	2 wks
25 Apr 58		SWEET LITTLE SIXTEEN London HLM 8585	16	5 wks
11 Jul 63		GO GO GO Pye International 7N 25209	38	6 wks
10 Oct 63	●	LET IT ROCK/ MEMPHIS TENNESSEE Pye International 7N 25218	6	13 wks
19 Dec 63		RUN RUDOLPH RUN Pye International 7N 25228	36	6 wks
13 Feb 64		NADINE (IS IT YOU) Pye International 7N 25236	27	6 wks
2 Apr 64		NADINE (IS IT YOU) (re-entry) Pye International 7N 25236	43	1 wk
7 May 64	●	NO PARTICULAR PLACE TO GO Pye International 7N 25242	3	12 wks
20 Aug 64		YOU NEVER CAN TELL Pye International 7N 25257	23	8 wks
14 Jan 65		PROMISED LAND Pye International 7N 25285	26	6 wks
28 Oct 72	★	MY DING-A-LING Chess 6145 019	1	17 wks
3 Feb 73		REELIN' AND ROCKIN' Chess 6145 020	18	7 wks

Dave BERRY UK, male vocalist   76 wks

19 Sep 63		MEMPHIS TENNESSEE Decca F 11734	19	13 wks
9 Jan 64		MY BABY LEFT ME Decca F 11803	41	1 wk
23 Jan 64		MY BABY LEFT ME (re-entry) Decca F 11803	37	8 wks
30 Apr 64		BABY IT'S YOU Decca F 11876	24	6 wks
6 Aug 64	●	THE CRYING GAME Decca F 11937	5	12 wks
26 Nov 64		ONE HEART BETWEEN TWO Decca F 12020	41	2 wks
25 Mar 65	●	LITTLE THINGS Decca F 12103	5	12 wks
22 Jul 65		THIS STRANGE EFFECT Decca F 12188	37	6 wks
30 Jun 66	●	MAMA Decca F 12435	5	16 wks

Billed as Dave Berry and the Cruisers on the first two hits.

Mike BERRY UK, male vocalist   51 wks

12 Oct 61		TRIBUTE TO BUDDY HOLLY HMV POP 912	24	6 wks
3 Jan 63	●	DON'T YOU THINK IT'S TIME HMV POP 1105	6	12 wks
11 Apr 63		MY LITTLE BABY HMV POP 1142	34	7 wks
2 Aug 80	●	THE SUNSHINE OF YOUR SMILE Polydor 2059 261	9	12 wks
29 Nov 80		IF I COULD ONLY MAKE YOU CARE Polydor POSP 202	37	9 wks
5 Sep 81		MEMORIES Polydor POSP 287	55	5 wks

HMV hits credited to Mike Berry with the Outlaws. See also Outlaws.

Nick BERRY UK, male vocalist   13 wks

| 4 Oct 86 | ★ | EVERY LOSER WINS BBC RESL 204 | 1 | 11 wks |
| 27 Dec 86 | | EVERY LOSER WINS (re-entry) BBC RESL 204 | 72 | 2 wks |

Adele BERTEI – See JELLYBEAN

BEVERLEY SISTERS UK, female vocal trio   34 wks

27 Nov 53		I SAW MOMMY KISSING SANTA CLAUS Philips PB 188	11	1 wk
11 Dec 53	●	I SAW MOMMY KISSING SANTA CLAUS (re-entry) Philips PB 188	6	4 wks
13 Apr 56		WILLIE CAN Decca F 10705	23	4 wks
1 Feb 57		I DREAMED Decca F 10832	24	2 wks
13 Feb 59	●	LITTLE DRUMMER BOY Decca F 11107	6	13 wks
20 Nov 59		LITTLE DONKEY Decca F 11172	14	7 wks
23 Jun 60		GREEN FIELDS Columbia DB 4444	48	1 wk
7 Jul 60		GREEN FIELDS (re-entry) Columbia DB 4444	29	2 wks

See also Various Artists - All Star Hit Parade No.2.

Frankie BEVERLY – See MAZE featuring Frankie BEVERLY

B-52s US, male/female vocal/instrumental group   39 wks

11 Aug 79		ROCK LOBSTER Island WIP 6506	37	5 wks
9 Aug 80		GIVE ME BACK MY MAN Island WIP 6579	61	3 wks
7 May 83		FUTURE GENERATION Island IS 107	63	2 wks
10 May 86		ROCK LOBSTER/ PLANET CLAIRE Island BFT 1	12	7 wks
3 Mar 90	●	LOVE SHACK Reprise W 9917	2	13 wks
19 May 90		ROAM Reprise W 9827	17	7 wks
18 Aug 90		CHANNEL Z Reprise W 9737	61	2 wks

On Island BFT 1 Planet Claire only listed from 17 May Rock Lobster was a re-issue.

BIBLE UK, male vocal/instrumental group   8 wks

| 20 May 89 | | GRACELAND Chrysalis BIB 4 | 51 | 4 wks |
| 26 Aug 89 | | HONEY BE GOOD Ensign BIB 5 | 54 | 4 wks |

BIDDU UK, orchestra   13 wks

2 Aug 75		SUMMER OF '42 Epic EPC 3318	14	8 wks
17 Apr 76		RAIN FOREST Epic EPC 4084	39	4 wks
11 Feb 78		JOURNEY TO THE MOON Epic EPC 5910	41	1 wk

BIG APPLE BAND – See Walter MURPHY and the BIG APPLE BAND

BIG AUDIO DYNAMITE   25 wks
UK/US, male vocal/instrumental group

22 Mar 86		E = MC2 CBS A 6963	11	9 wks
7 Jun 86		MEDICINE SHOW CBS A 7181	29	5 wks
18 Oct 86		C'MON EVERY BEATBOX CBS 650147	51	3 wks
21 Feb 87		V THIRTEEN CBS BAAD 2	49	5 wks
28 May 88		JUST PLAY MUSIC CBS BAAD 4	51	3 wks

BIG BAD HORNS – See LITTLE ANGELS

BIG BAM BOO UK, male vocal/instrumental duo   2 wks

| 28 Jan 89 | | SHOOTING FROM MY HEART MCA MCA 1281 | 61 | 2 wks |

BIG BEN BANJO BAND UK, instrumental group   6 wks

10 Dec 54 ●	LET'S GET TOGETHER NO. 1 Columbia DB 3549	6	4 wks
9 Dec 55 ●	LET'S GET TOGETHER AGAIN Columbia DB 3676	19	1 wk
30 Dec 55	LET'S GET TOGETHER AGAIN (re-entry)		
.	Columbia DB 3676	18	1 wk

These hits were both medleys as follows: Let's Get Together No.1: I'm Just Wild About Harry/April Showers/ Rock-a-Bye Your Baby/Swanee/Darktown Strutters Ball/For Me And My Gal/Oh You Beautiful Doll/Yes Sir That's My Baby. Let's Get Together Again: I'm Looking Over A Four-leafed Clover/By The Light Of The Silvery Moon/Oh Susannah/Baby Face/I'm Sitting On Top Of The World/My Mammy/Dixie's Land/Margie.

BIG BOPPER US, male vocalist   8 wks

| 26 Dec 58 | CHANTILLY LACE Mercury AMT 1002 | 30 | 1 wk |
| 9 Jan 59 | CHANTILLY LACE (re-entry) Mercury AMT 1002 | 12 | 7 wks |

BIG COUNTRY UK, male vocal/instrumental group   91 wks

26 Feb 83 ●	FIELDS OF FIRE (400 MILES) Mercury COUNT 2	10	12 wks
28 May 83	IN A BIG COUNTRY Mercury COUNT 3	17	7 wks
3 Sep 83 ●	CHANCE Mercury COUNT 4	9	9 wks
21 Jan 84 ●	WONDERLAND Mercury COUNT 5	8	8 wks
29 Sep 84	EAST OF EDEN Mercury MER 175	17	6 wks
1 Dec 84	WHERE THE ROSE IS SOWN Mercury MER 185	29	7 wks
19 Jan 85	JUST A SHADOW Mercury BCO 8	26	4 wks
12 Apr 86 ●	LOOK AWAY Mercury BIGC 1	7	8 wks
21 Jun 86	THE TEACHER Mercury BIGC 2	28	4 wks
20 Sep 86	ONE GREAT THING Mercury BIGC 3	19	6 wks
29 Nov 86	HOLD THE HEART Mercury BIGC 4	55	2 wks
20 Aug 88	KING OF EMOTION Mercury BIGC 5	16	5 wks
1 Oct 88	KING OF EMOTION (re-entry) Mercury BIGC 5	74	1 wk
5 Nov 88	BROKEN HEART (THIRTEEN VALLEYS)		
	Mercury BIGC 6	47	4 wks
4 Feb 89	PEACE IN OUR TIME Mercury BIGC 8	39	3 wks
12 May 90	SAVE ME Mercury BIGC 8	41	3 wks
21 Jul 90	HEART OF THE WORLD Mercury BIGC 9	50	2 wks

BIG DADDY US, male vocal/instrumental group   8 wks

| 9 Mar 85 | DANCING IN THE DARK Making Waves SURF 1033 | 21 | 8 wks |

BIG DADDY KANE US, male vocalist   6 wks

13 May 89	RAP SUMMARY/ WRATH OF KANE		
	Cold Chillin' W 2973	52	2 wks
26 Aug 89	SMOOTH OPERATOR Cold Chillin' W 2804	65	1 wk
13 Jan 90	AIN'T NO STOPPIN' US NOW Cold Chillin' W 2635	44	3 wks

BIG FAMILY – *See JT and the BIG FAMILY*

BIG FUN UK, male vocal group   27 wks

12 Aug 89 ●	BLAME IT ON THE BOOGIE Jive JIVE 217	4	11 wks
25 Nov 89 ●	CAN'T SHAKE THE FEELING Jive JIVE 234	8	9 wks
17 Mar 90	HANDFUL OF PROMISES Jive JIVE 243	21	6 wks
4 Aug 90	HEY THERE LONELY GIRL Jive JIVE 251	62	1 wk

See also Big Fun and Sonia.

BIG FUN and SONIA   6 wks
UK, male vocal group and female vocalist

| 23 Jun 90 | YOU'VE GOT A FRIEND Jive CHILD 90 | 14 | 6 wks |

See also Big Fun; Sonia.

BIG ROLL BAND – *See Zoot MONEY and the BIG ROLL BAND*

BIG SOUND – *See Simon DUPREE and the BIG SOUND*

BIG SOUND AUTHORITY   12 wks
UK, male/female vocal/instrumental group

19 Jan 85	THIS HOUSE (IS WHERE YOUR LOVE STANDS)		
	Source BSA 1	21	9 wks
8 Jun 85	A BAD TOWN Source BSA 2	54	3 wks

BIG SUPREME UK, male vocal group   5 wks

| 20 Sep 86 | DON'T WALK Polydor POSP 809 | 58 | 3 wks |
| 14 Mar 87 | PLEASE YOURSELF Polydor POSP 840 | 64 | 2 wks |

BIG THREE UK, vocal/instrumental group   17 wks

| 11 Apr 63 | SOME OTHER GUY Decca F 11614 | 37 | 7 wks |
| 11 Jul 63 | BY THE WAY Decca F 11689 | 22 | 10 wks |

Barry BIGGS Jamaica, male vocalist   46 wks

28 Aug 76	WORK ALL DAY Dynamic DYN 101	38	5 wks
4 Dec 76 ●	SIDESHOW Dynamic DYN 118	3	16 wks
23 Apr 77	YOU'RE MY LIFE Dynamic DYN 127	36	4 wks
9 Jul 77	THREE RING CIRCUS Dynamic DYN 128	22	8 wks
15 Dec 79	WHAT'S YOUR SIGN GIRL Dynamic DYN 150	55	7 wks
20 Jun 81	WIDE AWAKE IN A DREAM Dynamic DYN 10	44	6 wks

Ronald BIGGS – *See SEX PISTOLS*

Ivor BIGGUN UK, male vocalist   15 wks

| 2 Sep 78 | WINKER'S SONG (MISPRINT) Beggars Banquet BOP 1 | 22 | 12 wks |
| 12 Sep 81 | BRAS ON 45 (FAMILY VERSION) Dead Badger BOP 6 | 50 | 3 wks |

First hit gives minor credit to Ivor's backing group the Red Nosed Burglars (UK, male instrumental group). Second hit credited to Ivor Biggun and the D Cups.

BILBO UK, male vocal/instrumental group   7 wks

| 26 Aug 78 | SHE'S GONNA WIN Lightning Lig 548 | 42 | 7 wks |

Mr. Acker BILK   171 wks
UK, male jazz band leader, vocalist/instrumentalist - clarinet

22 Jan 60 ●	SUMMER SET Columbia DB 4382	5	19 wks
9 Jun 60	GOODNIGHT SWEET PRINCE Melodisc MEL 1547	50	1 wk
18 Aug 60	WHITE CLIFFS OF DOVER Columbia DB 4492	30	9 wks
8 Dec 60 ●	BUONA SERA Columbia DB 4544	7	18 wks
13 Jul 61 ●	THAT'S MY HOME Columbia DB 4673	7	17 wks
2 Nov 61	STARS AND STRIPES FOREVER/ CREOLE JAZZ		
	Columbia SCD 2155	22	10 wks
30 Nov 61 ●	STRANGER ON THE SHORE Columbia DB 4750	2	55 wks
15 Mar 62	FRANKIE AND JOHNNY Columbia DB 4795	42	2 wks
26 Jul 62	GOTTA SEE BABY TONIGHT Columbia SCD 2176	24	9 wks
27 Sep 62	LONELY Columbia DB 4897	14	11 wks
24 Jan 63	A TASTE OF HONEY Columbia DB 1949	16	9 wks
21 Aug 76 ●	ARIA Pye 7N 45607	5	11 wks

Stranger On The Shore, Lonely and A Taste Of Honey credit Mr Acker Bilk with the Leon Young String Chorale. Aria credits Acker Bilk, his Clarinet And Strings. All others Mr. Acker Bilk and his Paramount Jazz Band.

BILLY – *See S EXPRESS*

BIMBO JET *France, male/female vocal/instrumental group* **10 wks**

26 Jul 75	EL BIMBO *EMI 2317*	12	10 wks

Umberto BINDI *Italy, male vocalist* **1 wk**

10 Nov 60	IL NOSTRO CONCERTO *Oriole CB 1577*	47	1 wk

La BIONDA *Italy, male/female vocal group* **4 wks**

7 Oct 78	ONE FOR YOU ONE FOR ME *Philips 6198 227*	54	4 wks

BIRDLAND *UK, male vocal/instrumental group* **6 wks**

1 Apr 89	HOLLOW HEART *Lazy LAZY 13*	70	1 wk
8 Jul 89	PARADISE *Lazy LAZY 14*	70	1 wk
3 Feb 90	SLEEP WITH ME *Lazy LAZY 17*	32	3 wks
22 Sep 90	ROCK AND ROLL NIGGER *Lazy LAZY 20*	47	1 wk

BIRDS *UK, male vocal/instrumental group* **1 wk**

27 May 65	LEAVING HERE *Decca F 12140*	45	1 wk

Jane BIRKIN and Serge GAINSBOURG **34 wks**
UK/France, female/male vocal duo

30 Jul 69	● JE T'AIME. . . MOI NON PLUS *Fontana TF 1042*	2	11 wks
4 Oct 69	★ JE T'AIME. . . MOI NON PLUS (re-issue) *Major Minor MM 645*	1	14 wks
7 Dec 74	JE T'AIME. . . MOI NON PLUS (2nd re-issue) *Antic K 11511*	31	9 wks

Elvin BISHOP *US, male instrumentalist - guitar* **4 wks**

15 May 76	FOOLED AROUND AND FELL IN LOVE *Capricorn 2089 024*	34	4 wks

Hit has vocal (uncredited) by Mickey Thomas.

BIV – *See BELL BIV DEVOE*

BIZZ NIZZ *US/Belgium, male/female vocal/instrumental group* **11 wks**

31 Mar 90	● DON'T MISS THE PARTY LINE *Cooltempo COOL 203*	7	11 wks

BLACK *UK, male vocalist - Colin Vearncombe* **29 wks**

27 Sep 86	WONDERFUL LIFE *Ugly Man JACK 71*	72	1 wk
27 Jun 87	● SWEETEST SMILE *A & M AM 394*	8	10 wks
22 Aug 87	● WONDERFUL LIFE *A & M AM 402*	8	9 wks
16 Jan 88	PARADISE *A & M AM 422*	38	3 wks
24 Sep 88	THE BIG ONE *A & M AM 468*	54	4 wks
21 Jan 89	NOW YOU'RE GONE *A & M AM 491*	66	2 wks

Wonderful Life on A & M is a re-recording of his first hit.

Cilla BLACK *UK, female vocalist* **192 wks**

17 Oct 63	LOVE OF THE LOVED *Parlophone R 5065*	35	6 wks
6 Feb 64	★ ANYONE WHO HAD A HEART *Parlophone R 5101*	1	17 wks
7 May 64	★ YOU'RE MY WORLD *Parlophone R 5133*	1	17 wks
6 Aug 64	● IT'S FOR YOU *Parlophone R 5162*	7	10 wks
14 Jan 65	● YOU'VE LOST THAT LOVIN' FEELIN' *Parlophone R 5225*	2	9 wks
22 Apr 65	I'VE BEEN WRONG BEFORE *Parlophone R 5269*	17	8 wks
13 Jan 66	● LOVE'S JUST A BROKEN HEART *Parlophone R 5395*	5	11 wks
31 Mar 66	● ALFIE *Parlophone R 5427*	9	12 wks
9 Jun 66	● DON'T ANSWER ME *Parlophone R 5463*	6	10 wks
20 Oct 66	A FOOL AM I *Parlophone R 5515*	13	9 wks
8 Jun 67	WHAT GOOD AM I *Parlophone R 5608*	24	7 wks
29 Nov 67	I ONLY LIVE TO LOVE YOU *Parlophone R 5652*	26	11 wks
13 Mar 68	● STEP INSIDE LOVE *Parlophone R 5674*	8	9 wks
12 Jun 68	WHERE IS TOMORROW *Parlophone R 5706*	39	3 wks
12 Feb 69	● SURROUND YOURSELF WITH SORROW *Parlophone R 5759*	3	12 wks
9 Jul 69	● CONVERSATIONS *Parlophone R 5785*	7	12 wks
13 Dec 69	IF I THOUGHT YOU'D EVER CHANGE YOUR MIND *Parlophone R 5820*	20	9 wks
20 Nov 71	● SOMETHING TELLS ME (SOMETHING IS GONNA HAPPEN TONIGHT) *Parlophone R 5924*	3	14 wks
2 Feb 74	BABY WE CAN'T GO WRONG *EMI 2107*	36	6 wks

Jeanne BLACK *US, female vocalist* **4 wks**

23 Jun 60	HE'LL HAVE TO STAY *Capitol CL 15131*	41	4 wks

BLACK BOX *Italy, male/female vocal/instrumental group* **47 wks**

12 Aug 89	★ RIDE ON TIME *deConstruction PB 43055*	1	22 wks
17 Feb 90	● I DON'T KNOW ANYBODY ELSE *deConstruction PB 43479*	4	8 wks
2 Jun 90	EVERYBODY EVERYBODY *deConstruction PB 43715*	16	5 wks
3 Nov 90	● FANTASY *deConstruction PB 43895*	5†	9 wks
15 Dec 90	THE TOTAL MIX *deConstruction PB 44235*	15†	3 wks

BLACK CROWES *US, male vocal/instrumental group* **5 wks**

1 Sep 90	HARD TO HANDLE *Def American DEFA 6*	45	5 wks

BLACK GORILLA **6 wks**
UK, male/female vocal/instrumental group

27 Aug 77	GIMME DAT BANANA *Response SR 502*	29	6 wks

BLACK IVORY – *See CALIBRE CUTS*

BLACK LACE *UK, male vocal/instrumental group* **82 wks**

31 Mar 79	MARY ANN *EMI 2919*	42	4 wks
24 Sep 83	● SUPERMAN (GIOCA JOUER) *Flair FLA 105*	9	18 wks
30 Jun 84	● AGADOO *Flair FLA 107*	2	30 wks
24 Nov 84	● DO THE CONGA *Flair FLA 108*	10	9 wks
1 Jun 85	EL VINO COLLAPSO *Flair LACE 1*	42	5 wks
7 Sep 85	I SPEAKA DA LINGO *Flair LACE 2*	49	4 wks
7 Dec 85	HOKEY COKEY *Flair LACE 3*	31	6 wks
20 Sep 86	WIG WAM BAM *Flair LACE 5*	63	3 wks
26 Aug 89	I AM THE MUSIC MAN *Flair LACE 10*	52	3 wks

BLACK RIOT *US, male producer* **3 wks**

3 Dec 88	WARLOCK/ A DAY IN THE LIFE *Champion CHAMP 75*	68	3 wks

A Day In The Life only listed from 17 Dec 88.

BLACK SABBATH *UK/US, male vocal/instrumental group* **68 wks**

29 Aug 70	● PARANOID *Vertigo 6059 010*	4	18 wks
3 Jun 78	NEVER SAY DIE *Vertigo SAB 001*	21	8 wks
14 Oct 78	HARD ROAD *Vertigo SAB 002*	33	4 wks
5 Jul 80	NEON KNIGHTS *Vertigo SAB 3*	22	9 wks
16 Aug 80	PARANOID (re-issue) *Nems BSS 101*	14	12 wks
6 Dec 80	DIE YOUNG *Vertigo SAB 4*	41	7 wks
7 Nov 81	MOB RULES *Vertigo SAB 5*	46	4 wks
13 Feb 82	TURN UP THE NIGHT *Vertigo SAB 6*	37	5 wks

15 Apr 89   **HEADLESS CROSS** *IRS EIRS 107*............................. **62**   1 wk

Group UK only for first three hits and re-issue of Paranoid.

BLACK SLATE *UK/Jamaica, male vocal/instrumental group*   **15 wks**

20 Sep 80 ●	**AMIGO** *Ensign ENY 42*.............................	**9**	9 wks
6 Dec 80	**BOOM BOOM** *Ensign ENY 47*.................................	**51**	6 wks

---

BLACK UHURU *Jamaica, male vocal/instrumental group*   **9 wks**

8 Sep 84	**WHAT IS LIFE?** *Island IS 150*..................................	**56**	6 wks
31 May 86	**THE GREAT TRAIN ROBBERY**		
	Real Authentic Sound RAS 7018	**62**	3 wks

---

Band of the BLACK WATCH *UK, military band*   **22 wks**

30 Aug 75 ●	**SCOTCH ON THE ROCKS** *Spark SRL 1128*	**8**	14 wks
13 Dec 75	**DANCE OF THE CUCKOOS** *Spark SRL 1135*	**37**	8 wks

---

Tony BLACKBURN *UK, male vocalist*   **7 wks**

24 Jan 68	**SO MUCH LOVE** *MGM 1375*...................................	**31**	4 wks
26 Mar 69	**IT'S ONLY LOVE** *MGM 1467*	**42**	3 wks

---

BLACKBYRDS *US, male vocal/instrumental group*   **6 wks**

31 May 75	**WALKING IN RHYTHM** *Fantasy FTC 114*....................	**23**	6 wks

---

BLACKFOOT *US, male vocal/instrumental group*   **5 wks**

6 Mar 82	**DRY COUNTY** *Atco K 11686*	**43**	4 wks
18 Jun 83	**SEND ME AN ANGEL** *Atco B 9880*............................	**66**	1 wk

---

J. BLACKFOOT *US, male vocalist*   **4 wks**

17 Mar 84	**TAXI** *Allegiance ALES 2*	**48**	4 wks

---

BLACKFOOT SUE *UK, male vocal/instrumental group*   **15 wks**

12 Aug 72 ●	**STANDING IN THE ROAD** *Jam 13*	**4**	10 wks
16 Dec 72	**SING DON'T SPEAK** *Jam 29*	**36**	5 wks

---

BLACKHEARTS – *See Joan JETT and the BLACKHEARTS*

Honor BLACKMAN – *See Patrick MACNEE and Honor BLACKMAN*

Bill BLACK'S COMBO   **8 wks**
US, male instrumental group, Bill Black, bass

8 Sep 60	**WHITE SILVER SANDS** *London HLU 9090*...................	**50**	1 wk
3 Nov 60	**DON'T BE CRUEL** *London HLU 9212*........................	**32**	7 wks

---

BLACKWELLS *US, male vocal group*   **2 wks**

18 May 61	**LOVE OR MONEY** *London HLW 9334*.........................	**46**	2 wks

---

Vivian BLAINE *US, female vocalist*   **1 wk**

10 Jul 53	**BUSHEL AND A PECK** *Brunswick 05100*......................	**12**	1 wk

---

BLAIR – *See Terry HALL*

Joyce BLAIR – *See Miss X*

Peter BLAKE *UK, male vocalist*   **4 wks**

8 Oct 77	**LIPSMACKIN' ROCK 'N' ROLLIN'** *Pepper UP 36295*........	**40**	4 wks

---

BLANCMANGE *UK, male vocal/instrumental group*   **71 wks**

17 Apr 82	**GOD'S KITCHEN/ I'VE SEEN THE WORD**		
	London BLANC 1	**65**	2 wks
31 Jul 82	**FEEL ME** *London BLANC 2*................................	**46**	5 wks
30 Oct 82 ●	**LIVING ON THE CEILING** *London BLANC 3*	**7**	14 wks
19 Feb 83	**WAVES** *London BLANC 4*.................................	**19**	9 wks
7 May 83 ●	**BLIND VISION** *London BLANC 5*	**10**	8 wks
26 Nov 83	**THAT'S LOVE, THAT IT IS** *London BLANC 6*..............	**33**	8 wks
14 Apr 84 ●	**DON'T TELL ME** *London BLANC 7*........................	**8**	10 wks
21 Jul 84	**THE DAY BEFORE YOU CAME** *London BLANC 8*.........	**22**	8 wks
7 Sep 85	**WHAT'S YOUR PROBLEM?** *London BLANC 9*	**40**	5 wks
10 May 86	**I CAN SEE IT** *London BLANC 11*	**71**	2 wks

---

Billy BLAND *US, male vocalist*   **10 wks**

19 May 60	**LET THE LITTLE GIRL DANCE** *London HL 9096*..........	**15**	10 wks

---

BLOCKHEADS – *See Ian DURY and the BLOCKHEADS*

BLONDIE *US/UK, female/male vocal/instrumental group*   **145 wks**

18 Feb 78 ●	**DENIS** *Chrysalis CHS 2204*	**2**	14 wks
6 May 78 ●	**(I'M ALWAYS TOUCHED BY YOUR) PRESENCE**		
	DEAR *Chrysalis CHS 2217*............................	**10**	9 wks
26 Aug 78	**PICTURE THIS** *Chrysalis CHS 2242*	**12**	11 wks
11 Nov 78 ●	**HANGING ON THE TELEPHONE** *Chrysalis CHR 2266*	**5**	12 wks
27 Jan 79 ★	**HEART OF GLASS** *Chrysalis CHE 2275*....................	**1**	12 wks
19 May 79 ★	**SUNDAY GIRL** *Chrysalis CHS 2320*	**1**	13 wks
29 Sep 79 ●	**DREAMING** *Chrysalis CHS 2350*........................	**2**	8 wks
24 Nov 79	**UNION CITY BLUE** *Chrysalis CHS 2400*	**13**	10 wks
23 Feb 80 ★	**ATOMIC** *Chrysalis CHS 2410*	**1**	9 wks
12 Apr 80 ★	**CALL ME** *Chrysalis CHS 2414*..........................	**1**	9 wks
8 Nov 80 ★	**THE TIDE IS HIGH** *Chrysalis CHS 2465*	**1**	12 wks
24 Jan 81 ●	**RAPTURE** *Chrysalis CHS 2485*........................	**5**	8 wks
8 May 82	**ISLAND OF LOST SOULS** *Chrysalis CHS 2608*..........	**11**	9 wks
24 Jul 82	**WAR CHILD** *Chrysalis CHS 2624*	**39**	4 wks
3 Dec 88	**DENIS (re-mix)** *Chrysalis CHS 3328*...................	**50**	3 wks
11 Feb 89	**CALL ME (re-mix)** *Chrysalis CHS 3342*..................	**61**	2 wks

---

BLOOD SWEAT AND TEARS   **6 wks**
US/Canada, male vocal/instrumental group

30 Apr 69	**YOU'VE MADE ME SO VERY HAPPY** *CBS 4116*..........	**35**	6 wks

---

BLOODSTONE *US, male vocal/instrumental group*   **4 wks**

18 Aug 73	**NATURAL HIGH** *Decca F 13382*.............................	**40**	4 wks

---

Bobby BLOOM *US, male vocalist*   **24 wks**

29 Aug 70 ●	**MONTEGO BAY** *Polydor 2058 051*	**3**	14 wks
12 Dec 70	**MONTEGO BAY (re-entry)** *Polydor 2058 051*	**42**	3 wks
9 Jan 71	**HEAVY MAKES YOU HAPPY** *Polydor 2001 122*	**31**	5 wks
9 Jan 71	**MONTEGO BAY (2nd re-entry)** *Polydor 2058 051*	**47**	2 wks

BLOOMSBURY SET UK, male vocal/instrumental group   **3 wks**

25 Jun 83	HANGING AROUND WITH THE BIG BOYS *Stiletto STL 13*	56	3 wks

Kurtis BLOW US, male vocalist   **21 wks**

15 Dec 79	CHRISTMAS RAPPIN' *Mercury BLOW 7*	30	6 wks
11 Oct 80	THE BREAKS *Mercury BLOW 8*	47	4 wks
16 Mar 85	PARTY TIME (THE GO-GO EDIT) *Club JAB 12*	67	1 wk
18 Jan 86	IF I RULED THE WORLD *Club JAB 26*	24	8 wks
8 Nov 86	I'M CHILLIN' *Club JAB 42*	64	2 wks

See also Rene and Angela.

BLOW MONKEYS UK, male vocal/instrumental group   **46 wks**

1 Mar 86	DIGGING YOUR SCENE *RCA PB 40599*	12	10 wks
17 May 86	WICKED WAYS *RCA MONK 2*	60	2 wks
31 Jan 87	● IT DOESN'T HAVE TO BE THIS WAY *RCA MONK 4*	5	8 wks
28 Mar 87	OUT WITH HER *RCA MONK 5*	30	6 wks
30 May 87	(CELEBRATE) THE DAY AFTER YOU *RCA MONK 6*	52	2 wks
15 Aug 87	SOME KIND OF WONDERFUL *RCA MONK 7*	67	1 wk
6 Aug 88	THIS IS YOUR LIFE *RCA PB 42149*	70	2 wks
8 Apr 89	THIS IS YOUR LIFE (re-mix) *RCA PB 42695*	32	5 wks
15 Jul 89	CHOICE? *RCA PB 42885*	22	6 wks
14 Oct 89	SLAVES NO MORE *RCA PB 43201*	73	1 wk
26 May 90	SPRINGTIME FOR THE WORLD *RCA PB 43623*	69	2 wks

(Celebrate)The Day After You is with Curtis Mayfield. Choice? and Slaves No More feature vocals by Sylvia Tella - UK, female vocalist. See also Curtis Mayfield.

BLUE UK, male vocal/instrumental group   **8 wks**

30 Apr 77	GONNA CAPTURE YOUR HEART *Rocket ROKN 522*	18	8 wks

Babbity BLUE UK, female vocalist   **2 wks**

11 Feb 65	DON'T MAKE ME *Decca F 12053*	48	2 wks

Barry BLUE UK, male vocalist   **48 wks**

28 Jul 73	● (DANCING) ON A SATURDAY NIGHT *Bell 1295*	2	15 wks
3 Nov 73	● DO YOU WANNA DANCE *Bell 1336*	7	12 wks
2 Mar 74	SCHOOL LOVE *Bell 1345*	11	9 wks
3 Aug 74	MISS HIT AND RUN *Bell 1364*	26	7 wks
26 Oct 74	HOT SHOT *Bell 1379*	23	5 wks

BLUE AEROPLANES   **3 wks**
UK, male/female vocal/instrumental group

17 Feb 89	JACKET HANGS *Ensign ENY 628*	72	1 wk
26 May 89	... AND STONES *Ensign ENY 632*	63	2 wks

BLUE FEATHER Holland, male vocal/instrumental group   **4 wks**

3 Jul 82	LET'S FUNK TONIGHT *Mercury MER 109*	50	4 wks

BLUE FLAMES – *See Georgie FAME*

BLUE GRASS BOYS – *See Johnny DUNCAN and the BLUE GRASS BOYS*

BLUE HAZE UK, male vocal/instrumental group   **6 wks**

18 Mar 72	SMOKE GETS IN YOUR EYES *A &M AMS 891*	32	6 wks

BLUE JEANS – *See Bob B. SOXX and the BLUE JEANS*

BLUE MERCEDES UK, male vocal/instrumental duo   **18 wks**

10 Oct 87	I WANT TO BE YOUR PROPERTY *MCA BONA 1*	23	11 wks
13 Feb 88	SEE WANT MUST HAVE *MCA BONA 2*	57	2 wks
23 Jul 88	LOVE IS THE GUN *MCA BONA 3*	46	5 wks

BLUE MINK UK/US, male/female vocal/instrumental group   **83 wks**

15 Nov 69	● MELTING POT *Philips BF 1818*	3	15 wks
28 Mar 70	● GOOD MORNING FREEDOM *Philips BF 1838*	10	10 wks
19 Sep 70	OUR WORLD *Philips 6006 042*	17	9 wks
29 May 71	● BANNER MAN *Regal Zonophone RZ 3034*	3	14 wks
11 Nov 72	STAY WITH ME *Regal Zonophone RZ 3064*	11	13 wks
17 Feb 73	STAY WITH ME (re-entry) *Regal Zonophone RZ 3064*	43	2 wks
3 Mar 73	BY THE DEVIL *EMI 2007*	26	9 wks
23 Jun 73	● RANDY *EMI 2028*	9	11 wks

BLUE NILE UK, male vocal/instrumental group   **2 wks**

30 Sep 89	THE DOWNTOWN LIGHTS *Linn LKS 3*	67	1 wk
29 Sep 90	HEADLIGHTS ON THE PARADE *Linn LKS 4*	72	1 wk

BLUE OYSTER CULT   **14 wks**
US, male vocal/instrumental group

20 May 78	(DON'T FEAR) THE REAPER *CBS 6333*	16	14 wks

BLUE PEARL UK, male/female vocal/instrumental group   **18 wks**

7 Jul 90	● NAKED IN THE RAIN *Big Life BLR 32*	4	13 wks
3 Nov 90	LITTLE BROTHER *Big Life BLR 32*	31	5 wks

BLUE RONDO A LA TURK   **9 wks**
UK, male vocal/instrumental group

14 Nov 81	ME AND MR SANCHEZ *Virgin VS 463*	40	4 wks
13 Mar 82	KLACTOVEESEDSTEIN *Diable Noir VS 476*	50	5 wks

BLUE ZOO UK, male vocal/instrumental group   **17 wks**

12 Jun 82	I'M YOUR MAN *Magnet MAG 224*	55	3 wks
16 Oct 82	CRY BOY CRY *Magnet MAG 234*	13	10 wks
28 May 83	I JUST CAN'T (FORGIVE AND FORGET) *Magnet MAG 241*	60	4 wks

BLUEBELLS UK, male vocal/instrumental group   **37 wks**

12 Mar 83	CATH *London LON 20*	62	2 wks
9 Jul 83	SUGAR BRIDGE (IT WILL STAND) *London LON 27*	72	1 wk
24 Mar 84	I'M FALLING *London LON 45*	11	12 wks
23 Jun 84	● YOUNG AT HEART *London LON 49*	8	12 wks
1 Sep 84	CATH/ WILL SHE ALWAYS BE WAITING *London LON 54*	38	7 wks
9 Feb 85	ALL I AM (IS LOVING YOU) *London LON 58*	58	3 wks

LON 54 version of Cath *is a re-issue of LON 20.*

BLUENOTES – *See Harold MELVIN and the BLUENOTES*

BLUES BAND UK, male vocal/instrumental group   **2 wks**

12 Jul 80	BLUES BAND (EP) *Arista BOOT 2*	68	2 wks

Tracks on Blues Band EP: *Maggie's Farm/Ain't it Tuff/Diddy Wah Diddy/Back Door Man.*

Above: JON BON JOVI had his first solo hit from the soundtrack to the film *Young Guns II*.

DAVID BOWIE is the only artist to hit number one on his own and with each of two completely separate chart acts.

The Kon-rads

Benjamin Franklin Peay, better known as BROOK BENTON, had two dozen US Top Forty hits.

BLUES BROTHERS *US, male vocal duo* — 8 wks

| 7 Apr 89 | EVERYBODY NEEDS SOMEBODY TO LOVE | | |
| | *East West A7591* | 12 | 8 wks |

For the first two weeks, the flip side of 'Everybody Needs Somebody To Love' was listed as 'Think' by Aretha Franklin. See also Aretha Franklin.

Colin BLUNSTONE *UK, male vocalist* — 19 wks

12 Feb 72	SAY YOU DON'T MIND *Epic EPC 7765*	15	9 wks
11 Nov 72	I DON'T BELIEVE IN MIRACLES *Epic EPC 8434*	31	6 wks
17 Feb 73	HOW COULD WE DARE TO BE WRONG		
	Epic EPC 1197	45	2 wks
29 May 82	TRACKS OF MY TEARS *PRT 7P 236*	60	2 wks

See also Neil MacArthur; Dave Stewart.

BLUR *UK, male vocal/instrumental group* — 2 wks

| 27 Oct 90 | SHE'S SO HIGH *Food FOOD 26* | 48 | 2 wks |

B-MOVIE *UK, male vocal/instrumental group* — 7 wks

| 18 Apr 81 | REMEMBRANCE DAY *Deram DM 437* | 61 | 3 wks |
| 27 Mar 82 | NOWHERE GIRL *Some Bizzare BZZ 8* | 67 | 4 wks |

BOB and EARL *US, male vocal duo* — 13 wks

| 12 Mar 69 ● | HARLEM SHUFFLE *Island WIP 6053* | 7 | 13 wks |

BOB and MARCIA *Jamaica, male/female vocal duo* — 25 wks

| 14 Mar 70 ● | YOUNG GIFTED AND BLACK *Harry J HJ 6605* | 5 | 12 wks |
| 5 Jun 71 | PIED PIPER *Trojan TR 7818* | 11 | 13 wks |

BOBBYSOCKS *Norway/Sweden, female vocal duo* — 4 wks

| 25 May 85 | LET IT SWING *RCA PB 40127* | 44 | 4 wks |

BODYSNATCHERS *UK, female vocal/instrumental group* — 12 wks

| 15 Mar 80 | LET'S DO ROCK STEADY *2 Tone CHS TT 9* | 22 | 9 wks |
| 19 Jul 80 | EASY LIFE *2 Tone CHS TT 12* | 50 | 3 wks |

Humphrey BOGART – *See Dooley WILSON*

Hamilton BOHANNON
US, male vocalist/instrumentalist - drums — 38 wks

15 Feb 75	SOUTH AFRICAN MAN *Brunswick BR 16*	22	8 wks
24 May 75 ●	DISCO STOMP *Brunswick BR 19*	6	12 wks
5 Jul 75	FOOT STOMPIN' MUSIC *Brunswick BR 21*	23	6 wks
6 Sep 75	HAPPY FEELING *Brunswick BR 24*	49	3 wks
26 Aug 78	LET'S START THE DANCE *Mercury 6167 700*	56	4 wks
13 Feb 82	LET'S START TO DANCE AGAIN *London HL 10582*	49	5 wks

BOILING POINT *US, male vocal/instrumental group* — 6 wks

| 27 May 78 | LET'S GET FUNKTIFIED *Bang BANG 1312* | 41 | 6 wks |

Marc BOLAN – *See T. REX*

Michael BOLTON *US, male vocalist* — 25 wks

17 Feb 90 ●	HOW AM I SUPPOSED TO LIVE WITHOUT YOU		
	CBS 655397 7	3	10 wks
28 Apr 90 ●	HOW CAN WE BE LOVERS *CBS 655918 7*	10	10 wks
21 Jul 90	WHEN I'M BACK ON MY FEET AGAIN		
	CBS 656077 7	44	5 wks

BOMB THE BASS *UK, male producer - Tim Simenon* — 28 wks

20 Feb 88 ●	BEAT DIS *Mister-ron DOOD 1*	2	9 wks
27 Aug 88 ●	MEGABLAST/ DON'T MAKE ME WAIT		
	Mister-ron DOOD 2	6	9 wks
26 Nov 88 ●	SAY A LITTLE PRAYER *Rhythm King DOOD 3*	10	10 wks

Megablast features vocals by Merlin and Antonia - UK, male/female rap duo. Don't Make Me Wait features vocals by Lorraine - UK, female vocalist. Say A Little Prayer features Maureen - UK, female vocalist. See also Maureen.

BOMBALURINA *UK, male/female vocal group* — 19 wks

28 Jul 90 ★	ITSY BITSY TEENY WEENY YELLOW POLKA DOT		
	BIKINI *Carpet CRP 1*	1	13 wks
24 Nov 90	SEVEN LITTLE GIRLS SITTING IN THE BACKSEAT		
	Carpet CRPT 2	18†	6 wks

Seven Little Girls ... features Timmy Mallet.

BOMBERS *US, male/female vocal/instrumental group* — 10 wks

| 5 May 79 | (EVERYBODY) GET DANCIN' *Flamingo FM 1* | 37 | 7 wks |
| 18 Aug 79 | LET'S DANCE *Flamingo FM 4* | 58 | 3 wks |

BON JOVI *US, male vocal/instrumental group* — 71 wks

31 Aug 85	HARDEST PART IS THE NIGHT *Vertigo VER 22*	68	1 wk
9 Aug 86	YOU GIVE LOVE A BAD NAME *Vertigo VER 26*	14	10 wks
25 Oct 86 ●	LIVIN' ON A PRAYER *Vertigo VER 28*	4	15 wks
11 Apr 87	WANTED DEAD OR ALIVE *Vertigo JOV 1*	13	7 wks
15 Aug 87	NEVER SAY GOODBYE *Vertigo JOV 2*	21	5 wks
24 Sep 88	BAD MEDICINE *Vertigo JOV 3*	17	7 wks
10 Dec 88	BORN TO BE MY BABY *Vertigo JOV 4*	22	7 wks
29 Apr 89	I'LL BE THERE FOR YOU *Vertigo JOV 5*	18	7 wks
26 Aug 89	LAY YOUR HANDS ON ME *Vertigo JOV 6*	18	6 wks
9 Dec 89	LIVING IN SIN *Vertigo JOV 7*	35	6 wks

See also Jon Bon Jovi.

Jon BON JOVI *US, male vocalist* — 13 wks

| 4 Aug 90 | BLAZE OF GLORY *Vertigo JBJ 1* | 13 | 8 wks |
| 10 Nov 90 | MIRACLE *Vertigo JBVJ 2* | 29 | 5 wks |

See also Bon Jovi.

Ronnie BOND *UK, male vocalist* — 5 wks

| 31 May 80 | IT'S WRITTEN ON YOUR BODY *Mercury MER 13* | 52 | 5 wks |

Gary 'U.S.' BONDS *US, male vocalist* — 39 wks

19 Jan 61	NEW ORLEANS *Top Rank JAR 527*	16	11 wks
20 Jul 61 ●	QUARTER TO THREE *Top Rank JAR 575*	7	13 wks
30 May 81	THIS LITTLE GIRL *EMI America EA 122*	43	6 wks
22 Aug 81	JOLE BLON *EMI America EA 127*	51	3 wks
31 Oct 81	IT'S ONLY LOVE *EMI America EA 128*	43	3 wks
17 Jul 82	SOUL DEEP *EMI America EA 140*	59	3 wks

Known as U.S. Bonds on his 1961 hits.

Elbow BONES and the RACKETEERS   9 wks
US, male group leader and female backing group

14 Jan 84	**A NIGHT IN NEW YORK** *EMI America EA 165*		**33**	9 wks

BONEY M *Jamaica, Antilles, Montserrat, male/female vocal group*   155 wks

18 Dec 76	● **DADDY COOL** *Atlantic K 10827*		**6**	13 wks
12 Mar 77	● **SUNNY** *Atlantic K 10892*		**3**	10 wks
25 Jun 77	● **MA BAKER** *Atlantic K 10965*		**2**	13 wks
29 Oct 77	● **BELFAST** *Atlantic K 11020*		**8**	13 wks
29 Apr 78	★ **RIVERS OF BABYLON/ BROWN GIRL IN THE RING** *Atlantic/Hansa K 11120*		**1**	40 wks
7 Oct 78	● **RASPUTIN** *Atlantic/Hansa K 11192*		**2**	10 wks
2 Dec 78	★ **MARY'S BOY CHILD - OH MY LORD** *Atlantic/Hansa K 11221*		**1**	8 wks
3 Mar 79	● **PAINTER MAN** *Atlantic/Hansa K 11255*		**10**	6 wks
28 Apr 79	● **HOORAY HOORAY IT'S A HOLI-HOLIDAY** *Atlantic/Hansa K 11279*		**3**	9 wks
11 Aug 79	**GOTTA GO HOME/ EL LUTE** *Atlantic/Hansa K 11351*		**12**	11 wks
15 Dec 79	**I'M BORN AGAIN** *Atlantic/Hansa K 11410*		**35**	7 wks
26 Apr 80	**MY FRIEND JACK** *Atlantic/Hansa K 11463*		**57**	5 wks
14 Feb 81	**CHILDREN OF PARADISE** *Atlantic/Hansa K 11637*		**66**	2 wks
21 Nov 81	**WE KILL THE WORLD (DON'T KILL THE WORLD)** *Atlantic/Hansa K 11689*		**39**	5 wks
24 Dec 88	**MEGAMIX/ MARY'S BOY CHILD (re-mix)** *Ariola 111947*		**52**	3 wks

Brown Girl in The Ring only listed with Rivers of Babylon from 5 Aug 78. El Lute only listed with Gotta Go Home from 29 Sep 79.

Graham BONNET *UK, male vocalist*   15 wks

21 Mar 81	● **NIGHT GAMES** *Vertigo VER 1*		**6**	11 wks
13 Jun 81	**LIAR** *Vertigo VER 2*		**51**	4 wks

Graham BONNEY *UK, male vocalist*   8 wks

24 Mar 66	**SUPERGIRL** *Columbia DB 7843*		**19**	8 wks

BONNIE – *See DELANEY and BONNIE and FRIENDS featuring Eric CLAPTON*

BONO – *See CLANNAD*

BONZO DOG DOO-DAH BAND   14 wks
UK, male vocal/instrumental group

6 Nov 68	● **I'M THE URBAN SPACEMAN** *Liberty LBF 15144*		**5**	14 wks

Betty BOO *UK, female rapper*   27 wks

19 May 90	● **DOIN' THE DO** *Rhythm King LEFT 39*		**7**	12 wks
11 Aug 90	● **WHERE ARE YOU BABY** *Rhythm King LEFT 43*		**3**	10 wks
1 Dec 90	**24 HOURS** *Rhythm King LEFT 45*		**25†**	5 wks

See also Beatmasters.

BOO-YAA T.R.I.B.E. *US, male rap group*   3 wks

30 Jun 90	**PSYKO FUNK** *Fourth & Broadway BRW 179*		**43**	3 wks

BOOGIE BOX HIGH *UK, male vocal/instrumental duo*   11 wks

4 Jul 87	● **JIVE TALKIN'** *Hardback 7BOSS 4*		**7**	11 wks

BOOGIE DOWN PRODUCTIONS   2 wks
US, male rap/scratch duo

4 Jun 88	**MY PHILOSOPHY/ STOP THE VIOLENCE** *Jive JIVEX 170*		**69**	2 wks

BOOKER T. and the M.G.'s   43 wks
US, male instrumental group

11 Dec 68	**SOUL LIMBO** *Stax 102*		**30**	9 wks
7 May 69	● **TIME IS TIGHT** *Stax 119*		**4**	18 wks
30 Aug 69	**SOUL CLAP '69** *Stax 127*		**35**	4 wks
15 Dec 79	● **GREEN ONIONS** *Atlantic K 10109*		**7**	12 wks

BOOM BOOM ROOM   1 wk
UK, male vocal/instrumental group

8 Mar 86	**HERE COMES THE MAN** *Fun After All FUN 101*		**74**	1 wk

BOOMTOWN RATS   121 wks
Ireland, male vocal/instrumental group

27 Aug 77	**LOOKING AFTER NO. 1** *Ensign ENY 4*		**11**	9 wks
19 Nov 77	**MARY OF THE FOURTH FORM** *Ensign ENY 9*		**15**	9 wks
15 Apr 78	**SHE'S SO MODERN** *Ensign ENY 13*		**12**	11 wks
17 Jun 78	● **LIKE CLOCKWORK** *Ensign ENY 14*		**6**	13 wks
14 Oct 78	★ **RAT TRAP** *Ensign ENY 16*		**1**	15 wks
21 Jul 79	★ **I DON'T LIKE MONDAYS** *Ensign ENY 30*		**1**	12 wks
17 Nov 79	**DIAMOND SMILES** *Ensign ENY 33*		**13**	10 wks
26 Jan 80	● **SOMEONE'S LOOKING AT YOU** *Ensign ENY 34*		**4**	9 wks
22 Nov 80	● **BANANA REPUBLIC** *Ensign BONGO 1*		**3**	11 wks
31 Jan 81	**THE ELEPHANT'S GRAVEYARD (GUILTY)** *Ensign BONGO 2*		**26**	6 wks
12 Dec 81	**NEVER IN A MILLION YEARS** *Mercury MER 87*		**62**	4 wks
20 Mar 82	**HOUSE ON FIRE** *Mercury MER 91*		**24**	8 wks
18 Feb 84	**TONIGHT** *Mercury MER 154*		**73**	1 wk
19 May 84	**DRAG ME DOWN** *Mercury MER 163*		**50**	3 wks

Daniel BOONE *UK, male vocalist*   25 wks

14 Aug 71	**DADDY DON'T YOU WALK SO FAST** *Penny Farthing PEN 764*		**17**	15 wks
1 Apr 72	**BEAUTIFUL SUNDAY** *Penny Farthing PEN 781*		**48**	1 wk
15 Apr 72	**BEAUTIFUL SUNDAY (re-entry)** *Penny Farthing PEN 781*		**21**	9 wks

Debby BOONE *US, female vocalist*   2 wks

24 Dec 77	**YOU LIGHT UP MY LIFE** *Warner Bros. K 17043*		**48**	2 wks

Pat BOONE *US, male vocalist*   308 wks

18 Nov 55	● **AIN'T THAT A SHAME** *London HLD 8173*		**7**	9 wks
27 Apr 56	★ **I'LL BE HOME** *London HLD 8253*		**1**	22 wks
27 Jul 56	**LONG TALL SALLY** *London HLD 8291*		**27**	3 wks
17 Aug 56	**I ALMOST LOST MY MIND** *London HLD 8303*		**14**	7 wks
24 Aug 56	**LONG TALL SALLY (re-entry)** *London HLD 8291*		**18**	4 wks
7 Dec 56	● **FRIENDLY PERSUASION** *London HLD 8346*		**3**	21 wks
11 Jan 57	**AIN'T THAT A SHAME (re-entry)** *London HLD 8173*		**22**	2 wks
11 Jan 57	**I'LL BE HOME (re-entry)** *London HLD 8253*		**19**	2 wks
1 Feb 57	● **DON'T FORBID ME** *London HLD 8370*		**2**	16 wks
26 Apr 57	**WHY BABY WHY** *London HLD 8404*		**17**	7 wks
5 Jul 57	● **LOVE LETTERS IN THE SAND** *London HLD 8445*		**2**	21 wks
27 Sep 57	● **REMEMBER YOU'RE MINE/ THERE'S A GOLDMINE IN THE SKY** *London HLD 8479*		**5**	18 wks
6 Dec 57	● **APRIL LOVE** *London HLD 8512*		**7**	23 wks
13 Dec 57	**WHITE CHRISTMAS** *London HLD 8520*		**29**	1 wk
4 Apr 58	● **A WONDERFUL TIME UP THERE** *London HLD 8574*		**2**	17 wks

11 Apr 58 ●	IT'S TOO SOON TO KNOW *London HLD 8574*	7	12 wks
27 Jun 58 ●	SUGAR MOON *London HLD 8640*	6	12 wks
29 Aug 58	IF DREAMS CAME TRUE *London HLD 8675*	16	11 wks
5 Dec 58	GEE BUT IT'S LONELY *London HLD 8739*	30	1 wk
16 Jan 59	I'LL REMEMBER TONIGHT *London HLD 8775*	28	1 wk
6 Feb 59	I'LL REMEMBER TONIGHT (re-entry) *London HLD 8775*	21	1 wk
20 Feb 59	I'LL REMEMBER TONIGHT (2nd re-entry) *London HLD 8775*	18	7 wks
10 Apr 59	WITH THE WIND AND THE RAIN IN YOUR HAIR *London HLD 8824*	21	3 wks
22 May 59	FOR A PENNY *London HLD 8855*	28	3 wks
26 Jun 59	FOR A PENNY (re-entry) *London HLD 8855*	19	6 wks
31 Jul 59	'TWIXT TWELVE AND TWENTY *London HLD 8910*	18	6 wks
18 Sep 59	'TWIXT TWELVE AND TWENTY (re-entry) *London HLD 8910*	26	1 wk
23 Jun 60	WALKING THE FLOOR OVER YOU *London HLD 9138*	40	2 wks
14 Jul 60	WALKING THE FLOOR OVER YOU (re-entry) *London HLD 9138*	46	1 wk
4 Aug 60	WALKING THE FLOOR OVER YOU (2nd re-entry) *London HLD 9138*	39	2 wks
6 Jul 61	MOODY RIVER *London HLD 9350*	18	10 wks
7 Dec 61 ●	JOHNNY WILL *London HLD 9461*	4	13 wks
15 Feb 62	I'LL SEE YOU IN MY DREAMS *London HLD 9504*	27	9 wks
24 May 62	QUANDO QUANDO QUANDO *London HLD 9543*	41	1 wk
12 Jul 62 ●	SPEEDY GONZALES *London HLD 9573*	2	19 wks
15 Nov 62	THE MAIN ATTRACTION *London HLD 9620*	12	11 wks

There's A Goldmine In The Sky *was only credited for the week of 27 Sep 57.*

Duke BOOTEE – *See GRANDMASTER FLASH, Melle MEL and the FURIOUS FIVE*

Ken BOOTHE *Jamaica, male vocalist* **22 wks**

21 Sep 74 ★	EVERYTHING I OWN *Trojan TR 7920*	1	12 wks
14 Dec 74	CRYING OVER YOU *Trojan TR 7944*	11	10 wks

BOOTHILL FOOTAPPERS **3 wks**
UK, male/female vocal/instrumental group

14 Jul 84	GET YOUR FEET OUT OF MY SHOES *Go! Discs TAP 1*	64	3 wks

BOOTSY'S RUBBER BAND **3 wks**
US, male vocal/instrumental group

8 Jul 78	BOOTZILLA *Warner Bros. K 17196*	43	3 wks

BOOTZILLA ORCHESTRA – *See See Malcolm McCLAREN*

BOSTON *US, male vocal/instrumental group* **13 wks**

29 Jan 77	MORE THAN A FEELING *Epic EPC 4658*	22	8 wks
7 Oct 78	DON'T LOOK BACK *Epic EPC 6653*	43	5 wks

Eve BOSWELL *Hungary, female vocalist* **13 wks**

30 Dec 55 ●	PICKIN' A CHICKEN *Parlophone R 4082*	9	7 wks
2 Mar 56	PICKIN' A CHICKEN (re-entry) *Parlophone R 4082*	16	3 wks
6 Apr 56	PICKIN' A CHICKEN (2nd re-entry) *Parlophone R 4082*	20	3 wks

Judy BOUCHER *UK, female vocalist* **23 wks**

4 Apr 87 ●	CAN'T BE WITH YOU TONIGHT *Orbitone OR 721*	2	14 wks
4 Jul 87	YOU CAUGHT MY EYE *Orbitone OR 722*	18	9 wks

BOUNCING CZECKS **1 wk**
UK, male vocal/instrumental group

29 Dec 84	I'M A LITTLE CHRISTMAS CRACKER *RCA 463*	72	1 wk

BOURGEOIS TAGG *US, male vocal/instrumental duo* **6 wks**

6 Feb 88	I DON'T MIND AT ALL *Island IS 353*	35	6 wks

BOURGIE BOURGIE *UK, male vocal/instrumental group* **4 wks**

3 Mar 84	BREAKING POINT *MCA BOU 1*	48	4 wks

BOW WOW WOW **54 wks**
UK, female/male vocal/instrumental group

26 Jul 80	C30, C60, C90, GO *EMI 5088*	34	7 wks
6 Dec 80	YOUR CASSETTE PET *EMI WOW 1*	58	6 wks
28 Mar 81	W.O.R.K. (N.O. NAH NO NO MY DADDY DON'T) *EMI 5153*	62	3 wks
15 Aug 81	PRINCE OF DARKNESS *RCA 100*	58	4 wks
7 Nov 81	CHIHUAHUA *RCA 144*	51	4 wks
30 Jan 82 ●	GO WILD IN THE COUNTRY *RCA 175*	7	13 wks
1 May 82	SEE JUNGLE (JUNGLE BOY)/ TV SAVAGE *RCA 220*	45	3 wks
5 Jun 82 ●	I WANT CANDY *RCA 238*	9	8 wks
31 Jul 82	LOUIS QUATORZE *RCA 263*	66	2 wks
12 Mar 83	DO YOU WANNA HOLD ME *RCA 314*	47	4 wks

Your Cassette Pet *listed as Louis Quatorze on 6 Dec 80 only. Tracks on Your Cassette Pet (available only as a cassette) are: Louis Quatorze/Gold He Said/Umo-Sex-Al Apache/I Want My Baby On Mars/Sexy Eiffel Towers/Giant Sized Baby Thing/Fools Rush In/Radio G.String. RCA 263 is disc version of track on EMI WOW 1 Cassette.*

David BOWIE *UK, male vocalist* **366 wks**

6 Sep 69	SPACE ODDITY *Philips BF 1801*	48	1 wk
20 Sep 69 ●	SPACE ODDITY (re-entry) *Philips BF 1801*	5	13 wks
24 Jun 72 ●	STARMAN *RCA 2199*	10	11 wks
16 Sep 72	JOHN I'M ONLY DANCING *RCA 2263*	12	10 wks
9 Dec 72 ●	THE JEAN GENIE *RCA 2302*	2	13 wks
14 Apr 73 ●	DRIVE-IN SATURDAY *RCA 2352*	3	10 wks
30 Jun 73 ●	LIFE ON MARS *RCA 2316*	3	13 wks
15 Sep 73 ●	THE LAUGHING GNOME *Deram DM 123*	6	12 wks
20 Oct 73 ●	SORROW *RCA 2424*	3	15 wks
23 Feb 74 ●	REBEL REBEL *RCA LPBO 5009*	5	7 wks
20 Apr 74	ROCK AND ROLL SUICIDE *RCA LPBO 5021*	22	7 wks
22 Jun 74	DIAMOND DOGS *RCA APBO 0293*	21	6 wks
28 Sep 74 ●	KNOCK ON WOOD *RCA 2466*	10	6 wks
1 Mar 75	YOUNG AMERICANS *RCA 2523*	18	7 wks
2 Aug 75	FAME *RCA 2579*	17	8 wks
11 Oct 75 ★	SPACE ODDITY (re-issue) *RCA 2593*	1	10 wks
29 Nov 75 ●	GOLDEN YEARS *RCA 2640*	8	10 wks
22 May 76	TVC 15 *RCA 2682*	33	4 wks
19 Feb 77 ●	SOUND AND VISION *RCA PB 0905*	3	11 wks
15 Oct 77	HEROES *RCA PB 1121*	24	8 wks
21 Jan 78	BEAUTY AND THE BEAST *RCA PB 1190*	39	3 wks
2 Dec 78	BREAKING GLASS (EP) *RCA BOW 1*	54	7 wks
5 May 79 ●	BOYS KEEP SWINGING *RCA BOW 2*	7	10 wks
21 Jul 79	D.J. *RCA BOW 3*	29	5 wks
15 Dec 79	JOHN I'M ONLY DANCING (AGAIN) (1975)/ JOHN I'M ONLY DANCING (1972) *RCA BOW 4*	12	8 wks
1 Mar 80	ALABAMA SONG *RCA BOW 5*	23	5 wks
16 Aug 80 ★	ASHES TO ASHES *RCA BOW 6*	1	10 wks
1 Nov 80 ●	FASHION *RCA BOW 7*	5	12 wks
10 Jan 81	SCARY MONSTERS (AND SUPER CREEPS) *RCA BOW 8*	20	6 wks
28 Mar 81	UP THE HILL BACKWARDS *RCA BOW 9*	32	6 wks
28 Nov 81	WILD IS THE WIND *RCA BOW 10*	24	10 wks
6 Mar 82	BAAL'S HYMN (EP) *RCA BOW 11*	29	5 wks
10 Apr 82	CAT PEOPLE (PUTTING OUT FIRE) *MCA 770*	26	6 wks
26 Mar 83 ★	LET'S DANCE *EMI America EA 152*	1	14 wks
11 Jun 83 ●	CHINA GIRL *EMI America EA 157*	2	8 wks

24 Sep 83 ●	MODERN LOVE *EMI America EA 158*	2	8 wks
5 Nov 83	WHITE LIGHT, WHITE HEAT *RCA 372*	46	3 wks
22 Sep 84 ●	BLUE JEAN *EMI America EA 181*	6	8 wks
8 Dec 84	TONIGHT *EMI America EA 187*	53	4 wks
8 Jun 85	LOVING THE ALIEN *EMI America EA 195*	19	6 wks
27 Jul 85	LOVING THE ALIEN (re-entry) *EMI America EA 195*	67	1 wk
15 Mar 86 ●	ABSOLUTE BEGINNERS *Virgin VS 838*	2	9 wks
21 Jun 86	UNDERGROUND *EMI America EA 216*	21	6 wks
8 Nov 86	WHEN THE WIND BLOWS *Virgin VS 906*	44	4 wks
4 Apr 87	DAY-IN DAY-OUT *EMI America EA 230*	17	6 wks
27 Jun 87	TIME WILL CRAWL *EMI America EA 237*	33	4 wks
29 Aug 87	NEVER LET ME DOWN *EMI America EA 239*	34	6 wks
7 Apr 90	FAME (re-mix) *EMI-USA FAME 90*	28	4 wks

Tracks on Breaking Glass EP: Breaking Glass/Art Decade/Ziggy Stardust. All three versions of John I'm Only Dancing are different versions. Tracks on Baal's Hymn EP: Baal's Hymn/The Drowned Girl/Remembering Marie/The Dirty Song/Ballad of the Adventurers. See also Queen and David Bowie; David Bowie and Bing Crosby; David Bowie and Mick Jagger; David Bowie and the Pat Metheny Group.

David BOWIE and Bing CROSBY   8 wks
UK/US, male vocal duo

27 Nov 82 ●	PEACE ON EARTH - LITTLE DRUMMER BOY *RCA BOW 12*	3	8 wks

See also David Bowie; Bing Crosby.

David BOWIE and Mick JAGGER   12 wks
UK, male vocal duo

7 Sep 85 ★	DANCING IN THE STREET *EMI America EA 204*	1	12 wks

See also David Bowie; Mick Jagger.

David BOWIE and the Pat METHENY GROUP   7 wks
UK/US, male vocalist/male vocal/instrumental group

9 Feb 85	THIS IS NOT AMERICA *EMI America EA 190*	14	7 wks

See also David Bowie.

BOX TOPS   US, male vocal/instrumental group   33 wks

13 Sep 67 ●	THE LETTER *Stateside SS 2044*	5	12 wks
20 Mar 68	CRY LIKE A BABY *Bell 1001*	15	12 wks
23 Aug 69	SOUL DEEP *Bell 1068*	22	9 wks

BOY GEORGE   UK, male vocalist   34 wks

7 Mar 87 ★	EVERYTHING I OWN *Virgin BOY 100*	1	9 wks
6 Jun 87	KEEP ME IN MIND *Virgin BOY 101*	29	4 wks
18 Jul 87	SOLD *Virgin BOY 102*	24	5 wks
21 Nov 87	TO BE REBORN *Virgin BOY 103*	13	7 wks
5 Mar 88	LIVE MY LIFE *Virgin BOY 105*	62	2 wks
18 Jun 88	NO CLAUSE 28 *Virgin BOY 106*	57	3 wks
8 Oct 88	DON'T CRY *Virgin BOY 107*	60	2 wks
4 Mar 89	DON'T TAKE MY MIND ON A TRIP *Virgin BOY 108*	68	2 wks

BOY MEETS GIRL   US, male/female vocal duo   13 wks

3 Dec 88 ●	WAITING FOR A STAR TO FALL *RCA PB 49519*	9	13 wks

Jimmy BOYD   US, male vocalist   6 wks

27 Nov 53 ●	I SAW MOMMY KISSING SANTA CLAUS *Columbia DB 3365*	3	6 wks

See also Frankie Laine and Jimmy Boyd.

Jacqueline BOYER   France, female vocalist   2 wks

28 Apr 60	TOM PILLIBI *Columbia DB 4452*	33	2 wks

BOYS   US, male vocal group   3 wks

12 Nov 88	DIAL MY HEART *Motown ZB 42245*	61	2 wks
29 Sep 90	CRAZY *Motown ZB 44037*	57	1 wk

BOYSTOWN GANG   US, male/female vocal group   20 wks

22 Aug 81	AIN'T NO MOUNTAIN HIGH ENOUGH - REMEMBER ME (MEDLEY) *WEA DICK 1*	46	6 wks
31 Jul 82 ●	CAN'T TAKE MY EYES OFF YOU *ERC 101*	4	11 wks
9 Oct 82	SIGNED SEALED DELIVERED (I'M YOURS) *ERC 102*	50	3 wks

BOYZ – *See HEAVY D and the BOYZ*

Billy BRAGG   UK, male vocalist   33 wks

16 Mar 85	BETWEEN THE WARS (EP) *Go! Discs AGOEP 1*	15	6 wks
28 Dec 85	DAYS LIKE THESE *Go! Discs GOD 8*	43	5 wks
28 Jun 86	LEVI STUBBS TEARS *Go! Discs GOD 12*	29	6 wks
15 Nov 86	GREETINGS TO THE NEW BRUNETTE *Go! Discs GOD 15*	58	2 wks
14 May 88 ★	SHE'S LEAVING HOME *Childline CHILD 1*	1	11 wks
10 Sep 88	WAITING FOR THE GREAT LEAP FORWARDS *Go! Discs GOD 23*	52	3 wks

Tracks on EP: Between the Wars/Which Side Are You On/World Turned Upside Down/It Says Here. She's Leaving Home is with Cara Tivey - UK, female vocalist/instrumentalist - piano. It was listed with the flip side With A Little Help From My Friends by Wet Wet Wet. See also Wet Wet Wet; Norman Cook.

Wilfred BRAMBELL and Harry H. CORBETT   12 wks
UK, male vocal duo

28 Nov 63	AT THE PALACE (PARTS 1 & 2) *Pye 7N 15588*	25	12 wks

Johnny BRANDON   UK, male vocalist   12 wks

11 Mar 55 ●	TOMORROW *Polygon P 1131*	8	6 wks
29 Apr 55	TOMORROW (re-entry) *Polygon P 1131*	16	2 wks
1 Jul 55	DON'T WORRY *Polygon P 1163*	18	4 wks

Laura BRANIGAN   US, female vocalist   33 wks

18 Dec 82 ●	GLORIA *Atlantic K 11759*	6	13 wks
7 Jul 84 ●	SELF CONTROL *Atlantic A 9676*	5	17 wks
6 Oct 84	THE LUCKY ONE *Atlantic A 9636*	56	3 wks

BRASS CONSTRUCTION   35 wks
US, male vocal/instrumental group

3 Apr 76	MOVIN' *United Artists UP 36090*	23	6 wks
5 Feb 77	HA CHA CHA (FUNKTION) *United Artists UP 36205*	37	5 wks
26 Jan 80	MUSIC MAKES YOU FEEL LIKE DANCING *United Artists UP 615*	39	6 wks
28 May 83	WALKIN' THE LINE *Capitol CL 292*	47	3 wks
16 Jul 83	WE CAN WORK IT OUT *Capitol CL 299*	70	2 wks
7 Jul 84	PARTYLINE *Capitol CL 335*	56	4 wks
27 Oct 84	INTERNATIONAL *Capitol CL 341*	70	2 wks
9 Nov 85	GIVE AND TAKE *Capitol CL 377*	62	3 wks
28 May 88	MOVIN' 1988 (re-mix) *Syncopate SY 11*	24	4 wks

BRAT UK, male vocalist   **8 wks**

10 Jul 82	**CHALK DUST - THE UMPIRE STRIKES BACK** *Hansa SMASH 1*	**19**	8 wks

Los BRAVOS Spain/Germany, male vocal/instrumental group   **24 wks**

30 Jun 66 ●	**BLACK IS BLACK** *Decca F 22419*	**2**	13 wks
8 Sep 66	**I DON'T CARE** *Decca F 22484*	**16**	11 wks

Dhar BRAXTON US, female vocalist   **8 wks**

31 May 86	**JUMP BACK (SET ME FREE)** *Fourth & Broadway BRW 47*	**32**	8 wks

BREAD US, male vocal/instrumental group   **46 wks**

1 Aug 70 ●	**MAKE IT WITH YOU** *Elektra 2101 010*	**5**	14 wks
15 Jan 72	**BABY I'M A WANT YOU** *Elektra K 12033*	**14**	10 wks
29 Apr 72	**EVERYTHING I OWN** *Elektra K 12041*	**32**	6 wks
30 Sep 72	**GUITAR MAN** *Elektra K 12066*	**16**	9 wks
25 Dec 76	**LOST WITHOUT YOUR LOVE** *Elektra K 12241*	**27**	7 wks

BREAK MACHINE US, male vocal/dance group   **32 wks**

4 Feb 84 ●	**STREET DANCE** *Record Shack SOHO 13*	**3**	14 wks
12 May 84 ●	**BREAKDANCE PARTY** *Record Shack SOHO 20*	**9**	8 wks
14 Jul 84	**BREAKDANCE PARTY (re-entry)** *Record Shack SOHO 20*	**65**	2 wks
11 Aug 84	**ARE YOU READY?** *Record Shack SOHO 24*	**27**	8 wks

BREAKFAST CLUB US, male vocal/instrumental group   **3 wks**

27 Jun 87	**RIGHT ON TRACK** *MCA MCA 1146*	**54**	3 wks

BREATHE UK, male vocal/instrumental group   **27 wks**

30 Jul 88 ●	**HANDS TO HEAVEN** *Siren SRN 68*	**4**	12 wks
22 Oct 88	**JONAH** *Siren SRN 95*	**60**	3 wks
3 Dec 88	**HOW CAN I FALL** *Siren SRN 102*	**48**	7 wks
11 Mar 89	**DON'T TELL ME LIES** *Siren SRN 109*	**45**	5 wks

Freddy BRECK Germany, male vocalist   **4 wks**

13 Apr 74	**SO IN LOVE WITH YOU** *Decca F 13481*	**44**	4 wks

BRECKER BROTHERS   **5 wks**
US, male vocal/instrumental group

4 Nov 78	**EAST RIVER** *Arista ARIST 211*	**34**	5 wks

BREEKOUT KREW US, male vocal duo   **3 wks**

24 Nov 84	**MATT'S MOOD** *London LON 59*	**51**	3 wks

Ann BREEN Ireland, female vocalist   **2 wks**

19 Mar 83	**PAL OF MY CRADLE DAYS** *Homespun HS 052*	**69**	1 wk
7 Jan 84	**PAL OF MY CRADLE DAYS (re-entry)** *Homespun HS 052*	**74**	1 wk

BRENDON UK, male vocalist   **9 wks**

19 Mar 77	**GIMME SOME** *Magnet MAG 80*	**14**	9 wks

Rose BRENNAN Ireland, female vocalist   **9 wks**

7 Dec 61	**TALL DARK STRANGER** *Philips PB 1193*	**31**	9 wks

Walter BRENNAN US, male vocalist   **3 wks**

28 Jun 62	**OLD RIVERS** *Liberty LIB 55436*	**38**	3 wks

Tony BRENT UK, male vocalist   **52 wks**

19 Dec 52 ●	**WALKIN' TO MISSOURI** *Columbia DB 3147*	**9**	2 wks
2 Jan 53 ●	**MAKE IT SOON** *Columbia DB 3187*	**9**	4 wks
9 Jan 53 ●	**WALKIN' TO MISSOURI (re-entry)** *Columbia DB 3147*	**7**	5 wks
23 Jan 53	**GOT YOU ON MY MIND** *Columbia DB 3226*	**12**	1 wk
13 Mar 53 ●	**MAKE IT SOON (re-entry)** *Columbia DB 3187*	**9**	3 wks
30 Nov 56	**CINDY OH CINDY** *Columbia DB 3844*	**16**	6 wks
8 Feb 57	**CINDY OH CINDY (re-entry)** *Columbia DB 3844*	**30**	1 wk
28 Jun 57	**DARK MOON** *Columbia DB 3950*	**17**	14 wks
28 Feb 58	**THE CLOUDS WILL SOON ROLL BY** *Columbia DB 4066*	**24**	3 wks
9 May 58	**THE CLOUDS WILL SOON ROLL BY (re-entry)** *Columbia DB 4066*	**20**	2 wks
5 Sep 58	**GIRL OF MY DREAMS** *Columbia DB 4177*	**16**	7 wks
24 Jul 59	**WHY SHOULD I BE LONELY** *Columbia DB 4304*	**24**	4 wks

Bernard BRESSLAW UK, male vocalist   **11 wks**

5 Sep 58 ●	**MAD PASSIONATE LOVE** *HMV POP 522*	**6**	11 wks

See also Michael Medwin, Bernard Bresslaw, Alfie Bass and Leslie Fyson.

Teresa BREWER US, female vocalist   **53 wks**

11 Feb 55 ●	**LET ME GO LOVER** *Vogue/Coral Q 72043*	**9**	10 wks
13 Apr 56 ●	**A TEAR FELL** *Vogue/Coral Q 72146*	**2**	15 wks
13 Jul 56 ●	**SWEET OLD-FASHIONED GIRL** *Vogue/Coral Q 72172*	**3**	15 wks
10 May 57	**NORA MALONE** *Vogue/Coral Q 72224*	**26**	2 wks
23 Jun 60	**HOW DO YOU KNOW IT'S LOVE** *Coral Q 72396*	**21**	11 wks

BRIAN and MICHAEL UK, male vocal duo   **19 wks**

25 Feb 78 ★	**MATCHSTALK MEN AND MATCHSTALK CATS AND DOGS** *Pye 7N 46035*	**1**	19 wks

BRICK US, male vocal/instrumental group   **4 wks**

5 Feb 77	**DAZZ** *Bang 004*	**36**	4 wks

Edie BRICKELL and the NEW BOHEMIANS   **8 wks**
US, female/male vocal/instrumental group

4 Feb 89	**WHAT I AM** *Geffen GEF 49*	**31**	7 wks
27 May 89	**CIRCLE** *Geffen GEF 51*	**74**	1 wk

Alicia BRIDGES US, female vocalist   **10 wks**

11 Nov 78	**I LOVE THE NIGHT LIFE (DISCO ROUND)** *Polydor 2066 936*	**32**	10 wks

Left: Jason Donovan seems to be doing Zorba's dance as he guests with BROS.

Bottom Left: JAMES BROWN had twenty-six hits on the US R&B chart before his first UK success.

Left: Durga McBroom was the lead singer of BLUE PEARL.

Below: BOBBY BROWN, the artist with Most Weeks on Chart in 1989, is shown at the 1990 American Music Awards.

BRIGHOUSE AND RASTRICK BRASS BAND *UK, male brass band* — 13 wks

12 Nov 77 ●	THE FLORAL DANCE *Transatlantic BIG 548*	2	13 wks

Bette BRIGHT *UK, female vocalist* — 5 wks

8 Mar 80	HELLO I AM YOUR HEART *Korova KOW 3*	50	5 wks

Sarah BRIGHTMAN *UK, female vocalist* — 34 wks

11 Nov 78 ●	I LOST MY HEART TO A STARSHIP TROOPER *Ariola/Hansa AHA 527*	6	14 wks
7 Apr 79	THE ADVENTURES OF THE LOVE CRUSADER *Ariola/Hansa AHA 538*	53	5 wks
30 Jul 83	HIM *Polydor POSP 625*	55	4 wks
10 Jan 87 ●	WISHING YOU WERE SOMEHOW HERE AGAIN *Polydor POSP 803*	7	11 wks

First hit credited to Sarah Brightman and Hot Gossip, second to Sarah Brightman and the Starship Troopers. Him credited to Sarah Brightman and the Royal Philharmonic Orchestra. The listed flip side of Wishing You Were Somehow Here Again was The Music Of The Night by Michael Crawford. See also Sarah Brightman and Paul Miles-Kingston; Sarah Brightman and Steve Harley; Cliff Richard and Sarah Brightman; Michael Crawford.

Sarah BRIGHTMAN and Steve HARLEY *UK, female/male vocal duo* — 10 wks

11 Jan 86 ●	THE PHANTOM OF THE OPERA *Polydor POSP 800*	7	10 wks

See also Sarah Brightman; Steve Harley and Cockney Rebel.

Sarah BRIGHTMAN and Paul MILES-KINGSTON *UK, female/male vocal duo* — 8 wks

23 Mar 85 ●	PIE JESU *HMV WEBBER 1*	3	8 wks

Also credited: Winchester Cathedral Choir, Director Martin Neary; James Lancelot, organ; English Chamber Orchestra directed by Lorin Maazel. See also Sarah Brightman.

BRIGHTON AND HOVE ALBION F.C. *UK, male football team vocalists* — 2 wks

28 May 83	THE BOYS IN THE OLD BRIGHTON BLUE *Energy NRG 2*	65	2 wks

BRILLIANT *UK, male/female vocal/instrumental group* — 13 wks

19 Oct 85	IT'S A MAN'S MAN'S MAN'S WORLD *Food FOOD 5*	58	5 wks
22 Mar 86	LOVE IS WAR *Food FOOD 6*	64	4 wks
2 Aug 86	SOMEBODY *Food FOOD 7*	67	4 wks

Johnny BRISTOL *US, male vocalist* — 11 wks

24 Aug 74 ●	HANG ON IN THERE BABY *MGM 2006 443*	3	11 wks

See also Amii Stewart and Johnny Bristol.

BROKEN ENGLISH *UK, male vocal/instrumental group* — 13 wks

30 May 87	COMIN' ON STRONG *EMI EM 5*	18	10 wks
3 Oct 87	LOVE ON THE SIDE *EMI EM 55*	69	3 wks

BRONSKI BEAT *UK, male vocal/instrumental group* — 55 wks

2 Jun 84 ●	SMALLTOWN BOY *Forbidden Fruit BITE 1*	3	13 wks
22 Sep 84 ●	WHY? *Forbidden Fruit BITE 2*	6	10 wks
1 Dec 84	IT AIN'T NECESSARILY SO *Forbidden Fruit BITE 3*	16	11 wks
30 Nov 85 ●	HIT THAT PERFECT BEAT *Forbidden Fruit BITE 6*	3	14 wks
29 Mar 86	COME ON, COME ON *Forbidden Fruit BITE 7*	20	7 wks

See also Bronski Beat and Marc Almond; Eartha Kitt and Bronski Beat.

BRONSKI BEAT and Marc ALMOND *UK, male vocal/instrumental group with UK, male vocalist* — 12 wks

20 Apr 85 ●	I FEEL LOVE (MEDLEY) *Forbidden Fruit BITE 4*	3	12 wks

Tracks on medley: I Feel Love/Love To Love You Baby/Johnnie Remember Me. See also Bronski Beat; Marc Almond.

Jet BRONX and the FORBIDDEN *UK, male vocal/instrumental group* — 1 wk

17 Dec 77	AIN'T DOIN' NOTHIN' *Lightning L1G 50*	49	1 wk

BROOK BROTHERS *UK, male vocal duo* — 35 wks

30 Mar 61 ●	WARPAINT *Pye 7N 15333*	5	14 wks
24 Aug 61	AIN'T GONNA WASH FOR A WEEK *Pye 7N 15369*	13	10 wks
25 Jan 62	HE'S OLD ENOUGH TO KNOW BETTER *Pye 7N 15409*	37	1 wk
16 Aug 62	WELCOME HOME BABY *Pye 7N 15453*	33	6 wks
21 Feb 63	TROUBLE IS MY MIDDLE NAME *Pye 7N 15498*	38	4 wks

Bruno BROOKES – See Liz KERSHAW and Bruno BROOKES

BROOKLYN, BRONX and QUEENS – See BB and Q Band

Elkie BROOKS *UK, female vocalist* — 91 wks

2 Apr 77 ●	PEARL'S A SINGER *A&M AMS 7275*	8	9 wks
20 Aug 77 ●	SUNSHINE AFTER THE RAIN *A&M AMS 7306*	10	9 wks
25 Feb 78	LILAC WINE *A&M AMS 7333*	16	7 wks
3 Jun 78	ONLY LOVE CAN BREAK YOUR HEART *A&M AMS 7353*	43	5 wks
11 Nov 78	DON'T CRY OUT LOUD *A&M AMS 7395*	12	11 wks
5 May 79	THE RUNAWAY *A&M AMS 7428*	50	5 wks
16 Jan 82	FOOL IF YOU THINK IT'S OVER *A&M AMS 8187*	17	10 wks
1 May 82	OUR LOVE *A&M AMS 8214*	43	5 wks
17 Jul 82	NIGHTS IN WHITE SATIN *A&M AMS 8235*	33	5 wks
22 Jan 83	GASOLINE ALLEY *A&M AMS 8305*	52	5 wks
22 Nov 86 ●	NO MORE THE FOOL *Legend LM 4*	5	16 wks
4 Apr 87	BREAK THE CHAIN *Legend LM 8*	55	3 wks
11 Jul 87	WE'VE GOT TONIGHT *Legend LM 9*	69	1 wk

Mel BROOKS *US, male vocalist* — 10 wks

18 Feb 84	TO BE OR NOT TO BE (THE HITLER RAP) *Island IS 158*	12	10 wks

Norman BROOKS *US, male vocalist* — 1 wk

12 Nov 54	A SKY BLUE SHIRT AND A RAINBOW TIE *London L 1228*	17	1 wk

BROS *UK, male vocal/instrumental group* — 75 wks

5 Dec 87	WHEN WILL I BE FAMOUS *CBS ATOM 2*	62	2 wks
9 Jan 88 ●	WHEN WILL I BE FAMOUS (re-entry) *CBS ATOM 2*	2	13 wks

19 Mar 88	● DROP THE BOY *CBS ATOM 3*	2	10 wks
18 Jun 88	★ I OWE YOU NOTHING *CBS ATOM 4*	1	11 wks
17 Sep 88	● I QUIT *CBS ATOM 5*	4	8 wks
3 Dec 88	● CAT AMONG THE PIGEONS/ SILENT NIGHT		
	CBS ATOM 6	2	8 wks
29 Jul 89	● TOO MUCH *CBS ATOM 7*	2	7 wks
7 Oct 89	● CHOCOLATE BOX *CBS ATOM 8*	9	6 wks
16 Dec 89	● SISTER *CBS ATOM 9*	10	6 wks
10 Mar 90	MADLY IN LOVE *CBS ATOM 10*	14	4 wks

BROTHER BEYOND *UK, male vocal/instrumental group*   **56 wks**

4 Apr 87	HOW MANY TIMES *EMI EMI 5591*	62	3 wks
8 Aug 87	CHAIN-GANG SMILE *Parlophone R 6160*	57	3 wks
23 Jan 88	CAN YOU KEEP A SECRET *Parlophone R 6174*	56	4 wks
30 Jul 88	● THE HARDER I TRY *Parlophone R 6184*	2	14 wks
5 Nov 88	● HE AIN'T NO COMPETITION *Parlophone R 6193*	6	10 wks
21 Jan 89	BE MY TWIN *Parlophone R 6195*	14	6 wks
1 Apr 89	CAN YOU KEEP A SECRET (re-mix) *Parlophone R 6197*.....	22	5 wks
28 Oct 89	DRIVE ON *Parlophone R 6233*	39	4 wks
9 Dec 89	WHEN WILL I SEE YOU AGAIN *Parlophone R 6239*..........	43	5 wks
10 Mar 90	TRUST *Parlophone R 6245*	53	2 wks

BROTHERHOOD OF MAN   **97 wks**
UK, male/female vocal group

14 Feb 70	● UNITED WE STAND *Deram DM 284*	10	9 wks
4 Jul 70	WHERE ARE YOU GOING TO MY LOVE		
	Deram DM 298	22	10 wks
13 Mar 76	★ SAVE YOUR KISSES FOR ME *Pye 7N 45569*	1	16 wks
19 Jun 76	MY SWEET ROSALIE *Pye 7N 45602*	30	7 wks
26 Feb 77	● OH BOY (THE MOOD I'M IN) *Pye 7N 45656*	8	12 wks
9 Jul 77	★ ANGELO *Pye 7N 45699*	1	12 wks
14 Jan 78	★ FIGARO *Pye 7N 46037*	1	11 wks
27 May 78	BEAUTIFUL LOVER *Pye 7N 46071*	15	12 wks
30 Sep 78	MIDDLE OF THE NIGHT *Pye 7N 46117*	41	6 wks
3 Jul 82	LIGHTNING FLASH *EMI 5309*	67	2 wks

BROTHERLOVE – *See PRATT and McLAIN with BROTHERLOVE*

BROTHERS *UK, male vocal group*   **9 wks**

29 Jan 77	● SING ME *Bus Stop Bus 1054*	8	9 wks

BROTHERS FOUR *US, male vocal group*   **2 wks**

23 Jun 60	GREENFIELDS *Philips PB 1009*	49	1 wk
7 Jul 60	GREENFIELDS (re-entry) *Philips PB 1009*	40	1 wk

BROTHERS GRIMM – *See JAZZ and the BROTHERS GRIMM*

BROTHERS JOHNSON   **34 wks**
US, male vocal/instrumental duo

9 Jul 77	STRAWBERRY LETTER 23 *A & M AMS 7297*	35	5 wks
2 Sep 78	AIN'T WE FUNKIN' NOW *A & M AMS 7379*	43	6 wks
4 Nov 78	RIDE-O-ROCKET *A & M AMS 7400*	50	4 wks
23 Feb 80	● STOMP *A & M AMS 7509*	6	12 wks
31 May 80	LIGHT UP THE NIGHT *A & M AMS 7526*	47	4 wks
25 Jul 81	THE REAL THING *A & M AMS 8149*	50	3 wks

Edgar BROUGHTON BAND   **10 wks**
UK, male vocal/instrumental group

18 Apr 70	OUT DEMONS OUT *Harvest HAR 5015*	39	5 wks
23 Jan 71	APACHE DROPOUT *Harvest HAR 5032*	49	1 wk
6 Feb 71	APACHE DROPOUT (re-entry) *Harvest HAR 5032*	35	2 wks
13 Mar 71	APACHE DROPOUT (2nd re-entry) *Harvest HAR 5032*	35	1 wk

27 Mar 71	APACHE DROPOUT (3rd re-entry) *Harvest HAR 5032*......	33	1 wk

Bobby BROWN *US, male vocalist*   **70 wks**

6 Aug 88	DON'T BE CRUEL *MCA MCA 1268*	42	7 wks
7 Jan 89	● MY PEROGATIVE *MCA MCA 1299*	6	17 wks
25 Mar 89	DON'T BE CRUEL (re-issue) *MCA MCA 1310*	13	8 wks
20 May 89	EVERY LITTLE STEP *MCA MCA 1338*	6	9 wks
15 Jul 89	● ON OUR OWN (FROM GHOSTBUSTERS II)		
	MCA MCA 1350	4	9 wks
23 Sep 89	ROCK WIT'CHA *MCA MCA 1367*	33	6 wks
25 Nov 89	RONI *MCA MCA 1384*	21	7 wks
9 Jun 90	THE FREE STYLE MEGA-MIX *MCA MCA 1421*	14	7 wks

Carl BROWN – *See DOUBLE TROUBLE*

Crazy World of Arthur BROWN   **14 wks**
UK, male vocal/instrumental group

26 Jun 68	★ FIRE *Track 604 022*	1	14 wks

Dennis BROWN *Jamaica, male vocalist*   **18 wks**

3 Mar 79	MONEY IN MY POCKET *Lightning LV 5*	14	9 wks
3 Jul 82	LOVE HAS FOUND ITS WAY *A & M AMS 8226*	47	6 wks
11 Sep 82	HALFWAY UP HALFWAY DOWN *A & M AMS 8250*	56	3 wks

Diana BROWN and Barrie K. SHARPE   **8 wks**
UK, female/male vocal duo

2 Jun 90	THE MASTERPLAN *FFRR F 133*	39	6 wks
1 Sep 90	SUN WORSHIPPERS (POSITIVE THINKING)		
	FFRR F 144	61	2 wks

Errol BROWN *UK, male vocalist*   **10 wks**

4 Jul 87	PERSONAL TOUCH *WEA YZ 130*	25	8 wks
28 Nov 87	BODY ROCKIN' *WEA YZ 162*	51	2 wks

Gloria D. BROWN *US, female vocalist*   **3 wks**

8 Jun 85	THE MORE THEY KNOCK, THE MORE I LOVE YOU		
	10 TEN 52	57	3 wks

James BROWN *US, male vocalist*   **91 wks**

23 Sep 65	PAPA'S GOT A BRAND NEW BAG *London HL 9990*........	25	7 wks
24 Feb 66	I GOT YOU *Pye International 7N 25350*	29	6 wks
16 Jun 66	IT'S A MAN'S MAN'S MAN'S WORLD		
	Pye International 7N 25371	13	9 wks
10 Oct 70	GET UP I FEEL LIKE BEING A SEX MACHINE		
	Polydor 2001 071	32	7 wks
27 Nov 71	HEY AMERICA *Mojo 2093 006*	47	3 wks
18 Sep 76	GET UP OFFA THAT THING *Polydor 2066 687*..............	22	6 wks
29 Jan 77	BODY HEAT *Polydor 2066 763*	36	4 wks
10 Apr 81	RAPP PAYBACK (WHERE IZ MOSES?) *RCA 28*	39	5 wks
2 Jul 83	BRING IT ON ... BRING IT ON *Sonet SON 2258*	45	4 wks
27 Apr 85	FROGGY MIX *Boiling Point FROG 1*	50	3 wks
1 Jun 85	GET UP I FEEL LIKE BEING A SEX		
	MACHINE (re-issue) *Boiling Point POSP 751*	47	5 wks
25 Jan 86	● LIVING IN AMERICA *Scotti Brothers A 6701*	5	10 wks
1 Mar 86	GET UP I FEEL LIKE BEING A SEX		
	MACHINE (re-entry of re-issue)		
	Boiling Point POSP 751	46	4 wks
18 Oct 86	GRAVITY *Scotti Brothers 650059 7*	65	2 wks
30 Jan 88	SHE'S THE ONE *Urban URB 13*	45	3 wks
23 Apr 88	THE PAYBACK MIX *Urban URB 17*	12	6 wks
4 Jun 88	I'M REAL *Scotti Brothers JSB 1*	31	4 wks

23 Jul 88   **I GOT YOU (I FEEL GOOD) (re-issue)** *A & M AM 444* ..... **52**   3 wks

Billed as James Brown and The Famous Flames on the first three hits. Froggy Mix is a medley of twelve James Brown songs. I'm Real features Full Force. The listed flip side of I Got You (I Feel Good) was Nowhere To Run by Martha Reeves and the Vandellas. See also Afrika Bambaataa and James Brown; Martha Reeves and the Vandellas; Full Force.

Joanne BROWN – *See Tony OSBORNE*

Jocelyn BROWN *US, female vocalist*   **13 wks**

21 Apr 84	**SOMEBODY ELSE'S GUY** *Fourth & Broadway BRW 5*	**13**	9 wks
22 Sep 84	**I WISH YOU WOULD** *Fourth & Broadway BRW 14*	**51**	3 wks
15 Mar 86	**LOVE'S GONNA GET YOU** *Warner Bros. W 8889*	**70**	1 wk

Joe BROWN *UK, male vocalist/instrumentalist – guitar*   **92 wks**

17 Mar 60	**DARKTOWN STRUTTERS BALL** *Decca F 11207*	**34**	6 wks
26 Jan 61	**SHINE** *Pye 7N 15322*	**33**	6 wks
11 Jan 62	**WHAT A CRAZY WORLD WE'RE LIVING IN** *Piccadilly 7N 35024*	**37**	2 wks
17 May 62	● **A PICTURE OF YOU** *Piccadilly 7N 35047*	**2**	19 wks
13 Sep 62	**YOUR TENDER LOOK** *Piccadilly 7N 35058*	**31**	6 wks
15 Nov 62	● **IT ONLY TOOK A MINUTE** *Piccadilly 7N 35082*	**6**	13 wks
7 Feb 63	● **THAT'S WHAT LOVE WILL DO** *Piccadilly 7N 35106*	**3**	14 wks
21 Feb 63	**IT ONLY TOOK A MINUTE (re-entry)** *Piccadilly 7N 35082*	**50**	1 wk
27 Jun 63	**NATURE'S TIME FOR LOVE** *Piccadilly 7N 35129*	**26**	6 wks
26 Sep 63	**SALLY ANN** *Piccadilly 7N 35138*	**28**	9 wks
29 Jun 67	**WITH A LITTLE HELP FROM MY FRIENDS** *Pye 7N 17339*	**32**	4 wks
14 Apr 73	**HEY MAMA** *Ammo AMO 101*	**33**	6 wks

Joe Brown's male vocal/instrumental backing group, the Bruvvers, were credited on all his hits except Shine, With A Little Help From My Friends and Hey Mama.

Miquel BROWN *US, female vocalist*   **7 wks**

18 Feb 84	**HE'S A SAINT, HE'S A SINNER** *Record Shack SOHO 15*	**68**	4 wks
24 Aug 85	**CLOSE TO PERFECTION** *Record Shack SOHO 48*	**63**	3 wks

Peter BROWN *US, male vocalist*   **9 wks**

11 Feb 78	**DO YA WANNA GET FUNKY WITH ME** *TK TKR 6009*	**43**	4 wks
17 Jun 78	**DANCE WITH ME** *TK TKR 6027*	**57**	5 wks

Polly BROWN *UK, female vocalist*   **5 wks**

14 Sep 74	**UP IN A PUFF OF SMOKE** *GTO GT 2*	**43**	5 wks

Sam BROWN *UK, female vocalist*   **34 wks**

11 Jun 88	**STOP** *A & M AM 440*	**52**	3 wks
4 Feb 89	● **STOP (re-entry)** *A & M AM 440*	**4**	12 wks
13 May 89	**CAN I GET A WITNESS** *A & M AM 509*	**15**	7 wks
3 Mar 90	**WITH A LITTLE LOVE** *A & M AM 539*	**44**	4 wks
5 May 90	**KISSING GATE** *A&M AM 549*	**23**	8 wks

Sharon BROWN *US, female vocalist*   **9 wks**

17 Apr 82	**I SPECIALIZE IN LOVE** *Virgin VS 494*	**38**	9 wks

BROWN SAUCE *UK, male/female vocal group*   **12 wks**

12 Dec 81	**I WANNA BE A WINNER** *BBC RESL 101*	**15**	12 wks

Duncan BROWNE *UK, male vocalist*   **8 wks**

19 Aug 72	**JOURNEY** *RAK 135*	**23**	6 wks
22 Dec 84	**THEME FROM 'THE TRAVELLING MAN'** *Towerbell TOW 64*	**68**	2 wks

Jackson BROWNE *US, male vocalist*   **13 wks**

1 Jul 78	**STAY** *Asylum K 13128*	**12**	11 wks
18 Oct 86	**IN THE SHAPE OF A HEART** *Elektra EKR 42*	**66**	2 wks

Ronnie BROWNE – *See SCOTTISH RUGBY TEAM with Ronnie BROWNE*

Tom BROWNE *US, male vocalist*   **20 wks**

19 Jul 80	● **FUNKIN' FOR JAMAICA (N.Y.)** *Arista ARIST 357*	**10**	11 wks
25 Oct 80	**THIGHS HIGH (GRIP YOUR HIPS AND MOVE)** *Arista ARIST 367*	**45**	5 wks
30 Jan 82	**FUNGI MAMA (BEBOPAFUNKADISCOLYPSO)** *Arista ARIST 450*	**58**	4 wks

BROWNS *US, male/female vocal group*   **13 wks**

18 Sep 59	● **THE THREE BELLS** *RCA 1140*	**6**	13 wks

BROWNSVILLE STATION
US, male vocal/instrumental group   **6 wks**

2 Mar 74	**SMOKIN' IN THE BOYS' ROOM** *Philips 6073 834*	**27**	6 wks

Dave BRUBECK QUARTET
US, male instrumental group   **30 wks**

26 Oct 61	● **TAKE FIVE** *Fontana H 339*	**6**	15 wks
8 Feb 62	**IT'S A RAGGY WALTZ** *Fontana H 352*	**36**	3 wks
17 May 62	**UNSQUARE DANCE** *CBS AAG 102*	**14**	12 wks

Tommy BRUCE *UK, male vocalist*   **21 wks**

26 May 60	● **AIN'T MISBEHAVIN'** *Columbia DB 4453*	**3**	16 wks
8 Sep 60	**BROKEN DOLL** *Columbia DB 4498*	**36**	4 wks
22 Feb 62	**BABETTE** *Columbia DB 4776*	**50**	1 wk

First two hits credit the Bruisers, Tommy's backing group. See also Bruisers.

Claudia BRUCKEN *Germany, female vocalist*   **1 wk**

1 Aug 90	**ABSOLUT(E)** *Island IS 471*	**71**	1 wk

BRUFORD – *See ANDERSON BRUFORD WAKEMAN HOWE*

BRUISERS *UK, male vocal/instrumental group*   **7 wks**

8 Aug 63	**BLUE GIRL** *Parlophone R 5042*	**31**	6 wks
26 Sep 63	**BLUE GIRL (re-entry)** *Parlophone R 5042*	**47**	1 wk

See also Tommy Bruce.

BRUNO and LIZ – *See Liz KERSHAW and Bruno BROOKES*

Tyrone BRUNSON *US, male instrumentalist – bass*   **5 wks**

25 Dec 82	**THE SMURF** *Epic EPC A 3024*	**52**	5 wks

BRUVVERS – *See Joe BROWN*

Dora BRYAN *UK, female vocalist*   **6 wks**

5 Dec 63	ALL I WANT FOR CHRISTMAS IS A BEATLE *Fontana TF 427*	**20**	6 wks

Anita BRYANT *US, female vocalist*   **6 wks**

26 May 60	PAPER ROSES *London HLL 9144*	**49**	1 wk
30 Jun 60	PAPER ROSES (re-entry) *London HLL 9144*	**45**	1 wk
14 Jul 60	PAPER ROSES (2nd re-entry) *London HLL 9144*	**24**	2 wks
6 Oct 60	MY LITTLE CORNER OF THE WORLD *London HLL 9171*	**48**	2 wks

Peabo BRYSON and Roberta FLACK   **13 wks**
US, male/female vocal duo

20 Aug 83	● TONIGHT I CELEBRATE MY LOVE *Capitol CL 302*	**2**	13 wks

See also Roberta Flack.

B. T. EXPRESS *US, male instrumental/vocal group*   **10 wks**

29 Mar 75	EXPRESS *Pye International 7N 25674*	**34**	6 wks
26 Jul 80	DOES IT FEEL GOOD/ GIVE UP THE FUNK (LET'S DANCE) *Calibre CAB 503*	**52**	4 wks

BUBBLEROCK   **5 wks**
UK, male vocalist, Jonathan King under a false name

26 Jan 74	(I CAN'T GET NO) SATISFACTION *UK 53*	**29**	5 wks

See also Jonathan King.

Roy BUCHANAN *US, male instrumentalist - guitar*   **3 wks**

31 Mar 73	SWEET DREAMS *Polydor 2066 307*	**40**	3 wks

Lindsey BUCKINGHAM *US, male vocalist*   **7 wks**

16 Jan 82	TROUBLE *Mercury MER 85*	**31**	7 wks

BUCKS FIZZ *UK, male/female vocal group*   **150 wks**

28 Mar 81	★ MAKING YOUR MIND UP *RCA 56*	**1**	12 wks
6 Jun 81	PIECE OF THE ACTION *RCA 88*	**12**	9 wks
15 Aug 81	ONE OF THOSE NIGHTS *RCA 114*	**20**	10 wks
28 Nov 81	★ THE LAND OF MAKE BELIEVE *RCA 163*	**1**	16 wks
27 Mar 82	★ MY CAMERA NEVER LIES *RCA 202*	**1**	8 wks
19 Jun 82	● NOW THOSE DAYS ARE GONE *RCA 241*	**8**	9 wks
27 Nov 82	IF YOU CAN'T STAND THE HEAT *RCA 300*	**10**	11 wks
12 Mar 83	RUN FOR YOUR LIFE *RCA FIZ 1*	**14**	7 wks
18 Jun 83	● WHEN WE WERE YOUNG *RCA 342*	**10**	8 wks
1 Oct 83	LONDON TOWN *RCA 363*	**34**	6 wks
17 Dec 83	RULES OF THE GAME *RCA 380*	**57**	6 wks
25 Aug 84	TALKING IN YOUR SLEEP *RCA FIZ 2*	**15**	9 wks
27 Oct 84	GOLDEN DAYS *RCA FIZ 3*	**42**	4 wks
29 Dec 84	I HEAR TALK *RCA FIZ 4*	**34**	8 wks
22 Jun 85	YOU AND YOUR HEART SO BLUE *RCA PB 40233*	**43**	4 wks
14 Sep 85	MAGICAL *RCA PB 40367*	**57**	3 wks
7 Jun 86	● NEW BEGINNING (MAMBA SEYRA) *Polydor POSP 794*	**8**	10 wks
30 Aug 86	LOVE THE ONE YOU'RE WITH *Polydor POSP 813*	**47**	3 wks
15 Nov 86	KEEP EACH OTHER WARM *Polydor POSP 835*	**45**	4 wks
5 Nov 88	HEART OF STONE *RCA PB 42035*	**50**	3 wks

BUDGIE *UK, male vocal/instrumental group*   **2 wks**

3 Oct 81	KEEPING A RENDEZVOUS *RCA BUDGIE 3*	**71**	2 wks

BUGGLES *UK, male vocal/instrumental duo*   **28 wks**

22 Sep 79	★ VIDEO KILLED THE RADIO STAR *Island WIP 6524*	**1**	11 wks
26 Jan 80	THE PLASTIC AGE *Island WIP 6540*	**16**	8 wks
5 Apr 80	CLEAN CLEAN *Island WIP 6584*	**38**	5 wks
8 Nov 80	ELSTREE *Island WIP 6624*	**55**	4 wks

B. BUMBLE and the STINGERS   **26 wks**
US, male instrumental group

19 Apr 62	★ NUT ROCKER *Top Rank JAR 611*	**1**	15 wks
3 Jun 72	NUT ROCKER (re-issue) *Stateside SS 2203*	**19**	11 wks

BUNKER KRU – *See HARLEQUIN 4's/BUNKER KRU*

BUNNYMEN – *See ECHO and the BUNNYMEN*

Eric BURDON *UK, male vocalist*   **42 wks**

27 Oct 66	HELP ME GIRL *Decca F 12502*	**14**	10 wks
15 Jun 67	WHEN I WAS YOUNG *MGM 1340*	**45**	3 wks
6 Sep 67	GOOD TIMES *MGM 1344*	**20**	11 wks
18 Oct 67	● SAN FRANCISCAN NIGHTS *MGM 1359*	**7**	10 wks
14 Feb 68	SKY PILOT *MGM 1373*	**40**	3 wks
15 Jan 69	RING OF FIRE *MGM 1461*	**35**	5 wks

Help Me Girl, When I Was Young, Good Times *and* Ring Of Fire *are credited to Eric Burdon and the Animals. See also the Animals.*

Geoffrey BURGON *UK, orchestra*   **4 wks**

26 Dec 81	BRIDESHEAD THEME *Chrysalis CHS 2562*	**48**	4 wks

Keni BURKE *US, male vocalist*   **3 wks**

27 Jun 81	LET SOMEBODY LOVE YOU *RCA 93*	**59**	3 wks

Hank C. BURNETTE *Sweden, male multi-instrumentalist*   **8 wks**

30 Oct 76	SPINNING ROCK BOOGIE *Sonet SON 2094*	**21**	8 wks

Johnny BURNETTE *US, male vocalist*   **48 wks**

29 Sep 60	● DREAMIN' *London HLG 9172*	**5**	16 wks
12 Jan 61	● YOU'RE SIXTEEN *London HLG 9254*	**3**	12 wks
13 Apr 61	LITTLE BOY SAD *London HLG 9315*	**12**	12 wks
10 Aug 61	GIRLS *London HLG 9388*	**37**	5 wks
17 May 62	CLOWN SHOES *Liberty LIB 55416*	**35**	3 wks

Rocky BURNETTE *US, male vocalist*   **7 wks**

17 Nov 79	TIRED OF TOEIN' THE LINE *EMI 2992*	**58**	7 wks

Ray BURNS *UK, male vocalist*   **19 wks**

11 Feb 55	● MOBILE *Columbia DB 3563*	**4**	13 wks
26 Aug 55	THAT'S HOW A LOVE SONG WAS BORN *Columbia DB 3640*	**14**	6 wks

Malandra BURROWS UK, female vocalist   **5 wks**

1 Dec 90	**JUST THIS SIDE OF LOVE** Yorkshire Television DALE 1	**11**†	5 wks

Jenny BURTON US, female vocalist   **2 wks**

30 Mar 85	**BAD HABITS** Atlantic A 9583	**68**	2 wks

BURUNDI STEIPHENSON BLACK   **14 wks**
Burundi, drummers and chanters with orchestral additions by Mike Stei-phenson of France

13 Nov 71	**BURUNDI BLACK** Barclay BAR 3.............................	**31**	14 wks

Lou BUSCH US, orchestra   **17 wks**

27 Jan 56	● **ZAMBESI** Capitol CL 14504	**2**	17 wks

See also Joe 'Fingers' Carr.

Kate BUSH UK, female vocalist   **134 wks**

11 Feb 78	★ **WUTHERING HEIGHTS** EMI 2719	**1**	12 wks
13 May 78	**WUTHERING HEIGHTS (re-entry)** EMI 2719	**75**	1 wk
10 Jun 78	● **MAN WITH THE CHILD IN HIS EYES** EMI 2806...........	**6**	11 wks
11 Nov 78	**HAMMER HORROR** EMI 2887	**44**	6 wks
17 Mar 79	**WOW** EMI 2911	**14**	10 wks
15 Sep 79	● **KATE BUSH ON STAGE** (EP) EMI MIEP 2991	**10**	9 wks
26 Apr 80	**BREATHING** EMI 5058	**16**	7 wks
5 Jul 80	● **BABOOSHKA** EMI 5085	**5**	10 wks
4 Oct 80	**ARMY DREAMERS** EMI 5106	**16**	9 wks
6 Dec 80	**DECEMBER WILL BE MAGIC AGAIN** EMI 5121	**29**	7 wks
11 Jul 81	**SAT IN YOUR LAP** EMI 5201	**11**	7 wks
7 Aug 82	**THE DREAMING** EMI 5296	**48**	3 wks
17 Aug 85	● **RUNNING UP THAT HILL** EMI KB 1	**3**	11 wks
26 Oct 85	**CLOUDBUSTING** EMI KB 2................................	**20**	6 wks
1 Mar 86	**HOUNDS OF LOVE** EMI KB 3.............................	**18**	5 wks
10 May 86	**THE BIG SKY** EMI KB 4	**37**	3 wks
8 Nov 86	**EXPERIMENT IV** EMI KB 5..............................	**23**	4 wks
30 Sep 89	**THE SENSUAL WORLD** EMI EM 102	**12**	5 wks
2 Dec 89	**THIS WOMAN'S WORK** EMI EM 119	**25**	5 wks
10 Mar 90	**LOVE AND ANGER** EMI EM 134	**38**	3 wks

Tracks on On Stage EP: Them Heavy People/Don't Push Your Foot on the Heartbrake/James and the Cold Gun/L'Amour Looks Something Like You. See also Peter Gabriel and Kate Bush.

BUSTER UK, male vocal/instrumental group   **1 wk**

19 Jun 76	**SUNDAY** RCA 2678	**49**	1 wk

Prince BUSTER Jamaica, male vocalist   **13 wks**

23 Feb 67	**AL CAPONE** Blue Beat BB 324................................	**18**	13 wks

Jonathan BUTLER South Africa, male vocalist/instrumentalist - guitar   **11 wks**

8 Aug 87	**LIES** Jive JIVE 141	**18**	11 wks

BUTTERSCOTCH UK, male vocal group   **11 wks**

2 May 70	**DON'T YOU KNOW** RCA 1937.............................	**17**	11 wks

BUZZCOCKS UK, male vocal/instrumental group   **53 wks**

18 Feb 78	**WHAT DO I GET** United Artists UP 36348...............	**37**	3 wks
13 May 78	**I DON'T MIND** United Artists UP 36386	**55**	2 wks
15 Jul 78	**LOVE YOU MORE** United Artists UP 36433	**34**	6 wks
23 Sep 78	**EVER FALLEN IN LOVE (WITH SOMEONE YOU SHOULDN'T'VE)** United Artists UP 36455	**12**	11 wks
25 Nov 78	**PROMISES** United Artists UP 36471	**20**	10 wks
10 Mar 79	**EVERYBODY'S HAPPY NOWADAYS** United Artists UP 36499	**29**	6 wks
21 Jul 79	**HARMONY IN MY HEAD** United Artists UP 36541....	**32**	6 wks
25 Aug 79	**SPIRAL SCRATCH** (EP) New Hormones ORG 1	**31**	6 wks
6 Sep 80	**ARE EVERYTHING/ WHY SHE'S A GIRL FROM THE CHAINSTORE** United Artists BP 365	**61**	3 wks

Tracks on Spiral Scratch EP: Breakdown/Time's Up/Boredom/Friends Of Mine. Sleeve of EP (not the label) credits 'Buzzcocks with Howard Devoto'. Why She's A Girl From The Chainstore listed from 13 Sep 80.

BUZZY BUNCH – See Celi BEE and the BUZZY BUNCH

B.V.S.M.P. US, male vocal group   **12 wks**

23 Jul 88	● **I NEED YOU** Debut DEBT 3044................................	**3**	12 wks

BY ALL MEANS US, male vocal group   **2 wks**

18 Jun 88	**I SURRENDER TO YOUR LOVE** Fourth & Broadway BRW 102	**65**	2 wks

Max BYGRAVES UK, male vocalist   **131 wks**

14 Nov 52	**COWPUNCHER'S CANTATA** HMV B 10250	**11**	1 wk
2 Jan 53	● **COWPUNCHER'S CANTATA (re-entry)** HMV B 10250	**8**	1 wk
23 Jan 53	● **COWPUNCHER'S CANTATA (2nd re-entry)** HMV B 10250	**6**	5 wks
6 Mar 53	● **COWPUNCHER'S CANTATA (3rd re-entry)** HMV B 10250	**10**	1 wk
14 May 54	● **HEART OF MY HEART** HMV B 10654..................	**7**	8 wks
10 Sep 54	● **GILLY GILLY OSSENFEFFER KATZENELLEN BOGEN BY THE SEA** HMV B 10734	**7**	7 wks
5 Nov 54	**GILLY GILLY OSSENFEFFER KATZENELLEN BOGEN BY THE SEA (re-entry)** HMV B 10734	**20**	1 wk
21 Jan 55	**MR. SANDMAN** HMV B 10821............................	**16**	1 wk
18 Nov 55	● **MEET ME ON THE CORNER** HMV POP 116	**2**	11 wks
17 Feb 56	**BALLAD OF DAVY CROCKETT** HMV POP 153	**20**	1 wk
25 May 56	**OUT OF TOWN** HMV POP 164...........................	**18**	7 wks
5 Apr 57	**HEART** Decca F 10862....................................	**14**	8 wks
2 May 58	● **YOU NEED HANDS/ TULIPS FROM AMSTERDAM** Decca F 11004...	**3**	25 wks
22 Aug 58	**LITTLE TRAIN/ GOTTA HAVE RAIN** Decca F 11096.......	**28**	2 wks
2 Jan 59	**MY UKELELE** Decca F 11077	**19**	4 wks
18 Dec 59	● **JINGLE BELL ROCK** Decca F 11176....................	**7**	4 wks
10 Mar 60	● **FINGS AIN'T WOT THEY USED T'BE** Decca F 11214....	**5**	15 wks
28 Jul 60	**CONSIDER YOURSELF** Decca F 11251	**50**	1 wk
1 Jun 61	**BELLS OF AVIGNON** Decca F 11350	**36**	5 wks
19 Feb 69	**YOU'RE MY EVERYTHING** Pye 7N 17705	**50**	1 wk
5 Mar 69	**YOU'RE MY EVERYTHING (re-entry)** Pye 7N 17705	**34**	3 wks
6 Oct 73	**DECK OF CARDS** Pye 7N 45276..........................	**13**	15 wks
9 Dec 89	**WHITE CHRISTMAS** Parkfield PMS 5012	**71**	4 wks

See also Various Artists - All Star Hit Parade No. 2. Cowpuncher's Cantata is a medley with the following songs: Cry Of The Wild Goose/Riders In The Sky/Mule Train/Jezebel. You Need Hands was listed by itself on 2 May 58. Tulips From Amsterdam was first listed on 9 May 58 and both sides continued to be listed until the end of the record's chart run.

Charlie BYRD – See Stan GETZ and Charlie BYRD

Donald BYRD US, male vocalist/instrumentalist - trumpet   **6 wks**

26 Sep 81	**LOVE HAS COME AROUND/ LOVING YOU** Elektra K 12559	**41**	6 wks

Above: Just as Kiss had
nothing to do with Prince,
and Deep Purple were
unrelated to Nino Tempo
and April Stevens, BIG
FUN were uninvolved with
Kool and the Gang, who
had a hit with their group
name.

Far Right: 'Babooshka' was in
the chart when KATE
BUSH made this unusual
entrance.

Right: PHIL COLLINS and
wife Jill are shown at the
1989 Golden Globe Awards
at Beverly Hills.

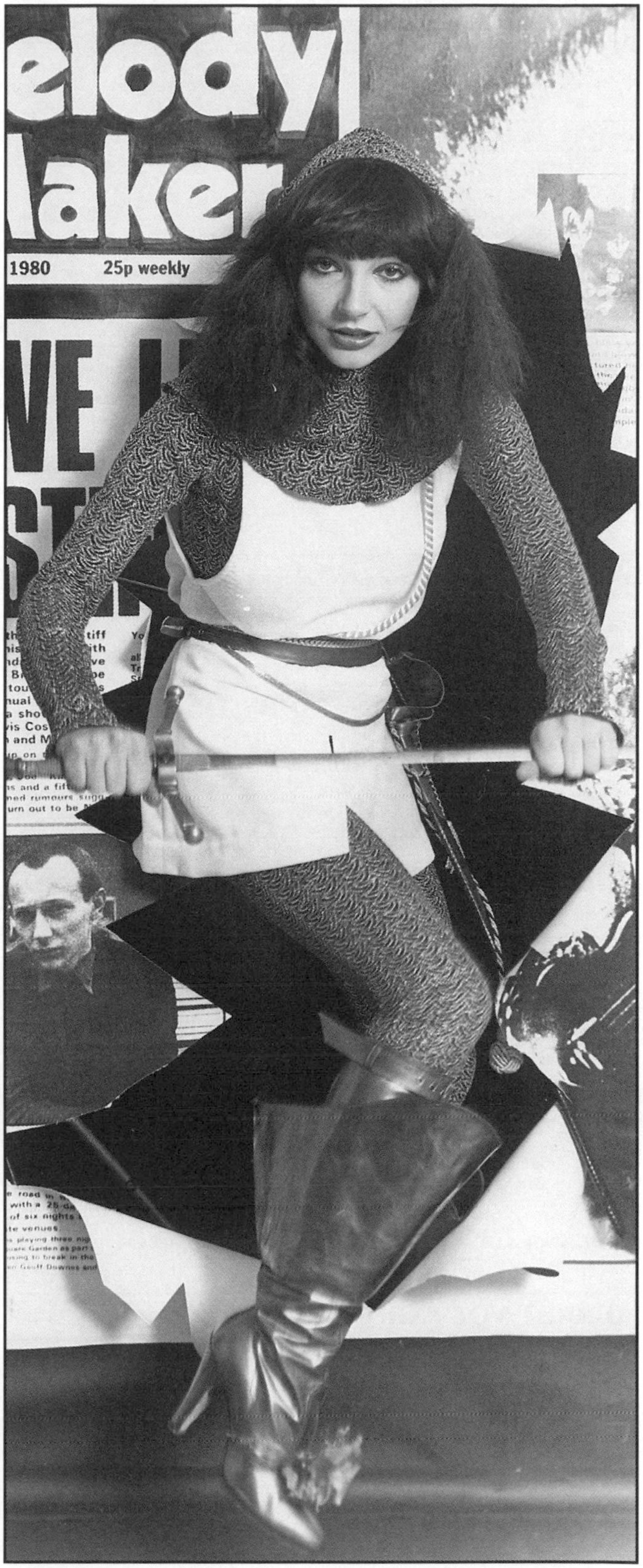

Gary BYRD and the GB EXPERIENCE
US, male vocalist and male/female instrumental group   **9 wks**

23 Jul 83 ●	THE CROWN *Motown TMGT 1312*	6	9 wks

BYRDS US, male vocal/instrumental group   **52 wks**

17 Jun 65 ★	MR. TAMBOURINE MAN *CBS 201765*	1	14 wks
12 Aug 65 ●	ALL I REALLY WANT TO DO *CBS 201796*	4	10 wks
11 Nov 65	TURN! TURN! TURN! *CBS 202008*	26	8 wks
5 May 66	EIGHT MILES HIGH *CBS 202067*	24	9 wks
5 Jun 68	YOU AIN'T GOIN' NOWHERE *CBS 3411*	45	3 wks
13 Feb 71	CHESTNUT MARE *CBS 5322*	19	8 wks

Edward BYRNES and Connie STEVENS   **8 wks**
US, male/female vocal duo

5 May 60	KOOKIE KOOKIE (LEND ME YOUR COMB) *Warner Bros. WB 5*	27	8 wks

See also Connie Stevens.

BYSTANDERS UK, male vocal/instrumental group   **1 wk**

9 Feb 67	98.6 *Piccadilly 7N 35363*	45	1 wk

C

Roy C US, male vocalist   **24 wks**

21 Apr 66 ●	SHOTGUN WEDDING *Island WI 273*	6	11 wks
25 Nov 72 ●	SHOTGUN WEDDING (re-issue) *UK 19*	8	13 wks

C & C MUSIC FACTORY   **3 wks**
US, male/female vocal/instrumental group

15 Dec 90	GONNA MAKE YOU SWEAT *CBS 6564540*	29†	3 wks

ÇA VA ÇA VA UK, male vocal/instrumental group   **8 wks**

18 Sep 82	WHERE'S ROMEO *Regard RG 103*	49	5 wks
19 Feb 83	BROTHER BRIGHT *Regard RG 105*	65	3 wks

Montserrat CABALLE – *See Freddie MERCURY and Montserrat CABALLE*

CABARET VOLTAIRE   **8 wks**
UK, male vocal/instrumental group

18 Jul 87	DON'T ARGUE *Parlophone R 6157*	69	2 wks
4 Nov 89	HYPNOTISED *Parlophone R 6227*	66	2 wks
12 May 90	KEEP ON *Parlophone R 6250*	55	2 wks
18 Aug 90	EASY LIFE *Parlophone R 6261*	61	2 wks

CACIQUE UK, male/female vocal/instrumental group   **1 wk**

1 Jun 85	DEVOTED TO YOU *Diamond Duel DISC 1*	69	1 wk

CACTUS WORLD NEWS   **7 wks**
Ireland, male vocal/instrumental group

8 Feb 86	YEARS LATER *MCA MCA 1024*	59	3 wks
26 Apr 86	WORLDS APART *MCA MCA 1040*	58	3 wks
20 Sep 86	THE BRIDGE *MCA MCA 1080*	74	1 wk

CADETS Ireland, male/female vocal group   **1 wk**

3 Jun 65	JEALOUS HEART *Pye 7N 15852*	42	1 wk

Hit has credit 'with Eileen Read lead vocal'.

Susan CADOGAN UK, female vocalist   **19 wks**

5 Apr 75 ●	HURT SO GOOD *Magnet MAG 23*	4	12 wks
19 Jul 75	LOVE ME BABY *Magnet MAG 36*	22	7 wks

Al CAIOLA US, orchestra   **6 wks**

15 Jun 61	THE MAGNIFICENT SEVEN *HMV POP 889*	34	6 wks

CALIBRE CUTS Montage of 16 other discs, see footnote   **2 wks**

17 May 80	CALIBRE CUTS *Calibre CAB 502*	75	2 wks

Calibre Cuts is a montage of 13 singles and three re-makes of hit titles by session musicians. The titles are: Big Apples Rock by Black Ivory, Don't Hold Back by Chanson, The River Drive by Jupiter Beyond, Dancing In The Disco by L.A.X., Mellow Mellow Right On by Lowrell, Pata Pata by Osibisa, I Like It by Players Association, We Got The Funk by Positive Force, Holdin' On by Tony Rallo and the Midnight Band, Can You Feel The Force by the Real Thing, Miami Heatwave by Seventh Avenue, Rappers Delight by Sugarhill Gang, Que Tal America by Two Man Sound. The three re-makes by session musicians are: Ain't No Stopping Us Now, Bad Girls and We Are Family. Act descriptions are, of course, various.

CALL US, male vocal/instrumental group   **6 wks**

30 Sep 89	LET THE DAY BEGIN *MCA MCA 1362*	42	6 wks

Eddie CALVERT UK, male instrumentalist - trumpet   **80 wks**

18 Dec 53 ★	OH MEIN PAPA *Columbia DB 3337*	1	21 wks
8 Apr 55 ★	CHERRY PINK & APPLE BLOSSOM WHITE *Columbia DB 3581*	1	21 wks
13 May 55	STRANGER IN PARADISE *Columbia DB 3594*	14	4 wks
29 Jul 55 ●	JOHN AND JULIE *Columbia DB 3624*	6	11 wks
2 Mar 56	ZAMBESI *Columbia DB 3747*	18	1 wk
23 Mar 56	ZAMBESI (re-entry) *Columbia DB 3747*	13	6 wks
7 Feb 58 ●	MANDY *Columbia DB 3956*	9	14 wks
20 Jun 58	LITTLE SERENADE *Columbia DB 4105*	28	2 wks

Donnie CALVIN – *See ROCKER'S REVENGE*

CAMEO US, male vocal/instrumental group   **66 wks**

31 Mar 84	SHE'S STRANGE *Club JAB 2*	37	8 wks
13 Jul 85	ATTACK ME WITH YOUR LOVE *Club JAB 16*	65	2 wks
14 Sep 85	SINGLE LIFE *Club JAB 21*	15	10 wks
7 Dec 85	SHE'S STRANGE (re-issue) *Club JAB 25*	22	8 wks
22 Mar 86	A GOODBYE *Club JAB 28*	65	2 wks
30 Aug 86 ●	WORD UP *Club JAB 38*	3	13 wks
29 Nov 86	CANDY *Club JAB 43*	27	9 wks
25 Apr 87	BACK AND FORTH *Club JAB 49*	11	9 wks
17 Oct 87	SHE'S MINE *Club JAB 57*	35	4 wks
29 Oct 88	YOU MAKE ME WORK *Club JAB 70*	74	1 wk

Andy CAMERON UK, male vocalist			**8 wks**
4 Mar 78	● ALLY'S TARTAN ARMY Klub 03	**6**	8 wks

Tony CAMILLO'S BAZUKA			**5 wks**
US, male instrumental/vocal group			
31 May 75	DYNOMITE (PART 1) A & M AMS 7168	**28**	5 wks

CAMOUFLAGE featuring MYSTI			**3 wks**
UK, male/female vocal/instrumental group			
24 Sep 77	BEE STING State STAT 58..	**48**	3 wks

Ethna CAMPBELL UK, female vocalist			**11 wks**
27 Dec 75	THE OLD RUGGED CROSS Philips 6006 475	**33**	11 wks

Glen CAMPBELL US, male vocalist			**84 wks**
29 Jan 69	● WICHITA LINEMAN Ember EMBS 261	**7**	13 wks
7 May 69	GALVESTON Ember EMBS 263	**14**	10 wks
7 Feb 70	TRY A LITTLE KINDNESS Capitol CL 15622	**45**	2 wks
9 May 70	● HONEY COME BACK Capitol CL 15638	**4**	19 wks
26 Sep 70	EVERYTHING A MAN COULD EVER NEED		
	Capitol CL 15653	**32**	5 wks
21 Nov 70	● IT'S ONLY MAKE BELIEVE Capitol CL 15663	**4**	14 wks
27 Mar 71	DREAM BABY Capitol CL 15674	**39**	3 wks
4 Oct 75	● RHINESTONE COWBOY Capitol CL 15824	**4**	12 wks
26 Mar 77	SOUTHERN NIGHTS Capitol CL 15907	**28**	6 wks

See also Bobbie Gentry and Glen Campbell.

Jo Ann CAMPBELL US, female vocalist			**3 wks**
8 Jun 61	MOTORCYCLE MICHAEL HMV POP 873.................	**41**	3 wks

Junior CAMPBELL UK, male vocalist			**18 wks**
14 Oct 72	● HALLELUJAH FREEDOM Deram DM 364	**10**	9 wks
2 Jun 73	SWEET ILLUSION Deram DM 387	**15**	9 wks

Pat CAMPBELL Ireland, male vocalist			**5 wks**
15 Nov 69	THE DEAL Major Minor MM 648	**31**	5 wks

Stan CAMPBELL UK, male vocalist			**3 wks**
6 Jun 87	YEARS GO BY WEA YZ 127	**65**	3 wks

Ian CAMPBELL FOLK GROUP			**5 wks**
UK, male vocal/instrumental group			
11 Mar 65	THE TIMES THEY ARE A-CHANGIN'		
	Transatlantic SP 5	**42**	2 wks
1 Apr 65	THE TIMES THEY ARE A-CHANGIN' (re-entry)		
	Transatlantic SP 5	**47**	1 wk
15 Apr 65	THE TIMES THEY ARE A-CHANGIN' (2nd re-entry)		
	Transatlantic SP 5	**46**	2 wks

CAN Germany, male vocal/instrumental group			**10 wks**
28 Aug 76	I WANT MORE Virgin VS 153	**26**	10 wks

CANDIDO US, male multi-instrumentalist			**3 wks**
18 Jul 81	JINGO Excaliber EXC 102	**55**	3 wks

CANDLEWICK GREEN UK, vocal/instrumental group			**8 wks**
23 Feb 74	WHO DO YOU THINK YOU ARE Decca F 13480...........	**21**	8 wks

CANDY FLIP UK, male vocal/instrumental duo			**14 wks**
17 Mar 90	● STRAWBERRY FIELDS FOREVER Debut DEBT 3092........	**3**	10 wks
14 Jul 90	THIS CAN BE REAL Debut DEBT 3099	**60**	4 wks

CANNED HEAT US, male vocal/instrumental group			**41 wks**
24 Jul 68	● ON THE ROAD AGAIN Liberty LBS 15090	**8**	15 wks
1 Jan 69	GOING UP THE COUNTRY Liberty LBF 15169	**19**	10 wks
17 Jan 70	● LET'S WORK TOGETHER Liberty LBF 15302	**2**	15 wks
11 Jul 70	SUGAR BEE Liberty LBF 15350...............................	**49**	1 wk

Freddy CANNON US, male vocalist			**51 wks**
14 Aug 59	TALLAHASSEE LASSIE Top Rank JAR 135	**17**	8 wks
1 Jan 60	● WAY DOWN YONDER IN NEW ORLEANS		
	Top Rank JAR 247	**3**	16 wks
10 Mar 60	CALIFORNIA HERE I COME Top Rank JAR 309	**33**	1 wk
17 Mar 60	INDIANA Top Rank JAR 309	**42**	1 wk
24 Mar 60	CALIFORNIA HERE I COME (re-entry)		
	Top Rank JAR 309	**46**	1 wk
19 May 60	THE URGE Top Rank JAR 369	**18**	10 wks
20 Apr 61	MUSKRAT RAMBLE Top Rank JAR 548	**32**	5 wks
28 Jun 62	PALISADES PARK Stateside SS 101	**20**	9 wks

Jim CAPALDI UK, male vocalist			**17 wks**
27 Jul 74	IT'S ALL UP TO YOU Island WIP 6198	**27**	6 wks
25 Oct 75	● LOVE HURTS Island WIP 6246...............................	**4**	11 wks

CAPPELLA Italy, male vocalist			**12 wks**
9 Apr 88	PUSH THE BEAT/ BAUHAUS Fast Globe FGL 1.............	**60**	2 wks
6 May 89	HELYOM HALIB Music Man MMMS 7004	**11**	9 wks
23 Sep 89	HOUSE ENERGY REVENGE Music Man MMPS 7009	**73**	1 wk

Tony CAPSTICK and the CARLTON MAIN/ FRICKLEY COLLIERY BAND			**8 wks**
UK, male vocalist and male instrumental band			
21 Mar 81	● THE SHEFFIELD GRINDER/ CAPSTICK COMES		
	HOME Dingles SID 27..	**3**	8 wks

CAPTAIN BEAKY – *See Keith MICHELL*

CAPTAIN HOLLYWOOD – *See TWENTY 4 SEVEN featuring CAPTAIN HOLLYWOOD*

CAPTAIN SENSIBLE UK, male vocalist			**30 wks**
26 Jun 82	★ HAPPY TALK A & M CAP 1	**1**	8 wks
14 Aug 82	WOT A & M CAP 2..	**26**	7 wks
24 Mar 84	● GLAD IT'S ALL OVER/ DAMNED ON 45 A & M CAP 6	**6**	10 wks
28 Jul 84	THERE ARE MORE SNAKES THAN LADDERS		
	A & M CAP 7..	**57**	5 wks

CAPTAIN and TENNILLE
US, male instrumentalist - keyboards and female vocalist **24 wks**

2 Aug 75		LOVE WILL KEEP US TOGETHER *A & M AMS 7165*	32	5 wks
24 Jan 76		THE WAY I WANT TO TOUCH YOU *A & M AMS 7203*	28	6 wks
4 Nov 78		YOU NEVER DONE IT LIKE THAT *A & M AMS 7384*	63	3 wks
16 Feb 80	●	DO THAT TO ME ONE MORE TIME *Casablanca CAN 175*	7	10 wks

Irene CARA *US, female vocalist* **33 wks**

3 Jul 82	★	FAME *RSO 90*	1	16 wks
4 Sep 82		OUT HERE ON MY OWN *RSO 66*	58	3 wks
4 Jun 83	●	FLASHDANCE ... WHAT A FEELING *Casablanca CAN 1016*	2	14 wks

CARAMBA **6 wks**
Sweden, male vocalist/multi-instrumentalist/dog impersonator, Michael Tretow under a false group name

| 12 Nov 83 | | FEDORA (I'LL BE YOUR DAWG) *Billco BILL 101* | 56 | 6 wks |

CARAVELLES *UK, female vocal duo* **13 wks**

| 8 Aug 63 | ● | YOU DON'T HAVE TO BE A BABY TO CRY *Decca F 11697* | 6 | 13 wks |

CARE *UK, male vocal/instrumental duo* **4 wks**

| 12 Nov 83 | | FLAMING SWORD *Arista KBIRD 2* | 48 | 4 wks |

Mariah CAREY *US, female vocalist* **20 wks**

| 4 Jul 90 | ● | VISION OF LOVE *CBS 6559320* | 9 | 12 wks |
| 10 Nov 90 | | LOVE TAKES TIME *CBS 6563647* | 37† | 8 wks |

Belinda CARLISLE *US, female vocalist* **85 wks**

12 Dec 87	★	HEAVEN IS A PLACE ON EARTH *Virgin VS 1036*	1	14 wks
27 Feb 88	●	I GET WEAK *Virgin VS 1046*	10	9 wks
7 May 88	●	CIRCLE IN THE SAND *Virgin VS 1074*	4	11 wks
6 Aug 88		MAD ABOUT YOU *IRS IRM 118*	67	3 wks
10 Sep 88		WORLD WITHOUT YOU *Virgin VS 1114*	34	6 wks
10 Dec 88		LOVE NEVER DIES... *Virgin VS 1150*	54	5 wks
7 Oct 89	●	LEAVE A LIGHT ON *Virgin VS 1210*	4	10 wks
9 Dec 89		LA LUNA *Virgin VS 1230*	38	6 wks
24 Feb 90		RUNAWAY HORSES *Virgin VS 1244*	40	5 wks
26 May 90		VISION OF YOU *Virgin VS 1264*	41	4 wks
13 Oct 90	●	(WE WANT) THE SAME THING *Virgin VS 1291*	6	10 wks
22 Dec 90		SUMMER RAIN *Virgin VS 1323*	41†	2 wks

Sara CARLSON – *See MANIC MC's featuring Sara CARLSON*

Carl CARLTON *US, male vocalist* **8 wks**

| 18 Jul 81 | | SHE'S A BAD MAMA JAMA (SHE'S BUILT, SHE'S STACKED) *20th Century TC 2488* | 34 | 8 wks |

Larry CARLTON – *See Mike POST*

CARLTON MAIN/ FRICKLEY COLLIERY BAND – *See Tony CAPSTICK and the CARLTON MAIN/FRICKLEY COLLIERY BAND*

CARMEL *UK, female/male vocal/instrumental group* **19 wks**

6 Aug 83		BAD DAY *London LON 29*	15	9 wks
11 Feb 84		MORE, MORE, MORE *London LON 44*	23	7 wks
14 Jun 86		SALLY *London LON 90*	60	3 wks

Eric CARMEN *US, male vocalist* **7 wks**

| 10 Apr 76 | | ALL BY MYSELF *Arista 42* | 12 | 7 wks |

Jean CARN – *See Bobby M*

Kim CARNES *US, female vocalist* **15 wks**

9 May 81	●	BETTE DAVIS EYES *EMI America EA 121*	10	9 wks
8 Aug 81		DRAW OF THE CARDS *EMI America EA 125*	49	4 wks
9 Oct 82		VOYEUR *EMI America EA 143*	68	2 wks

Renato CAROSONE and his SEXTET **1 wk**
Italy, male vocalist and instrumental backing group

| 4 Jul 58 | | TORERO - CHA CHA CHA *Parlophone R 4433* | 25 | 1 wk |

CARPENTERS *US, male/female vocal/instrumental duo* **168 wks**

5 Sep 70	●	(THEY LONG TO BE) CLOSE TO YOU *A & M AMS 800*	6	18 wks
9 Jan 71		WE'VE ONLY JUST BEGUN *A & M AMS 813*	28	7 wks
18 Sep 71		SUPERSTAR / FOR ALL WE KNOW *A & M AMS 864*	18	13 wks
1 Jan 72		MERRY CHRISTMAS DARLING *A & M AME 601*	45	1 wk
23 Sep 72	●	I WON'T LAST A DAY WITHOUT YOU/ GOODBYE TO LOVE *A & M AMS 7023*	9	16 wks
7 Jul 73	●	YESTERDAY ONCE MORE *A & M AMS 7073*	2	17 wks
20 Oct 73	●	TOP OF THE WORLD *A & M AMS 7086*	5	18 wks
2 Mar 74		JAMBALAYA (ON THE BAYOU)/ MR. GUDER *A & M AMS 7098*	12	11 wks
8 Jun 74		I WON'T LAST A DAY WITHOUT YOU (re-issue) *A & M AMS 7111*	32	5 wks
18 Jan 75	●	PLEASE MR. POSTMAN *A & M AMS 7141*	2	12 wks
19 Apr 75	●	ONLY YESTERDAY *A & M AMS 7159*	7	10 wks
30 Aug 75		SOLITAIRE *A & M AMS 7187*	32	5 wks
20 Dec 75		SANTA CLAUS IS COMIN' TO TOWN *A & M AMS 7144*	37	4 wks
27 Mar 76		THERE'S A KIND OF HUSH (ALL OVER THE WORLD) *A & M AMS 7219*	22	6 wks
3 Jul 76		I NEED TO BE IN LOVE *A & M AMS 7238*	36	5 wks
8 Oct 77	●	CALLING OCCUPANTS OF INTERPLANETARY CRAFT (THE RECOGNISED ANTHEM OF WORLD CONTACT DAY) *A & M AMS 7318*	9	9 wks
11 Feb 78		SWEET SWEET SMILE *A & M AMS 7327*	40	4 wks
22 Oct 83		MAKE BELIEVE IT'S YOUR FIRST TIME *A & M AM 147*	60	3 wks
8 Dec 90		MERRY CHRISTMAS DARLING/ CLOSE TO YOU (re-issues) *A & M AM 716*	25†	4 wks

I Won't Last A Day Without You AMS 703 listed by itself 23 Sep 72. Goodbye To Love, the other side, listed by itself from 30 Sep 72 until the end of the record's chart run. Mr Guder listed with Jambalaya from 16 Mar 74 until the end of the record's chart run.

Joe 'Fingers' CARR **5 wks**
US, male instrumentalist - piano, Lou Busch under a false name

| 29 Jun 56 | | PORTUGUESE WASHERWOMAN *Capitol CL 14587* | 20 | 5 wks |

See also Lou Busch.

Linda CARR and the LOVE SQUAD   8 wks
US, female vocalist, female vocal backing group

12 Jul 75	HIGHWIRE *Chelsea 2005 025*	15	8 wks

See also Linda and the Funky Boys - it's the same Linda.

Pearl CARR and Teddy JOHNSON   19 wks
UK, female/male vocal duo

20 Mar 59	SING LITTLE BIRDIE *Columbia DB 4275*	12	8 wks
6 Apr 61	HOW WONDERFUL TO KNOW *Columbia DB 4603*	23	11 wks

Valerie CARR *UK, female vocalist*   2 wks

4 Jul 58	WHEN THE BOYS TALK ABOUT THE GIRLS *Columbia DB 4131*	29	1 wk
18 Jul 58	WHEN THE BOYS TALK ABOUT THE GIRLS (re-entry) *Columbia DB 4131*	30	1 wk

Vikki CARR *US, female vocalist*   26 wks

1 Jun 67 ●	IT MUST BE HIM (SEUL SUR SON ETOILE) *Liberty LIB 55917*	2	20 wks
30 Aug 67	THERE I GO *Liberty LBF 15022*	50	1 wk
12 Mar 69	WITH PEN IN HAND *Liberty LBF 15166*	43	1 wk
26 Mar 69	WITH PEN IN HAND (re-entry) *Liberty LBF 15166*	40	2 wks
30 Apr 69	WITH PEN IN HAND (2nd re-entry) *Liberty LBF 15166*	40	2 wks

Raffaella CARRA *Italy, female vocalist*   12 wks

15 Apr 78 ●	DO IT DO IT AGAIN *Epic EPC 6094*	9	12 wks

Paul CARRACK *UK, male vocalist*   8 wks

16 May 87	WHEN YOU WALK IN THE ROOM *Chrysalis CHS 3109*	48	5 wks
18 Mar 89	DON'T SHED A TEAR *Chrysalis CHS 3164*	60	3 wks

Ronnie CARROLL *UK, male vocalist*   50 wks

27 Jul 56	WALK HAND IN HAND *Philips PB 603*	13	8 wks
29 Mar 57	THE WISDOM OF A FOOL *Philips PB 667*	20	2 wks
31 Mar 60	FOOTSTEPS *Philips PB 1004*	36	3 wks
22 Feb 62	RING A DING GIRL *Philips PB 1222*	46	3 wks
2 Aug 62 ●	ROSES ARE RED *Philips 326532 BF*	3	16 wks
15 Nov 62	IF ONLY TOMORROW *Philips 326550 BF*	33	4 wks
7 Mar 63 ●	SAY WONDERFUL THINGS *Philips 326574 BF*	6	14 wks

Jasper CARROTT *UK, male vocalist*   15 wks

16 Aug 75 ●	FUNKY MOPED/ MAGIC ROUNDABOUT *DJM DJS 388*	5	15 wks

CARS *US, male vocal/instrumental group*   51 wks

11 Nov 78 ●	MY BEST FRIEND'S GIRL *Elektra K 12301*	3	10 wks
17 Feb 79	JUST WHAT I NEEDED *Elektra K 12312*	17	10 wks
28 Jul 79	LET'S GO *Elektra K 12371*	51	4 wks
5 Jun 82	SINCE YOU'RE GONE *Elektra K 13177*	37	4 wks
29 Sep 84 ●	DRIVE *Elektra E 9706*	5	11 wks
3 Aug 85	DRIVE (re-entry) *Elektra E 9706*	4	12 wks

Clarence CARTER *US, male vocalist*   13 wks

10 Oct 70 ●	PATCHES *Atlantic 2091 030*	2	13 wks

CARVELLS   4 wks
UK, male vocalist/instrumentalist - Alan Carvell under a group name

26 Nov 77	THE L.A. RUN *Creole CR 143*	31	4 wks

CASCADES *US, male vocal group*   16 wks

28 Feb 63 ●	RHYTHM OF THE RAIN *Warner Bros. WB 88*	5	16 wks

Natalie CASEY *UK, female vocalist*   1 wk

7 Jan 84	CHICK CHICK CHICKEN *Polydor CHICK 1*	72	1 wk

Johnny CASH *US, male vocalist*   59 wks

3 Jun 65	IT AIN'T ME BABE *CBS 201760*	28	8 wks
6 Sep 69 ●	A BOY NAMED SUE *CBS 4460*	4	19 wks
23 May 70	WHAT IS TRUTH *CBS 4934*	21	11 wks
15 Apr 72 ●	A THING CALLED LOVE *CBS 7797*	4	13 wks
22 Jul 72	A THING CALLED LOVE (re-entry) *CBS 7797*	48	1 wk
3 Jul 76	ONE PIECE AT A TIME *CBS 4287*	32	7 wks

A Thing Called Love with the Evangel Temple Choir. One Piece At A Time with the Tennessee Three.

CASHFLOW *US, male vocal/instrumental group*   8 wks

24 May 86	MINE ALL MINE/ PARTY FREAK *Club JAB 30*	15	8 wks

CASHMERE *US, male vocal/instrumental group*   11 wks

19 Jan 85	CAN I *Fourth & Broadway BRW 19*	29	8 wks
23 Mar 85	WE NEED LOVE *Fourth & Broadway BRW 22*	52	3 wks

CASINOS *US, male vocal group*   7 wks

23 Feb 67	THEN YOU CAN TELL ME GOODBYE *President PT 123*	28	7 wks

Mama CASS *US, female vocalist*   27 wks

14 Aug 68	DREAM A LITTLE DREAM OF ME *RCA 1726*	11	12 wks
16 Aug 69 ●	IT'S GETTING BETTER *Stateside SS 8021*	8	15 wks

See also Mamas and the Papas.

David CASSIDY *US, male vocalist*   109 wks

8 Apr 72 ●	COULD IT BE FOREVER/ CHERISH *Bell 1224*	2	17 wks
16 Sep 72 ★	HOW CAN I BE SURE *Bell 1258*	1	11 wks
25 Nov 72	ROCK ME BABY *Bell 1268*	11	9 wks
24 Mar 73 ●	I'M A CLOWN/ SOME KIND OF A SUMMER *Bell MABEL 4*	3	12 wks
13 Oct 73 ★	DAYDREAMER/ THE PUPPY SONG *Bell 1334*	1	15 wks
11 May 74	IF I DIDN'T CARE *Bell 1350*	9	8 wks
27 Jul 74	PLEASE PLEASE ME *Bell 1371*	16	6 wks
5 Jul 75	I WRITE THE SONGS/ GET IT UP FOR LOVE *RCA 2571*	11	8 wks
25 Oct 75	DARLIN' *RCA 2622*	16	8 wks
23 Feb 85 ●	THE LAST KISS *Arista ARIST 589*	6	9 wks
11 May 85	ROMANCE (LET YOUR HEART GO) *Arista ARIST 620*	54	6 wks

See also Partridge Family starring Shirley Jones featuring David Cassidy.

CAST OF IDIOTS – *See Rick DEES and his CAST OF IDIOTS*

Roy CASTLE *UK, male vocalist* — **3 wks**

22 Dec 60	LITTLE WHITE BERRY *Philips PB 1087*	40	3 wks

CASUALS *UK, male vocal/instrumental group* — **26 wks**

14 Aug 68 ●	JESAMINE *Decca F 22784*	2	18 wks
4 Dec 68	TOY *Decca F 22852*	30	8 wks

CATCH *UK, male vocal/instrumental group* — **1 wk**

17 Nov 90	FREE (C'MON) *FFRR F 147*	70	1 wk

CATS *UK, male instrumental group* — **2 wks**

9 Apr 69	SWAN LAKE *BAF 1*	48	1 wk
21 May 69	SWAN LAKE (re-entry) *BAF 1*	50	1 wk

CATS U.K. *UK, female vocal group* — **8 wks**

6 Oct 79	LUTON AIRPORT *WEA K 18075*	22	8 wks

C. C. S. *UK, male vocal/instrumental group* — **55 wks**

31 Oct 70	WHOLE LOTTA LOVE *RAK 104*	13	13 wks
27 Feb 71 ●	WALKIN' *RAK 109*	7	16 wks
4 Sep 71 ●	TAP TURNS ON THE WATER *RAK 119*	5	13 wks
4 Mar 72	BROTHER *RAK 126*	25	8 wks
4 Aug 73	BAND PLAYED THE BOOGIE *RAK 154*	36	5 wks

CENTRAL LINE *UK, male vocal/instrumental group* — **30 wks**

31 Jan 81	(YOU KNOW) YOU CAN DO IT *Mercury LINE 7*	67	3 wks
15 Aug 81	WALKING INTO SUNSHINE *Mercury MER 78*	42	10 wks
30 Oct 82	DON'T TELL ME *Mercury MER 90*	55	3 wks
20 Nov 82	YOU'VE SAID ENOUGH *Mercury MER 117*	58	3 wks
22 Jan 83	NATURE BOY *Mercury MER 131*	21	8 wks
11 Jun 83	SURPRISE SURPRISE *Mercury MER 133*	48	3 wks

CERRONE *France, male producer/multi-instrumentalist* — **20 wks**

5 Mar 77	LOVE IN C MINOR *Atlantic K 10895*	31	4 wks
29 Jul 78 ●	SUPER NATURE *Atlantic K 11089*	8	12 wks
13 Jan 79	JE SUIS MUSIC *CBS 6918*	39	4 wks

A CERTAIN RATIO *UK, male vocal/instrumental group* — **3 wks**

16 Jun 90	WON'T STOP LOVING YOU *A &M ACR 540*	55	3 wks

Peter CETERA *US, male vocalist* — **13 wks**

2 Aug 86 ●	GLORY OF LOVE *Full Moon W 8662*	3	13 wks

Frank CHACKSFIELD *UK, orchestra* — **35 wks**

3 Apr 53 ●	LITTLE RED MONKEY *Parlophone R 3658*	10	3 wks
22 May 53 ●	LIMELIGHT *Decca F 10106*	2	24 wks
12 Feb 54 ●	EBB TIDE *Decca F 10122*	9	2 wks
24 Feb 56	IN OLD LISBON *Decca F 10689*	15	4 wks
31 Aug 56	DONKEY CART *Decca F 10743*	26	2 wks

Little Red Monkey credited to Frank Chacksfield's Tunesmiths.

CHAIRMEN OF THE BOARD *US, male vocal group* — **77 wks**

22 Aug 70 ●	GIVE ME JUST A LITTLE MORE TIME *Invictus INV 501*	3	13 wks
14 Nov 70 ●	YOU'VE GOT ME DANGLING ON A STRING *Invictus INV 504*	5	13 wks
20 Feb 71	EVERYTHING'S TUESDAY *Invictus INV 507*	12	9 wks
15 May 71	PAY TO THE PIPER *Invictus INV 511*	34	7 wks
4 Sep 71	CHAIRMAN OF THE BOARD *Invictus INV 516*	48	2 wks
15 Jul 72	WORKING ON A BUILDING OF LOVE *Invictus INV 519*	20	8 wks
7 Oct 72	ELMO JAMES *Invictus INV 524*	21	7 wks
16 Dec 72	I'M ON MY WAY TO A BETTER PLACE *Invictus INV 527*	38	1 wk
13 Jan 73	I'M ON MY WAY TO A BETTER PLACE (re-entry) *Invictus INV 527*	30	5 wks
23 Jun 73	FINDERS KEEPERS *Invictus INV 530*	21	9 wks
13 Sep 86	LOVERBOY *EMI EMI 5585*	56	3 wks

Label for EMI EMI 5585 credits lead singer General Johnson.

CHAKACHAS *Belgium, male/female vocal/instrumental group* — **8 wks**

11 Jan 62	TWIST TWIST *RCA 1264*	48	1 wk
27 May 72	JUNGLE FEVER *Polydor 2121 064*	29	7 wks

George CHAKIRIS *US, male vocalist* — **1 wk**

2 Jun 60	HEART OF A TEENAGE GIRL *Triumph RGM 1010*	49	1 wk

Richard CHAMBERLAIN *US, male vocalist* — **36 wks**

7 Jun 62	THEME FROM 'DR. KILDARE' (THREE STARS WILL SHINE TONIGHT) *MGM 1160*	12	10 wks
1 Nov 62	LOVE ME TENDER *MGM 1173*	15	11 wks
21 Feb 63	HI-LILI HI-LO *MGM 1189*	20	9 wks
18 Jul 63	TRUE LOVE *MGM 1205*	30	6 wks

CHAMELEONS – *See LORI and the CHAMELEONS*

CHAMPAIGN *US, male/female vocal/instrumental group* — **13 wks**

9 May 81 ●	HOW 'BOUT US *CBS A 1046*	5	13 wks

CHAMPION LEGEND *Record company montage* — **1 wk**

10 Feb 90	CAN YOU FEEL IT *Champion CHAMP 227*	62	1 wk

Hit was listed with Can You Feel It *by Raze. See also Raze.*

CHAMPS *US, male instrumental group* — **10 wks**

4 Apr 58 ●	TEQUILA *London HLU 8580*	5	9 wks
17 Mar 60	TOO MUCH TEQUILA *London HLH 9052*	49	1 wk

CHAMPS BOYS *France, male instrumental group* — **6 wks**

19 Jun 76	TUBULAR BELLS *Philips 6006 519*	41	6 wks

Gene CHANDLER *US, male vocalist* — **29 wks**

5 Jun 68	NOTHING CAN STOP ME *Soul City SC 102*	41	4 wks
3 Feb 79	GET DOWN *20th Century BTC 1040*	11	11 wks
1 Sep 79	WHEN YOU'RE NUMBER 1 *20th Century TC 2411*	43	5 wks

28 Jun 80	**DOES SHE HAVE A FRIEND** *20th Century TC 2451*	**28**	9 wks

CHANELLE *US, female vocalist*   **8 wks**

11 Mar 89	**ONE MAN** *Cooltempo COOL 183*	**16**	8 wks

CHANGE *US, male/female vocal/instrumental group*   **43 wks**

28 Jun 80	**A LOVER'S HOLIDAY/ GLOW OF LOVE** *WEA K 79141*	**14**	8 wks
6 Sep 80	**SEARCHING** *WEA K 79156*	**11**	10 wks
2 Jun 84	**CHANGE OF HEART** *WEA YZ 7*	**17**	10 wks
11 Aug 84	**YOU ARE MY MELODY** *WEA YZ 14*	**48**	4 wks
16 Mar 85	**LET'S GO TOGETHER** *Cooltempo COOL 107*	**37**	7 wks
25 May 85	**OH WHAT A FEELING** *Cooltempo COOL 109*	**56**	2 wks
13 Jul 85	**MUTUAL ATTRACTION** *Cooltempo COOL 111.* ...	**60**	2 wks

Although uncredited Luther Vandross is the vocalist on Searching. *See also Luther Vandross.*

Bruce CHANNEL *US, male vocalist*   **28 wks**

22 Mar 62	● **HEY! BABY** *Mercury AMT 1171*	**2**	12 wks
26 Jun 68	**KEEP ON** *Bell 1010*	**12**	16 wks

CHANSON *US, male/female vocal group*   **7 wks**

13 Jan 79	**DON'T HOLD BACK** *Ariola ARO 140*	**33**	7 wks

See also Calibre Cuts

CHANTAYS *US, male instrumental group*   **14 wks**

18 Apr 63	**PIPELINE** *London HLD 9696*	**16**	14 wks

CHANTER SISTERS *UK, female vocal group*   **5 wks**

17 Jul 76	**SIDE SHOW** *Polydor 2058 735*	**43**	5 wks

Harry CHAPIN *US, male vocalist*   **5 wks**

11 May 74	**W.O.L.D.** *Elektra K 12133*	**34**	5 wks

Tracy CHAPMAN *US, female vocalist*   **15 wks**

11 Jun 88	● **FAST CAR** *Elektra EKR 73*	**5**	12 wks
30 Sep 89	**CROSSROADS** *Elektra EKR 95*	**61**	3 wks

CHAQUITO   **1 wk**
UK, male arranger/conductor, Johnny Gregory, under false name

27 Oct 60	**NEVER ON SUNDAY** *Fontana H 265*	**50**	1 wk

CHARITY – *See FAITH, HOPE and CHARITY*

CHARLATANS *UK, male vocal/instrumental group*   **14 wks**

2 Jun 90	● **THE ONLY ONE I KNOW** *Situation Two SIT 70T*	**9**	9 wks
22 Sep 90	**THEN** *Situation Two SIT 74T*	**12**	5 wks

CHARLENE *US, female vocalist*   **12 wks**

15 May 82	★ **I'VE NEVER BEEN TO ME** *Motown TMG 1260*	**1**	12 wks

Don CHARLES *UK, male vocalist*   **5 wks**

22 Feb 62	**WALK WITH ME MY ANGEL** *Decca F 11424*	**39**	5 wks

Ray CHARLES *US, male vocalist/instrumentalist – piano*   **123 wks**

1 Dec 60	**GEORGIA ON MY MIND** *HMV POP 792*	**47**	1 wk
15 Dec 60	**GEORGIA ON MY MIND (re-entry)** *HMV POP 792*	**24**	7 wks
19 Oct 61	● **HIT THE ROAD JACK** *HMV POP 935*	**6**	12 wks
14 Jun 62	★ **I CAN'T STOP LOVING YOU** *HMV POP 1034*	**1**	17 wks
13 Sep 62	**YOU DON'T KNOW ME** *HMV POP 1064*	**9**	13 wks
13 Dec 62	**YOUR CHEATING HEART** *HMV POP 1099*	**13**	8 wks
28 Mar 63	**DON'T SET ME FREE** *HMV POP 1133.*	**37**	3 wks
16 May 63	● **TAKE THESE CHAINS FROM MY HEART** *HMV POP 1161.*	**5**	20 wks
12 Sep 63	**NO ONE** *HMV POP 1202*	**35**	7 wks
31 Oct 63	**BUSTED** *HMV POP 1221*	**21**	10 wks
24 Sep 64	**NO ONE TO CRY TO** *HMV POP 1333.*	**38**	3 wks
21 Jan 65	**MAKIN' WHOOPEE** *HMV POP 1383*	**42**	4 wks
10 Feb 66	**CRYIN' TIME** *HMV POP 1502.*	**50**	1 wk
21 Apr 66	**TOGETHER AGAIN** *HMV POP 1519.*	**48**	1 wk
5 Jul 67	**HERE WE GO AGAIN** *HMV POP 1595*	**38**	1 wk
19 Jul 67	**HERE WE GO AGAIN (re-entry)** *HMV POP 1595.* ...	**45**	2 wks
20 Dec 67	**YESTERDAY** *Stateside SS 2071*	**44**	4 wks
31 Jul 68	**ELEANOR RIGBY** *Stateside SS 2120.*	**36**	9 wks

See also Quincy Jones.

Tina CHARLES *UK, female vocalist*   **63 wks**

7 Feb 76	★ **I LOVE TO LOVE (BUT MY BABY LOVES TO DANCE)** *CBS 3937.*	**1**	12 wks
1 May 76	**LOVE ME LIKE A LOVER** *CBS 4237*	**28**	7 wks
21 Aug 76	● **DANCE LITTLE LADY DANCE** *CBS 4480* ...	**6**	13 wks
4 Dec 76	● **DR. LOVE** *CBS 4779*	**4**	10 wks
14 May 77	**RENDEZVOUS** *CBS 5174*	**27**	6 wks
29 Oct 77	**LOVE BUG-SWEETS FOR MY SWEET** (MEDLEY) *CBS 5680*	**26**	4 wks
11 Mar 78	**I'LL GO WHERE YOUR MUSIC TAKES ME** *CBS 6062*	**27**	8 wks
30 Aug 86	**I LOVE TO LOVE (re-mix)** *DMC DECK 1* ...	**67**	3 wks

Dick CHARLESWORTH and his CITY GENTS   **1 wk**
UK, male jazz band group, Dick Charlesworth clarinet

4 May 61	**BILLY BOY** *Top Rank JAR 558*	**43**	1 wk

CHARLEY – *See JOHNNY and CHARLEY*

CHARME *US, male/female vocal group*   **2 wks**

17 Nov 84	**GEORGY PORGY** *RCA 464.*	**68**	2 wks

CHARO and the SALSOUL ORCHESTRA   **4 wks**
US, female vocalist and orchestra

29 Apr 78	**DANCE A LITTLE BIT CLOSER** *Salsoul SSOL 101*	**44**	4 wks

CHAS and DAVE *UK, male vocal/instrumental duo*   **57 wks**

11 Nov 78	**STRUMMIN'** *EMI 2874*	**52**	3 wks
26 May 79	**GERTCHA** *EMI 2947*	**20**	8 wks
1 Sep 79	**THE SIDEBOARD SONG (GOT MY BEER IN THE SIDEBOARD HERE)** *EMI 2986*	**55**	3 wks
29 Nov 80	● **RABBIT** *Rockney 9*	**8**	11 wks
12 Dec 81	**STARS OVER 45** *Rockney KOR 12*	**21**	8 wks
13 Mar 82	**AIN'T NO PLEASING YOU** *Rockney KOR 14.*	**2**	11 wks
17 Jul 82	**MARGATE** *Rockney KOR 15*	**46**	4 wks
19 Mar 83	**LONDON GIRLS** *Rockney KOR 17.*	**63**	3 wks

In the last edition of *British Hit Singles* Donny Osmond was pictured with Billy Idol. This time around he meets TERENCE TRENT D'ARBY.

Far Left: The ALICE COOPER album *From the Inside*, a collaboration with lyricist Bernie Taupin, included the single 'How You Gonna See Me Now' and inspired a Marvel Comic.

Liberace finds RAY CHARLES has beaten him to the piano.

Bottom Left: SKEETER DAVIS revealed she sang 'The End Of The World' thinking of her former singing partner Betty Davis (no relation), who had died in a car crash in 1953.

3 Dec 83   **MY MELANCHOLY BABY** *Rockney KOR 21* .... **51**   6 wks

Strummin' credited to Chas and Dave with Rockney - UK, male instrumental group. See also Tottenham Hotspur FA Cup Squad; Matchroom Mob with Chas and Dave.

CHEAP TRICK *US, male vocal/instrumental group*   **14 wks**

5 May 79	**I WANT YOU TO WANT ME** *Epic EPC 7258*	**29**	9 wks
2 Feb 80	**WAY OF THE WORLD** *Epic EPC 8114*	**73**	2 wks
31 Jul 82	**IF YOU WANT MY LOVE** *Epic EPC A 2406*	**57**	3 wks

Oliver CHEATHAM *US, male vocalist*   **5 wks**

2 Jul 83   **GET DOWN SATURDAY NIGHT** *MCA 828* .... **38**   5 wks

CHECK 1-2 – *See Craig McCLACHLAN and CHECK 1-2*

Chubby CHECKER *US, male vocalist*   **97 wks**

22 Sep 60	**THE TWIST** *Columbia DB 4503*	**49**	1 wk
6 Oct 60	**THE TWIST (re-entry)** *Columbia DB 4503*	**44**	1 wk
30 Mar 61	**PONY TIME** *Columbia DB 4591*	**27**	6 wks
17 Aug 61	**LET'S TWIST AGAIN** *Columbia DB 4691*	**37**	3 wks
28 Dec 61	● **LET'S TWIST AGAIN (re-entry)** *Columbia DB 4691*	**2**	27 wks
11 Jan 62	**THE TWIST (2nd re-entry)** *Columbia DB 4503*	**14**	10 wks
5 Apr 62	**SLOW TWISTIN'** *Columbia DB 4808*	**23**	8 wks
9 Aug 62	**DANCIN' PARTY** *Columbia DB 4876*	**19**	13 wks
23 Aug 62	**LET'S TWIST AGAIN (2nd re-entry)** *Columbia DB 4691*	**46**	1 wk
13 Sep 62	**LET'S TWIST AGAIN (3rd re-entry)** *Columbia DB 4691*	**49**	3 wks
1 Nov 62	**LIMBO ROCK** *Cameo-Parkway P 849*	**32**	10 wks
31 Oct 63	**WHAT DO YA SAY** *Cameo-Parkway P 806*	**37**	4 wks
29 Nov 75	● **LET'S TWIST AGAIN/ THE TWIST (re-issue)** *London HL 10512*	**5**	10 wks

See also Chubby Checker and Bobby Rydell; Fat Boys.

Chubby CHECKER and Bobby RYDELL   **4 wks**
US, male vocal duo

19 Apr 62	**TEACH ME TO TWIST** *Columbia DB 4802*	**45**	1 wk
20 Dec 62	**JINGLE BELL ROCK** *Cameo-Parkway C 205*	**40**	3 wks

See also Chubby Checker; Bobby Rydell.

CHECKMATES – *See Emile FORD and the CHECKMATES*

CHECKMATES LTD. *US, male vocal/instrumental group*   **8 wks**

15 Nov 69   **PROUD MARY** *A &M AMS 769* .... **30**   8 wks

CHEETAHS *UK, male vocal/instrumental group*   **6 wks**

1 Oct 64	**MECCA** *Philips BF 1362*	**36**	3 wks
21 Jan 65	**SOLDIER BOY** *Philips BF 1383*	**39**	3 wks

CHELSEA F.C. *UK, male football team vocalists*   **12 wks**

26 Feb 72   ● **BLUE IS THE COLOUR** *Penny Farthing PEN 782* .... **5**   12 wks

CHEQUERS *UK, male vocal/instrumental group*   **10 wks**

18 Oct 75	**ROCK ON BROTHER** *Creole CR 111*	**21**	5 wks
28 Feb 76	**HEY MISS PAYNE** *Creole CR 116*	**32**	5 wks

CHER *US, female vocalist*   **94 wks**

19 Aug 65	● **ALL I REALLY WANT TO DO** *Liberty LIB 66114*	**9**	10 wks
31 Mar 66	● **BANG BANG (MY BABY SHOT ME DOWN)** *Liberty LIB 66160*	**3**	12 wks
4 Aug 66	**I FEEL SOMETHING IN THE AIR** *Liberty LIB 12034*	**43**	2 wks
22 Sep 66	**SUNNY** *Liberty LIB 12083*	**32**	5 wks
6 Nov 71	● **GYPSYS TRAMPS AND THIEVES** *MCA MU 1142*	**4**	13 wks
16 Feb 74	**DARK LADY** *MCA 101*	**36**	3 wks
16 Mar 74	**DARK LADY (re-entry)** *MCA 101*	**45**	1 wk
19 Dec 87	● **I FOUND SOMEONE** *Geffen GEF 31*	**5**	10 wks
2 Apr 88	**WE ALL SLEEP ALONE** *Geffen GEF 35*	**47**	5 wks
2 Sep 89	● **IF I COULD TURN BACK TIME** *Geffen GEF 59*	**6**	14 wks
13 Jan 90	**JUST LIKE JESSE JAMES** *Geffen GEF 69*	**11**	11 wks
7 Apr 90	**HEART OF STONE** *Geffen GEF 75*	**43**	5 wks
11 Aug 90	**YOU WOULDN'T KNOW LOVE** *Geffen GEF 77*	**55**	3 wks

See also Sonny and Cher; Meatloaf.

CHERELLE *US, female vocalist*   **5 wks**

1 Mar 86	**WILL YOU SATISFY?** *Tabu A 6927*	**57**	3 wks
6 May 89	**AFFAIR** *Tabu 654673 7*	**67**	2 wks

See also Cherelle with Alexander O'Neal; Alexander O'Neal.

CHERELLE with Alexander O'NEAL   **13 wks**
US, female/male vocal duo

28 Dec 85	● **SATURDAY LOVE** *Tabu A 6829*	**6**	11 wks
24 Mar 90	**SATURDAY LOVE (re-mix)** *Tabu 655680 7*	**55**	2 wks

See also Cherelle; Alexander O'Neal.

CHERI *Canada, female vocal duo*   **9 wks**

19 Jun 82   **MURPHY'S LAW** *Polydor POSP 459* .... **13**   9 wks

CHEROKEES *UK, male vocal/instrumental group*   **5 wks**

3 Sep 64   **SEVEN DAFFODILS** *Columbia DB 7341* .... **33**   5 wks

Don CHERRY *US, male vocalist*   **11 wks**

10 Feb 56   ● **BAND OF GOLD** *Philips PB 549* .... **6**   11 wks

Neneh CHERRY *US, female vocalist*   **41 wks**

10 Dec 88	● **BUFFALO STANCE** *Circa YR 21*	**3**	13 wks
20 May 89	● **MANCHILD** *Circa YR 30*	**5**	10 wks
12 Aug 89	**KISSES ON THE WIND** *Circa YR 33*	**20**	6 wks
23 Dec 89	**INNA CITY MAMMA** *Circa YR 42*	**31**	7 wks
29 Sep 90	**I'VE GOT YOU UNDER MY SKIN** *Circa YR 53*	**25**	5 wks

CHIC *US, male/female vocal/instrumental group*   **87 wks**

26 Nov 77	● **DANCE DANCE DANCE (YOWSAH YOWSAH YOWSAH)** *Atlantic K 11038*	**6**	12 wks
1 Apr 78	● **EVERYBODY DANCE** *Atlantic K 11097*	**9**	11 wks
18 Nov 78	● **LE FREAK** *Atlantic K 11209*	**7**	16 wks
24 Feb 79	● **I WANT YOUR LOVE** *Atlantic LV 16*	**4**	11 wks
30 Jun 79	● **GOOD TIMES** *Atlantic K 11310*	**5**	11 wks
13 Oct 79	**MY FORBIDDEN LOVER** *Atlantic K 11385*	**15**	8 wks
8 Dec 79	**MY FEET KEEP DANCING** *Atlantic K 11415*	**21**	9 wks
12 Mar 83	**HANGIN'** *Atlantic A 9898*	**64**	1 wk
19 Sep 87	**JACK LE FREAK** *Atlantic A 9198*	**19**	6 wks
14 Jul 90	**MEGACHIC - CHIC MEDLEY** *East West A 7949*	**58**	2 wks

CHICAGO *US, male vocal/instrumental group*   **81 wks**

10 Jan 70	●	**I'M A MAN** CBS 4715	**8**	11 wks
18 Jul 70	●	**25 OR 6 TO 4** CBS 5076	**7**	13 wks
9 Oct 76	★	**IF YOU LEAVE ME NOW** CBS 4603. ...	**1**	16 wks
5 Nov 77		**BABY WHAT A BIG SURPRISE** CBS 5672	**41**	3 wks
21 Aug 82	●	**HARD TO SAY I'M SORRY** Full Moon K 79301 ...	**4**	15 wks
27 Oct 84	●	**HARD HABIT TO BREAK** Full Moon W 9214 ...	**8**	13 wks
26 Jan 85		**YOU'RE THE INSPIRATION** Warner Bros. W 9126	**14**	10 wks

CHICKEN SHACK   **19 wks**
UK, male/female vocal/instrumental group

7 May 69	**I'D RATHER GO BLIND** Blue Horizon 57-3153 ...	**14**	13 wks
6 Sep 69	**TEARS IN THE WIND** Blue Horizon 57-3160 ...	**29**	6 wks

CHICORY TIP *UK, male vocal/instrumental group*   **34 wks**

29 Jan 72	★	**SON OF MY FATHER** CBS 7737. ...	**1**	13 wks
20 May 72		**WHAT'S YOUR NAME** CBS 8021 ...	**13**	8 wks
31 Mar 73		**GOOD GRIEF CHRISTINA** CBS 1258 ...	**17**	13 wks

CHIFFONS *US, female vocal group*   **40 wks**

11 Apr 63		**HE'S SO FINE** Stateside SS 172 ...	**16**	12 wks
18 Jul 63		**ONE FINE DAY** Stateside SS 202 ...	**29**	6 wks
26 May 66		**SWEET TALKIN' GUY** Stateside SS 512 ...	**31**	8 wks
18 Mar 72	●	**SWEET TALKIN' GUY** (re-issue) London HL 10271 ...	**4**	14 wks

CHILD *UK, male vocal/instrumental group*   **22 wks**

29 Apr 78		**WHEN YOU WALK IN THE ROOM** Ariola Hansa AHA 511 ...	**38**	5 wks
22 Jul 78	●	**IT'S ONLY MAKE BELIEVE** Ariola Hansa AHA 522 ...	**10**	12 wks
28 Apr 79		**ONLY YOU (AND YOU ALONE)** Ariola Hansa AHA 536 ...	**33**	5 wks

Jane CHILD *US, female vocalist*   **8 wks**

12 May 90	**DON'T WANNA FALL IN LOVE** Warner Bros. W 9817 ...	**22**	8 wks

CHILDREN OF THE NIGHT   **2 wks**
UK, male vocalist/producer

26 Nov 88	**IT'S A TRIP (TUNE IN, TURN ON, DROP OUT)** Jive JIVE 189 ...	**52**	2 wks

CHILDREN OF THE REVOLUTION – *See KLF featuring CHILDREN OF THE REVOLUTION*

Toni CHILDS *US, female vocalist*   **4 wks**

25 Mar 89	**DON'T WALK AWAY** A & M AM 462 ...	**53**	4 wks

CHI-LITES *US, male vocal group*   **89 wks**

28 Aug 71		**(FOR GOD'S SAKE) GIVE MORE POWER TO THE PEOPLE** MCA MU 1138 ...	**32**	6 wks
15 Jan 72	●	**HAVE YOU SEEN HER** MCA MU 1146 ...	**3**	12 wks
27 May 72		**OH GIRL** MCA MU 1156 ...	**14**	9 wks
23 Mar 74	●	**HOMELY GIRL** Brunswick BR 9 ...	**5**	13 wks
20 Jul 74		**I FOUND SUNSHINE** Brunswick BR 12 ...	**35**	5 wks
2 Nov 74	●	**TOO GOOD TO BE FORGOTTEN** Brunswick BR 13 ...	**10**	11 wks
21 Jun 75	●	**HAVE YOU SEEN HER/ OH GIRL** (re-issue) Brunswick BR 20 ...	**5**	9 wks

13 Sep 75	●	**IT'S TIME FOR LOVE** Brunswick BR 25 ...	**5**	10 wks
31 Jul 76	●	**YOU DON'T HAVE TO GO** Brunswick BR 34 ...	**3**	11 wks
13 Aug 83		**CHANGING FOR YOU** R & B RBS 215 ...	**61**	3 wks

CHILL FAC-TORR *US, male vocal/instrumental group*   **8 wks**

2 Apr 83	**TWIST (ROUND 'N' ROUND)** Phillyworld PWS 109 ...	**37**	8 wks

CHIMES *UK, male/female vocal/instrumental group*   **28 wks**

19 Aug 89		**1-2-3** CBS 655166 7. ...	**60**	3 wks
2 Dec 89		**HEAVEN** CBS 655432 7. ...	**66**	2 wks
6 Jan 90		**HEAVEN** (re-entry) CBS 655432 7. ...	**69**	3 wks
19 May 90	●	**STILL HAVEN'T FOUND WHAT I'M LOOKING FOR** CBS CHIM 1	**6**	9 wks
28 Jul 90		**TRUE LOVE** CBS CHIM 12. ...	**48**	3 wks
29 Sep 90		**HEAVEN** (re-issue) CBS CHIM 3. ...	**24**	6 wks
1 Dec 90		**LOVE COMES TO MIND** CBS CHIM 4. ...	**49**	2 wks

CHINA CRISIS *UK, male vocal/instrumental group*   **66 wks**

7 Aug 82		**AFRICAN AND WHITE** Inevitable INEV 011 ...	**45**	5 wks
22 Jan 83		**CHRISTIAN** Virgin VS 562 ...	**12**	9 wks
21 May 83		**TRAGEDY AND MYSTERY** Virgin VS 587 ...	**46**	6 wks
15 Oct 83		**WORKING WITH FIRE AND STEEL** Virgin VS 620 ...	**48**	5 wks
14 Jan 84	●	**WISHFUL THINKING** Virgin VS 647 ...	**9**	8 wks
10 Mar 84		**HANNA HANNA** Virgin VS 665 ...	**44**	3 wks
30 Mar 85		**BLACK MAN RAY** Virgin VS 752 ...	**14**	9 wks
1 Jun 85		**KING IN A CATHOLIC STYLE (WAKE UP)** Virgin VS 765 ...	**19**	9 wks
7 Sep 85		**YOU DID CUT ME** Virgin VS 799 ...	**54**	3 wks
8 Nov 86		**ARIZONA SKY** Virgin VS 898 ...	**47**	4 wks
24 Jan 87		**BEST KEPT SECRET** Virgin VS 926 ...	**36**	5 wks

Jonny CHINGAS *US, male vocalist*   **6 wks**

19 Feb 83	**PHONE HOME** CBS A 3121 ...	**43**	6 wks

CHIPMUNKS   **8 wks**
US, male vocalist, David Seville as himself and a chipmunk vocal trio

24 Jul 59	**RAGTIME COWBOY JOE** London HLU 8916 ...	**11**	8 wks

See also David Seville.

Ted CHIPPINGTON – *See VINDALOO SUMMER SPECIAL*

CHORDETTES *US, female vocal group*   **25 wks**

17 Dec 54		**MR. SANDMAN** Columbia DB 3553 ...	**11**	8 wks
31 Aug 56	●	**BORN TO BE WITH YOU** London HLA 8302 ...	**8**	9 wks
18 Apr 58	●	**LOLLIPOP** London HLA 8584 ...	**6**	8 wks

CHORDS *UK, male vocal/instrumental group*   **17 wks**

6 Oct 79	**NOW IT'S GONE** Polydor 2059 141 ...	**63**	2 wks
2 Feb 80	**MAYBE TOMORROW** Polydor POSP 101 ...	**40**	5 wks
26 Apr 80	**SOMETHING'S MISSING** Polydor POSP 146 ...	**55**	3 wks
12 Jul 80	**THE BRITISH WAY OF LIFE** Polydor 2059 258 ...	**54**	3 wks
18 Oct 80	**IN MY STREET** Polydor POSP 185 ...	**50**	4 wks

CHRIS – *See GLENN and CHRIS*

Neil CHRISTIAN *UK, male vocalist*   **10 wks**

7 Apr 66	**THAT'S NICE** Strike JH 301 ...	**14**	10 wks

Roger CHRISTIAN UK, male vocalist — 3 wks

30 Sep 89	TAKE IT FROM ME Island IS 427	63	3 wks

CHRISTIANS UK, male vocal/instrumental group — 67 wks

31 Jan 87	FORGOTTEN TOWN Island IS 291	22	11 wks
13 Jun 87	HOOVERVILLE (THEY PROMISED US THE WORLD) Island IS 326	21	10 wks
26 Sep 87	WHEN THE FINGERS POINT Island IS 335	34	7 wks
5 Dec 87	IDEAL WORLD Island IS 347	14	13 wks
23 Apr 88	BORN AGAIN Island IS 365	25	7 wks
15 Oct 88 ●	HARVEST FOR THE WORLD Island IS 395	8	7 wks
23 Dec 89	WORDS Island IS 450	18	8 wks
7 Apr 90	I FOUND OUT Island IS 453	56	2 wks
15 Sep 90	GREENBANK DRIVE Island IS 466	63	2 wks

See also Christians, Holly Johnson, Paul McCartney, Gerry Marsden and Stock Aitken Waterman.

CHRISTIANS, Holly JOHNSON, Paul McCARTNEY, Gerry MARSDEN and STOCK AITKEN WATERMAN — 7 wks
UK, male charity ensemble

20 May 89 ★	FERRY 'CROSS THE MERSEY PWL PWL 41	1	7 wks

See also Christians; Holly Johnson; Paul McCartney; Gerry and the Pacemakers; Stock Aitken Waterman.

CHRISTIE UK, male vocal/instrumental group — 37 wks

2 May 70 ★	YELLOW RIVER CBS 4911	1	22 wks
10 Oct 70	SAN BERNADINO CBS 5169	49	1 wk
24 Oct 70 ●	SAN BERNADINO (re-entry) CBS 5169	7	13 wks
25 Mar 72	IRON HORSE CBS 7747	47	1 wk

David CHRISTIE France, male vocalist — 12 wks

14 Aug 82 ●	SADDLE UP KR KR 9	9	12 wks

John CHRISTIE Australia, male vocalist — 6 wks

25 Dec 76	HERE'S TO LOVE (AULD LANG SYNE) EMI 2554	24	6 wks

Lou CHRISTIE US, male vocalist — 35 wks

24 Feb 66	LIGHTNIN' STRIKES MGM 1297	11	8 wks
28 Apr 66	RHAPSODY IN THE RAIN MGM 1308	37	2 wks
13 Sep 69 ●	I'M GONNA MAKE YOU MINE Buddah 201 057	2	17 wks
27 Dec 69	SHE SOLD ME MAGIC Buddah 201 073	25	8 wks

Tony CHRISTIE UK, male vocalist — 47 wks

9 Jan 71	LAS VEGAS MCA MK 5058	21	9 wks
8 May 71 ●	I DID WHAT I DID FOR MARIA MCA MK 5064	2	17 wks
20 Nov 71	IS THIS THE WAY TO AMARILLO MCA MKS 5073	18	13 wks
10 Feb 73	AVENUES AND ALLEYWAYS MCA MKS 5101	37	4 wks
17 Jan 76	DRIVE SAFELY DARLIN' MCA 219	35	4 wks

CHRISTMAS TREES – See SANTA CLAUS and the CHRISTMAS TREES

CHUCKS UK, male/female vocal group — 7 wks

24 Jan 63	LOO-BE-LOO Decca F 11569	22	7 wks

CINDERELLA US, male vocal/instrumental group — 6 wks

6 Aug 88	GYPSY ROAD Vertigo VER 40	54	2 wks
4 Mar 89	DON'T KNOW WHAT YOU GOT Vertigo VER 43	54	2 wks
17 Nov 90	SHELTER ME Vertigo VER 51	55	2 wks

CINDY and the SAFFRONS UK, female vocal group — 3 wks

15 Jan 83	PAST, PRESENT AND FUTURE Stilletto STL 9	56	3 wks

Gigliola CINQUETTI Italy, female vocalist — 27 wks

23 Apr 64	NON HO L'ETA PER AMARTI Decca F 21882	17	17 wks
4 May 74 ●	GO (BEFORE YOU BREAK MY HEART) CBS 2294	8	10 wks

CIRRUS UK, male vocal group — 1 wk

30 Sep 78	ROLLIN' ON Jet 123	62	1 wk

CITY BOY UK, male vocal/instrumental group — 20 wks

8 Jul 78 ●	5-7-0-5 Vertigo 6059 207	8	12 wks
28 Oct 78	WHAT A NIGHT Vertigo 6059 211	39	5 wks
15 Sep 79	THE DAY THE EARTH CAUGHT FIRE Vertigo 6059 238	67	3 wks

CITY GENTS – See Dick CHARLESWORTH and his CITY GENTS

C.J. & CO. US, male vocal/instrumental group — 2 wks

30 Jul 77	DEVIL'S GUN Atlantic K 10956	43	2 wks

Gary CLAIL UK, male producer — 2 wks

14 Jul 90	BEEF RCA PB 49265	64	2 wks

CLAIRE and FRIENDS — 11 wks
UK, female vocalist and young male/female friends

7 Jun 86	IT'S 'ORRIBLE BEING IN LOVE (WHEN YOU'RE 8 1/2) BBC RESL 189	13	11 wks

CLANNAD Ireland, male/female vocal group — 28 wks

6 Nov 82 ●	THEME FROM HARRY'S GAME RCA 292	5	10 wks
2 Jul 83	NEW GRANGE RCA 340	65	1 wk
12 May 84	ROBIN (THE HOODED MAN) RCA HOOD 1	42	5 wks
25 Jan 86	IN A LIFETIME RCA PB 40535	20	5 wks
10 Jun 89	IN A LIFETIME (re-issue) RCA PB 42873	17	7 wks

In A Lifetime features Bono, Ireland, male vocalist.

Jimmy CLANTON US, male vocalist — 1 wk

21 Jul 60	ANOTHER SLEEPLESS NIGHT Top Rank JAR 382	50	1 wk

Eric CLAPTON UK, male vocalist/instrumentalist - guitar — 66 wks

27 Jul 74 ●	I SHOT THE SHERIFF RSO 2090 132	9	9 wks
10 May 75	SWING LOW SWEET CHARIOT RSO 2090 158	19	9 wks
16 Aug 75	KNOCKIN' ON HEAVEN'S DOOR RSO 2090 166	38	4 wks
24 Dec 77	LAY DOWN SALLY RSO 2090 264	39	6 wks
21 Oct 78	PROMISES RSO 21	37	7 wks
5 Jun 82	I SHOT THE SHERIFF (re-issue) RSO 88	64	2 wks

23 Apr 83		THE SHAPE YOU'RE IN *Duck W 9701*	75	1 wk
16 Mar 85		FOREVER MAN *Warner Bros. W 9069*	51	4 wks
4 Jan 86		EDGE OF DARKNESS *BBC RESL 178*	65	3 wks
17 Jan 87		BEHIND THE MASK *Duck W 8461*	15	11 wks
27 Jan 90		BAD LOVE *Duck W 2644*	25	7 wks
14 Apr 90		NO ALIBIS *Duck W 9981*	53	3 wks

Edge of Darkness features Michael Kamen. See also Derek and the Dominos; Delaney and Bonnie and Friends featuring Eric Clapton; Eric Clapton and Tina Turner.

Eric CLAPTON and Tina TURNER   UK/US, male/female vocal/instrumental duo   **3 wks**

| 20 Jun 87 | | TEARING US APART *Duck W 8299* .... | 56 | 3 wks |

See also Eric Clapton; Tina Turner.

Dee CLARK   US, male vocalist   **9 wks**

| 2 Oct 59 | | JUST KEEP IT UP *London HL 8915* .... | 26 | 1 wk |
| 11 Oct 75 | | RIDE A WILD HORSE *Chelsea 2005 037* .... | 16 | 8 wks |

Petula CLARK   UK, female vocalist   **247 wks**

11 Jun 54		THE LITTLE SHOEMAKER *Polygon P 1117*	12	1 wk
25 Jun 54	●	THE LITTLE SHOEMAKER (re-entry) *Polygon P 1117*	7	9 wks
18 Feb 55		MAJORCA *Polygon P 1146*	12	4 wks
25 Mar 55		MAJORCA (re-entry) *Polygon P 1146*	18	1 wk
25 Nov 55	●	SUDDENLY THERE'S A VALLEY *Pye Nixa N 15013*	7	10 wks
26 Jul 57	●	WITH ALL MY HEART *Pye Nixa N 15096*	4	18 wks
15 Nov 57	●	ALONE *Pye Nixa N 15112*	8	12 wks
28 Feb 58		BABY LOVER *Pye Nixa N 15126*	12	7 wks
26 Jan 61	★	SAILOR *Pye 7N 15324*	1	15 wks
13 Apr 61		SOMETHING MISSING *Pye 7N 15337*	44	1 wk
13 Jul 61	●	ROMEO *Pye 7N 15361*	3	15 wks
16 Nov 61	●	MY FRIEND THE SEA *Pye 7N 15389*	7	13 wks
8 Feb 62		I'M COUNTING ON YOU *Pye 7N 15407*	41	2 wks
28 Jun 62		YA YA TWIST *Pye 7N 15448*	14	11 wks
20 Sep 62		YA YA TWIST (re-entry) *Pye 7N 15448*	45	2 wks
2 May 63		CASANOVA / CHARIOT *Pye 7N 15522*	39	7 wks
12 Nov 64	●	DOWNTOWN *Pye 7N 15722*	2	15 wks
11 Mar 65		I KNOW A PLACE *Pye 7N 15772*	17	8 wks
12 Aug 65		YOU BETTER COME HOME *Pye 7N 15864*	44	3 wks
14 Oct 65		ROUND EVERY CORNER *Pye 7N 15945*	43	3 wks
4 Nov 65		YOU'RE THE ONE *Pye 7N 15991*	23	9 wks
10 Feb 66	●	MY LOVE *Pye 7N 17038*	4	9 wks
21 Apr 66		A SIGN OF THE TIMES *Pye 7N 17071*	49	1 wk
30 Jun 66	●	I COULDN'T LIVE WITHOUT YOUR LOVE *Pye 7N 17133*	6	11 wks
2 Feb 67	★	THIS IS MY SONG *Pye 7N 17258*	1	14 wks
25 May 67		DON'T SLEEP IN THE SUBWAY *Pye 7N 17325*	12	11 wks
13 Dec 67		THE OTHER MAN'S GRASS *Pye 7N 17416*	20	9 wks
6 Mar 68		KISS ME GOODBYE *Pye 7N 17466*	50	1 wk
30 Jan 71		THE SONG OF MY LIFE *Pye 7N 45026*	41	1 wk
13 Feb 71		THE SONG OF MY LIFE (re-entry) *Pye 7N 45026*	32	11 wks
15 Jan 72		I DON'T KNOW HOW TO LOVE HIM *Pye 7N 45112* ...	47	1 wk
29 Jan 72		I DON'T KNOW HOW TO LOVE HIM (re-entry) *Pye 7N 45112*	49	1 wk
19 Nov 88	●	DOWNTOWN '88 (re-mix) *PRT PYS 19*	10	11 wks

Dave CLARK FIVE   UK, male vocal/instrumental group   **171 wks**

3 Oct 63		DO YOU LOVE ME *Columbia DB 7112*	30	6 wks
21 Nov 63	★	GLAD ALL OVER *Columbia DB 7154*	1	19 wks
20 Feb 64	●	BITS AND PIECES *Columbia DB 7210*	2	11 wks
28 May 64	●	CAN'T YOU SEE THAT SHE'S MINE *Columbia DB 7291*	10	11 wks
13 Aug 64		THINKING OF YOU BABY *Columbia DB 7335*	26	4 wks
22 Oct 64		ANYWAY YOU WANT IT *Columbia DB 7377*	25	5 wks
14 Jan 65		EVERYBODY KNOWS *Columbia DB 7453*	37	4 wks
11 Mar 65		REELIN' AND ROCKIN' *Columbia DB 7503*	24	8 wks
27 May 65		COME HOME *Columbia DB 7580*	16	8 wks
15 Jul 65	●	CATCH US IF YOU CAN *Columbia DB 7625*	5	11 wks
11 Nov 65		OVER AND OVER *Columbia DB 7744*	45	4 wks

19 May 66		LOOK BEFORE YOU LEAP *Columbia DB 7909*	50	1 wk
16 Mar 67		YOU GOT WHAT IT TAKES *Columbia DB 8152*	28	8 wks
1 Nov 67	●	EVERYBODY KNOWS *Columbia DB 8286*	2	14 wks
28 Feb 68		NO ONE CAN BREAK A HEART LIKE YOU *Columbia DB 8342*	28	7 wks
18 Sep 68	●	RED BALLOON *Columbia DB 8465*	7	11 wks
27 Nov 68		LIVE IN THE SKY *Columbia DB 8505*	39	6 wks
25 Oct 69		PUT A LITTLE LOVE IN YOUR HEART *Columbia DB 8624*	31	4 wks
6 Dec 69	●	GOOD OLD ROCK 'N ROLL *Columbia DB 8638*	7	12 wks
7 Mar 70	●	EVERYBODY GET TOGETHER *Columbia DB 8660*	8	8 wks
4 Jul 70		HERE COMES SUMMER *Columbia DB 8689*	44	3 wks
7 Nov 70		MORE GOOD OLD ROCK 'N ROLL *Columbia DB 8724*	34	6 wks

Everybody Knows on DB 7453 and Everybody Knows on DB 8286 are two different songs. The two Rock 'N Roll titles are medleys as follows: Good Old Rock 'N Roll/Sweet Little Sixteen/Long Tall Sally/Whole Lotta Shakin' Goin' On/Blue Suede Shoes/Lucille/Reelin' And Rockin'/Memphis Tennessee. More Good Old Rock and Roll: Rock And Roll Music/Blueberry Hill/Good Golly Miss Molly/My Blue Heaven/Keep A Knockin'/Loving You/One Night/Lawdy Miss Clawdy.

John Cooper CLARKE   UK, male vocalist   **3 wks**

| 10 Mar 79 | | GIMMIX! PLAY LOUD *Epic EPC 7009* .... | 39 | 3 wks |

Rick CLARKE   UK, male vocalist   **2 wks**

| 30 Apr 88 | | I'LL SEE YOU ALONG THE WAY *WA WA 1* .... | 63 | 2 wks |

Sharon D. CLARKE – *See FPI PROJECT*

Julian CLARY – *See JOAN COLLINS FAN CLUB*

CLASH   UK, male vocal/instrumental group   **118 wks**

2 Apr 77		WHITE RIOT *CBS 5058*	38	3 wks
8 Oct 77		COMPLETE CONTROL *CBS 5664*	28	2 wks
4 Mar 78		CLASH CITY ROCKERS *CBS 5834*	35	4 wks
24 Jun 78		(WHITE MAN) IN HAMMERSMITH PALAIS *CBS 6383*	32	7 wks
2 Dec 78		TOMMY GUN *CBS 6788*	19	10 wks
3 Mar 79		ENGLISH CIVIL WAR (JOHNNY COMES MARCHING HOME) *CBS 7082*	25	6 wks
19 May 79		THE COST OF LIVING (EP) *CBS 7324*	22	8 wks
15 Dec 79		LONDON CALLING *CBS 8087*	11	10 wks
9 Aug 80		BANKROBBER *CBS 8323*	12	10 wks
6 Dec 80		THE CALL UP *CBS 9339*	40	6 wks
24 Jan 81		HITSVILLE UK *CBS 9480*	56	4 wks
25 Apr 81		THE MAGNIFICENT SEVEN *CBS 1133*	34	5 wks
28 Nov 81		THIS IS RADIO CLASH *CBS A 1797*	47	6 wks
1 May 82		KNOW YOUR RIGHTS *CBS A 2309*	43	3 wks
26 Jun 82		ROCK THE CASBAH *CBS A 2429*	30	10 wks
25 Sep 82		SHOULD I STAY OR SHOULD I GO/ STRAIGHT TO HELL *CBS A 2646*	17	9 wks
12 Oct 85		THIS IS ENGLAND *CBS A 6122*	24	5 wks
12 Mar 88		I FOUGHT THE LAW *CBS CLASH 1*	29	5 wks
7 May 88		LONDON CALLING (re-issue) *CBS CLASH 2*	46	3 wks
21 Jul 90		RETURN TO BRIXTON *CBS 656072 7*	57	2 wks

Tracks on The Cost Of Living EP: I Fought The Law/Groovy Times/Gates Of The West/Capital Radio. CBS CLASH 1 is a re-issue of a track from The Cost of Living EP.

CLASS ACTION featuring Chris WILTSHIRE   US, female vocal group   **3 wks**

| 7 May 83 | | WEEKEND *Jive JIVE 35* .... | 49 | 3 wks |

CLASSICS IV   US, male vocal/instrumental group   **1 wk**

| 28 Feb 68 | | SPOOKY *Liberty LBS 15051* .... | 46 | 1 wk |

CLASSIX NOUVEAUX
UK, male vocal/instrumental group **34 wks**

28 Feb 81	**GUILTY** *Liberty BP 388*............................	**43** 7 wks
16 May 81	**TOKYO** *Liberty BP 397*............................	**67** 3 wks
8 Aug 81	**INSIDE OUTSIDE** *Liberty BP 403*................	**45** 5 wks
7 Nov 81	**NEVER AGAIN (THE DAYS TIME ERASED)**	
	Liberty BP 406	**44** 4 wks
13 Mar 82	**IS IT A DREAM** *Liberty BP 409*	**11** 9 wks
29 May 82	**BECAUSE YOU'RE YOUNG** *Liberty BP 411*............	**43** 4 wks
30 Oct 82	**THE END ... OR THE BEGINNING** *Liberty BP 414*	**60** 2 wks

Judy CLAY and William BELL
US, female/male vocal duo **14 wks**

20 Nov 68	● **PRIVATE NUMBER** *Stax 101*....................	**8** 14 wks

See also William Bell.

Merry CLAYTON *US, female vocalist* **1 wk**

21 May 88	**YES** *RCA PB 49563*	**70** 1 wk

CLAYTOWN TROUPE
UK, male vocal/instrumental group **2 wks**

16 Jun 90	**WAYS OF LOVE** *Island IS 464*	**57** 2 wks

Johnny CLEGG and SAVUKA *UK/South*
Africa, male vocal/instrumental group **1 wk**

16 May 87	**SCATTERLINGS OF AFRICA** *EMI EMI 5605*	**75** 1 wk

Jimmy CLIFF *Jamaica, male vocalist* **28 wks**

25 Oct 69	● **WONDERFUL WORLD BEAUTIFUL PEOPLE**	
	Trojan TR 690	**6** 13 wks
14 Feb 70	**VIETNAM** *Trojan TR 7722*	**47** 1 wk
28 Feb 70	**VIETNAM (re-entry)** *Trojan TR 7722*	**46** 2 wks
8 Aug 70	● **WILD WORLD** *Island WIP 6087*	**8** 12 wks

Buzz CLIFFORD *US, male vocalist* **13 wks**

2 Mar 61	**BABY SITTIN' BOOGIE** *Fontana H 297*.....................	**17** 13 wks

Linda CLIFFORD *US, female vocalist* **12 wks**

10 Jun 78	**IF MY FRIENDS COULD SEE ME NOW**	
	Curtom K 17163..........................	**50** 5 wks
5 May 79	**BRIDGE OVER TROUBLED WATER** *RSO 30*.............	**28** 7 wks

CLIMAX BLUES BAND
UK, male vocal/instrumental group **9 wks**

9 Oct 76	● **COULDN'T GET IT RIGHT** *BTM SBT 105*	**10** 9 wks

CLIMIE FISHER *UK, male vocal/instrumental duo* **44 wks**

5 Sep 87	**LOVE CHANGES (EVERYTHING)** *EMI EM 15*............	**67** 2 wks
12 Dec 87	● **RISE TO THE OCCASION** *EMI EM 33*	**10** 11 wks
12 Mar 88	● **LOVE CHANGES (EVERYTHING) (re-mix)**	
	EMI EM 47................................	**2** 12 wks
21 May 88	**THIS IS ME** *EMI EM 58*	**22** 5 wks
20 Aug 88	**I WON'T BLEED FOR YOU** *EMI EM 66*	**35** 4 wks

24 Dec 88	**LOVE LIKE A RIVER** *EMI EM 81*........................	**22** 7 wks
23 Sep 89	**FACTS OF LOVE** *EMI EMI 103*	**50** 3 wks

Patsy CLINE *US, female vocalist* **10 wks**

26 Apr 62	**SHE'S GOT YOU** *Brunswick 05866*	**43** 1 wk
29 Nov 62	**HEARTACHES** *Brunswick 05878*	**31** 5 wks
8 Dec 90	**CRAZY** *MCA MCA 1465*........................	**26**† 4 wks

George CLINTON *US, male vocalist* **7 wks**

4 Dec 82	**LOOPZILLA** *Capitol CL 271*......................	**57** 5 wks
26 Apr 86	**DO FRIES GO WITH THAT SHAKE** *Capitol CL 402*	**57** 2 wks

Rosemary CLOONEY *US, female vocalist* **81 wks**

14 Nov 52	● **HALF AS MUCH** *Columbia DB 3129*	**3** 9 wks
5 Feb 54	● **MAN** *Philips PB 220*	**7** 5 wks
8 Oct 54	★ **THIS OLE HOUSE** *Philips PB 336*	**1** 18 wks
17 Dec 54	★ **MAMBO ITALIANO** *Philips PB 382*	**1** 16 wks
20 May 55	● **WHERE WILL THE BABY'S DIMPLE BE** *Philips PB 428*	**6** 13 wks
30 Sep 55	● **HEY THERE** *Philips PB 494*	**4** 11 wks
29 Mar 57	**MANGOS** *Philips PB 671*..........................	**25** 2 wks
26 Apr 57	**MANGOS (re-entry)** *Philips PB 671*	**17** 7 wks

From 19 Feb 54 other side of Man, Woman *by José Ferrer was also credited. See José Ferrer.*

CLOUD *UK, male instrumental group* **1 wk**

31 Jan 81	**ALL NIGHT LONG/ TAKE IT TO THE TOP**	
	UK Champagne FUNK 1..................................	**72** 1 wk

CLOUT *South Africa, female vocal/instrumental group* **15 wks**

17 Jun 78	● **SUBSTITUTE** *Carrere EMI 2788*....................	**2** 15 wks

CLUB NOUVEAU
US, male/female vocal/instrumental group **12 wks**

21 Mar 87	● **LEAN ON ME** *King Jay W 8430*	**3** 12 wks

CLUBHOUSE *Italy, male vocal/instrumental group* **12 wks**

23 Jul 83	**DO IT AGAIN - BILLIE JEAN (MEDLEY)**	
	Island IS 132	**11** 6 wks
3 Dec 83	**SUPERSTITION - GOOD TIMES (MEDLEY)**	
	Island IS 147	**59** 3 wks
1 Jul 89	**I'M A MAN - YE KE YE KE (MEDLEY)**	
	Music Man MMPS 7003....................	**69** 3 wks

Jeremy CLYDE – *See Chad STUART and Jeremy CLYDE*

CLYDE VALLEY STOMPERS
UK, male instrumental group **8 wks**

9 Aug 62	**PETER AND THE WOLF** *Parlophone R 4928*	**25** 8 wks

COAST TO COAST *UK, male vocal/instrumental group* **22 wks**

31 Jan 81	● **(DO) THE HUCKLEBUCK** *Polydor POSP 214*.................	**5** 15 wks
23 May 81	**LET'S JUMP THE BROOMSTICK** *Polydor POSP 249*........	**28** 7 wks

COASTERS US, male vocal group — 28 wks

27 Sep 57	SEARCHIN' London HLE 8450	30	1 wk
15 Aug 58	YAKETY YAK London HLE 8665	12	8 wks
27 Mar 59	● CHARLIE BROWN London HLE 8819	6	12 wks
30 Oct 59	POISON IVY London HLE 8938	15	7 wks

Odia COATES – See Paul ANKA

Luis COBOS featuring Placido DOMINGO — 2 wks
Spain, male instrumental/vocal duo

16 Jun 90	NESSUN DORMA FROM 'TURANDOT' Epic 656005 7	59	2 wks

See also Placido Domingo and John Denver.

Eddie COCHRAN US, male vocalist — 90 wks

7 Nov 58	SUMMERTIME BLUES London HLU 8702	18	6 wks
13 Mar 59	● C'MON EVERYBODY London HLU 8792	6	13 wks
16 Oct 59	SOMETHIN' ELSE London HLU 8944	22	3 wks
22 Jan 60	HALLELUJAH I LOVE HER SO London HLW 9022	28	1 wk
5 Feb 60	HALLELUJAH I LOVE HER SO (re-entry) London HLW 9022	22	3 wks
12 May 60	★ THREE STEPS TO HEAVEN London HLG 9115	1	15 wks
6 Oct 60	SWEETIE PIE London HLG 9196	38	3 wks
3 Nov 60	LONELY London HLG 9196	41	1 wk
15 Jun 61	WEEKEND London HLG 9362	15	16 wks
30 Nov 61	JEANNIE, JEANNIE, JEANNIE London HLG 9460	31	4 wks
25 Apr 63	MY WAY Liberty LIB 10088	23	10 wks
24 Apr 68	SUMMERTIME BLUES (re-issue) Liberty LBF 15071	34	8 wks
13 Feb 88	C'MON EVERYBODY (re-issue) Liberty EDDIE 501	14	7 wks

COCK ROBIN US, male/female vocal/instrumental group — 12 wks

31 May 86	THE PROMISE YOU MADE CBS A 6764	28	12 wks

Joe COCKER UK, male vocalist — 37 wks

22 May 68	MARJORINE Regal-Zonophone RZ 3006	48	1 wk
2 Oct 68	★ WITH A LITTLE HELP FROM MY FRIENDS Regal-Zonophone RZ 3013	1	13 wks
27 Sep 69	● DELTA LADY Regal-Zonophone RZ 3024	10	11 wks
4 Jul 70	THE LETTER Regal-Zonophone RZ 3027	39	6 wks
14 Nov 87	UNCHAIN MY HEART Capitol CL 465	46	4 wks
13 Jan 90	WHEN THE NIGHT COMES Capitol CL 535	65	2 wks

See also Joe Cocker and Jennifer Warnes; Crusaders.

Joe COCKER and Jennifer WARNES — 13 wks
UK/US, male/female vocal duo

15 Jan 83	● UP WHERE WE BELONG Island WIP 6831	7	13 wks

See also Joe Cocker; Jennifer Warnes.

COCKEREL CHORUS UK, male vocal group — 12 wks

24 Feb 73	NICE ONE CYRIL Youngblood YB 1017	14	12 wks

COCKNEY REBEL – See Steve HARLEY

COCKNEY REJECTS UK, male vocal/instrumental group — 22 wks

1 Dec 79	I'M NOT A FOOL EMI 5008	65	2 wks
16 Feb 80	BADMAN EMI 5035	65	3 wks
26 Apr 80	THE GREATEST COCKNEY RIPOFF EMI Z 2	21	7 wks
17 May 80	I'M FOREVER BLOWING BUBBLES EMI Z 4	35	5 wks
12 Jul 80	WE CAN DO ANYTHING EMI Z 6	65	2 wks
25 Oct 80	WE ARE THE FIRM EMI Z 10	54	3 wks

CO-CO UK, male/female vocal/instrumental group — 7 wks

22 Apr 78	BAD OLD DAYS Ariola Hansa AHA 513	13	7 wks

El COCO US, male vocal/instrumental group — 4 wks

14 Jan 78	COCOMOTION Pye International 7N 25761	31	4 wks

COCONUTS US, female vocal group — 3 wks

11 Jun 83	DID YOU HAVE TO LOVE ME LIKE YOU DID EMI America EA 156	60	3 wks

See also Kid Creole and the Coconuts.

COCTEAU TWINS — 15 wks
UK, male/female vocal/instrumental group

28 Apr 84	PEARLY-DEWDROPS' DROPS 4AD 405	29	5 wks
30 Mar 85	AIKEA-GUINEA 4AD AD 501	41	3 wks
23 Nov 85	TINY DYNAMINE (EP) 4AD BAD 510	52	2 wks
7 Dec 85	ECHOES IN A SHALLOW BAY (EP) 4AD BAD 511	65	1 wk
25 Oct 86	LOVE'S EASY TEARS 4AD AD 610	53	1 wk
8 Sep 90	ICEBLINK LUCK 4AD AD 0011	38	3 wks

Tracks on Tiny Dynamine EP: Pink Orange Red/Ribbed and Veined/Plain Tiger/Sultitan Itan.
Tracks on Echoes In A Shallow Bay EP: Great Spangled Fritillary/Melonella/Pale Clouded White/Eggs and Their Shells.

C.O.D. US, male vocal/instrumental group — 2 wks

14 May 83	IN THE BOTTLE Streetwave WAVE 2	54	2 wks

COFFEE US, female vocal group — 13 wks

27 Sep 80	CASANOVA De-Lite MER 38	13	10 wks
6 Dec 80	SLIP AND DIP/I WANNA BE WITH YOU De-Lite DE 1	57	3 wks

Alma COGAN UK, female vocalist — 110 wks

19 Mar 54	● BELL BOTTOM BLUES HMV B 10653	4	9 wks
27 Aug 54	LITTLE THINGS MEAN A LOT HMV B 10717	11	2 wks
8 Oct 54	LITTLE THINGS MEAN A LOT (re-entry) HMV B 10717	19	1 wk
22 Oct 54	LITTLE THINGS MEAN A LOT (2nd re-entry) HMV B 10717	18	2 wks
3 Dec 54	● I CAN'T TELL A WALTZ FROM A TANGO HMV B 10786	6	11 wks
27 May 55	★ DREAMBOAT HMV B 10872	1	16 wks
23 Sep 55	BANJO'S BACK IN TOWN HMV B 10917	17	1 wk
14 Oct 55	GO ON BY HMV B 10917	16	4 wks
16 Dec 55	TWENTY TINY FINGERS HMV POP 129	17	1 wk
23 Dec 55	● NEVER DO A TANGO WITH AN ESKIMO HMV POP 129	6	5 wks
30 Mar 56	WILLIE CAN HMV POP 187	13	8 wks
13 Jul 56	THE BIRDS AND THE BEES HMV POP 223	25	4 wks
10 Aug 56	WHY DO FOOLS FALL IN LOVE HMV POP 223	22	3 wks
2 Nov 56	IN THE MIDDLE OF THE HOUSE HMV POP 261	26	1 wk
23 Nov 56	IN THE MIDDLE OF THE HOUSE (re-entry) HMV POP 261	20	3 wks
18 Jan 57	YOU ME AND US HMV POP 284	18	6 wks
29 Mar 57	WHATEVER LOLA WANTS HMV POP 317	26	2 wks
31 Jan 58	THE STORY OF MY LIFE HMV POP 433	25	2 wks
14 Feb 58	SUGARTIME HMV POP 450	16	10 wks
2 May 58	SUGARTIME (re-entry) HMV POP 450	30	1 wk

23 Jan 59		LAST NIGHT ON THE BACK PORCH		
		HMV POP 573	27	2 wks
18 Dec 59		WE GOT LOVE HMV POP 670	26	4 wks
12 May 60		DREAM TALK HMV POP 728	48	1 wk
11 Aug 60		TRAIN OF LOVE HMV POP 760	27	5 wks
20 Apr 61		COWBOY JIMMY JOE Columbia DB 4607	37	6 wks

Shaye COGAN US, female vocalist   1 wk

24 Mar 60		MEAN TO ME MGM 1063	43	1 wk

Izhar COHEN and ALPHABETA   7 wks
Israel, male/female vocal group

13 May 78		A BA NI BI Polydor 2001 781	20	7 wks

COLD JAM featuring GRACE   2 wks
US, male/female vocal/instrumental group

28 Jul 90		LAST NIGHT A DJ SAVED MY LIFE		
		Big Wave BWR 39	64	2 wks

COLDCUT UK, male production duo   32 wks

20 Feb 88	●	DOCTORIN' THE HOUSE Ahead Of Our Time CCUT 27	6	9 wks
10 Sep 88		STOP THIS CRAZY THING		
		Ahead Of Our Time CCUT 4	21	7 wks
25 Mar 89		PEOPLE HOLD ON Ahead Of Our Time CCUT 5	11	9 wks
3 Jun 89		MY TELEPHONE Ahead Of Our Time CCUT 6	52	2 wks
16 Dec 89		COLDCUT'S CHRISTMAS BREAK		
		Ahead Of Our Time CCUT 7	67	3 wks
26 May 90		FIND A WAY Ahead Of Our Time CCUT 8	52	2 wks

Doctorin' The House *features Yazz and the Plastic Population;* Stop This Crazy Thing *features Junior Reid - UK, male rapper;* People Hold On *features Lisa Stansfield;* Find A Way *features Queen Latifah. See also Yazz; Lisa Stansfield; Queen Latifah + De La Soul.*

Cozy COLE US, male instrumentalist - drums   1 wk

5 Dec 58		TOPSY (PARTS 1 AND 2) London HL 8750	29	1 wk

Lloyd COLE UK, male vocalist   54 wks

26 May 84		PERFECT SKIN Polydor COLE 1	71	1 wk
9 Jun 84		PERFECT SKIN (re-entry) Polydor COLE 1	26	8 wks
25 Aug 84		FOREST FIRE Polydor COLE 2	41	6 wks
17 Nov 84		RATTLESNAKES Poldor COLE 3	65	2 wks
14 Sep 85		BRAND NEW FRIEND Polydor COLE 4	19	8 wks
9 Nov 85		LOST WEEKEND Polydor COLE 5	17	7 wks
18 Jan 86		CUT ME DOWN Polydor COLE 6	38	4 wks
3 Oct 87		MY BAG Polydor COLE 7	46	4 wks
9 Jan 88		JENNIFER SHE SAID Polydor COLE 8	31	5 wks
23 Apr 88		FROM THE HIP (EP) Polydor COLE 9	59	2 wks
3 Feb 90		NO BLUE SKIES Polydor COLE 11	42	4 wks
7 Apr 90		DON'T LOOK BACK Polydor COLE 12	59	3 wks

Tracks on From The Hip EP: *From The Hip/Please/Lonely Mile/Love Your Wife. First nine singles credit the Commotions - UK, male instrumental group.*

Nat 'King' COLE US, male vocalist   233 wks

14 Nov 52	●	SOMEWHERE ALONG THE WAY Capitol CL 13774	3	7 wks
19 Dec 52	●	BECAUSE YOU'RE MINE Capitol CL 13811	6	2 wks
2 Jan 53		FAITH CAN MOVE MOUNTAINS Capitol CL 13811	11	1 wk
16 Jan 53		FAITH CAN MOVE MOUNTAINS (re-entry)		
		Capitol CL 13811	12	2 wks
23 Jan 53	●	BECAUSE YOU'RE MINE (re-entry) Capitol CL 13811	10	1 wk
6 Feb 53	●	FAITH CAN MOVE MOUNTAINS (2nd re-entry)		
		Capitol CL 13811	10	1 wk

13 Feb 53		BECAUSE YOU'RE MINE (2nd re-entry)		
		Capitol CL 13811	11	1 wk
24 Apr 53	●	PRETEND Capitol CL 13878	2	18 wks
14 Aug 53	●	CAN'T I? Capitol CL 13937	9	3 wks
18 Sep 53	●	CAN'T I? (re-entry) Capitol CL 13937	6	4 wks
18 Sep 53	●	MOTHER NATURE AND FATHER TIME		
		Capitol CL 13912	7	7 wks
30 Oct 53	●	CAN'T I? (2nd re-entry) Capitol CL 13937	10	1 wk
16 Apr 54	●	TENDERLY Capitol CL 14061	10	1 wk
10 Sep 54	●	SMILE Capitol CL 14149	2	14 wks
8 Oct 54		MAKE HER MINE Capitol CL 14149	11	2 wks
25 Feb 55	●	A BLOSSOM FELL Capitol CL 14235	3	10 wks
26 Aug 55		MY ONE SIN Capitol CL 14327	18	1 wk
16 Sep 55		MY ONE SIN (re-entry) Capitol CL 14327	17	1 wk
27 Jan 56	●	DREAMS CAN TELL A LIE Capitol CL 14513	10	9 wks
11 May 56	●	TOO YOUNG TO GO STEADY Capitol CL 14573	8	14 wks
14 Sep 56		LOVE ME AS IF THERE WERE NO TOMORROW		
		Capitol CL 14621	24	2 wks
5 Oct 56		LOVE ME AS IF THERE WERE NO		
		TOMORROW (re-entry) Capitol CL 14621	11	13 wks
19 Apr 57	●	WHEN I FALL IN LOVE Capitol CL 14709	2	20 wks
5 Jul 57		WHEN ROCK 'N ROLL CAME TO TRINIDAD		
		Capitol CL 14733	28	1 wk
18 Oct 57		MY PERSONAL POSSESSION Capitol CL 14765	21	2 wks
25 Oct 57		STARDUST Capitol CL 14787	24	2 wks
29 May 59		YOU MADE ME LOVE YOU Capitol CL 15017	22	3 wks
4 Sep 59		MIDNIGHT FLYER Capitol CL 15056	27	1 wk
18 Sep 59		MIDNIGHT FLYER (re-entry) Capitol CL 15056	23	3 wks
12 Feb 60		TIME AND THE RIVER Capitol CL 15111	29	2 wks
26 Feb 60		TIME AND THE RIVER (re-entry) Capitol CL 15111	23	2 wks
31 Mar 60		TIME AND THE RIVER (2nd re-entry)		
		Capitol CL 15111	47	1 wk
26 May 60	●	THAT'S YOU Capitol CL 15129	10	8 wks
10 Nov 60		JUST AS MUCH AS EVER Capitol CL 15163	18	10 wks
2 Feb 61		THE WORLD IN MY ARMS Capitol CL 15178	36	10 wks
16 Nov 61		LET TRUE LOVE BEGIN Capitol CL 15224	29	10 wks
22 Mar 62		BRAZILIAN LOVE SONG Capitol CL 15241	34	4 wks
31 May 62		THE RIGHT THING TO SAY Capitol CL 15250	42	4 wks
19 Jul 62		LET THERE BE LOVE Capitol CL 15257	11	14 wks
27 Sep 62	●	RAMBLIN' ROSE Capitol CL 15270	5	14 wks
20 Dec 62		DEAR LONELY HEARTS Capitol CL 15280	37	3 wks
12 Dec 87	●	WHEN I FALL IN LOVE (re-issue) Capitol CL 15975	4	7 wks

Let There Be Love *is with George Shearing. See also George Shearing.*

Natalie COLE US, female vocalist   78 wks

11 Oct 75		THIS WILL BE Capitol CL 15834	32	5 wks
8 Aug 87		JUMP START Manhattan MT 22	44	8 wks
26 Mar 88	●	PINK CADILLAC Manhattan MT 35	5	12 wks
25 Jun 88		EVERLASTING Manhattan MT 46	28	6 wks
20 Aug 88		JUMP START (re-issue) Manhattan MT 50	36	4 wks
26 Nov 88		I LIVE FOR YOUR LOVE Manhattan MT 57	23	14 wks
15 Apr 89	●	MISS YOU LIKE CRAZY EMI-USA MT 63	2	15 wks
22 Jul 89		BEST OF THE NIGHT EMI-USA MT 69	56	2 wks
16 Dec 89		STARTING OVER AGAIN EMI-USA MT 77	56	4 wks
21 Apr 90		WILD WOMEN DO EMI-USA MT 81	16	7 wks

John Ford COLEY – *See ENGLAND DAN and John Ford COLEY*

COLLAGE   5 wks
US/Canada/Philippines, male vocal/instrumental group

21 Sep 85		ROMEO WHERE'S JULIET? MCA MCA 1006	46	5 wks

Dave and Ansil COLLINS   27 wks
Jamaica, male vocal/instrumental duo

27 Mar 71	★	DOUBLE BARREL Technique TE 901	1	15 wks
26 Jun 71	●	MONKEY SPANNER Technique TE 914	7	12 wks

Edwyn COLLINS – *See Paul QUINN and Edwyn COLLINS*

Jeff COLLINS UK, male vocalist — 8 wks

18 Nov 72	**ONLY YOU** *Polydor 2058 287*	**40**	8 wks

Judy COLLINS US, female vocalist — 86 wks

17 Jan 70	**BOTH SIDES NOW** *Elektra EKSN 45043*	**14**	11 wks
5 Dec 70 ●	**AMAZING GRACE** *Elektra 2101 020*	**5**	32 wks
24 Jul 71	**AMAZING GRACE (re-entry)** *Elektra 2101 020*	**48**	1 wk
4 Sep 71	**AMAZING GRACE (2nd re-entry)** *Elektra 2101 020*	**40**	7 wks
20 Nov 71	**AMAZING GRACE (3rd re-entry)** *Elektra 2101 020*..........	**50**	1 wk
18 Dec 71	**AMAZING GRACE (4th re-entry)** *Elektra 2101 020*	**48**	2 wks
22 Apr 72	**AMAZING GRACE (5th re-entry)** *Elektra 2101 020*	**20**	19 wks
9 Sep 72	**AMAZING GRACE (6th re-entry)** *Elektra 2101 020*	**46**	2 wks
23 Dec 72	**AMAZING GRACE (7th re-entry)** *Elektra 2101 020*	**49**	3 wks
17 May 75 ●	**SEND IN THE CLOWNS** *Elektra K 12177*....................	**6**	8 wks

Phil COLLINS UK, male vocalist — 162 wks

17 Jan 81 ●	**IN THE AIR TONIGHT** *Virgin VSK 102*	**2**	10 wks
7 Mar 81	**I MISSED AGAIN** *Virgin VS 402*	**14**	8 wks
30 May 81	**IF LEAVING ME IS EASY** *Virgin VS 423*	**17**	8 wks
23 Oct 82	**THRU' THESE WALLS** *Virgin VS 524*	**56**	2 wks
4 Dec 82 ★	**YOU CAN'T HURRY LOVE** *Virgin VS 531*	**1**	16 wks
19 Mar 83	**DON'T LET HIM STEAL YOUR HEART AWAY** *Virgin VS 572*....................	**45**	5 wks
7 Apr 84 ●	**AGAINST ALL ODDS (TAKE A LOOK AT ME NOW)** *Virgin VS 674*....................	**2**	14 wks
26 Jan 85	**SUSSUDIO** *Virgin VS 736*........................	**12**	9 wks
13 Apr 85 ●	**ONE MORE NIGHT** *Virgin VS 755*..................	**4**	9 wks
27 Jul 85	**TAKE ME HOME** *Virgin VS 777*	**19**	9 wks
18 Jun 88 ●	**IN THE AIR TONIGHT (re-mix)** *Virgin VS 102*..........	**4**	9 wks
3 Sep 88 ★	**A GROOVY KIND OF LOVE** *Virgin VS 1117*	**1**	13 wks
26 Nov 88 ●	**TWO HEARTS** *Virgin VS 1141*	**6**	11 wks
4 Nov 89 ●	**ANOTHER DAY IN PARADISE** *Virgin VS 1234*..........	**2**	11 wks
27 Jan 90 ●	**I WISH IT WOULD RAIN DOWN** *Virgin VS 1240*	**7**	9 wks
28 Apr 90	**SOMETHING HAPPENED ON THE WAY TO HEAVEN** *Virgin VS 1251*.................	**15**	7 wks
28 Jul 90	**THAT'S JUST THE WAY IT IS** *Virgin VS 1277*...............	**26**	5 wks
6 Oct 90	**HANG IN LONG ENOUGH** *Virgin VS 1300*..................	**34**	3 wks
8 Dec 90	**DO YOU REMEMBER (LIVE)** *Virgin VS 1305*............	**57†**	4 wks

Don't Let Him Steal Your Heart Away *has credit: With the Martyn Ford Orchestra. See also Phil Collins and Marilyn Martin; Martyn Ford; Philip Bailey.*

Phil COLLINS and Marilyn MARTIN — 13 wks
UK/US, male/female vocal duo

23 Nov 85 ●	**SEPARATE LIVES** *Virgin VS 818*.................	**4**	13 wks

See also Phil Collins.

Rodger COLLINS US, male vocalist — 6 wks

3 Apr 76	**YOU SEXY SUGAR PLUM (BUT I LIKE IT)** *Fantasy FTC 132*.................	**22**	6 wks

Willie COLLINS US, male vocalist — 4 wks

28 Jun 86	**WHERE YOU GONNA BE TONIGHT?** *Capitol CL 410*.....	**46**	4 wks

Willie COLON US, male vocalist — 7 wks

28 Jun 86	**SET FIRE TO ME** *A & M AM 330*..................	**41**	7 wks

COLORADO UK, female vocal group — 3 wks

21 Oct 78	**CALIFORNIA DREAMIN'** *Pinnacle PIN 67*	**45**	3 wks

COLOUR FIELD UK, male vocal/instrumental group — 18 wks

21 Jan 84	**THE COLOUR FIELD** *Chrysalis COLF 1*.............	**43**	4 wks
28 Jul 84	**TAKE** *Chrysalis COLF 2*........................	**70**	1 wk
26 Jan 85	**THINKING OF YOU** *Chrysalis COLF 3*	**12**	10 wks
13 Apr 85	**CASTLES IN THE AIR** *Chrysalis COLF 4*	**51**	3 wks

COMETS – *See Bill HALEY and his COMETS*

COMMENTATORS — 7 wks
UK, male impressionist - Rory Bremner

22 Jun 85	**N-N-NINETEEN NOT OUT** *Oval 100*.....................	**13**	7 wks

COMMODORES US/UK, male vocal/instrumental group — 121 wks

24 Aug 74	**MACHINE GUN** *Tamla Motown TMG 902*	**20**	11 wks
23 Nov 74	**THE ZOO (THE HUMAN ZOO)** *Tamla Motown TMG 924.*	**44**	2 wks
2 Jul 77 ●	**EASY** *Motown TMG 1073*	**9**	10 wks
8 Oct 77	**BRICK HOUSE/ SWEET LOVE** *Motown TMG 1086*	**32**	6 wks
11 Mar 78	**TOO HOT TO TROT/ ZOOM** *Motown TMG 1096*..........	**38**	4 wks
24 Jun 78	**FLYING HIGH** *Motown TMG 1111*...................	**37**	7 wks
5 Aug 78 ★	**THREE TIMES A LADY** *Motown TMG 1113*	**1**	14 wks
25 Nov 78	**JUST TO BE CLOSE TO YOU** *Motown TMG 1127*..........	**62**	4 wks
25 Aug 79 ●	**SAIL ON** *Motown TMG 1155*	**8**	10 wks
3 Nov 79 ●	**STILL** *Motown TMG 1166*	**4**	11 wks
19 Jan 80	**WONDERLAND** *Motown TMG 1172*..................	**40**	4 wks
1 Aug 81	**LADY (YOU BRING ME UP)** *Motown TMG 1238*	**56**	5 wks
21 Nov 81	**OH NO** *Motown TMG 1245*	**44**	3 wks
26 Jan 85 ●	**NIGHTSHIFT** *Motown TMG 1371*	**3**	14 wks
11 May 85	**ANIMAL INSTINCT** *Motown ZB 40097*	**74**	1 wk
25 Oct 86	**GOIN' TO THE BANK** *Polydor POSPA 826*	**43**	4 wks
13 Aug 88	**EASY (re-issue)** *Motown ZB 41793*....................	**15**	11 wks

Group were US for first thirteen hits and the re-issue of Easy.

COMMOTIONS – *See Lloyd COLE*

COMMUNARDS UK, male vocal/instrumental duo — 76 wks

12 Oct 85	**YOU ARE MY WORLD** *London LON 77*	**30**	8 wks
24 May 86	**DISENCHANTED** *London LON 89*....................	**29**	5 wks
23 Aug 86 ★	**DON'T LEAVE ME THIS WAY** *London LON 103*	**1**	14 wks
29 Nov 86 ●	**SO COLD THE NIGHT** *London LON 110*	**8**	10 wks
21 Feb 87	**YOU ARE MY WORLD ('87) (re-mix)** *London LON 123*	**21**	6 wks
12 Sep 87	**TOMORROW** *London LON 143*....................	**23**	7 wks
7 Nov 87 ●	**NEVER CAN SAY GOODBYE** *London LON 158*	**4**	11 wks
20 Feb 88	**FOR A FRIEND** *London LON 166*	**28**	7 wks
11 Jun 88	**THERE'S MORE TO LOVE** *London LON 173*	**20**	8 wks

On Don't Leave Me This Way *billed as Communards with Sarah Jane Morris, UK, female vocalist.*

Perry COMO US, male vocalist — 294 wks

16 Jan 53 ★	**DON'T LET THE STARS GET IN YOUR EYES** *HMV B 10400*	**1**	15 wks
4 Jun 54 ●	**WANTED** *HMV B 10667*	**4**	14 wks
25 Jun 54 ●	**IDLE GOSSIP** *HMV B 10710*	**3**	15 wks
1 Oct 54	**WANTED (re-entry)** *HMV B 10667*................	**18**	1 wk
10 Dec 54	**PAPA LOVES MAMBO** *HMV B 10776*	**16**	1 wk
30 Dec 55	**TINA MARIE** *HMV POP 103*	**24**	1 wk
27 Apr 56	**JUKE BOX BABY** *HMV POP 191*	**22**	6 wks
25 May 56 ●	**HOT DIGGITY** *HMV POP 212*	**4**	13 wks
21 Sep 56 ●	**MORE** *HMV POP 240.*	**10**	11 wks
28 Sep 56	**GLENDORA** *HMV POP 240.*	**18**	6 wks
14 Dec 56	**MORE (re-entry)** *HMV POP 240.*	**29**	1 wk
7 Feb 58 ★	**MAGIC MOMENTS** *RCA 1036*	**1**	17 wks
7 Mar 58 ●	**CATCH A FALLING STAR** *RCA 1036*	**9**	10 wks
9 May 58 ●	**KEWPIE DOLL** *RCA 1055*	**9**	7 wks
30 May 58	**I MAY NEVER PASS THIS WAY AGAIN** *RCA 1062*	**15**	8 wks
5 Sep 58	**MOON TALK** *RCA 1071*	**17**	11 wks

7 Nov 58 ●	**LOVE MAKES THE WORLD GO ROUND** *RCA 1086*	**6**	14 wks
21 Nov 58	**MANDOLINS IN THE MOONLIGHT** *RCA 1086*	**13**	12 wks
27 Feb 59 ●	**TOMBOY** *RCA 1111*	**10**	12 wks
10 Jul 59	**I KNOW** *RCA 1126*	**13**	16 wks
26 Feb 60 ●	**DELAWARE** *RCA 1170*	**3**	13 wks
10 May 62	**CATERINA** *RCA 1283*	**37**	4 wks
14 Jun 62	**CATERINA (re-entry)** *RCA 1283*	**45**	2 wks
30 Jan 71 ●	**IT'S IMPOSSIBLE** *RCA 2043*	**4**	23 wks
15 May 71	**I THINK OF YOU** *RCA 2075*	**14**	11 wks
21 Apr 73 ●	**AND I LOVE YOU SO** *RCA 2346*	**3**	31 wks
25 Aug 73 ●	**FOR THE GOOD TIMES** *RCA 2402*	**7**	27 wks
8 Dec 73	**WALK RIGHT BACK** *RCA 2432*	**33**	10 wks
12 Jan 74	**AND I LOVE YOU SO (re-entry)** *RCA 2346*	**40**	4 wks
25 May 74	**I WANT TO GIVE** *RCA LPBO 7518*	**31**	6 wks

COMPAGNONS DE LA CHANSON — 3 wks

France, male vocal group

9 Oct 59	**THE THREE BELLS** *Columbia DB 4358*	**27**	1 wk
23 Oct 59	**THE THREE BELLS (re-entry)** *Columbia DB 4358*	**21**	2 wks

Song is sub-titled The Jimmy Brown Song.

COMSAT ANGELS UK, male vocal/instrumental group — 2 wks

21 Jan 84	**INDEPENDENCE DAY** *Jive JIVE 54*	**75**	1 wk
4 Feb 84	**INDEPENDENCE DAY (re-entry)** *Jive JIVE 54*	**71**	1 wk

CON FUNK SHUN US, male vocal/instrumental group — 2 wks

19 Jul 86	**BURNIN' LOVE** *Club JAB 32*	**68**	2 wks

CONCEPT US, male vocalist/instrumentalist - keyboards — 6 wks

14 Dec 85	**MR. DJ** *Fourth & Broadway BRW 40*	**27**	6 wks

CONFEDERATES – *See Elvis COSTELLO*

CONGREGATION UK, male/female choir — 14 wks

27 Nov 71 ●	**SOFTLY WHISPERING I LOVE YOU** *Columbia DB 8830*	**4**	14 wks

Arthur CONLEY US, male vocalist — 15 wks

27 Apr 67 ●	**SWEET SOUL MUSIC** *Atlantic 584 083*	**7**	14 wks
10 Apr 68	**FUNKY STREET** *Atlantic 583 175*	**46**	1 wk

Billy CONNOLLY UK, male vocalist — 31 wks

1 Nov 75 ★	**D.I.V.O.R.C.E.** *Polydor 2058 652*	**1**	10 wks
17 Jul 76	**NO CHANCE (NO CHARGE)** *Polydor 2058 748*	**24**	5 wks
25 Aug 79	**IN THE BROWNIES** *Polydor 2059 160*	**38**	7 wks
9 Mar 85	**SUPER GRAN** *Stiff BUY 218*	**32**	9 wks

Jess CONRAD UK, male vocalist — 13 wks

30 Jun 60	**CHERRY PIE** *Decca F 11236*	**39**	1 wk
26 Jan 61	**MYSTERY GIRL** *Decca F 11315*	**44**	1 wk
9 Feb 61	**MYSTERY GIRL (re-entry)** *Decca F 11315*	**18**	9 wks
11 Oct 62	**PRETTY JENNY** *Decca F 11511*	**50**	2 wks

CONSORTIUM UK, male vocal group — 9 wks

12 Feb 69	**ALL THE LOVE IN THE WORLD** *Pye 7N 17635*	**22**	9 wks

CONTOURS US, male vocal group — 6 wks

24 Jan 70	**JUST A LITTLE MISUNDERSTANDING** *Tamla Motown TMG 723*	**31**	6 wks

CONWAY BROTHERS US, male vocal group — 10 wks

22 Jun 85	**TURN IT UP** *10 TEN 57*	**11**	10 wks

Russ CONWAY UK, male instrumentalist - piano — 168 wks

29 Nov 57	**PARTY POPS** *Columbia DB 4031*	**24**	5 wks
29 Aug 58	**GOT A MATCH** *Columbia DB 4166*	**30**	1 wk
28 Nov 58 ●	**MORE PARTY POPS** *Columbia DB 4204*	**10**	7 wks
23 Jan 59	**THE WORLD OUTSIDE** *Columbia DB 4234*	**24**	1 wk
20 Feb 59 ★	**SIDE SADDLE** *Columbia DB 4256*	**1**	30 wks
6 Mar 59	**THE WORLD OUTSIDE (re-entry)** *Columbia DB 4234*	**24**	3 wks
15 May 59 ★	**ROULETTE** *Columbia DB 4298*	**1**	19 wks
21 Aug 59 ●	**CHINA TEA** *Columbia DB 4337*	**5**	13 wks
13 Nov 59 ●	**SNOW COACH** *Columbia DB 4368*	**7**	9 wks
20 Nov 59 ●	**MORE AND MORE PARTY POPS** *Columbia DB 4373*	**5**	8 wks
10 Mar 60	**ROYAL EVENT** *Columbia DB 4418*	**15**	7 wks
21 Apr 60	**FINGS AIN'T WOT THEY USED T'BE** *Columbia DB 4422*	**47**	1 wk
19 May 60	**LUCKY FIVE** *Columbia DB 4457*	**14**	9 wks
29 Sep 60	**PASSING BREEZE** *Columbia DB 4508*	**16**	10 wks
24 Nov 60	**EVEN MORE PARTY POPS** *Columbia DB 4535*	**27**	9 wks
19 Jan 61	**PEPE** *Columbia DB 4564*	**19**	9 wks
25 May 61	**PABLO** *Columbia DB 4649*	**45**	2 wks
30 Nov 61 ●	**TOY BALLOONS** *Columbia DB 4738*	**7**	11 wks
22 Feb 62	**LESSON ONE** *Columbia DB 4784*	**21**	7 wks
29 Nov 62	**ALWAYS YOU AND ME** *Columbia DB 4934*	**33**	4 wks
3 Jan 63	**ALWAYS YOU AND ME (re-entry)** *Columbia DB 4934*	**35**	3 wks

Always You And Me featured Russ Conway talking as well as playing piano. Several of the discs were medleys as follows: Party Pops: When You're Smiling/I'm Looking Over a Four-Leafed Clover/When You Wore a Tulip/Row Row Row/For Me And My Girl/Shine On Harvest Moon/By The Light Of The Silvery Moon/Side By Side. More Party Pops: Music Music Music/If You Were The Only Girl In The World/Nobody's Sweetheart/Yes Sir That's My Baby/Some Of These Days/Honeysuckle And The Bee/Hello Hello Who's Your Lady Friend/Shanty In Old Shanty Town. More And More Party Pops: Sheik of Araby/Who Were You With Last Night/Any Old Iron/Tiptoe Through The Tulips/If You Were The Only Girl In The World/When I Leave The World Behind. Even More Party Pops: Ain't She Sweet/I Can't Give You Anything But Love/Yes We Have No Bananas/I May Be Wrong/Happy Days And Lonely Nights/Glad Rag Doll. He really did feature If You Were The Only Girl In The World on two different hits. See also Dorothy Squires and Russ Conway.

Martin COOK – *See Richard DENTON and Martin COOK*

Norman COOK UK, male producer/multi-instrumentalist — 10 wks

8 Jul 89	**WON'T TALK ABOUT IT/ BLAME IT ON THE BASSLINE** *Go Beat GOD 33*	**29**	6 wks
21 Oct 89	**FOR SPACIOUS LIES** *Go Beat GOD 37*	**48**	4 wks

Won't Talk About It features Billy Bragg. Blame It On The Bassline features MC Wildski and For Spacious Lies features Lester - UK, male vocalist. See also Billy Bragg; MC Wildski.

Peter COOK UK, male vocalist — 5 wks

15 Jul 65	**THE BALLAD OF SPOTTY MULDOON** *Decca F 12182*	**34**	5 wks

See also Peter Cook and Dudley Moore.

Peter COOK and Dudley MOORE — 10 wks
UK, male vocal duo, Dudley Moore featured pianist

17 Jun 65	**GOODBYE-EE** *Decca F 12158*	**18**	10 wks

See also Peter Cook.

Brandon COOKE featuring Roxanne SHANTE US, male/female rap/scratch duo — 3 wks

29 Oct 88	**SHARP AS A KNIFE** Club JAB 73	45	3 wks

See also Roxanne Shante.

Sam COOKE US, male vocalist — 82 wks

17 Jan 58	**YOU SEND ME** London HLU 8506	29	1 wk
14 Aug 59	**ONLY SIXTEEN** HMV POP 642	23	4 wks
7 Jul 60	**WONDERFUL WORLD** HMV POP 754	27	8 wks
29 Sep 60 ●	**CHAIN GANG** RCA 1202	9	11 wks
27 Jul 61 ●	**CUPID** RCA 1242	7	14 wks
8 Mar 62 ●	**TWISTIN' THE NIGHT AWAY** RCA 1277	6	14 wks
16 May 63	**ANOTHER SATURDAY NIGHT** RCA 1341	23	12 wks
5 Sep 63	**FRANKIE AND JOHNNY** RCA 1361	30	6 wks
22 Mar 86 ●	**WONDERFUL WORLD (re-issue)** RCA PB 49871	2	11 wks
10 May 86	**ANOTHER SATURDAY NIGHT (re-issue)** RCA PB 49849	75	1 wk

COOKIE CREW UK, female vocal group — 17 wks

7 Jan 89	**BORN THIS WAY** FFRR FFR 19	23	5 wks
1 Apr 89	**GOT TO KEEP ON** FFRR FFR 25	17	9 wks
15 Jul 89	**COME AND GET SOME** FFRR F 110	42	3 wks

See also Beatmasters.

COOKIES US, female vocal group — 1 wk

10 Jan 63	**CHAINS** London HLU 9634	50	1 wk

COOL DOWN ZONE UK, male/female vocal/instrumental group — 4 wks

30 Jun 90	**HEAVEN KNOWS** 10 TEN 309	52	4 wks

Rita COOLIDGE US, female vocalist — 24 wks

25 Jun 77 ●	**WE'RE ALL ALONE** A & M AMS 7295	6	13 wks
15 Oct 77	**(YOUR LOVE HAS LIFTED ME) HIGHER AND HIGHER** A & M AMS 7315	49	1 wk
29 Oct 77	**(YOUR LOVE HAS LIFTED ME) HIGHER AND HIGHER (re-entry)** A & M AMS 7315	48	1 wk
4 Feb 78	**WORDS** A & M AMS 7330	25	8 wks
25 Jun 83	**ALL TIME HIGH** A & M AM 007	75	1 wk

COOLNOTES UK, male/female vocal/instrumental group — 28 wks

18 Aug 84	**YOU'RE NEVER TOO YOUNG** Abstract Dance AD 1	42	5 wks
17 Nov 84	**I FORGOT** Abstract Dance AD 2	63	2 wks
23 Mar 85	**SPEND THE NIGHT** Abstract Dance AD 3	11	9 wks
13 Jul 85	**IN YOUR CAR** Abstract Dance AD 4	13	9 wks
19 Oct 85	**HAVE A GOOD FOREVER** Abstract Dance AD 5	73	1 wk
17 May 86	**INTO THE MOTION** Abstract Dance AD 8	66	2 wks

Alice COOPER US, male vocalist — 87 wks

15 Jul 72 ★	**SCHOOL'S OUT** Warner Bros. K 16188	1	12 wks
7 Oct 72 ●	**ELECTED** Warner Bros. K 16214	4	10 wks
10 Feb 73 ●	**HELLO HURRAY** Warner Bros. K 16248	6	12 wks
21 Apr 73 ●	**NO MORE MR. NICE GUY** Warner Bros. K 16262	10	10 wks
19 Jan 74	**TEENAGE LAMENT '74** Warner Bros. K 16345	12	7 wks
21 May 77	**(NO MORE) LOVE AT YOUR CONVENIENCE** Warner Bros. K 16935	44	2 wks
23 Dec 78	**HOW YOU GONNA SEE ME NOW** Warner Bros. K 17270	61	6 wks
6 Mar 82	**SEVEN AND SEVEN IS** (LIVE VERSION) Warner Bros. K 17924	62	3 wks
8 May 82	**FOR BRITAIN ONLY/ UNDER MY WHEELS** Warner Bros. K 17940	66	2 wks
18 Oct 86	**HE'S BACK (THE MAN BEHIND THE MASK)** MCA MCA 1090	61	2 wks
9 Apr 88	**FREEDOM** MCA MCA 1241	50	3 wks
29 Jul 89 ●	**POISON** Epic 655061 7	2	11 wks
7 Oct 89	**BED OF NAILS** Epic ALICE 3	38	5 wks
2 Dec 89	**HOUSE OF FIRE** Epic ALICE 4	65	2 wks

For the first five hits, 'Alice Cooper' was the name of the entire group, not just the lead vocalist.

Tommy COOPER UK, male vocalist — 3 wks

29 Jun 61	**DON'T JUMP OFF THE ROOF DAD** Palette PG 9019	40	2 wks
20 Jul 61	**DON'T JUMP OFF THE ROOF DAD (re-entry)** Palette PG 9019	50	1 wk

Julian COPE UK, male vocalist — 37 wks

19 Nov 83	**SUNSHINE PLAYROOM** Mercury COPE 1	64	1 wk
31 Mar 84	**THE GREATNESS AND PERFECTION OF LOVE** Mercury MER 155	52	5 wks
27 Sep 86	**WORLD SHUT YOUR MOUTH** Island IS 290	19	8 wks
17 Jan 87	**TRAMPOLENE** Island IS 305	31	6 wks
11 Apr 87	**EVE'S VOLCANO (COVERED IN SIN)** Island IS 318	41	5 wks
24 Sep 88	**CHARLOTTE ANNE** Island IS 380	35	6 wks
21 Jan 89	**5 O'CLOCK WORLD** Island IS 399	42	4 wks
24 Jun 89	**CHINA DOLL** Island IS 406	53	2 wks

Harry H. CORBETT – *See Wilfred BRAMBELL and Harry H. CORBETT*

Frank CORDELL UK, orchestra — 4 wks

24 Aug 56	**SADIE'S SHAWL** HMV POP 229	29	2 wks
16 Feb 61	**BLACK BEAR** HMV POP 824	44	2 wks

Phil CORDELL – *See SPRINGWATER*

Louise CORDET France, female vocalist — 13 wks

5 Jul 62	**I'M JUST A BABY** Decca F 11476	13	13 wks

Don CORNELL US, male vocalist — 23 wks

3 Sep 54 ★	**HOLD MY HAND** Vogue Q 2013	1	21 wks
22 Apr 55	**STRANGER IN PARADISE** Vogue Q 72073	19	2 wks

Lynn CORNELL UK, female vocalist — 9 wks

20 Oct 60	**NEVER ON SUNDAY** Decca F 11277	30	9 wks

Charlotte CORNWELL – *See Julie COVINGTON, Rula LENSKA, Charlotte CORNWELL and Sue JONES-DAVIES*

Hugh CORNWELL UK, male vocalist/instrumentalist - guitar — 3 wks

24 Jan 87	**FACTS + FIGURES** Virgin VS 922	61	2 wks
7 May 88	**ANOTHER KIND OF LOVE** Virgin VS 945	71	1 wk

CORONETS UK, male/female vocal group — 1 wk

25 Nov 55	**TWENTY TINY FINGERS** Columbia DB 3671	20	1 wk

Vladimir COSMA *Hungary, orchestra* — **1 wk**

14 Jul 79	**DAVID'S SONG (MAIN THEME FROM 'KIDNAPPED')** *Decca FR 13841*	64	1 wk

Don COSTA *US, orchestra* — **10 wks**

13 Oct 60	**NEVER ON SUNDAY** *London HLT 9195*	27	9 wks
22 Dec 60	**NEVER ON SUNDAY (re-entry)** *London HLT 9195*	41	1 wk

Elvis COSTELLO and the ATTRACTIONS — **151 wks**
UK, male vocal/instrumental group

5 Nov 77	**WATCHING THE DETECTIVES** *Stiff BUY 20*	15	11 wks
11 Mar 78	**(I DON'T WANNA GO TO) CHELSEA** *Radar ADA 3*	16	10 wks
13 May 78	**PUMP IT UP** *Radar ADA 10*	24	10 wks
28 Oct 78	**RADIO RADIO** *Radar ADA 24*	29	7 wks
10 Feb 79 ●	**OLIVER'S ARMY** *Radar ADA 31*	2	12 wks
12 May 79	**ACCIDENTS WILL HAPPEN** *Radar ADA 35*	28	8 wks
16 Feb 80 ●	**I CAN'T STAND UP FOR FALLING DOWN** *F. Beat XX 1*	4	8 wks
12 Apr 80	**HI FIDELITY** *F. Beat XX 3*	30	5 wks
7 Jun 80	**NEW AMSTERDAM** *F. Beat XX 5*	36	6 wks
20 Dec 80	**CLUBLAND** *F. Beat XX 12*	60	4 wks
3 Oct 81 ●	**A GOOD YEAR FOR THE ROSES** *F. Beat XX 17*	6	11 wks
12 Dec 81	**SWEET DREAMS** *F. Beat XX 19*	42	8 wks
10 Apr 82	**I'M YOUR TOY** *F. Beat XX 21*	51	3 wks
19 Jun 82	**YOU LITTLE FOOL** *F. Beat XX 26*	52	3 wks
31 Jul 82	**MAN OUT OF TIME** *F. Beat XX 28*	58	2 wks
25 Sep 82	**FROM HEAD TO TOE** *F. Beat XX 30*	43	4 wks
11 Dec 82	**PARTY PARTY** *A & M AMS 8267*	48	6 wks
9 Jul 83	**EVERYDAY I WRITE THE BOOK** *F. Beat XX 32*	28	8 wks
17 Sep 83	**LET THEM ALL TALK** *F. Beat XX 33*	59	2 wks
16 Jun 84	**I WANNA BE LOVED / TURNING THE TOWN RED** *F. Beat XX 35*	25	6 wks
25 Aug 84	**THE ONLY FLAME IN TOWN** *F. Beat XX 37*	71	2 wks
4 May 85	**GREEN SHIRT** *F. Beat ZB 40085*	71	1 wk
18 May 85	**GREEN SHIRT (re-entry)** *F. Beat ZB 40085*	68	1 wk
1 Feb 86	**DON'T LET ME BE MISUNDERSTOOD** *F. Beat ZB 40555*	33	4 wks
30 Aug 86	**TOKYO STORM WARNING** *Imp IMP 007*	73	1 wk
4 Mar 89	**VERONICA** *Warner Bros. W 7558*	31	7 wks
20 May 89	**BABY PLAYS AROUND (EP)** *Warner Bros. W 2949*	65	1 wk

Billed as Elvis Costello on hits in 1977 and 1980 with the exception of Clubland. I'm Your Toy *credits Elvis Costello and the Attractions with the Royal Philharmonic Orchestra. Don't Let Me Be Misunderstood bills the Costello Show featuring the Confederates - US, male backing band. Tracks on Baby Plays Around (EP): Baby Plays Around/Poisoned Rose/Almost Blue/My Funny Valentine. See also Royal Philharmonic Orchestra; Imposter.*

COTTAGERS – *See Tony REES and the COTTAGERS*

Billy COTTON and his BAND — **25 wks**
UK, male bandleader, vocalist, with band and chorus

1 May 53 ●	**IN A GOLDEN COACH** *Decca F 10058*	3	10 wks
18 Dec 53	**I SAW MOMMY KISSING SANTA CLAUS** *Decca F 10206*	11	3 wks
30 Apr 54	**FRIENDS AND NEIGHBOURS** *Decca F 10299*	12	1 wk
14 May 54 ●	**FRIENDS AND NEIGHBOURS (re-entry)** *Decca F 10299*	3	11 wks

In A Golden Coach has the credit 'vocals by Doreen Stephens', but also featured Billy Cotton as unbilled narrator. I Saw Mommy Kissing Santa Claus has the credit 'vocals by the Mill Girls and the Bandits'. Friends And Neighbours vocal by the Bandits. See also Various Artists - All Star Hit Parade No.2.

Mike COTTON'S JAZZMEN — **4 wks**
UK, male instrumental band, Mike Cotton trumpet

20 Jun 63	**SWING THAT HAMMER** *Columbia DB 7029*	36	4 wks

John COUGAR – *See John Cougar MELLENCAMP*

COUGARS *UK, male instrumental group* — **8 wks**

28 Feb 63	**SATURDAY NITE AT THE DUCK POND** *Parlophone R 4989*	33	8 wks

COUNCIL COLLECTIVE — **6 wks**
UK/US, male/female vocal/instrumental group

22 Dec 84	**SOUL DEEP** (PART 1) *Polydor MINE 1*	24	6 wks

COUNTRYMEN *UK, male vocal group* — **2 wks**

3 May 62	**I KNOW WHERE I'M GOING** *Piccadilly 7N 35029*	45	2 wks

Don COVAY *US, male vocalist* — **6 wks**

7 Sep 74	**IT'S BETTER TO HAVE (AND DON'T NEED)** *Mercury 6052 634*	29	6 wks

COVENTRY CITY CUP FINAL SQUAD — **2 wks**
UK, male football team vocalists

23 May 87	**GO FOR IT!** *Sky Blue SKB 1*	61	2 wks

Julie COVINGTON *UK, female vocalist* — **29 wks**

25 Dec 76 ★	**DON'T CRY FOR ME ARGENTINA** *MCA 260*	1	15 wks
3 Dec 77	**ONLY WOMEN BLEED** *Virgin VS 196*	12	11 wks
15 Jul 78	**DON'T CRY FOR ME ARGENTINA (re-entry)** *MCA 260*	63	3 wks

See also Julie Covington, Rula Lenska, Charlotte Cornwell and Sue Jones-Davies.

Julie COVINGTON, Rula LENSKA, Charlotte CORNWELL and Sue JONES-DAVIES *UK, female vocal group* — **6 wks**

21 May 77 ●	**O.K?** *Polydor 2001 714*	10	6 wks

See also Julie Covington.

Warren COVINGTON – *See Tommy DORSEY ORCHESTRA starring Warren COVINGTON*

Patrick COWLEY – *See SYLVESTER with Patrick COWLEY*

Michael COX *UK, male vocalist* — **15 wks**

9 Jun 60 ●	**ANGELA JONES** *Triumph RGM 1011*	7	13 wks
20 Oct 60	**ALONG CAME CAROLINE** *HMV POP 789*	41	2 wks

Floyd CRAMER *US, male instrumentalist - piano* — **24 wks**

13 Apr 61 ★	**ON THE REBOUND** *RCA 1231*	1	14 wks
20 Jul 61	**SAN ANTONIO ROSE** *RCA 1241*	36	8 wks
23 Aug 62	**HOT PEPPER** *RCA 1301*	46	2 wks

CRAMPS US, male/female vocal/instrumental group — 4 wks

9 Nov 85	CAN YOUR PUSSY DO THE DOG? Big Beat NS 110	68	1 wk
10 Feb 90	BIKINI GIRLS WITH MACHINE GUNS Enigma ENV 17	35	3 wks

Les CRANE US, male vocalist — 14 wks

19 Feb 72 ●	DESIDERATA Warner Bros. K 16119	7	14 wks

Jimmy CRAWFORD UK, male vocalist — 11 wks

8 Jun 61	LOVE OR MONEY Columbia DB 4633	49	1 wk
16 Nov 61	I LOVE HOW YOU LOVE ME Columbia DB 4717	18	10 wks

Michael CRAWFORD UK, male vocalist — 11 wks

10 Jan 87 ●	THE MUSIC OF THE NIGHT Polydor POSP 803	7	11 wks

The flip side of The Music Of The Night was Wishing You Were Somehow Here Again by Sarah Brightman. See also Sarah Brightman.

Randy CRAWFORD US, female vocalist — 67 wks

21 Jun 80	LAST NIGHT AT DANCELAND Warner Bros. K 17631	61	2 wks
30 Aug 80 ●	ONE DAY I'LL FLY AWAY Warner Bros. K 17680	2	11 wks
30 May 81	YOU MIGHT NEED SOMEBODY Warner Bros. K 17803	11	13 wks
8 Aug 81	RAINY NIGHT IN GEORGIA Warner Bros. K 17840	18	9 wks
31 Oct 81	SECRET COMBINATION Warner Bros. K 17872	48	3 wks
30 Jan 82	IMAGINE Warner Bros. K 17906	60	1 wk
13 Feb 82	IMAGINE (re-entry) Warner Bros. K 17906	75	1 wk
5 Jun 82	ONE HELLO Warner Bros. K 17948	48	4 wks
19 Feb 83	HE REMINDS ME Warner Bros. K 17970	65	2 wks
8 Oct 83	NIGHT LINE Warner Bros. W 9530	51	4 wks
29 Nov 86 ●	ALMAZ Warner Bros. W 8583	4	17 wks

See also Crusaders.

Robert CRAY BAND US, male vocal/instrumental group — 4 wks

20 Jun 87	RIGHT NEXT DOOR (BECAUSE OF ME) Mercury CRAY 3	50	4 wks

CRAZY ELEPHANT US, male vocal group — 13 wks

21 May 69	GIMME GIMME GOOD LOVIN' Major Minor MM 609	12	13 wks

CRAZYHEAD UK, male vocal/instrumental group — 5 wks

16 Jul 88	TIME HAS TAKEN IT'S TOLL ON YOU Food FOOD 12	65	2 wks
25 Feb 89	HAVE LOVE, WILL TRAVEL (EP) Food SGE 2025	68	2 wks
9 Dec 89	LIKE PRINCES DO Food FOOD 23	63	1 wk

Tracks on EP: Have Love Will Travel/Out On A Limb (Live)/Baby Turpentine (Live)/Snake Eyes (Live). Like Princes Do was one track from the Food Christmas EP. The others were I Don't Want That Kind Of Love by Jesus Jones and Info Freako by Diesel Park West. See also Jesus Jones; Diesel Park West.

CREAM UK, male vocal/instrumental group — 59 wks

20 Oct 66	WRAPPING PAPER Reaction 591 007	34	6 wks
15 Dec 66	I FEEL FREE Reaction 591 011	11	12 wks
8 Jun 67	STRANGE BREW Reaction 591 015	17	9 wks
5 Jun 68	ANYONE FOR TENNIS (THE SAVAGE SEVEN THEME) Polydor 56 258	40	3 wks
9 Oct 68	SUNSHINE OF YOUR LOVE Polydor 56 286	25	7 wks
15 Jan 69	WHITE ROOM Polydor 56 300	28	8 wks
9 Apr 69	BADGE Polydor 56 315	18	10 wks
28 Oct 72	BADGE (re-issue) Polydor 2058 285	42	4 wks

CREATION UK, male vocal/instrumental group — 3 wks

7 Jul 66	MAKING TIME Planet PLF 116	49	1 wk
3 Nov 66	PAINTER MAN Planet PLF 119	36	2 wks

CREATURES UK, male/female vocal/instrumental group — 26 wks

3 Oct 81	MAD EYED SCREAMER Polydor POSPD 354	24	7 wks
23 Apr 83	MISS THE GIRL Wonderland SHE 1	21	7 wks
16 Jul 83	RIGHT NOW Wonderland SHE 2	14	10 wks
14 Oct 89	STANDING THERE Wonderland SHE 17	53	2 wks

CREEDENCE CLEARWATER REVIVAL US, male vocal/instrumental group — 93 wks

28 May 69 ●	PROUD MARY Liberty LBF 15223	8	13 wks
16 Aug 69 ★	BAD MOON RISING Liberty LBF 15230	1	15 wks
15 Nov 69	GREEN RIVER Liberty LBF 15250	19	11 wks
14 Feb 70	DOWN ON THE CORNER Liberty LBF 15283	31	6 wks
4 Apr 70	TRAVELLIN' BAND Liberty LBF 15310	8	12 wks
20 Jun 70 ●	UP AROUND THE BEND Liberty LBF 15354	3	12 wks
4 Jul 70	TRAVELLIN' BAND (re-entry) Liberty LBF 15310	46	1 wk
5 Sep 70	LONG AS I CAN SEE THE LIGHT Liberty LBF 15384	20	9 wks
20 Mar 71	HAVE YOU EVER SEEN THE RAIN Liberty LBF 15440	36	6 wks
24 Jul 71	SWEET HITCH-HIKER United Artists UP 35261	36	8 wks

Kid CREOLE and the COCONUTS US, male vocalist and female vocal group — 56 wks

13 Jun 81	ME NO POP I Ze WIP 6711	32	7 wks
15 May 82 ●	I'M A WONDERFUL THING, BABY Ze WIP 6756	4	11 wks
24 Jul 82 ●	STOOL PIGEON Ze WIP 6793	7	9 wks
9 Oct 82 ●	ANNIE I'M NOT YOUR DADDY Ze WIP 6801	2	8 wks
11 Dec 82	DEAR ADDY Ze WIP 6840	29	7 wks
10 Sep 83	THERE'S SOMETHING WRONG IN PARADISE Island IS 130	35	5 wks
19 Nov 83	THE LIFEBOAT PARTY Island IS 142	49	4 wks
14 Apr 89	THE SEX OF IT CBS 655698 7	29	5 wks

Me No Pop I billed as 'Kid Creole and the Coconuts present Coati Mundi' - US, male vocalist. See also Coconuts.

CREW CUTS Canada, male vocal group — 29 wks

1 Oct 54	SH-BOOM Mercury MB 3140	12	9 wks
15 Apr 55 ●	EARTH ANGEL Mercury MB 3202	4	20 wks

Bernard CRIBBINS UK, male vocalist — 29 wks

15 Feb 62 ●	HOLE IN THE GROUND Parlophone R 4869	9	13 wks
5 Jul 62 ●	RIGHT SAID FRED Parlophone R 4923	10	10 wks
13 Dec 62	GOSSIP CALYPSO Parlophone R 4961	25	6 wks

CRICKETS US, male vocal/instrumental group — 91 wks

27 Sep 57 ★	THAT'LL BE THE DAY Vogue Coral Q 72279	1	14 wks
27 Dec 57 ●	OH BOY Coral Q 72298	3	15 wks
10 Jan 58	THAT'LL BE THE DAY (re-entry) Vogue Coral Q 72279	29	1 wk
14 Mar 58 ●	MAYBE BABY Coral Q 72307	4	10 wks
25 Jul 58	THINK IT OVER Coral Q 72329	11	7 wks
24 Apr 59	LOVE'S MADE A FOOL OF YOU Coral Q 72365	26	1 wk
8 May 59	LOVE'S MADE A FOOL OF YOU (re-entry) Coral Q 72365	30	1 wk
15 Jan 60	WHEN YOU ASK ABOUT LOVE Coral Q 72382	27	1 wk
12 May 60	MORE THAN I CAN SAY Coral Q 72395	42	1 wk
26 May 60	BABY MY HEART Coral Q 72395	33	4 wks
21 Jun 62 ●	DON'T EVER CHANGE Liberty LIB 55441	5	13 wks

24 Jan 63	**MY LITTLE GIRL** Liberty LIB 10067	**17**	9 wks
6 Jun 63	**DON'T TRY TO CHANGE ME** Liberty LIB 10092	**37**	4 wks
2 Jul 64	**(THEY CALL HER) LA BAMBA** Liberty LIB 55696	**21**	10 wks

Although not credited on the records, Buddy Holly was featured on the first four hits. See also Buddy Holly.

CRIMINAL ELEMENT ORCHESTRA   3 wks
US, producer - Arthur Baker under an assumed group name

5 Sep 87	**PUT THE NEEDLE TO THE RECORD** Cooltempo COOL 150	**63**	3 wks

See also Wally Jump Jr. and the Criminal Element; Criminal Element Orchestra with Wendell Williams; Arthur Baker.

CRIMINAL ELEMENT ORCHESTRA and Wendell WILLIAMS   4 wks
US, male producer - Arthur Baker- with US, male rapper

6 Oct 90	**EVERYBODY (RAP)** deConstruction PB 44701	**30**	4 wks

See also Criminal Element Orchestra; Arthur Baker.

CRISPY AND COMPANY   11 wks
US, male vocal/instrumental group

16 Aug 75	**BRAZIL** Creole CR 109	**26**	5 wks
27 Dec 75	**GET IT TOGETHER** Creole CR 114	**21**	6 wks

CRITTERS *US, male vocal/instrumental group*   5 wks

30 Jun 66	**YOUNGER GIRL** London HL 10047	**38**	5 wks

Tony CROMBIE and his ROCKETS   2 wks
UK, male vocal/instrumental group, Tony Crombie drums

19 Oct 56	**TEACH YOU TO ROCK/ SHORT'NIN' BREAD** Columbia DB 3822	**25**	2 wks

Bing CROSBY *US, male vocalist*   53 wks

14 Nov 52	● **ISLE OF INNISFREE** Brunswick 04900	**3**	12 wks
19 Dec 52	● **SILENT NIGHT** Brunswick 03929	**8**	2 wks
19 Mar 54	● **CHANGING PARTNERS** Brunswick 05244	**10**	1 wk
2 Apr 54	● **CHANGING PARTNERS (re-entry)** Brunswick 05244	**9**	1 wk
23 Apr 54	**CHANGING PARTNERS (2nd re-entry)** Brunswick 05244	**11**	1 wk
7 Jan 55	**COUNT YOUR BLESSINGS** Brunswick 05339	**18**	1 wk
21 Jan 55	**COUNT YOUR BLESSINGS (re-entry)** Brunswick 05339	**11**	2 wks
29 Apr 55	**STRANGER IN PARADISE** Brunswick 05410	**17**	2 wks
27 Apr 56	**IN A LITTLE SPANISH TOWN** Brunswick 05543	**22**	3 wks
24 May 57	● **AROUND THE WORLD** Brunswick 05674	**5**	15 wks
9 Aug 75	**THAT'S WHAT LIFE IS ALL ABOUT** United Artists UP 35852	**41**	4 wks
3 Dec 77	● **WHITE CHRISTMAS** MCA 111	**5**	7 wks
21 Dec 85	**WHITE CHRISTMAS (re-issue)** MCA BING 1	**69**	2 wks

See also Bing Crosby and Grace Kelly; Bing Crosby and Jane Wyman; David Bowie and Bing Crosby.

Bing CROSBY and Grace KELLY   30 wks
US, male/female vocal duo

23 Nov 56	● **TRUE LOVE** Capitol CL 14645	**4**	27 wks
17 Dec 83	**TRUE LOVE (re-issue)** Capitol CL 315	**70**	3 wks

See also Bing Crosby.

Bing CROSBY and Jane WYMAN   2 wks
US, male/female vocal duo

5 Dec 52	● **ZING A LITTLE ZONG** Brunswick 04981	**10**	2 wks

See also Bing Crosby.

CROSBY, STILLS and NASH   9 wks
US/UK, male vocal/instrumental group

16 Aug 69	**MARRAKESH EXPRESS** Atlantic 584 283	**17**	9 wks

See also Crosby Stills Nash and Young; Stephen Stills.

CROSBY STILLS NASH and YOUNG   3 wks
US/UK/Canada, male vocal/instrumental group

21 Jan 89	**AMERICAN DREAM** Atlantic A 9003	**55**	3 wks

See also Stephen Stills; Neil Young; Crosby, Stills and Nash.

CROSS *UK/US, male vocal/instrumental group*   1 wk

17 Oct 87	**COWBOYS AND INDIANS** Virgin VS 1007	**74**	1 wk

Christopher CROSS *US, male vocalist*   27 wks

19 Apr 80	**RIDE LIKE THE WIND** Warner Bros. K 17582	**69**	1 wk
14 Feb 81	**SAILING** Warner Bros. K 17695	**48**	6 wks
17 Oct 81	**ARTHUR'S THEME (BEST THAT YOU CAN DO)** Warner Bros. K 17847	**56**	4 wks
9 Jan 82	● **ARTHUR'S THEME (BEST THAT YOU CAN DO) (re-entry)** Warner Bros. K 17847	**7**	11 wks
5 Feb 83	**ALL RIGHT** Warner Bros. W 9843	**51**	5 wks

CROWD   11 wks
Multi-national, male/female vocal/instrumental charity assembly

1 Jun 85	★ **YOU'LL NEVER WALK ALONE** Spartan BRAD 1	**1**	11 wks

CROWDED HOUSE *Australia/New Zealand, male vocal/instrumental group*   8 wks

6 Jun 87	**DON'T DREAM IT'S OVER** Capitol CL 438	**27**	8 wks

CROWN HEIGHTS AFFAIR   34 wks
US, male vocal/instrumental group

19 Aug 78	**GALAXY OF LOVE** Philips 6168 801	**24**	10 wks
11 Nov 78	**I'M GONNA LOVE YOU FOREVER** Mercury 6168 803	**47**	4 wks
14 Apr 79	**DANCE LADY DANCE** Mercury 6168 804	**44**	4 wks
3 May 80	● **YOU GAVE ME LOVE** De-Lite MER 9	**10**	12 wks
9 Aug 80	**YOU'VE BEEN GONE** De-Lite MER 28	**44**	4 wks

Julee CRUISE *US, female vocalist*   8 wks

10 Nov 90	● **FALLING** Warner Bros. W 9544	**7†**	8 wks

CRUISERS – See Dave BERRY

CRUSADERS US, male vocal/instrumental group   16 wks

18 Aug 79	●	STREET LIFE MCA 513	5	11 wks
26 Sep 81		I'M SO GLAD I'M STANDING HERE TODAY MCA 741	61	3 wks
7 Apr 84		NIGHT LADIES MCA MCA 853	55	2 wks

Vocalist on Street Life *was Randy Crawford, though uncredited.* I'm So Glad I'm Standing Here Today *credits 'featured vocalist Joe Cocker'. See also Randy Crawford; Joe Cocker.*

Bobby CRUSH UK, male instrumentalist - piano   4 wks

4 Nov 72	BORSALINO Philips 6006 248	37	4 wks

CRY BEFORE DAWN   2 wks
Ireland, male vocal/instrumental group

17 Jun 89	WITNESS FOR THE WORLD Epic GONE 3	67	2 wks

CRY SISCO!   9 wks
UK, male producer - Barry Blue under an assumed name.

2 Sep 89	AFRO DIZZI ACT Escape AWOL 1	42	8 wks
20 Jan 90	AFRO DIZZI ACT (re-entry) Escape AWOL 1	70	1 wk

CRYIN' SHAMES UK, male vocal/instrumental group   7 wks

31 Mar 66	PLEASE STAY Decca F 12340	26	7 wks

CRYPT-KICKERS – See Bobby 'Boris' PICKETT and the CRYPT-KICKERS

CRYSTAL PALACE UK, male football team vocalists   2 wks

12 May 90	GLAD ALL OVER/ WHERE EAGLES FLY Parkfield PMS 5019	50	2 wks

CRYSTALS US, female vocal group   54 wks

22 Nov 62		HE'S A REBEL London HLU 9611	19	13 wks
20 Jun 63	●	DA DOO RON RON London HLU 9732	5	16 wks
19 Sep 63	●	THEN HE KISSED ME London HLU 9773	2	14 wks
5 Mar 64		I WONDER London HLU 9852	36	3 wks
19 Oct 74		DA DOO RON RON (re-issue) Warner Spector K 19010	15	8 wks

CUFFLINKS US, male vocal group   30 wks

29 Nov 69	●	TRACY MCA MU 1101	4	16 wks
14 Mar 70	●	WHEN JULIE COMES AROUND MCA MU 1112	10	14 wks

CULT UK, male vocal/instrumental group   71 wks

22 Dec 84	RESURRECTION JOE Beggars Banquet BEG 122	74	2 wks
25 May 85	SHE SELLS SANCTUARY Beggars Banquet BEG 135	15	17 wks
28 Sep 85	SHE SELLS SANCTUARY (re-entry) Beggars Banquet BEG 135	61	2 wks
5 Oct 85	RAIN Beggars Banquet BEG 147	17	8 wks
30 Nov 85	REVOLUTION Beggars Banquet BEG 152	30	7 wks
28 Feb 87	LOVE REMOVAL MACHINE Beggars Banquet BEG 182	18	7 wks
2 May 87	LIL' DEVIL Beggars Banquet BEG 188	11	7 wks
22 Aug 87	WILD FLOWER (DOUBLE SINGLE) Beggars Banquet BEG 195D	24	2 wks
29 Aug 87	WILD FLOWER Beggars Banquet BEG 195	30	4 wks
1 Apr 89	FIRE WOMAN Beggars Banquet BEG 228	15	4 wks
8 Jul 89	EDIE (CIAO BABY) Beggars Banquet BEG 230	32	5 wks
18 Nov 89	SUN KING/ EDIE (CIAO BABY) (re-issue) Beggars Banquet BEG 235	39	2 wks

10 Mar 90	SWEET SOUL SISTER Beggars Banquet BEG 241	42	4 wks

Tracks on double single: Wild Flower/Love Trooper/Outlaw/Horse Nation.

CULT JAM – See LISA LISA and CULT JAM

CULTURE BEAT   3 wks
Germany, male/female vocal/instrumental group

3 Feb 90	(CHERRY LIPS) DER ERDBEERMUND Epic 655633 7	55	3 wks

CULTURE CLUB UK, male vocal/instrumental group   103 wks

18 Sep 82	★	DO YOU REALLY WANT TO HURT ME Virgin VS 518	1	18 wks
27 Nov 82	●	TIME (CLOCK OF THE HEART) Virgin VS 558	3	12 wks
9 Apr 83	●	CHURCH OF THE POISON MIND Virgin VS 571	2	9 wks
17 Sep 83	★	KARMA CHAMELEON Virgin VS 612	1	20 wks
10 Dec 83	●	VICTIMS Virgin VS 641	3	10 wks
24 Mar 84	●	IT'S A MIRACLE Virgin VS 662	4	9 wks
6 Oct 84	●	THE WAR SONG Virgin VS 694	2	8 wks
1 Dec 84		THE MEDAL SONG Virgin VS 730	32	4 wks
5 Jan 85		THE MEDAL SONG (re-entry) Virgin VS 730	74	1 wk
15 Mar 86	●	MOVE AWAY Virgin VS 845	7	7 wks
31 May 86		GOD THANK YOU WOMAN Virgin VS 861	31	5 wks

Smiley CULTURE UK, male vocalist   13 wks

15 Dec 84	POLICE OFFICER Fashion FAD 7012	12	10 wks
6 Apr 85	COCKNEY TRANSLATION Fashion FAD 7028	71	1 wk
13 Sep 86	SCHOOLTIME CHRONICLE Polydor POSP 815	59	2 wks

Larry CUNNINGHAM and the MIGHTY AVONS Ireland, male vocal/instrumental group   11 wks

10 Dec 64	TRIBUTE TO JIM REEVES King KG 1016	40	8 wks
25 Feb 65	TRIBUTE TO JIM REEVES (re-entry) King KG 1016	46	3 wks

CUPID'S INSPIRATION   19 wks
UK, male vocal/instrumental group

19 Jun 68	●	YESTERDAY HAS GONE Nems 56 3500	4	11 wks
2 Oct 68		MY WORLD Nems 56 3702	33	8 wks

CURE UK, male vocal/instrumental group   125 wks

12 Apr 80		A FOREST Fiction FICS 10	31	8 wks
4 Apr 81		PRIMARY Fiction FICS 12	43	6 wks
17 Oct 81		CHARLOTTE SOMETIMES Fiction FICS 14	44	4 wks
24 Jul 82		HANGING GARDEN Fiction FICS 15	34	4 wks
27 Nov 82		LET'S GO TO BED Fiction FICS 17	44	4 wks
8 Jan 83		LET'S GO TO BED (re-entry) Fiction FICS 17	75	1 wk
9 Jul 83		THE WALK Fiction FICS 18	12	8 wks
29 Oct 83	●	THE LOVE CATS Fiction FICS 19	7	11 wks
7 Apr 84		THE CATERPILLAR Fiction FICS 20	14	7 wks
27 Jul 85		IN BETWEEN DAYS Fiction FICS 22	15	10 wks
21 Sep 85		CLOSE TO ME Fiction FICS 23	24	8 wks
3 May 86		BOYS DON'T CRY Fiction FICS 24	22	6 wks
18 Apr 87		WHY CAN'T I BE YOU Fiction FICS 25	21	5 wks
4 Jul 87		CATCH Fiction FICS 26	27	6 wks
17 Oct 87		JUST LIKE HEAVEN Fiction FICS 27	29	5 wks
20 Feb 88		HOT HOT HOT!!! Fiction FICSX 28	45	3 wks
22 Apr 89	●	LULLABY Fiction FICS 29	5	6 wks
2 Sep 89		LOVESONG Fiction FICS 30	18	7 wks
31 Mar 90		PICTURES OF YOU Fiction FICS 34	24	6 wks
29 Sep 90		NEVER ENOUGH Fiction FICS 35	13	5 wks
3 Nov 90		CLOSE TO ME (re-mix) fiction FICS 36	13	5 wks

CURIOSITY KILLED THE CAT
UK, male vocal/instrumental group **45 wks**

13 Dec 86	● DOWN TO EARTH *Mercury CAT 2*	3	18 wks
4 Apr 87	ORDINARY DAY *Mercury CAT 3*	11	7 wks
20 Jun 87	● MISFIT *Mercury CAT 4*	7	9 wks
19 Sep 87	FREE *Mercury CAT 5*	56	2 wks
16 Sep 89	NAME AND NUMBER *Mercury CAT 6*	14	9 wks

Last hit credited simply to Curiosity.

CURLS – *See Paul EVANS and the CURLS*

Chantal CURTIS *France, female vocalist* **3 wks**

14 Jul 79	GET ANOTHER LOVE *Pye 7P 5003*	51	3 wks

T. C. CURTIS *Jamaica, male vocalist/instrumentalist* **4 wks**

23 Feb 85	YOU SHOULD HAVE KNOWN BETTER *Hot Melt VS 754*	50	4 wks

Features backing vocals by Galaxy. See also Phil Fearon and Galaxy.

CURVED AIR *UK, male/female vocal/instrumental group* **12 wks**

7 Aug 71	● BACK STREET LUV *Warner Bros. K 16092*	4	12 wks

Adge CUTLER and the WURZELS
UK, male vocal/instrumental group **1 wk**

2 Feb 67	DRINK UP THY ZIDER *Columbia DB 8081*	45	1 wk

See also Wurzels.

CUTTING CREW *UK, male vocal/instrumental group* **37 wks**

16 Aug 86	● (I JUST) DIED IN YOUR ARMS *Siren SIREN 21*	4	12 wks
25 Oct 86	I'VE BEEN IN LOVE BEFORE *Siren SIREN 29*	31	9 wks
10 Jan 87	I'VE BEEN IN LOVE BEFORE (re-entry) *Siren SIREN 29*	70	1 wk
7 Mar 87	ONE FOR THE MOCKINGBIRD *Siren SIREN 40*	52	5 wks
21 Nov 87	I'VE BEEN IN LOVE BEFORE (2nd re-entry) *Siren SIREN 29*	24	8 wks
22 Jul 89	(BETWEEN A) ROCK AND A HARD PLACE *Siren SRN 108*	66	2 wks

CYBERSONIK *US, male sampling group* **1 wk**

10 Nov 90	TECHNARCHY *Champion CHAMP 264*	73	1 wk

Johnny CYMBAL *UK, male vocalist* **10 wks**

14 Mar 63	MR. BASS MAN *London HLR 9682*	24	10 wks

D

Dimples D *US, female rapper* **7 wks**

17 Nov 90	SUCKER DJ *FBI FBI 1*	17†	7 wks

Longsy D *UK, male vocalist* **7 wks**

4 Mar 89	THIS IS SKA *Big One BIG 13*	56	7 wks

Nikki D – *See Alyson WILLIAMS*

Vicky D *US, female vocalist* **6 wks**

13 Mar 82	THIS BEAT IS MINE *Virgin VS 486*	42	6 wks

D, B, M and T *UK, male vocal/instrumental group* **8 wks**

1 Aug 70	MR. PRESIDENT *Fontana 6007 022*	33	8 wks

See also Dave Dee, Dozy, Beaky, Mick and Tich.

D CUPS – *See Ivor BIGGUN*

D MOB *UK, male producer* **43 wks**

15 Oct 88	● WE CALL IT ACIEED *FFRR FFR 13*	3	12 wks
3 Jun 89	● IT IS TIME TO GET FUNKY *FFRR F 107*	9	10 wks
21 Oct 89	C'MON AND GET MY LOVE *FFRR F 117*	15	10 wks
6 Jan 90	● PUT YOUR HANDS TOGETHER *London LON 124*	7	8 wks
7 Apr 90	THAT'S THE WAY OF THE WORLD *FFRR F 132*	48	3 wks

We Call It Acieed features Gary Haisman - UK, male vocalist. It Is Time To Get Funky features LRS - UK, male rap group; C'Mon And Get My Love and That's The Way Of The World feature Cathy Dennis - UK, female vocalist; Put Your Hands Together features Nuff Juice - UK, male vocal group. See also Various Artists - The Brits 1990.

D TRAIN *US, male vocal/instrumental duo* **36 wks**

6 Feb 82	YOU'RE THE ONE FOR ME *Epic EPC A 2016*	30	8 wks
8 May 82	WALK ON BY *Epic EPC A 2298*	44	6 wks
7 May 83	MUSIC PART 1 *Prelude A 3332*	23	7 wks
16 Jul 83	KEEP GIVING ME LOVE *Prelude A 3497*	65	2 wks
27 Jul 85	YOU'RE THE ONE FOR ME (re-mix) *Prelude ZB 40302*	15	11 wks
12 Oct 85	MUSIC *Prelude ZB 40431*	62	2 wks

Paul DA VINCI *UK, male vocalist* **8 wks**

20 Jul 74	YOUR BABY AIN'T YOUR BABY ANYMORE *Penny Farthing PEN 843*	20	8 wks

Terry DACTYL and the DINOSAURS **16 wks**
UK, male vocal/instrumental group

15 Jul 72	● SEASIDE SHUFFLE *UK 5*	2	12 wks
13 Jan 73	ON A SATURDAY NIGHT *UK 21*	45	4 wks

Terry Dactyl is Jona Lewie. See also Jona Lewie.

DAINTEES *UK, male vocal/instrumental group* **3 wks**

17 Jan 87	TROUBLE TOWN *Kitchenware SK 13*	58	3 wks

See also Martin Stephenson and the Daintees.

DAKOTAS *UK, male instrumental group* **13 wks**

11 Jul 63	THE CRUEL SEA *Parlophone R 5044*	18	13 wks

See also Billy J. Kramer and the Dakotas.

Left: What are all these DIRE STRAITS gold records good for? Mark Knopfler (far right) supplies a bin.

Bottom Far Left: BO DIDDLEY, rock 'n' roll pioneer of the Fifties, UK chart star of the Sixties, and writer of Craig McLachlan's 1990 hit 'Mona'.

Below Centre: Now accustomed to performing to stadium audiences, DEPECHE MODE here enjoy the silence.

Leslie Wonderman found fame as TAYLOR DAYNE.

Jim DALE UK, male vocalist — 22 wks

11 Oct 57	● BE MY GIRL *Parlophone R 4343*	2	16 wks
10 Jan 58	JUST BORN *Parlophone R 4376*	27	1 wk
17 Jan 58	CRAZY DREAM *Parlophone R 4376*	24	2 wks
7 Mar 58	SUGARTIME *Parlophone R 4402*	25	3 wks

DALE and GRACE US, male/female vocal duo — 2 wks

9 Jan 64	I'M LEAVING IT UP TO YOU *London HL 9807*	42	2 wks

DALE SISTERS UK, female vocal group — 6 wks

23 Nov 61	MY SUNDAY BABY *Ember S 140*	36	6 wks

DALI'S CAR UK, male vocal/instrumental duo — 2 wks

3 Nov 84	THE JUDGEMENT IS THE MIRROR *Paradox DOX 1*	66	2 wks

Roger DALTREY UK, male vocalist — 46 wks

14 Apr 73	● GIVING IT ALL AWAY *Track 2094 110*	5	11 wks
4 Aug 73	I'M FREE *Ode ODS 66302*	13	10 wks
14 May 77	WRITTEN ON THE WIND *Polydor 2121 319*	46	2 wks
2 Aug 80	FREE ME *Polydor 2001 980*	39	6 wks
11 Oct 80	WITHOUT YOUR LOVE *Polydor POSP 181*	55	4 wks
3 Mar 84	WALKING IN MY SLEEP *WEA U 9686*	56	3 wks
5 Oct 85	AFTER THE FIRE *10 TEN 69*	50	4 wks
8 Mar 86	UNDER A RAGING MOON *10 TEN 81*	43	5 wks

Carolina DAMAS – *See SUENO LATINO featuring Carolina DAMAS*

DAMIAN UK, male vocalist — 26 wks

26 Dec 87	THE TIME WARP 2 *Jive JIVE 160*	51	6 wks
27 Aug 88	THE TIME WARP 2 *Jive JIVE 182*	64	3 wks
19 Aug 89	● THE TIME WARP (re-mix) *Jive JIVE 209*	7	13 wks
16 Dec 89	WIG WAM BAM *Jive JIVE 236*	49	4 wks

DAMNED UK, male vocal/instrumental group — 77 wks

5 May 79	LOVE SONG *Chiswick CHIS 112*	20	8 wks
20 Oct 79	SMASH IT UP *Chiswick CHIS 116*	35	5 wks
1 Dec 79	I JUST CAN'T BE HAPPY TODAY *Chiswick CHIS 120*	46	5 wks
4 Oct 80	HISTORY OF THE WORLD (PART 1) *Chiswick CHIS 135*	51	4 wks
28 Nov 81	FRIDAY 13TH (EP) *Stale One TRY 1*	50	4 wks
10 Jul 82	LOVELY MONEY *Bronze BRO 149*	42	4 wks
9 Jun 84	THANKS FOR THE NIGHT *Damned DAMNED 1*	43	4 wks
30 Mar 85	GRIMLY FIENDISH *MCA GRIM 1*	21	7 wks
22 Jun 85	THE SHADOW OF LOVE *MCA GRIM 2*	25	8 wks
21 Sep 85	IS IT A DREAM *MCA GRIM 3*	34	4 wks
8 Feb 86	● ELOISE *MCA GRIM 4*	3	9 wks
19 Apr 86	ELOISE (re-entry) *MCA GRIM 4*	72	1 wk
22 Nov 86	ANYTHING *MCA GRIM 5*	32	4 wks
7 Feb 87	GIGOLO *MCA GRIM 6*	29	3 wks
25 Apr 87	ALONE AGAIN OR *MCA GRIM 7*	27	6 wks
28 Nov 87	IN DULCE DECORUM *MCA GRIM 8*	72	1 wk

Tracks on EP: Disco Man/Limit Club/Billy Bad Breaks/Citadel.

Kenny DAMON US, male vocalist — 1 wk

19 May 66	WHILE I LIVE *Mercury MF 907*	48	1 wk

Vic DAMONE US, male vocalist — 22 wks

6 Dec 57	AN AFFAIR TO REMEMBER *Philips PB 745*	29	1 wk
31 Jan 58	AN AFFAIR TO REMEMBER (re-entry) *Philips PB 745*	30	1 wk
9 May 58	★ ON THE STREET WHERE YOU LIVE *Philips PB 819*	1	17 wks
1 Aug 58	THE ONLY MAN ON THE ISLAND *Philips PB 837*	24	3 wks

DANA UK, female vocalist — 75 wks

4 Apr 70	★ ALL KINDS OF EVERYTHING *Rex R 11054*	1	15 wks
25 Jul 70	ALL KINDS OF EVERYTHING (re-entry) *Rex R 11054*	47	1 wk
13 Feb 71	WHO PUT THE LIGHTS OUT *Rex R 11062*	14	11 wks
25 Jan 75	● PLEASE TELL HIM THAT I SAID HELLO *GTO GT 6*	8	14 wks
13 Dec 75	● IT'S GONNA BE A COLD COLD CHRISTMAS *GTO GT 45*	4	6 wks
6 Mar 76	NEVER GONNA FALL IN LOVE AGAIN *GTO GT 55*	31	4 wks
16 Oct 76	FAIRYTALE *GTO GT 66*	13	16 wks
31 Mar 79	SOMETHING'S COOKIN' IN THE KITCHEN *GTO GT 243*	44	5 wks
15 May 82	I FEEL LOVE COMIN' ON *Creole CR 32*	66	3 wks

DAN-I UK, male vocalist — 9 wks

10 Nov 79	MONKEY CHOP *Island WIP 6520*	30	9 wks

Charlie DANIELS BAND
US, male vocal/instrumental group — 10 wks

22 Sep 79	THE DEVIL WENT DOWN TO GEORGIA *Epic EPC 7737*	14	10 wks

Johnny DANKWORTH — 33 wks
UK, male orchestral/group leader/instrumentalist – alto sax

22 Jun 56	● EXPERIMENTS WITH MICE *Parlophone R 4185*	7	12 wks
23 Feb 61	● AFRICAN WALTZ *Columbia DB 4590*	9	21 wks

DANNY and the JUNIORS US, male vocal group — 19 wks

17 Jan 58	● AT THE HOP *HMV POP 436*	3	14 wks
10 Jul 76	AT THE HOP (re-issue) *ABC 4123*	39	5 wks

DANNY WILSON UK, male vocal/instrumental group — 28 wks

22 Aug 87	MARY'S PRAYER *Virgin VS 934*	42	7 wks
2 Apr 88	● MARY'S PRAYER (re-entry) *Virgin VS 934*	3	11 wks
17 Jun 89	THE SECOND SUMMER OF LOVE *Virgin VS 1186*	23	9 wks
16 Sep 89	NEVER GONNA BE THE SAME *Virgin VS 1203*	69	1 wk

DANSE SOCIETY UK, male vocal/instrumental group — 5 wks

27 Aug 83	WAKE UP *Society SOC 5*	61	3 wks
5 Nov 83	HEAVEN IS WAITING *Society SOC 6*	60	2 wks

Steven DANTE UK, male vocalist — 6 wks

9 Jul 88	I'M TOO SCARED *Cooltempo DANTE 1*	34	6 wks

DANY – *See DOUBLE DEE featuring DANY*

Terence Trent D'ARBY US, male vocalist — 44 wks

14 Mar 87	● IF YOU LET ME STAY *CBS TRENT 1*	7	13 wks
20 Jun 87	● WISHING WELL *CBS TRENT 2*	4	11 wks

10 Oct 87		DANCE LITTLE SISTER (PART ONE)			
		CBS TRENT 3	20	7 wks	
9 Jan 88	●	SIGN YOUR NAME CBS TRENT 4	2	10 wks	
20 Jan 90		TO KNOW SOMEONE DEEPLY IS TO KNOW			
		SOMEONE SOFTLY CBS TRENT 6	55	3 wks	

Richard DARBYSHIRE – See JELLYBEAN

DARE UK, male vocal/instrumental group — 4 wks

| 29 Apr 89 | | THE RAINDANCE A & M AM 483 | 62 | 2 wks |
| 29 Jul 89 | | ABANDON A & M AM 519 | 71 | 2 wks |

Bobby DARIN US, male vocalist — 161 wks

1 Aug 58		SPLISH SPLASH London HLE 8666	28	1 wk
15 Aug 58		SPLISH SPLASH (re-entry) London HLE 8666	18	6 wks
9 Jan 59		QUEEN OF THE HOP London HLE 8737	24	2 wks
29 May 59	★	DREAM LOVER London HLE 8867	1	19 wks
25 Sep 59	★	MACK THE KNIFE London HLE 8939	1	16 wks
22 Jan 60		MACK THE KNIFE (re-entry) London HLE 8939	30	1 wk
29 Jan 60	●	LA MER (BEYOND THE SEA) London HLE 9034	8	10 wks
10 Mar 60		MACK THE KNIFE (2nd re-entry) London HLE 8939	50	1 wk
31 Mar 60	●	CLEMENTINE London HLK 9086	8	12 wks
21 Apr 60		LA MER (BEYOND THE SEA) (re-entry)		
		London HLE 9034	40	2 wks
30 Jun 60		BILL BAILEY London HLK 9142	36	1 wk
14 Jul 60		BILL BAILEY (re-entry) London HLK 9142	34	1 wk
16 Mar 61	●	LAZY RIVER London HLK 9303	2	13 wks
6 Jul 61		NATURE BOY London HLK 9375	24	7 wks
12 Oct 61	●	YOU MUST HAVE BEEN A BEAUTIFUL BABY		
		London HLK 9429	10	11 wks
26 Oct 61		COME SEPTEMBER London HLK 9407	50	1 wk
21 Dec 61	●	MULTIPLICATION London HLK 9474	5	13 wks
19 Jul 62	●	THINGS London HLK 9575	2	17 wks
4 Oct 62		IF A MAN ANSWERS Capitol CL 15272	24	6 wks
29 Nov 62		BABY FACE London HLK 9624	40	4 wks
25 Jul 63		EIGHTEEN YELLOW ROSES Capitol CL 15306	37	4 wks
13 Oct 66	●	IF I WERE A CARPENTER Atlantic 584 051	9	12 wks
14 Apr 79		DREAM LOVER/ MACK THE KNIFE (re-issue)		
		Lightning LIG 9017	64	1 wk

Come September is an instrumental credited to the Bobby Darin Orchestra.

DARLING BUDS UK, male/female vocal/instrumental group — 19 wks

8 Oct 88		BURST Epic BLOND 1	50	5 wks
7 Jan 89		HIT THE GROUND CBS BLOND 2	27	5 wks
25 Mar 89		LET'S GO ROUND THERE CBS BLOND 3	49	4 wks
22 Jul 89		YOU'VE GOT TO CHOOSE CBS BLOND 4	45	3 wks
2 Jun 90		TINY MACHINE CBS BLOND 5	60	2 wks

Guy DARRELL UK, male vocalist — 13 wks

| 18 Aug 73 | | I'VE BEEN HURT Santa Ponsa PNS 4 | 12 | 13 wks |

James DARREN US, male vocalist — 25 wks

11 Aug 60		BECAUSE THEY'RE YOUNG Pye International 7N 25059	29	7 wks
14 Dec 61		GOODBYE CRUEL WORLD Pye International 7N 25116	28	9 wks
29 Mar 62		HER ROYAL MAJESTY Pye International 7N 25125	36	3 wks
21 Jun 62		CONSCIENCE Pye International 7N 25138	30	6 wks

DARTS UK, male/female vocal/instrumental group — 117 wks

5 Nov 77	●	DADDY COOL - THE GIRL CAN'T HELP IT		
		Magnet MAG 100	6	13 wks
28 Jan 78	●	COME BACK MY LOVE Magnet MAG 110	2	12 wks
6 May 78	●	BOY FROM NEW YORK CITY Magnet MAG 116	2	13 wks
5 Aug 78	●	IT'S RAINING Magnet MAG 126	2	11 wks
11 Nov 78		DON'T LET IT FADE AWAY Magnet MAG 134	18	11 wks

10 Feb 79	●	GET IT Magnet MAG 140	10	9 wks
21 Jul 79	●	DUKE OF EARL Magnet MAG 147	6	11 wks
20 Oct 79		CAN'T GET ENOUGH OF YOUR LOVE		
		Magnet MAG 156	43	6 wks
1 Dec 79		REET PETITE Magnet MAG 160	51	7 wks
31 May 80		LET'S HANG ON Magnet MAG 174	11	14 wks
6 Sep 80		PEACHES Magnet MAG 179	66	3 wks
29 Nov 80		WHITE CHRISTMAS/ SH-BOOM (LIFE COULD BE A		
		DREAM) Magnet MAG 184	48	7 wks

DAVE – See CHAS and DAVE

DAVE – See SAM and DAVE

Anne-Marie DAVID France, female vocalist — 9 wks

| 28 Apr 73 | | WONDERFUL DREAM Epic EPC 1446 | 13 | 9 wks |

F.R. DAVID France, male vocalist — 13 wks

| 2 Apr 83 | ● | WORDS Carrere CAR 248 | 2 | 12 wks |
| 18 Jun 83 | | MUSIC Carrere CAR 282 | 71 | 1 wk |

DAVID and JONATHAN UK, male vocal duo — 22 wks

| 13 Jan 66 | | MICHELLE Columbia DB 7800 | 11 | 6 wks |
| 7 Jul 66 | ● | LOVERS OF THE WORLD UNITE Columbia DB 7950 | 7 | 16 wks |

Jim DAVIDSON UK, male vocalist — 4 wks

| 27 Dec 80 | | WHITE CHRISTMAS/ TOO RISKY Scratch SCR 001 | 52 | 4 wks |

Paul DAVIDSON Jamaica, male vocalist — 10 wks

| 27 Dec 75 | ● | MIDNIGHT RIDER Tropical ALO 56 | 10 | 10 wks |

Dave DAVIES UK, male vocalist — 17 wks

| 19 Jul 67 | ● | DEATH OF A CLOWN Pye 7N 17356 | 3 | 10 wks |
| 6 Dec 67 | | SUSANNAH'S STILL ALIVE Pye 7N 17429 | 20 | 7 wks |

Windsor DAVIES and Don ESTELLE — 16 wks
UK, male vocal duo

| 17 May 75 | ★ | WHISPERING GRASS EMI 2290 | 1 | 12 wks |
| 25 Oct 75 | | PAPER DOLL EMI 2361 | 41 | 4 wks |

Billie DAVIS UK, female vocalist — 23 wks

7 Feb 63	●	TELL HIM Decca F 11572	10	12 wks
30 May 63		HE'S THE ONE Decca F 11658	40	3 wks
9 Oct 68		I WANT YOU TO BE MY BABY Decca F 12823	33	8 wks

See also Mike Sarne.

Billy DAVIS Jr. – See Marilyn McCOO and Billy DAVIS Jr.

Darlene DAVIS US, female vocalist — 5 wks

| 7 Feb 87 | | I FOUND LOVE Serious 7OUS 1 | 55 | 5 wks |

John DAVIS and the MONSTER ORCHESTRA US, male vocal/instrumental group — 2 wks

10 Feb 79	AIN'T THAT ENOUGH FOR YOU Miracle M 2	70	2 wks

Mac DAVIS US, male vocalist — 22 wks

4 Nov 72	BABY DON'T GET HOOKED ON ME CBS 8250	29	6 wks
15 Nov 80	IT'S HARD TO BE HUMBLE Casablanca CAN 210	27	16 wks

Ruth DAVIS – See Bo KIRKLAND and Ruth DAVIS

Sammy DAVIS Jr. US, male vocalist — 25 wks

29 Jul 55	SOMETHING'S GOTTA GIVE Brunswick 05428	19	2 wks
19 Aug 55	SOMETHING'S GOTTA GIVE (re-entry) Brunswick 05428	11	5 wks
9 Sep 55	● LOVE ME OR LEAVE ME Brunswick 05428	8	6 wks
30 Sep 55	THAT OLD BLACK MAGIC Brunswick 05450	16	1 wk
7 Oct 55	HEY THERE Brunswick 05469	19	1 wk
4 Nov 55	LOVE ME OR LEAVE ME (re-entry) Brunswick 05428	18	2 wks
20 Apr 56	IN A PERSIAN MARKET Brunswick 05518	28	1 wk
28 Dec 56	ALL OF YOU Brunswick 05629	28	1 wk
22 Mar 62	WHAT KIND OF FOOL AM I?/ GONNA BUILD A MOUNTAIN Reprise R 20048	26	8 wks

See also Sammy Davis Jr. and Carmen McRae; Frank Sinatra and Sammy Davis Jr.

Sammy DAVIS Jr. and Carmen McRAE — 1 wk
US, male/female vocal duo

16 Jun 60	HAPPY TO MAKE YOUR ACQUAINTANCE Brunswick 05830	46	1 wk

See also Sammy Davis Jr.

Skeeter DAVIS US, female vocalist — 13 wks

14 Mar 63	END OF THE WORLD RCA 1328	18	13 wks

Spencer DAVIS GROUP — 71 wks
UK, male vocal/instrumental group

5 Nov 64	I CAN'T STAND IT Fontana TF 499	47	3 wks
25 Feb 65	EVERY LITTLE BIT HURTS Fontana TF 530	43	2 wks
18 Mar 65	EVERY LITTLE BIT HURTS (re-entry) Fontana TF 530	41	1 wk
10 Jun 65	STRONG LOVE Fontana TF 571	50	1 wk
24 Jun 65	STRONG LOVE (re-entry) Fontana TF 571	44	3 wks
2 Dec 65	★ KEEP ON RUNNING Fontana TF 632	1	14 wks
24 Mar 66	★ SOMEBODY HELP ME Fontana TF 679	1	10 wks
1 Sep 66	WHEN I COME HOME Fontana TF 739	12	9 wks
3 Nov 66	● GIMME SOME LOVING Fontana TF 762	2	12 wks
26 Jan 67	● I'M A MAN Fontana TF 785	9	7 wks
9 Aug 67	TIME SELLER Fontana TF 854	30	5 wks
10 Jan 68	MR. SECOND CLASS United Artists UP 1203	35	4 wks

DAVIS PINCKNEY PROJECT – See GO GO LORENZO and the DAVIS PINCKNEY PROJECT

DAWN US, male/female vocal group — 109 wks

16 Jan 71	● CANDIDA Bell 1118	9	11 wks
10 Apr 71	★ KNOCK THREE TIMES Bell 1146	1	27 wks
31 Jul 71	● WHAT ARE YOU DOING SUNDAY Bell 1169	3	12 wks
10 Mar 73	★ TIE A YELLOW RIBBON ROUND THE OLD OAK TREE Bell 1287	1	39 wks
4 Aug 73	SAY, HAS ANYBODY SEEN MY SWEET GYPSY ROSE Bell 1322	12	15 wks
5 Jan 74	TIE A YELLOW RIBBON ROUND THE OLD OAK TREE (re-entry) Bell 1287	41	1 wk
9 Mar 74	WHO'S IN THE STRAWBERRY PATCH WITH SALLY Bell 1343	37	4 wks

First two hits credit Dawn, the next three Dawn featuring Tony Orlando, and the final one Tony Orlando and Dawn. See also Tony Orlando.

Bobby DAY US, male vocalist — 2 wks

7 Nov 58	ROCKIN' ROBIN London HL 8726	29	2 wks

Doris DAY US, female vocalist — 122 wks

21 Nov 52	● MY LOVE AND DEVOTION Columbia DB 3157	10	2 wks
2 Apr 54	★ SECRET LOVE Philips PB 230	1	29 wks
27 Apr 54	● BLACK HILLS OF DAKOTA Philips PB 287	7	8 wks
1 Oct 54	● IF I GIVE MY HEART TO YOU Philips PB 325	4	11 wks
8 Apr 55	● READY WILLING AND ABLE Philips PB 402	7	9 wks
9 Sep 55	LOVE ME OR LEAVE ME Philips PB 479	20	1 wk
21 Oct 55	I'LL NEVER STOP LOVING YOU Philips PB 497	17	2 wks
25 Nov 55	I'LL NEVER STOP LOVING YOU (re-entry) Philips PB 497	19	1 wk
29 Jun 56	★ WHATEVER WILL BE WILL BE Philips PB 586	1	22 wks
13 Jun 58	A VERY PRECIOUS LOVE Philips PB 799	16	11 wks
15 Aug 58	EVERYBODY LOVES A LOVER Philips PB 843	25	3 wks
26 Sep 58	EVERYBODY LOVES A LOVER (re-entry) Philips PB 843	27	1 wk
12 Mar 64	● MOVE OVER DARLING CBS AAG 183	8	16 wks
18 Apr 87	MOVE OVER DARLING (re-issue) CBS LEGS 1	45	6 wks

See also Doris Day and Frankie Laine; Doris Day and Johnnie Ray.

Doris DAY and Frankie LAINE — 8 wks
US, female/male vocal duo

14 Nov 52	● SUGARBUSH Columbia DB 3123	8	2 wks
5 Dec 52	● SUGARBUSH (re-entry) Columbia DB 3123	8	6 wks

See also Doris Day; Frankie Laine.

Doris DAY and Johnnie RAY — 16 wks
US, female/male vocal duo

3 Apr 53	MA SAYS PA SAYS Columbia DB 3242	12	1 wk
17 Apr 53	FULL TIME JOB Columbia DB 3242	11	1 wk
24 Jul 53	● LET'S WALK THATA-WAY Philips PB 157	4	14 wks

See also Doris Day; Johnnie Ray.

Patti DAY US, female vocalist — 1 wk

9 Dec 89	RIGHT BEFORE MY EYES Debut DEBT 3080	69	1 wk

Taylor DAYNE US, female vocalist — 38 wks

23 Jan 88	● TELL IT TO MY HEART Arista 109616	3	13 wks
19 Mar 88	● PROVE YOUR LOVE Arista 109830	8	10 wks
11 Jun 88	I'LL ALWAYS LOVE YOU Arista 111536	41	7 wks
18 Nov 89	WITH EVERY BEAT OF MY HEART Arista 112760	53	2 wks
14 Apr 90	I'LL BE YOUR SHELTER Arista 112966	43	5 wks
4 Jul 90	LOVE WILL LEAD YOU BACK Arista 113277	69	1 wk

DAYTON US, male vocalist — 1 wk

10 Dec 83	THE SOUND OF MUSIC Capitol CL 318	75	1 wk

DAZZ BAND US, male vocal/instrumental group — 12 wks

3 Nov 84	LET IT ALL BLOW Motown TMG 1361	12	12 wks

D.B.M. Germany, male/female vocal/instrumental group — 3 wks

12 Nov 77	DISCO BEATLEMANIA Atlantic K 11027	45	3 wks

Nino DE ANGELO Germany, male vocalist — 5 wks

21 Jul 84	GUARDIAN ANGEL Carrere CAR 335	57	5 wks

Chris DE BURGH Ireland, male vocalist — 58 wks

23 Oct 82	DON'T PAY THE FERRYMAN A & M AMS 8256	48	5 wks
12 May 84	HIGH ON EMOTION A & M AM 190	44	5 wks
12 Jul 86	★ THE LADY IN RED A & M AM 331	1	14 wks
20 Sep 86	FATAL HESITATION A & M AM 348	44	4 wks
13 Dec 86	A SPACEMAN CAME TRAVELLING/ THE BALLROOM OF ROMANCE A & M AM 365	40	5 wks
21 Feb 87	THE LADY IN RED (re-entry) A & M AM 331	74	1 wk
12 Dec 87	THE SIMPLE TRUTH (A CHILD IS BORN) A & M AM 427	69	2 wks
2 Jan 88	THE SIMPLE TRUTH (A CHILD IS BORN) (re-entry) A & M AM 427	55	1 wk
29 Oct 88	● MISSING YOU A & M AM 474	3	12 wks
7 Jan 89	TENDER HANDS A & M AM 486	43	6 wks
14 Oct 89	THIS WAITING HEART A & M AM 528	59	3 wks

DE CASTRO SISTERS US, female vocal group — 1 wk

11 Feb 55	TEACH ME TONIGHT London HL 8104	20	1 wk

DE LA SOUL US, male rap/sampling group — 30 wks

8 Apr 89	ME MYSELF AND I Big Life BLR 7	22	8 wks
8 Jul 89	SAY NO GO Big Life BLR 10	18	7 wks
21 Oct 89	EYE KNOW Big Life BLR 13	14	7 wks
23 Dec 89	● THE MAGIC NUMBER/ BUDDY Big Life BLR 14	7	8 wks

Buddy only listed for first four weeks. See also Queen Latifah + De La Soul; Jungle Brothers.

Lynsey DE PAUL UK, female vocalist — 47 wks

19 Aug 72	● SUGAR ME MAM 81	5	11 wks
2 Dec 72	GETTING A DRAG MAM 88	18	8 wks
27 Oct 73	WON'T SOMEBODY DANCE WITH ME MAM 109	14	7 wks
8 Jun 74	OOH I DO Warner Bros. K 16401	25	6 wks
2 Nov 74	● NO HONESTLY Jet 747	7	11 wks
22 Mar 75	MY MAN AND ME Jet 750	40	4 wks

See also Lynsey De Paul and Mike Moran.

Lynsey DE PAUL and Mike MORAN — 7 wks
UK, female/male vocal/instrumental duo, pianos

26 Mar 77	ROCK BOTTOM Polydor 2058 859	19	7 wks

See also Lynsey De Paul.

Tullio DE PISCOPO Italy, male vocalist — 4 wks

28 Feb 87	STOP BAJON...PRIMAVERA Greyhound GREY 9	58	4 wks

Terri DE SARIO US, female vocalist — 5 wks

2 Sep 78	AIN'T NOTHIN' (GONNA KEEP ME FROM YOU) Casablanca CAN 128	52	5 wks

Stephanie DE SYKES UK, female vocalist — 17 wks

20 Jul 74	● BORN WITH A SMILE ON MY FACE Bradley's BRAD 7409	2	10 wks
19 Apr 75	WE'LL FIND OUR DAY Bradley's BRAD 7509	17	7 wks

Born With A Smile On My Face credits Stephanie De Sykes with Rain - UK, male vocal group.

William DE VAUGHN US, male vocalist — 10 wks

6 Jul 74	BE THANKFUL FOR WHAT YOU'VE GOT Chelsea 2005 002	31	5 wks
20 Sep 80	BE THANKFUL FOR WHAT YOU'VE GOT EMI 5101	44	5 wks

EMI version of hit is a new recording.

DEACON BLUE UK, male/female vocal/instrumental group — 66 wks

23 Jan 88	DIGNITY CBS DEAC 4	31	8 wks
9 Apr 88	WHEN WILL YOU MAKE MY TELEPHONE RING CBS DEAC 5	34	7 wks
16 Jul 88	CHOCOLATE GIRL CBS DEAC 6	43	7 wks
15 Oct 88	● REAL GONE KID CBS DEAC 7	8	13 wks
4 Mar 89	WAGES DAY CBS DEAC 8	18	6 wks
20 May 89	FERGUS SINGS THE BLUES CBS DEAC 9	14	6 wks
16 Sep 89	LOVE AND REGRET CBS DEAC 10	28	5 wks
6 Jan 90	QUEEN OF THE NEW YEAR CBS DEAC 11	21	5 wks
25 Aug 90	● FOUR BACHARACH AND DAVID SONGS EP CBS DEAC 12	2	9 wks

Tracks on Four Bacharach and David Songs EP: I'll Never Fall In Love Again/The Look Of Love/Message To Michael/Are You There (With Another Girl).

DEAD END KIDS UK, male vocal/instrumental group — 10 wks

26 Mar 77	● HAVE I THE RIGHT CBS 4972	6	10 wks

DEAD KENNEDYS US, male vocal/instrumental group — 9 wks

1 Nov 80	KILL THE POOR Cherry Red CHERRY 16	49	3 wks
30 May 81	TOO DRUNK TO FUCK Cherry Red CHERRY 24	36	6 wks

DEAD OR ALIVE UK, male vocal/instrumental group — 70 wks

24 Mar 84	THAT'S THE WAY (I LIKE IT) Epic A 4271	22	9 wks
1 Dec 84	★ YOU SPIN ME ROUND (LIKE A RECORD) Epic A 4861	1	23 wks
20 Apr 85	LOVER COME BACK TO ME Epic A 6086	11	8 wks
29 Jun 85	IN TOO DEEP Epic A 6360	14	8 wks
21 Sep 85	MY HEART GOES BANG (GET ME TO THE DOCTOR) Epic A 6571	23	6 wks
20 Sep 86	BRAND NEW LOVER Epic A 650075 7	31	4 wks
10 Jan 87	SOMETHING IN MY HOUSE Epic BURNS 1	12	7 wks
4 Apr 87	HOOKED ON LOVE Epic BURNS 2	69	2 wks
3 Sep 88	TURN ROUND AND COUNT 2 TEN Epic BURNS 4	70	1 wk
22 Jul 89	COME HOME WITH ME BABY Epic BURNS 5	62	2 wks

DEAN – See JAN and DEAN

Hazell DEAN UK, female vocalist — 70 wks

18 Feb 84	EVERGREEN/ JEALOUS LOVE Proto ENA 114	63	3 wks
21 Apr 84	● SEARCHIN' (I GOTTA FIND A MAN) Proto ENA 109	6	15 wks
28 Jul 84	● WHATEVER I DO (WHEREVER I GO) Proto ENA 119	4	11 wks
3 Nov 84	BACK IN MY ARMS(ONCE AGAIN) Proto ENA 122	41	4 wks

2 Mar 85	NO FOOL (FOR LOVE) *Proto ENA 123*	41	5 wks
12 Oct 85	THEY SAY IT'S GONNA RAIN *Parlophone R 6107*	58	4 wks
2 Apr 88	● WHO'S LEAVING WHO *EMI EM 45*	4	11 wks
25 Jun 88	MAYBE (WE SHOULD CALL IT A DAY) *EMI EM 62*	15	6 wks
24 Sep 88	TURN IT INTO LOVE *EMI EM 71*	21	7 wks
26 Aug 89	LOVE PAINS *Lisson DOLE 12*	48	4 wks

Jimmy DEAN US, *male vocalist*   17 wks

26 Oct 61	● BIG BAD JOHN *Philips PB 1187*	2	13 wks
8 Nov 62	LITTLE BLACK BOOK *CBS AAG 122*	33	4 wks

Letitia DEAN and Paul MEDFORD   7 wks
UK, *female/male vocal duo*

25 Oct 86	SOMETHING OUTA NOTHING *BBC RESL 203*	12	7 wks

DeBARGE US, *male/female vocal group*   17 wks

6 Apr 85	● RHYTHM OF THE NIGHT *Gordy TMG 1376*	4	14 wks
21 Sep 85	YOU WEAR IT WELL *Gordy ZB 40345*	54	3 wks

You Wear It Well *credited to El DeBarge with Debarge. See also El DeBarge.*

El DeBARGE US, *male vocalist*   2 wks

28 Jun 86	WHO'S JOHNNY ('SHORT CIRCUIT' THEME) *Gordy ELD 1*	60	2 wks

See also DeBarge; Quincy Jones.

Diana DECKER US, *female vocalist*   10 wks

23 Oct 53	● POPPA PICCOLINO *Columbia DB 3325*	2	8 wks
8 Jan 54	● POPPA PICCOLINO (re-entry) *Columbia DB 3325*	5	2 wks

Dave DEE UK, *male vocalist*   4 wks

14 Mar 70	MY WOMAN'S MAN *Fontana TF 1074*	42	4 wks

See also Dave Dee, Dozy, Beaky, Mick and Tich.

Dave DEE, DOZY, BEAKY, MICK and TICH 141 wks
UK, *male vocal/instrumental group*

23 Dec 65	YOU MAKE IT MOVE *Fontana TF 630*	26	8 wks
3 Mar 66	● HOLD TIGHT *Fontana TF 671*	4	17 wks
9 Jun 66	● HIDEAWAY *Fontana TF 711*	10	11 wks
15 Sep 66	● BEND IT *Fontana TF 746*	2	12 wks
8 Dec 66	● SAVE ME *Fontana TF 775*	4	10 wks
9 Mar 67	TOUCH ME TOUCH ME *Fontana TF 798*	13	9 wks
18 May 67	● OKAY! *Fontana TF 830*	4	11 wks
11 Oct 67	● ZABADAK! *Fontana TF 873*	3	14 wks
14 Feb 68	★ LEGEND OF XANADU *Fontana TF 903*	1	12 wks
3 Jul 68	● LAST NIGHT IN SOHO *Fontana TF 953*	8	11 wks
2 Oct 68	WRECK OF THE ANTOINETTE *Fontana TF 971*	14	9 wks
5 Mar 69	DON JUAN *Fontana TF 1000*	23	9 wks
14 May 69	SNAKE IN THE GRASS *Fontana TF 1020*	23	8 wks

See also Dave Dee; D, B, M and T.

Jazzy DEE US, *male vocalist*   5 wks

5 Mar 83	GET ON UP *Laurie LRS 101*	53	5 wks

Joey DEE and the STARLITERS   8 wks
US, *male vocal/instrumental group*

8 Feb 62	PEPPERMINT TWIST *Columbia DB 4758*	33	8 wks

Kiki DEE UK, *female vocalist*   55 wks

10 Nov 73	AMOUREUSE *Rocket PIG 4*	13	13 wks
7 Sep 74	I GOT THE MUSIC IN ME *Rocket PIG 12*	19	8 wks
12 Apr 75	(YOU DONT KNOW) HOW GLAD I AM *Rocket PIG 16*	33	4 wks
11 Sep 76	LOVING AND FREE/AMOUREUSE (re-issue) *Rocket ROKN 515*	13	8 wks
19 Feb 77	FIRST THING IN THE MORNING *Rocket ROKN 520*	32	5 wks
11 Jun 77	CHICAGO *Rocket ROKN 526*	28	4 wks
21 Feb 81	STAR *Ariola ARO 251*	13	10 wks
23 May 81	PERFECT TIMING *Ariola ARO 257*	66	3 wks

Amoureuse *when re-issued on the same record as a new title, Loving And Free, was only listed on the charts for 5 weeks of the record's 8-week run. On 18 Sep, 25 Sep and 2 Oct 1976, Loving And Free was the only title mentioned. I Got The Music In Me and (You Don't Know) How Glad I Am credited to the Kiki Dee Band. Chicago was one side of a double sided chart entry, the other being Bite Your Lip (Get Up And Dance) by Elton John. See also Elton John; Elton John and Kiki Dee.*

Nancy DEE – *See BENELUX and Nancy DEE*

DEEDEE – *See DICK and DEEDEE*

DEEE-LITE   19 wks
US/USSR/Japan, *male/female vocal/instrumental group*

18 Aug 90	● GROOVE IS IN THE HEART/WHAT IS LOVE *Elektra EKR 114*	2	13 wks
24 Nov 90	POWER OF LOVE/DEEE-LITE THEME *Elektra EKR 117*	25†	6 wks

What Is Love *only listed from 25 Aug 90.*

Carol DEENE UK, *female vocalist*   25 wks

26 Oct 61	SAD MOVIES *HMV POP 922*	44	3 wks
25 Jan 62	NORMAN *HMV POP 973*	24	8 wks
5 Jul 62	JOHNNY GET ANGRY *HMV POP 1027*	32	4 wks
23 Aug 62	SOME PEOPLE *HMV POP 1058*	25	10 wks

DEEP FEELING UK, *male vocal/instrumental group*   5 wks

25 Apr 70	DO YOU LOVE ME *Page One POF 165*	45	1 wk
9 May 70	DO YOU LOVE ME (re-entry) *Page One POF 165*	34	4 wks

DEEP PURPLE UK, *male vocal/instrumental group*   82 wks

15 Aug 70	● BLACK NIGHT *Harvest HAR 5020*	2	21 wks
27 Feb 71	● STRANGE KIND OF WOMAN *Harvest HAR 5033*	8	12 wks
13 Nov 71	FIREBALL *Harvest HAR 5045*	15	13 wks
1 Apr 72	NEVER BEFORE *Purple PUR 102*	35	6 wks
16 Apr 77	SMOKE ON THE WATER *Purple PUR 132*	21	7 wks
15 Oct 77	NEW LIVE AND RARE (EP) *Purple PUR 135*	31	4 wks
7 Oct 78	NEW LIVE AND RARE II (EP) *Purple PUR 137*	45	3 wks
2 Aug 80	BLACK NIGHT (re-issue) *Harvest HAR 5210*	43	6 wks
1 Nov 80	NEW LIVE AND RARE VOLUME 3 (EP) *Harvest SHEP 101*	48	3 wks
26 Jan 85	PERFECT STRANGERS *Polydor POSP 719*	48	3 wks
15 Jun 85	KNOCKING AT YOUR BACK DOOR/PERFECT STRANGERS *Polydor POSP 749*	68	1 wk
18 Jun 88	HUSH *Polydor PO 4*	62	2 wks
20 Oct 90	KING OF DREAMS *RCA PB 49247*	70	1 wk

Tracks on New Live And Rare EP: Black Night (Live)/Painted Horse/When A Blind Man Cries. New Live And Rare II EP: Burn (Edited Version)/Coronarias Redig/Mistreated (Live)/Rock Me Baby. New Live And Rare Volume 3 EP: Smoke On The Water/Bird Has Flown/Grabsplatter.

DEEP RIVER BOYS US, male vocal group — 1 wk

7 Dec 56	**THAT'S RIGHT** *HMV POP 263*	29	1 wk

Rick DEES and his CAST OF IDIOTS — 9 wks
US, male vocalist with male/female vocal/instrumental group

18 Sep 76	● **DISCO DUCK (PART ONE)** *RSO 2090 204*	6	9 wks

DEF LEPPARD UK, male vocal/instrumental group — 55 wks

17 Nov 79	**WASTED** *Vertigo 6059 247*	61	3 wks
23 Feb 80	**HELLO AMERICA** *Vertigo LEPP 1*	45	4 wks
5 Feb 83	**PHOTOGRAPH** *Vertigo VER 5*	66	3 wks
27 Aug 83	**ROCK OF AGES** *Vertigo VER 6*	41	4 wks
1 Aug 87	● **ANIMAL** *Bludgeon Riffola LEP 1*	6	9 wks
19 Sep 87	**POUR SOME SUGAR ON ME** *Bludgeon Riffola LEP 2*	18	6 wks
28 Nov 87	**HYSTERIA** *Bludgeon Riffola LEP 3*	26	5 wks
9 Jan 88	**HYSTERIA (re-entry)** *Bludgeon Riffola LEP 3*	74	1 wk
9 Apr 88	**ARMAGEDDON IT** *Bludgeon Riffola LEP 4*	20	5 wks
16 Jul 88	**LOVE BITES** *Bludgeon Riffola LEP 5*	11	8 wks
11 Feb 89	**ROCKET** *Bludgeon Riffola LEP 6*	15	7 wks

DEJA US, male/female vocal duo — 1 wk

29 Aug 87	**SERIOUS** *10 TEN 132*	75	1 wk

Desmond DEKKER and the ACES — 71 wks
Jamaica, male vocal/instrumental group

12 Jul 67	**007** *Pyramid PYR 6004*	14	11 wks
19 Mar 69	★ **ISRAELITES** *Pyramid PYR 6058*	1	14 wks
25 Jun 69	● **IT MIEK** *Pyramid PYR 6068*	7	11 wks
2 Jul 69	**ISRAELITES (re-entry)** *Pyramid PYR 6058*	45	1 wk
10 Jan 70	**PICKNEY GAL** *Pyramid PYR 6078*	42	3 wks
22 Aug 70	● **YOU CAN GET IT IF YOU REALLY WANT** *Trojan TR 7777*	2	15 wks
10 May 75	● **ISRAELITES (re-issue)** *Cactus CT 57*	10	9 wks
30 Aug 75	**SING A LITTLE SONG** *Cactus CT 73*	16	7 wks

You Can Get It If You Really Want *credited only to Desmond Dekker.*

DEL AMITRI UK, male vocal/instrumental group — 27 wks

19 Aug 89	**KISS THIS THING GOODBYE** *A & M AM 515*	59	2 wks
13 Jan 90	**NOTHING EVER HAPPENS** *A & M AM 536*	11	9 wks
24 Mar 90	**KISS THIS THING GOODBYE (re-issue)** *A & M AM 551*	43	4 wks
16 Jun 90	**MOVE AWAY JIMMY BLUE** *A & M AM 555*	36	6 wks
3 Nov 90	**SPIT IN THE RAIN** *A & M AM 589*	21	6 wks

DELAGE UK, female vocal group — 2 wks

15 Dec 90	**ROCK THE BOAT** *PWL/Polydor PO 113*	63	2 wks

DELANEY and BONNIE and FRIENDS featuring Eric CLAPTON — 9 wks
US/UK, male/female vocal/instrumental group

20 Dec 69	**COMIN' HOME** *Atlantic 584 308*	16	9 wks

See also Eric Clapton.

DELEGATION UK, male vocal/instrumental group — 7 wks

23 Apr 77	**WHERE IS THE LOVE (WE USED TO KNOW)** *State STAT 40*	22	6 wks
20 Aug 77	**YOU'VE BEEN DOING ME WRONG** *State STAT 55*	49	1 wk

DELFONICS US, male vocal group — 23 wks

10 Apr 71	**DIDN'T I (BLOW YOUR MIND THIS TIME)** *Bell 1099*	43	1 wk
24 Apr 71	**DIDN'T I (BLOW YOUR MIND THIS TIME) (re-entry)** *Bell 1099*	22	8 wks
10 Jul 71	**LA-LA MEANS I LOVE YOU** *Bell 1165*	19	10 wks
16 Oct 71	**READY OR NOT HERE I COME** *Bell 1175*	41	4 wks

'DELIVERANCE' SOUNDTRACK — 7 wks
US, male instrumental duo

31 Mar 73	**DUELLING BANJOS** *Warner Bros. K 16223*	17	7 wks

DELLS US, male vocal group — 9 wks

16 Jul 69	**I CAN SING A RAINBOW - LOVE IS BLUE** (MEDLEY) *Chess CRS 8099*	15	9 wks

DELRONS – *See REPARATA and the DELRONS*

DELUXE US, female vocalist — 1 wk

18 Mar 89	**JUST A LITTLE MORE** *Unyque UNQ 5*	74	1 wk

Terry DENE UK, male vocalist — 20 wks

7 Jun 57	**A WHITE SPORT COAT** *Decca F 10895*	18	6 wks
19 Jul 57	**START MOVIN'** *Decca F 10914*	15	8 wks
26 Jul 57	**A WHITE SPORT COAT (re-entry)** *Decca F 10895*	30	1 wk
16 May 58	**STAIRWAY OF LOVE** *Decca F 11016*	16	5 wks

Cathy DENNIS – *See D MOB*

Jackie DENNIS UK, male vocalist — 10 wks

14 Mar 58	● **LA DEE DAH** *Decca F 10992*	4	9 wks
27 Jun 58	**PURPLE PEOPLE EATER** *Decca F 11033*	29	1 wk

Stefan DENNIS Australia, male vocalist — 8 wks

6 May 89	**DON'T IT MAKE YOU FEEL GOOD** *Sublime LIME 105*	16	7 wks
7 Oct 89	**THIS LOVE AFFAIR** *Sublime LIME 113*	67	1 wk

DENNISONS UK, male vocal/instrumental group — 13 wks

15 Aug 63	**BE MY GIRL** *Decca F 11691*	46	6 wks
7 May 64	**WALKIN' THE DOG** *Decca F 11880*	36	7 wks

Richard DENTON and Martin COOK — 7 wks
UK, male orchestral leaders/instrumental duo, guitar and keyboards

15 Apr 78	**THEME FROM THE HONG KONG BEAT** *BBC RESL 52*	25	7 wks

John DENVER US, male vocalist | 13 wks

17 Aug 74	★ ANNIE'S SONG RCA APBO 0295	1	13 wks

See also Placido Domingo and John Denver.

Karl DENVER UK, male vocalist | 124 wks

22 Jun 61	● MARCHETA Decca F 11360	8	20 wks
19 Oct 61	● MEXICALI ROSE Decca F 11395	8	11 wks
25 Jan 62	● WIMOWEH Decca F 11420	4	17 wks
22 Feb 62	● NEVER GOODBYE Decca F 11431	9	18 wks
7 Jun 62	A LITTLE LOVE A LITTLE KISS Decca F 11470	19	10 wks
20 Sep 62	BLUE WEEKEND Decca F 11505	33	5 wks
21 Mar 63	CAN YOU FORGIVE ME Decca F 11608	32	8 wks
13 Jun 63	INDIAN LOVE CALL Decca F 11674	32	8 wks
22 Aug 63	STILL Decca F 11720	13	15 wks
5 Mar 64	MY WORLD OF BLUE Decca F 11828	29	6 wks
4 Jun 64	LOVE ME WITH ALL YOUR HEART Decca F 11905	37	6 wks

See also Happy Mondays and Karl Denver.

DEODATO US, orchestra | 9 wks

5 May 73	● ALSO SPRACH ZARATHUSTRA (2001) Creed Taylor CTI 4000	7	9 wks

DEPARTMENT S UK, male vocal/instrumental group | 13 wks

4 Apr 81	IS VIC THERE? Demon D 1003	22	10 wks
11 Jul 81	GOING LEFT RIGHT Stiff BUY 118	55	3 wks

DEPECHE MODE UK, male vocal/instrumental group | 189 wks

4 Apr 81	DREAMING OF ME Mute MUTE 013	57	4 wks
13 Jun 81	NEW LIFE Mute MUTE 014	11	15 wks
19 Sep 81	● JUST CAN'T GET ENOUGH Mute MUTE 016	8	10 wks
13 Feb 82	SEE YOU Mute MUTE 018	6	10 wks
8 May 82	THE MEANING OF LOVE Mute MUTE 022	12	8 wks
28 Aug 82	LEAVE IN SILENCE Mute BONG 1	18	10 wks
12 Feb 83	GET THE BALANCE RIGHT Mute 7 BONG 2	13	8 wks
23 Jul 83	● EVERYTHING COUNTS Mute 7 BONG 3	6	11 wks
1 Oct 83	LOVE IN ITSELF.2 Mute 7 BONG 4	21	7 wks
24 Mar 84	● PEOPLE ARE PEOPLE Mute 7 BONG 5	4	10 wks
1 Sep 84	● MASTER AND SERVANT Mute 7 BONG 6	9	9 wks
10 Nov 84	SOMEBODY / BLASPHEMOUS RUMOURS Mute 7 BONG 7	16	6 wks
11 May 85	SHAKE THE DISEASE Mute BONG 8	18	9 wks
28 Sep 85	IT'S CALLED A HEART Mute BONG 9	18	4 wks
22 Feb 86	STRIPPED Mute BONG 10	15	6 wks
26 Apr 86	A QUESTION OF LUST Mute BONG 11	28	5 wks
23 Aug 86	A QUESTION OF TIME Mute BONG 12	17	6 wks
9 May 87	STRANGELOVE Mute BONG 13	16	5 wks
5 Sep 87	NEVER LET ME DOWN AGAIN Mute BONG 14	22	4 wks
9 Jan 88	BEHIND THE WHEEL Mute BONG 15	21	5 wks
28 May 88	LITTLE 15 (import) Mute LITTLE 15	60	2 wks
25 Feb 89	EVERYTHING COUNTS Mute BONG 16	22	7 wks
9 Sep 89	PERSONAL JESUS Mute BONG 17	13	8 wks
17 Feb 90	● ENJOY THE SILENCE Mute BONG 18	6	9 wks
19 May 90	POLICY OF TRUTH Mute BONG 19	16	6 wks
29 Sep 90	WORLD IN MY EYES Mute BONG 20	17	6 wks

BONG 16 is a live version of BONG 3.

DEREK and the DOMINOS | 21 wks
UK/US, male vocal/instrumental group

12 Aug 72	● LAYLA Polydor 2058 130	7	11 wks
6 Mar 82	● LAYLA (re-issue) RSO 87	4	10 wks

Derek being Eric Clapton under a false name; see also Eric Clapton.

DESIRELESS France, female vocalist | 19 wks

31 Oct 87	VOYAGE VOYAGE CBS DESI 1	53	6 wks
14 May 88	● VOYAGE VOYAGE (re-mix) CBS DESI 2	5	13 wks

DESKEE UK, male instrumentalist | 3 wks

3 Feb 90	LET THERE BE HOUSE Big One VBIG 19	52	2 wks
8 Sep 90	DANCE, DANCE Big One VBIG 22	74	1 wk

DETROIT EMERALDS US, male vocal group | 44 wks

10 Feb 73	● FEEL THE NEED IN ME Janus 6146 020	4	15 wks
5 May 73	YOU WANT IT YOU GOT IT Westbound 6146 103	12	9 wks
11 Aug 73	I THINK OF YOU Westbound 6146 104	27	9 wks
18 Jun 77	FEEL THE NEED IN ME Atlantic K 10945	12	11 wks

The second Feel The Need In Me was a re-recording.

DETROIT SPINNERS US, male vocal group | 83 wks

14 Nov 70	IT'S A SHAME Tamla Motown TMG 755	20	11 wks
21 Apr 73	COULD IT BE I'M FALLING IN LOVE Atlantic K 10283	11	11 wks
29 Sep 73	● GHETTO CHILD Atlantic K 10359	7	10 wks
11 Sep 76	THE RUBBERBAND MAN Atlantic K 10807	16	11 wks
29 Jan 77	WAKE UP SUSAN Atlantic K 10799	29	6 wks
7 May 77	COULD IT BE I'M FALLING IN LOVE (EP) Atlantic K 10935	32	3 wks
23 Feb 80	★ WORKING MY WAY BACK TO YOU/ FORGIVE ME GIRL Atlantic K 11432	1	14 wks
10 May 80	BODY LANGUAGE Atlantic K 11392	40	7 wks
28 Jun 80	● CUPID - I'VE LOVED YOU FOR A LONG TIME (MEDLEY) Atlantic K 11498	4	10 wks

See also Dionne Warwick and the Detroit Spinners. Group is known simply as the Spinners in the US. On It's A Shame they were called the Motown Spinners in the UK. Tracks on Could It Be I'm Falling In Love EP: Could It Be I'm Falling In Love/You're Throwing A Good Love Away/Games People Play/Lazy Susan.

DETROIT WHEELS – *See Mitch RYDER and the DETROIT WHEELS*

Sidney DEVINE UK, male vocalist | 1 wk

1 Apr 78	SCOTLAND FOREVER Philips SCOT 1	48	1 wk

DEVO US, male vocal/instrumental group | 23 wks

22 Apr 78	(I CAN'T ME GET NO) SATISFACTION Stiff BOY 1	41	8 wks
13 May 78	JOCKO HOMO Stiff DEV 1	62	3 wks
12 Aug 78	BE STIFF Stiff BOY 2	71	1 wk
2 Sep 78	COME BACK JONEE Virgin VS 223	60	4 wks
22 Nov 80	WHIP IT Virgin VS 383	51	7 wks

DEVOE – *See BELL BIV DEVOE*

DEVOTIONS – *See BELLE and the DEVOTIONS*

Howard DEVOTO – *See BUZZCOCKS*

DEXY'S MIDNIGHT RUNNERS | 93 wks
UK, male vocal/instrumental group

19 Jan 80	DANCE STANCE Oddball Productions R 6028	40	6 wks
22 Mar 80	★ GENO Late Night Feelings R 6033	1	14 wks
12 Jul 80	● THERE THERE MY DEAR Late Night Feelings R 6038	7	9 wks
21 Mar 81	PLAN B Parlophone R 6046	58	2 wks
11 Jul 81	SHOW ME Mercury DEXYS 6	16	9 wks

20 Mar 82	THE CELTIC SOUL BROTHERS *Mercury DEXYS 8*	**45**	4 wks
3 Jul 82 ★	COME ON EILEEN *Mercury DEXYS 9*..............	**1**	17 wks
2 Oct 82 ●	JACKIE WILSON SAID *Mercury DEXYS 10*..............	**5**	7 wks
4 Dec 82	LET'S GET THIS STRAIGHT (FROM THE START)/ OLD *Mercury DEXYS 11*.............	**17**	9 wks
2 Apr 83	THE CELTIC SOUL BROTHERS *Mercury DEXYS 12*	**20**	6 wks
22 Nov 86	BECAUSE OF YOU *Mercury BRUSH 1*	**13**	10 wks

The first entries of The Celtic Soul Brothers and Come On Eileen are credited to Dexy's Midnight Runners with the Emerald Express (female vocal/instrumental group). Jackie Wilson Said, Let's Get This Straight and the new version of The Celtic Soul Brothers are credited to Kevin Rowland and Dexy's Midnight Runners. DEXYS 12 is a different version from DEXYS 8.

Jim DIAMOND *UK, male vocalist*   **30 wks**

3 Nov 84 ★	I SHOULD HAVE KNOWN BETTER *A & M AM 220*.......	**1**	13 wks
2 Feb 85	I SLEEP ALONE AT NIGHT *A & M AM 229*.............	**72**	1 wk
18 May 85	REMEMBER I LOVE YOU *A & M AM 247*...............	**42**	5 wks
22 Feb 86 ●	HI HO SILVER *A & M AM 296*....................	**5**	11 wks

Neil DIAMOND *US, male vocalist*   **107 wks**

7 Nov 70 ●	CRACKLIN' ROSIE *Uni UN 529*	**3**	17 wks
20 Feb 71 ●	SWEET CAROLINE *Uni UN 531*................	**8**	11 wks
8 May 71 ●	I AM . . . I SAID *Uni UN 532*..................	**4**	12 wks
13 May 72	SONG SUNG BLUE *Uni UN 538*	**14**	13 wks
14 Aug 76	IF YOU KNOW WHAT I MEAN *CBS 4398*	**35**	4 wks
23 Oct 76	BEAUTIFUL NOISE *CBS 4601*.............	**13**	9 wks
24 Dec 77	DESIREE *CBS 5869*................	**39**	6 wks
3 Mar 79	FOREVER IN BLUE JEANS *CBS 7047*	**16**	12 wks
15 Nov 80	LOVE ON THE ROCKS *Capitol CL 16173*	**17**	12 wks
14 Feb 81	HELLO AGAIN *Capitol CL 16176*	**51**	4 wks
20 Nov 82	HEARTLIGHT *CBS A 2814*	**47**	7 wks

See also Barbra and Neil.

Gregg DIAMOND BIONIC BOOGIE   **3 wks**
US, male/female vocal group

20 Jan 79	CREAM (ALWAYS RISES TO THE TOP) *Polydor POSP 18*.............	**61**	3 wks

DIAMOND HEAD *UK, male vocal/instrumental group*   **2 wks**

11 Sep 82	IN THE HEAT OF THE NIGHT *MCA DHM 102*	**67**	2 wks

DIAMONDS *Canada, male vocal group*   **17 wks**

31 May 57 ●	LITTLE DARLIN' *Mercury MT 148*	**3**	17 wks

DICK and DEEDEE *US, male/female vocal duo*   **3 wks**

26 Oct 61	THE MOUNTAIN'S HIGH *London HLG 9408*	**37**	3 wks

Charles DICKENS *UK, male vocalist*   **8 wks**

1 Jul 65	THAT'S THE WAY LOVE GOES *Pye 7N 15887*........	**37**	8 wks

Gwen DICKEY *US, female vocalist*   **2 wks**

27 Jan 90	CAR WASH *Swanyard SYR 7*	**72**	2 wks

Neville DICKIE *UK, male instrumentalist - piano*   **10 wks**

25 Oct 69	ROBIN'S RETURN *Major Minor MM 644*	**33**	7 wks
20 Dec 69	ROBIN'S RETURN (re-entry) *Major Minor MM 644*	**43**	3 wks

DICKIES *US, male vocal/instrumental group*   **28 wks**

16 Dec 78	SILENT NIGHT *A & M AMS 7403*..........	**47**	4 wks
21 Apr 79 ●	BANANA SPLITS (TRA LA LA SONG) *A & M AMS 7431*........	**7**	8 wks
21 Jul 79	PARANOID *A & M AMS 7368*...........	**45**	6 wks
15 Sep 79	NIGHTS IN WHITE SATIN *A & M AMS 7469* ...	**39**	5 wks
16 Feb 80	FAN MAIL *A & M AMS 7504*...........	**57**	3 wks
19 Jul 80	GIGANTOR *A & M AMS 7544*	**72**	2 wks

Bruce DICKINSON *UK, male vocalist*   **12 wks**

28 Apr 90	TATTOED MILLIONAIRE *EMI EM 138*......	**18**	5 wks
23 Jun 90	ALL THE YOUNG DUDES *EMI EM 142* ...	**23**	5 wks
25 Aug 90	DIVE! DIVE! DIVE! *EMI EM 151*.......	**45**	2 wks

Barbara DICKSON *UK, female vocalist*   **33 wks**

17 Jan 76 ●	ANSWER ME *RSO 2090 174*.............	**9**	7 wks
26 Feb 77	ANOTHER SUITCASE IN ANOTHER HALL *MCA 266*........	**18**	7 wks
19 Jan 80	CARAVAN SONG *Epic EPC 8103*........	**41**	7 wks
15 Mar 80	JANUARY FEBRUARY *Epic EPC 8115* ...	**11**	10 wks
14 Jun 80	IN THE NIGHT *Epic EPC 8593*........	**48**	2 wks

See also Elaine Paige and Barbara Dickson.

DICTATORS *US, male vocal/instrumental group*   **2 wks**

17 Sep 77	SEARCH AND DESTROY *Asylum K 13091*	**49**	1 wk
1 Oct 77	SEARCH AND DESTROY (re-entry) *Asylum K 13091*	**50**	1 wk

Bo DIDDLEY *US, male vocalist/instrumentalist - guitar*   **10 wks**

10 Oct 63	PRETTY THING *Pye International 7N 25217*......	**34**	6 wks
18 Mar 65	HEY GOOD LOOKIN' *Chess 8000*..........	**39**	4 wks

DIESEL PARK WEST *UK, male vocal/instrumental group*   **8 wks**

4 Feb 89	ALL THE MYTHS ON SUNDAY *Food FOOD 17*..........	**66**	2 wks
1 Apr 89	LIKE PRINCES DO *Food FOOD 19*	**58**	3 wks
5 Aug 89	WHEN THE HOODOO COMES *Food FOOD 20*	**62**	2 wks
9 Dec 89	INFO FREAKO *Food FOOD 23*.............	**63**	1 wk

Info Freako was one track from the Food Christmas EP. The others were: I Don't Want That Kind Of Love by Jesus Jones and Like Princes Do by Crazyhead. See also Jesus Jones; Crazyhead.

DIFFORD and TILBROOK   **2 wks**
UK, male vocal/instrumental duo

30 Jun 84	LOVE'S CRASHING WAVES *A & M AM 193*.........	**57**	2 wks

Paolo DINI – *See FPI PROJECT*

Mark DINNING *US, male vocalist*   **4 wks**

10 Mar 60	TEEN ANGEL *MGM 1053*.................	**37**	3 wks
7 Apr 60	TEEN ANGEL (re-entry) *MGM 1053*	**42**	1 wk

DINOSAURS – *See Terry DACTYL and the DINOSAURS*

DIO *UK/US, male vocal/instrumental group*   **22 wks**

20 Aug 83	HOLY DIVER *Vertigo DIO 1*.............	**72**	2 wks
29 Oct 83	RAINBOW IN THE DARK *Vertigo DIO 2* ...	**46**	3 wks
11 Aug 84	WE ROCK *Vertigo DIO 3*	**42**	3 wks
29 Sep 84	MYSTERY *Vertigo DIO 4*	**34**	4 wks

10 Aug 85	**ROCK 'N' ROLL CHILDREN** Vertigo DIO 5................	26	6 wks
2 Nov 85	**HUNGRY FOR HEAVEN** Vertigo DIO 6................	72	1 wk
17 May 86	**HUNGRY FOR HEAVEN (re-issue)** Vertigo DIO 7	56	2 wks
1 Aug 87	**I COULD HAVE BEEN A DREAMER** Vertigo DIO 8.........	69	1 wk

DION US, male vocalist   33 wks

19 Jan 61	**LONELY TEENAGER** Top Rank JAR 521....................	47	1 wk
2 Nov 61	**RUNAROUND SUE** Top Rank JAR 586..................	11	9 wks
15 Feb 62 ●	**THE WANDERER** HMV POP 971....................	10	12 wks
22 May 76	**THE WANDERER (re-issue)** Philips 6146 700................	16	9 wks
19 Aug 89	**KING OF THE NEW YORK STREET** Arista 112556	74	2 wks

See also Dion and the Belmonts.

DION and the BELMONTS US, male vocal group   2 wks

| 26 Jun 59 | **A TEENAGER IN LOVE** London HLU 8874.................. | 28 | 2 wks |

See also Dion.

DIONNE Canada, female vocalist   2 wks

| 23 Sep 89 | **COME GET MY LOVIN'** Citybeat CBC 745.................. | 69 | 2 wks |

DIPPY – *See Keith HARRIS and ORVILLE*

DIPSTICKS – *See Laurie LINGO and the DIPSTICKS*

DIRE STRAITS UK, male vocal/instrumental group   107 wks

10 Mar 79 ●	**SULTANS OF SWING** Vertigo 6059 206.....................	8	11 wks
28 Jul 79	**LADY WRITER** Vertigo 6059 230....................	51	6 wks
17 Jan 81 ●	**ROMEO AND JULIET** Vertigo MOVIE 1	8	11 wks
4 Apr 81	**SKATEAWAY** Vertigo MOVIE 2....................	37	5 wks
10 Oct 81	**TUNNEL OF LOVE** Vertigo MUSIC 3	54	3 wks
4 Sep 82 ●	**PRIVATE INVESTIGATIONS** Vertigo DSTR 1.	2	8 wks
22 Jan 83	**TWISTING BY THE POOL** Vertigo DSTR 2	14	7 wks
18 Feb 84	**LOVE OVER GOLD (LIVE)/ SOLID ROCK (LIVE)** Vertigo DSTR A12	50	3 wks
20 Apr 85	**SO FAR AWAY** Vertigo DSTR 9	20	6 wks
6 Jul 85 ●	**MONEY FOR NOTHING** Vertigo DSTR 10	4	16 wks
26 Oct 85	**BROTHERS IN ARMS** Vertigo DSTR 11	16	13 wks
11 Jan 86 ●	**WALK OF LIFE** Vertigo DSTR 12	2	11 wks
3 May 86	**YOUR LATEST TRICK** Vertigo DSTR 13.............	26	6 wks
5 Nov 88	**SULTANS OF SWING (re-issue)** Vertigo DSTR 15........	62	1 wk

DIRECT DRIVE UK, male/female vocal/instrumental group   3 wks

| 26 Jan 85 | **ANYTHING?** Polydor POSP 728............................. | 67 | 2 wks |
| 4 May 85 | **A.B.C. (FALLING IN LOVE'S NOT EASY)** Boiling Point POSP 742 .... | 75 | 1 wk |

DISCHARGE UK, male vocal/instrumental group   3 wks

| 24 Oct 81 | **NEVER AGAIN** Clay CLAY 6.................................. | 64 | 3 wks |

DISCO TEX and the SEX-O-LETTES   22 wks
US, male vocalist/female vocal group

| 23 Nov 74 ● | **GET DANCING** Chelsea 2005 013 .... | 8 | 12 wks |
| 26 Apr 75 ● | **I WANNA DANCE WIT CHOO** Chelsea 2005 024 .... | 6 | 10 wks |

Second hit has credit 'featuring Sir Monti Rock III' - the lead vocalist.

Sacha DISTEL France, male vocalist   27 wks

10 Jan 70	**RAINDROPS KEEP FALLING ON MY HEAD** Warner Bros. WB 7345.	50	1 wk
24 Jan 70 ●	**RAINDROPS KEEP FALLING ON MY HEAD (re-entry)** Warner Bros. WB 7345.	10	20 wks
27 Jun 70	**RAINDROPS KEEP FALLING ON MY HEAD (2nd re-entry)** Warner Bros. WB 7345	43	4 wks
1 Aug 70	**RAINDROPS KEEP FALLING ON MY HEAD (3rd re-entry)** Warner Bros. WB 7345	47	1 wk
15 Aug 70	**RAINDROPS KEEP FALLING ON MY HEAD (4th re-entry)** Warner Bros. WB 7345	44	1 wk

DIVERSIONS UK, male/female vocal/instrumental group   3 wks

| 20 Sep 75 | **FATTIE BUM BUM** Gull GULS 18............................ | 34 | 3 wks |

DIVINE US, male vocalist   24 wks

15 Oct 83	**LOVE REACTION** Design Communications DES 4	65	2 wks
14 Jul 84	**YOU THINK YOU'RE A MAN** Proto ENA 118	16	10 wks
20 Oct 84	**I'M SO BEAUTIFUL** Proto ENA 121................	52	2 wks
27 Apr 85	**WALK LIKE A MAN** Proto ENA 125	23	7 wks
20 Jul 85	**TWISTIN' THE NIGHT AWAY** Proto ENA 127	47	3 wks

DIXIE CUPS US, female vocal group   16 wks

| 18 Jun 64 | **CHAPEL OF LOVE** Pye International 7N 25245 .... | 22 | 8 wks |
| 13 May 65 | **IKO IKO** Red Bird RB 10024................................. | 23 | 8 wks |

DIZZY HEIGHTS UK, male vocal/instrumental group   4 wks

| 18 Dec 82 | **CHRISTMAS RAPPING** Polydor WRAP 1 .... | 49 | 4 wks |

DJ 'Fast' EDDIE US, male producer   11 wks

21 Jan 89	**HIP HOUSE/ I CAN DANCE** DJ International DJIN 5	47	4 wks
11 Mar 89	**YO YO GET FUNKY** DJ International DJIN 7...................	54	3 wks
28 Oct 89	**GIT ON UP** DJ International 655366 7	49	4 wks

Git On Up features Sundance - US, male rapper. See also Kenny 'Jammin" Jason and 'Fast' Eddie Smith.

D.J. E-Z ROCK – *See Rob BASE and D.J. E-Z ROCK*

DJ JAZZY JEFF and FRESH PRINCE   8 wks
US, male vocal/instrumental rap duo

| 4 Oct 86 | **GIRLS AIN'T NOTHING BUT TROUBLE** Champion CHAMP 18 .... | 21 | 8 wks |

DNA UK, male production duo   18 wks

| 28 Jul 90 ● | **TOM'S DINER** A &M AM 592 .... | 2 | 10 wks |
| 18 Aug 90 | **LA SERENISSIMA** Raw Bass RBASS 006..................... | 34† | 8 wks |

Tom's Diner features Suzanne Vega and is a re-mix of her hit on A &M VEGA 2. See also Suzanne Vega.

Carl DOBKINS Jr. US, male vocalist   1 wk

| 31 Mar 60 | **LUCKY DEVIL** Brunswick 05817................................. | 44 | 1 wk |

Anita DOBSON UK, female vocalist   13 wks

9 Aug 86	● ANYONE CAN FALL IN LOVE *BBC RESL 191*	4	9 wks
18 Jul 87	TALKING OF LOVE *Parlophone R 6159*	43	4 wks

First hit features the Simon May Orchestra. See also Simon May Orchestra.

DOCTOR and the MEDICS   25 wks
UK, male/female vocal/instrumental group

10 May 86	★ SPIRIT IN THE SKY *IRS IRM 113*	1	15 wks
9 Aug 86	BURN *IRS IRM 119*	29	6 wks
22 Nov 86	WATERLOO *IRS IRM 125*	45	4 wks

Waterloo features Roy Wood. See also Roy Wood.

DR. FEELGOOD UK, male vocal/instrumental group   29 wks

11 Jun 77	SNEAKIN' SUSPICION *United Artists UP 36255*	47	3 wks
24 Sep 77	SHE'S A WIND UP *United Artists UP 36304*	34	5 wks
30 Sep 78	DOWN AT THE DOCTOR'S *United Artists UP 36444*	48	5 wks
20 Jan 79	● MILK AND ALCOHOL *United Artists UP 36468*	9	9 wks
5 May 79	AS LONG AS THE PRICE IS RIGHT *United Artists YUP 36506*	40	6 wks
8 Dec 79	PUT HIM OUT OF YOUR MIND *United Artists BP 306*	73	1 wk

DR. HOOK US, male vocal/instrumental group   96 wks

24 Jun 72	● SYLVIA'S MOTHER *CBS 7929*	2	13 wks
26 Jun 76	● A LITTLE BIT MORE *Capitol CL 15871*	2	14 wks
30 Oct 76	● IF NOT YOU *Capitol CL 15885*	5	10 wks
25 Mar 78	MORE LIKE THE MOVIES *Capitol CL 15967*	14	10 wks
22 Sep 79	★ WHEN YOU'RE IN LOVE WITH A BEAUTIFUL WOMAN *Capitol CL 16039*	1	17 wks
5 Jan 80	● BETTER LOVE NEXT TIME *Capitol CL 16112*	8	8 wks
29 Mar 80	● SEXY EYES *Capitol CL 16127*	4	9 wks
23 Aug 80	YEARS FROM NOW *Capitol CL 16154*	47	6 wks
8 Nov 80	SHARING THE NIGHT TOGETHER *Capitol CL 16171*	43	4 wks
22 Nov 80	GIRLS CAN GET IT *Mercury MER 51*	40	5 wks

Group billed as Dr. Hook And The Medicine Show on CBS.

Ken DODD UK, male vocalist   233 wks

7 Jul 60	● LOVE IS LIKE A VIOLIN *Decca F 11248*	8	18 wks
15 Jun 61	ONCE IN EVERY LIFETIME *Decca F 11355*	28	7 wks
10 Aug 61	ONCE IN EVERY LIFETIME (re-entry) *Decca F 11355*	47	1 wk
24 Aug 61	ONCE IN EVERY LIFETIME (2nd re-entry) *Decca F 11355*	31	10 wks
1 Feb 62	PIANISSIMO *Decca F 11422*	21	15 wks
29 Aug 63	STILL *Columbia DB 7094*	35	10 wks
6 Feb 64	EIGHT BY TEN *Columbia DB 7191*	22	11 wks
23 Jul 64	HAPPINESS *Columbia DB 7325*	31	13 wks
26 Nov 64	SO DEEP IS THE NIGHT *Columbia DB 7398*	31	7 wks
2 Sep 65	★ TEARS *Columbia DB 7659*	1	24 wks
18 Nov 65	● THE RIVER (LE COLLINE SONO IN FIORO) *Columbia DB 7750*	3	14 wks
12 May 66	● PROMISES *Columbia DB 7914*	6	14 wks
4 Aug 66	MORE THAN LOVE *Columbia DB 7976*	14	11 wks
27 Oct 66	IT'S LOVE *Columbia DB 8031*	36	7 wks
19 Jan 67	LET ME CRY ON YOUR SHOULDER *Columbia DB 8101*	11	10 wks
30 Jul 69	TEARS WON'T WASH AWAY MY HEARTACHE *Columbia DB 8600*	22	11 wks
5 Dec 70	BROKEN HEARTED *Columbia DB 8725*	15	9 wks
13 Feb 71	BROKEN HEARTED (re-entry) *Columbia DB 8725*	38	1 wk
10 Jul 71	WHEN LOVE COMES ROUND AGAIN (L'ARCA DI NOE) *Columbia DB 8796*	19	16 wks
18 Nov 72	JUST OUT OF REACH (OF MY TWO EMPTY ARMS) *Columbia DB 8947*	29	11 wks
29 Nov 75	(THINK OF ME) WHEREVER YOU ARE *EMI 2342*	21	8 wks
26 Dec 81	HOLD MY HAND *Images IMGS 0002*	44	5 wks

Rory DODD – *See Jim STEINMAN*

DOGS D'AMOUR UK, male vocal instrumental group   14 wks

4 Feb 89	HOW COME IT NEVER RAINS *China CHINA 13*	44	3 wks
5 Aug 89	SATELLITE KID *China CHINA 17*	26	3 wks
14 Oct 89	TRAIL OF TEARS *China CHINA 20*	47	3 wks
23 Jun 90	VICTIMS OF SUCCESS *China CHINA 24*	36	3 wks
15 Sep 90	EMPTY WORLD *China CHINA 27*	61	2 wks

Joe DOLAN Ireland, male vocalist   40 wks

25 Jun 69	● MAKE ME AN ISLAND *Pye 7N 17738*	3	18 wks
1 Nov 69	TERESA *Pye 7N 17833*	20	7 wks
8 Nov 69	MAKE ME AN ISLAND (re-entry) *Pye 7N 17738*	48	1 wk
28 Feb 70	YOU'RE SUCH A GOOD LOOKING WOMAN *Pye 7N 17891*	17	13 wks
17 Sep 77	I NEED YOU *Pye 7N 45702*	43	1 wk

Thomas DOLBY UK, male vocalist/multi-instrumentalist   36 wks

3 Oct 81	EUROPA AND THE PIRATE TWINS *Parlophone R 6051*	48	3 wks
14 Aug 82	WINDPOWER *Venice In Peril VIPS 103*	31	8 wks
6 Nov 82	SHE BLINDED ME WITH SCIENCE *Venice In Peril VIPS 104*	49	4 wks
16 Jul 83	SHE BLINDED ME WITH SCIENCE (re-issue) *Venice In Peril VIP 105*	56	4 wks
21 Jan 84	HYPERACTIVE *Parlophone Odeon R 6065*	17	9 wks
31 Mar 84	I SCARE MYSELF *Parlophone Odeon R 6067*	46	5 wks
16 Apr 88	AIRHEAD *Manhattan MT 38*	53	3 wks

Joe DOLCE MUSIC THEATRE US, male vocalist   10 wks

7 Feb 81	★ SHADDAP YOU FACE *Epic EPC 9518*	1	10 wks

DOLL UK, male/female vocal/instrumental group   8 wks

13 Jan 79	DESIRE ME *Beggars Banquet BEG 11*	28	8 wks

DOLLAR UK, male/female vocal duo   128 wks

11 Nov 78	SHOOTING STAR *EMI 2871*	14	12 wks
19 May 79	WHO WERE YOU WITH IN THE MOONLIGHT *Carrere CAR 110*	14	12 wks
18 Aug 79	● LOVE'S GOTTA HOLD ON ME *Carrere CAR 122*	4	13 wks
24 Nov 79	● I WANNA HOLD YOUR HAND *Carrere CAR 131*	9	9 wks
25 Oct 80	TAKIN' A CHANCE ON YOU *WEA K 18353*	62	3 wks
15 Aug 81	HAND HELD IN BLACK AND WHITE *WEA BUCK 1*	19	12 wks
14 Nov 81	● MIRROR MIRROR (MON AMOUR) *WEA BUCK 2*	4	17 wks
20 Mar 82	RING RING *Carrere CAR 225*	61	2 wks
27 Mar 82	● GIVE ME BACK MY HEART *WEA BUCK 3*	4	9 wks
19 Jun 82	VIDEOTHEQUE *WEA BUCK 4*	17	10 wks
18 Sep 82	GIVE ME SOME KINDA MAGIC *WEA BUCK 5*	34	6 wks
16 Aug 86	WE WALKED IN LOVE *Arista DIME 1*	61	4 wks
26 Aug 87	● O L'AMOUR *London LON 146*	7	11 wks
16 Jul 88	IT'S NATURE'S WAY (NO PROBLEM) *London LON 179*	58	3 wks

Placido DOMINGO with John DENVER   9 wks
Spain, male vocalist with US, male vocalist/instrumentalist - guitar

12 Dec 81	PERHAPS LOVE *CBS A 1905*	46	9 wks

See also John Denver; Placido Domingo and Jennifer Rush.

Placido DOMINGO and Jennifer RUSH
Spain/US, male/female vocal duo **9 wks**

27 May 89	TILL I LOVED YOU *CBS 654843 7*	24	9 wks

See also Jennifer Rush; Placido Domingo with John Denver.

Fats DOMINO *US, male vocalist/instrumentalist - piano* **109 wks**

27 Jul 56	I'M IN LOVE AGAIN *London HLU 8280*	28	1 wk
17 Aug 56	I'M IN LOVE AGAIN (re-entry) *London HLU 8280*	12	13 wks
30 Nov 56	BLUEBERRY HILL *London HLU 8330*	26	1 wk
21 Dec 56 ●	BLUEBERRY HILL (re-entry) *London HLU 8330*	6	14 wks
25 Jan 57	AIN'T THAT A SHAME *London HLU 8173*	23	2 wks
1 Feb 57	HONEY CHILE *London HLU 8356*	29	1 wk
29 Mar 57	BLUE MONDAY *London HLP 8377*	23	1 wk
19 Apr 57	BLUE MONDAY (re-entry) *London HLP 8377*	30	1 wk
19 Apr 57	I'M WALKIN' *London HLP 8407*	19	7 wks
19 Jul 57	VALLEY OF TEARS *London HLP 8449*	25	1 wk
28 Mar 58	THE BIG BEAT *London HLP 8575*	20	4 wks
4 Jul 58	SICK AND TIRED *London HLP 8628*	26	1 wk
22 May 59	MARGIE *London HLP 8865*	18	5 wks
16 Oct 59	I WANT TO WALK YOU HOME *London HLP 8942*	14	5 wks
18 Dec 59	BE MY GUEST *London HLP 9005*	11	8 wks
19 Feb 60	BE MY GUEST (re-entry) *London HLP 9005*	19	3 wks
17 Mar 60	COUNTRY BOY *London HLP 9073*	19	11 wks
21 Jul 60	WALKING TO NEW ORLEANS *London HLP 9163*	19	10 wks
10 Nov 60	THREE NIGHTS A WEEK *London HLP 9198*	45	2 wks
5 Jan 61	MY GIRL JOSEPHINE *London HLP 9244*	32	4 wks
27 Jul 61	IT KEEPS RAININ' *London HLP 9374*	49	1 wk
30 Nov 61	WHAT A PARTY *London HLP 9456*	43	1 wk
29 Mar 62	JAMBALAYA *London HLP 9520*	41	1 wk
31 Oct 63	RED SAILS IN THE SUNSET *HMV POP 1219*	34	6 wks
24 Apr 76	BLUEBERRY HILL (re-issue) *United Artists UP 35797*	41	5 wks

DOMINOS – *See DEREK and the DOMINOS*

Don PABLO'S ANIMALS *Italy, male instrumental group* **10 wks**

19 May 90 ●	VENUS *Rumour RUMA*	4	10 wks

Lonnie DONEGAN *UK, male vocalist* **321 wks**

6 Jan 56 ●	ROCK ISLAND LINE *Decca F 10647*	8	13 wks
13 Apr 56	ROCK ISLAND LINE (re-entry) *Decca F 10647*	16	3 wks
20 Apr 56	STEWBALL *Pye Nixa N 15036*	27	1 wk
27 Apr 56 ●	LOST JOHN/ STEWBALL *Pye Nixa N 15036*	2	17 wks
11 May 56	ROCK ISLAND LINE (2nd re-entry) *Decca F 10647*	19	6 wks
6 Jul 56	SKIFFLE SESSION (EP) *Pye Nixa NJE 1017*	20	2 wks
7 Sep 56 ●	BRING A LITTLE WATER SYLVIE/ DEAD OR ALIVE *Pye Nixa N 15071*	7	12 wks
21 Dec 56	LONNIE DONEGAN SHOWCASE (LP) *Pye Nixa NPT 19012*	26	3 wks
11 Jan 57	BRING A LITTLE WATER SYLVIE/ DEAD OR ALIVE (re-entry) *Pye Nixa N 15071*	30	1 wk
18 Jan 57	DON'T YOU ROCK ME DADDY-O *Pye Nixa N 15080*	4	17 wks
5 Apr 57 ★	CUMBERLAND GAP *Pye Nixa B 15087*	1	12 wks
7 Jun 57 ★	GAMBLIN' MAN/ PUTTING ON THE STYLE *Pye Nixa N 15093*	1	19 wks
11 Oct 57	MY DIXIE DARLING *Pye Nixa N 15108*	10	15 wks
20 Dec 57	JACK O' DIAMONDS *Pye Nixa N 15116*	14	7 wks
11 Apr 58 ●	GRAND COOLIE DAM *Pye Nixa N 15129*	6	15 wks
11 Jul 58	SALLY DON'T YOU GRIEVE/ BETTY BETTY BETTY *Pye Nixa N 15148*	11	7 wks
26 Sep 58	LONESOME TRAVELLER *Pye Nixa N 15158*	28	1 wk
14 Nov 58	LONNIE'S SKIFFLE PARTY *Pye Nixa N 15165*	23	5 wks
21 Nov 58 ●	TOM DOOLEY *Pye Nixa 7N 15172*	3	14 wks
6 Feb 59 ●	DOES YOUR CHEWING GUM LOSE ITS FLAVOUR *Pye Nixa 7N 15181*	3	12 wks
8 May 59	FORT WORTH JAIL *Pye Nixa 7N 15198*	14	5 wks
26 Jun 59 ●	BATTLE OF NEW ORLEANS *Pye 7N 15206*	2	16 wks
11 Sep 59	SAL'S GOT A SUGAR LIP *Pye 7N 15223*	13	4 wks
4 Dec 59	SAN MIGUEL *Pye 7N 15237*	19	4 wks
24 Mar 60 ★	MY OLD MAN'S A DUSTMAN *Pye 7N 15256*	1	13 wks

26 May 60 ●	I WANNA GO HOME *Pye 7N 15267*	5	17 wks
25 Aug 60 ●	LORELEI *Pye 7N 15275*	10	8 wks
24 Nov 60	LIVELY *Pye 7N 15312*	13	6 wks
8 Dec 60	VIRGIN MARY *Pye 7N 15315*	27	5 wks
11 May 61 ●	HAVE A DRINK ON ME *Pye 7N 15354*	8	15 wks
31 Aug 61 ●	MICHAEL ROW THE BOAT/ LUMBERED *Pye 7N 15371*	6	11 wks
18 Jan 62	THE COMANCHEROS *Pye 7N 15410*	14	10 wks
5 Apr 62 ●	THE PARTY'S OVER *Pye 7N 15424*	9	12 wks
16 Aug 62	PICK A BALE OF COTTON *Pye 7N 15455*	11	10 wks

Stewball had one week on the chart by itself on 20 Apr 56. Lost John, the other side, replaced it on 27 Apr 56 but Stewball was given co-billing with Lost John for the weeks of 11, 18 and 25 May 56 only during Lost John's 17-week run. Dead Or Alive was not listed for the week 7 Sep 56 with Bring A Little Water Sylvie. Putting On The Style was not listed for the weeks of 7 and 14 Jun 56 with Gamblin' Man. Tracks on Skiffle Session EP: Railroad Bill/Stockalee/Ballad of Jesse James/Ol' Riley. Tracks on Lonnie Donegan Showcase LP: Wabash Cannonball/How Long How Long Blues/Nobody's Child/I Shall Not Be Moved/I'm Alabammy Bound/I'm A Rambling Man/Wreck Of The Old '97/Frankie And Johnny. Lonnie's Skiffle Party was a medley as follows: Little Liza Jane/Putting On The Style/Camptown Races/Knees Up Mother Brown/So Long/On Top Of Old Smokey/Down In The Valley/So Long. Yes, there are two versions of So Long on this disc.

DONNA – *See ALTHIA and DONNA*

Ral DONNER *US, male vocalist* **10 wks**

21 Sep 61	YOU DON'T KNOW WHAT YOU'VE GOT *Parlophone R 4820*	25	10 wks

DONOVAN *UK, male vocalist* **90 wks**

25 Mar 65 ●	CATCH THE WIND *Pye 7N 15801*	4	13 wks
3 Jun 65 ●	COLOURS *Pye 7N 15866*	4	12 wks
11 Nov 65	TURQUOISE *Pye 7N 15984*	30	6 wks
8 Dec 66 ●	SUNSHINE SUPERMAN *Pye 7N 17241*	2	11 wks
9 Feb 67 ●	MELLOW YELLOW *Pye 7N 17267*	8	8 wks
25 Oct 67 ●	THERE IS A MOUNTAIN *Pye 7N 17403*	8	11 wks
21 Feb 68 ●	JENNIFER JUNIPER *Pye 7N 17457*	5	11 wks
29 May 68 ●	HURDY GURDY MAN *Pye 7N 17537*	4	10 wks
4 Dec 68	ATLANTIS *Pye 7N 17660*	23	8 wks

See also Donovan with the Jeff Beck Group; Singing Corner Meets Donovan.

DONOVAN with the Jeff BECK GROUP **9 wks**
UK, male vocalist/instrumental group

9 Jul 69	GOO GOO BARABAJAGAL (LOVE IS HOT) *Pye 7N 17778*	12	9 wks

See also Donovan; Jeff Beck.

Jason DONOVAN *Australia, male vocalist* **79 wks**

10 Sep 88 ●	NOTHING CAN DIVIDE US *PWL PWL 17*	5	12 wks
4 Mar 89 ★	TOO MANY BROKEN HEARTS *PWL PWL 32*	1	13 wks
10 Jun 89 ●	SEALED WITH A KISS *PWL PWL 39*	1	10 wks
9 Sep 89 ●	EVERY DAY (I LOVE YOU MORE) *PWL PWL 43*	2	9 wks
9 Dec 89 ●	WHEN YOU COME BACK TO ME *PWL PWL 46*	2	11 wks
7 Apr 90 ●	HANG ON TO YOUR LOVE *PWL PWL 51*	8	7 wks
30 Jun 90	ANOTHER NIGHT *PWL PWL 58*	18	5 wks
1 Sep 90 ●	RHYTHM OF THE RAIN *PWL PWL 60*	9	6 wks
27 Oct 90	I'M DOING FINE *PWL PWL 69*	22	6 wks

See also Kylie Minogue and Jason Donovan.

DOOBIE BROTHERS *US, male vocal/instrumental group* **32 wks**

9 Mar 74	LISTEN TO THE MUSIC *Warner Bros. K 16208*	29	7 wks
7 Jun 75	TAKE ME IN YOUR ARMS *Warner Bros. K 16559*	29	5 wks
17 Feb 79	WHAT A FOOL BELIEVES *Warner Bros. K 17314*	31	10 wks
5 May 79	WHAT A FOOL BELIEVES (re-entry) *Warner Bros. K 17314*	72	1 wk
14 Jul 79	MINUTE BY MINUTE *Warner Bros. K 17411*	47	4 wks

24 Jan 87	**WHAT A FOOL BELIEVES (re-issue)**		
	Warner Bros. W 8451	**57**	3 wks
29 Jul 89	**THE DOCTOR** *Capitol CL 536*	**73**	2 wks

The re-issue of What A Fool Believes *has credit 'featuring Michael McDonald'. See also Michael McDonald.*

DOOLEYS *UK, male/female vocal/instrumental group*   **83 wks**

13 Aug 77	**THINK I'M GONNA FALL IN LOVE WITH YOU**		
	GTO GT 95	**13**	10 wks
12 Nov 77	● **LOVE OF MY LIFE** *GTO GT 110*	**9**	11 wks
13 May 78	**DON'T TAKE IT LYIN' DOWN** *GTO GT 220*	**60**	3 wks
2 Sep 78	**A ROSE HAS TO DIE** *GTO GT 229*	**11**	11 wks
10 Feb 79	**HONEY I'M LOST** *GTO GT 242*	**24**	9 wks
16 Jun 79	● **WANTED** *GTO GT 249*	**3**	14 wks
22 Sep 79	● **THE CHOSEN FEW** *GTO GT 258*	**7**	11 wks
8 Mar 80	**LOVE PATROL** *GTO GT 260*	**29**	7 wks
6 Sep 80	**BODY LANGUAGE** *GTO GT 276*	**46**	4 wks
10 Oct 81	**AND I WISH** *GTO GT 300*	**52**	3 wks

Val DOONICAN *Ireland, male vocalist*   **143 wks**

15 Oct 64	● **WALK TALL** *Decca F 11982*	**3**	21 wks
21 Jan 65	● **THE SPECIAL YEARS** *Decca F 12049*	**7**	12 wks
8 Apr 65	**I'M GONNA GET THERE SOMEHOW** *Decca F 12118*	**25**	5 wks
22 Apr 65	**THE SPECIAL YEARS (re-entry)** *Decca F 12049*	**49**	1 wk
17 Mar 66	● **ELUSIVE BUTTERFLY** *Decca F 12358*	**5**	12 wks
3 Nov 66	● **WHAT WOULD I BE** *Decca F 12505*	**2**	17 wks
23 Feb 67	**MEMORIES ARE MADE OF THIS** *Decca F 12566*	**11**	12 wks
25 May 67	**TWO STREETS** *Decca F 12608*	**39**	4 wks
18 Oct 67	● **IF THE WHOLE WORLD STOPPED LOVING**		
	Pye 7N 17396	**3**	19 wks
21 Feb 68	**YOU'RE THE ONLY ONE** *Pye 7N 17465*	**37**	4 wks
12 Jun 68	**NOW** *Pye 7N 17534*	**43**	2 wks
23 Oct 68	**IF I KNEW THEN WHAT I KNOW NOW**		
	Pye 7N 17616	**14**	13 wks
23 Apr 69	**RING OF BRIGHT WATER** *Pye 7N 17713*	**48**	1 wk
4 Dec 71	**MORNING** *Philips 6006 177*	**12**	13 wks
10 Mar 73	**HEAVEN IS MY WOMAN'S LOVE** *Philips 6028 031*	**34**	6 wks
28 Apr 73	**HEAVEN IS MY WOMAN'S LOVE (re-entry)**		
	Philips 6028 031	**47**	1 wk

DOORS *US, male vocal/instrumental group*   **31 wks**

16 Aug 67	**LIGHT MY FIRE** *Elektra EKSN 45014*	**49**	1 wk
28 Aug 68	**HELLO I LOVE YOU** *Elektra EKSN 45037*	**15**	12 wks
16 Oct 71	**RIDERS ON THE STORM** *Elektra K 12021*	**50**	1 wk
30 Oct 71	**RIDERS ON THE STORM (re-entry)** *Elektra K 12021*	**22**	10 wks
20 Mar 76	**RIDERS ON THE STORM (re-issue)** *Elektra K 12203*	**33**	5 wks
3 Feb 79	**HELLO I LOVE YOU (re-issue)** *Elektra K 12215*	**71**	2 wks

Charlie DORE *UK, female vocalist*   **2 wks**

17 Nov 79	**PILOT OF THE AIRWAVES** *Island WIP 6526*	**66**	2 wks

Lee DORSEY *US, male vocalist*   **36 wks**

3 Feb 66	**GET OUT OF MY LIFE WOMAN** *Stateside SS 485*	**22**	7 wks
5 May 66	**CONFUSION** *Stateside SS 506*	**38**	6 wks
11 Aug 66	● **WORKING IN THE COALMINE** *Stateside SS 528*	**8**	11 wks
27 Oct 66	● **HOLY COW** *Stateside SS 552*	**6**	12 wks

Tommy DORSEY ORCHESTRA starring Warren COVINGTON   **19 wks**

US, orchestra, Warren Covington, male leader

17 Oct 58	● **TEA FOR TWO CHA CHA** *Brunswick 05757*	**3**	19 wks

DOUBLE *Switzerland, male vocal/instrumental duo*   **10 wks**

25 Jan 86	● **THE CAPTAIN OF HER HEART** *Polydor POSP 779*	**8**	9 wks
5 Dec 87	**DEVIL'S BALL** *Polydor POSP 888*	**71**	1 wk

DOUBLE DEE featuring DANY   **2 wks**

US, male vocal/instrumental group

1 Dec 90	**FOUND LOVE** *Epic 6563766*	**63**	2 wks

DOUBLE TROUBLE   **7 wks**

UK, male instrumental/production duo

12 May 90	**TALK BACK** *Desire WANT 27*	**71**	1 wk
30 Jun 90	**LOVE DON'T LIVE HERE ANYMORE**		
	Desire WANT 32	**21**	6 wks

Both hits feature Janette Sewell - UK, female vocalist. Second hit also features Carl Brown - UK, male rapper. See also Double Trouble and the Rebel M.C.

DOUBLE TROUBLE and the REBEL M.C.   **26 wks**

UK, male vocal/instrumental group

27 May 89	**JUST KEEP ROCKIN'** *Desire WANT 9*	**11**	12 wks
7 Oct 89	● **STREET TUFF** *Desire WANT 18*	**3**	14 wks

Second hit bills act in reverse order. See also Double Trouble; Rebel M.C.; Various Artists - The Brits 1990.

Carl DOUGLAS *Jamaica, male vocalist*   **28 wks**

17 Aug 74	★ **KUNG FU FIGHTING** *Pye 7N 45377*	**1**	13 wks
30 Nov 74	**DANCE THE KUNG FU** *Pye 7N 45418*	**35**	5 wks
3 Dec 77	**RUN BACK** *Pye 7N 46018*	**25**	10 wks

Carol DOUGLAS *US, female vocalist*   **4 wks**

22 Jul 78	**NIGHT FEVER** *Gull GULS 61*	**66**	4 wks

Craig DOUGLAS *UK, male vocalist*   **112 wks**

12 Jun 59	**A TEENAGER IN LOVE** *Top Rank JAR 133*	**13**	11 wks
7 Aug 59	★ **ONLY SIXTEEN** *Top Rank JAR 159*	**1**	15 wks
22 Jan 60	● **PRETTY BLUE EYES** *Top Rank JAR 268*	**4**	14 wks
28 Apr 60	● **THE HEART OF A TEENAGE GIRL** *Top Rank JAR 340*	**10**	9 wks
11 Aug 60	**OH! WHAT A DAY** *Top Rank JAR 406*	**43**	1 wk
20 Apr 61	● **A HUNDRED POUNDS OF CLAY** *Top Rank JAR 555*	**9**	9 wks
29 Jun 61	● **TIME** *Top Rank JAR 569*	**9**	14 wks
22 Mar 62	● **WHEN MY LITTLE GIRL IS SMILING**		
	Top Rank JAR 610	**9**	13 wks
28 Jun 62	● **OUR FAVOURITE MELODIES** *Columbia DB 4854*	**9**	10 wks
18 Oct 62	**OH LONESOME ME** *Decca F 11523*	**15**	12 wks
28 Feb 63	**TOWN CRIER** *Decca F 11575*	**36**	4 wks

DOWLANDS *UK, male vocal duo*   **7 wks**

9 Jan 64	**ALL MY LOVING** *Oriole CB 1897*	**33**	7 wks

Don DOWNING *US, male vocalist*   **10 wks**

10 Nov 73	**LONELY DAYS, LONELY NIGHTS** *People PEO 102*	**32**	10 wks

Will DOWNING US, male vocalist — 27 wks

2 Apr 88	A LOVE SUPREME Fourth & Broadway BRW 90	14	10 wks
25 Jun 88	IN MY DREAMS Fourth & Broadway BRW 104	34	6 wks
1 Oct 88	FREE Fourth & Broadway BRW 112	58	5 wks
28 Oct 89	TEST OF TIME Fourth & Broadway BRW 146	67	2 wks
24 Feb 90	COME TOGETHER AS ONE Fourth & Broadway BRW 159	48	4 wks

See also Mica Paris and Will Downing.

Lamont DOZIER – *See HOLLAND-DOZIER*

DOZY – *See Dave DEE, DOZY, BEAKY, MICK and TICH*

Charlie DRAKE UK, male vocalist — 37 wks

8 Aug 58	● SPLISH SPLASH Parlophone R 4461	7	11 wks
24 Oct 58	VOLARE Parlophone R 4478	28	2 wks
27 Oct 60	MR. CUSTER Parlophone R 4701	12	12 wks
5 Oct 61	MY BOOMERANG WON'T COME BACK Parlophone R 4824	14	11 wks
1 Jan 72	PUCKWUDGIE Columbia DB 8829	47	1 wk

DRAMATIS UK, male vocal/instrumental group — 1 wk

13 Nov 82	I CAN SEE HER NOW Rocket XPRES 83	57	1 wk

See also Gary Numan.

Rusty DRAPER US, male vocalist — 4 wks

11 Aug 60	MULE SKINNER BLUES Mercury AMT 1101	39	4 wks

DREAD ZEPPELIN US, male vocal/instrumental group — 1 wk

1 Dec 90	YOUR TIME IS GONNA COME IRS DREAD 1	59	1 wk

DREAM ACADEMY
UK, male/female vocal/instrumental group — 10 wks

30 Mar 85	LIFE IN A NORTHERN TOWN blanco y negro NEG 10	15	8 wks
14 Sep 85	THE LOVE PARADE blanco y negro NEG 16	68	2 wks

DREAM WARRIORS Canada, male rap group — 14 wks

14 Jul 90	WASH YOUR FACE IN MY SINK Fourth & Broadway BRW 183	16	8 wks
24 Nov 90	MY DEFINITION OF A BOOMBASTIC JAZZ STYLE Fourth & Broadway BRW 197	13†	6 wks

DREAMERS – *See FREDDIE and the DREAMERS*

DREAMWEAVERS US, male/female vocal group — 18 wks

10 Feb 56	★ IT'S ALMOST TOMORROW Brunswick 05515	1	18 wks

DRELLS – *See Archie BELL and the DRELLS*

Eddie DRENNON and B.B.S. UNLIMITED — 6 wks
US, male vocal/instrumental group

28 Feb 76	LET'S DO THE LATIN HUSTLE Pyr International 7N 25702	20	6 wks

Alan DREW UK, male vocalist — 2 wks

26 Sep 63	ALWAYS THE LONELY ONE Columbia DB 7090	48	2 wks

DRIFTERS US, male vocal group — 176 wks

8 Jan 60	DANCE WITH ME London HLE 8988	17	4 wks
10 Mar 60	DANCE WITH ME (re-entry) London HLE 8988	35	1 wk
3 Nov 60	● SAVE THE LAST DANCE FOR ME London HLK 9201	2	18 wks
16 Mar 61	I COUNT THE TEARS London HLK 9287	28	6 wks
5 Apr 62	WHEN MY LITTLE GIRL IS SMILING London HLK 9522	31	3 wks
10 Oct 63	I'LL TAKE YOU HOME London HLK 9785	37	5 wks
24 Sep 64	UNDER THE BOARDWALK Atlantic AT 4001	45	4 wks
8 Apr 65	AT THE CLUB Atlantic AT 4019	35	7 wks
29 Apr 65	COME ON OVER TO MY PLACE Atlantic AT 4023	40	5 wks
2 Feb 67	BABY WHAT I MEAN Atlantic 584 065	49	1 wk
25 Mar 72	AT THE CLUB (re-issue) Atlantic K 10148	39	1 wk
8 Apr 72	● AT THE CLUB/ SATURDAY NIGHT AT THE MOVIES (re-entry of re-issue) Atlantic K 10148	3	19 wks
26 Aug 72	● COME ON OVER TO MY PLACE (re-issue) Atlantic K 10216	9	11 wks
4 Aug 73	● LIKE SISTER AND BROTHER Bell 1313	7	12 wks
15 Jun 74	● KISSIN' IN THE BACK ROW OF THE MOVIES Bell 1358	2	13 wks
12 Oct 74	● DOWN ON THE BEACH TONIGHT Bell 1381	7	9 wks
8 Feb 75	LOVE GAMES Bell 1396	33	6 wks
6 Sep 75	● THERE GOES MY FIRST LOVE Bell 1433	3	12 wks
29 Nov 75	● CAN I TAKE YOU HOME LITTLE GIRL Bell 1462	10	10 wks
13 Mar 76	HELLO HAPPINESS Bell 1469	12	8 wks
11 Sep 76	EVERY NITE'S A SATURDAY NIGHT WITH YOU Bell 1491	29	7 wks
18 Dec 76	● YOU'RE MORE THAN A NUMBER IN MY LITTLE RED BOOK Arista 78	5	12 wks
14 Apr 79	SAVE THE LAST DANCE FOR ME/ WHEN MY LITTLE GIRL IS SMILING (re-issue) Lightning LIG 9014	69	2 wks

Saturday Night At The Movies only received chart credit with At The Club after the re-issue's return to the chart on 8 Apr 72.

Julie DRISCOLL, Brian AUGER and the TRINITY UK, female vocalist/male instrumental group — 16 wks

17 Apr 68	● THIS WHEEL'S ON FIRE Marmalade 598 006	5	16 wks

DRIVER 67 UK, male vocalist — 12 wks

23 Dec 78	● CAR 67 Logo GO 336	7	12 wks

Driver 67 is Paul Phillips.

Frank D'RONE US, male vocalist — 6 wks

22 Dec 60	STRAWBERRY BLONDE Mercury AMT 1123	24	6 wks

DRUM THEATRE UK, male vocal/instrumental group — 8 wks

15 Feb 86	LIVING IN THE PAST Epic A 6798	67	2 wks
17 Jan 87	ELDORADO Epic EMU 1	44	6 wks

DRUPI Italy, male vocalist — 12 wks

1 Dec 73	VADO VIA A & M AMS 7083	17	12 wks

D-SHAKE Holland, male production duo — 6 wks

2 Jun 90	YAAAH/ TECHNO TRANCE Cooltempo COOL 213	20	6 wks

D.S.M. US, male rap group · 4 wks

7 Dec 85	WARRIOR GROOVE 10 DAZZ 45-7 68	4 wks

D T I US, male vocal/instrumental group · 1 wk

16 Apr 88	KEEP THIS FREQUENCY CLEAR/ KEEP IT CLEAR *Premiere UK GRE 501* 73	1 wk

John DU CANN UK, male vocalist · 6 wks

22 Sep 79	DON'T BE A DUMMY *Vertigo 6059 241* 33	6 wks

John DU PREZ – *See MODERN ROMANCE*

DUBLINERS Ireland, male vocal/instrumental group · 35 wks

30 Mar 67	● SEVEN DRUNKEN NIGHTS *Major Minor MM 506* 7	17 wks
30 Aug 67	BLACK VELVET BAND *Major Minor MM 530* 15	15 wks
20 Dec 67	NEVER WED AN OLD MAN *Major Minor MM 551* 43	3 wks

See also Pogues and the Dubliners.

DUFFO Australia, male vocalist · 2 wks

24 Mar 79	GIVE ME BACK ME BRAIN *Beggars Banquet BEG 15* 60	2 wks

Stephen 'Tin Tin' DUFFY UK, male vocalist · 24 wks

9 Jul 83	HOLD IT *Curve X 9763* 55	4 wks
2 Mar 85	● KISS ME *10 TIN 2* 4	11 wks
18 May 85	ICING ON THE CAKE *10 TIN 3* 14	9 wks

First hit credited to Tin Tin.

George DUKE US, male vocalist/instrumentalist · 6 wks

12 Jul 80	BRAZILIAN LOVE AFFAIR *Epic EPC 8751* 36	6 wks

DUKES UK, male vocal duo · 13 wks

17 Oct 81	MYSTERY GIRL *WEA K 18867* 47	7 wks
1 May 82	THANK YOU FOR THE PARTY *WEA K 19136* 53	6 wks

Candy DULFER Holland, female instrumentalist · 2 wks

4 Aug 90	SAXUALITY *RCA PB 43769* 60	2 wks

See also David A. Stewart.

Thuli DUMAKUDE South Africa, male vocalist · 1 wk

2 Jan 88	THE FUNERAL (SEPTEMBER 25, 1977) *MCA MCA 1228* 75	1 wk

The listed flip side of The Funeral was Cry Freedom by George Fenton and Jonas Gwangwa. See also George Fenton and Jonas Gwangwa.

John DUMMER and Helen APRIL · 3 wks
UK, male/female vocal duo

28 Aug 82	BLUE SKIES *Speed SPEED 8* 54	3 wks

Johnny DUNCAN and the BLUE GRASS BOYS US, male vocal/instrumental group · 20 wks

26 Jul 57	● LAST TRAIN TO SAN FERNANDO *Columbia DB 3959*...... 2	17 wks
25 Oct 57	BLUE BLUE HEARTACHES *Columbia DB 3996* 27	1 wk
29 Nov 57	FOOTPRINTS IN THE SNOW *Columbia DB 4029* 27	1 wk
3 Jan 58	FOOTPRINTS IN THE SNOW (re-entry) *Columbia DB 4029* 28	1 wk

David DUNDAS UK, male vocalist · 14 wks

24 Jul 76	● JEANS ON *Air CHS 2094*.................................. 3	9 wks
9 Apr 77	ANOTHER FUNNY HONEYMOON *Air CHS 2136*........ 29	5 wks

Erroll DUNKLEY Jamaica, male vocalist · 14 wks

22 Sep 79	O.K. FRED *Scope SC 6* 11	11 wks
2 Feb 80	SIT DOWN AND CRY *Scope SC 11*........................ 52	3 wks

Clive DUNN UK, male vocalist · 28 wks

28 Nov 70	★ GRANDAD *Columbia DB 8726*............................ 1	27 wks
26 Jun 71	GRANDAD (re-entry) *Columbia D8 8726* 50	1 wk

Simon DUPREE and the BIG SOUND · 16 wks
UK, male vocal/instrumental group

22 Nov 67	● KITES *Parlophone R 5646*................................. 9	13 wks
3 Apr 68	FOR WHOM THE BELL TOLLS *Parlophone R 5670*.......... 43	3 wks

DURAN DURAN UK, male vocal/instrumental group · 187 wks

21 Feb 81	PLANET EARTH *EMI 5137* 12	11 wks
9 May 81	CARELESS MEMORIES *EMI 5168*.......................... 37	7 wks
25 Jul 81	● GIRLS ON FILM *EMI 5206* 5	11 wks
28 Nov 81	MY OWN WAY *EMI 5254* 14	11 wks
15 May 82	● HUNGRY LIKE THE WOLF *EMI 5295*..................... 5	12 wks
21 Aug 82	● SAVE A PRAYER *EMI 5327* 2	9 wks
13 Nov 82	● RIO *EMI 5346* 9	11 wks
26 Mar 83	★ IS THERE SOMETHING I SHOULD KNOW *EMI 5371* 1	9 wks
29 Oct 83	● UNION OF THE SNAKE *EMI 5429* 3	7 wks
24 Dec 83	UNION OF THE SNAKE (re-entry) *EMI 5429* 66	4 wks
4 Feb 84	● NEW MOON ON MONDAY *EMI DURAN 1* 9	7 wks
28 Apr 84	★ THE REFLEX *EMI DURAN 2* 1	14 wks
3 Nov 84	● WILD BOYS *Parlophone DURAN 3*........................ 2	14 wks
18 May 85	● A VIEW TO A KILL *Parlophone DURAN 007* 2	16 wks
1 Nov 86	● NOTORIOUS *EMI DDN 45* 7	6 wks
3 Jan 87	NOTORIOUS (re-entry) *EMI DDN 5.* 73	1 wk
21 Feb 87	SKIN TRADE *EMI TRADE 1* 22	6 wks
25 Apr 87	MEET EL PRESIDENTE *EMI TOUR 1.* 24	5 wks
1 Oct 88	I DON'T WANT YOUR LOVE *EMI YOUR 1* 14	5 wks
7 Jan 89	● ALL SHE WANTS IS *EMI DD 11.* 9	5 wks
22 Apr 89	DO YOU BELIEVE IN SHAME *EMI DD 12* 30	4 wks
16 Dec 89	BURNING THE GROUND *EMI DD 13.* 31	5 wks
4 Aug 90	VIOLENCE OF SUMMER (LOVE'S TAKING OVER) *Parlophone DD 14* 20	4 wks
17 Nov 90	SERIOUS *Parlophone DD 15* 48	3 wks

Judith DURHAM Australia, female vocalist · 5 wks

15 Jun 67	OLIVE TREE *Columbia DB 8207* 33	5 wks

Ian DURY and the BLOCKHEADS · 54 wks
UK, male vocal/instrumental group

29 Apr 78	● WHAT A WASTE *Stiff BUY 27* 9	12 wks
9 Dec 78	★ HIT ME WITH YOUR RHYTHM STICK *Stiff BUY 38*....... 1	15 wks

4 Aug 79 ●	REASONS TO BE CHEERFUL (PT.3) *Stiff BUY 50*		3	8 wks
30 Aug 80	I WANT TO BE STRAIGHT *Stiff BUY 90*		22	7 wks
15 Nov 80	SUEEPERMAN'S BIG SISTER *Stiff BUY 100*		51	3 wks
25 May 85	HIT ME WITH YOUR RHYTHM STICK (re-mix) *Stiff BUY 214*		55	4 wks
26 Oct 85	PROFOUNDLY IN LOVE WITH PANDORA *EMI EMI 5534*		45	5 wks

Stiff BUY 38 credits Ian and the Blockheads. EMI 5534 only bills Ian Dury.

Slim DUSTY *Australia, male vocalist*   **15 wks**

30 Jan 59 ●	A PUB WITH NO BEER *Columbia DB 4212*		3	15 wks

DYKE – *See ASHTON, GARDNER and DYKE*

Bob DYLAN *US, male vocalist*   **133 wks**

25 Mar 65 ●	TIMES THEY ARE A-CHANGIN' *CBS 201751*		9	11 wks
29 Apr 65 ●	SUBTERRANEAN HOMESICK BLUES *CBS 201753*		9	9 wks
17 Jun 65	MAGGIE'S FARM *CBS 201781*		22	8 wks
19 Aug 65 ●	LIKE A ROLLING STONE *CBS 201811*		4	12 wks
28 Oct 65 ●	POSITIVELY FOURTH STREET *CBS 201824*		8	12 wks
27 Jan 66	CAN YOU PLEASE CRAWL OUT YOUR WINDOW *CBS 201900*		17	5 wks
14 Apr 66	ONE OF US MUST KNOW (SOONER OR LATER) *CBS 202053*		33	5 wks
12 May 66 ●	RAINY DAY WOMEN NOS. 12 & 35 *CBS 202307*		7	8 wks
21 Jul 66	I WANT YOU *CBS 202258*		16	9 wks
14 May 69	I THREW IT ALL AWAY *CBS 4219*		30	6 wks
13 Sep 69 ●	LAY LADY LAY *CBS 4434*		5	12 wks
10 Jul 71	WATCHING THE RIVER FLOW *CBS 7329*		24	9 wks
6 Oct 73	KNOCKIN' ON HEAVEN'S DOOR *CBS 1762*		14	9 wks
7 Feb 76	HURRICANE *CBS 3878*		43	4 wks
29 Jul 78	BABY STOP CRYING *CBS 6499*		13	11 wks
28 Oct 78	IS YOUR LOVE IN VAIN *CBS 6718*		56	3 wks

DYNAMIX II featuring TOO TOUGH TEE   **4 wks**
US, male vocal/instrumental group

8 Aug 87	JUST GIVE THE DJ A BREAK *Cooltempo COOL 151*		50	4 wks

DYNASTY *US, male vocal/instrumental group*   **20 wks**

13 Oct 79	I DON'T WANT TO BE A FREAK (BUT I CAN'T HELP MYSELF) *Solar FB 1694*		20	13 wks
9 Aug 80	I'VE JUST BEGUN TO LOVE YOU *Solar SO 10*		51	4 wks
21 May 83	DOES THAT RING A BELL *Solar E 9911*		53	3 wks

DYNASTY OF TWO featuring ROWETTA   **2 wks**
UK, male/female vocal/instrumental group

20 Jan 90	STOP THIS THING *deConstruction PT 43372*		64	2 wks

Stop This Thing was one track from the Further Adventures Of North EP. The others were Carino 90 by T-Coy, Dream 17 by Annette and The Way I Feel by Frequency 9. See also T-Coy; Annette; Frequency 9.

Ronnie DYSON *US, male vocalist*   **6 wks**

4 Dec 71	WHEN YOU GET RIGHT DOWN TO IT *CBS 7449*		34	6 wks

E

Liz E – *See FRESH 4 featuring LIZZ E*

Sheila E *US, female vocalist/instrumentalist – percussion*   **9 wks**

23 Feb 85	THE BELLE OF ST MARK *Warner Bros. W 9180*		18	9 wks

EAGLES *US, male vocal/instrumental group*   **50 wks**

9 Aug 75	ONE OF THESE NIGHTS *Asylum AYM 543*		23	7 wks
1 Nov 75	LYIN' EYES *Asylum AYM 548*		23	7 wks
6 Mar 76	TAKE IT TO THE LIMIT *Asylum K 13029*		12	7 wks
15 Jan 77	NEW KID IN TOWN *Asylum K 13069*		20	7 wks
16 Apr 77 ●	HOTEL CALIFORNIA *Asylum K 13079*		8	10 wks
16 Dec 78	PLEASE COME HOME FOR CHRISTMAS *Asylum K 13145*		30	5 wks
13 Oct 79	HEARTACHE TONIGHT *Asylum K 12394*		40	5 wks
1 Dec 79	THE LONG RUN *Elektra K 12404*		66	2 wks

EARL – *See BOB and EARL*

Robert EARL *UK, male vocalist*   **27 wks**

25 Apr 58	I MAY NEVER PASS THIS WAY AGAIN *Philips PB 805*		14	13 wks
24 Oct 58	MORE THAN EVER (COME PRIMA) *Philips PB 867*		26	2 wks
21 Nov 58	MORE THAN EVER (COME PRIMA) (re-entry) *Philips PB 867*		28	2 wks
13 Feb 59	WONDERFUL SECRET OF LOVE *Philips PB 891*		17	10 wks

Charles EARLAND *US, male instrumentalist – keyboards*   **5 wks**

19 Aug 78	LET THE MUSIC PLAY *Mercury 6167 703*		46	5 wks

Hit features uncredited male vocalist.

Steve EARLE *US, male vocalist/instrumentalist – guitar*   **7 wks**

15 Oct 88	COPPERHEAD ROAD *MCA MCA 1280*		45	6 wks
31 Dec 88	JOHNNY COME LATELY *MCA MCA 1301*		75	1 wk

EARLY MUSIC CONSORT, Directed by David MUNROW *UK, male/female instrumental group*   **1 wk**

3 Apr 71	MUSIC FROM 'THE SIX WIVES OF HENRY VIII' *BBC RESL 1*		49	1 wk

EARTH WIND AND FIRE   **112 wks**
US, male vocal/instrumental group

12 Feb 77	SATURDAY NITE *CBS 4835*		17	9 wks
11 Feb 78	FANTASY *CBS 6056*		14	10 wks
13 May 78	JUPITER *CBS 6267*		41	5 wks
29 Jul 78	MAGIC MIND *CBS 6490*		75	1 wk
12 Aug 78	MAGIC MIND (re-entry) *CBS 6490*		54	4 wks
7 Oct 78	GOT TO GET YOU INTO MY LIFE *CBS 6553*		33	7 wks
9 Dec 78 ●	SEPTEMBER *CBS 6922*		3	13 wks
28 Jul 79 ●	AFTER THE LOVE HAS GONE *CBS 7721*		4	10 wks
6 Oct 79	STAR *CBS 7092*		16	8 wks
15 Dec 79	CAN'T LET GO *CBS 8077*		46	7 wks
8 Mar 80	IN THE STONE *CBS 8252*		53	3 wks
11 Oct 80	LET ME TALK *CBS 8982*		29	5 wks
20 Dec 80	BACK ON THE ROAD *CBS 9377*		63	4 wks
7 Nov 81 ●	LET'S GROOVE *CBS A 1679*		3	13 wks
6 Feb 82	IVE HAD ENOUGH *CBS A 1959*		29	6 wks
5 Feb 83	FALL IN LOVE WITH ME *CBS A 2927*		47	4 wks
7 Nov 87	SYSTEM OF SURVIVAL *CBS EWF 1*		54	3 wks

See also Earth Wind and Fire with the Emotions.

EARTH WIND AND FIRE with the EMOTIONS   13 wks

US, male vocal/instrumental group with female vocal group

| 12 May 79 | ● BOOGIE WONDERLAND *CBS 7292* | 4 | 13 wks |

See also Earth Wind and Fire; Emotions.

EAST OF EDEN *UK, male instrumental group*   12 wks

| 17 Apr 71 | ● JIG A JIG *Deram DM 297* | 7 | 12 wks |

Sheena EASTON *UK, female vocalist*   91 wks

5 Apr 80	MODERN GIRL *EMI 5042*	56	3 wks
19 Jul 80	● 9 TO 5 *EMI 5066*	3	15 wks
9 Aug 80	● MODERN GIRL (re-entry) *EMI 5042*	8	12 wks
25 Oct 80	ONE MAN WOMAN *EMI 5114*	14	6 wks
14 Feb 81	TAKE MY TIME *EMI 5135*	44	5 wks
2 May 81	WHEN HE SHINES *EMI 5166*	12	8 wks
27 Jun 81	● FOR YOUR EYES ONLY *EMI 5195*	8	13 wks
12 Sep 81	JUST ANOTHER BROKEN HEART *EMI 5232*	33	8 wks
5 Dec 81	YOU COULD HAVE BEEN WITH ME *EMI 5252*	54	3 wks
31 Jul 82	MACHINERY *EMI 5326*	38	5 wks
21 Jan 89	THE LOVER IN ME *MCA MCA 1289*	15	8 wks
18 Mar 89	DAYS LIKE THIS *MCA MCA 1325*	43	3 wks
15 Jul 89	101 *MCA MCA 1348*	54	2 wks

See also Kenny Rogers and Sheena Easton; Prince.

EASTSIDE CONNECTION *US, disco aggregation*   3 wks

| 8 Apr 78 | YOU'RE SO RIGHT FOR ME *Creole CR 149* | 44 | 3 wks |

Clint EASTWOOD *US, male vocalist*   2 wks

| 7 Feb 70 | I TALK TO THE TREES *Paramount PARA 3004* | 18 | 2 wks |

*This is the flip of Wand'rin Star by Lee Marvin and was listed with Marvin's A-side for 2 weeks only.
See also Lee Marvin; do not see Clint Eastwood and General Saint.*

Clint EASTWOOD and General SAINT   3 wks

UK, male vocal duo

| 29 Sep 84 | LAST PLANE (ONE WAY TICKET) *MCA MCA 910* | 51 | 3 wks |

Do not see Clint Eastwood.

EASYBEATS *Australia, male vocal/instrumental group*   24 wks

| 27 Oct 66 | ● FRIDAY ON MY MIND *United Artists UP 1157* | 6 | 15 wks |
| 10 Apr 68 | HELLO HOW ARE YOU *United Artists UP 2209* | 20 | 9 wks |

Cleveland EATON *US, male instrumentalist - keyboards*   6 wks

| 23 Sep 78 | BAMA BOOGIE WOOGIE *Gull GULS 63* | 35 | 6 wks |

EAV *Austria, male vocal/instrumental group*   4 wks

| 27 Sep 86 | BA-BA-BANKROBBERY (ENGLISH VERSION??) *Columbia DB 9139* | 63 | 4 wks |

EAV is short for Erste Allgemeine Verunsicherung.

ECHO and the BUNNYMEN   69 wks

UK, male vocal/instrumental group

17 May 80	RESCUE *Korova KOW 1*	62	1 wk
18 Apr 81	CROCODILES *Korova ECHO 1*	37	4 wks
18 Jul 81	A PROMISE *Korova KOW 15*	49	4 wks
29 May 82	THE BACK OF LOVE *Korova KOW 24*	19	7 wks
22 Jan 83	● THE CUTTER *Korova KOW 26*	8	8 wks
16 Jul 83	NEVER STOP *Korova KOW 28*	15	7 wks
28 Jan 84	● THE KILLING MOON *Korova KOW 32*	9	6 wks
21 Apr 84	SILVER *Korova KOW 34*	30	5 wks
14 Jul 84	SEVEN SEAS *Korova KOW 35*	16	7 wks
19 Oct 85	BRING ON THE DANCING HORSES *Korova KOW 43*	21	7 wks
13 Jun 87	THE GAME *WEA YZ 134*	28	4 wks
1 Aug 87	LIPS LIKE SUGAR *WEA YZ 144*	36	4 wks
20 Feb 88	PEOPLE ARE STRANGE *WEA YZ 175*	29	5 wks

Billy ECKSTINE *US, male vocalist*   31 wks

| 12 Nov 54 | ● NO ONE BUT YOU *MGM 763* | 3 | 17 wks |
| 13 Feb 59 | ● GIGI *Mercury AMT 1018* | 8 | 14 wks |

See also Billy Eckstine and Sarah Vaughan.

Billy ECKSTINE and Sarah VAUGHAN   17 wks

US, male/female vocal duo

| 27 Sep 57 | PASSING STRANGERS *Mercury MT 164* | 22 | 2 wks |
| 12 Mar 69 | PASSING STRANGERS (re-issue) *Mercury MF 1082* | 20 | 15 wks |

See also Billy Eckstine; Sarah Vaughan.

EDDIE and the HOTRODS   26 wks

UK, male vocal/instrumental group

11 Sep 76	LIVE AT THE MARQUEE (EP) *Island IEP 2*	43	5 wks
13 Nov 76	TEENAGE DEPRESSION *Island WIP 6354*	35	4 wks
23 Apr 77	I MIGHT BE LYING *Island WIP 6388*	44	3 wks
13 Aug 77	● DO ANYTHING YOU WANNA DO *Island WIP 6401*	9	10 wks
21 Jan 78	QUIT THIS TOWN *Island WIP 6411*	36	4 wks

Do Anything You Wanna Do credited simply to Rods. Tracks on EP: 96 Tears/Get Out Of Denver/Medley: Gloria/Satisfaction.

Duane EDDY *US, male instrumentalist - guitar*   187 wks

5 Sep 58	REBEL ROUSER *London HL 8669*	19	10 wks
2 Jan 59	CANNONBALL *London HL 8764*	22	4 wks
19 Jun 59	● PETER GUNN THEME *London HLW 8879*	6	10 wks
24 Jul 59	YEP *London HLW 8879*	17	5 wks
4 Sep 59	FORTY MILES OF BAD ROAD *London HLW 8929*	11	9 wks
11 Sep 59	PETER GUNN THEME (re-entry) *London HLW 8879*	27	1 wk
18 Dec 59	SOME KINDA EARTHQUAKE *London HLW 9007*	12	5 wks
19 Feb 60	BONNIE CAME BACK *London HLW 9050*	12	10 wks
28 Apr 60	● SHAZAM! *London HLW 9104*	4	13 wks
21 Jul 60	● BECAUSE THEY'RE YOUNG *London HLW 9162*	2	18 wks
10 Nov 60	KOMMOTION *London HLW 9225*	13	10 wks
12 Jan 61	● PEPE *London HLW 9257*	2	14 wks
20 Apr 61	● THEME FROM DIXIE *London HLW 9324*	7	10 wks
22 Jun 61	RING OF FIRE *London HLW 9370*	17	10 wks
14 Sep 61	DRIVIN' HOME *London HLW 9406*	30	4 wks
5 Oct 61	CARAVAN *Parlophone R 4826*	42	3 wks
24 May 62	DEEP IN THE HEART OF TEXAS *RCA 1288*	19	8 wks
23 Aug 62	● BALLAD OF PALADIN *RCA 1300*	10	10 wks
8 Nov 62	● DANCE WITH THE GUITAR MAN *RCA 1316*	4	16 wks
14 Feb 63	BOSS GUITAR *RCA 1329*	27	8 wks
30 May 63	LONELY BOY LONELY GUITAR *RCA 1344*	35	4 wks
29 Aug 63	YOUR BABY'S GONE SURFIN' *RCA 1357*	49	1 wk
8 Mar 75	● PLAY ME LIKE YOU PLAY YOUR GUITAR *GTO GT 11*	9	9 wks

The London hits featured Duane Eddy and the Rebels. Dance With The Guitar Man, Boss Guitar and Play Me Like You Play Your Guitar featured Duane Eddy and the Rebelettes. See also Art of Noise.

EDDY and the SOUL BAND   7 wks
US, male vocal/instrumental group

23 Feb 85	**THE THEME FROM SHAFT** *Club JAB 11*.................. **13**	7 wks

Randy EDELMAN *US, male vocalist*   18 wks

6 Mar 76	**CONCRETE AND CLAY** *20th Century BTC 2261*............ **11**	7 wks
18 Sep 76	**UPTOWN UPTEMPO WOMAN** *20th Century BTC 2225*..... **25**	7 wks
15 Jan 77	**YOU** *20th Century BTC 2253* **49**	2 wks
17 Jul 82	**NOBODY MADE ME** *Rocket XPRES 81* **60**	2 wks

EDELWEISS *Switzerland, male/female vocal/instrumental group*   10 wks

29 Apr 89 ●	**BRING ME EDELWEISS** *WEA YZ 353*........................ **5**	10 wks

EDISON LIGHTHOUSE   13 wks
UK, male vocal/instrumental group

24 Jan 70 ★	**LOVE GROWS (WHERE MY ROSEMARY GOES)** *Bell 1091*.................................. **1**	12 wks
30 Jan 71	**IT'S UP TO YOU PETULA** *Bell 1136* **49**	1 wk

Dave EDMUNDS *UK, male vocalist/multi-instrumentalist*   87 wks

21 Nov 70 ★	**I HEAR YOU KNOCKING** *MAM 1*........................ **1**	14 wks
20 Jan 73 ●	**BABY I LOVE YOU** *Rockfield ROC 1* **8**	13 wks
9 Jun 73 ●	**BORN TO BE WITH YOU** *Rockfield ROC 2*................... **5**	12 wks
2 Jul 77	**I KNEW THE BRIDE** *Swan Song SSK 19411*............... **26**	8 wks
30 Jun 79 ●	**GIRLS TALK** *Swan Song SSK 19418*..................... **4**	11 wks
22 Sep 79	**QUEEN OF HEARTS** *Swansong SSK 19419*.................. **11**	9 wks
24 Nov 79	**CRAWLING FROM THE WRECKAGE** *Swan Song SSK 19420*........................... **59**	4 wks
9 Feb 80	**SINGING THE BLUES** *Swan Song SSK 19422* **28**	8 wks
28 Mar 81	**ALMOST SATURDAY NIGHT** *Swan Song SSK 19424* **58**	3 wks
26 Mar 83	**SLIPPING AWAY** *Arista ARIST 522* **60**	4 wks
7 Apr 90	**KING OF LOVE** *Capitol CL 568* **68**	1 wk

See also Dave Edmunds and the Stray Cats.

Dave EDMUNDS and the STRAY CATS   6 wks
UK, male vocalist/instrumentalist and US, male vocal/instrumental group

20 Jun 81	**THE RACE IS ON** *Swansong SSK 19425* **34**	6 wks

See also Dave Edmunds; Stray Cats.

Alton EDWARDS *South Africa, male vocalist*   9 wks

9 Jan 82	**I JUST WANNA (SPEND SOME TIME WITH YOU)** *Streetwave STRA 1897*.................... **20**	9 wks

Dennis EDWARDS *US, male vocalist*   10 wks

24 Mar 84	**DON'T LOOK ANY FURTHER** *Gordy TMG 1334*........... **45**	5 wks
20 Jun 87	**DON'T LOOK ANY FURTHER (re-entry)** *Gordy TMG 1334*.................... **55**	5 wks

Hit features Siedah Garrett - US, female vocalist.

Rupie EDWARDS *Jamaica, male vocalist*   16 wks

23 Nov 74 ●	**IRE FEELINGS (SKANGA)** *Cactus CT 38* **9**	10 wks
8 Feb 75	**LEGO SKANGA** *Cactus CT 51* **32**	6 wks

Tommy EDWARDS *US, male vocalist*   18 wks

3 Oct 58 ★	**IT'S ALL IN THE GAME** *MGM 989*............... **1**	17 wks
7 Aug 59	**MY MELANCHOLY BABY** *MGM 1020* **29**	1 wk

808 STATE *UK, male instrumental group*   18 wks

18 Nov 89 ●	**PACIFIC STATE** *ZTT ZANG 1*........................... **10**	9 wks
31 Mar 90	**THE EXTENDED PLEASURE OF DANCE** (EP) *ZTT 2T*............ **56**	1 wk
10 Nov 90 ●	**CUBIK/ OLYMPIC** *ZTT ZANG 5*..................... **10†**	8 wks

Tracks on The Extended Pleasure Of Dance EP: Ancodia, Cubik, Cuba Bora. Cubik is a re-issue of one of the tracks from The Extended Pleasures Of Dance EP. See also MC Tunes versus 808 State; Various Artists - The Brits 1990.

EIGHTH WONDER   25 wks
UK, male/female vocal/instrumental group

2 Nov 85	**STAY WITH ME** *CBS A 6594*............................ **65**	2 wks
20 Feb 88 ●	**I'M NOT SCARED** *CBS SCARE 1*........................... **7**	13 wks
25 Jun 88	**CROSS MY HEART** *CBS 651552 7*....................... **13**	8 wks
1 Oct 88	**BABY BABY** *CBS BABE 1*................................ **65**	2 wks

EINSTEIN – *See Simon HARRIS; TECHNOTRONIC*

Donnie ELBERT *US, male vocalist*   29 wks

8 Jan 72 ●	**WHERE DID OUR LOVE GO?** *London HL 10352*............ **8**	10 wks
26 Feb 72	**I CAN'T HELP MYSELF** *Avco 6105 009* **11**	10 wks
29 Apr 72	**LITTLE PIECE OF LEATHER** *London HL 10370* **27**	9 wks

ELECTRA *UK, male vocal/instrumental group*   7 wks

6 Aug 88	**JIBARO** *FFRR FFR 9*................................... **54**	3 wks
30 Dec 89	**IT'S YOUR DESTINY/ AUTUMN LOVE** *London F 121* **51**	4 wks

ELECTRIBE 101   13 wks
UK/Germany, male/female vocal/instrumental group

28 Oct 89	**TELL ME WHEN THE FEVER ENDED** *Mercury MER 310*.................... **32**	5 wks
24 Feb 90	**TALKING WITH MYSELF** *Mercury MER 316*.............. **23**	5 wks
22 Sep 90 ●	**YOU'RE WALKING** *Mercury MER 328* **50**	3 wks

ELECTRIC LIGHT ORCHESTRA   243 wks
UK, male vocal/instrumental group

29 Jul 72 ●	**10538 OVERTURE** *Harvest HAR 5053* **9**	8 wks
27 Jan 73 ●	**ROLL OVER BEETHOVEN** *Harvest HAR 5063* **6**	10 wks
6 Oct 73	**SHOWDOWN** *Harvest HAR 5077* **12**	10 wks
9 Mar 74	**MA-MA-MA-BELLE** *Warner Bros. K 16349*............ **22**	8 wks
10 Jan 76 ●	**EVIL WOMAN** *Jet 764* **10**	8 wks
3 Jul 76	**STRANGE MAGIC** *Jet 779* **38**	3 wks
13 Nov 76 ●	**LIVIN' THING** *Jet UP 36184* **4**	12 wks
19 Feb 77 ●	**ROCKARIA!** *Jet UP 36209* **9**	9 wks
21 May 77 ●	**TELEPHONE LINE** *Jet UP 36254* **8**	10 wks
29 Oct 77	**TURN TO STONE** *Jet UP 36313*..................... **18**	12 wks
28 Jan 78 ●	**MR. BLUE SKY** *Jet UP 36342* **6**	11 wks
10 Jun 78 ●	**WILD WEST HERO** *Jet JET 109* **6**	14 wks
7 Oct 78 ●	**SWEET TALKIN' WOMAN** *Jet 121*.................... **6**	9 wks
9 Dec 78	**ELO EP** (EP) *Jet ELO 1* **34**	8 wks
19 May 79 ●	**SHINE A LITTLE LOVE** *Jet 144*..................... **6**	10 wks
21 Jul 79 ●	**THE DIARY OF HORACE WIMP** *Jet 150* **8**	9 wks
1 Sep 79 ●	**DON'T BRING ME DOWN** *Jet 153* **3**	9 wks
17 Nov 79 ●	**CONFUSION / LAST TRAIN TO LONDON** *Jet 166* **8**	10 wks
24 May 80	**I'M ALIVE** *Jet 179* **20**	9 wks
2 Aug 80	**ALL OVER THE WORLD** *Jet 195*...................... **11**	8 wks

22 Nov 80		DON'T WALK AWAY *Jet 7004*	**21**	10 wks
1 Aug 81	●	HOLD ON TIGHT *Jet 7011*	**4**	12 wks
24 Oct 81		TWILIGHT *Jet 7015*	**30**	7 wks
9 Jan 82		TICKET TO THE MOON/ HERE IS THE NEWS		
		Jet 7018	**24**	8 wks
18 Jun 83		ROCK 'N' ROLL IS KING *Jet A 3500*	**13**	9 wks
3 Sep 83		SECRET MESSAGES *Jet A 3720*	**48**	3 wks
1 Mar 86		CALLING AMERICA *Epic A 6844*	**28**	7 wks

Here Is The News *listed from 16 Jan 82. Tracks on ELO EP: Out of My Head/Strange Magic/Ma-Ma-Ma-Belle/Evil Woman. See also Olivia Newton-John and Electric Light Orchestra.*

ELECTRIC PRUNES *US, male vocal/instrumental group*   **5 wks**

9 Feb 67		I HAD TOO MUCH TO DREAM LAST NIGHT		
		Reprise RS 20532	**49**	1 wk
11 May 67		GET ME TO THE WORLD ON TIME *Reprise RS 20564*	**42**	4 wks

ELECTRONIC *UK, male vocal/instrumental group*   **9 wks**

| 16 Dec 89 | | GETTING AWAY WITH IT *Factory FAC 2577* .... | **12** | 9 wks |

ELECTRONICAS *Holland, male instrumental group*   **8 wks**

| 19 Sep 81 | | ORIGINAL BIRD DANCE *Polydor POSP 360* .... | **22** | 8 wks |

ELEGANTS *US, male vocal group*   **2 wks**

| 26 Sep 58 | | LITTLE STAR *HMV POP 520* .... | **25** | 2 wks |

ELGINS *US, male/female vocal group*   **20 wks**

1 May 71	●	HEAVEN MUST HAVE SENT YOU		
		Tamla Motown TMG 771	**3**	13 wks
9 Oct 71		PUT YOURSELF IN MY PLACE		
		Tamla Motown TMG 787	**28**	7 wks

ELIAS and his ZIGZAG JIVE FLUTES *South Africa,*   **14 wks**
male instrumental group

| 25 Apr 58 | ● | TOM HARK *Columbia DB 4109* .... | **2** | 14 wks |

Yvonne ELLIMAN *US, female vocalist*   **44 wks**

29 Jan 72		I DON'T KNOW HOW TO LOVE HIM		
		MCA MMKS 5077	**47**	1 wk
6 Nov 76	●	LOVE ME *RSO 2090 205*	**6**	13 wks
7 May 77		HELLO STRANGER *RSO 2090 236*	**26**	5 wks
13 Aug 77		I CAN'T GET YOU OUT OF MY MIND		
		RSO 2090 251	**17**	13 wks
6 May 78	●	IF I CAN'T HAVE YOU *RSO 2090 266*	**4**	12 wks

I Don't Know How To Love Him *was one of four tracks on a Maxi-Single, two of which were credited during the disc's one week on the chart. The other track credited was* Superstar *by Murray Head. See also Murray Head.*

Duke ELLINGTON *US, orchestra*   **4 wks**

| 5 Mar 54 | ● | SKIN DEEP *Philips PB 243* .... | **7** | 4 wks |

Ray ELLINGTON *UK, orchestra*   **4 wks**

| 15 Nov 62 | | THE MADISON *Ember S 102* .... | **41** | 2 wks |
| 20 Dec 62 | | THE MADISON (re-entry) *Ember S 102* .... | **36** | 2 wks |

Bern ELLIOTT and the FENMEN   **22 wks**
UK, male vocalist, male vocal/instrumental backing group

| 21 Nov 63 | | MONEY *Decca F 11770* .... | **14** | 13 wks |
| 19 Mar 64 | | NEW ORLEANS *Decca F 11852* .... | **24** | 9 wks |

ELLIS, BEGGS AND HOWARD   **8 wks**
UK, male vocal/instrumental group

2 Jul 88		BIG BUBBLES, NO TROUBLES *RCA PB 42089*	**59**	3 wks
11 Mar 89		BIG BUBBLES, NO TROUBLES (re-entry)		
		RCA PB 42089	**41**	5 wks

Shirley ELLIS *US, female vocalist*   **17 wks**

| 6 May 65 | ● | THE CLAPPING SONG *London HLR 9961* .... | **6** | 13 wks |
| 8 Jul 78 | | THE CLAPPING SONG (EP) *MCA MCEP 1* .... | **59** | 4 wks |

Tracks on The Clapping Song EP: The Clapping Song/Ever See a Diver Kiss His Wife While The Bubbles Bounce Above The Water/The Name Game/The Nitty Gritty. The Clapping Song *itself qualifies as a re-issue.*

Keith EMERSON *UK, male instrumentalist - piano*   **5 wks**

| 10 Apr 76 | | HONKY TONK TRAIN BLUES *Manticore K 13513* .... | **21** | 5 wks |

See also Emerson, Lake and Palmer.

EMERSON, LAKE AND PALMER   **13 wks**
UK, male instrumental group

| 4 Jun 77 | ● | FANFARE FOR THE COMMON MAN *Atlantic K 10946* ...... | **2** | 13 wks |

See also Keith Emerson; Greg Lake.

Dick EMERY *UK, male vocalist*   **8 wks**

| 26 Feb 69 | | IF YOU LOVE HER *Pye 7N 17644* .... | **32** | 4 wks |
| 13 Jan 73 | | YOU ARE AWFUL *Pye 7N 45202* .... | **43** | 4 wks |

EMF *UK, male vocal/instrumental group*   **9 wks**

| 3 Nov 90 | ● | UNBELIEVABLE *Parlophone R6273* .... | **3†** | 9 wks |

EMMA *UK, female vocalist*   **6 wks**

| 28 Apr 90 | | GIVE A LITTLE LOVE BACK TO THE WORLD | | |
| | | *Big Wave BWR 33* .... | **33** | 6 wks |

An EMOTIONAL FISH   **5 wks**
UK, male vocal/instrumental group

| 23 Jun 90 | | CELEBRATE *East West YZ 489* .... | **46** | 5 wks |

EMOTIONS *US, female vocal group*   **15 wks**

| 10 Sep 77 | ● | BEST OF MY LOVE *CBS 5555* .... | **4** | 10 wks |
| 24 Dec 77 | | I DON'T WANNA LOSE YOUR LOVE *CBS 5819* .... | **40** | 5 wks |

See also Earth Wind and Fire with the Emotions.

EN VOGUE *US, female vocal/instrumental group*   **15 wks**

| 5 May 90 | ● | HOLD ON *East West A 7908* .... | **5** | 11 wks |
| 21 Jul 90 | | LIES *East West A 7893* .... | **44** | 4 wks |

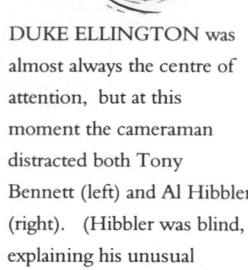

DUKE ELLINGTON was almost always the centre of attention, but at this moment the cameraman distracted both Tony Bennett (left) and Al Hibbler (right). (Hibbler was blind, explaining his unusual expression).

Below Left: HARRY ENFIELD (left) is shown with famous friends Hugh Laurie and Stephen Fry.

Left: After his recovery from his motorcycle accident, BOB DYLAN shed his rebellious image and briefly became a country crooner, so all-American in appeal he even made the cover of the mainstream magazine *Saturday Evening Post*.

Below: EN VOGUE were just that in mid-1990.

ENERGY ORCHARD   6 wks
Ireland, male vocal/instrumental group

27 Jan 90	**BELFAST** *MCA MCA 1392*	**52**	4 wks
7 Apr 90	**SAILORTOWN** *MCA MCA 1402*	**73**	2 wks

Harry ENFIELD *UK, male vocalist*   7 wks

7 May 88	● **LOADSAMONEY (DOIN' UP THE HOUSE)** *Mercury DOSH 1*	**4**	7 wks

ENGLAND DAN and John Ford COLEY   12 wks
US, male vocal duo

25 Sep 76	**I'D REALLY LOVE TO SEE YOU TONIGHT** *Atlantic K 10810*	**26**	7 wks
23 Jun 79	**LOVE IS THE ANSWER** *Big Tree K 11296*	**45**	5 wks

ENGLAND SISTERS *UK, female vocal group*   1 wk

17 Mar 60	**HEARTBEAT** *HMV POP 710*	**33**	1 wk

ENGLAND WORLD CUP SQUAD   34 wks
UK, male football team vocalists

18 Apr 70	★ **BACK HOME** *Pye 7N 17920*	**1**	16 wks
15 Aug 70	**BACK HOME (re-entry)** *Pye 7N 17920*	**46**	1 wk
10 Apr 82	● **THIS TIME (WE'LL GET IT RIGHT)/ ENGLAND WE'LL FLY THE FLAG** *England ER 1*	**2**	13 wks
19 Apr 86	**WE'VE GOT THE WHOLE WORLD AT OUR FEET/ WHEN WE ARE FAR FROM HOME** *Columbia DB 9128*	**66**	2 wks
21 May 88	**ALL THE WAY** *MCA GOAL 1*	**64**	2 wks

All The Way billed as England Football Team and credits 'the 'sound' of Stock, Aitken & Waterman'.
See also Englandneworder, Stock Aitken & Waterman.

ENGLANDNEWORDER   12 wks
UK, male football team vocalists and male/female vocal/instrumental group

2 Jun 90	★ **WORLD IN MOTION...** *Factory FAC 2937*	**1**	12 wks

See also England World Cup Squad; New Order.

Scott ENGLISH *US, male vocalist*   10 wks

9 Oct 71	**BRANDY** *Horse HOSS 7*	**12**	10 wks

ENGLISH CHAMBER ORCHESTRA – *See Sarah BRIGHTMAN and Paul MILES-KINGSTON*

ENIGMA *UK, male vocal/instrumental group*   15 wks

23 May 81	**AIN'T NO STOPPING** *Creole CR 9*	**11**	8 wks
8 Aug 81	**I LOVE MUSIC** *Creole CR 14*	**25**	7 wks

ENIGMA   3 wks
Germany/Yugoslavia, male/female vocal/instrumental group

15 Dec 90	● **SADNESS PART 1** *Virgin International DINS 101*	**4†**	3 wks

ENYA *Ireland, female vocalist*   21 wks

15 Oct 88	★ **ORINOCO FLOW** *WEA YZ 312*	**1**	13 wks
24 Dec 88	**EVENING FALLS...** *WEA YZ 356*	**20**	4 wks
10 Jun 89	**STORMS IN AFRICA (PART II)** *WEA YZ 368*	**41**	4 wks

EQUALS *UK/Guyana, male vocal/instrumental group*   69 wks

21 Feb 68	**I GET SO EXCITED** *President PT 180*	**44**	4 wks
1 May 68	**BABY COME BACK** *President PT 135*	**50**	1 wk
15 May 68	★ **BABY COME BACK (re-entry)** *President PT 135*	**1**	17 wks
21 Aug 68	**LAUREL AND HARDY** *President PT 200*	**35**	5 wks
27 Nov 68	**SOFTLY SOFTLY** *President PT 222*	**48**	3 wks
2 Apr 69	**MICHAEL AND THE SLIPPER TREE** *President PT 240*	**24**	7 wks
30 Jul 69	● **VIVA BOBBY JOE** *President PT 260*	**6**	14 wks
27 Dec 69	**RUB A DUB DUB** *President PT 275*	**34**	7 wks
19 Dec 70	● **BLACK SKIN BLUE EYED BOYS** *President PT 325*	**9**	11 wks

ERASURE *UK, male vocal/instrumental duo*   119 wks

5 Oct 85	**WHO NEEDS LOVE LIKE THAT** *Mute MUTE 40*	**55**	2 wks
25 Oct 86	● **SOMETIMES** *Mute MUTE 51*	**2**	17 wks
28 Feb 87	**IT DOESN'T HAVE TO BE** *Mute MUTE 56*	**12**	9 wks
30 May 87	● **VICTIM OF LOVE** *Mute MUTE 61*	**7**	9 wks
3 Oct 87	● **THE CIRCUS** *Mute MUTE 66*	**6**	10 wks
5 Mar 88	● **SHIP OF FOOLS** *Mute MUTE 74*	**6**	8 wks
11 Jun 88	● **CHAINS OF LOVE** *Mute MUTE 83*	**11**	7 wks
1 Oct 88	● **A LITTLE RESPECT** *Mute MUTE 85*	**4**	10 wks
10 Dec 88	● **CRACKERS INTERNATIONAL** (EP) *Mute MUTE 93*	**2**	13 wks
30 Sep 89	● **DRAMA!** *Mute MUTE 89*	**4**	8 wks
9 Dec 89	**YOU SURROUND ME** *Mute MUTE 99*	**15**	9 wks
10 Mar 90	● **BLUE SAVANNAH** *Mute MUTE 109*	**3**	10 wks
2 Jun 90	**STAR** *Mute MUTE 111*	**11**	7 wks

Tracks on Crackers International EP: Stop/The Hardest Part/Knocking On Your Door/She Won't Be Home.

ERIC and the GOOD GOOD FEELING   1 wk
UK, male/female vocal/instrumental group

3 Jun 89	**GOOD GOOD FEELING** *Equinox EQN 1*	**73**	1 wk

See also S Express.

EROTIC DRUM BAND   3 wks
Canada, male/female vocal/instrumental group

9 Jun 79	**LOVE DISCO STYLE** *Scope SC 1*	**47**	3 wks

ERUPTION *US, male/female vocal/instrumental group*   21 wks

18 Feb 78	● **I CAN'T STAND THE RAIN** *Atlantic K 11068*	**5**	11 wks
21 Apr 79	● **ONE WAY TICKET** *Atlantic/Hansa K 11266*	**9**	10 wks

I Can't Stand The Rain has credit 'Eruption featuring Precious Wilson' - US, female vocalist.

ESCORTS *UK, male vocal/instrumental group*   2 wks

2 Jul 64	**THE ONE TO CRY** *Fontana TF 474*	**49**	2 wks

ESSEX *US, male/female vocal group*   5 wks

8 Aug 63	**EASIER SAID THAN DONE** *Columbia DB 7077*	**41**	5 wks

David ESSEX *UK, male vocalist*   196 wks

18 Aug 73	● **ROCK ON** *CBS 1693*	**3**	11 wks
10 Nov 73	● **LAMPLIGHT** *CBS 1902*	**7**	15 wks

11 May 74	AMERICA *CBS 2176*	32	5 wks
12 Oct 74	★ GONNA MAKE YOU A STAR *CBS 2492*	1	17 wks
14 Dec 74	● STARDUST *CBS 2828*	7	10 wks
5 Jul 75	ROLLIN' STONE *CBS 3425*	5	7 wks
13 Sep 75	★ HOLD ME CLOSE *CBS 3572*	1	10 wks
6 Dec 75	IF I COULD *CBS 3776*	13	8 wks
20 Mar 76	CITY LIGHTS *CBS 4050*	24	4 wks
16 Oct 76	COMING HOME *CBS 4486*	24	6 wks
17 Sep 77	COOL OUT TONIGHT *CBS 5495*	23	6 wks
11 Mar 78	STAY WITH ME BABY *CBS 6063*	45	5 wks
19 Aug 78	● OH WHAT A CIRCUS *Mercury 6007 185*	3	11 wks
21 Oct 78	BRAVE NEW WORLD *CBS 6705*	55	3 wks
3 Mar 79	IMPERIAL WIZARD *Mercury 6007 202*	32	8 wks
5 Apr 80	● SILVER DREAM MACHINE (PART 1) *Mercury BIKE 1*	4	11 wks
14 Jun 80	HOT LOVE *Mercury HOT 11*	57	4 wks
26 Jun 82	ME AND MY GIRL (NIGHT-CLUBBING) *Mercury MER 107*	13	10 wks
11 Dec 82	● A WINTER'S TALE *Mercury MER 127*	2	10 wks
4 Jun 83	THE SMILE *Mercury ESSEX 1*	52	4 wks
27 Aug 83	★ TAHITI *Mercury BOUNT 1*	8	11 wks
26 Nov 83	YOU'RE IN MY HEART *Mercury ESSEX 2*	67	2 wks
17 Dec 83	YOU'RE IN MY HEART (re-entry) *Mercury ESSEX 2*	59	4 wks
23 Feb 85	FALLING ANGELS RIDING *Mercury ESSEX 5*	29	7 wks
18 Apr 87	MYFANWY *Arista RIS 11*	41	7 wks

Gloria ESTEFAN *US, female vocalist*   **108 wks**

11 Aug 84	● DR BEAT *Epic A 4614*	6	14 wks
17 May 86	BAD BOY *Epic A 6537*	16	11 wks
16 Jul 88	● ANYTHING FOR YOU *Epic 651673 7*	10	16 wks
22 Oct 88	1-2-3 *Epic 652958 7*	9	9 wks
17 Dec 88	RHYTHM IS GONNA GET YOU *Epic 654514 7*	16	9 wks
31 Dec 88	1-2-3 (re-entry) *Epic 652958 7*	72	1 wk
11 Feb 89	● CAN'T STAY AWAY FROM YOU *Epic 651444 7*	7	12 wks
15 Jul 89	● DON'T WANNA LOSE YOU *Epic 655054 0*	6	10 wks
16 Sep 89	OYE MI CANTO (HEAR MY VOICE) *Epic 655287 7*	16	8 wks
25 Nov 89	GET ON YOUR FEET *Epic 655450 7*	23	7 wks
3 Mar 90	HERE WE ARE *Epic 655473 9*	23	6 wks
26 May 90	CUTS BOTH WAYS *Epic 655982 7*	49	5 wks

First two hits credited to Miami Sound Machine, the next four to Gloria Estefan and Miami Sound Machine, from then on simply Gloria Estefan although there was no significant change to the line-up of the group.

Don ESTELLE – *See Windsor DAVIES and Don ESTELLE*

Deon ESTUS *US, male vocalist/instrumentalist - bass*   **4 wks**

29 Apr 89	HEAVEN HELP ME *Mika MIKA 2*	41	4 wks

ETHIOPIANS *Jamaica, male vocal/instrumental group*   **6 wks**

13 Sep 67	TRAIN TO SKAVILLE *Rio RIO 130*	40	6 wks

Tony ETORIA *UK, male vocalist*   **8 wks**

4 Jun 77	I CAN PROVE IT *GTO GT 89*	21	8 wks

E.U. – *See SALT 'N' PEPA*

EUROPE *Sweden, male vocal/instrumental group*   **37 wks**

1 Nov 86	★ THE FINAL COUNTDOWN *Epic A 7127*	1	15 wks
31 Jan 87	ROCK THE NIGHT *Epic EUR 1*	12	9 wks
18 Apr 87	CARRIE *Epic EUR 2*	22	8 wks
20 Aug 88	SUPERSTITIOUS *Epic EUR 3*	34	5 wks

EURYTHMICS *UK, male/female vocal/instrumental duo*   **182 wks**

4 Jul 81	NEVER GONNA CRY AGAIN *RCA 68*	63	3 wks
20 Nov 82	LOVE IS A STRANGER *RCA DA 1*	54	5 wks
12 Feb 83	● SWEET DREAMS (ARE MADE OF THIS) *RCA DA 2*	2	14 wks
9 Apr 83	● LOVE IS A STRANGER (re-entry) *RCA DA 1*	6	8 wks
9 Jul 83	● WHO'S THAT GIRL? *RCA DA 3*	3	10 wks
5 Nov 83	● RIGHT BY YOUR SIDE *RCA DA 4*	10	11 wks
21 Jan 84	● HERE COMES THE RAIN AGAIN *RCA DA 5*	8	8 wks
3 Nov 84	● SEXCRIME (NINETEEN EIGHTY FOUR) *Virgin VS 728*	4	13 wks
19 Jan 85	JULIA *Virgin VS 734*	44	4 wks
20 Apr 85	WOULD I LIE TO YOU? *RCA PB 40101*	17	8 wks
6 Jul 85	★ THERE MUST BE AN ANGEL (PLAYING WITH MY HEART) *RCA PB 40247*	1	13 wks
11 Jan 86	IT'S ALRIGHT (BABY'S COMING BACK) *RCA PB 40375*	12	8 wks
14 Jun 86	WHEN TOMORROW COMES *RCA DA 7*	30	6 wks
6 Sep 86	● THORN IN MY SIDE *RCA DA 8*	5	11 wks
29 Nov 86	THE MIRACLE OF LOVE *RCA DA 9*	23	9 wks
28 Feb 87	MISSIONARY MAN *RCA DA 10*	31	4 wks
24 Oct 87	BEETHOVEN (I LOVE TO LISTEN TO) *RCA DA 11*	25	5 wks
26 Dec 87	SHAME *RCA DA 14*	41	6 wks
9 Apr 88	I NEED A MAN *RCA DA 15*	26	5 wks
11 Jun 88	YOU HAVE PLACED A CHILL IN MY HEART *RCA DA 16*	16	8 wks
26 Aug 89	REVIVAL *RCA DA 17*	26	6 wks
4 Nov 89	DON'T ASK ME WHY *RCA DA 19*	25	6 wks
3 Feb 90	THE KING AND QUEEN OF AMERICA *RCA DA 24*	29	5 wks
12 May 90	ANGEL *RCA DA 21*	23	6 wks

See also Eurythmics and Aretha Franklin.

EURYTHMICS and Aretha FRANKLIN   **11 wks**
UK, male/female vocal/instrumental duo and US, female vocalist

2 Nov 85	● SISTERS ARE DOIN' IT FOR THEMSELVES *RCA PB 40339*	9	11 wks

See also Eurythmics; Aretha Franklin.

EVANGEL TEMPLE CHOIR – *See Johnny CASH*

EVANS – *See ZAGER and EVANS*

Maureen EVANS *UK, female vocalist*   **37 wks**

22 Jan 60	THE BIG HURT *Oriole CB 1533*	26	2 wks
17 Mar 60	LOVE KISSES AND HEARTACHES *Oriole CB 1540*	44	1 wk
2 Jun 60	PAPER ROSES *Oriole CB 1550*	40	5 wks
29 Nov 62	● LIKE I DO *Oriole CB 1760*	3	18 wks
27 Feb 64	I LOVE HOW YOU LOVE ME *Oriole CB 1906*	34	10 wks
14 May 64	I LOVE HOW YOU LOVE ME (re-entry) *Oriole CB 1906*	50	1 wk

Paul EVANS *US, male vocalist*   **14 wks**

27 Nov 59	SEVEN LITTLE GIRLS SITTING IN THE BACK SEAT *London HLL 8968*	25	1 wk
31 Mar 60	MIDNIGHT SPECIAL *London HLL 9045*	41	1 wk
16 Dec 78	● HELLO THIS IS JOANIE (THE TELEPHONE ANSWERING MACHINE SONG) *Spring 2066 932*	6	12 wks

Seven Little Girls Sitting In The Back Seat credits Paul Evans and The Curls, The Curls being a US, female vocal group.

EVASIONS *UK, male/female vocal/instrumental group*   **8 wks**

13 Jun 81	WIKKA WRAP *Groove GP 107*	20	8 wks

Right: GLORIA ESTEFAN attends a party at Spago in West Hollywood following the 1990 American Music Awards.

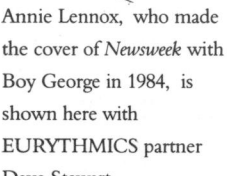

Far Right: Resembling neither Warren Beatty nor Faye Dunaway did not deter GEORGIE FAME from achieving his third number one.

Annie Lennox, who made the cover of *Newsweek* with Boy George in 1984, is shown here with EURYTHMICS partner Dave Stewart.

Below: ERASURE were kept out of number one first by Berlin and then by Kylie and Jason.

Betty EVERETT US, female vocalist   **14 wks**

| 14 Jan 65 | GETTING MIGHTY CROWDED Fontana TF 520 | 29 | 7 wks |
| 30 Oct 68 | IT'S IN HIS KISS President PT 215 | 34 | 7 wks |

Kenny EVERETT UK, male vocalist   **8 wks**

| 26 Mar 83 ● | SNOT RAP RCA KEN 1 | 9 | 8 wks |

See also Kenny Everett and Mike Vickers.

Kenny EVERETT and Mike VICKERS   **4 wks**
UK, male vocalist and vocalist/multi-instrumentalist

| 12 Nov 77 | CAPTAIN KREMMEN (RETRIBUTION) DJM DJS 10810 | 32 | 4 wks |

See also Kenny Everett.

Phil EVERLY US, male vocalist   **6 wks**

| 6 Nov 82 | LOUISE Capitol CL 266 | 47 | 6 wks |

See also Everly Brothers; Phil Everly and Cliff Richard.

Phil EVERLY and Cliff RICHARD   **9 wks**
US/UK, male vocal duo

| 19 Feb 83 ● | SHE MEANS NOTHING TO ME Capitol CL 276 | 9 | 9 wks |

See also Cliff Richard; Phil Everly.

EVERLY BROTHERS US, male vocal duo   **344 wks**

12 Jul 57 ●	BYE BYE LOVE London HLA 8440	6	16 wks
8 Nov 57 ●	WAKE UP LITTLE SUSIE London HLA 8498	2	13 wks
23 May 58 ★	ALL I HAVE TO DO IS DREAM/ CLAUDETTE London HLA 8618	1	21 wks
12 Sep 58 ●	BIRD DOG London HLA 8685	2	16 wks
23 Jan 59 ●	PROBLEMS London HLA 8781	6	12 wks
22 May 59	TAKE A MESSAGE TO MARY London HLA 8863	29	1 wk
29 May 59	POOR JENNY London HLA 8863	14	11 wks
19 Jun 59	TAKE A MESSAGE TO MARY (re-entry) London HLA 8863	27	1 wk
3 Jul 59	TAKE A MESSAGE TO MARY (2nd re-entry) London HLA 8863	20	8 wks
11 Sep 59 ●	('TIL) I KISSED YOU London HLA 8934	2	15 wks
12 Feb 60	LET IT BE ME London HLA 9039	13	5 wks
31 Mar 60	LET IT BE ME (re-entry) London HLA 9039	26	4 wks
14 Apr 60 ★	CATHY'S CLOWN Warner Bros. WB 1	1	18 wks
14 Jul 60 ●	WHEN WILL I BE LOVED London HLA 9157	4	16 wks
22 Sep 60 ●	LUCILLE / SO SAD (TO WATCH GOOD LOVE GO BAD) Warner Bros. WB 19	4	15 wks
15 Dec 60	LIKE STRANGERS London HLA 9250	11	10 wks
9 Feb 61 ★	WALK RIGHT BACK/ EBONY EYES Warner Bros. WB 33	1	16 wks
15 Jun 61 ★	TEMPTATION Warner Bros. WB 42	1	15 wks
5 Oct 61	MUSKRAT/ DON'T BLAME ME Warner Bros. WB 50	20	6 wks
18 Jan 62 ●	CRYIN' IN THE RAIN Warner Bros. WB 56	6	15 wks
17 May 62	HOW CAN I MEET HER Warner Bros. WB 67	12	10 wks
25 Oct 62	NO ONE CAN MAKE MY SUNSHINE SMILE Warner Bros. WB 79	11	11 wks
21 Mar 63	SO IT WILL ALWAYS BE Warner Bros. WB 94	23	11 wks
13 Jun 63	IT'S BEEN NICE Warner Bros. WB 99	26	5 wks
17 Oct 63	THE GIRL SANG THE BLUES Warner Bros. WB 109	25	9 wks
16 Jul 64	FERRIS WHEEL Warner Bros. WB 135	22	10 wks
3 Dec 64	GONE GONE GONE Warner Bros. WB 146	36	7 wks
6 May 65	THAT'LL BE THE DAY Warner Bros. WB 158	30	4 wks
20 May 65 ●	THE PRICE OF LOVE Warner Bros. WB 161	2	14 wks
26 Aug 65	I'LL NEVER GET OVER YOU Warner Bros. WB 5639	35	5 wks
21 Oct 65	LOVE IS STRANGE Warner Bros. WB 5649	11	9 wks
8 May 68	IT'S MY TIME Warner Bros. WB 7192	39	6 wks
22 Sep 84	ON THE WINGS OF A NIGHTINGALE Mercury MER 170	41	9 wks

All I Have To Do Is Dream was listed without Claudette for its first week on the chart, but from 30 May 58 both sides were charted for 20 more weeks. See also Phil Everly.

EVERTON 1985 UK, male football team vocalists   **5 wks**

| 11 May 85 | HERE WE GO Columbia DB 9106 | 14 | 5 wks |

EVERYTHING BUT THE GIRL   **32 wks**
UK, male/female vocal/instrumental group

12 May 84	EACH AND EVERYONE blanco y negro NEG 1	28	7 wks
21 Jul 84	MINE blanco y negro NEG 3	58	2 wks
6 Oct 84	NATIVE LAND blanco y negro NEG 6	73	2 wks
2 Aug 86	COME ON HOME blanco y negro NEG 21	44	7 wks
11 Oct 86	DON'T LEAVE ME BEHIND blanco y negro NEG 23	72	2 wks
13 Feb 88	THESE EARLY DAYS blanco y negro NEG 30	75	1 wk
9 Jul 88 ●	I DON'T WANT TO TALK ABOUT IT blanco y negro NEG 34	3	9 wks
27 Jan 90	DRIVING blanco y negro NEG 40	54	2 wks

EX PISTOLS UK, male vocal/instrumental group   **2 wks**

| 2 Feb 85 | LAND OF HOPE AND GLORY Virginia PISTOL 76 | 69 | 2 wks |

This is an early recording by the Sex Pistols. See also Sex Pistols.

EXCITERS US, male/female vocal group   **7 wks**

| 21 Feb 63 | TELL HIM United Artists UP 1011 | 46 | 1 wk |
| 4 Oct 75 | REACHING FOR THE BEST 20th Century BTC 1005 | 31 | 6 wks |

EXILE US, male vocal/instrumental group   **18 wks**

19 Aug 78 ●	KISS YOU ALL OVER RAK 279	6	12 wks
12 May 79	HOW COULD THIS GO WRONG RAK 293	67	2 wks
12 Sep 81	HEART AND SOUL RAK 333	54	4 wks

EXPLOITED UK, male vocal/instrumental group   **12 wks**

18 Apr 81	DOGS OF WAR Secret SHH 110	63	4 wks
17 Oct 81	DEAD CITIES Secret SHH 120	31	5 wks
8 May 82	ATTACK Secret SHH 130	50	3 wks

See also Exploited and Anti-Pasti.

EXPLOITED and ANTI-PASTI   **1 wk**
UK, male vocal/instrumental group

| 5 Dec 81 | DON'T LET 'EM GRIND YOU DOWN Superville EXP 1003 | 70 | 1 wk |

See also Exploited.

EXPRESSOS UK, male/female vocal/instrumental group   **5 wks**

| 21 Jun 80 | HEY GIRL WEA K 18246 | 60 | 3 wks |
| 14 Mar 81 | TANGO IN MONO WEA K 18431 | 70 | 2 wks |

E-ZEE POSSE UK, male/female vocal/instrumental group   **15 wks**

26 Aug 89	EVERYTHING STARTS WITH AN 'E' More Protein PROT 1	69	1 wk
20 Jan 90	LOVE ON LOVE More Protein PROT 3	59	3 wks
17 Mar 90	EVERYTHING STARTS WITH AN 'E' (re-entry) More Protein PROT 1	15	8 wks
30 Jun 90	THE SUN MACHINE More Protein PROT 4	62	3 wks

F

FAB UK, male producers   11 wks

7 Jul 90	●	THUNDERBIRDS ARE GO *Brothers Organisation FAB 1*........	5	8 wks
20 Oct 90		THE PRISONER *Brothers Organisation FAB 6*	56	2 wks
1 Dec 90		THE STINGRAY MEGAMIX *Brothers Organisation FAB 2*	66	1 wk

Thunderbirds Are Go features MC Parker, The Prisoner features MC Number 6, The Stingray Megamix features Aqua Marina. All are UK, male producers.

Shelley FABARES US, female vocalist   4 wks

| 26 Apr 62 | | JOHNNY ANGEL *Pye International 7N 25132*................... | 41 | 4 wks |

FABIAN US, male vocalist   1 wk

| 10 Mar 60 | | HOUND DOG MAN *HMV POP 695*......................... | 46 | 1 wk |

FACES UK, male vocal/instrumental group   46 wks

18 Dec 71	●	STAY WITH ME *Warner Bros. K 16136*	6	14 wks
17 Feb 73	●	CINDY INCIDENTALLY *Warner Bros. K 16247*........	2	9 wks
8 Dec 73	●	POOL HALL RICHARD/ I WISH IT WOULD RAIN		
		Warner Bros. K 16341........................	8	11 wks
7 Dec 74		YOU CAN MAKE ME DANCE SING OR ANYTHING		
		Warner Bros. K 16136	12	9 wks
4 Jun 77		THE FACES (EP) *Riva 8*.........................	41	3 wks

Tracks on The Faces EP: Memphis/You Can Make Me Dance Sing Or Anything/Stay With Me/Cindy Incidentally. You Can Make Me Dance Sing Or Anything credited to Rod Stewart and the Faces. See also Rod Stewart; Small Faces.

Joe FAGIN UK, male vocalist   20 wks

7 Jan 84	●	THAT'S LIVIN' ALRIGHT *Towerbell TOW 46*	3	11 wks
5 Apr 86		BACK WITH THE BOYS AGAIN/ GET IT RIGHT		
		Towerbell TOW 84	53	9 wks

Yvonne FAIR US, female vocalist   11 wks

| 24 Jan 76 | ● | IT SHOULD HAVE BEEN ME *Tamla Motown TMG 1013* ..... | 5 | 11 wks |

FAIR WEATHER UK, male vocal/instrumental group   12 wks

| 18 Jul 70 | ● | NATURAL SINNER *RCA 1977*................................ | 6 | 12 wks |

Fair Weather is led by Andy Fairweather-Low. See also Andy Fairweather-Low.

FAIRGROUND ATTRACTION   27 wks
UK, female/male vocal/instrumental group

16 Apr 88	★	PERFECT *RCA PB 41845*..................................	1	13 wks
30 Jul 88	●	FIND MY LOVE *RCA PB 42079*	7	10 wks
19 Nov 88		A SMILE IN A WHISPER *RCA PB 42249*	75	1 wk
28 Jan 89		CLARE *RCA PB 42607*................................	49	3 wks

FAIRPORT CONVENTION   9 wks
UK, male/female vocal/instrumental group

| 23 Jul 69 | | SI TU DOIS PARTIR *Island WIP 6064* .... | 21 | 8 wks |
| 27 Sep 69 | | SI TU DOIS PARTIR (re-entry) *Island WIP 6064* .... | 49 | 1 wk |

Andy FAIRWEATHER-LOW UK, male vocalist   18 wks

| 21 Sep 74 | ● | REGGAE TUNE *A &M AMS 7129*............................. | 10 | 8 wks |
| 6 Dec 75 | ● | WIDE EYED AND LEGLESS *A &M AMS 7202* .... | 6 | 10 wks |

See also Fair Weather.

Adam FAITH UK, male vocalist   251 wks

20 Nov 59	★	WHAT DO YOU WANT *Parlophone R 4591*................	1	19 wks
22 Jan 60	★	POOR ME *Parlophone R 4623*.........................	1	17 wks
14 Apr 60		SOMEONE ELSE'S BABY *Parlophone R 4643*..............	2	13 wks
30 Jun 60	●	WHEN JOHNNY COMES MARCHING HOME/ MADE		
		YOU *Parlophone R 4665*	5	13 wks
15 Sep 60	●	HOW ABOUT THAT *Parlophone R 4689*..............	4	14 wks
17 Nov 60	●	LONELY PUP (IN A CHRISTMAS SHOP)		
		Parlophone R 4708	4	11 wks
9 Feb 61	●	THIS IS IT / WHO AM I *Parlophone R 4735*	5	14 wks
27 Apr 61		EASY GOING ME *Parlophone R 4766*	12	10 wks
20 Jul 61		DON'T YOU KNOW IT *Parlophone R 4807*	12	10 wks
26 Oct 61	●	THE TIME HAS COME *Parlophone R 4837*	4	14 wks
18 Jan 62		LONESOME *Parlophone R 4864*	12	9 wks
3 May 62	●	AS YOU LIKE IT *Parlophone R 4896*	5	15 wks
30 Aug 62	●	DON'T THAT BEAT ALL *Parlophone R 4930*	8	11 wks
13 Dec 62		BABY TAKE A BOW *Parlophone R 4964*	22	6 wks
31 Jan 63		WHAT NOW *Parlophone R 4990*	31	5 wks
11 Jul 63		WALKIN' TALL *Parlophone R 5039*	23	6 wks
19 Sep 63	●	THE FIRST TIME *Parlophone R 5061*	5	13 wks
12 Dec 63		WE ARE IN LOVE *Parlophone R 5091*	11	12 wks
12 Mar 64		IF HE TELLS YOU *Parlophone R 5109*	25	9 wks
28 May 64		I LOVE BEING IN LOVE WITH YOU		
		Parlophone R 5138	33	6 wks
26 Nov 64		MESSAGE TO MARTHA (KENTUCKY BLUEBIRD)		
		Parlophone R 5201	12	11 wks
11 Feb 65		STOP FEELING SORRY FOR YOURSELF		
		Parlophone R 5235	23	6 wks
17 Jun 65		SOMEONE'S TAKEN MARIA AWAY *Parlophone R 5289*.....	34	5 wks
20 Oct 66		CHERYL'S GOIN' HOME *Parlophone R 5516*................	46	2 wks

The following hits featured the Roulettes, UK, male vocal/instrumental group, backing Adam Faith: The First Time, We Are In Love, If He Tells You, I Love Being In Love With You.

Horace FAITH Jamaica, male vocalist   10 wks

| 12 Sep 70 | | BLACK PEARL *Trojan TR 7790* .... | 13 | 10 wks |

Percy FAITH US, orchestra   30 wks

| 10 Mar 60 | ● | THEME FROM 'A SUMMER PLACE' *Philips PB 989*........ | 2 | 30 wks |

FAITH BROTHERS UK, male vocal/instrumental group   6 wks

| 13 Apr 85 | | THE COUNTRY OF THE BLIND *Siren SIREN 2* .... | 63 | 3 wks |
| 6 Jul 85 | | A STRANGER ON HOME GROUND *Siren SIREN 4* .... | 69 | 3 wks |

FAITH, HOPE and CHARITY   4 wks
US, male/female vocal group

| 31 Jan 76 | | JUST ONE LOOK *RCA 2632* .... | 38 | 4 wks |

FAITH, HOPE AND CHARITY   3 wks
UK, female vocal group

| 23 Jun 90 | | BATTLE OF THE SEXES *WEA YZ 480* .... | 53 | 3 wks |

FAITH NO MORE US, male vocal/instrumental group   21 wks

| 6 Feb 88 | | WE CARE A LOT *Slash LASH 17* .... | 53 | 3 wks |
| 10 Feb 90 | | EPIC *Slash LASH 21*.................................. | 37 | 4 wks |

14 Apr 90		FROM OUT OF NOWHERE *Slash LASH 24*	**23**	6 wks
14 Jul 90		FALLING TO PIECES *Slash LASH 25*	**41**	3 wks
8 Sep 90		EPIC (re-issue) *Slash LASH 26*	**25**	5 wks

Marianne FAITHFULL *UK, female vocalist*   **59 wks**

13 Aug 64	●	AS TEARS GO BY *Decca F 11923*	**9**	13 wks
18 Feb 65	●	COME AND STAY WITH ME *Decca F 12075*	**4**	13 wks
6 May 65	●	THIS LITTLE BIRD *Decca F 12162*	**6**	11 wks
22 Jul 65	●	SUMMER NIGHTS *Decca F 12193*	**10**	10 wks
4 Nov 65		YESTERDAY *Decca F 12268*	**36**	4 wks
9 Mar 67		IS THIS WHAT I GET FOR LOVING YOU *Decca F 22524*	**43**	2 wks
24 Nov 79		THE BALLAD OF LUCY JORDAN *Island WIP 6491*	**48**	6 wks

FALCO *Austria, male vocalist*   **26 wks**

22 Mar 86	★	ROCK ME AMADEUS *A & M AM 278*	**1**	15 wks
31 May 86	●	VIENNA CALLING *A & M AM 318*	**10**	8 wks
2 Aug 86		JEANNY *A & M AM 333*	**68**	1 wk
27 Sep 86		THE SOUND OF MUSIK *WEA U 8591*	**61**	2 wks

FALL *UK/US, male/female vocal/instrumental group*   **19 wks**

13 Sep 86		MR. PHARMACIST *Beggars Banquet BEG 168*	**75**	1 wk
20 Dec 86		HEY! LUCIANI *Beggars Banquet BEG 176*	**59**	1 wk
9 May 87		THERE'S A GHOST IN MY HOUSE *Beggars Banquet BEG 187*	**30**	4 wks
31 Oct 87		HIT THE NORTH *Beggars Banquet BEG 200*	**57**	5 wks
30 Jan 88		VICTORIA *Beggars Banquet BEG 206*	**35**	3 wks
26 Nov 88		BIG NEW PRINZ/ JERUSALEM (double single) *Beggars Banquet FALL 2/3*	**59**	2 wks
27 Jan 90		TELEPHONE THING *Cog Sinister SIN 4*	**58**	1 wk
8 Sep 90		WHITE LIGHTNING *Cog Sinister SIN 6*	**56**	2 wks

Tracks on Big New Prinz/ Jerusalem double single: Big New Prinz/Wrong Place Right Time Number Two/Jerusalem/Acid Priest 2088.

Harold FALTERMEYER   **23 wks**
Germany, male instrumentalist - keyboards

23 Mar 85		AXEL F *MCA MCA 949*	**62**	4 wks
1 Jun 85	●	AXEL F (re-entry) *MCA MCA 949*	**2**	18 wks
24 Aug 85		FLETCH THEME *MCA MCA 991*	**74**	1 wk

Agnetha FALTSKOG *Sweden, female vocalist*   **12 wks**

28 May 83		THE HEAT IS ON *Epic A 3436*	**35**	6 wks
13 Aug 83		WRAP YOUR ARMS AROUND ME *Epic A 3622*	**44**	5 wks
22 Oct 83		CAN'T SHAKE LOOSE *Epic A 3812*	**63**	1 wk

Georgie FAME *UK, male vocalist*   **105 wks**

17 Dec 64	★	YEH YEH *Columbia DB 7428*	**1**	12 wks
4 Mar 65		IN THE MEANTIME *Columbia DB 7494*	**22**	8 wks
29 Jul 65		LIKE WE USED TO BE *Columbia DB 7633*	**33**	7 wks
28 Oct 65		SOMETHING *Columbia DB 7727*	**23**	7 wks
23 Jun 66	★	GET AWAY *Columbia DB 7946*	**1**	11 wks
22 Sep 66		SUNNY *Columbia DB 8015*	**13**	8 wks
22 Dec 66		SITTING IN THE PARK *Columbia DB 8096*	**12**	10 wks
23 Mar 67		BECAUSE I LOVE YOU *CBS 202587*	**15**	8 wks
13 Sep 67		TRY MY WORLD *CBS 2945*	**37**	5 wks
13 Dec 67	★	BALLAD OF BONNIE AND CLYDE *CBS 3124*	**1**	13 wks
9 Jul 69		PEACEFUL *CBS 4295*	**16**	9 wks
13 Dec 69		SEVENTH SON *CBS 4659*	**25**	7 wks

All Columbia hits except Sunny *credit The Blue Flames backing Georgie Fame. See also Fame and Price Together.*

FAME and PRICE TOGETHER   **10 wks**
UK, male vocal/instrumental duo - piano

10 Apr 71		ROSETTA *CBS 7108*	**11**	10 wks

See also Georgie Fame; Alan Price.

FAMILY *UK, male vocal/instrumental group*   **44 wks**

1 Nov 69		NO MULE'S FOOL *Reprise RS 27001*	**29**	7 wks
22 Aug 70		STRANGE BAND *Reprise RS 27009*	**11**	12 wks
17 Jul 71	●	IN MY OWN TIME *Reprise K 14090*	**4**	13 wks
23 Sep 72		BURLESQUE *Reprise K 14196*	**13**	12 wks

FAMILY – *See Afrika BAMBAATAA with UB40 and FAMILY*

FAMILY COOKIN' – *See LIMMIE and the FAMILY COOKIN'*

FAMILY DOGG *UK, male/female vocal group*   **14 wks**

28 May 69	●	WAY OF LIFE *Bell 1055*	**6**	14 wks

FAMILY STAND *US, male/female vocal/instrumental group*   **11 wks**

31 Mar 90	●	GHETTO HEAVEN *East West A 7997*	**10**	11 wks

FAMILY STONE – *See SLY and the FAMILY STONE*

FAMOUS FLAMES – *See James BROWN*

FANTASTIC FOUR *US, male vocal group*   **4 wks**

24 Feb 79		B.Y.O.F. (BRING YOUR OWN FUNK) *Atlantic LV 14*	**62**	4 wks

FANTASTICS *US, male vocal group*   **12 wks**

27 Mar 71	●	SOMETHING OLD, SOMETHING NEW *Bell 1141*	**9**	12 wks

FANTASY U.F.O. *UK, male instrumental group*   **3 wks**

29 Sep 90		FANTASY *XL Recording XLT 15*	**56**	3 wks

FAR CORPORATION   **11 wks**
UK/US/Germany/Switzerland, male vocal/instrumental group

26 Oct 85	●	STAIRWAY TO HEAVEN *Arista ARIST 639*	**8**	11 wks

Don FARDON *UK, male vocalist*   **22 wks**

18 Apr 70		BELFAST BOY *Young Blood YB 1010*	**32**	5 wks
10 Oct 70	●	INDIAN RESERVATION *Young Blood YB 1015*	**3**	17 wks

Chris FARLOWE *UK, male vocalist*   **36 wks**

27 Jan 66		THINK *Immediate IM 023*	**49**	1 wk
10 Feb 66		THINK (re-entry) *Immediate IM 023*	**37**	2 wks
23 Jun 66	★	OUT OF TIME *Immediate IM 035*	**1**	13 wks
27 Oct 66		RIDE ON BABY *Immediate IM 038*	**31**	7 wks
16 Feb 67		MY WAY OF GIVING IN *Immediate IM 041*	**48**	1 wk

29 Jun 67	MOANIN' *Immediate IM 056*	46	2 wks
13 Dec 67	HANDBAGS AND GLADRAGS *Immediate IM 065*	33	6 wks
27 Sep 75	OUT OF TIME (re-issue) *Immediate IMS 101*	44	4 wks

FARM UK, *male vocal/instrumental group*   **18 wks**

5 May 90	STEPPING STONE/ FAMILY OF MAN *Produce MILK 101*	58	4 wks
1 Sep 90	● GROOVY TRAIN *Produce MILK 102*	6	10 wks
8 Dec 90	● ALL TOGETHER NOW *Produce MILK 103*	4†	4 wks

FARMERS BOYS UK, *male vocal/instrumental group*   **17 wks**

9 Apr 83	MUCK IT OUT *EMI 5380*	48	6 wks
30 Jul 83	FOR YOU *EMI 5401*	66	3 wks
4 Aug 84	IN THE COUNTRY *EMI FAB 2*	44	5 wks
3 Nov 84	PHEW WOW *EMI FAB 3*	59	3 wks

John FARNHAM Australia, *male vocalist*   **17 wks**

| 25 Apr 87 | ● YOU'RE THE VOICE *Wheatley PB 41093* | 6 | 17 wks |

Joe FARRELL US, *male instrumentalist - saxophone*   **4 wks**

| 16 Dec 78 | NIGHT DANCING *Warner Bros. LV 2* | 57 | 4 wks |

Gene FARROW and G.F. BAND   **8 wks**
UK, *male vocal/instrumental group*

1 Apr 78	MOVE YOUR BODY *Magnet MAG 109*	33	5 wks
13 May 78	MOVE YOUR BODY (re-entry) *Magnet MAG 109*	67	1 wk
5 Aug 78	DON'T STOP NOW *Magnet MAG 125*	71	1 wk
19 Aug 78	DON'T STOP NOW (re-entry) *Magnet MAG 125*	74	1 wk

FASCINATIONS US, *female vocal group*   **6 wks**

| 3 Jul 71 | GIRLS ARE OUT TO GET YOU *Mojo 2092 004* | 32 | 6 wks |

FASHION UK, *male vocal/instrumental group*   **12 wks**

3 Apr 82	STREETPLAYER (MECHANIK) *Arista ARIST 456*	46	5 wks
21 Aug 82	LOVE SHADOW *Arista ARIST 483*	51	5 wks
18 Feb 84	EYE TALK *De Stijl A 4106*	69	2 wks

Susan FASSBENDER UK, *female vocalist*   **8 wks**

| 17 Jan 81 | TWILIGHT CAFE *CBS 9468* | 21 | 8 wks |

FASTWAY UK, *male vocal/instrumental group*   **1 wk**

| 2 Apr 83 | EASY LIVIN' *CBS A 3196* | 74 | 1 wk |

FAT BOYS US, *male vocal rap group*   **29 wks**

4 May 85	JAIL HOUSE RAP *Sultra U 9123*	63	2 wks
22 Aug 87	● WIPEOUT *Urban URB 5*	2	12 wks
18 Jun 88	● THE TWIST (YO, TWIST) *Urban URB 20*	2	11 wks
5 Nov 88	LOUIE LOUIE *Urban URB 26*	46	4 wks

Wipeout features the Beach Boys as co-vocalists. The Twist (Yo, Twist) features Chubby Checker as co-vocalist. See also Beach Boys; Chubby Checker.

FAT LARRY'S BAND US, *male vocal/instrumental group*   **22 wks**

2 Jul 77	CENTER CITY *Atlantic K 10951*	31	5 wks
18 Aug 79	LOOKING FOR LOVE TONIGHT *Fantasy FTC 179*	46	6 wks
18 Sep 82	ZOOM *Virgin VS 546*	2	11 wks

See also F.L.B.

FATBACK BAND US, *male vocal/instrumental group*   **67 wks**

6 Sep 75	YUM YUM (GIMME SOME) *Polydor 2066 590*	40	6 wks
6 Dec 75	(ARE YOU READY) DO THE BUS STOP *Polydor 2066 637*	18	10 wks
21 Feb 76	● (DO THE) SPANISH HUSTLE *Polydor 2066 656*	10	7 wks
29 May 76	PARTY TIME *Polydor 2066 682*	41	4 wks
14 Aug 76	NIGHT FEVER *Spring 2066 706*	38	4 wks
12 Mar 77	DOUBLE DUTCH *Spring 2066 777*	31	4 wks
9 Aug 80	BACKSTROKIN' *Spring POSP 149*	41	9 wks
23 Jun 84	I FOUND LOVIN' *Master Mix CME 8401*	49	4 wks
4 May 85	GIRLS ON MY MIND *Atlantic/Cotillion FBACK 1*	69	2 wks
6 Sep 86	I FOUND LOVIN' (re-mix) *Important TAN 10*	55	5 wks
5 Sep 87	I FOUND LOVIN' (re-entry) *Master Mix CME 8401*	7	12 wks

Backstrokin' and Girls On My Mind credited simply to Fatback.

FBI – *See REDHEAD KINGPIN and the FBI*

Phil FEARON and GALAXY   **63 wks**
UK, *male/female vocal/instrumental group*

23 Apr 83	● DANCING TIGHT *Ensign ENY 501*	4	11 wks
30 Jul 83	WAIT UNTIL TONIGHT (MY LOVE) *Ensign ENY 503*	20	8 wks
22 Oct 83	FANTASY REAL *Ensign ENY 507*	41	6 wks
10 Mar 84	● WHAT DO I DO *Ensign ENY 510*	5	10 wks
14 Jul 84	● EVERYBODY'S LAUGHING *Ensign ENY 514*	10	10 wks
15 Jun 85	YOU DON'T NEED A REASON *Ensign ENY 517*	42	4 wks
27 Jul 85	THIS KIND OF LOVE *Ensign ENY 521*	70	3 wks
2 Aug 86	● I CAN PROVE IT *Ensign PF 1*	8	9 wks
15 Nov 86	AIN'T NOTHING BUT A HOUSEPARTY *Ensign PF 2*	60	2 wks

First two hits credited to Galaxy featuring Phil Fearon. This Kind of Love credits Dee Galdes, female vocalist. Ensign PF1 and PF2 just credit Phil Fearon. See also T.C. Curtis.

Wilton FELDER US, *male instrumentalist - tenor sax*   **7 wks**

| 1 Nov 80 | INHERIT THE WIND *MCA 646* | 39 | 5 wks |
| 16 Feb 85 | (NO MATTER HOW HIGH I GET) I'LL STILL BE LOOKIN' UP TO YOU *MCA MCA 919* | 63 | 2 wks |

Bobby Womack sang lead vocals on MCA 646. MCA 919 features Bobby Womack and Altrina Grayson. See also Bobby Womack.

José FELICIANO US, *male vocalist/instrumentalist - guitar*   **23 wks**

| 18 Sep 68 | ● LIGHT MY FIRE *RCA 1715* | 6 | 16 wks |
| 18 Oct 69 | AND THE SUN WILL SHINE *RCA 1871* | 25 | 7 wks |

Julie FELIX US, *female vocalist*   **19 wks**

| 18 Apr 70 | IF I COULD (EL CONDOR PASA) *RAK 101* | 19 | 11 wks |
| 17 Oct 70 | HEAVEN IS HERE *RAK 105* | 22 | 8 wks |

FELLY – *See TECHNOTRONIC*

FEMME FATALE US, *male/female vocal/instrumental group*   **2 wks**

| 11 Feb 89 | FALLING IN AND OUT OF LOVE *MCA MCA 1309* | 69 | 2 wks |

FENDERMEN US, male vocal/instrumental duo - guitars   **9 wks**

18 Aug 60	**MULE SKINNER BLUES** *Top Rank JAR 395* **50**	1 wk
1 Sep 60	**MULE SKINNER BLUES (re-entry)** *Top Rank JAR 395* **37**	2 wks
29 Sep 60	**MULE SKINNER BLUES (2nd re-entry)**	
	Top Rank JAR 395 .... **32**	6 wks

FENMEN – See Bern ELLIOTT and the FENMEN

George FENTON and Jonas GWANGWA   **1 wk**
UK/South Africa, male instrumental production duo

2 Jan 88	**CRY FREEDOM** *MCA MCA 1228* **75**	1 wk

The listed flip side of Cry Freedom *was* The Funeral *by Thuli Dumakude. See also Thuli Dumakude.*

Peter FENTON UK, male vocalist   **3 wks**

10 Nov 66	**MARBLE BREAKS IRON BENDS** *Fontana TF 748* **46**	3 wks

Shane FENTON and the FENTONES   **28 wks**
UK, male vocal/instrumental group

26 Oct 61	**I'M A MOODY GUY** *Parlophone R 4827* **22**	8 wks
1 Feb 62	**WALK AWAY** *Parlophone R 4866* **38**	5 wks
5 Apr 62	**IT'S ALL OVER NOW** *Parlophone R 4883* **29**	7 wks
12 Jul 62	**CINDY'S BIRTHDAY** *Parlophone R 4921*..................... **19**	8 wks

Fenton later became Alvin Stardust - see also Alvin Stardust; Fentones.

FENTONES UK, male instrumental group   **4 wks**

19 Apr 62	**THE MEXICAN** *Parlophone R 4899* **41**	3 wks
27 Sep 62	**THE BREEZE AND I** *Parlophone R 4937* **48**	1 wk

See also Shane Fenton and the Fentones.

FERKO STRING BAND   **2 wks**
US, male vocal/instrumental group

12 Aug 55	**ALABAMA JUBILEE** *London HL 8140* **20**	2 wks

Luisa FERNANDEZ Spain, female vocalist   **8 wks**

11 Nov 78	**LAY LOVE ON YOU** *Warner Bros. K 17061* **31**	8 wks

FERRANTE and TEICHER   **18 wks**
US, male instrumental duo - pianos

18 Aug 60	**THEME FROM 'THE APARTMENT'**	
	London HLT 9164 .... **44**	1 wk
9 Mar 61	● **THEME FROM 'EXODUS'**	
	London HLT 9298 and HMV POP 881............................ **6**	17 wks

Theme From Exodus *available first on London, then on HMV when the American label, United Artists, changed its UK outlet.*

José FERRER US, male vocalist   **3 wks**

19 Feb 54	● **WOMAN** *Philips PB 220* **7**	3 wks

Woman *coupled with* Man *by Rosemary Clooney. See Rosemary Clooney.*

FERRY AID International, male/female charity ensemble   **7 wks**

4 Apr 87	★ **LET IT BE** *The Sun AID 1* **1**	7 wks

Bryan FERRY UK, male vocalist   **119 wks**

29 Sep 73	● **A HARD RAIN'S GONNA FALL** *Island WIP 6170*............ **10**	9 wks
25 May 74	**THE IN CROWD** *Island WIP 6196* **13**	6 wks
31 Aug 74	**SMOKE GETS IN YOUR EYES** *Island WIP 6205* **17**	8 wks
5 Jul 75	**YOU GO TO MY HEAD** *Island WIP 6234* **33**	3 wks
12 Jun 76	● **LET'S STICK TOGETHER** *Island WIP 6307*.................... **4**	10 wks
7 Aug 76	● **EXTENDED PLAY** (EP) *Island IEP 1* **7**	9 wks
5 Feb 77	● **THIS IS TOMORROW** *Polydor 2001 704*..................... **9**	9 wks
14 May 77	**TOKYO JOE** *Polydor 2001 714* **15**	7 wks
13 May 78	**WHAT GOES ON** *Polydor POSP 3* **67**	2 wks
5 Aug 78	**SIGN OF THE TIMES** *Polydor 2001 798* **37**	8 wks
11 May 85	● **SLAVE TO LOVE** *EG FERRY 1*............................... **10**	9 wks
31 Aug 85	**DON'T STOP THE DANCE** *EG FERRY 2*................... **21**	7 wks
7 Dec 85	**WINDSWEPT** *EG FERRY 3*.................................. **46**	3 wks
29 Mar 86	**IS YOUR LOVE STRONG ENOUGH?** *EG FERRY 4* **22**	7 wks
10 Oct 87	**THE RIGHT STUFF** *Virgin VS 940* **37**	6 wks
13 Feb 88	**KISS AND TELL** *Virgin VS 1034* **41**	5 wks
29 Oct 88	**LET'S STICK TOGETHER (re-mix)** *EG EGO 44* **12**	7 wks
11 Feb 89	**THE PRICE OF LOVE (re-mix)** *EG EGO 46*................. **49**	3 wks
22 Apr 89	**HE'LL HAVE TO GO** *EG EGO 48*.......................... **63**	1 wk

Tracks on EP: Price Of Love/Shame Shame Shame/Heart On My Sleeve/It's Only Love.

Karel FIALKA UK, male vocalist/multi-instrumentalist   **12 wks**

17 May 80	**THE EYES HAVE IT** *Blueprint BLU 2005* **52**	4 wks
5 Sep 87	● **HEY MATTHEW** *IRS IRM 140* **9**	8 wks

FIAT LUX UK, male vocal/instrumental group   **4 wks**

28 Jan 84	**SECRETS** *Polydor FIAT 2* **65**	3 wks
17 Mar 84	**BLUE EMOTION** *Polydor FIAT 3* **59**	1 wk

FICTION FACTORY UK, male vocal/instrumental group   **11 wks**

14 Jan 84	● **(FEELS LIKE) HEAVEN** *CBS A 3996* **6**	9 wks
17 Mar 84	**GHOST OF LOVE** *CBS A 3819*................................ **64**	2 wks

FIDDLER'S DRAM   **9 wks**
UK, male/female vocal/instrumental group

15 Dec 79	● **DAY TRIP TO BANGOR (DIDN'T WE HAVE A**	
	LOVELY TIME) *Dingles SID 211*.............................. **3**	9 wks

FIDELFATTI featuring RONNETTE   **1 wk**
Italy, male producer and female vocalist

27 Jan 90	**JUST WANNA TOUCH ME** *Urban URB 46* **65**	1 wk

Billy FIELD Australia, male vocalist   **3 wks**

12 Jun 82	**YOU WEREN'T IN LOVE WITH ME** *CBS A 2344* **67**	3 wks

Ernie FIELDS US, orchestra   **8 wks**

25 Dec 59	**IN THE MOOD** *London HL 8985* **13**	8 wks

Gracie FIELDS UK, female vocalist   **15 wks**

31 May 57	● **AROUND THE WORLD** Columbia DB 3953	8	8 wks
2 Aug 57	**AROUND THE WORLD (re-entry)** Columbia DB 3953	24	1 wk
6 Nov 59	**LITTLE DONKEY** Columbia DB 4360.	30	1 wk
20 Nov 59	**LITTLE DONKEY (re-entry)** Columbia DB 4360.	20	5 wks

FIELDS OF THE NEPHILIM   **9 wks**
UK, male vocal/instrumental group

24 Oct 87	**BLUE WATER** Situation Two SIT 48	75	1 wk
4 Jun 88	**MOONCHILD** Situation Two SIT 52	28	3 wks
27 May 89	**PSYCHONAUT** Situation Two ST 57	35	3 wks
4 Aug 90	**FOR HER LIGHT** Beggars Banquet BEG 244T	54	1 wk
24 Nov 90	**SUMERLAND (DREAMED)** Beggars Banquet BEG 250........	37	1 wk

Richard 'Dimples' FIELDS US, male vocalist   **4 wks**

20 Feb 82	**I'VE GOT TO LEARN TO SAY NO** Epic EPC A 1918	56	4 wks

FIFTH DIMENSION US, male/female vocal group   **21 wks**

16 Apr 69	**(MEDLEY)** Liberty LBF 15193	11	12 wks
17 Jan 70	**WEDDING BELL BLUES** Liberty LBF 15288..................	16	9 wks

52ND STREET UK, male/female vocal/instrumental group   **13 wks**

2 Nov 85	**TELL ME (HOW IT FEELS)** 10 TEN 74......................	54	5 wks
11 Jan 86	**YOU'RE MY LAST CHANCE** 10 TEN 89	49	4 wks
8 Mar 86	**I CAN'T LET YOU GO** 10 TEN 114	57	4 wks

53RD and 3RD   **4 wks**
UK, male vocal group plus Jonathan King much in evidence on vocals

20 Sep 75	**CHICK A BOOM (DON'T YA JES LOVE IT)** UK 2012 002	36	4 wks

Hit featured 'The Sound Of Shag'. See also Shag; Jonathan King.

FINE YOUNG CANNIBALS   **76 wks**
UK, male vocal/instrumental group

8 Jun 85	● **JOHNNY COME HOME** London LON 68......................	8	13 wks
9 Nov 85	**BLUE** London LON 79.	41	6 wks
11 Jan 86	● **SUSPICIOUS MINDS** London LON 82......................	8	9 wks
12 Apr 86	**FUNNY HOW LOVE IS** London LON 88	58	4 wks
21 Mar 87	● **EVER FALLEN IN LOVE** London LON 121	9	10 wks
7 Jan 89	● **SHE DRIVES ME CRAZY** London LON 199	5	11 wks
15 Apr 89	● **GOOD THING** London LON 218	7	8 wks
19 Aug 89	**DON'T LOOK BACK** London LON 220	34	4 wks
18 Nov 89	**I'M NOT THE MAN I USED TO BE** London LON 244......	20	8 wks
24 Feb 90	**I'M NOT SATISFIED** London LON 252	46	3 wks

FINK BROTHERS UK, male vocal/instrumental duo   **4 wks**

9 Feb 85	**MUTANTS IN MEGA CITY ONE** Zarjazz JAZZ 2	50	4 wks

Elisa FIORILLO US, female vocalist   **4 wks**

13 Feb 88	**HOW CAN I FORGET YOU** Chrysalis ELISA 1	50	4 wks

See also Jellybean.

FIRE INC. – See Jim STEINMAN

FIREBALLS US, male instrumental group   **9 wks**

27 Jul 61	**QUITE A PARTY** Pye International 7N 25092..................	29	9 wks

See also Jimmy Gilmer and the Fireballs.

FIRM UK, male vocal/instrumental group   **21 wks**

17 Jul 82	**ARTHUR DALEY ('E'S ALRIGHT)** Bark HID 1	14	9 wks
6 Jun 87	★ **STAR TREKKIN'** Bark TREK 1	1	12 wks

FIRST CHOICE US, female vocal group   **21 wks**

19 May 73	**ARMED AND EXTREMELY DANGEROUS** Bell 1297......	16	10 wks
4 Aug 73	● **SMARTY PANTS** Bell 1324	9	11 wks

FIRST CLASS UK, male vocal group   **10 wks**

15 Jun 74	**BEACH BABY** UK 66	13	10 wks

FIRST EDITION – See Kenny ROGERS

FIRST LIGHT UK, male vocal/instrumental duo   **5 wks**

21 May 83	**EXPLAIN THE REASONS** London LON 26	65	3 wks
28 Jan 84	**WISH YOU WERE HERE** London LON 43	71	2 wks

FISCHER-Z UK, male vocal/instrumental group   **7 wks**

26 May 79	**THE WORKER** United Artists UP 36509........................	53	5 wks
3 May 80	**SO LONG** United Artists BP 342	72	2 wks

FISH UK, male vocalist   **10 wks**

28 Oct 89	**STATE OF MIND** EMI EM 109...............................	32	3 wks
6 Jan 90	**BIG WEDGE** EMI EM 125....................................	25	4 wks
17 Mar 90	**A GENTLEMAN'S EXCUSE ME** EMI EM 135...............	30	3 wks

See also Fish and Tony Banks.

FISH and Tony BANKS   **1 wk**
UK, male vocalist and UK, male instrumentalist - keyboards

18 Oct 86	**SHORT CUT TO SOMEWHERE** Charisma CB 426	75	1 wk

See also Fish.

Eddie FISHER US, male vocalist   **105 wks**

2 Jan 53	★ **OUTSIDE OF HEAVEN** HMV B 10362	1	16 wks
23 Jan 53	**EVERYTHING I HAVE IS YOURS** HMV B 10398	12	1 wk
6 Feb 53	● **EVERYTHING I HAVE IS YOURS (re-entry)** HMV B 10398	8	4 wks
1 May 53	● **DOWNHEARTED** HMV B 10450.............................	3	15 wks
1 May 53	**OUTSIDE OF HEAVEN (re-entry)** HMV B 10362	12	1 wk
22 May 53	★ **I'M WALKING BEHIND YOU** HMV B 10489.................	1	18 wks
6 Nov 53	● **WISH YOU WERE HERE** HMV B 10564......................	8	9 wks
22 Jan 54	● **OH MEIN PAPA** HMV B 10614..............................	9	1 wk
5 Feb 54	**OH MEIN PAPA (re-entry)** HMV B 10614.....................	11	1 wk
26 Feb 54	**OH MEIN PAPA (2nd re-entry)** HMV B 10614...............	10	1 wk
12 Mar 54	**OH MEIN PAPA (3rd re-entry)** HMV B 10614...............	11	1 wk
29 Oct 54	**I NEED YOU NOW** HMV B 10755	16	2 wks
19 Nov 54	**I NEED YOU NOW (re-entry)** HMV B 10755	13	7 wks
21 Jan 55	**I NEED YOU NOW (2nd re-entry)** HMV B 10755	19	1 wk
18 Mar 55	● **WEDDING BELLS** HMV B 10839.............................	5	11 wks
23 Nov 56	● **CINDY OH CINDY** HMV POP 273..........................	5	16 wks

'Good Thing' by FINE YOUNG CANNIBALS was originally performed in the film *Tin Men*.

Bottom Left: Not until Diana Ross overtook her in 1982 did an American female vocalist spend more weeks on chart than CONNIE FRANCIS.

Bottom Right: 'Oh Mein Papa' star EDDIE FISHER is now the famous father of actress/ novelist Carrie Fisher, whose *Postcards From the Edge* became a major film recently.

Below: ARETHA FRANKLIN won the Grammy Award for Best Rhythm and Blues Vocal Performance (Female) every year from 1967 to 1974.

Mark FISHER featuring Dotty GREEN
UK, male instrumentalist - keyboards, featuring UK, female vocalist   **2 wks**

29 Jun 85   **LOVE SITUATION** *Total Control TOCO 3* .... **59**   2 wks

Toni FISHER *US, female vocalist*   **1 wk**

12 Feb 60   **THE BIG HURT** *Top Rank JAR 261* .... **30**   1 wk

Ella FITZGERALD *US, female vocalist*   **29 wks**

23 May 58	**SWINGIN' SHEPHERD BLUES** *HMV POP 486*	**15**	5 wks
16 Oct 59	**BUT NOT FOR ME** *HMV POP 657*	**25**	2 wks
25 Dec 59	**BUT NOT FOR ME (re-entry)** *HMV POP 657*	**29**	1 wk
21 Apr 60	**MACK THE KNIFE** *HMV POP 736*	**19**	9 wks
6 Oct 60	**HOW HIGH THE MOON** *HMV POP 782*	**46**	1 wk
22 Nov 62	**DESAFINADO** *Verve VS 502*	**38**	4 wks
27 Dec 62	**DESAFINADO (re-entry)** *Verve VS 502*	**41**	2 wks
30 Apr 64	**CAN'T BUY ME LOVE** *Verve VS 519*	**34**	5 wks

Scott FITZGERALD *UK, male vocalist*   **2 wks**

7 May 88   **GO** *PRT PYS 10* .... **52**   2 wks

See also Scott Fitzgerald and Yvonne Keely.

Scott FITZGERALD and Yvonne KEELY   **10 wks**
UK/Holland, male/female vocal duo

14 Jan 78 ● **IF I HAD WORDS** *Pepper UP 36333* .... **3**   10 wks

Hit credits St. Thomas More School Choir. See also Scott Fitzgerald.

FIVE SMITH BROTHERS *UK, male vocal group*   **1 wk**

22 Jul 55   **I'M IN FAVOUR OF FRIENDSHIP** *Decca F 10527* .... **20**   1 wk

FIVE STAR *UK, male/female vocal group*   **140 wks**

4 May 85	**ALL FALL DOWN** *Tent PB 40039*	**15**	12 wks
20 Jul 85	**LET ME BE THE ONE** *Tent PB 40193*	**18**	9 wks
14 Sep 85	**LOVE TAKE OVER** *Tent PB 40353*	**25**	9 wks
16 Nov 85	**R.S.V.P.** *Tent PB 40445*	**45**	5 wks
11 Jan 86 ●	**SYSTEM ADDICT** *Tent PB 40515*	**3**	11 wks
12 Apr 86 ●	**CAN'T WAIT ANOTHER MINUTE** *Tent PB 40697*	**7**	10 wks
26 Jul 86 ●	**FIND THE TIME** *Tent PB 40799*	**7**	10 wks
13 Sep 86 ●	**RAIN OR SHINE** *Tent PB 40901*	**2**	11 wks
22 Nov 86	**IF I SAY YES** *Tent PB 40981*	**15**	9 wks
7 Feb 87 ●	**STAY OUT OF MY LIFE** *Tent PB 41131*	**9**	8 wks
18 Apr 87 ●	**THE SLIGHTEST TOUCH** *Tent PB 41265*	**4**	9 wks
22 Aug 87	**WHENEVER YOU'RE READY** *Tent PB 41477*	**11**	6 wks
10 Oct 87	**STRONG AS STEEL** *Tent PB 41565*	**16**	7 wks
5 Dec 87	**SOMEWHERE SOMEBODY** *Tent PB 41661*	**23**	6 wks
4 Jun 88	**ANOTHER WEEKEND** *Tent PB 42081*	**18**	4 wks
6 Aug 88	**ROCK MY WORLD** *Tent PB 42145*	**28**	4 wks
17 Sep 88	**THERE'S A BRAND NEW WORLD** *Tent PB 42235*	**61**	2 wks
19 Nov 88	**LET ME BE YOURS** *Tent PB 42343*	**51**	3 wks
8 Apr 89	**WITH EVERY HEARTBEAT** *Tent PB 42693*	**49**	2 wks
10 Mar 90	**TREAT ME LIKE A LADY** *Tent FIVE 1*	**54**	2 wks
7 Jul 90	**HOT LOVE** *Tent FIVE 2*	**68**	1 wk

FIVE THIRTY *UK, male vocal/instrumental group*   **1 wk**

4 Aug 90   **ABSTAIN** *East West YZ 530* .... **75**   1 wk

5000 VOLTS *UK, male/female vocal/instrumental group*   **18 wks**

6 Sep 75 ●	**I'M ON FIRE** *Philips 6006 464*	**4**	9 wks
24 Jul 76 ●	**DR. KISS KISS** *Philips 6006 533*	**8**	9 wks

FIXX *UK, male vocal/instrumental group*   **8 wks**

24 Apr 82	**STAND OR FALL** *MCA FIXX 2*	**54**	4 wks
17 Jul 82	**RED SKIES** *MCA FIXX 3*	**57**	4 wks

Roberta FLACK *US, female vocalist*   **44 wks**

27 May 72	**THE FIRST TIME EVER I SAW YOUR FACE** *Atlantic K 10161*	**14**	14 wks
17 Feb 73 ●	**KILLING ME SOFTLY WITH HIS SONG** *Atlantic K 10282*	**6**	14 wks
24 Aug 74	**FEEL LIKE MAKING LOVE** *Atlantic K 10467*	**34**	7 wks
30 Aug 80	**DON'T MAKE ME WAIT TOO LONG** *Atlantic K 11555*	**44**	7 wks
29 Jul 89	**UH-UH OOH OOH LOOK OUT (HERE IT COMES)** *Atlantic A 8941*	**72**	2 wks

See also Peabo Bryson and Roberta Flack; Roberta Flack and Donny Hathaway.

Roberta FLACK and Donny HATHAWAY   **22 wks**
US, female/male vocal duo

5 Aug 72	**WHERE IS THE LOVE** *Atlantic K 10202*	**29**	7 wks
6 May 78	**THE CLOSER I GET TO YOU** *Atlantic K 11099*	**42**	4 wks
17 May 80 ●	**BACK TOGETHER AGAIN** *Atlantic K 11481*	**3**	11 wks

See also Roberta Flack.

FLAMINGOS *US, male vocal group*   **5 wks**

4 Jun 69   **BOOGALOO PARTY** *Philips BF 1786* .... **26**   5 wks

Michael FLANDERS *UK, male vocalist*   **3 wks**

27 Feb 59	**LITTLE DRUMMER BOY** *Parlophone R 4528*	**20**	2 wks
17 Apr 59	**LITTLE DRUMMER BOY (re-entry)** *Parlophone R 4528*	**24**	1 wk

FLASH AND THE PAN   **15 wks**
Australia, male vocal/instrumental group

23 Sep 78	**AND THE BAND PLAYED ON (DOWN AMONG THE DEAD MEN)** *Ensign ENY 15*	**54**	4 wks
21 May 83 ●	**WAITING FOR A TRAIN** *Easybeat EASY 1*	**7**	11 wks

Lester FLATT and Earl SCRUGGS   **6 wks**
US, male instrumental duo - banjos

15 Nov 67   **FOGGY MOUNTAIN BREAKDOWN** *CBS 3038 and Mercury MF 1007* .... **39**   6 wks

The versions on the two labels were not the same cuts; CBS had a 1965 recording, Mercury a 1967. The chart did not differentiate and listed both together.

Fogwell FLAX and the ANKLEBITERS from FREEHOLD JUNIOR SCHOOL   **2 wks**
UK, male vocalist and school choir

26 Dec 81   **ONE NINE FOR SANTA** *EMI 5255* .... **68**   2 wks

F.L.B. US, male vocal/instrumental group   4 wks

| 10 Mar 79 | BOOGIE TOWN Fantasy FTC 168 | 46 | 4 wks |

See also Fat Larry's Band.

FLEE-REKKERS UK, male instrumental group   13 wks

| 19 May 60 | GREEN JEANS Triumph RGM 1008 | 23 | 13 wks |

FLEETWOOD MAC   223 wks
UK/US, male/female vocal/instrumental group

10 Apr 68	BLACK MAGIC WOMAN Blue Horizon 57 3138	37	7 wks
17 Jul 68	NEED YOUR LOVE SO BAD Blue Horizon 57 3139	31	13 wks
4 Dec 68 ★	ALBATROSS Blue Horizon 57 3145	1	20 wks
16 Apr 69 ●	MAN OF THE WORLD Immediate IM 080	2	14 wks
23 Jul 69	NEED YOUR LOVE SO BAD (re-issue) Blue Horizon 57 3157	32	6 wks
13 Sep 69	NEED YOUR LOVE SO BAD (re-entry of re-issue) Blue Horizon 57 3157	42	3 wks
4 Oct 69 ●	OH WELL Reprise RS 27000	2	16 wks
23 May 70 ●	THE GREEN MANALISHI (WITH THE TWO-PRONG CROWN) Reprise RS 27007	10	12 wks
12 May 73 ●	ALBATROSS (re-issue) CBS 8306	2	15 wks
13 Nov 76	SAY YOU LOVE ME Reprise K 14447	40	4 wks
19 Feb 77	GO YOUR OWN WAY Warner Bros. K 16872	38	4 wks
30 Apr 77	DON'T STOP Warner Bros. K 16930	32	5 wks
9 Jul 77	DREAMS Warner Bros. K 16969	24	9 wks
22 Oct 77	YOU MAKE LOVING FUN Warner Bros. K 17013	45	2 wks
11 Mar 78	RHIANNON Reprise K 14430	46	3 wks
6 Oct 79 ●	TUSK Warner Bros. K 17468	6	10 wks
22 Dec 79	SARA Warner Bros. K 17533	37	8 wks
25 Sep 82	GYPSY Warner Bros. K 17997	46	3 wks
18 Dec 82 ●	OH DIANE Warner Bros. FLEET 1	9	15 wks
4 Apr 87 ●	BIG LOVE Warner Bros. W 8398	9	12 wks
11 Jul 87	SEVEN WONDERS Warner Bros. W 8317	56	4 wks
26 Sep 87 ●	LITTLE LIES Warner Bros. W 8291	5	12 wks
26 Dec 87	FAMILY MAN Warner Bros. W 8114	54	5 wks
2 Apr 88 ●	EVERYWHERE Warner Bros. W 8143	4	10 wks
18 Jun 88	ISN'T IT MIDNIGHT Warner Bros. W 7860	60	2 wks
17 Dec 88	AS LONG AS YOU FOLLOW Warner Bros. W 7644	66	3 wks
5 May 90	SAVE ME Warner Bros. W 9866	53	3 wks
25 Aug 90	IN THE BACK OF MY MIND Warner Bros. W 9739	58	3 wks

Group were UK and male only up to and including the re-issue of Albatross.

FLEETWOODS US, male/female vocal group   8 wks

| 24 Apr 59 ● | COME SOFTLY TO ME London HL 8841 | 6 | 8 wks |

La FLEUR Holland, male/female vocal/instrumental group   4 wks

| 30 Jul 83 | BOOGIE NIGHTS Proto ENA 111 | 51 | 4 wks |

K.C. FLIGHTT US, male rapper   4 wks

| 1 Apr 89 | PLANET E RCA PT 49404 | 48 | 4 wks |

Berni FLINT UK, male vocalist   11 wks

| 19 Mar 77 ● | I DON'T WANT TO PUT A HOLD ON YOU EMI 2599 | 3 | 10 wks |
| 23 Jul 77 | SOUTHERN COMFORT EMI 2621 | 48 | 1 wk |

FLINTLOCK UK, male vocal/instrumental group   5 wks

| 29 May 76 | DAWN Pinnacle P 8419 | 30 | 5 wks |

F.L.O. – *See Rahni HARRIS and F.L.O.*

FLOATERS US, male vocal/instrumental group   11 wks

| 23 Jul 77 ★ | FLOAT ON ABC 4187 | 1 | 11 wks |

A FLOCK OF SEAGULLS   46 wks
UK, male vocal/instrumental group

27 Mar 82	I RAN Jive JIVE 14	43	6 wks
12 Jun 82	SPACE AGE LOVE SONG Jive JIVE 17	34	6 wks
6 Nov 82 ●	WISHING (IF I HAD A PHOTOGRAPH OF YOU) Jive JIVE 25	10	12 wks
23 Apr 83	NIGHTMARES Jive JIVE 33	53	3 wks
25 Jun 83	TRANSFER AFFECTION Jive JIVE 41	38	5 wks
14 Jul 84	THE MORE YOU LIVE, THE MORE YOU LOVE Jive JIVE 62	26	11 wks
19 Oct 85	WHO'S THAT GIRL (SHE'S GOT IT) Jive JIVE 106	66	3 wks

FLOWERED UP UK, male vocal/instrumental group   5 wks

| 28 Jul 90 | IT'S ON Heavenly HVN 3 | 54 | 4 wks |
| 24 Nov 90 | PHOBIA Heavenly HVN 7 | 75 | 1 wk |

FLOWERPOT MEN UK, male vocal group   12 wks

| 23 Aug 67 ● | LET'S GO TO SAN FRANCISCO Deram DM 142 | 4 | 12 wks |

Eddie FLOYD US, male vocalist   29 wks

2 Feb 67	KNOCK ON WOOD Atlantic 584 041	50	1 wk
2 Mar 67	KNOCK ON WOOD (re-entry) Atlantic 584 041	19	17 wks
16 Mar 67	RAISE YOUR HAND Stax 601 001	42	3 wks
9 Aug 67	THINGS GET BETTER Stax 601 016	31	8 wks

FLYING LIZARDS   16 wks
UK, male/female vocal/instrumental group

| 4 Aug 79 ● | MONEY Virgin VS 276 | 5 | 10 wks |
| 9 Feb 80 | T.V. Virgin VS 325 | 43 | 6 wks |

FLYING PICKETS UK, male vocal group   20 wks

26 Nov 83 ★	ONLY YOU 10 TEN 14	1	11 wks
21 Apr 84 ●	WHEN YOU'RE YOUNG AND IN LOVE 10 TEN 20	7	8 wks
8 Dec 84	WHO'S THAT GIRL 10 GIRL 1	71	1 wk

FM UK, male vocal/instrumental group   11 wks

31 Jan 87	FROZEN HEART Portrait DIDGE 1	64	2 wks
20 Jun 87	LET LOVE BE THE LEADER Portrait MERV 1	71	2 wks
5 Aug 89	BAD LUCK Epic 655031 7	54	4 wks
7 Oct 89	SOMEDAY (YOU'LL COME RUNNING) CBS DINK 1	64	2 wks
10 Feb 90	EVERYTIME I THINK OF YOU Epic DINK 2	73	1 wk

FOCUS Holland, male instrumental group   21 wks

| 20 Jan 73 | HOCUS POCUS Polydor 2001 211 | 20 | 10 wks |
| 27 Jan 73 ● | SYLVIA Polydor 2001 422 | 4 | 11 wks |

Dan FOGELBERG US, male vocalist   4 wks

15 Mar 80	LONGER Epic EPC 8230	59	4 wks

Claudia FONTAINE – See BEATMASTERS

Wayne FONTANA UK, male vocalist   31 wks

9 Dec 65	IT WAS EASIER TO HURT HER Fontana TF 642	36	6 wks
21 Apr 66	COME ON HOME Fontana TF 684	16	12 wks
25 Aug 66	GOODBYE BLUEBIRD Fontana TF 737	49	1 wk
8 Dec 66	PAMELA PAMELA Fontana TF 770	11	12 wks

See also Wayne Fontana and the Mindbenders.

Wayne FONTANA and the MINDBENDERS   45 wks
UK, male vocalist, male vocal/instrumental backing group

11 Jul 63	HELLO JOSEPHINE Fontana TF 404	46	2 wks
28 May 64	STOP LOOK AND LISTEN Fontana TF 451	37	4 wks
8 Oct 64	● UM UM UM UM UM UM Fontana TF 497	5	15 wks
4 Feb 65	● GAME OF LOVE Fontana TF 535	2	11 wks
17 Jun 65	JUST A LITTLE BIT TOO LATE Fontana TF 579	20	7 wks
30 Sep 65	SHE NEEDS LOVE Fontana TF 611	32	6 wks

See also Wayne Fontana; Mindbenders.

Bill FORBES UK, male vocalist   1 wk

15 Jan 60	TOO YOUNG Columbia DB 4386	29	1 wk

FORBIDDEN – See Jet BRONX and the FORBIDDEN

FORCE M.D.s US, male vocal group   9 wks

12 Apr 86	TENDER LOVE Tommy Boy IS 269	23	9 wks

Baby FORD UK, male instrumentalist - keyboards   16 wks

10 Sep 88	OOCHY KOOCHY Rhythm King 7BFORD 1	58	6 wks
24 Dec 88	CHIKKI CHIKKI AHH AHH Rhythm King 7BFORD 2	75	1 wk
7 Jan 89	CHIKKI CHIKKI AHH AHH (re-entry) Rhythm King 7BFORD 2	54	3 wks
17 Jun 89	CHILDREN OF THE REVOLUTION Rhythm King 7BFORD 4	53	4 wks
17 Feb 90	BEACH BUMP Rhythm King 7BFORD 6	68	2 wks

Clinton FORD UK, male vocalist   25 wks

23 Oct 59	OLD SHEP Oriole CB 1500	27	1 wk
17 Aug 61	TOO MANY BEAUTIFUL GIRLS Oriole CB 1623	48	1 wk
8 Mar 62	FANLIGHT FANNY Oriole CB 1706	22	10 wks
5 Jan 67	RUN TO THE DOOR Piccadilly 7N 35361	25	13 wks

Emile FORD and the CHECKMATES   87 wks
UK, male vocal/instrumental group

30 Oct 59	★ WHAT DO YOU WANT TO MAKE THOSE EYES AT ME FOR Pye 7N 15225	1	25 wks
5 Feb 60	● ON A SLOW BOAT TO CHINA Pye 7N 15245	3	14 wks
26 May 60	YOU'LL NEVER KNOW WHAT YOU'RE MISSING Pye 7N 15268	12	9 wks
1 Sep 60	THEM THERE EYES Pye 7N 15282	18	16 wks
8 Dec 60	● COUNTING TEARDROPS Pye 7N 15314	4	12 wks
2 Mar 61	WHAT AM I GONNA DO Pye 7N 15331	33	6 wks
18 May 61	HALF OF MY HEART Piccadilly 7N 35003	50	1 wk
22 Jun 61	HALF OF MY HEART (re-entry) Piccadilly 7N 35003	42	3 wks
8 Mar 62	I WONDER WHO'S KISSING HER NOW Piccadilly 7N 35033	43	1 wk

Checkmates not on Them There Eyes or the two Piccadilly hits.

Lita FORD US, female vocalist   4 wks

17 Dec 88	KISS ME DEADLY RCA PB 49575	75	1 wk
20 May 89	CLOSE MY EYES FOREVER Dreamland PB 49409	47	3 wks

Close My Eyes Forever has credit 'duet with Ozzy Osbourne'. See also Ozzy Osbourne.

Martyn FORD UK, orchestra   3 wks

14 May 77	LET YOUR BODY GO DOWNTOWN Mountain TOP 26	38	3 wks

See also Phil Collins.

Mary FORD – See Les PAUL and Mary FORD

Pennye FORD US, female vocalist   5 wks

4 May 85	DANGEROUS Total Experience FB 49975	43	5 wks

Tennessee Ernie FORD US, male vocalist   42 wks

21 Jan 55	★ GIVE ME YOUR WORD Capitol CL 14005	1	24 wks
6 Jan 56	★ SIXTEEN TONS Capitol CL 14500	1	11 wks
13 Jan 56	● THE BALLAD OF DAVY CROCKETT Capitol CL 14506	3	7 wks

Julia FORDHAM UK, female vocalist   14 wks

2 Jul 88	HAPPY EVER AFTER Circa YR 15	27	9 wks
25 Feb 89	WHERE DOES THE TIME GO Circa YR 23	41	5 wks

FOREIGNER UK/US, male vocal/instrumental group   77 wks

6 May 78	FEELS LIKE THE FIRST TIME Atlantic K 11086	39	6 wks
15 Jul 78	COLD AS ICE Atlantic K 10986	24	10 wks
28 Oct 78	HOT BLOODED Atlantic K 11167	42	3 wks
24 Feb 79	BLUE MORNING BLUE DAY Atlantic K 11236	45	4 wks
29 Aug 81	URGENT Atlantic K 11665	54	4 wks
10 Oct 81	JUKE BOX HERO Atlantic K 11678	48	4 wks
12 Dec 81	● WAITING FOR A GIRL LIKE YOU Atlantic K 11696	8	13 wks
8 May 82	URGENT (re-issue) Atlantic K 11728	45	5 wks
8 Dec 84	★ I WANT TO KNOW WHAT LOVE IS Atlantic A 9596	1	16 wks
6 Apr 85	THAT WAS YESTERDAY Atlantic A 9571	28	6 wks
22 Jun 85	COLD AS ICE (re-mix) Atlantic A 9539	64	2 wks
19 Dec 87	SAY YOU WILL Atlantic A 9169	71	4 wks

FORMATIONS US, male vocal group   11 wks

31 Jul 71	AT THE TOP OF THE STAIRS Mojo 2027 001	50	1 wk
14 Aug 71	AT THE TOP OF THE STAIRS (re-entry) Mojo 2027 001	28	10 wks

George FORMBY UK, male vocalist/instrumentalist - ukelele   3 wks

21 Jul 60	HAPPY GO LUCKY ME/ BANJO BOY Pye 7N 15269	40	3 wks

FORREST US, male vocalist   20 wks

26 Feb 83	● ROCK THE BOAT CBS A 3121	4	10 wks
14 May 83	FEEL THE NEED IN ME CBS A 3411	17	8 wks
17 Sep 83	ONE LOVER (DON'T STOP THE SHOW) CBS A 3734	67	2 wks

Lance FORTUNE UK, male vocalist — 17 wks

19 Feb 60	● BE MINE *Pye 7N 15240*	4	12 wks
5 May 60	THIS LOVE I HAVE FOR YOU *Pye 7N 15260*	26	5 wks

FORTUNES UK, male vocal/instrumental group — 65 wks

8 Jul 65	● YOU'VE GOT YOUR TROUBLES *Decca F 12173*	2	14 wks
7 Oct 65	● HERE IT COMES AGAIN *Decca F 12243*	4	14 wks
3 Feb 66	THIS GOLDEN RING *Decca F 12321*	15	9 wks
11 Sep 71	● FREEDOM COME FREEDOM GO *Capitol CL 15693*	6	17 wks
29 Jan 72	● STORM IN A TEACUP *Capitol CL 15707*	7	11 wks

45 KING US, male producer — 6 wks

28 Oct 89	THE KING IS HERE/ THE 900 NUMBER *Dance Trax DRX 9*	60	5 wks
11 Aug 90	THE KING IS HERE/ THE 900 NUMBER (re-entry) *Dance Trax DRX 9*	73	1 wk

49ers Italy, male producer — 22 wks

16 Dec 89	● TOUCH ME *Fourth & Broadway BRW 157*	3	13 wks
17 Mar 90	DON'T YOU LOVE ME *Fourth & Broadway BRW 167*	12	6 wks
9 Jun 90	GIRL TO GIRL *Fourth & Broadway BRW 174*	31	3 wks

FOSTER and ALLEN Ireland, male vocal duo — 47 wks

27 Feb 82	A BUNCH OF THYME *Ritz RITZ 5*	18	11 wks
30 Oct 82	OLD FLAMES *Ritz RITZ 028*	51	8 wks
19 Feb 83	MAGGIE *Ritz RITZ 025*	27	9 wks
29 Oct 83	I WILL LOVE YOU ALL MY LIFE *Ritz RITZ 056*	49	6 wks
30 Jun 84	JUST FOR OLD TIME'S SAKE *Ritz RITZ 066*	47	6 wks
29 Mar 86	AFTER ALL THESE YEARS *Ritz RITZ 106*	43	7 wks

FOUNDATIONS UK, male vocal/instrumental group — 56 wks

27 Sep 67	★ BABY NOW THAT I'VE FOUND YOU *Pye 7N 17366*	1	16 wks
24 Jan 68	BACK ON MY FEET AGAIN *Pye 7N 17417*	18	10 wks
1 May 68	ANY OLD TIME *Pye 7N 17503*	48	1 wk
15 May 68	ANY OLD TIME (re-entry) *Pye 7N 17503*	50	1 wk
20 Nov 68	● BUILD ME UP BUTTERCUP *Pye 7N 17636*	2	15 wks
12 Mar 69	● IN THE BAD BAD OLD DAYS *Pye 7N 17702*	8	10 wks
13 Sep 69	BORN TO LIVE AND BORN TO DIE *Pye 7N 17809*	46	3 wks

FOUR ACES US, male vocal group — 40 wks

30 Jul 54	● THREE COINS IN THE FOUNTAIN *Brunswick 05308*	5	5 wks
22 Oct 54	THREE COINS IN THE FOUNTAIN (re-entry) *Brunswick 05308*	17	1 wk
7 Jan 55	● MR. SANDMAN *Brunswick 05355*	9	5 wks
20 May 55	● STRANGER IN PARADISE *Brunswick 05418*	6	6 wks
18 Nov 55	● LOVE IS A MANY SPLENDOURED THING *Brunswick 05480*	2	13 wks
19 Oct 56	● WOMAN IN LOVE *Brunswick 05589*	19	3 wks
4 Jan 57	FRIENDLY PERSUASION *Brunswick 05623*	29	1 wk
23 Jan 59	THE WORLD OUTSIDE *Brunswick 05773*	18	6 wks

FOUR BUCKETEERS UK, male/female vocal group — 6 wks

3 May 80	BUCKET OF WATER SONG *CBS 8393*	26	6 wks

FOUR ESQUIRES US, male vocal group — 2 wks

31 Jan 58	LOVE ME FOREVER *London HLO 8533*	23	2 wks

4 HERO UK, male instrumental group — 2 wks

24 Nov 90	MR. KIRK'S NIGHTMARE *Reinforced RIVET 1203*	73	2 wks

400 BLOWS UK, male vocal/instrumental duo — 4 wks

29 Jun 85	MOVIN' *Illuminated ILL 61*	54	4 wks

FOUR KNIGHTS US, male vocal group — 11 wks

4 Jun 54	● I GET SO LONELY *Capitol CL 14076*	5	7 wks
30 Jul 54	● I GET SO LONELY (re-entry) *Capitol CL 14076*	10	4 wks

FOUR LADS Canada, male vocal group — 4 wks

28 Apr 60	STANDING ON THE CORNER *Philips PB 1000*	34	4 wks

FOUR PENNIES UK, male vocal/instrumental group — 56 wks

16 Jan 64	DO YOU WANT ME TO *Philips BF 1296*	47	1 wk
6 Feb 64	DO YOU WANT ME TO (re-entry) *Philips BF 1296*	49	1 wk
2 Apr 64	★ JULIET *Philips BF 1322*	1	15 wks
16 Jul 64	I FOUND OUT THE HARD WAY *Philips BF 1349*	14	11 wks
29 Oct 64	BLACK GIRL *Philips BF 1366*	20	12 wks
7 Oct 65	UNTIL IT'S TIME FOR YOU TO GO *Philips BF 1435*	19	11 wks
17 Feb 66	TROUBLE IS MY MIDDLE NAME *Philips BF 1469*	32	5 wks

FOUR PREPS US, male vocal group — 23 wks

13 Jun 58	● BIG MAN *Capitol CL 14873*	2	13 wks
19 Sep 58	BIG MAN (re-entry) *Capitol CL 14873*	22	1 wk
26 May 60	GOT A GIRL *Capitol CL 15128*	28	6 wks
14 Jul 60	GOT A GIRL (re-entry) *Capitol CL 15128*	47	1 wk
2 Nov 61	MORE MONEY FOR YOU AND ME (MEDLEY) *Capitol CL 15217*	39	2 wks

Tracks of medley: Mr. Blue/Alley Oop/Smoke Gets In Your Eyes/In This Whole Wide World/A Worried Man/Tom Dooley/A Teenager In Love, all with new lyrics.

FOUR SEASONS US, male vocal group — 151 wks

4 Oct 62	● SHERRY *Stateside SS 122*	8	16 wks
17 Jan 63	BIG GIRLS DON'T CRY *Stateside SS 145*	13	10 wks
28 Mar 63	WALK LIKE A MAN *Stateside SS 169*	12	12 wks
27 Jun 63	AIN'T THAT A SHAME *Stateside SS 194*	38	3 wks
27 Aug 64	● RAG DOLL *Philips BF 1347*	2	13 wks
18 Nov 65	● LET'S HANG ON *Philips BF 1439*	4	16 wks
31 Mar 66	WORKIN' MY WAY BACK TO YOU *Philips BF 1474*	50	3 wks
2 Jun 66	OPUS 17 (DON'T YOU WORRY 'BOUT ME) *Philips BF 1493*	20	9 wks
29 Sep 66	I'VE GOT YOU UNDER MY SKIN *Philips BF 1511*	12	11 wks
12 Jan 67	TELL IT TO THE RAIN *Philips BF 1538*	37	5 wks
19 Apr 75	● NIGHT *Mowest MW 3024*	7	9 wks
20 Sep 75	● WHO LOVES YOU *Warner Bros. K 16602*	6	9 wks
31 Jan 76	★ DECEMBER '63 (OH WHAT A NIGHT) *Warner Bros. K 16688*	1	10 wks
24 Apr 76	● SILVER STAR *Warner Bros. K 16742*	3	9 wks
27 Nov 76	WE CAN WORK IT OUT *Warner Bros. K 16845*	34	4 wks
18 Jun 77	RHAPSODY *Warner Bros. K 16932*	37	3 wks
20 Aug 77	DOWN THE HALL *Warner Bros. K 16982*	34	5 wks
29 Oct 88	DECEMBER '63 (OH WHAT A NIGHT) (re-mix) *BR 45277*	49	4 wks

First two Philips hits 'with the sound of Frankie Valli', last four Philips hits 'with Frankie Valli'. Mowest and BR hits credit Frankie Valli and the Four Seasons. See also Frankie Valli.

FOUR TOPS US, male vocal group — 298 wks

1 Jul 65	I CAN'T HELP MYSELF *Tamla Motown TMG 515*	23	9 wks
2 Sep 65	IT'S THE SAME OLD SONG *Tamla Motown TMG 528*	34	8 wks

21 Jul 66		LOVING YOU IS SWEETER THAN EVER		
		Tamla Motown TMG 568	21	12 wks
13 Oct 66	★	REACH OUT I'LL BE THERE Tamla Motown TMG 579	1	16 wks
12 Jan 67	●	STANDING IN THE SHADOWS OF LOVE		
		Tamla Motown TMG 589	6	8 wks
30 Mar 67	●	BERNADETTE Tamla Motown TMG 601	8	10 wks
15 Jun 67		SEVEN ROOMS OF GLOOM Tamla Motown TMG 612	12	9 wks
11 Oct 67		YOU KEEP RUNNING AWAY Tamla Motown TMG 623	26	7 wks
13 Dec 67	●	WALK AWAY RENEE Tamla Motown TMG 634	3	11 wks
13 Mar 68		IF I WERE A CARPENTER Tamla Motown TMG 647	7	11 wks
21 Aug 68		YESTERDAY'S DREAMS Tamla Motown TMG 665	23	15 wks
13 Nov 68		I'M IN A DIFFERENT WORLD		
		Tamla Motown TMG 675	27	13 wks
28 May 69		WHAT IS A MAN Tamla Motown TMG 698	16	11 wks
27 Sep 69		DO WHAT YOU GOTTA DO Tamla Motown TMG 710	11	11 wks
21 Mar 70	●	I CAN'T HELP MYSELF (re-issue)		
		Tamla Motown TMG 732	10	11 wks
30 May 70	●	IT'S ALL IN THE GAME Tamla Motown TMG 736	5	14 wks
12 Sep 70		IT'S ALL IN THE GAME (re-entry)		
		Tamla Motown TMG 736	48	2 wks
3 Oct 70	●	STILL WATER (LOVE) Tamla Motown TMG 752	10	10 wks
19 Dec 70		STILL WATER (LOVE) (re-entry)		
		Tamla Motown TMG 752	44	2 wks
1 May 71		JUST SEVEN NUMBERS (CAN STRAIGHTEN OUT		
		MY LIFE) Tamla Motown TMG 770	36	5 wks
25 Sep 71	●	SIMPLE GAME Tamla Motown TMG 785	3	11 wks
11 Mar 72		BERNADETTE (re-issue) Tamla Motown TMG 803	23	7 wks
5 Aug 72		WALK WITH ME TALK WITH ME DARLING		
		Tamla Motown TMG 823	32	6 wks
18 Nov 72		KEEPER OF THE CASTLE Probe PRO 575	18	9 wks
10 Nov 73		SWEET UNDERSTANDING LOVE Probe PRO 604	29	10 wks
17 Oct 81	●	WHEN SHE WAS MY GIRL Casablanca CAN 1005	3	10 wks
19 Dec 81		DON'T WALK AWAY Casablanca CAN 1006	16	11 wks
6 Mar 82		TONIGHT I'M GONNA LOVE YOU ALL OVER		
		Casablanca CAN 1008	43	4 wks
26 Jun 82		BACK TO SCHOOL AGAIN RSO 89	62	2 wks
23 Jul 88		REACH OUT I'LL BE THERE (re-mix)		
		Motown ZB 41943	11	9 wks
17 Sep 88		INDESTRUCTIBLE Arista 111717	55	4 wks
3 Dec 88	●	LOCO IN ACAPULCO Arista 111850	7	13 wks
25 Feb 89		INDESTRUCTIBLE Arista 112074	30	7 wks

The original US recording of Indestructible was not issued until after the chart run of the UK-only mix. The latter features Smokey Robinson. See also Supremes and the Four Tops; Smokey Robinson.

FOURMOST UK, male vocal/instrumental group   **64 wks**

12 Sep 63	●	HELLO LITTLE GIRL Parlophone R 5056	9	17 wks
26 Dec 63		I'M IN LOVE Parlophone R 5078	17	12 wks
23 Apr 64	●	A LITTLE LOVING Parlophone R 5128	6	13 wks
13 Aug 64		HOW CAN I TELL HER Parlophone R 5157	33	4 wks
26 Nov 64		BABY I NEED YOUR LOVIN' Parlophone R 5194	24	12 wks
9 Dec 65		GIRLS GIRLS GIRLS Parlophone R 5379	33	6 wks

14-18 UK, male vocalist, Peter Waterman, under false group name   **4 wks**

1 Nov 75		GOODBYE-EE Magnet MAG 48	33	4 wks

See also Stock Aitken Waterman.

FOX UK/US, male/female vocal/instrumental group   **29 wks**

15 Feb 75	●	ONLY YOU CAN GTO GT 8	3	11 wks
10 May 75		IMAGINE ME IMAGINE YOU GTO GT 21	15	8 wks
10 Apr 76	●	S-S-S-SINGLE BED GTO GT 57	4	10 wks

Noosha FOX UK, female vocalist   **6 wks**

12 Nov 77		GEORGINA BAILEY GTO GT 106	31	6 wks

Samantha FOX UK, female vocalist   **71 wks**

22 Mar 86	●	TOUCH ME (I WANT YOUR BODY) Jive FOXY 1	3	10 wks
28 Jun 86	●	DO YA DO YA (WANNA PLEASE ME) Jive FOXY 2	10	7 wks
6 Sep 86		HOLD ON TIGHT Jive FOXY 3	26	5 wks
13 Dec 86		I'M ALL YOU NEED Jive FOXY 4	41	6 wks
30 May 87	●	NOTHING'S GONNA STOP ME NOW Jive FOXY 5	8	9 wks
25 Jul 87		I SURRENDER (TO THE SPIRIT OF THE NIGHT)		
		Jive FOXY 6	25	7 wks
17 Oct 87		I PROMISE YOU (GET READY) Jive FOXY 7	58	3 wks
19 Dec 87		TRUE DEVOTION Jive FOXY 8	62	3 wks
21 May 88		NAUGHTY GIRLS Jive FOXY 9	31	5 wks
19 Nov 88		LOVE HOUSE Jive FOXY 10	32	6 wks
28 Jan 89		I ONLY WANNA BE WITH YOU Jive FOXY 11	16	8 wks
17 Jun 89		I WANNA HAVE SOME FUN Jive FOXY 12	63	2 wks

Naughty Girls features Full Force. See also Full Force.

Bruce FOXTON UK, male vocalist   **9 wks**

30 Jul 83		FREAK Arista BFOX 1	23	5 wks
29 Oct 83		THIS IS THE WAY Arista BFOX 2	56	3 wks
21 Apr 84		IT MAKES ME WONDER Arista BFOX 3	74	1 wk

Inez FOXX US, female vocalist   **3 wks**

23 Jul 64		HURT BY LOVE Sue WI 323	40	3 wks

See also Inez and Charlie Foxx.

Inez and Charlie FOXX   **5 wks**

US, female/male vocal/instrumental duo, Charlie Foxx guitar

19 Feb 69		MOCKINGBIRD United Artists UP 2269	36	2 wks
19 Mar 69		MOCKINGBIRD (re-entry) United Artists UP 2269	34	3 wks

See also Inez Foxx.

John FOXX UK, male vocalist   **31 wks**

26 Jan 80		UNDERPASS Virgin VS 318	31	8 wks
29 Mar 80		NO-ONE DRIVING (DOUBLE SINGLE) Virgin VS 338	32	4 wks
19 Jul 80		BURNING CAR Virgin VS 360	35	7 wks
8 Nov 80		MILES AWAY Virgin VS 382	51	3 wks
29 Aug 81		EUROPE (AFTER THE RAIN) Virgin VS 393	40	5 wks
2 Jul 83		ENDLESSLY Virgin VS 543	66	3 wks
17 Sep 83		YOUR DRESS Virgin VS 615	61	1 wk

Tracks on double single: No-One Driving/Glimmer/Mr. No/This City.

FPI PROJECT Italy, male instrumental group   **12 wks**

9 Dec 89	●	GOING BACK TO MY ROOTS/ RICH IN PARADISE		
		Rumour RUMAT 9	9	12 wks

Going Back To My Roots was a vocal track available in two formats and featured either Paolo Dini - Italy, male vocalist, or Sharon D. Clarke - UK, female vocalist.

FRAGGLES UK/US, puppets   **8 wks**

18 Feb 84		FRAGGLE ROCK THEME RCA 389	33	8 wks

Peter FRAMPTON UK, male vocalist   **24 wks**

1 May 76	●	SHOW ME THE WAY A &M AMS 7218	10	12 wks
11 Sep 76		BABY I LOVE YOUR WAY A &M AMS 7246	43	5 wks
6 Nov 76		DO YOU FEEL LIKE WE DO A &M AMS 7260	39	4 wks
23 Jul 77		I'M IN YOU A &M AMS 7298	41	3 wks

Connie FRANCIS US, female vocalist   241 wks

4 Apr 58	★ WHO'S SORRY NOW MGM 975	1	25 wks
27 Jun 58	I'M SORRY I MADE YOU CRY MGM 982	11	10 wks
22 Aug 58	★ CAROLINA MOON/ STUPID CUPID MGM 985	1	19 wks
31 Oct 58	I'LL GET BY MGM 993	19	6 wks
21 Nov 58	FALLIN' MGM 993	20	5 wks
26 Dec 58	YOU ALWAYS HURT THE ONE YOU LOVE MGM 998	13	7 wks
13 Feb 59	● MY HAPPINESS MGM 1001	4	14 wks
29 May 59	MY HAPPINESS (re-entry) MGM 1001	30	1 wk
3 Jul 59	● LIPSTICK ON YOUR COLLAR MGM 1018	3	16 wks
11 Sep 59	PLENTY GOOD LOVIN' MGM 1036	18	10 wks
4 Dec 59	AMONG MY SOUVENIRS MGM 1046	11	10 wks
17 Mar 60	● VALENTINO MGM 1060	27	8 wks
19 May 60	● MAMA / ROBOT MAN MGM 1076	2	19 wks
18 Aug 60	● EVERYBODY'S SOMEBODY'S FOOL MGM 1086	5	13 wks
3 Nov 60	● MY HEART HAS A MIND OF ITS OWN MGM 1100	3	15 wks
12 Jan 61	MANY TEARS AGO MGM 1111	12	9 wks
16 Mar 61	● WHERE THE BOYS ARE/ BABY ROO MGM 1121	5	14 wks
15 Jun 61	BREAKIN' IN A BRAND NEW BROKEN HEART MGM 1136	12	11 wks
14 Sep 61	● TOGETHER MGM 1138	6	11 wks
14 Dec 61	BABY'S FIRST CHRISTMAS MGM 1145	30	4 wks
26 Apr 62	DON'T BREAK THE HEART THAT LOVES YOU MGM 1157	39	3 wks
2 Aug 62	● VACATION MGM 1165	10	9 wks
20 Dec 62	I'M GONNA BE WARM THIS WINTER MGM 1185	48	1 wk
10 Jun 65	MY CHILD MGM 1271	26	6 wks
20 Jan 66	JEALOUS HEART MGM 1293	44	2 wks

Claude FRANCOIS France, male vocalist   4 wks

10 Jan 76	TEARS ON THE TELEPHONE Bradley's BRAD 7528	35	4 wks

Joe FRANK – See HAMILTON, Joe FRANK and REYNOLDS

FRANKIE GOES TO HOLLYWOOD   117 wks
UK, male vocal/instrumental group

26 Nov 83	★ RELAX ZTT ZTAS 1	1	48 wks
16 Jun 84	★ TWO TRIBES ZTT ZTAS 3	1	20 wks
10 Nov 84	TWO TRIBES (re-entry) ZTT ZTAS 3	73	1 wk
1 Dec 84	★ THE POWER OF LOVE ZTT ZTAS 5	1	11 wks
16 Feb 85	RELAX (re-entry) ZTT ZTAS 1	58	4 wks
23 Feb 85	THE POWER OF LOVE (re-entry) ZTT ZTAS 5	64	1 wk
30 Mar 85	● WELCOME TO THE PLEASURE DOME ZTT ZTAS 7	2	11 wks
6 Sep 86	● RAGE HARD ZTT ZTAS 22	4	7 wks
22 Nov 86	WARRIORS (OF THE WASTELAND) ZTT ZTAS 25	19	8 wks
7 Mar 87	WATCHING THE WILDLIFE ZTT ZTAS 26	28	6 wks

Aretha FRANKLIN US, female vocalist   131 wks

8 Jun 67	● RESPECT Atlantic 584 115	10	14 wks
23 Aug 67	BABY I LOVE YOU Atlantic 584 127	39	4 wks
20 Dec 67	CHAIN OF FOOLS/ SATISFACTION Atlantic 584 157	43	2 wks
10 Jan 68	SATISFACTION (re-entry) Atlantic 584 157	37	5 wks
13 Mar 68	SINCE YOU'VE BEEN GONE Atlantic 584 172	47	1 wk
22 May 68	THINK Atlantic 584 186	26	9 wks
7 Aug 68	● I SAY A LITTLE PRAYER Atlantic 584 206	4	14 wks
22 Aug 70	DON'T PLAY THAT SONG Atlantic 2091 027	13	11 wks
2 Oct 71	SPANISH HARLEM Atlantic 2091 138	14	9 wks
8 Sep 73	ANGEL Atlantic K 10346	37	5 wks
16 Feb 74	UNTIL YOU COME BACK TO ME (THAT'S WHAT I'M GONNA DO) Atlantic K 10399	26	8 wks
6 Dec 80	WHAT A FOOL BELIEVES Arista ARIST 377	46	7 wks
4 Sep 82	JUMP TO IT Arista ARIST 479	42	5 wks
23 Jul 83	GET IT RIGHT Arista ARIST 537	74	2 wks
13 Jul 85	FREEWAY OF LOVE Arista ARIST 624	68	5 wks
23 Nov 85	WHO'S ZOOMIN' WHO Arista ARIST 633	11	14 wks
22 Feb 86	ANOTHER NIGHT Arista ARIST 657	54	6 wks
10 May 86	FREEWAY OF LOVE (re-entry) Arista ARIST 624	51	3 wks
25 Oct 86	JUMPIN' JACK FLASH Arista ARIST 678	58	3 wks

14 Mar 87	JIMMY LEE Arista RIS 6	46	4 wks
7 Apr 90	THINK East West A 7951	31	2 wks

Think on East West is a re-recording. It was the flip side of Everybody Needs Somebody To Love by Blues Brothers and was listed for the first two weeks of the record's run. See also Aretha Franklin and George Benson; Aretha Franklin and Elton John; Aretha Franklin and George Michael; Eurythmics and Aretha Franklin; Aretha Franklin and Whitney Houston; Blues Brothers.

Aretha FRANKLIN and George BENSON   3 wks
US, female vocalist and male vocalist/instrumentalist - guitar

19 Sep 81	LOVE ALL THE HURT AWAY Arista ARIST 428	49	3 wks

See also Aretha Franklin; George Benson.

Aretha FRANKLIN and Whitney HOUSTON   5 wks
US, female vocal duo

9 Sep 89	IT ISN'T, IT WASN'T, IT AIN'T NEVER GONNA BE Arista 112545	29	5 wks

See also Aretha Franklin; Whitney Houston.

Aretha FRANKLIN and Elton JOHN   3 wks
US/UK, female/male vocal duo

6 May 89	THROUGH THE STORM Arista 112185	41	3 wks

See also Aretha Franklin; Elton John.

Aretha FRANKLIN and George MICHAEL   9 wks
US/UK, female/male vocal duo

31 Jan 87	★ I KNEW YOU WERE WAITING (FOR ME) Epic DUET 2	1	9 wks

See also Aretha Franklin; George Michael.

Rodney FRANKLIN US, male instrumentalist - piano   9 wks

19 Apr 80	● THE GROOVE CBS 8529	7	9 wks

FRANTIC FIVE – See Don LANG

FRANTIQUE US, female vocal group   12 wks

11 Aug 79	● STRUT YOUR FUNKY STUFF Philadelphia International PIR 7728	10	12 wks

Elizabeth FRASER – See Ian McCULLOCH

Wendy FRASER – See Patrick SWAYZE featuring Wendy FRASER

FRAZIER CHORUS   12 wks
UK, male/female vocal/instrumental group

4 Feb 89	DREAM KITCHEN Virgin VS 1145	57	3 wks
15 Apr 89	TYPICAL! Virgin VS 1174	53	2 wks
15 Jul 89	SLOPPY HEART Virgin VS 1192	73	1 wk
9 Jun 90	CLOUD 8 Virgin VS 1252	52	3 wks
25 Aug 90	NOTHING Virgin VS 1284	51	3 wks

Stan FREBERG US, male vocalist   5 wks

19 Nov 54	SH-BOOM Capitol CL 14187	15	2 wks
27 Jul 56	ROCK ISLAND LINE/ HEARTBREAK HOTEL Capitol CL 14608	24	1 wk

| 10 Aug 56 | ROCK ISLAND LINE/ HEARTBREAK HOTEL (re-entry) Capitol CL 14608 | 29 | 1 wk |
| 12 May 60 | THE OLD PAYOLA ROLL BLUES Capitol CL 15122 | 40 | 1 wk |

John FRED and the PLAYBOY BAND
US, male vocal/instrumental group — **12 wks**

| 3 Jan 68 ● | JUDY IN DISGUISE (WITH GLASSES) Pye International 7N 25442 | 3 | 12 wks |

FREDDIE and the DREAMERS
UK, male vocal/instrumental group — **85 wks**

9 May 63 ●	IF YOU GOTTA MAKE A FOOL OF SOMEBODY Columbia DB 7032	3	14 wks
8 Aug 63 ●	I'M TELLING YOU NOW Columbia DB 7086	2	11 wks
7 Nov 63 ●	YOU WERE MADE FOR ME Columbia DB 7147	3	15 wks
20 Feb 64	OVER YOU Columbia DB 7214	13	11 wks
14 May 64	I LOVE YOU BABY Columbia DB 7286	16	8 wks
16 Jul 64	JUST FOR YOU Columbia DB 7322	41	3 wks
5 Nov 64 ●	I UNDERSTAND Columbia DB 7381	5	15 wks
22 Apr 65	A LITTLE YOU Columbia DB 7526	26	5 wks
4 Nov 65	THOU SHALT NOT STEAL Columbia DB 7720	44	3 wks

FREDERICK – See NINA and FREDERICK

FREE *UK, male vocal/instrumental group* — **66 wks**

6 Jun 70 ●	ALL RIGHT NOW Island WIP 6082	2	16 wks
1 May 71 ●	MY BROTHER JAKE Island WIP 6100	4	11 wks
27 May 72	LITTLE BIT OF LOVE Island WIP 6129	13	10 wks
13 Jan 73 ●	WISHING WELL Island WIP 6146	7	10 wks
21 Jul 73	ALL RIGHT NOW (re-entry) Island WIP 6082	15	9 wks
18 Feb 78	FREE (EP) Island IEP 6	11	7 wks
23 Oct 82	FREE (EP) (re-entry) Island IEP 6	57	3 wks

Tracks on Free EP: All Right Now/My Brother Jake/Wishing Well.

FREEEZ *UK, male vocal/instrumental group* — **48 wks**

7 Jun 80	KEEP IN TOUCH Calibre CAB 103	49	3 wks
7 Feb 81 ●	SOUTHERN FREEEZ Beggars Banquet BEG 51	8	11 wks
18 Apr 81	FLYING HIGH Beggars Banquet BEG 55	35	5 wks
18 Jun 83 ●	I.O.U. Beggars Banquet BEG 96	2	15 wks
1 Oct 83	POP GOES MY LOVE Beggars Banquet BEG 98	26	6 wks
17 Jan 87	I.O.U. (re-mix) Citybeat CBE 709	23	6 wks
30 May 87	SOUTHERN FREEEZ (re-mix) Total Control TOCO 14	63	2 wks

The re-mix of I.O.U. has credit 'featuring John Rocca'.

FREEHOLD JUNIOR SCHOOL – See Fogwell FLAX and the ANKLEBITERS from FREEHOLD JUNIOR SCHOOL

FREIHEIT *Germany, male vocal/instrumental duo* — **8 wks**

| 17 Dec 88 | KEEPING THE DREAM ALIVE CBS 652989 7 | 14 | 8 wks |

FREQUENCY 9 *UK, male vocal/instrumental group* — **2 wks**

| 20 Jan 90 | THE WAY I FEEL deConstruction PT 43372 | 64 | 2 wks |

The Way I Feel was one track from the Further Adventures Of North EP. The others tracks were: Carino 90 by T-Coy, Dream 17 by Annette and Stop This Thing by Dynasty Of Two featuring Rowetta. See also T-Coy; Annette; Dynasty Of Two featuring Rowetta.

Doug E. FRESH and the GET FRESH CREW
US, male vocalist and rap/scratch group — **11 wks**

| 9 Nov 85 ● | THE SHOW Cooltempo COOL 116 | 7 | 11 wks |

FRESH 4 featuring Lizz E
UK, male scratch group and female vocal group — **9 wks**

| 7 Oct 89 ● | WISHING ON A STAR 10 TEN 287 | 10 | 9 wks |

FRESH PRINCE – See DJ JAZZY JEFF and FRESH PRINCE

FRESHIES *UK, male vocal/instrumental group* — **3 wks**

| 14 Feb 81 | I'M IN LOVE WITH THE GIRL ON A CERTAIN MANCHESTER MEGASTORE CHECKOUT DESK MCA 670 | 54 | 3 wks |

Matt FRETTON *UK, male vocalist* — **5 wks**

| 11 Jun 83 | IT'S SO HIGH Chrysalis MATT 1 | 50 | 5 wks |

'FREUR' *UK, male vocal/instrumental group* — **4 wks**

| 23 Apr 83 | DOOT DOOT CBS A 3141 | 59 | 4 wks |

Glenn FREY *US, male vocalist* — **20 wks**

| 2 Mar 85 | THE HEAT IS ON MCA MCA 941 | 12 | 12 wks |
| 22 Jun 85 | SMUGGLER'S BLUES BBC RESL 170 | 22 | 8 wks |

FRIDA *Norway, female vocalist* — **7 wks**

| 21 Aug 82 | I KNOW THERE'S SOMETHING GOING ON Epic EPC A2603 | 43 | 7 wks |

See also Frida and B.A. Robertson.

FRIDA and B.A. ROBERTSON
Norway/UK, female/male vocal duo — **5 wks**

| 17 Dec 83 | TIME Epic A 3983 | 45 | 5 wks |

See also Frida; B.A. Robertson.

Dean FRIEDMAN *US, male vocalist* — **22 wks**

3 Jun 78	WOMAN OF MINE Lifesong LS 401	52	5 wks
23 Sep 78 ●	LUCKY STARS Lifesong LS 402	3	10 wks
18 Nov 78	LYDIA Lifesong LS 403	31	7 wks

FRIENDS AGAIN *UK, male vocal/instrumental group* — **3 wks**

| 4 Aug 84 | THE FRIENDS AGAIN (EP) Mercury FA 1 | 59 | 3 wks |

Tracks on EP: Lullaby On Board/Wand You Wave/Thank You For Being an Angel.

FRIJID PINK *US, male vocal/instrumental group* — **16 wks**

| 28 Mar 70 ● | HOUSE OF THE RISING SUN Deram DM 288 | 4 | 16 wks |

Jane FROMAN *US, female vocalist* — **4 wks**

| 17 Jun 55 | I WONDER Capitol CL 14254 | 14 | 4 wks |

FULL CIRCLE *US, male vocal group* — **5 wks**

| 7 Mar 87 | WORKIN' UP A SWEAT EMI America EA 229 | 41 | 5 wks |

FULL FORCE US, male vocal/instrumental group — **11 wks**

| 21 Dec 85 | ● ALICE I WANT YOU JUST FOR ME CBS A 6640............ | 9 | 11 wks |

See also Lisa Lisa and Cult Jam; James Brown; Samantha Fox.

Bobby FULLER FOUR — **4 wks**
US, male vocal/instrumental group

| 14 Apr 66 | I FOUGHT THE LAW London HL 10030..................... | 33 | 4 wks |

FUN BOY THREE UK, male vocal/instrumental group — **50 wks**

7 Nov 81	THE LUNATICS (HAVE TAKEN OVER THE ASYLUM) Chrysalis CHS 2563.................................	20	12 wks
8 May 82	THE TELEPHONE ALWAYS RINGS Chrysalis CHS 2609.......................................	17	9 wks
31 Jul 82	SUMMERTIME Chrysalis CHS 2629.........................	18	8 wks
15 Jan 83	THE MORE I SEE (THE LESS I BELIEVE) Chrysalis CHS 2554....................................	68	1 wk
5 Feb 83	● TUNNEL OF LOVE Chrysalis CHS 2678.....................	10	10 wks
30 Apr 83	● OUR LIPS ARE SEALED Chrysalis FUNB 1...................	7	10 wks

See also Fun Boy Three and Bananarama.

FUN BOY THREE and BANANARAMA — **10 wks**
UK, male vocal group and female vocal group

| 13 Feb 82 | ● IT AIN'T WHAT YOU DO IT'S THE WAY THAT YOU DO IT Chrysalis CHS 2570.......................... | 4 | 10 wks |

See also Fun Boy Three; Bananarama.

Farley 'Jackmaster' FUNK US, male producer — **14 wks**

| 23 Aug 86 | ● LOVE CAN'T TURN AROUND D.J. International LON 105.. | 10 | 12 wks |
| 11 Feb 89 | AS ALWAYS Champion CHAMP 90........................... | 49 | 2 wks |

Vocals on first hit were by Darryl Pandy - US, male vocalist.

FUNK MASTERS UK, male/female vocal/instrumental group — **12 wks**

| 18 Jun 83 | ● IT'S OVER Master Funk Records 7MP 004........................ | 8 | 12 wks |

FUNKADELIC US, male vocal/instrumental group — **12 wks**

| 9 Dec 78 | ● ONE NATION UNDER A GROOVE (PART 1) Warner Bros. K 17246................................ | 9 | 12 wks |

FUNKAPOLITAN UK, male vocal/instrumental group — **7 wks**

| 22 Aug 81 | AS TIME GOES BY (VOCALS) London LON 001............. | 41 | 7 wks |

A FUNKI DREDD – See A HOMEBOY, A HIPPIE and A FUNKI DREDD

FUNKY BOYS – See LINDA and the FUNKY BOYS

FUNKY WORM UK, male/female vocal/instrumental group — **14 wks**

30 Jul 88	HUSTLE! (TO THE MUSIC...) Fon FON 15................	13	8 wks
26 Nov 88	THE SPELL! Fon FON 16................................	61	3 wks
20 May 89	U + ME = LOVE Fon FON 19.............................	46	3 wks

FUREYS Ireland, male vocal group — **14 wks**

| 10 Oct 81 | WHEN YOU WERE SWEET SIXTEEN Ritz RITZ 003...... | 14 | 11 wks |
| 3 Apr 82 | I WILL LOVE YOU (EV'RY TIME WHEN WE ARE GONE) Ritz RITZ 012... | 54 | 3 wks |

When You Were Sweet Sixteen credits the Fureys with Davey Arthur.

FURIOUS FIVE – See GRANDMASTER FLASH, Melle MEL and the FURIOUS FIVE

FURNITURE UK, male/female vocal/instrumental group — **10 wks**

| 14 Jun 86 | BRILLIANT MIND Stiff BUY 251............................. | 21 | 10 wks |

Billy FURY UK, male vocalist — **281 wks**

27 Feb 59	MAYBE TOMORROW Decca F 11102.........................	22	3 wks
27 Mar 59	MAYBE TOMORROW (re-entry) Decca F 11102.............	18	6 wks
26 Jun 59	MARGO Decca F 11128...................................	28	1 wk
10 Mar 60	● COLETTE Decca F 11200................................	9	10 wks
26 May 60	THAT'S LOVE Decca F 11237..............................	19	11 wks
22 Sep 60	WONDROUS PLACE Decca F 11267.........................	25	9 wks
19 Jan 61	A THOUSAND STARS Decca F 11311.......................	14	10 wks
27 Apr 61	DON'T WORRY Decca F 11334.............................	40	2 wks
11 May 61	● HALFWAY TO PARADISE Decca F 11349.....................	3	23 wks
7 Sep 61	● JEALOUSY Decca F 11384..............................	2	12 wks
14 Dec 61	● I'D NEVER FIND ANOTHER YOU Decca F 11409...........	5	15 wks
15 Mar 62	LETTER FULL OF TEARS Decca F 11437...................	32	6 wks
3 May 62	● LAST NIGHT WAS MADE FOR LOVE Decca F 11458........	4	16 wks
19 Jul 62	● ONCE UPON A DREAM Decca F 11485....................	7	13 wks
25 Oct 62	BECAUSE OF LOVE Decca F 11508........................	18	14 wks
14 Feb 63	● LIKE I'VE NEVER BEEN GONE Decca F11582..............	3	15 wks
16 May 63	● WHEN WILL YOU SAY I LOVE YOU Decca F 11655.........	3	12 wks
25 Jul 63	● IN SUMMER Decca F 11701.............................	5	11 wks
3 Oct 63	SOMEBODY ELSE'S GIRL Decca F 11744..................	18	7 wks
2 Jan 64	DO YOU REALLY LOVE ME TOO Decca F 11792............	13	10 wks
30 Apr 64	I WILL Decca F 11888...................................	14	12 wks
23 Jul 64	● IT'S ONLY MAKE BELIEVE Decca F 11939................	10	10 wks
14 Jan 65	I'M LOST WITHOUT YOU Decca F 12048...................	16	10 wks
22 Jul 65	● IN THOUGHTS OF YOU Decca F 12178....................	9	11 wks
16 Sep 65	RUN TO MY LOVIN' ARMS Decca F 12230.................	25	7 wks
10 Feb 66	I'LL NEVER QUITE GET OVER YOU Decca F 12325.......	35	5 wks
4 Aug 66	GIVE ME YOUR WORD Decca F 12459......................	27	7 wks
4 Sep 82	LOVE OR MONEY Polydor POSP 488.......................	57	5 wks
13 Nov 82	DEVIL OR ANGEL Polydor POSP 528......................	58	4 wks
4 Jun 83	FORGET HIM Polydor POSP 558............................	59	4 wks

FUZZBOX – See WE'VE GOT A FUZZBOX AND WE'RE GONNA USE IT

Leslie FYSON – See Michael MEDWIN, Bernard BRESSLAW, Alfie BASS and Leslie FYSON

Bobby G UK, male vocalist — **12 wks**

1 Dec 84	BIG DEAL BBC RESL 151.................................	75	1 wk
15 Dec 84	BIG DEAL (re-entry) BBC RESL 151........................	65	5 wks
19 Oct 85	BIG DEAL (2nd re-entry) BBC RESL 151...................	46	6 wks

Kenny G US, male instrumentalist - saxophone — **12 wks**

21 Apr 84	HI! HOW YA DOIN'? Arista ARIST 561.......................	70	3 wks
30 Aug 86	WHAT DOES IT TAKE (TO WIN YOUR LOVE) Arista ARIST 672..	64	2 wks
4 Jul 87	SONGBIRD Arista RIS 18..................................	22	7 wks

Peter GABRIEL UK, male vocalist 74 wks

9 Apr 77	SOLSBURY HILL Charisma CB 301	13	9 wks
9 Feb 80 ●	GAMES WITHOUT FRONTIERS Charisma CB 354	4	11 wks
10 May 80	NO SELF CONTROL Charisma CB 360	33	6 wks
23 Aug 80	BIKO Charisma CB 370	38	3 wks
25 Sep 82	SHOCK THE MONKEY Charisma SHOCK 1	58	5 wks
9 Jul 83	I DON'T REMEMBER Charisma GAB 1	62	3 wks
2 Jun 84	WALK THROUGH THE FIRE Virgin VS 689	69	3 wks
26 Apr 86 ●	SLEDGEHAMMER Virgin PGS 1	4	16 wks
28 Mar 87	BIG TIME Charisma PGS 3	13	7 wks
11 Jul 87	RED RAIN Charisma PGS 4	46	3 wks
21 Nov 87	BIKO (LIVE) Charisma PGS 6	49	6 wks
22 Dec 90	SOLSBURY HILL (re-issue) Virgin VS 1322	57†	2 wks

Solsbury Hill on Virgin was coupled with Shaking The Tree by Youssou N'Dour and Peter Gabriel. See also Youssou N'Dour and Peter Gabriel; Peter Gabriel and Kate Bush.

Peter GABRIEL and Kate BUSH 11 wks
UK, male/female vocal duo

1 Nov 86 ●	DON'T GIVE UP Virgin PGS 2	9	11 wks

See also Peter Gabriel; Kate Bush.

Yvonne GAGE US, female vocalist 4 wks

16 Jun 84	DOIN' IT IN A HAUNTED HOUSE Epic A 4519	45	4 wks

Serge GAINSBOURG – See Jane BIRKIN and Serge GAINSBOURG

GALAXY – See Phil FEARON and GALAXY

Dee GALDES – See Phil FEARON and GALAXY

Eve GALLAGHER UK, female vocalist 4 wks

1 Dec 90	LOVE COME DOWN More Protein PROT 6	61	3 wks
29 Dec 90	LOVE COME DOWN (re-entry) More Protein PROT 6	68†	1 wk

GALLAGHER and LYLE 27 wks
UK, male vocal/instrumental duo

28 Feb 76 ●	I WANNA STAY WITH YOU A &M AMS 7211	6	9 wks
22 May 76 ●	HEART ON MY SLEEVE A &M AMS 7227	6	10 wks
11 Sep 76	BREAKAWAY A &M AMS 7245	35	4 wks
29 Jan 77	EVERY LITTLE TEARDROP A &M AMS 7274	32	4 wks

Patsy GALLANT Canada, female vocalist 9 wks

10 Sep 77 ●	FROM NEW YORK TO L.A. EMI 2620	6	9 wks

James GALWAY UK, male instrumentalist - flute 13 wks

27 May 78 ●	ANNIE'S SONG RCA Red Seal RB 5085	3	13 wks

GANG OF FOUR UK, male vocal/instrumental group 5 wks

16 Jun 79	AT HOME HE'S A TOURIST EMI 2956	58	3 wks
22 May 82	I LOVE A MAN IN UNIFORM EMI 5299	65	2 wks

GANG STARR US, male rap group 2 wks

13 Oct 90	JAZZ THING CBS 356377 7	66	2 wks

GAP BAND US, male vocal/instrumental group 82 wks

12 Jul 80 ●	OOPS UP SIDE YOUR HEAD Mercury MER 22	6	14 wks
27 Sep 80	PARTY LIGHTS Mercury MER 37	30	8 wks
27 Dec 80	BURN RUBBER ON ME (WHY YOU WANNA HURT ME) Mercury MER 52	22	11 wks
11 Apr 81	HUMPIN' Mercury MER 63	36	6 wks
27 Jun 81	YEARNING FOR YOUR LOVE Mercury MER 73	47	4 wks
5 Jun 82	EARLY IN THE MORNING Mercury MER 97	55	3 wks
19 Feb 83	OUTSTANDING Total Experience TE 001	68	2 wks
31 Mar 84	SOMEDAY Total Experience TE 5	17	8 wks
23 Jun 84	JAMMIN' IN AMERICA Total Experience TE 6	64	2 wks
13 Dec 86 ●	BIG FUN Total Experience FB 49779	4	12 wks
14 Mar 87	HOW MUSIC CAME ABOUT (BOP B DA B DA DA) Total Experience FB 49755	61	2 wks
11 Jul 87	OOPS UPSIDE YOUR HEAD (re-mix) Club JAB 54	20	8 wks
18 Feb 89	I'M GONNA GIT YOU SUCKA Arista 112016	63	2 wks

Boris GARDINER Jamaica, male vocalist/instrumentalist 38 wks

17 Jan 70	ELIZABETHAN REGGAE Duke DU 39	48	1 wk
31 Jan 70	ELIZABETHAN REGGAE (re-entry) Duke DU 39	14	13 wks
26 Jul 86 ★	I WANT TO WAKE UP WITH YOU Revue REV 733	1	15 wks
4 Oct 86	YOU'RE EVERYTHING TO ME Revue REV 735	11	8 wks
27 Dec 86	THE MEANING OF CHRISTMAS Revue REV 740	69	1 wk

The first copies of Elizabethan Reggae, an instrumental, were printed with the label incorrectly crediting Byron Lee as the performer. The charts for the first entry, and the first four weeks of the re-entry, all reprinted this error. All charts and discs printed after 28 Feb 1970 gave Boris Gardiner the credit he deserved.

Paul GARDINER UK, male instrumentalist - bass 4 wks

25 Jul 81	STORMTROOPER IN DRAG Beggars Banquet BEG 61	49	4 wks

Featuring Gary Numan on vocals. See also Gary Numan.

GARDNER – See ASHTON, GARDNER and DYKE

Art GARFUNKEL US, male vocalist 37 wks

13 Sep 75 ★	I ONLY HAVE EYES FOR YOU CBS 3575	1	11 wks
3 Mar 79 ★	BRIGHT EYES CBS 6947	1	19 wks
7 Jul 79	SINCE I DON'T HAVE YOU CBS 7371	38	7 wks

See also Simon and Garfunkel

Judy GARLAND US, female vocalist 2 wks

10 Jun 55	THE MAN THAT GOT AWAY Philips PB 366	18	2 wks

Lee GARRETT US, male vocalist 7 wks

29 May 76	YOU'RE MY EVERYTHING Chrysalis CHS 2087	15	7 wks

Leif GARRETT US, male vocalist 14 wks

20 Jan 79 ●	I WAS MADE FOR DANCIN' Scotti Brothers K 11202	4	10 wks
21 Apr 79	FEEL THE NEED Scotti Brothers K 11274	38	4 wks

Siedah GARRETT – See Dennis EDWARDS; Michael JACKSON

David GARRICK UK, male vocalist 16 wks

9 Jun 66	LADY JANE Piccadilly 7N 35317	28	7 wks
22 Sep 66	DEAR MRS. APPLEBEE Piccadilly 7N 35335	22	9 wks

GARY'S GANG US, male vocal/instrumental group — 18 wks

24 Feb 79	●	KEEP ON DANCIN' CBS 7109	8	10 wks
2 Jun 79		LET'S LOVE DANCE TONIGHT CBS 7328	49	4 wks
6 Nov 82		KNOCK ME OUT Arista ARIST 499	45	4 wks

Barbara GASKIN – See Dave STEWART with Barbara GASKIN

David GATES US, male vocalist — 2 wks

22 Jul 78	TOOK THE LAST TRAIN Elektra K 12307	50	2 wks

GAY GORDON and the MINCE PIES — 5 wks
UK, male/female vocal/instrumental group

6 Dec 86	THE ESSENTIAL WALLY PARTY MEDLEY Lifestyle XY 2	60	5 wks

GAYE BYKERS ON ACID — 2 wks
UK, male vocal/instrumental group

31 Oct 87	GIT DOWN (SHAKE YOUR THANG) Purple Fluid VS 1008	54	2 wks

Marvin GAYE US, male vocalist — 101 wks

10 Dec 64		HOW SWEET IT IS Stateside SS 360	49	1 wk
29 Sep 66		LITTLE DARLIN' Tamla Motown TMG 574	50	1 wk
12 Feb 69	★	I HEARD IT THROUGH THE GRAPEVINE Tamla Motown TMG 686	1	15 wks
23 Jul 69	●	TOO BUSY THINKING 'BOUT MY BABY Tamla Motown TMG 705	5	16 wks
9 May 70	●	ABRAHAM MARTIN AND JOHN Tamla Motown TMG 734	9	14 wks
11 Dec 71		SAVE THE CHILDREN Tamla Motown TMG 796	41	6 wks
22 Sep 73		LET'S GET IT ON Tamla Motown TMG 868	31	7 wks
7 May 77	●	GOT TO GIVE IT UP Motown TMG 1069	7	10 wks
30 Oct 82	●	(SEXUAL) HEALING CBS A 2855	4	14 wks
8 Jan 83		MY LOVE IS WAITING CBS A 3048	34	5 wks
18 May 85		SANCTIFIED LADY CBS A 4894	51	4 wks
26 Apr 86	●	I HEARD IT THRU THE GRAPEVINE (re-issue) Tamla Motown ZB 40701	8	8 wks

See also Diana Ross and Marvin Gaye; Marvin Gaye and Tammi Terrell; Marvin Gaye and Mary Wells; Marvin Gaye and Kim Weston; Diana Ross, Marvin Gaye, Smokey Robinson and Stevie Wonder.

Marvin GAYE and Tammi TERRELL — 61 wks
US, male/female vocal duo

17 Jan 68	IF I COULD BUILD MY WHOLE WORLD AROUND YOU Tamla Motown TMG 635	41	7 wks
12 Jun 68	AIN'T NOTHIN' LIKE THE REAL THING Tamla Motown TMG 655	34	7 wks
2 Oct 68	YOU'RE ALL I NEED TO GET BY Tamla Motown TMG 668	19	19 wks
22 Jan 69	YOU AIN'T LIVIN' TILL YOU'RE LOVIN' Tamla Motown TMG 681	21	8 wks
4 Jun 69	GOOD LOVIN' AIN'T EASY TO COME BY Tamla Motown TMG 697	26	7 wks
30 Jul 69	GOOD LOVIN' AIN'T EASY TO COME BY (re-entry) Tamla Motown TMG 697	48	1 wk
15 Nov 69	● ONION SONG Tamla Motown TMG 715	9	12 wks

See also Marvin Gaye.

Marvin GAYE and Mary WELLS — 1 wk
US, male/female vocal duo

30 Jul 64	ONCE UPON A TIME Stateside SS 316	50	1 wk

See also Marvin Gaye; Mary Wells.

Marvin GAYE and Kim WESTON — 11 wks
US, male/female vocal duo

26 Jan 67	IT TAKES TWO Tamla Motown TMG 590	16	11 wks

See also Marvin Gaye.

Crystal GAYLE US, female vocalist — 28 wks

12 Nov 77	● DON'T IT MAKE MY BROWN EYES BLUE United Artists UP 36307	5	14 wks
26 Aug 78	TALKING IN YOUR SLEEP United Artists UP 36422	11	14 wks

Roy GAYLE – See MIRAGE

Gloria GAYNOR US, female vocalist — 62 wks

7 Dec 74	●	NEVER CAN SAY GOODBYE MGM 2006 463	2	13 wks
8 Mar 75		REACH OUT I'LL BE THERE MGM 2006 499	14	8 wks
9 Aug 75		ALL I NEED IS YOUR SWEET LOVIN' MGM 2006 531	44	3 wks
17 Jan 76		HOW HIGH THE MOON MGM 2006 558	33	4 wks
3 Feb 79	★	I WILL SURVIVE Polydor 2095 017	1	15 wks
6 Oct 79		LET ME KNOW (I HAVE A RIGHT) Polydor STEP 5	32	7 wks
24 Dec 83		I AM WHAT I AM Chrysalis CHS 2765	13	12 wks

GAZ US, male vocal/instrumental group — 4 wks

24 Feb 79	SING SING Salsoul SSOL 116	60	4 wks

GAZZA UK, male vocalist - Paul Gascoigne — 2 wks

22 Dec 90	GEORDIE BOYS (GAZZA RAP) Best ZB 44229	34†	2 wks

GAZZA and LINDISFARNE — 8 wk
UK, male vocalist and male vocal/instrumental group

10 Nov 90	● FOG ON THE TYNE Best ZB 44083	2	8 wks

See also Gazza; Lindisfarne.

GB EXPERIENCE – See Gary BYRD and the GB EXPERIENCE

GBH UK, male vocal/instrumental group — 5 wks

6 Feb 82	NO SURVIVORS Clay CLAY 8	63	2 wks
20 Nov 82	GIVE ME FIRE Clay CLAY 16	69	3 wks

G-CLEFS US, male vocal group — 12 wks

30 Nov 61	I UNDERSTAND London HLU 9433	17	12 wks

J. GEILS BAND US, male vocal/instrumental group — 20 wks

9 Jun 79		ONE LAST KISS EMI America AM 507	74	1 wk
13 Feb 82	●	CENTERFOLD EMI America EA 135	3	9 wks
10 Apr 82		FREEZE-FRAME EMI America EA 134	27	7 wks
26 Jun 82		ANGEL IN BLUE EMI America EA 138	55	3 wks

Far Left: Only months before his death, MARVIN GAYE stretches out in a setting appropriate to his friend Smokey Robinson's 'Tears Of A Clown'.

Left: The fans were phoning for DEBBIE GIBSON at a 1989 New York radiothon for AIDS relief.

Left: 'It's My Party' by LESLEY GORE was Quincy Jones' first US number one production.

THE FOUR TOPS, the longest running major group with no personnel change, have been together since 1954. This photo was taken in 1966.

Bob GELDOF *Ireland, male vocalist* **14 wks**

1 Nov 86	THIS IS THE WORLD CALLING *Mercury BOB 101*	25	5 wks
21 Feb 87	LOVE LIKE A ROCKET *Mercury BOB 102*	61	3 wks
23 Jun 90	THE GREAT SONG OF INDIFFERENCE *Mercury BOB 104*	15	6 wks

GENE AND JIM ARE INTO SHAKES **2 wks**
UK, male vocal/instrumental duo

| 19 Mar 88 | SHAKE! (HOW ABOUT A SAMPLING GENE) *Rough Trade RT 216* | 68 | 2 wks |

GENE LOVES JEZEBEL **7 wks**
UK, male vocal/instrumental group

29 Mar 86	SWEETEST THING *Beggars Banquet BEG 156*	75	1 wk
14 Jun 86	HEARTACHE *Beggars Banquet BEG 161*	71	2 wks
5 Sep 87	THE MOTION OF LOVE *Beggars Banquet BEG 192*	56	3 wks
5 Dec 87	GORGEOUS *Beggars Banquet BEG 202*	68	1 wk

GENERAL PUBLIC *UK, male vocal/instrumental group* **3 wks**

| 10 Mar 84 | GENERAL PUBLIC *Virgin VS 659* | 60 | 3 wks |

GENERATION X *UK, male vocal/instrumental group* **31 wks**

17 Sep 77	YOUR GENERATION *Chrysalis CHS 2165*	36	4 wks
11 Mar 78	READY STEADY GO *Chrysalis CHS 2207*	47	3 wks
20 Jan 79	KING ROCKER *Chrysalis CHS 2261*	11	9 wks
7 Apr 79	VALLEY OF THE DOLLS *Chrysalis CHS 2310*	23	7 wks
30 Jun 79	FRIDAY'S ANGELS *Chrysalis CHS 2330*	62	2 wks
18 Oct 80	DANCING WITH MYSELF *Chrysalis CHS 2444*	62	2 wks
24 Jan 81	DANCING WITH MYSELF (EP) *Chrysalis CHS 2488*	60	4 wks

On Dancing With Myself, *group is billed as Gen X. Dancing With Myself EP contains the following tracks: Dancing With Myself/Untouchables/Rock On/King Rocker.*

GENESIS *UK, male vocal/instrumental group* **148 wks**

6 Apr 74	I KNOW WHAT I LIKE (IN YOUR WARDROBE) *Charisma CB 224*	21	7 wks
26 Feb 77	YOUR OWN SPECIAL WAY *Charisma CB 300*	43	3 wks
28 May 77	SPOT THE PIGEON (EP) *Charisma GEN 001*	14	7 wks
11 Mar 78	● FOLLOW YOU FOLLOW ME *Charisma CB 309*	7	13 wks
8 Jul 78	MANY TOO MANY *Charisma CB 315*	43	5 wks
15 Mar 80	TURN IT ON AGAIN *Charisma CB 356*	8	10 wks
17 May 80	DUCHESS *Charisma CB 363*	46	5 wks
13 Sep 80	MISUNDERSTANDING *Charisma CB 369*	42	5 wks
22 Aug 81	★ ABACAB *Charisma CB 388*	9	8 wks
31 Oct 81	KEEP IT DARK *Charisma CB 391*	33	4 wks
13 Mar 82	MAN ON THE CORNER *Charisma CB 393*	41	5 wks
22 May 82	● 3 X 3 (EP) *Charisma GEN 1*	10	8 wks
3 Sep 83	● MAMA *Charisma/Virgin MAMA 1*	4	10 wks
12 Nov 83	THAT'S ALL *Charisma/Virgin TATA 1*	16	11 wks
11 Feb 84	ILLEGAL ALIEN *Charisma/Virgin AL1*	46	3 wks
10 Mar 84	ILLEGAL ALIEN (re-entry) *Charisma/Virgin AL1*	70	1 wk
31 May 86	INVISIBLE TOUCH *Virgin GENS 1*	15	8 wks
30 Aug 86	IN TOO DEEP *Virgin GENS 2*	19	9 wks
22 Nov 86	LAND OF CONFUSION *Virgin GENS 3*	14	12 wks
14 Mar 87	TONIGHT TONIGHT TONIGHT *Virgin GENS 4*	18	6 wks
20 Jun 87	THROWING IT ALL AWAY *Virgin GENS 5*	22	8 wks

Tracks on Spot The Pigeon EP: Match Of The Day/Pigeons/Inside and Out. Tracks on 3 X 3 EP: Paperlate/You Might Recall/Me And Virgil.

GENEVIEVE *France, female vocalist* **1 wk**

| 5 May 66 | ONCE *CBS 202061* | 43 | 1 wk |

Bobbie GENTRY *US, female vocalist* **34 wks**

13 Sep 67	ODE TO BILLY JOE *Capitol CL 15511*	13	11 wks
30 Aug 69	★ I'LL NEVER FALL IN LOVE AGAIN *Capitol CL 15606*	1	19 wks
21 Feb 70	RAINDROPS KEEP FALLIN' ON MY HEAD *Capitol CL 15626*	40	4 wks

See also Bobbie Gentry and Glen Campbell.

Bobbie GENTRY and Glen CAMPBELL **14 wks**
US, female/male vocal duo

| 6 Dec 69 | ● ALL I HAVE TO DO IS DREAM *Capitol CL 15619* | 3 | 14 wks |

See also Bobbie Gentry; Glen Campbell.

GEORDIE *UK, vocal/instrumental group* **35 wks**

2 Dec 72	DON'T DO THAT *Regal Zonophone RZ 3067*	32	7 wks
17 Mar 73	● ALL BECAUSE OF YOU *EMI 2008*	6	13 wks
16 Jun 73	CAN YOU DO IT *EMI 2031*	13	9 wks
25 Aug 73	ELECTRIC LADY *EMI 2048*	32	6 wks

Robin GEORGE *UK, male vocalist/instrumentalist - guitar* **2 wks**

| 27 Apr 85 | HEARTLINE *Bronze BRO 191* | 68 | 2 wks |

Sophia GEORGE *Jamaica, female vocalist* **11 wks**

| 7 Dec 85 | ● GIRLIE GIRLIE *Winner WIN 01* | 7 | 11 wks |

GEORGIA SATELLITES **8 wks**
US, male vocal/instrumental group

7 Feb 87	KEEP YOUR HANDS TO YOURSELF *Elektra EKR 50*	69	1 wk
16 May 87	BATTLESHIP CHAINS *Elektra EKR 58*	44	4 wks
21 Jan 89	HIPPY HIPPY SHAKE *Elektra EKR 86*	63	3 wks

GEORGIO *US, male vocalist* **3 wks**

| 20 Feb 88 | LOVER'S LANE *Motown ZB 41611* | 54 | 3 wks |

Danyel GERARD *France, male vocalist* **12 wks**

| 18 Sep 71 | BUTTERFLY *CBS 7454* | 11 | 12 wks |

GERRY and the PACEMAKERS **114 wks**
UK, male vocal/instrumental group

14 Mar 63	★ HOW DO YOU DO IT? *Columbia DB 4987*	1	18 wks
30 May 63	★ I LIKE IT *Columbia DB 7041*	1	15 wks
10 Oct 63	★ YOU'LL NEVER WALK ALONE *Columbia DB 7126*	1	19 wks
16 Jan 64	● I'M THE ONE *Columbia DB 7189*	2	15 wks
16 Apr 64	● DON'T LET THE SUN CATCH YOU CRYING *Columbia DB 7268*	6	11 wks
3 Sep 64	IT'S GONNA BE ALL RIGHT *Columbia DB 7353*	24	7 wks
17 Dec 64	● FERRY ACROSS THE MERSEY *Columbia DB 7437*	8	13 wks
25 Mar 65	I'LL BE THERE *Columbia DB 7504*	15	9 wks
18 Nov 65	WALK HAND IN HAND *Columbia DB 7738*	29	7 wks

GET FRESH CREW – *See Doug E. FRESH and the GET FRESH CREW*

Stan GETZ and Charlie BYRD
US, male instrumental duo - sax and guitar   **13 wks**

8 Nov 62	**DESAFINADO** *HMV POP 1061*	**11**	13 wks

See also Stan Getz and Joao Gilberto.

Stan GETZ and Joao GILBERTO
US/Brazil, male instrumentalists - tenor sax/male vocalist   **10 wks**

23 Jul 64	**THE GIRL FROM IPANEMA (GAROTA DE IPANEMA)** *Verve VS 520*	**29**	10 wks

Joao Gilberto did not actually appear on this hit. The vocalist is in fact Astrud, his wife. See also Astrud Gilberto; Stan Getz and Charlie Byrd.

G. F. BAND – *See Gene FARROW and G. F. BAND*

GHOST DANCE *UK, male vocal/instrumental group*   **2 wks**

17 Jun 89	**DOWN TO THE WIRE** *Chrysalis CHS 3376*	**66**	2 wks

Andy GIBB *UK, male vocalist*   **30 wks**

25 Jun 77	**I JUST WANNA BE YOUR EVERYTHING** *RSO 2090 237*	**26**	7 wks
13 May 78	**SHADOW DANCING** *RSO 001*	**42**	6 wks
12 Aug 78	● **AN EVERLASTING LOVE** *RSO 015*	**10**	10 wks
27 Jan 79	**(OUR LOVE) DON'T THROW IT ALL AWAY** *RSO 26*	**32**	7 wks

Barry GIBB – *See Barbra STREISAND and Barry GIBB*

Robin GIBB *UK, male vocalist*   **21 wks**

9 Jul 69	● **SAVED BY THE BELL** *Polydor 56-337*	**2**	16 wks
15 Nov 69	**SAVED BY THE BELL (re-entry)** *Polydor 56-337*	**49**	1 wk
7 Feb 70	**AUGUST OCTOBER** *Polydor 56-371*	**45**	3 wks
11 Feb 84	**ANOTHER LONELY NIGHT IN NEW YORK** *Polydor POSP 668*	**71**	1 wk

Steve GIBBONS BAND   **14 wks**
UK, male vocal/instrumental group

6 Aug 77	**TULANE** *Polydor 2058 889*	**12**	10 wks
13 May 78	**EDDY VORTEX** *Polydor 2059 017*	**56**	4 wks

Georgia GIBBS *US, female vocalist*   **2 wks**

22 Apr 55	**TWEEDLE DEE** *Mercury MB 3196*	**20**	1 wk
13 Jul 56	**KISS ME ANOTHER** *Mercury MT 110*	**24**	1 wk

Debbie GIBSON *US, female vocalist*   **61 wks**

26 Sep 87	**ONLY IN MY DREAMS** *Atlantic A 9322*	**54**	5 wks
23 Jan 88	● **SHAKE YOUR LOVE** *Atlantic A 9187*	**7**	8 wks
19 Mar 88	**ONLY IN MY DREAMS (re-entry)** *Atlantic A 9322*	**11**	7 wks
7 May 88	**OUT OF THE BLUE** *Atlantic A 9091*	**19**	7 wks
9 Jul 88	● **FOOLISH BEAT** *Atlantic A 9059*	**9**	9 wks
15 Oct 88	**STAYING TOGETHER** *Atlantic A 9020*	**53**	2 wks
28 Jan 89	**LOST IN YOUR EYES** *Atlantic A 8970*	**34**	7 wks
29 Apr 89	**ELECTRIC YOUTH** *Atlantic A 8919*	**14**	8 wks
19 Aug 89	**WE COULD BE TOGETHER** *Atlantic A 8896*	**22**	8 wks

Don GIBSON *US, male vocalist*   **16 wks**

31 Aug 61	**SEA OF HEARTBREAK** *RCA 1243*	**14**	13 wks
1 Feb 62	**LONESOME NUMBER ONE** *RCA 1272*	**47**	3 wks

Wayne GIBSON *UK, male vocalist*   **13 wks**

3 Sep 64	**KELLY** *Pye 7N 15680*	**48**	2 wks
23 Nov 74	**UNDER MY THUMB** *Pye Disco Demand DDS 2001*	**17**	11 wks

GIBSON BROTHERS   **54 wks**
Martinique, male vocal/instrumental group

10 Mar 79	**CUBA** *Island WIP 6483*	**41**	9 wks
21 Jul 79	● **OOH! WHAT A LIFE** *Island WIP 6503*	**10**	12 wks
17 Nov 79	● **QUE SERA MI VIDA (IF YOU SHOULD GO)** *Island WIP 6525*	**5**	11 wks
23 Feb 80	**CUBA (re-issue)/ BETTER DO IT SALSA** *Island WIP 6561*	**12**	9 wks
12 Jul 80	**MARIANA** *Island WIP 6617*	**11**	10 wks
9 Jul 83	**MY HEART'S BEATING WILD (TIC TAC TIC TAC)** *Stiff BUY 184*	**56**	3 wks

GIDEA PARK   **19 wks**
UK, male vocal/instrumentalist, Adrian Baker under false group name

4 Jul 81	**BEACHBOY GOLD** *Stone SON 2162*	**11**	13 wks
12 Sep 81	**SEASONS OF GOLD** *Polo POLO 14*	**28**	6 wks

See also Adrian Baker.

Astrud GILBERTO *Brazil, female vocalist*   **6 wks**

25 Aug 84	**THE GIRL FROM IPANEMA** *Verve IPA 1*	**55**	6 wks

Re-issue of The Girl From Ipanema (Garota De Ipanema) on Verve VS 520 by Stan Getz and Joao Gilberto. See also Stan Getz and Joao Gilberto.

Joao GILBERTO – *See Stan GETZ and Joao GILBERTO*

GILLAN *UK, male vocal/instrumental group*   **46 wks**

14 Jun 80	**SLEEPIN' ON THE JOB** *Virgin VS 355*	**55**	3 wks
4 Oct 80	**TROUBLE** *Virgin VS 377*	**14**	6 wks
14 Feb 81	**MUTUALLY ASSURED DESTRUCTION** *Virgin VS 103*	**32**	5 wks
21 Mar 81	**NEW ORLEANS** *Virgin VS 406*	**17**	10 wks
20 Jun 81	**NO LAUGHING IN HEAVEN** *Virgin VS 425*	**31**	6 wks
10 Oct 81	**NIGHTMARE** *Virgin VS 441*	**36**	6 wks
23 Jan 82	**RESTLESS** *Virgin VS 465*	**25**	7 wks
4 Sep 82	**LIVING FOR THE CITY** *Virgin VS 519*	**50**	3 wks

Stuart GILLIES *UK, male vocalist*   **10 wks**

31 Mar 73	**AMANDA** *Philips 6006 293*	**13**	10 wks

Jimmy GILMER and the FIREBALLS   **8 wks**
US, male vocal/instrumental group

14 Nov 63	**SUGAR SHACK** *London HLD 9789*	**45**	4 wks
19 Dec 63	**SUGAR SHACK (re-entry)** *London HLD 9789*	**46**	4 wks

See also Fireballs.

James GILREATH *US, male vocalist*   **10 wks**

2 May 63	**LITTLE BAND OF GOLD** *Pye International 7N 25190*	**29**	10 wks

Jim GILSTRAP US, male vocalist   **11 wks**

| 15 Mar 75 | ● | SWING YOUR DADDY *Chelsea 2005 021*..................... | **4** | 11 wks |

Gordon GILTRAP UK, male instrumentalist - guitar   **10 wks**

| 14 Jan 78 | | HEARTSONG *Electric WOT 19*................................. | **21** | 7 wks |
| 28 Apr 79 | | FEAR OF THE DARK *Electric WOT 29* .... | **58** | 3 wks |

Fear Of The Dark *credited to the Gordon Giltrap Band.*

GINGERBREADS – *See GOLDIE and the GINGERBREADS*

GIRL UK, male vocal/instrumental group   **3 wks**

| 12 Apr 80 | | HOLLYWOOD TEASE *Jet 176*................................ | **50** | 3 wks |

GIRLSCHOOL UK, female vocal/instrumental group   **17 wks**

2 Aug 80		RACE WITH THE DEVIL *Bronze BRO 100*	**49**	6 wks
11 Apr 81		HIT AND RUN *Bronze BRO 118*..............................	**32**	6 wks
11 Jul 81		C'MON LET'S GO *Bronze BRO 126*	**42**	3 wks
3 Apr 82		WILDLIFE (EP) *Bronze BRO 144*	**58**	2 wks

Tracks on Wildlife EP: Don't Call It Love/Wildlife/Don't Stop. See also Motorhead and Girlschool.

Junior GUISCOMBE – *See JUNIOR*

GLADIATORS – *See NERO and the GLADIATORS*

GLASS TIGER Canada/UK, male vocal/instrumental group   **11 wks**

| 18 Oct 86 | | DON'T FORGET ME (WHEN I'M GONE) *Manhattan MT 13* .... | **29** | 9 wks |
| 31 Jan 87 | | SOMEDAY *Manhattan MT 17* .... | **66** | 2 wks |

Mayson GLEN ORCHESTRA – *See Paul HENRY and the Mayson GLEN ORCHESTRA*

GLENN and CHRIS UK, male vocal duo   **8 wks**

| 18 Apr 87 | | DIAMOND LIGHTS *Record Shack KICK 1* .... | **12** | 8 wks |

Gary GLITTER UK, male vocalist   **163 wks**

10 Jun 72	●	ROCK AND ROLL (PARTS 1 & 2) *Bell 1216*	**2**	15 wks
23 Sep 72	●	I DIDN'T KNOW I LOVED YOU (TILL I SAW YOU ROCK 'N' ROLL) *Bell 1259*	**4**	11 wks
20 Jan 73	●	DO YOU WANNA TOUCH ME? (OH YEAH) *Bell 1280*	**2**	11 wks
7 Apr 73	●	HELLO HELLO I'M BACK AGAIN *Bell 1299*	**2**	14 wks
21 Jul 73	★	I'M THE LEADER OF THE GANG (I AM) *Bell 1321*	**1**	12 wks
17 Nov 73	★	I LOVE YOU LOVE ME LOVE *Bell 1337*	**1**	14 wks
30 Mar 74		REMEMBER ME THIS WAY *Bell 1349*......................	**3**	8 wks
15 Jun 74	★	ALWAYS YOURS *Bell 1359*..................................	**1**	9 wks
23 Nov 74	●	OH YES! YOU'RE BEAUTIFUL *Bell 1391*....................	**2**	10 wks
3 May 75	●	LOVE LIKE YOU AND ME *Bell 1423*	**10**	6 wks
21 Jun 75	●	DOING ALRIGHT WITH THE BOYS *Bell 1429*.............	**6**	7 wks
8 Nov 75		PAPA OOM MOW MOW *Bell 1451*.........................	**38**	5 wks
13 Mar 76		YOU BELONG TO ME *Bell 1473*............................	**40**	5 wks
22 Jan 77		IT TAKES ALL NIGHT LONG *Arista 85*	**25**	6 wks
16 Jul 77		A LITTLE BOOGIE WOOGIE IN THE BACK OF MY MIND *Arista 112*	**31**	5 wks
20 Sep 80		GARY GLITTER (EP) *GTO GT 282*..........................	**57**	3 wks
10 Oct 81		AND THEN SHE KISSED ME *Bell BELL 1497*...............	**39**	5 wks
5 Dec 81		ALL THAT GLITTERS *Bell BELL 1498*......................	**48**	5 wks
23 Jun 84		DANCE ME UP *Arista ARIST 570*...........................	**25**	5 wks
1 Dec 84	●	ANOTHER ROCK AND ROLL CHRISTMAS *Arista ARIST 592*	**7**	7 wks

Rock And Roll Part 1 *not listed with Part 2 for weeks of 10 and 17 Jan 72. Tracks on Gary Glitter EP: I'm The Leader Of The Gang (I Am)/Rock And Roll (Part 2)/Hello Hello I'm Back Again/Do You Wanna Touch Me?(Oh Yeah). All were re-issues.*

GLITTER BAND UK, male vocal/instrumental group   **60 wks**

23 Mar 74	●	ANGEL FACE *Bell 1348*	**4**	10 wks
3 Aug 74	●	JUST FOR YOU *Bell 1368*	**10**	8 wks
19 Oct 74	●	LET'S GET TOGETHER AGAIN *Bell 1383*	**8**	8 wks
18 Jan 75	●	GOODBYE MY LOVE *Bell 1395*............................	**2**	9 wks
12 Apr 75	●	THE TEARS I CRIED *Bell 1416*	**8**	8 wks
9 Aug 75	●	LOVE IN THE SUN *Bell 1437*	**15**	8 wks
28 Feb 76	●	PEOPLE LIKE YOU AND PEOPLE LIKE ME *Bell 1471*.....	**5**	9 wks

GLOVE UK, male vocal/instrumental group   **3 wks**

| 20 Aug 83 | | LIKE AN ANIMAL *Wonderland SHE 3* .... | **52** | 3 wks |

GO GO LORENZO and the DAVIS PINCKNEY PROJECT   **8 wks**
US, male vocal/instrumental group

| 6 Dec 86 | | YOU CAN DANCE (IF YOU WANT TO) *Boiling Point POSP 836* .... | **46** | 8 wks |

GO-GOS US, female vocal/instrumental group   **6 wks**

| 15 May 82 | | OUR LIPS ARE SEALED *IRS GDN 102* .... | **47** | 6 wks |

GO WEST UK, male vocal/instrumental duo   **63 wks**

23 Feb 85	●	WE CLOSE OUR EYES *Chrysalis CHS 2850*	**5**	14 wks
11 May 85		CALL ME *Chrysalis GOW 1*	**12**	10 wks
3 Aug 85		GOODBYE GIRL *Chrysalis GOW 2*	**25**	7 wks
23 Nov 85		DON'T LOOK DOWN - THE SEQUEL *Chrysalis GOW 3*	**13**	10 wks
29 Nov 86		TRUE COLOURS *Chrysalis GOW 4*..........................	**48**	7 wks
9 May 87		I WANT TO HEAR IT FROM YOU *Chrysalis GOW 5*........	**43**	3 wks
12 Sep 87		THE KING IS DEAD *Chrysalis GOW 6*	**67**	2 wks
28 Jul 90		THE KING OF WISHFUL THINKING *Chrysalis GOW 8*	**18**	10 wks

GODIEGO Japan/US, male vocal/instrumental group   **11 wks**

| 15 Oct 77 | | THE WATER MARGIN *BBC RESL 50*........................ | **37** | 4 wks |
| 16 Feb 80 | | GANDHARA *BBC RESL 66*.................................. | **56** | 7 wks |

The Water Margin *is the English version of the song, which shared chart credit with the Japanese language version by Peter MacJunior. See also Peter MacJunior.*

GODLEY and CREME UK, male vocal/instrumental duo   **36 wks**

12 Sep 81	●	UNDER YOUR THUMB *Polydor POSP 322*....................	**3**	11 wks
21 Nov 81	●	WEDDING BELLS *Polydor POSP 369*	**7**	11 wks
30 Mar 85		CRY *Polydor POSP 732*.....................................	**19**	11 wks
16 Aug 86		CRY (re-entry) *Polydor POSP 732*..........................	**66**	3 wks

Andrew GOLD US, male vocalist/instrumentalist - piano   **36 wks**

2 Apr 77		LONELY BOY *Asylum K 13076*	**11**	9 wks
25 Mar 78	●	NEVER LET HER SLIP AWAY *Asylum K 13112*	**5**	13 wks
24 Jun 78		HOW CAN THIS BE LOVE *Asylum K 13126*................	**19**	10 wks
14 Oct 78		THANK YOU FOR BEING A FRIEND *Asylum K 13135*	**42**	4 wks

GOLDEN EARRING
Holland, male vocal/instrumental group   **16 wks**

8 Dec 73 ●	RADAR LOVE *Track 2094 116*	**7**	13 wks
8 Oct 77	RADAR LOVE *Polydor 2121 335.*	**44**	3 wks

These are two different recordings of the same song.

GOLDIE *UK, male vocal/instrumental group*   **11 wks**

27 May 78 ●	MAKING UP AGAIN *Bronze BRO 50*	**7**	11 wks

GOLDIE and the GINGERBREADS
US, female vocal/instrumental group   **5 wks**

25 Feb 65	CAN'T YOU HEAR MY HEART BEAT? *Decca F 12070*	**25**	5 wks

Bobby GOLDSBORO *US, male vocalist*   **47 wks**

17 Apr 68 ●	HONEY *United Artists UP2215*	**2**	15 wks
4 Aug 73 ●	SUMMER (THE FIRST TIME) *United Artists UP35558*	**9**	10 wks
3 Aug 74	HELLO SUMMERTIME *United Artists UP35705*	**14**	10 wks
29 Mar 75 ●	HONEY (re-issue) *United Artists UP35633*	**2**	12 wks

Glen GOLDSMITH *US, male vocalist*   **24 wks**

7 Nov 87	I WON'T CRY *Reproduction PB 41493*	**34**	7 wks
12 Mar 88	DREAMING *Reproduction PB 41711*	**12**	11 wks
11 Jun 88	WHAT YOU SEE IS WHAT YOU GET *Reproduction PB 42075.*	**33**	5 wks
3 Sep 88	SAVE A LITTLE BIT *Reproduction PB 42147*	**73**	1 wk

Leroy GOMEZ – *See SANTA ESMERALDA and Leroy GOMEZ*

GONZALEZ *UK/US, male vocal/instrumental group*   **11 wks**

31 Mar 79	HAVEN'T STOPPED DANCING YET *Sidewalk SID 102.*	**15**	11 wks

GOOD GOOD FEELING – *See ERIC and the GOOD GOOD FEELING*

GOODBYE MR. MACKENZIE
UK, male/female vocal/instrumental group   **13 wks**

20 Aug 88	GOODBYE MR MACKENZIE *Capitol CL 501*	**62**	2 wks
11 Mar 89	THE RATTLER *Capitol CL 522*	**37**	6 wks
29 Jul 89	GOODWILL CITY/ I'M SICK OF YOU *Capitol CL 538*	**49**	2 wks
21 Apr 90	LOVE CHILD *Parlophone R 6247.*	**52**	2 wks
23 Jun 90	BLACKER THAN BLACK *Parlophone R 6257.*	**61**	1 wk

GOODIES *UK, male vocal group*   **38 wks**

7 Dec 74 ●	THE IN BETWEENIES/ FATHER CHRISTMAS DO NOT TOUCH ME *Bradley's BRAD 7421*	**7**	9 wks
15 Mar 75 ●	FUNKY GIBBON/ SICK MAN BLUES *Bradley's BRAD 7504.*	**4**	10 wks
21 Jun 75	BLACK PUDDING BERTHA *Bradley's BRAD 7517.*	**19**	7 wks
27 Sep 75	NAPPY LOVE/ WILD THING *Bradley's BRAD 7524*	**21**	6 wks
13 Dec 75	MAKE A DAFT NOISE FOR CHRISTMAS *Bradley's BRAD 7533.*	**20**	6 wks

Cuba GOODING *US, male vocalist*   **2 wks**

19 Nov 83	HAPPINESS IS JUST AROUND THE BEND *London LON 41*	**72**	2 wks

Ron GOODWIN *UK, orchestra*   **24 wks**

15 May 53 ●	LIMELIGHT *Parlophone R 3686*	**3**	23 wks
28 Oct 55	BLUE STAR (THE MEDIC THEME) *Parlophone R 4074*	**20**	1 wk

GOODY GOODY *US, female vocal duo*   **5 wks**

2 Dec 78	NUMBER ONE DEE JAY *Atlantic LV 3*	**55**	5 wks

GOOMBAY DANCE BAND
Germany/Montserrat, male/female vocal/instrumental group   **16 wks**

27 Feb 82 ★	SEVEN TEARS *Epic EPC A 1242*	**1**	12 wks
15 May 82	SUN OF JAMAICA *Epic EPC A 2345.*	**50**	4 wks

GOONS *UK, male vocal group*   **30 wks**

29 Jun 56 ●	I'M WALKING BACKWARDS FOR CHRISTMAS/ BLUEBOTTLE BLUES *Decca F 10756*	**4**	10 wks
14 Sep 56 ●	BLOODNOK'S ROCK N ROLL/ YING TONG SONG *Decca E 10780.*	**3**	10 wks
21 Jul 73 ●	YING TONG SONG (re-issue) *Decca F 13414.*	**9**	10 wks

Bluebottle Blues only listed from 13 Jul 56.

GORDON – *See PETER and GORDON*

Lonnie GORDON *US, female vocalist*   **13 wks**

27 Jan 90 ●	HAPPENIN' ALL OVER AGAIN *Supreme SUPE 159.*	**4**	10 wks
11 Aug 90	BEYOND YOUR WILDEST DREAMS *Supreme SUPE 167.*	**48**	2 wks
17 Nov 90	IF I HAVE TO STAND ALONE *Supreme SUPE 181.*	**68**	1 wk

See also Simon Harris.

Lesley GORE *US, female vocalist*   **20 wks**

20 Jun 63 ●	IT'S MY PARTY *Mercury AMT 1205*	**9**	12 wks
24 Sep 64	MAYBE I KNOW *Mercury MF 829*	**20**	8 wks

Eydie GORMÉ *US, female vocalist*   **20 wks**

24 Jan 58	LOVE ME FOREVER *HMV POP 432.*	**21**	5 wks
21 Jun 62 ●	YES MY DARLING DAUGHTER *CBS AAG 105*	**10**	9 wks
31 Jan 63	BLAME IT ON THE BOSSA NOVA *CBS AAG 131*	**32**	6 wks

See also Steve and Eydie.

G.O.S.H. *UK, male/female charity ensemble*   **11 wks**

28 Nov 87	THE WISHING WELL *MBS GOSH 1.*	**22**	11 wks

Nigel GOULDING – *See Abigail MEAD and Nigel GOULDING*

Graham GOULDMAN *UK, male vocalist*   **4 wks**

23 Jun 79	SUNBURN *Mercury SUNNY 1.*	**52**	4 wks

G.Q. *US, male vocal/instrumental group*   **6 wks**

10 Mar 79	DISCO NIGHTS (ROCK FREAK) *Arista ARIST 245*	**42**	6 wks

GRACE – *See COLD JAM featuring GRACE*

GRACE – *See DALE and GRACE*

Charlie GRACIE *US, male vocalist* **39 wks**

19 Apr 57	**BUTTERFLY** *Parlophone R 4290*	12	8 wks
14 Jun 57	● **FABULOUS** *Parlophone R 4313*	8	16 wks
23 Aug 57	**I LOVE YOU SO MUCH IT HURTS/WANDERIN'**		
	EYES *London HL 8467*	14	2 wks
6 Sep 57	● **WANDERIN' EYES** *London HL 8467*	6	12 wks
6 Sep 57	**I LOVE YOU SO MUCH IT HURTS** *London HL 8467*	20	2 wks
10 Jan 58	**COOL BABY** *London HLU 8521*	26	1 wk

I Love You So Much It Hurts and Wanderin' Eyes were listed together for 2 weeks, then listed separately for a further 2 and 12 weeks respectively.

Eve GRAHAM – *See NEW SEEKERS*

Jaki GRAHAM *UK, female vocalist* **50 wks**

29 Jun 85	● **ROUND AND ROUND** *EMI JAKI 4*	9	11 wks
31 Aug 85	**HEAVEN KNOWS** *EMI JAKI 5*	59	3 wks
3 May 86	● **SET ME FREE** *EMI JAKI 7*	7	12 wks
9 Aug 86	**BREAKING AWAY** *EMI JAKI 8*	16	8 wks
15 Nov 86	**STEP RIGHT UP** *EMI JAKI 9*	15	12 wks
9 Jul 88	**NO MORE TEARS** *EMI JAKI 12*	60	2 wks
24 Jun 89	**FROM NOW ON** *EMI JAKI 15*	73	2 wks

See also David Grant and Jaki Graham.

Larry GRAHAM *US, male vocalist* **4 wks**

3 Jul 82	**SOONER OR LATER** *Warner Bros. K 17925*	54	4 wks

Ron GRAINER ORCHESTRA *UK, orchestra* **7 wks**

9 Dec 78	**A TOUCH OF VELVET A STING OF BRASS**		
	Casino Classics CC 5	60	7 wks

GRAND FUNK RAILROAD **1 wk**
US, male vocal/instrumental group

6 Feb 71	**INSIDE LOOKING OUT** *Capitol CL 15668*	40	1 wk

GRAND PLAZ *UK, male producers* **4 wks**

8 Sep 90	**WOW WOW - NA NA** *Urban URB 60*	41	4 wks

GRAND PRIX *UK, male vocal/instrumental group* **1 wk**

27 Feb 82	**KEEP ON BELIEVING** *RCA 162*	75	1 wk

GRANDMASTER FLASH, Melle MEL and the FURIOUS FIVE **84 wks**
US, male vocal duo and male vocal group

28 Aug 82	● **THE MESSAGE** *Sugarhill SHL 117*	8	9 wks
22 Jan 83	**MESSAGE II (SURVIVAL)** *Sugarhill SH 119*	74	2 wks
19 Nov 83	**WHITE LINES (DON'T DON'T DO IT)**		
	Sugarhill SH 130	60	3 wks
11 Feb 84	● **WHITE LINES (DON'T DON'T DO IT) (re-entry)**		
	Sugarhill SH 130	7	38 wks
30 Jun 84	**BEAT STREET BREAKDOWN** *Atlantic A9659*	42	7 wks
22 Sep 84	**WE DON'T WORK FOR FREE** *Sugarhill SH 136*	45	4 wks
24 Nov 84	**WHITE LINES (DON'T DON'T DO IT) (2nd re-entry)**		
	Sugarhill SH 130	75	1 wk
15 Dec 84	● **STEP OFF (PART 1)** *Sugarhill SH 139*	8	12 wks
5 Jan 85	**WHITE LINES (DON'T DON'T DO IT) (3rd re-entry)**		
	Sugarhill SH 130	73	1 wk
16 Feb 85	**SIGN OF THE TIMES** *Elektra E 9677*	72	1 wk
16 Mar 85	**PUMP ME UP** *Sugarhill SH 141*	45	6 wks

Act billed as Grandmaster Flash and the Furious Five on The Message; as Melle Mel and Duke Bootee on Message II (Survival); as Grandmaster Flash and Melle Mel on White Lines (Don't Don't Do It); as Grandmaster Flash on Sign Of The Times and as Grandmaster Melle Mel and the Furious Five on other hits.

GRANDMIXER *US, male 'scratch' DJ* **3 wks**

24 Dec 83	**CRAZY CUTS** *Island IS 146*	73	2 wks
14 Jan 84	**CRAZY CUTS (re-entry)** *Island IS 146*	71	1 wk

GRANGE HILL CAST **6 wks**
UK, male/female vocal charity assembly

19 Apr 86	● **JUST SAY NO** *BBC RESL 183*	5	6 wks

Gerri GRANGER *US, female vocalist* **3 wks**

30 Sep 78	**I GO TO PIECES (EVERYTIME)** *Casino Classics CC3*	50	3 wks

Boysie GRANT – *See Ezz RECO and the LAUNCHERS with Boysie GRANT*

David GRANT *UK, male vocalist* **38 wks**

30 Apr 83	**STOP AND GO** *Chrysalis GRAN 1*	19	9 wks
16 Jul 83	● **WATCHING YOU WATCHING ME** *Chrysalis GRAN 2*	10	13 wks
8 Oct 83	**LOVE WILL FIND A WAY** *Chrysalis GRAN 3*	24	6 wks
26 Nov 83	**ROCK THE MIDNIGHT** *Chrysalis GRAN 4*	46	4 wks
1 Aug 87	**CHANGE** *Polydor POSP 871*	55	4 wks
12 May 90	**KEEP IT TOGETHER** *Fourth & Broadway BRW 169*	56	2 wks

See also David Grant and Jaki Graham.

David GRANT AND Jaki GRAHAM **21 wks**
UK, male/female vocal duo

23 Mar 85	● **COULD IT BE I'M FALLING IN LOVE**		
	Chrysalis GRAN 6	5	11 wks
16 Nov 85	**MATED** *EMI JAKI 6*	20	10 wks

See also David Grant; Jaki Graham.

Eddy GRANT *Guyana, male vocalist/instrumentalist* **94 wks**

2 Jun 79	**LIVING ON THE FRONT LINE** *Ensign ENY 26*	11	11 wks
15 Nov 80	● **DO YOU FEEL MY LOVE** *Ensign ENY 45*	8	11 wks
4 Apr 81	**CAN'T GET ENOUGH OF YOU** *Ensign ENY 207*	13	10 wks
25 Jul 81	**I LOVE YOU, YES I LOVE YOU** *Ensign ENY 216*	37	6 wks
16 Oct 82	★ **I DON'T WANNA DANCE** *Ice ICE 56*	1	15 wks
15 Jan 83	● **ELECTRIC AVENUE** *Ice ICE 57*	2	9 wks
19 Mar 83	**LIVING ON THE FRONTLINE/ DO YOU FEEL MY**		
	LOVE (re-issues) *Mercury MER 135*	47	4 wks
23 Apr 83	**WAR PARTY** *Ice ICE 58*	42	4 wks
29 Oct 83	**TILL I CAN'T TAKE LOVE NO MORE** *Ice ICE 60*	42	7 wks
19 May 84	**ROMANCING THE STONE** *Ice ICE 61*	52	3 wks
23 Jan 88	● **GIMME HOPE JO'ANNA** *Ice ICE 78701*	7	12 wks
27 May 89	**WALKING ON SUNSHINE** *Blue Wave R 6217*	63	2 wks

Gogi GRANT *US, female vocalist* **11 wks**

29 Jun 56	● **WAYWARD WIND** *London HLB 8282*	9	11 wks

Julie GRANT *UK, female vocalist* — **17 wks**

3 Jan 63	**UP ON THE ROOF** *Pye 7N 15483*	33	3 wks
28 Mar 63	**COUNT ON ME** *Pye 7N 15508*	24	9 wks
24 Sep 64	**COME TO ME** *Pye 7N 15684*	31	5 wks

Rudy GRANT *Guyana, male vocalist* — **3 wks**

14 Feb 81	**LATELY** *Ensign ENY 202*	58	3 wks

GRAPEFRUIT *UK, male vocal/instrumental group* — **19 wks**

14 Feb 68	**DEAR DELILAH** *RCA 1656*	21	9 wks
14 Aug 68	**C'MON MARIANNE** *RCA 1716*	31	10 wks

Dobie GRAY *US, male vocalist* — **11 wks**

25 Feb 65	**THE IN CROWD** *London HL 9953*	25	7 wks
27 Sep 75	**OUT ON THE FLOOR** *Black Magic BM 107*	42	4 wks

Dorian GRAY *UK, male vocalist* — **7 wks**

27 Mar 68	**I'VE GOT YOU ON MY MIND** *Parlophone R 5667*	36	7 wks

Les GRAY *UK, male vocalist* — **5 wks**

26 Feb 77	**A GROOVY KIND OF LOVE** *Warner Bros. K 16883*	32	5 wks

Barry GRAY ORCHESTRA *UK, orchestra* — **8 wks**

11 Jul 81	**THUNDERBIRDS** *PRT 7P 216*	61	2 wks
14 Jun 86	**JOE 90/ CAPTAIN SCARLET THEME** *PRT 7PX 345*	53	6 wks

PRT 7PX 345 credits Peter Beckett – keyboards.

Altrina GRAYSON – *See Wilton FELDER*

GREAT WHITE *US, male vocal/instrumental group* — **2 wks**

24 Feb 90	**HOUSE OF BROKEN LOVE** *Capitol CL 562*	44	2 wks

Buddy GRECO *US, male vocalist* — **8 wks**

7 Jul 60	**LADY IS A TRAMP** *Fontana H 225*	26	8 wks

GREEDIES *Ireland/UK/US, male vocal/instrumental group* — **5 wks**

15 Dec 79	**A MERRY JINGLE** *Vertigo GREED 1*	28	5 wks

GREEK SERENADERS – *See MAKADOPOULOS and his GREEK SERENADERS*

Al GREEN *US, male vocalist* — **53 wks**

9 Oct 71	● **TIRED OF BEING ALONE** *London HL 10337*	4	13 wks
8 Jan 72	● **LET'S STAY TOGETHER** *London HL 10348*	7	12 wks
20 May 72	**LOOK WHAT YOU DONE FOR ME** *London HL 10369*	44	4 wks
19 Aug 72	**I'M STILL IN LOVE WITH YOU** *London HL 10382*	35	5 wks
16 Nov 74	**SHA-LA-LA (MAKE ME HAPPY)** *London HL 10470*	20	11 wks
15 Mar 75	**L. O. V. E.** *London HL 10482*	24	8 wks

See also Annie Lennox and Al Green; Arthur Baker.

Dotty GREEN – *See Mark FISHER featuring Dotty GREEN*

Jesse GREEN *US, male vocalist* — **26 wks**

7 Aug 76	**NICE AND SLOW** *EMI 2492*	17	12 wks
18 Dec 76	**FLIP** *EMI 2564*	26	8 wks
11 Jun 77	**COME WITH ME** *EMI 2615*	29	6 wks

Norman GREENBAUM *US, male vocalist* — **20 wks**

21 Mar 70	★ **SPIRIT IN THE SKY** *Reprise RS 20885*	1	20 wks

Lorne GREENE *US, male vocalist* — **8 wks**

17 Dec 64	**RINGO** *RCA 1428*	22	8 wks

Lee GREENWOOD *US, male vocalist* — **6 wks**

19 May 84	**THE WIND BENEATH MY WINGS** *MCA 877*	49	6 wks

Iain GREGORY *UK, male vocalist* — **2 wks**

4 Jan 62	**CAN'T YOU HEAR THE BEAT OF A BROKEN HEART** *Pye 7N 15397*	39	2 wks

Johnny GREGORY – *See CHAQUITO*

Band of the GRENADIER GUARDS – *See ST. JOHN'S COLLEGE SCHOOL CHOIR and the Band of the GRENADIER GUARDS*

GREYHOUND *Jamaica, male vocal/instrumental group* — **33 wks**

26 Jun 71	● **BLACK AND WHITE** *Trojan TR 7820*	6	13 wks
8 Jan 72	**MOON RIVER** *Trojan TR 7848*	12	11 wks
25 Mar 72	**I AM WHAT I AM** *Trojan TR 7853*	20	9 wks

GRID *UK, male vocal/instrumental duo* — **6 wks**

7 Jul 90	**FLOATATION** *East West YZ 475*	60	2 wks
29 Sep 90	**A BEAT CALLED LOVE** *East West YZ 498*	65	4 wks

Zaine GRIFF *New Zealand, male vocalist* — **6 wks**

16 Feb 80	**TONIGHT** *Automatic K 17547*	54	3 wks
31 May 80	**ASHES AND DIAMONDS** *Automatic K 17610*	68	3 wks

Billy GRIFFIN *US, male vocalist* — **12 wks**

8 Jan 83	**HOLD ME TIGHTER IN THE RAIN** *CBS A 2935*	17	9 wks
14 Jan 84	**SERIOUS** *CBS A 4053*	64	3 wks

Clive GRIFFIN *UK, male vocalist* — **2 wks**

24 Jun 89	**HEAD ABOVE WATER** *Mercury STEP 4*	60	2 wks

Ronnie GRIFFITH *US, female vocalist* — **4 wks**

30 Jun 84	**(THE BEST PART OF) BREAKING UP** *Making Waves SURF 101*	63	4 wks

GRIMETHORPE COLLIERY BAND – *See Peter SKELLERN*

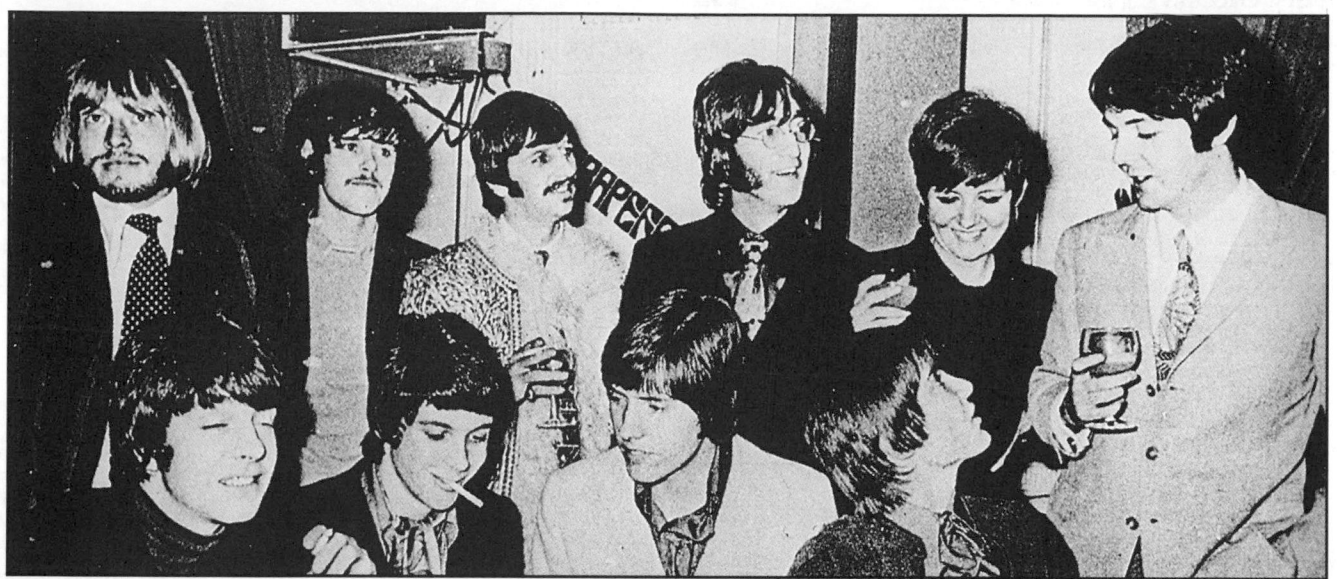

Above: Celebrating the launch of GRAPEFRUIT are (top, left to right) Brian Jones, Donovan, Ringo Starr, John Lennon, Cilla Black and Paul McCartney.

GRAHAM GOULDMAN wrote hits for the Yardbirds, Hollies and Herman's Hermits, starred with 10 C. C. and Wax, and sampled solo success.

Far Left: Christian James of HALO JAMES shone in 1990.

Left: As AL GREEN used to tell interviewers, the titles of his hits told a story. 'I'm tired of being alone, so let's stay together. Look what you done for me! I'm still in love with you . . . '

Henry GROSS US, male vocalist — 4 wks

28 Aug 76	SHANNON *Life Song ELS 45002*	32	4 wks

Boring Bob GROVER – *See PIRANHAS*

G.T.O. *Holland, male instrumental group* — 3 wks

4 Aug 90	PURE *Cooltempo COOL 218*	57	3 wks

GUESS WHO *Canada, male vocal/instrumental group* — 14 wks

16 Feb 67	HIS GIRL *King KG 1044*	45	1 wk
9 May 70	AMERICAN WOMAN *RCA 1943*	45	2 wks
30 May 70	AMERICAN WOMAN (re-entry) *RCA 1943*	19	11 wks

GUN *UK, male vocal/instrumental group* — 11 wks

20 Nov 68 ●	RACE WITH THE DEVIL *CBS 3734*	8	11 wks

GUN *UK, male vocal/instrumental group* — 20 wks

1 Jul 89	BETTER DAYS *A &M AM 505*	33	9 wks
16 Sep 89	MONEY (EVERYBODY LOVES HER) *A &M AM 520*	73	2 wks
11 Nov 89	INSIDE OUT *A &M AM 531*	57	2 wks
10 Feb 90	TAKING ON THE WORLD *A &M AM 541*	50	3 wks
14 Jul 90	SHAME ON YOU *A &M AM 573*	33	4 wks

GUNS N' ROSES *US, male vocal/instrumental group* — 45 wks

3 Oct 87	WELCOME TO THE JUNGLE *Geffen GEF 30*	67	2 wks
20 Aug 88	SWEET CHILD O' MINE *Geffen GEF 43*	24	8 wks
29 Oct 88	WELCOME TO THE JUNGLE (re-issue)/ NIGHTTRAIN *Geffen GEF 47*	24	5 wks
18 Mar 89 ●	PARADISE CITY *Geffen GEF 50*	6	9 wks
3 Jun 89 ●	SWEET CHILD O' MINE (re-mix) *Geffen GEF 55*	6	9 wks
1 Jul 89 ●	PATIENCE *Geffen GEF 56*	10	7 wks
2 Sep 89	NIGHTTRAIN (re-issue) *Geffen GEF 60*	17	5 wks

GURU JOSH *UK, male vocal/instrumental group* — 14 wks

24 Feb 90 ●	INFINITY *deConstruction PB 43475*	5	10 wks
16 Jun 90	WHOSE LAW (IS IT ANYWAY) *deConstruction PB 43647*	26	4 wks

Adrian GURVITZ *UK, male vocalist* — 16 wks

30 Jan 82 ●	CLASSIC *RAK 339*	8	13 wks
12 Jun 82	YOUR DREAM *RAK 343*	61	3 wks

Gwen GUTHRIE *US, female vocalist* — 23 wks

19 Jul 86 ●	AIN'T NOTHING GOIN' ON BUT THE RENT *Boiling Point POSP 807*	5	12 wks
11 Oct 86	(THEY LONG TO BE) CLOSE TO YOU *Boiling Point POSP 822*	25	7 wks
14 Feb 87	GOOD TO GO LOVER/ OUTSIDE IN THE RAIN *Boiling Point POSP 841*	37	4 wks

A GUY CALLED GERALD — 23 wks
UK, male vocalist/multi-instrumentalist

8 Apr 89	VOODOO RAY *Rham! RS 804*	55	8 wks
24 Jun 89	VOODOO RAY (re-entry) *Rham! RS 804*	12	10 wks
16 Dec 89	FX/ EYES OF SORROW *Subscape AGCG 1*	52	5 wks

See also Various Artists - The Brits 1990.

GUYS and DOLLS *UK, male/female vocal group* — 33 wks

1 Mar 75 ●	THERE'S A WHOLE LOT OF LOVING *Magnet MAG 20*	2	11 wks
17 May 75	HERE I GO AGAIN *Magnet MAG 30*	33	5 wks
21 Feb 76 ●	YOU DON'T HAVE TO SAY YOU LOVE ME *Magnet MAG 50*	5	8 wks
6 Nov 76	STONEY GROUND *Magnet MAG 76*	38	4 wks
13 May 78	ONLY LOVIN' DOES IT *Magnet MAG 115*	42	5 wks

Jonas GWANGA – *See George FENTON and Jonas GWANGA*

HABIT *UK, male vocal/instrumental group* — 2 wks

30 Apr 88	LUCY *Virgin VS 1063*	56	2 wks

Steve HACKETT *UK, male vocalist/instrumentalist - guitar* — 2 wks

2 Apr 83	CELL 151 *Charisma CELL 1*	66	2 wks

Sammy HAGAR *US, male vocalist/instrumentalist - guitar* — 15 wks

15 Dec 79	THIS PLANET'S ON FIRE/ SPACE STATION NO.5 *Capitol CL 16114*	52	5 wks
16 Feb 80	I'VE DONE EVERYTHING FOR YOU *Capitol CL 16120*	36	5 wks
24 May 80	HEARTBEAT / LOVE OR MONEY *Capitol RED 1*	67	2 wks
16 Jan 82	PIECE OF MY HEART *Geffen GEFA 1884*	67	1 wk
30 Jan 82	PIECE OF MY HEART (re-entry) *Geffen GEFA 1884*	67	2 wks

Paul HAIG *UK, male vocalist* — 3 wks

28 May 83	HEAVEN SENT *Island IS 111*	74	3 wks

HAIRCUT 100 *UK, male vocal/instrumental group* — 47 wks

24 Oct 81 ●	FAVOURITE SHIRTS (BOY MEETS GIRL) *Arista CLIP 1*	4	14 wks
30 Jan 82 ●	LOVE PLUS ONE *Arista CLIP 2*	3	12 wks
10 Apr 82 ●	FANTASTIC DAY *Arista CLIP 3*	9	9 wks
21 Aug 82 ●	NOBODY'S FOOL *Arista CLIP 4*	9	7 wks
6 Aug 83	PRIME TIME *Polydor HC 1*	46	5 wks

Curtis HAIRSTON *US, male vocalist* — 16 wks

15 Oct 83	I WANT YOU (ALL TONIGHT) *RCA 368*	44	5 wks
27 Apr 85	I WANT YOUR LOVIN' (JUST A LITTLE BIT) *London LON 66*	13	7 wks
6 Dec 86	CHILLIN' OUT *Atlantic A 9335*	57	4 wks

Gary HAISMAN – *See D MOB*

Bill HALEY and his COMETS — 199 wks
US, male vocal/instrumental group

17 Dec 54 ●	SHAKE RATTLE AND ROLL *Brunswick 05338*	4	14 wks
7 Jan 55	ROCK AROUND THE CLOCK *Brunswick 05317*	17	2 wks
15 Apr 55	MAMBO ROCK *Brunswick 05405*	14	2 wks

Date		Title / Label	Pos	Wks

14 Oct 55 ★ **ROCK AROUND THE CLOCK (re-entry)**
Brunswick 05317 .... **1** 17 wks
30 Dec 55 ● **ROCK-A-BEATIN' BOOGIE** *Brunswick 05509* .... **4** 9 wks
9 Mar 56 ● **SEE YOU LATER ALLIGATOR** *Brunswick 05530* .... **7** 13 wks
25 May 56 ● **THE SAINTS ROCK 'N ROLL** *Brunswick 05565* .... **5** 24 wks
17 Aug 56 ● **ROCKIN' THROUGH THE RYE** *Brunswick 05582* .... **3** 18 wks
14 Sep 56 **RAZZLE DAZZLE** *Brunswick 05453* .... **13** 8 wks
21 Sep 56 ● **ROCK AROUND THE CLOCK (2nd re-entry)**
Brunswick 05317 .... **5** 11 wks
21 Sep 56 **SEE YOU LATER ALLIGATOR (re-entry)**
Brunswick 05530 .... **12** 8 wks
9 Nov 56 ● **RIP IT UP** *Brunswick 05615* .... **4** 18 wks
9 Nov 56 **ROCK 'N ROLL STAGE SHOW** (LP)
Brunswick LAT 8139 .... **30** 1 wk
23 Nov 56 **RUDY'S ROCK** *Brunswick 05616* .... **30** 1 wk
14 Dec 56 **ROCK AROUND THE CLOCK (3rd re-entry)**
Brunswick 05317 .... **24** 2 wks
14 Dec 56 **RUDY'S ROCK (re-entry)** *Brunswick 05616* .... **26** 4 wks
4 Jan 57 **ROCK AROUND THE CLOCK (4th re-entry)**
Brunswick 05317 .... **25** 2 wks
4 Jan 57 **ROCKIN' THROUGH THE RYE (re-entry)**
Brunswick 05582 .... **19** 5 wks
25 Jan 57 **ROCK AROUND THE CLOCK (5th re-entry)**
Brunswick 05317 .... **22** 2 wks
1 Feb 57 **ROCK THE JOINT** *London HLF 8371* .... **20** 4 wks
8 Feb 57 ● **DON'T KNOCK THE ROCK** *Brunswick 05640* .... **7** 8 wks
3 Apr 68 **ROCK AROUND THE CLOCK (re-issue)**
MCA MU 1013 .... **20** 11 wks
16 Mar 74 **ROCK AROUND THE CLOCK (2nd re-issue)**
MCA 128 .... **12** 10 wks
25 Apr 81 **HALEY'S GOLDEN MEDLEY** *MCA 694* .... **50** 5 wks

Tracks on Rock 'N Roll Stage Show LP: Calling All Comets/Rockin' Through The Rye/A Rockin' Little Tune/Hide And Seek/Hey There Now/Goofin' Around/Hook Line and Sinker/Rudy's Rock/Choo Choo Ch'Boogie/Blue Comets Rock/Hot Dog Buddy Buddy/Tonight's The Night. Occasionally, some of the Rock Around The Clock labels billed the song as (We're Gonna) Rock Around The Clock.

Audrey HALL *Jamaica, female vocalist* 20 wks

25 Jan 86 **ONE DANCE WON'T DO** *Germain DG7-1985* .... **20** 11 wks
5 Jul 86 **SMILE** *Germain DG 15* .... **14** 9 wks

Daryl HALL *US, male vocalist* 8 wks

2 Aug 86 **DREAMTIME** *RCA HALL 1* .... **28** 8 wks

See also Daryl Hall and John Oates.

Daryl HALL and John OATES 83 wks
US, male vocal/instrumental duo

16 Oct 76 **SHE'S GONE** *Atlantic K 10828* .... **42** 4 wks
14 Jun 80 **RUNNING FROM PARADISE** *RCA RUN 1* .... **41** 6 wks
20 Sep 80 **YOU'VE LOST THAT LOVIN' FEELIN'** *RCA 1* .... **55** 3 wks
15 Nov 80 **KISS ON MY LIST** *RCA 15* .... **33** 8 wks
23 Jan 82 ● **I CAN'T GO FOR THAT (NO CAN DO)** *RCA 172* ...... **8** 10 wks
10 Apr 82 **PRIVATE EYES** *RCA 134* .... **32** 7 wks
30 Oct 82 ● **MANEATER** *RCA 290* .... **6** 11 wks
22 Jan 83 **ONE ON ONE** *RCA 305* .... **63** 3 wks
30 Apr 83 **FAMILY MAN** *RCA 323* .... **15** 7 wks
12 Nov 83 **SAY IT ISN'T SO** *RCA 375* .... **69** 3 wks
10 Mar 84 **ADULT EDUCATION** *RCA 396* .... **63** 2 wks
20 Oct 84 **OUT OF TOUCH** *RCA 449* .... **48** 5 wks
9 Feb 85 **METHOD OF MODERN LOVE** *RCA RCA 472* .... **21** 8 wks
22 Jun 85 **OUT OF TOUCH (re-mix)** *RCA PB 49967* .... **62** 3 wks
21 Sep 85 **A NIGHT AT THE APOLLO LIVE!** *RCA PB 49935* ...... **58** 2 wks
29 Sep 90 **SO CLOSE** *Arista 113600* .... **69** 1 wk

A Night At The Apollo Live! is a medley of The Way You Do The Things You Do/ My Girl. David Ruffin and Eddie Kendricks are both credited on the label. So Close credited simply to Hall & Oates. See also Daryl Hall; David Ruffin; Eddie Kendricks.

Pam HALL *Jamaica, female vocalist* 4 wks

16 Aug 86 **DEAR BOOPSIE** *Bluemountain BM 027* .... **54** 4 wks

Terry HALL *UK, male vocalist* 1 wk

11 Nov 89 **MISSING** *Chrysalis CHS 3381* .... **75** 1 wk

The sleeve, not the label of Missing credits Terry, Blair and Anouchka.

HALO JAMES *UK, male vocal/instrumental group* 24 wks

7 Oct 89 **WANTED** *Epic HALO 1* .... **45** 5 wks
23 Dec 89 ● **COULD HAVE TOLD YOU SO** *Epic HALO 2* .... **6** 12 wks
17 Mar 90 **BABY** *Epic HALO 3* .... **43** 4 wks
19 May 90 **MAGIC HOUR** *Epic HALO 4* .... **59** 3 wks

HAMILTON, Joe FRANK and REYNOLDS 6 wks
US, male vocal group

13 Sep 75 **FALLIN' IN LOVE** *Pye International 7N 25690* .... **33** 6 wks

George HAMILTON IV *US, male vocalist* 13 wks

7 Mar 58 **WHY DON'T THEY UNDERSTAND** *HMV POP 429* ..... **22** 9 wks
18 Jul 58 **I KNOW WHERE I'M GOING** *HMV POP 505* .... **29** 1 wk
8 Aug 58 **I KNOW WHERE I'M GOING (re-entry)**
HMV POP 505 .... **23** 3 wks

Lynne HAMILTON *Australia, female vocalist* 11 wks

29 Apr 89 ● **ON THE INSIDE (THEME FROM 'PRISONER CELL BLOCK H')** *A.1. A1 311* .... **3** 11 wks

Russ HAMILTON *UK, male vocalist* 26 wks

24 May 57 ● **WE WILL MAKE LOVE** *Oriole CB 1359* .... **2** 20 wks
27 Sep 57 **WEDDING RING** *Oriole CB 1388* .... **20** 6 wks

Marvin HAMLISCH *US, male instrumentalist – piano* 13 wks

30 Mar 74 **THE ENTERTAINER** *MCA 121* .... **25** 13 wks

Jan HAMMER 20 wks
Czechoslovakia, male instrumentalist – keyboards

12 Oct 85 ● **MIAMI VICE THEME** *MCA MCA 1000* .... **5** 8 wks
19 Sep 87 ● **CROCKETT'S THEME** *MCA MCA 1193* .... **2** 12 wks

Albert HAMMOND *UK, male vocalist* 11 wks

30 Jun 73 **FREE ELECTRIC BAND** *Mums 1494* .... **19** 11 wks

Beres HAMMOND – *See Maxi PRIEST*

Herbie HANCOCK 41 wks
US, male vocalist/instrumentalist – keyboards

26 Aug 78 **I THOUGHT IT WAS YOU** *CBS 6530* .... **15** 9 wks
3 Feb 79 **YOU BET YOUR LOVE** *CBS 7010* .... **18** 10 wks
30 Jul 83 ● **ROCKIT** *CBS A 3577* .... **8** 12 wks
8 Oct 83 **AUTO DRIVE** *CBS A 3802* .... **33** 4 wks
21 Jan 84 **FUTURE SHOCK** *CBS A 4075* .... **54** 3 wks
4 Aug 84 **HARDROCK** *CBS A 4616* .... **65** 3 wks

HANDLEY FAMILY UK, male/female vocal group — 7 wks

7 Apr 73	**WAM BAM** GL 100	**30**	7 wks

HANDS OF DR. TELENY – *See Peter STRAKER and the HANDS OF DR. TELENY*

HANOI ROCKS Finland/UK, male vocal/instrumental group — 2 wks

7 Jul 84	**UP AROUND THE BEND** CBS A 4513	**61**	2 wks

HAPPENINGS US, male vocal group — 14 wks

18 May 67	**I GOT RHYTHM** Stateside SS 2013	**28**	9 wks
16 Aug 67	**MY MAMMY**		
	Pye International 7N 25501 and B.T. Puppy BTS 45530	**34**	5 wks

Pye gave the American B.T. Puppy label its own identification halfway through the success of My Mammy.

HAPPY MONDAYS UK, male vocal/instrumental group — 34 wks

30 Sep 89	**WFL** Factory FAC 2327	**68**	2 wks
25 Nov 89	**MADCHESTER RAVE ON** (EP) Factory FAC 2427	**19**	14 wks
7 Apr 90 ●	**STEP ON** Factory FAC 2727	**5**	11 wks
20 Oct 90 ●	**KINKY AFRO** Factory FAC 3027	**5**	7 wks

Tracks on Madchester Rave On EP: Hallelujah/Holy Ghost/Clap Your Hands/Rave On. See also Happy Mondays and Karl Denver.

HAPPY MONDAYS and Karl DENVER — 3 wks
UK, male vocal/instrumental group and male vocalist

9 Jun 90	**LAZYITIS - ONE ARMED BOXER** Factory FAC 2227	**46**	3 wks

See also Happy Mondays; Karl Denver.

Paul HARDCASTLE — 66 wks
UK, male producer/instrumentalist - keyboards

7 Apr 84	**YOU'RE THE ONE FOR ME - DAYBREAK - A.M.**		
	Total Control TOCO 1	**41**	4 wks
28 Jul 84	**GUILTY** Total Control TOCO 2	**55**	3 wks
22 Sep 84	**RAIN FOREST** Bluebird BR 8	**41**	5 wks
17 Nov 84	**EAT YOUR HEART OUT** Cooltempo COOL 102	**59**	4 wks
4 May 85 ★	**NINETEEN** Chrysalis CHS 2860	**1**	16 wks
15 Jun 85	**RAIN FOREST** (re-issue) Bluebird 10 BR 15	**53**	4 wks
9 Nov 85	**JUST FOR MONEY** Chrysalis CASH 1	**19**	5 wks
1 Feb 86 ●	**DON'T WASTE MY TIME** Chrysalis PAUL 1	**8**	11 wks
21 Jun 86	**FOOLIN' YOURSELF** Chrysalis PAUL 2	**51**	3 wks
11 Oct 86	**THE WIZARD** Chrysalis PAUL 3	**15**	6 wks
9 Apr 88	**WALK IN THE NIGHT** Chrysalis PAUL 4	**54**	3 wks
4 Jun 88	**40 YEARS** Chrysalis PAUL 5	**53**	2 wks

Just for Money features the voices of Laurence Olivier, Bob Hoskins, Ed O'Ross and Alan Talbot. Don't Waste My Time features Carol Kenyon - UK, female vocalist. See also Silent Underdog.

Tim HARDIN US, male vocalist — 1 wk

5 Jan 67	**HANG ON TO A DREAM** Verve VS 1504	**50**	1 wk

Mike HARDING UK, male vocalist — 8 wks

2 Aug 75	**ROCHDALE COWBOY** Rubber ADUB 3	**22**	8 wks

Francoise HARDY France, female vocalist — 26 wks

25 Jun 64	**TOUS LES GARCONS ET LES FILLES** Pye 7N 15653	**36**	7 wks
7 Jan 65	**ET MEME** Pye 7N 15740	**31**	4 wks
25 Mar 65	**ALL OVER THE WORLD** Pye 7N 15802	**16**	15 wks

HARLEM COMMUNITY CHOIR – *See John LENNON*

HARLEQUIN 4's/ BUNKER KRU — 4 wks
US, male vocal/instrumental group with UK, male production duo

19 Mar 88	**SET IT OFF** Champion CHAMP 64	**55**	4 wks

Steve HARLEY and COCKNEY REBEL — 54 wks
UK, male vocalist and male vocal/instrumental backing group

11 May 74 ●	**JUDY TEEN** EMI 2128	**5**	11 wks
10 Aug 74	**MR. SOFT** EMI 2191	**8**	9 wks
8 Feb 75 ★	**MAKE ME SMILE (COME UP AND SEE ME)**		
	EMI 2263	**1**	9 wks
7 Jun 75	**MR. RAFFLES (MAN IT WAS MEAN)** EMI 2299	**13**	6 wks
31 Jul 76 ●	**HERE COMES THE SUN** EMI 2505	**10**	7 wks
6 Nov 76	**LOVE'S A PRIMA DONNA** EMI 2539	**41**	4 wks
20 Oct 79	**FREEDOM'S PRISONER** EMI 2994	**58**	3 wks
13 Aug 83	**BALLERINA (PRIMA DONNA)** Stilleto STL 14	**51**	5 wks

First two hits are credited simply to Cockney Rebel, the next two to Steve Harley and Cockney Rebel, the remaining hits to Steve Harley. See also Sarah Brightman and Steve Harley.

HARLEY QUINNE UK, male vocal group — 8 wks

14 Oct 72	**NEW ORLEANS** Bell 1255	**19**	8 wks

HARMONY GRASS UK, male vocal/instrumental group — 7 wks

29 Jan 69	**MOVE IN A LITTLE CLOSER** RCA 1772	**24**	7 wks

Charlie HARPER UK, male vocalist — 1 wk

19 Jul 80	**BARMY LONDON ARMY** Gem GEMS 35	**68**	1 wk

HARPERS BIZARRE US, male vocal group — 13 wks

30 Mar 67	**59TH STREET BRIDGE SONG (FEELING GROOVY)**		
	Warner Bros. WB 5890	**34**	7 wks
4 Oct 67	**ANYTHING GOES** Warner Bros. WB 7063	**33**	6 wks

HARPO Sweden, male vocalist — 6 wks

17 Apr 76	**MOVIE STAR** DJM DJS 400	**24**	6 wks

T. HARRINGTON – *See Rahni HARRIS and F.L.O.*

Anita HARRIS UK, female vocalist — 50 wks

29 Jun 67 ●	**JUST LOVING YOU** CBS 2724	**6**	30 wks
11 Oct 67	**PLAYGROUND** CBS 2991	**46**	3 wks
24 Jan 68	**ANNIVERSARY WALTZ** CBS 3211	**21**	9 wks
14 Aug 68	**DREAM A LITTLE DREAM OF ME** CBS 3637	**33**	8 wks

Emmylou HARRIS US, female vocalist — 6 wks

6 Mar 76	**HERE THERE AND EVERYWHERE** Reprise K 14415	**30**	6 wks

HAPPY MONDAYS seem to be contemplating a prop from *This Is Spinal Tap*.

M. C. HAMMER couldn't be touched atop the US album chart in the summer of 1990.

Far Right: OFRA HAZA is the most successful female soloist from Israel.

Jet HARRIS UK, male instrumentalist - bass guitar   **18 wks**

24 May 62	**BESAME MUCHO** Decca F 11466		**22**	7 wks
16 Aug 62	**MAIN TITLE THEME FROM 'MAN WITH THE GOLDEN ARM'** Decca F 11488		**12**	11 wks

See also Jet Harris and Tony Meehan.

Jet HARRIS and Tony MEEHAN   **39 wks**
UK, male instrumental duo - bass guitar and drums

10 Jan 63	★ **DIAMONDS** Decca F 11563		**1**	13 wks
25 Apr 63	● **SCARLETT O'HARA** Decca F 11644		**2**	13 wks
5 Sep 63	● **APPLEJACK** Decca F 11710		**4**	13 wks

See also Jet Harris; Tony Meehan.

Keith HARRIS and ORVILLE   **20 wks**
UK, male ventriloquist vocalist with feathered dummy

18 Dec 82	● **ORVILLE'S SONG** BBC RESL 124		**4**	11 wks
24 Dec 83	● **COME TO MY PARTY** BBC RESL 138		**44**	4 wks
14 Dec 85	**WHITE CHRISTMAS** Columbia DB 9121		**40**	5 wks

Come To My Party also credits Dippy (Prehistoric Dummy).

Major HARRIS US, male vocalist   **9 wks**

9 Aug 75	**LOVE WON'T LET ME WAIT** Atlantic K 10585		**37**	7 wks
5 Nov 83	**ALL MY LIFE** London LON 37		**61**	2 wks

Max HARRIS UK, orchestra   **10 wks**

1 Dec 60	**GURNEY SLADE** Fontana H 282		**11**	10 wks

Rahni HARRIS and F.L.O. US, male instrumental group   **7 wks**

16 Dec 78	**SIX MILLION STEPS (WEST RUNS SOUTH)** Mercury 6007 198		**43**	7 wks

Hit has credit 'vocals by T. Harrington and O. Rasbury'.

Richard HARRIS Ireland, male vocalist   **18 wks**

26 Jun 68	● **MACARTHUR PARK** RCA 1699		**4**	12 wks
8 Jul 72	**MACARTHUR PARK (re-issue)** Probe GFF 101		**38**	6 wks

Rolf HARRIS Australia, male vocalist   **64 wks**

21 Jul 60	● **TIE ME KANGAROO DOWN SPORT** Columbia DB 4483		**9**	13 wks
25 Oct 62	● **SUN ARISE** Columbia DB 4888		**3**	16 wks
28 Feb 63	**JOHNNY DAY** Columbia DB 4979		**44**	2 wks
16 Apr 69	**BLUER THAN BLUE** Columbia DB 8553		**30**	8 wks
22 Nov 69	★ **TWO LITTLE BOYS** Columbia DB 8630		**1**	24 wks
20 Jun 70	**TWO LITTLE BOYS (re-entry)** Columbia DB 8630		**50**	1 wk

Ronnie HARRIS UK, male vocalist   **3 wks**

24 Sep 54	**STORY OF TINA** Columbia DB 3499		**12**	3 wks

Sam HARRIS US, male vocalist   **2 wks**

9 Feb 85	**HEARTS ON FIRE/ OVER THE RAINBOW** Motown TMG 1370		**67**	2 wks

Simon HARRIS US, male producer   **17 wks**

19 Mar 88	**BASS (HOW LOW CAN YOU GO)** FFRR FFR 4		**12**	6 wks
29 Oct 88	**HERE COMES THAT SOUND** FFRR FFR 12		**38**	4 wks
24 Jun 89	**(I'VE GOT YOUR) PLEASURE CONTROL** FFRR F 106		**60**	3 wks
18 Nov 89	**ANOTHER MONSTERJAM** FFRR F 116		**65**	1 wk
10 Mar 90	**RAGGA HOUSE (ALL NIGHT LONG)** Living Beat 7SMASH 9		**56**	3 wks

(I've Got Your) Pleasure Control features Lonnie Gordon; Another Monsterjam features Einstein - UK, male rapper. See also Lonnie Gordon.

George HARRISON UK, male vocalist   **82 wks**

23 Jan 71	★ **MY SWEET LORD** Apple R 5884		**1**	17 wks
14 Aug 71	● **BANGLA DESH** Apple R 5912		**10**	9 wks
2 Jun 73	● **GIVE ME LOVE (GIVE ME PEACE ON EARTH)** Apple R 5988		**8**	10 wks
21 Dec 74	**DING DONG** Apple R 6002		**38**	5 wks
11 Oct 75	**YOU** Apple R 6007		**38**	5 wks
10 Mar 79	**BLOW AWAY** Dark Horse K 17327		**51**	5 wks
23 May 81	**ALL THOSE YEARS AGO** Dark Horse 3 K 17807		**13**	7 wks
24 Oct 87	● **GOT MY MIND SET ON YOU** Dark Horse W 8178		**2**	14 wks
6 Feb 88	**WHEN WE WAS FAB** Dark Horse W 8131		**25**	7 wks
25 Jun 88	**THIS IS LOVE** Dark Horse W 7913		**55**	3 wks

Noel HARRISON UK, male vocalist   **14 wks**

26 Feb 69	● **WINDMILLS OF YOUR MIND** Reprise RS 20758		**8**	14 wks

HARRY – *See ALFI and HARRY*

Deborah HARRY US, female vocalist   **42 wks**

1 Aug 81	**BACKFIRED** Chrysalis CHS 2526		**32**	6 wks
15 Nov 86	● **FRENCH KISSIN' IN THE USA** Chrysalis CHS 3066		**8**	10 wks
28 Feb 87	**FREE TO FALL** Chrysalis CHS 3093		**46**	4 wks
9 May 87	**IN LOVE WITH LOVE** Chrysalis CHS 3128		**45**	5 wks
7 Oct 89	**I WANT THAT MAN** Chrysalis CHS 3369		**13**	10 wks
2 Dec 89	**BRITE SIDE** Chrysalis CHS 3452		**59**	4 wks
31 Mar 90	**SWEET AND LOW** Chrysalis CHS 3491		**57**	3 wks

Billed as Debbie Harry on first four hits.

HARRY J. ALL STARS Jamaica, male instrumental group   **25 wks**

25 Oct 69	● **LIQUIDATOR** Trojan TR 675		**9**	20 wks
29 Mar 80	**LIQUIDATOR (re-issue)** Trojan TRO 9063		**42**	5 wks

Re-issue of Liquidator coupled with re-issue of Long Shot Kick De Bucket by the Pioneers. See also Pioneers.

Richard HARTLEY and the Michael REED ORCHESTRA   **10 wks**
UK, male instrumentalist - synthesizer, and orchestra

25 Feb 84	● **THE MUSIC OF TORVILL AND DEAN EP** Safari SKATE 1		**9**	10 wks

Tracks on EP: Bolero/Capriccio Espagnole Opus. 34 (Nos.4 and 5) by Richard Hartley; Barnum On Ice/Discoskate by the Michael Reed Orchestra.

Dan HARTMAN US, male vocalist   **33 wks**

21 Oct 78	● **INSTANT REPLAY** Sky 6706		**8**	15 wks
13 Jan 79	**THIS IS IT** Blue Sky SKY 6999		**17**	8 wks
18 May 85	**SECOND NATURE** MCA MCA 957		**66**	2 wks
24 Aug 85	**I CAN DREAM ABOUT YOU** MCA MCA 988		**12**	8 wks

Sensational Alex HARVEY BAND
UK, male vocal/instrumental group   **25 wks**

26 Jul 75	● **DELILAH** *Vertigo ALEX 001*.....................................	**7**	7 wks
22 Nov 75	**GAMBLIN' BAR ROOM BLUES** *Vertigo ALEX 002*..........	**38**	8 wks
19 Jun 76	**THE BOSTON TEA PARTY** *Mountain TOP 12*..............	**13**	10 wks

Steve HARVEY *UK, male vocalist*   **6 wks**

28 May 83	**SOMETHING SPECIAL** *London LON 25*	**46**	4 wks
29 Oct 83	**TONIGHT** *London LON 36*..................................	**63**	2 wks

Tony HATCH *UK, orchestra*   **1 wk**

4 Oct 62	**OUT OF THIS WORLD** *Pye 7N 15460*	**50**	1 wk

Donny HATHAWAY – *See Roberta FLACK and Donny HATHAWAY*

Lalah HATHAWAY *US, female vocalist*   **2 wks**

1 Sep 90	**HEAVEN KNOWS** *Virgin America VUS 28*....................	**66**	2 wks

Edwin HAWKINS SINGERS
US, male/female vocal group   **13 wks**

21 May 69	● **OH HAPPY DAY** *Buddah 201 048*	**2**	12 wks
23 Aug 69	**OH HAPPY DAY (re-entry)** *Buddah 201 048*	**43**	1 wk

Hit credits soloist Dorothy Combs Morrison - US, female vocalist.

HAWKWIND
UK, male vocal/instrumental group with female dancer   **28 wks**

1 Jul 72	● **SILVER MACHINE** *United Artists UP 35381*....................	**3**	15 wks
11 Aug 73	**URBAN GUERRILLA** *United Artists UP 35566*	**39**	3 wks
21 Oct 78	**SILVER MACHINE (re-entry)** *United Artists UP 35381*........	**34**	5 wks
19 Jul 80	**SHOT DOWN IN THE NIGHT** *Bronze BRO 98*..............	**59**	3 wks
15 Jan 83	**SILVER MACHINE (2nd re-entry)** *United Artists UP 35381*	**67**	2 wks

Bill HAYES *US, male vocalist*   **9 wks**

6 Jan 56	● **BALLAD OF DAVY CROCKETT** *London HLA 8220*..........	**2**	9 wks

Isaac HAYES *US, male vocalist/multi-instrumentalist*   **21 wks**

4 Dec 71	● **THEME FROM 'SHAFT'** *Stax 2025 069*	**4**	12 wks
3 Apr 76	● **DISCO CONNECTION** *ABC 4100*	**10**	9 wks

Billed as Isaac Hayes Movement on Disco Connection.

HAYSI FANTAYZEE *UK, male/female vocal duo*   **25 wks**

24 Jul 82	**JOHN WAYNE IS BIG LEGGY** *Regard RG 100*	**11**	10 wks
13 Nov 82	**HOLY JOE** *Regard RG 104*	**51**	3 wks
22 Jan 83	**SHINY SHINY** *Regard RG 106*	**16**	10 wks
25 Jun 83	**SISTER FRICTION** *Regard RG 108*	**62**	2 wks

Justin HAYWARD *UK, male vocalist*   **13 wks**

8 Jul 78	● **FOREVER AUTUMN** *CBS 6368*..............................	**5**	13 wks

See also Justin Hayward and John Lodge.

Justin HAYWARD and John LODGE
UK, male vocal/instrumental duo   **7 wks**

25 Oct 75	● **BLUE GUITAR** *Threshold TH 21*..............................	**8**	7 wks

See also Justin Hayward.

Leon HAYWOOD *US, male vocalist*   **11 wks**

15 Mar 80	**DON'T PUSH IT, DON'T FORCE IT** *20th Century Fox TC 2443*...	**12**	11 wks

HAYWOODE *UK, female vocalist*   **31 wks**

17 Sep 83	**A TIME LIKE THIS** *CBS A 3651*	**48**	7 wks
29 Sep 84	**I CAN'T LET YOU GO** *CBS A 4664*	**63**	4 wks
13 Apr 85	**ROSES** *CBS A 6069*	**65**	3 wks
5 Oct 85	**GETTING CLOSER** *CBS A 6582*..............................	**67**	2 wks
21 Jun 86	**ROSES (re-issue)** *CBS A 7224*	**11**	11 wks
13 Sep 86	**I CAN'T LET YOU GO (re-issue)** *CBS 650076 7*............	**50**	4 wks

Ofra HAZA *Israel, female vocalist*   **8 wks**

30 Apr 88	**IM NIN'ALU** *WEA YZ 190*	**15**	8 wks

Lee HAZLEWOOD – *See Nancy SINATRA and Lee HAZLEWOOD*

Murray HEAD *UK, male vocalist*   **15 wks**

29 Jan 72	**SUPERSTAR** *MCA MMKS 5077*	**47**	1 wk
10 Nov 84	**ONE NIGHT IN BANGKOK** *RCA CHESS 1*...................	**12**	13 wks
16 Feb 85	**ONE NIGHT IN BANGKOK (re-entry)** *RCA CHESS 1*.....	**74**	1 wk

Superstar was one of four tracks on a maxi-single, two of which were credited during the disc's one week on the chart. The other track credited was I Don't Know How To Love Him by Yvonne Elliman. See also Yvonne Elliman.

Roy HEAD *US, male vocalist*   **5 wks**

4 Nov 65	**TREAT HER RIGHT** *Vocalion V-P 9248*	**30**	5 wks

HEADBANGERS *UK, male vocal/instrumental group*   **3 wks**

10 Oct 81	**STATUS ROCK** *Magnet MAG 206*.............................	**60**	3 wks

HEADBOYS *UK, male vocal/instrumental group*   **8 wks**

22 Sep 79	**THE SHAPE OF THINGS TO COME** *RSO 40*..............	**45**	8 wks

HEADGIRL – *See MOTORHEAD and GIRLSCHOOL*

Max HEADROOM – *See ART OF NOISE*

HEADS *UK, male instrumental group*   **4 wks**

21 Jun 86	**AZTEC LIGHTNING (THEME FROM BBC WORLD CUP GRANDSTAND)** *BBC RESL 184*	**45**	4 wks

HEAR 'N AID
International, male/female vocal/instrumental charity assembly   **6 wks**

19 Apr 86	**STARS** *Vertigo HEAR 1*	**26**	6 wks

Above: THE JIMI HENDRIX EXPERIENCE got 1967 off to a psychedelic start in the year's very first week.

DON HENLEY attends a ball honouring Lana Turner with actress Maren Jensen.

Far Right: DEBBIE HARRY did a lot of kissing during her 1986 comeback.

HEART were US chart stars for a full ten years before their British breakthrough.

HEART US, female/male vocal/instrumental group — 70 wks

Date	Title	Pos	Wks
29 Mar 86	THESE DREAMS Capitol CL 394	62	4 wks
13 Jun 87	● ALONE Capitol CL 448	3	16 wks
19 Sep 87	WHO WILL YOU RUN TO Capitol CL 457	30	7 wks
12 Dec 87	THERE'S THE GIRL Capitol CL 473	34	7 wks
5 Mar 88	● NEVER/ THESE DREAMS (re-issue) Capitol CL 482	8	9 wks
14 May 88	WHAT ABOUT LOVE Capitol CL 487	14	6 wks
22 Oct 88	NOTHIN' AT ALL Capitol CL 507	38	3 wks
24 Mar 90	● ALL I WANNA DO IS MAKE LOVE TO YOU Capitol CL 569	8	13 wks
28 Jul 90	I DIDN'T WANT TO NEED YOU Capitol CL 580	47	3 wks
17 Nov 90	STRANDED Capitol CL 595	60	2 wks

HEARTBEAT UK, male/female vocal/instrumental group — 5 wks

Date	Title	Pos	Wks
24 Oct 87	TEARS FROM HEAVEN Priority P 17	32	4 wks
23 Apr 88	THE WINNER Priority P 19	70	1 wk

HEARTBREAKERS – See Stevie NICKS with Tom PETTY and the HEARTBREAKERS; Tom PETTY

Ted HEATH UK, orchestra — 56 wks

Date	Title	Pos	Wks
16 Jan 53	VANESSA Decca F 9983	11	1 wk
3 Jul 53	● HOT TODDY Decca F 10093	6	11 wks
23 Oct 53	DRAGNET Decca F 10176	12	1 wk
27 Nov 53	● DRAGNET (re-entry) Decca F 10176	9	1 wk
11 Dec 53	DRAGNET (2nd re-entry) Decca F 10176	11	1 wk
15 Jan 54	DRAGNET (3rd re-entry) Decca F 10176	11	1 wk
5 Feb 54	DRAGNET (4th re-entry) Decca F 10176	12	1 wk
12 Feb 54	● SKIN DEEP Decca F 10246	9	3 wks
6 Jul 56	THE FAITHFUL HUSSAR Decca F 10746	18	9 wks
14 Mar 58	● SWINGIN' SHEPHERD BLUES Decca F 11000	3	14 wks
11 Apr 58	TEQUILA Decca F 11003	21	6 wks
4 Jul 58	TOM HARK Decca F 11025	24	2 wks
5 Oct 61	SUCU SUCU Decca F 11392	36	4 wks
9 Nov 61	SUCU SUCU (re-entry) Decca F 11392	47	1 wk

HEATWAVE UK/US, male vocal/instrumental group — 80 wks

Date	Title	Pos	Wks
22 Jan 77	● BOOGIE NIGHTS GTO GT 77	2	14 wks
7 May 77	TOO HOT TO HANDLE/ SLIP YOUR DISC TO THIS GTO GT 91	15	11 wks
14 Jan 78	THE GROOVE LINE GTO GT 115	12	8 wks
3 Jun 78	MIND BLOWING DECISIONS GTO GT 226	12	11 wks
4 Nov 78	● ALWAYS AND FOREVER/ MIND BLOWING DECISIONS (re-mix) GTO GT 236	9	14 wks
26 May 79	RAZZLE DAZZLE GTO GT 248	43	5 wks
17 Jan 81	GANGSTERS OF THE GROOVE GTO GT 285	19	8 wks
21 Mar 81	JITTERBUGGIN' GTO GT 290	34	7 wks
1 Sep 90	MIND BLOWING DECISIONS (re-issue of re-mix) Brothers Organisation HW 1	65	2 wks

Mind Blowing Decisions on GT 236 is an extended remixed version of GT 226.

HEAVEN 17 UK, male vocal/instrumental group — 73 wks

Date	Title	Pos	Wks
21 Mar 81	(WE DON'T NEED THIS) FASCIST GROOVE THANG Virgin VS 400	45	5 wks
5 Sep 81	PLAY TO WIN Virgin VS 433	46	7 wks
14 Nov 81	PENTHOUSE AND PAVEMENT Virgin VS 455	57	3 wks
30 Oct 82	LET ME GO Virgin VS 532	41	6 wks
16 Apr 83	● TEMPTATION Virgin VS 570	2	13 wks
25 Jun 83	● COME LIVE WITH ME Virgin VS 607	5	11 wks
10 Sep 83	CRUSHED BY THE WHEELS OF INDUSTRY Virgin VS 628	17	7 wks
1 Sep 84	SUNSET NOW Virgin VS 708	24	6 wks
27 Oct 84	THIS IS MINE Virgin VS 722	23	7 wks
19 Jan 85	...(AND THAT'S NO LIE) Virgin VS 740	52	5 wks
17 Jan 87	TROUBLE Virgin VS 920	51	3 wks

Carol Kenyon - UK, female vocalist - is the uncredited vocalist on Temptation.

HEAVY D. and the BOYZ — 10 wks
Jamaica/US, male vocal/instrumental group

Date	Title	Pos	Wks
6 Dec 86	MR. BIG STUFF MCA MCA 1106	61	8 wks
15 Jul 89	WE GOT OUR OWN THANG MCA MCA 23942	69	2 wks

HEAVY PETTIN' UK, male vocal/instrumental group — 2 wks

Date	Title	Pos	Wks
17 Mar 84	LOVE TIMES LOVE Polydor HEP 3	69	2 wks

Bobby HEBB US, male vocalist — 15 wks

Date	Title	Pos	Wks
8 Sep 66	SUNNY Philips BF 1503	12	9 wks
19 Aug 72	LOVE LOVE LOVE Philips 6051 023	32	6 wks

HEDGEHOPPERS ANONYMOUS — 12 wks
UK, male vocal/instrumental group

Date	Title	Pos	Wks
30 Sep 65	● IT'S GOOD NEWS WEEK Decca F 12241	5	12 wks

Neal HEFTI US, male orchestra — 4 wks

Date	Title	Pos	Wks
9 Apr 88	BATMAN THEME RCA PB 49571	55	4 wks

Den HEGARTY UK, male vocalist — 2 wks

Date	Title	Pos	Wks
31 Mar 79	VOODOO VOODOO Magnet MAG 143	73	2 wks

Anita HEGERLAND – See Mike OLDFIELD

HEINZ UK, male vocalist — 35 wks

Date	Title	Pos	Wks
8 Aug 63	● JUST LIKE EDDIE Decca F 11693	5	15 wks
28 Nov 63	COUNTRY BOY Decca F 11768	26	9 wks
27 Feb 64	YOU WERE THERE Decca F 11831	26	8 wks
15 Oct 64	QUESTIONS I CAN'T ANSWER Columbia DB 7374	39	2 wks
18 Mar 65	DIGGIN' MY POTATOES Columbia DB 7482	49	1 wk

HELLO UK, male vocal/instrumental group — 21 wks

Date	Title	Pos	Wks
9 Nov 74	● TELL HIM Bell 1377	6	12 wks
18 Oct 75	● NEW YORK GROOVE Bell 1438	9	9 wks

HELLOWEEN US, male vocal/instrumental group — 5 wks

Date	Title	Pos	Wks
27 Aug 88	DR STEIN Noise International 7HELLO 1	57	3 wks
12 Nov 88	I WANT OUT Noise International 7HELLO 2	69	2 wks

Bobby HELMS US, male vocalist — 7 wks

Date	Title	Pos	Wks
29 Nov 57	MY SPECIAL ANGEL Brunswick 05721	22	3 wks
21 Feb 58	NO OTHER BABY Brunswick 05730	30	1 wk
1 Aug 58	JACQUELINE Brunswick 05748	20	3 wks

Jimmy HELMS UK, male vocalist — 10 wks

Date	Title	Pos	Wks
24 Feb 73	● GONNA MAKE YOU AN OFFER YOU CAN'T REFUSE Cube BUG 27	8	10 wks

Eddie HENDERSON
US, male vocalist/instrumentalist - trumpet   **6 wks**

28 Oct 78	PRANCE ON *Capitol CL 16015*	44	6 wks

Joe 'Mr. Piano' HENDERSON
UK, male instrumentalist - piano   **23 wks**

3 Jun 55	SING IT WITH JOE *Polygon P 1167*	14	4 wks
2 Sep 55	SING IT AGAIN WITH JOE *Polygon P 1184*	18	3 wks
25 Jul 58	TRUDIE *Pye Nixa N 15147*	14	12 wks
24 Oct 58	TRUDIE (re-entry) *Pye Nixa N 15147*	23	2 wks
23 Oct 59	TREBLE CHANCE *Pye 7N 15224*	28	1 wk
24 Mar 60	OOH LA LA *Pye 7N 15257*	46	1 wk

*First two hits are medley as follows: Sing It With Joe: Margie/I'm Nobody's
Sweetheart/Somebody Stole My Gal/Moonlight Bay/By The Light Of The Silvery Moon/Cuddle
Up A Little Closer. Sing It Again With Joe: Put Your Arms Around Me Honey/Ain't She
Sweet/When You're Smiling/Shine On Harvest Moon/My Blue Heaven/Show Me The Way To
Go Home.*

Wayne HENDERSON – *See Roy AYERS and Wayne HENDERSON*

Jimi HENDRIX EXPERIENCE
*US/UK, male vocal/instrumental group, Jimi Hendrix, vocalist/
instrumentalist - guitar*   **87 wks**

5 Jan 67	● HEY JOE *Polydor 56 139*	6	10 wks
23 Mar 67	● PURPLE HAZE *Track 604 001*	3	14 wks
11 May 67	● THE WIND CRIES MARY *Track 604 004*	6	11 wks
30 Aug 67	BURNING OF THE MIDNIGHT LAMP *Track 604 007*	18	9 wks
23 Oct 68	● ALL ALONG THE WATCHTOWER *Track 604 025*	5	11 wks
16 Apr 69	CROSSTOWN TRAFFIC *Track 604 029*	37	3 wks
7 Nov 70	★ VOODOO CHILE *Track 2095 001*	1	13 wks
30 Oct 71	GYPSY EYES/ REMEMBER *Track 2094 010*	35	5 wks
12 Feb 72	JOHNNY B. GOODE *Polydor 2001 277*	35	5 wks
21 Apr 90	CROSSTOWN TRAFFIC (re-issue) *Polydor PO 71*	61	3 wks
20 Oct 90	ALL ALONG THE WATCHTOWER (EP) *Polydor PO 100*	52	3 wks

*On Polydor the act is simply billed as Jimi Hendrix. Tracks on All Along The Watchtower
EP: All Along The Watchtower/Voodoo Chile/Hey Joe.*

Nona HENDRYX *US, female vocalist*   **2 wks**

16 May 87	WHY SHOULD I CRY *EMI America EA 234*	60	2 wks

HENHOUSE FIVE PLUS TOO – *See Ray STEVENS*

Don HENLEY *US, male vocalist*   **18 wks**

12 Feb 83	DIRTY LAUNDRY *Asylum E 9894*	59	3 wks
9 Feb 85	THE BOYS OF SUMMER *Geffen A 4945*	12	10 wks
29 Jul 89	THE END OF THE INNOCENCE *Geffen GEF 57*	48	5 wks

Clarence 'Frogman' HENRY *US, male vocalist*   **33 wks**

4 May 61	● BUT I DO *Pye International 7N 25078*	3	19 wks
13 Jul 61	● YOU ALWAYS HURT THE ONE YOU LOVE *Pye International 7N 25089*	6	12 wks
21 Sep 61	LONELY STREET/ WHY CAN'T YOU *Pye International 7N 25108*	42	2 wks

Paul HENRY and the Mayson GLEN ORCHESTRA *UK, male vocalist/orchestra*   **2 wks**

14 Jan 78	BENNY'S THEME *Pye 7N 46027*	39	2 wks

HERB – *See PEACHES and HERB*

HERD *UK, male vocal/instrumental group*   **35 wks**

13 Sep 67	● FROM THE UNDERWORLD *Fontana TF 856*	6	13 wks
20 Dec 67	PARADISE LOST *Fontana TF 887*	15	9 wks
10 Apr 68	● I DON'T WANT OUR LOVING TO DIE *Fontana TF 925*	5	13 wks

HERMAN'S HERMITS   **211 wks**
UK, male vocal/instrumental group

20 Aug 64	★ I'M INTO SOMETHING GOOD *Columbia DB 7338*	1	15 wks
19 Nov 64	SHOW ME GIRL *Columbia DB 7408*	19	9 wks
18 Feb 65	● SILHOUETTES *Columbia DB 7475*	3	12 wks
29 Apr 65	● WONDERFUL WORLD *Columbia DB 7546*	7	9 wks
2 Sep 65	JUST A LITTLE BIT BETTER *Columbia DB 7670*	15	9 wks
23 Dec 65	● A MUST TO AVOID *Columbia DB 7791*	6	11 wks
24 Mar 66	YOU WON'T BE LEAVING *Columbia DB 7861*	20	7 wks
23 Jun 66	THIS DOOR SWINGS BOTH WAYS *Columbia DB 7947*	18	7 wks
6 Oct 66	NO MILK TODAY *Columbia DB 8012*	7	11 wks
1 Dec 66	EAST WEST *Columbia DB 8076*	37	7 wks
9 Feb 67	● THERE'S A KIND OF HUSH *Columbia DB 8123*	7	11 wks
17 Jan 68	I CAN TAKE OR LEAVE YOUR LOVING *Columbia DB 8327*	11	9 wks
1 May 68	SLEEPY JOE *Columbia DB 8404*	12	10 wks
17 Jul 68	● SUNSHINE GIRL *Columbia DB 8446*	8	14 wks
18 Dec 68	● SOMETHING'S HAPPENING *Columbia DB 8504*	6	15 wks
23 Apr 69	● MY SENTIMENTAL FRIEND *Columbia DB 8563*	2	12 wks
8 Nov 69	HERE COMES THE STAR *Columbia DB 8626*	33	9 wks
7 Feb 70	● YEARS MAY COME, YEARS MAY GO *Columbia DB 8656*	7	11 wks
2 May 70	YEARS MAY COME, YEARS MAY GO (re-entry) *Columbia DB 8656*	45	1 wk
23 May 70	BET YER LIFE I DO *RAK 102*	22	10 wks
14 Nov 70	LADY BARBARA *RAK 106*	13	12 wks

On Lady Barbara billed as Peter Noone and Herman's Hermits. See also Peter Noone.

HERNANDEZ *UK, male vocalist*   **3 wks**

15 Apr 89	ALL MY LOVE *Epic HER 1*	58	3 wks

Patrick HERNANDEZ *Guadeloupe, male vocalist*   **14 wks**

16 Jun 79	● BORN TO BE ALIVE *Gem GEM 4*	10	14 wks

HERREYS *Sweden, male vocal group*   **3 wks**

26 May 84	DIGGI LOO-DIGGI LEY *Panther PAN 5*	46	3 wks

Nick HEYWARD *UK, male vocalist*   **57 wks**

19 Mar 83	WHISTLE DOWN THE WIND *Arista HEY 1*	13	8 wks
4 Jun 83	TAKE THAT SITUATION *Arista HEY 2*	11	10 wks
24 Sep 83	BLUE HAT FOR A BLUE DAY *Arista HEY 3*	14	8 wks
3 Dec 83	ON A SUNDAY *Arista HEY 4*	52	5 wks
2 Jun 84	LOVE ALL DAY *Arista HEY 5*	31	6 wks
3 Nov 84	WARNING SIGN *Arista HEY 6*	25	8 wks
5 Jan 85	WARNING SIGN (re-entry) *Arista HEY 6*	72	1 wk
8 Jun 85	LAURA *Arista HEY 8*	45	4 wks
10 May 86	OVER THE WEEKEND *Arista HEY 9*	43	5 wks
10 Sep 88	YOU'RE MY WORLD *Warner Bros. W 7758*	67	2 wks

HI GLOSS *US, disco aggregation*   **13 wks**

8 Aug 81	YOU'LL NEVER KNOW *Epic EPC A 1387*	12	13 wks

HI POWER Germany, male rap group — 1 wk

1 Sep 90	**CULT OF SNAP/ SIMBA GROOVE** *Rumour RUMAT 24*	73	1 wk

HI TENSION UK, male vocal/instrumental group — 23 wks

6 May 78	**HI TENSION** *Island WIP 6422*	13	12 wks
12 Aug 78 ●	**BRITISH HUSTLE/ PEACE ON EARTH** *Island WIP 6446*	8	11 wks

Peace On Earth credited with British Hustle from 2 Sep 78 to end of record's chart run.

Al HIBBLER US, male vocalist — 17 wks

13 May 55 ●	**UNCHAINED MELODY** *Brunswick 05420*	2	17 wks

Bertie HIGGINS US, male vocalist — 4 wks

5 Jun 82	**KEY LARGO** *Epic EPC A 2168*	60	4 wks

HIGH UK, male vocal group — 6 wks

25 Aug 90	**UP AND DOWN** *London LON 272*	53	4 wks
27 Oct 90	**TAKE YOUR TIME** *London LON 280*	56	2 wks

HIGH NUMBERS UK, male vocal/instrumental group — 4 wks

5 Apr 80	**I'M THE FACE** *Back Door DOOR 4*	49	4 wks

The High Numbers were an early version of the Who. See also the Who.

HIGH SOCIETY UK, male vocal/instrumental group — 4 wks

15 Nov 80	**I NEVER GO OUT IN THE RAIN** *Eagle ERS 002*	53	4 wks

HIGHLY LIKELY UK, male vocal/instrumental group — 4 wks

21 Apr 73	**WHATEVER HAPPENED TO YOU (LIKELY LADS THEME)** *BBC RESL 10*	35	4 wks

HIGHWAYMEN US, male vocal group — 18 wks

7 Sep 61 ★	**MICHAEL** *HMV POP 910*	1	14 wks
7 Dec 61	**GYPSY ROVER** *HMV POP 948*	41	3 wks
11 Jan 62	**GYPSY ROVER (re-entry)** *HMV POP 948*	43	1 wk

HIJACK UK, male producer — 3 wks

6 Jan 90	**THE BADMAN IS ROBBIN'** *Rhyme Syndicate 655517 7*	56	3 wks

Benny HILL UK, male vocalist — 39 wks

16 Feb 61	**GATHER IN THE MUSHROOMS** *Pye 7N 15327*	12	8 wks
1 Jun 61	**TRANSISTOR RADIO** *Pye 7N 15359*	24	6 wks
16 May 63	**HARVEST OF LOVE** *Pye 7N 15520*	20	8 wks
13 Nov 71 ★	**ERNIE (THE FASTEST MILKMAN IN THE WEST)** *Columbia DB 8833*	1	17 wks

Chris HILL UK, male vocalist plus extracts from other hit records — 14 wks

6 Dec 75 ●	**RENTA SANTA** *Philips 6006 491*	10	7 wks
4 Dec 76 ●	**BIONIC SANTA** *Philips 6006 551*	10	7 wks

Dan HILL Canada, male vocalist — 13 wks

18 Feb 78	**SOMETIMES WHEN WE TOUCH** *20th Century BTC 2355*	46	1 wk
4 Mar 78	**SOMETIMES WHEN WE TOUCH (re-entry)** *20th Century BTC 2355*	13	12 wks

Lonnie HILL US, male vocalist — 4 wks

22 Mar 86	**GALVESTON BAY** *10 TEN 111*	51	4 wks

Roni HILL US, female vocalist — 4 wks

7 May 77	**YOU KEEP ME HANGIN' ON - STOP IN THE NAME OF LOVE** (MEDLEY) *Creole CR 138*	36	4 wks

Vince HILL UK, male vocalist — 91 wks

7 Jun 62	**THE RIVER'S RUN DRY** *Piccadilly 7N 35043*	49	1 wk
28 Jun 62	**THE RIVER'S RUN DRY (re-entry)** *Piccadilly 7N 35043*	41	1 wk
6 Jan 66	**TAKE ME TO YOUR HEART AGAIN** *Columbia DB 7781*	13	11 wks
17 Mar 66	**HEARTACHES** *Columbia DB 7852*	28	5 wks
2 Jun 66	**MERCI CHERI** *Columbia DB 7924*	36	6 wks
9 Feb 67 ●	**EDELWEISS** *Columbia DB 8127*	2	17 wks
11 May 67	**ROSES OF PICARDY** *Columbia DB 8185*	13	11 wks
27 Sep 67	**LOVE LETTERS IN THE SAND** *Columbia DB 8268*	23	9 wks
26 Jun 68	**IMPORTANCE OF YOUR LOVE** *Columbia DB 8414*	32	12 wks
12 Feb 69	**DOESN'T ANYBODY KNOW MY NAME?** *Columbia DB 8515*	50	1 wk
25 Oct 69	**LITTLE BLUE BIRD** *Columbia DB 8616*	42	1 wk
25 Sep 71	**LOOK AROUND** *Columbia DB 8804*	12	16 wks

HILLTOPPERS US, male vocal group — 30 wks

27 Jan 56 ●	**ONLY YOU** *London HLD 8221*	3	22 wks
10 Aug 56	**ONLY YOU (re-entry)** *London HLD 8221*	24	1 wk
14 Sep 56	**TRYIN'** *London HLD 8298*	30	1 wk
5 Apr 57	**MARIANNE** *London HLD 8381*	20	2 wks
26 Apr 57	**MARIANNE (re-entry)** *London HLD 8381*	23	4 wks

Ronnie HILTON UK, male vocalist — 128 wks

26 Nov 54 ●	**I STILL BELIEVE** *HMV B 10785*	3	14 wks
10 Dec 54	**VENI VIDI VICI** *HMV B 10785*	12	8 wks
11 Mar 55 ●	**A BLOSSOM FELL** *HMV B 10808*	10	5 wks
26 Aug 55	**STARS SHINE IN YOUR EYES** *HMV B 10901*	13	7 wks
11 Nov 55	**YELLOW ROSE OF TEXAS** *HMV B 10924*	15	2 wks
10 Feb 56	**YOUNG AND FOOLISH** *HMV POP 154*	17	1 wk
24 Feb 56	**YOUNG AND FOOLISH (re-entry)** *HMV POP 154*	20	1 wk
9 Mar 56	**YOUNG AND FOOLISH (2nd re-entry)** *HMV POP 154*	19	1 wk
20 Apr 56 ★	**NO OTHER LOVE** *HMV POP 198*	1	14 wks
29 Jun 56 ●	**WHO ARE WE** *HMV POP 221*	6	12 wks
21 Sep 56	**WOMAN IN LOVE** *HMV POP 248*	30	1 wk
9 Nov 56	**TWO DIFFERENT WORLDS** *HMV POP 274*	13	13 wks
24 May 57 ●	**AROUND THE WORLD** *HMV POP 338*	4	18 wks
2 Aug 57	**WONDERFUL WONDERFUL** *HMV POP 364*	27	2 wks
21 Feb 58	**MAGIC MOMENTS** *HMV POP 446*	22	2 wks
18 Apr 58	**I MAY NEVER PASS THIS WAY AGAIN** *HMV POP 468*	30	1 wk
2 May 58	**I MAY NEVER PASS THIS WAY AGAIN (re-entry)** *HMV POP 468*	30	1 wk
6 Jun 58	**I MAY NEVER PASS THIS WAY AGAIN (2nd re-entry)** *HMV POP 468*	27	1 wk
9 Jan 59	**THE WORLD OUTSIDE** *HMV POP 559*	18	6 wks
21 Aug 59	**THE WONDER OF YOU** *HMV POP 638*	22	3 wks
21 May 64	**DON'T LET THE RAIN COME DOWN** *HMV POP 1291*	21	10 wks
11 Feb 65	**A WINDMILL IN OLD AMSTERDAM** *HMV POP 1378*	23	13 wks

HINDSIGHT UK, male vocal/instrumental group — 3 wks

5 Sep 87	**LOWDOWN** Circa YR 5..	62	3 wks

Gregory HINES – See Luther VANDROSS

A HIPPIE – See A HOMEBOY, A HIPPIE and A FUNKI DREDD

HIPSWAY UK, male vocal/instrumental group — 21 wks

13 Jul 85	**THE BROKEN YEARS** Mercury MER 193.....................	72	3 wks
14 Sep 85	**ASK THE LORD** Mercury MER 195.........................	72	1 wk
22 Feb 86	**THE HONEYTHIEF** Mercury MER 212.......................	17	9 wks
10 May 86	**ASK THE LORD** Mercury LORD 1	50	5 wks
20 Sep 86	**LONG WHITE CAR** Mercury MER 230........................	55	2 wks
1 Apr 89	**YOUR LOVE** Mercury MER 279	66	1 wk

LORD 1 was a re-recording of MER 195.

HISTORY featuring Q-TEE
US, male/female rap group — 5 wks

21 Apr 90	**AFRIKA** SBK SBK 7008..	42	5 wks

Carol HITCHCOCK Australia, female vocalist — 5 wks

30 May 87	**GET READY** A & M AM 391	56	5 wks

HI-TEK featuring YA KID K
Belgium, male/female vocal/instrumental group — 9 wks

3 Feb 90	**SPIN THAT WHEEL** Brothers Organisation BORG 1...........	69	3 wks
29 Sep 90	**SPIN THAT WHEEL (TURTLES GET REAL)** (re-issue) Brothers Organisation BORG 16...................................	15	6 wks

See also Technotronic.

HITHOUSE Holland, male producer - Peter Slaghuis — 13 wks

5 Nov 88	**JACK TO THE SOUND OF THE UNDERGROUND** Supreme SUPE 137..	14	12 wks
19 Aug 89	**MOVE YOUR FEET TO THE RHYTHM OF THE BEAT** Supreme SUPE 149....................................	69	1 wk

HITMAN HOWIE TEE – See REAL ROXANNE

Edmund HOCKRIDGE Canada, male vocalist — 18 wks

17 Feb 56	● **YOUNG AND FOOLISH** Nixa N 15039.....................	10	7 wks
13 Apr 56	**YOUNG AND FOOLISH** (re-entry) Nixa N 15039...........	28	1 wk
4 May 56	**YOUNG AND FOOLISH** (2nd re-entry) Nixa N 15039........	26	1 wk
11 May 56	**NO OTHER LOVE** Nixa N 15046..........................	24	2 wks
1 Jun 56	**NO OTHER LOVE** (re-entry) Nixa N 15046................	29	1 wk
15 Jun 56	**NO OTHER LOVE** (2nd re-entry) Nixa N 15046............	30	1 wk
31 Aug 56	**BY THE FOUNTAINS OF ROME** Pye Nixa N 15063	17	5 wks

Eddie HODGES US, male vocalist — 10 wks

28 Sep 61	**I'M GONNA KNOCK ON YOUR DOOR** London HLA 9369	37	6 wks
9 Aug 62	**MADE TO LOVE (GIRLS GIRLS GIRLS)** London HLA 9576	37	4 wks

HOLLAND-DOZIER US, male vocal duo — 5 wks

28 Oct 72	**WHY CAN'T WE BE LOVERS** Invictus INV 525..............	29	5 wks

Hit has credit 'featuring Lamont Dozier'.

Jennifer HOLLIDAY US, female vocalist — 6 wks

4 Sep 82	**AND I'M TELLING YOU I'M NOT GOING** Geffen GEF A 2644	32	6 wks

Michael HOLLIDAY UK, male vocalist — 63 wks

30 Mar 56	**NOTHIN' TO DO** Columbia DB 3746.......................	20	1 wk
27 Apr 56	**NOTHIN' TO DO** (re-entry) Columbia DB 3746............	23	2 wks
15 Jun 56	**GAL WITH THE YALLER SHOES** Columbia DB 3783	13	3 wks
22 Jun 56	**HOT DIGGITY** Columbia DB 3783	14	5 wks
3 Aug 56	**HOT DIGGITY/ GAL WITH THE YALLER SHOES** (re-entry) Columbia DB 3783...............	17	3 wks
5 Oct 56	**TEN THOUSAND MILES** Columbia DB 3813.................	24	3 wks
17 Jan 58	★ **THE STORY OF MY LIFE** Columbia DB 4058............	1	15 wks
14 Mar 58	**IN LOVE** Columbia DB 4087..............................	26	3 wks
16 May 58	● **STAIRWAY OF LOVE** Columbia DB 4121...............	3	13 wks
11 Jul 58	**I'LL ALWAYS BE IN LOVE WITH YOU** Columbia DB 4155..	27	1 wk
1 Jan 60	★ **STARRY EYED** Columbia DB 4378.....................	1	12 wks
14 Apr 60	**SKYLARK** Columbia DB 4437............................	39	3 wks
1 Sep 60	**LITTLE BOY LOST** Columbia DB 4475.....................	50	1 wk

When Hot Diggity/ Gal With The Yaller Shoes re-entered the chart on 3 Aug 56 Hot
Diggity was listed by itself on 3 Aug and 10 Aug. Both sides were listed on 17 Aug.

HOLLIES UK, male vocal/instrumental group — 316 wks

30 May 63	**JUST LIKE ME** Parlophone R 5030........................	25	10 wks
29 Aug 63	**SEARCHIN'** Parlophone R 5052...........................	12	14 wks
21 Nov 63	● **STAY** Parlophone R 5077..............................	8	16 wks
27 Feb 64	● **JUST ONE LOOK** Parlophone R 5104..................	2	13 wks
21 May 64	● **HERE I GO AGAIN** Parlophone R 5137................	4	12 wks
17 Sep 64	● **WE'RE THROUGH** Parlophone R 5178.................	7	11 wks
28 Jan 65	● **YES I WILL** Parlophone R 5232.......................	9	13 wks
27 May 65	★ **I'M ALIVE** Parlophone R 5287........................	1	14 wks
2 Sep 65	● **LOOK THROUGH ANY WINDOW** Parlophone R 5322.......	4	11 wks
9 Dec 65	**IF I NEEDED SOMEONE** Parlophone R 5392..............	20	9 wks
24 Feb 66	● **I CAN'T LET GO** Parlophone R 5409..................	2	10 wks
23 Jun 66	● **BUS STOP** Parlophone R 5469........................	5	9 wks
13 Oct 66	● **STOP STOP STOP** Parlophone R 5508.................	2	12 wks
16 Feb 67	● **ON A CAROUSEL** Parlophone R 5562..................	4	11 wks
1 Jun 67	● **CARRIE-ANNE** Parlophone R 5602....................	3	11 wks
27 Sep 67	**KING MIDAS IN REVERSE** Parlophone R 5637.............	18	8 wks
27 Mar 68	● **JENNIFER ECCLES** Parlophone R 5680.................	7	11 wks
2 Oct 68	**LISTEN TO ME** Parlophone R 5733.......................	11	11 wks
5 Mar 69	● **SORRY SUZANNE** Parlophone R 5765.................	3	12 wks
4 Oct 69	● **HE AIN'T HEAVY, HE'S MY BROTHER** Parlophone R 5806..	3	15 wks
18 Apr 70	● **I CAN'T TELL THE BOTTOM FROM THE TOP** Parlophone R 5837.......................................	7	10 wks
3 Oct 70	**GASOLINE ALLEY BRED** Parlophone R 5862..............	14	7 wks
22 May 71	**HEY WILLY** Parlophone R 5905..........................	22	7 wks
26 Feb 72	**THE BABY** Polydor 2058 199	26	6 wks
2 Sep 72	**LONG COOL WOMAN IN A BLACK DRESS** Parlophone R 5939..	32	8 wks
13 Oct 73	**THE DAY THAT CURLY BILLY SHOT CRAZY SAM McGHEE** Polydor 2058 403	24	6 wks
9 Feb 74	● **THE AIR THAT I BREATHE** Polydor 2058 435	2	13 wks
14 Jun 80	**SOLDIER'S SONG** Polydor 2059 246	58	3 wks
29 Aug 81	**HOLLIEDAZE** (MEDLEY) EMI 5229........................	28	7 wks
3 Sep 88	★ **HE AIN'T HEAVY, HE'S MY BROTHER** (re-issue) EMI EM 74..	1	11 wks
3 Dec 88	**THE AIR THAT I BREATHE** (re-issue) EMI EM 80	60	5 wks

Buddy HOLLY US, male vocalist   190 wks

6 Dec 57	●	**PEGGY SUE** Coral Q 72293	6	17 wks
14 Mar 58		**LISTEN TO ME** Coral Q 72288	16	2 wks
20 Jun 58	●	**RAVE ON** Coral Q 72325	5	14 wks
29 Aug 58		**EARLY IN THE MORNING** Coral Q 72333	17	4 wks
16 Jan 59		**HEARTBEAT** Coral Q 72346	30	1 wk
27 Feb 59	★	**IT DOESN'T MATTER ANYMORE** Coral Q 72360	1	21 wks
31 Jul 59		**MIDNIGHT SHIFT** Brunswick 05800	26	3 wks
11 Sep 59		**PEGGY SUE GOT MARRIED** Coral Q 72376	13	10 wks
28 Apr 60		**HEARTBEAT (re-issue)** Coral Q 72392	30	3 wks
26 May 60		**TRUE LOVE WAYS** Coral Q 72397	25	7 wks
20 Oct 60		**LEARNIN' THE GAME** Coral Q 72411	36	3 wks
26 Jan 61		**WHAT TO DO** Coral Q 72419	34	6 wks
6 Jul 61		**BABY I DON'T CARE/VALLEY OF TEARS** Coral Q 72432	12	14 wks
15 Mar 62		**LISTEN TO ME (re-issue)** Coral Q 72449	48	1 wk
13 Sep 62		**REMINISCING** Coral Q 72455	17	11 wks
14 Mar 63	●	**BROWN-EYED HANDSOME MAN** Coral Q 72459	3	17 wks
6 Jun 63	●	**BO DIDDLEY** Coral Q 72463	4	12 wks
5 Sep 63	●	**WISHING** Coral Q 72466	10	11 wks
19 Dec 63		**WHAT TO DO** Coral Q 72469	27	8 wks
14 May 64		**YOU'VE GOT LOVE** Coral Q 72472	40	6 wks
10 Sep 64		**LOVE'S MADE A FOOL OF YOU** Coral Q 72475	39	6 wks
3 Apr 68		**PEGGY SUE/RAVE ON (re-issue)** MCA MU 1012	32	9 wks
10 Dec 88		**TRUE LOVE WAYS (re-issue)** MCA MCA 1302	65	4 wks

Buddy Holly's version of Love's Made A Fool Of You *is not the same version as the Crickets' hit of 1959, on which Holly did not appear.* You've Got Love *was released with credit to Buddy Holly and the Crickets.* Valley Of Tears *was not listed together with* Baby I Don't Care *until 13 Jul 61.* What To Do *on Q 72469 was a re-recording. See also Crickets.*

HOLLY and the IVYS
UK, male/female vocal/instrumental group   4 wks

19 Dec 81		**CHRISTMAS ON 45** Decca SANTA 1	40	4 wks

HOLLYWOOD ARGYLES US, male vocal group   10 wks

21 Jul 60		**ALLEY OOP** London HLU 9146	24	10 wks

HOLLYWOOD BEYOND UK, male vocalist   14 wks

12 Jul 86	●	**WHAT'S THE COLOUR OF MONEY?** WEA YZ 76	7	10 wks
20 Sep 86		**NO MORE TEARS** WEA YZ 81	47	4 wks

Eddie HOLMAN US, male vocalist   13 wks

19 Oct 74	●	**(HEY THERE) LONELY GIRL** ABC 4012	4	13 wks

Rupert HOLMES US, male vocalist   14 wks

12 Jan 80		**ESCAPE (THE PINA COLADA SONG)** Infinity INF 120	23	7 wks
22 Mar 80		**HIM** MCA 565	31	7 wks

John HOLT Jamaica, male vocalist   14 wks

14 Dec 74	●	**HELP ME MAKE IT THROUGH THE NIGHT** Trojan TR 7909	6	14 wks

A HOMEBOY, A HIPPIE and A FUNKI DREDD UK, male vocal/instrumental group   4 wks

13 Oct 90		**TOTAL CONFUSION** Tam Tam 7TTT 031	56	3 wks
29 Dec 90		**FREEDOM** Tam Tam TTT 039	73†	1 wk

HONEYBUS UK, male vocal/instrumental group   12 wks

20 Mar 68	●	**I CAN'T LET MAGGIE GO** Deram DM 182	8	12 wks

HONEYCOMBS UK, male/female vocal/instrumental group   39 wks

23 Jul 64	★	**HAVE I THE RIGHT** Pye 7N 15664	1	15 wks
22 Oct 64		**IS IT BECAUSE** Pye 7N 15705	38	6 wks
29 Apr 65		**SOMETHING BETTER BEGINNING** Pye 7N 15827	39	4 wks
5 Aug 65		**THAT'S THE WAY** Pye 7N 15890	12	14 wks

HONEYDRIPPERS
UK/US, male vocal/instrumental group   3 wks

2 Feb 85		**SEA OF LOVE** Es Paranza YZ 33 YZ 33	56	3 wks

HONKY UK, male vocal/instrumental group   5 wks

28 May 77		**JOIN THE PARTY** Creole CR 137	28	5 wks

Frank HOOKER and POSITIVE PEOPLE   4 wks
US, male vocal/instrumental group

5 Jul 80		**THIS FEELIN'** DJM DJS 10947	48	4 wks

John Lee HOOKER US, male vocalist   10 wks

11 Jun 64		**DIMPLES** Stateside SS 297	23	10 wks

HOOTERS US, male vocal/instrumental group   9 wks

21 Nov 87		**SATELLITE** CBS 651168 7	22	9 wks

HOPE – *See FAITH, HOPE and CHARITY*

Mary HOPKIN UK, female vocalist   74 wks

4 Sep 68	★	**THOSE WERE THE DAYS** Apple 2	1	21 wks
2 Apr 69	●	**GOODBYE** Apple 10	2	14 wks
31 Jan 70	●	**TEMMA HARBOUR** Apple 22	6	11 wks
28 Mar 70	●	**KNOCK KNOCK WHO'S THERE** Apple 26	2	14 wks
31 Oct 70		**THINK ABOUT YOUR CHILDREN** Apple 30	19	7 wks
2 Jan 71		**THINK ABOUT YOUR CHILDREN (re-entry)** Apple 30	46	2 wks
31 Jul 71		**LET MY NAME BE SORROW** Apple 34	46	1 wk
20 Mar 76		**IF YOU LOVE ME** Good Earth GD 2	32	4 wks

Anthony HOPKINS UK, male vocalist   1 wk

27 Dec 86		**DISTANT STAR** Juice AA 5	75	1 wk

Bruce HORNSBY and the RANGE   15 wks
US, male vocal/instrumental group

2 Aug 86		**THE WAY IT IS** RCA PB 49805	15	10 wks
25 Apr 87		**MANDOLIN RAIN** RCA PB 49769	70	1 wk
28 May 88		**THE VALLEY ROAD** RCA PB 49561	44	4 wks

HORSE UK, male/female vocal/instrumental group   3 wks

24 Nov 90		**CAREFUL** Capitol CL 587	52	3 wks

Above: They had two classic hits in the chart at the same time, 'Oh Boy' credited to the Crickets and 'Peggy Sue' to BUDDY HOLLY (centre).

Right: Cousins Dionne Warwick (left) and WHITNEY HOUSTON pose at the 1990 United Negro College Fund dinner in New York where Whitney was honoured.

Top Far Right: THE HERREYS hurried their chart career after their 1984 Eurovision Song Contest win.

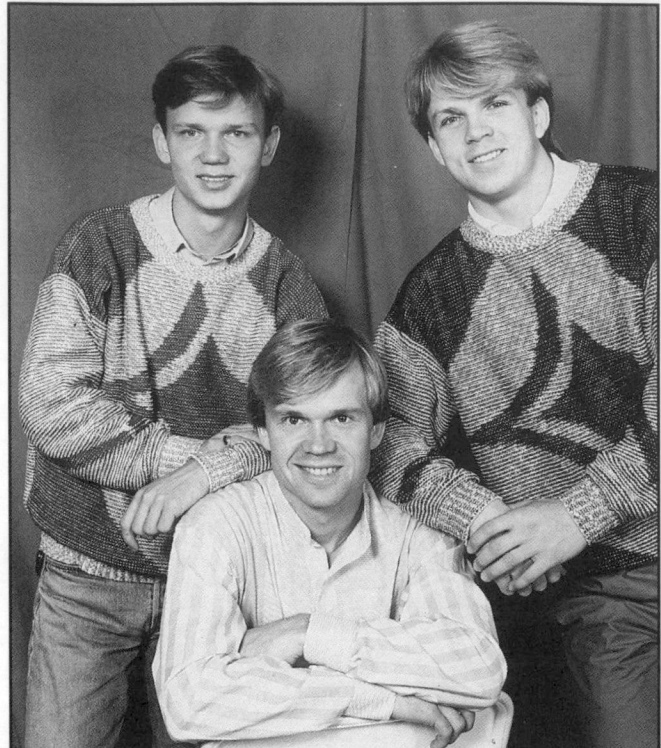

THE HERD went overground in 1967.

Johnny HORTON US, male vocalist — 15 wks

Date	Title	Pos	Wks
26 Jun 59	BATTLE OF NEW ORLEANS *Philips PB 932*	16	4 wks
19 Jan 61	NORTH TO ALASKA *Philips PB 1062*	23	11 wks

Bob HOSKINS – *See Paul HARDCASTLE*

HOT BLOOD France, male instrumental group — 5 wks

Date	Title	Pos	Wks
9 Oct 76	SOUL DRACULA *Creole CR 132*	32	5 wks

HOT BUTTER US, male instrumental group — 19 wks

Date	Title	Pos	Wks
22 Jul 72 ●	POPCORN *Pye International 7N 25583*	5	16 wks
23 Dec 72	POPCORN (re-entry) *Pye International 7N 25583*	50	3 wks

HOT CHOCOLATE UK, male vocal/instrumental group — 267 wks

Date	Title	Pos	Wks
15 Aug 70 ●	LOVE IS LIFE *RAK 103*	6	12 wks
6 Mar 71	YOU COULD HAVE BEEN A LADY *RAK 110*	22	9 wks
28 Aug 71	I BELIEVE (IN LOVE) *RAK 118*	8	11 wks
28 Oct 72	YOU'LL ALWAYS BE A FRIEND *RAK 139*	23	8 wks
14 Apr 73 ●	BROTHER LOUIE *RAK 149*	7	10 wks
18 Aug 73	RUMOURS *RAK 157*	44	3 wks
16 Mar 74 ●	EMMA *RAK 168*	3	10 wks
30 Nov 74	CHERI BABE *RAK 188*	31	9 wks
24 May 75	DISCO QUEEN *RAK 202*	11	7 wks
9 Aug 75 ●	A CHILD'S PRAYER *RAK 212*	7	10 wks
8 Nov 75 ●	YOU SEXY THING *RAK 221*	2	12 wks
20 Mar 76	DON'T STOP IT NOW *RAK 230*	11	8 wks
26 Jun 76	MAN TO MAN *RAK 238*	14	8 wks
21 Aug 76	HEAVEN IS IN THE BACK SEAT OF MY CADILLAC *RAK 240*	25	8 wks
18 Jun 77 ★	SO YOU WIN AGAIN *RAK 259*	1	11 wks
26 Nov 77 ●	PUT YOUR LOVE IN ME *RAK 266*	10	9 wks
4 Mar 78	EVERY 1'S A WINNER *RAK 270*	12	11 wks
2 Dec 78	I'LL PUT YOU TOGETHER AGAIN *RAK 286*	13	11 wks
19 May 79	MINDLESS BOOGIE *RAK 292*	46	5 wks
28 Jul 79	GOING THROUGH THE MOTIONS *RAK 296*	53	4 wks
3 May 80 ●	NO DOUBT ABOUT IT *RAK 310*	2	11 wks
19 Jul 80	ARE YOU GETTING ENOUGH OF WHAT MAKES YOU HAPPY *RAK 318*	17	7 wks
13 Dec 80	LOVE ME TO SLEEP *RAK 324*	50	5 wks
30 May 81	YOU'LL NEVER BE SO WRONG *RAK 331*	52	4 wks
17 Apr 82 ●	GIRL CRAZY *RAK 341*	7	11 wks
10 Jul 82 ●	IT STARTED WITH A KISS *RAK 344*	5	12 wks
25 Sep 82	CHANCES *RAK 350*	32	5 wks
7 May 83 ●	WHAT KINDA BOY YOU LOOKING FOR (GIRL) *RAK 357*	10	9 wks
17 Sep 83	TEARS ON THE TELEPHONE *RAK 363*	37	5 wks
4 Feb 84	I GAVE YOU MY HEART (DIDN'T I) *RAK 369*	13	10 wks
17 Jan 87 ●	YOU SEXY THING (re-mix) *EMI 5592*	10	10 wks
4 Apr 87	EVERY 1'S A WINNER (re-mix) *EMI 5607*	69	2 wks

HOT GOSSIP – *See Sarah BRIGHTMAN*

HOT HOUSE UK, male/female vocal/instrumental group — 3 wks

Date	Title	Pos	Wks
14 Feb 87	DON'T COME TO STAY *deConstruction CHEZ 1*	74	1 wk
24 Sep 88	DON'T COME TO STAY (re-issue) *de Construction PB 42233*	70	2 wks

HOT STREAK US, male vocal/instrumental group — 8 wks

Date	Title	Pos	Wks
10 Sep 83	BODY WORK *Polydor POSP 642*	19	8 wks

HOTHOUSE FLOWERS
Ireland, male vocal/instrumental group — 25 wks

Date	Title	Pos	Wks
14 May 88	DON'T GO *London LON 174*	11	8 wks
23 Jul 88	I'M SORRY *London LON 187*	53	3 wks
12 May 90	GIVE IT UP *London LON 258*	30	5 wks
28 Jul 90	I CAN SEE CLEARLY NOW *London LON 269*	23	7 wks
20 Oct 90	MOVIES *London LON 276*	68	2 wks

HOTLEGS UK, male vocal/instrumental group — 14 wks

Date	Title	Pos	Wks
4 Jul 70 ●	NEANDERTHAL MAN *Fontana 6007 019*	2	14 wks

HOTRODS – *See EDDIE and the HOTRODS*

HOTSHOTS UK, male vocal group — 15 wks

Date	Title	Pos	Wks
2 Jun 73 ●	SNOOPY VS. THE RED BARON *Mooncrest MOON 5*	4	15 wks

HOUSE ENGINEERS UK, male vocal/instrumental duo — 2 wks

Date	Title	Pos	Wks
5 Dec 87	GHOST HOUSE *Syncopate SY 8*	69	2 wks

HOUSE OF LOVE UK, male vocal/instrumental group — 13 wks

Date	Title	Pos	Wks
22 Apr 89	NEVER *Fontana HOL 1*	41	2 wks
18 Nov 89	I DON'T KNOW WHY I LOVE YOU *Fontana HOL 2*	41	3 wks
3 Feb 90	SHINE ON *Fontana HOL 3*	20	4 wks
7 Apr 90	BEATLES AND THE STONES *Fontana HOL 4*	36	4 wks

HOUSEMARTINS UK, male vocal/instrumental group — 59 wks

Date	Title	Pos	Wks
8 Mar 86	SHEEP *Go! Discs GOD 9*	54	3 wks
5 Apr 86	SHEEP (re-entry) *Go! Discs GOD 9*	71	1 wk
7 Jun 86 ●	HAPPY HOUR *Go! Discs GOD 11*	3	13 wks
4 Oct 86	THINK FOR A MINUTE *Go! Discs GOD 13*	18	8 wks
6 Dec 86 ★	CARAVAN OF LOVE *Go! Discs GOD 16*	1	11 wks
23 May 87	FIVE GET OVER EXCITED *Go! Discs GOD 18*	11	6 wks
5 Sep 87	ME AND THE FARMER *Go! Discs GOD 19*	15	5 wks
21 Nov 87	BUILD *Go! Discs GOD 21*	15	8 wks
23 Apr 88	THERE IS ALWAYS SOMETHING THERE TO REMIND ME *Go! Discs GOD 22*	35	4 wks

HOUSEMASTER BOYZ and the RUDE BOY OF HOUSE US, male vocal/instrumental group — 14 wks

Date	Title	Pos	Wks
9 May 87	HOUSE NATION *Magnetic Dance MAGD 1*	48	6 wks
12 Sep 87 ●	HOUSE NATION (re-entry) *Magnetic Dance MAGD 1*	8	8 wks

Thelma HOUSTON US, female vocalist — 20 wks

Date	Title	Pos	Wks
5 Feb 77	DON'T LEAVE ME THIS WAY *Motown TMG 1060*	13	8 wks
27 Jun 81	IF YOU FEEL IT *RCA 77*	48	4 wks
1 Dec 84	YOU USED TO HOLD ME SO TIGHT *MCA MCA 932*	49	8 wks

Whitney HOUSTON US, female vocalist — 113 wks

Date	Title	Pos	Wks
16 Nov 85 ★	SAVING ALL MY LOVE FOR YOU *Arista ARIST 640*	1	16 wks
25 Jan 86 ●	HOW WILL I KNOW *Arista ARIST 656*	5	12 wks
12 Apr 86 ●	GREATEST LOVE OF ALL *Arista ARIST 658*	8	11 wks
23 May 87 ★	I WANNA DANCE WITH SOMEBODY (WHO LOVES ME) *Arista RIS 1*	1	16 wks
22 Aug 87	DIDN'T WE ALMOST HAVE IT ALL *Arista RIS 31*	14	8 wks
14 Nov 87 ●	SO EMOTIONAL *Arista RIS 43*	5	11 wks

12 Mar 88	WHERE DO BROKEN HEARTS GO *Arista 109793*	14	8 wks
28 May 88	● LOVE WILL SAVE THE DAY *Arista 111516*	10	7 wks
24 Sep 88	★ ONE MOMENT IN TIME *Arista 111613*	1	12 wks
20 Oct 90	● I'M YOUR BABY TONIGHT *Arista 113594*	5	9 wks
22 Dec 90	ALL THE MAN THAT I NEED *Arista 114000*	22†	2 wks
29 Dec 90	I'M YOUR BABY TONIGHT (re-entry) *Arista 113594*	69†	1 wk

See also Teddy Pendergrass with Whitney Houston; Aretha Franklin and Whitney Houston.

HOWARD – See ELLIS, BEGGS and HOWARD

Billy HOWARD *UK, male vocalist* — 12 wks

13 Dec 75	● KING OF THE COPS *Penny Farthing PEN 892*	6	12 wks

Miki HOWARD *US, female vocalist* — 2 wks

26 May 90	UNTIL YOU COME BACK (THAT'S WHAT I'M GONNA DO) *East West 7935*	67	2 wks

Robert HOWARD and Kym MAZELLE — 10 wks
UK/US, male/female vocal duo

14 Jan 89	● WAIT *RCA PB 42595*	7	10 wks

See also Kym Mazelle.

HOWLIN' WOLF *US, male vocalist* — 5 wks

4 Jun 64	SMOKESTACK LIGHTNIN' *Pye International 7N 25244*	42	5 wks

H₂O *UK, male vocal/instrumental group* — 16 wks

21 May 83	DREAM TO SLEEP *RCA 330*	17	10 wks
13 Aug 83	JUST OUTSIDE OF HEAVEN *RCA 349*	38	6 wks

Al HUDSON and the PARTNERS — 14 wks
US, male/female vocal/instrumental group

9 Sep 78	DANCE, GET DOWN/ HOW DO YOU DO *ABC 4229*	57	4 wks
15 Sep 79	YOU CAN DO IT *MCA 511*	15	10 wks

First hit credited to Al Hudson. See also One Way featuring Al Hudson.

Lavine HUDSON *UK, female vocalist* — 3 wks

21 May 88	INTERVENTION *Virgin VS 1067*	57	3 wks

HUDSON-FORD *UK, male vocal/instrumental duo* — 20 wks

18 Aug 73	● PICK UP THE PIECES *A & M AMS 7078*	8	9 wks
16 Feb 74	BURN BABY BURN *A & M AMS 7096*	15	9 wks
29 Jun 74	FLOATING IN THE WIND *A & M AMS 7116*	35	2 wks

See also Monks.

HUE AND CRY *UK, male vocal/instrumental duo* — 48 wks

13 Jun 87	● LABOUR OF LOVE *Circa YR 4*	6	16 wks
19 Sep 87	STRENGTH TO STRENGTH *Circa YR 6*	46	5 wks
30 Jan 88	I REFUSE *Circa YR 8*	47	3 wks
22 Oct 88	ORDINARY ANGEL *Circa YR 18*	42	6 wks
28 Jan 89	LOOKING FOR LINDA *Circa YR 24*	15	9 wks
6 May 89	VIOLENTLY (EP) *Circa YR 29*	21	6 wks
30 Sep 89	SWEET INVISIBILITY *Circa YR 37*	55	3 wks

Tracks on Violently *EP: Violently/The Man With The Child In His Eyes/Calamity John.*

HUES CORPORATION *US, male/female vocal group* — 16 wks

27 Jul 74	● ROCK THE BOAT *RCA APBO 0232*	6	10 wks
19 Oct 74	ROCKIN' SOUL *RCA PB 10066*	24	6 wks

David HUGHES *UK, male vocalist* — 1 wk

21 Sep 56	BY THE FOUNTAINS OF ROME *Philips PB 606*	27	1 wk

HUGO and LUIGI *US, male vocal duo* — 2 wks

24 Jul 59	LA PLUME DE MA TANTE *RCA 1127*	29	2 wks

HUMAN LEAGUE — 131 wks
UK, male/female vocal/instrumental group

3 May 80	HOLIDAY 80 (DOUBLE SINGLE) (re-entry) *Virgin SV 105*	56	5 wks
21 Jun 80	EMPIRE STATE HUMAN *Virgin VS 351*	62	2 wks
28 Feb 81	BOYS AND GIRLS *Virgin VS 395*	48	4 wks
2 May 81	THE SOUND OF THE CROWD *Virgin VS 416*	12	10 wks
8 Aug 81	● LOVE ACTION (I BELIEVE IN LOVE) *Virgin VS 435*	3	13 wks
10 Oct 81	● OPEN YOUR HEART *Virgin VS 453*	6	9 wks
5 Dec 81	★ DON'T YOU WANT ME *Virgin VS 466*	1	13 wks
9 Jan 82	● BEING BOILED *EMI FAST 4*	6	9 wks
6 Feb 82	HOLIDAY 80 (DOUBLE SINGLE) (re-entry) *Virgin SV 105*	46	5 wks
20 Nov 82	● MIRROR MAN *Virgin VS 522*	2	10 wks
23 Apr 83	● (KEEP FEELING) FASCINATION *Virgin VS 569*	2	9 wks
5 May 84	THE LEBANON *Virgin VS 672*	11	6 wks
23 Jun 84	THE LEBANON (re-entry) *Virgin VS 672*	75	1 wk
30 Jun 84	LIFE ON YOUR OWN *Virgin VS 688*	16	6 wks
17 Nov 84	LOUISE *Virgin VS 723*	13	10 wks
23 Aug 86	● HUMAN *Virgin VS 880*	8	8 wks
22 Nov 86	I NEED YOUR LOVING *Virgin VS 900*	72	1 wk
15 Oct 88	LOVE IS ALL THAT MATTERS *Virgin VS 1025*	41	5 wks
18 Aug 90	HEART LIKE A WHEEL *Virgin VS 1262*	29	5 wks

Tracks on double single: Being Boiled/Marianne/Rock And Roll - Nightclubbing/Dancevision.

HUMANOID *UK, male producer* — 10 wks

26 Nov 88	STAKKER HUMANOID *Westside WSR 12*	17	8 wks
22 Apr 89	SLAM *Westside WSR 14*	54	2 wks

HUMBLE PIE *UK, male vocal/instrumental group* — 10 wks

23 Aug 69	● NATURAL BORN BUGIE *Immediate IM 082*	4	10 wks

Engelbert HUMPERDINCK *UK, male vocalist* — 235 wks

26 Jan 67	★ RELEASE ME *Decca F 12541*	1	56 wks
25 May 67	● THERE GOES MY EVERYTHING *Decca F 12610*	2	29 wks
23 Aug 67	★ THE LAST WALTZ *Decca F 12655*	1	27 wks
10 Jan 68	● AM I THAT EASY TO FORGET *Decca F 12722*	3	13 wks
24 Apr 68	● A MAN WITHOUT LOVE *Decca F 12770*	2	15 wks
25 Sep 68	● LES BICYCLETTES DE BELSIZE *Decca F 12834*	5	15 wks
5 Feb 69	● THE WAY IT USED TO BE *Decca F 12879*	3	14 wks
9 Aug 69	I'M A BETTER MAN *Decca F 12957*	15	13 wks
15 Nov 69	● WINTER WORLD OF LOVE *Decca F 12980*	7	13 wks
30 May 70	MY MARIE *Decca F 13032*	31	7 wks
12 Sep 70	SWEETHEART *Decca F 13068*	22	6 wks
31 Oct 70	SWEETHEART (re-entry) *Decca F 13068*	50	1 wk
11 Sep 71	ANOTHER TIME ANOTHER PLACE *Decca F 13212*	13	12 wks
4 Mar 72	TOO BEAUTIFUL TO LAST *Decca F 13281*	14	10 wks
20 Oct 73	LOVE IS ALL *Decca F 13443*	44	3 wks
17 Nov 73	LOVE IS ALL (re-entry) *Decca F 13443*	45	1 wk

Geraldine HUNT	Canada, female vocalist		5 wks
25 Oct 80	CAN'T FAKE THE FEELING *Champagne FIZZ 501*	44	5 wks

Marsha HUNT	US, female vocalist		3 wks
21 May 69	WALK ON GILDED SPLINTERS *Track 604 030*	46	2 wks
2 May 70	KEEP THE CUSTOMER SATISFIED *Track 604 037*	41	1 wk

Tommy HUNT	US, male vocalist		17 wks
11 Oct 75	CRACKIN' UP *Spark SRL 1132*	39	5 wks
21 Aug 76	LOVING ON THE LOSING SIDE *Spark SRL 1146*	28	9 wks
4 Dec 76	ONE FINE MORNING *Spark SRL 1148*	44	3 wks

Ian HUNTER	UK, male vocalist		10 wks
3 May 75	ONCE BITTEN TWICE SHY *CBS 3194*	14	10 wks

Tab HUNTER	US, male vocalist		30 wks
8 Feb 57	★ YOUNG LOVE *London HLD 8380*	1	18 wks
12 Apr 57	● 99 WAYS *London HLD 8410*	5	11 wks
5 Jul 57	99 WAYS (re-entry) *London HLD 8410*	29	1 wk

Steve 'Silk' HURLEY	US, male vocalist		9 wks
10 Jan 87	★ JACK YOUR BODY *DJ International LON 117*	1	9 wks

HURRICANES – *See JOHNNY and the HURRICANES*

Phil HURTT	US, male vocalist		5 wks
11 Nov 78	GIVING IT BACK *Fantasy FTC 161*	36	5 wks

Willie HUTCH	US, male vocalist		8 wks
4 Dec 82	IN AND OUT *Motown TMG 1285*	51	7 wks
6 Jul 85	KEEP ON JAMMIN' *Motown ZB 40173*	73	1 wk

June HUTTON	US, female vocalist		7 wks
7 Aug 53	● SAY YOU'RE MINE AGAIN *Capitol CL 13918*	10	3 wks
4 Sep 53	● SAY YOU'RE MINE AGAIN (re-entry) *Capitol CL 13918*	6	4 wks

Brian HYLAND	US, male vocalist		72 wks
7 Jul 60	● ITSY BITSY TEENY WEENY YELLOW POLKA DOT BIKINI *London HLR 9161*	8	13 wks
20 Oct 60	FOUR LITTLE HEELS *London HLR 9203*	29	6 wks
10 May 62	● GINNY COME LATELY *HMV POP 1013*	5	15 wks
2 Aug 62	● SEALED WITH A KISS *HMV POP 1051*	3	15 wks
8 Nov 62	WARMED OVER KISSES *HMV POP 1079*	28	6 wks
27 Mar 71	GYPSY WOMAN *Uni UN 530*	45	1 wk
10 Apr 71	GYPSY WOMAN (re-entry) *Uni UN 530*	42	5 wks
28 Jun 75	● SEALED WITH A KISS (re-issue) *ABC 4059*	7	11 wks

Sheila HYLTON	Jamaica, female vocalist		12 wks
15 Sep 79	BREAKFAST IN BED *United Artists BP 304*	57	5 wks
17 Jan 81	THE BED'S TOO BIG WITHOUT YOU *Island WIP 6671*	35	7 wks

Phyllis HYMAN	US, female vocalist		9 wks
16 Feb 80	YOU KNOW HOW TO LOVE ME *Arista ARIST 323*	47	6 wks
12 Sep 81	YOU SURE LOOK GOOD TO ME *Arista ARIST 424*	56	3 wks

Dick HYMAN TRIO			10 wks
US, male instrumental group, Dick Hyman, keyboards			
16 Mar 56	● THEME FROM 'THE THREEPENNY OPERA' *MGM 890*	9	10 wks

HYSTERICS	UK, male vocal/instrumental group		5 wks
12 Dec 81	JINGLE BELLS LAUGHING ALL THE WAY *Record Delivery KA 5*	44	5 wks

Janis IAN	US, female vocalist		10 wks
17 Nov 79	FLY TOO HIGH *CBS 7936*	44	7 wks
28 Jun 80	THE OTHER SIDE OF THE SUN *CBS 8611*	44	3 wks

ICEHOUSE	New Zealand, male vocal/instrumental group		28 wks
5 Feb 83	HEY LITTLE GIRL *Chrysalis CHS 2670*	17	10 wks
23 Apr 83	STREET CAFE *Chrysalis COOL 1*	62	4 wks
3 May 86	NO PROMISES *Chrysalis CHS 2978*	72	1 wk
29 Aug 87	CRAZY *Chrysalis CHS 3156*	74	1 wk
13 Feb 88	CRAZY (re-entry) *Chrysalis CHS 3156*	38	8 wks
14 May 88	ELECTRIC BLUE *Chrysalis CHS 3239*	53	4 wks

ICE-T	US, male rapper		4 wks
18 Mar 89	HIGH ROLLERS *Sire W 7574*	63	2 wks
17 Feb 90	YOU PLAYED YOURSELF *Sire W 9994*	64	2 wks

See also Curtis Mayfield and Ice-T.

ICICLE WORKS	UK, male vocal/instrumental group		28 wks
24 Dec 83	LOVE IS A WONDERFUL COLOUR *Beggars Banquet BEG 99*	15	8 wks
10 Mar 84	BIRDS FLY (WHISPER TO A SCREAM)/ IN THE CAULDRON OF LOVE *Beggars Banquet BEG 108*	53	4 wks
26 Jul 86	UNDERSTANDING JANE *Beggars Banquet BEG 160*	52	3 wks
4 Oct 86	WHO DO YOU WANT FOR YOUR LOVE *Beggars Banquet BEG 172*	54	4 wks
14 Feb 87	EVANGELINE *Beggars Banquet BEG 181*	53	4 wks
30 Apr 88	LITTLE GIRL LOST *Beggars Banquet BEG 215*	59	4 wks
17 Mar 90	MOTORCYCLE RIDER *Epic WORKS 100*	73	1 wk

IDES OF MARCH	US, male vocal/instrumental group		9 wks
6 Jun 70	VEHICLE *Warner Bros. WB 7378*	31	9 wks

Billy IDOL	UK, male vocalist		99 wks
11 Sep 82	HOT IN THE CITY *Chrysalis CHS 2625*	58	4 wks
24 Mar 84	REBEL YELL *Chrysalis IDOL 2*	62	2 wks
30 Jun 84	EYES WITHOUT A FACE *Chrysalis IDOL 3*	18	11 wks
29 Sep 84	FLESH FOR FANTASY *Chrysalis IDOL 4*	54	3 wks
13 Jul 85	● WHITE WEDDING *Chrysalis IDOL 5*	6	15 wks

HOTHOUSE FLOWERS
are shown at a 1988 New
York party with the stars of a
previous century.

Once he had moved to
America, it took time for
BILLY IDOL to be taken
seriously at home. His first
two Top Ten hits were
reissues of songs initially
released during this problem
period.

14 Sep 85	● REBEL YELL (re-issue) *Chrysalis IDOL 6*	6	12 wks
4 Oct 86	TO BE A LOVER *Chrysalis IDOL 8*	22	8 wks
7 Mar 87	DON'T NEED A GUN *Chrysalis IDOL 9*	26	5 wks
13 Jun 87	SWEET SIXTEEN *Chrysalis IDOL 10*	17	9 wks
3 Oct 87	● MONY MONY *Chrysalis IDOL 11*	7	10 wks
16 Jan 88	HOT IN THE CITY (re-mix) *Chrysalis IDOL 12*	13	9 wks
13 Aug 88	CATCH MY FALL *Chrysalis IDOL 13*	63	3 wks
28 Apr 90	CRADLE OF LOVE *Chrysalis IDOL 14*	34	4 wks
11 Aug 90	L.A. WOMAN *Chrysalis IDOL 15*	70	2 wks
22 Dec 90	PRODIGAL BLUES *Chrysalis IDOL 16*	47†	2 wks

Frank IFIELD *UK, male vocalist*   **158 wks**

19 Feb 60	LUCKY DEVIL *Columbia DB 4399*	22	5 wks
7 Apr 60	LUCKY DEVIL (re-entry) *Columbia DB 4399*	33	2 wks
29 Sep 60	GOTTA GET A DATE *Columbia DB 4496*	49	1 wk
5 Jul 62	★ I REMEMBER YOU *Columbia DB 4856*	1	28 wks
25 Oct 62	★ LOVESICK BLUES *Columbia DB 4913*	1	17 wks
24 Jan 63	★ WAYWARD WIND *Columbia DB 4960*	1	13 wks
11 Apr 63	● NOBODY'S DARLIN' BUT MINE *Columbia DB 7007*	4	16 wks
27 Jun 63	★ CONFESSIN' *Columbia DB 7062*	1	16 wks
17 Oct 63	MULE TRAIN *Columbia DB 7131*	22	6 wks
9 Jan 64	● DON'T BLAME ME *Columbia DB 7184*	8	13 wks
23 Apr 64	ANGRY AT THE BIG OAK TREE *Columbia DB 7263*	25	8 wks
23 Jul 64	I SHOULD CARE *Columbia DB 7319*	33	3 wks
1 Oct 64	SUMMER IS OVER *Columbia DB 7355*	25	6 wks
19 Aug 65	PARADISE *Columbia DB 7655*	26	9 wks
23 Jun 66	NO ONE WILL EVER KNOW *Columbia DB 7940*	25	4 wks
8 Dec 66	CALL HER YOUR SWEETHEART *Columbia DB 8078*	24	11 wks

Julio IGLESIAS *Spain, male vocalist*   **48 wks**

24 Oct 81	★ BEGIN THE BEGUINE (VOLVER A EMPEZAR) *CBS A 1612*	1	14 wks
6 Mar 82	● QUIEREME MUCHO (YOURS) *CBS A 1939*	3	9 wks
9 Oct 82	AMOR *CBS A 2801*	32	7 wks
9 Apr 83	HEY! *CBS JULIO 1*	31	7 wks
6 Aug 88	● MY LOVE *CBS JULIO 2*	5	11 wks

My Love features Stevie Wonder. See also Stevie Wonder; Julio Iglesias and Willie Nelson; Julio Iglesias and Diana Ross.

Julio IGLESIAS and Willie NELSON   **10 wks**
Spain/US, male vocal duo

7 Apr 84	TO ALL THE GIRLS I'VE LOVED BEFORE *CBS A 4252*	17	10 wks

See also Julio Iglesias; Willie Nelson.

Julio IGLESIAS and Diana ROSS   **8 wks**
Spain/US, male/female vocal duo

7 Jul 84	ALL OF YOU *CBS A 4522*	43	8 wks

See also Julio Iglesias; Diana Ross.

I-LEVEL *UK, male vocal/instrumental group*   **9 wks**

16 Apr 83	MINEFIELD *Virgin VS 563*	52	6 wks
18 Jun 83	TEACHER *Virgin VS 595*	56	3 wks

IMAGINATION *UK, male vocal/instrumental group*   **105 wks**

16 May 81	● BODY TALK *R & B RBS 201*	4	18 wks
5 Sep 81	IN AND OUT OF LOVE *R & B RBS 202*	16	9 wks
14 Nov 81	FLASHBACK *R & B RBS 206*	16	13 wks
6 Mar 82	● JUST AN ILLUSION *R & B RBS 208*	2	11 wks
26 Jun 82	● MUSIC AND LIGHTS *R & B RBS 210*	5	9 wks
25 Sep 82	IN THE HEAT OF THE NIGHT *R & B RBS 211*	22	8 wks
11 Dec 82	CHANGES *R & B RBS 213*	31	8 wks
4 Jun 83	LOOKING AT MIDNIGHT *R & B RBS 214*	29	7 wks

5 Nov 83	NEW DIMENSIONS *R & B RBS 216*	56	3 wks
26 May 84	STATE OF LOVE *R & B RBS 218*	67	2 wks
24 Nov 84	THANK YOU MY LOVE *R & B RBS 219*	22	15 wks
16 Jan 88	INSTINCTUAL *RCA PB 41697*	62	2 wks

IMMACULATE FOOLS   **4 wks**
UK, male vocal/instrumental group

26 Jan 85	IMMACULATE FOOLS *A & M AM 227*	51	4 wks

IMPALAS *US, male vocal group*   **1 wk**

21 Aug 59	SORRY (I RAN ALL THE WAY HOME) *MGM 1015*	28	1 wk

IMPEDANCE *UK, male producer*   **4 wks**

11 Nov 89	TAINTED LOVE *Jumpin' & Pumpin' TOT 4*	54	4 wks

IMPERIALS *US, male vocal group*   **9 wks**

24 Dec 77	WHO'S GONNA LOVE ME *Power Exchange PX 266*	17	9 wks

See also Little Anthony and the Imperials.

IMPOSTER   **7 wks**
UK, male vocalist, Elvis Costello under an assumed name

11 Jun 83	PILLS AND SOAP *Imp IMP 001*	16	4 wks
28 Apr 84	PEACE IN OUR TIME *Imposter TRUCE 1*	48	3 wks

See also Elvis Costello and the Attractions.

IMPRESSIONS *US, male vocal group*   **10 wks**

22 Nov 75	FIRST IMPRESSIONS *Curtom K 16638*	16	10 wks

IN CROWD *UK, male vocal/instrumental group*   **1 wk**

20 May 65	THAT'S HOW STRONG MY LOVE IS *Parlophone R 5276*	48	1 wk

IN TUA NUA *Ireland, male/female vocal/instrumental group*   **2 wks**

14 May 88	ALL I WANTED *Virgin VS 1072*	69	2 wks

INCANTATION *UK, male instrumental group*   **12 wks**

4 Dec 82	CACHARPAYA (ANDES PUMPSA DAESI) *Beggars Banquet BEG 84*	12	12 wks

INCOGNITO *France, male instrumental group*   **2 wks**

15 Nov 80	PARISIENNE GIRL *Ensign ENY 44*	73	2 wks

INDEEP *US, male/female vocal duo*   **11 wks**

22 Jan 83	LAST NIGHT A DJ SAVED MY LIFE *Sound of New York SNY 1*	13	9 wks
14 May 83	WHEN BOYS TALK *Sound of New York SNY 3*	67	2 wks

Los INDIOS TABAJARAS
Brazil, male instrumental duo - guitars

				17 wks
31 Oct 63	● MARIA ELENA *RCA 1365*	**5**	17 wks

INGRAM *US, male vocal/instrumental group*

				2 wks
11 Jun 83	SMOOTHIN' GROOVIN' *Streetwave WAVE 3*	**56**	2 wks

James INGRAM with Michael McDONALD
US, male vocal duo

				16 wks
18 Feb 84	YAH MO B THERE *Qwest W 9394*	**44**	5 wks
7 Apr 84	YAH MO B THERE (re-entry) *Qwest W 9394*	**69**	3 wks
12 Jan 85	YAH MO B THERE (2nd re-entry) *Qwest W 9394*	**12**	8 wks

The 85 entry is a re-mix of the original hit, with the same catalogue number. See also Patti Austin and James Ingram; Linda Ronstadt and James Ingram; Quincy Jones; Michael McDonald.

INK SPOTS *US, male vocal group*

				4 wks
29 Apr 55	● MELODY OF LOVE *Parlophone MSP 6152*	**10**	4 wks

John INMAN *UK, male vocalist*

				6 wks
25 Oct 75	ARE YOU BEING SERVED SIR *DJM DJS 602*	**39**	6 wks

INMATES *UK, male vocal/instrumental group*

				9 wks
8 Dec 79	THE WALK *Radar ADA 47*	**36**	9 wks

INNER CIRCLE *Jamaica, male vocal/instrumental group*

				11 wks
24 Feb 79	EVERYTHING IS GREAT *Island WIP 6472*	**37**	8 wks
12 May 79	STOP BREAKING MY HEART *Island WIP 6488*	**50**	3 wks

INNER CITY *US, male/female vocal/instrumental group*

				53 wks
3 Sep 88	● BIG FUN *10 TEN 240*	**8**	14 wks
10 Dec 88	● GOOD LIFE *10 TEN 249*	**4**	12 wks
22 Apr 89	● AIN'T NOBODY BETTER *10 TEN 252*	**10**	7 wks
29 Jul 89	DO YOU LOVE WHAT YOU FEEL *10 TEN 237*	**16**	7 wks
18 Nov 89	WATCHA GONNA DO WITH MY LOVIN' *10 TEN 290*	**12**	9 wks
13 Oct 90	THAT MAN (HE'S ALL MINE) *10 TEN 334*	**42**	4 wks

Big Fun features Kevin Saunderson.

INNOCENCE *UK, male/female vocal/instrumental group*

				22 wks
3 Mar 90	NATURAL THING *Cooltempo COOL 201*	**16**	7 wks
21 Jul 90	SILENT VOICE *Cooltempo COOL 212*	**37**	5 wks
13 Oct 90	LET'S PUSH IT *Cooltempo COOL 220*	**25**	6 wks
8 Dec 90	A MATTER OF FACT *Cooltempo COOL 223*	**37†**	4 wks

INSPIRAL CARPETS *UK, male vocal/instrumental group* 20 wks

18 Nov 89	MOVE *Cow DUNG 6*	**49**	2 wks
17 Mar 90	THIS IS HOW IT FEELS *Cow DUNG 7*	**14**	8 wks
30 Jun 90	SHE COMES IN THE FALL *Cow DUNG 10*	**27**	6 wks
17 Nov 90	ISLAND HEAD (EP) *Cow DUNG 11*	**21**	4 wks

Tracks on Island Head EP: *Biggest Mountain/Weakness/I'll Keep It In Mind/Gold Top.*

INSPIRATIONAL CHOIR *US, male/female choir*

				11 wks
22 Dec 84	ABIDE WITH ME *Epic A 4997*	**44**	5 wks
14 Dec 85	ABIDE WITH ME (re-issue) *Portrait A 4997*	**36**	6 wks

Label credits the Royal Choral Society.

INSTANT FUNK *US, male vocal/instrumental group*

				5 wks
20 Jan 79	GOT MY MIND MADE UP *Salsoul SSOL 114*	**46**	5 wks

INTELLIGENT HOODLUM *US, male rap group*

				3 wks
6 Oct 90	BACK TO REALITY *A & M AM 598*	**55**	3 wks

INTRUDERS *US, male vocal group*

				21 wks
13 Apr 74	I'LL ALWAYS LOVE MY MAMA *Philadelphia International PIR 2149*	**32**	7 wks
6 Jul 74	(WIN PLACE OR SHOW) SHE'S A WINNER *Philadelphia International PIR 2212*	**14**	9 wks
22 Dec 84	WHO DO YOU LOVE? *Streetwave KHAN 34*	**65**	5 wks

INVISIBLE GIRLS – *See Pauline MURRAY and the INVISIBLE GIRLS*

INXS *Australia, male vocal/instrumental group* 65 wks

19 Apr 86	WHAT YOU NEED *Mercury INXS 5*	**51**	6 wks
28 Jun 86	LISTEN LIKE THIEVES *Mercury INXS 6*	**46**	7 wks
30 Aug 86	KISS THE DIRT (FALLING DOWN THE MOUNTAIN) *Mercury INXS 7*	**54**	3 wks
24 Oct 87	NEED YOU TONIGHT *Mercury INXS 8*	**58**	3 wks
9 Jan 88	NEW SENSATION *Mercury INXS 9*	**25**	6 wks
12 Mar 88	DEVIL INSIDE *Mercury INXS 10*	**47**	5 wks
25 Jun 88	NEVER TEAR US APART *Mercury INXS 11*	**24**	7 wks
12 Nov 88	● NEED YOU TONIGHT (re-issue) *Mercury INXS 12*	**2**	11 wks
8 Apr 89	MYSTIFY *Mercury INXS 13*	**14**	7 wks
15 Sep 90	SUICIDE BLONDE *Mercury INXS 14*	**11**	6 wks
8 Dec 90	DISAPPEAR *Mercury INXS 15*	**21†**	4 wks

Tippa IRIE *UK, male vocalist*

				10 wks
22 Mar 86	HELLO DARLING *Greensleeves/UK Bubblers TIPPA 4*	**22**	7 wks
19 Jul 86	HEARTBEAT *Greensleeves/UK Bubblers TIPPA 5*	**59**	3 wks

IRON MAIDEN *UK, male vocal/instrumental group* 119 wks

23 Feb 80	RUNNING FREE *EMI 5032*	**34**	5 wks
7 Jun 80	SANCTUARY *EMI 5065*	**29**	5 wks
8 Nov 80	WOMEN IN UNIFORM *EMI 5105*	**35**	4 wks
14 Mar 81	TWILIGHT ZONE/ WRATH CHILD *EMI 5145*	**31**	5 wks
27 Jun 81	PURGATORY *EMI 5184*	**52**	3 wks
26 Sep 81	MAIDEN JAPAN *EMI 5219*	**43**	4 wks
20 Feb 82	● RUN TO THE HILLS *EMI 5263*	**7**	10 wks
15 May 82	THE NUMBER OF THE BEAST *EMI 5287*	**18**	8 wks
23 Apr 83	FLIGHT OF ICARUS *EMI 5378*	**11**	6 wks
2 Jul 83	THE TROOPER *EMI 5397*	**12**	7 wks
18 Aug 84	2 MINUTES TO MIDNIGHT *EMI 5849*	**11**	6 wks
3 Nov 84	ACES HIGH *EMI 5502*	**20**	5 wks
5 Oct 85	RUNNING FREE (LIVE) *EMI 5532*	**19**	5 wks
14 Dec 85	RUN TO THE HILLS (LIVE) *EMI 5542*	**26**	6 wks
6 Sep 86	WASTED YEARS *EMI EMI 5583*	**18**	4 wks
22 Nov 86	STRANGER IN A STRANGE LAND *EMI EMI 5589*	**22**	4 wks
27 Dec 86	STRANGER IN A STRANGE LAND (re-entry) *EMI EMI 5589*	**71**	2 wks
26 Mar 88	● CAN I PLAY WITH MADNESS *EMI EM 49*	**3**	6 wks
13 Aug 88	● THE EVIL THAT MEN DO *EMI EM 64*	**5**	6 wks
19 Nov 88	● THE CLAIRVOYANT *EMI EM 79*	**6**	6 wks
18 Nov 89	● INFINITE DREAMS *EMI EM 117*	**6**	5 wks
30 Dec 89	INFINITE DREAMS (re-entry) *EMI EM 117*	**74**	1 wk

22 Sep 90 ●	HOLY SMOKE *EMI EM 153*	3	4 wks

IRONHORSE *Canada, male vocal/instrumental group* **3 wks**

5 May 79	SWEET LUI-LOUISE *Scotti Brothers K 11271*	60	3 wks

Big Dee IRWIN *US, male vocalist* **17 wks**

21 Nov 63 ●	SWINGING ON A STAR *Colpix PX 11010*	7	17 wks

This hit was in fact a vocal duet by Big Dee Irwin and Little Eva, though Little Eva was not credited. See also Little Eva.

Chris ISAAK *US, male vocalist/instrumentalist* **6 wks**

24 Nov 90 ●	WICKED GAME *London LON 279*	10†	6 wks

ISLEY – *See Rod STEWART*

ISLEY BROTHERS *US, male vocal/instrumental group* **108 wks**

25 Jul 63	TWIST AND SHOUT *Stateside SS 112*	42	1 wk
28 Apr 66	THIS OLD HEART OF MINE *Tamla Motown TMG 555*	47	1 wk
1 Sep 66	I GUESS I'LL ALWAYS LOVE YOU *Tamla Motown TMG 572*	45	2 wks
23 Oct 68 ●	THIS OLD HEART OF MINE (re-entry) *Tamla Motown TMG 555*	3	16 wks
15 Jan 69	I GUESS I'LL ALWAYS LOVE YOU (re-issue) *Tamla Motown TMG 683*	11	9 wks
16 Apr 69 ●	BEHIND A PAINTED SMILE *Tamla Motown TMG 693*	5	12 wks
25 Jun 69	IT'S YOUR THING *Major Minor MM 621*	30	5 wks
30 Aug 69	PUT YOURSELF IN MY PLACE *Tamla Motown TMG 708*	13	11 wks
22 Sep 73	THAT LADY *Epic EPC 1704*	14	9 wks
19 Jan 74	HIGHWAY OF MY LIFE *Epic EPC 1980*	25	8 wks
25 May 74	SUMMER BREEZE *Epic EPC 2244*	16	8 wks
10 Jul 76 ●	HARVEST FOR THE WORLD *Epic EPC 4369*	10	8 wks
13 May 78	TAKE ME TO THE NEXT PHASE *Epic EPC 6292*	50	4 wks
3 Nov 79	IT'S A DISCO NIGHT (ROCK DON'T STOP) *Epic EPC 7911*	14	11 wks
16 Jul 83	BETWEEN THE SHEETS *Epic A 3513*	52	3 wks

ISLEY JASPER ISLEY *US, male vocal/instrumental group* **5 wks**

23 Nov 85	CARAVAN OF LOVE *Epic A 6612*	52	5 wks

IT BITES *UK, male vocal/instrumental group* **21 wks**

12 Jul 86 ●	CALLING ALL THE HEROES *Virgin VS 872*	6	12 wks
18 Oct 86	WHOLE NEW WORLD *Virgin VS 896*	54	3 wks
23 May 87	THE OLD MAN AND THE ANGEL *Virgin VS 941*	72	1 wk
13 May 89	STILL TOO YOUNG TO REMEMBER *Virgin VS 1184*	66	3 wks
24 Feb 90	STILL TOO YOUNG TO REMEMBER (re-issue) *Virgin VS 1238*	60	2 wks

IT'S IMMATERIAL *UK, male vocal/instrumental group* **10 wks**

12 Apr 86	DRIVING AWAY FROM HOME (JIM'S TUNE) *Siren SIREN 15*	18	7 wks
2 Aug 86	ED'S FUNKY DINER (FRIDAY NIGHT, SATURDAY MORNING) *Siren SIREN 24*	65	3 wks

Burl IVES *US, male vocalist* **25 wks**

25 Jan 62 ●	A LITTLE BITTY TEAR *Brunswick 05863*	9	15 wks
17 May 62	FUNNY WAY OF LAUGHIN' *Brunswick 05868*	29	10 wks

IVY LEAGUE *UK, male vocal group* **31 wks**

4 Feb 65 ●	FUNNY HOW LOVE CAN BE *Piccadilly 7N 35222*	8	9 wks
6 May 65	THAT'S WHY I'M CRYING *Piccadilly 7N 35228*	22	8 wks
24 Jun 65 ●	TOSSING AND TURNING *Piccadilly 7N 35251*	3	13 wks
14 Jul 66	WILLOW TREE *Piccadilly 7N 35326*	50	1 wk

IVYS – *See HOLLY and the IVYS*

IZIT *UK, male/female vocal/instrumental group* **3 wks**

2 Dec 89	STORIES *FFRR F 122*	52	3 wks

J

JACK 'N' CHILL *UK, male instrumental group* **21 wks**

6 Jun 87	THE JACK THAT HOUSE BUILT *Oval TEN 174*	48	5 wks
9 Jan 88 ●	THE JACK THAT HOUSE BUILT (re-entry) *Oval TEN 174*	6	11 wks
9 Jul 88	BEATIN' THE HEAT *10 TEN 234*	42	5 wks

Terry JACKS *Canada, male vocalist* **21 wks**

23 Mar 74 ★	SEASONS IN THE SUN *Bell 1344*	1	12 wks
29 Jun 74 ●	IF YOU GO AWAY *Bell 1362*	8	9 wks

Chad JACKSON *UK, male producer* **10 wks**

2 Jun 90 ●	HEAR THE DRUMMER (GET WICKED) *Big Wave BWR 36*	3	10 wks

Dee D. JACKSON *UK, female vocalist* **14 wks**

22 Apr 78 ●	AUTOMATIC LOVER *Mercury 6007 171*	4	9 wks
2 Sep 78	METEOR MAN *Mercury 6007 182*	48	5 wks

Freddie JACKSON *US, male vocalist* **25 wks**

23 Nov 85	YOU ARE MY LADY *Capitol CL 379*	49	4 wks
22 Feb 86	ROCK ME TONIGHT (FOR OLD TIME'S SAKE) *Capitol CL 358*	18	9 wks
11 Oct 86	TASTY LOVE *Capitol CL 428*	73	1 wk
7 Feb 87	HAVE YOU EVER LOVED SOMEBODY *Capitol CL 437*	33	6 wks
9 Jul 88	NICE 'N' SLOW *Capitol CL 502*	56	2 wks
15 Oct 88	CRAZY (FOR ME) *Capitol CL 510*	41	3 wks

Janet JACKSON *US, female vocalist* **96 wks**

22 Mar 86 ●	WHAT HAVE YOU DONE FOR ME LATELY *A & M AM 308*	3	14 wks
31 May 86	NASTY *A & M AM 316*	19	9 wks
9 Aug 86 ●	WHEN I THINK OF YOU *A & M AM 337*	10	10 wks
1 Nov 86	CONTROL *A & M AM 359*	42	5 wks
21 Mar 87 ●	LET'S WAIT AWHILE *A & M AM 601*	3	10 wks
13 Jun 87	PLEASURE PRINCIPLE *Breakout USA 604*	24	5 wks
14 Nov 87	FUNNY HOW TIME FLIES (WHEN YOU'RE HAVING FUN) *Breakout USA 613*	59	2 wks
2 Sep 89	MISS YOU MUCH *Breakout USA 663*	25	5 wks
4 Nov 89	RHYTHM NATION *Breakout USA 673*	23	5 wks
27 Jan 90	COME BACK TO ME *Breakout USA 681*	20	7 wks
31 Mar 90	ESCAPADE *Breakout USA 684*	17	7 wks

MICHAEL JACKSON received an Honorary Doctorate from the United Negro College Fund in a 1988 ceremony attended by his producer Quincy Jones (left) and Whitney Houston.

Relief pitchers on the 1990 baseball champion Cincinnati Reds called themselves the 'Nasty Boys' after the 1986 hit by JANET JACKSON, shown here with date Rene Elizando.

(continued)

7 Jul 90		**ALRIGHT** *A & M USA 693*	**20** 5 wks
8 Sep 90		**BLACK CAT** *A & M AM 587*........................	**15** 6 wks
27 Oct 90		**LOVE WILL NEVER DO (WITHOUT YOU)** *A & M AM 700*	**34** 4 wks

See also Herb Alpert.

Jermaine JACKSON *US, male vocalist* **41 wks**

10 May 80	●	**LET'S GET SERIOUS** *Motown TMG 1183*	**8** 11 wks
26 Jul 80		**BURNIN' HOT** *Motown TMG 1194*	**32** 6 wks
30 May 81		**YOU LIKE ME DON'T YOU** *Motown TMG 1222*	**41** 5 wks
12 May 84		**SWEETEST SWEETEST** *Arista JJK 1*	**52** 4 wks
16 Feb 85	●	**DO WHAT YOU DO** *Arista ARIST 609*	**6** 13 wks
21 Oct 89		**DON'T TAKE IT PERSONAL** *Arista 112634*..............	**69** 2 wks

See also Jackson Five; Jermaine Jackson and Pia Zadora.

Jermaine JACKSON and Pia ZADORA **2 wks**
US, male/female vocal duo

27 Oct 84		**WHEN THE RAIN BEGINS TO FALL** *Arista ARIST 584*	**68** 2 wks

See also Jermaine Jackson; Pia.

Joe JACKSON *UK, male vocalist* **40 wks**

4 Aug 79		**IS SHE REALLY GOING OUT WITH HIM?** *A & M AMS 7459*........................	**13** 9 wks
12 Jan 80	●	**IT'S DIFFERENT FOR GIRLS** *A & M AMS 7493*..............	**5** 9 wks
4 Jul 81		**JUMPIN' JIVE** *A & M AMS 8145*	**43** 5 wks
8 Jan 83	●	**STEPPIN' OUT** *A & M AMS 8262*	**6** 8 wks
12 Mar 83		**BREAKING US IN TWO** *A & M AM 101*..............	**59** 4 wks
28 Apr 84		**HAPPY ENDING** *A & M AM 186*	**58** 3 wks
7 Jul 84		**BE MY NUMBER TWO** *A & M AM 200*	**70** 2 wks

Jumpin' Jive credited to Joe Jackson's Jumpin' Jive. See also Suzanne Vega.

Michael JACKSON *US, male vocalist* **272 wks**

12 Feb 72	●	**GOT TO BE THERE** *Tamla Motown TMG 797*	**5** 11 wks
20 May 72	●	**ROCKIN' ROBIN** *Tamla Motown TMG 816*	**3** 14 wks
19 Aug 72	●	**AIN'T NO SUNSHINE** *Tamla Motown TMG 826*	**8** 11 wks
25 Nov 72	●	**BEN** *Tamla Motown TMG 834*........................	**7** 14 wks
15 Sep 79		**DON'T STOP TILL YOU GET ENOUGH** *Epic EPC 7763*	**3** 12 wks
24 Nov 79	●	**OFF THE WALL** *Epic EPC 8045*	**7** 10 wks
9 Feb 80	●	**ROCK WITH YOU** *Epic EPC 8206*	**7** 9 wks
3 May 80	●	**SHE'S OUT OF MY LIFE** *Epic EPC 8384*	**3** 9 wks
26 Jul 80		**GIRLFRIEND** *Epic EPC 8782*........................	**41** 5 wks
23 May 81	★	**ONE DAY IN YOUR LIFE** *Motown TMG 976*........	**1** 14 wks
1 Aug 81		**WE'RE ALMOST THERE** *Motown TMG 977*........	**46** 3 wks
29 Jan 83	★	**BILLIE JEAN** *Epic EPC A 3084*........................	**1** 15 wks
9 Apr 83	●	**BEAT IT** *Epic EPC A 3258*	**3** 12 wks
11 Jun 83	●	**WANNA BE STARTIN' SOMETHING** *Epic A 3427*	**8** 9 wks
23 Jul 83		**HAPPY (LOVE THEME FROM 'LADY SINGS THE BLUES')** *Tamla Motown TMG 986*........................	**52** 3 wks
19 Nov 83	●	**THRILLER** *Epic A 3643*	**10** 18 wks
31 Mar 84		**P.Y.T. (PRETTY YOUNG THING)** *Epic A 4136*..............	**11** 8 wks
2 Jun 84	●	**FAREWELL MY SUMMER LOVE** *Motown TMG 1342*	**7** 12 wks
11 Aug 84		**GIRL YOU'RE SO TOGETHER** *Motown TMG 1355*	**33** 5 wks
8 Aug 87	★	**I JUST CAN'T STOP LOVING YOU** *Epic 650202 7*..........	**1** 9 wks
26 Sep 87	●	**BAD** *Epic 651155 7*........................	**3** 11 wks
5 Dec 87	●	**THE WAY YOU MAKE ME FEEL** *Epic 651275 7*	**3** 10 wks
20 Feb 88		**MAN IN THE MIRROR** *Epic 651388 7*	**21** 8 wks
16 Jul 88	●	**DIRTY DIANA** *Epic 651546 7*........................	**4** 8 wks
10 Sep 88		**ANOTHER PART OF ME** *Epic 652844 7*........................	**15** 6 wks
26 Nov 88	●	**SMOOTH CRIMINAL** *Epic 653026 7*..............	**8** 10 wks
25 Feb 89	●	**LEAVE ME ALONE** *Epic 654672 7*........................	**2** 9 wks
15 Jul 89		**LIBERIAN GIRL** *Epic 654947 0*........................	**13** 6 wks

I Just Can't Stop Loving You features Siedah Garrett. See also Jackson Five; Jacksons; Diana Ross and Michael Jackson; Michael Jackson and Paul McCartney; Stevie Wonder and Michael Jackson.

Michael JACKSON and Paul McCARTNEY **25 wks**
US/UK, male vocal duo

6 Nov 82	●	**THE GIRL IS MINE** *Epic EPC A2729*........................	**8** 9 wks
15 Jan 83		**THE GIRL IS MINE (re-entry)** *Epic EPC 2729*	**75** 1 wk
15 Oct 83	●	**SAY SAY SAY** *Parlophone R 6062*	**2** 15 wks

See also Michael Jackson; Paul McCartney. Second hit bills artists in reverse order.

Mick JACKSON *UK, male vocalist* **16 wks**

30 Sep 78		**BLAME IT ON THE BOOGIE** *Atlantic K 11102*..............	**15** 8 wks
3 Feb 79		**WEEKEND** *Atlantic K 11224*........................	**38** 8 wks

Millie JACKSON *US, female vocalist* **3 wks**

18 Nov 72		**MY MAN A SWEET MAN** *Mojo 2093 022*	**50** 1 wk
10 Mar 84		**I FEEL LIKE WALKIN' IN THE RAIN** *Sire W 9348*........	**55** 2 wks

Stonewall JACKSON *US, male vocalist* **2 wks**

17 Jul 59		**WATERLOO** *Philips PB 941*	**24** 2 wks

Tony JACKSON and the VIBRATIONS **3 wks**
UK, male vocal/instrumental group

8 Oct 64		**BYE BYE BABY** *Pye 7N 15685*........................	**38** 3 wks

Wanda JACKSON *US, female vocalist* **11 wks**

1 Sep 60		**LET'S HAVE A PARTY** *Capitol CL 15147*	**32** 8 wks
26 Jan 61		**MEAN MEAN MAN** *Capitol CL 15176*	**46** 1 wk
9 Feb 61		**MEAN MEAN MAN (re-entry)** *Capitol CL 15176*	**40** 2 wks

JACKSON FIVE *US, male vocal group* **113 wks**

31 Jan 70	●	**I WANT YOU BACK** *Tamla Motown TMG 724*..............	**2** 13 wks
16 May 70	●	**ABC** *Tamla Motown TMG 738*	**8** 11 wks
1 Aug 70	●	**THE LOVE YOU SAVE** *Tamla Motown TMG 746*........	**7** 9 wks
21 Nov 70	●	**I'LL BE THERE** *Tamla Motown TMG 758*	**4** 16 wks
10 Apr 71		**MAMA'S PEARL** *Tamla Motown TMG 769*	**25** 7 wks
17 Jul 71		**NEVER CAN SAY GOODBYE** *Tamla Motown TMG 778*......	**33** 7 wks
11 Nov 72	●	**LOOKIN' THROUGH THE WINDOWS** *Tamla Motown TMG 833*........................	**9** 11 wks
23 Dec 72		**SANTA CLAUS IS COMING TO TOWN** *Tamla Motown TMG 837*........................	**43** 3 wks
17 Feb 73	●	**DOCTOR MY EYES** *Tamla Motown TMG 842*	**9** 10 wks
9 Jun 73		**HALLELUJAH DAY** *Tamla Motown TMG 856*	**20** 9 wks
8 Sep 73		**SKYWRITER** *Tamla Motown TMG 865*	**25** 8 wks
16 Apr 88	●	**I WANT YOU BACK (re-mix)** *Motown ZB 41913*	**8** 9 wks

Eighty per cent of the group became part of the Jacksons and moved to Epic records. The remix of I Want You Back is credited to Michael Jackson with the Jackson Five. See also Jacksons; Michael Jackson; Jermaine Jackson.

JACKSON SISTERS *US, female vocal group* **2 wks**

20 Jun 87		**I BELIEVE IN MIRACLES** *Urban URB 4*	**72** 2 wks

JACKSONS *US, male vocal group* **122 wks**

9 Apr 77		**ENJOY YOURSELF** *Epic EPC 5063*........................	**42** 4 wks
4 Jun 77	★	**SHOW YOU THE WAY TO GO** *Epic EPC 5266*	**1** 10 wks
13 Aug 77		**DREAMER** *Epic EPC 5458*	**22** 9 wks
5 Nov 77		**GOIN' PLACES** *Epic EPC 5732*	**26** 7 wks
11 Feb 78		**EVEN THOUGH YOU'VE GONE** *Epic EPC 5919*	**31** 4 wks
23 Sep 78	●	**BLAME IT ON THE BOOGIE** *Epic EPC 6683*..............	**8** 12 wks

3 Feb 79	DESTINY *Epic EPC 6983*	39	6wks
24 Mar 79 ●	SHAKE YOUR BODY (DOWN TO THE GROUND)		
	Epic EPC 7181.	4	12wks
25 Oct 80	LOVELY ONE *Epic EPC 9302*	29	6wks
13 Dec 80	HEARTBREAK HOTEL *Epic EPC 9391*	44	6wks
28 Feb 81 ●	CAN YOU FEEL IT *Epic EPC 9554*	6	15wks
4 Jul 81 ●	WALK RIGHT NOW *Epic EPC A 1294*	7	11wks
7 Jul 84	STATE OF SHOCK *Epic A 4431*	14	8wks
8 Sep 84	TORTURE *Epic A 4675*	26	6wks
13 May 89	NOTHIN' (THAT COMPARES 2 U) *EPIC 654808 7* 33		6wks

The Jacksons were the Jackson Five minus Jermaine, plus other relatives too young to perform in Jackson Five days. Jermaine Jackson did appear on Torture. State Of Shock *credits lead vocal to Mick Jagger and Michael Jackson. See also Jackson Five; Michael Jackson; Mick Jagger.*

JACKY – *See Jackie LEE*

JAGGED EDGE *UK, male vocal/instrumental group* — 2 wks

15 Sep 90	YOU DON'T LOVE ME *Polydor PO 97*	66	2 wks

Mick JAGGER *UK, male vocalist* — 18 wks

14 Nov 70	MEMO FROM TURNER *Decca F 13067*	32	5 wks
16 Feb 85	JUST ANOTHER NIGHT *CBS A 4722*	32	6 wks
12 Sep 87	LET'S WORK *CBS 651028 7*	31	7 wks

See also David Bowie and Mick Jagger; Jacksons.

JAGS *UK, male vocal/instrumental group* — 11 wks

8 Sep 79	BACK OF MY HAND *Island WIP 6501*	17	10 wks
2 Feb 80	WOMAN'S WORLD *Island WIP 6531*	75	1 wk

J.A.L.N. BAND *UK/Jamaica, male vocal/instrumental group* — 17 wks

11 Sep 76	DISCO MUSIC/ I LIKE IT *Magnet MAG 73*	21	9 wks
27 Aug 77	I GOT TO SING *Magnet MAG 97*	40	4 wks
1 Jul 78	GET UP *Magnet MAG 118*	53	4 wks

JAM *UK, male vocal/instrumental group* — 201 wks

7 May 77	IN THE CITY *Polydor 2058 866*	40	6 wks
23 Jul 77	ALL AROUND THE WORLD *Polydor 2058 903*	13	8 wks
5 Nov 77	THE MODERN WORLD *Polydor 2058 945*	36	4 wks
11 Mar 78	NEWS OF THE WORLD *Polydor 2058 995*	27	5 wks
26 Aug 78	DAVID WATTS/ 'A' BOMB IN WARDOUR STREET		
	Polydor 2059 054	25	8 wks
21 Oct 78	DOWN IN THE TUBE STATION AT MIDNIGHT		
	Polydor POSP 8	15	7 wks
17 Mar 79	STRANGE TOWN *Polydor POSP 34*	15	9 wks
25 Aug 79	WHEN YOU'RE YOUNG *Polydor POSP 69*	17	7 wks
3 Nov 79 ●	THE ETON RIFLES *Polydor POSP 83*	3	12 wks
22 Mar 80 ★	GOING UNDERGROUND/ DREAMS OF CHILDREN		
	Polydor POSP 113	1	9 wks
26 Apr 80	ALL AROUND THE WORLD (re-entry)		
	Polydor 2058 903	43	3 wks
26 Apr 80	DAVID WATTS/ 'A'BOMB IN WARDOUR STREET (re-entry) *Polydor 2059 054*	54	3 wks
26 Apr 80	IN THE CITY (re-entry) *Polydor 2058 866*	40	4 wks
26 Apr 80	NEWS OF THE WORLD (re-entry) *Polydor 2058 995*	53	3 wks
26 Apr 80	STRANGE TOWN (re-entry) *Polydor POSP 34*	44	4 wks
26 Apr 80	THE MODERN WORLD (re-entry) *Polydor 2058 945*	52	3 wks
23 Aug 80 ★	START *Polydor 2059 266*	1	8 wks
7 Feb 81	THAT'S ENTERTAINMENT (IMPORT)		
	Metronome 0030 364	21	7 wks
6 Jun 81 ●	FUNERAL PYRE *Polydor POSP 257*	4	6 wks
24 Oct 81 ●	ABSOLUTE BEGINNERS *Polydor POSP 350*	4	6 wks
13 Feb 82 ★	TOWN CALLED MALICE/ PRECIOUS		
	Polydor POSP 400	1	8 wks
3 Jul 82 ●	JUST WHO IS THE FIVE O'CLOCK HERO		
	Polydor 2059 504	8	5 wks

18 Sep 82 ●	THE BITTEREST PILL (I EVER HAD TO SWALLOW)		
	Polydor POSP 505	2	7 wks
4 Dec 82 ★	BEAT SURRENDER *Polydor POSP 540*	1	9 wks
22 Jan 83	ALL AROUND THE WORLD (2nd re-entry)		
	Polydor 2058 903	38	4 wks
22 Jan 83	DAVID WATTS/ 'A'BOMB IN WARDOUR STREET (2nd re-entry) *Polydor 2059 054*	50	4 wks
22 Jan 83	DOWN IN THE TUBE STATION AT MIDNIGHT (re-entry) *Polydor POSP 8.*	30	6 wks
22 Jan 83	GOING UNDERGROUND/ DREAMS OF CHILDREN (re-entry) *Polydor POSP 113*	21	6 wks
22 Jan 83	IN THE CITY (2nd re-entry) *Polydor 2058 866*	47	4 wks
22 Jan 83	NEWS OF THE WORLD (2nd re-entry)		
	Polydor 2058 995	39	4 wks
22 Jan 83	STRANGE TOWN (2nd re-entry) *Polydor POSP 34*	42	5 wks
22 Jan 83	THE MODERN WORLD (2nd re-entry)		
	Polydor 2058 945	51	4 wks
22 Jan 83	WHEN YOU'RE YOUNG (re-entry) *Polydor POSP 69*	53	4 wks
29 Jan 83	THAT'S ENTERTAINMENT (re-issue)		
	Polydor POSP 482	60	3 wks
5 Feb 83	START (re-entry) *Polydor 2059 266*	62	2 wks
5 Feb 83	THE ETON RIFLES (re-entry) *Polydor POSP 83*	54	3 wks
5 Feb 83	TOWN CALLED MALICE/ PRECIOUS (re-entry)		
	Polydor POSP 400	73	1 wk

Dreams of Children was only listed with the re-entry of Going Underground from 5 Feb 83.

JAM MACHINE *Italy/US, male vocal/instrumental group* — 1 wk

23 Dec 89	EVERYDAY *deConstruction PB 43299*	68	1 wk

JAM ON THE MUTHA — 2 wks
UK, male vocal/instrumental group

11 Aug 90	HOTEL CALIFORNIA *M & G MAGS 3.*	62	2 wks

JAM TRONIK *Germany, male/female vocal/instrumental group* — 7 wks

24 Mar 90	ANOTHER DAY IN PARADISE *Debut DEBT 3093*	19	7 wks

JAMES *UK, male vocal/instrumental group* — 11 wks

12 May 90	HOW WAS IT FOR YOU *Fontana JIM 5*	32	3 wks
7 Jul 90	COME HOME *Fontana JIM 6*	32	4 wks
8 Dec 90	LOSE CONTROL *Fontana JIM 7*	38†	4 wks

JAMES – *See BELL and JAMES*

Dick JAMES *UK, male vocalist* — 13 wks

20 Jan 56	ROBIN HOOD *Parlophone R 4117*	14	8 wks
18 May 56	ROBIN HOOD (re-entry)/ BALLAD OF DAVY CROCKETT *Parlophone R 4117*	29	1 wk
11 Jan 57	GARDEN OF EDEN *Parlophone R 4255*	18	4 wks

Freddie JAMES *US, male vocalist* — 3 wks

24 Nov 79	GET UP AND BOOGIE *Warner Bros. K 17478*	54	3 wks

Jimmy JAMES and the VAGABONDS — 25 wks
UK, male vocal/instrumental group

11 Sep 68	RED RED WINE *Pye 7N 17579*	36	8 wks
24 Apr 76	I'LL GO WHERE YOUR MUSIC TAKES ME		
	Pye 7N 45585	23	8 wks
17 Jul 76 ●	NOW IS THE TIME *Pye 7N 45606*	5	9 wks

Joni JAMES US, female vocalist   **2 wks**

| 6 Mar 53 | WHY DON'T YOU BELIEVE ME *MGM 582* | 11 | 1 wk |
| 30 Jan 59 | THERE MUST BE A WAY *MGM 1002* | 24 | 1 wk |

Rick JAMES US, male vocalist   **19 wks**

8 Jul 78	YOU AND I *Motown TMG 1110*	46	7 wks
6 Sep 80	BIG TIME *Motown TMG 1198*	41	6 wks
4 Jul 81	GIVE IT TO ME BABY *Motown TMG 1229*	47	3 wks
3 Jul 82	DANCE WIT' ME *Motown TMG 1266*	53	3 wks

See also Teena Marie; Temptations.

Sonny JAMES US, male vocalist   **8 wks**

| 30 Nov 56 | THE CAT CAME BACK *Capitol CL 14635* | 30 | 1 wk |
| 8 Feb 57 | YOUNG LOVE *Capitol CL 14683* | 11 | 7 wks |

Tommy JAMES and the SHONDELLS   **25 wks**
US, male vocal/instrumental group

| 21 Jul 66 | HANKY PANKY *Roulette RK 7000* | 38 | 7 wks |
| 5 Jun 68 | ★ MONY MONY *Major Minor MM 567* | 1 | 18 wks |

JAMES BOYS UK, male vocal duo   **6 wks**

| 19 May 73 | OVER AND OVER *Penny Farthing PEN 806* | 39 | 6 wks |

JAMMERS US, male vocal/instrumental group   **2 wks**

| 29 Jan 83 | BE MINE TONIGHT *Salsoul SAL 101* | 65 | 2 wks |

JAN and DEAN US, male vocal duo   **18 wks**

| 24 Aug 61 | HEART AND SOUL *London HLH 9395* | 24 | 8 wks |
| 15 Aug 63 | SURF CITY *Liberty LIB 55580* | 26 | 10 wks |

JAN and KJELD Denmark, male vocal duo   **4 wks**

| 21 Jul 60 | BANJO BOY *Ember S 101* | 36 | 4 wks |

Horst JANKOWSKI Germany, male instrumentalist - piano   **18 wks**

| 29 Jul 65 | ● A WALK IN THE BLACK FOREST *Mercury MF 861* | 3 | 18 wks |

Philip JAP UK, male vocalist   **8 wks**

| 31 Jul 82 | SAVE US *A & M AMS 8217* | 53 | 4 wks |
| 25 Sep 82 | TOTAL ERASURE *A & M JAP 1* | 41 | 4 wks |

JAPAN UK, male vocal/instrumental group   **81 wks**

18 Oct 80	GENTLEMEN TAKE POLAROIDS *Virgin VS 379*	60	2 wks
9 May 81	THE ART OF PARTIES *Virgin VS 409*	48	5 wks
19 Sep 81	QUIET LIFE *Hansa HANSA 6*	19	9 wks
7 Nov 81	VISIONS OF CHINA *Virgin VS 436*	32	12 wks
23 Jan 82	EUROPEAN SON *Hansa HANSA 10*	31	6 wks
20 Mar 82	● GHOSTS *Virgin VS 472*	5	8 wks
22 May 82	CANTONESE BOY *Virgin VS 502*	24	6 wks
3 Jul 82	● I SECOND THAT EMOTION *Hansa HANSA 12*	9	11 wks
9 Oct 82	LIFE IN TOKYO *Hansa HANSA 17*	28	6 wks
20 Nov 82	NIGHT PORTER *Virgin VS 554*	29	9 wks
12 Mar 83	ALL TOMORROW'S PARTIES *Hansa HANSA 18*	38	4 wks

| 21 May 83 | CANTON (LIVE) *Virgin VS 581* | 42 | 3 wks |

Jean-Michel JARRE France, male instrumentalist/producer   **25 wks**

27 Aug 77	● OXYGENE PART IV *Polydor 2001 721*	4	9 wks
20 Jan 79	EQUINOXE PART 5 *Polydor POSP 20*	45	5 wks
23 Aug 86	FOURTH RENDEZ-VOUS *Polydor POSP 788*	65	4 wks
5 Nov 88	REVOLUTIONS *Polydor PO 25*	52	2 wks
7 Jan 89	LONDON KID *Polydor PO 32*	52	3 wks
7 Oct 89	OXYGENE PART IV (re-mix) *Polydor PO 55*	65	2 wks

London Kid features Hank Marvin. See also Hank Marvin.

Al JARREAU US, male vocalist   **26 wks**

26 Sep 81	WE'RE IN THIS LOVE TOGETHER *Warner Bros. K 17849*	55	4 wks
14 May 83	MORNIN' *WEA U9929*	28	6 wks
16 Jul 83	TROUBLE IN PARADISE *WEA Int. U9871*	36	5 wks
24 Sep 83	BOOGIE DOWN *WEA U9814*	63	3 wks
7 Mar 87	● 'MOONLIGHTING' THEME *WEA U8407*	8	8 wks

See also Shakatak; Melissa Manchester and Al Jarreau.

Kenny 'Jammin' JASON and 'Fast' Eddie SMITH US, male production duo   **4 wks**

| 11 Apr 87 | CAN U DANCE *Champion CHAMP 41* | 71 | 2 wks |
| 14 Nov 87 | CAN U DANCE (re-entry) *Champion CHAMP 41* | 67 | 2 wks |

See also DJ 'Fast' Eddie.

JAVELLS featuring Nosmo KING   **8 wks**
UK, male/female vocal group

| 9 Nov 74 | GOODBYE NOTHING TO SAY *Pye Disco Demand DDS 2003* | 26 | 8 wks |

Peter JAY and the JAYWALKERS   **11 wks**
UK, male instrumental group, Peter Jay, drums

| 8 Nov 62 | CAN CAN 62 *Decca F 11531* | 31 | 11 wks |

JAZZ and the BROTHERS GRIMM   **2 wks**
UK, male vocal/instrumental group

| 9 Jul 88 | (LET'S ALL GO BACK) DISCO NIGHTS *Ensign ENY 616* | 57 | 2 wks |

JB's ALL STARS UK, male/female vocal/instrumental group   **4 wks**

| 11 Feb 84 | BACKFIELD IN MOTION *RCA Victor RCA 384* | 48 | 4 wks |

JEFFERSON UK, male vocalist   **8 wks**

| 9 Apr 69 | COLOUR OF MY LOVE *Pye 7N 17706* | 22 | 8 wks |

JEFFERSON STARSHIP   **9 wks**
US, male vocal/instrumental group

| 26 Jan 80 | JANE *Grunt FB 1750* | 21 | 9 wks |

See also Starship.

JELLYBEAN US, male producer   47 wks

1 Feb 86	**SIDEWALK TALK** EMI America EA 210	**47**	4 wks
26 Sep 87	**THE REAL THING** Chrysalis CHS 3167	**13**	10 wks
28 Nov 87 ●	**WHO FOUND WHO** Chrysalis CHS JEL 1	**10**	10 wks
12 Dec 87	**JINGO** Chrysalis JEL 2	**12**	10 wks
12 Mar 88	**JUST A MIRAGE** Chrysalis JEL 3	**13**	10 wks
20 Aug 88	**COMING BACK FOR MORE** Chrysalis JEL 4	**41**	3 wks

Jellybean utilises the talents of the following vocalists: on Sidewalk Talk - Catherine Buchanan (US, female); The Real Thing - Steven Dante (UK, male); Who Found Who - Elisa Fiorillo (US, female); Just A Mirage - Adele Bertei (US, female); Coming Back For More - Richard Darbyshire (UK, male). See also Steven Dante; Elisa Fiorillo.

JERRY – *See OLLIE and JERRY*

JESUS AND MARY CHAIN   37 wks
UK, male vocal/instrumental group

2 Mar 85	**NEVER UNDERSTAND** blanco y negro NEG 8	**47**	4 wks
8 Jun 85	**YOU TRIP ME UP** blanco y negro NEG 13	**55**	3 wks
12 Oct 85	**JUST LIKE HONEY** blanco y negro NEG 17	**45**	3 wks
26 Jul 86	**SOME CANDY TALKING** blanco y negro NEG 19	**13**	5 wks
2 May 87 ●	**APRIL SKIES** blanco y negro NEG 24	**8**	6 wks
15 Aug 87	**HAPPY WHEN IT RAINS** blanco y negro NEG 25	**25**	5 wks
7 Nov 87	**DARKLANDS** blanco y negro NEG 29	**33**	4 wks
9 Apr 88	**SIDEWALKING** blanco y negro NEG 32	**30**	3 wks
23 Sep 89	**BLUES FROM A GUN** blanco y negro NEG 41	**32**	2 wks
18 Nov 89	**HEAD ON** blanco y negro NEG 42	**57**	2 wks
8 Sep 90	**ROLLERCOASTER** (EP) blanco y negro NEG 45	**46**	2 wks

Tracks on Rollercoaster EP: Rollercoaster/Silverblade/Lowlife/Tower Of Song.

JESUS JONES UK, male vocal/instrumental group   22 wks

25 Feb 89	**INFO-FREAKO** Food FOOD 18	**42**	3 wks
8 Jul 89	**NEVER ENOUGH** Food FOOD 21	**42**	3 wks
23 Sep 89	**BRING IT ON DOWN** Food FOOD 22	**46**	3 wks
9 Dec 89	**I DON'T WANT THAT KIND OF LOVE** Food FOOD 23	**63**	1 wk
7 Apr 90	**REAL REAL REAL** Food FOOD 24	**19**	8 wks
6 Oct 90	**RIGHT HERE RIGHT NOW** Food FOOD 25	**31**	4 wks

I Don't Want That Kind Of Love was one track from the Food Christmas EP. The others were: Like Princes Do by Crazyhead and Info-Freako by Diesel Park West. See also Crazyhead and Diesel Park West.

JESUS LOVES YOU UK, male vocalist   2 wks

11 Nov 89	**AFTER THE LOVE** More Protein PROT 2	**68**	2 wks

JETHRO TULL UK, male vocal/instrumental group   62 wks

1 Jan 69	**LOVE STORY** Island WIP 6048	**29**	8 wks
14 May 69 ●	**LIVING IN THE PAST** Island WIP 6056	**3**	14 wks
1 Nov 69 ●	**SWEET DREAM** Chrysalis WIP 6070	**7**	11 wks
24 Jan 70 ●	**THE WITCH'S PROMISE/ TEACHER** Chrysalis WIP 6077	**4**	9 wks
18 Sep 71	**LIFE IS A LONG SONG/ UP THE POOL** Chrysalis WIP 6106	**11**	8 wks
11 Dec 76	**RING OUT SOLSTICE BELLS**[CF43] (EP) Chrysalis CXP 2	**28**	6 wks
15 Sep 84	**LAP OF LUXURY** Chrysalis TULL 1	**70**	2 wks
16 Jan 87	**SAID SHE WAS A DANCER** Chrysalis TULL 4	**55**	4 wks

Tracks on EP: Ring Out Solstice Bells/March the Mad Scientist/The Christmas Song/Pan Dance.

JETS UK, male vocal/instrumental group   38 wks

22 Aug 81	**SUGAR DOLL** EMI 5211	**55**	3 wks
31 Oct 81	**YES TONIGHT JOSEPHINE** EMI 5247	**25**	11 wks
6 Feb 82	**LOVE MAKES THE WORLD GO ROUND** EMI 5262	**21**	9 wks

24 Apr 82	**THE HONEYDRIPPER** EMI 5289	**58**	3 wks
9 Oct 82	**SOMEBODY TO LOVE** EMI 5342	**56**	3 wks
6 Aug 83	**BLUE SKIES** EMI 5405	**53**	3 wks
17 Dec 83	**ROCKIN' AROUND THE CHRISTMAS TREE** PRT 7P 297	**62**	4 wks
13 Oct 84	**PARTY DOLL** PRT JETS 2	**72**	2 wks

JETS US, male/female vocal/instrumental group   19 wks

31 Jan 87 ●	**CRUSH ON YOU** MCA MCA 1048	**5**	13 wks
25 Apr 87	**CURIOSITY** MCA MCA 1119	**41**	4 wks
28 May 88	**ROCKET 2 U** MCA MCA 1226	**69**	2 wks

Joan JETT and the BLACKHEARTS   20 wks
US, female vocalist with male vocal/instrumental group

24 Apr 82 ●	**I LOVE ROCK 'N' ROLL** Epic EPC A 2087	**4**	10 wks
10 Jul 82	**CRIMSON AND CLOVER** Epic EPC A 2485	**60**	3 wks
20 Aug 88	**I HATE MYSELF FOR LOVING YOU** London LON 195	**46**	6 wks
31 Mar 90	**DIRTY DEEDS** Chrysalis CHS 3518	**73**	1 wk

Last hit gives no credit to the Blackhearts.

JIGSAW UK, male vocal/instrumental group   16 wks

1 Nov 75 ●	**SKY HIGH** Splash CPI 1	**9**	11 wks
6 Aug 77	**IF I HAVE TO GO AWAY** Splash CP 11	**36**	5 wks

JILTED JOHN UK, male vocalist   12 wks

12 Aug 78 ●	**JILTED JOHN** EMI International INT 567	**4**	12 wks

JIMMY THE HOOVER   8 wks
UK, male/female vocal/instrumental group

25 Jun 83	**TANTALISE (WO WO EE YEH YEH)** Innervision A 3406	**18**	8 wks

JINGLE BELLS US/UK, female vocal group   4 wks

17 Dec 83	**CHRISTMAS SPECTRE** Passion PASH 14	**37**	4 wks

JIVE BUNNY and the MASTERMIXERS   56 wks
UK, male production/mixing group

15 Jul 89 ★	**SWING THE MOOD** Music Factory Dance MFD 001	**1**	19 wks
14 Oct 89 ★	**THAT'S WHAT I LIKE** Music Factory Dance MFD 002	**1**	12 wks
16 Dec 89 ★	**LET'S PARTY** Music Factory Dance MFD 003	**1**	6 wks
17 Mar 90 ●	**THAT SOUNDS GOOD TO ME** Music Factory Dance MFD 004	**4**	6 wks
25 Aug 90 ●	**CAN CAN YOU PARTY** Music Factory Dance MFD 007	**8**	6 wks
17 Nov 90	**LET'S SWING AGAIN** Music Factory Dance MFD 009	**19**	5 wks
22 Dec 90	**THE CRAZY PARTY MIXES** Music Factory Dance MFD 010	**13†**	2 wks

See also Liz Kershaw and Bruno Brookes.

JKD BAND UK, male vocal/instrumental group   4 wks

1 Jul 78	**DRAGON POWER** Satril SAT 132	**58**	4 wks

J.M.D. – *See TYREE*

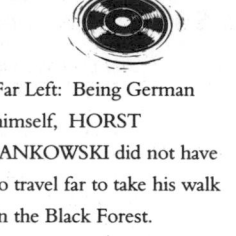

Far Left: Being German himself, HORST JANKOWSKI did not have to travel far to take his walk in the Black Forest.

Left: By topping the chart with 'Sacrifice', ELTON JOHN ceased leading a less likeable list, Most Top Ten Hits Without a Number One. His only previous visit to the top spot had been in a duet with Kiki Dee.

In this remarkable photo of the JESUS AND MARY CHAIN hardly anybody looks interested, on or off stage.

J.M. SILK US, male vocal/instrumental duo   **6 wks**

| 25 Oct 86 | I CAN'T TURN AROUND RCA PB 49793 | 62 | 3 wks |
| 7 Mar 87 | LET THE MUSIC TAKE CONTROL RCA PB 49767 | 47 | 3 wks |

JO BOXERS UK, male vocal/instrumental group   **33 wks**

19 Feb 83	● BOXER BEAT RCA BOXX 1	3	15 wks
21 May 83	● JUST GOT LUCKY RCA BOXX 2	7	9 wks
13 Aug 83	JOHNNY FRIENDLY RCA BOXX 3	31	8 wks
12 Nov 83	JEALOUS LOVE RCA BOXX 4	72	1 wk

JO JO GUNNE US, male vocal/instrumental group   **12 wks**

| 25 Mar 72 | ● RUN RUN RUN Asylum AYM 501 | 6 | 12 wks |

JOAN COLLINS FAN CLUB   **3 wks**
UK, male vocalist - Julian Clary

| 18 Jun 88 | LEADER OF THE PACK 10 TEN 227 | 60 | 3 wks |

John Paul JOANS UK, male vocalist   **7 wks**

| 19 Dec 70 | MAN FROM NAZARETH RAK 107 | 41 | 3 wks |
| 16 Jan 71 | MAN FROM NAZARETH (re-entry) RAK 107 | 25 | 4 wks |

JOCKMASTER B.A. – See MAD JOCKS featuring JOCKMASTER B.A.

JOCKO US, male vocalist   **3 wks**

| 23 Feb 80 | RHYTHM TALK Philadelphia International PIR 8222 | 56 | 3 wks |

Billy JOEL US, male vocalist/instrumentalist - piano   **121 wks**

11 Feb 78	JUST THE WAY YOU ARE CBS 5872	19	9 wks
24 Jun 78	MOVIN' OUT (ANTHONY'S SONG) CBS 6412	35	6 wks
2 Dec 78	MY LIFE CBS 6821	12	15 wks
28 Apr 79	UNTIL THE NIGHT CBS 7242	50	3 wks
12 Apr 80	ALL FOR LEYNA CBS 8325	40	4 wks
9 Aug 80	IT'S STILL ROCK AND ROLL TO ME CBS 8753	14	11 wks
15 Oct 83	★ UPTOWN GIRL CBS A 3775	1	17 wks
10 Dec 83	TELL HER ABOUT IT CBS A 3655	4	10 wks
18 Feb 84	AN INNOCENT MAN CBS A 4142	8	10 wks
28 Apr 84	THE LONGEST TIME CBS A 4280	25	8 wks
23 Jun 84	LEAVE A TENDER MOMENT ALONE/ GOODNIGHT SAIGON CBS A 4521	29	7 wks
22 Feb 86	SHE'S ALWAYS A WOMAN/ JUST THE WAY YOU ARE CBS A 6862	53	1 wk
20 Sep 86	A MATTER OF TRUST CBS 650057 7	52	4 wks
30 Sep 89	● WE DIDN'T START THE FIRE CBS JOEL 1	7	10 wks
16 Dec 89	LENINGRAD CBS JOEL 1	53	4 wks
10 Mar 90	I GO TO EXTREMES CBS JOEL 2	70	2 wks

Goodnight Saigon only listed from 30 Jun 84. Just The Way You Are on the double A-side CBS A 6862 was a re-issue.

Elton JOHN UK, male vocalist/instrumentalist - piano   **392 wks**

23 Jan 71	● YOUR SONG DJM DJS 233	7	12 wks
22 Apr 72	● ROCKET MAN DJM DJX 501	2	13 wks
9 Sep 72	HONKY CAT DJM DJS	31	6 wks
4 Nov 72	● CROCODILE ROCK DJM DJS 271	5	14 wks
20 Jan 73	● DANIEL DJM DJS 275	4	10 wks
7 Jul 73	● SATURDAY NIGHT'S ALRIGHT FOR FIGHTING DJM DJX 502	7	9 wks
29 Sep 73	● GOODBYE YELLOW BRICK ROAD DJM DJS 285	6	16 wks
8 Dec 73	STEP INTO CHRISTMAS DJM DJS 290	24	7 wks
2 Mar 74	CANDLE IN THE WIND DJM DJS 297	11	9 wks
1 Jun 74	DON'T LET THE SUN GO DOWN ON ME DJM DJS 302	16	8 wks
14 Sep 74	THE BITCH IS BACK DJM DJS 322	15	7 wks
23 Nov 74	● LUCY IN THE SKY WITH DIAMONDS DJM DJS 340	10	10 wks
8 Mar 75	PHILADELPHIA FREEDOM DJM DJS 354	12	9 wks
28 Jun 75	SOMEONE SAVED MY LIFE TONIGHT DJM DJS 385	22	5 wks
4 Oct 75	ISLAND GIRL DJM DJS 610	14	8 wks
20 Mar 76	● PINBALL WIZARD DJM DJS 652	7	7 wks
25 Sep 76	BENNIE AND THE JETS DJM DJS 10705	37	5 wks
13 Nov 76	SORRY SEEMS TO BE THE HARDEST WORD Rocket ROKN 517	11	10 wks
26 Feb 77	CRAZY WATER Rocket ROKN 521	27	6 wks
11 Jun 77	BITE YOUR LIP (GET UP AND DANCE) Rocket ROKN 526	28	4 wks
15 Apr 78	EGO Rocket ROKN 538	34	6 wks
21 Oct 78	PART TIME LOVE Rocket XPRES 1	15	13 wks
16 Dec 78	● SONG FOR GUY Rocket XPRES 5	4	10 wks
12 May 79	ARE YOU READY FOR LOVE Rocket XPRES 13	42	6 wks
24 May 80	LITTLE JEANNIE Rocket XPRES 32	33	7 wks
23 Aug 80	SARTORIAL ELOQUENCE Rocket XPRES 41	44	5 wks
23 May 81	NOBODY WINS Rocket XPRES 54	42	5 wks
27 Mar 82	● BLUE EYES Rocket XPRES 71	8	10 wks
12 Jun 82	EMPTY GARDEN Rocket XPRES 77	51	4 wks
30 Apr 83	● I GUESS THAT'S WHY THEY CALL IT THE BLUES Rocket XPRES 91	5	15 wks
30 Jul 83	● I'M STILL STANDING Rocket EJS 1	4	11 wks
15 Oct 83	KISS THE BRIDE Rocket EJS 2	20	7 wks
10 Dec 83	COLD AS CHRISTMAS Rocket EJS 3	33	6 wks
26 May 84	SAD SONGS (SAY SO MUCH) Rocket PH 7	7	12 wks
11 Aug 84	● PASSENGERS Rocket EJS 5	5	11 wks
20 Oct 84	WHO WEARS THESE SHOES Rocket EJS 6	50	3 wks
2 Mar 85	BREAKING HEARTS (AIN'T WHAT IT USED TO BE) Rocket EJS 7	59	3 wks
12 Oct 85	● NIKITA Rocket EJS 9	3	13 wks
7 Dec 85	WRAP HER UP Rocket EJS 10	12	10 wks
1 Mar 86	CRY TO HEAVEN Rocket EJS 11	47	4 wks
4 Oct 86	HEARTACHE ALL OVER THE WORLD Rocket EJS 12	45	4 wks
16 Jan 88	● CANDLE IN THE WIND Rocket EJS 15	5	11 wks
4 Jun 88	I DON'T WANNA GO ON WITH YOU LIKE THAT Rocket EJS 16	30	8 wks
3 Sep 88	TOWN OF PLENTY Rocket EJS 17	74	1 wk
26 Aug 89	HEALING HANDS Rocket EJS 19	45	5 wks
4 Nov 89	SACRIFICE Rocket EJS 20	55	3 wks
9 Jun 90	★ SACRIFICE/ HEALING HANDS (re-issues) Rocket EJS 22	1	15 wks
18 Aug 90	CLUB AT THE END OF THE STREET/ WHISPERS Rocket EJS 23	47	3 wks
20 Oct 90	YOU GOTTA LOVE SOMEONE Rocket EJS 24	33	4 wks
15 Dec 90	EASIER TO WALK AWAY Rocket EJS 25	67	1 wk
29 Dec 90	EASIER TO WALK AWAY (re-entry) Rocket EJS 25	63†	1 wk

Philadelphia Freedom credits the Elton John Band. Bite Your Lip (Get Up and Dance) was one side of a double-sided chart entry, the other being Chicago by Kiki Dee. Wrap Her Up features George Michael as uncredited co-vocalist. The 1988 version of Candle In The Wind was a live recording. See also Elton John and Kiki Dee; Elton John and Millie Jackson; Elton John Band featuring John Lennon and the Muscle Shoals Horns; Elton John and Cliff Richard; Dionne Warwick and Friends; Jennifer Rush and Elton John; Aretha Franklin and Elton John; Elton John and George Michael.

Elton JOHN and Kiki DEE UK, male/female vocal duo   **14 wks**

| 3 Jul 76 | ★ DON'T GO BREAKING MY HEART Rocket ROKN 512 | 1 | 14 wks |

See also Elton John; Kiki Dee.

Elton JOHN and Millie JACKSON   **5 wks**
UK/US, male/female vocal duo

| 15 Jun 85 | ACT OF WAR Rocket EJS 8 | 32 | 5 wks |

See also Elton John; Millie Jackson.

Elton JOHN and Cliff RICHARD   8 wks
UK, male vocal duo

29 Nov 86	**SLOW RIVERS** *Rocket EJS 13*	**44**	8 wks

See also Elton John; Cliff Richard.

Elton JOHN BAND featuring John LENNON and the MUSCLE SHOALS HORNS   4 wks
UK, male vocalists/instrumentalists with US, male instrumental group

21 Mar 81	**I SAW HER STANDING THERE** *DJM DJS 10965*	**40**	4 wks

See also Elton John; John Lennon.

Robert JOHN *US, male vocalist*   13 wks

17 Jul 68	**IF YOU DON'T WANT MY LOVE** *CBS 3436*..............	**42**	5 wks
20 Oct 79	**SAD EYES** *EMI American EA 101*	**31**	8 wks

JOHNNY – *See SANTO and JOHNNY*

JOHNNY and CHARLEY *Spain, male vocal duo*   1 wk

14 Oct 65	**LA YENKA** *Pye International 7N 25326*	**49**	1 wk

JOHNNY HATES JAZZ   45 wks
UK, male vocal/instrumental group

11 Apr 87	● **SHATTERED DREAMS** *Virgin VS 948*	**5**	14 wks
29 Aug 87	**I DON'T WANT TO BE A HERO** *Virgin VS 1000*	**11**	10 wks
21 Nov 87	**TURN BACK THE CLOCK** *Virgin VS 1017*.................	**12**	11 wks
27 Feb 88	**HEART OF GOLD** *Virgin VS 1045*	**19**	7 wks
9 Jul 88	**DON'T SAY IT'S LOVE** *Virgin VS 1081*	**48**	3 wks

JOHNNY and the HURRICANES   88 wks
US, male instrumental group

9 Oct 59	● **RED RIVER ROCK** *London HL 8948*	**3**	16 wks
25 Dec 59	**REVEILLE ROCK** *London HL 9017*	**14**	5 wks
17 Mar 60	● **BEATNIK FLY** *London HLI 9072*	**8**	19 wks
16 Jun 60	● **DOWN YONDER** *London HLX 9134*.....................	**8**	11 wks
29 Sep 60	● **ROCKING GOOSE** *London HLX 9190*	**3**	20 wks
2 Mar 61	**JA-DA** *London HLX 9289*	**14**	9 wks
6 Jul 61	**OLD SMOKEY/ HIGH VOLTAGE** *London HLX 9378*........	**24**	8 wks

Bryan JOHNSON *UK, male vocalist*   11 wks

10 Mar 60	**LOOKING HIGH HIGH HIGH** *Decca F 11213*	**20**	11 wks

Carey JOHNSON *Australia, male vocalist*   8 wks

25 Apr 87	**REAL FASHION REGGAE STYLE** *Oval TEN 170*	**19**	8 wks

Don JOHNSON *US, male vocalist*   5 wks

18 Oct 86	**HEARTBEAT** *Epic 650064 7*	**46**	5 wks

See also Barbra Streisand and Don Johnson.

General JOHNSON – *See CHAIRMAN OF THE BOARD*

Holly JOHNSON *UK, male vocalist*   29 wks

14 Jan 89	● **LOVE TRAIN** *MCA MCA 1306*	**4**	11 wks
1 Apr 89	● **AMERICANOS** *MCA MCA 1323*	**4**	11 wks
24 Jun 89	**ATOMIC CITY** *MCA MCA 1342*.............................	**18**	4 wks
30 Sep 89	**HEAVEN'S HERE** *MCA MCA 1365*...........................	**62**	2 wks
1 Dec 90	**WHERE HAS LOVE GONE** *MCA MCA 1460*.................	**73**	1 wk

See also Christians, Holly Johnson, Paul McCartney, Gerry Marsden and Stock Aitken Waterman.

Howard JOHNSON *US, male vocalist*   6 wks

4 Sep 82	**KEEPIN' LOVE NEW/ SO FINE** *A & M USA 1221*	**45**	6 wks

Keepin' Love New listed 4 Sep only.

Johnny JOHNSON and the BANDWAGON   50 wks
US, male vocal group

16 Oct 68	● **BREAKIN' DOWN THE WALLS OF HEARTACHE** *Direction 58-3670*	**4**	15 wks
5 Feb 69	**YOU** *Direction 58-3923*	**34**	4 wks
28 May 69	**LET'S HANG ON** *Direction 58-4180*.........................	**36**	6 wks
25 Jul 70	● **SWEET INSPIRATION** *Bell 1111*...........................	**10**	12 wks
24 Oct 70	**SWEET INSPIRATION (re-entry)** *Bell 1111*..................	**46**	1 wk
28 Nov 70	● **BLAME IT ON THE PONY EXPRESS** *Bell 1128*	**7**	12 wks

Listed as Bandwagon on Direction hits.

Kevin JOHNSON *Australia, male vocalist*   6 wks

11 Jan 75	**ROCK 'N ROLL (I GAVE YOU THE BEST YEARS OF MY LIFE)** *UK UKR 84*.......................................	**23**	6 wks

Laurie JOHNSON *UK, orchestra*   12 wks

28 Sep 61	● **SUCU SUCU** *Pye 7N 15383*..................................	**9**	12 wks

L. J. JOHNSON *US, male vocalist*   6 wks

7 Feb 76	**YOUR MAGIC PUT A SPELL ON ME** *Philips 6006 492*	**27**	6 wks

Lou JOHNSON *US, male vocalist*   2 wks

26 Nov 64	**MESSAGE TO MARTHA** *London HL 9929*...................	**36**	2 wks

Marv JOHNSON *US, male vocalist*   39 wks

12 Feb 60	● **YOU GOT WHAT IT TAKES** *London HLT 9013*	**5**	16 wks
5 May 60	**I LOVE THE WAY YOU LOVE** *London HLT 9109*...........	**35**	3 wks
11 Aug 60	**AIN'T GONNA BE THAT WAY** *London HLT 9165*	**50**	1 wk
22 Jan 69	● **I'LL PICK A ROSE FOR MY ROSE** *Tamla Motown TMG 680*..................................	**10**	11 wks
25 Oct 69	**I MISS YOU BABY** *Tamla Motown TMG 713*	**25**	8 wks

Paul JOHNSON *UK, male vocalist*   7 wks

21 Feb 87	**WHEN LOVE COMES CALLING** *CBS PJOHN 1*	**52**	5 wks
25 Feb 89	**NO MORE TOMORROWS** *CBS PJOHN 7*	**67**	2 wks

Teddy JOHNSON – *See Pearl CARR and Teddy JOHNSON*

Bruce JOHNSTON *US, male instrumentalist - keyboards*   4 wks

27 Aug 77	**PIPELINE** *CBS 5514*	**33**	4 wks

JOHNSTON BROTHERS *UK, male vocal group*   **30 wks**

3 Apr 53	●	OH HAPPY DAY *Decca F 10071*	4	8 wks
7 Oct 55	★	HERNANDO'S HIDEAWAY *Decca F 10608*	1	13 wks
30 Dec 55	●	JOIN IN AND SING AGAIN *Decca F 10636*	9	1 wk
13 Apr 56		NO OTHER LOVE *Decca F 10721*	22	1 wk
30 Nov 56		IN THE MIDDLE OF THE HOUSE *Decca F 10781*	27	1 wk
7 Dec 56		JOIN IN AND SING (NO. 3) *Decca F 10814*	30	1 wk
28 Dec 56		JOIN IN AND SING (NO. 3) (re-entry) *Decca F 10814*	24	1 wk
8 Feb 57		GIVE HER MY LOVE *Decca F 10828*	27	1 wk
19 Apr 57		HEART *Decca F 10860*	23	3 wks

The following two hits were medleys: Join In And Sing Again: Sheik Of Araby/Yes Sir That's My Baby/California Here I Come/Some Of These Days/Charleston/Margie. Join In And Sing (No.3): Coal Black Morning/When You're Smiling/Alexander's Ragtime Band/Sweet Sue Just You/When You Wore A Tulip/If You Were The Only Girl In The World. See also Joan Regan and the Johnston Brothers; Various Artists - All Star Hit Parade No. 2.

JOLLY BROTHERS *Jamaica, male vocal/instrumental group*   **7 wks**

28 Jul 79		CONSCIOUS MAN *United Artists UP 36415*	46	7 wks

JOLLY ROGER *UK, male vocalist*   **12 wks**

10 Sep 88		ACID MAN *10 TEN 236*	23	12 wks

JOMANDA *US, female vocal group*   **3 wks**

22 Apr 89		MAKE MY BODY ROCK *RCA PB 42749*	44	3 wks

JON and VANGELIS   **28 wks**
UK, male vocalist/Greece, male multi-instrumentalist

5 Jan 80	●	I HEAR YOU NOW *Polydor POSP 96*	8	11 wks
12 Dec 81	●	I'LL FIND MY WAY HOME *Polydor JV 1*	6	13 wks
30 Jul 83		HE IS SAILING *Polydor JV 4*	61	2 wks
18 Aug 84		STATE OF INDEPENDENCE *Polydor JV 5*	67	2 wks

See also Vangelis.

JONATHAN – *See DAVID and JONATHAN*

Aled JONES *UK, male vocalist*   **18 wks**

20 Jul 85		MEMORY *BBC RESL 175*	42	4 wks
30 Nov 85	●	WALKING IN THE AIR *HMV ALED 1*	5	11 wks
20 Dec 86		A WINTER STORY *HMV ALED 2*	51	3 wks

See also Mike Oldfield.

Barbara JONES *Jamaica, female vocalist*   **7 wks**

31 Jan 81		JUST WHEN I NEEDED YOU MOST *Sonet SON 2221*	31	7 wks

Grace JONES *US, female vocalist*   **43 wks**

26 Jul 80		PRIVATE LIFE *Island WIP 6629*	17	8 wks
20 Jun 81		PULL UP TO THE BUMPER *Island WIP 6696*	53	4 wks
30 Oct 82		THE APPLE STRETCHING/ NIPPLE TO THE BOTTLE *Island WIP 6779*	50	4 wks
9 Apr 83		MY JAMAICAN GUY *Island IS 103*	56	3 wks
12 Oct 85		SLAVE TO THE RHYTHM *ZTT IS 206*	12	8 wks
18 Jan 86		PULL UP TO THE BUMPER (re-issue)/ LA VIE EN ROSE *Island IS 240*	12	9 wks
1 Mar 86		LOVE IS THE DRUG *Island IS 266*	35	4 wks
15 Nov 86		I'M NOT PERFECT (BUT I'M PERFECT FOR YOU) *Manhattan MT 15*	56	3 wks

La Vie En Rose was only listed from 1 Feb 86.

Howard JONES *UK, male vocalist*   **100 wks**

17 Sep 83	●	NEW SONG *WEA HOW 1*	3	12 wks
26 Nov 83	●	WHAT IS LOVE *WEA HOW 2*	2	15 wks
14 Jan 84		NEW SONG (re-entry) *WEA HOW 1*	60	3 wks
18 Feb 84		HIDE AND SEEK *WEA HOW 3*	12	9 wks
26 May 84	●	PEARL IN THE SHELL *WEA HOW 4*	7	10 wks
11 Aug 84	●	LIKE TO GET TO KNOW YOU WELL *WEA HOW 5*	4	12 wks
9 Feb 85	●	THINGS CAN ONLY GET BETTER *WEA HOW 6*	6	8 wks
20 Apr 85	●	LOOK MAMA *WEA HOW 7*	10	6 wks
29 Jun 85		LIFE IN ONE DAY *WEA HOW 8*	14	7 wks
15 Mar 86		NO ONE IS TO BLAME *WEA HOW 9*	16	7 wks
4 Oct 86		ALL I WANT *WEA HOW 10*	35	4 wks
29 Nov 86		YOU KNOW I LOVE YOU...DON'T YOU? *WEA HOW 11*	43	3 wks
21 Mar 87		A LITTLE BIT OF SNOW *WEA HOW 12*	70	1 wk
4 Mar 89		EVERLASTING LOVE *WEA HOW 13*	62	3 wks

Janie JONES *UK, female vocalist*   **3 wks**

27 Jan 66		WITCHES' BREW *HMV POP 1495*	46	3 wks

Jimmy JONES *US, male vocalist*   **47 wks**

17 Mar 60	●	HANDY MAN *MGM 1051*	3	21 wks
16 Jun 60	★	GOOD TIMIN' *MGM 1078*	1	15 wks
18 Aug 60		HANDY MAN (re-entry) *MGM 1051*	32	3 wks
8 Sep 60		I JUST GO FOR YOU *MGM 1091*	35	4 wks
17 Nov 60		READY FOR LOVE *MGM 1103*	46	1 wk
30 Mar 61		I TOLD YOU SO *MGM 1123*	33	3 wks

Juggy JONES *US, male multi-instrumentalist*   **4 wks**

7 Feb 76		INSIDE AMERICA *Contempo CS 2080*	39	4 wks

Oran 'Juice' JONES *US, male vocalist*   **14 wks**

15 Nov 86	●	THE RAIN *Def Jam A 7303*	4	14 wks

Paul JONES *UK, male vocalist*   **34 wks**

6 Oct 66	●	HIGH TIME *HMV POP 1554*	4	15 wks
19 Jan 67	●	I'VE BEEN A BAD BAD BOY *HMV POP 1576*	5	9 wks
23 Aug 67		THINKIN' AIN'T FOR ME *HMV POP 1602*	47	1 wk
13 Sep 67		THINKIN' AIN'T FOR ME (re-entry) *HMV POP 1602*	32	7 wks
5 Feb 69		AQUARIUS *Columbia DB 8514*	45	2 wks

See also Manfred Mann.

Quincy JONES *US, male producer/instrumentalist - keyboards*   **39 wks**

29 Jul 78		STUFF LIKE THAT *A & M AMS 7367*	34	9 wks
11 Apr 81		AI NO CORRIDA (I-NO-KO-REE-DA) *A & M AMS 8109*	14	10 wks
20 Jun 81		RAZZAMATAZZ *A & M AMS 8140*	11	9 wks
5 Sep 81		BETCHA' WOULDN'T HURT ME *A & M AMS 8157*	52	3 wks
13 Jan 90		I'LL BE GOOD TO YOU *Qwest W 2697*	21	7 wks
31 Mar 90		SECRET GARDEN *Qwest W 9992*	67	1 wk

Vocals on AMS 7367 were by Ashford and Simpson and Chaka Khan, on AMS 8109 they were by Dune - US male vocalist, and on AMS 8140 they were by Patti Austin. I'll Be Good To You features Ray Charles and Chaka Khan. Secret Garden features Al B. Sure!, James Ingram, El DeBarge and Barry White. See Ashford and Simpson; Chaka Khan; Patti Austin and James Ingram; Ray Charles; El DeBarge; James Ingram with Michael McDonald; Al B. Sure!; Barry White.

Rickie Lee JONES *US, female vocalist*   **9 wks**

23 Jun 79		CHUCK E.'S IN LOVE *Warner Bros. K 17390*	18	9 wks

Shirley JONES – *See PARTRIDGE FAMILY starring Shirley JONES featuring David CASSIDY; VARIOUS ARTISTS* - Carousel Soundtrack.

Tammy JONES *UK, female vocalist* — 10 wks

26 Apr 75	● LET ME TRY AGAIN *Epic EPC 3211*	5	10 wks

Tom JONES *UK, male vocalist* — 330 wks

11 Feb 65	★ IT'S NOT UNUSUAL *Decca F 12062*	1	14 wks
6 May 65	ONCE UPON A TIME *Decca F 12121*	32	4 wks
8 Jul 65	WITH THESE HANDS *Decca F 12191*	13	11 wks
12 Aug 65	WHAT'S NEW PUSSYCAT *Decca F 12203*	11	10 wks
13 Jan 66	THUNDERBALL *Decca F 12292*	35	4 wks
19 May 66	ONCE THERE WAS A TIME/ NOT RESPONSIBLE *Decca F 12390*	18	9 wks
18 Aug 66	THIS AND THAT *Decca F 12461*	44	3 wks
10 Nov 66	★ GREEN GREEN GRASS OF HOME *Decca F 22511*	1	22 wks
16 Feb 67	● DETROIT CITY *Decca F 22555*	8	10 wks
13 Apr 67	● FUNNY FAMILIAR FORGOTTEN FEELINGS *Decca F 12599*	7	15 wks
26 Jul 67	● I'LL NEVER FALL IN LOVE AGAIN *Decca F 12639*	2	25 wks
22 Nov 67	● I'M COMING HOME *Decca F 12693*	2	16 wks
28 Feb 68	● DELILAH *Decca F 12747*	2	17 wks
17 Jul 68	● HELP YOURSELF *Decca F 12812*	5	26 wks
27 Nov 68	A MINUTE OF YOUR TIME *Decca F 12854*	14	15 wks
14 May 69	● LOVE ME TONIGHT *Decca F 12924*	9	12 wks
13 Dec 69	● WITHOUT LOVE *Decca F 12990*	10	11 wks
14 Mar 70	WITHOUT LOVE (re-entry) *Decca F 12990*	49	1 wk
18 Apr 70	● DAUGHTER OF DARKNESS *Decca F 13013*	5	15 wks
15 Aug 70	I (WHO HAVE NOTHING) *Decca F 13061*	16	8 wks
17 Oct 70	I (WHO HAVE NOTHING) (re-entry) *Decca F 13061*	47	3 wks
16 Jan 71	SHE'S A LADY *Decca F 13113*	13	9 wks
27 Mar 71	SHE'S A LADY (re-entry) *Decca F 13113*	47	1 wk
5 Jun 71	PUPPET MAN *Decca F 13183*	49	1 wk
19 Jun 71	PUPPET MAN (re-entry) *Decca F 13183*	50	1 wk
23 Oct 71	● TILL *Decca F 13236*	2	15 wks
1 Apr 72	THE YOUNG NEW MEXICAN PUPPETEER *Decca F 13298*	6	12 wks
14 Apr 73	LETTER TO LUCILLE *Decca F 13393*	31	8 wks
7 Sep 74	SOMETHING 'BOUT YOU BABY I LIKE *Decca F 13550*	36	5 wks
16 Apr 77	SAY YOU'LL STAY UNTIL TOMORROW *EMI 2583*	40	3 wks
18 Apr 87	● A BOY FROM NOWHERE *Epic OLE 1*	2	12 wks
30 May 87	IT'S NOT UNUSUAL (re-issue) *Decca F 103*	17	8 wks
2 Jan 88	I WAS BORN TO BE ME *Epic OLE 4*	61	1 wk
29 Apr 89	MOVE CLOSER *Jive JIVE 203*	49	3 wks

See also Art Of Noise.

Sue JONES-DAVIES – *See Julie COVINGTON, Rula LENSKA, Charlotte CORNWELL and Sue JONES-DAVIES*

Dick JORDAN *UK, male vocalist* — 4 wks

17 Mar 60	HALLELUJAH I LOVE HER SO *Oriole CB 1534*	47	1 wk
9 Jun 60	LITTLE CHRISTINE *Oriole CB 1548*	39	3 wks

David JOSEPH *UK, male vocalist* — 16 wks

26 Feb 83	YOU CAN'T HIDE (YOUR LOVE FROM ME) *Island IS 101*	13	9 wks
28 May 83	LET'S LIVE IT UP (NITE PEOPLE) *Island IS 116*	26	5 wks
18 Feb 84	JOYS OF LIFE *Island IS 153*	61	2 wks

See also Chris Paul.

JOURNEY *US, male vocal/instrumental group* — 9 wks

27 Feb 82	DON'T STOP BELIEVIN' *CBS A 1728*	62	4 wks
11 Sep 82	WHO'S CRYING NOW *CBS A 2725*	46	5 wks

Ruth JOY *UK, female vocalist* — 2 wks

26 Aug 89	DON'T PUSH IT *MCA RJOY 1*	66	2 wks

JOY DIVISION *UK, male vocal/instrumental group* — 21 wks

28 Jun 80	LOVE WILL TEAR US APART *Factory FAC 23*	13	9 wks
29 Oct 83	LOVE WILL TEAR US APART (re-entry) *Factory FAC 23*	19	7 wks
18 Jun 88	ATMOSPHERE *Factory FAC 2137*	34	5 wks

JOY STRINGS *UK, male/female vocal/instrumental group* — 11 wks

27 Feb 64	IT'S AN OPEN SECRET *Regal-Zonophone RZ 501*	32	7 wks
17 Dec 64	A STARRY NIGHT *Regal-Zonophone RZ 504*	35	4 wks

JT and the BIG FAMILY
Italy, male/female vocal/instrumental group — 8 wks

3 Mar 90	● MOMENTS IN SOUL *Champion CHAMP 237*	7	8 wks

JUDAS PRIEST *UK, male vocal/instrumental group* — 49 wks

20 Jan 79	TAKE ON THE WORLD *CBS 6915*	14	10 wks
12 May 79	EVENING STAR *CBS 7312*	53	4 wks
29 Mar 80	LIVING AFTER MIDNIGHT *CBS 8379*	12	7 wks
7 Jun 80	BREAKING THE LAW *CBS 8644*	12	6 wks
23 Aug 80	UNITED *CBS 8897*	26	8 wks
21 Feb 81	DON'T GO *CBS 9520*	51	3 wks
25 Apr 81	HOT ROCKIN' *CBS 1153*	60	3 wks
21 Aug 82	YOU'VE GOT ANOTHER THING COMIN' *CBS A 2611*	66	2 wks
21 Jan 84	FREEWHEEL BURNIN' *CBS A 4054*	42	3 wks
23 Apr 88	JOHNNY. B. GOODE *Atlantic A 9114*	64	2 wks
15 Sep 90	PAINKILLER *CBS 656273 7*	74	1 wk

JUDGE DREAD *UK, male vocalist* — 95 wks

26 Aug 72	BIG SIX *Big Shot BI 608*	11	27 wks
9 Dec 72	● BIG SEVEN *Big Shot BI 613*	8	18 wks
21 Apr 73	BIG EIGHT *Big Shot BI 619*	14	10 wks
5 Jul 75	● JE T'AIME (MOI NON PLUS) *Cactus CT 65*	9	9 wks
27 Sep 75	BIG TEN *Cactus CT 77*	14	7 wks
6 Dec 75	CHRISTMAS IN DREADLAND/ COME OUTSIDE *Cactus CT 80*	14	7 wks
8 May 76	THE WINKLE MAN *Cactus CT 90*	35	4 wks
28 Aug 76	Y VIVA SUSPENDERS *Cactus CT 99*	27	4 wks
2 Apr 77	5TH ANNIVERSARY[CF43] (EP) *Cactus CT 98*	31	4 wks
14 Jan 78	UP WITH THE COCK/ BIG PUNK *Cactus CT 110*	49	1 wk
16 Dec 78	HOKEY COKEY/ JINGLE BELLS *EMI 2881*	59	4 wks

Tracks on 5th Anniversary EP: Jamaica Jerk (off)/Bring Back The Skins/End Of The World/Big Everything.

JUICY *US, male/female vocal duo* — 5 wks

22 Feb 86	SUGAR FREE *Epic A 6917*	45	5 wks

JUICY LUCY *UK, male vocal/instrumental group* — 17 wks

7 Mar 70	WHO DO YOU LOVE *Vertigo V 1*	14	12 wks
10 Oct 70	PRETTY WOMAN *Vertigo 6059 015*	45	2 wks
31 Oct 70	PRETTY WOMAN (re-entry) *Vertigo 6059 015*	44	3 wks

JULIA and COMPANY US, male/female vocal group — 10 wks

3 Mar 84	BREAKIN' DOWN (SUGAR SAMBA) London LON 46	15	8 wks
23 Feb 85	I'M SO HAPPY Next Plateau LON 61	56	2 wks

JULUKA South Africa, male/female vocal/instrumental group — 4 wks

12 Feb 83	SCATTERLINGS OF AFRICA Safari ZULU 1	44	4 wks

Wally JUMP Jr. and the CRIMINAL ELEMENT — 12 wks
US, male producer - Arthur Baker under a false group name

28 Feb 87	TURN ME LOOSE London LON 126	60	2 wks
12 Dec 87	TIGHTEN UP - I JUST CAN'T STOP DANCING Breakout USA 621	24	7 wks
19 Mar 88	PRIVATE PARTY Breakout USA 624	57	3 wks

See also the Criminal Element Orchestra; Arthur Baker.

JUMPING JACKS – See Danny PEPPERMINT and the JUMPING JACKS

Rosemary JUNE US, female vocalist — 9 wks

23 Jan 59	APPLE BLOSSOM TIME Pye International 7N 25005	14	9 wks

JUNGLE BROTHERS US, male rap group — 12 wks

18 Mar 89	BLACK IS BLACK/ STRAIGHT OUT OF THE JUNGLE Gee Street GEE 15	72	1 wk
31 Mar 90	WHAT 'U' WAITIN' '4' Eternal W 9865	35	5 wks
21 Jul 90	DOIN' OUR OWN DANG Eternal W 9754	33	6 wks

Although uncredited, Doin' Our Own Dang features De La Soul and Monie Love. See also Richie Rich meets the Jungle Brothers; De La Soul; Monie Love.

JUNIOR UK, male vocalist — 40 wks

24 Apr 82	● MAMA USED TO SAY (AMERICAN REMIX) Mercury MER 98	7	13 wks
10 Jul 82	TOO LATE Mercury MER 112	20	9 wks
25 Sep 82	LET ME KNOW/ I CAN'T HELP IT Mercury MER 116	53	3 wks
23 Apr 83	COMMUNICATION BREAKDOWN Mercury MER 134	57	3 wks
8 Sep 84	SOMEBODY London LON 50	64	2 wks
9 Feb 85	DO YOU REALLY (WANT MY LOVE) London LON 60	47	4 wks
30 Nov 85	OH LOUISE London LON 75	74	3 wks
25 Aug 90	STEP OFF MCA MCA 1432	63	3 wks

Step Off credited to Junior Giscombe. See also Kim Wilde and Junior.

JUNIORS – See DANNY and the JUNIORS

JUPITER BEYOND – See CALIBRE CUTS

Jimmy JUSTICE UK, male vocalist — 35 wks

29 Mar 62	● WHEN MY LITTLE GIRL IS SMILING Pye 7N 15421	9	13 wks
14 Jun 62	● AIN'T THAT FUNNY Pye 7N 15443	8	11 wks
23 Aug 62	SPANISH HARLEM Pye 7N 15457	20	11 wks

Bill JUSTIS US, male instrumentalist - alto sax — 8 wks

10 Jan 58	RAUNCHY London HLS 8517	24	2 wks
31 Jan 58	RAUNCHY (re-entry) London HLS 8517	11	6 wks

Patrick JUVET France, male vocalist — 19 wks

2 Sep 78	GOT A FEELING Casablanca CAN 127	34	7 wks
4 Nov 78	I LOVE AMERICA Casablanca CAN 132	12	12 wks

Leila K – See ROB 'N' RAZ featuring Leila K

Bert KAEMPFERT Germany, orchestra — 10 wks

23 Dec 65	BYE BYE BLUES Polydor BM 56 504	24	10 wks

KAJAGOOGOO UK, male vocal/instrumental group — 50 wks

22 Jan 83	★ TOO SHY EMI 5359	1	13 wks
2 Apr 83	● OOH TO BE AH EMI 5383	7	8 wks
4 Jun 83	HANG ON NOW EMI 5394	13	7 wks
17 Sep 83	● BIG APPLE EMI 5423	8	8 wks
3 Mar 84	THE LION'S MOUTH EMI 5449	25	7 wks
5 May 84	TURN YOUR BACK ON ME EMI 5646	47	4 wks
21 Sep 85	SHOULDN'T DO THAT Parlophone R 6106	63	3 wks

Act changed name to Kaja for last hit.

KALIN TWINS US, male vocal duo — 18 wks

18 Jul 58	★ WHEN Brunswick 05751	1	18 wks

Kitty KALLEN US, female vocalist — 23 wks

2 Jul 54	★ LITTLE THINGS MEAN A LOT Brunswick 05287	1	23 wks

Gunther KALLMAN CHOIR — 3 wks
Germany, male/female vocal group

24 Dec 64	ELISABETH SERENADE Polydor NH 24678	45	3 wks

Nick KAMEN UK, male vocalist — 33 wks

8 Nov 86	● EACH TIME YOU BREAK MY HEART WEA YZ 90	5	12 wks
28 Feb 87	LOVING YOU IS SWEETER THAN EVER WEA YZ 106	16	9 wks
16 May 87	NOBODY ELSE WEA YZ 122	47	3 wks
28 May 88	TELL ME WEA YZ 184	40	5 wks
28 Apr 90	I PROMISED MYSELF WEA YZ 454	50	4 wks

KANDIDATE UK, male vocal/instrumental group — 28 wks

19 Aug 78	DON'T WANNA SAY GOODNIGHT RAK 280	47	6 wks
17 Mar 79	I DON'T WANNA LOSE YOU RAK 289	11	12 wks
4 Aug 79	GIRLS GIRLS GIRLS RAK 295	34	7 wks
22 Mar 80	LET ME ROCK YOU RAK 306	58	3 wks

Eden KANE UK, male vocalist — 73 wks

1 Jun 61	★ WELL I ASK YOU Decca F 11353	1	21 wks
14 Sep 61	● GET LOST Decca F 11381	10	11 wks
18 Jan 62	● FORGET ME NOT Decca F 11418	3	14 wks
10 May 62	● I DON'T KNOW WHY Decca F 11460	7	13 wks
30 Jan 64	● BOYS CRY Fontana TF 438	8	14 wks

Far Right: NICK KAMEN, model turned singer, became one of Italy's top pop stars.

Right: GURU JOSH proclaimed the new decade 'time for the guru' on his first hit.

In 1987 TOM JONES overtook Shirley Bassey as the all-time top Welsh chart star.

Right: FERN KINNEY covered Steve Allan's minor hit to score a 1980 number one.

Far Right: JOHNNY KEMP (right) attends the annual Soul Train awards.

...ANE GANG UK, male vocal/instrumental group   37 wks

9 May 84	SMALL TOWN CREED *Kitchenware SK 11*	60	2 wks
7 Jul 84	CLOSEST THING TO HEAVEN *Kitchenware SK 15*	12	11 wks
10 Nov 84	RESPECT YOURSELF *Kitchenware SK 16*	21	10 wks
26 Jan 85	RESPECT YOURSELF (re-entry) *Kitchenware SK 16*	75	1 wk
9 Mar 85	GUN LAW *Kitchenware SK 20*	53	4 wks
27 Jun 87	MOTORTOWN *Kitchenware SK 30*	45	5 wks
16 Apr 88	DON'T LOOK ANY FURTHER *Kitchenware SK 33*	52	4 wks

KANSAS US, male vocal/instrumental group   7 wks

1 Jul 78	CARRY ON WAYWARD SON *Kirshner KIR 4932*	51	7 wks

Mory KANTE Guinea, male vocalist   9 wks

23 Jul 88	YE KE YE KE *London LON 171*	29	9 wks

KAOMA France, male/female vocal/instrumental group   20 wks

21 Oct 89	● LAMBADA *CBS 650011 7*	4	18 wks
27 Jan 90	DANCANADO LAMBADA *CBS 655235 7*	62	2 wks

KARIYA US, female vocalist   9 wks

8 Jul 89	LET ME LOVE YOU FOR TONIGHT *Sleeping Bag SBUK 4*	44	6 wks
21 Oct 89	LET ME LOVE YOU FOR TONIGHT (re-entry) *Sleeping Bag SBUK 4*	57	3 wks

Mick KARN featuring David SYLVIAN   2 wks
UK, male vocal/instrumental duo

17 Jan 87	BUOY *Virgin VS 910*	63	2 wks

See also David Sylvian; Midge Ure and Mick Karn.

KARTOON KREW US, male vocal/instrumental group   6 wks

7 Dec 85	INSPECTOR GADGET *Champion CHAMP 6*	58	6 wks

KASENETZ-KATZ SINGING ORCHESTRAL CIRCUS   15 wks
US, male vocal/instrumental group

20 Nov 68	QUICK JOEY SMALL (RUN JOEY RUN) *Buddah 201 022*	19	15 wks

KATRINA and the WAVES   21 wks
UK/US, male/female vocal/instrumental group

4 May 85	● WALKING ON SUNSHINE *Capitol CL 354*	8	12 wks
5 Jul 86	SUN STREET *Capitol CL 407*	22	9 wks

Janet KAY UK, female vocalist   17 wks

9 Jun 79	● SILLY GAMES *Scope SC 2*	2	14 wks
11 Aug 90	SILLY GAMES (re-mix) *Music Factory Dance MFD 006*	62	3 wks

See also Lindy Layton featuring Janet Kay.

Danny KAYE US, male vocalist

27 Feb 53	● WONDERFUL COPENHAGEN *Brunswick 05023*		

KAYE SISTERS UK, female vocal group   20 wks

3 Jan 58	SHAKE ME I RATTLE/ ALONE *Philips PB 752*	27	1 wk
7 Jul 60	● PAPER ROSES *Philips PB 1024*	7	19 wks

See also Frankie Vaughan and the Kaye Sisters; Three Kayes.

KC and the SUNSHINE BAND   102 wks
US, male vocal/instrumental group

17 Aug 74	● QUEEN OF CLUBS *Jayboy BOY 88*	7	12 wks
23 Nov 74	SOUND YOUR FUNKY HORN *Jayboy BOY 83*	17	9 wks
29 Mar 75	GET DOWN TONIGHT *Jayboy BOY 93*	21	9 wks
2 Aug 75	● THAT'S THE WAY (I LIKE IT) *Jayboy BOY 99*	4	10 wks
22 Nov 75	I'M SO CRAZY *Jayboy BOY 101*	34	3 wks
17 Jul 76	(SHAKE SHAKE SHAKE) SHAKE YOUR BOOTY *Jayboy BOY 110*	22	8 wks
11 Dec 76	KEEP IT COMIN' LOVE *Jayboy BOY 112*	31	8 wks
30 Apr 77	I'M YOUR BOOGIE MAN *TK XB 2167*	41	4 wks
6 May 78	BOOGIE SHOES *TK TKR 6025*	34	5 wks
22 Jul 78	IT'S THE SAME OLD SONG *TK TKR 6037*	49	5 wks
8 Dec 79	● PLEASE DON'T GO *TK TKR 7558*	3	12 wks
16 Jul 83	★ GIVE IT UP *Epic EPC A 3017*	1	14 wks
24 Sep 83	(YOU SAID) YOU'D GIMME SOME MORE *Epic A 2760*	41	3 wks

Ernie K-DOE US, male vocalist   7 wks

11 May 61	MOTHER-IN-LAW *London HLU 9330*	29	7 wks

Johnny KEATING UK, orchestra   14 wks

1 Mar 62	● THEME FROM 'Z CARS' *Piccadilly 7N 35032*	8	14 wks

Kevin KEEGAN UK, male vocalist   6 wks

9 Jun 79	HEAD OVER HEELS IN LOVE *EMI 2965*	31	6 wks

Yvonne KEELY – *See Scott FITZGERALD and Yvonne KEELY*

Nelson KEENE UK, male vocalist   5 wks

25 Aug 60	IMAGE OF A GIRL *HMV POP 771*	37	4 wks
29 Sep 60	IMAGE OF A GIRL (re-entry) *HMV POP 771*	45	1 wk

KEITH US, male vocalist   8 wks

26 Jan 67	98.6 *Mercury MF 955*	24	7 wks
16 Mar 67	TELL ME TO MY FACE *Mercury MF 968*	50	1 wk

Jerry KELLER US, male vocalist   14 wks

28 Aug 59	★ HERE COMES SUMMER *London HLR 8890*	1	14 wks

Frank KELLY Ireland, male vocalist   5 wks

24 Dec 83	CHRISTMAS COUNTDOWN *Ritz RITZ 062*	26	4 wks
29 Dec 84	CHRISTMAS COUNTDOWN (re-entry) *Ritz RITZ 062*	54	1 wk

Frankie KELLY *US, male vocalist/instrumentalist* — **2 wks**

2 Nov 85	**AIN'T THAT THE TRUTH** 10 TEN 87	65	2 wks

Grace KELLY – *See Bing CROSBY and Grace KELLY*

Keith KELLY *UK, male vocalist* — **5 wks**

5 May 60	**TEASE ME** Parlophone R 4640	46	1 wk
19 May 60	**TEASE ME (re-entry)** Parlophone R 4640	27	3 wks
18 Aug 60	**LISTEN LITTLE GIRL** Parlophone R 4676	47	1 wk

Roberta KELLY *US, female vocalist* — **3 wks**

21 Jan 78	**ZODIACS** Oasis/Hansa 3	48	1 wk
4 Feb 78	**ZODIACS (re-entry)** Oasis/Hansa 3	44	2 wks

Johnny KEMP *Barbados, male vocalist* — **1 wk**

27 Aug 88	**JUST GOT PAID** CBS 651470 7	68	1 wk

Graham KENDRICK *UK, male vocalist* — **4 wks**

9 Sep 89	**LET THE FLAME BURN BRIGHTER** Power P 30	55	4 wks

Eddie KENDRICKS *US, male vocalist* — **18 wks**

3 Nov 73	**KEEP ON TRUCKIN'** Tamla Motown TMG 873	18	14 wks
16 Mar 74	**BOOGIE DOWN** Tamla Motown TMG 888	39	4 wks

See also Daryl Hall and John Oates.

Jane KENNAWAY and STRANGE BEHAVIOUR *UK, female vocalist, male instrumental group* — **3 wks**

24 Jan 81	**I.O.U.** Deram DM 436	65	3 wks

KENNY *Ireland, male vocalist* — **16 wks**

3 Mar 73	**HEART OF STONE** RAK 144	11	13 wks
30 Jun 73	**GIVE IT TO ME NOW** RAK 153	38	3 wks

KENNY *UK, male vocal/instrumental group* — **39 wks**

7 Dec 74	● **THE BUMP** RAK 186	3	15 wks
8 Mar 75	● **FANCY PANTS** RAK 196	4	9 wks
7 Jun 75	**BABY I LOVE YOU OK** RAK 207	12	7 wks
16 Aug 75	● **JULIE ANN** RAK 214	10	8 wks

Gerard KENNY *US, male vocalist* — **21 wks**

9 Dec 78	**NEW YORK, NEW YORK** RCA PB 5117	43	8 wks
21 Jun 80	**FANTASY** RCA PB 5256	65	1 wk
5 Jul 80	**FANTASY (re-entry)** RCA PB 5256	34	5 wks
18 Feb 84	**THE OTHER WOMAN, THE OTHER MAN** Impression IMS 3	69	4 wks
4 May 85	**NO MAN'S LAND** WEA YZ 38	56	3 wks

Klark KENT *US, male vocalist/multi-instrumentalist* — **4 wks**

26 Aug 78	**DON'T CARE** A & M AMS 7376	48	4 wks

Carol KENYON – *See Paul HARDCASTLE*

KERRI and MICK *Australia, female/male vocal duo* — **3 wks**

28 Apr 84	**SONS AND DAUGHTERS THEME** A-1 A1 286	68	3 wks

Liz KERSHAW and Bruno BROOKES *UK, male/female vocal duo* — **3 wks**

2 Dec 89	**IT TAKES TWO BABY** Spartan CIN 101	53	2 wks
1 Dec 90	**LET'S DANCE** Jive BRUNO 1	54	1 wk

First hit credited to Liz Kershaw, Bruno Brookes, Jive Bunny and Londonbeat. Second hit to Bruno and Liz and the Radio 1 DJ Posse (UK, male/female vocal group). See also Jive Bunny and the Mastermixers; Londonbeat.

Nik KERSHAW *UK, male vocalist* — **87 wks**

19 Nov 83	**I WON'T LET THE SUN GO DOWN ON ME** MCA MCA 816	47	5 wks
28 Jan 84	● **WOULDN'T IT BE GOOD** MCA NIK 2	4	14 wks
14 Apr 84	**DANCING GIRLS** MCA NIK 3	13	9 wks
16 Jun 84	● **I WON'T LET THE SUN GO DOWN ON ME (re-issue)** MCA NIK 4	2	13 wks
15 Sep 84	**HUMAN RACING** MCA NIK 5	19	7 wks
17 Nov 84	● **THE RIDDLE** MCA NIK 6	3	11 wks
16 Mar 85	● **WIDE BOY** MCA NIK 7	9	8 wks
3 Aug 85	● **DON QUIXOTE** MCA NIK 8	10	7 wks
30 Nov 85	**WHEN A HEART BEATS** MCA NIK 9	27	7 wks
11 Oct 86	**NOBODY KNOWS** MCA NIK 10	44	3 wks
13 Dec 86	**RADIO MUSICOLA** MCA NIK 11	43	2 wks
4 Feb 89	**ONE STEP AHEAD** MCA NIK 12	55	1 wk

KEVIN THE GERBIL *UK, male gerbil vocalist* — **6 wks**

4 Aug 84	**SUMMER HOLIDAY** Magnet RAT 3	50	6 wks

Chaka KHAN *US, female vocalist* — **58 wks**

2 Dec 78	**I'M EVERY WOMAN** Warner Bros. K 17269	11	13 wks
20 Oct 84	★ **I FEEL FOR YOU** Warner Bros. W 9209	1	16 wks
19 Jan 85	**THIS IS MY NIGHT** Warner Bros. W 9097	14	6 wks
20 Apr 85	**EYE TO EYE** Warner Bros. W 9009	16	7 wks
12 Jul 86	**LOVE OF A LIFETIME** Warner Bros. W 8671	52	4 wks
21 Jan 89	**IT'S MY PARTY** Warner Bros. W 7678	71	2 wks
6 May 89	● **I'M EVERY WOMAN (re-mix)** Warner Bros. W 2963	8	8 wks
7 Oct 89	**I FEEL FOR YOU (re-mix)** Warner Bros. W 2764	45	2 wks

See also Rufus and Chaka Khan; Quincy Jones.

KICK SQUAD *UK/Germany, male vocal/instrumental group* — **2 wks**

10 Nov 90	**SOUND CLASH (CHAMPION SOUND)** Kickin KICK 2	59	2 wks

KICKING BACK with TAXMAN *UK, male/female vocal/instrumental duo with male rapper* — **8 wks**

17 Mar 90	**DEVOTION** 10 TEN 297	47	4 wks
7 Jul 90	**EVERYTHING** 10 TEN 307	54	4 wks

K.I.D. *Antilles, male/female vocal/instrumental group* — **4 wks**

28 Feb 81	**DON'T STOP** EMI 5143	49	4 wks

KID 'N' PLAY *US, male vocal/instrumental duo* — **7 wks**

18 Jul 87	**LAST NIGHT** Cooltempo COOL 148	71	1 wk
26 Mar 88	**DO THIS MY WAY** Cooltempo COOL 164	48	3 wks

17 Sep 88	GITTIN' FUNKY *Cooltempo COOL 168*	55	3 wks

Johnny KIDD and the PIRATES   62 wks
UK, male vocal/instrumental group

12 Jun 59	PLEASE DON'T TOUCH *HMV POP 615*	26	3 wks
17 Jul 59	PLEASE DON'T TOUCH (re-entry) *HMV POP 615*	25	2 wks
12 Feb 60	YOU GOT WHAT IT TAKES *HMV POP 698*	25	3 wks
16 Jun 60 ★	SHAKIN' ALL OVER *HMV POP 753*	1	19 wks
6 Oct 60	RESTLESS *HMV POP 790*	22	7 wks
13 Apr 61	LINDA LU *HMV POP 853*	47	1 wk
10 Jan 63	SHOT OF RHYTHM AND BLUES *HMV POP 1088*	48	1 wk
25 Jul 63 ●	I'LL NEVER GET OVER YOU *HMV POP 1173*	4	15 wks
28 Nov 63	HUNGRY FOR LOVE *HMV POP 1228*	20	10 wks
30 Apr 64	ALWAYS AND EVER *HMV POP 1269*	46	1 wk

Please Don't Touch *without the Pirates.*

KIDS FROM 'FAME' *US, male/female vocal group*   36 wks

14 Aug 82 ●	HI-FIDELITY *RCA 254*	5	10 wks
2 Oct 82 ●	STARMAKER *RCA 280*	3	10 wks
11 Dec 82	MANNEQUIN *RCA 299*	50	6 wks
9 Apr 83	FRIDAY NIGHT (LIVE VERSION) *RCA 320*	13	10 wks

Hi-Fidelity *is 'featuring Valerie Landsberg'.* Mannequin *is 'featuring Gene Anthony Ray'.*

Greg KIHN BAND *US, male vocal/instrumental group*   2 wks

23 Apr 83	JEOPARDY *Beserkley E 9847*	63	2 wks

KILLING JOKE *UK, male vocal/instrumental group*   41 wks

23 May 81	FOLLOW THE LEADERS *Malicious Damage EGMDS 101*	55	5 wks
20 Mar 82	EMPIRE SONG *Malicious Damage EGO 4*	43	4 wks
30 Oct 82	BIRDS OF A FEATHER *EG EGO 10*	64	2 wks
25 Jun 83	LET'S ALL (GO TO THE FIRE DANCES) *EG EGO 11*	51	3 wks
15 Oct 83	ME OR YOU? *EG EGO 14*	57	1 wk
7 Apr 84	EIGHTIES *EG EGO 16*	60	5 wks
21 Jul 84	A NEW DAY *EG EGO 17*	56	2 wks
2 Feb 85	LOVE LIKE BLOOD *EG EGO 20*	16	9 wks
30 Mar 85	KINGS AND QUEENS *EG EGO 21*	58	3 wks
16 Aug 86	ADORATIONS *EG EGO 27*	42	6 wks
18 Oct 86	SANITY *EG EGO 30*	70	1 wk

KIM – *See MEL and KIM; Kim APPLEBY*

Andy KIM *Canada, male vocalist*   12 wks

24 Aug 74 ●	ROCK ME GENTLY *Capitol CL 15787*	2	12 wks

KING *UK/Ireland, male vocal/instrumental group*   44 wks

12 Jan 85 ●	LOVE AND PRIDE *CBS A 4988*	2	14 wks
23 Mar 85	WON'T YOU HOLD MY HAND NOW *CBS A 6094*	24	8 wks
17 Aug 85 ●	ALONE WITHOUT YOU *CBS A 6308*	8	9 wks
19 Oct 85	THE TASTE OF YOUR TEARS *CBS A 6618*	11	9 wks
11 Jan 86	TORTURE *CBS A 6761*	23	4 wks

See also Paul King.

Albert KING – *See Gary MOORE*

B.B. KING – *See U2 with B.B. KING*

Ben E. KING *US, male vocalist*   35 wks

2 Feb 61	FIRST TASTE OF LOVE *London HLK 9258*	27	11 wks
22 Jun 61	STAND BY ME *London HLK 9358*	50	1 wk
6 Jul 61	STAND BY ME (re-entry) *London HLK 9358*	27	6 wks
5 Oct 61	AMOR AMOR *London HLK 9416*	38	4 wks
14 Feb 87 ★	STAND BY ME (re-issue) *Atlantic A 9361*	1	11 wks
4 Jul 87	SAVE THE LAST DANCE FOR ME *Manhattan MT 25*	69	2 wks

Carole KING *US, female vocalist*   29 wks

20 Sep 62 ●	IT MIGHT AS WELL RAIN UNTIL SEPTEMBER *London HLU 9591*	3	13 wks
7 Aug 71 ●	IT'S TOO LATE *A & M AMS 849*	6	12 wks
28 Oct 72	IT MIGHT AS WELL RAIN UNTIL SEPTEMBER (re-issue) *London HL 10391*	43	4 wks

Dave KING *Canada, male vocalist*   29 wks

17 Feb 56 ●	MEMORIES ARE MADE OF THIS *Decca F 10684*	5	15 wks
13 Apr 56	YOU CAN'T BE TRUE TO TWO *Decca F 10720*	11	9 wks
21 Dec 56	CHRISTMAS AND YOU *Decca F 10791*	23	2 wks
24 Jan 58	THE STORY OF MY LIFE *Decca F 10973*	20	3 wks

See also Various Artists - All Star Hit Parade.

Evelyn 'Champagne' KING *US, female vocalist*   75 wks

13 May 78	SHAME *RCA PC 1122*	39	23 wks
3 Feb 79	I DON'T KNOW IF IT'S RIGHT *RCA PB 1386*	67	2 wks
27 Jun 81	I'M IN LOVE *RCA 95*	27	11 wks
26 Sep 81	IF YOU WANT MY LOVIN' *RCA 131*	43	6 wks
28 Aug 82 ●	LOVE COME DOWN *RCA 249*	7	13 wks
20 Nov 82	BACK TO LOVE *RCA 287*	40	4 wks
19 Feb 83	GET LOOSE *RCA 315*	45	5 wks
9 Nov 85	YOUR PERSONAL TOUCH *RCA PB 49915*	37	5 wks
29 Mar 86	HIGH HORSE *RCA PB 49891*	55	3 wks
23 Jul 88	HOLD ON TO WHAT YOU'VE GOT *Manhattan MT 49*	47	3 wks

Billed simply as Evelyn King on all hits from I'm In Love *to* Get Loose *inclusive.*

Jonathan KING *UK, male vocalist*   67 wks

29 Jul 65 ●	EVERYONE'S GONE TO THE MOON *Decca F 12187*	4	11 wks
10 Jan 70	LET IT ALL HANG OUT *Decca F 12988*	26	7 wks
29 May 71	LAZY BONES *Decca F 13177*	23	8 wks
20 Nov 71	HOOKED ON A FEELING *Decca F 13241*	23	10 wks
5 Feb 72	FLIRT *Decca F 13276*	22	9 wks
6 Sep 75 ●	UNA PALOMA BLANCA *UK 105*	5	11 wks
7 Oct 78	ONE FOR YOU ONE FOR ME *GTO GT 237*	29	6 wks
16 Jun 79	YOU'RE THE GREATEST LOVER *UK International INT 586*	67	2 wks
3 Nov 79	GLORIA *Ariola ARO 198*	65	3 wks

See also Father Abraphart and the Smurps; Bubblerock; 53rd and 3rd; One Hundred Ton and A Feather; Sakkarin; Shag; Sound 9418; Weathermen.

Nosmo KING – *See JAVELLS featuring Nosmo KING*

Paul KING *UK, male vocalist*   3 wks

2 May 87	I KNOW *CBS PKING 1*	59	3 wks

See also King.

Solomon KING *US, male vocalist*   28 wks

3 Jan 68 ●	SHE WEARS MY RING *Columbia DB 8325*	3	18 wks
1 May 68	WHEN WE WERE YOUNG *Columbia DB 8402*	21	10 wks

KING BROTHERS *UK, male vocal/instrumental group*   **74 wks**

31 May 57	●	A WHITE SPORT COAT *Parlophone R 4310*	6	14 wks
9 Aug 57		IN THE MIDDLE OF AN ISLAND *Parlophone R 4338*	19	13 wks
6 Dec 57		WAKE UP LITTLE SUSIE *Parlophone R 4367*	22	3 wks
31 Jan 58		PUT A LIGHT IN THE WINDOW *Parlophone R 4389*	29	1 wk
14 Feb 58		PUT A LIGHT IN THE WINDOW (re-entry) *Parlophone R 4389*	28	1 wk
28 Feb 58		PUT A LIGHT IN THE WINDOW (2nd re-entry) *Parlophone R 4389*	25	2 wks
14 Apr 60	●	STANDING ON THE CORNER *Parlophone R 4639*	4	11 wks
28 Jul 60		MAIS OUI *Parlophone R 4672*	16	10 wks
12 Jan 61		DOLL HOUSE *Parlophone R 4715*	21	8 wks
2 Mar 61		76 TROMBONES *Parlophone R 4737*	19	11 wks

KING KURT *UK, male vocal/instrumental group*   **16 wks**

15 Oct 83	DESTINATION ZULULAND *Stiff BUY 189*	36	6 wks
28 Apr 84	MACK THE KNIFE *Stiff BUY 199*	55	4 wks
4 Aug 84	BANANA BANANA *Stiff BUY 206*	54	4 wks
15 Nov 86	AMERICA *Polydor KURT 1*	73	1 wk
2 May 87	THE LAND OF RING DANG DO *Polydor KURT 2*	67	1 wk

KING SUN-D'MOET *US, male rap/scratch duo*   **3 wks**

11 Jul 87	HEY LOVE *Flame MELT 5*	66	3 wks

KING TRIGGER *UK, male/female vocal/instrumental group*   **4 wks**

14 Aug 82	THE RIVER *Chrysalis CHS 2623*	57	4 wks

KINGDOM COME *US, male vocal/instrumental group*   **2 wks**

16 Apr 88	GET IT ON *Polydor KCS 1*	75	1 wk
6 May 89	DO YOU LIKE IT *Polydor KCS 3*	73	1 wk

KINGS OF SWING ORCHESTRA   **5 wks**
Australia, orchestra

1 May 82	SWITCHED ON SWING *Philips Swing 1*	48	5 wks

KINGSMEN *US, male vocal/instrumental group*   **7 wks**

30 Jan 64	LOUIE LOUIE *Pye International 7N 25231*	26	7 wks

KINGSTON TRIO *US, male vocal/instrumental group*   **15 wks**

21 Nov 58	●	TOM DOOLEY *Capitol CL 14951*	5	14 wks
4 Dec 59		SAN MIGUEL *Capitol CL 15073*	29	1 wk

KINKS *UK, male vocal/instrumental group*   **213 wks**

13 Aug 64	★	YOU REALLY GOT ME *Pye 7N 15673*	1	12 wks
29 Oct 64	●	ALL DAY AND ALL OF THE NIGHT *Pye 7N 15714*	2	14 wks
21 Jan 65	★	TIRED OF WAITING FOR YOU *Pye 7N 15759*	1	10 wks
25 Mar 65		EVERYBODY'S GONNA BE HAPPY *Pye 7N 15813*	17	8 wks
27 May 65	●	SET ME FREE *Pye 7N 15854*	9	11 wks
5 Aug 65	●	SEE MY FRIEND *Pye 7N 15919*	10	9 wks
2 Dec 65	●	TILL THE END OF THE DAY *Pye 7N 15981*	8	12 wks
3 Mar 66	●	DEDICATED FOLLOWER OF FASHION *Pye 7N 17064*	4	11 wks
9 Jun 66	★	SUNNY AFTERNOON *Pye 7N 17125*	1	13 wks
24 Nov 66	●	DEAD END STREET *Pye 7N 17222*	5	11 wks
11 May 67	●	WATERLOO SUNSET *Pye 7N 17321*	2	11 wks
18 Oct 67	●	AUTUMN ALMANAC *Pye 7N 17400*	3	11 wks
17 Apr 68		WONDERBOY *Pye 7N 17468*	36	5 wks
17 Jul 68		DAYS *Pye 7N 17573*	12	10 wks

16 Apr 69		PLASTIC MAN *Pye 7N 17724*	31	4 wks
10 Jan 70		VICTORIA *Pye 7N 17865*	33	4 wks
4 Jul 70	●	LOLA *Pye 7N 17961*	2	14 wks
12 Dec 70	●	APEMAN *Pye 7N 45016*	5	14 wks
27 May 72		SUPERSONIC ROCKET SHIP *RCA 2211*	16	8 wks
27 Jun 81		BETTER THINGS *Arista ARIST 415*	46	5 wks
6 Aug 83		COME DANCING *Arista ARIST 502*	12	9 wks
15 Oct 83		DON'T FORGET TO DANCE *Arista ARIST 524*	58	3 wks
15 Oct 83		YOU REALLY GOT ME (re-issue) *PRT KD1*	47	4 wks

Fern KINNEY *US, female vocalist*   **11 wks**

16 Feb 80	★	TOGETHER WE ARE BEAUTIFUL *WEA K 79111*	1	11 wks

KINSHASA BAND – *See Johnny WAKELIN*

Kathy KIRBY *UK, female vocalist*   **54 wks**

15 Aug 63		DANCE ON *Decca F 11682*	11	13 wks
7 Nov 63	●	SECRET LOVE *Decca F 11759*	4	18 wks
20 Feb 64	●	LET ME GO LOVER *Decca F 11832*	10	11 wks
7 May 64		YOU'RE THE ONE *Decca F 11892*	17	9 wks
4 Mar 65		I BELONG *Decca F 12087*	36	3 wks

Bo KIRKLAND and Ruth DAVIS   **9 wks**
US, male/female vocal duo

4 Jun 77	YOU'RE GONNA GET NEXT TO ME *EMI International INT 532*	12	9 wks

KISS *US, male vocal/instrumental group*   **47 wks**

30 Jun 79		I WAS MADE FOR LOVIN' YOU *Casablanca CAN 152*	50	7 wks
20 Feb 82		A WORLD WITHOUT HEROES *Casablanca KISS 002*	55	3 wks
30 Apr 83		CREATURES OF THE NIGHT *Casablanca KISS 4*	34	4 wks
29 Oct 83		LICK IT UP *Vertigo KISS 5*	31	5 wks
8 Sep 84		HEAVEN'S ON FIRE *Vertigo VER 12*	43	3 wks
9 Nov 85		TEARS ARE FALLING *Vertigo KISS 6*	57	2 wks
3 Oct 87	●	CRAZY CRAZY NIGHTS *Vertigo KISS 7*	4	9 wks
5 Dec 87		REASON TO LIVE *Vertigo KISS 8*	33	7 wks
10 Sep 88		TURN ON THE NIGHT *Vertigo KISS 9*	41	3 wks
18 Nov 89		HIDE YOUR HEART *Vertigo KISS 10*	59	2 wks
31 Mar 90		FOREVER *Vertigo KISS 11*	65	2 wks

KISS AMC *UK, female vocal duo*   **5 wks**

1 Jul 89	A BIT OF... *Syncopate SY 29*	58	2 wks
19 Aug 89	A BIT OF U2 (re-entry) *Syncopate SY 29*	58	2 wks
3 Feb 90	MY DOCS *Syncopate XAMC 1*	66	1 wk

Before the re-entry of A Bit Of U2, copyright problems meant that the disc was unable to be given its full title.

KISSING THE PINK   **14 wks**
UK, male/female vocal/instrumental group

5 Mar 83	LAST FILM *Magnet KTP 3*	19	14 wks

Mac and Katie KISSOON *UK, male/female vocal duo*   **33 wks**

19 Jun 71		CHIRPY CHIRPY CHEEP CHEEP *Young Blood YB 1026*	41	1 wk
18 Jan 75	●	SUGAR CANDY KISSES *Polydor 2058 531*	3	10 wks
3 May 75	●	DON'T DO IT BABY *State STAT 4*	9	8 wks
30 Aug 75		LIKE A BUTTERFLY *State STAT 9*	18	9 wks
15 May 76		THE TWO OF US *State STAT 21*	46	5 wks

Kevin KITCHEN UK, male vocalist · 3 wks

| 20 Apr 85 | PUT MY ARMS AROUND YOU China WOK 1 | 64 | 3 wks |

Eartha KITT US, female vocalist · 25 wks

1 Apr 55 ●	UNDER THE BRIDGES OF PARIS HMV B 10647	7	9 wks
10 Jun 55	UNDER THE BRIDGES OF PARIS (re-entry) HMV B 10647	20	1 wk
3 Dec 83	WHERE IS MY MAN Record Shack SOHO 11	36	11 wks
7 Jul 84	I LOVE MEN Record Shack SOHO 21	50	3 wks
12 Apr 86	THIS IS MY LIFE Record Shack SOHO 61	73	1 wk

See also Eartha Kitt and Bronski Beat.

Eartha KITT and BRONSKI BEAT · 7 wks
US, female vocalist and UK, male vocal/instrumental group

| 1 Jul 89 | CHA CHA HEELS Arista 112331 | 32 | 7 wks |

See also Eartha Kitt; Bronski Beat.

KJELD – *See JAN and KJELD*

KLAXONS Belgium, male vocal/instrumental group · 6 wks

| 10 Dec 83 | THE CLAP CLAP SOUND PRT 7P 290 | 45 | 6 wks |

KLEEER US, male/female vocal/instrumental group · 10 wks

| 17 Mar 79 | KEEEP YOUR BODY WORKING Atlantic LV 21 | 51 | 6 wks |
| 14 Mar 81 | GET TOUGH Atlantic 11560 | 49 | 4 wks |

KLF featuring the CHILDREN OF THE REVOLUTION UK, male vocal/instrumental group · 12 wks

| 11 Aug 90 ● | WHAT TIME IS LOVE (LIVE AT TRANCENTRAL) KLF Commmunications KLF 004 | 5 | 12 wks |

KNACK US, male vocal/instrumental group · 12 wks

| 30 Jun 79 ● | MY SHARONA Capitol CL 16087 | 6 | 10 wks |
| 13 Oct 79 | GOOD GIRLS DON'T Capitol CL 16097 | 66 | 2 wks |

Frederick KNIGHT US, male vocalist · 10 wks

| 10 Jun 72 | I'VE BEEN LONELY SO LONG Stax 2025 098 | 22 | 10 wks |

Gladys KNIGHT and the PIPS · 176 wks
US, female vocalist and male vocal backing group

8 Jun 67	TAKE ME IN YOUR ARMS AND LOVE ME Tamla Motown TMG 604	13	15 wks
27 Dec 67	I HEARD IT THROUGH THE GRAPEVINE Tamla Motown TMG 629	47	1 wk
17 Jun 72	JUST WALK IN MY SHOES Tamla Motown TMG 813	35	8 wks
25 Nov 72	HELP ME MAKE IT THROUGH THE NIGHT Tamla Motown TMG 830	11	17 wks
3 Mar 73	LOOK OF LOVE Tamla Motown TMG 844	21	9 wks
26 May 73	NEITHER ONE OF US Tamla Motown TMG 855	31	7 wks
5 Apr 75 ●	THE WAY WE WERE/ TRY TO REMEMBER Buddah BDS 428	4	15 wks
2 Aug 75 ●	BEST THING THAT EVER HAPPENED TO ME Buddah BDS 432	7	10 wks
15 Nov 75	PART TIME LOVER Buddah BDS 438	30	5 wks
8 May 76 ●	MIDNIGHT TRAIN TO GEORGIA Buddah BDS 444	10	9 wks
21 Aug 76	MAKE YOURS A HAPPY HOME Buddah BDS 447	35	4 wks
6 Nov 76	SO SAD THE SONG Buddah BDS 448	20	9 wks
15 Jan 77	NOBODY BUT YOU Buddah BDS 451	34	2 wks
28 May 77 ●	BABY DON'T CHANGE YOUR MIND Buddah BDS 458	4	12 wks
24 Sep 77	HOME IS WHERE THE HEART IS Buddah BDS 460	35	4 wks
8 Apr 78	THE ONE AND ONLY Buddah BDS 470	32	4 wks
13 May 78	THE ONE AND ONLY (re-entry) Buddah BDS 470	66	1 wk
24 Jun 78	COME BACK AND FINISH WHAT YOU STARTED Buddah BDS 473	15	13 wks
30 Sep 78	IT'S A BETTER THAN GOOD TIME Buddah BDS 478	59	4 wks
30 Aug 80	TASTE OF BITTER LOVE CBS 8890	35	6 wks
8 Nov 80	BOURGIE BOURGIE CBS 9081	32	6 wks
16 Jan 88	LOVE OVERBOARD MCA MCA 1223	42	4 wks
10 Jun 89 ●	LICENCE TO KILL MCA MCA 1339	6	11 wks

Licence To Kill credits only Gladys Knight. See also Johnny Mathis and Gladys Knight; Dionne Warwick and Friends.

Robert KNIGHT US, male vocalist · 26 wks

17 Jan 68	EVERLASTING LOVE Monument MON 1008	40	2 wks
24 Nov 73 ●	LOVE ON A MOUNTAIN TOP Monument MNT 1875	10	16 wks
9 Mar 74	EVERLASTING LOVE (re-issue) Monument MNT 2106	19	8 wks

Mark KNOPFLER UK, male vocalist/instrumentalist - guitar · 3 wks

| 12 Mar 83 | GOING HOME (THEME OF 'LOCAL HERO') Vertigo DSTR 4 | 56 | 3 wks |

Buddy KNOX US, male vocalist · 5 wks

| 10 May 57 | PARTY DOLL Columbia DB 3914 | 29 | 3 wks |
| 16 Aug 62 | SHE'S GONE Liberty LIB 55473 | 45 | 2 wks |

Frankie KNUCKLES US, male producer · 7 wks

| 17 Jun 89 | TEARS FFRR F 108 | 50 | 3 wks |
| 21 Oct 89 | YOUR LOVE Trax TRAXT 3 | 59 | 4 wks |

Tears has the credit 'presents Satoshi Tomiie' - Japan, male vocalist.

Moe KOFFMAN QUARTETTE · 2 wks
Canada, male instrumental group, Moe Koffman, flute

| 28 Mar 58 | SWINGIN' SHEPHERD BLUES London HLJ 8549 | 23 | 2 wks |

KOKOMO US, male instrumentalist - piano · 7 wks

| 13 Apr 62 | ASIA MINOR London HLU 9305 | 35 | 7 wks |

KOKOMO UK, male/female vocal/instrumental group · 3 wks

| 29 May 82 | A LITTLE BIT FURTHER AWAY CBS A 2064 | 45 | 3 wks |

KON KAN Canada, male vocal/instrumental duo · 13 wks

| 4 Mar 89 ● | I BEG YOUR PARDON Atlantic A 8969 | 5 | 13 wks |

John KONGOS South · 25 wks
Africa, male vocalist/multi-instrumentalist

| 22 May 71 ● | HE'S GONNA STEP ON YOU AGAIN Fly BUG 8 | 4 | 14 wks |
| 20 Nov 71 ● | TOKOLOSHE MAN Fly BUG 14 | 4 | 11 wks |

KOOL and the GANG US, male vocal/instrumental group — 206 wks

27 Oct 79	● LADIES NIGHT Mercury KOOL 7	9	12 wks
19 Jan 80	TOO HOT Mercury KOOL 8	23	8 wks
12 Jul 80	HANGIN' OUT De-Lite KOOL 9	52	4 wks
1 Nov 80	● CELEBRATION De-Lite KOOL 10	7	13 wks
21 Feb 81	JONES VS JONES/ SUMMER MADNESS De-Lite KOOL 11	17	11 wks
30 May 81	TAKE IT TO THE TOP De-Lite DE 2	15	9 wks
31 Oct 81	STEPPIN' OUT De-Lite DE 4	12	13 wks
19 Dec 81	● GET DOWN ON IT De-Lite DE 5	3	12 wks
6 Mar 82	TAKE MY HEART (YOU CAN HAVE IT IF YOU WANT IT) De-Lite DE 6	29	7 wks
7 Aug 82	BIG FUN De-Lite DE 7	14	8 wks
16 Oct 82	● OOH LA LA LA (LET'S GO DANCIN') De-Lite DE 9	6	9 wks
4 Dec 82	HI DE HI, HI DE HO De-Lite DE 14	29	8 wks
10 Dec 83	STRAIGHT AHEAD De-Lite DE 15	15	10 wks
11 Feb 84	● JOANNA / TONIGHT De-Lite DE 16	2	11 wks
14 Apr 84	(WHEN YOU SAY YOU LOVE SOMEBODY) IN THE HEART De-Lite DE 17	7	8 wks
24 Nov 84	FRESH De-Lite DE 18	11	12 wks
9 Feb 85	MISLED De-Lite DE 19	28	5 wks
11 May 85	● CHERISH De-Lite DE 20	4	22 wks
2 Nov 85	EMERGENCY De-Lite DE 21	50	3 wks
22 Nov 86	VICTORY Club JAB 44	67	2 wks
20 Dec 86	VICTORY (re-entry) Club JAB 44	30	10 wks
21 Mar 87	STONE LOVE Club JAB 47	45	4 wks
31 Dec 88	CELEBRATION (re-mix) Club JAB 78	56	5 wks

Funky Stuff and Hollywood Swinging *only appeared on 12-inch and EP versions of Kool 11, although the chart listed all four songs.*

KOOL ROCK STEADY – *See TYREE*

KORGIS UK, male vocal/instrumental duo — 27 wks

23 Jun 79	IF I HAD YOU Rialto TREB 103	13	12 wks
24 May 80	● EVERYBODY'S GOT TO LEARN SOMETIME Rialto TREB 115	5	12 wks
30 Aug 80	IF IT'S ALRIGHT WITH YOU BABY Rialto TREB 118	56	3 wks

KRAFTWERK Germany, male instrumental/vocal group — 63 wks

10 May 75	AUTOBAHN Vertigo 6147 012	11	9 wks
28 Oct 78	NEON LIGHTS Capitol CL 15998	53	3 wks
9 May 81	POCKET CALCULATOR EMI 5175	39	6 wks
11 Jul 81	COMPUTER LOVE/ THE MODEL EMI 5207	36	8 wks
26 Dec 81	★ COMPUTER LOVE/ THE MODEL (re-entry) EMI 5207	1	13 wks
20 Feb 82	SHOWROOM DUMMIES EMI 5272	25	5 wks
6 Aug 83	TOUR DE FRANCE EMI 5413	22	8 wks
25 Aug 84	TOUR DE FRANCE (re-entry) EMI 5413	24	11 wks

Billy J. KRAMER and the DAKOTAS — 71 wks
UK, male vocalist and male instrumental backing group

2 May 63	● DO YOU WANT TO KNOW A SECRET? Parlophone R 5023	2	15 wks
1 Aug 63	★ BAD TO ME Parlophone R 5049	1	14 wks
7 Nov 63	● I'LL KEEP YOU SATISFIED Parlophone R 5073	4	13 wks
27 Feb 64	★ LITTLE CHILDREN Parlophone R 5105	1	13 wks
23 Jul 64	FROM A WINDOW Parlophone R 5156	10	8 wks
20 May 65	TRAINS AND BOATS AND PLANES Parlophone R 5285	12	8 wks

See also Dakotas.

KRANKIES UK, male/female vocal duo — 6 wks

7 Feb 81	FAN'DABI'DOZI Monarch MON 21	71	1 wk
7 Mar 81	FAN'DABI'DOZI (re-entry) Monarch MON 21	46	5 wks

Lenny KRAVITZ US, male vocalist — 6 wks

2 Jun 90	MR. CABDRIVER Virgin America VUS 20	58	2 wks
4 Aug 90	LET LOVE RULE Virgin America VUS 26	39	4 wks

KRAZE US, male/female vocal/instrumental group — 6 wks

22 Oct 88	THE PARTY MCA MCA 1288	29	5 wks
17 Jun 89	LET'S PLAY HOUSE MCA MCA 1337	71	1 wk

KREW-KATS UK, male instrumental group — 10 wks

9 Mar 61	TRAMBONE HMV POP 840	33	9 wks
18 May 61	TRAMBONE (re-entry) HMV POP 840	49	1 wk

Marty KRISTIAN – *See NEW SEEKERS*

KROKUS Switzerland/Malta, male vocal/instrumental group — 2 wks

16 May 81	INDUSTRIAL STRENGTH (EP) Ariola ARO 258	62	2 wks

Tracks on Industrial Strength EP: Bedside Radio/Easy Rocker/Celebration/Bye Bye Baby.

KRUSH UK, male/female vocal/instrumental group — 15 wks

5 Dec 87	● HOUSE ARREST Club JAB 63	3	15 wks

Charlie KUNZ US, male instrumentalist - piano — 4 wks

17 Dec 54	PIANO MEDLEY NO. 114 Decca F 10419	20	3 wks
14 Jan 55	PIANO MEDLEY NO. 114 (re-entry) Decca F 10419	16	1 wk

Medley titles: There Must Be A Reason/Hold My Hand/If I Give My Heart To You/Little Things Mean A Lot/Make Her Mine/My Son My Son.

KURSAAL FLYERS UK, male vocal/instrumental group — 10 wks

20 Nov 76	LITTLE DOES SHE KNOW CBS 4689	14	10 wks

L.A. MIX UK, male/female vocal/instrumental duo — 22 wks

10 Oct 87	DON'T STOP (JAMMIN') Breakout USA 615	47	4 wks
21 May 88	● CHECK THIS OUT Breakout USA 629	6	7 wks
8 Jul 89	GET LOOSE Breakout USA 659	25	6 wks
16 Sep 89	LOVE TOGETHER Breakout USA 662	66	2 wks
15 Sep 90	COMING BACK FOR MORE A &M AM 579	50	3 wks

LA NA NEE NEE NOO NOO – *See BANANARAMA/LA NA NEE NEE NOO NOO*

Danny LA RUE UK, male vocalist — 9 wks

18 Dec 68	ON MOTHER KELLY'S DOORSTEP Page One POF 108	33	9 wks

Denise LA SALLE US, female vocalist — 13 wks

15 Jun 85	● MY TOOT TOOT Epic A 6334	6	13 wks

LABELLE US, female vocal group   9 wks

| 22 Mar 75 | LADY MARMALADE (VOULEZ-VOUS COUCHER AVEC MOI CE SOIR?) Epic EPC 2852 | 17 | 9 wks |

See also Patti Labelle.

Patti LABELLE US, female vocalist   6 wks

| 2 Aug 86 | OH, PEOPLE MCA MCA 1075 | 26 | 6 wks |

See also Patti Labelle and Michael McDonald; Labelle.

Patti LABELLE and Michael McDONALD   13 wks
US, female/male vocal duo

| 3 May 86 ● | ON MY OWN MCA MCA 1045 | 2 | 13 wks |

See also Patti Labelle; Michael McDonald.

LADIES CHOICE UK, male vocalist   4 wks

| 25 Jan 86 | FUNKY SENSATION Sure Delight SD 01 | 41 | 4 wks |

LAID BACK Norway, male vocal/instrumental duo   4 wks

| 5 May 90 | BAKERMAN Arista 112356 | 44 | 4 wks |

Cleo LAINE UK, female vocalist   14 wks

| 29 Dec 60 | LET'S SLIP AWAY Fontana H 269 | 42 | 1 wk |
| 14 Sep 61 ● | YOU'LL ANSWER TO ME Fontana H 326 | 5 | 13 wks |

Frankie LAINE US, male vocalist   253 wks

14 Nov 52 ●	HIGH NOON Columbia DB 3113	7	7 wks
20 Mar 53	GIRL IN THE WOOD Columbia DB 2907	11	1 wk
3 Apr 53 ★	I BELIEVE Philips PB 117	1	36 wks
4 Sep 53 ●	WHERE THE WIND BLOWS Philips PB 167	2	12 wks
16 Oct 53 ★	HEY JOE Philips PB 172	1	8 wks
30 Oct 53 ●	ANSWER ME Philips PB 196	1	17 wks
8 Jan 54 ●	BLOWING WILD Philips PB 207	2	12 wks
26 Mar 54 ●	GRANADA Philips PB 242	10	1 wk
9 Apr 54 ●	GRANADA (re-entry) Philips PB 242	9	1 wk
16 Apr 54 ●	THE KID'S LAST FIGHT Philips PB 258	3	10 wks
13 Aug 54 ●	MY FRIEND Philips PB 316	3	15 wks
8 Oct 54 ●	THERE MUST BE A REASON Philips PB 306	9	9 wks
22 Oct 54 ●	RAIN RAIN RAIN Philips PB 311	8	16 wks
11 Mar 55	IN THE BEGINNING Philips PB 404	20	1 wk
24 Jun 55 ●	COOL WATER Philips PB 465	2	22 wks
15 Jul 55 ●	STRANGE LADY IN TOWN Philips PB 478	6	13 wks
11 Nov 55	HUMMING BIRD Philips PB 498	16	1 wk
25 Nov 55 ●	HAWKEYE Philips PB 519	7	8 wks
20 Jan 56 ●	SIXTEEN TONS Philips PB 539	10	3 wks
4 May 56	HELL HATH NO FURY Philips PB 585	28	1 wk
7 Sep 56 ★	A WOMAN IN LOVE Philips PB 617	1	21 wks
28 Dec 56 ●	MOONLIGHT GAMBLER Philips PB 638	13	12 wks
29 Mar 57	MOONLIGHT GAMBLER (re-entry) Philips PB 638	28	1 wk
26 Apr 57	LOVE IS A GOLDEN RING Philips PB 676	19	5 wks
13 Nov 59 ●	RAWHIDE Philips PB 965	6	17 wks
31 Mar 60	RAWHIDE (re-entry) Philips PB 965	41	2 wks
11 May 61	GUNSLINGER Philips PB 1135	50	1 wk

See also Frankie Laine and Jimmy Boyd; Frankie Laine and Johnnie Ray; Doris Day and Frankie Laine.

Frankie LAINE and Jimmy BOYD   16 wks
US, male vocal duo

| 8 May 53 ● | TELL ME A STORY Philips PB 126 | 5 | 15 wks |
| 11 Sep 53 | TELL ME A STORY (re-entry) Philips PB 126 | 12 | 1 wk |

See also Frankie Laine; Jimmy Boyd.

Frankie LAINE and Johnnie RAY   4 wks
US, male vocal duo

| 4 Oct 57 | GOOD EVENING FRIENDS/ UP ABOVE MY HEAD Philips PB 708 | 25 | 4 wks |

See also Frankie Laine; Johnnie Ray.

Greg LAKE UK, male vocalist   12 wks

6 Dec 75 ●	I BELIEVE IN FATHER CHRISTMAS Manticore K 13511	2	7 wks
25 Dec 82	I BELIEVE IN FATHER CHRISTMAS (re-entry) Manticore K 13511	72	3 wks
24 Dec 83	I BELIEVE IN FATHER CHRISTMAS (2nd re-entry) Manticore K 13511	65	2 wks

See also Emerson, Lake and Palmer.

Annabel LAMB UK, female vocalist   7 wks

| 27 Aug 83 | RIDERS ON THE STORM A & M AM 131 | 27 | 7 wks |

LAMBRETTAS UK, male vocal/instrumental group   24 wks

1 Mar 80 ●	POISON IVY Rocket XPRESS 25	7	12 wks
24 May 80	D-A-A-ANCE Rocket XPRESS 33	12	8 wks
23 Aug 80	ANOTHER DAY (ANOTHER GIRL) Rocket XPRESS 36	49	4 wks

LANCASTRIANS UK, male vocal/instrumental group   2 wks

| 24 Dec 64 | WE'LL SING IN THE SUNSHINE Pye 7N 15732 | 47 | 2 wks |

Major LANCE US, male vocalist   2 wks

| 13 Feb 64 | UM UM UM UM UM UM Columbia DB 7205 | 40 | 2 wks |

James LANCELOT – *See Sarah BRIGHTMAN and Paul MILES-KINGSTON*

Valerie LANDSBERG – *See KIDS FROM FAME*

LANDSCAPE UK, male vocal/instrumental group   20 wks

| 28 Feb 81 ● | EINSTEIN A GO-GO RCA 22 | 5 | 13 wks |
| 23 May 81 | NORMAN BATES RCA 60 | 40 | 7 wks |

Ronnie LANE UK, male vocalist   12 wks

| 12 Jan 74 | HOW COME GM GMS 011 | 11 | 8 wks |
| 15 Jun 74 | THE POACHER GM GMS 024 | 36 | 4 wks |

Both hits have the credit 'accompanied by the band Slim Chance'.

Don LANG UK, male vocalist   18 wks

4 Nov 55	CLOUDBURST HMV POP 115	16	2 wks
2 Dec 55	CLOUDBURST (re-entry) HMV POP 115	18	1 wk
13 Jan 56	CLOUDBURST (2nd re-entry) HMV POP 115	20	1 wk

5 Jul 57	SCHOOL DAY *HMV POP 350*..............................	26	2 wks
23 May 58 ●	WITCH DOCTOR *HMV POP 488*	5	11 wks
10 Mar 60	SINK THE BISMARCK *HMV POP 714*	43	1 wk

School Day *and* Witch Doctor *credit Don Lang and his Frantic Five.*

Thomas LANG *UK, male vocalist*   3 wks

30 Jan 88	THE HAPPY MAN *Epic VOW 4*	67	3 wks

Mario LANZA *US, male vocalist*   32 wks

14 Nov 52 ●	BECAUSE YOU'RE MINE *HMV DA 2017*....................	3	24 wks
4 Feb 55	DRINKING SONG *HMV DA 2065*	13	1 wk
18 Feb 55	I'LL WALK WITH GOD *HMV DA 2062*	18	1 wk
22 Apr 55	SERENADE *HMV DA 2065*	19	1 wk
6 May 55	I'LL WALK WITH GOD (re-entry) *HMV DA 2062*.........	20	1 wk
6 May 55	SERENADE (re-entry) *HMV DA 2065*	15	2 wks
14 Sep 56	SERENADE *HMV DA 2085*	25	1 wk
12 Oct 56	SERENADE (re-entry) *HMV DA 2085*	29	1 wk

DA 2065 and DA 2085 are two different songs.

Julius LAROSA *US, male vocalist*   9 wks

4 Jul 58	TORERO *RCA 1063*	15	9 wks

LA'S *UK, male vocal/instrumental group*   15 wks

14 Jan 89	THERE SHE GOES *Go! Discs GOLAS 2*	59	4 wks
15 Sep 90	TIMELESS MELODY *Go! Discs GOLAS 4*	57	2 wks
3 Nov 90	THERE SHE GOES (re-issue) *Go! Discs GOLAS 5*	13†	9 wks

James LAST BAND *Germany, male orchestra*   4 wks

3 May 80	THE SEDUCTION (LOVE THEME) *Polydor PD 2071*.......	48	4 wks

LATE SHOW *UK, male vocal/instrumental group*   6 wks

3 Mar 79	BRISTOL STOMP *Decca F 13822*	40	6 wks

LATIN QUARTER
UK, male/female vocal/instrumental group   10 wks

18 Jan 86	RADIO AFRICA *Rockin' Horse RH 102*	19	9 wks
18 Apr 87	NOMZAMO (ONE PEOPLE ONE CAUSE) *Rockin' Horse RH 113*....................................	73	1 wk

Gino LATINO *Italy, male producer*   7 wks

20 Jan 90	WELCOME *FFRR F 126*	17	7 wks

LATINO RAVE *Multinational, album sampler*   13 wks

25 Nov 89	DEEP HEAT '89 *Deep Heat DEEP 10*.....................	12	11 wks
28 Apr 90	THE SIXTH SENSE *Deep Heat DEEP 12*	49	2 wks

Deep Heat '89 *featured* Pump Up The Jam *by* Technotronic, Stakker Humanoid *by* Humanoid, A Day In The Life *by* Black Riot, Work It To The Bone *by* LNR, I Can Make U Dance *by DJ 'Fast' Eddie,* Voodoo Ray *by* A Guy Called Gerald, Numero Uno *by* Starlight, Bango (To The Batmobile) *by* Todd Terry, Break 4 Love *by* Raze *and* Don't Scandalize Minc *by* Sugar Bear. *See also separate lists of these artists.*

Stacy LATTISAW *US, female vocalist*   14 wks

14 Jun 80 ●	JUMP TO THE BEAT *Atlantic/Cotillion K 11496*...............	3	11 wks
30 Aug 80	DYNAMITE *Atlantic K 11554*............................	51	3 wks

LAUNCHERS – *See Ezz RECO and the LAUNCHERS with Boysie GRANT*

Cyndi LAUPER *US, female vocalist*   69 wks

14 Jan 84 ●	GIRLS JUST WANT TO HAVE FUN *Portrait A 3943*.........	2	12 wks
24 Mar 84	TIME AFTER TIME *Portrait A 4290*......................	54	4 wks
16 Jun 84 ●	TIME AFTER TIME (re-entry) *Portrait A 4290*	3	13 wks
1 Sep 84	SHE BOP *Portrait A 4620*	46	5 wks
17 Nov 84	ALL THROUGH THE NIGHT *Portrait A 4849*	64	2 wks
20 Sep 86	TRUE COLOURS *Portrait 650026 7*	12	11 wks
27 Dec 86	CHANGE OF HEART *Portrait CYNDI 1*..................	74	1 wk
10 Jan 87	CHANGE OF HEART (re-entry) *Portrait CYNDI 1*...........	67	1 wk
28 Mar 87	WHAT'S GOING ON *Portrait CYN 1*	57	3 wks
20 May 89 ●	I DROVE ALL NIGHT *Epic CYN 4*.......................	7	12 wks
5 Aug 89	MY FIRST NIGHT WITHOUT YOU *Epic CYN 5*	53	4 wks
30 Dec 89	HEADING WEST *Epic CYN 6*	68	1 wk

LAUREL and HARDY *UK, male vocal/instrumental duo*   2 wks

2 Apr 83	CLUNK CLINK *CBS A 3213*...............................	65	2 wks

LAUREL and HARDY with the AVALON   10 wks
BOYS *UK/US, male vocal duo with US, male vocal group*

22 Nov 75 ●	THE TRAIL OF THE LONESOME PINE *United Artists UP 36026*	2	10 wks

Has credit: featuring Chill Wills.

Joanna LAW *UK, female vocalist*   3 wks

7 Jul 90	FIRST TIME EVER *Citybeat CBE 752*	67	3 wks

Lee LAWRENCE *UK, male vocalist*   10 wks

20 Nov 53	CRYING IN THE CHAPEL *Decca F 10177*................	11	1 wk
11 Dec 53 ●	CRYING IN THE CHAPEL (re-entry) *Decca F 10177*........	7	5 wks
2 Dec 55	SUDDENLY THERE'S A VALLEY *Columbia DB 3681*	19	1 wk
16 Dec 55	SUDDENLY THERE'S A VALLEY (re-entry) *Columbia DB 3681*...................................	14	3 wks

Steve LAWRENCE *US, male vocalist*   14 wks

21 Apr 60 ●	FOOTSTEPS *HMV POP 726*............................	4	13 wks
18 Aug 60	GIRLS GIRLS GIRLS *London HLT 9166*......................	49	1 wk

See also Steve and Eydie.

L.A.X. – *See CALIBRE CUTS*

Lindy LAYTON featuring Janet KAY   7 wks
UK, female vocal duo

11 Aug 90	SILLY GAMES *Arista 113452*................................	22	7 wks

See also Beats International; Janet Kay.

Doug LAZY *US, male vocalist*   9 wks

15 Jul 89	LET IT ROLL *Atlantic A 8866*............................	27	5 wks
4 Nov 89	LET THE RHYTHM PUMP *Atlantic A 8784*	45	3 wks
26 May 90	LET THE RHYTHM PUMP (re-mix) *East West A 7919*	63	1 wk

Keith LE BLANC – *See Malcolm X*

Vicky LEANDROS *Greece, female vocalist*   **29 wks**

8 Apr 72	●	COME WHAT MAY *Philips 6000 049*	**2**	16 wks
23 Dec 72		THE LOVE IN YOUR EYES *Philips 6000 081*	**48**	3 wks
20 Jan 73		THE LOVE IN YOUR EYES (re-entry) *Philips 6000 081*	**40**	4 wks
7 Apr 73		THE LOVE IN YOUR EYES (2nd re-entry) *Philips 6000 081.*	**46**	1 wk
7 Jul 73		WHEN BOUZOUKIS PLAYED *Philips 6000 111*	**44**	2 wks
28 Jul 73		WHEN BOUZOUKIS PLAYED (re-entry) *Philips 6000 111.*	**45**	3 wks

LEE – *See PETERS and LEE*

Brenda LEE *US, female vocalist*   **210 wks**

17 Mar 60		SWEET NOTHIN'S *Brunswick 05819.*	**45**	1 wk
7 Apr 60	●	SWEET NOTHIN'S (re-entry) *Brunswick 05819.*	**4**	18 wks
30 Jun 60		I'M SORRY *Brunswick 05833*	**12**	16 wks
20 Oct 60		I WANT TO BE WANTED *Brunswick 05839*	**31**	6 wks
19 Jan 61		LET'S JUMP THE BROOMSTICK *Brunswick 05823*	**12**	15 wks
6 Apr 61		EMOTIONS *Brunswick 05847*	**45**	1 wk
20 Jul 61		DUM DUM *Brunswick 05854*	**22**	8 wks
16 Nov 61		FOOL NUMBER ONE *Brunswick 05860*	**38**	3 wks
8 Feb 62		BREAK IT TO ME GENTLY *Brunswick 05864*	**46**	2 wks
5 Apr 62	●	SPEAK TO ME PRETTY *Brunswick 05867*	**3**	12 wks
21 Jun 62	●	HERE COMES THAT FEELING *Brunswick 05871*	**5**	12 wks
13 Sep 62		IT STARTED ALL OVER AGAIN *Brunswick 05876*	**15**	11 wks
29 Nov 62	●	ROCKIN' AROUND THE CHRISTMAS TREE *Brunswick 05880.*	**6**	7 wks
17 Jan 63	●	ALL ALONE AM I *Brunswick 05882.*	**7**	17 wks
28 Mar 63	●	LOSING YOU *Brunswick 05886.*	**10**	16 wks
18 Jul 63		I WONDER *Brunswick 05891.*	**14**	9 wks
31 Oct 63		SWEET IMPOSSIBLE YOU *Brunswick 05896.*	**28**	6 wks
9 Jan 64	●	AS USUAL *Brunswick 05899.*	**5**	15 wks
9 Apr 64		THINK *Brunswick 05903.*	**26**	8 wks
10 Sep 64		IS IT TRUE *Brunswick 05915.*	**17**	8 wks
10 Dec 64		CHRISTMAS WILL BE JUST ANOTHER LONELY DAY *Brunswick 05921.*	**29**	5 wks
4 Feb 65		THANKS A LOT *Brunswick 05927.*	**41**	2 wks
29 Jul 65		TOO MANY RIVERS *Brunswick 05936.*	**22**	12 wks

Byron LEE – *See Boris GARDINER*

Curtis LEE *US, male vocalist*   **2 wks**

31 Aug 61		PRETTY LITTLE ANGEL EYES *London HLX 9397.*	**47**	1 wk
14 Sep 61		PRETTY LITTLE ANGEL EYES (re-entry) *London HLX 9397.*	**48**	1 wk

Dee C. LEE *UK, female vocalist*   **17 wks**

9 Nov 85	●	SEE THE DAY *CBS A 6570*	**3**	12 wks
8 Mar 86		COME HELL OR WATERS HIGH *CBS A 6869*	**46**	5 wks

Jackie LEE *UK, female vocalist*   **31 wks**

10 Apr 68	●	WHITE HORSES *Philips BF 1674*	**10**	14 wks
2 Jan 71		RUPERT *Pye 7N 45003*	**14**	17 wks

Artist billed on White Horses *as Jacky.*

Leapy LEE *UK, male vocalist*   **28 wks**

21 Aug 68	●	LITTLE ARROWS *MCA MU 1028.*	**2**	21 wks
20 Dec 69		GOOD MORNING *MCA MK 5021*	**47**	1 wk
10 Jan 70		GOOD MORNING (re-entry) *MCA MK 5021*	**29**	6 wks

Peggy LEE *US, female vocalist*   **28 wks**

24 May 57	●	MR. WONDERFUL *Brunswick 05671*	**5**	13 wks
15 Aug 58	●	FEVER *Capitol CL 14902.*	**5**	11 wks
23 Mar 61		TILL THERE WAS YOU *Capitol CL 15184*	**40**	1 wk
6 Apr 61		TILL THERE WAS YOU (re-entry) *Capitol CL 15184*	**30**	3 wks

Toney LEE *US, male vocalist*   **4 wks**

29 Jan 83		REACH UP *TMT TMT 2.*	**64**	4 wks

LEEDS UNITED FC *UK, male football team vocalists*   **10 wks**

29 Apr 72	●	LEEDS UNITED *Chapter One SCH 168*	**10**	10 wks

Raymond LEFEVRE *France, orchestra*   **2 wks**

15 May 68		SOUL COAXING *Major Minor MM 559*	**46**	2 wks

Paul LEKAKIS *US, male vocalist*   **4 wks**

30 May 87		BOOM BOOM (LET'S GO BACK TO MY ROOM) *Champion CHAMP 43.*	**60**	4 wks

LEMON PIPERS *US, male vocal/instrumental group*   **16 wks**

7 Feb 68	●	GREEN TAMBOURINE *Pye International 7N 25444.*	**7**	11 wks
1 May 68		RICE IS NICE *Pye International 7N 25454.*	**41**	5 wks

John LENNON *UK, male vocalist*   **180 wks**

9 Jul 69	●	GIVE PEACE A CHANCE *Apple 13*	**2**	13 wks
1 Nov 69		COLD TURKEY *Apple APPLES 1001*	**14**	8 wks
21 Feb 70	●	INSTANT KARMA *Apple APPLES 1003*	**5**	9 wks
20 Mar 71	●	POWER TO THE PEOPLE *Apple R 5892*	**7**	9 wks
9 Dec 72	●	HAPPY XMAS (WAR IS OVER) *Apple R 5970*	**4**	8 wks
24 Nov 73		MIND GAMES *Apple R 5994.*	**26**	9 wks
19 Oct 74		WHATEVER GETS YOU THROUGH THE NIGHT *Apple R 5998.*	**36**	4 wks
4 Jan 75		HAPPY XMAS (WAR IS OVER) (re-entry) *Apple R 5970.*	**48**	1 wk
8 Feb 75		NUMBER 9 DREAM *Apple R 6003.*	**23**	8 wks
3 May 75		STAND BY ME *Apple R 6005.*	**30**	7 wks
1 Nov 75	●	IMAGINE *Apple R 6009.*	**6**	11 wks
8 Nov 80	★	(JUST LIKE) STARTING OVER *Geffen K 79186*	**1**	15 wks
20 Dec 80	●	HAPPY XMAS (WAR IS OVER) (2nd re-entry) *Apple R 5970.*	**2**	9 wks
27 Dec 80	★	IMAGINE (re-entry) *Apple R 6009.*	**1**	13 wks
24 Jan 81	★	WOMAN *Geffen K 79195.*	**1**	11 wks
24 Jan 81		GIVE PEACE A CHANCE (re-entry) *Apple 13*	**33**	5 wks
4 Apr 81		WATCHING THE WHEELS *Geffen K 79207.*	**30**	6 wks
19 Dec 81		HAPPY XMAS (WAR IS OVER) (3rd re-entry) *Apple R 5970.*	**28**	5 wks
20 Nov 82		LOVE *Parlophone R 6059.*	**41**	7 wks
25 Dec 82		HAPPY XMAS (WAR IS OVER) (4th re-entry) *Apple R 5970.*	**56**	3 wks
21 Jan 84	●	NOBODY TOLD ME *Ono Music/Polydor POSP 700.*	**6**	6 wks
17 Mar 84		BORROWED TIME *Polydor POSP 701.*	**32**	6 wks
30 Nov 85		JEALOUS GUY *Parlophone R 6117*	**65**	2 wks
10 Dec 88		IMAGINE/ JEALOUS GUY/ HAPPY XMAS (WAR IS OVER) (re-issues) *Parlophone R 6199.*	**45**	5 wks

Instant Karma *is by* Lennon, Ono and the Plastic Ono Band, Power To The People *by John Lennon/Plastic Ono Band*, Happy Xmas (War Is Over) *by John and Yoko/Plastic Ono Band with The Harlem Community Choir*, Whatever Gets You Through The Night *by John Lennon with The Plastic Ono Nuclear Band, and the others simply to John Lennon. The Yoko and the Ono in these credits refer to Yoko Ono. See also Elton John Band featuring John Lennon and the Muscle Shoals Horns; Yoko Ono.*

Far Left: ROBERT KNIGHT doesn't look too happy that Love Affair's version of 'Everlasting Love' has been a bigger British hit than his original.

Left: CYNDI LAUPER had most of her fun in 1984.

They bled for their art: the members of KISS had drops of their blood mixed with the printer's ink of their 1977 Marvel Comic.

1962 was the year BRENDA LEE had three Top Ten hits and one comic book.

The top chart star of the Eighties, MADONNA has had more number ones than any female soloist ever.

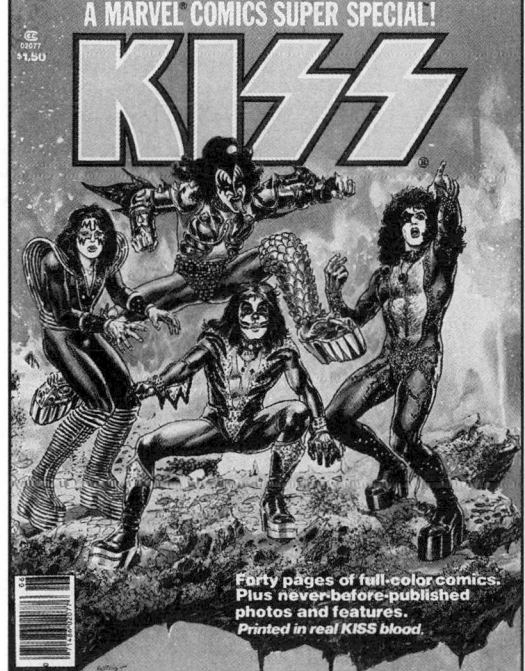

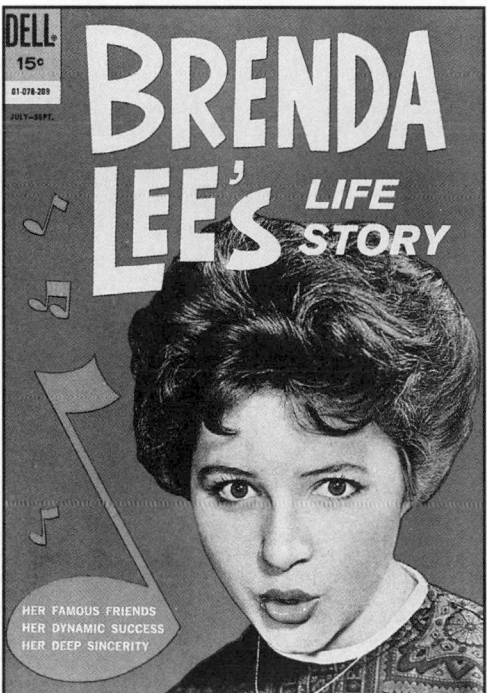

Julian LENNON UK, male vocalist — 28 wks

Date	Title	Pos	Wks
6 Oct 84 ●	TOO LATE FOR GOODBYES Charisma JL 1	6	11 wks
15 Dec 84	VALOTTE Charisma JL 2	55	6 wks
9 Mar 85	SAY YOU'RE WRONG Charisma JL 3	75	1 wk
7 Dec 85	BECAUSE EMI 5538	40	7 wks
11 Mar 89	NOW YOU'RE IN HEAVEN Virgin VS 1154	59	3 wks

Annie LENNOX and Al GREEN UK/US, female/male vocal duo — 8 wks

Date	Title	Pos	Wks
3 Dec 88	PUT A LITTLE LOVE IN YOUR HEART A & M AM 484	28	8 wks

See also Al Green.

Rula LENSKA – See Julie COVINGTON, Rula LENSKA, Charlotte CORNWELL and Sue JONES-DAVIES

LESTER – See Norman COOK

Ketty LESTER US, female vocalist — 16 wks

Date	Title	Pos	Wks
19 Apr 62 ●	LOVE LETTERS London HLN 9527	4	12 wks
19 Jul 62	BUT NOT FOR ME London HLN 9574	45	4 wks

LETTERMEN US, male vocal group — 3 wks

Date	Title	Pos	Wks
23 Nov 61	THE WAY YOU LOOK TONIGHT Capitol CL 15222	36	3 wks

LEVEL 42 UK, male vocal/instrumental group — 161 wks

Date	Title	Pos	Wks
30 Aug 80	LOVE MEETING LOVE Polydor POSP 170	61	4 wks
18 Apr 81	LOVE GAMES Polydor POSP 234	38	6 wks
8 Aug 81	TURN IT ON Polydor POSP 286	57	6 wks
14 Nov 81	STARCHILD Polydor POSP 343	47	4 wks
8 May 82	ARE YOU HEARING (WHAT I HEAR)? Polydor POSP 396	49	5 wks
2 Oct 82	WEAVE YOUR SPELL Polydor POSP 500	43	4 wks
15 Jan 83	THE CHINESE WAY Polydor POSP 538	24	8 wks
16 Apr 83	OUT OF SIGHT, OUT OF MIND Polydor POSP 570	41	4 wks
30 Jul 83 ●	THE SUN GOES DOWN (LIVING IT UP) Polydor POSP 622	10	12 wks
22 Oct 83	MICRO KIDS Polydor POSP 643	37	5 wks
1 Sep 84	HOT WATER Polydor POSP 697	18	9 wks
3 Nov 84	THE CHANT HAS BEGUN Polydor POSP 710	41	5 wks
21 Sep 85 ●	SOMETHING ABOUT YOU Polydor POSP 759	6	17 wks
7 Dec 85	LEAVING ME NOW Polydor POSP 776	15	11 wks
26 Apr 86 ●	LESSONS IN LOVE Polydor POSP 790	3	13 wks
14 Feb 87 ●	RUNNING IN THE FAMILY Polydor POSP 842	6	10 wks
25 Apr 87 ●	TO BE WITH YOU AGAIN Polydor POSP 855	10	7 wks
12 Sep 87 ●	IT'S OVER Polydor POSP 900	10	8 wks
12 Dec 87	CHILDREN SAY Polydor POSP 911	22	6 wks
3 Sep 88	HEAVEN IN MY HANDS Polydor PO 14	12	5 wks
29 Oct 88	TAKE A LOOK Polydor PO 24	32	4 wks
21 Jan 89	TRACIE Polydor PO 34	25	5 wks
28 Oct 89	TAKE CARE OF YOURSELF Polydor PO 58	39	3 wks

LEVERT UK, male vocal group — 10 wks

Date	Title	Pos	Wks
22 Aug 87 ●	CASANOVA Atlantic A 9217	9	10 wks

Hank LEVINE US, orchestra — 4 wks

Date	Title	Pos	Wks
21 Dec 61	IMAGE HMV POP 947	45	4 wks

Barrington LEVY Jamaica, male vocalist — 4 wks

Date	Title	Pos	Wks
2 Feb 85	HERE I COME London LON 62	41	4 wks

Jona LEWIE UK, male vocalist — 20 wks

Date	Title	Pos	Wks
10 May 80	YOU'LL ALWAYS FIND ME IN THE KITCHEN AT PARTIES Stiff BUY 73	16	9 wks
29 Nov 80 ●	STOP THE CAVALRY Stiff BUY 104	3	11 wks

On some copies first title was simply Kitchen At Parties. See also Terry Dactyl and the Dinosaurs.

Dee LEWIS UK, female vocalist — 5 wks

Date	Title	Pos	Wks
18 Jun 88	BEST OF MY LOVE Mercury DEE 3	47	5 wks

Gary LEWIS and the PLAYBOYS US, male vocal/instrumental group — 7 wks

Date	Title	Pos	Wks
8 Feb 75	MY HEART'S SYMPHONY United Artists UP 35780	36	7 wks

Huey LEWIS and the NEWS US, male vocal/instrumental group — 66 wks

Date	Title	Pos	Wks
27 Oct 84	IF THIS IS IT Chrysalis CHS 2829	39	6 wks
31 Aug 85	THE POWER OF LOVE Chrysalis HUEY 1	11	10 wks
23 Nov 85	HEART AND SOUL (EP) Chrysalis HUEY 2	61	4 wks
8 Feb 86 ●	THE POWER OF LOVE (re-entry)/ DO YOU BELIEVE IN LOVE Chrysalis HUEY 1	9	12 wks
10 May 86	THE HEART OF ROCK AND ROLL Chrysalis HUEY 4	49	3 wks
23 Aug 86	STUCK WITH YOU Chrysalis HUEY 5	12	12 wks
6 Dec 86	HIP TO BE SQUARE Chrysalis HUEY 6	41	8 wks
21 Mar 87	SIMPLE AS THAT Chrysalis HUEY 7	47	5 wks
16 Jul 88	PERFECT WORLD Chrysalis HUEY 10	48	6 wks

Tracks on EP: Heart and Soul/Hope You Love Me Like You Say You Do/Heart of Rock And Roll/Buzz Buzz Buzz. Do You Believe In Love only listed from 15 Feb 86.

Jerry LEWIS US, male vocalist — 8 wks

Date	Title	Pos	Wks
8 Feb 57	ROCK-A-BYE YOUR BABY (WITH A DIXIE MELODY) Brunswick 05636	12	7 wks
5 Apr 57	ROCK-A-BYE YOUR BABY (WITH A DIXIE MELODY) (re-entry) Brunswick 05636	22	1 wk

Jerry Lee LEWIS US, male vocalist/instrumentalist - piano — 68 wks

Date	Title	Pos	Wks
27 Sep 57 ●	WHOLE LOTTA SHAKIN' GOIN' ON London HLS 8457	8	10 wks
20 Dec 57 ★	GREAT BALLS OF FIRE London HLS 8529	1	12 wks
27 Dec 57	WHOLE LOTTA SHAKIN' GOIN' ON (re-entry) London HLS 8457	26	1 wk
11 Apr 58 ●	BREATHLESS London HLS 8592	8	7 wks
23 Jan 59	HIGH SCHOOL CONFIDENTIAL London HLS 8780	12	6 wks
1 May 59	LOVIN' UP A STORM London HLS 8840	28	1 wk
9 Jun 60	BABY BABY BYE BYE London HLS 9131	47	1 wk
4 May 61 ●	WHAT'D I SAY London HLS 9335	10	12 wks
3 Aug 61	WHAT'D I SAY (re-entry) London HLS 9335	49	2 wks
6 Sep 62	SWEET LITTLE SIXTEEN London HLS 9584	38	5 wks
14 Mar 63	GOOD GOLLY MISS MOLLY London HLS 9688	31	6 wks
6 May 72	CHANTILLY LACE Mercury 6052 141	33	5 wks

Linda LEWIS UK, female vocalist — 30 wks

Date	Title	Pos	Wks
2 Jun 73	ROCK-A-DOODLE-DOO Raft RA 18502	15	11 wks
12 Jul 75 ●	IT'S IN HIS KISS Arista 17	6	8 wks
17 Apr 76	BABY I'M YOURS Arista 43	33	6 wks

2 Jun 79	I'D BE SURPRISINGLY GOOD FOR YOU		
	Ariola ARO 166	40	5 wks

Ramsey LEWIS US, male instrumentalist - piano   8 wks

15 Apr 72	WADE IN THE WATER Chess 6145 004	31	8 wks

Shirley LEWIS – See Arthur BAKER

John LEYTON UK, male vocalist   70 wks

3 Aug 61	★ JOHNNY REMEMBER ME Top Rank JAR 577	1	15 wks
5 Oct 61	● WILD WIND Top Rank JAR 585	2	10 wks
28 Dec 61	SON THIS IS SHE HMV POP 956	15	10 wks
15 Mar 62	LONE RIDER HMV POP 992	40	5 wks
3 May 62	LONELY CITY HMV POP 1014	14	11 wks
23 Aug 62	DOWN THE RIVER NILE HMV POP 1054	42	3 wks
21 Feb 63	CUPBOARD LOVE HMV POP 1122	22	12 wks
18 Jul 63	I'LL CUT YOUR TAIL OFF HMV POP 1175	50	1 wk
8 Aug 63	I'LL CUT YOUR TAIL OFF (re-entry) HMV POP 1175	36	2 wks
20 Feb 64	MAKE LOVE TO ME HMV POP 1264	49	1 wk

LEYTON BUZZARDS   5 wks
UK, male vocal/instrumental group

3 Mar 79	SATURDAY NIGHT (BENEATH THE PLASTIC PALM TREES) Chrysalis CHS 2288	53	5 wks

LFO UK, male instrumental group   10 wks

14 Jul 90	LFO Warp WAP 5	12	10 wks

LIBERACE US, male instrumentalist - piano   2 wks

17 Jun 55	UNCHAINED MELODY Philips PB 430	20	1 wk
19 Oct 56	I DON'T CARE Columbia DB 3834	28	1 wk

I Don't Care featured Liberace as vocalist too.

LICK THE TINS UK, male/female vocal/instrumental group   8 wks

29 Mar 86	CAN'T HELP FALLING IN LOVE Sedition EDIT 3308	42	8 wks

Ben LIEBRAND Holland, male producer/multi-instrumentalist   2 wks

9 Jun 90	PULS(T)AR Epic LIEB 1	68	2 wks

See also Jeff Wayne's War Of The World.

LIEUTENANT PIGEON   29 wks
UK, male/female instrumental group

16 Sep 72	★ MOULDY OLD DOUGH Decca F 13278	1	19 wks
16 Dec 72	DESPERATE DAN Decca F 13365	17	10 wks

LIGHT OF THE WORLD   25 wks
UK, male vocal/instrumental group

14 Apr 79	SWINGIN' Ensign ENY 22	45	5 wks
14 Jul 79	MIDNIGHT GROOVIN' Ensign ENY 29	72	1 wk
18 Oct 80	LONDON TOWN Ensign ENY 43	41	5 wks
17 Jan 81	I SHOT THE SHERIFF Ensign ENY 46	40	5 wks
28 Mar 81	I'M SO HAPPY Ensign MER 64	35	6 wks
21 Nov 81	RIDE THE LOVE TRAIN EMI 5242	49	3 wks

Gordon LIGHTFOOT Canada, male vocalist   26 wks

19 Jun 71	IF YOU COULD READ MY MIND Reprise RS 20974	30	9 wks
3 Aug 74	SUNDOWN Reprise K 14327	33	7 wks
15 Jan 77	THE WRECK OF THE EDMUND FITZGERALD Reprise K 14451	40	4 wks
16 Sep 78	DAYLIGHT KATY Warner Bros. K 17214	41	6 wks

Terry LIGHTFOOT and his NEW ORLEANS JAZZMEN   17 wks
UK, male jazz band, Terry Lightfoot vocalist/instrumentalist - clarinet

7 Sep 61	TRUE LOVE Columbia DB 4696	33	4 wks
23 Nov 61	KING KONG Columbia SCD 2165	29	12 wks
3 May 62	TAVERN IN THE TOWN Columbia DB 4822	49	1 wk

LIGHTNING SEEDS UK, male vocalist - Ian Broudie   8 wks

22 Jul 89	PURE Ghetto GTG 4	16	8 wks

LIL LOUIS US, male producer   17 wks

29 Jul 89	● FRENCH KISS FFRR FX 115	2	11 wks
13 Jan 90	I CALLED U FFRR F 123	16	6 wks

LIMAHL UK, male vocalist   25 wks

5 Nov 83	ONLY FOR LOVE EMI LML 1	16	7 wks
7 Jan 84	ONLY FOR LOVE (re-entry) EMI LML 1	75	1 wk
2 Jun 84	TOO MUCH TROUBLE EMI LML 2	64	3 wks
13 Oct 84	● NEVER ENDING STORY EMI LML 3	4	14 wks

LIMIT Holland, male vocal/instrumental duo   8 wks

5 Jan 85	SAY YEAH Portrait A 4808	17	8 wks

LIMMIE and the FAMILY COOKIN'   28 wks
US, male/female vocal group

21 Jul 73	● YOU CAN DO MAGIC Avco 6105 019	3	13 wks
20 Oct 73	DREAMBOAT Avco 6105 025	31	5 wks
6 Apr 74	● A WALKIN' MIRACLE Avco 6105 027	6	10 wks

Bob LIND US, male vocalist   10 wks

10 Mar 66	● ELUSIVE BUTTERFLY Fontana TF 670	5	9 wks
26 May 66	REMEMBER THE RAIN Fontana TF 702	46	1 wk

LINDA and the FUNKY BOYS   4 wks
US, female vocalist, male vocal/instrumental backing group

5 Jun 76	SOLD MY ROCK 'N ROLL (GAVE IT FOR FUNKY SOUL) Spark SRL 1139	36	4 wks

Linda is Linda Carr. See also Linda Carr and the Love Squad.

LINDISFARNE UK, male vocal/instrumental group   46 wks

26 Feb 72	● MEET ME ON THE CORNER Charisma CB 173	5	11 wks
13 May 72	● LADY ELEANOR Charisma CB 153	3	11 wks
23 Sep 72	ALL FALL DOWN Charisma CB 191	34	5 wks
3 Jun 78	● RUN FOR HOME Mercury 6007 177	10	15 wks
7 Oct 78	JUKE BOX GYPSY Mercury 6007 187	56	4 wks

See also Gazza and Lindisfarne.

LINER UK, male vocal/instrumental group — 6 wks

| 10 Mar 79 | KEEP REACHING OUT FOR LOVE Atlantic K 11235 .... | 49 | 3 wks |
| 26 May 79 | YOU AND ME Atlantic K 11285 .... | 44 | 3 wks |

Laurie LINGO and the DIPSTICKS — 7 wks
UK, male vocal duo, disc jockeys Dave Lee Travis and Paul Burnett

| 17 Apr 76 ● | CONVOY G. B. State STAT 23 .... | 4 | 7 wks |

See also the Pee Bee Squad.

LINX UK, male vocal/instrumental duo — 45 wks

20 Sep 80	YOU'RE LYING Chrysalis CHS 2461	15	10 wks
7 Mar 81 ●	INTUITION Chrysalis CHS 2500	7	11 wks
13 Jun 81	THROW AWAY THE KEY Chrysalis CHS 2519	21	9 wks
5 Sep 81	SO THIS IS ROMANCE Chrysalis CHS 2546	15	9 wks
21 Nov 81	CAN'T HELP MYSELF Chrysalis CHS 2565	55	3 wks
10 Jul 82	PLAYTHING Chrysalis CHS 2621	48	3 wks

LIPPS INC. US, male/female vocal/instrumental group — 13 wks

| 17 May 80 ● | FUNKYTOWN Casablanca CAN 194............................ | 2 | 13 wks |

LIQUID GOLD UK, male/female vocal/instrumental group — 46 wks

2 Dec 78	ANYWAY YOU DO IT Creole CR 159............................	41	7 wks
23 Feb 80 ●	DANCE YOURSELF DIZZY Polo POLO 1	2	14 wks
31 May 80 ●	SUBSTITUTE Polo POLO 4...	8	9 wks
1 Nov 80	THE NIGHT THE WINE AND THE ROSES Polo POLO 6.....	32	7 wks
28 Mar 81	DON'T PANIC Polo POLO 8	42	5 wks
21 Aug 82	WHERE DID WE GO WRONG Polo POLO 23	56	4 wks

LIQUID OXYGEN US, male producer — 2 wks

| 28 Apr 90 | THE PLANET DANCE Champion CHAMP 242.............. | 56 | 2 wks |

LISA LISA AND CULT JAM — 21 wks
US, female/male vocal/instrumental group

4 May 85	I WONDER IF I TAKE YOU HOME CBS A 6057............	53	6 wks
3 Aug 85	I WONDER IF I TAKE YOU HOME (re-entry) CBS A 6057	12	11 wks
31 Oct 87	LOST IN EMOTION CBS 651036 7............................	58	4 wks

First hit credits Full Force. See also Full Force.

LISA MARIE – See Malcolm McLAREN

LITTLE ANGELS UK, male vocal/instrumental group — 12 wks

4 Mar 89	BIG BAD (EP) Polydor LTLEP 2................................	74	1 wk
24 Feb 90	KICKING UP DUST Polydor LTL 5............................	46	4 wks
12 May 90	RADICAL YOUR LOVER Polydor LTL 6.......................	34	4 wks
4 Aug 90	SHE'S A LITTLE ANGEL Polydor LTL 7.....................	21	3 wks

Tracks on Big Bad EP: She's A Little Angel/Don't Waste My Time/Better Than The Rest/Sex In Cars. Radical Your Lover features the Big Bad Horns - US, male instrumental group.

De Etta LITTLE and Nelson PIGFORD — 5 wks
US, female/male vocal duo

| 13 Aug 77 | YOU TAKE MY HEART AWAY United Artists UP 36257...... | 35 | 5 wks |

LITTLE ANTHONY and the IMPERIALS — 4 wks
US, male vocal group

| 31 Jul 76 | BETTER USE YOUR HEAD United Artists UP 36141 .... | 15 | 4 wks |

See also Imperials.

LITTLE BENNY and the MASTERS — 7 wks
US, male rapper/instrumentalist - trumpet, and male instrumental group

| 2 Feb 85 | WHO COMES TO BOOGIE Bluebird 10 BR 13................ | 33 | 7 wks |

LITTLE CAESAR UK, male vocalist — 3 wks

| 9 Jun 90 | THE WHOLE OF THE MOON A1 EAU 1................... | 68 | 3 wks |

LITTLE EVA US, female vocalist — 45 wks

6 Sep 62 ●	THE LOCO-MOTION London HL 9581	2	17 wks
3 Jan 63	KEEP YOUR HANDS OFF MY BABY London HLU 9633..	30	5 wks
7 Mar 63	LET'S TURKEY TROT London HLU 9687	13	12 wks
29 Jul 72	THE LOCO-MOTION (re-entry) London HL 9581..........	11	11 wks

See also Big Dee Irwin.

LITTLE RICHARD — 108 wks
US, male vocalist/instrumentalist - piano

14 Dec 56	RIP IT UP London HLO 8336	30	1 wk
8 Feb 57 ●	LONG TALL SALLY London HLO 8366	3	16 wks
22 Feb 57	TUTTI FRUTTI London HLO 8366	29	1 wk
8 Mar 57	SHE'S GOT IT London HLO 8382	15	7 wks
15 Mar 57 ●	THE GIRL CAN'T HELP IT London HLO 8382	9	11 wks
24 May 57	SHE'S GOT IT (re-entry) London HLO 8382	28	2 wks
28 Jun 57 ●	LUCILLE London HLO 8446	10	9 wks
13 Sep 57	JENNY JENNY London HLO 8470	11	5 wks
29 Nov 57	KEEP A KNOCKIN' London HLO 8509	21	7 wks
28 Feb 58 ●	GOOD GOLLY MISS MOLLY London HLU 8560	8	9 wks
11 Jul 58	OOH MY SOUL London HLO 8647	30	1 wk
25 Jul 58	OOH MY SOUL (re-entry) London HLO 8647	22	3 wks
2 Jan 59 ●	BABY FACE London HLU 8770	2	15 wks
3 Apr 59	BY THE LIGHT OF THE SILVERY MOON London HLU 8831..	17	5 wks
5 Jun 59	KANSAS CITY London HLU 8868	26	5 wks
11 Oct 62	HE GOT WHAT HE WANTED Mercury AMT 1189	38	4 wks
4 Jun 64	BAMA LAMA BAMA LOO London HL 9896	20	7 wks
2 Jul 77	GOOD GOLLY MISS MOLLY/ RIP IT UP Creole CR 140..	37	4 wks
14 Jun 86	GREAT GOSH A'MIGHTY (IT'S A MATTER OF TIME) MCA MCA 1049	62	2 wks
25 Oct 86	OPERATOR WEA YZ 89	67	2 wks

The versions of Good Golly Miss Molly and Rip It Up on Creole are re-recordings.

LITTLE STEVEN US, male vocalist/instrumentalist - guitar — 3 wks

| 23 May 87 | BITTER FRUIT Manhattan MT 21............................. | 66 | 3 wks |

LITTLE TONY Italy, male vocalist — 3 wks

| 15 Jan 60 | TOO GOOD Decca F 11190 .... | 19 | 3 wks |

LIVE REPORT UK, male vocal/instrumental group — 1 wk

| 20 May 89 | WHY DO I ALWAYS GET IT WRONG Brouhaha CUE 7.. | 73 | 1 wk |

LIVERPOOL EXPRESS   26 wks
UK, male vocal/instrumental group

26 Jun 76	**YOU ARE MY LOVE** Warner Bros. K 16743	11	9 wks
16 Oct 76	**HOLD TIGHT** Warner Bros. K 16799	46	2 wks
18 Dec 76	**EVERY MAN MUST HAVE A DREAM** Warner Bros. K 16854	17	11 wks
4 Jun 77	**DREAMIN'** Warner Bros. K 16933	40	4 wks

LIVERPOOL FC *UK, male football team vocalists*   16 wks

28 May 77	**WE CAN DO IT** State STAT 50	15	4 wks
23 Apr 83	**LIVERPOOL (WE'RE NEVER GONNA...)/ LIVERPOOL (ANTHEM)** Mean MEAN 102	54	4 wks
17 May 86	**SITTING ON THE TOP OF THE WORLD** Columbia DB 9116	50	2 wks
14 May 88	● **ANFIELD RAP (RED MACHINE IN FULL EFFECT)** Virgin LFC 1	3	6 wks

Tracks on We Can Do It EP: We Can Do It/Liverpool Lou/We Shall Not Be Moved/You'll Never Walk Alone.

LIVIN' BASS – See Jay MONDI and the LIVIN' BASS

LIVING COLOUR   1 wk
US, male/female vocal instrumental group

27 Oct 90	**TYPE** Epic LCL 7	75	1 wk

LIVING IN A BOX *UK, male vocal/instrumental group*   62 wks

4 Apr 87	● **LIVING IN A BOX** Chrysalis LIB 1	5	13 wks
13 Jun 87	**SCALES OF JUSTICE** Chrysalis LIB 2	30	6 wks
26 Sep 87	**SO THE STORY GOES** Chrysalis LIB 3	34	8 wks
30 Jan 88	**LOVE IS THE ART** Chrysalis LIB 4	45	4 wks
18 Feb 89	● **BLOW THE HOUSE DOWN** Chrysalis LIB 5	10	9 wks
10 Jun 89	**GATECRASHING** Chrysalis LIB 6	36	6 wks
23 Sep 89	● **ROOM IN YOUR HEART** Chrysalis LIB 7	5	13 wks
30 Dec 89	**DIFFERENT AIR** Chrysalis LIB 8	64	1 wk
13 Jan 90	**DIFFERENT AIR (re-entry)** Chrysalis LIB 8	57	2 wks

So The Story Goes features Bobby Womack; see also Bobby Womack.

Dandy LIVINGSTONE *Jamaica, male vocalist*   19 wks

2 Sep 72	**SUZANNE BEWARE OF THE DEVIL** Horse HOSS 16	14	11 wks
13 Jan 73	**BIG CITY/ THINK ABOUT THAT** Horse HOSS 25	26	8 wks

LL COOL J *US, male rapper*   26 wks

4 Jul 87	**I'M BAD** Def Jam 650856 7	71	1 wk
12 Sep 87	● **I NEED LOVE** Def Jam 651101 7	8	10 wks
21 Nov 87	**GO CUT CREATOR GO** Def Jam LLCJ 1	66	2 wks
13 Feb 88	**GOING BACK TO CALI/ JACK THE RIPPER** Def Jam LLCJ 2	37	4 wks
10 Jun 89	**I'M THAT TYPE OF GUY** Def Jam LLCJ 3	43	5 wks
1 Dec 90	**AROUND THE WAY GIRL/ MAMA SAID KNOCK YOU OUT** Def Jam 6564470	41	4 wks

Jack The Ripper only listed from 27 Feb 88.

LNR *US, male vocal/instrumental duo*   2 wks

3 Jun 89	**WORK IT TO THE BONE** Kool Kat KOOL 501	64	2 wks

LOBO *US, male vocalist*   25 wks

19 Jun 71	● **ME AND YOU AND A DOG NAMED BOO** Philips 6073 801	4	14 wks

8 Jun 74	● **I'D LOVE YOU TO WANT ME** UK 68	5	11 wks

LOBO *Holland, male vocalist*   11 wks

25 Jul 81	● **THE CARIBBEAN DISCO SHOW** Polydor POSP 302	8	11 wks

Los LOBOS *US, male vocal/instrumental group*   24 wks

6 Apr 85	**DON'T WORRY BABY/ WILL THE WOLF SURVIVE** London LASH 4	57	4 wks
18 Jul 87	★ **LA BAMBA** Slash LASH 13	1	11 wks
26 Sep 87	**COME ON LET'S GO** Slash LASH 14	18	9 wks

Tone LOC *US, male rapper*   19 wks

11 Feb 89	**WILD THING/ LOC'ED AFTER DARK** Fourth & Broadway BRW 121	21	8 wks
20 May 89	**FUNKY COLD MEDINA** Fourth & Broadway BRW 129	13	9 wks
5 Aug 89	**I GOT IT GOIN' ON** Fourth & Broadway BRW 140	55	2 wks

Hank LOCKLIN *US, male vocalist*   41 wks

11 Aug 60	● **PLEASE HELP ME I'M FALLING** RCA 1188	9	19 wks
15 Feb 62	**FROM HERE TO THERE TO YOU** RCA 1273	44	3 wks
15 Nov 62	**WE'RE GONNA GO FISHIN'** RCA 1305	18	11 wks
5 May 66	**I FEEL A CRY COMING ON** RCA 1510	28	8 wks

LOCKSMITH *US, male vocal/instrumental group*   6 wks

23 Aug 80	**UNLOCK THE FUNK** Arista ARIST 364	42	6 wks

LOCOMOTIVE *UK, male vocal/instrumental group*   8 wks

16 Oct 68	**RUDI'S IN LOVE** Parlophone R 5718	25	8 wks

John LODGE – See Justin HAYWARD and John LODGE

Nils LOFGREN *US, male vocalist/instrumentalist - guitar*   3 wks

8 Jun 85	**SECRETS IN THE STREET** Towerbell TOW 68	53	3 wks

Johnny LOGAN *Australia, male vocalist*   24 wks

3 May 80	★ **WHAT'S ANOTHER YEAR** Epic EPC 8572	1	8 wks
23 May 87	● **HOLD ME NOW** Epic LOG 1	2	11 wks
22 Aug 87	**I'M NOT IN LOVE** Epic LOG 2	51	5 wks

Kenny LOGGINS *US, male vocalist*   21 wks

28 Apr 84	● **FOOTLOOSE** CBS A 4101	6	10 wks
1 Nov 86	**DANGER ZONE** CBS A 7188	45	11 wks

LOLA *US, female vocalist*   1 wk

28 Mar 87	**WAX THE VAN** Syncopate SY 1	65	1 wk

Alain LOMBARD – See Mady MESPLÉ and Danielle MILLET

Julie LONDON *US, female vocalist*   3 wks

5 Apr 57	**CRY ME A RIVER** London HLU 8240	22	3 wks

Right: THE LOOK had a brief look at the Top Ten in early 1981.

Below Right: It would seem they are trying to comment on their own success, but in fact LIVING IN A BOX are celebrating the first birthday in 1987 of the British Telecom Dial-a-Hit service.

Right: The 1958 US smash 'Tears On My Pillow' by LITTLE ANTHONY AND THE IMPERIALS became a UK number one in 1990 for Kylie Minogue.

Below: Two members of LEVERT were sons of the O'Jays' Eddie Levert.

Laurie LONDON UK, male vocalist   **12 wks**

8 Nov 57	HE'S GOT THE WHOLE WORLD IN HIS HANDS *Parlophone R 4359*	12	12 wks

LONDON BOYS UK, male vocal duo   **44 wks**

10 Dec 88	REQUIEM *WEA YZ 345*	59	6 wks
1 Apr 89 ●	REQUIEM (re-entry) *WEA YZ 345*	4	15 wks
1 Jul 89 ●	LONDON NIGHTS *WEA YZ 393*	2	9 wks
16 Sep 89	HARLEM DESIRE *WEA YZ 415*	17	7 wks
2 Dec 89	MY LOVE *WEA YZ 433*	46	6 wks
16 Jun 90	CHAPEL OF LOVE *East West YZ 458*	75	1 wk

LONDON COMMUNITY GOSPEL CHOIR – *See Sal SOLO*

LONDON STRING CHORALE UK, orchestra/choir   **13 wks**

15 Dec 73	GALLOPING HOME *Polydor 2058 280*	49	3 wks
19 Jan 74	GALLOPING HOME (re-entry) *Polydor 2058 280*	31	10 wks

LONDON SYMPHONY ORCHESTRA
UK, orchestra   **5 wks**

6 Jan 79	THEME FROM 'SUPERMAN' (MAIN TITLE) *Warner Bros. K 17292*	32	5 wks

Orchestra conducted by John Williams.

LONDONBEAT UK/US, male vocal group   **30 wks**

26 Nov 88	9 A.M. (THE COMFORT ZONE) *AnXious ANX 008*	21	10 wks
18 Feb 89	FAILING IN LOVE AGAIN *AnXious ANX 007*	60	2 wks
1 Sep 90 ●	I'VE BEEN THINKING ABOUT YOU *AnXious ANX 14*	2	13 wks
24 Nov 90	A BETTER LOVE *AnXious ANX 21*	52	5 wks

See also Liz Kershaw and Bruno Brookes.

LONE JUSTICE US, female/male vocal/instrumental group   **4 wks**

7 Mar 87	I FOUND LOVE *Geffen GEF 18*	45	4 wks

Shorty LONG US, male vocalist   **7 wks**

17 Jul 68	HERE COMES THE JUDGE *Tamla Motown TMG 663*	30	7 wks

LONG AND THE SHORT   **8 wks**
UK, male vocal/instrumental group

10 Sep 64	THE LETTER *Decca F 11964*	30	5 wks
24 Dec 64	CHOC ICE *Decca F 12043*	49	3 wks

LONG RYDERS US, male vocal/instrumental group   **4 wks**

5 Oct 85	LOOKING FOR LEWIS AND CLARK *Island IS 237*	59	4 wks

LOOK UK, male vocal/instrumental group   **15 wks**

20 Dec 80 ●	I AM THE BEAT *MCA 647*	6	12 wks
29 Aug 81	FEEDING TIME *MCA 736*	50	3 wks

LOOSE ENDS UK, male/female vocal/instrumental group   **70 wks**

25 Feb 84	TELL ME WHAT YOU WANT *Virgin VS 658*	74	1 wk
28 Apr 84	EMERGENCY (DIAL 999) *Virgin VS 677*	41	6 wks
21 Jul 84	CHOOSE ME (RESCUE ME) *Virgin VS 697*	59	3 wks
23 Feb 85	HANGIN' ON A STRING (CONTEMPLATING) *Virgin VS 748*	13	13 wks
11 May 85	MAGIC TOUCH *Virgin VS 761*	16	7 wks
27 Jul 85	GOLDEN YEARS *Virgin VS 795*	59	4 wks
14 Jun 86	STAY A LITTLE WHILE, CHILD *Virgin VS 819*	52	5 wks
20 Sep 86	SLOW DOWN *Virgin VS 884*	27	7 wks
29 Nov 86	NIGHTS OF PLEASURE *Virgin VS 919*	42	7 wks
4 Jun 88	MR BACHELOR *Virgin VS 1080*	50	4 wks
25 Aug 90	DON'T BE A FOOL *10 TEN 312*	13	9 wks
17 Nov 90	LOVE'S GOT ME *10 TEN 330*	40	4 wks

Trini LOPEZ US, male vocalist   **37 wks**

12 Sep 63 ●	IF I HAD A HAMMER *Reprise R 20198*	4	17 wks
12 Dec 63	KANSAS CITY *Reprise R 20236*	35	5 wks
12 May 66	I'M COMING HOME CINDY *Reprise R 20455*	28	5 wks
6 Apr 67	GONNA GET ALONG WITHOUT YA NOW *Reprise R 20547*	41	5 wks
19 Dec 81	TRINI TRACKS *RCA 154*	59	5 wks

LORD TANAMO Trinidad, male vocalist   **2 wks**

1 Dec 90	I'M IN THE MOOD FOR LOVE *Mooncrest MOON 1009*	58	2 wks

Jerry LORDAN UK, male vocalist   **15 wks**

8 Jan 60	I'LL STAY SINGLE *Parlophone R 4588*	26	2 wks
26 Feb 60	WHO COULD BE BLUER *Parlophone R 4627*	17	9 wks
10 Mar 60	I'LL STAY SINGLE (re-entry) *Parlophone R 4588*	41	1 wk
19 May 60	WHO COULD BE BLUER (re-entry) *Parlophone R 4627*	45	1 wk
2 Jun 60	SING LIKE AN ANGEL *Parlophone R 4653*	36	2 wks

Sophia LOREN – *See Peter SELLERS and Sophia LOREN*

LORI and the CHAMELEONS   **1 wk**
UK, female/male vocal/instrumental group

8 Dec 79	TOUCH *Sire SIR 4025*	70	1 wk

LORRAINE – *See BOMB THE BASS*

Joe LOSS UK, orchestra   **53 wks**

29 Jun 61	WHEELS CHA CHA *HMV POP 880*	21	21 wks
19 Oct 61	SUCU SUCU *HMV POP 937*	48	1 wk
29 Mar 62	THE MAIGRET THEME *HMV POP 995*	20	10 wks
1 Nov 62	MUST BE MADISON *HMV POP 1075*	20	13 wks
5 Nov 64	MARCH OF THE MODS *HMV POP 1351*	35	4 wks
24 Dec 64	MARCH OF THE MODS (re-entry) *HMV POP 1351*	31	4 wks

LOTUS EATERS UK, male vocal/instrumental duo   **16 wks**

2 Jul 83	FIRST PICTURE OF YOU *Sylvan SYL 1*	15	12 wks
8 Oct 83	YOU DON'T NEED SOMEONE NEW *Sylvan SYL 2*	53	4 wks

Bonnie LOU US, female vocalist   **10 wks**

5 Feb 54 ●	TENNESSEE WIG WALK *Parlophone R 3730*	4	10 wks

John D. LOUDERMILK US, male vocalist — 10 wks

4 Jan 62	THE LANGUAGE OF LOVE RCA 1269	13	10 wks

Geoff LOVE – See MANUEL and his MUSIC OF THE MOUNTAINS

Monie LOVE UK, female rapper — 29 wks

4 Feb 89	I CAN DO THIS Cooltempo COOL 177	37	4 wks
24 Jun 89	GRANDPA'S PARTY Cooltempo COOL 184	16	9 wks
14 Jul 90	MONIE IN THE MIDDLE Cooltempo COOL 210	46	3 wks
22 Sep 90	IT'S A SHAME (MY SISTER) Cooltempo COOL 219	12	8 wks
1 Dec 90	DOWN TO EARTH Cooltempo COOL 222	31†	5 wks

See also Jungle Brothers.

Vikki LOVE – See NUANCE featuring Vikki LOVE

LOVE AFFAIR UK, male vocal/instrumental group — 56 wks

3 Jan 68	★ EVERLASTING LOVE CBS 3125	1	12 wks
17 Apr 68	● RAINBOW VALLEY CBS 3366	5	13 wks
11 Sep 68	● A DAY WITHOUT LOVE CBS 3674	6	12 wks
19 Feb 69	ONE ROAD CBS 3994	16	9 wks
16 Jul 69	● BRINGING ON BACK THE GOOD TIMES CBS 4300	9	10 wks

LOVE AND MONEY UK, male vocal/instrumental group — 21 wks

24 May 86	CANDYBAR EXPRESS Mercury MONEY 1	56	4 wks
25 Apr 87	LOVE AND MONEY Mercury MONEY 4	68	4 wks
17 Sep 88	HALLELUJAH MAN Fontana MONEY 5	63	4 wks
14 Jan 89	STRANGE KIND OF LOVE Fontana MONEY 6	45	5 wks
25 Mar 89	JOCELYN SQUARE Fontana MONEY 7	51	4 wks

LOVE DECREE UK, male vocal/instrumental group — 4 wks

16 Sep 89	SOMETHING SO REAL (CHINHEADS THEME) Ariola 112642	61	4 wks

LOVE REACTION – See Zodiac MINDWARP and the LOVE REACTION

LOVE SCULPTURE UK, instrumental group — 14 wks

27 Nov 68	● SABRE DANCE Parlophone R 5744	5	14 wks

LOVE SQUAD – See Linda CARR and the LOVE SQUAD

LOVE UNLIMITED US, female vocal group — 19 wks

17 Jun 72	WALKIN' IN THE RAIN WITH THE ONE I LOVE Uni UN 539	14	10 wks
25 Jan 75	IT MAY BE WINTER OUTSIDE (BUT IN MY HEART IT'S SPRING) 20th Century BTC 2149	11	9 wks

LOVE UNLIMITED ORCHESTRA US, orchestra — 10 wks

2 Feb 74	● LOVE'S THEME Pye International 7N 25635	10	10 wks

LOVEBUG STARSKI US, male vocalist — 9 wks

31 May 86	AMITYVILLE (THE HOUSE ON THE HILL) Epic A 7182	12	9 wks

Bill LOVELADY UK, male vocalist — 10 wks

18 Aug 79	REGGAE FOR IT NOW Charisma CB 337	12	10 wks

LOVER SPEAKS UK, male vocal/instrumental duo — 5 wks

16 Aug 86	NO MORE 'I LOVE YOU'S' A &M AM 326	58	5 wks

Michael LOVESMITH US, male vocalist — 1 wk

5 Oct 85	AIN'T NOTHIN' LIKE IT Motown ZB 40369	75	1 wk

Lene LOVICH US, female vocalist — 38 wks

17 Feb 79	● LUCKY NUMBER Stiff BUY 42	3	11 wks
12 May 79	SAY WHEN Stiff BUY 46	19	10 wks
20 Oct 79	BIRD SONG Stiff BUY 53	39	7 wks
29 Mar 80	WHAT WILL I DO WITHOUT YOU Stiff BUY 69	58	3 wks
14 Mar 81	NEW TOY Stiff BUY 97	53	5 wks
27 Nov 82	IT'S YOU, ONLY YOU (MEIN SCHMERZ) Stiff BUY 164	68	2 wks

LOVIN' SPOONFUL — 33 wks
US/Canada, male vocal/instrumental group

14 Apr 66	● DAYDREAM Pye International 7N 25361	2	13 wks
14 Jul 66	● SUMMER IN THE CITY Kama Sutra KAS 200	8	11 wks
5 Jan 67	NASHVILLE CATS Kama Sutra KAS 204	26	7 wks
9 Mar 67	DARLING BE HOME SOON Kama Sutra KAS 207	44	2 wks

LOVINDEER UK, male vocalist — 3 wks

27 Sep 86	MAN SHORTAGE TSOJ TS 1	69	3 wks

Gary LOW Italy, male vocalist — 3 wks

8 Oct 83	I WANT YOU Savoir Faire FAIS 004	52	3 wks

Jim LOWE US, male vocalist — 9 wks

26 Oct 56	● THE GREEN DOOR London HLD 8317	8	9 wks

Nick LOWE UK, male vocalist — 27 wks

11 Mar 78	● I LOVE THE SOUND OF BREAKING GLASS Radar ADA 1	7	8 wks
9 Jun 79	CRACKIN' UP Radar ADA 34	34	5 wks
25 Aug 79	CRUEL TO BE KIND Radar ADA 43	12	11 wks
26 May 84	HALF A BOY HALF A MAN F. Beat XX 34	53	3 wks

LOWRELL US, male vocalist — 9 wks

24 Nov 79	MELLOW MELLOW RIGHT ON AVI AVIS 108	37	9 wks

See also Calibre Cuts.

LRS – See D MOB

L.T.D. US, male vocal/instrumental group — 3 wks

9 Sep 78	HOLDING ON (WHEN LOVE IS GONE) A &M AMS 7378	70	3 wks

Carrie LUCAS US, female vocalist — 6 wks

16 Jun 79	DANCE WITH YOU *Solar FB 1482*	40	6 wks

LUIGI – See HUGO and LUIGI

Robin LUKE US, male vocalist — 6 wks

17 Oct 58	SUSIE DARLIN' *London HLD 8676*	24	3 wks
21 Nov 58	SUSIE DARLIN' (re-entry) *London HLD 8676*	23	1 wk
5 Dec 58	SUSIE DARLIN' (2nd re-entry) *London HLD 8676*	23	2 wks

LUKK featuring Felicia COLLINS — 1 wk
US, male/female vocal/instrumental group

28 Sep 85	ON THE ONE *Important TAN 6*	72	1 wk

LULU UK, female vocalist — 134 wks

14 May 64	● SHOUT *Decca F 11884*	7	13 wks
12 Nov 64	HERE COMES THE NIGHT *Decca F 12017*	50	1 wk
17 Jun 65	● LEAVE A LITTLE LOVE *Decca F 12169*	8	11 wks
2 Sep 65	TRY TO UNDERSTAND *Decca F 12214*	25	8 wks
13 Apr 67	● THE BOAT THAT I ROW *Columbia DB 8169*	6	11 wks
29 Jun 67	LET'S PRETEND *Columbia DB 8221*	11	11 wks
8 Nov 67	LOVE LOVES TO LOVE LOVE *Columbia DB 8295*	32	6 wks
28 Feb 68	● ME THE PEACEFUL HEART *Columbia DB 8358*	9	9 wks
5 Jun 68	BOY *Columbia DB 8425*	15	7 wks
6 Nov 68	● I'M A TIGER *Columbia DB 8500*	9	13 wks
12 Mar 69	● BOOM BANG-A-BANG *Columbia DB 8550*	2	13 wks
22 Nov 69	OH ME OH MY (I'M A FOOL FOR YOU BABY) *Atco 226 008*	47	2 wks
26 Jan 74	● THE MAN WHO SOLD THE WORLD *Polydor 2001 490*	3	9 wks
19 Apr 75	TAKE YOUR MAMA FOR A RIDE *Chelsea 2005 022*	37	4 wks
12 Dec 81	I COULD NEVER MISS YOU (MORE THAN I DO) *Alfa ALFA 1700*	62	4 wks
16 Jan 82	I COULD NEVER MISS YOU (MORE THAN I DO) (re-entry) *Alfa ALFA 1700*	63	1 wk
19 Jul 86	● SHOUT *Jive LULU 1/Decca SHOUT 1*	8	10 wks

The newly recorded Shout entered the chart 19 Jul 86, and the next week the original Decca version by Lulu and the Luvvers also charted. For all subsequent weeks Gallup amalgamated both versions under one entry.

Bob LUMAN US, male vocalist — 21 wks

8 Sep 60	● LET'S THINK ABOUT LIVING *Warner Bros. WB 18*	6	18 wks
15 Dec 60	WHY WHY BYE BYE *Warner Bros. WB 28*	46	1 wk
4 May 61	THE GREAT SNOWMAN *Warner Bros. WB 37*	49	2 wks

LURKERS UK, male vocal/instrumental group — 11 wks

3 Jun 78	AIN'T GOT A CLUE *Beggars Banquet BEG 6*	45	3 wks
5 Aug 78	I DON'T NEED TO TELL HER *Beggars Banquet BEG 9*	49	4 wks
3 Feb 79	JUST THIRTEEN *Beggars Banquet BEG 14*	66	2 wks
9 Jun 79	OUT IN THE DARK/ CYANIDE *Beggars Banquet BEG 19*	72	1 wk
17 Nov 79	NEW GUITAR IN TOWN *Beggars Banquet BEG 28*	72	1 wk

LUSH UK, male vocal/instrumental group — 3 wks

10 Mar 90	MAD LOVE (EP) *4AD BAD 0003*	55	1 wk
27 Oct 90	SWEETNESS AND LIGHT *4AD AD 0013*	47	2 wks

Tracks on Mad Love EP: De-Luxe/Leaves Me Cold/Downer/Thoughtforms.

LUVVERS – See LULU

John LYDON – See TIME ZONE

LYLE See GALLAGHER and LYLE

Frankie LYMON and the TEENAGERS — 33 wks
US, male vocal group

29 Jun 56	★ WHY DO FOOLS FALL IN LOVE *Columbia DB 3772*	1	16 wks
29 Mar 57	I'M NOT A JUVENILE DELINQUENT *Columbia DB 3878*	12	7 wks
12 Apr 57	● BABY BABY *Columbia DB 3878*	4	12 wks
20 Sep 57	GOODY GOODY *Columbia DB 3983*	24	3 wks

First hit billed the group as The Teenagers Featuring Frankie Lymon.

Kenny LYNCH UK, male vocalist — 59 wks

30 Jun 60	MOUNTAIN OF LOVE *HMV POP 751*	33	3 wks
13 Sep 62	PUFF *HMV POP 1057*	33	5 wks
25 Oct 62	PUFF (re-entry) *HMV POP 1057*	46	1 wk
6 Dec 62	● UP ON THE ROOF *HMV POP 1090*	10	12 wks
20 Jun 63	● YOU CAN NEVER STOP ME LOVING YOU *HMV POP 1165*	10	14 wks
16 Apr 64	STAND BY ME *HMV POP 1280*	39	7 wks
27 Aug 64	WHAT AM I TO DO *HMV POP 1321*	37	4 wks
1 Oct 64	WHAT AM I TO DO (re-entry) *HMV POP 1321*	44	2 wks
17 Jun 65	I'LL STAY BY YOU *HMV POP 1430*	29	7 wks
20 Aug 83	HALF THE DAY'S GONE AND WE HAVEN'T EARNT A PENNY *Satril SAT 510*	50	4 wks

Cheryl LYNN US, female vocalist — 2 wks

8 Sep 84	ENCORE *Streetwave KHAN 23*	68	2 wks

Patti LYNN UK, female vocalist — 5 wks

10 May 62	JOHNNY ANGEL *Fontana H 391*	37	5 wks

Tami LYNN US, female vocalist — 20 wks

22 May 71	● I'M GONNA RUN AWAY FROM YOU *Mojo 2092 001*	4	14 wks
3 May 75	I'M GONNA RUN AWAY FROM YOU (re-issue) *Contempo Raries CS 9026*	36	6 wks

Vera LYNN UK, female vocalist — 46 wks

14 Nov 52	● AUF WIEDERSEHEN *Decca F 9927*	10	1 wk
14 Nov 52	● FORGET ME NOT *Decca F 9985*	7	1 wk
14 Nov 52	● HOMING WALTZ *Decca F 9959*	9	3 wks
28 Nov 52	● FORGET ME NOT (re-entry) *Decca F 9985*	5	5 wks
5 Jun 53	WINDSOR WALTZ *Decca F 10092*	11	1 wk
15 Oct 54	★ MY SON MY SON *Decca F 10372*	1	14 wks
8 Jun 56	WHO ARE WE *Decca F 10715*	30	1 wk
26 Oct 56	A HOUSE WITH LOVE IN IT *Decca F 10799*	17	13 wks
15 Mar 57	THE FAITHFUL HUSSAR (DON'T CRY MY LOVE) *Decca F 10846*	29	2 wks
21 Jun 57	TRAVELLIN' HOME *Decca F 10903*	20	5 wks

Jeff LYNNE UK, male vocalist — 4 wks

30 Jun 90	EVERY LITTLE THING *Reprise W 9799*	59	4 wks

Philip LYNOTT Ireland, male vocalist — 26 wks

5 Apr 80	DEAR MISS LONELY HEARTS *Vertigo SOLO 1*	32	6 wks
21 Jun 80	KING'S CALL *Vertigo SOLO 2*	35	6 wks
21 Mar 81	YELLOW PEARL *Vertigo SOLO 3*	56	1 wk
26 Dec 81	YELLOW PEARL (re-entry) *Vertigo SOLO 3*	14	9 wks
24 Jan 87	KING'S CALL (re-mix) *Vertigo LYN 1*	68	2 wks

See Gary Moore and Phil Lynott.

LYNYRD SKYNYRD US, male vocal/instrumental group   21 wks

11 Sep 76	**FREE BIRD** MCA 251	**31**	4 wks
22 Dec 79	**FREE BIRD** (re-entry) MCA 251................	**43**	8 wks
19 Jun 82	**FREE BIRD** (2nd re-entry) MCA 251	**21**	9 wks

Tracks on EP: Free Bird/Sweet Home Alabama/Double Trouble.

Barbara LYON US, female vocalist   12 wks

24 Jun 55	**STOWAWAY** Columbia DB 3619	**12**	8 wks
21 Dec 56	**LETTER TO A SOLDIER** Columbia DB 3685	**27**	4 wks

Humphrey LYTTELTON BAND   6 wks
UK, male jazz band, Humphrey Lyttelton - trumpet

13 Jul 56	**BAD PENNY BLUES** Parlophone R 4184	**19**	6 wks

M UK, male vocalist/multi-instrumentalist   39 wks

7 Apr 79 ●	**POP MUZIK** MCA 413	**2**	14 wks
8 Dec 79	**MOONLIGHT AND MUZAK** MCA 541	**33**	9 wks
15 Mar 80	**THAT'S THE WAY THE MONEY GOES** MCA 570	**45**	5 wks
22 Nov 80	**OFFICIAL SECRETS** MCA 650	**64**	2 wks
10 Jun 89	**POP MUZIK** (re-mix) Freestyle FRS 1	**15**	9 wks

M is Robin Scott.

Bobby M US, male/female vocal/instrumental duo   3 wks

29 Jan 83	**LET'S STAY TOGETHER** Gordy TMG 1288................	**53**	3 wks

Hit has credit: featuring Jean Carn.

M + M Canada, male/female vocal duo   4 wks

28 Jul 84	**BLACK STATIONS WHITE STATIONS** RCA 426	**46**	4 wks

See also Martha and the Muffins.

M and O BAND UK, male vocal/instrumental group   6 wks

28 Feb 76	**LET'S DO THE LATIN HUSTLE** Creole CR 120	**16**	6 wks

Lorin MAAZEL – *See PHILHARMONIA ORCHESTRA, conductor Lorin MAAZEL; Sarah BRIGHTMAN and Paul MILES-KINGSTON*

MAC BAND featuring the McCAMPBELL BROTHERS US, male vocal group   17 wks

18 Jun 88 ●	**ROSES ARE RED** MCA MCA 1264	**8**	13 wks
10 Sep 88	**STALEMATE** MCA MCA 1271................	**40**	4 wks

Stalemate credits the McCampbell Brothers on the sleeve only, not on the label.

Neil MacARTHUR UK, male vocalist   5 wks

5 Feb 69	**SHE'S NOT THERE** Deram DM 225........................	**34**	5 wks

Neil MacArthur is Colin Blunstone under a false name. See also Colin Blunstone; Dave Stewart.

David MacBETH UK, male vocalist   4 wks

30 Oct 59	**MR. BLUE** Pye 7N 15231........................	**18**	4 wks

Frankie McBRIDE Ireland, male vocalist   15 wks

9 Aug 67	**FIVE LITTLE FINGERS** Emerald MD 1081........	**19**	15 wks

Dan McCAFFERTY UK, male vocalist   3 wks

13 Sep 75	**OUT OF TIME** Mountain TOP 1	**41**	3 wks

C.W. McCALL US, male vocalist   10 wks

14 Feb 76 ●	**CONVOY** MGM 2006 560	**2**	10 wks

David McCALLUM UK, male vocalist   4 wks

14 Apr 66	**COMMUNICATION** Capitol CL 15439	**32**	4 wks

McCAMPBELL BROTHERS – *See MAC BAND featuring the McCAMPBELL BROTHERS*

Linda McCARTNEY – *See Paul McCARTNEY*

Paul McCARTNEY UK, male vocalist   345 wks

27 Feb 71 ●	**ANOTHER DAY** Apple R 5889	**2**	12 wks
28 Aug 71	**BACK SEAT OF MY CAR** Apple R 5914	**39**	5 wks
26 Feb 72	**GIVE IRELAND BACK TO THE IRISH** Apple R5936........	**16**	8 wks
27 May 72 ●	**MARY HAD A LITTLE LAMB** Apple R 5949........	**9**	11 wks
9 Dec 72 ●	**HI HI HI/ C MOON** Apple R 5973	**5**	13 wks
7 Apr 73 ●	**MY LOVE** Apple R 5985	**9**	11 wks
9 Jun 73 ●	**LIVE AND LET DIE** Apple R 5987	**9**	13 wks
15 Sep 73	**LIVE AND LET DIE** (re-entry) Apple R 5987	**49**	1 wk
3 Nov 73	**HELEN WHEELS** Apple R 5993	**12**	12 wks
2 Mar 74 ●	**JET** Apple R 5996	**7**	9 wks
6 Jul 74 ●	**BAND ON THE RUN** Apple R 5997	**3**	11 wks
9 Nov 74	**JUNIOR'S FARM** Apple R 5999	**16**	10 wks
31 May 75 ●	**LISTEN TO WHAT THE MAN SAID** Capitol R 6006	**6**	8 wks
18 Oct 75	**LETTING GO** Capitol R 6008	**41**	3 wks
15 May 76 ●	**SILLY LOVE SONGS** Parlophone R 6014	**2**	11 wks
7 Aug 76 ●	**LET 'EM IN** Parlophone R 6015	**2**	10 wks
19 Feb 77	**MAYBE I'M AMAZED** Parlophone R 6017	**28**	5 wks
19 Nov 77 ★	**MULL OF KINTYRE/ GIRLS' SCHOOL** Capitol R 6018	**1**	17 wks
1 Apr 78 ●	**WITH A LITTLE LUCK** Parlophone R 6019	**5**	9 wks
1 Jul 78	**I'VE HAD ENOUGH** Parlophone R 6020	**42**	7 wks
9 Sep 78	**LONDON TOWN** Parlophone R 6021............	**60**	4 wks
7 Apr 79 ●	**GOODNIGHT TONIGHT** Parlophone R 6023	**5**	10 wks
16 Jun 79	**OLD SIAM SIR** MPL R 6026	**35**	6 wks
1 Sep 79	**GETTING CLOSER/ BABY'S REQUEST** R 6027	**60**	3 wks
1 Dec 79 ●	**WONDERFUL CHRISTMASTIME** Parlophone R 6029........	**6**	8 wks
19 Apr 80 ●	**COMING UP** Parlophone R 6035	**2**	9 wks
21 Jun 80	**WATERFALLS** Parlophone R 6037	**9**	8 wks
3 Jul 82	**TAKE IT AWAY** Parlophone R 6056	**15**	10 wks
9 Oct 82	**TUG OF WAR** Parlophone R 6057	**53**	3 wks
17 Dec 83 ★	**PIPES OF PEACE** Parlophone R 6064	**1**	12 wks
6 Oct 84 ●	**NO MORE LONELY NIGHTS (BALLADS)** Parlophone R 6080	**2**	15 wks
24 Nov 84 ●	**WE ALL STAND TOGETHER** Parlophone R 6086............	**3**	13 wks
30 Nov 85	**SPIES LIKE US** Parlophone R 6118	**16**	10 wks
21 Dec 85	**WE ALL STAND TOGETHER** (re-entry) Parlophone R 6086	**32**	5 wks
26 Jul 86	**PRESS** Parlophone R 6133	**25**	8 wks
13 Dec 86	**ONLY LOVE REMAINS** Parlophone R 6148	**34**	5 wks
28 Nov 87 ●	**ONCE UPON A LONG AGO** Parlophone R 6170	**10**	7 wks
20 May 89	**MY BRAVE FACE** Parlophone R 6213	**18**	8 wks
29 Jul 89	**THIS ONE** Parlophone R 6223	**18**	6 wks
25 Nov 89	**FIGURE OF EIGHT** Parlophone R 6225	**42**	3 wks
17 Feb 90	**PUT IT THERE** Parlophone R 6246	**32**	2 wks

| 20 Oct 90 | **BIRTHDAY** *Parlophone R 6271*..................... | **29** | 3 wks |
| 8 Dec 90 | **ALL MY TRIALS** *Parlophone R 6278*................. | **35†** | 4 wks |

My Love, Helen Wheels, Jet, Band on the Run *and* Junior's Farm *credited to Paul McCartney and Wings. R6027 no label at all, although the number is a Parlophone one. All other songs between Feb 72 and Sep 79 were credited to Wings.* Back Seat Of My Car *was credited to Paul and Linda McCartney.* We All Stand Together *credited to Paul McCartney and the Frog Chorus. See also Paul McCartney with Stevie Wonder; Michael Jackson and Paul McCartney; Christians, Holly Johnson, Paul McCartney, Gerry Marsden and Stock Aitken Waterman.*

Paul McCARTNEY with Stevie WONDER   10 wks
UK/US, male vocal duo

| 10 Apr 82 | ★ **EBONY AND IVORY** *Parlophone R 6054* .... | **1** | 10 wks |

See also Paul McCartney; Stevie Wonder.

Kirsty MacCOLL *UK, female vocalist*   34 wks

13 Jun 81	**THERE'S A GUY WORKS DOWN THE CHIPSHOP SWEARS HE'S ELVIS** *Polydor POSP 250*.............	**14**	9 wks
19 Jan 85	● **A NEW ENGLAND** *Stiff BUY 216*................	**7**	10 wks
8 Apr 89	**FREE WORLD** *Virgin KMA 1*...................	**43**	6 wks
1 Jul 89	**DAYS** *Virgin KMA 2*	**12**	9 wks

See also Pogues.

Marilyn McCOO and Billy DAVIS Jr.   9 wks
US, female/male vocal duo

| 19 Mar 77 | ● **YOU DON'T HAVE TO BE A STAR (TO BE IN MY SHOW)** *ABC 4147* .... | **7** | 9 wks |

Van McCOY *US, orchestra*   36 wks

31 May 75	● **THE HUSTLE** *Avco 6105 038*..................	**3**	12 wks
1 Nov 75	**CHANGE WITH THE TIMES** *Avco 6105 042*............	**36**	4 wks
12 Feb 77	**SOUL CHA CHA** *H & L 6105 065*...............	**34**	6 wks
9 Apr 77	● **THE SHUFFLE** *H & L 6105 076*..............	**4**	14 wks

First hit featured the Soul City Symphony.

McCOYS *US, male vocal/instrumental group*   18 wks

| 2 Sep 65 | ● **HANG ON SLOOPY** *Immediate IM 001* .... | **5** | 14 wks |
| 16 Dec 65 | **FEVER** *Immediate IM 021*................. | **44** | 4 wks |

George McCRAE *US, male vocalist*   62 wks

29 Jun 74	★ **ROCK YOUR BABY** *Jayboy BOY 85*................	**1**	14 wks
5 Oct 74	● **I CAN'T LEAVE YOU ALONE** *Jayboy BOY 90*........	**9**	9 wks
14 Dec 74	**YOU CAN HAVE IT ALL** *Jayboy BOY 92*..........	**23**	9 wks
22 Mar 75	**SING A HAPPY SONG** *Jayboy BOY 95*	**38**	4 wks
19 Jul 75	● **IT'S BEEN SO LONG** *Jayboy BOY 100*..........	**4**	11 wks
18 Oct 75	**I AIN'T LYIN'** *Jayboy BOY 105*.............	**12**	7 wks
24 Jan 76	**HONEY I** *Jayboy BOY 107*.............	**33**	4 wks
25 Feb 84	**ONE STEP CLOSER (TO LOVE)** *President PT 522*.......	**57**	4 wks

Gwen McCRAE *US, female vocalist*   2 wks

| 30 Apr 88 | **ALL THIS LOVE THAT I'M GIVING** *Flame MELT 7* ...... | **63** | 2 wks |

MacCRARYS *US, male vocal/instrumental group*   4 wks

| 31 Jul 82 | **LOVE ON A SUMMER NIGHT** *Capitol CL 251* .... | **52** | 4 wks |

Ian McCULLOCH *UK, male vocalist*   10 wks

15 Dec 84	**SEPTEMBER SONG** *Korova KOW 40*................	**51**	5 wks
2 Sep 89	**PROUD TO FALL** *WEA YZ 417*................	**51**	4 wks
12 May 90	**CANDLELAND (THE SECOND COMING)** *East West YZ 452*....................	**75**	1 wk

Candleland (The Second Coming) *features Elizabeth Fraser - UK, female vocalist.*

Gene McDANIELS *US, male vocal*   2 wks

| 16 Nov 61 | **TOWER OF STRENGTH** *London HLG 9448*.......... | **49** | 1 wk |
| 30 Nov 61 | **TOWER OF STRENGTH (re-entry)** *London HLG 9448*...... | **49** | 1 wk |

Charles McDEVITT SKIFFLE GROUP featuring Nancy WHISKEY   20 wks
UK, male/female vocal/instrumental group

12 Apr 57	● **FREIGHT TRAIN** *Oriole CB 1352*..............	**5**	17 wks
14 Jun 57	**GREENBACK DOLLAR** *Oriole CB 1371*	**28**	1 wk
5 Jul 57	**GREENBACK DOLLAR (re-entry)** *Oriole CB 1371*	**30**	1 wk
20 Sep 57	**FREIGHT TRAIN (re-entry)** *Oriole CB 1352*..............	**27**	1 wk

Michael McDONALD *US, male vocalist*   16 wks

| 26 Jul 86 | **I KEEP FORGETTIN'** *Warner Bros K 17992*................ | **43** | 6 wks |
| 6 Sep 86 | **SWEET FREEDOM** *MCA MCA 1073*............... | **12** | 10 wks |

See also James Ingram with Michael McDonald; Patti Labelle and Michael McDonald; Doobie Brothers.

Carrie McDOWELL *US, female vocalist*   3 wks

| 26 Sep 87 | **UH UH NO NO CASUAL SEX** *Motown ZV 41501*........... | **68** | 3 wks |

MACEO and the MACS   5 wks
US, male vocal/instrumental group

| 16 May 87 | **CROSS THE TRACK (WE BETTER GO BACK)** *Urban URBX 1* .... | **54** | 5 wks |

McFADDEN and WHITEHEAD *US, male vocal duo*   10 wks

| 19 May 79 | ● **AIN'T NO STOPPIN' US NOW** *Philadelphia International PIR 7365* .... | **5** | 10 wks |

Bobby McFERRIN *US, male vocalist*   15 wks

| 24 Sep 88 | ● **DON'T WORRY BE HAPPY** *Manhattan MT 56* .... | **2** | 11 wks |
| 17 Dec 88 | **THINKIN' ABOUT YOUR BODY** *Manhattan BLUE 6*....... | **46** | 4 wks |

Mike McGEAR *UK, male vocalist*   4 wks

| 5 Oct 74 | **LEAVE IT** *Warner Bros. K 16446* .... | **36** | 4 wks |

Maureen McGOVERN *US, female vocalist*   8 wks

| 5 Jun 76 | **THE CONTINENTAL** *20th Century BTC 2222* .... | **16** | 8 wks |

Freddie McGREGOR *Jamaica, male vocalist*   16 wks

| 27 Jun 87 | ● **JUST DON'T WANT TO BE LONELY** *Germain DG 24*...... | **9** | 11 wks |
| 19 Sep 87 | **THAT GIRL (GROOVY SITUATION)** *Polydor POSP 884* .... | **47** | 5 wks |

Mary MacGREGOR US, female vocalist   10 wks

19 Feb 77 ● TORN BETWEEN TWO LOVERS *Ariola America AA 111*...... 4 10 wks

McGUINNESS FLINT   26 wks
UK, male vocal/instrumental group

21 Nov 70 ● WHEN I'M DEAD AND GONE *Capitol CL 15662*............. 2 14 wks
1 May 71 ● MALT AND BARLEY BLUES *Capitol CL 15682*............. 5 12 wks

Barry McGUIRE US, male vocalist   13 wks

9 Sep 65 ● EVE OF DESTRUCTION *RCA 1469*.......................... 3 13 wks

McGUIRE SISTERS US, female vocal group   24 wks

1 Apr 55	NO MORE *Vogue Coral Q 72050*	20	1 wk
15 Jul 55	SINCERELY *Vogue Coral Q 72050*	14	4 wks
1 Jun 56	DELILAH JONES *Vogue Coral Q 72161*	24	2 wks
14 Feb 58	SUGARTIME *Coral Q 72305*	14	6 wks
1 May 59	MAY YOU ALWAYS *Coral Q 72356*	15	10 wks
17 Jul 59	MAY YOU ALWAYS (re-entry) *Coral Q 72356*	28	1 wk

Peter MacJUNIOR US, male vocalist   4 wks

15 Oct 77 THE WATER MARGIN *BBC RESL 50*....................... 37 4 wks

This is the Japanese version of the song which shared chart credit with the English language version by Godiego. See also Godiego.

Lonnie MACK US, male instrumentalist - guitar   3 wks

14 Apr 79 MEMPHIS *Lightning LIG 9011* .... 47 3 wks

Memphis was coupled with Let's Dance by Chris Montez as a double A-side. See also Chris Montez.

Maria McKEE US, female vocalist   14 wks

15 Sep 90 ★ SHOW ME HEAVEN *Epic 656303 7*............................ 1 14 wks

Kenneth McKELLAR UK, male vocalist   4 wks

10 Mar 66 A MAN WITHOUT LOVE *Decca F 12341* .... 30 4 wks

Gisele McKENZIE Canada, female vocalist   6 wks

17 Jul 53	SEVEN LONELY DAYS *Capitol CL 13920*	12	1 wk
31 Jul 53	SEVEN LONELY DAYS (re-entry) *Capitol CL 13920*	11	1 wk
21 Aug 53	● SEVEN LONELY DAYS (2nd re-entry) *Capitol CL 13920*	6	4 wks

Scott McKENZIE US, male vocalist   18 wks

12 Jul 67 ★ SAN FRANCISCO (BE SURE TO WEAR FLOWERS IN
            YOUR HAIR) *CBS 2816*....................................... 1 17 wks
1 Nov 67 LIKE AN OLD TIME MOVIE *CBS 3009* .... 50 1 wk

Second hit credited to The Voice Of Scott McKenzie.

Ken MACKINTOSH UK, orchestra   9 wks

15 Jan 54	THE CREEP *HMV BD 1295*	12	1 wk
29 Jan 54	● THE CREEP (re-entry) *HMV BD 1295*	10	1 wk
7 Feb 58	RAUNCHY *HMV POP 426*	19	6 wks
10 Mar 60	NO HIDING PLACE *HMV POP 713*	45	1 wk

Craig McCLACHLAN and CHECK 1-2   20 wks
Australia, male vocal/instrumental group

16 Jun 90	● MONA *Epic 655784 7*	2	11 wks
4 Aug 90	AMANDA *Epic 656170 7*	19	6 wks
10 Nov 90	I ALMOST FELT LIKE CRYING *Epic 656310 7*	50	3 wks

McLAIN – *See PRATT and McLAIN with BROTHERLOVE*

Tommy McLAIN US, male vocalist   1 wk

8 Sep 66 SWEET DREAMS *London HL 10065* .... 49 1 wk

Malcolm McLAREN UK, male vocalist   60 wks

4 Dec 82	● BUFFALO GALS *Charisma MALC 1*	9	12 wks
26 Feb 83	SOWETO *Charisma MALC 2*	32	5 wks
2 Jul 83	● DOUBLE DUTCH *Charisma MALC 3*	3	13 wks
17 Dec 83	DUCK FOR THE OYSTER *Charisma MALC 4*	54	5 wks
1 Sep 84	MADAM BUTTERFLY (UN BEL DI VEDREMO) *Charisma MALC 5*	13	9 wks
27 May 89	WALTZ DARLING *Epic WALTZ 2*	31	8 wks
19 Aug 89	SOMETHING'S JUMPIN' IN YOUR SHIRT *Epic WALTZ 3*	29	7 wks
25 Nov 89	HOUSE OF THE BLUE DANUBE *Epic WALTZ 4*	73	1 wk

First hit credited to Malcolm McLaren and the World's Famous Supreme Team, second to Malcolm McLaren and the McLarenettes. Waltz Darling credits the Bootzilla Orchestra. Something's Jumpin' In Your Shirt credits the Bootzilla Orchestra and Lisa Marie. See also World's Famous Supreme Team Show.

Don McLEAN US, male vocalist   58 wks

22 Jan 72	● AMERICAN PIE *United Artists UP 35325*	2	16 wks
13 May 72	★ VINCENT *United Artists UP 35359*	1	15 wks
14 Apr 73	EVERYDAY *United Artists UP 35519*	38	5 wks
10 May 80	★ CRYING *EMI 5051*	1	14 wks
17 Apr 82	CASTLES IN THE AIR *EMI 5258*	47	8 wks

Jackie McLEAN US, male instrumentalist - alto sax   4 wks

7 Jul 79 DR. JACKYLL AND MISTER FUNK *RCA PB 1575* .... 53 4 wks

Phil McLEAN US, male vocalist   4 wks

18 Jan 62 SMALL SAD SAM *Top Rank JAR 597*........................... 34 4 wks

MACNEAL – *See MOUTH and MACNEAL*

Patrick MACNEE and Honor BLACKMAN   5 wks
UK, male/female vocal duo

1 Dec 90 ● KINKY BOOTS *Deram KINKY 1* .... 5† 5 wks

Rita McNEIL Canada, female vocalist   10 wks

6 Oct 90 WORKING MAN *Polydor PO 98* .... 11 10 wks

Clyde McPHATTER US, male vocalist   1 wk

24 Aug 56 TREASURE OF LOVE *London HLE 8293*...................... 27 1 wk

Carmen McRAE – *See Sammy DAVIS Jr. and Carmen McRAE*

Gordon MacRAE – See VARIOUS ARTISTS (Carousel Soundtrack)

Ralph McTELL *UK, male vocalist*   **18 wks**

7 Dec 74	●	STREETS OF LONDON *Reprise K 14380*.....................	2	12 wks
20 Dec 75		DREAMS OF YOU *Warner Bros. K 16648*..................	36	6 wks

MAD JOCKS featuring JOCKMASTER B.A.   **5 wks**
UK, male vocal/instrumental group

19 Dec 87	JOCK MIX 1 *Debut DEBT 3037*................................	46	5 wks

Danny MADDEN *US, male vocalist*   **2 wks**

14 Jul 90	THE FACTS OF LIFE *Eternal YZ 473*.......................	72	2 wks

MADNESS *UK, male vocal/instrumental group*   **237 wks**

1 Sep 79		THE PRINCE *2-Tone TT 3*..............................	16	11 wks
10 Nov 79	●	ONE STEP BEYOND *Stiff BUY 56*......................	7	14 wks
5 Jan 80	●	MY GIRL *Stiff BUY 62*................................	3	10 wks
5 Apr 80	●	WORK REST AND PLAY (EP) *Stiff BUY 71*............	6	8 wks
13 Sep 80	●	BAGGY TROUSERS *Stiff BUY 84*.....................	3	20 wks
22 Nov 80	●	EMBARRASSMENT *Stiff BUY 102*....................	4	12 wks
24 Jan 81	●	THE RETURN OF THE LOS PALMAS SEVEN *Stiff BUY 108*............................	7	11 wks
25 Apr 81	●	GREY DAY *Stiff BUY 112*.............................	4	10 wks
26 Sep 81	●	SHUT UP *Stiff BUY 126*..............................	7	9 wks
5 Dec 81	●	IT MUST BE LOVE *Stiff BUY 134*....................	4	12 wks
20 Feb 82		CARDIAC ARREST *Stiff BUY 140*....................	14	10 wks
22 May 82	★	HOUSE OF FUN *Stiff BUY 146*.......................	1	9 wks
24 Jul 82	●	DRIVING IN MY CAR *Stiff BUY 153*.................	4	8 wks
27 Nov 82	●	OUR HOUSE *Stiff BUY 163*...........................	5	13 wks
19 Feb 83	●	TOMORROW'S (JUST ANOTHER DAY)/ MADNESS (IS ALL IN THE MIND) *Stiff BUY 169*............	8	9 wks
20 Aug 83	●	WINGS OF A DOVE *Stiff BUY 181*...................	2	10 wks
5 Nov 83	●	THE SUN AND THE RAIN *Stiff BUY 192*............	5	10 wks
11 Feb 84		MICHAEL CAINE *Stiff BUY 196*.....................	11	8 wks
2 Jun 84		ONE BETTER DAY *Stiff BUY 201*....................	17	7 wks
31 Aug 85		YESTERDAY'S MEN *Zarjazz JAZZ 5*.................	18	7 wks
26 Oct 85		UNCLE SAM *Zarjazz JAZZ 7*..........................	21	11 wks
1 Feb 86		SWEETEST GIRL *Zarjazz JAZZ 8*....................	35	6 wks
8 Nov 86		(WAITING FOR) THE GHOST TRAIN *Zarjazz JAZZ 9*...................................	18	7 wks
3 Jan 87		(WAITING FOR) THE GHOST TRAIN (re-entry) *Zarjazz JAZZ 9*...................................	74	1 wk
19 Mar 88		I PRONOUNCE YOU *Virgin VS 1054*..............	44	4 wks

Tracks on Work Rest and Play EP: Night Boat to Cairo/Deceives The Eye/The Young And The Old/Don't Quote Me On That. Act billed as The Madness on I Pronounce You.

MADONNA *US, female vocalist*   **285 wks**

14 Jan 84	●	HOLIDAY *Sire W 9405*................................	6	11 wks
17 Mar 84		LUCKY STAR *Sire W 9522*............................	14	9 wks
2 Jun 84		BORDERLINE *Sire W 9260*...........................	56	4 wks
17 Nov 84	●	LIKE A VIRGIN *Sire W 9210*........................	3	18 wks
2 Mar 85	●	MATERIAL GIRL *Sire W 9083*......................	3	10 wks
8 Jun 85	●	CRAZY FOR YOU *Geffen A 6323*....................	2	15 wks
27 Jul 85	★	INTO THE GROOVE *Sire W 8934*..................	1	14 wks
3 Aug 85	●	HOLIDAY (re-entry) *Sire W 9405*.................	2	10 wks
21 Sep 85	●	ANGEL *Sire W 8881*...................................	5	9 wks
12 Oct 85	●	GAMBLER *Geffen A 6585*.............................	4	11 wks
7 Dec 85	●	DRESS YOU UP *Sire W 8848*........................	5	11 wks
4 Jan 86		GAMBLER (re-entry) *Geffen A 6585*	61	1 wk
25 Jan 86	●	BORDERLINE (re-entry) *Sire W 9260*	2	9 wks
26 Apr 86	●	LIVE TO TELL *Sire W 8717*..........................	2	12 wks
28 Jun 86	★	PAPA DON'T PREACH *Sire W 8636*................	1	14 wks
4 Oct 86	★	TRUE BLUE *Sire W 8550*.............................	1	15 wks
13 Dec 86	●	OPEN YOUR HEART *Sire W 8480*..................	4	9 wks
4 Apr 87	★	LA ISLA BONITA *Sire W 8378*......................	1	11 wks

18 Jul 87	★	WHO'S THAT GIRL *Sire W 8341*....................	1	10 wks
19 Sep 87	●	CAUSING A COMMOTION *Sire W 8224*...........	4	9 wks
12 Dec 87	●	THE LOOK OF LOVE *Sire W 8115*..................	9	7 wks
18 Mar 89	★	LIKE A PRAYER *Sire W 7539*.......................	1	12 wks
3 Jun 89	●	EXPRESS YOURSELF *Sire W 2948*.................	5	10 wks
16 Sep 89	●	CHERISH *Sire W 2883*...............................	3	8 wks
16 Dec 89	●	DEAR JESSIE *Sire W 2668*..........................	5	9 wks
7 Apr 90	★	VOGUE *Sire W 9851*..................................	1	14 wks
21 Jul 90	●	HANKY PANKY *Sire W 9789*........................	2	9 wks
8 Dec 90	●	JUSTIFY MY LOVE *Sire W 9000*....................	2†	4 wks

MAGAZINE *UK, male vocal/instrumental group*   **7 wks**

11 Feb 78	SHOT BY BOTH SIDES *Virgin VS 200*..................	41	4 wks
26 Jul 80	SWEET HEART CONTRACT *Virgin VS 368*	54	3 wks

MAGIC LADY *US, female vocal duo*   **3 wks**

14 May 88	BETCHA CAN'T LOSE (WITH MY LOVE) *Motown ZB 42003*	58	3 wks

MAGIC LANTERNS *UK, male vocal/instrumental group*   **3 wks**

7 Jul 66	EXCUSE ME BABY *CBS 202094*	46	1 wk
28 Jul 66	EXCUSE ME BABY (re-entry) *CBS 202094*	44	1 wk
11 Aug 66	EXCUSE ME BABY (2nd re-entry) *CBS 202094*	46	1 wk

MAGNUM *UK, male vocal/instrumental group*   **26 wks**

22 Mar 80	MAGNUM (DOUBLE SINGLE) *Jet 175*............	47	6 wks
12 Jul 86	LONELY NIGHT *Polydor POSP 798*	70	2 wks
19 Mar 88	DAYS OF NO TRUST *Polydor POSP 910*...........	32	4 wks
7 May 88	START TALKING LOVE *Polydor POSP 920*	22	4 wks
2 Jul 88	IT MUST HAVE BEEN LOVE *Polydor POSP 930*...	33	4 wks
23 Jun 90	ROCKIN' CHAIR *Polydor PO 88*	27	4 wks
25 Aug 90	HEARTBROKE AND BUSTED *Polydor PO 94*	49	2 wks

Tracks on double single: Invasion/Kingdom of Madness/All Of My Life/Great Adventure.

MAHLATHINI and the MAHOTELLA QUEENS – See ART OF NOISE

MAI TAI *Holland, female vocal group*   **30 wks**

25 May 85	●	HISTORY *Virgin VS 773*	8	13 wks
3 Aug 85	●	BODY AND SOUL *Virgin VS 801*	9	13 wks
15 Feb 86		FEMALE INTUITION *Virgin VS 844*..............	54	4 wks

MAIN INGREDIENT *US, male vocal group*   **7 wks**

29 Jun 74	JUST DON'T WANT TO BE LONELY *RCA APBO 0205*	27	7 wks

MAISONETTES *UK, male/female vocal group*   **12 wks**

11 Dec 82	●	HEARTACHE AVENUE *Ready Steady Go! RSG 1*..............	7	12 wks

Raven MAIZE *US, male vocalist*   **1 wk**

5 Aug 89	FOREVER TOGETHER *Republic LIC 014*	67	1 wk

MAJORS – See Morris MINOR and the MAJORS

MAKADOPULOS and his GREEK SERENADERS *Greece, male vocal/instrumental group*   **14 wks**

20 Oct 60	**NEVER ON SUNDAY** *Palette PG 9005*		**36**	14 wks

Jack E. MAKOSSA *Kenya, male producer*   **5 wks**

12 Sep 87	**THE OPERA HOUSE** *Champion CHAMP 50*		**48**	5 wks

Carl MALCOLM *Jamaica, male vocalist*   **8 wks**

13 Sep 75	● **FATTIE BUM BUM** *UK 108*		**8**	8 wks

Timmy MALLET – *See BOMBALURINA*

MAMAS and the PAPAS *US, female/male vocal group*   **64 wks**

28 Apr 66	**CALIFORNIA DREAMIN'** *RCA 1503*		**23**	9 wks
12 May 66	● **MONDAY MONDAY** *RCA 1516*		**3**	13 wks
28 Jul 66	**I SAW HER AGAIN** *RCA 1533*		**11**	4 wks
9 Feb 67	**WORDS OF LOVE** *RCA 1564*		**47**	3 wks
6 Apr 67	● **DEDICATED TO THE ONE I LOVE** *RCA 1576*		**2**	17 wks
26 Jul 67	● **CREEQUE ALLEY** *RCA 1613*		**9**	11 wks

See also Mama Cass.

MAMBAS – *See MARC and the MAMBAS*

A MAN CALLED ADAM
UK, male/female vocal/instrumental group   **4 wks**

29 Sep 90	**BAREFOOT IN THE HEAD** *Big Life BLR 28*		**70**	2 wks
20 Oct 90	**BAREFOOT IN THE HEAD** (re-entry) *Big Life BLR 28*		**60**	2 wks

MAN TO MAN *US, male vocal/instrumental duo*   **19 wks**

13 Sep 86	**MALE STRIPPER** *Bolts BOLTS 4*		**64**	3 wks
3 Jan 87	**MALE STRIPPER** (re-entry) *Bolts BOLTS 4*		**63**	1 wk
7 Feb 87	● **MALE STRIPPER** (2nd re-entry) *Bolts BOLTS 4*		**4**	12 wks
4 Jul 87	**I NEED A MAN / ENERGY IS EUROBEAT** *Bolts BOLTS 5*		**43**	3 wks

On first hit act billed as Man 2 Man meet Man Parrish. See also Man Parrish.

Melissa MANCHESTER and Al JARREAU   **1 wk**
US, male/female vocal duo

5 Apr 86	**THE MUSIC OF GOODBYE (LOVE THEME FROM OUT OF AFRICA)** *MCA MCA 1038*		**75**	1 wk

See also Al Jarreau.

MANCHESTER UNITED FOOTBALL CLUB *UK, male football team vocalists*   **11 wks**

8 May 76	**MANCHESTER UNITED** *Decca F 13633*		**50**	1 wk
21 May 83	**GLORY GLORY MAN. UNITED** *EMI 5390*		**13**	5 wks
18 May 85	● **WE ALL FOLLOW MAN. UNITED** *Columbia DB 9107*		**10**	5 wks

Henry MANCINI *US, orchestra/chorus*   **23 wks**

7 Dec 61	**MOON RIVER** *RCA 1256*		**46**	2 wks
28 Dec 61	**MOON RIVER** (re-entry) *RCA 1256*		**44**	1 wk
24 Sep 64	● **HOW SOON** *RCA 1414*		**10**	12 wks
25 Mar 72	**THEME FROM 'CADE'S COUNTY'** *RCA 2182*		**42**	1 wk

11 Feb 84	**MAIN THEME FROM 'THE THORNBIRDS'** *Warner Bros. 9677*		**23**	7 wks

Steve MANDELL – *See 'DELIVERANCE' SOUNDTRACK*

MANFRED MANN *South Africa/UK, male vocal/instrumental group*   **176 wks**

23 Jan 64	● **5-4-3-2-1** *HMV POP 1252*		**5**	13 wks
16 Apr 64	**HUBBLE BUBBLE TOIL AND TROUBLE** *HMV POP 1282*		**11**	8 wks
16 Jul 64	★ **DO WAH DIDDY DIDDY** *HMV POP 1320*		**1**	14 wks
15 Oct 64	● **SHA LA LA** *HMV POP 1346*		**3**	12 wks
14 Jan 65	● **COME TOMORROW** *HMV POP 1381*		**4**	9 wks
15 Apr 65	● **OH NO NOT MY BABY** *HMV POP 1413*		**11**	10 wks
16 Sep 65	● **IF YOU GOTTA GO GO NOW** *HMV POP 1466*		**2**	12 wks
21 Apr 66	★ **PRETTY FLAMINGO** *HMV POP 1523*		**1**	12 wks
7 Jul 66	**YOU GAVE ME SOMEBODY TO LOVE** *HMV POP 1541*		**36**	4 wks
4 Aug 66	● **JUST LIKE A WOMAN** *Fontana TF 730*		**10**	10 wks
27 Oct 66	● **SEMI-DETACHED SUBURBAN MR. JAMES** *Fontana TF 757*		**2**	12 wks
30 Mar 67	● **HA HA SAID THE CLOWN** *Fontana TF 812*		**4**	11 wks
25 May 67	**SWEET PEA** *Fontana TF 828*		**36**	4 wks
24 Jan 68	★ **MIGHTY QUINN** *Fontana TF 897*		**1**	11 wks
12 Jun 68	● **MY NAME IS JACK** *Fontana TF 943*		**8**	11 wks
18 Dec 68	● **FOX ON THE RUN** *Fontana TF 985*		**5**	12 wks
30 Apr 69	● **RAGAMUFFIN MAN** *Fontana TF 1013*		**8**	11 wks

The HMV hits featured Paul Jones as lead vocalist and the Fontana hits Mike d'Abo, except for Sweet Pea, an instrumental disc. See also Paul Jones; Manfred Mann's Earth Band.

MANFRED MANN'S EARTH BAND *South Africa/UK, male vocal/instrumental group*   **41 wks**

8 Sep 73	● **JOYBRINGER** *Vertigo 6059 083*		**9**	10 wks
28 Aug 76	● **BLINDED BY THE LIGHT** *Bronze BRO 29*		**6**	10 wks
20 May 78	● **DAVY'S ON THE ROAD AGAIN** *Bronze BRO 52*		**6**	12 wks
17 Mar 79	**YOU ANGEL YOU** *Bronze BRO 68*		**54**	5 wks
7 Jul 79	**DON'T KILL IT CAROL** *Bronze BRO 77*		**45**	4 wks

See also Manfred Mann.

MANHATTAN TRANSFER *US, male/female vocal group*   **72 wks**

7 Feb 76	**TUXEDO JUNCTION** *Atlantic K 10670*		**24**	6 wks
5 Feb 77	★ **CHANSON D'AMOUR** *Atlantic K 10886*		**1**	13 wks
28 May 77	**DON'T LET GO** *Atlantic K 10930*		**32**	6 wks
18 Feb 78	**WALK IN LOVE** *Atlantic K 11075*		**48**	1 wk
4 Mar 78	**WALK IN LOVE** (re-entry) *Atlantic K 11075*		**12**	11 wks
20 May 78	**ON A LITTLE STREET IN SINGAPORE** *Atlantic K 11136*		**20**	9 wks
16 Sep 78	**WHERE DID OUR LOVE GO/ JE VOULAIS TE DIRE (QUE JE T'ATTENDS)** *Atlantic K 11182*		**40**	4 wks
23 Dec 78	**WHO WHAT WHEN WHERE WHY** *Atlantic K 11233*		**49**	6 wks
17 May 80	**TWILIGHT ZONE-TWILIGHT TONE** (MEDLEY) *Atlantic K 11476*		**25**	8 wks
21 Jan 84	**SPICE OF LIFE** *Atlantic A 9728*		**19**	8 wks

MANHATTANS *US, male vocal group*   **31 wks**

19 Jun 76	● **KISS AND SAY GOODBYE** *CBS 4317*		**4**	11 wks
2 Oct 76	● **HURT** *CBS 4562*		**4**	11 wks
23 Apr 77	**IT'S YOU** *CBS 5093*		**43**	3 wks
26 Jul 80	**SHINING STAR** *CBS 8624*		**45**	4 wks
6 Aug 83	**CRAZY** *CBS A 3578*		**63**	2 wks

MANIC MC's featuring Sara CARLSON
UK, male production duo and female vocalist   **5 wks**

12 Aug 89	**MENTAL** *RCA PB 43037*	30	5 wks

Barry MANILOW *US, male vocalist*   **128 wks**

22 Feb 75	**MANDY** *Arista 1*	11	9 wks
6 May 78	**CAN'T SMILE WITHOUT YOU** *Arista 176*	43	7 wks
29 Jul 78	**SOMEWHERE IN THE NIGHT/ COPACABANA (AT THE COPA)** *Arista 196*	42	10 wks
23 Dec 78	**COULD IT BE MAGIC** *Arista ARIST 229*.............	25	10 wks
8 Nov 80	**LONELY TOGETHER** *Arista ARIST 373*	21	13 wks
7 Feb 81	**I MADE IT THROUGH THE RAIN** *Arista ARIST 384*	37	6 wks
11 Apr 81	**BERMUDA TRIANGLE** *Arista ARIST 406*.............	15	9 wks
26 Sep 81	**LET'S HANG ON** *Arista ARIST 429*....................	12	11 wks
12 Dec 81	**THE OLD SONGS** *Arista ARIST 443*.............	48	8 wks
20 Feb 82	**IF I SHOULD LOVE AGAIN** *Arista ARIST 453*	66	2 wks
17 Apr 82	**STAY** *Arista ARIST 464*...............	23	8 wks
16 Oct 82	● **I WANNA DO IT WITH YOU** *Arista ARIST 495* ...	8	8 wks
4 Dec 82	**I'M GONNA SIT RIGHT DOWN AND WRITE MYSELF A LETTER** *Arista ARIST 503*....................	36	7 wks
25 Jun 83	**SOME KIND OF FRIEND** *Arista ARIST 516*	48	2 wks
27 Aug 83	**YOU'RE LOOKING HOT TONIGHT** *Arista ARIST 542*	47	6 wks
10 Dec 83	**READ 'EM AND WEEP** *Arista ARIST 551*.............	17	7 wks
8 Apr 89	**PLEASE DON'T BE SCARED** *Arista 112186*................	35	5 wks

ARIST 464 was available as both a live and studio recording.

MANKIND *UK, male instrumental group*   **12 wks**

25 Nov 78	**DR. WHO** *Pinnacle PIN 71*	25	12 wks

Aimee MANN – *See RUSH*

Johnny MANN SINGERS *US, male/female vocal group*   **13 wks**

12 Jul 67	● **UP, UP AND AWAY** *Liberty LIB 55972*	6	13 wks

MANTOVANI *UK, orchestra*   **52 wks**

19 Dec 52	● **WHITE CHRISTMAS** *Decca F 10017*.............	6	3 wks
29 May 53	★ **MOULIN ROUGE** *Decca F 10094*	1	21 wks
23 Oct 53	● **SWEDISH RHAPSODY** *Decca F 10168*.............	2	17 wks
13 Nov 53	● **MOULIN ROUGE (re-entry)** *Decca F 10094*	10	1 wk
4 Dec 53	**MOULIN ROUGE (2nd re-entry)** *Decca F 10094*........	12	1 wk
26 Feb 54	**SWEDISH RHAPSODY (re-entry)** *Decca F 10168*	12	1 wk
11 Feb 55	**LONELY BALLERINA** *Decca F 10395*	16	3 wks
18 Mar 55	**LONELY BALLERINA (re-entry)** *Decca F 10395*	18	1 wk
31 May 57	**AROUND THE WORLD** *Decca F 10888*......................	20	4 wks

See David Whitfield.

MANTRONIX *US/Jamaica, male vocal/instrumental duo*   **42 wks**

22 Feb 86	**LADIES** *10 TEN 116*	55	4 wks
17 May 86	**BASSLINE** *10 TEN 118*	34	6 wks
7 Feb 87	**WHO IS IT** *10 TEN 137*	40	6 wks
4 Jul 87	**SCREAM (PRIMAL SCREAM)** *10 TEN 169*	46	4 wks
30 Jan 88	**SING A SONG (BREAK IT DOWN)** *10 TEN 206*...........	61	2 wks
12 Mar 88	**SIMPLE SIMON (YOU GOTTA REGARD)** *10 TEN 217*	72	2 wks
6 Jan 90	● **GOT TO HAVE YOUR LOVE** *Capitol CL 559*	4	11 wks
12 May 90	● **TAKE YOUR TIME** *Capitol CL 573*	10	7 wks

Got To Have Your Love and Take Your Time feature Wondress – UK, female vocalist.

MANUEL and his MUSIC OF THE MOUNTAINS *UK, orchestra, leader Geoff Love*   **31 wks**

28 Aug 59	**THEME FROM HONEYMOON** *Columbia DB 4323*.........	29	2 wks
25 Sep 59	**THEME FROM HONEYMOON (re-entry)** *Columbia DB 4323*	22	5 wks
6 Nov 59	**THEME FROM HONEYMOON (2nd re-entry)** *Columbia DB 4323*	27	2 wks
13 Oct 60	**NEVER ON SUNDAY** *Columbia DB 4515*..............	29	10 wks
13 Oct 66	**SOMEWHERE MY LOVE** *Columbia DB 7969*...............	42	2 wks
31 Jan 76	● **RODRIGO'S GUITAR CONCERTO DE ARANJUEZ (THEME FROM 2ND MOVEMENT)** *EMI 2383*............	3	10 wks

MARAUDERS *UK, male vocal/instrumental group*   **4 wks**

8 Aug 63	**THAT'S WHAT I WANT** *Decca F 11695*	48	1 wk
22 Aug 63	**THAT'S WHAT I WANT (re-entry)** *Decca F 11695*	43	3 wks

MARBLES *UK, male vocal duo*   **18 wks**

25 Sep 68	● **ONLY ONE WOMAN** *Polydor 56 272*	5	12 wks
26 Mar 69	**THE WALLS FELL DOWN** *Polydor 56 310*	28	6 wks

MARC and the MAMBAS
UK, male/female vocal/instrumental group   **3 wks**

2 Jun 83	**BLACK HEART** *Some Bizzare BZS 19*	49	3 wks

See also Marc Almond.

MARCELS *US, male vocal group*   **17 wks**

13 Apr 61	★ **BLUE MOON** *Pye International 7N 25073*...................	1	13 wks
8 Jun 61	**SUMMERTIME** *Pye International 7N 25083*...............	46	4 wks

Little Peggy MARCH *US, female vocalist*   **7 wks**

12 Sep 63	**HELLO HEARTACHE GOODBYE LOVE** *RCA 1362*.......	29	7 wks

MARCIA – *See BOB and MARCIA*

MARDI GRAS *UK, male vocal/instrumental group*   **9 wks**

5 Aug 72	**TOO BUSY THINKING 'BOUT MY BABY** *Bell 1226*.......	19	9 wks

Kelly MARIE *UK, female vocalist*   **36 wks**

2 Aug 80	★ **FEELS LIKE I'M IN LOVE** *Calibre PLUS 1*.......	1	16 wks
18 Oct 80	**LOVING JUST FOR FUN** *Calibre PLUS 4*	21	7 wks
7 Feb 81	**HOT LOVE** *Calibre PLUS 5*....................	22	10 wks
30 May 81	**LOVE TRIAL** *Calibre PLUS 7*....................	51	3 wks

Teena MARIE *US, female vocalist*   **28 wks**

7 Jul 79	**I'M A SUCKER FOR YOUR LOVE** *Motown TMG 1146*	43	8 wks
31 May 80	● **BEHIND THE GROOVE** *Motown TMG 1185*	6	10 wks
11 Oct 80	**I NEED YOUR LOVIN'** *Motown TMG 1203*	28	6 wks
26 Mar 88	**OO LA LA LA** *Epic 651423 7*............................	74	2 wks
10 Nov 90	**SINCE DAY ONE** *Epic 656429 7*	69	2 wks

First hit has credit 'Co-lead vocals: Rick James'. See also Rick James.

MARILLION UK, male vocal/instrumental group   **79 wks**

20 Nov 82		MARKET SQUARE HEROES EMI 5351........................	60	2 wks
12 Feb 83		HE KNOWS YOU KNOW EMI 5362......................	35	4 wks
16 Apr 83		MARKET SQUARE HEROES (re-entry) EMI 5351.........	53	6 wks
18 Jun 83		GARDEN PARTY EMI 5393...........................	16	5 wks
11 Feb 84		PUNCH AND JUDY EMI MARIL 1.....................	29	4 wks
12 May 84		ASSASSING EMI MARIL 2...........................	22	5 wks
18 May 85	●	KAYLEIGH EMI MARIL 3............................	2	14 wks
7 Sep 85	●	LAVENDER EMI MARIL 4............................	5	9 wks
30 Nov 85		HEART OF LOTHIAN EMI MARIL 5...................	29	6 wks
23 May 87	●	INCOMMUNICADO EMI MARIL 6.....................	6	5 wks
25 Jul 87		SUGAR MICE EMI MARIL 7..........................	22	5 wks
7 Nov 87		WARM WET CIRCLES EMI MARIL 8..................	22	4 wks
26 Nov 88		FREAKS (LIVE) EMI MARIL 9........................	24	3 wks
9 Sep 89		HOOKS IN YOU Capitol MARIL 10...................	30	3 wks
9 Dec 89		UNINVITED GUEST EMI MARIL 11..................	53	2 wks
14 Apr 90		EASTER EMI MARIL 12.............................	34	2 wks

MARILYN UK, male vocalist   **26 wks**

5 Nov 83	●	CALLING YOUR NAME Mercury MAZ 1	4	12 wks
11 Feb 84		CRY AND BE FREE Mercury MAZ 2	31	6 wks
21 Apr 84		YOU DON'T LOVE ME Mercury MAZ 3...............	40	7 wks
13 Apr 85		BABY U LEFT ME (IN THE COLD) Mercury MAZ 4........	70	1 wk

Marino MARINI Italy, male vocalist   **17 wks**

3 Oct 58		VOLARE Durium DC 16632..........................	13	7 wks
10 Oct 58	●	COME PRIMA Durium DC 16632	2	14 wks
20 Mar 59		CIAO CIAO BAMBINA Durium DC 16636	25	1 wk
3 Apr 59		CIAO CIAO BAMBINA (re-entry) Durium DC 16636	24	1 wk

Pigmeat MARKHAM US, male vocalist   **8 wks**

17 Jul 68		HERE COMES THE JUDGE Chess CRS 8077................	19	8 wks

Biz MARKIE US, male rapper   **2 wks**

26 Mar 90		JUST A FRIEND Cold Chillin' W 9823	55	2 wks

Yannis MARKOPOULOS Greece, orchestra   **8 wks**

17 Dec 77		WHO PAYS THE FERRYMAN BBC RESL 51	11	8 wks

Guy MARKS Australia, male vocalist   **8 wks**

13 May 78		LOVING YOU HAS MADE ME BANANAS ABC 4211	25	8 wks

Bob MARLEY and the WAILERS   **121 wks**
Jamaica, male vocal/instrumental group

27 Sep 75		NO WOMAN NO CRY Island WIP 6244......................	22	7 wks
25 Jun 77		EXODUS Island WIP 6390............................	14	9 wks
10 Sep 77		WAITING IN VAIN Island WIP 6402..................	27	6 wks
10 Dec 77	●	JAMMING/ PUNKY REGGAE PARTY Island WIP 6410	9	12 wks
25 Feb 78	●	IS THIS LOVE Island WIP 6420.....................	9	9 wks
10 Jun 78		SATISFY MY SOUL Island WIP 6440	21	10 wks
20 Oct 79		SO MUCH TROUBLE IN THE WORLD		
		Island WIP 6510	56	4 wks
21 Jun 80	●	COULD YOU BE LOVED Island WIP 6610	5	12 wks
13 Sep 80		THREE LITTLE BIRDS Island WIP 6641.............	17	9 wks
13 Jun 81	●	NO WOMAN NO CRY (re-entry) Island WIP 6244......	8	11 wks
7 May 83		BUFFALO SOLDIER Island/Tuff Gong IS 108	4	12 wks
21 Apr 84	●	ONE LOVE/ PEOPLE GET READY Island IS 169........	5	11 wks
23 Jun 84		WAITING IN VAIN (re-issue) Island IS 180	31	7 wks
8 Dec 84		COULD YOU BE LOVED (re-issue) Island IS 210...........	71	2 wks

Ziggy MARLEY and the MELODY MAKERS   **11 wks**
Jamaica, male/female vocal/instrumental group

11 Jun 88		TOMORROW PEOPLE Virgin VS 1049	22	10 wks
23 Sep 89		LOOK WHO'S DANCING Virgin America VUS 5.............	65	1 wk

MARMALADE UK, male vocal/instrumental group   **130 wks**

22 May 68	●	LOVIN' THINGS CBS 3412	6	13 wks
23 Oct 68		WAIT FOR ME MARIANNE CBS 3708.................	30	5 wks
4 Dec 68	★	OB-LA-DI OB-LA-DA CBS 3892	1	20 wks
11 Jun 69	●	BABY MAKE IT SOON CBS 4287	9	13 wks
20 Dec 69		REFLECTIONS OF MY LIFE Decca F 12982............	3	12 wks
18 Jul 70	●	RAINBOW Decca F 13035...........................	3	14 wks
27 Mar 71		MY LITTLE ONE Decca F 13135....................	15	11 wks
4 Sep 71	●	COUSIN NORMAN Decca F 13214...................	6	11 wks
27 Nov 71		BACK ON THE ROAD Decca F 13251.................	35	7 wks
22 Jan 72		BACK ON THE ROAD (re-entry) Decca F 13251........	50	1 wk
1 Apr 72	●	RADANCER Decca F 13297..........................	6	12 wks
21 Feb 76	●	FALLING APART AT THE SEAMS Target TGT 105.........	9	11 wks

M/ A/ R/ R/ S UK, male instrumental/scratch group   **14 wks**

5 Sep 87	★	PUMP UP THE VOLUME/ ANITINA (THE FIRST		
		TIME I SEE SHE DANCE) 4AD AD 70...................	1	14 wks

The 'B' side of this record was listed on the chart at the record company's request without evidence of consumer interest.

Gerry MARSDEN – *See CHRISTIANS, Holly JOHNSON, Paul McCARTNEY, Gerry MARSDEN and STOCK AITKEN WATERMAN; GERRY and the PACEMAKERS*

Stevie MARSH UK, female vocalist   **4 wks**

4 Dec 59		THE ONLY BOY IN THE WORLD Decca F 11181..........	29	2 wks
25 Dec 59		THE ONLY BOY IN THE WORLD (re-entry)		
		Decca F 11181....................................	24	2 wks

Joy MARSHALL UK, female vocalist   **2 wks**

23 Jun 66		THE MORE I SEE YOU Decca F 12422	34	2 wks

Keith MARSHALL UK, male vocalist   **10 wks**

4 Apr 81		ONLY CRYING Arrival PIK 2	12	10 wks

MARSHALL HAIN   **19 wks**
UK, male/female vocal/instrumental duo

3 Jun 78	●	DANCING IN THE CITY Harvest HAR 5157	3	15 wks
14 Oct 78		COMING HOME Harvest HAR 5168	39	4 wks

Lena MARTELL UK, female vocalist   **18 wks**

29 Sep 79	★	ONE DAY AT A TIME Pye 7N 46021........................	1	18 wks

MARTHA and the MUFFINS   **10 wks**
Canada, female/male vocal/instrumental group

1 Mar 80	●	ECHO BEACH Dindisc DIN 9................................	10	10 wks

See also M + M, who are Martha and a Muffin.

MARTHA and the VANDELLAS – *See Martha REEVES and the VANDELLAS*

MARTIKA *US, female vocalist* — **35 wks**

28 Jul	89	● TOY SOLDIERS *CBS 655049 7*	5	11 wks
14 Oct	89	● I FEEL THE EARTH MOVE *CBS 655294 7*	7	14 wks
13 Jan	90	MORE THAN YOU KNOW *CBS 655526 7*	15	7 wks
17 Mar	90	WATER *CBS 655731 7*	59	3 wks

Dean MARTIN *US, male vocalist* — **154 wks**

18 Sep	53	● KISS *Capitol CL 13893*	9	1 wk
2 Oct	53	● KISS (re-entry) *Capitol CL 13893*	5	7 wks
22 Jan	54	● THAT'S AMORE *Capitol CL 14008.*	2	11 wks
1 Oct	54	● SWAY *Capitol CL 14138.*	6	7 wks
22 Oct	54	HOW DO YOU SPEAK TO AN ANGEL *Capitol CL 14150*	15	2 wks
19 Nov	54	HOW DO YOU SPEAK TO AN ANGEL (re-entry) *Capitol CL 14150*	17	4 wks
28 Jan	55	● NAUGHTY LADY OF SHADY LANE *Capitol CL 14226*	5	10 wks
4 Feb	55	MAMBO ITALIANO *Capitol CL 14227*	14	2 wks
25 Feb	55	● LET ME GO LOVER *Capitol CL 14226*	3	9 wks
1 Apr	55	● UNDER THE BRIDGES OF PARIS *Capitol CL 14255.*	6	8 wks
10 Feb	56	★ MEMORIES ARE MADE OF THIS *Capitol CL 14523*	1	16 wks
2 Mar	56	YOUNG AND FOOLISH *Capitol CL 14519*	20	1 wk
27 Apr	56	INNAMORATA *Capitol CL 14507*	21	3 wks
22 Mar	57	THE MAN WHO PLAYS THE MANDOLINO *Capitol CL 14690*	21	2 wks
13 Jun	58	● RETURN TO ME *Capitol CL 14844*	2	22 wks
29 Aug	58	● VOLARE *Capitol CL 14910*	2	14 wks
27 Aug	64	EVERYBODY LOVES SOMEBODY *Reprise R 20281*	11	13 wks
12 Nov	64	THE DOOR IS STILL OPEN TO MY HEART *Reprise R 20307*	42	4 wks
5 Feb	69	● GENTLE ON MY MIND *Reprise RS 23343*	2	23 wks
30 Aug	69	GENTLE ON MY MIND (re-entry) *Reprise RS 23343*	49	1 wk

Juan MARTIN *Spain, male instrumentalist - guitar* — **7 wks**

28 Jan	84	● LOVE THEME FROM 'THE THORN BIRDS' *WEA X 9518*	10	7 wks

Marilyn MARTIN – See Phil COLLINS and Marilyn MARTIN

Ray MARTIN *UK, orchestra* — **11 wks**

14 Nov	52	● BLUE TANGO *Columbia DB 3051.*	8	1 wk
28 Nov	52	● BLUE TANGO (re-entry) *Columbia DB 3051.*	10	3 wks
4 Dec	53	● SWEDISH RHAPSODY *Columbia DB 3346.*	10	1 wk
18 Dec	53	● SWEDISH RHAPSODY (re-entry) *Columbia DB 3346.*	4	3 wks
15 Jun	56	CAROUSEL WALTZ *Columbia DB 3771.*	28	1 wk
3 Aug	56	CAROUSEL WALTZ (re-entry) *Columbia DB 3771.*	24	2 wks

Tony MARTIN *US, male vocalist* — **28 wks**

22 Apr	55	● STRANGER IN PARADISE *HMV B 10849*	6	13 wks
13 Jul	56	● WALK HAND IN HAND *HMV POP 222*	2	15 wks

Vince MARTIN *US, male vocalist* — **1 wk**

14 Dec	56	CINDY OH CINDY *London HLN 8340*	26	1 wk

Wink MARTINDALE *US, male vocalist* — **41 wks**

4 Dec	59	DECK OF CARDS *London HLD 8962.*	18	5 wks
15 Jan	60	DECK OF CARDS (re-entry) *London HLD 8962.*	28	2 wks
31 Mar	60	DECK OF CARDS (2nd re-entry) *London HLD 8962.*	45	1 wk
18 Apr	63	● DECK OF CARDS (3rd re-entry) *London HLD 8962.*	5	21 wks
20 Oct	73	DECK OF CARDS (re-issue) *Dot DOT 109*	22	12 wks

Al MARTINO *US, male vocalist* — **87 wks**

14 Nov	52	★ HERE IN MY HEART *Capitol CL 13779*	1	18 wks
21 Nov	52	● TAKE MY HEART *Capitol CL 13769*	9	1 wk
30 Jan	53	● NOW *Capitol CL 13835*	3	12 wks
10 Jul	53	● RACHEL *Capitol CL 13879*	10	4 wks
11 Sep	53	RACHEL (re-entry) *Capitol CL 13879*	12	1 wk
4 Jun	54	WANTED *Capitol CL 14128*	12	1 wk
18 Jun	54	● WANTED (re-entry) *Capitol CL 14128*	4	14 wks
1 Oct	54	● THE STORY OF TINA *Capitol CL 14163.*	10	8 wks
1 Oct	54	WANTED (2nd re-entry) *Capitol CL 14128*	17	1 wk
23 Sep	55	THE MAN FROM LARAMIE *Capitol CL 14347.*	19	2 wks
28 Oct	55	THE MAN FROM LARAMIE (re-entry) *Capitol CL 14347*	20	1 wk
31 Mar	60	SUMMERTIME *Top Rank JAR 312*	49	1 wk
29 Aug	63	I LOVE YOU BECAUSE *Capitol CL 15300*	48	1 wk
22 Aug	70	SPANISH EYES *Capitol CL 15430*	49	1 wk
14 Jul	73	● SPANISH EYES (re-entry) *Capitol CL 15430*	5	21 wks

MARVELETTES *US, female vocal group* — **10 wks**

15 Jun	67	WHEN YOU'RE YOUNG AND IN LOVE *Tamla Motown TMG 609.*	13	10 wks

Hank MARVIN *UK, male vocalist/instrumentalist - guitar* — **4 wks**

6 Mar	82	DON'T TALK *Polydor POSP 420*	49	4 wks

See also Cliff Richard; Cliff Richard and the Young Ones; Jean-Michel Jarre.

Lee MARVIN *US, male vocalist* — **23 wks**

7 Feb	70	★ WAND'RIN' STAR *Paramount PARA 3004*	1	18 wks
20 Jun	70	WAND'RIN' STAR (re-entry) *Paramount PARA 3004.*	42	3 wks
15 Aug	70	WAND'RIN' STAR (2nd re-entry) *Paramount PARA 3004.*	47	2 wks

I Talk To The Trees by Clint Eastwood, the flip side of Wand'rin' Star was listed with Wand'rin' Star for 7 Feb 70 and 14 Feb 70 only. See also Clint Eastwood.

MARVIN THE PARANOID ANDROID — **4 wks**
UK, robot

16 May	81	MARVIN *Polydor POSP 261*	53	4 wks

Richard MARX *US, male vocalist* — **33 wks**

27 Feb	88	SHOULD'VE KNOWN BETTER *Manhattan MT 32*	50	5 wks
14 May	88	ENDLESS SUMMER NIGHTS *Manhattan MT 39*	50	3 wks
17 Jun	89	SATISFIED *EMI-USA MT 64*	52	4 wks
2 Sep	89	● RIGHT HERE WAITING *EMI-USA MT 72*	2	10 wks
11 Nov	89	ANGELIA *EMI-USA MT 74*	45	4 wks
24 Mar	90	TOO LATE TO SAY GOODBYE *EMI-USA MT 80*	38	3 wks
7 Jul	90	CHILDREN OF THE NIGHT *EMI-USA MT 84*	54	2 wks
1 Sep	90	ENDLESS SUMMER NIGHTS (re-issue)/ HOLD ON TO THE NIGHTS *EMI-USA MT 89*	60	2 wks

MARY – *See PETER, PAUL and MARY*

MARY JANE GIRLS *US, female vocal group* — **14 wks**

21 May	83	CANDY MAN *Motown TMG 1301.*	60	4 wks
25 Jun	83	ALL NIGHT LONG *Gordy TMG 1309.*	13	9 wks
8 Oct	83	BOYS *Gordy TMG 1315*	74	1 wk

Carolyne MAS *US, female vocalist* — **2 wks**

2 Feb	80	QUOTE GOODBYE QUOTE *Mercury 6167 873*	71	2 wks

MIREILLE MATHIEU is welcomed to Brussels by music publisher Peter Plum.

Far Right: RICHARD MARX wrote the 1984 US hit 'What About Me' by Kenny Rogers, Kim Carnes and James Ingram, then waited five years for his own UK Top Ten success.

Bottom Right: Frankie Vaughan had a number one with his cover of 'Tower of Strength' by GENE McDANIELS.

Right: BARRY MANILOW had eleven Top Ten singles in America but only one in Britain.

Below: The singles of easy listening stars JOHNNY MATHIS (left) and Andy Williams spent a total of over six and a half years on the chart.

MASH US, male vocal/instrumental group ___ 12 wks

| 10 May 80 | ★ THEME FROM M*A*S*H (SUICIDE IS PAINLESS) CBS 8536 | 1 | 12 wks |

Barbara MASON US, female vocalist ___ 5 wks

| 21 Jan 84 | ANOTHER MAN Streetwave KHAN 3 | 45 | 5 wks |

Glen MASON UK, male vocalist ___ 7 wks

| 28 Sep 56 | GLENDORA Parlophone R 4203 | 28 | 2 wks |
| 16 Nov 56 | GREEN DOOR Parlophone R 4244 | 24 | 5 wks |

Mary MASON UK, female vocalist ___ 6 wks

| 8 Oct 77 | ANGEL OF THE MORNING - ANY WAY THAT YOU WANT ME (MEDLEY) Epic EPC 5552 | 27 | 6 wks |

MASQUERADE UK, male/female vocal group ___ 10 wks

11 Jan 86	ONE NATION Streetwave KHAN 59	54	6 wks
5 Jul 86	(SOLUTION TO) THE PROBLEM Streetwave KHAN 67	65	2 wks
26 Jul 86	(SOLUTION TO) THE PROBLEM (re-entry) Streetwave KHAN 67	64	2 wks

MASS MEDIA – See STEINSKI and MASS MEDIA

MASS PRODUCTION
US, male vocal/instrumental group ___ 7 wks

| 12 Mar 77 | WELCOME TO OUR WORLD (OF MERRY MUSIC) Atlantic K 10898 | 44 | 3 wks |
| 17 May 80 | SHANTE Atlantic K 11475 | 59 | 4 wks |

MASSIEL Spain, female vocalist ___ 4 wks

| 24 Apr 68 | LA LA LA Philips BF 1667 | 35 | 4 wks |

MASSIVO featuring TRACY
UK, male/female vocal/instrumental group ___ 11 wks

| 26 May 90 | LOVING YOU Debut DEBT 3097 | 25 | 11 wks |

MASTER SINGERS UK, male vocal group ___ 7 wks

| 14 Apr 66 | HIGHWAY CODE Parlophone R 5428 | 25 | 6 wks |
| 17 Nov 66 | WEATHER FORECAST Parlophone R 5523 | 50 | 1 wk |

MASTERMIXERS – See JIVE BUNNY and the MASTERMIXERS

Sammy MASTERS US, male vocalist ___ 5 wks

| 9 Jun 60 | ROCKIN' RED WING Warner Bros. WB 10 | 36 | 5 wks |

MATCH UK, male vocal/instrumental group ___ 3 wks

| 16 Jun 79 | BOOGIE MAN Flamingo FM 2 | 48 | 3 wks |

MATCHBOX UK, male vocal/instrumental group ___ 66 wks

3 Nov 79	ROCKABILLY REBEL Magnet MAG 155	18	12 wks
19 Jan 80	BUZZ BUZZ A DIDDLE IT Magnet MAG 157	22	8 wks
10 May 80	MIDNITE DYNAMOS Magnet MAG 169	14	12 wks
27 Sep 80	● WHEN YOU ASK ABOUT LOVE Magnet MAG 191	4	12 wks
29 Nov 80	OVER THE RAINBOW - YOU BELONG TO ME (MEDLEY) Magnet MAG 192	15	11 wks
4 Apr 81	BABES IN THE WOOD Magnet MAG 193	46	6 wks
1 Aug 81	LOVE'S MADE A FOOL OF YOU Magnet MAG 194	63	3 wks
29 May 82	ONE MORE SATURDAY NIGHT Magnet MAG 223	63	2 wks

MATCHROOM MOB with CHAS and DAVE ___ 9 wks
UK, male vocalists with male vocal/instrumental duo

| 3 May 86 | ● SNOOKER LOOPY Rockney POT 14 | 6 | 9 wks |

See also Chas and Dave.

Mireille MATHIEU France, female vocalist ___ 7 wks

| 13 Dec 67 | LA DERNIERE VALSE Columbia DB 8323 | 26 | 7 wks |

Johnny MATHIS US, male vocalist ___ 115 wks

23 May 58	TEACHER TEACHER Fontana H 130	27	5 wks
26 Sep 58	A CERTAIN SMILE Fontana H 142	4	16 wks
19 Dec 58	WINTER WONDERLAND Fontana H 165	17	3 wks
7 Aug 59	● SOMEONE Fontana H 199	6	15 wks
27 Nov 59	THE BEST OF EVERYTHING Fontana H 218	30	1 wk
29 Jan 60	MISTY Fontana H 219	12	9 wks
24 Mar 60	YOU ARE BEAUTIFUL Fontana H 234	38	8 wks
14 Apr 60	MISTY (re-entry) Fontana H 219	46	2 wks
26 May 60	YOU ARE BEAUTIFUL (re-entry) Fontana H 234	46	1 wk
28 Jul 60	STARBRIGHT Fontana H 254	47	2 wks
6 Oct 60	● MY LOVE FOR YOU Fontana H 267	9	18 wks
4 Apr 63	WHAT WILL MARY SAY CBS AAG 135	49	1 wk
25 Jan 75	● I'M STONE IN LOVE WITH YOU CBS 2653	10	12 wks
13 Nov 76	★ WHEN A CHILD IS BORN (SOLEADO) CBS 4599	1	12 wks
11 Aug 79	GONE GONE GONE CBS 7730	15	10 wks

See also Johnny Mathis and Gladys Knight; Johnny Mathis and Deniece Williams.

Johnny MATHIS and Gladys KNIGHT ___ 2 wks
US, male/female vocal duo

| 26 Dec 81 | WHEN A CHILD IS BORN CBS S 1758 | 74 | 2 wks |

See also Johnny Mathis; Gladys Knight and the Pips.

Johnny MATHIS and Deniece WILLIAMS ___ 20 wks
US, male/female vocal duo

| 25 Mar 78 | ● TOO MUCH TOO LITTLE TOO LATE CBS 6164 | 3 | 14 wks |
| 29 Jul 78 | YOU'RE ALL I NEED TO GET BY CBS 6483 | 45 | 6 wks |

See also Johnny Mathis; Deniece Williams.

MATT BIANCO UK, male vocalist ___ 65 wks

11 Feb 84	GET OUT OF YOUR LAZY BED WEA BIANCO 1	15	8 wks
14 Apr 84	SNEAKING OUT THE BACK DOOR/ MATT'S MOOD WEA YZ 3	44	7 wks
10 Nov 84	HALF A MINUTE WEA YZ 26	23	10 wks
2 Mar 85	MORE THAN I CAN BEAR WEA YZ 34	50	7 wks
5 Oct 85	YEH YEH WEA YZ 46	13	10 wks
1 Mar 86	JUST CAN'T STAND IT WEA YZ 62	66	2 wks
14 Jun 86	DANCING IN THE STREET WEA YZ 72	64	3 wks
4 Jun 88	DON'T BLAME IT ON THAT GIRL/ WAP-BAM-BOOGIE WEA YZ 188	11	13 wks
27 Aug 88	GOOD TIMES WEA YZ 302	55	3 wks

BOBBY McFERRIN is genuinely happy after his Grammy sweep in 1989.

Far Left: CRAIG McLACHLAN was the fourth member of the *Neighbours* cast to have singles success.

GEORGE MICHAEL greets Axl Rose of Guns n' Roses at a 1988 Beverly Hills party.

Below: BARRY McGUIRE sang with the New Christy Minstrels before becoming a protest singer.

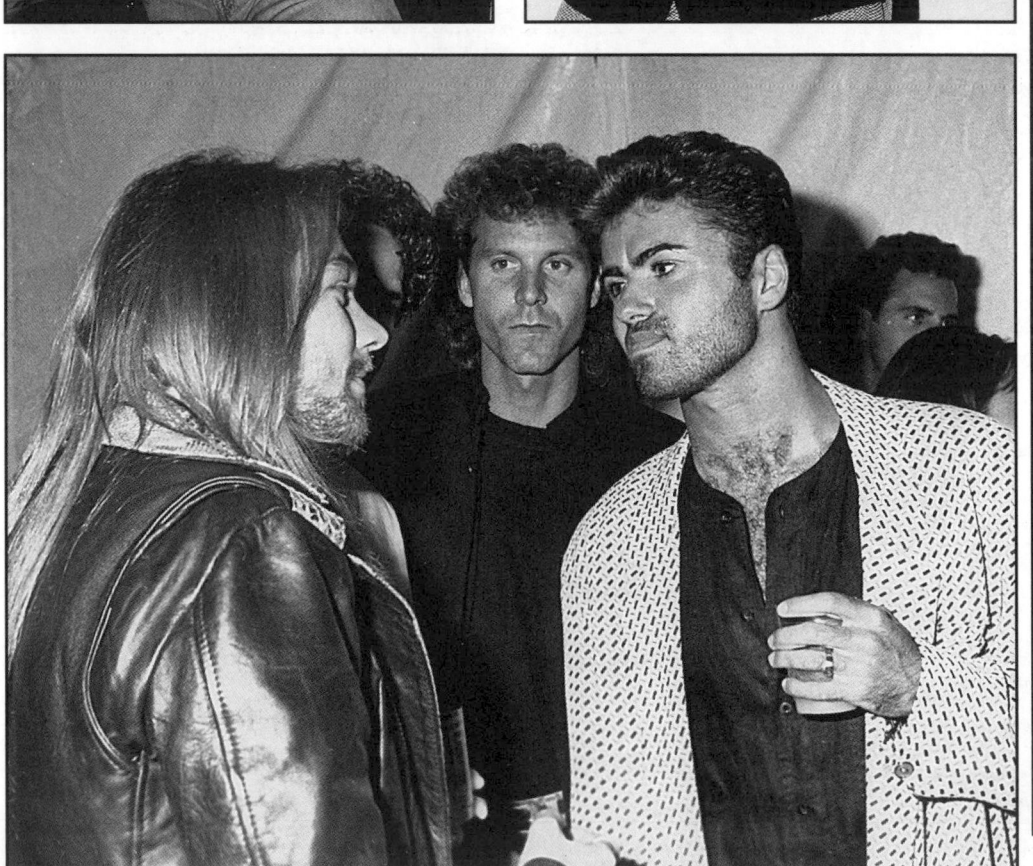

4 Feb 89	**NERVOUS/ WAP BAM BOOGIE (re-mix)**	
	WEA YZ 328 .... **59**	2 wks

Matt's Mood *only credited from 5 May 84. Act was a UK/Poland male/female vocal/instrumental group on first five hits. See also Basia.*

Al MATTHEWS *US, male vocalist*   **8 wks**

23 Aug 75	**FOOL** *CBS 3429*.. **16**	8 wks

MATTHEWS SOUTHERN COMFORT   **18 wks**
UK, male vocal/instrumental group

26 Sep 70	★ **WOODSTOCK** *Uni UNS 526* **1**	18 wks

MATUMBI *UK, male vocal/instrumental group*   **7 wks**

29 Sep 79	**POINT OF VIEW** *Matumbi RIC 101* **35**	7 wks

Susan MAUGHAN *UK, female vocalist*   **25 wks**

11 Oct 62	● **BOBBY'S GIRL** *Philips 326544 BF* **3**	19 wks
14 Feb 63	**HAND A HANDKERCHIEF TO HELEN**	
	Philips 326562 BF **41**	3 wks
9 May 63	**SHE'S NEW TO YOU** *Philips 326586 BF*...................... **45**	3 wks

MAUREEN *UK, female vocalist*   **9 wks**

16 Jun 90	**THINKING OF YOU** *Urban URB 55* **11**	9 wks

Some copies are credited to the fuller name of Maureen Walsh. See also Bomb The Bass.

Paul MAURIAT *France, orchestra*   **14 wks**

21 Feb 68	**LOVE IS BLUE (L'AMOUR EST BLEU)**	
	Philips BF 1637 .... **12**	14 wks

MAX Q *Australia, male vocal/instrumental duo*   **3 wks**

17 Feb 90	**SOMETIMES** *Mercury MXQ 2* **53**	3 wks

Billy MAY *US, orchestra*   **10 wks**

27 Apr 56	● **MAIN TITLE THEME FROM MAN WITH THE**	
	GOLDEN ARM *Capitol CL 14551* **9**	10 wks

Brian MAY and FRIENDS   **3 wks**
UK, male vocalist/instrumentalist - guitar, and male instrumental group

5 Nov 83	**STAR FLEET** *EMI 5436* **65**	3 wks

Mary MAY *UK, female vocalist*   **1 wk**

27 Feb 64	**ANYONE WHO HAD A HEART** *Fontana TF 110* **19**	1 wk

Simon MAY *UK, male vocalist*   **10 wks**

9 Oct 76	● **SUMMER OF MY LIFE** *Pye 7N 45627* **7**	8 wks
21 May 77	**WE'LL GATHER LILACS - ALL MY LOVING**	
	(MEDLEY) *Pye 7N 45688* **49**	1 wk
4 Jun 77	**WE'LL GATHER LILACS - ALL MY LOVING**	
	(MEDLEY) (re-entry) *Pye 7N 45688* **50**	1 wk

See also Simon May Orchestra.

Simon MAY ORCHESTRA *UK, orchestra*   **11 wks**

26 Oct 85	**HOWARD'S WAY** *BBC RESL 174* **21**	11 wks

See also Simon May; Anita Dobson; Marti Webb.

Curtis MAYFIELD *US, male vocalist*   **13 wks**

31 Jul 71	**MOVE ON UP** *Buddah 2011 080* **12**	10 wks
2 Dec 78	**NO GOODBYES** *Atlantic LV 1*................................. **65**	3 wks

See also Curtis Mayfield and Ice-T; Blow Monkeys.

Curtis MAYFIELD and ICE-T *US, male vocalist with*   **3 wks**
US, male rapper

29 Sep 90	**SUPERFLY 1990** *Capitol CL* **48**	3 wks

See also Curtis Mayfield; Ice-T.

MAYTALS *Jamaica, male vocal/instrumental group*   **4 wks**

25 Apr 70	**MONKEY MAN** *Trojan TR 7711*................................ **50**	1 wk
9 May 70	**MONKEY MAN (re-entry)** *Trojan TR 7711*................... **47**	3 wks

MAZE featuring Frankie BEVERLY   **14 wks**
US, male vocal/instrumental group

20 Jul 85	**TOO MANY GAMES** *Capitol CL 363* **36**	7 wks
23 Aug 86	**I WANNA BE WITH YOU** *Capitol CL 421*.................... **55**	3 wks
27 May 89	**JOY AND PAIN** *Capitol CL 531* **57**	4 wks

Joy And Pain gives no credit to Frankie Beverly.

Kym MAZELLE *US, female vocalist*   **18 wks**

12 Nov 88	**USELESS (I DON'T NEED YOU NOW)**	
	Syncopate SY 18 .... **53**	3 wks
25 Mar 89	**GOT TO GET YOU BACK** *Syncopate SY 25* **29**	4 wks
7 Oct 89	**LOVE STRAIN** *Syncopate SY 30*............................. **52**	3 wks
20 Jan 90	**WAS THAT ALL IT WAS** *Syncopate SY 32* **33**	6 wks
26 Mar 90	**USELESS (I DON'T NEED YOU NOW) (re-mix)**	
	Syncopate SY 36 .... **48**	2 wks

See also Robert Howard and Kym Mazelle; Soul II Soul.

M.C. DUKE *US, male rapper*   **1 wk**

11 Mar 89	**I'M RIFFIN (ENGLISH RASTA)**	
	Music Of Life 7NOTE 25...................................... **75**	1 wk

MC ERIC – *See TECHNOTRONIC*

MC HAMMER *US, male rapper*   **27 wks**

9 Jun 90	● **U CAN'T TOUCH THIS** *Capitol CL 578* **3**	16 wks
6 Oct 90	● **HAVE YOU SEEN HER** *Capitol CL 590* **8**	7 wks
8 Dec 90	● **PRAY** *Capitol CL 599* .... **9†**	4 wks

M.C. MIKER 'G' and Deejay SVEN   **7 wks**
Holland, male vocal/instrumental rap duo

6 Sep 86	● **HOLIDAY RAP** *Debut DEBT 3008* **6**	7 wks

MC NUMBER 6 – *See FAB*

MC PARKER – *See FAB*

MC TUNES versus 808 STATE
UK, male rapper and instrumental group **17 wks**

2 Jun 90	●	THE ONLY RHYME THAT BITES *ZTT ZANG 3*	10	9 wks
15 Sep 90		TUNES SPLITS THE ATOM *ZTT ZANG 6*	18	7 wks
1 Dec 90		PRIMARY RHYMING *ZTT ZANG 10*	67	1 wk

Primary Rhyming gives no 808 State credit. See also 808 State.

MC WILDSKI *UK, male rapper* **4 wks**

| 3 Mar 90 | WARRIOR *Arista 112956* | 49 | 4 wks |

See also Norman Cook.

ME AND YOU *Jamaica/UK, male/female vocal duo* **9 wks**

| 28 Jul 79 | YOU NEVER KNOW WHAT YOU'VE GOT *Laser LAS 8* | 31 | 9 wks |

Has credit: featuring We The People Band.

Abigail MEAD and Nigel GOULDING
UK/US, female/male producers **10 wks**

| 26 Sep 87 | ● | FULL METAL JACKET (I WANNA BE YOUR DRILL INSTRUCTOR) *Warner Bros. W 8187* | 2 | 10 wks |

MEAT LOAF *US, male vocalist* **80 wks**

20 May 78		YOU TOOK THE WORDS RIGHT OUT OF MY MOUTH *Epic EPC 5980*	33	8 wks
19 Aug 78		TWO OUT OF THREE AIN'T BAD *Epic EPC 6281*	32	8 wks
10 Feb 79		BAT OUT OF HELL *Epic EPC 7018*	15	7 wks
26 Sep 81		I'M GONNA LOVE HER FOR BOTH OF US *Epic EPCA 1580*	62	3 wks
28 Nov 81	●	DEAD RINGER FOR LOVE *Epic EPCA 1697*	5	17 wks
28 May 83		IF YOU REALLY WANT TO *Epic A 3357*	59	2 wks
24 Sep 83		MIDNIGHT AT THE LOST AND FOUND *Epic A 3748*	17	8 wks
14 Jan 84		RAZOR'S EDGE *Epic A 4080*	41	3 wks
6 Oct 84		MODERN GIRL *Arista ARIST 585*	17	9 wks
22 Dec 84		NOWHERE FAST *Arista ARIST 600*	67	4 wks
23 Mar 85		PIECE OF THE ACTION *Arista ARIST 603*	47	5 wks
30 Aug 86		ROCK 'N' ROLL MERCENARIES *Arista ARIST 666*	31	6 wks

Dead Ringer For Love features Cher as uncredited co-vocalist. Rock 'n' Roll Mercenaries features John Parr. See also Cher; John Parr.

MECHANICS – *See MIKE + the MECHANICS*

MECO *US, orchestra* **9 wks**

| 1 Oct 77 | ● | STAR WARS THEME-CANTINA BAND *RCA XB 1028* | 7 | 9 wks |

Glenn MEDEIROS *US, male vocalist* **26 wks**

18 Jun 88	★	NOTHING'S GONNA CHANGE MY LOVE FOR YOU *London LON 184*	1	13 wks
3 Sep 88		LONG AND LASTING LOVE (ONCE IN A LIFETIME) *London LON 202*	42	4 wks
30 Jun 90		SHE AIN'T WORTH IT *London LON 265*	12	9 wks

She Ain't Worth It features Bobby Brown. See also Bobby Brown.

MEDICINE HEAD *UK, male vocal/instrumental duo* **37 wks**

| 26 Jun 71 | | (AND THE) PICTURES IN THE SKY *Dandelion DAN 7003* | 22 | 8 wks |
| 5 May 73 | ● | ONE AND ONE IS ONE *Polydor 2001 432* | 3 | 13 wks |

| 4 Aug 73 | | RISING SUN *Polydor 2058 389* | 11 | 9 wks |
| 9 Feb 74 | | SLIP AND SLIDE *Polydor 2058 436* | 22 | 7 wks |

MEDICINE SHOW – *See DR. HOOK*

Bill MEDLEY *US, male vocalist* **6 wks**

| 27 Aug 88 | HE AIN'T HEAVY, HE'S MY BROTHER *Scotti Brothers PO 10* | 25 | 6 wks |

See also Bill Medley and Jennifer Warnes.

Bill MEDLEY and Jennifer WARNES
US, male/female vocal duo **15 wks**

| 31 Oct 87 | ● | (I'VE HAD) THE TIME OF MY LIFE *RCA PB 49625* | 6 | 12 wks |
| 15 Dec 90 | | (I'VE HAD) THE TIME OF MY LIFE (re-issue) *RCA PB 49625* | 43† | 3 wks |

See also Bill Medley; Jennifer Warnes.

Michael MEDWIN, Bernard BRESSLAW, Alfie BASS and Leslie FYSON *UK, male vocal group* **9 wks**

| 30 May 58 | ● | THE SIGNATURE TUNE OF THE ARMY GAME *HMV POP 490* | 5 | 9 wks |

See also Bernard Bresslaw.

Tony MEEHAN COMBO
UK, male instrumentalist - drums **4 wks**

| 16 Jan 64 | SONG OF MEXICO *Decca F 11801* | 39 | 4 wks |

See also Jet Harris and Tony Meehan.

MEGABASS *UK, record company album sampler* **8 wks**

| 10 Nov 90 | TIME TO MAKE THE FLOOR BURN *Megabass MEGAX 1* | 16† | 8 wks |

MEGADETH *US, male vocal/instrumental group* **16 wks**

19 Dec 87		WAKE UP DEAD *Capitol CL 476*	65	2 wks
27 Feb 88		ANARCHY IN THE UK *Capitol CL 480*	45	3 wks
21 May 88		MARY JANE *Capitol CL 489*	46	2 wks
13 Jan 90		NO MORE MR. NICE GUY *SBK SBK 4*	13	6 wks
29 Sep 90		HOLY WARS...THE PUNISHMENT DUE *Capitol CLP 588*	24	3 wks

Melle MEL – *See GRANDMASTERFLASH, Melle MEL and the FURIOUS FIVE*

MEL and KIM *UK, female vocal duo* **51 wks**

20 Sep 86	●	SHOWING OUT (GET FRESH AT THE WEEKEND) *Supreme SUPE 107*	3	19 wks
7 Mar 87	★	RESPECTABLE *Supreme SUPE 111*	1	15 wks
11 Jul 87	●	F.L.M. *Supreme SUPE 113*	7	10 wks
27 Feb 88	●	THAT'S THE WAY IT IS *Supreme SUPE 117*	10	7 wks

See also Kim Appleby.

MEL and KIM *UK, male/female vocal duo* **7 wks**

| 5 Dec 87 | ● | ROCKIN' AROUND THE CHRISTMAS TREE *10 TEN 2* | 3 | 7 wks |

This Mel and Kim are Mel Smith, UK male vocalist and Kim Wilde; see also Kim Wilde.

MELACHRINO ORCHESTRA 9 wks
UK, orchestra, conductor George Melachrino

12 Oct 56	**AUTUMN CONCERTO** *HMV B 10958*		**18**	9 wks

MELANIE *US, female vocalist* 35 wks

26 Sep 70	● **RUBY TUESDAY** *Buddah 2011 038*		**9**	14 wks
9 Jan 71	**RUBY TUESDAY (re-entry)** *Buddah 2011 038*		**43**	1 wk
16 Jan 71	**WHAT HAVE THEY DONE TO MY SONG MA** *Buddah 2011 038*		**39**	1 wk
1 Jan 72	● **BRAND NEW KEY** *Buddah 2011 105*		**4**	12 wks
16 Feb 74	**WILL YOU LOVE ME TOMORROW** *Neighbourhood NBH 9*		**37**	5 wks
24 Sep 83	**EVERY BREATH OF THE WAY** *Neighbourhood HOOD NB1*		**70**	2 wks

MELISSA – *See TECHNOTRONIC*

John Cougar MELLENCAMP *US, male vocalist* 15 wks

23 Oct 82	**JACK AND DIANE** *Riva RIVA 37*		**25**	8 wks
1 Feb 86	**SMALL TOWN** *Riva JCM 5*		**53**	4 wks
10 May 86	**R.O.C.K. IN THE U.S.A.** *Riva JCM 6*		**67**	3 wks

Billed as John Cougar on first hit.

MELODIANS *Jamaica, male vocal/instrumental group* 1 wk

10 Jan 70	**SWEET SENSATION** *Trojan TR 695*		**41**	1 wk

MELODY MAKERS – *See Ziggy MARLEY and the MELODY MAKERS*

Harold MELVIN and the BLUENOTES 52 wks
US, male vocal group

13 Jan 73	● **IF YOU DON'T KNOW ME BY NOW** *CBS 8496*		**9**	9 wks
12 Jan 74	**THE LOVE I LOST** *Philadelphia International PIR 1879*		**21**	8 wks
13 Apr 74	**SATISFACTION GUARANTEED (OR TAKE YOUR LOVE BACK)** *Philadelphia International PIR 2187*		**32**	6 wks
31 May 75	**GET OUT** *Route RT 06*		**35**	5 wks
28 Feb 76	**WAKE UP EVERYBODY** *Philadelphia PIR 3866*		**23**	7 wks
22 Jan 77	● **DON'T LEAVE ME THIS WAY** *Philadelphia International PIR 4909*		**5**	10 wks
2 Apr 77	**REACHING FOR THE WORLD** *ABC 4161*		**48**	1 wk
28 Apr 84	**DON'T GIVE ME UP** *London LON 47*		**59**	4 wks
4 Aug 84	**TODAY'S YOUR LUCKY DAY** *London LON 52*		**66**	2 wks

MEMBERS *UK, male vocal/instrumental group* 14 wks

3 Feb 79	**THE SOUND OF THE SUBURBS** *Virgin VS 242*		**12**	9 wks
7 Apr 79	**OFFSHORE BANKING BUSINESS** *Virgin VS 248*		**31**	5 wks

MEN AT WORK *Australia, male vocal/instrumental group* 39 wks

30 Oct 82	**WHO CAN IT BE NOW?** *Epic EPC A 2392*		**45**	5 wks
8 Jan 83	★ **DOWN UNDER** *Epic EPC A 1980*		**1**	12 wks
9 Apr 83	**OVERKILL** *Epic EPC A 3220*		**21**	10 wks
2 Jul 83	**IT'S A MISTAKE** *Epic EPC A 3475*		**33**	6 wks
10 Sep 83	**DR. HECKYLL AND MR. JIVE** *Epic EPC A 3668*		**31**	6 wks

MEN THEY COULDN'T HANG 4 wks
UK, male vocal/instrumental group

2 Apr 88	**THE COLOURS** *Magnet SELL 6*		**61**	4 wks

MEN WITHOUT HATS 11 wks
Canada, male vocal/instrumental group

8 Oct 83	● **THE SAFETY DANCE** *Statik TAK 1*		**6**	11 wks

Sergio MENDES *Brazil, male conductor* 5 wks

9 Jul 83	**NEVER GONNA LET YOU GO** *A & M AM 118*		**45**	5 wks

Uncredited vocals by Joe Pizzulo and Leza Miller.

MENTAL AS ANYTHING 13 wks
Australia, male vocal/instrumental group

7 Feb 87	● **LIVE IT UP** *Epic ANY 1*		**3**	13 wks

Freddie MERCURY *UK, male vocalist* 39 wks

22 Sep 84	● **LOVE KILLS** *CBS A 4735*		**10**	8 wks
20 Apr 85	**I WAS BORN TO LOVE YOU** *CBS A 6019*		**11**	10 wks
13 Jul 85	**MADE IN HEAVEN** *CBS A 6413*		**57**	4 wks
21 Sep 85	**LIVING ON MY OWN** *CBS A 6555*		**50**	3 wks
24 May 86	**TIME** *EMI EMI 5559*		**32**	5 wks
7 Mar 87	● **THE GREAT PRETENDER** *Parlophone R 6151*		**4**	9 wks

See also Freddie Mercury and Montserrat Caballe.

Freddie MERCURY and Montserrat 9 wks
CABALLE *UK/Spain, male/female vocal duo*

7 Nov 87	● **BARCELONA** *Polydor POSP 887*		**8**	9 wks

See also Freddie Mercury.

MERCY MERCY *UK, male vocal/instrumental group* 2 wks

21 Sep 85	**WHAT ARE WE GONNA DO ABOUT IT?** *Ensign ENY 522*		**59**	2 wks

MERLIN – *See BEATMASTERS, BOMB THE BASS*

MERLIN and ANTONIA – *See BOMB THE BASS*

Tony MERRICK *UK, male vocalist* 1 wk

2 Jun 66	**LADY JANE** *Columbia DB 7913*		**49**	1 wk

MERSEYBEATS *UK, male vocal/instrumental group* 64 wks

12 Sep 63	**IT'S LOVE THAT REALLY COUNTS** *Fontana TF 412*		**24**	12 wks
16 Jan 64	● **I THINK OF YOU** *Fontana TF 431*		**5**	17 wks
16 Apr 64	**DON'T TURN AROUND** *Fontana TF 459*		**13**	11 wks
9 Jul 64	**WISHIN' AND HOPIN'** *Fontana TF 482*		**13**	10 wks
5 Nov 64	**LAST NIGHT** *Fontana TF 504*		**40**	3 wks
14 Oct 65	**I LOVE YOU, YES I DO** *Fontana TF 607*		**22**	8 wks
20 Jan 66	**I STAND ACCUSED** *Fontana TF 645*		**38**	3 wks

MERSEYS *UK, male vocal duo* 13 wks

28 Apr 66	● **SORROW** *Fontana TF 694*		**4**	13 wks

MERTON PARKAS *UK, male vocal/instrumental group* 6 wks

4 Aug 79	**YOU NEED WHEELS** *Beggars Banquet BEG 22*		**40**	6 wks

Mady MESPLÉ and the Danielle MILLET PARIS OPERA-COMIQUE ORCHESTRA conducted by Alain LOMBARD

France, female vocal duo and orchestra   **4 wks**

6 Apr 85	FLOWER DUET (FROM LAKME) *EMI 5481*	47	4 wks

METAL GURUS *UK, male vocal/instrumental group*   **2 wks**

8 Dec 90	MERRY XMAS EVERYBODY *Mercury GURU 1*	55	2 wks

METALLICA *US/Denmark, male vocal/instrumental group*   **14 wks**

22 Aug 87	THE $5.98 E.P. - GARAGE DAYS REVISITED *Vertigo METAL 112*	27	4 wks
3 Sep 88	HARVESTER OF SORROW *Vertigo METAL 212*	20	3 wks
22 Apr 89	ONE *Vertigo METAL 5*	13	7 wks

Tracks on The $5.98 E.P.: Garage Days Revisited/Helpless/Crash Course in Brain Surgery/The Small Hours/Last Caress/Green Hell.

METEORS *UK, male vocal/instrumental group*   **2 wks**

26 Feb 83	JOHNNY REMEMBER ME *I.D. EYE 1*	66	2 wks

MEZZOFORTE *Iceland, male instrumental group*   **10 wks**

5 Mar 83	GARDEN PARTY *Steinar STE 705*	17	9 wks
11 Jun 83	ROCKALL *Steinar STE 710*	75	1 wk

MFSB *US, orchestra*   **18 wks**

27 Apr 74	TSOP (THE SOUND OF PHILADELPHIA) *Philadelphia International PIR 2289*	22	9 wks
26 Jul 75	SEXY *Philadelphia International PIR 3381*	37	5 wks
31 Jan 81	MYSTERIES OF THE WORLD *The Sound of Philadelphia PIR 9501*	41	4 wks

TSOP billed as MFSB featuring the Three Degrees. See also Three Degrees.

M.G.'s – *See BOOKER T. and the M.G.'s*

MIAMI SOUND MACHINE – *See Gloria ESTEFAN*

George MICHAEL *UK, male vocalist*   **89 wks**

4 Aug 84	★ CARELESS WHISPER *Epic A 4603*	1	17 wks
5 Apr 86	★ A DIFFERENT CORNER *Epic A 7033*	1	10 wks
13 Jun 87	● I WANT YOUR SEX *Epic LUST 1*	3	10 wks
24 Oct 87	● FAITH *Epic EMU 3*	2	12 wks
9 Jan 88	FATHER FIGURE *Epic EMU 4*	11	6 wks
23 Apr 88	● ONE MORE TRY *Epic EMU 5*	8	7 wks
16 Jul 88	MONKEY *Epic EMU 6*	13	6 wks
3 Dec 88	KISSING A FOOL *Epic EMU 7*	18	6 wks
25 Aug 90	● PRAYING FOR TIME *Epic GEO 1*	6	7 wks
27 Oct 90	WAITING FOR THAT DAY *Epic GEO 2*	23	5 wks
15 Dec 90	FREEDOM! *Epic GEO 3*	28†	3 wks

I Want Your Sex is subtitled Rhythm 1 Lust. See also Aretha Franklin and George Michael; Elton John.

MICHAELA *UK, female vocalist*   **6 wks**

2 Sep 89	-H-A-P-P-Y-RADIO *London H 1*	62	4 wks
28 Apr 90	TAKE GOOD CARE OF MY HEART *London WAC 90*	66	2 wks

Keith MICHELL *Australia, male vocalist*   **25 wks**

27 Mar 71	I'LL GIVE YOU THE EARTH (TOUS LES BATEAUX, TOUS LES OISEAUX) *Spark SRL 1046*	43	1 wk
17 Apr 71	I'LL GIVE YOU THE EARTH (TOUS LES BATEAUX, TOUS LES OISEAUX) (re-entry) *Spark SRL 1046*	30	10 wks
26 Jan 80	● CAPTAIN BEAKY/ WILFRED THE WEASEL *Polydor POSP 106*	5	10 wks
29 Mar 80	THE TRIAL OF HISSING SID *Polydor HISS 1*	53	4 wks

Last hit credited to Keith Michell, Captain Beaky and his Band.

Lloyd MICHELS – *See MISTURA*

MICK – *See Dave DEE, DOZY, BEAKY, MICK and TICH*

MICK – *See KERRI and MICK*

MICK – *See PAT and MICK*

MICROBE *UK, male vocalist*   **7 wks**

14 May 69	GROOVY BABY *CBS 4158*	29	7 wks

MICRODISNEY *Ireland, male vocal/instrumental group*   **3 wks**

21 Feb 87	TOWN TO TOWN *Virgin VS 927*	55	3 wks

MIDDLE OF THE ROAD   **76 wks**

UK, male/female vocal/instrumental group

5 Jun 71	★ CHIRPY CHIRPY CHEEP CHEEP *RCA 2047*	1	34 wks
4 Sep 71	● TWEEDLE DEE TWEEDLE DUM *RCA 2110*	2	17 wks
11 Dec 71	● SOLEY SOLEY *RCA 2151*	5	12 wks
25 Mar 72	SACRAMENTO *RCA 2184*	49	1 wk
8 Apr 72	SACRAMENTO (re-entry) *RCA 2184*	23	6 wks
29 Jul 72	SAMSON AND DELILAH *RCA 2237*	26	6 wks

Bette MIDLER *US, female vocalist*   **17 wks**

17 Jun 89	● WIND BENEATH MY WINGS *Atlantic A 8972*	5	12 wks
13 Oct 90	FROM A DISTANCE *Atlantic A 7820*	45	5 wks

MIDNIGHT BAND – *See Tony RALLO and the MIDNIGHT BAND*

MIDNIGHT COWBOY SOUNDTRACK   **4 wks**

US, orchestra

8 Nov 80	MIDNIGHT COWBOY *United Artists UP 634*	47	4 wks

MIDNIGHT OIL *Australia, male vocal/instrumental group*   **26 wks**

23 Apr 88	BEDS ARE BURNING *Sprint OIL 1*	48	5 wks
2 Jul 88	THE DEAD HEART *Sprint OIL 2*	68	2 wks
25 Mar 89	● BEDS ARE BURNING (re-issue) *Sprint OIL 3*	6	13 wks
1 Jul 89	THE DEAD HEART (re-issue) *Sprint OIL 4*	62	4 wks
10 Feb 90	BLUE SKY MINE *CBS OIL 5*	66	2 wks

MIDNIGHT STAR   **26 wks**

US, male/female vocal/instrumental group

23 Feb 85	OPERATOR *Solar MCA 942*	66	2 wks
28 Jun 86	HEADLINES *Solar MCA 1065*	16	8 wks
4 Oct 86	● MIDAS TOUCH *Solar MCA 1096*	8	10 wks
7 Feb 87	ENGINE NO.9 *Solar MCA 1117*	64	3 wks

2 May 87	WET MY WHISTLE Solar MCA 1127	60	3 wks

MIGHTY AVENGERS UK, male vocal/instrumental group   2 wks

26 Nov 64	SO MUCH IN LOVE Decca F 11962...........................	46	2 wks

MIGHTY AVONS – *See Larry CUNNINGHAM and the MIGHTY AVONS*

MIGHTY LEMON DROPS   6 wks
UK, male vocal/instrumental group

13 Sep 86	THE OTHER SIDE OF YOU Blue Guitar AZUR 1............	67	1 wk
18 Apr 87	OUT OF HAND Blue Guitar AZUR 4	66	3 wks
23 Jan 88	INSIDE OUT Blue Guitar AZUR 6............................	74	2 wks

MIGHTY WAH UK, male vocal/instrumental group   26 wks

25 Dec 82	● THE STORY OF THE BLUES Eternal JF 1....................	3	12 wks
19 Mar 83	HOPE (I WISH YOU'D BELIEVE ME) WEA X 9880	37	5 wks
30 Jun 84	COME BACK Beggars Banquet BEG 111	20	9 wks

Act billed as Wah! for first two hits.

MIGIL FIVE UK, male vocal/instrumental group   20 wks

19 Mar 64	● MOCKINGBIRD HILL Pye 7N 15597	10	13 wks
4 Jun 64	NEAR YOU Pye 7N 15645	31	7 wks

MIKE + the MECHANICS   24 wks
UK, male vocal/instrumental group

15 Feb 86	SILENT RUNNING (ON DANGEROUS GROUND) WEA U 8908	21	9 wks
31 May 86	ALL I NEED IS A MIRACLE WEA U 8765	53	4 wks
14 Jan 89	● THE LIVING YEARS WEA U 7717...........................	2	11 wks

MIKI and GRIFF UK, female/male vocal duo   25 wks

2 Oct 59	HOLD BACK TOMORROW Pye 7N 15213.................	26	2 wks
13 Oct 60	ROCKIN' ALONE Pye 7N 15296............................	44	3 wks
1 Feb 62	LITTLE BITTY TEAR Pye 7N 15412........................	16	13 wks
22 Aug 63	I WANNA STAY HERE Pye 7N 15555.......................	23	7 wks

John MILES UK, male vocalist/multi-instrumentalist   30 wks

18 Oct 75	HIGH FLY Decca F 13595	17	6 wks
20 Mar 76	● MUSIC Decca F 13627	3	9 wks
16 Oct 76	REMEMBER YESTERDAY Decca F 13667.................	32	5 wks
18 Jun 77	● SLOW DOWN Decca F 13709	10	10 wks

June MILES-KINGSTON – *See Jimmy SOMERVILLE*

Paul MILES-KINGSTON – *See Sarah BRIGHTMAN and Paul MILES-KINGSTON*

MILK AND HONEY   8 wks
Israel, male/female vocal/instrumental group

14 Apr 79	● HALLELUJAH Polydor 2001 870	5	8 wks

Hit has credit 'featuring Gali Atari', Israeli female vocalist.

MILL GIRLS – *See Billy COTTON*

Frankie MILLER UK, male vocalist   26 wks

4 Jun 77	BE GOOD TO YOURSELF Chrysalis CHS 2147...............	27	6 wks
14 Oct 78	● DARLIN' Chrysalis CHS 2255	6	15 wks
20 Jan 79	WHEN I'M AWAY FROM YOU Chrysalis CHS 2276	42	5 wks

Gary MILLER UK, male vocalist   35 wks

21 Oct 55	YELLOW ROSE OF TEXAS Nixa N 15004	13	5 wks
13 Jan 56	● ROBIN HOOD Nixa N 15020	10	6 wks
11 Jan 57	GARDEN OF EDEN Pye Nixa N 15070......................	14	6 wks
1 Mar 57	GARDEN OF EDEN (re-entry) Pye Nixa N 15070...........	27	1 wk
19 Jul 57	WONDERFUL WONDERFUL Pye Nixa N 15094	29	1 wk
17 Jan 58	STORY OF MY LIFE Pye Nixa N 15120......................	14	6 wks
21 Dec 61	THERE GOES THAT SONG AGAIN/ THE NIGHT IS YOUNG Pye 7N 15404	29	9 wks
1 Mar 62	THERE GOES THAT SONG AGAIN (re-entry) Pye 7N 15404..	48	1 wk

The Night Is Young only listed with There Goes That Song Again for weeks 21 and 28 Dec 61 and 4 Jan 62.

Glenn MILLER US, orchestra, Glenn Miller, trombone   9 wks

12 Mar 54	MOONLIGHT SERENADE HMV BD 5942	12	1 wk
24 Jan 76	MOONLIGHT SERENADE/ LITTLE BROWN JUG/ IN THE MOOD (re-issue) RCA 2644...........................	13	8 wks

Jody MILLER US, female vocalist   1 wk

21 Oct 65	HOME OF THE BRAVE Capitol CL 15415	49	1 wk

Leza MILLER – *See Sergio MENDES*

Mitch MILLER US, orchestra and chorus   13 wks

7 Oct 55	● YELLOW ROSE OF TEXAS Philips PB 505	2	13 wks

Ned MILLER US, male vocalist   22 wks

14 Feb 63	● FROM A JACK TO A KING London HL 9658	2	21 wks
18 Feb 65	DO WHAT YOU DO DO WELL London HL 9937............	48	1 wk

Roger MILLER US, male vocalist   42 wks

18 Mar 65	★ KING OF THE ROAD Philips BF 1397	1	15 wks
3 Jun 65	ENGINE ENGINE NO. 9 Philips BF 1416	33	5 wks
21 Oct 65	KANSAS CITY STAR Philips BF 1437	48	1 wk
16 Dec 65	ENGLAND SWINGS Philips BF 1456.........................	45	1 wk
6 Jan 66	ENGLAND SWINGS (re-entry) Philips BF 1456	13	7 wks
27 Mar 68	LITTLE GREEN APPLES Mercury MF 1021	19	10 wks
2 Apr 69	LITTLE GREEN APPLES (re-entry) Mercury MF 1021.......	48	1 wk
7 May 69	LITTLE GREEN APPLES (2nd re-entry) Mercury MF 1021	39	2 wks

Suzi MILLER UK, female vocalist   2 wks

21 Jan 55	HAPPY DAYS AND LONELY NIGHTS Decca F 10389	14	2 wks

Steve MILLER BAND US, male vocal/instrumental group   36 wks

23 Oct 76	ROCK 'N ME Mercury 6078 804	11	9 wks
19 Jun 82	● ABRACADABRA Mercury STEVE 3	2	11 wks
4 Sep 82	KEEPS ME WONDERING WHY Mercury STEVE 4	52	3 wks
11 Aug 90	★ THE JOKER Capitol CL 583...................................	1	13 wks

MILLI VANILLI
France/Germany, male vocal/instrumental duo   **50 wks**

1 Oct 88	● **GIRL YOU KNOW IT'S TRUE** *Cooltempo COOL 170*	3	13 wks
17 Dec 88	**BABY DON'T FORGET MY NUMBER**		
	Cooltempo COOL 178	16	11 wks
22 Jul 89	**BLAME IT ON THE RAIN** *Cooltempo COOL 180*	53	5 wks
30 Sep 89	● **GIRL I'M GONNA MISS YOU** *Cooltempo COOL 191*	2	15 wks
2 Dec 89	**BLAME IT ON THE RAIN** (re-entry)		
	Cooltempo COOL 180	52	5 wks
10 Mar 90	**ALL OR NOTHING** *Cooltempo COOL 199*	74	1 wk

MILLICAN and NESBITT
UK, male vocal duo   **14 wks**

1 Dec 73	**VAYA CON DIOS** *Pye 7N 45310*	20	11 wks
18 May 74	**FOR OLD TIME'S SAKE** *Pye 7N 45357*	38	3 wks

MILLIE
Jamaica, female vocalist   **33 wks**

12 Mar 64	● **MY BOY LOLLIPOP** *Fontana TF 449*	2	18 wks
25 Jun 64	**SWEET WILLIAM** *Fontana TF 479*	30	9 wks
11 Nov 65	**BLOODSHOT EYES** *Fontana TF 617*	48	1 wk
25 Jul 87	**MY BOY LOLLIPOP** (re-issue) *Island WIP 6574*	46	5 wks

Garry MILLS
UK, male vocalist   **31 wks**

7 Jul 60	● **LOOK FOR A STAR** *Top Rank JAR 336*	7	14 wks
20 Oct 60	**TOP TEEN BABY** *Top Rank JAR 500*	24	12 wks
22 Jun 61	**I'LL STEP DOWN** *Decca F 11358*	39	5 wks

Hayley MILLS
UK, female vocalist   **11 wks**

19 Oct 61	**LET'S GET TOGETHER** *Decca F 21396*	17	11 wks

Mrs. MILLS
UK, female instrumentalist - piano   **5 wks**

14 Dec 61	**MRS MILLS' MEDLEY** *Parlophone R 4856*	18	5 wks

Mrs Mills' Medley consisted of the following tunes: I Want To Be Happy/Sheik Of Araby/Baby Face/Somebody Stole My Gal/Ma (He's Making Eyes At Me)/Swanee/Ain't She Sweet/California Here I Come.

Stephanie MILLS
US, female vocalist   **30 wks**

18 Oct 80	● **NEVER KNEW LOVE LIKE THIS BEFORE**		
	20th Century TC 2460	4	14 wks
23 May 81	**TWO HEARTS** *20th Century TC 2492*	49	5 wks
15 Sep 84	**THE MEDICINE SONG** *Club JAB 8*	29	9 wks
5 Sep 87	**(YOU'RE PUTTIN') A RUSH ON ME**		
	MCA MCA 1187	62	2 wks

Two Hearts features Teddy Pendergrass. See Teddy Pendergrass.

Warren MILLS
Zambia, male vocalist   **1 wk**

28 Sep 85	**SUNSHINE** *Jive JIVE 99*	74	1 wk

MILLS BROTHERS
US, male vocal group   **1 wk**

30 Jan 53	● **GLOW WORM** *Brunswick 05007*	10	1 wk

Garnet MIMMS and TRUCKIN' CO.
US, male vocalist and male instrumental group   **1 wk**

25 Jun 77	**WHAT IT IS** *Arista 109*	44	1 wk

MINCE PIES – *See GAY GORDON and the MINCE PIES*

MINDBENDERS
UK, male vocal/instrumental group   **34 wks**

13 Jan 66	● **A GROOVY KIND OF LOVE** *Fontana TF 644*	2	14 wks
5 May 66	**CAN'T LIVE WITH YOU (CAN'T LIVE WITHOUT**		
	YOU) *Fontana TF 697*	28	7 wks
25 Aug 66	**ASHES TO ASHES** *Fontana TF 731*	14	9 wks
20 Sep 67	**THE LETTER** *Fontana TF 869*	42	4 wks

See also Wayne Fontana and the Mindbenders.

Zodiac MINDWARP and the LOVE REACTION
UK, male/female vocal/instrumental group   **11 wks**

9 May 87	**PRIME MOVER** *Mercury ZOD 1*	18	6 wks
14 Nov 87	**BACKSEAT EDUCATION** *Mercury ZOD 2*	49	3 wks
2 Apr 88	**PLANET GIRL** *Mercury ZOD 3*	63	2 wks

Sal MINEO
US, male vocalist   **11 wks**

12 Jul 57	**START MOVIN'** *Philips PB 707*	16	11 wks

Marcello MINEREBI
Italy, orchestra   **16 wks**

22 Jul 65	● **ZORBA'S DANCE** *Durium DRS 54001*	6	16 wks

MINI POPS
UK, male/female vocal group   **2 wks**

26 Dec 87	**SONGS FOR CHRISTMAS '87** (EP) *Bright BULB 9*	39	2 wks

Tracks on Songs For Christmas '87 EP: Thanks For Giving Us Christmas/The Man In Red/Christmas Time Around The World/Shine On.

MINK DE VILLE
US, male vocal/instrumental group   **9 wks**

6 Aug 77	**SPANISH STROLL** *Capitol CLX 103*	20	9 wks

Liza MINNELLI
US, female vocalist   **15 wks**

12 Aug 89	● **LOSING MY MIND** *Epic ZEE 1*	6	7 wks
7 Oct 89	**DON'T DROP BOMBS** *Epic ZEE 2*	46	3 wks
25 Nov 89	**SO SORRY I SAID** *Epic ZEE 3*	62	2 wks
3 Mar 90	**LOVE PAINS** *Epic ZEE 4*	41	3 wks

Kylie MINOGUE
Australia, female vocalist   **108 wks**

23 Jan 88	★ **I SHOULD BE SO LUCKY** *PWL PWL 8*	1	16 wks
14 May 88	● **GOT TO BE CERTAIN** *PWL PWL 12*	2	12 wks
6 Aug 88	● **THE LOCO-MOTION** *PWL PWL 14*	2	11 wks
22 Oct 88	● **JE NE SAIS PAS POURQUOI** *PWL PWL 21*	2	13 wks
6 May 89	★ **HAND ON YOUR HEART** *PWL PWL 35*	1	11 wks
5 Aug 89	● **WOULDN'T CHANGE A THING** *PWL PWL 42*	2	9 wks
4 Nov 89	● **NEVER TOO LATE** *PWL PWL 45*	4	10 wks
20 Jan 90	★ **TEARS ON MY PILLOW** *PWL PWL 47*	1	8 wks
12 May 90	● **BETTER THE DEVIL YOU KNOW** *PWL PWL 56*	2	10 wks
3 Nov 90	● **STEP BACK IN TIME** *PWL PWL 64*	4	8 wks

See also Kylie Minogue and Jason Donovan.

Kylie MINOGUE and Jason DONOVAN
Australia, female/male vocal duo   **14 wks**

7 Jan 89	★ **ESPECIALLY FOR YOU** *PWL PWL 24*	1	14 wks

See also Kylie Minogue; Jason Donovan.

The first six singles by KYLIE MINOGUE all reached the top two, the best start by any solo artist.

Far Left: MILLI VANILLI had three number ones in America in 1989. They were stripped of their Best New Artist Grammy award in 1990 when they admitted they had not personally performed on any of them.

MICK AND PAT (Mick Brown, right, and Pat Sharp) haven't stopped raising money for Help A London Child.

Far Left: KYLIE MINOGUE AND JASON DONOVAN are shown as they appeared in the television series *Neighbours*.

Morris MINOR and the MAJORS
UK, male vocal group   **11 wks**

19 Dec 87 ● STUTTER RAP (NO SLEEP 'TIL BEDTIME)
     10 TEN 203 .... **4** 11 wks

Sugar MINOTT *UK, male vocalist*   **16 wks**

28 Mar 81 ● GOOD THING GOING (WE'VE GOT A GOOD
     THING GOING) *RCA 58*.............................. **4** 12 wks
17 Oct 81   NEVER MY LOVE *RCA 138* .... **52** 4 wks

MINT JULEPS *UK, female vocal group*   **7 wks**

22 Mar 86   ONLY LOVE CAN BREAK YOUR HEART
     Stiff BUY 241 .... **62** 2 wks
30 May 87   EVERY KINDA PEOPLE *Stiff BUY 257* .... **58** 5 wks

MIRACLES *US, male vocal group*   **10 wks**

10 Jan 76 ● LOVE MACHINE *Tamla Motown TMG 1015* .... **3** 10 wks

See also Smokey Robinson and the Miracles.

MIRAGE *UK, male vocal/instrumental group*   **35 wks**

14 Jan 84   GIVE ME THE NIGHT (MEDLEY) *Passion PASH 15* .... **49** 4 wks
9 May 87 ● JACK MIX II/ III *Debut DEBT 3022*............................... **4** 11 wks
25 Jul 87   SERIOUS MIX *Debut DEBT 3028* .... **42** 4 wks
7 Nov 87 ● JACK MIX IV *Debut DEBT 3035*.................................. **8** 10 wks
27 Feb 88   JACK MIX VII *Debut DEBT 3042* .... **50** 3 wks
2 Jul 88   PUSH THE BEAT *Debut DEBT 3050* .... **67** 2 wks
11 Nov 89   LATINO HOUSE *Debut DEBT 3085* .... **70** 1 wk

First hit features Roy Gayle. Jack Mix III only listed with Jack Mix II from 6 Jun 87.

Danny MIRROR *Holland, male vocalist*   **9 wks**

17 Sep 77 ● I REMEMBER ELVIS PRESLEY (THE KING IS DEAD)
     Sonet SON 2121 .... **4** 9 wks

MISSION *UK, male vocal/instrumental group*   **46 wks**

14 Jun 86   SERPENTS KISS *Chapter 22 CHAP 6* .... **70** 3 wks
26 Jul 86   GARDEN OF DELIGHT/ LIKE A HURRICANE
     Chapter 22 CHAP 7 .... **50** 4 wks
18 Oct 86   STAY WITH ME *Mercury MYTH 1* .... **30** 4 wks
17 Jan 87   WASTELAND *Mercury MYTH 2* .... **11** 6 wks
14 Mar 87   SEVERINA *Mercury MYTH 3* .... **25** 5 wks
13 Feb 88   TOWER OF STRENGTH *Mercury MYTH 4* .... **12** 7 wks
23 Apr 88   BEYOND THE PALE *Mercury MYTH 6* .... **32** 4 wks
13 Jan 90   BUTTERFLY ON A WHEEL *Mercury MYTH 8* .... **12** 4 wks
10 Mar 90   DELIVERANCE *Mercury MYTH 9*.......................... **27** 4 wks
2 Jun 90   INTO THE BLUE *Mercury MYTH 10* .... **32** 3 wks
17 Nov 90   HAND ACROSS THE OCEAN *Mercury MYTH 11* .... **28** 2 wks

MISTA E *UK, male producer*   **5 wks**

10 Dec 88   DON'T BELIEVE THE HYPE *Urban URB 28* .... **41** 5 wks

MR. BIG *UK, male vocal/instrumental group*   **14 wks**

12 Feb 77 ● ROMEO *EMI 2567* .... **4** 10 wks
21 May 77   FEEL LIKE CALLING HOME *EMI 2610* .... **35** 4 wks

MR. BLOE *UK, male instrumentalist – harmonica*   **18 wks**

9 May 70 ● GROOVIN' WITH MR. BLOE *DJM DJS 216* .... **2** 18 wks

MR. FINGERS *US, male producer*   **1 wk**

17 Mar 90   WHAT ABOUT THIS LOVE *FFRR F 131* .... **74** 1 wk

MR. FOOD *UK, male vocalist*   **3 wks**

9 Jun 90   ...AND THAT'S BEFORE ME TEA! *Tangible TGB 005*....... **62** 3 wks

MR. LEE *US, male producer*   **6 wks**

6 Aug 88   PUMP UP LONDON *Breakout USA 639*..................... **64** 2 wks
11 Nov 89   GET BUSY *Jive JIVE 231*.................................... **71** 1 wk
24 Feb 90   GET BUSY (re-entry) *Jive JIVE 231*.......................... **41** 3 wks

MR. MISTER *US, male vocal/instrumental group*   **22 wks**

21 Dec 85 ● BROKEN WINGS *RCA PB 49945*............................. **4** 13 wks
1 Mar 86   KYRIE *RCA PB 49927* .... **11** 9 wks

MISTURA *US, male instrumental group*   **10 wks**

15 May 76   THE FLASHER *Route RT 30*................................. **23** 10 wks

Has credit: Featuring Lloyd Michels (trumpet).

Cameron MITCHELL – *See VARIOUS ARTISTS (Carousel Soundtrack)*

Guy MITCHELL *US, male vocalist*   **164 wks**

14 Nov 52 ● FEET UP *Columbia DB 3151* .... **2** 10 wks
13 Feb 53 ★ SHE WEARS RED FEATHERS *Columbia DB 3238*............. **1** 15 wks
24 Apr 53 ● PRETTY LITTLE BLACK EYED SUSIE
     Columbia DB 3255 .... **2** 11 wks
12 Jun 53   SHE WEARS RED FEATHERS (re-entry)
     Columbia DB 3238 .... **12** 1 wk
28 Aug 53 ★ LOOK AT THAT GIRL *Philips PB 162* .... **1** 14 wks
6 Nov 53 ● CHICKA BOOM *Philips PB 178* .... **5** 9 wks
18 Dec 53 ● CLOUD LUCKY SEVEN *Philips PB 210*...................... **2** 16 wks
15 Jan 54   CHICKA BOOM (re-entry) *Philips PB 178* .... **4** 6 wks
19 Feb 54   CUFF OF MY SHIRT *Philips PB 225* .... **9** 1 wk
26 Feb 54   SIPPIN' SODA *Philips PB 210* .... **11** 1 wk
19 Mar 54   CUFF OF MY SHIRT (re-entry) *Philips PB 225* .... **12** 1 wk
2 Apr 54   CUFF OF MY SHIRT (2nd re-entry) *Philips PB 225* ...... **11** 1 wk
30 Apr 54 ● DIME AND A DOLLAR *Philips PB 248*..................... **8** 1 wk
14 May 54 ● DIME AND A DOLLAR (re-entry) *Philips PB 248*.......... **8** 4 wks
7 Dec 56 ★ SINGING THE BLUES *Philips PB 650* .... **1** 22 wks
15 Feb 57 ● KNEE DEEP IN THE BLUES *Philips PB 669* .... **3** 12 wks
26 Apr 57 ★ ROCK-A-BILLY *Philips PB 685* .... **1** 14 wks
26 Jul 57   IN THE MIDDLE OF A DARK DARK NIGHT/ SWEET
     STUFF *Philips PB 712* .... **27** 2 wks
23 Aug 57   IN THE MIDDLE OF A DARK DARK NIGHT/ SWEET
     STUFF (re-entry) *Philips PB 712* .... **25** 2 wks
11 Oct 57   CALL ROSIE ON THE PHONE *Philips PB 743* .... **17** 6 wks
27 Nov 59   HEARTACHES BY THE NUMBER *Philips PB 964* .... **26** 2 wks
18 Dec 59 ● HEARTACHES BY THE NUMBER (re-entry)
     Philips PB 964 .... **5** 13 wks

Joni MITCHELL *Canada, female vocalist*   **15 wks**

13 Jun 70   BIG YELLOW TAXI *Reprise RS 20906*...................... **11** 15 wks

Willie MITCHELL US, male instrumentalist – guitar — 3 wks

24 Apr 68	SOUL SERENADE London HLU 10186	43	1 wk
11 Dec 76	THE CHAMPION London HL 10545	47	2 wks

MIXMASTER Italy, male producer — 10 wks

4 Nov 89 ●	GRAND PIANO BCM BCM 344	9	10 wks

MIXTURES Australia, male vocal/instrumental group — 21 wks

16 Jan 71 ●	THE PUSHBIKE SONG Polydor 2058 083	2	21 wks

Hank MIZELL US, male vocalist — 13 wks

20 Mar 76 ●	JUNGLE ROCK Charly CS 1005	3	13 wks

MOBILES UK, male/female vocal/instrumental group — 14 wks

9 Jan 82 ●	DROWNING IN BERLIN Rialto RIA 3	9	10 wks
27 Mar 82	AMOUR AMOUR Rialto RIA 5	45	4 wks

MODERN LOVERS US, male vocal/instrumental group — 4 wks

21 Jan 78	MORNING OF OUR LIVES Beserkley BZZ 7	29	4 wks

See also Jonathan Richman and the Modern Lovers.

MODERN ROMANCE — 77 wks
UK, male vocal/instrumental group

15 Aug 81	EVERYBODY SALSA WEA K 18815	12	10 wks
7 Nov 81 ●	AY AY AY AY MOOSEY WEA K 18883	10	12 wks
30 Jan 82	QUEEN OF THE RAPPING SCENE (NOTHING EVER GOES THE WAY YOU PLAN) WEA K 18928	37	8 wks
14 Aug 82	CHERRY PINK AND APPLE BLOSSOM WHITE WEA K 19245	15	8 wks
13 Nov 82 ●	BEST YEARS OF OUR LIVES WEA ROM 1	4	13 wks
26 Feb 83 ●	HIGH LIFE WEA ROM 2	8	8 wks
7 May 83	DON'T STOP THAT CRAZY RHYTHM WEA ROM 3	14	6 wks
6 Aug 83 ●	WALKING IN THE RAIN WEA X 9733	7	12 wks

Cherry Pink And Apple Blossom White has credit 'featuring John du Prez'.

MODERN TALKING — 22 wks
Germany, male vocal/instrumental duo

15 Jun 85	YOU'RE MY HEART, YOU'RE MY SOUL Magnet MAG 277	69	2 wks
17 Aug 85	YOU'RE MY HEART, YOU'RE MY SOUL (re-entry) Magnet MAG 277	56	5 wks
12 Oct 85	YOU CAN WIN IF YOU WANT Magnet MAG 282	70	2 wks
16 Aug 86 ●	BROTHER LOUIE RCA PB 40875	4	10 wks
4 Oct 86	ATLANTIS IS CALLING (S.O.S. FOR LOVE) RCA PB 40969	55	3 wks

MODETTES UK, female vocal/instrumental group — 6 wks

12 Jul 80	PAINT IT BLACK Deram DET-R 1	42	5 wks
18 Jul 81	TONIGHT Deram DET 3	68	1 wk

Domenico MODUGNO Italy, male vocalist — 13 wks

5 Sep 58 ●	VOLARE Oriole CB 5000	10	12 wks
27 Mar 59	CIAO CIAO BAMBINA Oriole CB 1489	29	1 wk

MOHAWKS Jamaica, male vocal/instrumental group — 2 wks

24 Jan 87	THE CHAMP Pama PM 1	58	2 wks

MOJO UK, male instrumental group — 3 wks

22 Aug 81	DANCE ON Creole CR 17	70	3 wks

MOJOS UK, male vocal/instrumental group — 26 wks

26 Mar 64 ●	EVERYTHING'S ALRIGHT Decca F 11853	9	11 wks
11 Jun 64	WHY NOT TONIGHT Decca F 11918	25	10 wks
10 Sep 64	SEVEN DAFFODILS Decca F 11959	30	5 wks

MOMENTS US, male vocal group — 22 wks

19 Jul 75 ●	DOLLY MY LOVE All Platinum 6146 306	10	9 wks
25 Oct 75	LOOK AT ME (I'M IN LOVE) All Platinum 6146 309	42	4 wks
22 Jan 77 ●	JACK IN THE BOX All Platinum 6146 318	7	9 wks

See also Moments and Whatnauts.

MOMENTS and WHATNAUTS — 10 wks
US, male vocal group, male instrumental group

8 Mar 75 ●	GIRLS All Platinum 6146 302	3	10 wks

See also Moments.

Jay MONDI and the LIVING BASS — 3 wks
US, male/female vocal/instrumental group

24 Mar 90	ALL NIGHT LONG 10 TEN 304	63	3 wks

MONDO KANE UK, male vocal/instrumental group — 2 wks

16 Aug 86	NEW YORK AFTERNOON Lisson DOLE 2	70	2 wks

Zoot MONEY and the BIG ROLL BAND — 8 wks
UK, male vocalist/instrumentalist - keyboards and male instrumental backing group

18 Aug 66	BIG TIME OPERATOR Columbia DB 7975	25	8 wks

T.S. MONK US, male/female vocal/instrumental group — 6 wks

7 Mar 81	BON BON VIE Mirage K 11653	63	2 wks
25 Apr 81	CANDIDATE FOR LOVE Mirage K 11648	58	4 wks

MONKEES US/UK, male vocal/instrumental group — 101 wks

5 Jan 67 ★	I'M A BELIEVER RCA 1560	1	17 wks
26 Jan 67	LAST TRAIN TO CLARKSVILLE RCA 1547	23	7 wks
6 Apr 67 ●	A LITTLE BIT ME A LITTLE BIT YOU RCA 1580	3	12 wks
22 Jun 67 ●	ALTERNATE TITLE RCA 1604	2	12 wks
16 Aug 67	PLEASANT VALLEY SUNDAY RC 1620	11	8 wks
15 Nov 67 ●	DAYDREAM BELIEVER RCA 1645	5	17 wks
27 Mar 68	VALLERI RCA 1673	12	8 wks
26 Jun 68	D.W. WASHBURN RCA 1706	17	6 wks
26 Mar 69	TEARDROP CITY RCA 1802	46	1 wk
25 Jun 69	SOMEDAY MAN RCA 1824	47	1 wk
15 Mar 80	THE MONKEES EP Arista ARIST 326	33	9 wks
18 Oct 86	THAT WAS THEN, THIS IS NOW Arista ARIST 673	68	1 wk
1 Apr 89	THE MONKEES (EP) Arista 112157	62	2 wks

Tracks on Arista 326 EP: I'm a Believer/Daydream Believer/Last Train to Clarksville/A Little

Bit Me A Little Bit You. Tracks on Arista 112157 EP: Daydream Believer/Monkees Theme/Last Train To Clarksville.

MONKS UK, *male vocal/instrumental duo* — 9 wks

21 Apr 79	**NICE LEGS SHAME ABOUT HER FACE** *Carrere CAR 104*		**19**	9 wks

The Monks are Hudson-Ford under new name. See also Hudson-Ford.

Matt MONRO UK, *male vocalist* — 127 wks

15 Dec 60	● **PORTRAIT OF MY LOVE** *Parlophone R 4714*		**3**	16 wks
9 Mar 61	● **MY KIND OF GIRL** *Parlophone R 4755*		**5**	12 wks
18 May 61	**WHY NOT NOW/ CAN THIS BE LOVE** *Parlophone R 4775*		**24**	9 wks
28 Sep 61	**GONNA BUILD A MOUNTAIN** *Parlophone R 4819*		**44**	3 wks
8 Feb 62	● **SOFTLY AS I LEAVE YOU** *Parlophone R 4868*		**10**	18 wks
14 Jun 62	**WHEN LOVE COMES ALONG** *Parlophone R 4911*		**46**	3 wks
8 Nov 62	**MY LOVE AND DEVOTION** *Parlophone R 4954*		**29**	5 wks
14 Nov 63	**FROM RUSSIA WITH LOVE** *Parlophone R 5068*		**20**	13 wks
17 Sep 64	● **WALK AWAY** *Parlophone R 5171*		**4**	20 wks
24 Dec 64	**FOR MAMA** *Parlophone R 5215*		**36**	4 wks
25 Mar 65	**WITHOUT YOU** *Parlophone R 5251*		**37**	4 wks
21 Oct 65	**YESTERDAY** *Parlophone R 5348*		**8**	12 wks
24 Nov 73	● **AND YOU SMILED** *EMI 2091*		**28**	8 wks

Gerry MONROE UK, *male vocalist* — 57 wks

23 May 70	● **SALLY** *Chapter One CH 122*		**4**	20 wks
19 Sep 70	**CRY** *Chapter One CH 128*		**38**	5 wks
14 Nov 70	● **MY PRAYER** *Chapter One CH 132*		**9**	12 wks
17 Apr 71	**IT'S A SIN TO TELL A LIE** *Chapter One CH 144*		**13**	10 wks
21 Aug 71	**LITTLE DROPS OF SILVER** *Chapter One CH 152*		**37**	6 wks
12 Feb 72	**GIRL OF MY DREAMS** *Chapter One CH 159*		**43**	2 wks

MONSOON UK, *male/female vocal/instrumental group* — 12 wks

3 Apr 82	**EVER SO LONELY** *Mobile Suit Corp CORP 2*		**12**	9 wks
5 Jun 82	**SHAKTI (THE MEANING OF WITHIN)** *Mobile Suit Corp CORP 4*		**41**	3 wks

MONSTER ORCHESTRA – *See John DAVIS and the MONSTER ORCHESTRA*

MONTANA SEXTET
US, *male/female vocal/instrumental group* — 1 wk

15 Jan 83	**HEAVY VIBES** *Virgin VS 560*		**59**	1 wk

Hugo MONTENEGRO US, *orchestra* — 26 wks

11 Sep 68	★ **THE GOOD THE BAD AND THE UGLY** *RCA 1727*		**1**	24 wks
8 Jan 69	**HANG 'EM HIGH** *RCA 1771*		**50**	1 wk
19 Mar 69	**THE GOOD THE BAD AND THE UGLY (re-entry)** *RCA 1727*		**48**	1 wk

Chris MONTEZ US, *male vocalist* — 61 wks

4 Oct 62	● **LET'S DANCE** *London HLU 9596*		**2**	18 wks
17 Jan 63	● **SOME KINDA FUN** *London HLU 9650*		**10**	9 wks
30 Jun 66	● **THE MORE I SEE YOU** *Pye International 7N 25369*		**3**	13 wks
22 Sep 66	**THERE WILL NEVER BE ANOTHER YOU** *Pye International 7N 25381*		**37**	4 wks
14 Oct 72	● **LET'S DANCE (re-issue)** *London HL 10205*		**9**	14 wks
14 Apr 79	**LET'S DANCE (2nd re-issue)** *Lightning LIG 9011*		**47**	3 wks

The second re-issue of Let's Dance on Lightning was coupled with Memphis by Lonnie Mack as a double A-side. See also Lonnie Mack.

MONTROSE US, *male vocal/instrumental group* — 2 wks

28 Jun 80	**SPACE STATION NO. 5/ GOOD ROCKIN' TONIGHT** *WB HM 9*		**71**	2 wks

MONYAKA US/Jamaica, *male vocal/instrumental group* — 8 wks

10 Sep 83	**GO DEH YAKA (GO TO THE TOP)** *Polydor POSP 641*		**14**	8 wks

MOOD UK, *male vocal/instrumental group* — 10 wks

6 Feb 82	**DON'T STOP** *RCA 171*		**59**	4 wks
22 May 82	**PARIS IS ONE DAY AWAY** *RCA 211*		**42**	5 wks
30 Oct 82	**PASSION IN DARK ROOMS** *RCA 276*		**74**	1 wk

MOODY BLUES UK, *male vocal/instrumental group* — 114 wks

10 Dec 64	★ **GO NOW** *Decca F 12022*		**1**	14 wks
4 Mar 65	**I DON'T WANT TO GO ON WITHOUT YOU** *Decca F 12095*		**33**	9 wks
10 Jun 65	**FROM THE BOTTOM OF MY HEART** *Decca F 12166*		**22**	9 wks
18 Nov 65	**EVERYDAY** *Decca F 12266*		**44**	2 wks
27 Dec 67	**NIGHTS IN WHITE SATIN** *Deram DM 161*		**19**	11 wks
7 Aug 68	**VOICES IN THE SKY** *Deram DM 196*		**27**	10 wks
4 Dec 68	**RIDE MY SEE-SAW** *Deram DM 213*		**42**	1 wk
2 May 70	● **QUESTION** *Threshold TH 4*		**2**	12 wks
6 May 72	**ISN'T LIFE STRANGE** *Threshold TH 9*		**13**	10 wks
2 Dec 72	**NIGHTS IN WHITE SATIN (re-entry)** *Deram DM 161*		**9**	11 wks
10 Feb 73	**I'M JUST A SINGER (IN A ROCK 'N' ROLL BAND)** *Threshold TH 13*		**36**	4 wks
10 Nov 79	**NIGHTS IN WHITE SATIN (2nd re-entry)** *Deram DM 161*		**14**	12 wks
20 Aug 83	**BLUE WORLD** *Threshold TH 30*		**35**	5 wks
25 Jun 88	**I KNOW YOU'RE OUT THERE SOMEWHERE** *Polydor POSP 921*		**52**	4 wks

MOONTREKKERS UK, *male instrumental group* — 1 wk

2 Nov 61	**NIGHT OF THE VAMPIRE** *Parlophone R 4814*		**50**	1 wk

Dorothy MOORE US, *female vocalist* — 24 wks

19 Jun 76	● **MISTY BLUE** *Contempo CS 2087*		**5**	12 wks
16 Oct 76	**FUNNY HOW TIME SLIPS AWAY** *Contempo CS 2092*		**38**	3 wks
15 Oct 77	**I BELIEVE YOU** *Epic EPC 5573*		**20**	9 wks

Dudley MOORE – *See Peter COOK and Dudley MOORE*

Gary MOORE UK, *male vocalist/instrumentalist - guitar* — 74 wks

21 Apr 79	● **PARISIENNE WALKWAYS** *MCA 419*		**8**	11 wks
21 Jan 84	**HOLD ON TO LOVE** *10 TEN 13*		**65**	4 wks
11 Aug 84	**EMPTY ROOMS** *10 TEN 25*		**51**	5 wks
27 Jul 85	**EMPTY ROOMS (re-issue)** *10 TEN 58*		**23**	8 wks
20 Dec 86	**OVER THE HILLS AND FAR AWAY** *10 TEN 134*		**20**	8 wks
28 Feb 87	**WILD FRONTIER** *10 TEN 159*		**35**	5 wks
9 May 87	**FRIDAY ON MY MIND** *10 TEN 164*		**26**	6 wks
29 Aug 87	**THE LONER** *10 TEN 178*		**53**	5 wks
5 Dec 87	**TAKE A LITTLE TIME (DOUBLE SINGLE)** *10 TEN 190*		**75**	1 wk
14 Jan 89	**AFTER THE WAR** *Virgin GMS 1*		**37**	4 wks
18 Mar 89	**READY FOR LOVE** *Virgin GMS 2*		**56**	2 wks
24 Mar 90	**OH PRETTY WOMAN** *Virgin VS 1233*		**48**	3 wks
12 May 90	**STILL GOT THE BLUES (FOR YOU)** *Virgin VS 1267*		**31**	4 wks
18 Aug 90	**WALKING BY MYSELF** *Virgin VS 1281*		**48**	5 wks
15 Dec 90	**TOO TIRED** *Virgin VS 1306*		**71**	1 wk

Parisienne Walkways features vocals by Phil Lynott. Tracks on double single: Take A Little Time/Out In The Fields/All Messed Up/Thunder Rising. Oh Pretty Woman features Albert King - US, male instrumentalist - guitarist. See also Gary Moore and Phil Lynott.

Gary MOORE and Phil LYNOTT — 10 wks
UK/Ireland, male vocal/instrumental duo

| 18 May 85 | ● OUT IN THE FIELDS *10 TEN 49* | 5 | 10 wks |

See also Gary Moore; Phil Lynott.

Jackie MOORE — 5 wks
US, female vocalist

| 15 Sep 79 | THIS TIME BABY *CBS 7722* | 49 | 5 wks |

Melba MOORE — 29 wks
US, female vocalist

15 May 76	● THIS IS IT *Buddah BDS 443*	9	8 wks
26 May 79	PICK ME UP I'LL DANCE *Epic EPC 7234*	48	5 wks
9 Oct 82	LOVE'S COMIN' AT YA *EMI America EA 146*	15	8 wks
15 Jan 83	MIND UP TONIGHT *Capitol CL 272*	22	6 wks
5 Mar 83	UNDERLOVE *Capitol CL 281*	60	2 wks

Ray MOORE — 9 wks
UK, male vocalist

| 29 Nov 86 | O' MY FATHER HAD A RABBIT *Play PLAY 213* | 24 | 7 wks |
| 5 Dec 87 | BOG EYED JOG *Play PLAY 224* | 61 | 2 wks |

Sam MOORE and Lou REED — 10 wks
US, male vocal duo

| 17 Jan 87 | SOUL MAN *A & M AM 364* | 30 | 10 wks |

See also Lou Reed; Sam and Dave.

Mike MORAN – *See Lynsey DE PAUL and Mike MORAN*

MORE — 2 wks
UK, male vocal/instrumental group

| 14 Mar 81 | WE ARE THE BAND *Atlantic K 11561* | 59 | 2 wks |

Derrick MORGAN — 1 wk
Jamaica, male vocalist

| 17 Jan 70 | MOON HOP *Crab 32* | 49 | 1 wk |

Jamie J. MORGAN — 6 wks
US, male vocalist

| 10 Feb 90 | WALK ON THE WILD SIDE *Tabu 655596 7* | 27 | 6 wks |

Jane MORGAN — 22 wks
US, female vocalist

5 Dec 58	★ THE DAY THE RAINS CAME *London HLR 8751*	1	16 wks
22 May 59	IF ONLY I COULD LIVE MY LIFE AGAIN *London HLR 8810*	27	1 wk
21 Jul 60	ROMANTICA *London HLR 9120*	39	5 wks

Meli'sa MORGAN — 7 wks
US, female vocalist

| 9 Aug 86 | FOOL'S PARADISE *Capitol CL 415* | 41 | 5 wks |
| 25 Jun 88 | GOOD LOVE *Capitol CL 483* | 59 | 2 wks |

Ray MORGAN — 6 wks
UK, male vocalist

| 25 Jul 70 | THE LONG AND WINDING ROAD *B & C CB 128* | 32 | 6 wks |

Giorgio MORODER — 16 wks
Italy, male instrumentalist - synthesisers

| 24 Sep 77 | FROM HERE TO ETERNITY *Oasis 1* | 16 | 10 wks |
| 17 Mar 79 | CHASE *Casablanca CAN 144* | 48 | 6 wks |

First hit credited simply to Giorgio. See also Giorgio Moroder and Phil Oakey.

Giorgio MORODER and Phil OAKEY — 18 wks
Italy/UK, male instrumental/vocal duo

| 22 Sep 84 | ● TOGETHER IN ELECTRIC DREAMS *Virgin VS 713* | 3 | 13 wks |
| 29 Jun 85 | GOODBYE BAD TIMES *Virgin VS 772* | 44 | 5 wks |

See also Giorgio Moroder.

Ennio MORRICONE *Italy, orchestra* — 12 wks

| 11 Apr 81 | ● CHI MAI (THEME FROM THE TV SERIES THE LIFE AND TIMES OF DAVID LLOYD GEORGE) *BBC RESL 92* | 2 | 12 wks |

Sarah Jane MORRIS – *See COMMUNARDS*

Diana MORRISON – *See Michael BALL and Diana MORRISON*

Dorothy Combs MORRISON – *See Edwin HAWKINS SINGERS*

Van MORRISON — 10 wks
UK, male vocalist

20 Oct 79	BRIGHT SIDE OF THE ROAD *Mercury 6001 121*	63	3 wks
1 Jul 89	HAVE I TOLD YOU LATELY *Polydor VANS 1*	74	1 wk
9 Dec 89	WHENEVER GOD SHINES HIS LIGHT *Polydor VANS 2*	20	6 wks

Whenever God Shines His Light is with Cliff Richard. See also Cliff Richard.

MORRISSEY — 31 wks
UK, male vocalist

27 Feb 88	● SUEDEHEAD *HMV POP 1618*	5	6 wks
11 Jun 88	● EVERYDAY IS LIKE SUNDAY *HMV POP 1619*	9	6 wks
11 Feb 89	LAST OF THE FAMOUS INTERNATIONAL PLAYBOYS *HMV POP 1620*	6	5 wks
29 Apr 89	● INTERESTING DRUG *HMV POP 1621*	9	4 wks
25 Nov 89	OUIJA BOARD OUIJA BOARD *HMV POP 1622*	18	4 wks
5 May 90	NOVEMBER SPAWNED A MONSTER *HMV POP 1623*	12	4 wks
20 Oct 90	PICCADILLY PALARE *HMV POP 1624*	18	2 wks

MORRISTON ORPHEUS MALE VOICE CHOIR – *See ALARM*

Buddy MORROW — 1 wk
US, orchestra

| 20 Mar 53 | NIGHT TRAIN *HMV B 10347* | 12 | 1 wk |

Mickie MOST — 1 wk
UK, male vocalist

| 25 Jul 63 | MISTER PORTER *Decca F 11664* | 45 | 1 wk |

MOTELS — 7 wks
US/UK, male/female vocal/instrumental group

| 11 Oct 80 | WHOSE PROBLEM? *Capitol CL 16162* | 42 | 4 wks |
| 10 Jan 81 | DAYS ARE O.K. *Capitol CL 16149* | 41 | 3 wks |

MOTLEY CRUE US, male vocal/instrumental group | 21 wks

24 Aug 85	SMOKIN' IN THE BOYS ROOM Elektra EKR 16...............	71	2 wks
8 Feb 86	HOME SWEET HOME/ SMOKIN' IN THE BOYS		
	ROOM Elektra EKR 33.................	51	3 wks
1 Aug 87	GIRLS GIRLS GIRLS Elektra EKR 59	26	6 wks
16 Jan 88	YOU'RE ALL I NEED/ WILD SIDE Elektra EKR 65	23	4 wks
4 Nov 89	DR. FEELGOOD Elektra EKR 97.................	50	4 wks
12 May 90	WITHOUT YOU Elektra EKR 109.............	39	3 wks

Smokin' In the Boys Room *was re-issued on Elektra EKR 33. Wild Side only listed with
You're All I Need from 30 Jan 88.*

MOTORHEAD UK, male vocal/instrumental group | 62 wks

16 Sep 78	LOUIE LOUIE Bronze BRO 60	75	1 wk
30 Sep 78	LOUIE LOUIE (re-entry) Bronze BRO 60	68	1 wk
10 Mar 79	OVERKILL Bronze BRO 67	39	4 wks
14 Apr 79	OVERKILL (re-entry) Bronze BRO 67	57	3 wks
30 Jun 79	NO CLASS Bronze BRO 78.	61	4 wks
1 Dec 79	BOMBER Bronze BRO 85	34	7 wks
3 May 80	● THE GOLDEN YEARS (EP) Bronze BRO 92	8	7 wks
1 Nov 80	ACE OF SPADES Bronze BRO 106	15	12 wks
22 Nov 80	BEER DRINKERS AND HELL RAISERS		
	Big Beat SWT 61.	43	4 wks
11 Jul 81	● MOTORHEAD LIVE Bronze BRO 124.........	6	7 wks
3 Apr 82	IRON FIST Bronze BRO 146.........	29	5 wks
21 May 83	I GOT MINE Bronze BRO 165.........	46	2 wks
30 Jul 83	SHINE Bronze BRO 167	59	2 wks
1 Sep 84	KILLED BY DEATH Bronze BRO 185	51	2 wks
5 Jul 86	DEAF FOREVER GWR GWR 2	67	1 wk

Tracks on EP: Dead Men Tell No Tales/Too Late Too Late/Leaving Here/Stone Dead Forever.
See also Motorhead and Girlschool.

MOTORHEAD and GIRLSCHOOL | 8 wks
UK, male/female vocal/instrumental group

| 21 Feb 81 | ● ST. VALENTINE'S DAY MASSACRE (EP) | | |
| | Bronze BRO 116................. | 5 | 8 wks |

Tracks on St. Valentine's Day Massacre EP: Please Don't Touch/Emergency/Bomber. Group
also known as Headgirl. See Motorhead; Girlschool.

MOTORS UK, male vocal/instrumental group | 29 wks

24 Sep 77	DANCING THE NIGHT AWAY Virgin VS 186..............	42	4 wks
10 Jun 78	● AIRPORT Virgin VS 219.................	4	13 wks
19 Aug 78	FORGET ABOUT YOU Virgin VS 222.................	13	9 wks
12 Apr 80	LOVE AND LONELINESS Virgin VS 263.................	58	3 wks

MOTOWN SPINNERS – See DETROIT SPINNERS

MOTT THE HOOPLE | 55 wks
UK, male vocal/instrumental group

12 Aug 72	● ALL THE YOUNG DUDES CBS 8271	3	11 wks
16 Jun 73	HONALOOCHIE BOOGIE CBS 1530.............	12	9 wks
8 Sep 73	● ALL THE WAY FROM MEMPHIS CBS 1764.............	10	8 wks
24 Nov 73	● ROLL AWAY THE STONE CBS 1895.............	8	12 wks
30 Mar 74	GOLDEN AGE OF ROCK AND ROLL CBS 2177	16	7 wks
22 Jun 74	FOXY FOXY CBS 2439.............	33	5 wks
2 Nov 74	SATURDAY GIG CBS 2754.............	41	3 wks

Nana MOUSKOURI Greece, female vocalist | 11 wks

| 11 Jan 86 | ● ONLY LOVE Philips PH 38............. | 2 | 11 wks |

MOUTH and MACNEAL | 10 wks
Holland, male/female vocal duo

| 4 May 74 | ● I SEE A STAR Decca F 13504................. | 8 | 10 wks |

MOVE UK, male vocal/instrumental group | 110 wks

5 Jan 67	● NIGHT OF FEAR Deram DM 109.................	2	10 wks
6 Apr 67	● I CAN HEAR THE GRASS GROW Deram DM 117...........	5	10 wks
6 Sep 67	● FLOWERS IN THE RAIN Regal Zonophone RZ3001	2	13 wks
7 Feb 68	● FIRE BRIGADE Regal Zonophone RZ3005	3	11 wks
25 Dec 68	★ BLACKBERRY WAY Regal Zonophone RZ3015 ...	1	12 wks
23 Jul 69	CURLY Regal Zonophone RZ3021	12	12 wks
25 Apr 70	● BRONTOSAURUS Regal Zonophone RZ3026 ...	7	10 wks
3 Jul 71	TONIGHT Harvest HAR 5038.................	11	10 wks
23 Oct 71	CHINATOWN Harvest HAR 5043.................	23	8 wks
13 May 72	● CALIFORNIA MAN Harvest HAR 5050.................	7	14 wks

MOVEMENT 98 featuring Carroll | 8 wks
THOMPSON UK, male/female vocal/instrumental group

| 19 May 90 | JOY AND HEARTBREAK Circa YR 45 .... | 27 | 5 wks |
| 15 Sep 90 | SUNRISE Circa YR 51................. | 58 | 3 wks |

See also Courtney Pine featuring Carroll Thompson.

Alison MOYET UK, female vocalist | 82 wks

23 Jun 84	● LOVE RESURRECTION CBS A 4497.................	10	11 wks
13 Oct 84	● ALL CRIED OUT CBS A 4757.................	8	11 wks
1 Dec 84	INVISIBLE CBS A 4930.................	21	10 wks
16 Mar 85	● THAT OLE DEVIL CALLED LOVE CBS A 6044.............	2	10 wks
29 Nov 86	● IS THIS LOVE? CBS MOYET 1	3	16 wks
7 Mar 87	● WEAK IN THE PRESENCE OF BEAUTY		
	CBS MOYET 2	6	10 wks
30 May 87	ORDINARY GIRL CBS MOYET 3	43	4 wks
28 Nov 87	● LOVE LETTERS CBS MOYET 5	4	10 wks

MTUME US, male/female vocal/instrumental group | 12 wks

| 14 May 83 | JUICY FRUIT Epic A 3424................. | 34 | 9 wks |
| 22 Sep 84 | PRIME TIME Epic A 4720................. | 57 | 3 wks |

MUD UK, male vocal/instrumental group | 139 wks

10 Mar 73	CRAZY RAK 146.................	12	12 wks
23 Jun 73	HYPNOSIS RAK 152.................	16	13 wks
27 Oct 73	● DYNA-MITE RAK 159.................	4	12 wks
19 Jan 74	★ TIGER FEET RAK 166.................	1	11 wks
13 Apr 74	● THE CAT CREPT IN RAK 170	2	9 wks
27 Jul 74	● ROCKET RAK 178.................	6	9 wks
30 Nov 74	★ LONELY THIS CHRISTMAS RAK 187	1	10 wks
15 Feb 75	● THE SECRETS THAT YOU KEEP RAK 194	3	9 wks
26 Apr 75	★ OH BOY RAK 201.................	1	9 wks
21 Jun 75	● MOONSHINE SALLY RAK 208.........	10	7 wks
2 Aug 75	ONE NIGHT RAK 213.................	32	4 wks
4 Oct 75	● L-L-LUCY Private Stock PVT 41.........	10	6 wks
29 Nov 75	● SHOW ME YOU'RE A WOMAN Private Stock PVT 45	8	8 wks
15 May 76	SHAKE IT DOWN Private Stock PVT 65	12	8 wks
27 Nov 76	● LEAN ON ME Private Stock PVT 85	7	9 wks
21 Dec 85	LONELY THIS CHRISTMAS (re-entry) RAK 187	61	3 wks

MUDLARKS UK, male/female vocal group | 19 wks

2 May 58	● LOLLIPOP Columbia DB 4099.................	2	9 wks
6 Jun 58	● BOOK OF LOVE Columbia DB 4133.................	8	9 wks
27 Feb 59	THE LOVE GAME Columbia DB 4250	30	1 wk

MUFFINS – See MARTHA and the MUFFINS

MINT JULEPS were a unique chart act, an all-female *a capella* group.

As songwriter Jerry Samuels, he penned Sammy Davis Jr.'s US Top Forty hit 'Shelter of Your Arms'. As NAPOLEON XIV he was taken away in October 1966.

Far Right: HANK MIZELL was a middle-aged rockabilly when he found top three success with his vintage recording.

Vince Neil of MOTLEY CRUE (centre) is shown with two members of the Stray Cats before a 1988 charity softball game at the University of Southern California.

Idris MUHAMMAD US, male vocalist   3 wks

17 Sep 77	COULD HEAVEN EVER BE LIKE THIS Kudu 935 42	3 wks

Maria MULDAUR US, female vocalist   8 wks

29 Jun 74	MIDNIGHT AT THE OASIS Reprise K 14331 21	8 wks

Arthur MULLARD – See Hylda BAKER and Arthur MULLARD

Coati MUNDI – See Kid CREOLE and the COCONUTS

MUNGO JERRY UK, male vocal/instrumental group   87 wks

6 Jun 70	★ IN THE SUMMERTIME Dawn DNX 2502 1	20 wks
6 Feb 71	BABY JUMP Dawn DNX 2505 32	1 wk
20 Feb 71	★ BABY JUMP (re-entry) Dawn DNX 2505 1	12 wks
29 May 71	● LADY ROSE Dawn DNX 2510. 5	12 wks
18 Sep 71	YOU DON'T HAVE TO BE IN THE ARMY TO FIGHT IN THE WAR Dawn DNX 2513 13	8 wks
22 Apr 72	OPEN UP Dawn DNX 2514 21	8 wks
7 Jul 73	● ALRIGHT ALRIGHT ALRIGHT Dawn DNS 1037 3	12 wks
10 Nov 73	WILD LOVE Dawn DNS 1051 32	5 wks
6 Apr 74	LONGLEGGED WOMAN DRESSED IN BLACK Dawn DNS 1061 13	9 wks

MUNICH MACHINE Germany, male instrumental group   8 wks

10 Dec 77	GET ON THE FUNK TRAIN Oasis 2 41	4 wks
4 Nov 78	A WHITER SHADE OF PALE Oasis OASIS 5 42	4 wks

A Whiter Shade Of Pale billed as Munich Machine introducing Chris Bennett.

David MUNROW – See EARLY MUSIC CONSORT

MUPPETS US, puppets   15 wks

28 May 77	● HALFWAY DOWN THE STAIRS Pye 7N 45698 7	8 wks
17 Dec 77	THE MUPPET SHOW MUSIC HALL EP PYE 7NX 8004 19	7 wks

Halfway Down the Stairs is sung by Jerry Nelson as Kermit the Frog's nephew, Robin. Tracks
on EP: Don't Dilly Dally On The Way/Waiting At The Church/The Boy In The
Gallery/Wotcher (Knocked 'Em In The Old Kent Road).

Lydia MURDOCK US, female vocalist   9 wks

24 Sep 83	SUPERSTAR Korova KOW 30 14	9 wks

Shirley MURDOCK US, female vocalist   2 wks

12 Apr 86	TRUTH OR DARE Elektra EKR 36 60	2 wks

Noel MURPHY Ireland, male vocalist   4 wks

27 Jun 87	MURPHY AND THE BRICKS Murphy's STACK 1 57	4 wks

Walter MURPHY and the BIG APPLE BAND US, orchestra   9 wks

10 Jul 76	A FIFTH OF BEETHOVEN Private Stock PVT 59. 28	9 wks

Anne MURRAY Canada, female vocalist   40 wks

24 Oct 70	SNOWBIRD Capitol CL 15654 23	17 wks
21 Oct 72	DESTINY Capitol CL 15734 41	4 wks
9 Dec 78	YOU NEEDED ME Capitol CL 16011 22	14 wks
21 Apr 79	I JUST FALL IN LOVE AGAIN Capitol CL 16069. 58	2 wks
19 Apr 80	DAYDREAM BELIEVER Capitol CL 16123 61	3 wks

Pauline MURRAY and the INVISIBLE GIRLS   2 wks
UK, female vocalist with male (really) vocal/instrumental group

2 Aug 80	DREAM SEQUENCE (ONE) Illusive IVE 1 67	2 wks

Ruby MURRAY UK, female vocalist   114 wks

3 Dec 54	● HEARTBEAT Columbia DB 3542 3	16 wks
28 Jan 55	★ SOFTLY SOFTLY Columbia DB 3558 1	22 wks
4 Feb 55	● HAPPY DAYS AND LONELY NIGHTS Columbia DB 3577 6	8 wks
4 Mar 55	● LET ME GO LOVER Columbia DB 3577 5	7 wks
18 Mar 55	● IF ANYONE FINDS THIS I LOVE YOU Columbia DB 3580 4	11 wks
1 Jul 55	● EVERMORE Columbia DB 3617 3	17 wks
8 Jul 55	SOFTLY SOFTLY (re-entry) Columbia DB 3558 20	1 wk
14 Oct 55	● I'LL COME WHEN YOU CALL Columbia DB 3643 6	7 wks
31 Aug 56	YOU ARE MY FIRST LOVE Columbia DB 3770. 16	4 wks
5 Oct 56	YOU ARE MY FIRST LOVE (re-entry) Columbia DB 3770 21	1 wk
12 Dec 58	REAL LOVE Columbia DB 4192 18	6 wks
5 Jun 59	● GOODBYE JIMMY GOODBYE Columbia DB 4305. 10	13 wks
9 Oct 59	GOODBYE JIMMY GOODBYE (re-entry) Columbia DB 4305 26	1 wk

Junior MURVIN Jamaica, male vocalist   9 wks

3 May 80	POLICE AND THIEVES Island WIP 6539 23	9 wks

MUSICAL YOUTH UK, male vocal/instrumental group   55 wks

25 Sep 82	★ PASS THE DUTCHIE MCA YOU 1 1	12 wks
20 Nov 82	YOUTH OF TODAY MCA YOU 2 13	9 wks
8 Jan 83	PASS THE DUTCHIE (re-entry) MCA YOU 1 65	1 wk
12 Feb 83	● NEVER GONNA GIVE YOU UP MCA YOU 3. 6	10 wks
16 Apr 83	HEARTBREAKER MCA YOU 4 44	3 wks
9 Jul 83	TELL MY WHY MCA YOU 5 33	6 wks
22 Oct 83	007 MCA YOU 6 26	6 wks
14 Jan 84	SIXTEEN MCA YOU 7 23	8 wks

See also Donna Summer.

MUSIQUE US, female vocal group   12 wks

18 Nov 78	IN THE BUSH CBS 6791 16	12 wks

MUSTAFAS – See STAIFFI and his MUSTAFAS

MXM Italy, male/female vocal/instrumental group   1 wk

2 Jun 90	NOTHING COMPARES 2 U London LON 267 68	1 wk

MY BLOODY VALENTINE   3 wks
UK, male/female vocal/instrumental group

5 May 90	SOON Creation CRE 073 41	3 wks

Tim MYCROFT – *See SOUNDS NICE*

Alicia MYERS *US, female vocalist* **3 wks**

1 Sep 84	YOU GET THE BEST FROM ME (SAY SAY SAY) *MCA MCA 914*	58	3 wks

Richard MYHILL *UK, male vocalist* **9 wks**

1 Apr 78	IT TAKES TWO TO TANGO *Mercury 6007 167*	17	9 wks

Alannah MYLES *Canada, female vocalist* **17 wks**

17 Mar 90	● BLACK VELVET *East West A 8742*..............................	2	15 wks
16 Jun 90	LOVE IS *East West A 8918*	61	2 wks

Marie MYRIAM *France, female vocalist* **4 wks**

28 May 77	L'OISEAU ET L'ENFANT *Polydor 2056 634*...................	42	4 wks

MYSTERIANS – *See ?(QUESTION MARK) and the MYSTERIANS*

MYSTI – *See CAMOUFLAGE featuring MYSTI*

MYSTIC MERLIN **9 wks**
US, male vocal/instrumental and magic group

26 Apr 80	JUST CAN'T GIVE YOU UP *Capitol CL 16133*	20	9 wks

Jimmy NAIL *UK, male vocalist* **11 wks**

27 Apr 85	● LOVE DON'T LIVE HERE ANYMORE *Virgin VS 764*........	3	11 wks

NAKED EYES *UK, male vocal/instrumental duo* **3 wks**

23 Jul 83	ALWAYS SOMETHING THERE TO REMIND ME *RCA 348*	59	3 wks

NAPOLEON XIV *US, male vocalist* **10 wks**

4 Aug 66	● THEY'RE COMING TO TAKE ME AWAY HA-HAAA! *Warner Bros WB 5831*	4	10 wks

NARADA *US, male vocalist/instrumentalist – drums* **28 wks**

23 Feb 80	TONIGHT I'M ALL RIGHT *Atlantic K 11437*	34	9 wks
26 Apr 80	● I SHOULDA LOVED YA *Atlantic K 11413*	8	9 wks
23 Apr 88	● DIVINE EMOTIONS *Reprise W 7967*	8	10 wks

First two hits credited to Narada Michael Walden.

NASH – *See CROSBY, STILLS and NASH*

Johnny NASH *US, male vocalist* **106 wks**

7 Aug 68	● HOLD ME TIGHT *Regal Zonophone RZ 3010*..............	5	16 wks
8 Jan 69	● YOU GOT SOUL *Major Minor MM 586*	6	12 wks
2 Apr 69	● CUPID *Major Minor MM 603*	6	11 wks
25 Jun 69	CUPID (re-entry) *Major Minor MM 603*	50	1 wk
1 Apr 72	STIR IT UP *CBS 7800*	13	12 wks
24 Jun 72	● I CAN SEE CLEARLY NOW *CBS 8113*....................	5	15 wks
7 Oct 72	● THERE ARE MORE QUESTIONS THAN ANSWERS *CBS 8351*	9	9 wks
14 Jun 75	★ TEARS ON MY PILLOW *CBS 3220*	1	11 wks
11 Oct 75	LET'S BE FRIENDS *CBS 3597*	42	3 wks
12 Jun 76	(WHAT A) WONDERFUL WORLD *Epic EPC 4294*..........	25	7 wks
9 Nov 85	ROCK ME BABY *2000 A.D. FED 19*	47	4 wks
15 Apr 89	I CAN SEE CLEARLY NOW (re-mix) *Epic JN 1*	54	5 wks

NASHVILLE TEENS *UK, male vocal/instrumental group* **37 wks**

9 Jul 64	● TOBACCO ROAD *Decca F 11930*	6	13 wks
22 Oct 64	● GOOGLE EYE *Decca F 12000*	10	11 wks
4 Mar 65	FIND MY WAY BACK HOME *Decca F 12089*	34	6 wks
20 May 65	THIS LITTLE BIRD *Decca F 12143*	38	4 wks
3 Feb 66	THE HARD WAY *Decca F 12316*	45	2 wks
24 Feb 66	THE HARD WAY (re-entry) *Decca F 12316*	48	1 wk

NATASHA *UK, female vocalist* **16 wks**

5 Jun 82	● IKO IKO *Towerbell TOW 22*	10	11 wks
4 Sep 82	THE BOOM BOOM ROOM *Towerbell TOW 25*..............	44	5 wks

Ultra NATÉ *US, female vocalist* **3 wks**

9 Dec 89	IT'S OVER NOW *Eternal YZ 440*	62	3 wks

NATURALS *UK, male vocal/instrumental group* **9 wks**

20 Aug 64	I SHOULD HAVE KNOWN BETTER *Parlophone R 5165*......................................	24	9 wks

David NAUGHTON *US, male vocalist* **6 wks**

25 Aug 79	MAKIN' IT *RSO 32*....................................	44	6 wks

NAZARETH *UK, male vocal/instrumental group* **75 wks**

5 May 73	● BROKEN DOWN ANGEL *Mooncrest MOON 1*................	9	11 wks
21 Jul 73	● BAD BAD BOY *Mooncrest MOON 9*	10	9 wks
13 Oct 73	THIS FLIGHT TONIGHT *Mooncrest MOON 14*	11	13 wks
23 Mar 74	SHANGHAI'D IN SHANGHAI *Mooncrest MOON 22*..........	41	4 wks
14 Jun 75	MY WHITE BICYCLE *Mooncrest MOON 47*	14	8 wks
15 Nov 75	HOLY ROLLER *Mountain TOP 3*	36	4 wks
24 Sep 77	HOT TRACKS (EP) *Mountain NAZ 1*	15	11 wks
18 Feb 78	GONE DEAD TRAIN *Mountain NAZ 002*	49	2 wks
13 May 78	PLACE IN YOUR HEART *Mountain TOP 37*	70	1 wk
27 May 78	PLACE IN YOUR HEART (re-entry) *Mountain TOP 37*	74	1 wk
27 Jan 79	MAY THE SUN SHINE *Mountain NAZ 003*	22	8 wks
28 Jul 79	STAR *Mountain TOP 45*	54	3 wks

Tracks on Hot Tracks EP: Love Hurts/This Flight Tonight/Broken Down Angel/Hair of the Dog.

Youssou N'DOUR and Peter GABRIEL **5 wks**
Senegal/UK, male vocal/instrumental duo

3 Jun 89	SHAKING THE TREE *Virgin VS 1167*........................	61	3 wks
22 Dec 90	SHAKING THE TREE (re-issue) *Virgin VS 1132* ....57†		2 wks

The re-issue of Shaking The Tree was listed with Solsbury Hill by Peter Gabriel. See also Peter Gabriel.

NED'S ATOMIC DUSTBIN — 4 wks
UK, male vocal/instrumental group

14 Jul 90	**KILL YOUR TELEVISION** *Chapter 22 CHAP 48*	53	2 wks
27 Oct 90	**UNTIL YOU FIND OUT** *Chapter 22 CHAP 52*	51	2 wks

NEIL – *See BARBRA and NEIL; Neil DIAMOND*

neil — 10 wks
UK, male vocalist

14 Jul 84	● **HOLE IN MY SHOE** *WEA YZ 10*	2	10 wks

NELSON — 3 wks
US, male vocal duo

27 Oct 90	**(CAN'T LIVE WITHOUT YOUR) LOVE AND AFFECTION** *DGC GEF 82*	54	3 wks

Bill NELSON — 12 wks
UK, male vocalist/instrumentalist - guitars and synthesizers

24 Feb 79	**FURNITURE MUSIC** *Harvest HAR 5176*	59	3 wks
5 May 79	**REVOLT INTO STYLE** *Harvest HAR 5183*	69	2 wks
5 Jul 80	**DO YOU DREAM IN COLOUR?** *Cocteau COQ 1*	52	4 wks
13 Jun 81	**YOUTH OF NATION ON FIRE** *Mercury WILL 2*	73	3 wks

Furniture Music and Revolt Into Style credited to Bill Nelson's Red Noise.

Phyllis NELSON — 21 wks
US, female vocalist

23 Feb 85	★ **MOVE CLOSER** *Carrere CAR 337*	1	21 wks

Rick NELSON *US, male vocalist* — 132 wks

21 Feb 58	**STOOD UP** *London HLP 8542*	27	1 wk
7 Mar 58	**STOOD UP (re-entry)** *London HLP 8542*	29	1 wk
22 Aug 58	● **POOR LITTLE FOOL** *London HLP 8670*	4	13 wks
7 Nov 58	**SOMEDAY** *London HLP 8732*	9	13 wks
21 Nov 58	**I GOT A FEELING** *London HLP 8732*	27	1 wk
28 Nov 58	**POOR LITTLE FOOL (re-entry)** *London HLP 8670*	28	1 wk
17 Apr 59	● **IT'S LATE** *London HLP 8817*	3	20 wks
15 May 59	**NEVER BE ANYONE ELSE BUT YOU** *London HLP 8817*	19	1 wk
5 Jun 59	**NEVER BE ANYONE ELSE BUT YOU (re-entry)** *London HLP 8817*	14	9 wks
4 Sep 59	**SWEETER THAN YOU** *London HLP 8927*	19	3 wks
11 Sep 59	**JUST A LITTLE TOO MUCH** *London HLP 8927*	11	8 wks
15 Jan 60	**I WANNA BE LOVED** *London HLP 9021*	30	1 wk
7 Jul 60	**YOUNG EMOTIONS** *London HLP 9121*	48	1 wk
1 Jun 61	● **HELLO MARY LOU/ TRAVELLIN' MAN** *London HLP 9347*	2	18 wks
16 Nov 61	**EVERLOVIN'** *London HLP 9440*	23	5 wks
29 Mar 62	**YOUNG WORLD** *London HLP 9524*	19	13 wks
30 Aug 62	**TEENAGE IDOL** *London HLP 9583*	39	4 wks
17 Jan 63	**IT'S UP TO YOU** *London HLP 9648*	22	9 wks
17 Oct 63	**FOOLS RUSH IN** *Brunswick 05895*	12	9 wks
30 Jan 64	**FOR YOU** *Brunswick 05900*	14	10 wks
21 Oct 72	**GARDEN PARTY** *MCA MU 1165*	41	4 wks

Billed as Ricky Nelson on all the hits up to and including Hello Mary Lou/ Travellin' Man.

Sandy NELSON *US, male instrumentalist - drums* — 42 wks

6 Nov 59	● **TEEN BEAT** *Top Rank JAR 197*	9	11 wks
5 Feb 60	**TEEN BEAT (re-entry)** *Top Rank JAR 197*	25	1 wk
14 Dec 61	● **LET THERE BE DRUMS** *London HLP 9466*	3	16 wks
22 Mar 62	**DRUMS ARE MY BEAT** *London HLP 9521*	30	6 wks
7 Jun 62	**DRUMMIN' UP A STORM** *London HLP 9558*	39	8 wks

Willie NELSON *US, male vocalist* — 3 wks

31 Jul 82	**ALWAYS ON MY MIND** *CBS A 2511*	49	3 wks

See also Julio Iglesias and Willie Nelson.

NENA *Germany, female/male vocal/instrumental group* — 14 wks

4 Feb 84	★ **99 RED BALLOONS** *Epic A 4074*	1	12 wks
5 May 84	**JUST A DREAM** *Epic H 3249*	70	2 wks

NERO and the GLADIATORS — 6 wks
UK, male instrumental group

23 Mar 61	**ENTRY OF THE GLADIATORS** *Decca F 11329*	50	1 wk
6 Apr 61	**ENTRY OF THE GLADIATORS (re-entry)** *Decca F 11329*	37	4 wks
27 Jul 61	**IN THE HALL OF THE MOUNTAIN KING** *Decca F 11367*	48	1 wk

NESBITT – *See MILLICAN and NESBITT*

Michael NESMITH *US, male vocalist* — 6 wks

26 Mar 77	**RIO** *Island WIP 6373*	28	6 wks

NEVADA *UK, male/female vocal/instrumental group* — 1 wk

8 Jan 83	**IN THE BLEAK MID WINTER** *Polydor POSP 203*	71	1 wk

Robbie NEVIL *US, male vocalist* — 24 wks

20 Dec 86	● **C'EST LA VIE** *Manhattan MT 14*	3	11 wks
2 May 87	**DOMINOES** *Manhattan MT 19*	26	6 wks
11 Jul 87	**WOT'S IT TO YA** *Manhattan MT 24*	43	7 wks

Aaron NEVILLE – *See Linda RONSTADT*

NEVILLE BROTHERS — 7 wks
US, male vocal/instrumental group

25 Nov 89	**WITH GOD ON OUR SIDE** *A & M AM 545*	47	6 wks
7 Jul 90	**BIRD ON A WIRE** *A & M AM 568*	72	1 wk

NEW BOHEMIANS – *See Edie BRICKELL and the NEW BOHEMIANS*

NEW EDITION *US, male vocal group* — 28 wks

16 Apr 83	★ **CANDY GIRL** *London LON 21*	1	13 wks
13 Aug 83	**POPCORN LOVE** *London LON 31*	43	5 wks
23 Feb 85	**MR TELEPHONE MAN** *MCA MCA 938*	19	9 wks
15 Apr 89	**CRUCIAL** *MCA MCA 23934*	70	1 wk

NEW GENERATION *UK, male vocal/instrumental group* — 5 wks

26 Jun 68	**SMOKEY BLUES AWAY** *Spark SRL 1007*	38	5 wks

NEW KIDS ON THE BLOCK *US, male vocal group* — 68 wks

16 Sep 89	**HANGIN' TOUGH** *CBS BLOCK 1*	52	4 wks
11 Nov 89	★ **YOU GOT IT (THE RIGHT STUFF)** *CBS BLOCK 2*	1	13 wks
6 Jan 90	★ **HANGIN' TOUGH (re-issue)** *CBS BLOCK 3*	1	9 wks
17 Mar 90	● **I'LL BE LOVING YOU (FOREVER)** *CBS BLOCK 4*	5	8 wks

Three generations of hitmakers and two generations of comic characters, the Nelson family included Thirties bandleader Ozzie, his featured singer and wife Harriet, and their son RICKY NELSON, whose twin boys hit the American Top Ten in 1990 under the name Nelson. *The Adventures Of Ozzie And Harriet* comic book, based on the popular radio show with young sons Ricky and David, was published in 1949 and 1950, while Ricky got comics of his own from 1958 to 1961. The issue shown is now worth over £50.

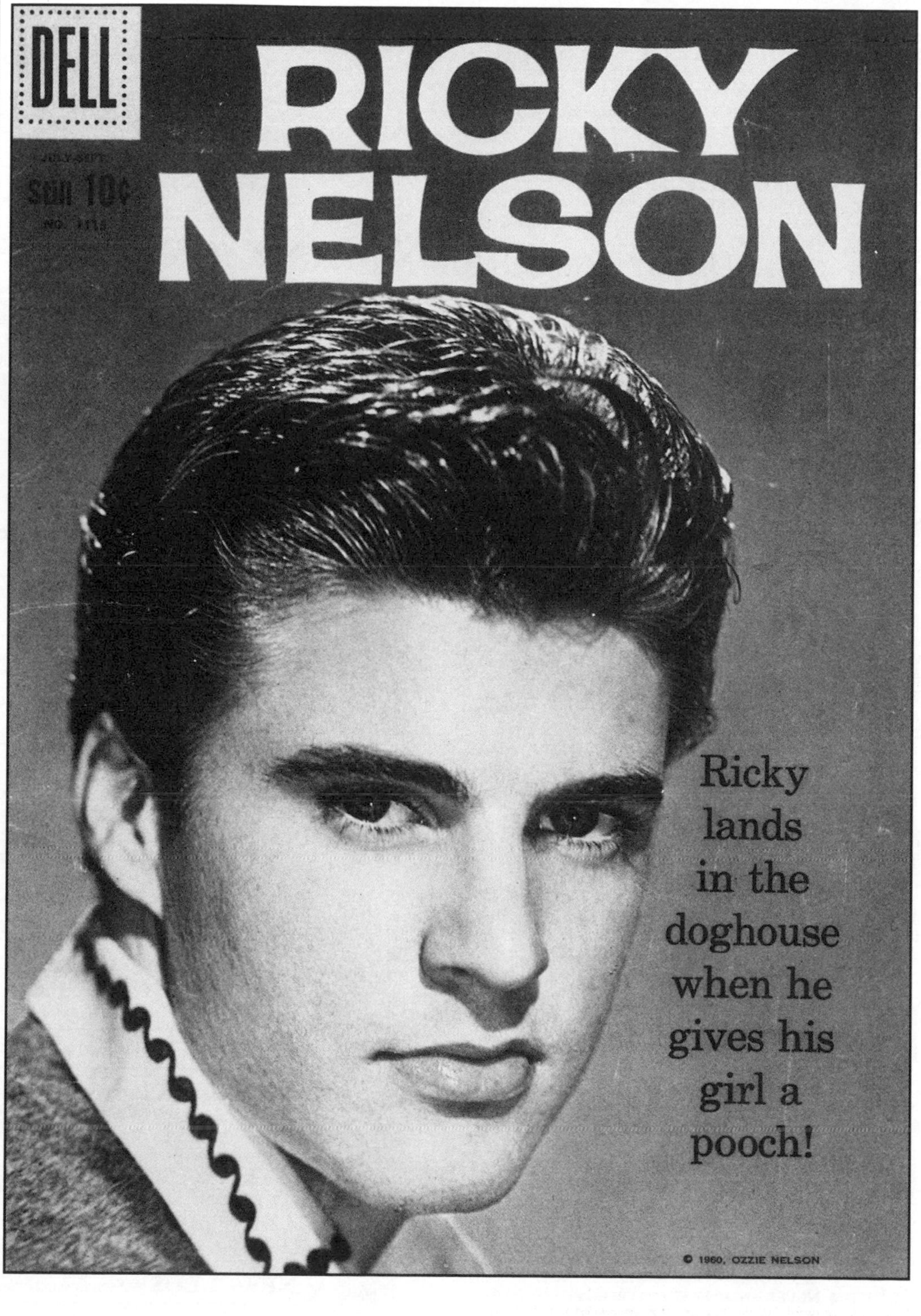

DELL

JULY-SEPT.
Sun 10¢
NO. 1115

RICKY NELSON

Ricky lands in the doghouse when he gives his girl a pooch!

© 1960, OZZIE NELSON

12 May 90 ●	COVER GIRL *CBS BLOCK 5*	4	8 wks
16 Jun 90 ●	STEP BY STEP *CBS BLOCK 6*	2	7 wks
4 Aug 90 ●	TONIGHT *CBS BLOCK 7*	3	10 wks
13 Oct 90 ●	LET'S TRY AGAIN/ DIDN'T I BLOW YOUR MIND *CBS BLOCK 8*	8	5 wks
8 Dec 90 ●	THIS ONE'S FOR THE CHILDREN *CBS BLOCK 9*	9†	4 wks

NEW MODEL ARMY *UK, male vocal/instrumental group*   **28 wks**

27 Apr 85	NO REST *EMI NMA 1*	28	5 wks
3 Aug 85	BETTER THAN THEM/ NO SENSE *EMI NMA 2*	49	2 wks
30 Nov 85	BRAVE NEW WORLD *EMI NMA 3*	57	1 wk
8 Nov 86	FIFTY-FIRST STATE *EMI NMA 4*	71	2 wks
28 Feb 87	POISON STREET *EMI NMA 5*	64	1 wk
26 Sep 87	WHITE COATS (EP) *EMI NMA 6*	50	3 wks
21 Jan 89	STUPID QUESTION *EMI NMA 7*	31	3 wks
11 Mar 89	VAGABONDS *EMI NMA 8*	37	3 wks
10 Jun 89	GREEN AND GREY *EMI NMA 9*	37	3 wks
8 Sep 90	GET ME OUT *EMI NMA 10*	34	3 wks
3 Nov 90	PURITY *EMI NMA 11*	61	2 wks

Tracks on White Coats *EP: The Charge/Chinese Whispers/My Country.*

NEW MUSIK *UK, male vocal/instrumental group*   **27 wks**

6 Oct 79	STRAIGHT LINES *GTO GT 255*	53	5 wks
19 Jan 80	LIVING BY NUMBERS *GTO GT 261*	13	8 wks
26 Apr 80	THIS WORLD OF WATER *GTO GT 268*	31	7 wks
12 Jul 80	SANCTUARY *GTO GT 275*	31	7 wks

NEW ORDER *UK, male/female vocal/instrumental group*   **131 wks**

14 Mar 81	CEREMONY *Factory FAC 33*	34	5 wks
3 Oct 81	PROCESSION/ EVERYTHING'S GONE GREEN *Factory FAC 53*	38	5 wks
22 May 82	TEMPTATION *Factory FAC 63*	29	7 wks
19 Mar 83	BLUE MONDAY *Factory FAC 73*	12	17 wks
13 Aug 83 ●	BLUE MONDAY (re-entry) *Factory FAC 73*	9	17 wks
3 Sep 83	CONFUSION *Factory FAC 93*	12	4 wks
7 Jan 84	BLUE MONDAY (2nd re-entry) *Factory FAC 73*	52	4 wks
28 Apr 84	THIEVES LIKE US *Factory FAC 103*	18	5 wks
25 May 85	THE PERFECT KISS *Factory FAC 123*	46	4 wks
9 Nov 85	SUB-CULTURE *Factory FAC 133*	63	4 wks
29 Mar 86	SHELLSHOCK *Factory FAC 143*	28	5 wks
27 Sep 86	STATE OF THE NATION *Factory FAC 153*	30	3 wks
27 Sep 86	THE PEEL SESSIONS (1ST JUNE 1982) *Strange Fruit SFPS 001*	54	1 wk
15 Nov 86	BIZARRE LOVE TRIANGLE *Factory FAC 163*	56	2 wks
1 Aug 87 ●	TRUE FAITH *Factory FAC 183/7*	4	10 wks
19 Dec 87	TOUCHED BY THE HAND OF GOD *Factory FAC 1937*	20	7 wks
7 May 88 ●	BLUE MONDAY 1988 (re-mix) *Factory FAC 737*	3	11 wks
10 Dec 88	FINE TIME *Factory FAC 2237*	11	8 wks
11 Mar 89	ROUND AND ROUND *Factory FAC 2637*	21	7 wks
9 Sep 89	RUN 2 *Factory FAC 273*	49	2 wks

Group male only on first hit. Blue Monday 1988 is a re-mixed version of the original 1983 hit which was made available on 7 inch for the first time, hence the slight difference in catalogue number. Sales for the re-mix and the original were combined from 7 May 1988 onwards when calculating its chart position. See also Englandneworder.

NEW ORLEANS JAZZMEN – *See Terry LIGHTFOOT and his NEW ORLEANS JAZZMEN*

NEW SEEKERS *UK, male/female vocal/instrumental group*   **143 wks**

17 Oct 70	WHAT HAVE THEY DONE TO MY SONG MA *Philips 6006 027*	48	1 wk
31 Oct 70	WHAT HAVE THEY DONE TO MY SONG MA (re-entry) *Philips 6006 027*	44	1 wk
10 Jul 71 ●	NEVER ENDING SONG OF LOVE *Philips 6006 125*	2	19 wks
18 Dec 71 ★	I'D LIKE TO TEACH THE WORLD TO SING *Polydor 2058 184*	1	21 wks
4 Mar 72 ●	BEG STEAL OR BORROW *Polydor 2058 201*	2	13 wks
10 Jun 72 ●	CIRCLES *Polydor 2058 242*	4	16 wks
2 Dec 72 ●	COME SOFTLY TO ME *Polydor 2058 315*	20	11 wks
24 Feb 73	PINBALL WIZARD - SEE ME FEEL ME (MEDLEY) *Polydor 2058 338*	16	8 wks
7 Apr 73	NEVERTHELESS *Polydor 2068 340*	34	5 wks
16 Jun 73	GOODBYE IS JUST ANOTHER WORD *Polydor 2058 368*	36	5 wks
24 Nov 73 ★	YOU WON'T FIND ANOTHER FOOL LIKE ME *Polydor 2058 421*	1	16 wks
9 Mar 74 ●	I GET A LITTLE SENTIMENTAL OVER YOU *Polydor 2058 439*	5	9 wks
14 Aug 76	IT'S SO NICE (TO HAVE YOU HOME) *CBS 4391*	44	4 wks
29 Jan 77	I WANNA GO BACK *CBS 4786*	25	4 wks
15 Jul 78	ANTHEM (ONE DAY IN EVERY WEEK) *CBS 6413*	21	10 wks

Come Softly To Me *has credit 'featuring Marty Kristian'. Nevertheless billed as 'by Eve Graham and the New Seekers'.*

NEW VAUDEVILLE BAND   **43 wks**
UK, male vocal/instrumental group

8 Sep 66 ●	WINCHESTER CATHEDRAL *Fontana TF 741*	4	19 wks
26 Jan 67 ●	PEEK-A-BOO *Fontana TF 784*	7	11 wks
11 May 67	FINCHLEY CENTRAL *Fontana TF 824*	11	9 wks
2 Aug 67	GREEN STREET GREEN *Fontana TF 853*	37	4 wks

Peek-A-Boo *has credit: Featuring Tristram.*

NEW WORLD *Australia, male vocal/instrumental group*   **53 wks**

27 Feb 71	ROSE GARDEN *RAK 111*	15	11 wks
3 Jul 71 ●	TOM TOM TURNAROUND *RAK 117*	6	15 wks
4 Dec 71	KARA KARA *RAK 123*	17	13 wks
13 May 72 ●	SISTER JANE *RAK 130*	9	13 wks
12 May 73	ROOF TOP SINGING *RAK 148*	50	1 wk

NEW YORK CITY *US, male vocal group*   **11 wks**

21 Jul 73	I'M DOING FINE NOW *RCA 2351*	20	11 wks

NEW YORK SKYY   **2 wks**
US, male/female vocal/instrumental group

16 Jan 82	LET'S CELEBRATE *Epic EPC A 1898*	71	1 wk
30 Jan 82	LET'S CELEBRATE (re-entry) *Epic EPC A 1898*	67	1 wk

NEWBEATS *US, male vocal group*   **22 wks**

10 Sep 64	BREAD AND BUTTER *Hickory 1269*	15	9 wks
23 Oct 71 ●	RUN BABY RUN *London HL 10341*	10	13 wks

Booker NEWBURY III *US, male vocalist*   **11 wks**

28 May 83 ●	LOVE TOWN *Polydor POSP 613*	6	8 wks
8 Oct 83	TEDDY BEAR *Polydor POSP 637*	44	3 wks

Mickey NEWBURY *US, male vocalist*   **5 wks**

1 Jul 72	AMERICAN TRILOGY *Elektra K 12047*	42	5 wks

NEWCLEUS *US, male vocal/instrumental group*   **6 wks**

3 Sep 83	JAM ON REVENGE (THE WIKKI WIKKI SONG) *Beckett BKS 8*	44	6 wks

Anthony NEWLEY UK, male vocalist — 129 wks

1 May 59	●	I'VE WAITED SO LONG Decca F 11127	3	15 wks
8 May 59		IDLE ON PARADE (EP) Decca DFE 6566	13	4 wks
12 Jun 59	●	PERSONALITY Decca F 11142	6	12 wks
15 Jan 60	★	WHY Decca F 11194	1	17 wks
24 Mar 60	★	DO YOU MIND Decca F 11220	1	15 wks
14 Jul 60	●	IF SHE SHOULD COME TO YOU Decca F 11254	6	15 wks
24 Nov 60	●	STRAWBERY FAIR Decca F 11295	3	11 wks
16 Mar 61	●	AND THE HEAVENS CRIED Decca F 11331	6	12 wks
15 Jun 61		POP GOES THE WEASEL/ BEE BOM Decca F 11362	12	9 wks
3 Aug 61		WHAT KIND OF FOOL AM I? Decca F 11376	36	8 wks
25 Jan 62		D-DARLING Decca F 11419	25	6 wks
26 Jul 62		THAT NOISE Decca F 11486	34	5 wks

Bee Bom *only listed together with* Pop Goes The Weasel *for weeks of 15 and 22 June 61.*
Tracks on Idle On Parade *EP: I've Waited So Long/Idle Rock-A-Boogie/Idle On Parade/Saturday Night Rock-A-Boogie.*

Alfred NEWMAN – *See VARIOUS ARTISTS (Carousel Soundtrack)*

Brad NEWMAN UK, male vocalist — 1 wk

| 22 Feb 62 | SOMEBODY TO LOVE Fontana H 357 | 47 | 1 wk |

Dave NEWMAN UK, male vocalist — 6 wks

| 15 Apr 72 | THE LION SLEEPS TONIGHT Pye 7N 45134 | 48 | 1 wk |
| 29 Apr 72 | THE LION SLEEPS TONIGHT (re-entry) Pye 7N 45134 | 34 | 5 wks |

NEWS – *See Huey LEWIS and the NEWS*

NEWS US, male vocal/instrumental group — 3 wks

| 29 Aug 81 | AUDIO VIDEO George GEORGE 1 | 52 | 3 wks |

Juice NEWTON US, female vocalist — 6 wks

| 2 May 81 | ANGEL OF THE MORNING Capitol CL 16189 | 43 | 6 wks |

Olivia NEWTON-JOHN UK, female vocalist — 145 wks

20 Mar 71	●	IF NOT FOR YOU Pye International 7N 25543	7	11 wks
23 Oct 71	●	BANKS OF THE OHIO Pye International 7N 25568	6	17 wks
11 Mar 72		WHAT IS LIFE Pye International 7N 25575	16	8 wks
13 Jan 73		TAKE ME HOME COUNTRY ROADS Pye International 7N 25599	15	13 wks
16 Mar 74		LONG LIVE LOVE Pye International 7N 25638	11	8 wks
12 Oct 74		I HONESTLY LOVE YOU EMI 2216	22	6 wks
11 Jun 77	●	SAM EMI 2616	6	11 wks
4 Nov 78	●	HOPELESSLY DEVOTED TO YOU RSO 17	2	11 wks
16 Dec 78	●	A LITTLE MORE LOVE EMI 2879	4	12 wks
30 Jun 79		DEEPER THAN THE NIGHT EMI 2954	64	3 wks
23 Aug 80		MAGIC Jet 196	32	7 wks
10 Oct 81	●	PHYSICAL EMI 5234	7	16 wks
16 Jan 82		LANDSLIDE EMI 5257	18	9 wks
17 Apr 82		MAKE A MOVE ON ME EMI 5291	43	3 wks
23 Oct 82		HEART ATTACK EMI 5347	46	4 wks
15 Jan 83		I HONESTLY LOVE YOU (re-issue) EMI 5360	52	4 wks
12 Nov 83		TWIST OF FATE EMI 5438	57	2 wks

See also Olivia Newton-John and Electric Light Orchestra; Olivia Newton-John and Cliff Richard; John Travolta and Olivia Newton-John.

Olivia NEWTON-JOHN and ELECTRIC LIGHT ORCHESTRA — 11 wks
UK, female vocalist, male vocal/instrumental group

| 21 Jun 80 | ★ | XANADU Jet 185 | 1 | 11 wks |

See also Olivia Newton-John; Electric Light Orchestra.

Olivia NEWTON-JOHN and Cliff RICHARD — 7 wks
UK, female/male vocal duo

| 25 Oct 80 | SUDDENLY Jet 7002 | 15 | 7 wks |

See also Olivia Newton-John; Cliff Richard.

NICE UK, male instrumental group — 15 wks

| 10 Jul 68 | AMERICA Immediate IM 068 | 21 | 15 wks |

Paul NICHOLAS UK, male vocalist — 31 wks

17 Apr 76		REGGAE LIKE IT USED TO BE RSO 2090 185	17	8 wks
9 Oct 76	●	DANCING WITH THE CAPTAIN RSO 2090 206	8	9 wks
4 Dec 76	●	GRANDMA'S PARTY RSO 2090 216	9	11 wks
9 Jul 77		HEAVEN ON THE 7TH FLOOR RSO 2090 249	40	3 wks

Sue NICHOLLS UK, female vocalist — 8 wks

| 3 Jul 68 | WHERE WILL YOU BE Pye 7N 17565 | 17 | 8 wks |

Stevie NICKS US, female vocalist — 17 wks

25 Jan 86	I CAN'T WAIT Parlophone R 6110	54	4 wks
29 Mar 86	TALK TO ME Parlophone R 6124	68	2 wks
6 May 89	ROOMS ON FIRE EMI EM 90	16	7 wks
12 Aug 89	LONG WAY TO GO EMI EM 97	60	2 wks
11 Nov 89	WHOLE LOTTA TROUBLE EMI EM 114	62	2 wks

See also Stevie Nicks with Tom Petty and the Heartbreakers.

Stevie NICKS with Tom PETTY and the HEARTBREAKERS — 4 wks
US, female vocalist with male vocal/instrumental group

| 15 Aug 81 | STOP DRAGGIN' MY HEART AROUND WEA K 79231 | 50 | 4 wks |

See also Stevie Nicks; Tom Petty.

NICOLE Germany, female vocalist — 10 wks

| 8 May 82 | ★ | A LITTLE PEACE CBS A 2365 | 1 | 9 wks |
| 21 Aug 82 | | GIVE ME MORE TIME CBS A 2467 | 75 | 1 wk |

NICOLE with Timmy THOMAS — 7 wks
US, female/male vocal duo

| 28 Dec 85 | NEW YORK EYES Portrait A 6805 | 41 | 7 wks |

See also Timmy Thomas.

Maxine NIGHTINGALE UK, female vocalist — 16 wks

| 1 Nov 75 | ● | RIGHT BACK WHERE WE STARTED FROM United Artists UP 36015 | 8 | 8 wks |
| 12 Mar 77 | | LOVE HIT ME United Artists UP 36215 | 11 | 8 wks |

NIGHTINGALES – *See VINDALOO SUMMER SPECIAL*

NIGHTMARES ON WAX *UK, male instrumental group*   **5 wks**

27 Oct 90	AFTERMATH/ I'M FOR REAL *Warp WAP 6*	38	5 wks

NILSSON *US, male vocalist*   **51 wks**

27 Sep 69	EVERYBODY'S TALKIN' *RCA 1876*	50	1 wk
11 Oct 69	EVERYBODY'S TALKIN' (re-entry) *RCA 1876*	23	9 wks
14 Mar 70	EVERYBODY'S TALKIN' (2nd re-entry) *RCA 1876*	39	5 wks
5 Feb 72 ★	WITHOUT YOU *RCA 2165*	1	20 wks
3 Jun 72	COCONUT *RCA 2214*	42	5 wks
16 Oct 76	WITHOUT YOU (re-issue) *RCA 2733*	22	8 wks
20 Aug 77	ALL I THINK ABOUT IS YOU *RCA PB 9104*	43	3 wks

NINA and FREDERICK *Denmark, female/male vocal duo*   **29 wks**

18 Dec 59	MARY'S BOY CHILD *Columbia DB 4375*	26	1 wk
10 Mar 60	LISTEN TO THE OCEAN *Columbia DB 4332*	47	1 wk
7 Apr 60	LISTEN TO THE OCEAN (re-entry) *Columbia DB 4332*	46	1 wk
17 Nov 60 ●	LITTLE DONKEY *Columbia DB 4536*	3	10 wks
28 Sep 61	LONGTIME BOY *Columbia DB 4703*	43	3 wks
5 Oct 61	SUCU SUCU *Columbia DB 4632*	23	13 wks

999 *UK, male vocal/instrumental group*   **13 wks**

25 Nov 78	HOMICIDE *United Artists UP 36467*	40	3 wks
27 Oct 79	FOUND OUT TOO LATE *Radar ADA 46*	69	2 wks
16 May 81	OBSESSED *Albion ION 1011*	71	1 wk
18 Jul 81	LIL RED RIDING HOOD *Albion ION 1017*	59	3 wks
14 Nov 81	INDIAN RESERVATION *Albion ION 1023*	51	4 wks

9.9 *US, female/male vocal group*   **3 wks**

6 Jul 85	ALL OF ME FOR ALL OF YOU *RCA PB 49951*	53	3 wks

1910 FRUITGUM CO. *US, male vocal/instrumental group*   **16 wks**

20 Mar 68 ●	SIMON SAYS *Pye International 7N 25447*	2	16 wks

1927 *Australia, male vocal/instrumental group*   **6 wks**

22 Apr 89	THAT'S WHEN I THINK OF YOU *WEA YZ 351*	46	6 wks

NIRVANA *UK/Ireland, male vocal/instrumental duo*   **6 wks**

15 May 68	RAINBOW CHASER *Island WIP 6029*	34	6 wks

NITRO DELUXE *US, male multi-instrumentalist*   **16 wks**

14 Feb 87	THIS BRUTAL HOUSE *Cooltempo COOL 142*	47	7 wks
13 Jun 87	THIS BRUTAL HOUSE (re-entry) *Cooltempo COOL 142*	62	4 wks
6 Feb 88	LET'S GET BRUTAL *Cooltempo COOL 142*	24	5 wks

Let's Get Brutal *is a re-mixed version of* This Brutal House.

N-JOI *UK, male instrumental group*   **5 wks**

27 Oct 90	ANTHEM *deConstruction PB 44041*	45	5 wks

NO DICE *UK, male vocal/instrumental group*   **2 wks**

5 May 79	COME DANCING *EMI 2927*	65	2 wks

NO SWEAT *US, male vocal/instrumental group*   **4 wks**

13 Oct 90	HEART AND SOUL *London LON 274*	64	4 wks

NO WAY JOSE *US, male instrumental group*   **6 wks**

3 Aug 85	TEQUILA *Fourth & Broadway BRW 28*	47	6 wks

NOLANS *Ireland, female vocal group*   **89 wks**

6 Oct 79	SPIRIT BODY AND SOUL *Epic EPC 7796*	34	6 wks
22 Dec 79 ●	I'M IN THE MOOD FOR DANCING *Epic EPC 8068*	3	15 wks
12 Apr 80	DON'T MAKE WAVES *Epic EPC 8349*	12	11 wks
13 Sep 80 ●	GOTTA PULL MYSELF TOGETHER *Epic EPC 8878*	9	13 wks
6 Dec 80	WHO'S GONNA ROCK YOU *Epic EPC 9325*	12	11 wks
14 Mar 81 ●	ATTENTION TO ME *Epic EPC 9571*	9	13 wks
15 Aug 81	CHEMISTRY *Epic EPC A1485*	15	8 wks
20 Feb 82	DON'T LOVE ME TOO HARD *Epic EPC A 1927*	14	12 wks

First hit billed as Nolan Sisters.

Peter NOONE *UK, male vocalist*   **9 wks**

22 May 71	OH YOU PRETTY THING *RAK 114*	12	9 wks

See also Herman's Hermits.

Chris NORMAN – *See Suzi QUATRO and Chris NORMAN*

NORTHSIDE *UK, male vocal/instrumental group*   **8 wks**

9 Jun 90	SHALL WE TAKE A TRIP/ MOODY PLACES *Factory FAC 268*	50	5 wks
3 Nov 90	MY RISING STAR *Factory FAC 2987*	32	3 wks

Freddie NOTES and the RUDIES   **2 wks**
Jamaica, male vocal/instrumental group

10 Oct 70	MONTEGO BAY *Trojan TR 7791*	45	2 wks

NOTTINGHAM FOREST F.C. and PAPER   **6 wks**
LACE *UK, football team vocalists and male vocal/instrumental group*

4 Mar 78	WE'VE GOT THE WHOLE WORLD IN OUR HANDS *Warner Bros. K 17110*	24	6 wks

See also Paper Lace.

Nancy NOVA *UK, female vocalist*   **2 wks**

4 Sep 82	NO NO NO *EMI 5328*	63	2 wks

N.T. GANG *Germany, male vocal/instrumental group*   **1 wk**

2 Apr 88	WAM BAM *Cooltempo COOL 163*	71	1 wk

NU SHOOZ *US, male/female vocal duo*   **17 wks**

24 May 86 ●	I CAN'T WAIT *Atlantic A 9446*	2	14 wks
26 Jul 86	POINT OF NO RETURN *Atlantic A 9392*	48	3 wks

Lining up before a five night stand at the Universal Amphitheatre in Los Angeles are the five member of NEW KIDS ON THE BLOCK (left to right: Jordan Knight, Danny Wood, Donnie Wahlberg, Joe McIntyre, and Jonathan Knight).

Bottom Left: SINEAD O'CONNOR arrives at Los Angeles International Airport for the 1990 MTV Awards, where she won multiple prizes for 'Nothing Compares 2 U'.

Don't criticize the dance technique of ALEXANDER O'NEAL.

Below: Did DES O'CONNOR get this scarf on the Kings Road?

NUANCE featuring Vikki LOVE
US, male/female vocal/instrumental group　　　3 wks

| 19 Jan 85 | LOVERIDE *Fourth and Broadway BRW 20* | 59 | 3 wks |

NUFF JUICE – *See D MOB*

Gary NUMAN
UK, male vocalist　　　131 wks

19 May 79	★ ARE 'FRIENDS' ELECTRIC *Beggars Banquet BEG 18*	1	16 wks
1 Sep 79	★ CARS *Beggars Banquet BEG 23*	1	11 wks
24 Nov 79	● COMPLEX *Beggars Banquet BEG 29*	6	9 wks
24 May 80	● WE ARE GLASS *Beggars Banquet BEG 35*	5	7 wks
30 Aug 80	● I DIE: YOU DIE *Beggars Banquet BEG 46*	6	7 wks
20 Dec 80	THIS WRECKAGE *Beggars Banquet BEG 50*	20	7 wks
29 Aug 81	● SHE'S GOT CLAWS *Beggars Banquet BEG 62*	6	6 wks
5 Dec 81	LOVE NEEDS NO DISGUISE *Beggars Banquet BEG 68*	33	7 wks
6 Mar 82	MUSIC FOR CHAMELEONS *Beggars Banquet BEG 70*	19	7 wks
19 Jun 82	● WE TAKE MYSTERY (TO BED) *Beggars Banquet BEG 77*	9	4 wks
28 Aug 82	WHITE BOYS AND HEROES *Beggars Banquet BEG 81*	20	4 wks
3 Sep 83	WARRIORS *Beggars Banquet BEG 95*	20	5 wks
22 Oct 83	SISTER SURPRISE *Beggars Banquet BEG 101*	32	5 wks
3 Nov 84	BERSERKER *Numa NU 4*	32	5 wks
22 Dec 84	MY DYING MACHINE *Numa NU 6*	66	1 wk
25 May 85	THE LIVE EP *Numa NUM 7*	27	4 wks
10 Aug 85	YOUR FASCINATION *Numa NU 9*	46	5 wks
21 Sep 85	CALL OUT THE DOGS *Numa NU 11*	49	2 wks
16 Nov 85	MIRACLES *Numa NU 13*	49	3 wks
19 Apr 86	THIS IS LOVE *Numa NU 16*	28	3 wks
28 Jun 86	I CAN'T STOP *Numa NU 17*	27	4 wks
6 Dec 86	I STILL REMEMBER *Numa NU 21*	74	1 wk
19 Sep 87	CARS (E REG MODEL)/ ARE 'FRIENDS' ELECTRIC (re-mix) *Beggars Banquet BEG 199*	16	7 wks
1 Oct 88	NEW ANGER *Illegal ILS 1003*	46	2 wks
3 Dec 88	AMERICA *Illegal ILS 1004*	49	1 wk

Are 'Friends' Electric *by Gary Numan under the group name Tubeway Army. Love Needs No Disguise credited to Gary Numan and Dramatis. The Live EP tracks are: Are 'Friends' Electric/Berserker/Cars/We Are Glass. See also Sharpe and Numan; Radio Heart featuring Gary Numan; Dramatis.*

Bobby NUNN
US, male vocalist/multi-instrumentalist　　　3 wks

| 4 Feb 84 | DON'T KNOCK IT (UNTIL YOU TRY IT) *Motown TMG 1323* | 65 | 3 wks |

N.W.A.
US, male rap group　　　13 wks

9 Sep 89	EXPRESS YOURSELF *Fourth & Broadway BRW 144*	50	4 wks
26 May 90	EXPRESS YOURSELF (re-entry) *Fourth & Broadway BRW 144*	26	5 wks
1 Sep 90	GANGSTA, GANGSTA *Fourth & Broadway BRW 191*	70	1 wk
10 Nov 90	100 MILES AND RUNNIN' *Fourth & Broadway BRW 200*	38	3 wks

Phil OAKEY – *See Georgio MORODER and Phil OAKEY*

John OATES – *See Daryl HALL and John OATES*

OBERNKIRCHEN CHILDREN'S CHOIR
Germany, children's choir　　　26 wks

| 22 Jan 54 | ● HAPPY WANDERER *Parlophone R 3799* | 2 | 23 wks |
| 9 Jul 54 | ● HAPPY WANDERER (re-entry) *Parlophone R 3799* | 8 | 3 wks |

Dermot O'BRIEN
Ireland, male vocalist　　　2 wks

| 20 Oct 66 | THE MERRY PLOUGHBOY *Envoy ENV 016* | 46 | 1 wk |
| 3 Nov 66 | THE MERRY PLOUGHBOY (re-entry) *Envoy ENV 016* | 50 | 1 wk |

Billy OCEAN
UK, male vocalist　　　151 wks

21 Feb 76	● LOVE REALLY HURTS WITHOUT YOU *GTO GT 52*	2	10 wks
10 Jul 76	L.O.D. (LOVE ON DELIVERY) *GTO GT 62*	19	8 wks
13 Nov 76	STOP ME (IF YOU'VE HEARD IT ALL BEFORE) *GTO GT 72*	12	11 wks
19 Mar 77	● RED LIGHT SPELLS DANGER *GTO GT 85*	2	10 wks
1 Sep 79	AMERICAN HEARTS *GTO GT 244*	54	5 wks
19 Jan 80	ARE YOU READY *GTO GT 259*	42	7 wks
13 Oct 84	● CARIBBEAN QUEEN (NO MORE LOVE ON THE RUN) *Jive Jive 77*	6	14 wks
19 Jan 85	LOVERBOY *Jive JIVE 80*	15	10 wks
11 May 85	● SUDDENLY *Jive JIVE 90*	4	14 wks
17 Aug 85	MYSTERY LADY *Jive JIVE 98*	49	4 wks
25 Jan 86	★ WHEN THE GOING GETS TOUGH, THE TOUGH GET GOING *Jive JIVE 114*	1	13 wks
12 Apr 86	THERE'LL BE SAD SONGS (TO MAKE YOU CRY) *Jive JIVE 117*	12	13 wks
9 Aug 86	LOVE ZONE *Jive JIVE 124*	49	4 wks
11 Oct 86	BITTERSWEET *Jive JIVE 133*	44	4 wks
10 Jan 87	LOVE IS FOREVER *Jive JIVE 134*	34	7 wks
6 Feb 88	● GET OUTTA MY DREAMS GET INTO MY CAR *Jive BOS 1*	3	11 wks
7 May 88	CALYPSO CRAZY *Jive BOS 2*	35	4 wks
6 Aug 88	THE COLOUR OF LOVE *Jive BOS 3*	65	3 wks

Des O'CONNOR
UK, male vocalist　　　107 wks

1 Nov 67	● CARELESS HANDS *Columbia DB 8275*	6	17 wks
8 May 68	★ I PRETEND *Columbia DB 8397*	1	36 wks
20 Nov 68	1-2-3 O'LEARY *Columbia DB 8492*	4	11 wks
7 May 69	DICK-A-DUM-DUM (KING'S ROAD) *Columbia DB 8566*	14	10 wks
29 Nov 69	LONELINESS *Columbia DB 8632*	18	11 wks
14 Mar 70	I'LL GO ON HOPING *Columbia DB 8661*	30	7 wks
26 Sep 70	THE TIPS OF MY FINGERS *Columbia DB 8713*	15	15 wks

See also Roger Whittaker and Des O'Connor.

Hazel O'CONNOR
UK, female vocalist　　　46 wks

16 Aug 80	● EIGHTH DAY *A & M AMS 7553*	5	11 wks
25 Oct 80	GIVE ME AN INCH *A & M AMS 7569*	41	4 wks
21 Mar 81	● D-DAYS *Albion ION 1009*	10	9 wks
23 May 81	● WILL YOU *A & M AMS 8131*	8	10 wks
1 Aug 81	(COVER PLUS) WE'RE ALL GROWN UP *Albion ION 1018*	41	6 wks
3 Oct 81	HANGING AROUND *Albion ION 1022*	45	3 wks
23 Jan 82	CALLS THE TUNE *A & M AMS 8203*	60	3 wks

Sinead O'CONNOR
Ireland, female vocalist　　　32 wks

16 Jan 88	MANDINKA *Ensign ENY 611*	17	9 wks
20 Jan 90	★ NOTHING COMPARES 2 U *Ensign ENY 630*	1	14 wks
21 Jul 90	THE EMPEROR'S NEW CLOTHES *Ensign ENY 633*	31	5 wks
20 Oct 90	THREE BABIES *Ensign ENY 635*	42	4 wks

Alan O'DAY
US, male vocalist　　　3 wks

| 2 Jul 77 | UNDERCOVER ANGEL *Atlantic K 10926* | 43 | 3 wks |

ODETTA – *See Harry BELAFONTE and ODETTA*

ODYSSEY US, male/female vocal group — 82 wks

24 Dec 77	● NATIVE NEW YORKER RCA PC 1129	5	11 wks
21 Jun 80	★ USE IT UP AND WEAR IT OUT RCA PB 1962	1	12 wks
13 Sep 80	● IF YOU'RE LOOKIN' FOR A WAY OUT RCA 5	6	15 wks
17 Jan 81	HANG TOGETHER RCA 23	36	7 wks
30 May 81	● GOING BACK TO MY ROOTS RCA 85	4	12 wks
19 Sep 81	IT WILL BE ALRIGHT RCA 128	43	5 wks
12 Jun 82	● INSIDE OUT RCA 226	3	11 wks
11 Sep 82	MAGIC TOUCH RCA 275	41	5 wks
17 Aug 85	(JOY) I KNOW IT Mirror BUTCH 12	51	4 wks

Esther and Abi OFARIM Israel, female/male vocal duo — 22 wks

14 Feb 68	★ CINDERELLA ROCKEFELLA Philips BF 1640	1	13 wks
19 Jun 68	ONE MORE DANCE Philips BF 1678	13	9 wks

OFF-SHORE Germany, male production duo — 2 wks

22 Dec 90	I CAN'T TAKE THE POWER CBS 6565707	51†	2 wks

OH WELL Germany, male producer — 7 wks

14 Oct 89	OH WELL Parlophone R 6236	28	6 wks
3 Mar 90	RADAR LOVE Parlophone R 6244	65	1 wk

OHIO EXPRESS US, male vocal/instrumental group — 15 wks

5 Jun 68	● YUMMY YUMMY YUMMY Pye International 7N 25459	5	15 wks

OHIO PLAYERS US, male vocal/instrumental group — 4 wks

10 Jul 76	WHO'D SHE COO Mercury PLAY 001	43	4 wks

O'JAYS US, male vocal group — 72 wks

23 Sep 72	BACK STABBERS CBS 8270	14	9 wks
3 Mar 73	● LOVE TRAIN CBS 1181	9	13 wks
31 Jan 76	I LOVE MUSIC Philadelphia International PIR 3879	13	9 wks
12 Feb 77	DARLIN' DARLIN' BABY (SWEET, TENDER, LOVE) Philadelphia International PIR 4834	24	6 wks
8 Apr 78	I LOVE MUSIC (re-issue) Philadelphia International PIR 6093	36	3 wks
17 Jun 78	USED TA BE MY GIRL Philadelphia International PIR 6332	12	12 wks
30 Sep 78	BRANDY Philadelphia International PIR 6658	21	9 wks
29 Sep 79	SING A HAPPY SONG Philadelphia International PIR 7825	39	6 wks
30 Jul 83	PUT OUR HEADS TOGETHER Philadelphia International A 3642	45	5 wks

See also Philadelphia International All-Stars.

Mike OLDFIELD UK, male multi-instrumentalist/vocalist — 92 wks

13 Jul 74	MIKE OLDFIELD'S SINGLE (THEME FROM TUBULAR BELLS) Virgin VS 101	31	6 wks
20 Dec 75	● IN DULCE JUBILO/ ON HORSEBACK Virgin VS 131	4	10 wks
27 Nov 76	● PORTSMOUTH Virgin VS 163	3	12 wks
23 Dec 78	TAKE 4 (EP) Virgin VS 238	72	3 wks
21 Apr 79	GUILTY Virgin VS 245	22	8 wks
8 Dec 79	BLUE PETER Virgin VS 317	19	9 wks
20 Mar 82	FIVE MILES OUT Virgin VS 464	43	5 wks
12 Jun 82	FAMILY MAN Virgin VS 489	45	6 wks
28 May 83	● MOONLIGHT SHADOW Virgin VS 586	4	17 wks
14 Jan 84	CRIME OF PASSION Virgin VS 648	61	3 wks
30 Jun 84	TO FRANCE Virgin VS 686	48	7 wks
14 Dec 85	PICTURES IN THE DARK Virgin VS 836	50	6 wks

Tracks on Take 4 EP: Portsmouth/In Dulce Jubilo/Wrekorder Wrondo/Sailors Hornpipe.
Pictures In The Dark features Aled Jones, Anita Hegerland and Barry Palmer. Hits from Five Miles Out to To France feature Maggie Reilly.

Sally OLDFIELD UK, female vocalist — 13 wks

9 Dec 78	MIRRORS Bronze BRO 66	19	13 wks

OLIVER US, male vocalist — 18 wks

9 Aug 69	● GOOD MORNING STARSHINE CBS 4435	6	16 wks
27 Dec 69	GOOD MORNING STARSHINE (re-entry) CBS 4435	39	2 wks

Laurence OLIVIER – See Paul HARDCASTLE

OLLIE and JERRY US, male vocal duo — 14 wks

23 Jun 84	● BREAKIN'...THERE'S NO STOPPING US Polydor POSP 690	5	11 wks
9 Mar 85	ELECTRIC BOOGALOO Polydor POSP 730	57	3 wks

OLYMPIC ORCHESTRA UK, orchestra — 15 wks

1 Oct 83	REILLY Red Bus RBUS 82	26	15 wks

OLYMPIC RUNNERS UK, male vocal/instrumental group — 21 wks

13 May 78	WHATEVER IT TAKES RCA PC 5078	61	2 wks
14 Oct 78	GET IT WHILE YOU CAN Polydor RUN 7	35	6 wks
20 Jan 79	SIR DANCEALOT Polydor POSP 17	35	6 wks
28 Jul 79	THE BITCH Polydor POSP 63	37	7 wks

OLYMPICS US, male vocal group — 9 wks

3 Oct 58	WESTERN MOVIES HMV POP 528	12	8 wks
19 Jan 61	I WISH I COULD SHIMMY LIKE MY SISTER KATE Vogue V 9174	45	1 wk

ONE HUNDRED TON AND A FEATHER UK, male vocalist, Jonathan King under false name — 9 wks

26 Jun 76	● IT ONLY TAKES A MINUTE UK 135	9	9 wks

See also Jonathan King.

ONE THE JUGGLER UK, male vocal/instrumental group — 1 wk

19 Feb 83	PASSION KILLER Regard RG 107	71	1 wk

ONE 2 MANY Norway, male/female vocal/instrumental group — 11 wks

12 Nov 88	DOWNTOWN A &M AM 476	65	4 wks
3 Jun 89	DOWNTOWN (re-issue) A &M AM 456	43	7 wks

ONE WAY featuring Al HUDSON US, male/female vocal/instrumental group — 8 wks

8 Dec 79	MUSIC MCA 542	56	6 wks
29 Jun 85	LET'S TALK MCA 972	64	2 wks

See also Al Hudson and the Partners.

Alexander O'NEAL US, male vocalist — 72 wks

15 Feb 86	IF YOU WERE HERE TONIGHT Tabu A 6391	13	10 wks
5 Apr 86	A BROKEN HEART CAN MEND Tabu A 6244	53	4 wks

6 Jun 87	FAKE *Tabu 650891 7*	33	6 wks
31 Oct 87	● CRITICIZE *Tabu 651211 7*	4	14 wks
6 Feb 88	NEVER KNEW LOVE LIKE THIS *Tabu 651382 7*	26	7 wks
28 May 88	THE LOVERS *Tabu 651595 7*	28	4 wks
23 Jul 88	(WHAT CAN I SAY) TO MAKE YOU LOVE ME *Tabu 652852 7*	27	5 wks
24 Sep 88	FAKE '88 (re-mix) *Tabu 652949 7*	16	7 wks
10 Dec 88	CHRISTMAS SONG/ THANK YOU FOR A GOOD YEAR *Tabu 653182 7*	30	5 wks
25 Feb 89	HEARSAY '89 *Tabu 654466 7*	56	2 wks
2 Sep 89	SUNSHINE *Tabu 655191 7*	72	1 wk
9 Dec 89	HITMIX (OFFICIAL BOOTLEG MEGA-MIX) *Tabu 655504 7*	19	7 wks

Never Knew Love Like This *features Cherelle. See also Cherelle with Alexander O'Neal; Cherelle.*

Yoko ONO *Japan, female vocalist*   5 wks

| 28 Feb 81 | WALKING ON THIN ICE *Geffen K 79202* | 35 | 5 wks |

See also John Lennon.

ONSLAUGHT *UK, male vocal/instrumental group*   3 wks

| 6 May 89 | LET THERE BE ROCK *London LON 224* | 50 | 3 wks |

OPUS *Austria, male vocal/instrumental group*   15 wks

| 15 Jun 85 | ● LIVE IS LIFE *Polydor POSP 743* | 6 | 15 wks |

ORANGE JUICE *UK, male vocal/instrumental group*   34 wks

7 Nov 81	L.O.V.E...LOVE *Polydor POSP 357*	65	2 wks
30 Jan 82	FELICITY *Polydor POSP 386*	63	3 wks
21 Aug 82	TWO HEARTS TOGETHER/ HOKOYO *Polydor POSP 470*	60	2 wks
23 Oct 82	I CAN'T HELP MYSELF *Polydor POSP 522*	42	3 wks
19 Feb 83	● RIP IT UP *Polydor POSP 547*	8	11 wks
4 Jun 83	FLESH OF MY FLESH *Polydor OJ 4*	41	6 wks
25 Feb 84	BRIDGE *Polydor OJ 5*	67	2 wks
12 May 84	WHAT PRESENCE? *Polydor OJ 6*	47	4 wks
27 Oct 84	LEAN PERIOD *Polydor OJ 7*	74	1 wk

Roy ORBISON *US, male vocalist*   324 wks

28 Jul 60	ONLY THE LONELY *London HLU 9149*	36	1 wk
11 Aug 60	★ ONLY THE LONELY (re-entry) *London HLU 9149*	1	23 wks
27 Oct 60	BLUE ANGEL *London HLU 9207*	11	16 wks
25 May 61	● RUNNING SCARED *London HLU 9342*	9	15 wks
21 Sep 61	CRYIN' *London HLU 9405*	25	9 wks
8 Mar 62	● DREAM BABY *London HLU 9511*	2	14 wks
28 Jun 62	THE CROWD *London HLU 9561*	40	4 wks
8 Nov 62	WORKIN' FOR THE MAN *London HLU 9607*	50	1 wk
28 Feb 63	● IN DREAMS *London HLU 9676*	6	23 wks
30 May 63	FALLING *London HLU 9727*	9	11 wks
19 Sep 63	● BLUE BAYOU/ MEAN WOMAN BLUES *London HLU 9777*	3	19 wks
20 Feb 64	BORNE ON THE WIND *London HLU 9845*	15	10 wks
30 Apr 64	★ IT'S OVER *London HLU 9882*	1	18 wks
10 Sep 64	★ OH PRETTY WOMAN *London HLU 9919*	1	18 wks
19 Nov 64	● PRETTY PAPER *London HLU 9930*	6	11 wks
11 Feb 65	GOODNIGHT *London HLU 9951*	14	9 wks
22 Jul 65	(SAY) YOU'RE MY GIRL *London HLU 9978*	23	8 wks
9 Sep 65	RIDE AWAY *London HLU 9986*	34	6 wks
4 Nov 65	CRAWLIN' BACK *London HLU 10000*	19	9 wks
27 Jan 66	BREAKIN' UP IS BREAKIN' MY HEART *London HL 10015*	22	6 wks
7 Apr 66	TWINKLE TOES *London HLU 10034*	29	5 wks
16 Jun 66	LANA *London HL 10051*	15	9 wks
18 Aug 66	● TOO SOON TO KNOW *London HLU 10067*	3	17 wks
1 Dec 66	THERE WON'T BE MANY COMING HOME *London HL 10096*	18	9 wks

23 Feb 67	SO GOOD *London HL 10113*	32	6 wks
24 Jul 68	WALK ON *London HLU 10206*	39	10 wks
25 Sep 68	HEARTACHE *London HLU 10222*	44	4 wks
30 Apr 69	MY FRIEND *London HL 10261*	35	4 wks
13 Sep 69	PENNY ARCADE *London HL 10285*	40	3 wks
11 Oct 69	PENNY ARCADE (re-entry) *London HL 10285*	27	11 wks
14 Jan 89	● YOU GOT IT *Virgin VS 1166*	3	10 wks
1 Apr 89	SHE'S A MYSTERY TO ME *Virgin VS 1173*	27	5 wks

ORBITAL *UK, male instrumental duo*   10 wks

| 24 Mar 90 | CHIME *FFRR F 135* | 17 | 7 wks |
| 22 Sep 90 | OMEN *FFRR F 145* | 46 | 3 wks |

ORCHESTRA ON THE HALF SHELL   3 wks
US, male vocal/instrumetal group

| 15 Dec 90 | TURTLE RHAPSODY *SBK SBK 17* | 38† | 3 wks |

ORCHESTRAL MANOEUVRES IN THE DARK   153 wks
UK, male vocal/instrumental duo

9 Feb 80	RED FRAME WHITE LIGHT *Dindisc DIN 6*	67	2 wks
10 May 80	MESSAGES *Dindisc DIN 15*	13	11 wks
4 Oct 80	● ENOLA GAY *Dindisc DIN 22*	8	15 wks
29 Aug 81	● SOUVENIR *Dindisc DIN 24*	3	12 wks
24 Oct 81	● JOAN OF ARC *Dindisc DIN 36*	5	14 wks
23 Jan 82	● MAID OF ORLEANS (THE WALTZ JOAN OF ARC) *Dindisc DIN 40*	4	10 wks
19 Feb 83	GENETIC ENGINEERING *Virgin VS 527*	20	8 wks
9 Apr 83	TELEGRAPH *Virgin VS 580*	42	4 wks
14 Apr 84	● LOCOMOTION *Virgin VS 660*	5	11 wks
16 Jun 84	TALKING LOUD AND CLEAR *Virgin VS 685*	11	10 wks
8 Sep 84	TESLA GIRLS *Virgin VS 705*	21	8 wks
10 Nov 84	NEVER TURN AWAY *Virgin VS 727*	70	4 wks
25 May 85	SO IN LOVE *Virgin VS 766*	27	7 wks
20 Jul 85	SECRET *Virgin VS 796*	34	7 wks
26 Oct 85	LA FEMME ACCIDENT *Virgin VS 811*	42	4 wks
3 May 86	IF YOU LEAVE *Virgin VS 843*	48	4 wks
6 Sep 86	(FOREVER) LIVE AND DIE *Virgin VS 888*	11	10 wks
15 Nov 86	WE LOVE YOU *Virgin VS 911*	54	5 wks
2 May 87	SHAME *Virgin VS 938*	52	3 wks
6 Feb 88	DREAMING *Virgin VS 987*	50	3 wks
2 Jul 88	DREAMING (re-entry) *Virgin VS 987*	60	3 wks

ORCHESTRE DE CHAMBRE Jean-Francois   3 wks
PAILLARD *France, male conductor and orchestra*

| 20 Aug 88 | THEME FROM 'VIETNAM' (CANON IN D) *Debut DEBT 3053* | 61 | 3 wks |

Raul ORELLANA *Italy, male producer*   8 wk

| 30 Sep 89 | THE REAL WILD HOUSE *RCA BCM 322* | 29 | 8 wks |

Tony ORLANDO *US, male vocalist*   11 wks

| 5 Oct 61 | ● BLESS YOU *Fontana H 330* | 5 | 11 wks |

See also Dawn.

ORLONS *US, female/male vocal group*   3 wks

| 27 Dec 62 | DON'T HANG UP *Cameo Parkway C 231* | 50 | 1 wk |
| 10 Jan 63 | DON'T HANG UP (re-entry) *Cameo Parkway C 231* | 39 | 2 wks |

Ed O'ROSS – *See Paul HARDCASTLE*

ORVILLE – See Keith HARRIS

Jeffrey OSBORNE US, male vocalist — 35 wks

17 Sep 83	DON'T YOU GET SO MAD A & M AM 140	54	2 wks
14 Apr 84	STAY WITH ME TONIGHT A & M AM 188	18	11 wks
23 Jun 84	ON THE WINGS OF LOVE A & M AM 198	11	14 wks
20 Oct 84	DON'T STOP A & M AM 222	61	3 wks
26 Jul 86	SOWETO A & M AM 334	44	5 wks
6 Sep 86	SOWETO (re-entry) A & M AM 334	75	1 wk

See also Dionne Warwick and Jeffrey Osborne.

Tony OSBORNE SOUND UK, orchestra — 3 wks

| 23 Feb 61 | MAN FROM MADRID HMV POP 827 | 50 | 1 wk |
| 3 Feb 73 | THE SHEPHERD'S SONG Philips 6006 266 | 46 | 2 wks |

First hit has credit: 'featuring Joanne Brown' (UK, female vocalist).

Ozzy OSBOURNE UK, male vocalist — 31 wks

13 Sep 80	CRAZY TRAIN Jet 197	49	4 wks
15 Nov 80	MR. CROWLEY Jet 7003	46	3 wks
26 Nov 83	BARK AT THE MOON Epic A 3915	21	8 wks
2 Jun 84	SO TIRED Epic A 4452	20	9 wks
1 Feb 86	SHOT IN THE DARK Epic A 6859	20	6 wks
9 Aug 86	THE ULTIMATE SIN/ LIGHTNING STRIKES Epic A 7311	72	1 wk

Act billed as Ozzy Osbourne's Blizzard of Ozz for first two hits. See also Lita Ford.

OSIBISA Ghana/Nigeria, male vocal/instrumental group — 12 wks

| 17 Jan 76 | SUNSHINE DAY Bronze BRO 20 | 17 | 6 wks |
| 5 Jun 76 | DANCE THE BODY MUSIC Bronze BRO 26 | 31 | 6 wks |

See also Calibre Cuts.

Donny OSMOND US, male vocalist — 116 wks

17 Jun 72	★ PUPPY LOVE MGM 2006 104	1	17 wks
16 Sep 72	● TOO YOUNG MGM 2006 113	5	12 wks
21 Oct 72	PUPPY LOVE (re-entry) MGM 2006 104	45	2 wks
11 Nov 72	● WHY MGM 2006 119	3	20 wks
23 Dec 72	PUPPY LOVE (2nd re-entry) MGM 2006 104	46	3 wks
23 Dec 72	TOO YOUNG (re-entry) MGM 2006 113	47	3 wks
27 Jan 73	PUPPY LOVE (3rd re-entry) MGM 2006 104	48	1 wk
10 Mar 73	THE TWELFTH OF NEVER MGM 2006 199	1	14 wks
18 Aug 73	★ YOUNG LOVE MGM 2006 300	1	10 wks
10 Nov 73	● WHEN I FALL IN LOVE MGM 2006 365	4	13 wks
9 Nov 74	WHERE DID ALL THE GOOD TIMES GO MGM 2006 468	18	10 wks
26 Sep 87	I'M IN IT FOR LOVE Virgin VS 994	70	1 wk
6 Aug 88	SOLDIER OF LOVE Virgin VS 1094	29	8 wks
12 Nov 88	IF IT'S LOVE THAT YOU WANT Virgin VS 1140	70	2 wks

See also Donny and Marie Osmond; Osmonds.

Donny and Marie OSMOND — 37 wks
US, male/female vocal duo

3 Aug 74	● I'M LEAVING IT (ALL) UP TO YOU MGM 2006 446	2	12 wks
14 Dec 74	● MORNING SIDE OF THE MOUNTAIN MGM 2006 274	5	12 wks
21 Jun 75	MAKE THE WORLD GO AWAY MGM 2006 523	18	6 wks
17 Jan 76	DEEP PURPLE MGM 2006 561	25	7 wks

See also Donny Osmond; Marie Osmond.

Little Jimmy OSMOND US, male vocalist — 50 wks

25 Nov 72	★ LONG HAIRED LOVER FROM LIVERPOOL MGM 2006 109	1	24 wks
31 Mar 73	● TWEEDLE DEE MGM 2006 175	4	13 wks
19 May 73	LONG HAIRED LOVER FROM LIVERPOOL (re-entry) MGM 2006 109	41	3 wks
23 Mar 74	I'M GONNA KNOCK ON YOUR DOOR MGM 2006 389	11	10 wks

Marie OSMOND US, female vocalist — 15 wks

| 17 Nov 73 | ● PAPER ROSES MGM 2006 315 | 2 | 15 wks |

See also Donny and Marie Osmond.

OSMONDS US, male vocal/instrumental group — 91 wks

25 Mar 72	DOWN BY THE LAZY RIVER MGM 2006 096	40	5 wks
11 Nov 72	● CRAZY HORSES MGM 2006 142	2	18 wks
14 Jul 73	● GOING HOME MGM 2006 288	4	10 wks
27 Oct 73	● LET ME IN MGM 2006 321	2	14 wks
20 Apr 74	I CAN'T STOP MCA 129	12	10 wks
24 Aug 74	★ LOVE ME FOR A REASON MGM 2006 458	1	9 wks
1 Mar 75	HAVING A PARTY MGM 2006 492	28	8 wks
24 May 75	● THE PROUD ONE MGM 2006 520	5	8 wks
15 Nov 75	I'M STILL GONNA NEED YOU MGM 2006 551	32	4 wks
30 Oct 76	I CAN'T LIVE A DREAM Polydor 2066 726	37	5 wks

Gilbert O'SULLIVAN Ireland, male vocalist — 145 wks

28 Nov 70	● NOTHING RHYMED MAM 3	8	11 wks
3 Apr 71	UNDERNEATH THE BLANKET GO MAM 13	40	1 wk
17 Apr 71	UNDERNEATH THE BLANKET GO (re-entry) MAM 13	42	3 wks
24 Jul 71	WE WILL MAM 30	16	11 wks
27 Nov 71	● NO MATTER HOW I TRY MAM 53	5	15 wks
4 Mar 72	● ALONE AGAIN (NATURALLY) MAM 66	3	12 wks
17 Jun 72	● OOH-WAKKA-DOO-WAKKA-DAY MAM 78	8	11 wks
21 Oct 72	★ CLAIR MAM 84	1	14 wks
17 Mar 73	★ GET DOWN MAM 96	1	13 wks
15 Sep 73	OOH BABY MAM 107	18	7 wks
10 Nov 73	● WHY OH WHY OH WHY MAM 111	6	14 wks
9 Feb 74	HAPPINESS IS ME AND YOU MAM 114	19	7 wks
24 Aug 74	A WOMAN'S PLACE MAM 122	42	3 wks
14 Dec 74	CHRISTMAS SONG MAM 124	12	6 wks
14 Jun 75	I DON'T LOVE YOU BUT I THINK I LIKE YOU MAM 130	14	6 wks
27 Sep 80	WHAT'S IN A KISS? CBS 8929	19	9 wks
24 Feb 90	SO WHAT Dover ROJ 3	70	2 wks

Johnny OTIS SHOW US, orchestra and chorus — 22 wks

| 22 Nov 57 | ● MA HE'S MAKING EYES AT ME Capitol CL 14794 | 2 | 15 wks |
| 10 Jan 58 | BYE BYE BABY Capitol CL 14817 | 20 | 7 wks |

Ma He's Making Eyes At Me *credits Johnny Otis and his orchestra with Marie Adams and the Three Tons of Joy.* Bye Bye Baby *features vocals by Marie Adams and Johnny Otis.*

OTTAWAN Guadaloupe, male/female vocal duo — 45 wks

13 Sep 80	● D.I.S.C.O. Carrere CAR 161	2	18 wks
13 Dec 80	YOU'RE O.K. Carrere CAR 168	56	6 wks
29 Aug 81	● HANDS UP (GIVE ME YOUR HEART) Carrere CAR 183	3	15 wks
5 Dec 81	HELP, GET ME SOME HELP! Carrere CAR 215	49	6 wks

John OTWAY and Wild Willy BARRETT — 12 wks
UK, male vocal/instrumental duo

| 3 Dec 77 | REALLY FREE Polydor 2058 951 | 27 | 8 wks |
| 5 Jul 80 | DK 50-80 Polydor 2059 250 | 45 | 4 wks |

DK 50-80 *credited simply to Otway and Barrett.*

OUR DAUGHTER'S WEDDING   6 wks
US, male vocal/instrumental group

1 Aug 81	LAWNCHAIRS EMI America EA 124	49	6 wks

OUR KID   UK, male vocal group   11 wks

29 May 76	● YOU JUST MIGHT SEE ME CRY Polydor 2058 729	2	11 wks

OUTLAWS   UK, male instrumental group   4 wks

13 Apr 61	SWINGIN' LOW HMV POP 844	46	2 wks
8 Jun 61	AMBUSH HMV POP 877	43	2 wks

See also Mike Berry with the Outlaws.

OVERLANDERS   UK, male vocal/instrumental group   10 wks

13 Jan 66	★ MICHELLE Pye 7N 17034	1	10 wks

Reg OWEN   UK, orchestra   10 wks

27 Feb 59	MANHATTAN SPIRITUAL Pye International 7N 25009	20	8 wks
27 Oct 60	OBSESSION Palette PG 9004	43	2 wks

P

Jazzi P   US, female vocalist   2 wks

9 Jun 90	FEEL THE RHYTHM A & M AM USA 691	51	2 wks

Thom PACE   US, male vocalist   15 wks

19 May 79	MAYBE RSO 34	14	15 wks

PACEMAKERS – See GERRY and the PACEMAKERS

PACK featuring Nigel BENN   2 wks
UK, male vocal/instrumental group

8 Dec 90	STAND AND FIGHT IQ ZB 44237	61	2 wks

PACKABEATS   UK, male instrumental group   1 wk

23 Feb 61	GYPSY BEAT Parlophone R 4729	49	1 wk

Hal PAGE and the WHALERS   1 wk
US, male vocal/instrumental group

25 Aug 60	GOING BACK TO MY HOME TOWN Melodisc MEL 1553	50	1 wk

Patti PAGE   US, female vocalist   5 wks

27 Mar 53	● (HOW MUCH IS) THAT DOGGIE IN THE WINDOW Oriole CB 1156	9	5 wks

Tommy PAGE   US, male vocalist   3 wks

26 May 90	I'LL BE YOUR EVERYTHING Sire W 9959	53	3 wks

PAGLIARO   Canada, male vocalist   6 wks

19 Feb 72	LOVING YOU AIN'T EASY Pye 7N 45111	31	6 wks

Elaine PAIGE   UK, female vocalist   22 wks

21 Oct 78	DON'T WALK AWAY TILL I TOUCH YOU EMI 2862	46	5 wks
6 Jun 81	● MEMORY Polydor POSP 279	6	12 wks
30 Jan 82	MEMORY (re-entry) Polydor POSP 279	67	3 wks
14 Apr 84	SOMETIMES (THEME FROM 'CHAMPIONS') Island IS 174	72	1 wk
21 Nov 87	THE SECOND TIME (THEME FROM 'BILITIS') WEA YZ 163	69	1 wk

See also Elaine Paige and Barbara Dickson.

Elaine PAIGE and Barbara DICKSON   16 wks
UK, female vocal duo

5 Jan 85	★ I KNOW HIM SO WELL RCA CHESS 3	1	16 wks

See Elaine Paige; Barbara Dickson.

PALE FOUNTAINS   UK, male vocal/instrumental group   6 wks

27 Nov 82	THANK YOU Virgin VS 557	48	6 wks

Barry PALMER – See Mike OLDFIELD

Robert PALMER   UK, male vocalist   89 wks

20 May 78	EVERY KINDA PEOPLE Island WIP 6425	53	4 wks
7 Jul 79	BAD CASE OF LOVIN' YOU (DOCTOR DOCTOR) Island WIP 6481	61	2 wks
6 Sep 80	JOHNNY AND MARY Island WIP 6638	44	8 wks
22 Nov 80	LOOKING FOR CLUES Island WIP 6651	33	9 wks
13 Feb 82	SOME GUYS HAVE ALL THE LUCK Island WIP 6754	16	8 wks
2 Apr 83	YOU ARE IN MY SYSTEM Island IS 104	53	4 wks
18 Jun 83	YOU CAN HAVE IT (TAKE MY HEART) Island IS 121	66	2 wks
10 May 86	● ADDICTED TO LOVE Island IS 270	5	15 wks
19 Jul 86	● I DIDN'T MEAN TO TURN YOU ON Island IS 283	9	9 wks
1 Nov 86	DISCIPLINE OF LOVE Island IS 242	68	1 wk
26 Mar 88	SWEET LIES Island IS 352	58	3 wks
11 Jun 88	SIMPLY IRRESISTIBLE EMI EM 61	44	4 wks
15 Oct 88	● SHE MAKES MY DAY EMI EM 65	6	12 wks
13 May 89	CHANGE HIS WAYS EMI EM 85	28	7 wks
26 Aug 89	IT COULD HAPPEN TO YOU EMI EM 99	71	1 wk

See also Robert Palmer with UB40.

Robert PALMER and UB40   9 wks
UK, male vocalist and male vocal/instrumental group

3 Nov 90	● I'LL BE YOUR BABY TONIGHT EMI EM 167	6†	9 wks

See also Robert Palmer; UB40.

PANDORA'S BOX   3 wks
US, male/female vocal/instrumental group

21 Oct 89	IT'S ALL COMING BACK TO ME NOW Virgin VS 1216	51	3 wks

THE OSMONDS, with
Donny in front, guest on
Andy Williams' TV show.

ELAINE PAIGE suggests to
Cliff Richard that anything
Olivia Newton-John and
Sarah Brightman and Sheila
Walsh and Phil Everly and
Elton John and the Shadows
and the Young Ones can
do. . .

Darryl PANDY – *See Farley 'Jackmaster' Funk*

PAPER DOLLS *UK, female vocal group*   **13 wks**

13 Mar 68	**SOMETHING HERE IN MY HEART (KEEPS A-TELLIN' ME NO)** *Pye 7N 17456*	**11**	13 wks

PAPER LACE *UK, male vocal/instrumental group*   **35 wks**

23 Feb 74	★ **BILLY DON'T BE A HERO** *Bus Stop BUS 1014*	**1**	14 wks
4 May 74	● **THE NIGHT CHICAGO DIED** *Bus Stop BUS 1016*	**3**	11 wks
24 Aug 74	**THE BLACK EYED BOYS** *Bus Stop BUS 1019*	**11**	10 wks

See also Nottingham Forest F.C. with Paper Lace

Vanessa PARADIS *France, female vocalist*   **10 wks**

13 Feb 88	● **JOE LE TAXI** *FA Productions POSP 902*	**3**	10 wks

PARADISE *UK, male vocal/instrumental group*   **4 wks**

10 Sep 83	**ONE MIND, TWO HEARTS** *Priority P 1*	**42**	4 wks

PARADOX *UK, male instrumental duo*   **2 wks**

24 Feb 90	**JAILBREAK** *Ronin 7R2*	**66**	2 wks

Norrie PARAMOR *UK, orchestra*   **8 wks**

17 Mar 60	**THEME FROM 'A SUMMER PLACE'** *Columbia DB 4419*	**36**	2 wks
22 Mar 62	**THEME FROM 'Z CARS'** *Columbia DB 4789*	**33**	6 wks

PARAMOUNT JAZZ BAND – *See Mr. Acker BILK*

PARAMOUNTS *UK, male vocal/instrumental group*   **7 wks**

16 Jan 64	**POISON IVY** *Parlophone R 5093*	**35**	7 wks

PARCHMENT *UK, male/female vocal/instrumental group*   **5 wks**

16 Sep 72	**LIGHT UP THE FIRE** *Pye 7N 45178*	**31**	5 wks

PARIS *UK, male/female vocal group*   **4 wks**

19 Jun 82	**NO GETTING OVER YOU** *RCA 222*	**49**	4 wks

Mica PARIS *UK, female vocalist*   **32 wks**

7 May 88	● **MY ONE TEMPTATION** *Fourth & Broadway BRW 85*	**7**	11 wks
30 Jul 88	**LIKE DREAMERS DO** *Fourth & Broadway BRW 108*	**26**	5 wks
22 Oct 88	**BREATHE LIFE INTO ME** *Fourth & Broadway BRW 115*	**26**	10 wks
6 Oct 90	**CONTRIBUTION** *Fourth & Broadway BRW 188*	**33**	4 wks
1 Dec 90	**SOUTH OF THE RIVER** *Fourth & Broadway BRW 199*	**50**	2 wks

Like Dreamers Do features Courtney Pine - UK, male saxophonist. See also Mica Paris and Will Downing; Courtney Pine featuring Carroll Thompson.

Mica PARIS and Will DOWNING   **7 wks**
UK/US, female/male vocal duo

21 Jan 89	**WHERE IS THE LOVE** *Fourth + Broadway BRW 122*	**19**	7 wks

See also Mica Paris; Will Downing.

Ryan PARIS *France, male vocalist*   **10 wks**

3 Sep 83	● **DOLCE VITA** *Carrere CAR 289*	**5**	10 wks

PARIS ANGELS *Ireland, male vocal/instrumental group*   **1 wk**

3 Nov 90	**SCOPE** *Sheer Joy SHEER 0047*	**75**	1 wk

Simon PARK *UK, orchestra*   **23 wk**

25 Nov 72	**EYE LEVEL** *Columbia DB 8946*	**41**	2 wks
15 Sep 73	★ **EYE LEVEL (re-entry)** *Columbia DB 8946*	**1**	21 wks

Graham PARKER *UK, male vocalist*   **4 wks**

20 Mar 82	**TEMPORARY BEAUTY** *RCA PARK 100*	**50**	4 wks

See also Graham Parker and the Rumour.

Graham PARKER and the RUMOUR   **12 wks**
UK, male vocal and instrumental group

19 Mar 77	**THE PINK PARKER** (EP) *Vertigo PARK 001*	**24**	5 wks
22 Apr 78	**HEY LORD DON'T ASK ME QUESTIONS** *Vertigo PARK 002*	**32**	7 wks

Tracks on The Pink Parker EP: Hold Back The Night/(Let Me Get) Sweet On You/White Honey/Soul Shoes. See also Graham Parker.

Ray PARKER Jr *US, male vocalist*   **47 wks**

25 Aug 84	● **GHOSTBUSTERS** *Arista ARIST 580*	**2**	31 wks
18 Jan 86	**GIRLS ARE MORE FUN** *Arista ARIST 641*	**46**	4 wks
3 Oct 87	**I DON'T THINK THAT MAN SHOULD SLEEP ALONE** *Geffen GEF 27*	**13**	10 wks
30 Jan 88	**OVER YOU** *Geffen GEF 33*	**65**	2 wks

Robert PARKER *US, male vocalist*   **8 wks**

4 Aug 66	**BAREFOOTIN'** *Island WI 286*	**24**	8 wks

Jimmy PARKINSON *Australia, male vocalist*   **19 wks**

2 Mar 56	● **THE GREAT PRETENDER** *Columbia DB 3729*	**9**	13 wks
17 Aug 56	**WALK HAND IN HAND** *Columbia DB 3775*	**30**	1 wk
5 Oct 56	**WALK HAND IN HAND (re-entry)** *Columbia DB 3775*	**26**	1 wk
9 Nov 56	**IN THE MIDDLE OF THE HOUSE** *Columbia DB 3833*	**26**	2 wks
30 Nov 56	**IN THE MIDDLE OF THE HOUSE (re-entry)** *Columbia DB 3833*	**20**	2 wks

John PARR *UK, male vocalist*   **16 wks**

14 Sep 85	● **ST ELMOS'S FIRE (MAN IN MOTION)** *London LON 73*	**6**	13 wks
18 Jan 86	**NAUGHTY NAUGHTY** *London LON 80*	**58**	3 wks

See also Meat Loaf.

Dean PARRISH *US, male vocalist*   **5 wks**

8 Feb 75	**I'M ON MY WAY** *UK USA 2*	**38**	5 wks

Man PARRISH *US, mixer* — **10 wks**

26 Mar 83	HOP HOP, BE BOP (DON'T STOP) *Polydor POSP 575*	41	6 wks
23 Mar 85	BOOGIE DOWN (BRONX) *Boiling Point POSP 731*	56	4 wks

See also Man To Man.

Bill PARSONS *US, male vocalist* — **2 wks**

10 Apr 59	ALL AMERICAN BOY *London HL 8798*	22	2 wks

Alan PARSONS PROJECT — **4 wks**
UK, male vocal/instrumental group

15 Jan 83	OLD AND WISE *Arista ARIST 494*	74	1 wk
10 Mar 84	DON'T ANSWER ME *Arista ARIST 553*	58	3 wks

PARTNERS – *See Al HUDSON and the PARTNERS*

PARTNERS IN KRYME — **10 wks**
US, male vocal/instrumental group

21 Jul 90	★ TURTLE POWER *SBK TURTLE 1*	1	10 wks

David PARTON *UK, male vocalist* — **9 wks**

15 Jan 77	● ISN'T SHE LOVELY *Pye 7N 45663*	4	9 wks

Dolly PARTON *US, female vocalist* — **16 wks**

15 May 76	● JOLENE *RCA 2675*	7	10 wks
21 Feb 81	9 TO 5 *RCA 25*	47	5 wks
7 Apr 84	HERE YOU COME AGAIN *RCA 395*	75	1 wk

See also Kenny Rogers and Dolly Parton.

Stella PARTON *US, female vocalist* — **4 wks**

22 Oct 77	THE DANGER OF A STRANGER *Elektra K 12272*	35	4 wks

Don PARTRIDGE *UK, male vocalist* — **32 wks**

7 Feb 68	● ROSIE *Columbia DB 8330*	4	12 wks
29 May 68	● BLUE EYES *Columbia DB 8416*	3	13 wks
19 Feb 69	BREAKFAST ON PLUTO *Columbia DB 8538*	26	7 wks

PARTRIDGE FAMILY starring Shirley JONES featuring David CASSIDY — **53 wks**
US, male/female vocal group

13 Feb 71	I THINK I LOVE YOU *Bell 1130*	18	9 wks
26 Feb 72	IT'S ONE OF THOSE NIGHTS (YES LOVE) *Bell 1203*	11	11 wks
8 Jul 72	● BREAKING UP IS HARD TO DO *Bell MABEL 1*	3	13 wks
3 Feb 73	● LOOKING THROUGH THE EYES OF LOVE *Bell 1278*	9	9 wks
19 May 73	● WALKING IN THE RAIN *Bell 1293*	10	11 wks

Last two hits are simply starring David Cassidy - no Shirley Jones credit. See also David Cassidy;
Various Artists - Carousel Soundtrack on which Shirley Jones appears.

PASADENAS *UK, male vocal group* — **35 wks**

28 May 88	● TRIBUTE (RIGHT ON) *CBS PASA 1*	5	14 wks
17 Sep 88	RIDING ON A TRAIN *CBS PASA 2*	13	9 wks
26 Nov 88	ENCHANTED LADY *CBS PASA 3*	31	6 wks
12 May 90	LOVE THING *CBS PASA 4*	22	5 wks

14 Jul 90	REELING *CBS PASA 5*	75	1 wk

PASSIONS *UK, male/female vocal/instrumental group* — **8 wks**

31 Jan 81	I'M IN LOVE WITH A GERMAN FILM STAR *Polydor POSP 222*	25	8 wks

PAT and MICK *UK, male vocal duo* — **23 wks**

9 Apr 88	LET'S ALL CHANT/ ON THE NIGHT *PWL PWL 10*	11	9 wks
25 Mar 89	● I HAVEN'T STOPPED DANCING YET *PWL PWL 33*	9	8 wks
14 Apr 90	USE IT UP AND WEAR IT OUT *PWL PWL 55*	22	6 wks

First hit bills act in reverse order. On The Night only listed from 4 Jun 88.

PATIENCE and PRUDENCE *US, female vocal duo* — **8 wks**

2 Nov 56	TONIGHT YOU BELONG TO ME *London HLU 8321*	28	3 wks
1 Mar 57	GONNA GET ALONG WITHOUT YA NOW *London HLU 8369*	22	4 wks
12 Apr 57	GONNA GET ALONG WITHOUT YA NOW (re-entry) *London HLU 8369*	24	1 wk

Kellee PATTERSON *US, female vocalist* — **7 wks**

18 Feb 78	IF IT DON'T FIT DON'T FORCE IT *EMI International INT 544*	44	7 wks

PAUL – *See PETER, PAUL and MARY*

Billy PAUL *US, male vocalist* — **44 wks**

13 Jan 73	ME AND MRS JONES *Epic EPC 1055*	12	9 wks
12 Jan 74	THANKS FOR SAVING MY LIFE *Philadelphia International PIR 1928*	33	6 wks
22 May 76	LET'S MAKE A BABY *Philadelphia International PIR 4144*	30	5 wks
30 Apr 77	LET 'EM IN *Philadelphia International PIR 5143*	26	5 wks
16 Jul 77	YOUR SONG *Philadelphia International PIR 5391*	37	7 wks
19 Nov 77	ONLY THE STRONG SURVIVE *Philadelphia International PIR 5699*	33	7 wks
14 Jul 79	BRING THE FAMILY BACK *Philadelphia International PIR 7456*	51	5 wks

See also Philadelphia International All-Stars.

Chris PAUL *UK, male instrumentalist - guitar* — **8 wks**

31 May 86	EXPANSIONS '86 (EXPAND YOUR MIND) *Fourth & Broadway BRW 48*	58	5 wks
21 Nov 87	BACK IN MY ARMS *Syncopate SY 5*	74	2 wks
13 Aug 88	TURN THE MUSIC UP *Syncopate SY 13*	73	1 wk

First hit features David Joseph; see also David Joseph.

Les PAUL and Mary FORD — **4 wks**
US, male instrumentalist - guitar, and female vocalist

20 Nov 53	● VAYA CON DIOS *Capitol CL 13943*	7	4 wks

Lyn PAUL *UK, female vocalist* — **6 wks**

28 Jun 75	IT OUGHTA SELL A MILLION *Polydor 2058 602*	37	6 wks

Owen PAUL *UK, male vocalist* — **14 wks**

31 May 86	● MY FAVOURITE WASTE OF TIME *Epic A 7125*	3	14 wks

Above: Although Elvis Presley had the bigger UK version, CARL PERKINS originated 'Blue Suede Shoes'.

VANESSA PARADIS rode to the Top Three in 1988.

Top Left: Never mind the World Cup, LUCIANO PAVAROTTI wants to know what's on the plate.

DOLLY PARTON was a regular on the Porter Wagoner TV show from 1967 to 1974, the year her solo 'Jolene' hit number one on the country charts. Porter and Dolly had twenty-one hit country duets; 'Jolene' made the UK lists in 1976.

PAUL and PAULA US, male/female vocal duo — **31 wks**

Date	Title	Pos	Wks
14 Feb 63	● HEY PAULA *Philips 304012 BF*	8	12 wks
18 Apr 63	● YOUNG LOVERS *Philips 304016 BF*	9	14 wks
16 May 63	HEY PAULA (re-entry) *Philips 304012 BF*	37	5 wks

Luciano PAVAROTTI Italy, male operatic vocalist — **11 wks**

Date	Title	Pos	Wks
16 Jun 90	● NESSUN DORMA *Decca PAV 03*	2	11 wks

Rita PAVONE Italy, female vocalist — **19 wks**

Date	Title	Pos	Wks
1 Dec 66	HEART *RCA 1553*	27	12 wks
19 Jan 67	YOU ONLY YOU *RCA 1561*	21	7 wks

Freda PAYNE US, female vocalist — **30 wks**

Date	Title	Pos	Wks
5 Sep 70	★ BAND OF GOLD *Invictus INV 502*	1	19 wks
21 Nov 70	DEEPER AND DEEPER *Invictus INV 505*	33	9 wks
27 Mar 71	CHERISH WHAT IS DEAR TO YOU *Invictus INV 509*	46	2 wks

PEACHES and HERB US, female/male vocal duo — **23 wks**

Date	Title	Pos	Wks
20 Jan 79	SHAKE YOUR GROOVE THING *Polydor 2066 992*	26	10 wks
21 Apr 79	● REUNITED *Polydor POSP 43*	4	13 wks

PEARLS UK, female vocal duo — **24 wks**

Date	Title	Pos	Wks
27 May 72	THIRD FINGER, LEFT HAND *Bell 1217*	31	6 wks
23 Sep 72	YOU CAME YOU SAW YOU CONQUERED *Bell 1254*	32	5 wks
24 Mar 73	YOU ARE EVERYTHING *Bell 1284*	41	3 wks
1 Jun 74	● GUILTY *Bell 1352*	10	10 wks

Johnny PEARSON — **15 wks**
UK, orchestra, Johnny Pearson featured pianist

Date	Title	Pos	Wks
18 Dec 71	● SLEEPY SHORES *Penny Farthing PEN 778*	8	15 wks

PEBBLES US, female vocalist — **17 wks**

Date	Title	Pos	Wks
19 Mar 88	● GIRLFRIEND *MCA MCA 1233*	8	11 wks
28 May 88	MERCEDES BOY *MCA MCA 1248*	42	4 wks
27 Oct 90	GIVING YOU THE BENEFIT *MCA MCA 1448*	73	2 wks

PEDDLERS UK, male vocal/instrumental group — **14 wks**

Date	Title	Pos	Wks
7 Jan 65	LET THE SUNSHINE IN *Philips BF 1375*	50	1 wk
23 Aug 69	BIRTH *CBS 4449*	17	9 wks
31 Jan 70	GIRLIE *CBS 4720*	34	4 wks

PEE BEE SQUAD UK, male vocalist — **3 wks**

Date	Title	Pos	Wks
5 Oct 85	RUGGED AND MEAN, BUTCH AND ON SCREEN *Project PRO 3*	52	3 wks

Pee Bee Squad is disc jockey Paul Burnett under a false name. See also Laurie Lingo and the Dipsticks.

Ann PEEBLES US, female vocalist — **3 wks**

Date	Title	Pos	Wks
20 Apr 74	I CAN'T STAND THE RAIN *London HL 10428*	50	1 wk
4 May 74	I CAN'T STAND THE RAIN (re-entry) *London HL 10428*	41	2 wks

PEECH BOYS UK, male vocal/instrumental group — **3 wks**

Date	Title	Pos	Wks
30 Oct 82	DON'T MAKE ME WAIT *TMT TMT 7001*	49	3 wks

Donald PEERS UK, male vocalist — **27 wks**

Date	Title	Pos	Wks
18 Dec 68	● PLEASE DON'T GO *Columbia DB 8502*	3	18 wks
30 Apr 69	PLEASE DON'T GO (re-entry) *Columbia DB 8502*	38	3 wks
24 Jun 72	GIVE ME ONE MORE CHANCE *Decca F 13302*	36	6 wks

Teddy PENDERGRASS US, male vocalist — **12 wks**

Date	Title	Pos	Wks
21 May 77	THE WHOLE TOWN'S LAUGHING AT ME *Philadelphia International PIR 5116*	44	3 wks
28 Oct 78	ONLY YOU / CLOSE THE DOOR *Philadelphia International S PIR 6713*	41	6 wks
28 May 88	JOY *Elektra EKR 75*	58	3 wks

See also Philadelphia International All-Stars; Teddy Pendergrass with Whitney Houston; Stephanie Mills.

Teddy PENDERGRASS with Whitney HOUSTON US, male/female vocal duo — **5 wks**

Date	Title	Pos	Wks
25 Jan 86	HOLD ME *Asylum EKR 32*	44	5 wks

See also Teddy Pendergrass; Whitney Houston.

Barbara PENNINGTON US, female vocalist — **8 wks**

Date	Title	Pos	Wks
27 Apr 85	FAN THE FLAME *Record Shack SOHO 37*	62	3 wks
27 Jul 85	ON A CROWDED STREET *Record Shack SOHO 49*	57	5 wks

PENTANGLE UK, male/female vocal/instrumental group — **4 wks**

Date	Title	Pos	Wks
28 May 69	ONCE I HAD A SWEETHEART *Big T BIG 124*	46	1 wk
14 Feb 70	LIGHT FLIGHT *Big T BIG 128*	43	1 wk
28 Feb 70	LIGHT FLIGHT (re-entry) *Big T BIG 128*	45	2 wks

PENTHOUSE 4 UK, male vocal/instrumental duo — **3 wks**

Date	Title	Pos	Wks
23 Apr 88	BUST THIS HOUSE DOWN *Syncopate SY 10*	56	3 wks

PEOPLES – *See YARBROUGH and PEOPLES*

PEOPLES CHOICE US, male vocal/instrumental group — **9 wks**

Date	Title	Pos	Wks
20 Sep 75	DO IT ANYWAY YOU WANNA *Philadelphia International PIR 3500*	36	5 wks
21 Jan 78	JAM JAM JAM *Philadelphia International PIR 5891*	40	4 wks

PEPA – *See SALT 'N' PEPA*

Danny PEPPERMINT and the JUMPING JACKS US, male vocal/instrumental group — **8 wks**

Date	Title	Pos	Wks
18 Jan 62	PEPPERMINT TWIST *London HLL 9478*	26	8 wks

PEPPERS France, male instrumental group — **12 wks**

Date	Title	Pos	Wks
26 Oct 74	● PEPPER BOX *Spark SRL 1100*	6	12 wks

PEPSI and SHIRLIE UK, female vocal duo   **24 wks**

17 Jan 87	●	HEARTACHE *Polydor POSP 837*	2	12 wks
30 May 87	●	GOODBYE STRANGER *Polydor POSP 865*	9	7 wks
26 Sep 87		CAN'T GIVE ME LOVE *Polydor POSP 885*	58	3 wks
12 Dec 87		ALL RIGHT NOW *Polydor POSP 896*	50	2 wks

Lance PERCIVAL UK, male vocalist   **3 wks**

28 Oct 65	SHAME AND SCANDAL IN THE FAMILY *Parlophone R 5335*	37	3 wks

PERFECT DAY UK, male vocal/instrumental group   **4 wks**

21 Jan 89	LIBERTY TOWN *London LON 214*	58	3 wks
1 Apr 89	JANE *London LON 188*	68	1 wk

PERFECTLY ORDINARY PEOPLE   **3 wks**
UK, male vocal/instrumental group

22 Oct 88	THEME FROM P.O.P. *Urban URB 25*	61	3 wks

Emilio PERICOLI Italy, male vocalist   **14 wks**

28 Jun 62	AL DI LA *Warner Bros. WB 69*	30	14 wks

Carl PERKINS US, male vocalist   **8 wks**

18 May 56	●	BLUE SUEDE SHOES *London HLU 8271*	10	8 wks

Steve PERRY UK, male vocalist   **1 wk**

4 Aug 60	STEP BY STEP *HMV POP 745*	41	1 wk

Jon PERTWEE UK, male vocalist   **7 wks**

1 Mar 80	WORZEL'S SONG *Decca F 13885*	33	7 wks

PET SHOP BOYS UK, male vocal/instrumental duo   **116 wks**

23 Nov 85	★	WEST END GIRLS *Parlophone R 6115*	1	15 wks
8 Mar 86		LOVE COMES QUICKLY *Parlophone R 6116*	19	9 wks
31 May 86		OPPORTUNITIES (LET'S MAKE LOTS OF MONEY) *Parlophone R 6129*	11	8 wks
4 Oct 86	●	SUBURBIA *Parlophone R 6140*	8	9 wks
27 Jun 87	★	IT'S A SIN *Parlophone R 6158*	1	11 wks
24 Oct 87	●	RENT *Parlophone R 6168*	8	7 wks
12 Dec 87	★	ALWAYS ON MY MIND *Parlophone R 6171*	1	11 wks
2 Apr 88	★	HEART *Parlophone R 6177*	1	10 wks
24 Sep 88	●	DOMINO DANCING *Parlophone R 6190*	7	8 wks
26 Nov 88	●	LEFT TO MY OWN DEVICES *Parlophone R 6198*........	4	8 wks
8 Jul 89	●	IT'S ALRIGHT *Parlophone R 6220*	5	8 wks
6 Oct 90	●	SO HARD *Parlophone R 6269*	4	6 wks
24 Nov 90		BEING BORING *Parlophone R 6275*	20†	6 wks

See also Pet Shop Boys and Dusty Springfield.

PET SHOP BOYS and Dusty SPRINGFIELD   **9 wks**
UK, male vocal/instrumental duo and UK, female vocalist

22 Aug 87	●	WHAT HAVE I DONE TO DESERVE THIS *Parlophone R 6163*	2	9 wks

See also Pet Shop Boys; Dusty Springfield.

PETER and GORDON UK, male vocal duo   **77 wks**

12 Mar 64	★	A WORLD WITHOUT LOVE *Columbia DB 7225*	1	14 wks
4 Jun 64	●	NOBODY I KNOW *Columbia DB 7292*....................	10	11 wks
8 Apr 65	●	TRUE LOVE WAYS *Columbia DB 7524*	2	15 wks
24 Jun 65	●	TO KNOW YOU IS TO LOVE YOU *Columbia DB 7617*	5	10 wks
21 Oct 65		BABY I'M YOURS *Columbia DB 7729*..................	19	9 wks
24 Feb 66		WOMAN *Columbia DB 7834*..........................	28	7 wks
22 Sep 66		LADY GODIVA *Columbia DB 8003*....................	16	11 wks

PETER, PAUL and MARY   **38 wks**
US, male/female vocal/instrumental group

10 Oct 63	BLOWING IN THE WIND *Warner Bros. WB 104*..............	13	16 wks
16 Apr 64	TELL IT ON THE MOUNTAIN *Warner Bros. WB 127*	33	4 wks
15 Oct 64	THE TIMES THEY ARE A-CHANGIN' *Warner Bros. WB 142*	44	2 wks
17 Jan 70 ●	LEAVIN' ON A JET PLANE *Warner Bros. WB 7340*	2	16 wks

PETERS and LEE UK, male/female vocal duo   **57 wks**

26 May 73	★	WELCOME HOME *Philips 6006 307*	1	24 wks
3 Nov 73		BY YOUR SIDE *Philips 6006 339*	39	4 wks
20 Apr 74	●	DON'T STAY AWAY TOO LONG *Philips 6006 388*...........	3	15 wks
17 Aug 74		RAINBOW *Philips 6006 406*	17	7 wks
6 Mar 76		HEY MR. MUSIC MAN *Philips 6006 502*	16	7 wks

Ray PETERSON US, male vocalist   **9 wks**

4 Sep 59	THE WONDER OF YOU *RCA 1131*	23	1 wk
24 Mar 60	ANSWER ME *RCA 1175*.............................	47	1 wk
19 Jan 61	CORRINE, CORRINA *London HLX 9246*	48	1 wk
2 Feb 61	CORRINE, CORRINA (re-entry) *London HLX 9246*	41	6 wks

Tom PETTY US, male vocal/instrumental group   **28 wks**

25 Jun 77	ANYTHING THAT'S ROCK 'N' ROLL *Shelter WIP 6396*	36	3 wks
13 Aug 77	AMERICAN GIRL *Shelter WIP 6403*....................	40	5 wks
13 Apr 85	DON'T COME AROUND HERE NO MORE *MCA MCA 926*	50	4 wks
13 May 89	I WON'T BACK DOWN *MCA MCA 1334*...................	28	10 wks
12 Aug 89	RUNNIN' DOWN A DREAM *MCA MCA 1359*	55	4 wks
25 Nov 89	FREE FALLIN' *MCA MCA 1381*	64	2 wks

First three hits credit the Heartbreakers - US, male instrumental group. See also Stevie Nicks with Tom Petty and the Heartbreakers.

PHARAOHS – *See SAM THE SHAM and the PHARAOHS*

PHASE II US, male vocal group   **1 wk**

18 Mar 89	REACHIN' *Republic LIC 006*	70	1 wk

PhD UK, male vocal/instrumental duo   **14 wks**

3 Apr 82	●	I WON'T LET YOU DOWN *WEA K 79209*	3	14 wks

PHILADELPHIA INTERNATIONAL ALL-STARS   **8 wks**
US, amalgamation of various acts

13 Aug 77	LET'S CLEAN UP THE GHETTO *Philadelphia International PIR 5451*	34	8 wks

The All-Stars include Archie Bell, Dee Dee Sharp Gamble, O'Jays, Billy Paul, Teddy Pendergrass and Lou Rawls. See also the separate hit lists of of each of these artists: Dee Dee Sharpe Gamble, see Dee Dee Sharp; Archie Bell, see Archie Bell and the Drells.

IGGY POP will bend over
backwards for his fans.

THOM PACE models the
latest in Mickey Mouse
fashions.

Far Right: ROY ORBISON
had at least one hit every
year of the Sixties.

PHILHARMONIA ORCHESTRA, conductor Lorin MAAZEL UK, orchestra, US, male conductor

7 wks

30 Jul 69	**THUS SPAKE ZARATHUSTRA** Columbia DB 8607	33	7 wks

See also Sarah Brightman and Paul Miles-Kingston.

Esther PHILLIPS US, female vocalist

8 wks

4 Oct 75	● **WHAT A DIFFERENCE A DAY MADE** Kudu 925	6	8 wks

Paul PHILLIPS – See DRIVER 67

Paul PHOENIX UK, male vocalist

4 wks

3 Nov 79	**NUNC DIMITTIS** Different HAVE 20	56	4 wks

Full artist credit on hit as follows: Paul Phoenix (treble) with Instrumental Ensemble - James Watson (trumpet), John Scott (organ), conducted by Barry Rose.

PHOTOS UK, male/female vocal/instrumental group

4 wks

17 May 80	**IRENE** Epic EPC 8517	56	4 wks

PIA US, female vocalist

4 wks

12 Nov 88	**DANCE OUT OF MY HEAD** Epic 652886 1	65	4 wks

Pia is Pia Zadora. See also Jermaine Jackson and Pia Zadora.

Edith PIAF France, female vocalist

15 wks

12 May 60	**MILORD** Columbia DC 754	41	4 wks
3 Nov 60	**MILORD (re-entry)** Columbia DC 754	24	11 wks

Bobby 'Boris' PICKETT and the CRYPT-KICKERS

US, male vocalist, male vocal/instrumental backing group

13 wks

1 Sep 73	● **MONSTER MASH** London HL 10320	3	13 wks

Wilson PICKETT US, male vocalist

61 wks

23 Sep 65	**IN THE MIDNIGHT HOUR** Atlantic AT 4036	12	11 wks
25 Nov 65	**DON'T FIGHT IT** Atlantic AT 4052	29	8 wks
10 Mar 66	**634-5789** Atlantic AT 4072	36	5 wks
1 Sep 66	**LAND OF 1000 DANCES** Atlantic 584-039	22	9 wks
15 Dec 66	**MUSTANG SALLY** Atlantic 584-066	28	7 wks
27 Sep 67	**FUNKY BROADWAY** Atlantic 584-130	43	3 wks
11 Sep 68	**I'M A MIDNIGHT MOVER** Atlantic 584-203	38	6 wks
8 Jan 69	**HEY JUDE** Atlantic 584-236	16	9 wks
21 Nov 87	**IN THE MIDNIGHT HOUR** Motown ZB 41583	62	3 wks

In The Midnight Hour on Motown is a re-recording.

PICKETTYWITCH UK, male/female vocal/instrumental group

34 wks

28 Feb 70	● **THAT SAME OLD FEELING** Pye 7N 17887	5	14 wks
4 Jul 70	**(IT'S LIKE A) SAD OLD KINDA MOVIE** Pye 7N 17951	16	10 wks
7 Nov 70	**BABY I WON'T LET YOU DOWN** Pye 7N 45002	27	10 wks

PIGBAG UK, male instrumental group

20 wks

7 Nov 81	**SUNNY DAY** Y Records Y 12	53	3 wks
27 Feb 82	**GETTING UP** Y Records Y 16	61	3 wks
3 Apr 82	● **PAPA'S GOT A BRAND NEW PIGBAG** Y Records Y 10	3	11 wks
10 Jul 82	**THE BIG BEAN** Y Records Y 24	40	3 wks

Nelson PIGFORD – See De Etta LITTLE and Nelson PIGFORD

PIGLETS UK, female vocal group

12 wks

6 Nov 71	● **JOHNNY REGGAE** Bell 1180	3	12 wks

Dick PIKE – See Ruby WRIGHT

P.I.L. – See PUBLIC IMAGE LTD.

PILOT UK, male vocal/instrumental group

29 wks

2 Nov 74	**MAGIC** EMI 2217	11	11 wks
18 Jan 75	★ **JANUARY** EMI 2255	1	10 wks
19 Apr 75	**CALL ME ROUND** EMI 2287	34	4 wks
27 Sep 75	**JUST A SMILE** EMI 2338	31	4 wks

PILTDOWN MEN US, male instrumental group

36 wks

8 Sep 60	**MACDONALD'S CAVE** Capitol CL 15149	14	18 wks
12 Jan 61	**PILTDOWN RIDES AGAIN** Capitol CL 15175	14	10 wks
9 Mar 61	**GOODNIGHT MRS. FLINTSTONE** Capitol CL 15186	18	8 wks

Courtney PINE featuring Carroll THOMPSON UK, male/female instrumental/vocal duo

1 wk

7 Jul 90	**I'M STILL WAITING** Mango MNG 749	66	1 wk

See also Movement 98 featuring Carroll Thompson; Mica Paris.

PING PING and Al VERLAINE

Belgium, male vocal duo

4 wks

28 Sep 61	**SUCU SUCU** Oriole CB 1589	41	4 wks

PINK FLOYD UK, male vocal/instrumental group

48 wks

30 Mar 67	**ARNOLD LAYNE** Columbia DB 8156	20	8 wks
22 Jun 67	● **SEE EMILY PLAY** Columbia DB 8214	6	12 wks
1 Dec 79	★ **ANOTHER BRICK IN THE WALL** (PART 2) Harvest HAR 5194	1	12 wks
7 Aug 82	**WHEN THE TIGERS BROKE FREE** Harvest HAR 5222	39	5 wks
7 May 83	**NOT NOW JOHN** Harvest HAR 5224	30	4 wks
19 Dec 87	**ON THE TURNING AWAY** EMI EM 34	55	4 wks
25 Jun 88	**ONE SLIP** EMI EM 52	50	3 wks

PINKEES UK, male vocal/instrumental group

9 wks

18 Sep 82	● **DANGER GAMES** Creole CR 39	8	9 wks

PINKERTON'S ASSORTED COLOURS UK, male vocal/instrumental group

12 wks

13 Jan 66	● **MIRROR MIRROR** Decca F 12307	9	11 wks
21 Apr 66	**DON'T STOP LOVIN' ME BABY** Decca F 12377	50	1 wk

PIONEERS Jamaica, male vocal/instrumental group

34 wks

18 Oct 69	**LONG SHOT KICK DE BUCKET** Trojan TR 672	21	10 wks
10 Jan 70	**LONG SHOT KICK DE BUCKET (re-entry)** Trojan TR 672	40	1 wk

31 Jul 71	● LET YOUR YEAH BE YEAH *Trojan TR 7825*	5	12 wks
15 Jan 72	GIVE AND TAKE *Trojan TR 7846*	35	6 wks
29 Mar 80	LONG SHOT KICK DE BUCKET (re-issue) *Trojan TRO 9063*	42	5 wks

Re-issue of Long Shot Kick De Bucket *coupled with re-issue of* Liquidator *by Harry J. All Stars. See also Harry J. All Stars.*

PIPKINS *UK, male vocal duo* **10 wks**

28 Mar 70	● GIMME DAT DING *Columbia DB 8662*	6	10 wks

PIPS – *See Gladys KNIGHT and the PIPS*

PIRANHAS *UK, male vocal/instrumental group* **21 wks**

2 Aug 80	● TOM HARK *Sire SIR 4044*	6	12 wks
16 Oct 82	ZAMBESI *Dakota DAK 6*	17	9 wks

Zambesi *has credit 'featuring Boring Bob Grover'.*

PIRATES – *See Johnny KIDD and the PIRATES*

Gene PITNEY *US, male vocalist* **200 wks**

23 Mar 61	I WANNA LOVE MY LIFE AWAY *London HL 9270*	26	11 wks
8 Mar 62	TOWN WITHOUT PITY *HMV POP 952*	32	6 wks
5 Dec 63	● TWENTY FOUR HOURS FROM TULSA *United Artists UP 1035*	5	19 wks
5 Mar 64	● THAT GIRL BELONGS TO YESTERDAY *United Artists UP 1045*	7	12 wks
15 Oct 64	IT HURTS TO BE IN LOVE *United Artists UP 1063*	36	4 wks
12 Nov 64	● I'M GONNA BE STRONG *Stateside SS 358*	2	14 wks
18 Feb 65	● I MUST BE SEEING THINGS *Stateside SS 390*	6	10 wks
10 Jun 65	● LOOKING THROUGH THE EYES OF LOVE *Stateside SS 420*	3	12 wks
4 Nov 65	● PRINCESS IN RAGS *Stateside SS 471*	9	12 wks
17 Feb 66	● BACKSTAGE *Stateside SS 490*	4	10 wks
9 Jun 66	● NOBODY NEEDS YOUR LOVE *Stateside SS 518*	2	13 wks
10 Nov 66	● JUST ONE SMILE *Stateside SS 558*	8	12 wks
23 Feb 67	COLD LIGHT OF DAY *Stateside SS 597*	38	6 wks
15 Nov 67	● SOMETHING'S GOTTEN HOLD OF MY HEART *Stateside SS 2060*	5	13 wks
3 Apr 68	SOMEWHERE IN THE COUNTRY *Stateside SS 2103*	19	9 wks
27 Nov 68	YOURS UNTIL TOMORROW *Stateside SS 2131*	34	7 wks
5 Mar 69	MARIA ELENA *Stateside SS 2142*	25	6 wks
14 Mar 70	A STREET CALLED HOPE *Stateside SS 2164*	37	5 wks
3 Oct 70	SHADY LADY *Stateside SS 2177*	29	8 wks
28 Apr 73	24 SYCAMORE *Pye International 7N 25606*	34	7 wks
2 Nov 74	BLUE ANGEL *Bronze BRO 11*	49	1 wk
16 Nov 74	BLUE ANGEL (re-entry) *Bronze BRO 11*	39	3 wks

See also Marc Almond.

PIXIES *US, male/female vocal/instrumental group* **8 wks**

1 Apr 89	MONKEY GONE TO HEAVEN *4AD AD 904*	60	3 wks
1 Jul 89	HERE COMES YOUR MAN *4AD AD 909*	54	1 wk
28 Jul 90	VELOURIA *4AD AD 0009*	28	3 wks
10 Nov 90	DIG FOR FIRE *4AD AD 0014*	62	1 wk

Joe PIZZULO – *See Sergio MENDES*

PLANET PATROL *US, male vocal/instrumental group* **3 wks**

17 Sep 83	CHEAP THRILLS *Polydor POSP 639*	64	3 wks

PLANETS *UK, male vocal/instrumental group* **8 wks**

18 Aug 79	LINES *Rialto TREB 104*	36	6 wks
25 Oct 80	DON'T LOOK DOWN *Rialto TREB 116*	66	2 wks

Robert PLANT *UK, male vocalist* **19 wks**

9 Oct 82	BURNING DOWN ONE SIDE *Swansong SSK 19429*	73	1 wk
16 Jul 83	BIG LOG *WEA B 9848*	11	10 wks
30 Jan 88	HEAVEN KNOWS *Es Paranza A 9373*	33	5 wks
28 Apr 90	HURTING KIND (I'VE GOT MY EYES ON YOU) *Es Paranza A 9985*	45	3 wks

PLASMATICS *US, female/male vocal/instrumental group* **4 wks**

26 Jul 80	BUTCHER BABY *Stiff BUY 76*	55	4 wks

PLASTIC BERTRAND *Belgium, male vocalist* **17 wks**

13 May 78	● CA PLANE POUR MOI *Sire 6078 616*	8	12 wks
5 Aug 78	SHA LA LA LA LEE *Vertigo 6059 209*	39	5 wks

PLASTIC ONO BAND – *See John LENNON*

PLASTIC ONO NUCLEAR BAND – *See John LENNON*

PLASTIC PENNY *UK, male vocal/instrumental group* **10 wks**

3 Jan 68	● EVERYTHING I AM *Page One POF 051*	6	10 wks

PLASTIC POPULATION – *See YAZZ; COLDCUT*

PLATINUM HOOK *US, male vocal/instrumental group* **1 wk**

2 Sep 78	STANDING ON THE VERGE (OF GETTING IT ON) *Motown TMG 1115*	72	1 wk

PLATTERS *US, male/female vocal group* **91 wks**

7 Sep 56	● THE GREAT PRETENDER/ ONLY YOU *Mercury MT 117*	5	12 wks
2 Nov 56	● MY PRAYER *Mercury MT 120*	4	10 wks
7 Dec 56	THE GREAT PRETENDER/ ONLY YOU (re-entry) *Mercury MT 117*	21	1 wk
18 Jan 57	MY PRAYER (re-entry) *Mercury MT 120*	28	2 wks
25 Jan 57	YOU'LL NEVER NEVER KNOW/ IT ISN'T RIGHT *Mercury MT 130*	23	1 wk
8 Feb 57	YOU'LL NEVER NEVER KNOW/ IT ISN'T RIGHT (re-entry) *Mercury MT 130*	29	1 wk
29 Mar 57	MY PRAYER (2nd re-entry) *Mercury MT 120*	22	1 wk
29 Mar 57	ONLY YOU (2nd re-entry) *Mercury MT 117*	18	3 wks
12 Apr 57	YOU'LL NEVER NEVER KNOW/ IT ISN'T RIGHT (2nd re-entry) *Mercury MT 130*	29	1 wk
17 May 57	I'M SORRY *Mercury MT 145*	18	6 wks
5 Jul 57	I'M SORRY (re-entry) *Mercury MT 145*	23	1 wk
19 Jul 57	I'M SORRY (2nd re-entry) *Mercury MT 145*	22	1 wk
16 May 58	TWILIGHT TIME *Mercury MT 214*	3	18 wks
16 Jan 59	★ SMOKE GETS IN YOUR EYES *Mercury AMT 1016*	1	20 wks
28 Aug 59	REMEMBER WHEN *Mercury AMT 1053*	25	2 wks
29 Jan 60	HARBOUR LIGHTS *Mercury AMT 1081*	11	11 wks

PLAYBOY BAND – *See John FRED and the PLAYBOY BAND*

PLAYBOYS – *See Gary LEWIS and the PLAYBOYS*

PLAYER *US/UK, male vocal/instrumental group* **7 wks**

25 Feb 78	BABY COME BACK *RSO 2090 254*	32	7 wks

PLAYERS ASSOCIATION

17 wks

US, male/female vocal/instrumental group

10 Mar 79	● TURN THE MUSIC UP *Vanguard VS 5011*	8	9 wks
5 May 79	RIDE THE GROOVE *Vanguard VS 5012*	42	5 wks
9 Feb 80	WE GOT THE GROOVE *Vanguard VS 5016*	61	3 wks

See also Calibre Cuts.

PLUS ONE featuring SIRRON

4 wks

UK, male/female vocal/instrumental group

19 May 90	IT'S HAPPENIN' *MCA MCA 1405*	40	4 wks

PLUTO – *See Pluto SHERVINGTON*

POETS *UK, male vocal/instrumental group*

5 wks

29 Oct 64	NOW WE'RE THRU *Decca F 11995*	31	5 wks

POGUES *Ireland, male/female vocal/instrumental group*

45 wks

6 Apr 85	A PAIR OF BROWN EYES *Stiff BUY 220*	72	2 wks
22 Jun 85	SALLY MACLENNANE *Stiff BUY 224*	51	4 wks
14 Sep 85	DIRTY OLD TOWN *Stiff BUY 229*	62	3 wks
8 Mar 86	POGUETRY IN MOTION (EP) *Stiff BUY 243*	29	6 wks
30 Aug 86	HAUNTED *MCA MCA 1084*	42	4 wks
5 Dec 87	● FAIRYTALE OF NEW YORK *Pogue Mahone NY 7*	2	9 wks
5 Mar 88	IF I SHOULD FALL FROM GRACE WITH GOD *Pogue Mahone PG 1*	58	3 wks
16 Jul 88	FIESTA *Pogue Mahone PG 2*	24	5 wks
17 Dec 88	YEAH YEAH YEAH YEAH *Pogue Mahone YZ 355*	43	4 wks
8 Jul 89	MISTY MORNING, ALBERT BRIDGE *Pogue Mahone YZ 407*	41	3 wks
15 Sep 90	SUMMER IN SIAM *Pogue Mahone YZ 519*	64	7 wks

Tracks on EP: London Girl/The Body of an American/A Rainy Night in Soho/Planxty Noel Hill. Fairytale Of New York features Kirsty MacColl. See also Kirsty MacColl; Pogues and the Dubliners.

POGUES and the DUBLINERS

10 wks

Ireland, two male vocal/instrumental groups

28 Mar 87	● THE IRISH ROVER *Stiff BUY 258*	8	8 wks
16 Jun 90	JACK'S HEROES/ WHISKEY IN THE JAR *Pogue Mahone YZ 500*	63	2 wks

See also Pogues; Dubliners.

POINTER SISTERS *US, female vocal group*

87 wks

3 Feb 79	EVERYBODY IS A STAR *Planet K 12324*	61	3 wks
17 Mar 79	FIRE *Planet K 12339*	34	8 wks
22 Aug 81	● SLOWHAND *Planet K 12530*	10	11 wks
5 Dec 81	SHOULD I DO IT? *Reprise K 12578*	50	5 wks
14 Apr 84	● AUTOMATIC *Planet RPS 105*	2	15 wks
23 Jun 84	● JUMP (FOR MY LOVE) *Planet RPS 106*	6	10 wks
11 Aug 84	I NEED YOU *Planet RPS 107*	25	9 wks
27 Oct 84	I'M SO EXCITED *Planet RPS 108*	11	11 wks
12 Jan 85	NEUTRON DANCE *Planet RPS 109*	31	7 wks
20 Jul 85	DARE ME *RCA PB 49957*	17	8 wks

POISON *US, male vocal/instrumental group*

35 wks

23 May 87	TALK DIRTY TO ME *Music For Nations KUT 125*	67	1 wk
7 May 88	NOTHIN' BUT A GOOD TIME *Capitol CL 486*	35	3 wks
5 Nov 88	FALLEN ANGEL *Capitol CL 500*	59	1 wk
11 Feb 89	EVERY ROSE HAS ITS THORN *Capitol CL 520*	13	9 wks
29 Apr 89	YOUR MAMA DON'T DANCE *Capitol CL 523*	13	7 wks
23 Sep 89	NOTHIN' BUT A GOOD TIME *Capitol CL 539*	48	3 wks

30 Jun 90	UNSKINNY BOP *Capitol CL 582*	15	7 wks
27 Oct 90	SOMETHING TO BELIEVE IN *Enigma CL 594*	35	4 wks

POLECATS *UK, male vocal/instrumental group*

18 wks

7 Mar 81	JOHN I'M ONLY DANCING/ BIG GREEN CAR *Mercury POLE 1*	35	8 wks
16 May 81	ROCKABILLY GUY *Mercury POLE 2*	35	6 wks
22 Aug 81	JEEPSTER/ MARIE CELESTE *Mercury POLE 3*	53	4 wks

POLICE *UK/US, male vocal/instrumental group*

142 wks

7 Oct 78	CAN'T STAND LOSING YOU *A & M AMS 7381*	42	5 wks
28 Apr 79	ROXANNE *A & M AMS 7348*	12	9 wks
7 Jul 79	● CAN'T STAND LOSING YOU (re-entry) *A & M AMS 7381*	2	11 wks
22 Sep 79	★ MESSAGE IN A BOTTLE *A & M AMS 7474*	1	11 wks
17 Nov 79	FALL OUT *Illegal IL 001*	47	4 wks
1 Dec 79	● WALKING ON THE MOON *A & M AMS 7494*	1	10 wks
16 Feb 80	● SO LONELY *A & M AMS 7402*	6	10 wks
14 Jun 80	SIX PACK *A & M AMPP 6001*	17	4 wks
27 Sep 80	★ DON'T STAND SO CLOSE TO ME *A & M AMS 7564*	1	10 wks
13 Dec 80	● DE DO DO DO, DE DA DA DA *A & M AMS 7578*	5	8 wks
26 Sep 81	● INVISIBLE SUN *A & M AMS 8164*	2	8 wks
24 Oct 81	★ EVERY LITTLE THING SHE DOES IS MAGIC *A & M AMS 8174*	1	13 wks
12 Dec 81	SPIRITS IN THE MATERIAL WORLD *A & M AMS 8194*	12	8 wks
28 May 83	★ EVERY BREATH YOU TAKE *A & M AM 117*	1	11 wks
23 Jul 83	● WRAPPED AROUND YOUR FINGER *A & M AM 127*	7	7 wks
5 Nov 83	SYNCHRONICITY II *A & M AM 153*	17	4 wks
14 Jan 84	KING OF PAIN *A & M AM 176*	17	5 wks
11 Oct 86	DON'T STAND SO CLOSE TO ME '86 (re-mix) *A & M AM 354*	24	4 wks

Six Pack consists of six separate Police singles as follows: The Bed's Too Big Without You/Roxanne/Message In A Bottle/Walking On The Moon/So Lonely/Can't Stand Losing You. The last five titles were re-issues.

Su POLLARD *UK, female vocalist*

11 wks

5 Oct 85	COME TO ME (I AM WOMAN) *Rainbow RBR 1*	71	1 wk
1 Feb 86	● STARTING TOGETHER *Rainbow RBR 4*	2	10 wks

PONI-TAILS *US, female vocal group*

14 wks

19 Sep 58	● BORN TOO LATE *HMV POP 516*	5	11 wks
10 Apr 59	EARLY TO BED *HMV POP 596*	26	3 wks

Brian POOLE and the TREMELOES

90 wks

UK, male vocalist, male vocal/instrumental backing group

4 Jul 63	● TWIST AND SHOUT *Decca F 11694*	4	14 wks
12 Sep 63	★ DO YOU LOVE ME *Decca F 11739*	1	14 wks
28 Nov 63	I CAN DANCE *Decca F 11771*	31	8 wks
30 Jan 64	● CANDY MAN *Decca F 11823*	6	13 wks
7 May 64	● SOMEONE SOMEONE *Decca F 11893*	2	17 wks
20 Aug 64	TWELVE STEPS TO LOVE *Decca F 11951*	32	7 wks
7 Jan 65	THREE BELLS *Decca F 12037*	17	9 wks
22 Jul 65	I WANT CANDY *Decca F 12197*	25	8 wks

See also Tremeloes.

Glyn POOLE *UK, male vocalist*

8 wks

20 Oct 73	MILLY MOLLY MANDY *York SYK 565*	35	8 wks

Iggy POP US, male vocalist   16 wks

13 Dec 86	● REAL WILD CHILD (WILD ONE) A &M AM 368	10	11 wks
10 Feb 90	LIVIN' ON THE EDGE OF THE NIGHT		
	Virgin America VUS 18	51	4 wks
13 Oct 90	CANDY Virgin America VUS 29	67	1 wk

POP TOPS Spain, male vocal group   6 wks

9 Oct 71	MAMY BLUE A &M AMS 859	34	6 wks

POP WILL EAT ITSELF   21 wks
UK, male vocal/instrumental group

30 Jan 88	THERE IS NO LOVE BETWEEN US ANYMORE		
	Chapter 22 CHAP 20	66	1 wk
23 Jul 88	DEF. CON ONE Chapter 22 PWE 001	63	4 wks
11 Feb 89	CAN U DIG IT RCA PB 42621	38	4 wks
22 Apr 89	WISE UP! SUCKER RCA PB 42761	41	3 wks
2 Sep 89	VERY METAL NOISE POLLUTION (EP)		
	RCA PB 42883	45	3 wks
9 Jun 90	TOUCHED BY THE HAND OF CICCIOLINA		
	RCA PB 43735	28	4 wks
13 Oct 90	DANCE OF THE MAD RCA PB 44023	32	2 wks

Tracks on Very Metal Noise Pollution EP: Def Con. 1989 AD including the Twilight Zone/Preaching To The Perverted/P.W.E.I.-zation/92F.

POPPY FAMILY   14 wks
Canada, male/female vocal/instrumental group

15 Aug 70	● WHICH WAY YOU GOIN' BILLY Decca F 22976	7	14 wks

Gary PORTNOY US, male vocalist   3 wks

25 Feb 84	THEME FROM 'CHEERS' Starblend CHEER 1	58	3 wks

PORTSMOUTH SINFONIA UK, orchestra   4 wks

12 Sep 81	CLASSICAL MUDDLEY Island WIP 6736	38	4 wks

Sandy POSEY US, female vocalist   32 wks

15 Sep 66	BORN A WOMAN MGM 1321	24	11 wks
5 Jan 67	SINGLE GIRL MGM 1330	15	13 wks
13 Apr 67	WHAT A WOMAN IN LOVE WON'T DO MGM 1335	48	3 wks
6 Sep 75	SINGLE GIRL MGM 2006 533	35	5 wks

POSITIVE FORCE US, female vocal duo   9 wks

22 Dec 79	WE GOT THE FUNK Sugarhill SHL 102	18	9 wks

See also Calibre Cuts.

POSITIVE PEOPLE – See Frank HOOKER and POSITIVE PEOPLE

Mike POST US, orchestra   18 wks

9 Aug 75	AFTERNOON OF THE RHINO Warner Bros. K 16588	48	1 wk
23 Aug 75	AFTERNOON OF THE RHINO (re-entry)		
	Warner Bros. K 16588	47	1 wk
16 Jan 82	THEME FROM 'HILL STREET BLUES'		
	Elektron K 12576	25	11 wks
29 Sep 84	THE A TEAM RCA 443	45	5 wks

First hit credited to 'Mike Post Coalition'. Theme From Hill Street Blues features Larry Carlton - US, male instrumentalist - guitar.

POTTERS UK, male vocal group   2 wks

1 Apr 72	WE'LL BE WITH YOU Pye JT 100	34	2 wks

Cozy POWELL UK, male instrumentalist - drums   35 wks

8 Dec 73	● DANCE WITH THE DEVIL RAK 164	3	15 wks
25 May 74	THE MAN IN BLACK RAK 173	18	8 wks
10 Aug 74	● NA NA NA RAK 180	10	10 wks
10 Nov 79	THEME ONE Ariola ARO 189	62	2 wks

POWER STATION UK/US, male vocal/instrumental group   16 wks

16 Mar 85	SOME LIKE IT HOT Parlophone R 6091	14	8 wks
11 May 85	GET IT ON Parlophone R 6096	22	7 wks
9 Nov 85	COMMUNICATION Parlophone R 6114	75	1 wk

Will POWERS   9 wks
US, female vocalist, Lyn Goldsmith under assumed name

1 Oct 83	KISSING WITH CONFIDENCE Island IS 134	17	9 wks

Hit features vocals by Carly Simon. See also Carly Simon.

Perez PRADO Cuba, orchestra   33 wks

25 Mar 55	★ CHERRY PINK AND APPLE BLOSSOM WHITE		
	HMV B 10833	1	17 wks
25 Jul 58	● PATRICIA RCA 1067	8	16 wks

Billed on first hit as Perez 'Prez' Prado and His Orchestra, the King of the Mambo.

PRATT and McLAIN with BROTHERLOVE   6 wks
US, male vocal duo with male instrumental group

1 Oct 77	HAPPY DAYS Reprise K 14435	31	6 wks

PRAYING MANTIS UK, male vocal/instrumental group   2 wks

31 Jan 81	CHEATED Arista ARIST 378	69	2 wks

PREFAB SPROUT   38 wks
UK, male/female vocal/instrumental group

28 Jan 84	DON'T SING Kitchenware SK 9	64	2 wks
20 Jul 85	FARON YOUNG Kitchenware SK 22	74	1 wk
9 Nov 85	WHEN LOVE BREAKS DOWN Kitchenware SK 21	25	10 wks
8 Feb 86	JOHNNY JOHNNY Kitchenware SK 24	64	2 wks
13 Feb 88	CARS AND GIRLS Kitchenware SK 35	44	5 wks
30 Apr 88	● THE KING OF ROCK 'N' ROLL Kitchenware SK 37	7	10 wks
23 Jul 88	HEY MANHATTAN! Kitchenware SK 38	72	2 wks
18 Aug 90	LOOKING FOR ATLANTIS Kitchenware SK 47	51	3 wks
20 Oct 90	WE LET THE STARS GO Kitchenware SK 48	50	3 wks

PRELUDE UK, male/female vocal group   26 wks

26 Jan 74	AFTER THE GOLDRUSH Dawn DNS 1052	21	9 wks
26 Apr 80	PLATINUM BLONDE EMI 5046	45	7 wks
22 May 82	AFTER THE GOLDRUSH After Hours AFT 02	28	7 wks
31 Jul 82	ONLY THE LONELY After Hours AFT 06	55	3 wks

AFT 02 was a re-recording of DNS 1052. Both songs are a capella.

ELVIS PRESLEY had four
number ones in each of two
years in a row (1961-62).
No other artist has achieved
this feat.

LLOYD PRICE staggered
into the British charts in
1959, but his 'Lawdy Miss
Clawdy' had topped the US
R&B table in 1952.

Elvis PRESLEY US, male vocalist   1141 wks

Date	Title	Pos	Wks
11 May 56	● HEARTBREAK HOTEL *HMV POP 182*	2	21 wks
25 May 56	● BLUE SUEDE SHOES *HMV POP 213*	9	8 wks
13 Jul 56	I WANT YOU I NEED YOU I LOVE YOU *HMV POP 235*	25	2 wks
3 Aug 56	I WANT YOU I NEED YOU I LOVE YOU (re-entry) *HMV POP 235*	14	9 wks
17 Aug 56	BLUE SUEDE SHOES (re-entry) *HMV POP 213*	26	2 wks
21 Sep 56	● HOUND DOG *HMV POP 249*	2	23 wks
26 Oct 56	HEARTBREAK HOTEL (re-entry) *HMV POP 182*	23	1 wk
16 Nov 56	● BLUE MOON *HMV POP 272*	9	11 wks
23 Nov 56	I DON'T CARE IF THE SUN DON'T SHINE *HMV POP 272*	29	1 wk
7 Dec 56	LOVE ME TENDER *HMV POP 253*	11	9 wks
21 Dec 56	I DON'T CARE IF THE SUN DON'T SHINE (re-entry) *HMV POP 272*	23	3 wks
15 Feb 57	MYSTERY TRAIN *HMV POP 295*	25	5 wks
8 Mar 57	RIP IT UP *HMV POP 305*	27	1 wk
10 May 57	● TOO MUCH *HMV POP 330*	6	8 wks
14 Jun 57	ALL SHOOK UP *HMV POP 359*	24	1 wk
28 Jun 57	★ ALL SHOOK UP (re-entry) *HMV POP 359*	1	20 wks
12 Jul 57	● TEDDY BEAR *RCA 1013*	3	19 wks
12 Jul 57	TOO MUCH (re-entry) *HMV POP 330*	26	1 wk
30 Aug 57	PARALYSED *HMV POP 378*	8	10 wks
4 Oct 57	● PARTY *RCA 1020*	2	15 wks
18 Oct 57	GOT A LOT O' LIVIN' TO DO *RCA 1020*	17	4 wks
1 Nov 57	LOVING YOU *RCA 1013*	24	4 wks
1 Nov 57	TRYING TO GET TO YOU *HMV POP 408*	16	4 wks
8 Nov 57	LAWDY MISS CLAWDY *HMV POP 408*	15	5 wks
15 Nov 57	● SANTA BRING MY BABY BACK TO ME *RCA 1025*	7	8 wks
17 Jan 58	I'M LEFT YOU'RE RIGHT SHE'S GONE *HMV POP 428*	21	2 wks
24 Jan 58	★ JAILHOUSE ROCK *RCA 1028*	1	14 wks
31 Jan 58	JAILHOUSE ROCK (EP) *RCA RCX 106*	18	5 wks
7 Feb 58	I'M LEFT YOU'RE RIGHT SHE'S GONE (re-entry) *HMV POP 428*	29	1 wk
28 Feb 58	● DON'T *RCA 1043*	2	11 wks
2 May 58	● WEAR MY RING AROUND YOUR NECK *RCA 1058*	3	10 wks
25 Jul 58	● HARD HEADED WOMAN *RCA 1070*	2	11 wks
3 Oct 58	● KING CREOLE *RCA 1081*	2	15 wks
23 Jan 59	★ ONE NIGHT/ I GOT STUNG *RCA 1100*	1	12 wks
24 Apr 59	★ A FOOL SUCH AS I/ I NEED YOUR LOVE TONIGHT *RCA 1113*	1	15 wks
24 Jul 59	● A BIG HUNK O' LOVE *RCA 1136*	4	9 wks
12 Feb 60	STRICTLY ELVIS (EP) *RCA RCX 175*	26	1 wk
7 Apr 60	● STUCK ON YOU *RCA 1187*	3	14 wks
28 Jul 60	● A MESS OF BLUES *RCA 1194*	2	18 wks
3 Nov 60	★ IT'S NOW OR NEVER *RCA 1207*	1	19 wks
19 Jan 61	★ ARE YOU LONESOME TONIGHT *RCA 1216*	1	15 wks
9 Mar 61	★ WOODEN HEART *RCA 1226*	1	27 wks
25 May 61	★ SURRENDER *RCA 1227*	1	15 wks
7 Sep 61	● WILD IN THE COUNTRY/ I FEEL SO BAD *RCA 1244*	4	12 wks
2 Nov 61	★ HIS LATEST FLAME/ LITTLE SISTER *RCA 1258*	1	13 wks
1 Feb 62	★ ROCK A HULA BABY/ CAN'T HELP FALLING IN LOVE *RCA 1270*	1	20 wks
10 May 62	★ GOOD LUCK CHARM *RCA 1280*	1	17 wks
21 Jun 62	FOLLOW THAT DREAM (EP) *RCA RCX 211*	34	2 wks
30 Aug 62	★ SHE'S NOT YOU *RCA 1303*	1	14 wks
29 Nov 62	★ RETURN TO SENDER *RCA 1320*	1	14 wks
28 Feb 63	ONE BROKEN HEART FOR SALE *RCA 1337*	12	9 wks
4 Jul 63	★ DEVIL IN DISGUISE *RCA 1355*	1	12 wks
24 Oct 63	BOSSA NOVA BABY *RCA 1374*	13	8 wks
19 Dec 63	KISS ME QUICK *RCA 1375*	14	10 wks
12 Mar 64	VIVA LAS VEGAS *RCA 1390*	17	12 wks
25 Jun 64	● KISSIN' COUSINS *RCA 1404*	10	11 wks
20 Aug 64	SUCH A NIGHT *RCA 1411*	13	10 wks
29 Oct 64	AIN'T THAT LOVIN' YOU BABY *RCA 1422*	15	8 wks
3 Dec 64	BLUE CHRISTMAS *RCA 1430*	11	7 wks
11 Mar 65	DO THE CLAM *RCA 1443*	19	8 wks
27 May 65	★ CRYING IN THE CHAPEL *RCA 1455*	1	15 wks
11 Nov 65	TELL ME WHY *RCA 1489*	15	10 wks
24 Feb 66	BLUE RIVER *RCA 1504*	22	7 wks
7 Apr 66	FRANKIE AND JOHNNY *RCA 1509*	21	9 wks
7 Jul 66	● LOVE LETTERS *RCA 1526*	6	10 wks
13 Oct 66	ALL THAT I AM *RCA 1545*	18	8 wks
1 Dec 66	IF EVERY DAY WAS LIKE CHRISTMAS *RCA 1557*	13	7 wks
9 Feb 67	INDESCRIBABLY BLUE *RCA 1565*	21	5 wks
11 May 67	YOU GOTTA STOP/ LOVE MACHINE *RCA 1593*	38	5 wks
16 Aug 67	LONG LEGGED GIRL *RCA RCA 1616*	49	2 wks
21 Feb 68	GUITAR MAN *RCA 1663*	19	9 wks
15 May 68	U. S. MALE *RCA 1688*	15	8 wks
17 Jul 68	YOUR TIME HASN'T COME YET BABY *RCA 1714*	22	11 wks
16 Oct 68	YOU'LL NEVER WALK ALONE *RCA 1747*	44	3 wks
26 Feb 69	IF I CAN DREAM *RCA 1795*	11	10 wks
11 Jun 69	● IN THE GHETTO *RCA 1831*	2	16 wks
6 Sep 69	CLEAN UP YOUR OWN BACK YARD *RCA 1869*	21	7 wks
18 Oct 69	IN THE GHETTO (re-entry) *RCA 1831*	50	1 wk
29 Nov 69	● SUSPICIOUS MINDS *RCA 1900*	2	14 wks
28 Feb 70	● DON'T CRY DADDY *RCA 1916*	8	11 wks
16 May 70	KENTUCKY RAIN *RCA 1949*	21	11 wks
11 Jul 70	★ THE WONDER OF YOU *RCA 1974*	1	20 wks
8 Aug 70	KENTUCKY RAIN (re-entry) *RCA 1949*	46	1 wk
14 Nov 70	● I'VE LOST YOU *RCA 1999*	9	12 wks
9 Jan 71	● YOU DON'T HAVE TO SAY YOU LOVE ME *RCA 2046*	9	7 wks
23 Jan 71	THE WONDER OF YOU (re-entry) *RCA 1974*	47	1 wk
6 Mar 71	YOU DON'T HAVE TO SAY YOU LOVE ME (re-entry) *RCA 2046*	35	3 wks
20 Mar 71	● THERE GOES MY EVERYTHING *RCA 2060*	6	11 wks
15 May 71	RAGS TO RICHES *RCA 2084*	9	11 wks
17 Jul 71	● HEARTBREAK HOTEL/ HOUND DOG (re-issue) *RCA Maximillion 2104*	10	12 wks
2 Oct 71	I'M LEAVIN' *RCA 2125*	23	9 wks
4 Dec 71	● I JUST CAN'T HELP BELIEVING *RCA 2158*	6	16 wks
11 Dec 71	JAILHOUSE ROCK (re-issue) *RCA Maximillion 2153*	42	5 wks
1 Apr 72	● UNTIL IT'S TIME FOR YOU TO GO *RCA 2188*	5	9 wks
17 Jun 72	● AMERICAN TRILOGY *RCA 2229*	8	11 wks
30 Sep 72	● BURNING LOVE *RCA 2267*	7	9 wks
16 Dec 72	● ALWAYS ON MY MIND *RCA 2304*	9	13 wks
26 May 73	POLK SALAD ANNIE *RCA 2359*	23	7 wks
11 Aug 73	FOOL *RCA 2393*	15	10 wks
24 Nov 73	RAISED ON ROCK *RCA 2435*	36	7 wks
16 Mar 74	I'VE GOT A THING ABOUT YOU BABY *RCA APBO 0196*	33	5 wks
13 Jul 74	IF YOU TALK IN YOUR SLEEP *RCA APBO 0280*	40	3 wks
16 Nov 74	● MY BOY *RCA 2458*	5	13 wks
18 Jan 75	● PROMISED LAND *RCA PB 10074*	9	8 wks
24 May 75	T. R. O. U. B. L. E. *RCA 2562*	31	4 wks
29 Nov 75	GREEN GREEN GRASS OF HOME *RCA 2635*	29	7 wks
1 May 76	HURT *RCA 2674*	37	5 wks
4 Sep 76	● GIRL OF MY BEST FRIEND *RCA 2729*	9	12 wks
25 Dec 76	● SUSPICION *RCA 2768*	9	12 wks
5 Mar 77	● MOODY BLUE *RCA PB 0857*	6	9 wks
13 Aug 77	★ WAY DOWN *RCA PB 0998*	1	13 wks
3 Sep 77	ALL SHOOK UP (re-issue) *RCA PB 2694*	41	2 wks
3 Sep 77	ARE YOU LONESOME TONIGHT (re-issue) *RCA PB 2699*	46	1 wk
3 Sep 77	CRYING IN THE CHAPEL (re-issue) *RCA PB 2708*	43	2 wks
3 Sep 77	IT'S NOW OR NEVER (re-issue) *RCA PB 2698*	39	2 wks
3 Sep 77	JAILHOUSE ROCK (2nd re-issue) *RCA PB 2695*	44	2 wks
3 Sep 77	RETURN TO SENDER (re-issue) *RCA PB 2706*	42	3 wks
3 Sep 77	THE WONDER OF YOU (re-issue) *RCA PB 2709*	48	1 wk
3 Sep 77	WOODEN HEART (re-issue) *RCA PB 2700*	49	1 wk
10 Dec 77	● MY WAY *RCA PB 1165*	9	8 wks
24 Jun 78	DON'T BE CRUEL *RCA PB 9265*	24	12 wks
15 Dec 79	IT WON'T SEEM LIKE CHRISTMAS (WITHOUT YOU) *RCA PB 9464*	13	6 wks
30 Aug 80	● IT'S ONLY LOVE/ BEYOND THE REEF *RCA 4*	3	10 wks
6 Dec 80	SANTA CLAUS IS BACK IN TOWN *RCA 16*	41	6 wks
14 Feb 81	GUITAR MAN *RCA 43*	43	4 wks
18 Apr 81	LOVING ARMS *RCA 48*	47	4 wks
13 Mar 82	ARE YOU LONESOME TONIGHT *RCA 196*	25	7 wks
26 Jun 82	THE SOUND OF YOUR CRY *RCA 232*	59	2 wks
5 Feb 83	JAILHOUSE ROCK (re-issue) *RCA 1028*	27	6 wks
7 May 83	BABY I DON'T CARE *RCA 332*	61	3 wks
3 Dec 83	I CAN HELP *RCA 369*	30	9 wks
10 Nov 84	THE LAST FAREWELL *RCA 459*	48	6 wks
19 Jan 85	THE ELVIS MEDLEY *RCA 476*	51	3 wks
10 Aug 85	ALWAYS ON MY MIND *RCA PB 49944*	59	4 wks
11 Apr 87	AIN'T THAT LOVIN' YOU BABY/ BOSSA NOVA BABY *RCA ARON 1*	47	5 wks
22 Aug 87	LOVE ME TENDER/ IF I CAN DREAM (re-issue) *RCA ARON 2*	56	3 wks
16 Jan 88	STUCK ON YOU (re-issue) *RCA PB 49595*	58	2 wks

Tracks on Jailhouse Rock EP: Jailhouse Rock/Young And Beautiful/I Want To Be Free/Don't
Leave Me Now/Baby I Don't Care. On Strictly Elvis EP: Old Shep/Any Place Is

Paradise/Paralysed/Is It So Strange. On Follow That Dream EP: Follow That Dream/Angel/What A Wonderful Life/I'm Not The Marrying Kind. On 5 July 62 a note on the Top 50 for that week stated 'Due to difficulties in assessing returns of Follow That Dream EP, it has been decided not to include it in Britain's Top 50. It is of course No.1 in the EP charts'. Therefore this EP only had a 2 week chart when its sales would certainly have justified a much longer one. Beyond The Reef listed only 30 Aug to 13 Sep 80. Are You Lonesome Tonight on RCA 196 is a live version. Can't Help Falling In Love credited from 1 Mar 62. Tracks on The Elvis Medley: Jailhouse Rock/Teddy Bear/Hound Dog/Don't Be Cruel/Burning Love/Suspicious Minds. Both sides of RCA ARON 1 are alternate versions to the original hits. RCA PB 49944 is also an alternate version.

Billy PRESTON US, male vocalist/instrumentalist - keyboards   13 wks

2 Jul 69	THAT'S THE WAY GOD PLANNED IT Apple 12	11	10 wks
16 Sep 72	OUTA SPACE A & M AMS 7007	44	3 wks

See also Beatles; Billy Preston and Syreeta.

Billy PRESTON and SYREETA   15 wks
US, male/female vocal duo

15 Dec 79 ●	WITH YOU I'M BORN AGAIN Motown TMG 1159	2	11 wks
8 Mar 80	IT WILL COME IN TIME Motown TMG 1175	47	4 wks

See also Billy Preston; Syreeta.

Johnny PRESTON US, male vocalist   45 wks

12 Feb 60 ★	RUNNING BEAR Mercury AMT 1079	1	14 wks
21 Apr 60 ●	CRADLE OF LOVE Mercury AMT 1092	2	16 wks
2 Jun 60	RUNNING BEAR (re-entry) Mercury AMT 1079	41	1 wk
28 Jul 60	I'M STARTING TO GO STEADY Mercury AMT 1104	49	1 wk
11 Aug 60	FEEL SO FINE Mercury AMT 1104	18	10 wks
8 Dec 60	CHARMING BILLY Mercury AMT 1114	34	1 wk
22 Dec 60	CHARMING BILLY (re-entry) Mercury AMT 1114	42	2 wks

Mike PRESTON UK, male vocalist   33 wks

30 Oct 59	MR. BLUE Decca F 11167	12	8 wks
25 Aug 60	I'D DO ANYTHING Decca F 11255	23	10 wks
22 Dec 60	TOGETHERNESS Decca F 11287	41	5 wks
9 Mar 61	MARRY ME Decca F 11335	14	10 wks

PRETENDERS UK/US, male/female vocal/instrumental group   110 wks

10 Feb 79	STOP YOUR SOBBING Real ARE 6	34	9 wks
14 Jul 79	KID Real ARE 9	33	7 wks
17 Nov 79 ★	BRASS IN POCKET Real ARE 11	1	17 wks
5 Apr 80 ●	TALK OF THE TOWN Real ARE 12	8	8 wks
14 Feb 81	MESSAGE OF LOVE Real ARE 15	11	7 wks
12 Sep 81	DAY AFTER DAY Real ARE 17	45	4 wks
14 Nov 81 ●	I GO TO SLEEP Real ARE 18	7	10 wks
2 Oct 82	BACK ON THE CHAIN GANG Real ARE 19	17	9 wks
26 Nov 83	2000 MILES Real ARE 20	15	9 wks
9 Jun 84	THIN LINE BETWEEN LOVE AND HATE Real ARE 22	49	3 wks
11 Oct 86 ●	DON'T GET ME WRONG Real YZ 85	10	9 wks
13 Dec 86	HYMN TO HER Real YZ 93	8	12 wks
15 Aug 87	IF THERE WAS A MAN Real YZ 149	49	6 wks

On YZ 149 act billed as Pretenders For 007.

PRETTY BOY FLOYD   1 wk
US, male vocal/instrumental group

10 Mar 90	ROCK AND ROLL (IS GONNA SET THE NIGHT ON FIRE) MCA MCA 1393	75	1 wk

PRETTY THINGS UK, male vocal/instrumental group   41 wks

18 Jun 64	ROSALYN Fontana TF 469	41	5 wks
22 Oct 64 ●	DON'T BRING ME DOWN Fontana TF 503	10	11 wks
25 Feb 65	HONEY I NEED Fontana TF 537	13	10 wks
15 Jul 65	CRY TO ME Fontana TF 585	28	7 wks
20 Jan 66	MIDNIGHT TO SIX MAN Fontana TF 647	46	1 wk
5 May 66	COME SEE ME Fontana TF 688	43	5 wks
21 Jul 66	A HOUSE IN THE COUNTRY Fontana TF 722	50	1 wk
4 Aug 66	A HOUSE IN THE COUNTRY (re-entry) Fontana TF 722	50	1 wk

Alan PRICE UK, male vocalist/instrumentalist - keyboards   78 wks

31 Mar 66 ●	I PUT A SPELL ON YOU Decca F 12367	9	10 wks
14 Jul 66	HI LILI HI LO Decca F 12442	11	12 wks
2 Mar 67 ●	SIMON SMITH AND HIS AMAZING DANCING BEAR Decca F 12570	4	12 wks
2 Aug 67	THE HOUSE THAT JACK BUILT Decca F 12641	4	10 wks
15 Nov 67	SHAME Decca F 12691	45	2 wks
31 Jan 68	DON'T STOP THE CARNIVAL Decca F 12731	13	8 wks
25 May 74 ●	JARROW SONG Warner Bros. K 16372	6	9 wks
29 Apr 78	JUST FOR YOU Jet UP 36358	43	8 wks
17 Feb 79	BABY OF MINE/ JUST FOR YOU (re-issue) Jet 135	32	3 wks
30 Apr 88	CHANGES Ariola 109911	54	4 wks

The Decca hits are credited to the Alan Price Set. See also Fame and Price Together.

Lloyd PRICE US, male vocalist   36 wks

13 Feb 59 ●	STAGGER LEE HMV POP 580	7	14 wks
15 May 59	WHERE WERE YOU HMV POP 598	15	6 wks
12 Jun 59 ●	PERSONALITY HMV POP 626	9	8 wks
14 Aug 59	PERSONALITY (re-entry) HMV POP 626	25	2 wks
11 Sep 59	I'M GONNA GET MARRIED HMV POP 650	23	5 wks
21 Apr 60	LADY LUCK HMV POP 712	45	1 wk

Dickie PRIDE UK, male vocalist   1 wk

30 Oct 59	PRIMROSE LANE Columbia DB 4340	28	1 wk

Maxi PRIEST UK, male vocalist   69 wks

29 Mar 86	STROLLIN' ON 10 TEN 84	32	9 wks
12 Jul 86	IN THE SPRINGTIME 10 TEN 127	54	3 wks
8 Nov 86	CRAZY LOVE 10 TEN 135	67	5 wks
4 Apr 87	LET ME KNOW 10 TEN 156	49	4 wks
24 Oct 87	SOME GUYS HAVE ALL THE LUCK 10 TEN 198	12	12 wks
20 Feb 88	HOW CAN WE EASE THE PAIN 10 TEN 207	41	6 wks
4 Jun 88 ●	WILD WORLD 10 TEN 221	5	9 wks
27 Aug 88	GOODBYE TO LOVE AGAIN 10 TEN 238	57	3 wks
9 Jun 90 ●	CLOSE TO YOU 10 TEN 294	7	10 wks
1 Sep 90	PEACE THROUGHOUT THE WORLD 10 TEN 317	41	4 wks
1 Dec 90	HUMAN WORK OF ART 10 TEN 328	75	1 wk
15 Dec 90	HUMAN WORK OF ART (re-entry) 10 TEN 328	71†	3 wks

How Can We Ease The Pain features Beres Hammond.

Louis PRIMA US, male vocalist   1 wk

21 Feb 58	BUONA SERA Capitol CL 14841	25	1 wk

PRIMA DONNA UK, male/female vocal group   4 wks

26 Apr 80	LOVE ENOUGH FOR TWO Ariola ARO 221	48	4 wks

PRIMAL SCREAM UK, male vocal/instrumental group   15 wks

3 Mar 90	LOADED Creation CRE 070	16	9 wks
18 Aug 90	COME TOGETHER Creation CRE 0778	26	6 wks

PRIME MOVERS US, male vocal/instrumental group   **1 wk**

8 Feb 86	ON THE TRAIL *Island IS 263*	74	1 wk

PRIMITIVES UK, male/female vocal/instrumental group   **25 wks**

27 Feb 88	● CRASH *Lazy PB 41761*	5	10 wks
30 Apr 88	OUT OF REACH *Lazy PB 42011*	25	4 wks
3 Sep 88	WAY BEHIND ME *Lazy PB 42209*	36	4 wks
29 Jul 89	SICK OF IT *Lazy PB 42947*	24	4 wks
30 Sep 89	SECRETS *Lazy PB 43173*	49	3 wks

PRINCE US, male vocalist   **189 wks**

19 Jan 80	I WANNA BE YOUR LOVER *Warner Bros. K 17537*	41	3 wks
29 Jan 83	1999 *Warner Bros. W 9896*	25	7 wks
30 Apr 83	LITTLE RED CORVETTE *Warner Bros. W 9688*	34	6 wks
26 Nov 83	LITTLE RED CORVETTE (re-issue)		
	Warner Bros. W 9436	66	2 wks
30 Jun 84	● WHEN DOVES CRY *Warner Bros. W 9286*	4	15 wks
22 Sep 84	● PURPLE RAIN *Warner Bros. W 9174*	8	9 wks
8 Dec 84	I WOULD DIE 4 U *Warner Bros. W 9121*	58	6 wks
19 Jan 85	1999/ LITTLE RED CORVETTE (re-issues)		
	Warner Bros. W 1999	2	10 wks
23 Feb 85	● LET'S GO CRAZY/ TAKE ME WITH YOU		
	Warner Bros. W 2000	7	9 wks
25 May 85	PAISLEY PARK *WEA W 9052*	18	10 wks
27 Jul 85	RASPBERRY BERET *WEA W 8929*	25	8 wks
26 Oct 85	POP LIFE *Paisley Park W 8858*	60	2 wks
8 Mar 86	● KISS *Paisley Park W 8751*	6	9 wks
14 Jun 86	MOUNTAINS *Paisley Park W 8711*	45	4 wks
16 Aug 86	GIRLS AND BOYS *Paisley Park W 8586*	11	8 wks
1 Nov 86	ANOTHERLOVERHOLENYOHEAD		
	Paisley Park W 8521	36	3 wks
14 Mar 87	● SIGN 'O' THE TIMES *Paisley Park W 8399*	10	9 wks
20 Jun 87	IF I WAS YOUR GIRLFRIEND *Paisley Park W 8334*	20	6 wks
15 Aug 87	U GOT THE LOOK *Paisley Park W 8289*	11	9 wks
28 Nov 87	I COULD NEVER TAKE THE PLACE OF YOUR MAN		
	Paisley Park W 8288	29	6 wks
7 May 88	● ALPHABET STREET *Paisley Park W 7900*	9	6 wks
23 Jul 88	GLAM SLAM *Paisley Park W 7806*	29	4 wks
5 Nov 88	I WISH U HEAVEN *Paisley Park W 7745*	24	5 wks
24 Jun 89	● BATDANCE *Warner Bros. W 2924*	2	12 wks
9 Sep 89	PARTYMAN *Warner Bros. W 2814*	14	3 wks
18 Nov 89	THE ARMS OF ORION *Warner Bros. W 2757*	27	5 wks
4 Aug 90	● THIEVES IN THE TEMPLE *Paisley Park W 9751*	7	6 wks
10 Nov 90	NEW POWER GENERATION *Paisley Park W 9525*	26	4 wks

The Revolution, US male/female vocal/instrumental group, are credited on all hits from Purple Rain to Anotherloverholenyohead. The Arms Of Orion is with Sheena Easton, who also vocalises on U Got The Look, although uncredited. See also Sheena Easton.

PRINCE CHARLES and the CITY BEAT BAND US, male vocalist with US male vocal/instrumental group   **2 wks**

22 Feb 86	WE CAN MAKE IT HAPPEN *PRT 7P 348*	56	2 wks

PRINCESS UK, female vocalist   **44 wks**

3 Aug 85	● SAY I'M YOU'RE NO. 1 *Supreme SUPE 101*	7	12 wks
9 Nov 85	AFTER THE LOVE HAS GONE *Supreme SUPE 103*	28	13 wks
19 Apr 86	I'LL KEEP ON LOVING YOU *Supreme SUPE 105*	16	8 wks
5 Jul 86	TELL ME TOMORROW *Supreme SUPE 106*	34	5 wks
25 Oct 86	IN THE HEAT OF A PASSIONATE MOMENT		
	Supreme SUPE 109	74	1 wk
13 Jun 87	RED HOT *Polydor POSP 868*	58	5 wks

PRINCESS IVORI US, female rapper   **2 wks**

17 Mar 90	WANTED *Supreme SUPE 163*	69	2 wks

PRIVATE LIVES UK, male vocal/instrumental duo   **4 wks**

11 Feb 84	LIVING IN A WORLD (TURNED UPSIDE DOWN)		
	EMI PRIV 2	53	4 wks

P. J. PROBY US, male vocalist   **89 wks**

28 May 64	● HOLD ME *Decca F 11904*	3	15 wks
3 Sep 64	● TOGETHER *Decca F 11967*	8	11 wks
10 Dec 64	SOMEWHERE *Liberty LIB 10182*	6	12 wks
25 Feb 65	I APOLOGISE *Liberty LIB 10188*	11	8 wks
8 Jul 65	LET THE WATER RUN DOWN *Liberty LIB 10206*	19	8 wks
30 Sep 65	THAT MEANS A LOT *Liberty LIB 10215*	30	6 wks
25 Nov 65	● MARIA *Liberty LIB 10218*	8	9 wks
10 Feb 66	YOU'VE COME BACK *Liberty LIB 10223*	25	7 wks
16 Jun 66	TO MAKE A BIG MAN CRY *Liberty LIB 10236*	34	3 wks
27 Oct 66	I CAN'T MAKE IT ALONE *Liberty LIB 10250*	37	5 wks
6 Mar 68	IT'S YOUR DAY TODAY *Liberty LBF 15046*	32	5 wks

PROCLAIMERS UK, male vocal/instrumental duo   **39 wks**

14 Nov 87	● LETTER FROM AMERICA *Chrysalis CHS 3178*	3	10 wks
5 Mar 88	MAKE MY HEART FLY *Chrysalis CLAIM 1*	63	3 wks
27 Aug 88	I'M GONNA BE *Chrysalis CLAIM 2*	11	11 wks
12 Nov 88	SUNSHINE ON LEITH *Chrysalis CLAIM 3*	41	5 wks
11 Feb 89	I'M ON MY WAY *Chrysalis CLAIM 4*	43	4 wks
24 Nov 90	● KING OF THE ROAD (EP) *Chrysalis CLAIM 5*	9†	6 wks

Tracks on King Of The Road EP: King Of The Road/Long Black Veil/Lulu Selling/Not Ever.

PROCOL HARUM UK, male vocal/instrumental group   **56 wks**

25 May 67	★ A WHITER SHADE OF PALE *Deram DM 126*	1	15 wks
4 Oct 67	● HOMBURG *Regal Zonophone RZ 3003*	6	10 wks
24 Apr 68	QUITE RIGHTLY SO *Regal Zonophone RZ 3007*	50	1 wk
18 Jun 69	SALTY DOG *Regal Zonophone RZ 3019*	44	1 wk
2 Jul 69	SALTY DOG (re-entry) *Regal Zonophone RZ 3019*	44	1 wk
16 Jul 69	SALTY DOG (2nd re-entry) *Regal Zonophone RZ 3019*	44	1 wk
22 Apr 72	A WHITER SHADE OF PALE *Magnifly ECHO 10*	13	13 wks
5 Aug 72	CONQUISTADOR *Chrysalis CHS 2003*	22	7 wks
23 Aug 75	PANDORA'S BOX *Chrysalis CHS 2073*	16	7 wks

PROFESSIONALS UK, male vocal/instrumental group   **4 wks**

11 Oct 80	1-2-3 *Virgin VS 376*	43	4 wks

PROPAGANDA
Germany, male/female vocal/instrumental group   **35 wks**

17 Mar 84	DR MABUSE *ZTT ZTAS 2*	27	9 wks
4 May 85	DUEL *ZTT ZTAS 8*	21	12 wks
10 Aug 85	P MACHINERY *ZTT ZTAS 12*	50	5 wks
28 Apr 90	HEAVEN GIVE ME WORDS *Virgin VS 1245*	36	5 wks
8 Sep 90	ONLY ONE WORD *Virgin VS 1271*	73	4 wks

Brian PROTHEROE UK, male vocalist   **6 wks**

7 Sep 74	PINBALL *Chrysalis CHS 2043*	22	6 wks

Dorothy PROVINE US, female vocalist   **15 wks**

7 Dec 61	DON'T BRING LULU *Warner Bros. WB 53*	17	12 wks
28 Jun 62	CRAZY WORDS CRAZY TUNE *Warner Bros. WB 70*	45	3 wks

PRUDENCE – *See PATIENCE and PRUDENCE*

PSEUDO ECHO *Australia, male vocal/instrumental group*   **12 wks**

| 18 Jul 87 | ● **FUNKY TOWN** *RCA PB 49705* .... | **8** | 12 wks |

PSYCHEDELIC FURS   **31 wks**
UK, male vocal/instrumental group

2 May 81	**DUMB WAITERS** *CBS 1166*	**59**	2 wks
27 Jun 81	**PRETTY IN PINK** *CBS A 1327*	**43**	5 wks
31 Jul 82	**LOVE MY WAY** *CBS A 2549*	**42**	6 wks
31 Mar 84	**HEAVEN** *CBS A 4300.*	**29**	6 wks
16 Jun 84	**GHOST IN YOU** *CBS A 4470.*	**68**	2 wks
23 Aug 86	**PRETTY IN PINK** *CBS A 7242*	**18**	9 wks
9 Jul 88	**ALL THAT MONEY WANTS** *CBS FURS 4.*	**75**	1 wk

A 7242 was a re-recording of A 1327.

PSYCHIC TV *UK, male/female vocal/instrumental group*   **4 wks**

| 26 Apr 86 | **GODSTAR** *Temple TOPY 009.* .... | **67** | 2 wks |
| 20 Sep 86 | **GOOD VIBRATIONS/ ROMAN P.** *Temple TOPY 23.* ...... | **65** | 2 wks |

Label on first hit credits the Angels of Light.

PUBLIC ENEMY *US, male rap duo*   **35 wks**

21 Nov 87	**REBEL WITHOUT A PAUSE** *Def Jam 651245 7*	**37**	5 wks
2 Jan 88	**REBEL WITHOUT A PAUSE (re-entry)**		
	Def Jam 651245 7	**71**	2 wks
9 Jan 88	**BRING THE NOISE** *Def Jam 651335 7.*	**32**	5 wks
2 Jul 88	**DON'T BELIEVE THE HYPE** *Def Jam 652833 7*	**18**	5 wks
15 Oct 88	**NIGHT OF THE LIVING BASEHEADS**		
	Def Jam 6530460	**63**	2 wks
24 Jun 89	**FIGHT THE POWER** *Motown ZB 42877.*	**29**	5 wks
20 Jan 90	**WELCOME TO THE TERRORDOME**		
	Def Jam 655476 0	**18**	4 wks
7 Apr 90	**911 IS A JOKE** *Def Jam 655830 7*	**41**	3 wks
23 Jun 90	**BROTHERS GONNA WORK IT OUT**		
	Def Jam 656018 1	**46**	2 wks
3 Nov 90	**CAN'T DO NUTTIN' FOR YA MAN** *Def Jam 656385 7*	**53**	2 wks

PUBLIC IMAGE LTD.   **59 wks**
UK, male vocal/instrumental group

21 Oct 78	● **PUBLIC IMAGE** *Virgin VS 228.*	**9**	8 wks
7 Jul 79	**DEATH DISCO** (PARTS 1 & 2) *Virgin VS 274*	**20**	7 wks
20 Oct 79	**MEMORIES** *Virgin VS 299.*	**60**	2 wks
4 Apr 81	**FLOWERS OF ROMANCE** *Virgin VS 397*	**24**	7 wks
17 Sep 83	● **THIS IS NOT A LOVE SONG** *Virgin VS 529.*	**5**	10 wks
19 May 84	**BAD LIFE** *Virgin VS 675.*	**71**	2 wks
1 Feb 86	**RISE** *Virgin VS 841.*	**11**	8 wks
3 May 86	**HOME** *Virgin VS 855.*	**75**	1 wk
22 Aug 87	**SEATTLE** *Virgin VS 988.*	**47**	4 wks
6 May 89	**DISAPPOINTED** *Virgin VS 1181.*	**38**	5 wks
20 Oct 90	**DON'T ASK ME** *Virgin VS 1231.*	**22**	5 wks

Act billed as P.I.L. on all but first hit.

Gary PUCKETT and the UNION GAP   **47 wks**
US, male vocalist, male vocal/instrumental backing group

17 Apr 68	★ **YOUNG GIRL** *CBS 3365.*	**1**	17 wks
7 Aug 68	● **LADY WILLPOWER** *CBS 3551.*	**5**	16 wks
28 Aug 68	**WOMAN WOMAN** *CBS 3110*	**48**	1 wk
15 Jun 74	● **YOUNG GIRL** *CBS 8202.*	**6**	13 wks

Billed as The Union Gap featuring Gary Puckett on the original issue of Young Girl and Lady Willpower.

James and Bobby PURIFY *US, male vocal duo*   **16 wks**

| 24 Apr 76 | **I'M YOUR PUPPET** *Mercury 6167 324* .... | **12** | 10 wks |
| 7 Aug 76 | **MORNING GLORY** *Mercury 6167 380* .... | **27** | 6 wks |

PURPLE HEARTS *UK, male vocal/instrumental group*   **5 wks**

| 22 Sep 79 | **MILLIONS LIKE US** *Fiction FICS 003* .... | **57** | 3 wks |
| 8 Mar 80 | **JIMMY** *Fiction FICS 9.* .... | **60** | 2 wks |

PUSSYCAT *Holland, male/female vocal/instrumental group*   **30 wks**

| 28 Aug 76 | ★ **MISSISSIPPI** *Sonet SON 2077* .... | **1** | 22 wks |
| 25 Dec 76 | **SMILE** *Sonet SON 2096.* .... | **24** | 8 wks |

PYRAMIDS *Jamaica, male vocal/instrumental group*   **4 wks**

| 22 Nov 67 | **TRAIN TOUR TO RAINBOW CITY** *President PT 161* .... | **35** | 4 wks |

PYTHON LEE JACKSON   **12 wks**
Australia, male vocal/instrumental group

| 30 Sep 72 | ● **IN A BROKEN DREAM** *Youngblood YB 1002* .... | **3** | 12 wks |

Lead vocals by Rod Stewart, not a member of the group. See also Rod Stewart.

Q-TEE – *See HISTORY featuring Q-TEE*

QUADS *UK, male vocal/instrumental group*   **2 wks**

| 22 Sep 79 | **THERE MUST BE THOUSANDS** *Big Bear BB 23.* .... | **66** | 2 wks |

QUANTUM JUMP *UK, male vocal/instrumental group*   **10 wks**

| 2 Jun 79 | ● **THE LONE RANGER** *Electric WOT 33* .... | **5** | 10 wks |

QUARTERFLASH   **5 wks**
US, male/female vocal/instrumental group

| 27 Feb 82 | **HARDEN MY HEART** *Geffen GEF A 1838* .... | **49** | 5 wks |

Jackie QUARTZ *France, female vocalist*   **3 wks**

| 11 Mar 89 | **A LA VIE, A L'AMOUR** *PWL PWL 30* .... | **55** | 3 wks |

QUARTZ featuring STEPZ   **2 wks**
UK, male instrumental group with female rapper

| 17 Mar 90 | **WE'RE COMIN' AT YA** *Mercury ITMR 2* .... | **65** | 2 wks |

Suzi QUATRO   **114 wks**
US, female vocalist/instrumentalist - bass guitar

19 May 73	★ **CAN THE CAN** *RAK 150*	**1**	14 wks
28 Jul 73	● **48 CRASH** *RAK 158.*	**3**	9 wks
27 Oct 73	**DAYTONA DEMON** *RAK 161*	**14**	13 wks

In 1959, the year of his first number ones, CLIFF RICHARD made a broadcast from Radio Luxembourg's London studios.

Far Left: PRINCE seems surprised by the fringe benefits of the pop life.

JIM REEVES had more hits after his death in a plane crash (31/7/64) than before.

Below: CHRIS REA seems surprised to hear that this *is* the road to hell.

Below Left: QUEEN are shown in 1989, a miraculous year for them.

9 Feb 74	★ DEVIL GATE DRIVE RAK 167	1	11 wks
29 Jun 74	TOO BIG RAK 175	14	6 wks
9 Nov 74	● THE WILD ONE RAK 185	7	10 wks
8 Feb 75	YOUR MAMA WON'T LIKE ME RAK 191	31	5 wks
5 Mar 77	TEAR ME APART RAK 248	27	6 wks
18 Mar 78	● IF YOU CAN'T GIVE ME LOVE RAK 271	4	13 wks
22 Jul 78	THE RACE IS ON RAK 278	43	5 wks
20 Oct 79	SHE'S IN LOVE WITH YOU RAK 299	11	9 wks
19 Jan 80	MAMA'S BOY RAK 303	34	5 wks
5 Apr 80	I'VE NEVER BEEN IN LOVE RAK 307	56	3 wks
25 Oct 80	ROCK HARD Dreamland DLSP 6	68	2 wks
13 Nov 82	HEART OF STONE Polydor POSP 477	60	3 wks

See Suzi Quatro and Chris Norman.

Suzi QUATRO and Chris NORMAN   8 wks
US/UK, female/male vocal duo

11 Nov 78	STUMBLIN' IN RAK RAK 285	41	8 wks

See also Suzi Quatro.

QUEEN *UK, male vocal/instrumental group*   295 wks

9 Mar 74	● SEVEN SEAS OF RHYE EMI 2121	10	10 wks
26 Oct 74	● KILLER QUEEN EMI 2229	2	12 wks
25 Jan 75	NOW I'M HERE EMI 2256	11	7 wks
8 Nov 75	★ BOHEMIAN RHAPSODY EMI 2375	1	17 wks
3 Jul 76	● YOU'RE MY BEST FRIEND EMI 2494	7	8 wks
27 Nov 76	● SOMEBODY TO LOVE EMI 2565	2	9 wks
19 Mar 77	TIE YOUR MOTHER DOWN EMI 2593	31	4 wks
4 Jun 77	QUEEN'S FIRST EP (EP) EMI 2623	17	10 wks
22 Oct 77	● WE ARE THE CHAMPIONS EMI 2708	2	11 wks
25 Feb 78	SPREAD YOUR WINGS EMI 2757	34	4 wks
28 Oct 78	BICYCLE RACE/ FAT BOTTOMED GIRLS EMI 2870	11	12 wks
10 Feb 79	● DON'T STOP ME NOW EMI 2910	9	12 wks
14 Jul 79	LOVE OF MY LIFE EMI 2959	63	2 wks
20 Oct 79	● CRAZY LITTLE THING CALLED LOVE EMI 5001	2	14 wks
2 Feb 80	SAVE ME EMI 5022	11	6 wks
14 Jun 80	PLAY THE GAME EMI 5076	14	8 wks
6 Sep 80	● ANOTHER ONE BITES THE DUST EMI 5102	7	9 wks
6 Dec 80	● FLASH EMI 5126	10	13 wks
1 May 82	BODY LANGUAGE EMI 5293	25	6 wks
12 Jun 82	LAS PALABRAS DE AMOR EMI 5316	17	8 wks
21 Aug 82	BACKCHAT EMI 5325	40	4 wks
4 Feb 84	● RADIO GAGA EMI QUEEN 1	2	9 wks
14 Apr 84	● I WANT TO BREAK FREE EMI QUEEN 2	3	15 wks
28 Jul 84	● IT'S A HARD LIFE EMI QUEEN 3	6	9 wks
22 Sep 84	HAMMER TO FALL EMI QUEEN 4	13	7 wks
8 Dec 84	THANK GOD IT'S CHRISTMAS EMI QUEEN 5	21	6 wks
16 Nov 85	● ONE VISION EMI QUEEN 6	7	10 wks
29 Mar 86	● A KIND OF MAGIC EMI QUEEN 7	3	11 wks
21 Jun 86	FRIENDS WILL BE FRIENDS EMI QUEEN 8	14	8 wks
27 Sep 86	WHO WANTS TO LIVE FOREVER EMI QUEEN 9	24	5 wks
13 May 89	● I WANT IT ALL Parlophone QUEEN 10	3	7 wks
1 Jul 89	● BREAKTHRU' Parlophone QUEEN 11	7	7 wks
19 Aug 89	THE INVISIBLE MAN Parlophone QUEEN 12	12	6 wks
21 Oct 89	SCANDAL Parlophone QUEEN 14	25	4 wks
9 Dec 89	THE MIRACLE Parlophone QUEEN 15	21	5 wks

See also Queen and David Bowie. Tracks on Queen's First EP: Good Old Fashioned Lover Boy/Death On Two Legs (Dedicated To...)/Tenement Funster/White Queen (As it Began).

QUEEN and David BOWIE   11 wks
UK, male vocal/instrumental group and male vocalist

14 Nov 81	★ UNDER PRESSURE EMI 5250	1	11 wks

See also Queen; David Bowie.

QUEEN LATIFAH + DE LA SOUL   7 wks
US, female rapper and male rap group

24 Mar 90	MAMA GAVE BIRTH TO THE SOUL CHILDREN Gee Street GEE 26	14	7 wks

See also De La Soul; Coldcut.

QUEENSRYCHE *US, male vocal/instrumental group*   2 wks

13 May 89	EYES OF A STRANGER EMI USA MT 65	59	1 wk
10 Nov 90	EMPIRE EMI USA MT 90	61	1 wk

? (QUESTION MARK) and the MYSTERIANS *US, male vocal/instrumental group*   4 wks

17 Nov 66	96 TEARS Cameo Parkway C428	37	4 wks

QUESTIONS *UK, male vocal/instrumental group*   8 wks

23 Apr 83	PRICE YOU PAY Respond KOB 702	56	3 wks
17 Sep 83	TEAR SOUP Respond KOB 705	66	1 wk
10 Mar 84	TUESDAY SUNSHINE Respond KOB 707	46	4 wks

QUICK *UK, male vocal/instrumental group*   7 wks

15 May 82	RHYTHM OF THE JUNGLE Epic EPC A 2013	41	7 wks

Tommy QUICKLY *UK, male vocalist*   8 wks

22 Oct 64	WILD SIDE OF LIFE Pye 7N 15708	33	8 wks

QUIET FIVE *UK, male vocal/instrumental group*   3 wks

13 May 65	WHEN THE MORNING SUN DRIES THE DEW Parlophone R 5273	45	1 wk
21 Apr 66	HOMEWARD BOUND Parlophone R 5421	44	2 wks

QUIET RIOT *US, male vocal/instrumental group*   5 wks

3 Dec 83	METAL HEALTH/ CUM ON FEEL THE NOIZE Epic A 3968	45	5 wks

Cum on Feel the Noize only credited from 10 Dec 83.

Paul QUINN and Edwyn COLLINS   2 wks
UK, male vocal duo

11 Aug 84	PALE BLUE EYES Swamplands SWP 1	72	2 wks

QUIREBOYS *UK, male vocal/instrumental group*   21 wks

4 Nov 89	7 O'CLOCK Parlophone R 6230	36	4 wks
6 Jan 90	HEY YOU Parlophone R 6241	14	7 wks
7 Apr 90	I DON'T LOVE YOU ANYMORE Parlophone R 6248	24	6 wks
8 Sep 90	THERE SHE GOES AGAIN/ MISLED Parlophone R 6267	37	4 wks

QUIVER – *See SUTHERLAND BROTHERS*

Eddie RABBITT *US, male vocalist*   14 wks

27 Jan 79	EVERY WHICH WAY BUT LOOSE Elektra K 12331	41	9 wks
28 Feb 81	I LOVE A RAINY NIGHT Elektra K 12498	53	5 wks

Steve RACE UK, male instrumentalist - piano   9 wks

28 Feb 63		PIED PIPER (THE BEEJE) Parlophone R 4981	29	9 wks

RACEY UK, male vocal/instrumental group   44 wks

25 Nov 78	●	LAY YOUR LOVE ON ME RAK 284	3	14 wks
31 Mar 79	●	SOME GIRLS RAK 291	2	11 wks
18 Aug 79		BOY OH BOY RAK 297	22	9 wks
20 Dec 80		RUNAROUND SUE RAK 325	13	10 wks

RACING CARS UK, male vocal/instrumental group   7 wks

12 Feb 77	THEY SHOOT HORSES DON'T THEY Chrysalis CHS 2129	14	7 wks

RACKETEERS – See Elbow BONES and the RACKETEERS

Jimmy RADCLIFFE US, male vocalist   2 wks

4 Feb 65	LONG AFTER TONIGHT IS ALL OVER Stateside SS 374	40	2 wks

RADHA KRISHNA TEMPLE Oxford Street,   17 wks
male/female vocal/instrumental group

13 Sep 69	HARE KRISHNA MANTRA Apple 15	12	9 wks
28 Mar 70	GOVINDA Apple 25	23	8 wks

RADIO HEART featuring Gary NUMAN   8 wks
UK, male vocal/instrumental group

28 Mar 87	RADIO HEART GFM GFM 109	35	6 wks
13 Jun 87	LONDON TIMES GFM GFM 112	48	2 wks

See also Gary Numan.

RADIO 1 DJ POSSE – See Liz KERSHAW and Bruno BROOKES

RADIO REVELLERS – See Anthony STEEL and the RADIO REVELLERS

RADIO STARS UK, male vocal/instrumental group   3 wks

4 Feb 78	NERVOUS WRECK Chiswick NS 23	39	3 wks

Fonda RAE US, female vocalist   4 wks

6 Oct 84	TUCH ME Streetwave KHAN 28	49	4 wks

Jesse RAE UK, male vocalist   2 wks

11 May 85	OVER THE SEA Scotland-Video YZ 36	65	2 wks

Gerry RAFFERTY UK, male vocalist   47 wks

18 Feb 78	●	BAKER STREET United Artists UP 36346	3	15 wks
26 May 79	●	NIGHT OWL United Artists UP 36512	5	13 wks
18 Aug 79		GET IT RIGHT NEXT TIME United Artists BP 301	30	9 wks
22 Mar 80		BRING IT ALL HOME United Artists BP 340	54	4 wks
21 Jun 80		ROYAL MILE United Artists BP 354	67	2 wks
10 Mar 90		BAKER STREET (re-mix) EMI EM 132	53	4 wks

RAGGA TWINS UK, male vocal group   2 wks

10 Nov 90	ILLEGAL GUNSHOT/SPLIFFHEAD Shut Up And Dance SUAD 7	51	2 wks

RAGTIMERS UK, male instrumental group   8 wks

16 Mar 74	THE STING Pye 7N 45323	46	1 wk
30 Mar 74	THE STING (re-entry) Pye 7N 45323	31	7 wks

RAH BAND UK, male/female vocal/instrumental group   50 wks

9 Jul 77	●	THE CRUNCH Good Earth GD 7	6	12 wks
1 Nov 80		FALCON DJM DJS 10954	35	4 wks
7 Feb 81		SLIDE DJM DJS 10964	50	7 wks
1 May 82		PERFUMED GARDEN KR KR 5	45	7 wks
9 Jul 83		MESSAGES FROM THE STARS TMT TMT 5	42	5 wks
19 Jan 85		ARE YOU SATISFIED? (FUNKA NOVA) RCA RCA 470	70	2 wks
30 Mar 85	●	CLOUDS ACROSS THE MOON RCA PB 40025	6	10 wks

RAILWAY CHILDREN   5 wks
UK, male vocal/instrumental group

24 Mar 90	EVERY BEAT OF THE HEART Virgin VS 1237	68	2 wks
2 Jun 90	MUSIC STOP Virgin VS 1255	66	2 wks
20 Oct 90	SO RIGHT Virgin VS 1289	68	1 wk

RAIN – See Stephanie DE SYKES

RAINBOW UK, male vocal/instrumental group   62 wks

17 Sep 77		KILL THE KING Polydor 2066 845	44	3 wks
8 Apr 78		LONG LIVE ROCK 'N' ROLL Polydor 2066 913	33	3 wks
30 Sep 78		L. A. CONNECTION Polydor 2066 968	40	4 wks
15 Sep 79	●	SINCE YOU'VE BEEN GONE Polydor POSP 70	6	10 wks
16 Feb 80	●	ALL NIGHT LONG Polydor POSP 104	5	11 wks
31 Jan 81	●	I SURRENDER Polydor POSP 221	3	10 wks
20 Jun 81		CAN'T HAPPEN HERE Polydor POSP 251	20	8 wks
11 Jul 81		KILL THE KING (re-issue) Polydor POSP 274	41	4 wks
3 Apr 82		STONE COLD Polydor POSP 421	34	4 wks
27 Aug 83		STREET OF DREAMS Polydor POSP 631	52	3 wks
5 Nov 83		CAN'T LET YOU GO Polydor POSP 654	43	2 wks

RAINBOW COTTAGE   4 wks
UK, male vocal/instrumental group

6 Mar 76	SEAGULL Penny Farthing PEN 906	33	4 wks

RAINMAKERS US, male vocal/instrumental group   11 wks

7 Mar 87	LET MY PEOPLE GO-GO Mercury MER 238	18	11 wks

Marvin RAINWATER US, male vocalist   22 wks

7 Mar 58	★	WHOLE LOTTA WOMAN MGM 974	1	15 wks
6 Jun 58		I DIG YOU BABY MGM 980	19	7 wks

RAKIM – See Eric B. and RAKIM

Tony RALLO and the MIDNIGHT BAND   8 wks
France/US, male vocal/instrumental group

23 Feb 80	HOLDIN' ON Calibre CAB 150	34	8 wks

See also Calibre Cuts.

Sheryl Lee RALPH US, female vocalist — 2 wks

26 Jan 85	IN THE EVENING Arista ARIST 595	64	2 wks

RAM JAM US, male vocal/instrumental group — 20 wks

10 Sep 77	● BLACK BETTY Epic EPC 5492	7	12 wks
17 Feb 90	BLACK BETTY (re-mix) Epic 655430 7	13	8 wks

RAM JAM BAND – See Geno WASHINGTON and the RAM JAM BAND

RAMBLERS (from the Abbey Hey Junior School) UK, children's choir — 15 wks

13 Oct 79	THE SPARROW Decca F 13860	11	15 wks

RAMONES US, male vocal/instrumental group — 30 wks

21 May 77	SHEENA IS A PUNK ROCKER Sire RAM 001	22	7 wks
6 Aug 77	SWALLOW MY PRIDE Sire 6078 607	36	3 wks
30 Sep 78	DON'T COME CLOSE Sire SRE 1031	39	5 wks
8 Sep 79	ROCK 'N' ROLL HIGH SCHOOL Sire SIR 4021	67	2 wks
26 Jan 80	● BABY I LOVE YOU Sire SIR 4031	8	9 wks
19 Apr 80	DO YOU REMEMBER ROCK 'N' ROLL RADIO Sire SIR 4037	54	3 wks
10 May 86	SOMEBODY PUT SOMETHING IN MY DRINK/ SOMETHING TO BELIEVE IN Beggars Banquet BEG 157	69	1 wk

RAMRODS US, male/female instrumental group — 12 wks

23 Feb 61	● RIDERS IN THE SKY London HLU 9282	8	12 wks

RANGE – See Bruce HORNSBY and the RANGE

RANKING ANN – See SCRITTI POLITTI

RARE BIRD UK, male vocal/instrumental group — 8 wks

14 Feb 70	SYMPATHY Charisma CB 120	27	8 wks

O. RASBURY – See Rahni HARRIS and F.L.O.

Roland RAT SUPERSTAR UK, male rat vocalist — 20 wks

19 Nov 83	RAT RAPPING Rodent RAT 1	14	12 wks
28 Apr 84	LOVE ME TENDER Rodent RAT 2	32	7 wks
2 Mar 85	NO. 1 RAT FAN Rodent RAT 4	72	1 wk

RATTLES Germany, male vocal/instrumental group — 15 wks

3 Oct 70	● THE WITCH Decca F 23058	8	15 wks

RAW SILK US, female vocal group — 12 wks

16 Oct 82	DO IT TO THE MUSIC KR KR 14	18	9 wks
10 Sep 83	JUST IN TIME West End WEND 2	49	3 wks

Lou RAWLS US, male vocalist — 10 wks

31 Jul 76	● YOU'LL NEVER FIND ANOTHER LOVE LIKE MINE Philadelphia International PIR 4372	10	10 wks

See also Philadelphia International All-Stars.

Gene Anthony RAY – See KIDS FROM FAME

Johnnie RAY US, male vocalist — 132 wks

14 Nov 52	WALKING MY BABY BACK HOME Columbia DB 3060	12	1 wk
19 Dec 52	● FAITH CAN MOVE MOUNTAINS Columbia DB 3154	7	2 wks
9 Jan 53	● FAITH CAN MOVE MOUNTAINS (re-entry) Columbia DB 3154	9	1 wk
10 Apr 53	● SOMEBODY STOLE MY GAL Philips PB 123	6	1 wk
24 Apr 53	● SOMEBODY STOLE MY GAL (re-entry) Philips PB 123	6	4 wks
29 May 53	SOMEBODY STOLE MY GAL (2nd re-entry) Philips PB 123	12	1 wk
7 Aug 53	SOMEBODY STOLE MY GAL (3rd re-entry) Philips PB 123	11	1 wk
9 Apr 54	★ SUCH A NIGHT Philips PB 244	1	18 wks
8 Apr 55	IF YOU BELIEVE Philips PB 379	15	1 wk
13 May 55	● IF YOU BELIEVE (re-entry) Philips PB 379	7	10 wks
20 May 55	PATHS OF PARADISE Philips PB 441	20	1 wk
7 Oct 55	HERNANDO'S HIDEAWAY Philips PB 495	11	5 wks
14 Oct 55	● HEY THERE Philips PB 495	5	9 wks
28 Oct 55	● SONG OF THE DREAMER Philips PB 516	10	5 wks
17 Feb 56	WHO'S SORRY NOW Philips PB 546	17	2 wks
20 Apr 56	AIN'T MISBEHAVIN' Philips PB 580	17	6 wks
8 Jun 56	AIN'T MISBEHAVIN' (re-entry) Philips PB 580	24	1 wk
12 Oct 56	★ JUST WALKIN' IN THE RAIN Philips PB 624	1	19 wks
18 Jan 57	YOU DON'T OWE ME A THING Philips PB 655	12	15 wks
8 Feb 57	● LOOK HOMEWARD ANGEL Philips PB 655	7	16 wks
10 May 57	★ YES TONIGHT JOSEPHINE Philips PB 686	1	16 wks
6 Sep 57	BUILD YOUR LOVE Philips PB 721	17	7 wks
4 Dec 59	I'LL NEVER FALL IN LOVE AGAIN Philips PB 952	26	4 wks
8 Jan 60	I'LL NEVER FALL IN LOVE AGAIN (re-entry) Philips PB 952	26	1 wk
5 Feb 60	I'LL NEVER FALL IN LOVE AGAIN (2nd re-entry) Philips PB 952	28	1 wk

See also Doris Day and Johnnie Ray; Frankie Laine and Johnnie Ray. The chart history of You Don't Owe Me A Thing/ Look Homeward Angel is complicated, as follows: You Don't Owe Me A Thing entered the chart by itself on 18 Jan 57. On 8 and 15 Feb 57 Look Homeward Angel was coupled with You Don't Owe Me A Thing but from 22 Feb 57 the two sides went their individual ways on the chart and were listed separately, You Don't Owe Me A Thing for a further 10 weeks and Look Homeward Angel for a further 14.

RAYDIO US, male/female vocal/instrumental group — 21 wks

8 Apr 78	JACK AND JILL Arista 161	11	12 wks
8 Jul 78	IS THIS A LOVE THING Arista 193	27	9 wks

RAZ – See ROB 'N' RAZ

RAZE US, male/female vocal/instrumental group — 40 wks

1 Nov 86	JACK THE GROOVE Champion CHAMP 23	57	7 wks
3 Jan 87	JACK THE GROOVE (re-entry) Champion CHAMP 23	20	8 wks
28 Feb 87	LET THE MUSIC MOVE U Champion CHAMP 27	57	3 wks
31 Dec 88	BREAK 4 LOVE Champion CHAMP 67	28	11 wks
2 Sep 89	BREAK 4 LOVE (re-entry) Champion CHAMP 67	61	5 wks
27 Jan 90	ALL 4 LOVE (BREAK 4 LOVE 1990) Champion CHAMP 228	30	5 wks
10 Feb 90	CAN YOU FEEL IT Champion CHAMP 227	62	1 wk

Can You Feel It was listed with Can You Feel It by Champion Legend. See also Champion Legend.

Chris REA UK, male vocalist — 85 wks

7 Oct 78	FOOL (IF YOU THINK IT'S OVER) Magnet MAG 111	30	7 wks
21 Apr 79	DIAMONDS Magnet MAG 144	44	3 wks

27 Mar 82	LOVING YOU *Magnet MAG 215*	65	3 wks
1 Oct 83	I CAN HEAR YOUR HEARTBEAT *Magnet MAG 244*	60	2 wks
17 Mar 84	I DON'T KNOW WHAT IT IS BUT I LOVE IT *Magnet MAG 255*	65	2 wks
30 Mar 85	STAINSBY GIRLS *Magnet MAG 276*	27	10 wks
29 Jun 85	JOSEPHINE *Magnet MAG 280*	67	4 wks
29 Mar 86	IT'S ALL GONE *Magnet MAG 283*	69	1 wk
31 May 86	ON THE BEACH *Magnet MAG 294*	57	3 wks
28 Jun 86	ON THE BEACH (re-entry) *Magnet MAG 294*	75	1 wk
12 Jul 86	ON THE BEACH (2nd re-entry) *Magnet MAG 294*	66	4 wks
6 Jun 87	LET'S DANCE *Magnet MAG 299*	12	10 wks
29 Aug 87	LOVING YOU AGAIN *Magnet MAG 300*	47	4 wks
5 Dec 87	JOYS OF CHRISTMAS *Magnet MAG 314*	67	1 wk
13 Feb 88	QUE SERA *Magnet MAG 318*	73	2 wks
13 Aug 88	ON THE BEACH SUMMER '88 *WEA YZ 195*	12	6 wks
22 Oct 88	I CAN HEAR YOUR HEARTBEAT *WEA YZ 320*	74	2 wks
17 Dec 88	DRIVING HOME FOR CHRISTMAS (EP) *WEA YZ 825*	53	3 wks
18 Feb 89	WORKING ON IT *WEA YZ 50*	53	3 wks
14 Oct 89	● THE ROAD TO HELL (PART 2) *WEA YZ 431*	10	9 wks
10 Feb 90	TELL ME THERE'S A HEAVEN *East West YZ 455*	24	6 wks
5 May 90	TEXAS *East West YZ 468*	69	1 wk

Both On The Beach Summer '88 *and* I Can Hear Your Heartbeat *in 1988 are re-recordings.*
Tracks on Driving Home For Christmas *EP: Driving Home For Christmas/Footsteps In The Snow/Joys Of Christmas/Smile.*

Eileen READ – *See* CADETS

READY FOR THE WORLD
US, male vocal/instrumental group   **8 wks**

26 Oct 85	OH SHEILA *MCA MCA 1005*	50	5 wks
14 Mar 87	LOVE YOU DOWN *MCA MCA 1110*	60	3 wks

REAL ROXANNE *US, female vocalist*   **10 wks**

28 Jun 86	BANG ZOOM (LET'S GO GO) *Cooltempo COOL 124*	11	9 wks
12 Nov 88	RESPECT *Cooltempo COOL 176*	71	1 wk

First hit is with Hitman Howie Tee, US, male scratcher.

REAL THING *UK, male vocal/instrumental group*   **114 wks**

5 Jun 76	★ YOU TO ME ARE EVERYTHING *Pye International 7N 25709*	1	11 wks
4 Sep 76	● CAN'T GET BY WITHOUT YOU *Pye 7N 45618*	2	10 wks
12 Feb 77	YOU'LL NEVER KNOW WHAT YOU'RE MISSING *Pye 7N 45662*	16	9 wks
30 Jul 77	LOVE'S SUCH A WONDERFUL THING *Pye 7N 45701*	33	5 wks
4 Mar 78	WHENEVER YOU WANT MY LOVE *Pye 7N 46045*	18	9 wks
3 Jun 78	LET'S GO DISCO *Pye 7N 46078*	39	7 wks
12 Aug 78	RAININ' THROUGH MY SUNSHINE *Pye 7N 46113*	40	8 wks
17 Feb 79	● CAN YOU FEEL THE FORCE *Pye 7N 46147*	5	11 wks
21 Jul 79	BOOGIE DOWN (GET FUNKY NOW) *Pye 7P 109*	33	6 wks
22 Nov 80	SHE'S A GROOVY FREAK *Calibre CAB 105*	52	4 wks
8 Mar 86	● YOU TO ME ARE EVERYTHING (THE DECADE REMIX 76-86) *PRT 7P 349*	5	12 wks
24 May 86	● CAN'T GET BY WITHOUT YOU (THE SECOND DECADE REMIX) *PRT 7P 352*	6	13 wks
7 Jun 86	YOU TO ME ARE EVERYTHING (THE DECADE REMIX 76-86) (re-entry) *PRT 7P 349*	72	1 wk
2 Aug 86	CAN YOU FEEL THE FORCE ('86 REMIX) *PRT 7P 358*	24	6 wks
25 Oct 86	STRAIGHT TO THE HEART *Jive JIVE 129*	71	2 wks

See also Calibre Cuts.

REAL TO REEL *US, male vocal/instrumental group*   **2 wks**

21 Apr 84	LOVE ME LIKE THIS *Arista ARIST 565*	68	2 wks

REBEL M.C. *UK, male vocalist*   **8 wks**

31 Mar 90	BETTER WORLD *Desire WANT 25*	20	6 wks
2 Jun 90	REBEL MUSIC *Desire WANT 31*	53	2 wks

See also Double Trouble and the Rebel M.C.

REBEL ROUSERS – *See Cliff BENNETT and the REBEL ROUSERS*

REBELETTES – *See Duane EDDY*

REBELS – *See Duane EDDY*

Ezz RECO and the LAUNCHERS with Boysie GRANT *Jamaica, male vocal/instrumental group*   **4 wks**

5 Mar 64	KING OF KINGS *Columbia DB 7217*	44	4 wks

RED BOX *UK, male vocal/instrumental duo*   **28 wks**

24 Aug 85	● LEAN ON ME (AH-LI-AYO) *Sire W 8926*	3	14 wks
25 Oct 86	● FOR AMERICA *Sire YZ 84*	10	12 wks
31 Jan 87	HEART OF THE SUN *Sire YZ 100*	71	2 wks

RED HOT CHILLI PEPPPERS
US, male vocal/instrumental group   **9 wks**

10 Feb 90	HIGHER GROUND *EMI-USA MT 75*	55	3 wks
23 Jun 90	TASTE THE PAIN *EMI-USA MT 85*	29	3 wks
8 Sep 90	HIGHER GROUND (re-issue) *EMI-USA MT 88*	54	3 wks

RED NOSED BURGLARS – *See Ivor BIGGUN*

REDBONE *US, male vocal/instrumental group*   **12 wks**

25 Sep 71	● WITCH QUEEN OF NEW ORLEANS *Epic EPC 7351*	2	12 wks

Sharon REDD *US, female vocalist*   **27 wks**

28 Feb 81	CAN YOU HANDLE IT *Epic EPC 9572*	31	8 wks
2 Oct 82	NEVER GIVE YOU UP *Prelude PRL A2755*	20	9 wks
15 Jan 83	IN THE NAME OF LOVE *Prelude PRL A2905*	31	5 wks
22 Oct 83	LOVE HOW YOU FEEL *Prelude A3868*	39	5 wks

Otis REDDING *US, male vocalist*   **108 wks**

25 Nov 65	MY GIRL *Atlantic AT 4050*	11	16 wks
7 Apr 66	SATISFACTION *Atlantic AT 4080*	33	4 wks
14 Jul 66	MY LOVER'S PRAYER *Atlantic 584 019*	37	6 wks
25 Aug 66	I CAN'T TURN YOU LOOSE *Atlantic 584 030*	29	8 wks
24 Nov 66	FA FA FA FA FA (SAD SONG) *Atlantic 584 049*	23	9 wks
26 Jan 67	TRY A LITTLE TENDERNESS *Atlantic 584 070*	46	4 wks
23 Mar 67	DAY TRIPPER *Stax 601 005*	43	6 wks
4 May 67	LET ME COME ON HOME *Stax 601 007*	48	1 wk
15 Jun 67	SHAKE *Stax 601 011*	28	10 wks
14 Feb 68	MY GIRL (re-issue) *Atlantic 584 092*	36	9 wks
21 Feb 68	● (SITTIN' ON) THE DOCK OF THE BAY *Stax 601 031*	3	15 wks
29 May 68	HAPPY SONG *Stax 601 040*	24	5 wks
31 Jul 68	HARD TO HANDLE *Atlantic 584 199*	15	12 wks
9 Jul 69	LOVE MAN *Atco 226 001*	43	3 wks

See also Otis Redding and Carla Thomas.

Otis REDDING and Carla THOMAS
US, male/female vocal duo   **16 wks**

19 Jul 67		TRAMP Stax 601 012	18	11 wks
11 Oct 67		KNOCK ON WOOD Stax 601 021	35	5 wks

See also Otis Redding.

Helen REDDY *Australia, female vocalist*   **18 wks**

18 Jan 75	●	ANGIE BABY Capitol CL 15799	5	10 wks
28 Nov 81		I CAN'T SAY GOODBYE TO YOU MCA 744	43	8 wks

REDHEAD KINGPIN and the FBI   **11 wks**
US, male vocalist

22 Jul 89		DO THE RIGHT THING 10 TEN 271	13	10 wks
2 Dec 89		SUPERBAD SUPERSLICK 10 TEN 286	68	1 wk

REDSKINS *UK, male vocal/instrumental duo*   **12 wks**

10 Nov 84		KEEP ON KEEPIN' ON Decca F 1	43	5 wks
22 Jun 85		BRING IT DOWN (THIS INSANE THING) Decca F 2	33	5 wks
22 Feb 86		THE POWER IS YOURS Decca F 3	59	2 wks

Jimmy REED *US, male vocalist*   **2 wks**

10 Sep 64		SHAME SHAME SHAME Stateside SS 330	45	2 wks

Lou REED *US, male vocalist*   **9 wks**

12 May 73	●	WALK ON THE WILD SIDE RCA 2303	10	9 wks

See also Sam Moore and Lou Reed.

Michael REED ORCHESTRA – *See Richard HARTLEY and the Michael REED ORCHESTRA*

Dan REED NETWORK   **13 wks**
US, male vocal/instrumental group

20 Jan 90		COME BACK BABY Mercury DRN 2	51	3 wks
17 Mar 90		RAINBOW CHILD Mercury DRN 3	60	3 wks
21 Jul 90		STARDATE 1990/ RAINBOW CHILD (re-issue) Mercury DRN 4	39	4 wks
8 Sep 90		LOVER/ MONEY Mercury DRN 5	45	3 wks

Tony REES and the COTTAGERS   **1 wk**
UK, male vocal group

10 May 75		VIVA EL FULHAM Sonet SON 2059	46	1 wk

Jim REEVES *US, male vocalist*   **322 wks**

24 Mar 60		HE'LL HAVE TO GO RCA 1168	36	1 wk
7 Apr 60		HE'LL HAVE TO GO (re-entry) RCA 1168	12	30 wks
16 Mar 61		WHISPERING HOPE RCA 1223	50	1 wk
23 Nov 61		YOU'RE THE ONLY GOOD THING RCA 1261	17	19 wks
28 Jun 62		ADIOS AMIGO RCA 1293	23	21 wks
22 Nov 62		I'M GONNA CHANGE EVERYTHING RCA 1317	42	2 wks
13 Jun 63	●	WELCOME TO MY WORLD RCA 1342	6	15 wks
17 Oct 63		GUILTY RCA 1364	29	7 wks
20 Feb 64	●	I LOVE YOU BECAUSE RCA 1385	5	39 wks
18 Jun 64	●	I WON'T FORGET YOU RCA 1400	3	25 wks
5 Nov 64	●	THERE'S A HEARTACHE FOLLOWING ME RCA 1423	6	13 wks
7 Jan 65		I WON'T FORGET YOU (re-entry) RCA 1400	47	1 wk
4 Feb 65	●	IT HURTS SO MUCH RCA 1437	8	10 wks
15 Apr 65		NOT UNTIL THE NEXT TIME RCA 1446	13	12 wks
6 May 65		HOW LONG HAS IT BEEN RCA 1445	45	5 wks
15 Jul 65		THIS WORLD IS NOT MY HOME RCA 1412	22	9 wks
11 Nov 65		IS IT REALLY OVER RCA 1488	17	9 wks
18 Aug 66	★	DISTANT DRUMS RCA 1537	1	25 wks
2 Feb 67		I WON'T COME IN WHILE HE'S THERE RCA 1563	12	11 wks
26 Jul 67		TRYING TO FORGET RCA 1611	33	5 wks
22 Nov 67		I HEARD A HEART BREAK LAST NIGHT RCA 1643	38	6 wks
27 Mar 68		PRETTY BROWN EYES RCA 1672	33	5 wks
25 Jun 69		WHEN TWO WORLDS COLLIDE RCA 1830	17	17 wks
6 Dec 69		BUT YOU LOVE ME DADDY RCA 1899	15	16 wks
21 Mar 70		NOBODY'S FOOL RCA 1915	32	5 wks
12 Sep 70		ANGELS DON'T LIE RCA 1997	44	1 wk
26 Sep 70		ANGELS DON'T LIE (re-entry) RCA 1997	32	2 wks
26 Jun 71		I LOVE YOU BECAUSE/ HE'LL HAVE TO GO (re-issues)/ MOONLIGHT & ROSES RCA Maximillion 2092	34	8 wks
19 Feb 72		YOU'RE FREE TO GO (re-issue) RCA 2174	48	2 wks

Martha REEVES and the VANDELLAS   **85 wks**
US, female vocal group

29 Oct 64		DANCING IN THE STREET Stateside SS 345	28	8 wks
1 Apr 65		NOWHERE TO RUN Tamla Motown TMG 502	26	8 wks
1 Dec 66		I'M READY FOR LOVE Tamla Motown TMG 582	29	8 wks
30 Mar 67		JIMMY MACK Tamla Motown TMG 599	21	9 wks
17 Jan 68		HONEY CHILE Tamla Motown TMG 636	30	9 wks
15 Jan 69	●	DANCING IN THE STREET (re-issue) Tamla Motown TMG 684	4	12 wks
16 Apr 69		NOWHERE TO RUN (re-issue) Tamla Motown TMG 694	42	3 wks
29 Aug 70		JIMMY MACK (re-entry) Tamla Motown TMG 599	21	12 wks
13 Feb 71		FORGET ME NOT Tamla Motown TMG 762	11	8 wks
8 Jan 72		BLESS YOU Tamla Motown TMG 794	33	5 wks
23 Jul 88		NOWHERE TO RUN (2nd re-issue) A & M AM 444	52	3 wks

The group is billed as Martha and the Vandellas - no Reeves - for Dancing In The Street on Stateside, Nowhere To Run on Tamla Motown TMG 502, I'm Ready For Love and Jimmy Mack. The listed flip side of Nowhere To Run in 1988 was I Got You (I Feel Good) by James Brown. See also James Brown.

RE-FLEX *UK, male vocal/instrumental group*   **9 wks**

28 Jan 84		THE POLITICS OF DANCING EMI FLEX 2	28	9 wks

Joan REGAN *UK, female vocalist*   **61 wks**

11 Dec 53	●	RICOCHET Decca F 10193	8	1 wk
8 Jan 54	●	RICOCHET (re-entry) Decca F 10193	9	4 wks
14 May 54	●	SOMEONE ELSE'S ROSES Decca F 10257	5	8 wks
1 Oct 54		IF I GIVE MY HEART TO YOU Decca F 10373	20	1 wk
29 Oct 54	●	IF I GIVE MY HEART TO YOU (re-entry) Decca F 10373	3	10 wks
25 Mar 55	●	PRIZE OF GOLD Decca F 10432	6	8 wks
6 May 55		OPEN UP YOUR HEART Decca F 10474	19	1 wk
1 May 59	●	MAY YOU ALWAYS HMV POP 593	9	16 wks
5 Feb 60		HAPPY ANNIVERSARY Pye 7N 15238	29	1 wk
19 Feb 60		HAPPY ANNIVERSARY (re-entry) Pye 7N 15238	29	1 wk
28 Jul 60		PAPA LOVES MAMA Pye 7N 15278	29	8 wks
24 Nov 60		ONE OF THE LUCKY ONES Pye 7N 15310	47	1 wk
5 Jan 61		MUST BE SANTA Pye 7N 15303	42	1 wk

Ricochet credited to Joan Regan with the Squadronaires. See also Joan Regan and the Johnston Brothers; Various Artists - All Star Hit Parade.

Joan REGAN and the JOHNSTON BROTHERS   **1 wk**
UK, female vocalist and male vocal group

5 Nov 54		WAIT FOR ME Decca F 10362	18	1 wk

See also Joan Regan; Johnston Brothers.

REGENTS UK, male/female vocal/instrumental group   14 wks

| 22 Dec 79 | | 7 TEEN Rialto TREB 111 | 11 | 12 wks |
| 7 Jun 80 | | SEE YOU LATER Arista ARIST 350 | 55 | 2 wks |

REGGAE PHILHARMONIC ORCHESTRA   11 wks
UK, male/female vocal/instrumental group

| 19 Nov 88 | | MINNIE THE MOOCHER Mango IS 378 | 35 | 9 wks |
| 28 Jul 90 | | LOVELY THING Mango MNG 742 | 71 | 2 wks |

REGINA US, female vocalist   3 wks

| 1 Feb 86 | | BABY LOVE Funkin' Marvellous MARV 01 | 50 | 3 wks |

REID UK, male vocal group   12 wks

8 Oct 88		ONE WAY OUT Syncopate SY 16	66	2 wks
11 Feb 89		REAL EMOTION Syncopate SY 24	65	2 wks
15 Apr 89		GOOD TIMES Syncopate SY 27	55	6 wks
21 Oct 89		LOVIN' ON THE SIDE Syncopate REID 1	71	2 wks

Junior REID – See COLDCUT; SOUPDRAGONS

Mike REID UK, male vocalist   8 wks

| 22 Mar 75 | ● | THE UGLY DUCKLING Pye 7N 45434 | 10 | 8 wks |

Neil REID UK, male vocalist   26 wks

1 Jan 72	●	MOTHER OF MINE Decca F 13264	2	20 wks
8 Apr 72		THAT'S WHAT I WANT TO BE Decca F 13300	49	1 wk
22 Apr 72		THAT'S WHAT I WANT TO BE (re-entry) Decca F 13300	45	5 wks

Keith RELF UK, male vocalist   1 wk

| 26 May 66 | | MR. ZERO Columbia DB 7920 | 50 | 1 wk |

R.E.M US, male vocal/instrumental group   20 wks

28 Nov 87	●	THE ONE I LOVE IRS IRM 46	51	8 wks
30 Apr 88		FINEST WORKSONG IRS IRM 161	50	21 wks
4 Feb 89		STAND Warner Bros. W 7577	51	3 wks
3 Jun 89		ORANGE CRUSH Warner Bros. W 2960	28	5 wks
12 Aug 89		STAND (re-issue) Warner Bros. W 2833	48	2 wks

RENAISSANCE UK, male/female vocal/instrumental group   11 wks

| 15 Jul 78 | ● | NORTHERN LIGHTS Warner Bros. K 17177 | 10 | 11 wks |

RENE and ANGELA US, male/female vocal duo   15 wks

15 Jun 85		SAVE YOUR LOVE (FOR NUMBER 1) Club JAB 14	66	2 wks
7 Sep 85		I'LL BE GOOD Club JAB 18	22	10 wks
2 Nov 85		SECRET RENDEZVOUS Champion CHAMP 5	54	3 wks

JAB 14 features Kurtis Blow. See also Kurtis Blow.

RENE and YVETTE UK, male/female vocal duo   4 wks

| 22 Nov 86 | | JE T'AIME (ALLO ALLO)/ RENE D.M.C. (DEVASTATING MACHO CHARISMA) Sedition EDIT 3319 | 57 | 4 wks |

RENÉE and RENATO UK/Italy, female/male vocal duo   22 wks

| 30 Oct 82 | ★ | SAVE YOUR LOVE Hollywood HWD 003 | 1 | 16 wks |
| 12 Feb 83 | | JUST ONE MORE KISS Hollywood HWD 006 | 48 | 6 wks |

RENEGADE SOUNDWAVE   6 wks
UK, male vocal/instrumental group

| 3 Feb 90 | | PROBABLY A ROBBERY Mute MUTE 102 | 38 | 6 wks |

REO SPEEDWAGON US, male vocal/instrumental group   38 wks

11 Apr 81	●	KEEP ON LOVING YOU Epic EPC 9544	7	14 wks
27 Jun 81		TAKE IT ON THE RUN Epic EPC A 1207	19	14 wks
16 Mar 85		CAN'T FIGHT THIS FEELING Epic A 4880	16	10 wks

REPARATA US, female vocalist   2 wks

| 18 Oct 75 | | SHOES Dart 2066 562 | 43 | 2 wks |

See also Reparata and the Delrons.

REPARATA and the DELRONS   10 wks
US, female vocal group

| 20 Mar 68 | | CAPTAIN OF YOUR SHIP Bell 1002 | 13 | 10 wks |

See also Reparata.

REUNION US, male vocal group   4 wks

| 21 Sep 74 | | LIFE IS A ROCK (BUT THE RADIO ROLLED ME) RCA PB 10056 | 33 | 4 wks |

REVILLOS – See REZILLOS

REVOLUTION – See PRINCE

REYNOLDS – See HAMILTON, Joe FRANK and REYNOLDS

Debbie REYNOLDS US, female vocalist   17 wks

| 30 Aug 57 | ● | TAMMY Vogue-Coral Q 72274 | 2 | 17 wks |

Jody REYNOLDS US, male vocalist   1 wk

| 14 Apr 79 | | ENDLESS SLEEP Lightning LIG 9015 | 66 | 1 wk |

Endless Sleep was coupled with To Know Him Is To Love Him by the Teddy Bears as a double A-side. See also the Teddy Bears.

L.J. REYNOLDS US, male vocalist   3 wks

| 30 Jun 84 | | DON'T LET NOBODY HOLD YOU DOWN Club JAB 5 | 53 | 3 wks |

REYNOLDS GIRLS UK, female vocal duo   12 wks

| 25 Feb 89 | ● | I'D RATHER JACK PWL PWL 25 | 8 | 12 wks |

REZILLOS *UK, male/female vocal/instrumental group* · **21 wks**

Date	Title	Pos	Wks
12 Aug 78	TOP OF THE POPS *Sire SIR 4001*	17	9 wks
25 Nov 78	DESTINATION VENUS *Sire SIR 4008*	43	4 wks
18 Aug 79	I WANNA BE YOUR MAN/ I CAN'T STAND MY BABY *Sensible SAB 1*	71	1 wk
1 Sep 79	I WANNA BE YOUR MAN/ I CAN'T STAND MY BABY (re-entry) *Sensible SAB 1*	75	1 wk
26 Jan 80	MOTORBIKE BEAT *Dindisc DIN 5*	45	6 wks

Motorbike Beat credited to the Revillos.

RHODA with the SPECIAL A.K.A. · **5 wks**
UK, female vocalist with male vocal/instrumental group

Date	Title	Pos	Wks
23 Jan 82	THE BOILER *2-Tone CHSTT 18*	35	5 wks

See also Specials.

RHYTHM IS RHYTHM *US, male instrumental duo* · **1 wk**

Date	Title	Pos	Wks
11 Nov 89	STRINGS OF LIFE '89 *Kool Kat KOOL 509*	74	1 wk

RHYTHMATIC *UK, male instrumental group* · **3 wks**

Date	Title	Pos	Wks
12 May 90	TAKE ME BACK *Network NWK 8*	74	1 wk
26 May 90	TAKE ME BACK (re-entry) *Network NWK 8*	71	1 wk
3 Nov 90	FREQUENCY *Network NWK 13*	62	1 wk

Charlie RICH *US, male vocalist* · **29 wks**

Date	Title	Pos	Wks
16 Feb 74	● THE MOST BEAUTIFUL GIRL *CBS 1897*	2	14 wks
13 Apr 74	BEHIND CLOSED DOORS *Epic EPC 1539*	16	10 wks
1 Feb 75	WE LOVE EACH OTHER *Epic EPC 2868*	37	5 wks

Richie RICH *UK, male vocalist* · **7 wks**

Date	Title	Pos	Wks
16 Jul 88	TURN IT UP *Club JAB 68*	48	3 wks
10 Dec 88	MY DJ (PUMP IT UP SOME) *Gee Street GEE 7*	74	1 wk
2 Sep 89	SALSA HOUSE *FFRR F 113*	50	3 wks

See also Richie Rich meets the Jungle Brothers.

Richie RICH meets the JUNGLE BROTHERS · **5 wks**
UK, male vocalist with US, male rap/scratch group

Date	Title	Pos	Wks
22 Oct 88	I'LL HOUSE YOU *Gee Street GEE 003*	22	5 wks

See also Richie Rich; Jungle Brothers.

RICH KIDS *UK, male vocal/instrumental group* · **5 wks**

Date	Title	Pos	Wks
28 Jan 78	RICH KIDS *EMI 2738*	24	5 wks

Cliff RICHARD *UK, male vocalist* · **998 wks**

Date	Title	Pos	Wks
12 Sep 58	● MOVE IT *Columbia DB 4178*	2	17 wks
21 Nov 58	● HIGH CLASS BABY *Columbia DB 4203*	7	10 wks
30 Jan 59	LIVIN' LOVIN' DOLL *Columbia DB 4249*	20	6 wks
8 May 59	● MEAN STREAK *Columbia DB 4290*	10	9 wks
15 May 59	NEVER MIND *Columbia DB 4290*	21	2 wks
10 Jul 59	★ LIVING DOLL *Columbia DB 4306*	1	21 wks
9 Oct 59	★ TRAVELLIN' LIGHT *Columbia DB 4351*	1	17 wks
9 Oct 59	DYNAMITE *Columbia DB 4351*	16	2 wks
30 Oct 59	DYNAMITE (re-entry) *Columbia DB 4351*	21	2 wks
11 Dec 59	LIVING DOLL (re-entry) *Columbia DB 4306*	26	1 wk
1 Jan 60	LIVING DOLL (2nd re-entry) *Columbia DB 4306*	28	1 wk
15 Jan 60	EXPRESSO BONGO (EP) *Columbia SEG 7971*	14	7 wks
22 Jan 60	● VOICE IN THE WILDERNESS (re-entry) *Columbia DB 4398*	2	13 wks
24 Mar 60	● FALL IN LOVE WITH YOU *Columbia DB 4431*	2	15 wks
5 May 60	VOICE IN THE WILDERNESS *Columbia DB 4398*	36	2 wks
30 Jun 60	★ PLEASE DON'T TEASE *Columbia DB 4479*	1	18 wks
22 Sep 60	● NINE TIMES OUT OF TEN *Columbia DB 4506*	3	12 wks
1 Dec 60	★ I LOVE YOU *Columbia DB 4547*	1	16 wks
2 Mar 61	● THEME FOR A DREAM *Columbia DB 4593*	3	14 wks
30 Mar 61	● GEE WHIZ IT'S YOU *Columbia DC 756*	4	14 wks
22 Jun 61	● A GIRL LIKE YOU *Columbia DB 4667*	3	14 wks
19 Oct 61	● WHEN THE GIRL IN YOUR ARMS IS THE GIRL IN YOUR HEART *Columbia DB 4716*	3	15 wks
11 Jan 62	★ THE YOUNG ONES *Columbia DB 4761*	1	21 wks
10 May 62	● I'M LOOKING OUT THE WINDOW/ DO YOU WANNA DANCE *Columbia DB 4828*	2	17 wks
6 Sep 62	● IT'LL BE ME *Columbia DB 4886*	2	12 wks
6 Dec 62	★ THE NEXT TIME/ BACHELOR BOY *Columbia DB 4950*	1	18 wks
21 Feb 63	● SUMMER HOLIDAY *Columbia DB 4977*	1	18 wks
9 May 63	● LUCKY LIPS *Columbia DB 7034*	4	15 wks
22 Aug 63	● IT'S ALL IN THE GAME *Columbia DB 7089*	2	13 wks
7 Nov 63	● DON'T TALK TO HIM *Columbia DB 7150*	2	13 wks
6 Feb 64	● I'M THE LONELY ONE *Columbia DB 7203*	8	10 wks
13 Feb 64	DON'T TALK TO HIM (re-entry) *Columbia DB 7150*	50	1 wk
30 Apr 64	● CONSTANTLY *Columbia DB 7272*	4	13 wks
2 Jul 64	● ON THE BEACH *Columbia DB 7305*	7	13 wks
8 Oct 64	● THE TWELFTH OF NEVER *Columbia DB 7372*	8	11 wks
10 Dec 64	● I COULD EASILY FALL *Columbia DB 7420*	9	11 wks
11 Mar 65	★ THE MINUTE YOU'RE GONE *Columbia DB 7496*	1	14 wks
10 Jun 65	ON MY WORD *Columbia DB 7596*	12	10 wks
19 Aug 65	THE TIME IN BETWEEN *Columbia DB 7660*	22	8 wks
4 Nov 65	● WIND ME UP (LET ME GO) *Columbia DB 7745*	2	16 wks
24 Mar 66	BLUE TURNS TO GREY *Columbia DB 7866*	15	9 wks
21 Jul 66	● VISIONS *Columbia DB 7968*	7	12 wks
13 Oct 66	● TIME DRAGS BY *Columbia DB 8017*	10	10 wks
15 Dec 66	● IN THE COUNTRY *Columbia DB 8094*	6	10 wks
16 Mar 67	● IT'S ALL OVER *Columbia DB 8150*	9	10 wks
8 Jun 67	I'LL COME RUNNING *Columbia DB 8210*	26	8 wks
16 Aug 67	THE DAY I MET MARIE *Columbia DB 8245*	10	14 wks
15 Nov 67	● ALL MY LOVE *Columbia DB 8293*	6	12 wks
20 Mar 68	★ CONGRATULATIONS *Columbia DB 8376*	1	13 wks
26 Jun 68	I'LL LOVE YOU FOREVER TODAY *Columbia DB 8437*	27	6 wks
25 Sep 68	MARIANNE *Columbia DB 8476*	22	8 wks
27 Nov 68	DON'T FORGET TO CATCH ME *Columbia DB 8503*	21	10 wks
26 Feb 69	GOOD TIMES (BETTER TIMES) *Columbia DB 8548*	12	11 wks
28 May 69	● BIG SHIP *Columbia DB 8581*	8	10 wks
13 Sep 69	● THROW DOWN A LINE *Columbia DB 8615*	7	9 wks
6 Dec 69	WITH THE EYES OF A CHILD *Columbia DB 8641*	20	11 wks
21 Feb 70	JOY OF LIVING *Columbia DB 8657*	25	8 wks
6 Jun 70	● GOODBYE SAM HELLO SAMANTHA *Columbia DB 8685*	6	15 wks
5 Sep 70	I AIN'T GOT TIME ANYMORE *Columbia DB 8708*	21	7 wks
23 Jan 71	SUNNY HONEY GIRL *Columbia DB 8747*	19	8 wks
10 Apr 71	SILVERY RAIN *Columbia DB 8774*	27	6 wks
17 Jul 71	FLYING MACHINE *Columbia DB 8797*	37	7 wks
13 Nov 71	SING A SONG OF FREEDOM *Columbia DB 8836*	13	12 wks
11 Mar 72	JESUS *Columbia DB 8864*	35	3 wks
26 Aug 72	LIVING IN HARMONY *Columbia DB 8917*	12	10 wks
17 Mar 73	● POWER TO ALL OUR FRIENDS *EMI 2012*	4	12 wks
12 May 73	HELP IT ALONG/ TOMORROW RISING *EMI 2022*	29	6 wks
1 Dec 73	TAKE ME HIGH *EMI 2088*	27	12 wks
18 May 74	(YOU KEEP ME) HANGIN' ON *EMI 2150*	13	8 wks
7 Feb 76	MISS YOU NIGHTS *EMI 2376*	15	10 wks
8 May 76	● DEVIL WOMAN *EMI 2458*	9	8 wks
21 Aug 76	I CAN'T ASK FOR ANYMORE THAN YOU *EMI 2499*	17	8 wks
4 Dec 76	HEY MR. DREAM MAKER *EMI 2559*	31	5 wks
5 Mar 77	MY KINDA LIFE *EMI 2584*	15	8 wks
16 Jul 77	WHEN TWO WORLDS DRIFT APART *EMI 2633*	46	3 wks
31 Mar 79	GREEN LIGHT *EMI 2920*	57	3 wks
21 Jul 79	★ WE DON'T TALK ANYMORE *EMI 2975*	1	14 wks
3 Nov 79	HOT SHOT *EMI 5003*	46	5 wks
2 Feb 80	CARRIE *EMI 5006*	4	10 wks
16 Aug 80	● DREAMIN' *EMI 5095*	8	10 wks
24 Jan 81	A LITTLE IN LOVE *EMI 5123*	15	8 wks
29 Aug 81	● WIRED FOR SOUND *EMI 5221*	4	9 wks
21 Nov 81	DADDY'S HOME *EMI 5251*	2	12 wks
17 Jul 82	● THE ONLY WAY OUT *EMI 5318*	10	9 wks
25 Sep 82	WHERE DO WE GO FROM HERE *EMI 5341*	60	3 wks
4 Dec 82	LITTLE TOWN *EMI 5348*	11	7 wks
16 Apr 83	● TRUE LOVE WAYS *EMI 5385*	8	8 wks

3 Sep 83		NEVER SAY DIE (GIVE A LITTLE BIT MORE)		
		EMI 5415...............................	**15**	7 wks
26 Nov 83	●	PLEASE DON'T FALL IN LOVE *EMI 5437*..................	**7**	9 wks
31 Mar 84		BABY YOU'RE DYNAMITE/ OCEAN DEEP		
		EMI 5457...............................	**27**	6 wks
19 May 84		OCEAN DEEP/ BABY YOU'RE DYNAMITE (re-entry)		
		EMI 5457...............................	**72**	1 wk
3 Nov 84		SHOOTING FROM THE HEART *EMI RICH 1*.............	**51**	4 wks
9 Feb 85		HEART USER *EMI RICH 2*	**46**	3 wks
14 Sep 85		SHE'S SO BEAUTIFUL *EMI 5531*............	**17**	9 wks
7 Dec 85		IT'S IN EVERY ONE OF US *EMI 5537*..........	**45**	6 wks
20 Jun 87	●	MY PRETTY ONE *EMI EM 4*	**6**	10 wks
29 Aug 87	●	SOME PEOPLE *EMI EM 18*	**3**	10 wks
31 Oct 87		REMEMBER ME *EMI EM 31*..............	**35**	4 wks
13 Feb 88		TWO HEARTS *EMI EM 42*	**34**	3 wks
3 Dec 88	★	MISTLETOE AND WINE *EMI EM 78*...........	**1**	8 wks
10 Jun 89	●	THE BEST OF ME *EMI EM 78*............	**2**	7 wks
26 Aug 89	●	I JUST DON'T HAVE THE HEART *EMI EM 101*.........	**3**	8 wks
14 Oct 89		LEAN ON YOU *EMI EM 105*...............	**17**	6 wks
24 Feb 90		STRONGER THAN THAT *EMI EM 129*........	**14**	5 wks
25 Aug 90	●	SILHOUETTES *EMI EM 155*............	**10**	7 wks
13 Oct 90		FROM A DISTANCE *EMI EM 155*............	**11**	6 wks
8 Dec 90	★	SAVIOUR'S DAY *EMI XMAS 90*............	**1†**	4 wks

The Shadows appear on all Cliff's hits from Move It *to* A Girl Like You. *After that they are on the following hits:* The Young Ones, Do You Wanna Dance, It'll Be Me, The Next Time, Bachelor Boy, Summer Holiday, Lucky Lips, Don't Talk To Him, I'm The Lonely One, On The Beach, I Could Easily Fall, The Time In Between, Blue Turns To Grey, Time Drags By, In The Country *and* Don't Forget To Catch Me. Throw Down A Line *and* Joy Of Living *are credited to 'Cliff and Hank', Hank being Hank B. Marvin of the Shadows, who played guitar and sang on these two hits. The tracks on the* Expresso Bongo *EP:* Love/A Voice in The Wilderness/The Shrine On The Second Floor/Bongo Blues. Bongo Blues *features only the Shadows. The Shadows were the Drifters on Cliff's hits before* Living Doll. True Love Ways *credits the London Philharmonic Orchestra.* Ocean Deep *listed from 28 Apr 84 onwards. See also the Shadows, Hank Marvin. See also Olivia Newton-John and Cliff Richard; Phil Everly and Cliff Richard; Sheila Walsh and Cliff Richard; Cliff Richard and the Young Ones. Cliff Richard and Sarah Brightman; Elton John and Cliff Richard; Van Morrison.*

Cliff RICHARD and Sarah BRIGHTMAN   16 wks
UK, *male/female vocal duo*

| 4 Oct 86 | ● | ALL I ASK OF YOU *Polydor POSP 802*.................... | **3** | 16 wks |

See also Cliff Richard; Sarah Brightman.

Cliff RICHARD and the YOUNG ONES   11 wks
UK, *male vocal charity assembly*

| 22 Mar 86 | ★ | LIVING DOLL *WEA YZ 65* .... | **1** | 11 wks |

Features Hank B. Marvin on guitar. See also Cliff Richard; Bad News; Hank Marvin.

Wendy RICHARD – *See Mike SARNE*

Lionel RICHIE   US, *male vocalist*   124 wks

20 Nov 82	●	TRULY *Motown TMG 1284*	**6**	11 wks
29 Jan 83		YOU ARE *Motown TMG 1290*....................	**43**	7 wks
7 May 83		MY LOVE *Motown TMG 1300*	**70**	3 wks
1 Oct 83	●	ALL NIGHT LONG (ALL NIGHT) *Motown TMG 1319*	**2**	16 wks
3 Dec 83	●	RUNNING WITH THE NIGHT *Motown TMG 1324*.........	**9**	12 wks
10 Mar 84	★	HELLO *Motown TMG 1330*................	**1**	15 wks
23 Jun 84		STUCK ON YOU *Motown TMG 1341*...........	**12**	12 wks
20 Oct 84		PENNY LOVER *Motown TMG 1356*..........	**18**	7 wks
16 Nov 85	●	SAY YOU, SAY ME *Motown ZB 40421*	**8**	11 wks
26 Jul 86	●	DANCING ON THE CEILING *Motown L10 1*...........	**7**	11 wks
11 Oct 86		LOVE WILL CONQUER ALL *Motown L10 2*	**45**	5 wks
20 Dec 86		BALLERINA GIRL/ DEEP RIVER WOMAN		
		Motown L10 3....................	**17**	8 wks
28 Mar 87		SELA *Motown L10 4*....................	**43**	6 wks

See also Diana Ross and Lionel Richie. Deep River Woman only listed with Ballerina Girl from 17 Jan 87. It has the credit: 'background vocal: Alabama' (US, male vocal group).

Jonathan RICHMAN and the MODERN LOVERS   23 wks
US, *male vocal/instrumental group*

| 16 Jul 77 | | ROADRUNNER *Beserkley BZZ 1*............. | **11** | 9 wks |
| 29 Oct 77 | ● | EGYPTIAN REGGAE *Beserkley BZZ 2*......... | **5** | 14 wks |

See also Modern Lovers.

RICO – *See SPECIALS*

RIDE   UK, *male vocal/instrumental group*   8 wks

27 Jan 90		RIDE (EP) *Creation CRE 072T*....................	**71**	2 wks
14 Apr 90		PLAY (EP) *Creation CRE 075T*....................	**32**	3 wks
29 Oct 90		FALL (EP) *Creation CRE 087T*....................	**34**	3 wks

Tracks on Ride EP: Chelsea Girl/Drive Blind/All I See/Close My Eyes. Tracks on Play EP: Like A Daydream/Silver/Furthest Sense/ Perfect Time. Tracks on Fall EP: Dreams Burn Down/Taste/Hear And Now/Nowhere.

Andrew RIDGELEY   UK, *male vocalist*   3 wks

| 31 Mar 90 | | SHAKE *Epic AJR 1*.................... | **58** | 3 wks |

Stan RIDGWAY   US, *male vocalist*   12 wks

| 5 Jul 86 | ● | CAMOUFLAGE *IRS IRM 114*.................... | **4** | 12 wks |

RIGHEIRA   Spain, *male vocal duo*   3 wks

| 24 Sep 83 | | VAMOS A LA PLAYA *A &M AM 137* .... | **53** | 3 wks |

RIGHTEOUS BROTHERS   US, *male vocal duo*   76 wks

14 Jan 65	★	YOU'VE LOST THAT LOVIN' FEELIN'		
		London HLU 9943....................	**1**	10 wks
12 Aug 65		UNCHAINED MELODY *London HL 9975*	**14**	12 wks
13 Jan 66		EBB TIDE *London HL 10011*....................	**48**	2 wks
14 Apr 66		(YOU'RE MY) SOUL AND INSPIRATION		
		Verve VS 535....................	**15**	10 wks
10 Nov 66		WHITE CLIFFS OF DOVER *London HL 10086*	**21**	9 wks
22 Dec 66		ISLAND IN THE SUN *Verve VS 547*	**36**	5 wks
12 Feb 69	●	YOU'VE LOST THAT LOVIN' FEELIN' (re-issue)		
		London HL 10241....................	**10**	11 wks
19 Nov 77		YOU'VE LOST THAT LOVIN' FEELIN' (2nd re-issue)		
		Phil Spector International 2010 022	**42**	4 wks
27 Oct 90	★	UNCHAINED MELODY *Verve/Polydor PO 101*............	**1†**	10 wks
15 Dec 90	●	YOU'VE LOST THAT LOVIN' FEELIN' (3rd re-issue)/ EBB TIDE (re-issue) *Verve/Polydor PO 116*.........	**3†**	3 wks

Cheryl Pepsii RILEY   US, *female vocalist*   1 wk

| 28 Jan 89 | | THANKS FOR MY CHILD *CBS 653153 7*.................... | **75** | 1 wk |

Jeannie C. RILEY   US, *female vocalist*   15 wks

| 16 Oct 68 | | HARPER VALLEY P. T. A. *Polydor 56748* .... | **12** | 15 wks |

RIMSHOTS   US, *male instrumental/vocal group*   5 wks

| 19 Jul 75 | | 7-6-5-4-3-2-1 (BLOW YOUR WHISTLE) | | |
| | | *All Platinum 6146 304* .... | **26** | 5 wks |

Miguel RIOS   Spain, *male vocalist*   12 wks

| 11 Jul 70 | | SONG OF JOY *A &M AMS 790*.................... | **16** | 12 wks |

Waldo de los RIOS *Argentina, orchestra* **16 wks**

10 Apr 71	● MOZART SYMPHONY NO.40 IN G MINOR K550 1ST MOVEMENT (ALLEGRO MOLTO) *A & M AMS 836*	**5**	16 wks

Minnie RIPERTON *US, female vocalist* **10 wks**

12 Apr 75	● LOVING YOU *Epic EPC 3121*	**2**	10 wks

RITCHIE FAMILY *US, female vocal group* **19 wks**

23 Aug 75	BRAZIL *Polydor 2058 625*	**41**	4 wks
18 Sep 76	● THE BEST DISCO IN TOWN *Polydor 2058 777*	**10**	9 wks
17 Feb 79	AMERICAN GENERATION *Mercury 6007 199*	**49**	6 wks

Tex RITTER *US, male vocalist* **14 wks**

22 Jun 56	● WAYWARD WIND *Capitol CL 14581*	**8**	14 wks

RIVER CITY PEOPLE
UK, male/female vocal/instrumental group **18 wks**

12 Aug 89	(WHAT'S WRONG WITH) DREAMING *EMI EM 95*	**70**	3 wks
3 Mar 90	WALKING ON ICE *EMI EM 130*	**62**	2 wks
30 Jun 90	CARRY THE BLAME/ CALIFORNIA DREAMIN' *EMI EM 145*	**13**	10 wks
22 Sep 90	(WHAT'S WRONG WITH) DREAMING (re-issue) *EMI EM 156*	**40**	3 wks

RIVER DETECTIVES *UK, male vocal/instrumental duo* **4 wks**

29 Jul 89	CHAINS *WEA YZ 383*	**51**	4 wks

Danny RIVERS *UK, male vocalist* **3 wks**

12 Jan 61	CAN'T YOU HEAR MY HEART *Decca F 11294*	**36**	3 wks

ROACHFORD *UK, male vocalist* **24 wks**

18 Jun 88	CUDDLY TOY *CBS ROA 2*	**61**	4 wks
14 Jan 89	● CUDDLY TOY (re-issue) *CBS ROA 4*	**4**	9 wks
18 Mar 89	FAMILY MAN *CBS ROA 5*	**25**	6 wks
1 Jul 89	KATHLEEN *CBS ROA 6*	**43**	5 wks

ROB N' RAZ featuring Leila K **17 wks**
Sweden, male production duo with female vocalist

25 Nov 89	● GOT TO GET *Arista 112696*	**8**	14 wks
17 Mar 90	ROK THE NATION *Arista 112971*	**41**	3 wks

ROBBIE – *See SLY and ROBBIE*

Kate ROBBINS *UK, female vocalist* **10 wks**

30 May 81	● MORE THAN IN LOVE *RCA 69*	**2**	10 wks

Marty ROBBINS *US, male vocalist* **32 wks**

29 Jan 60	EL PASO *Fontana H 233*	**19**	7 wks
7 Apr 60	EL PASO (re-entry) *Fontana H 233*	**44**	1 wk
26 May 60	BIG IRON *Fontana H 229*	**48**	1 wk
27 Sep 62	● DEVIL WOMAN *CBS AAG 114*	**5**	17 wks
17 Jan 63	RUBY ANN *CBS AAG 128*	**24**	6 wks

Austin ROBERTS *US, male vocalist* **7 wks**

25 Oct 75	ROCKY *Private Stock PVT 33*	**22**	7 wks

Malcolm ROBERTS *UK, male vocalist* **29 wks**

11 May 67	TIME ALONE WILL TELL *RCA 1578*	**45**	2 wks
30 Oct 68	● MAY I HAVE THE NEXT DREAM WITH YOU *Major Minor MM 581*	**8**	14 wks
12 Feb 69	MAY I HAVE THE NEXT DREAM WITH YOU (re-entry) *Major Minor MM 581*	**45**	1 wk
22 Nov 69	LOVE IS ALL *Major Minor MM 637*	**12**	12 wks

B.A. ROBERTSON *UK, male vocalist* **47 wks**

28 Jul 79	● BANG BANG *Asylum K 13152*	**2**	12 wks
27 Oct 79	● KNOCKED IT OFF *Asylum K 12396*	**8**	12 wks
1 Mar 80	● KOOL IN THE KAFTAN *Asylum K 12427*	**17**	12 wks
31 May 80	● TO BE OR NOT TO BE *Asylum K 12449*	**9**	11 wks

See also B.A. Robertson and Maggie Bell; Frida and B.A. Robertson.

B.A. ROBERTSON and Maggie BELL **8 wks**
UK, male/female vocal duo

17 Oct 81	HOLD ME *Swansong BAM 1*	**11**	8 wks

See also B.A. Robertson; Maggie Bell.

Don ROBERTSON **9 wks**
US, male instrumentalist - piano and whistler

11 May 56	● THE HAPPY WHISTLER *Capitol CL 14575*	**8**	9 wks

Robbie ROBERTSON *Canada, male vocalist* **10 wks**

23 Jul 88	SOMEWHERE DOWN THE CRAZY RIVER *Geffen GEF 40*	**15**	10 wks

Ivo ROBIC *Yugoslavia, male vocalist* **1 wk**

6 Nov 59	MORGEN *Polydor 23 923*	**23**	1 wk

Floyd ROBINSON *US, male vocalist* **9 wks**

16 Oct 59	● MAKIN' LOVE *RCA 1146*	**9**	9 wks

Smokey ROBINSON *US, male vocalist* **29 wks**

23 Feb 74	JUST MY SOUL RESPONDING *Tamla Motown TMG 883*	**35**	6 wks
9 May 81	★ BEING WITH YOU *Motown TMG 1223*	**1**	13 wks
13 Mar 82	TELL ME TOMORROW *Motown TMG 1255*	**51**	4 wks
28 Mar 87	JUST TO SEE HER *Motown ZB 41147*	**52**	6 wks

See also Smokey Robinson and the Miracles; Diana Ross, Marvin Gaye, Smokey Robinson and Stevie Wonder; Four Tops.

Smokey ROBINSON and the MIRACLES **71 wks**
US, male vocal group

24 Feb 66	GOING TO A GO-GO *Tamla Motown TMG 547*	**44**	5 wks
22 Dec 66	(COME 'ROUND HERE) I'M THE ONE YOU NEED *Tamla Motown TMG 584*	**45**	2 wks
27 Dec 67	I SECOND THAT EMOTION *Tamla Motown TMG 631*	**27**	11 wks
3 Apr 68	IF YOU CAN WANT *Tamla Motown TMG 648*	**50**	1 wk

7 May 69 ●	**TRACKS OF MY TEARS** *Tamla Motown TMG 696*	**9**	13 wks
1 Aug 70 ★	**TEARS OF A CLOWN** *Tamla Motown TMG 745*	**1**	14 wks
30 Jan 71	**(COME 'ROUND HERE) I'M THE ONE YOU NEED** (re-issue) *Tamla Motown TMG 761*	**13**	9 wks
5 Jun 71	**I DON'T BLAME YOU AT ALL** *Tamla Motown TMG 774*	**11**	10 wks
2 Oct 76	**TEARS OF A CLOWN** (re-issue) *Tamla Motown TMG 1048*	**34**	6 wks

See also Miracles; Smokey Robinson.

Tom ROBINSON *UK, male vocalist* — 41 wks

22 Oct 77 ●	**2-4-6-8 MOTORWAY** *EMI 2715*	**5**	9 wks
18 Feb 78	**DON'T TAKE NO FOR AN ANSWER** *EMI 2749*	**18**	6 wks
13 May 78	**UP AGAINST THE WALL** *EMI 2787*	**33**	6 wks
17 Mar 79	**BULLY FOR YOU** *EMI 2916*	**68**	2 wks
25 Jun 83 ●	**WAR BABY** *Panic NIC 2*	**6**	9 wks
12 Nov 83	**LISTEN TO THE RADIO: ATMOSPHERICS** *Panic NIC 3*	**39**	6 wks
15 Sep 84	**RIKKI DON'T LOSE THAT NUMBER** *Castaway TR 2*	**58**	3 wks

First four singles bill Tom Robinson Band - UK, male vocal/instrumental group.

John ROCCA – *See FREEEZ*

ROCHELLE *US, female vocalist* — 6 wks

1 Feb 86	**MY MAGIC MAN** *Warner Bros. W 8838*	**27**	6 wks

ROCK AID ARMENIA
UK, male vocal/instrumental charity ensemble — 5 wks

16 Dec 89	**SMOKE ON THE WATER** *Life Aid Armenia ARMEN 001*	**39**	5 wks

ROCK CANDY *UK, male vocal/instrumental group* — 6 wks

11 Sep 71	**REMEMBER** *MCA MK 5069*	**32**	6 wks

ROCK GODDESS *UK, female vocal/instrumental group* — 5 wks

5 Mar 83	**MY ANGEL** *A & M AMS 8311*	**64**	2 wks
24 Mar 84	**I DIDN'T KNOW I LOVED YOU (TILL I SAW YOU ROCK 'N' ROLL)** *A & M AMS 185*	**57**	3 wks

Sir Monti ROCK III – *See DISCO TEX and the SEX-O-LETTES*

ROCKER'S REVENGE — 20 wks
US, male/female vocal/instrumental group

14 Aug 82 ●	**WALKING ON SUNSHINE** *London LON 11*	**4**	13 wks
29 Jan 83	**THE HARDER THEY COME** *London LON 18*	**30**	7 wks

First hit has credit: 'Featuring Donnie Calvin'.

ROCKETS – *See Tony CROMBIE and his ROCKETS.*

ROCKIN' BERRIES *UK, male vocal/instrumental group* — 41 wks

1 Oct 64	**I DIDN'T MEAN TO HURT YOU** *Piccadilly 7N 35197*	**43**	1 wk
15 Oct 64 ●	**HE'S IN TOWN** *Piccadilly 7N 35203*	**3**	13 wks
21 Jan 65	**WHAT IN THE WORLD'S COME OVER YOU** *Piccadilly 7N 35217*	**23**	7 wks
13 May 65 ●	**POOR MAN'S SON** *Piccadilly 7N 35236*	**5**	11 wks
26 Aug 65	**YOU'RE MY GIRL** *Piccadilly 7N 35254*	**40**	7 wks
6 Jan 66	**THE WATER IS OVER MY HEAD** *Piccadilly 7N 35270*	**43**	1 wk
20 Jan 66	**THE WATER IS OVER MY HEAD** (re-entry) *Piccadilly 7N 35270*	**50**	1 wk

Lord ROCKINGHAM'S XI — 20 wks
UK, male instrumental group

24 Oct 58 ★	**HOOTS MON** *Decca F 11059*	**1**	17 wks
6 Feb 59	**WEE TOM** *Decca F 11104*	**16**	3 wks

Both of the group's hits contain a little spoken Scottish.

ROCKNEY – *See CHAS and DAVE*

ROCKSTEADY CREW *US, male/female vocal group* — 16 wks

1 Oct 83 ●	**(HEY YOU) THE ROCKSTEADY CREW** *Charisma/Virgin RSC 1*	**6**	12 wks
5 May 84	**UPROCK** *Charisma/Virgin RSC 2*	**64**	4 wks

ROCKWELL *US, male vocalist* — 11 wks

4 Feb 84 ●	**SOMEBODY'S WATCHING ME** *Motown TMG 1331*	**6**	11 wks

ROCOCO *UK/Italy, male/female vocal/instrumental group* — 5 wks

16 Dec 89	**ITALO HOUSE MIX** *Mercury MER 314*	**54**	5 wks

Clodagh RODGERS *Ireland, female vocalist* — 59 wks

26 Mar 69 ●	**COME BACK AND SHAKE ME** *RCA 1792*	**3**	14 wks
9 Jul 69 ●	**GOODNIGHT MIDNIGHT** *RCA 1852*	**4**	11 wks
4 Oct 69	**GOODNIGHT MIDNIGHT** (re-entry) *RCA 1852*	**48**	1 wk
8 Nov 69	**BILJO** *RCA 1891*	**22**	9 wks
4 Apr 70	**EVERYBODY GO HOME THE PARTY'S OVER** *RCA 1930*	**47**	2 wks
20 Mar 71 ●	**JACK IN THE BOX** *RCA 2066*	**4**	10 wks
9 Oct 71	**LADY LOVE BUG** *RCA 2117*	**28**	12 wks

Jimmie RODGERS *US, male vocalist* — 37 wks

1 Nov 57	**HONEYCOMB** *Columbia DB 3986*	**30**	1 wk
20 Dec 57 ●	**KISSES SWEETER THAN WINE** *Columbia DB 4052*	**7**	11 wks
28 Mar 58	**OH OH, I'M FALLING IN LOVE AGAIN** *Columbia DB 4078*	**18**	6 wks
19 Dec 58	**WOMAN FROM LIBERIA** *Columbia DB 4206*	**18**	6 wks
14 Jun 62 ●	**ENGLISH COUNTRY GARDEN** *Columbia DB 4847*	**5**	13 wks

RODS – *See EDDIE and the HOT RODS*

Tommy ROE *US, male vocalist* — 74 wks

6 Sep 62 ●	**SHEILA** *HMV POP 1060*	**3**	14 wks
6 Dec 62	**SUSIE DARLIN'** *HMV POP 1092*	**37**	5 wks
21 Mar 63 ●	**THE FOLK SINGER** *HMV POP 1138*	**4**	13 wks
26 Sep 63 ●	**EVERYBODY** *HMV POP 1207*	**9**	11 wks
19 Dec 63	**EVERYBODY** (re-entry) *HMV POP 1207*	**49**	3 wks
16 Apr 69 ★	**DIZZY** *Stateside SS 2143*	**1**	19 wks
23 Jul 69	**HEATHER HONEY** *Stateside SS 2152*	**24**	9 wks

ROGER *US, male vocalist* — 4 wks

17 Oct 87	**I WANT TO BE YOUR MAN** *Reprise W 8229*	**61**	4 wks

See also Scritti Politti.

Julie ROGERS *UK, female vocalist* — 38 wks

13 Aug 64 ●	**THE WEDDING** *Mercury MF 820*	**3**	23 wks
10 Dec 64	**LIKE A CHILD** *Mercury MF 838*	**21**	9 wks
25 Mar 65	**HAWAIIAN WEDDING SONG** *Mercury MF 849*	**31**	6 wks

Kenny ROGERS US, male vocalist — 87 wks

18 Oct 69	● RUBY DON'T TAKE YOUR LOVE TO TOWN *Reprise RS 20829*	2	23 wks
7 Feb 70	● SOMETHING'S BURNING *Reprise RS 20888*	8	14 wks
30 Apr 77	★ LUCILLE *United Artists UP 36242*	1	14 wks
17 Sep 77	DAYTIME FRIENDS *United Artists UP 36289*	39	4 wks
2 Jun 79	SHE BELIEVES IN ME *United Artists UP 36533*	42	7 wks
26 Jan 80	★ COWARD OF THE COUNTY *United Artists UP 614*	1	12 wks
15 Nov 80	LADY *United Artists UP 635*	12	12 wks
22 Oct 83	EYES THAT SEE IN THE DARK *RCA 358*	61	1 wk

First two hits credit Kenny Rogers and the First Edition, US, male/female vocal/instrumental group. See also Kenny Rogers and Sheena Easton; Kenny Rogers and Dolly Parton.

Kenny ROGERS and Sheena EASTON — 7 wks
US/UK, male/female vocal duo

12 Feb 83	WE'VE GOT TONIGHT *Liberty UP 658*	28	7 wks

See also Kenny Rogers; Sheena Easton.

Kenny ROGERS and Dolly PARTON — 15 wks
US, male/female vocal duo

12 Nov 83	● ISLANDS IN THE STREAM *RCA 378*	7	15 wks

See also Kenny Rogers; Dolly Parton.

ROKOTTO UK, male vocal/instrumental group — 10 wks

22 Oct 77	BOOGIE ON UP *State STAT 62*	40	4 wks
10 Jun 78	FUNK THEORY *State STAT 80*	49	6 wks

ROLLING STONES UK, male vocal/instrumental group — 334 wks

25 Jul 63	COME ON *Decca F 11675*	21	14 wks
14 Nov 63	I WANNA BE YOUR MAN *Decca F 11764*	12	16 wks
27 Feb 64	● NOT FADE AWAY *Decca F 11845*	3	15 wks
2 Jul 64	★ IT'S ALL OVER NOW *Decca F 11934*	1	15 wks
19 Nov 64	★ LITTLE RED ROOSTER *Decca F 12014*	1	12 wks
4 Mar 65	★ THE LAST TIME *Decca F 12104*	1	13 wks
26 Aug 65	★ (I CAN'T GET NO) SATISFACTION *Decca F 12220*	1	12 wks
28 Oct 65	★ GET OFF OF MY CLOUD *Decca F 12263*	1	12 wks
10 Feb 66	● NINETEENTH NERVOUS BREAKDOWN *Decca F 12331*	2	8 wks
19 May 66	★ PAINT IT, BLACK *Decca F 12395*	1	10 wks
29 Sep 66	● HAVE YOU SEEN YOUR MOTHER BABY STANDING IN THE SHADOW *Decca F 12497*	5	8 wks
19 Jan 67	● LET'S SPEND THE NIGHT TOGETHER/RUBY TUESDAY *Decca F 12546*	3	10 wks
23 Aug 67	● WE LOVE YOU / DANDELION *Decca F 12654*	8	8 wks
29 May 68	★ JUMPING JACK FLASH *Decca F 12782*	1	11 wks
9 Jul 69	★ HONKY TONK WOMEN *Decca F 12952*	1	17 wks
24 Apr 71	● BROWN SUGAR/ BITCH/ LET IT ROCK *Rolling Stones RS 19100*	2	13 wks
3 Jul 71	STREET FIGHTING MAN *Decca F 13195*	21	8 wks
29 Apr 72	● TUMBLING DICE *Rolling Stones RS 19103*	5	8 wks
1 Sep 73	● ANGIE *Rolling Stones RS 19105*	5	10 wks
3 Aug 74	● IT'S ONLY ROCK AND ROLL *Rolling Stones RS 19114*	10	7 wks
20 Sep 75	OUT OF TIME *Decca F 13597*	45	2 wks
1 May 76	● FOOL TO CRY *Rolling Stones RS 19121*	6	10 wks
3 Jun 78	● MISS YOU/ FAR AWAY EYES *Rolling Stones EMI 2802*	3	13 wks
30 Sep 78	RESPECTABLE *Rolling Stones EMI 2861*	23	8 wks
5 Jul 80	● EMOTIONAL RESCUE *Rolling Stones RSR 105*	9	8 wks
4 Oct 80	SHE'S SO COLD *Rolling Stones RSR 106*	33	6 wks
29 Aug 81	● START ME UP *Rolling Stones RSR 108*	7	9 wks
12 Dec 81	WAITING ON A FRIEND *Rolling Stones RSR 109*	50	6 wks
12 Jun 82	GOING TO A GO GO *Rolling Stones RSR 110*	26	6 wks
2 Oct 82	TIME IS ON MY SIDE *Rolling Stones RSR 111*	62	2 wks
12 Nov 83	UNDERCOVER OF THE NIGHT *Rolling Stones RSR 113*	11	9 wks
11 Feb 84	SHE WAS HOT *Rolling Stones RSR 114*	42	4 wks
21 Jul 84	BROWN SUGAR (re-issue) *Rolling Stones SUGAR 1*	58	2 wks
15 Mar 86	HARLEM SHUFFLE *Rolling Stones A 6864*	13	7 wks
2 Sep 89	MIXED EMOTIONS *Rolling Stones 655193 7*	36	5 wks
2 Dec 89	ROCK AND A HARD PLACE *Rolling Stones 655422 7*	63	1 wk
23 Jun 90	PAINT IT, BLACK (re-issue) *London LON 264*	61	3 wks
30 Jun 90	ALMOST HEAR YOU SIGH *Rolling Stones 656065 7*	31	5 wks

Far Away Eyes credited from 15 Jul 78 until end of record's run.

ROMAN HOLLIDAY UK, male vocal/instrumental group — 19 wks

2 Apr 83	STAND BY *Jive JIVE 31*	61	3 wks
2 Jul 83	DON'T TRY TO STOP IT *Jive JIVE 39*	14	9 wks
24 Sep 83	MOTORMANIA *Jive JIVE 49*	40	7 wks

ROMANTICS – *See RUBY and the ROMANTICS*

Max ROMEO Jamaica, male vocalist — 25 wks

28 May 69	● WET DREAM *Unity UN 503*	10	24 wks
29 Nov 69	WET DREAM (re-entry) *Unity UN 503*	50	1 wk

RONDO VENEZIANA Italy, orchestra — 3 wks

22 Oct 83	LA SERENISSIMA (THEME FROM 'VENICE IN PERIL') *Ferroway 7 RON 1*	58	3 wks

RONETTES US, female vocal group — 34 wks

17 Oct 63	● BE MY BABY *London HLU 9793*	4	13 wks
9 Jan 64	BABY I LOVE YOU *London HLU 9826*	11	14 wks
27 Aug 64	BEST PART OF BREAKING UP *London HLU 9905*	43	3 wks
8 Oct 64	DO I LOVE YOU *London HLU 9922*	35	4 wks

RONNETTE – *See FIDELFATTI featuring RONNETTE*

Linda RONSTADT US, female vocalist — 21 wks

8 May 76	TRACKS OF MY TEARS *Asylum K 13034*	42	3 wks
28 Jan 78	BLUE BAYOU *Asylum K 13106*	35	4 wks
26 May 79	ALISON *Asylum K 13149*	66	2 wks
11 Nov 89	● DON'T KNOW MUCH *Elektra EKR 100*	2	12 wks

See also Linda Ronstadt and James Ingram.

Linda RONSTADT and James INGRAM — 13 wks
US, female/male vocal duo

11 Jul 87	● SOMEWHERE OUT THERE *MCA MCA 1132*	8	13 wks

See also Linda Ronstadt; James Ingram with Michael McDonald.

ROOFTOP SINGERS US, male/female vocal group — 12 wks

31 Jan 63	● WALK RIGHT IN *Fontana TF 271700*	10	12 wks

Barry ROSE – *See Paul PHOENIX*

ROSE MARIE UK, female vocalist — 5 wks

19 Nov 83	WHEN I LEAVE MY WORLD BEHIND *A1 284*	75	1 wk
3 Dec 83	WHEN I LEAVE MY WORLD BEHIND (re-entry) *A1 284*	63	2 wks
24 Dec 83	WHEN I LEAVE MY WORLD BEHIND (2nd re-entry) *A1 284*	66	2 wks

Above: Members of the 'We Are The World' cast at the 1986 Grammy Awards included (left to right) Stevie Wonder, producer Quincy Jones, Dionne Warwick, and the song's co-writers Michael Jackson and LIONEL RICHIE.

LINDA RONSTADT and Aaron Neville won Grammy Awards for 'Don't Know Much'.

Centre Left: If you had seen these mothers, baby, standing in the shadow, would you have guessed they were the ROLLING STONES?

Bottom Left: The ROCKSTEADY CREW had their biggest hit with their eponymous single.

ROSE OF ROMANCE ORCHESTRA

UK, orchestra

1 wk

9 Jan 82	TARA'S THEME FROM 'GONE WITH THE WIND' *BBC RESL 108*........................	71	1 wk

ROSE ROYCE *US, male/female vocal/instrumental group*

110 wks

25 Dec 76	● CAR WASH *MCA 267*	9	12 wks
22 Jan 77	PUT YOUR MONEY WHERE YOUR MOUTH IS *MCA 259*........................	44	5 wks
2 Apr 77	I WANNA GET NEXT TO YOU *MCA 278*........	14	8 wks
24 Sep 77	DO YOUR DANCE *Whitfield K 17006*........	30	6 wks
14 Jan 78	● WISHING ON A STAR *Warner Bros. K 17060*....	3	14 wks
6 May 78	IT MAKES YOU FEEL LIKE DANCIN' *Warner Bros. K 17148*........................	16	10 wks
16 Sep 78	LOVE DON'T LIVE HERE ANYMORE *Whitfield K 17236*........................	2	10 wks
3 Feb 79	I'M IN LOVE (AND I LOVE THE FEELING) *Whitfield K 17291*........................	51	4 wks
17 Nov 79	IS IT LOVE YOU'RE AFTER *Whitfield K 17456*....	13	13 wks
8 Mar 80	OOH BOY *Whitfield K 17575*........................	46	7 wks
21 Nov 81	ROSE ROYCE EXPRESS *Warner Bros. K 17875*....	52	3 wks
1 Sep 84	MAGIC TOUCH *Streetwave KHAN 21*........	43	8 wks
6 Apr 85	LOVE ME RIGHT NOW *Streetwave KHAN 39*....	60	3 wks
11 Jun 88	CAR WASH/ IS IT LOVE YOU'RE AFTER (re-issues) *MCA MCA 1253*........................	20	7 wks

ROSE TATTOO *Australia, male vocal/instrumental group*

4 wks

11 Jul 81	ROCK 'N' ROLL OUTLAW *Carrere CAR 200*........	60	4 wks

Jimmy ROSELLI *US, male vocalist*

8 wks

5 Mar 83	WHEN YOUR OLD WEDDING RING WAS NEW *A1 282*........................	51	5 wks
20 Jun 87	WHEN YOUR OLD WEDDING RING WAS NEW (re-issue) *First Night SCORE 9*........	52	3 wks

Diana ROSS *US, female vocalist*

310 wks

18 Jul 70	REACH OUT AND TOUCH *Tamla Motown TMG 743*......	33	5 wks
12 Sep 70	● AIN'T NO MOUNTAIN HIGH ENOUGH *Tamla Motown TMG 751*........................	6	12 wks
3 Apr 71	● REMEMBER ME *Tamla Motown TMG 768*........	7	12 wks
31 Jul 71	★ I'M STILL WAITING *Tamla Motown TMG 781*........	1	14 wks
30 Oct 71	● SURRENDER *Tamla Motown TMG 792*........	10	11 wks
13 May 72	DOOBEDOOD'NDOOBE DOOBEDOOD'NDOOBE *Tamla Motown TMG 812*........................	12	9 wks
14 Jul 73	● TOUCH ME IN THE MORNING *Tamla Motown TMG 861*........................	9	12 wks
13 Oct 73	TOUCH ME IN THE MORNING (re-entry) *Tamla Motown TMG 861*........................	50	1 wk
5 Jan 74	● ALL OF MY LIFE *Tamla Motown TMG 880*........	9	13 wks
4 May 74	LAST TIME I SAW HIM *Tamla Motown TMG 893*........	35	4 wks
28 Sep 74	LOVE ME *Tamla Motown TMG 917*........	38	5 wks
29 Mar 75	SORRY DOESN'T ALWAYS MAKE IT RIGHT *Tamla Motown TMG 941*........................	23	9 wks
3 Apr 76	● THEME FROM MAHOGANY (DO YOU KNOW WHERE YOU'RE GOING TO) *Tamla Motown TMG 1010*........................	5	8 wks
24 Apr 76	● LOVE HANGOVER *Tamla Motown TMG 1024*........	10	10 wks
10 Jul 76	I THOUGHT IT TOOK A LITTLE TIME *Tamla Motown TMG 1032*........................	32	5 wks
16 Oct 76	I'M STILL WAITING (re-issue) *Tamla Motown TMG 1041*........................	41	4 wks
19 Nov 77	GETTIN' READY FOR LOVE *Motown TMG 1090*........	23	7 wks
22 Jul 78	LOVIN' LIVIN' AND GIVIN' *Motown TMG 1112*........	54	6 wks
21 Jul 79	THE BOSS *Motown TMG 1150*........	40	7 wks
6 Oct 79	NO ONE GETS THE PRIZE *Motown TMG 1160*........	59	3 wks
24 Nov 79	IT'S MY HOUSE *Motown TMG 1169*........	32	10 wks
19 Jul 80	● UPSIDE DOWN *Motown TMG 1195*........	2	12 wks
20 Sep 80	● MY OLD PIANO *Motown TMG 1202*........	5	9 wks
15 Nov 80	I'M COMING OUT *Motown TMG 1210*........	13	10 wks
17 Jan 81	IT'S MY TURN *Motown TMG 1217*........	16	8 wks
28 Mar 81	ONE MORE CHANCE *Motown TMG 1227*........	49	5 wks
13 Jun 81	CRYIN' MY HEART OUT FOR YOU *Motown TMG 1233*........................	58	3 wks
7 Nov 81	● WHY DO FOOLS FALL IN LOVE *Capitol CL 226*....	4	12 wks
23 Jan 82	TENDERNESS *Motown TMG 1248*........	73	1 wk
30 Jan 82	MIRROR MIRROR *Capitol CL 234*........	36	5 wks
6 Feb 82	TENDERNESS (re-entry) *Motown TMG 1248*........	75	1 wk
29 May 82	● WORK THAT BODY *Capitol CL 241*........	7	11 wks
7 Aug 82	IT'S NEVER TOO LATE *Capitol CL 256*........	41	4 wks
23 Oct 82	MUSCLES *Capitol CL 268*........	15	9 wks
15 Jan 83	SO CLOSE *Capitol CL 277*........	43	4 wks
23 Jul 83	PIECES OF ICE *Capitol CL 298*........	46	3 wks
15 Sep 84	TOUCH BY TOUCH *Capitol CL 337*........	47	6 wks
28 Sep 85	EATEN ALIVE *Capitol CL 372*........	71	1 wk
25 Jan 86	★ CHAIN REACTION *Capitol CL 386*........	1	17 wks
3 May 86	EXPERIENCE *Capitol CL 400*........	47	3 wks
13 Jun 87	DIRTY LOOKS *EMI EM 2*........	49	3 wks
8 Oct 88	MR. LEE *EMI EM 73*........	58	2 wks
26 Nov 88	LOVE HANGOVER (re-mix) *Motown ZB 42307*........	75	1 wk
6 May 89	WORKIN' OVERTIME *EMI EM 91*........	32	5 wks
29 Jul 89	PARADISE *EMI EM 94*........	61	2 wks
7 Jul 90	I'M STILL WAITING (re-mix) *Motown ZB 43781*........	21	6 wks

See also Supremes; Supremes and the Four Tops; Diana Ross and Michael Jackson; Diana Ross and the Supremes and the Temptations; Diana Ross and Marvin Gaye; Diana Ross, Marvin Gaye, Smokey Robinson and Stevie Wonder; Diana Ross and Lionel Richie; Julio Iglesias and Diana Ross.

Diana ROSS and Marvin GAYE

US, female/male vocal duo

20 wks

23 Mar 74	● YOU ARE EVERYTHING *Tamla Motown TMG 890*........	5	12 wks
20 Jul 74	STOP LOOK LISTEN (TO YOUR HEART) *Tamla Motown TMG 906*........................	25	8 wks

See also Marvin Gaye; Diana Ross.

Diana ROSS, Marvin GAYE, Smokey ROBINSON and Stevie WONDER

US, female/male vocal group

5 wks

24 Feb 79	POPS, WE LOVE YOU *Motown TMG 1136*........	66	5 wks

See also Diana Ross; Marvin Gaye; Smokey Robinson; Stevie Wonder.

Diana ROSS and Michael JACKSON

US, female/male vocal duo

4 wks

18 Nov 78	EASE ON DOWN THE ROAD *MCA 396*........	45	4 wks

See also Diana Ross; Michael Jackson.

Diana ROSS and Lionel RICHIE

US, female/male vocal duo

12 wks

12 Sep 81	● ENDLESS LOVE *Motown TMG 1240*........	7	12 wks

See also Diana Ross; Lionel Richie.

Diana ROSS and the SUPREMES and the TEMPTATIONS *US, female and male vocal groups*

27 wks

29 Jan 69	● I'M GONNA MAKE YOU LOVE ME *Tamla Motown TMG 685*........................	3	11 wks
23 Apr 69	I'M GONNA MAKE YOU LOVE ME (re-entry) *Tamla Motown TMG 685*........................	49	1 wk
20 Sep 69	I SECOND THAT EMOTION *Tamla Motown TMG 709*......	18	8 wks
21 Mar 70	WHY (MUST WE FALL IN LOVE) *Tamla Motown TMG 730*........................	31	7 wks

See also Diana Ross; Supremes; Temptations.

Francis ROSSI and Bernard FROST   4 wks
UK, male vocal/instrumental duo

11 May 85	MODERN ROMANCE (I WANT TO FALL IN LOVE AGAIN) *Vertigo FROS 1*........................	54	4 wks

Laurent ROSSI – *See BIMBO JET*

Nini ROSSO *Italy, male instrumentalist - trumpet*   14 wks

26 Aug 65	● IL SILENZIO *Durium DRS 54000*	8	14 wks

David Lee ROTH *US, male vocalist*   10 wks

23 Feb 85	CALIFORNIA GIRLS *Warner Bros. W 9102*.....................	68	2 wks
5 Mar 88	JUST LIKE PARADISE *Warner Bros. W 8119*..................	27	7 wks
3 Sep 88	DAMN GOOD/ STAND UP *Warner Bros. W 7753*............	72	1 wk

ROULETTES – *See Adam FAITH*

Robert ROUNSEVILLE – *See VARIOUS ARTISTS (Carousel Soundtrack)*

Demis ROUSSOS *Greece, male vocalist*   44 wks

22 Nov 75	● HAPPY TO BE ON AN ISLAND IN THE SUN *Philips 6042 033*...	5	10 wks
28 Feb 76	CAN'T SAY HOW MUCH I LOVE YOU *Philips 6042 114*...	35	5 wks
26 Jun 76	★ THE ROUSSOS PHENOMENON (EP) *Philips DEMIS 001*	1	12 wks
2 Oct 76	● WHEN FOREVER HAS GONE *Philips 6042 186*	2	10 wks
19 Mar 77	BECAUSE *Philips 6042 245*	39	4 wks
18 Jun 77	KYRILA (EP) *Philips Demis 002*	33	3 wks

Tracks on The Roussos Phenomenon EP: Forever And Ever/Sing An Ode To Love/So Dreamy/My Friend The Wind. Tracks on Kyrila EP: Kyrila/I'm Gonna Fall In Love/I Dig You/Sister Emilyne.

ROUTERS *US, male instrumental group*   7 wks

27 Dec 62	LET'S GO *Warner Bros. WB 77*	32	7 wks

ROWETTA – *See DYNASTY OF TWO featuring ROWETTA*

John ROWLES *New Zealand, male vocalist*   28 wks

13 Mar 68	● IF I ONLY HAD TIME *MCA MU 1000*...........................	3	18 wks
19 Jun 68	HUSH NOT A WORD TO MARY *MCA MU 1023*............	12	10 wks

ROXETTE *Sweden, male/female vocal/instrumental duo*   48 wks

22 Apr 89	● THE LOOK *EMI EM 87*	7	10 wks
15 Jul 89	DRESSED FOR SUCCESS *EMI EM 96*	48	5 wks
28 Oct 89	LISTEN TO YOUR HEART *EMI EM 108*	62	3 wks
2 Jun 90	● IT MUST HAVE BEEN LOVE *EMI EM 141*....................	3	14 wks
11 Aug 90	● LISTEN TO YOUR HEART (re-issue)/ DANGEROUS *EMI EM 149*	6	9 wks
27 Oct 90	DRESSED FOR SUCCESS (re-issue) *EMI EM 162*..........	18	7 wks

ROXY MUSIC *UK, male vocal/instrumental group*   153 wks

19 Aug 72	● VIRGINIA PLAIN *Island WIP 6144*..............................	4	12 wks
10 Mar 73	● PYJAMARAMA *Island WIP 6159*..................................	10	12 wks
17 Nov 73	● STREET LIFE *Island WIP 6173*...................................	9	12 wks
12 Oct 74	ALL I WANT IS YOU *Island WIP 6208*........................	12	8 wks
11 Oct 75	● LOVE IS THE DRUG *Island WIP 6248*..........................	2	10 wks
27 Dec 75	BOTH ENDS BURNING *Island WIP 6262*	25	7 wks
22 Oct 77	VIRGINIA PLAIN (re-issue) *Polydor 2001 739*............	11	6 wks
3 Mar 79	TRASH *Polydor POSP 32*	40	6 wks
28 Apr 79	● DANCE AWAY *Polydor POSP 44*	2	14 wks
11 Aug 79	● ANGEL EYES *Polydor POSP 67*	4	11 wks
17 May 80	● OVER YOU *Polydor POSP 93*	5	9 wks
2 Aug 80	● OH YEAH (ON THE RADIO) *Polydor 2001 972*............	5	8 wks
8 Nov 80	THE SAME OLD SCENE *Polydor ROXY 1*	12	7 wks
21 Feb 81	★ JEALOUS GUY *EG ROXY 2*	1	11 wks
3 Apr 82	● MORE THAN THIS *EG ROXY 3*...................................	6	8 wks
19 Jun 82	AVALON *EG ROXY 4*	13	6 wks
25 Sep 82	TAKE A CHANCE WITH ME *EG ROXY 5*.....................	26	6 wks

Billy Joe ROYAL *US, male vocalist*   4 wks

7 Oct 65	DOWN IN THE BOONDOCKS *CBS 201802*	38	4 wks

The Central Band of the ROYAL AIR FORCE, Conductor W/ Cdr. A.E. Sims O.B.E.   1 wk
UK, military band

21 Oct 55	● THE DAMBUSTERS MARCH *HMV B 10877*.................	18	1 wks

ROYAL GUARDSMEN   17 wks
US, male vocal/instrumental group

19 Jan 67	● SNOOPY VS. THE RED BARON *Stateside SS 574*	8	13 wks
6 Apr 67	RETURN OF THE RED BARON *Stateside SS 2010*..........	37	4 wks

ROYAL HOUSE *US, male/female vocal/instrumental group*   18 wks

10 Sep 88	CAN YOU PARTY *Champion CHAMP 79*.....................	14	14 wks
7 Jan 89	YEAH! BUDDY *Champion CHAMP 91*	35	4 wks

ROYAL PHILHARMONIC ORCHESTRA arranged and conducted by Louis CLARK   19 wks
UK, orchestra and conductor

25 Jul 81	● HOOKED ON CLASSICS *RCA 109*.............................	2	11 wks
24 Oct 81	HOOKED ON CAN-CAN *RCA 151*	47	3 wks
10 Jul 82	BBC WORLD CUP GRANDSTAND *BBC RESL 116*	61	3 wks
7 Aug 82	IF YOU KNEW SOUSA (AND FRIENDS) *RCA 256*........	71	2 wks

See also Elvis Costello. Louis Clark did not conduct the third hit.

The Pipes and Drums and Military Band of the ROYAL SCOTS DRAGOON GUARDS   43 wks
UK, military band

1 Apr 72	★ AMAZING GRACE *RCA 2191*..................................	1	24 wks
19 Aug 72	HEYKENS SERENADE/ THE DAY IS OVER *RCA 2251*	30	7 wks
2 Dec 72	LITTLE DRUMMER BOY *RCA 2301*	13	9 wks
23 Dec 72	AMAZING GRACE (re-entry) *RCA 2191*.....................	42	3 wks

ROYALLE DELITE *US, female vocal group*   6 wks

14 Sep 85	(I'LL BE A) FREAK FOR YOU *Streetwave KHAN 51*	45	6 wks

Lita ROZA *UK, female vocalist*   18 wks

13 Mar 53	★ (HOW MUCH IS) THAT DOGGIE IN THE WINDOW *Decca F 10070*..	1	11 wks
7 Oct 55	HEY THERE *Decca F 10611*......................................	17	2 wks
23 Mar 56	JIMMY UNKNOWN *Decca F 10679*	15	5 wks

See also Various Artists - All Star Hit Parade.

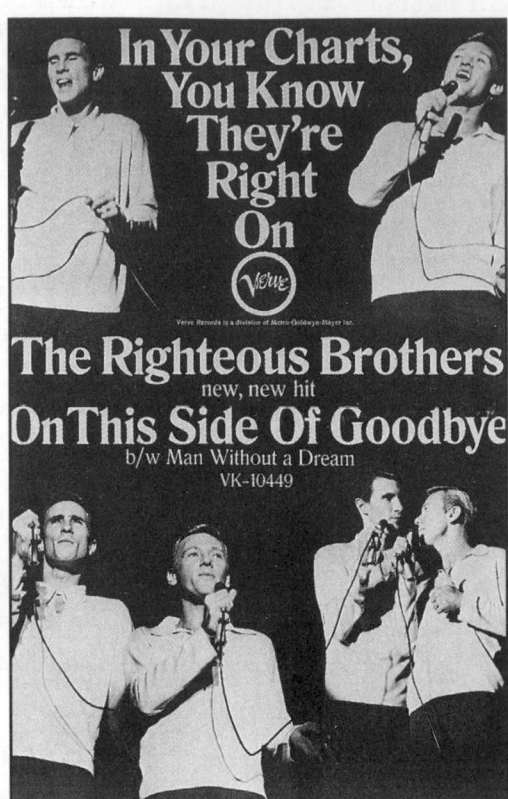

With the re-issue success of 'Unchained Melody' the RIGHTEOUS BROTHERS have set the new record for Gap Between Number One Hits.

Top Left: DIANA ROSS has charted every year since she went solo in 1970, the longest such streak of a still active artist. She is shown at her 1987 birthday party.

Bottom Left: Post-Frankie and post-moustache, PAUL RUTHERFORD got real.

Left: S EXPRESS (leader Mark Moore) is the only act to name check itself in the title of a number one.

Below: BARRY RYAN is the only artist of whom it can be truthfully said that part of his material was really 'Kitsch'.

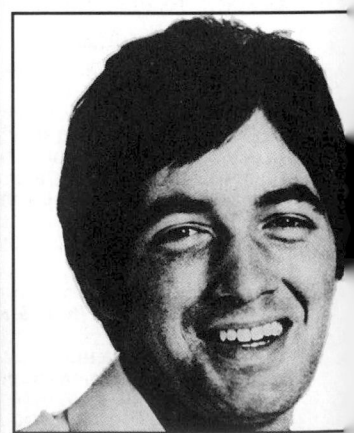

RUBETTES *UK, male vocal/instrumental group*   **68 wks**

4 May 74	★ SUGAR BABY LOVE *Polydor 2058 442*	**1**	10 wks
13 Jul 74	TONIGHT *Polydor 2058 499*	**12**	9 wks
16 Nov 74	● JUKE BOX JIVE *Polydor 2058 529*	**3**	12 wks
8 Mar 75	● I CAN DO IT *State STAT 1*	**7**	9 wks
21 Jun 75	FOE-DEE-O-DEE *State STAT 7*	**15**	6 wks
22 Nov 75	LITTLE DARLING *State STAT 13*	**30**	5 wks
1 May 76	YOU'RE THE REASON WHY *State STAT 20*	**28**	4 wks
25 Sep 76	UNDER ONE ROOF *State STAT 27*	**40**	3 wks
12 Feb 77	● BABY I KNOW *State STAT 37*	**10**	10 wks

RUBY and the ROMANTICS
US, female/male vocal group   **6 wks**

| 28 Mar 63 | OUR DAY WILL COME *London HLR 9679* | **38** | 6 wks |

RUDE BOY OF HOUSE – *See HOUSEMASTER BOYZE and the RUDE BOY OF HOUSE*

RUDIES – *See Freddie NOTES and the RUDIES*

Bruce RUFFIN *Jamaica, male vocalist*   **23 wks**

| 1 May 71 | RAIN *Trojan TR 7814* | **19** | 11 wks |
| 24 Jun 72 | ● MAD ABOUT YOU *Rhino RNO 101* | **9** | 12 wks |

David RUFFIN *US, male vocalist*   **8 wks**

| 17 Jan 76 | ● WALK AWAY FROM LOVE *Tamla Motown TMG 1017* | **10** | 8 wks |

See also Daryl Hall and John Oates.

Jimmy RUFFIN *US, male vocalist*   **106 wks**

27 Oct 66	● WHAT BECOMES OF THE BROKEN HEARTED *Tamla Motown TMG 577.*	**10**	15 wks
9 Feb 67	I'VE PASSED THIS WAY BEFORE *Tamla Motown TMG 593.*	**29**	7 wks
20 Apr 67	GONNA GIVE HER ALL THE LOVE I'VE GOT *Tamla Motown TMG 603.*	**26**	6 wks
9 Aug 69	I'VE PASSED THIS WAY BEFORE (re-issue) *Tamla Motown TMG 703.*	**33**	6 wks
28 Feb 70	● FAREWELL IS A LONELY SOUND *Tamla Motown TMG 726.*	**8**	16 wks
4 Jul 70	● I'LL SAY FOREVER MY LOVE *Tamla Motown TMG 740*	**7**	12 wks
17 Oct 70	● IT'S WONDERFUL *Tamla Motown TMG 753*	**6**	14 wks
27 Jul 74	● WHAT BECOMES OF THE BROKEN HEARTED (re-issue) *Tamla Motown TMG 911*	**4**	12 wks
2 Nov 74	FAREWELL IS A LONELY SOUND (re-issue) *Tamla Motown TMG 922.*	**30**	5 wks
16 Nov 74	TELL ME WHAT YOU WANT *Polydor 2058 433.*	**39**	4 wks
3 May 80	● HOLD ON TO MY LOVE *RSO 57.*	**7**	8 wks
26 Jan 85	THERE WILL NEVER BE ANOTHER YOU *EMI 5541*	**68**	1 wk

RUFUS and Chaka KHAN   **21 wks**
US, male instrumental group and female vocalist

| 31 Mar 84 | ● AIN'T NOBODY *Warner Bros. RCK 1* | **8** | 12 wks |
| 8 Jul 89 | ● AIN'T NOBODY (re-mix) *Warner Bros W 2880* | **6** | 9 wks |

See also Chaka Khan; Quincy Jones.

Barbara RUICK – *See VARIOUS ARTISTS (Carousel Soundtrack)*

RUMOUR – *See Graham PARKER and the RUMOUR*

RUMPLE-STILTS-SKIN   **4 wks**
US, male/female vocal/instrumental group

| 24 Sep 83 | I THINK I WANT TO DANCE WITH YOU *Polydor POSP 649* | **51** | 4 wks |

RUN D.M.C. *US, male rap group*   **36 wks**

19 Jul 86	MY ADIDAS/ PETER PIPER *London LON 101*	**62**	2 wks
6 Sep 86	● WALK THIS WAY *London LON 104*	**8**	10 wks
7 Feb 87	YOU BE ILLIN' *Profile LON 118*	**42**	4 wks
30 May 87	IT'S TRICKY *Profile LON 130*	**16**	7 wks
12 Dec 87	CHRISTMAS IN HOLLIS *Profile LON 163*	**56**	4 wks
21 May 88	RUN'S HOUSE *London LON 177*	**37**	4 wks
2 Sep 89	GHOSTBUSTERS *MCA Profile MCA 1360*	**65**	2 wks
1 Dec 90	WHAT'S IT ALL ABOUT *Profile PROF 315*	**48**	3 wks

Todd RUNDGREN *US, male vocalist*   **6 wks**

| 30 Jun 73 | I SAW THE LIGHT *Bearsville K 15506* | **36** | 6 wks |

See also Bonnie Tyler.

RUNRIG *UK, male vocal/instrumental group*   **2 wks**

| 29 Sep 90 | CAPTURE THE HEART (EP) *Chrysalis CHS 3594* | **49** | 2 wks |

Tracks on Capture The Heart *EP: Stepping Down The Glory Road/Satellite Flood/Harvest Moon/The Apple Came Down.*

RUSH *Canada, male vocal/instrumental group*   **42 wks**

11 Feb 78	CLOSER TO THE HEART *Mercury RUSH 7.*	**36**	3 wks
15 Mar 80	SPIRIT OF RADIO *Mercury RADIO 7.*	**13**	7 wks
28 Mar 81	VITAL SIGNS/ A PASSAGE TO BANGKOK *Mercury VITAL 7*	**41**	4 wks
31 Oct 81	TOM SAWYER *Exit EXIT 7*	**25**	6 wks
4 Sep 82	NEW WORLD MAN *Mercury RUSH 8*	**42**	3 wks
30 Oct 82	SUBDIVISIONS *Mercury RUSH 9*	**53**	2 wks
7 May 83	COUNTDOWN/ NEW WORLD MAN *Mercury RUSH 10.*	**36**	5 wks
26 May 84	THE BODY ELECTRIC *Vertigo RUSH 11.*	**56**	3 wks
12 Oct 85	THE BIG MONEY *Vertigo RUSH 12*	**46**	3 wks
31 Oct 87	TIME STAND STILL *Vertigo RUSH 13*	**42**	3 wks
23 Apr 88	PRIME MOVER *Vertigo RUSH 14*	**43**	3 wks

New World Man on RUSH 10 is a live version of RUSH 8. Time Stand Still is with Aimee Mann.

Jennifer RUSH *US, female vocalist*   **46 wks**

29 Jun 85	★ THE POWER OF LOVE *CBS A 5003*	**1**	32 wks
14 Dec 85	RING OF ICE *CBS A 4745*	**14**	10 wks
20 Dec 86	THE POWER OF LOVE (re-entry) *CBS A 5003*	**55**	4 wks

See also Jennifer Rush and Elton John; Placido Domingo and Jennifer Rush.

Jennifer RUSH and Elton JOHN   **3 wks**
US/UK, female/male vocal duo

| 20 Jun 87 | FLAMES OF PARADISE *CBS 650865 7* | **59** | 3 wks |

See also Jennifer Rush; Elton John.

Patrice RUSHEN *US, female vocalist*   **25 wks**

1 Mar 80	HAVEN'T YOU HEARD *Elektra K 12414*	**62**	3 wks
24 Jan 81	NEVER GONNA GIVE YOU UP (WON'T LET YOU BE) *Elektra K 12494*	**66**	3 wks
24 Apr 82	● FORGET ME NOTS *Elektra K 13173*	**8**	11 wks
10 Jul 82	I WAS TIRED OF BEING ALONE *Elektra K 13184*	**39**	5 wks

9 Jun 84	FEELS SO REAL (WON'T LET GO) Elektra E 9742	**51**	3 wks

Brenda RUSSELL US, female vocalist   **17 wks**

19 Apr 80	SO GOOD SO RIGHT/ IN THE THICK OF IT		
	A & M AM 7515	**51**	5 wks
12 Mar 88	PIANO IN THE DARK Breakout USA 623	**23**	12 wks

Paul RUTHERFORD UK, male vocalist   **6 wks**

8 Oct 88	GET REAL Fourth & Broadway BRW 113	**47**	3 wks
19 Aug 89	OH WORLD Fourth & Broadway BRW 136	**61**	3 wks

RUTHLESS RAP ASSASSINS UK, male rappers   **2 wks**

9 Jun 90	JUST MELLOW Syncopate SY 35	**75**	1 wk
1 Sep 90	AND IT WASN'T A DREAM Syncopate SY 38	**75**	1 wk

RUTLES UK, male vocal group   **4 wks**

15 Apr 78	I MUST BE IN LOVE Warner Bros. K 17125	**39**	3 wks
13 May 78	I MUST BE IN LOVE (re-entry) Warner Bros. K 17125	**64**	1 wk

RUTS UK, male vocal/instrumental group   **28 wks**

16 Jun 79	● BABYLON'S BURNING Virgin VS 271	**7**	11 wks
8 Sep 79	SOMETHING THAT I SAID Virgin VS 285	**29**	5 wks
19 Apr 80	STARING AT THE RUDE BOYS Virgin VS 327	**22**	8 wks
30 Aug 80	WEST ONE (SHINE ON ME) Virgin VS 370	**43**	4 wks

Barry RYAN UK, male vocalist   **33 wks**

23 Oct 68	● ELOISE MGM 1442	**2**	12 wks
19 Feb 69	LOVE IS LOVE MGM 1464	**25**	4 wks
4 Oct 69	HUNT Polydor 56 348	**34**	5 wks
21 Feb 70	MAGICAL SPIEL Polydor 56 370	**49**	1 wk
16 May 70	KITSCH Polydor 2001 035	**37**	6 wks
15 Jan 72	CAN'T LET YOU GO Polydor 2001 256	**32**	5 wks

See also Paul and Barry Ryan.

Marion RYAN UK, female vocalist   **11 wks**

24 Jan 58	● LOVE ME FOREVER Pye Nixa N 15121	**5**	11 wks

Paul and Barry RYAN UK, male vocal duo   **43 wks**

11 Nov 65	DON'T BRING ME YOUR HEARTACHES		
	Decca F 12260	**13**	9 wks
3 Feb 66	HAVE PITY ON THE BOY Decca F 12319	**18**	6 wks
12 May 66	I LOVE HER Decca F 12391	**17**	8 wks
14 Jul 66	I LOVE HOW YOU LOVE ME Decca F 12445	**21**	7 wks
29 Sep 66	HAVE YOU EVER LOVED SOMEBODY Decca F 12494	**49**	1 wk
8 Dec 66	MISSY MISSY Decca F 12520	**43**	4 wks
2 Mar 67	KEEP IT OUT OF SIGHT Decca F 12567	**30**	6 wks
29 Jun 67	CLAIRE Decca F 12633	**47**	2 wks

See also Barry Ryan.

Bobby RYDELL US, male vocalist   **56 wks**

10 Mar 60	● WILD ONE Columbia DB 4429	**7**	14 wks
23 Jun 60	WILD ONE (re-entry) Columbia DB 4429	**47**	1 wk
30 Jun 60	SWINGING SCHOOL Columbia DB 4471	**44**	1 wk
1 Sep 60	VOLARE Columbia DB 4495	**46**	1 wk
15 Sep 60	VOLARE (re-entry) Columbia DB 4495	**22**	5 wks
15 Dec 60	SWAY Columbia DB 4545	**12**	13 wks
23 Mar 61	GOOD TIME BABY Columbia DB 4600	**42**	7 wks

23 May 63	FORGET HIM Cameo Parkway C 108	**13**	14 wks

See also Chubby Checker and Bobby Rydell.

Mitch RYDER and the DETROIT WHEELS   **5 wks**
US, male vocalist, male vocal/instrumental backing group

10 Feb 66	JENNY TAKE A RIDE Stateside SS 481	**44**	1 wk
24 Feb 66	JENNY TAKE A RIDE (re-entry) Stateside SS 481	**33**	4 wks

S

S EXPRESS UK, male/female vocal/instrumental group   **44 wks**

16 Apr 88	★ THEME FROM S-EXPRESS Rhythm King LEFT 2	**1**	13 wks
23 Jul 88	● SUPERFLY GUY Rhythm King LEFT 28	**5**	9 wks
18 Feb 89	● HEY MUSIC LOVER Rhythm King LEFT 30	**6**	10 wks
16 Sep 89	MANTRA FOR A STATE OF MIND		
	Rhythm King LEFT 35	**21**	8 wks
15 Sep 90	NOTHING TO LOSE Rhythm King SEXY 01	**32**	4 wks

LEFT 30 features Eric & Billy. See also Eric and the Good Good Feeling; Various Artists - The Brits 1990.

SABRES – See Denny SEYTON and the SABRES

SABRINA Italy, female vocalist   **22 wks**

6 Feb 88	BOYS (SUMMERTIME LOVE) IBIZA IBIZ 1	**60**	3 wks
11 Jun 88	● BOYS (SUMMERTIME LOVE) (re-entry) IBIZA IBIZ 1	**3**	11 wks
1 Oct 88	ALL OF ME PWL PWL 19	**25**	7 wks
1 Jul 89	LIKE A YO-YO Videogram DCUP 1	**72**	1 wk

SAD CAFE UK, male vocal/instrumental group   **44 wks**

22 Sep 79	● EVERY DAY HURTS RCA PB 5180	**3**	12 wks
19 Jan 80	STRANGE LITTLE GIRL RCA PB 5202	**32**	5 wks
15 Mar 80	MY OH MY RCA SAD 3	**14**	11 wks
21 Jun 80	NOTHING LEFT TOULOUSE RCA SAD 4	**62**	4 wks
27 Sep 80	LA-DI-DA RCA SAD 5	**41**	6 wks
20 Dec 80	I'M IN LOVE AGAIN RCA SAD 6	**40**	6 wks

SADE UK, female/male vocal/instrumental group   **45 wks**

25 Feb 84	● YOUR LOVE IS KING Epic A 4137	**6**	11 wks
19 May 84	YOUR LOVE IS KING (re-entry) Epic A 4137	**75**	1 wk
26 May 84	WHEN AM I GONNA MAKE A LIVING Epic A 4437	**36**	5 wks
15 Sep 84	SMOOTH OPERATOR Epic A 4655	**19**	10 wks
12 Oct 85	THE SWEETEST TABOO Epic A 6609	**31**	5 wks
11 Jan 86	IS IT A CRIME Epic A 6742	**49**	3 wks
2 Apr 88	LOVE IS STRONGER THAN PRIDE Epic SADE 1	**44**	3 wks
4 Jun 88	PARADISE Epic SADE 2	**29**	7 wks

Staff Sergeant Barry SADLER US, male vocalist   **8 wks**

24 Mar 66	BALLAD OF THE GREEN BERETS RCA 1506	**24**	8 wks

SAFFRONS – See CINDY and the SAFFRONS

Mike SAGAR UK, male vocalist   **5 wks**

8 Dec 60	DEEP FEELING HMV POP 819	**44**	5 wks

Carole Bayer SAGER *US, female vocalist*　**9 wks**

28 May 77 ● **YOU'RE MOVING OUT TODAY** *Elektra K 12257*............ **6**　9 wks

SAILOR *UK, male vocal/instrumental group*　**24 wks**

6 Dec 75 ● **GLASS OF CHAMPAGNE** *Epic EPC 3770*.................... **2**　12 wks
27 Mar 76 ● **GIRLS GIRLS GIRLS** *Epic EPC 3858* .... **7**　8 wks
19 Feb 77 　 **ONE DRINK TOO MANY** *Epic EPC 4804* .... **35**　4 wks

General SAINT – *See Clint EASTWOOD and General SAINT*

ST. ANDREWS CHORALE *UK, church choir*　**5 wks**

14 Feb 76 　 **CLOUD 99** *Decca F 13617*............................ **31**　5 wks

ST. CECILIA *UK, male vocal/instrumental group*　**17 wks**

19 Jun 71 　 **LEAP UP AND DOWN (WAVE YOUR KNICKERS IN
　　　　　　　 THE AIR)** *Polydor 2058 104* .... **12**　17 wks

Barry ST. JOHN *UK, female vocalist*　**1 wk**

9 Dec 65 　 **COME AWAY MELINDA** *Columbia DB 7783*................ **47**　1 wk

ST. JOHN'S COLLEGE SCHOOL CHOIR and the Band of the GRENADIER GUARDS　**3 wks**
UK, school choir and military band

3 May 86 　 **THE QUEEN'S BIRTHDAY SONG** *Columbia Q1*........... **40**　3 wks

ST. LOUIS UNION *UK, male vocal/instrumental group*　**10 wks**

13 Jan 66 　 **GIRL** *Decca F 12318*................................ **11**　10 wks

Crispian ST. PETERS *UK, male vocalist*　**31 wks**

6 Jan 66 ● **YOU WERE ON MY MIND** *Decca F 12287* .... **2**　14 wks
31 Mar 66 ● **PIED PIPER** *Decca F 12359* .... **5**　13 wks
15 Sep 66 　 **CHANGES** *Decca F 12480*............................. **49**　1 wk
29 Sep 66 　 **CHANGES (re-entry)** *Decca F 12480* .... **47**　3 wks

ST. PHILIPS CHOIR *UK, choir*　**4 wks**

12 Dec 87 　 **SING FOR EVER** *BBC RESL 222*........................... **49**　4 wks

ST. THOMAS MORE SCHOOL CHOIR – *See Scott FITZGERALD and Yvonne KEELY*

ST. WINIFRED'S SCHOOL CHOIR　**11 wks**
UK, school choir

22 Nov 80 ★ **THERE'S NO ONE QUITE LIKE GRANDMA**
　　　　　　 MFP FP 900. .... **1**　11 wks

Buffy SAINTE-MARIE *US, female vocalist*　**23 wks**

17 Jul 71 ● **SOLDIER BLUE** *RCA 2081* .... **7**　18 wks
18 Mar 72 　 **I'M GONNA BE A COUNTRY GIRL AGAIN**
　　　　　　 Vanguard VRS 35143 .... **34**　5 wks

SAINTS *Australia, male vocal/instrumental group*　**4 wks**

16 Jul 77 　 **THIS PERFECT DAY** *Harvest HAR 5130* .... **34**　4 wks

Kyu SAKAMOTO *Japan, male vocalist*　**13 wks**

27 Jun 63 ● **SUKIYAKI** *HMV POP 1171*............................... **6**　13 wks

SAKKARIN　**14 wks**
UK, male vocalist, Jonathan King under a false name

3 Apr 71 　 **SUGAR SUGAR** *RCA 2064*................................ **12**　14 wks
See also Jonathan King.

SALFORD JETS *UK, male vocal/instrumental group*　**2 wks**

31 May 80 　 **WHO YOU LOOKING AT** *RCA PB 5239*.................... **72**　2 wks

SALSOUL ORCHESTRA – *See CHARO and the SALSOUL ORCHESTRA*

SALT 'N' PEPA *US, female rap duo*　**42 wks**

26 Mar 88 　 **PUSH IT/ I AM DOWN** *FFRR FFR 2*........................ **41**　6 wks
25 Jun 88 ● **PUSH IT/ TRAMP** *Champion/CHAMP51 FFRR FFR2* .... **2**　13 wks
3 Sep 88 　 **SHAKE YOUR THANG (IT'S YOUR THING)**
　　　　　　 FFRR FFR 11 .... **22**　8 wks
12 Nov 88 ● **TWIST AND SHOUT** *FFRR FFR 16* .... **4**　9 wks
14 Apr 90 　 **EXPRESSION** *London F 127*............................ **40**　6 wks

I Am Down *only listed from 2 April 88. The disc re-entered on 25 June when it was made available on* Champion *with a different flip side. Sales for both discs were amalgamated.* Shake Your Thang (It's Your Thing) *features E.U. - US, male instrumental group.*

SAM and DAVE *US, male vocal duo*　**39 wks**

16 Mar 67 　 **SOOTHE ME** *Stax 601 004* .... **48**　2 wks
13 Apr 67 　 **SOOTHE ME (re-entry)** *Stax 601 004* .... **35**　6 wks
1 Nov 67 　 **SOUL MAN** *Stax 601 023* .... **24**　14 wks
13 Mar 68 　 **I THANK YOU** *Stax 601 030* .... **34**　9 wks
29 Jan 69 　 **SOUL SISTER BROWN SUGAR** *Atlantic 584 237*............ **15**　8 wks
See also Sam Moore and Lou Reed.

SAM THE SHAM and the PHARAOHS　**18 wks**
US, male vocal/instrumental group

24 Jun 65 　 **WOOLY BULLY** *MGM 1269*............................... **11**　15 wks
4 Aug 66 　 **LIL' RED RIDING HOOD** *MGM 1315* .... **48**　1 wk
18 Aug 66 　 **LIL' RED RIDING HOOD (re-entry)** *MGM 1315* .... **46**　2 wks

Mike SAMMES SINGERS *UK, male/female vocal group*　**38 wks**

15 Sep 66 　 **SOMEWHERE MY LOVE** *HMV POP 1546* .... **22**　19 wks
12 Jul 67 　 **SOMEWHERE MY LOVE (re-entry)** *HMV POP 1546* .... **14**　19 wks

Dave SAMPSON *UK, male vocalist*　**6 wks**

19 May 60 　 **SWEET DREAMS** *Columbia DB 4449*...................... **48**　1 wk
2 Jun 60 　 **SWEET DREAMS (re-entry)** *Columbia DB 4449*.............. **29**　5 wks

SAMSON *UK, male vocal/instrumental group*　**6 wks**

4 Jul 81 　 **RIDING WITH THE ANGELS** *RCA 67* .... **55**　3 wks
24 Jul 82 　 **LOSING MY GRIP** *Polydor POSP 471*..................... **63**　2 wks
5 Mar 83 　 **RED SKIES** *Polydor POSP 554* .... **65**　1 wk

SAN JOSE UK, male instrumental group — 8 wks

17 Jun 78	**ARGENTINE MELODY (CANCION DE ARGENTINA)** *MCA 369*.....................	**14**	8 wks

Hit has credit 'featuring Rodriguez Argentina', who is Rod Argent. See also Argent; Silsoe.

SAN REMO STRINGS US, orchestra — 8 wks

18 Dec 71	**FESTIVAL TIME** *Tamla Motown TMG 795*..................	**39**	8 wks

Chris SANDFORD UK, male vocalist — 9 wks

12 Dec 63	**NOT TOO LITTLE NOT TOO MUCH** *Decca F 11778*......	**17**	9 wks

SANDPIPERS US, male vocal group — 33 wks

15 Sep 66	● **GUANTANAMERA** *Pye International 7N 25380*................	**7**	17 wks
5 Jun 68	**QUANDO M'INNAMORO (A MAN WITHOUT LOVE)** *A & M AMS 723*................	**33**	6 wks
26 Mar 69	**KUMBAYA** *A & M AMS 744*....................	**39**	1 wk
9 Apr 69	**KUMBAYA (re-entry)** *A & M AMS 744*...............	**49**	1 wk
27 Nov 76	**HANG ON SLOOPY** *Satril SAT 114*................	**32**	8 wks

SANDRA Germany, female vocalist — 8 wks

17 Dec 88	**EVERLASTING LOVE** *Siren SRN 85*............	**45**	8 wks

Jodie SANDS US, female vocalist — 10 wks

17 Oct 58	**SOMEDAY** *HMV POP 533*	**14**	10 wks

Tommy SANDS US, male vocalist — 7 wks

4 Aug 60	**OLD OAKEN BUCKET** *Capitol CL 15143*..............	**25**	7 wks

Samantha SANG Australia, female vocalist — 13 wks

4 Feb 78	**EMOTIONS** *Private Stock PVT 128*............	**11**	13 wks

SANTA CLAUS and the CHRISTMAS TREES UK, male vocal/instrumental group — 10 wks

11 Dec 82	**SINGALONG-A-SANTA** *Polydor IVY 1*..........	**19**	5 wks
10 Dec 83	**SINGALONG-A-SANTA AGAIN** *Polydor IVY 2*..........	**39**	5 wks

SANTA ESMERALDA and Leroy GOMEZ US/France, male/female vocal/instrumental group — 5 wks

12 Nov 77	**DON'T LET ME BE MISUNDERSTOOD** *Philips 6042 325*..................	**41**	5 wks

SANTANA US, male vocal/instrumental group — 25 wks

28 Sep 74	**SAMBA PA TI** *CBS 2561*................	**27**	7 wks
15 Oct 77	**SHE'S NOT THERE** *CBS 5671*..............	**11**	12 wks
25 Nov 78	**WELL ALL RIGHT** *CBS 6755*............	**53**	3 wks
22 Mar 80	**ALL I EVER WANTED** *CBS 8160*................	**57**	3 wks

SANTO and JOHNNY US, male instrumental duo - steel and electric guitars — 5 wks

16 Oct 59	**SLEEP WALK** *Pye International 7N 25037*..............	**22**	4 wks
31 Mar 60	**TEARDROP** *Parlophone R 4619*.............	**50**	1 wk

Mike SARNE UK, male vocalist — 43 wks

10 May 62	★ **COME OUTSIDE** *Parlophone R 4902*	**1**	19 wks
30 Aug 62	**WILL I WHAT** *Parlophone R 4932*	**18**	10 wks
10 Jan 63	**JUST FOR KICKS** *Parlophone R 4974*	**22**	7 wks
28 Mar 63	**CODE OF LOVE** *Parlophone R 5010*	**29**	7 wks

Come Outside - Mike Sarne with Wendy Richard; Will I What with Billie Davis. See also Billie Davis.

Joy SARNEY UK, female vocalist — 6 wks

7 May 77	**NAUGHTY NAUGHTY NAUGHTY** *Alaska ALA 2005*	**26**	6 wks

SARR BAND Italy/UK/France, male/female vocal/instrumental group — 1 wk

16 Sep 78	**MAGIC MANDRAKE** *Calendar Day 111*.............	**68**	1 wk

Peter SARSTEDT UK, male vocalist — 25 wks

5 Feb 69	★ **WHERE DO YOU GO TO MY LOVELY** *United Artists UP 2262*	**1**	16 wks
4 Jun 69	● **FROZEN ORANGE JUICE** *United Artists UP 35021*	**10**	9 wks

Robin SARSTEDT UK, male vocalist — 9 wks

8 May 76	● **MY RESISTANCE IS LOW** *Decca F 13624*................	**3**	9 wks

SATURDAY NIGHT BAND US, male vocal/instrumental group — 9 wks

1 Jul 78	**COME ON DANCE DANCE** *CBS 6367*..............	**16**	9 wks

Kevin SAUNDERSON – *See INNER CITY*

Edna SAVAGE UK, female vocalist — 1 wk

13 Jan 56	**ARRIVEDERCI DARLING** *Parlophone R 4097*................	**19**	1 wk

Telly SAVALAS US, male vocalist — 12 wks

22 Feb 75	★ **IF** *MCA 174*...................	**1**	9 wks
31 May 75	**YOU'VE LOST THAT LOVIN' FEELING** *MCA 189*........	**47**	3 wks

SAVANNA US, male vocalist/instrumentalist - guitar — 4 wks

10 Oct 81	**I CAN'T TURN AWAY** *R & B RBS 203*..................	**61**	4 wks

SAVUKA – *See Johnny CLEGG and SAVUKA*

SAXON UK, male vocal/instrumental group — 61 wks

22 Mar 80	**WHEELS OF STEEL** *Carrere CAR 143*	**20**	11 wks
21 Jun 80	**747 (STRANGERS IN THE NIGHT)** *Carrere CAR 151*.......	**13**	9 wks
28 Jun 80	**BACKS TO THE WALL** *Carrere HM 6*............	**64**	2 wks

28 Jun 80	BIG TEASER/ RAINBOW THEME *Carrere HM 5*	66	2 wks
29 Nov 80	STRONG ARM OF THE LAW *Carrere CAR 170*	63	3 wks
11 Apr 81	AND THE BANDS PLAYED ON *Carrere CAR 180*...........	12	8 wks
18 Jul 81	NEVER SURRENDER *Carrere CAR 204*	18	6 wks
31 Oct 81	PRINCESS OF THE NIGHT *Carrere CAR 208*	57	3 wks
23 Apr 83	POWER AND THE GLORY *RCA SAXON 1*	32	5 wks
30 Jul 83	NIGHTMARE *Carrere CAR 284*....................	50	3 wks
31 Aug 85	BACK ON THE STREETS *Parlophone R 6103*	75	1 wk
29 Mar 86	ROCK 'N' ROLL GYPSY *Parlophone R 6112*	71	1 wk
30 Aug 86	WAITING FOR THE NIGHT *EMI EMI 5575*	66	2 wks
5 Mar 88	RIDE LIKE THE WIND *EMI EM 43*	52	4 wks
30 Apr 88	I CAN'T WAIT ANYMORE *EMI EM 54*	71	1 wk

Al SAXON *UK, male vocalist*   10 wks

16 Jan 59	YOU'RE THE TOP CHA *Fontana H 164*	17	4 wks
28 Aug 59	ONLY SIXTEEN *Fontana H 205*....................	24	3 wks
22 Dec 60	BLUE-EYED BOY *Fontana H 278*	39	2 wks
7 Sep 61	THERE I'VE SAID IT AGAIN *Piccadilly 7N 35011*	48	1 wk

Leo SAYER *UK, male vocalist*   146 wks

15 Dec 73 ●	THE SHOW MUST GO ON *Chrysalis CHS 2023*..............	2	13 wks
15 Jun 74 ●	ONE MAN BAND *Chrysalis CHS 2045*	6	9 wks
14 Sep 74 ●	LONG TALL GLASSES *Chrysalis CHS 2052*..........	4	9 wks
30 Aug 75 ●	MOONLIGHTING *Chrysalis CHS 2076*	2	8 wks
30 Oct 76 ●	YOU MAKE ME FEEL LIKE DANCING *Chrysalis CHS 2119*	2	12 wks
29 Jan 77 ★	WHEN I NEED YOU *Chrysalis CHS 2127*.........	1	13 wks
9 Apr 77 ●	HOW MUCH LOVE *Chrysalis CHS 2140*..........	10	8 wks
10 Sep 77	THUNDER IN MY HEART *Chrysalis CHS 2163*	22	8 wks
16 Sep 78 ●	I CAN'T STOP LOVIN' YOU (THOUGH I TRY) *Chrysalis CHS 2240*	6	11 wks
25 Nov 78	RAINING IN MY HEART *Chrysalis CHS 2277*	21	10 wks
5 Jul 80 ●	MORE THAN I CAN SAY *Chrysalis CHS 2442*..........	2	11 wks
13 Mar 82 ●	HAVE YOU EVER BEEN IN LOVE *Chrysalis CHS 2596*	10	9 wks
19 Jun 82	HEART (STOP BEATING IN TIME) *Chrysalis CHS 2616*	22	10 wks
12 Mar 83	ORCHARD ROAD *Chrysalis CHS 2677*	16	8 wks
15 Oct 83	TILL YOU COME BACK TO ME *Chrysalis LEO 01*	51	3 wks
8 Feb 86	UNCHAINED MELODY *Chrysalis LEO 3*	54	4 wks

Alexei SAYLE *UK, male vocalist*   8 wks

25 Feb 84	'ULLO JOHN GOT A NEW MOTOR? *Island IS 162*	15	8 wks

SCAFFOLD *UK, male vocal group*   62 wks

22 Nov 67 ●	THANK U VERY MUCH *Parlophone R 5643*	4	12 wks
27 Mar 68	DO YOU REMEMBER *Parlophone R 5679*....................	34	5 wks
6 Nov 68 ★	LILY THE PINK *Parlophone R 5734*....................	1	24 wks
1 Nov 69	GIN GAN GOOLIE *Parlophone R 5812*	38	11 wks
24 Jan 70	GIN GAN GOOLIE (re-entry) *Parlophone R 5812*	50	1 wk
1 Jun 74 ●	LIVERPOOL LOU *Warner Bros. K 16400*	7	9 wks

Boz SCAGGS *US, male vocalist*   31 wks

30 Oct 76	LOWDOWN *CBS 4563*	28	4 wks
22 Jan 77 ●	WHAT CAN I SAY *CBS 4869*....................	10	10 wks
14 May 77	LIDO SHUFFLE *CBS 5136*	13	9 wks
10 Dec 77	HOLLYWOOD *CBS 5836*....................	33	8 wks

SCARLET FANTASTIC
UK, male/female vocal/instrumental group   12 wks

3 Oct 87	NO MEMORY *Arista RIS 36*	24	10 wks
23 Jan 88	PLUG ME IN (TO THE CENTRAL LOVE LINE) *Arista 109693*	67	2 wks

SCARLET PARTY *UK, male vocal/instrumental group*   5 wks

16 Oct 82	101 DAM-NATIONS *Parlophone R 6058*	44	5 wks

Michael SCHENKER GROUP   9 wks
Germany/UK, male vocal/instrumental group

13 Sep 80	ARMED AND READY *Chrysalis CHS 2455*	53	3 wks
8 Nov 80	CRY FOR THE NATIONS *Chrysalis CHS 2471*	56	3 wks
11 Sep 82	DANCER *Chrysalis CHS 2636*	52	3 wks

Lalo SCHIFRIN *US, orchestra*   9 wks

9 Oct 76	JAWS *CTI CTSP 005*	14	9 wks

Peter SCHILLING *Germany, male vocalist*   6 wks

5 May 84	MAJOR TOM (COMING HOME) *PSP/WEA X 9438*	42	5 wks
16 Jun 84	MAJOR TOM (COMING HOME) (re-entry) *PSP/WEA X 9438*	73	1 wk

SCIENTIST *UK, male instrumentalist*   9 wks

6 Oct 90	THE EXORCIST *Kickin' KICK 1*.......................	62	3 wks
1 Dec 90	THE EXORCIST (re-mix) *Kickin' KICK 1TR.*.................	46	3 wks
15 Dec 90	THE BEE *Kickin' KICK 3S*	52†	3 wks

SCORPIONS *Germany, male vocal/instrumental group*   18 wks

26 May 79	IS THERE ANYBODY THERE/ ANOTHER PIECE OF MEAT *Harvest HAR 5185*.......................................	39	4 wks
25 Aug 79	LOVEDRIVE *Harvest HAR 5188*........................	69	2 wks
31 May 80	MAKE IT REAL *Harvest HAR 5206*	72	2 wks
20 Sep 80	THE ZOO *Harvest HAR 5212*	75	1 wk
3 Apr 82	NO ONE LIKE YOU *Harvest HAR 5219*...............	65	3 wks
1 May 82	NO ONE LIKE YOU (re-entry) *Harvest HAR 5219*............	64	1 wk
17 Jul 82	CAN'T LIVE WITHOUT YOU *Harvest HAR 5221*	63	2 wks
4 Jun 88	RHYTHM OF LOVE *Harvest HAR 5240*.................	59	2 wks
18 Feb 89	PASSION RULES THE GAME *Harvest 5242*	74	1 wk

SCOTLAND WORLD CUP SQUAD   16 wks
UK, male football team vocalists

22 Jun 74	EASY EASY *Polydor 2058 452*........................	20	4 wks
1 May 82 ●	WE HAVE A DREAM *WEA K 19145*.......................	5	9 wks
9 Jun 90	SAY IT WITH PRIDE *RCA PB 43791*	45	3 wks

See also Rod Stewart.

Jack SCOTT *Canada, male vocalist*   28 wks

10 Oct 58 ●	MY TRUE LOVE *London HLU 8626*	9	10 wks
25 Sep 59	THE WAY I WALK *London HLL 8912*.................	30	1 wk
10 Mar 60	WHAT IN THE WORLD'S COME OVER YOU *Top Rank JAR 280*	11	15 wks
2 Jun 60	BURNING BRIDGES *Top Rank JAR 375*....................	32	2 wks

John SCOTT – *See Paul PHOENIX*

Linda SCOTT *US, female vocalist*   14 wks

18 May 61 ●	I'VE TOLD EVERY LITTLE STAR *Columbia DB 4638*........	7	13 wks
14 Sep 61	DON'T BET MONEY HONEY *Columbia DB 4692*	50	1 wk

Millie SCOTT US, female vocalist — **11 wks**

12 Apr 86	PRISONER OF LOVE Fourth & Broadway BRW 45	52	4 wks
23 Aug 86	AUTOMATIC Fourth & Broadway BRW 51	56	3 wks
21 Feb 87	EV'RY LITTLE BIT Fourth & Broadway BRW 58	63	4 wks

Simon SCOTT UK, male vocalist — **8 wks**

| 13 Aug 64 | MOVE IT BABY Parlophone R 5164 | 37 | 8 wks |

Tony SCOTT US, male vocalist — **6 wks**

| 15 Apr 89 | THAT'S HOW I'M LIVING/ THE CHIEF Champion CHAMP 97 | 48 | 4 wks |
| 10 Feb 90 | GET INTO THAT/ THAT'S HOW I'M LIVING (re-issue) Champion CHAMP 232 | 63 | 2 wks |

The Chief only listed from 6 May 89.

SCOTTISH RUGBY TEAM with Ronnie BROWNE UK, male rugby team vocalists — **1 wk**

| 2 Jun 90 | FLOWER OF SCOTLAND Greentrax STRAX 1001 | 73 | 1 wk |

SCREAMING BLUE MESSIAHS
UK, male vocal/instrumental group — **6 wks**

| 16 Jan 88 | I WANNA BE A FLINTSTONE WEA YZ 166 | 28 | 6 wks |

SCRITTI POLITTI UK, male vocal/instrumental group — **67 wks**

21 Nov 81	THE SWEETEST GIRL Rough Trade RT 091	64	3 wks
22 May 82	FAITHLESS Rough Trade RT 101	56	4 wks
7 Aug 82	ASYLUMS IN JERUSALEM/ JACQUES DERRIDA Rough Trade RT 111	43	5 wks
10 Mar 84 ●	WOOD BEEZ (PRAY LIKE ARETHA FRANKLIN) Virgin VS 657	10	12 wks
9 Jun 84	ABSOLUTE Virgin VS 680	17	9 wks
17 Nov 84	HYPNOTIZE Virgin VS 725	68	2 wks
11 May 85 ●	THE WORD GIRL Virgin VS 747	6	12 wks
7 Sep 85	PERFECT WAY Virgin VS 780	48	5 wks
7 May 88	OH PATTI (DON'T FEEL SORRY FOR LOVERBOY) Virgin VS 1006	13	9 wks
27 Aug 88	FIRST BOY IN THIS TOWN (LOVE SICK) Virgin VS 1082	63	3 wks
12 Nov 88	BOOM! THERE SHE WAS Virgin VS 1143	55	3 wks

The Word Girl credits Ranking Ann - UK, female vocalist. Boom! There She Was features Roger. See also Roger.

Earl SCRUGGS – See Lester FLATT and Earl SCRUGGS

SEA LEVEL US, male instrumental group — **4 wks**

| 17 Feb 79 | FIFTY-FOUR Capricorn POSP 28 | 63 | 4 wks |

SEAL UK, male vocalist — **4 wks**

| 8 Dec 90 | CRAZY ZTT ZANG 8 | 15† | 4 wks |

See also Adamski.

SEARCHERS UK, male vocal/instrumental group — **128 wks**

27 Jun 63 ★	SWEETS FOR MY SWEET Pye 7N 15533	1	16 wks
10 Oct 63	SWEET NOTHINS Philips BF 1274	48	2 wks
24 Oct 63 ●	SUGAR AND SPICE Pye 7N 15566	2	13 wks
16 Jan 64 ★	NEEDLES AND PINS Pye 7N 15594	1	15 wks
16 Apr 64 ★	DON'T THROW YOUR LOVE AWAY Pye 7N 15630	1	11 wks
16 Jul 64	SOMEDAY WE'RE GONNA LOVE AGAIN Pye 7N 15670	11	8 wks
17 Sep 64 ●	WHEN YOU WALK IN THE ROOM Pye 7N 15694	3	12 wks
3 Dec 64	WHAT HAVE THEY DONE TO THE RAIN Pye 7N 15739	13	11 wks
4 Mar 65 ●	GOODBYE MY LOVE Pye 7N 15794	4	11 wks
8 Jul 65	HE'S GOT NO LOVE Pye 7N 15878	12	10 wks
14 Oct 65	WHEN I GET HOME Pye 7N 15950	35	3 wks
16 Dec 65	TAKE ME FOR WHAT I'M WORTH Pye 7N 15992	20	8 wks
21 Apr 66	TAKE IT OR LEAVE IT Pye 7N 17094	31	6 wks
13 Oct 66	HAVE YOU EVER LOVED SOMEBODY Pye 7N 17170	48	2 wks

SEASHELLS UK, female vocal group — **5 wks**

| 9 Sep 72 | MAYBE I KNOW CBS 8218 | 32 | 5 wks |

Harry SECOMBE UK, male vocalist — **35 wks**

9 Dec 55	ON WITH THE MOTLEY Philips PB 523	16	3 wks
3 Oct 63	IF I RULED THE WORLD Philips BF 1261	44	2 wks
21 Nov 63	IF I RULED THE WORLD (re-entry) Philips BF 1261	18	15 wks
23 Feb 67 ●	THIS IS MY SONG Philips BF 1539	2	15 wks

SECOND CITY SOUND UK, male instrumental group — **8 wks**

| 20 Jan 66 | TCHAIKOVSKY ONE Decca F 12310 | 22 | 7 wks |
| 2 Apr 69 | DREAM OF OLWEN Major Minor MM 600 | 43 | 1 wk |

SECOND IMAGE UK, male vocal/instrumental group — **11 wks**

24 Jul 82	STAR Polydor POSP 457	60	2 wks
2 Apr 83	BETTER TAKE TIME Polydor POSP 565	67	2 wks
26 Nov 83	DON'T YOU MCA 848	68	2 wks
11 Aug 84	SING AND SHOUT MCA MCA 882	53	3 wks
2 Feb 85	STARTING AGAIN MCA 936	65	2 wks

SECRET AFFAIR UK, male vocal/instrumental group — **34 wks**

1 Sep 79	TIME FOR ACTION I-Spy SEE 1	13	10 wks
10 Nov 79	LET YOUR HEART DANCE I-Spy SEE 3	32	6 wks
8 Mar 80	MY WORLD I-Spy SEE 5	16	9 wks
23 Aug 80	SOUND OF CONFUSION I-Spy SEE 8	45	5 wks
17 Oct 81	DO YOU KNOW I-Spy SEE 10	57	4 wks

Neil SEDAKA US, male vocalist — **190 wks**

24 Apr 59 ●	I GO APE RCA 1115	9	13 wks
13 Nov 59 ●	OH CAROL RCA 1152	3	17 wks
14 Apr 60 ●	STAIRWAY TO HEAVEN RCA 1178	8	15 wks
1 Sep 60	YOU MEAN EVERYTHING TO ME RCA 1198	45	3 wks
2 Feb 61 ●	CALENDAR GIRL RCA 1220	8	14 wks
18 May 61 ●	LITTLE DEVIL RCA 1236	9	12 wks
21 Dec 61 ●	HAPPY BIRTHDAY SWEET SIXTEEN RCA 1266	3	18 wks
19 Apr 62	KING OF CLOWNS RCA 1282	23	11 wks
19 Jul 62 ●	BREAKING UP IS HARD TO DO RCA 1298	7	16 wks
22 Nov 62	NEXT DOOR TO AN ANGEL RCA 1319	29	4 wks
30 May 63	LET'S GO STEADY AGAIN RCA 1343	42	1 wk
13 Jun 63	LET'S GO STEADY AGAIN (re-entry) RCA 1343	43	2 wks
7 Oct 72	OH CAROL/ BREAKING UP IS HARD TO DO/ LITTLE DEVIL (re-issues) RCA Maximillion 2259	19	14 wks
4 Nov 72	BEAUTIFUL YOU RCA 2269	43	3 wks
24 Feb 73	THAT'S WHEN THE MUSIC TAKES ME RCA 2310	18	10 wks
2 Jun 73	STANDING ON THE INSIDE MGM 2006 267	26	9 wks
25 Aug 73	OUR LAST SONG TOGETHER MGM 2006 307	31	8 wks
9 Feb 74	A LITTLE LOVIN' Polydor 2058 434	34	6 wks
22 Jun 74	LAUGHTER IN THE RAIN Polydor 2058 494	15	9 wks
22 Mar 75	THE QUEEN OF 1964 Polydor 2058 546	35	5 wks

SEDUCTION US, female vocal group   **1 wk**

21 Apr 90	HEARTBEAT *Breakout USA 685*	75	1 wk

SEEKERS Australia/Sri Lanka, male/female vocal group   **120 wks**

7 Jan 65	★ I'LL NEVER FIND ANOTHER YOU *Columbia DB 7431*	1	23 wks
15 Apr 65	● A WORLD OF OUR OWN *Columbia DB 7532*	3	18 wks
28 Oct 65	★ THE CARNIVAL IS OVER *Columbia DB 7711*	1	17 wks
24 Mar 66	SOMEDAY ONE DAY *Columbia DB 7867*	11	11 wks
8 Sep 66	● WALK WITH ME *Columbia DB 8000*	10	12 wks
24 Nov 66	● MORNINGTOWN RIDE *Columbia DB 8060*	2	15 wks
23 Feb 67	● GEORGY GIRL *Columbia DB 8134*	3	11 wks
20 Sep 67	WHEN WILL THE GOOD APPLES FALL *Columbia DB 8273*	11	12 wks
13 Dec 67	EMERALD CITY *Columbia DB 8313*	50	1 wk

Bob SEGER and the SILVER BULLET BAND US, male vocal/instrumental group   **21 wks**

30 Sep 78	HOLLYWOOD NIGHTS *Capitol CL 16004*	42	6 wks
3 Feb 79	WE'VE GOT TONITE *Capitol CL 16028*	41	6 wks
24 Oct 81	HOLLYWOOD NIGHTS (re-issue) *Capitol CL 223*	49	3 wks
6 Feb 82	WE'VE GOT TONITE (re-issue) *Capitol CL 235*	60	4 wks
9 Apr 83	EVEN NOW *Capitol CL 284*	73	2 wks

SEIKO and Donnie WAHLBERG Japan/US, female/male vocal duo   **5 wks**

18 Aug 90	THE RIGHT COMBINATION *Epic 656203 7*	44	5 wks

SELECTER UK, male/female vocal/instrumental group   **28 wks**

13 Oct 79	● ON MY RADIO *2 Tone CHSTT 4*	8	9 wks
2 Feb 80	THREE MINUTE HERO *2 Tone CHS TT 8*	16	6 wks
29 Mar 80	MISSING WORDS *2 Tone CHS TT 10*	23	8 wks
23 Aug 80	THE WHISPER *Chrysalis CHSS 1*	36	5 wks

Peter SELLERS UK, male vocalist   **18 wks**

2 Aug 57	ANY OLD IRON *Parlophone R 4337*	21	3 wks
6 Sep 57	ANY OLD IRON (re-entry) *Parlophone R 4337*	17	8 wks
23 Dec 65	A HARD DAY'S NIGHT *Parlophone R 5393*	14	7 wks

See also Peter Sellers and Sophia Loren.

Peter SELLERS and Sophia LOREN UK/Italy, male/female vocal duo   **19 wks**

10 Nov 60	● GOODNESS GRACIOUS ME *Parlophone R 4702*	4	14 wks
12 Jan 61	BANGERS AND MASH *Parlophone R 4724*	22	5 wks

See also Peter Sellers.

Michael SEMBELLO US, male vocalist   **6 wks**

20 Aug 83	MANIAC *Casablanca CAN 1017*	43	6 wks

SEMPRINI UK, orchestra   **8 wks**

16 Mar 61	THEME FROM 'EXODUS' *HMV POP 842*	25	8 wks

SERIOUS INTENTION US, male vocal/instrumental group   **6 wks**

16 Nov 85	YOU DON'T KNOW (OH-OH-OH) *Important TAN 8*	75	1 wk
5 Apr 86	SERIOUS *Pow Wow LON 93*	51	5 wks

SET THE TONE UK, male vocal/instrumental group   **4 wks**

22 Jan 83	DANCE SUCKER *Island WIP 6836*	62	2 wks
26 Mar 83	RAP YOUR LOVE *Island IS 110*	67	2 wks

SETTLERS UK, male/female vocal/instrumental group   **5 wks**

16 Oct 71	THE LIGHTNING TREE *York SYK 505*	36	5 wks

Taja SEVELLE US, female vocalist   **13 wks**

20 Feb 88	● LOVE IS CONTAGIOUS *Paisley Park W 8257*	7	9 wks
14 May 88	WOULDN'T YOU LOVE TO LOVE ME *Paisley Park W 8127*	59	4 wks

SEVENTH AVENUE – *See CALIBRE CUTS*

7TH HEAVEN UK, male vocal group   **5 wks**

14 Sep 85	HOT FUN *Mercury MER 199*	47	5 wks

SEVERINE France, female vocalist   **11 wks**

24 Apr 71	● UN BANC, UN ARBRE, UNE RUE *Philips 6009 135*	9	11 wks

David SEVILLE US, male vocalist   **6 wks**

23 May 58	WITCH DOCTOR *London HLU 8619*	11	6 wks

See also Chipmunks; Alfi and Harry.

Janette SEWELL – *See DOUBLE TROUBLE*

SEX PISTOLS UK, male vocal/instrumental group   **80 wks**

11 Dec 76	ANARCHY IN THE U.K. *EMI 2566*	38	4 wks
4 Jun 77	● GOD SAVE THE QUEEN *Virgin VS 181*	2	9 wks
9 Jul 77	● PRETTY VACANT *Virgin VS 184*	6	8 wks
22 Oct 77	● HOLIDAYS IN THE SUN *Virgin VS 191*	8	6 wks
8 Jul 78	● NO ONE IS INNOCENT/ MY WAY *Virgin VS 220*	7	10 wks
3 Mar 79	● SOMETHING ELSE/ FRIGGIN' IN THE RIGGIN' *Virgin VS 240*	3	12 wks
7 Apr 79	● SILLY THING/WHO KILLED BAMBI *Virgin VS 256*	6	8 wks
30 Jun 79	● C'MON EVERYBODY *Virgin VS 272*	3	9 wks
13 Oct 79	THE GREAT ROCK 'N'ROLL SWINDLE/ ROCK AROUND THE CLOCK *Virgin VS 290*	21	6 wks
14 Jun 80	(I'M NOT YOUR) STEPPING STONE *Virgin VS 339*	21	8 wks

Rock Around The Clock *and* Who Killed Bambi *credited to* Ten Pole Tudor. No One Is Innocent *is described as a 'Punk Prayer By Ronald Biggs'. See also Ten Pole Tudor; The Ex Pistols.*

SEX-O-LETTES – *See DISCO TEX and the SEX-O-LETTES*

Denny SEYTON and the SABRES UK, male vocal/instrumental group   **1 wk**

17 Sep 64	THE WAY YOU LOOK TONIGHT *Mercury MF 824*	48	1 wk

THE SHADOWS have had
more number ones than any
other instrumental act.

Getting a number one
wasn't simple for SIMPLE
MINDS - they waited over a
decade.

Hats off to DEL
SHANNON, the much-
loved star who died in 1990.

SHADOWS UK, male instrumental/vocal group — 359 wks

21 Jul 60	★ APACHE Columbia DB 4484	1	21 wks
10 Nov 60	● MAN OF MYSTERY/ THE STRANGER Columbia DB 4530	5	15 wks
9 Feb 61	● F. B. I. Columbia DB 4580	6	19 wks
11 May 61	● FRIGHTENED CITY Columbia DB 4637	3	20 wks
7 Sep 61	★ KON-TIKI Columbia DB 4698	1	10 wks
16 Nov 61	● THE SAVAGE Columbia DB 4726	10	8 wks
23 Nov 61	KON-TIKI (re-entry) Columbia DB 4698	37	2 wks
1 Mar 62	★ WONDERFUL LAND Columbia DB 4790	1	19 wks
2 Aug 62	● GUITAR TANGO Columbia DB 4870	4	15 wks
13 Dec 62	★ DANCE ON Columbia DB 4948	1	15 wks
7 Mar 63	★ FOOT TAPPER Columbia DB 4984	1	16 wks
6 Jun 63	● ATLANTIS Columbia DB 7047	2	17 wks
19 Sep 63	● SHINDIG Columbia DB 7106	6	12 wks
5 Dec 63	GERONIMO Columbia DB 7163	11	12 wks
5 Mar 64	THEME FOR YOUNG LOVERS Columbia DB 7231	12	10 wks
7 May 64	● THE RISE AND FALL OF FLINGEL BUNT Columbia DB 7261	5	14 wks
3 Sep 64	RHYTHM AND GREENS Columbia DB 7342	22	7 wks
3 Dec 64	GENIE WITH THE LIGHT BROWN LAMP Columbia DB 7416	17	10 wks
11 Feb 65	MARY ANNE Columbia DB 7476	17	10 wks
10 Jun 65	STINGRAY Columbia DB 7588	19	7 wks
5 Aug 65	● DON'T MAKE MY BABY BLUE Columbia DB 7650	10	10 wks
25 Nov 65	WAR LORD Columbia DB 7769	18	9 wks
17 Mar 66	I MET A GIRL Columbia DB 7853	22	5 wks
7 Jul 66	A PLACE IN THE SUN Columbia DB 7952	24	6 wks
3 Nov 66	THE DREAMS I DREAM Columbia DB 8034	42	6 wks
13 Apr 67	MAROC 7 Columbia DB 8170	24	8 wks
8 Mar 75	LET ME BE THE ONE EMI 2269	12	9 wks
16 Dec 78	● DON'T CRY FOR ME ARGENTINA EMI 2890	5	14 wks
28 Apr 79	● THEME FROM THE DEER HUNTER (CAVATINA) EMI 2939	9	14 wks
26 Jan 80	RIDERS IN THE SKY EMI 5027	12	12 wks
23 Aug 80	EQUINOXE (PART V) Polydor POSP 148	50	3 wks
2 May 81	THE THIRD MAN Polydor POSP 255	44	4 wks

All the above hits were instrumentals except for Mary Anne, Don't Make My Baby Blue, I Met A Girl, The Dream I Dream and Let Me Be The One. See also Cliff Richard.

SHAG UK, male vocalist, Jonathan King under a false name — 13 wks

14 Oct 72	● LOOP DI LOVE UK 7	4	13 wks

See also Jonathan King; 53rd and 3rd.

SHAKATAK UK, male/female vocal/instrumental group — 85 wks

8 Nov 80	FEELS LIKE THE RIGHT TIME Polydor POSP 188	41	5 wks
7 Mar 81	LIVING IN THE U.K. Polydor POSP 230	52	4 wks
25 Jul 81	BRAZILIAN DAWN Polydor POSP 282	48	3 wks
21 Nov 81	EASIER SAID THAN DONE Polydor POSP 375	12	17 wks
3 Apr 82	● NIGHT BIRDS Polydor POSP 407	9	8 wks
19 Jun 82	STREETWALKIN' Polydor POSP 452	38	6 wks
4 Sep 82	INVITATIONS Polydor POSP 502	24	7 wks
6 Nov 82	STRANGER Polydor POSP 530	43	3 wks
4 Jun 83	DARK IS THE NIGHT Polydor POSP 595	15	8 wks
27 Aug 83	IF YOU COULD SEE ME NOW Polydor POSP 635	49	4 wks
7 Jul 84	● DOWN ON THE STREET Polydor POSP 688	9	11 wks
15 Sep 84	DON'T BLAME IT ON LOVE Polydor POSP 699	55	3 wks
16 Nov 85	DAY BY DAY Polydor POSP 770	53	3 wks
24 Oct 87	MR. MANIC AND SISTER COOL Polydor MANIC 1	56	3 wks

Day By Day credits Al Jarreau. See also Al Jarreau.

SHAKESPEAR'S SISTER — 13 wks
UK/US, female vocal/instrumental duo

29 Jul 89	● YOU'RE HISTORY FFRR F 112	7	9 wks
14 Oct 89	RUN SILENT FFRR F 119	54	3 wks
10 Mar 90	DIRTY MIND FFRR F 128	71	1 wk

SHAKY and BONNIE UK, male/female vocal duo — 9 wks

7 Jan 84	● A ROCKIN' GOOD WAY Epic A 4071	5	9 wks

See also Shakin' Stevens; Bonnie Tyler.

SHALAMAR US, male/female vocal group — 134 wks

14 May 77	UPTOWN FESTIVAL Soul Train FB 0885	30	5 wks
9 Dec 78	TAKE THAT TO THE BANK RCA FB 1379	20	12 wks
24 Nov 79	THE SECOND TIME AROUND Solar FB 1709	45	9 wks
9 Feb 80	RIGHT IN THE SOCKET Solar SO2	44	6 wks
30 Aug 80	I OWE YOU ONE Solar SO 11	13	10 wks
28 Mar 81	MAKE THAT MOVE Solar SO 17	30	10 wks
27 Mar 82	● I CAN MAKE YOU FEEL GOOD Solar K 12599	7	11 wks
12 Jun 82	● A NIGHT TO REMEMBER Solar K 13162	5	12 wks
4 Sep 82	● THERE IT IS Solar K 13194	5	10 wks
27 Nov 82	FRIENDS Solar CHUM 1	12	10 wks
11 Jun 83	● DEAD GIVEAWAY Solar E 9818	8	10 wks
13 Aug 83	DISAPPEARING ACT Solar E 9807	18	8 wks
15 Oct 83	OVER AND OVER Solar E 9792	23	6 wks
24 Mar 84	DANCING IN THE SHEETS CBS A 4171	41	3 wks
31 Mar 84	DEADLINE USA MCA MCA 866	52	3 wks
24 Nov 84	AMNESIA Solar/MCA SHAL 1	61	2 wks
2 Feb 85	MY GIRL LOVES ME MCA SHAL 2	45	3 wks
26 Apr 86	A NIGHT TO REMEMBER (re-mix) MCA SHAL 3	52	4 wks

SHAM 69 UK, male vocal/instrumental group — 53 wks

13 May 78	ANGELS WITH DIRTY FACES Polydor 2059 023	19	10 wks
29 Jul 78	● IF THE KIDS ARE UNITED Polydor 2059 050	9	9 wks
14 Oct 78	● HURRY UP HARRY Polydor POSP 7	10	8 wks
24 Mar 79	QUESTIONS AND ANSWERS Polydor POSP 27	18	9 wks
4 Aug 79	● HERSHAM BOYS Polydor POSP 64	6	9 wks
27 Oct 79	YOU'RE A BETTER MAN THAN I Polydor POSP 82	49	5 wks
12 Apr 80	TELL THE CHILDREN Polydor POSP 136	45	3 wks

SHAMEN UK, male vocal/instrumental duo — 9 wks

7 Apr 90	PRO-GEN One Little Indian 36 TP7	55	4 wks
22 Sep 90	MAKE IT MINE One Little Indian 46 TP7	42	5 wks

Jimmy SHAND UK, male dance band — 2 wks

23 Dec 55	BLUEBELL POLKA Parlophone F 3436	20	2 wks

Paul SHANE and the YELLOWCOATS — 5 wks
UK, male vocalist with male/female vocal group

16 May 81	HI DE HI (HOLIDAY ROCK) EMI 5180	36	5 wks

SHANGRI-LAS US, female vocal group — 48 wks

8 Oct 64	REMEMBER (WALKIN' IN THE SAND) Red Bird RB 10008	14	13 wks
14 Jan 65	LEADER OF THE PACK Red Bird RB 10014	11	9 wks
11 Oct 72	● LEADER OF THE PACK (re-issue) Kama Sutra 2013 024	3	14 wks
5 Jun 76	● LEADER OF THE PACK (2nd re-issue) Charly CS 1009	7	11 wks
12 Jun 76	● LEADER OF THE PACK (3rd re-issue) Contempo CS 9032	7	10 wks

From 19 Jun 76 until 14 Aug 76, the last week of the disc's chart run, the Charly and Contempo releases of Leader Of The Pack were bracketed together on the chart.

SHANNON US, female vocalist — 36 wks

19 Nov 83	LET THE MUSIC PLAY Club LET 1	51	3 wks
28 Jan 84	LET THE MUSIC PLAY (re-entry) Club LET 1	14	12 wks
7 Apr 84	GIVE ME TONIGHT Club JAB 1	24	7 wks

| 30 Jun 84 | SWEET SOMEBODY *Club JAB 3* | 25 | 8 wks |
| 20 Jul 85 | STRONGER TOGETHER *Club JAB 15* | 46 | 6 wks |

Del SHANNON *US, male vocalist* — 147 wks

27 Apr 61	★ RUNAWAY *London HLX 9317*	1	22 wks
14 Sep 61	● HATS OFF TO LARRY *London HLX 9402*	6	12 wks
7 Dec 61	● SO LONG BABY *London HLX 9462*	10	11 wks
15 Mar 62	● HEY LITTLE GIRL *London HLX 9515*	2	15 wks
6 Sep 62	CRY MYSELF TO SLEEP *London HLX 9587*	29	6 wks
11 Oct 62	● SWISS MAID *London HLX 9609*	2	17 wks
17 Jan 63	● LITTLE TOWN FLIRT *London HLX 9653*	4	13 wks
25 Apr 63	● TWO KINDS OF TEARDROPS *London HLX 9710*	5	13 wks
22 Aug 63	TWO SILHOUETTES *London HLX 9761*	23	8 wks
24 Oct 63	SUE'S GOTTA BE MINE *London HLU 9800*	21	8 wks
12 Mar 64	MARY JANE *Stateside SS 269*	35	5 wks
30 Jul 64	HANDY MAN *Stateside SS 317*	36	4 wks
14 Jan 65	● KEEP SEARCHIN' (WE'LL FOLLOW THE SUN) *Stateside SS 368*	3	11 wks
18 Mar 65	STRANGER IN TOWN *Stateside SS 395*	40	2 wks

Roxanne SHANTE *US, female rapper* — 7 wks

1 Aug 87	HAVE A NICE DAY *Breakout USA 612*	58	3 wks
4 Jun 88	GO ON GIRL *Breakout USA 633*	55	3 wks
17 Apr 90	GO ON GIRL (re-mix) *Breakout USA 689*	74	1 wk

See also Brandon Cooke featuring Roxanne Shante.

Helen SHAPIRO *UK, female vocalist* — 119 wks

23 Mar 61	● DON'T TREAT ME LIKE A CHILD *Columbia DB 4589*	3	20 wks
29 Jun 61	★ YOU DON'T KNOW *Columbia DB 4670*	1	23 wks
28 Sep 61	★ WALKIN' BACK TO HAPPINESS *Columbia DB 4715*	1	19 wks
15 Feb 62	● TELL ME WHAT HE SAID *Columbia DB 4782*	2	15 wks
3 May 62	LET'S TALK ABOUT LOVE *Columbia DB 4824*	23	7 wks
12 Jul 62	● LITTLE MISS LONELY *Columbia DB 4869*	8	11 wks
18 Oct 62	KEEP AWAY FROM OTHER GIRLS *Columbia DB 4908*	40	6 wks
7 Feb 63	QUEEN FOR TONIGHT *Columbia DB 4966*	33	5 wks
25 Apr 63	WOE IS ME *Columbia DB 7026*	35	6 wks
24 Oct 63	LOOK WHO IT IS *Columbia DB 7130*	47	3 wks
23 Jan 64	FEVER *Columbia DB 7190*	38	4 wks

Feargal SHARKEY *UK, male vocalist* — 50 wks

13 Oct 84	LISTEN TO YOUR FATHER *Zarjazz JAZZ 1*	23	7 wks
29 Jun 85	LOVING YOU *Virgin VS 770*	26	10 wks
12 Oct 85	★ A GOOD HEART *Virgin VS 808*	1	16 wks
4 Jan 86	● YOU LITTLE THIEF *Virgin VS 840*	5	9 wks
5 Apr 86	SOMEONE TO SOMEBODY *Virgin VS 828*	64	3 wks
16 Jan 88	MORE LOVE *Virgin VS 922*	44	5 wks

SHARONETTES *UK, female vocal group* — 8 wks

| 26 Apr 75 | PAPA OOM MOW MOW *Black Magic BM 102* | 26 | 5 wks |
| 12 Jul 75 | GOING TO A GO-GO *Black Magic BM 104* | 46 | 3 wks |

Dee Dee SHARP *US, female vocalist* — 2 wks

| 25 Apr 63 | DO THE BIRD *Cameo Parkway C 244* | 46 | 2 wks |

See also Philadelphia All-Stars.

Barrie K. SHARPE – *See Diana BROWN and Barrie K. SHARPE*

SHARPE and NUMAN *UK, male vocal/instrumental duo* — 16 wks

9 Feb 85	CHANGE YOUR MIND *Polydor POSP 722*	17	8 wks
4 Oct 86	NEW THING FROM LONDON TOWN *Numa NU 19*	52	3 wks
30 Jan 88	NO MORE LIES *Polydor POSP 894*	34	3 wks

| 3 Jun 89 | I'M ON AUTOMATIC *Polydor PO 43* | 44 | 2 wks |

See also Gary Numan.

Rocky SHARPE and the REPLAYS — 41 wks
UK, male/female vocal group

16 Dec 78	RAMA LAMA DING DONG *Chiswick CHIS 104*	17	10 wks
24 Mar 79	IMAGINATION *Chiswick CHIS 110*	39	6 wks
25 Aug 79	LOVE WILL MAKE YOU FAIL IN SCHOOL *Chiswick CHIS 114*	60	4 wks
9 Feb 80	MARTIAN HOP *Chiswick CHIS 121*	55	4 wks
17 Apr 82	SHOUT SHOUT (KNOCK YOURSELF OUT) *Chiswick DKE 3*	19	9 wks
7 Aug 82	CLAP YOUR HANDS *RAK 345*	54	3 wks
26 Feb 83	IF YOU WANNA BE HAPPY *Polydor POSP 560*	46	5 wks

Third and fourth hits feature the Top Liners.

Mark SHAW *UK, male vocalist/instrumentalist* — 1 wk

| 17 Nov 90 | LOVE SO BRIGHT *EMI EM 161* | 54 | 1 wk |

Sandie SHAW *UK, female vocalist* — 163 wks

8 Oct 64	★ (THERE'S) ALWAYS SOMETHING THERE TO REMIND ME *Pye 7N 15704*	1	11 wks
10 Dec 64	● GIRL DON'T COME *Pye 7N 15743*	3	12 wks
18 Feb 65	● I'LL STOP AT NOTHING *Pye 7N 15783*	4	11 wks
13 May 65	★ LONG LIVE LOVE *Pye 7N 15841*	1	14 wks
23 Sep 65	● MESSAGE UNDERSTOOD *Pye 7N 15940*	6	10 wks
18 Nov 65	HOW CAN YOU TELL *Pye 7N 15987*	21	9 wks
27 Jan 66	● TOMORROW *Pye 7N 17036*	9	9 wks
19 May 66	NOTHING COMES EASY *Pye 7N 17086*	14	9 wks
8 Sep 66	RUN *Pye 7N 17163*	32	5 wks
24 Nov 66	THINK SOMETIMES ABOUT ME *Pye 7N 17212*	32	4 wks
19 Jan 67	I DON'T NEED ANYTHING *Pye 7N 17239*	50	1 wk
16 Mar 67	★ PUPPET ON A STRING *Pye 7N 17272*	1	18 wks
12 Jul 67	TONIGHT IN TOKYO *Pye 7N 17346*	21	6 wks
4 Oct 67	YOU'VE NOT CHANGED *Pye 7N 17378*	18	12 wks
7 Feb 68	TODAY *Pye 7N 17441*	27	7 wks
12 Feb 69	● MONSIEUR DUPONT *Pye 7N 17675*	6	15 wks
14 May 69	THINK IT ALL OVER *Pye 7N 17726*	42	4 wks
21 Apr 84	HAND IN GLOVE *Rough Trade RT 130*	27	5 wks
14 Jun 86	ARE YOU READY TO BE HEARTBROKEN *Polydor POSP 793*	68	1 wk

Winifred SHAW *US, female vocalist* — 4 wks

| 14 Aug 76 | LULLABY OF BROADWAY *United Artists UP 36131* | 42 | 4 wks |

SHE ROCKERS *UK, female vocal duo* — 2 wks

| 13 Jan 90 | JAM IT JAM *Jive JIVE 233* | 58 | 2 wks |

George SHEARING *UK, male instrumentalist - piano* — 1 wk

| 4 Oct 62 | BAUBLES BANGLES AND BEADS *Capitol CL 15269* | 49 | 1 wk |

See also Nat 'King' Cole.

Gary SHEARSTON *Australia, male vocalist* — 8 wks

| 5 Oct 74 | ● I GET A KICK OUT OF YOU *Charisma CB 234* | 7 | 8 wks |

SHEER ELEGANCE *UK, male vocal group* — 23 wks

| 20 Dec 75 | MILKY WAY *Pye International 7N 25697* | 18 | 10 wks |
| 3 Apr 76 | ● LIFE IS TOO SHORT GIRL *Pye International 7N 25703* | 9 | 9 wks |

| 24 Jul 76 | | IT'S TEMPTATION *Pye International 7N 25715* .... | 41 | 4 wks |

SHEILA and B. DEVOTION   33 wks
France, female vocalist and US/Jamaica, male vocal/instrumental group

11 Mar 78		SINGIN' IN THE RAIN PART 1 *Carrere EMI 2751*............	11	13 wks
22 Jul 78		YOU LIGHT MY FIRE *Carrere EMI 2828*	44	6 wks
24 Nov 79		SPACER *Carrere CAR 128*	18	14 wks

First two hits have no 'and' in the act's name.

Doug SHELDON *UK, male vocalist*   15 wks

9 Nov 61		RUNAROUND SUE *Decca F 11398*	36	3 wks
4 Jan 62		YOUR MA SAID YOU CRIED IN YOUR SLEEP LAST NIGHT *Decca F 11416*.................	29	6 wks
7 Feb 63		I SAW LINDA YESTERDAY *Decca F 11564*	36	6 wks

Pete SHELLEY *UK, male vocalist*   1 wk

| 12 Mar 83 | | TELEPHONE OPERATOR *Genetic XX1*...................... | 66 | 1 wk |

Peter SHELLEY *UK, male vocalist*   20 wks

| 14 Sep 74 | ● | GEE BABY *Magnet MAG 12*....................................... | 4 | 10 wks |
| 22 Mar 75 | ● | LOVE ME LOVE MY DOG *Magnet MAG 22* .... | 3 | 10 wks |

Anne SHELTON *UK, female vocalist*   31 wks

16 Dec 55		ARRIVEDERCI DARLING *HMV POP 146*	17	4 wks
13 Apr 56		SEVEN DAYS *Philips PB 567*	20	4 wks
24 Aug 56	★	LAY DOWN YOUR ARMS *Philips PB 616*................	1	14 wks
20 Nov 59		VILLAGE OF ST. BERNADETTE *Philips PB 969*	27	1 wk
26 Jan 61	●	SAILOR *Philips PB 1096*.....................................	10	8 wks

SHEPHERD SISTERS *US, female vocal group*   6 wks

| 15 Nov 57 | | ALONE *HMV POP 411* .... | 14 | 5 wks |
| 3 Jan 58 | | ALONE (re-entry) *HMV POP 411* .... | 22 | 1 wk |

SHERBET *Australia, male vocal/instrumental group*   10 wks

| 25 Sep 76 | ● | HOWZAT *Epic EPC 4574*....................................... | 4 | 10 wks |

Tony SHERIDAN and the BEATLES   1 wk
UK, male vocalist, male instrumental backing group

| 6 Jun 63 | | MY BONNIE *Polydor NH 66833* .... | 48 | 1 wk |

See also Beatles.

Allan SHERMAN *US, male vocalist*   10 wks

| 12 Sep 63 | | HELLO MUDDAH HELLO FADDAH *Warner Bros. WB 106*................................. | 14 | 10 wks |

Bobby SHERMAN *US, male vocalist*   4 wks

| 31 Oct 70 | | JULIE DO YA LOVE ME *CBS 5144*............................. | 28 | 4 wks |

SHERRICK *US, male vocalist*   10 wks

| 1 Aug 87 | | JUST CALL *Warner Bros. W 8380*................................. | 23 | 8 wks |
| 21 Nov 87 | | LET'S BE LOVERS TONIGHT *Warner Bros. W 8146* .... | 63 | 2 wks |

Pluto SHERVINGTON *Jamaica, male vocalist*   20 wks

7 Feb 76	●	DAT *Opal PAL 5*...	6	8 wks
10 Apr 76		RAM GOAT LIVER *Trojan TR 7978*............................	43	4 wks
6 Mar 82		YOUR HONOUR *KR KR 4*	19	8 wks

Your Honour credited to Pluto.

Holly SHERWOOD *US, female vocalist*   7 wks

| 5 Feb 72 | | DAY BY DAY *Bell 1182* .... | 29 | 7 wks |

Tony SHEVETON *UK, male vocalist*   1 wk

| 13 Feb 64 | | MILLION DRUMS *Oriole CB 1895*........................... | 49 | 1 wk |

SHIRELLES *US, female vocal group*   29 wks

9 Feb 61	●	WILL YOU LOVE ME TOMORROW *Top Rank JAR 540*......	4	15 wks
31 May 62		SOLDIER BOY *HMV POP 1019*	23	9 wks
23 May 63		FOOLISH LITTLE GIRL *Stateside SS 181*	38	5 wks

SHIRLEY and COMPANY   9 wks
US, female vocalist and male vocal/instrumental backing group

| 8 Feb 75 | ● | SHAME SHAME SHAME *All Platinum 6146 301*................ | 6 | 9 wks |

SHIRLIE – *See PEPSI and SHIRLIE*

SHO NUFF *US, male vocal/instrumental group*   4 wks

| 24 May 80 | | IT'S ALRIGHT *Ensign ENY 37* .... | 53 | 4 wks |

Michelle SHOCKED *US, female vocalist*   10 wks

8 Oct 88		ANCHORAGE *Cooking Vinyl LON 193*........................	60	4 wks
14 Jan 89		IF LOVE WAS A TRAIN *Cooking Vinyl LON 212*	63	3 wks
11 Mar 89		WHEN I GROW UP *Cooking Vinyl LON 219*	67	3 wks

SHOCKING BLUE   14 wks
Holland, male/female vocal/instrumental group

| 17 Jan 70 | ● | VENUS *Penny Farthing PEN 702*................................. | 8 | 11 wks |
| 25 Apr 70 | | MIGHTY JOE *Penny Farthing PEN 713* .... | 43 | 3 wks |

Troy SHONDELL *US, male vocalist*   11 wks

| 2 Nov 61 | | THIS TIME *London HLG 9432* .... | 22 | 11 wks |

SHONDELLS – *See Tommy JAMES and the SHONDELLS*

SHOOTING PARTY *UK, male vocal duo*   2 wks

| 31 Mar 90 | | LET'S HANG ON *Lisson DOLE 15* .... | 66 | 2 wks |

SHOWADDYWADDY *UK, male vocal/instrumental group* 209 wks

18 May 74	●	HEY ROCK AND ROLL *Bell 1357*	2	14 wks
17 Aug 74		ROCK 'N' ROLL LADY *Bell 1374*	15	9 wks
30 Nov 74		HEY MR. CHRISTMAS *Bell 1387*............................	13	8 wks
22 Feb 75		SWEET MUSIC *Bell 1403*......................................	14	9 wks
17 May 75	●	THREE STEPS TO HEAVEN *Bell 1426*........................	2	11 wks
6 Sep 75	●	HEARTBEAT *Bell 1450*......................................	7	7 wks

15 Nov 75	HEAVENLY Bell 1460	34	6 wks
29 May 76	TROCADERO Bell 1476	32	3 wks
6 Nov 76	★ UNDER THE MOON OF LOVE Bell 1495	1	15 wks
5 Mar 77	● WHEN Arista 91	3	11 wks
23 Jul 77	● YOU GOT WHAT IT TAKES Arista 126	2	10 wks
5 Nov 77	● DANCIN' PARTY Arista 149	4	11 wks
25 Mar 78	● I WONDER WHY Arista 174	2	11 wks
24 Jun 78	● A LITTLE BIT OF SOAP Arista 191	5	12 wks
4 Nov 78	● PRETTY LITTLE ANGEL EYES Arista ARIST 222	5	12 wks
31 Mar 79	REMEMBER THEN Arista 247	17	8 wks
28 Jul 79	SWEET LITTLE ROCK 'N' ROLLER Arista 278	15	9 wks
10 Nov 79	A NIGHT AT DADDY GEE'S Arista 314	39	5 wks
27 Sep 80	WHY DO LOVERS BREAK EACH OTHER'S HEARTS Arista ARIST 359	22	10 wks
29 Nov 80	BLUE MOON Arista ARIST 379	32	9 wks
13 Jun 81	MULTIPLICATION Arista ARIST 416	39	4 wks
28 Nov 81	FOOTSTEPS Bell BELL 1499	31	9 wks
28 Aug 82	WHO PUT THE BOMP (IN THE BOMP-A-BOMP-A-BOMP) RCA 236	37	6 wks

SHOWDOWN US, male vocal/instrumental group   3 wks

| 17 Dec 77 | KEEP DOIN' IT State STAT 63 | 41 | 3 wks |

SHOWSTOPPERS US, male vocal group   25 wks

13 Mar 68	AIN'T NOTHING BUT A HOUSEPARTY Beacon 3-100	11	15 wks
13 Nov 68	EENY MEENY MGM 1436	33	7 wks
30 Jan 71	AIN'T NOTHING BUT A HOUSEPARTY (re-issue) Beacon BEA 100	43	1 wk
13 Feb 71	AIN'T NOTHING BUT A HOUSEPARTY (re-entry of re-issue) Beacon BEA 100	33	1 wk
27 Feb 71	AIN'T NOTHING BUT A HOUSEPARTY (2nd re-entry of re-issue) Beacon BEA 100	36	1 wk

SHRIEKBACK UK, male vocal/instrumental group   4 wks

| 28 Jul 84 | HAND ON MY HEART Arista SHRK 1 | 52 | 4 wks |

SHUT UP AND DANCE   5 wks
UK, male vocal/instrumental group

| 21 Apr 90 | 20 TO GET IN Shut Up And Dance SUAD 3 | 56 | 3 wks |
| 28 Jul 90 | LAMBORGHINI Shut Up And Dance SUAD 4 | 55 | 2 wks |

SHY UK, male vocal/instrumental group   3 wks

| 19 Apr 80 | GIRL (IT'S ALL I HAVE) Gallery GA 1 | 60 | 3 wks |

Labi SIFFRE UK, male vocalist   44 wks

27 Nov 71	IT MUST BE LOVE Pye International 7N 25572	14	12 wks
25 Mar 72	CRYING LAUGHING LOVING LYING Pye International 7N 25576	11	9 wks
29 Jul 72	WATCH ME Pye International 7N 25586	29	6 wks
4 Apr 87	● (SOMETHING INSIDE) SO STRONG China WOK 12	4	13 wks
21 Nov 87	NOTHIN'S GONNA CHANGE China WOK 16	52	4 wks

SIGUE SIGUE SPUTNIK   20 wks
UK, male vocal/instrumental group

1 Mar 86	● LOVE MISSILE F1-11 Parlophone SSS 1	3	9 wks
7 Jun 86	TWENTY-FIRST CENTURY BOY Parlophone SSS 2	20	5 wks
19 Nov 88	SUCCESS Parlophone SSS 3	31	3 wks
1 Apr 89	DANCERAMA Parlophone SSS 5	50	2 wks
20 May 89	ALBINONI VS STAR WARS Parlophone SSS 4	75	1 wk

SILENCERS UK, male vocal/instrumental group   6 wks

| 25 Jun 88 | PAINTED MOON RCA HUSH 1 | 57 | 4 wks |
| 27 May 89 | SCOTTISH RAIN RCA PB 42701 | 71 | 2 wks |

SILENT UNDERDOG   1 wk
UK, male instrumentalist - keyboards

| 16 Feb 85 | PAPA'S GOT A BRAND NEW PIGBAG Kaz KAZ 50 | 73 | 1 wk |

Paul Hardcastle under a false name. See also Paul Hardcastle.

SILJE Norway, female vocalist   3 wks

| 15 Dec 90 | TELL ME WHERE YOU'RE GOING EMI EM 159 | 63† | 3 wks |

SILKIE UK, male/female vocal/instrumental group   6 wks

| 23 Sep 65 | YOU'VE GOT TO HIDE YOUR LOVE AWAY Fontana TF 603 | 28 | 6 wks |

SILSOE UK, male instrumentalist - keyboards   4 wks

| 21 Jun 86 | AZTEC GOLD CBS A 7231 | 48 | 4 wks |

Aztec Gold was the ITV theme to the 1986 World Cup Finals and was performed by Rod Argent under the title Silsoe. See also Argent; San Jose.

SILVER BULLET UK, male vocal/instrumental duo   16 wks

2 Sep 89	BRING FORTH THE GUILLOTINE Tam Tam TTT 013	70	1 wk
9 Dec 89	20 SECONDS TO COMPLY Tam Tam 7TTT 019	11	10 wks
3 Mar 90	BRING FORTH THE GUILLOTINE (re-entry) Tam Tam TTT 013	45	5 wks

SILVER BULLET BAND – See Bob SEGER and the SILVER BULLET BAND

SILVER CONVENTION   35 wks
Germany/US, female vocal group

5 Apr 75	SAVE ME Magnet MAG 26	30	7 wks
15 Nov 75	FLY ROBIN FLY Magnet MAG 43	28	8 wks
3 Apr 76	● GET UP AND BOOGIE Magnet MAG 55	7	11 wks
19 Jun 76	TIGER BABY/ NO NO JOE Magnet MAG 69	41	4 wks
29 Jan 77	EVERYBODY'S TALKIN' 'BOUT LOVE Magnet MAG 81	25	5 wks

Dooley SILVERSPOON US, male vocalist   3 wks

| 31 Jan 76 | LET ME BE THE NUMBER ONE Seville SEV 1020 | 44 | 3 wks |

Harry SIMEONE CHORALE US, choir   14 wks

13 Feb 59	LITTLE DRUMMER BOY Top Rank JAR 101	13	7 wks
22 Dec 60	ONWARD CHRISTIAN SOLDIERS Ember EMBS 118	35	1 wk
5 Jan 61	ONWARD CHRISTIAN SOLDIERS (re-entry) Ember EMBS 118	38	1 wk
21 Dec 61	ONWARD CHRISTIAN SOLDIERS (2nd re-entry) Ember EMBS 118	36	3 wks
20 Dec 62	ONWARD CHRISTIAN SOLDIERS (re-issue) Ember EMBS 144	38	2 wks

Gene SIMMONS *US, male vocalist* — **4 wks**

27 Jan 79		RADIOACTIVE *Casablanca CAN 134*	**41**	4 wks

Carly SIMON *US, female vocalist* — **66 wks**

16 Dec 72	●	YOU'RE SO VAIN *Elektra K 12077*	**3**	15 wks
31 Mar 73		THE RIGHT THING TO DO *Elektra K 12095*	**17**	9 wks
6 Aug 77	●	NOBODY DOES IT BETTER *Elektra K 12261*	**7**	12 wks
21 Aug 82	●	WHY *WEA K 79300*	**10**	13 wks
24 Jan 87	●	COMING AROUND AGAIN *Arista ARIST 687*	**10**	12 wks
10 Jun 89		WHY (re-issue) *WEA U 7501*	**56**	5 wks

See also Carly Simon and James Taylor; Will Powers.

Carly SIMON and James TAYLOR — **5 wks**
US, female/male duo

16 Mar 74		MOCKINGBIRD *Elektra K 12134*	**34**	5 wks

See also Carly Simon; James Taylor.

Joe SIMON *US, male vocalist* — **10 wks**

16 Jun 73		STEP BY STEP *Mojo 2093 030*	**14**	10 wks

Paul SIMON *US, male vocalist* — **83 wks**

19 Feb 72	●	MOTHER AND CHILD REUNION *CBS 7793*	**5**	12 wks
29 Apr 72		ME AND JULIO DOWN BY THE SCHOOLYARD *CBS 7964*	**15**	9 wks
16 Jun 73	●	TAKE ME TO THE MARDI GRAS *CBS 1578*	**7**	11 wks
22 Sep 73		LOVES ME LIKE A ROCK *CBS 1700*	**39**	4 wks
10 Jan 76		50 WAYS TO LEAVE YOUR LOVER *CBS 3887*	**23**	6 wks
3 Dec 77		SLIP SLIDIN' AWAY *CBS 5770*	**36**	5 wks
6 Sep 80		LATE IN THE EVENING *Warner Bros. K 17666*	**58**	4 wks
13 Sep 86	●	YOU CAN CALL ME AL *Warner Bros. W 8667*	**4**	13 wks
13 Dec 86		THE BOY IN THE BUBBLE *Warner Bros. W 8509*	**26**	8 wks
6 Oct 90		THE OBVIOUS CHILD *Warner Bros W 9549*	**15**	10 wks

See also Simon and Garfunkel.

Tito SIMON *Jamaica, male vocalist* — **4 wks**

8 Feb 75		THIS MONDAY MORNING FEELING *Horse HOSS 57*	**45**	4 wks

SIMON and GARFUNKEL *US, male vocal duo* — **80 wks**

24 Mar 66	●	HOMEWARD BOUND *CBS 202045*	**9**	12 wks
16 Jun 66		I AM A ROCK *CBS 202303*	**17**	10 wks
10 Jul 68	●	MRS. ROBINSON *CBS 3443*	**4**	12 wks
8 Jan 69	●	MRS. ROBINSON (EP) *CBS EP 6400*	**9**	5 wks
30 Apr 69	●	THE BOXER *CBS 4162*	**6**	14 wks
21 Feb 70	★	BRIDGE OVER TROUBLED WATER *CBS 4790*	**1**	19 wks
15 Aug 70		BRIDGE OVER TROUBLED WATER (re-entry) *CBS 4790*	**45**	1 wk
7 Oct 72		AMERICA *CBS 8336*	**25**	7 wks

Titles on Mrs. Robinson EP: Mrs. Robinson/Scarborough Fair - Canticle/Sounds of Silence/April Come She Will. This EP would have stayed more than 5 weeks on chart had a decision to exclude EP from chart in Feb 69 not been taken. See also Paul Simon; Art Garfunkel.

Nina SIMONE *US, female vocalist* — **43 wks**

5 Aug 65		I PUT A SPELL ON YOU *Philips BF 1415*	**49**	1 wk
16 Oct 68	●	AIN'T GOT NO - I GOT LIFE/ DO WHAT YOU GOTTA DO *RCA 1743*	**2**	18 wks
15 Jan 69	●	TO LOVE SOMEBODY *RCA 1779*	**5**	9 wks
15 Jan 69		I PUT A SPELL ON YOU (re-issue) *Philips BF 1736*	**28**	4 wks
31 Oct 87	●	MY BABY JUST CARES FOR ME *Charly CYZ 7112*	**5**	11 wks

Do What You Gotta Do was only credited on the charts for 8 weeks of the 18, its highest position being 7.

SIMPLE MINDS *UK, male vocal/instrumental group* — **150 wks**

12 May 79		LIFE IN A DAY *Zoom ZUM 10*	**62**	2 wks
23 May 81		THE AMERICAN *Virgin VS 410*	**59**	3 wks
15 Aug 81		LOVE SONG *Virgin VS 434*	**47**	4 wks
7 Nov 81		SWEAT IN BULLET *Virgin VS 451*	**52**	3 wks
10 Apr 82		PROMISED YOU A MIRACLE *Virgin VS 488*	**13**	11 wks
28 Aug 82		GLITTERING PRIZE *Virgin VS 511*	**16**	11 wks
13 Nov 82		SOMEONE SOMEWHERE (IN SUMMERTIME) *Virgin VS 538*	**36**	5 wks
26 Nov 83		WATERFRONT *Virgin VS 636*	**13**	10 wks
28 Jan 84		SPEED YOUR LOVE TO ME *Virgin VS 649*	**20**	4 wks
24 Mar 84		UP ON THE CATWALK *Virgin VS 661*	**27**	5 wks
20 Apr 85	●	DON'T YOU (FORGET ABOUT ME) *Virgin VS 749*	**7**	11 wks
17 Aug 85		DON'T YOU (FORGET ABOUT ME) (re-entry) *Virgin VS 749*	**61**	8 wks
12 Oct 85	●	ALIVE AND KICKING *Virgin VS 817*	**7**	9 wks
28 Dec 85		DON'T YOU (FORGET ABOUT ME) (2nd re-entry) *Virgin VS 749*	**74**	1 wk
4 Jan 86		ALIVE AND KICKING (re-entry) *Virgin VS 817*	**60**	2 wks
1 Feb 86	●	SANCTIFY YOURSELF *Virgin SM 1*	**10**	7 wks
15 Feb 86		DON'T YOU (FORGET ABOUT ME) (3rd re-entry) *Virgin VS 779*	**62**	3 wks
15 Mar 86		DON'T YOU (FORGET ABOUT ME) (4th re-entry) *Virgin VS 779*	**68**	1 wk
12 Apr 86	●	ALL THE THINGS SHE SAID *Virgin VS 860*	**9**	8 wks
14 Jun 86		ALL THE THINGS SHE SAID (re-entry) *Virgin VS 860*	**73**	1 wk
15 Nov 86		GHOSTDANCING *Virgin VS 907*	**13**	6 wks
3 Jan 87		GHOSTDANCING (re-entry) *Virgin VS 907*	**68**	2 wks
20 Jun 87		PROMISED YOU A MIRACLE *Virgin SM 2*	**19**	7 wks
18 Feb 89	★	BELFAST CHILD *Virgin SM 3*	**1**	11 wks
22 Apr 89		THIS IS YOUR LAND *Virgin SMX4*	**13**	4 wks
29 Jul 89		KICK IT IN *Virgin SM 5*	**15**	5 wks
9 Dec 89		THE AMSTERDAM EP *Virgin SMX 6*	**18**	6 wks

The 1987 version of Promised You A Miracle *was a live recording. Tracks on* The Amsterdam *EP: Let It All Come Down/Jerusalem/Sign Of The Times.*

SIMPLICIOUS *US, male vocal group* — **9 wks**

29 Sep 84		LET HER FEEL IT *Fourth and Broadway BRW 13*	**65**	3 wks
2 Feb 85		LET HER FEEL IT (re-issue) *Fourth & Broadway BRW 18*	**34**	6 wks

The re-issue of Let Her Feel It *was coupled with* Personality *by Eugene Wilde. See also Eugene Wilde.*

SIMPLY RED *UK, male vocal/instrumental group* — **94 wks**

15 Jun 85		MONEY'S TOO TIGHT (TO MENTION) *Elektra EKR 9*	**13**	12 wks
21 Sep 85		COME TO MY AID *Elektra EKR 19*	**66**	2 wks
16 Nov 85		HOLDING BACK THE YEARS *Elektra EKR 29*	**51**	4 wks
8 Mar 86		JERICHO *WEA YZ 63*	**53**	3 wks
17 May 86	●	HOLDING BACK THE YEARS (re-issue) *WEA YZ 70*	**2**	13 wks
9 Aug 86		OPEN UP THE RED BOX *WEA YZ 75*	**61**	4 wks
14 Feb 87		THE RIGHT THING *WEA YZ 103*	**11**	10 wks
23 May 87		INFIDELITY *Elektra YZ 114*	**31**	5 wks
28 Nov 87		EV'RY TIME WE SAY GOODBYE *Elektra YZ 161*	**11**	9 wks
13 Mar 88		I WON'T FEEL BAD *Elektra YZ 172*	**68**	3 wks
28 Jan 89		IT'S ONLY LOVE *Elektra YZ 349*	**13**	8 wks
8 Apr 89	●	IF YOU DON'T KNOW ME BY NOW *Elektra YZ 377*	**2**	10 wks
8 Jul 89		A NEW FLAME *WEA YZ 404*	**17**	8 wks
28 Oct 89		YOU'VE GOT IT *Elektra YZ 424*	**46**	3 wks

SIMPSON – *See* **ASHFORD** *and* **SIMPSON**

Paul SIMPSON featuring ADEVA

US, male producer and female vocalist   **8 wks**

25 Mar 89		MUSICAL FREEDOM (MOVING ON UP) *Cooltempo COOL 182*	22	8 wks

See also Adeva.

Joyce SIMS *US, female vocalist*   **35 wks**

19 Apr 86		ALL AND ALL *London LON 94*	16	10 wks
13 Jun 87		LIFETIME LOVE *London LON 137*	34	6 wks
9 Jan 88	●	COME INTO MY LIFE *London LON 161*	7	9 wks
23 Apr 88		WALK AWAY *London LON 176*	24	6 wks
17 Jun 89		LOOKING FOR A LOVE *FFRR F 109*	39	4 wks

W/ Cdr A.E. SIMS – *See Central Band of the ROYAL AIR FORCE, conductor W/Cdr A.E. SIMS, OBE*

Frank SINATRA *US, male vocalist*   **401 wks**

9 Jul 54		YOUNG AT HEART *Capitol CL 14064*	12	1 wk
16 Jul 54	★	THREE COINS IN THE FOUNTAIN *Capitol CL 14120*	1	19 wks
10 Jun 55		YOU MY LOVE *Capitol CL 14240*	13	3 wks
22 Jul 55		YOU MY LOVE (re-entry) *Capitol CL 14240*	17	2 wks
5 Aug 55	●	LEARNIN' THE BLUES *Capitol CL 14296*	2	13 wks
12 Aug 55		YOU MY LOVE (2nd re-entry) *Capitol CL 14240*	17	2 wks
2 Sep 55		NOT AS A STRANGER *Capitol CL 14326*	18	1 wk
13 Jan 56	●	LOVE AND MARRIAGE *Capitol CL 14503*	3	8 wks
20 Jan 56	●	THE TENDER TRAP *Capitol CL 14511*	2	9 wks
15 Jun 56		SONGS FOR SWINGING LOVERS (LP) *Capitol LCT 6106*	12	8 wks
22 Nov 57		ALL THE WAY *Capitol CL 14800*	29	1 wk
29 Nov 57		CHICAGO *Capitol CL 14800*	25	1 wk
6 Dec 57		ALL THE WAY/ CHICAGO (re-entry) *Capitol CL 14800*	21	1 wk
13 Dec 57	●	ALL THE WAY (2nd re-entry) *Capitol CL 14800*	3	17 wks
7 Feb 58		WITCHCRAFT *Capitol CL 14819*	12	8 wks
14 Nov 58		MR. SUCCESS *Capitol CL 14956*	29	1 wk
12 Dec 58		MR. SUCCESS (re-entry) *Capitol CL 14956*	25	2 wks
2 Jan 59		MR. SUCCESS (2nd re-entry) *Capitol CL 14956*	26	1 wk
10 Apr 59		FRENCH FOREIGN LEGION *Capitol CL 14997*	18	5 wks
15 May 59		COME DANCE WITH ME (LP) *Capitol LCT 6179*	30	1 wk
28 Aug 59		HIGH HOPES *Capitol CL 15052*	28	1 wk
11 Sep 59	●	HIGH HOPES (re-entry) *Capitol CL 15052*	6	13 wks
10 Mar 60		HIGH HOPES (2nd re-entry) *Capitol CL 15052*	42	1 wk
7 Apr 60		IT'S NICE TO GO TRAV'LING *Capitol CL 15116*	48	2 wks
16 Jun 60		RIVER STAY 'WAY FROM MY DOOR *Capitol CL 15135*	18	9 wks
8 Sep 60		NICE 'N EASY *Capitol CL 15150*	15	12 wks
24 Nov 60		OL' MACDONALD *Capitol CL 15168*	11	8 wks
20 Apr 61		MY BLUE HEAVEN *Capitol CL 15193*	33	7 wks
28 Sep 61		GRANADA *Reprise R 20010*	15	8 wks
23 Nov 61		THE COFFEE SONG *Reprise R 20035*	39	3 wks
5 Apr 62		EVERYBODY'S TWISTING *Reprise R 20063*	22	12 wks
7 Mar 63		MY KIND OF GIRL *Reprise R 20148*	35	6 wks
24 Sep 64		HELLO DOLLY *Reprise R 20351*	47	1 wk
12 May 66	★	STRANGERS IN THE NIGHT *Reprise R 23052*	1	20 wks
29 Sep 66		SUMMER WIND *Reprise RS 20509*	36	5 wks
15 Dec 66		THAT'S LIFE *Reprise RS 20531*	46	5 wks
23 Aug 67		THE WORLD WE KNEW *Reprise RS 20610*	33	11 wks
2 Apr 69	●	MY WAY *Reprise RS 20817*	5	42 wks
4 Oct 69	●	LOVE'S BEEN GOOD TO ME *Reprise RS 20852*	8	18 wks
31 Jan 70		MY WAY (re-entry) *Reprise RS 20817*	49	1 wk
28 Feb 70		MY WAY (2nd re-entry) *Reprise RS 20817*	30	5 wks
11 Apr 70		MY WAY (3rd re-entry) *Reprise RS 20817*	33	9 wks
27 Jun 70		MY WAY (4th re-entry) *Reprise RS 20817*	28	21 wks
28 Nov 70		MY WAY (5th re-entry) *Reprise RS 20817*	18	16 wks
6 Mar 71		I WILL DRINK THE WINE *Reprise RS 23487*	16	12 wks
27 Mar 71		MY WAY (6th re-entry) *Reprise RS 20817*	22	19 wks
4 Sep 71		MY WAY (7th re-entry) *Reprise RS 20817*	39	8 wks
1 Jan 72		MY WAY (8th re-entry) *Reprise RS 20817*	50	1 wk
20 Dec 75		I BELIEVE I'M GONNA LOVE YOU *Reprise K 14400*	34	7 wks
9 Aug 80		THEME FROM NEW YORK, NEW YORK *Reprise K 14502*	59	4 wks
22 Feb 86	●	THEME FROM NEW YORK NEW YORK (re-entry) *Reprise K 14502*	4	10 wks

My Kind Of Girl and Hello Dolly with Count Basie. Tracks on Songs For Swinging Lovers LP: You Make Me Feel So Young/It Happened In Monterey/You're Getting To Be A Habit With Me/You Brought A New Kind Of Love To Me/Too Marvellous For Words/Old Devil Moon/Pennies From Heaven/Love Is Here To Stay/I've Got You Under My Skin/I Thought About You/We'll Be Together Again/Making Whoopee/Swingin' Down The Lane/Anything Goes/How About You. On Come Dance With Me LP: Something's Gotta Give/Just In Time/Dancing In The Dark/Too Close For Comfort/I Could Have Danced All Night/Saturday Night Is The Loneliest Night Of The Week/Day In Day Out/Cheek To Cheek/Baubles Bangles And Beads/The Song Is You/The Last Dance. All The Way and Chicago, Capitol CL 14800, were at first billed separately, then together for one week, then All The Way on its own. See also Frank Sinatra and Sammy Davis Jr.; Nancy Sinatra and Frank Sinatra.

Frank SINATRA and Sammy DAVIS Jr.

US, male vocal duo   **9 wks**

13 Dec 62		ME AND MY SHADOW *Reprise R 20128*	20	7 wks
7 Feb 63		ME AND MY SHADOW (re-entry) *Reprise R 20128*	47	2 wks

See also Frank Sinatra; Sammy Davis Jr.

Nancy SINATRA *US, female vocalist*   **61 wks**

27 Jan 66	★	THESE BOOTS ARE MADE FOR WALKING *Reprise R 20432*	1	14 wks
28 Apr 66		HOW DOES THAT GRAB YOU DARLIN' *Reprise R 20461*	19	8 wks
19 Jan 67	●	SUGAR TOWN *Reprise RS 20527*	8	10 wks
5 Jul 67		YOU ONLY LIVE TWICE *Reprise RS 20595*	11	19 wks
29 Nov 69		HIGHWAY SONG *Reprise RS 20869*	21	10 wks

See also Nancy Sinatra and Frank Sinatra; Nancy Sinatra and Lee Hazlewood.

Nancy SINATRA and Lee HAZLEWOOD

US, female/male vocal duo   **38 wks**

12 Jul 67		JACKSON *Reprise RS 20595*	11	18 wks
8 Nov 67		LADYBIRD *Reprise RS 20629*	47	1 wk
21 Aug 71	●	DID YOU EVER *Reprise K 14093*	2	19 wks

Did You Ever bills the duo simply as Nancy and Lee. Jackson was listed with You Only Live Twice by Nancy Sinatra on a double A-side. See also Nancy Sinatra

Nancy SINATRA and Frank SINATRA

US, female/male vocal duo   **18 wks**

23 Mar 67	★	SOMETHIN' STUPID *Reprise RS 23166*	1	18 wks

See also Nancy Sinatra; Frank Sinatra.

SINE *US, disco aggregation*   **9 wks**

10 Jun 78		JUST LET ME DO MY THING *CBS 6351*	33	9 wks

SINFONIA OF LONDON – *See Peter AUTY and the SINFONIA OF LONDON*

SINGING CORNER meets DONOVAN

UK, male vocalists   **1 wk**

1 Dec 90		JENNIFER JUNIPER *Fontana SYP 1*	68	1 wk

See also Donovan.

SINGING DOGS *Denmark, canine vocal group*   **4 wks**

25 Nov 55		THE SINGING DOGS (MEDLEY) *Nixa N 15009*	13	4 wks

Medley songs: Pat-a-cake/Three Blind Mice/Jingle Bells/Oh Susanna.

SINGING NUN (Soeur Sourire)   14 wks
Belgium, female vocalist

| 5 Dec 63 | ● DOMINIQUE *Philips BF 1293* .... 7 | 14 wks |

SINGING SHEEP *UK, computerized sheep noises*   5 wks

| 18 Dec 82 | BAA BAA BLACK SHEEP *Sheep BAA 1* .... 42 | 5 wks |

Maxine SINGLETON *US, female vocalist*   3 wks

| 2 Apr 83 | YOU CAN'T RUN FROM LOVE *Creole CR 50* .... 57 | 3 wks |

SINITTA *US, female vocalist*   98 wks

8 Mar 86	SO MACHO/ CRUISING *Fanfare FAN 7* 47	11 wks
28 Jun 86	● SO MACHO/ CRUISING (re-entry) *Fanfare FAN 7*........... 2	17 wks
11 Oct 86	FEELS LIKE THE FIRST TIME *Fanfare FAN 8*.............. 45	5 wks
25 Jul 87	★ TOY BOY *Fanfare FAN 12*........................... 4	14 wks
12 Dec 87	G.T.O *Fanfare FAN 14* 15	9 wks
19 Mar 88	● CROSS MY BROKEN HEART *Fanfare FAN 15*............. 6	9 wks
24 Sep 88	I DON'T BELIEVE IN MIRACLES *Fanfare FAN 16*......... 22	8 wks
3 Jun 89	● RIGHT BACK WHERE WE STARTED FROM	
	Fanfare FAN 18 4	10 wks
7 Oct 89	LOVE ON A MOUNTAIN TOP *Fanfare FAN 21* 20	6 wks
21 Apr 90	HITCHIN' A RIDE *Fanfare FAN 24* 24	6 wks
22 Sep 90	LOVE AND AFFECTION *Fanfare FAN 31* 62	3 wks

SIOUXSIE and the BANSHEES   135 wks
UK, female/male vocal/instrumental group

26 Aug 78	● HONG KONG GARDEN *Polydor 2059 052* 7	10 wks
31 Mar 79	THE STAIRCASE (MYSTERY) *Polydor POSP 9* 24	8 wks
7 Jul 79	PLAYGROUND TWIST *Polydor POSP 59*................... 28	6 wks
29 Sep 79	MITTAGEISEN (METAL POSTCARD)	
	Polydor 2059 151.................................. 47	3 wks
15 Mar 80	HAPPY HOUSE *Polydor POSP 117*....................... 17	8 wks
7 Jun 80	CHRISTINE *Polydor 2059 249*........................... 24	8 wks
6 Dec 80	ISRAEL *Polydor POSP 205*............................ 41	8 wks
30 May 81	SPELLBOUND *Polydor POSP 273*......................... 22	8 wks
1 Aug 81	ARABIAN KNIGHTS *Polydor POSP 309*.................... 32	7 wks
29 May 82	FIRE WORKS *Polydor POSPG 450*........................ 22	6 wks
9 Oct 82	SLOWDIVE *Polydor POSP 510*.......................... 41	4 wks
4 Dec 82	MELT/ IL EST NE LE DIVIN ENFANT	
	Polydor POSP 539.................................. 49	5 wks
1 Oct 83	● DEAR PRUDENCE *Wonderland SHE 4* 3	8 wks
24 Mar 84	SWIMMING HORSES *Wonderland SHE 6*.................... 28	4 wks
2 Jun 84	DAZZLE *Wonderland SHE 7*............................ 33	4 wks
27 Oct 84	THE THORN (EP) *Wonderland SHEEP 8*.................. 47	3 wks
26 Oct 85	CITIES IN DUST *Wonderland SHE 9*..................... 21	6 wks
8 Mar 86	CANDYMAN *Wonderland SHE 10*........................ 34	5 wks
17 Jan 87	THIS WHEEL'S ON FIRE *Wonderland SHE 11* 14	6 wks
28 Mar 87	THE PASSENGER *Wonderland SHE 12* 41	6 wks
25 Jul 87	SONG FROM THE EDGE OF THE WORLD	
	Wonderland SHE 13................................. 59	3 wks
30 Jul 88	PEEK-A-BOO *Wonderland SHE 14*....................... 16	6 wks
8 Oct 88	THE KILLING JAR *Wonderland SHE 15*.................. 41	3 wks
3 Dec 88	THE LAST BEAT OF MY HEART *Wonderland SHE 16* 44	1 wk

Tracks on EP: Overground/Voices/Placebo Effect/Red Over White. See also Creatures.

SIR DOUGLAS QUINTET   10 wks
US, male vocal/instrumental group

| 17 Jun 65 | SHE'S ABOUT A MOVER *London HLU 9964* .... 15 | 10 wks |

SIRRON – *See PLUS ONE featuring SIRRON*

SISTER SLEDGE *US, female vocal group*   94 wks

21 Jun 75	MAMA NEVER TOLD ME *Atlantic K 10619*................. 20	6 wks
17 Mar 79	● HE'S THE GREATEST DANCER	
	Atlantic/Cotillion K 11257............................ 6	11 wks
26 May 79	● WE ARE FAMILY *Atlantic/Cotillion K 11293*............. 8	10 wks
11 Aug 79	LOST IN MUSIC *Atlantic/Cotillion K 11337* 17	10 wks
19 Jan 80	GOT TO LOVE SOMEBODY *Atlantic/Cotillion K 11404*.... 34	4 wks
28 Feb 81	ALL AMERICAN GIRLS *Atlantic K 11656* 41	5 wks
26 May 84	THINKING OF YOU *Cotillion/Atlantic B 9744* 11	13 wks
8 Sep 84	● LOST IN MUSIC (re-mix) *Cotillion/Atlantic B 9718* 4	12 wks
17 Nov 84	WE ARE FAMILY (re-mix) *Cotillion/Atlantic B 9692*.... 33	4 wks
1 Jun 85	★ FRANKIE *Atlantic A 9547*............................ 1	16 wks
31 Aug 85	DANCING ON THE JAGGED EDGE *Atlantic A 9520*........ 50	3 wks

SISTERS OF MERCY   30 wks
UK, male/female vocal/instrumental duo

16 Jun 84	BODY AND SOUL/ TRAIN *Merciful Release MR 029*.......... 46	3 wks
20 Oct 84	WALK AWAY *Merciful Release MR 033* 45	3 wks
9 Mar 85	NO TIME TO CRY *Merciful Release MR 035* 63	2 wks
3 Oct 87	● THIS CORROSION *Merciful Release MR 39*.............. 7	6 wks
27 Feb 88	DOMINION *Merciful Release MR 43* 13	6 wks
18 Jun 88	LUCRETIA MY REFLECTION *Merciful Release MR 45*....... 20	4 wks
13 Oct 90	MORE *Merciful Release MR 47* 21	4 wks
22 Dec 90	DOCTOR JEEP *Merciful Release MR 51*....................... 37†	2 wks

SISTERS OF SOUL – *See Steve WRIGHT*

SIVUCA *Brazil, male vocalist*   3 wks

| 28 Jul 84 | AIN'T NO SUNSHINE *London LON 51*..................... 56 | 3 wks |

SKATALITES *Jamaica, male instrumental group*   6 wks

| 20 Apr 67 | GUNS OF NAVARONE *Island WI 168*....................... 36 | 6 wks |

Peter SKELLERN *UK, male vocalist*   24 wks

23 Sep 72	● YOU'RE A LADY *Decca F 13333*................................ 3	11 wks
29 Mar 75	HOLD ON TO LOVE *Decca F 13568*.......................... 14	9 wks
28 Oct 78	LOVE IS THE SWEETEST THING *Mercury 6008 603*........ 60	4 wks

Last hit has credit: 'Featuring Grimethorpe Colliery Band'.

SKID ROW *US, male/female vocal/instrumental group*   13 wks

18 Nov 89	YOUTH GONE WILD *Atlantic A 8935* 42	3 wks
3 Feb 90	18 AND LIFE *Atlantic A 8883* 12	6 wks
31 Mar 90	I REMEMBER YOU *East West A 8836* 36	4 wks

SKIDS *UK, male vocal/instrumental group*   60 wks

23 Sep 78	SWEET SUBURBIA *Virgin VS 227* 70	1 wk
7 Oct 78	SWEET SUBURBIA (re-entry) *Virgin VS 227* 71	2 wks
4 Nov 78	THE SAINTS ARE COMING *Virgin VS 232* 48	3 wks
17 Feb 79	● INTO THE VALLEY *Virgin VS 241* 10	11 wks
26 May 79	MASQUERADE *Virgin VS 262*.......................... 14	9 wks
29 Sep 79	CHARADE *Virgin VS 288* 31	6 wks
24 Nov 79	WORKING FOR THE YANKEE DOLLAR	
	Virgin VS 306 20	11 wks
1 Mar 80	ANIMATION *Virgin VS 323* 56	4 wks
16 Aug 80	CIRCUS GAMES *Virgin VS 359* 32	7 wks
18 Oct 80	GOODBYE CIVILIAN *Virgin VS 373* 52	4 wks
6 Dec 80	WOMEN IN WINTER *Virgin VSK 101* 49	3 wks

SINITTA attends the 1988 recording of the Children In Need Appeal song.

Far Left: FRANK SINATRA first charted in the United States as the lead vocalist on Tommy Dorsey's 1940 hit 'Polka Dots and Moonbeams'.

NANCY SINATRA really did have a swinging Sixties, recording a James Bond theme ('You Only Live Twice'), acting with Elvis Presley *(Speedway)* and having number ones both on her own and with famous father Frank.

SKIPWORTH and TURNER US, male vocal duo — 12 wks

27 Apr 85	**THINKING ABOUT YOUR LOVE** Fourth & Broadway BRW 23	**24**	10 wks
21 Jan 89	**MAKE IT LAST** Fourth & Broadway BRW 118	**60**	2 wks

SKY UK/Australia, male instrumental group — 11 wks

5 Apr 80	● **TOCCATA** Ariola ARO 300	**5**	11 wks

SKYHOOKS Australia, male vocal/instrumental group — 1 wk

9 Jun 79	**WOMEN IN UNIFORM** United Artists UP 36508	**73**	1 wk

SLADE UK, male vocal/instrumental group — 271 wks

19 Jun 71	**GET DOWN AND GET WITH IT** Polydor 2058 112	**16**	14 wks
30 Oct 71	★ **COZ I LUV YOU** Polydor 2058 155	**1**	15 wks
5 Feb 72	● **LOOK WOT YOU DUN** Polydor 2058 195	**4**	10 wks
3 Jun 72	★ **TAKE ME BAK 'OME** Polydor 2058 231	**1**	13 wks
2 Sep 72	★ **MAMA WEER ALL CRAZEE NOW** Polydor 2058 274	**1**	10 wks
25 Nov 72	● **GUDBUY T'JANE** Polydor 2058 312	**2**	13 wks
3 Mar 73	★ **CUM ON FEEL THE NOIZE** Polydor 2058 339	**1**	12 wks
30 Jun 73	★ **SKWEEZE ME PLEEZE ME** Polydor 2058 377	**1**	10 wks
6 Oct 73	● **MY FREND STAN** Polydor 2058 407	**2**	8 wks
15 Dec 73	★ **MERRY XMAS EVERYBODY** Polydor 2058 422	**1**	9 wks
6 Apr 74	● **EVERYDAY** Polydor 2058 453	**3**	7 wks
6 Jul 74	● **BANGIN' MAN** Polydor 2058 492	**3**	7 wks
19 Oct 74	● **FAR FAR AWAY** Polydor 2058 522	**2**	6 wks
15 Feb 75	**HOW DOES IT FEEL** Polydor 2058 547	**15**	7 wks
17 May 75	● **THANKS FOR THE MEMORY (WHAM BAM THANK YOU MAM)** Polydor 2058 585	**7**	7 wks
22 Nov 75	**IN FOR A PENNY** Polydor 2058 663	**11**	8 wks
7 Feb 76	**LET'S CALL IT QUITS** Polydor 2058 690	**11**	7 wks
5 Feb 77	**GYPSY ROAD HOG** Barn 2014 105	**48**	2 wks
29 Oct 77	**MY BABY LEFT ME - THAT'S ALL RIGHT** (MEDLEY) Barn 2014 114	**32**	4 wks
18 Oct 80	**SLADE ALIVE AT READING '80** (EP) Cheapskate CHEAP 5	**44**	5 wks
27 Dec 80	**MERRY XMAS EVERYBODY** Cheapskate CHEAP 11	**70**	2 wks
31 Jan 81	● **WE'LL BRING THE HOUSE DOWN** Cheapskate CHEAP 16	**10**	9 wks
4 Apr 81	**WHEELS AIN'T COMING DOWN** Cheapskate CHEAP 21	**60**	3 wks
19 Sep 81	**LOCK UP YOUR DAUGHTERS** RCA 124	**29**	8 wks
19 Dec 81	**MERRY XMAS EVERYBODY** (re-entry) Polydor 2058 422	**32**	4 wks
27 Mar 82	**RUBY RED** RCA 191	**51**	3 wks
27 Nov 82	**(AND NOW - THE WALTZ) C'EST LA VIE** RCA 291	**50**	6 wks
25 Dec 82	**MERRY XMAS EVERYBODY** (2nd re-entry) Polydor 2058 422	**67**	3 wks
19 Nov 83	● **MY OH MY** RCA 373	**2**	11 wks
10 Dec 83	**MERRY XMAS EVERYBODY** (3rd re-entry) Polydor 2058 422	**20**	5 wks
4 Feb 84	● **RUN RUN AWAY** RCA 385	**7**	10 wks
17 Nov 84	**ALL JOIN HANDS** RCA 455	**15**	9 wks
15 Dec 84	**MERRY XMAS EVERYBODY** (4th re-entry) Polydor 2058 422	**47**	4 wks
26 Jan 85	**7 YEAR BITCH** RCA 475	**60**	4 wks
23 Mar 85	**MYZSTERIOUS MIZTER JONES** RCA PB 40027	**50**	5 wks
30 Nov 85	**DO YOU BELIEVE IN MIRACLES** RCA PB 40449	**54**	6 wks
21 Dec 85	**MERRY XMAS EVERYBODY** (re-issue) Polydor POSP 780	**48**	3 wks
27 Dec 86	**MERRY XMAS EVERYBODY** (re-entry of re-issue) Polydor POSP 780	**71**	1 wk
21 Feb 87	**STILL THE SAME** RCA PB 41137	**73**	2 wks

Tracks on Slade Live At Reading EP: When I'm Dancin' I Ain't Fightin'/Born To Be Wild/Somethin' Else/Pistol Packin' Mama/Keep A Rollin'. Merry Xmas Everybody on Cheapskate is credited to Slade and the Reading Choir and is a re-recording.

SLAUGHTER US, male vocal/instrumental group — 1 wk

29 Sep 90	**UP ALL NIGHT** Chrysalis CHS 3556	**62**	1 wk

SLAVE US, male vocal/instrumental group — 3 wks

8 Mar 80	**JUST A TOUCH OF LOVE** Atlantic/Cotillion K 11442	**64**	3 wks

SLAYER US, male vocal/instrumental group — 1 wk

13 Jun 87	**CRIMINALLY INSANE** Def Jam LON 133	**64**	1 wk

Percy SLEDGE US, male vocalist — 34 wks

12 May 66	● **WHEN A MAN LOVES A WOMAN** Atlantic 584 001	**4**	17 wks
4 Aug 66	**WARM AND TENDER LOVE** Atlantic 584 034	**34**	7 wks
14 Feb 87	● **WHEN A MAN LOVES A WOMAN** (re-issue) Atlantic YZ 96	**2**	10 wks

SLICK US, male/female vocal/instrumental group — 15 wks

16 Jun 79	**SPACE BASS** Fantasy FTC 176	**16**	10 wks
15 Sep 79	**SEXY CREAM** Fantasy FTC 182	**47**	5 wks

Grace SLICK US, female vocalist — 4 wks

24 May 80	**DREAMS** RCA PB 9534	**50**	4 wks

SLIK UK, male vocal/instrumental group — 18 wks

17 Jan 76	★ **FOREVER AND EVER** Bell 1464	**1**	9 wks
8 May 76	**REQUIEM** Bell 1478	**24**	9 wks

SLIM CHANCE – See Ronnie LANE

SLITS UK, female vocal/instrumental group — 3 wks

13 Oct 79	**TYPICAL GIRLS/ I HEARD IT THROUGH THE GRAPEVINE** Island WIP 6505	**60**	3 wks

P. F. SLOAN US, male vocalist — 3 wks

4 Nov 65	**SINS OF THE FAMILY** RCA 1482	**38**	3 wks

SLY and the FAMILY STONE — 42 wks
US, male/female vocal/instrumental group, Sly Stone, vocals and keyboards

10 Jul 68	● **DANCE TO THE MUSIC** Direction 58 3568	**7**	14 wks
2 Oct 68	**M'LADY** Direction 58 3707	**32**	7 wks
19 Mar 69	**EVERYDAY PEOPLE** Direction 58 3938	**36**	1 wk
9 Apr 69	**EVERYDAY PEOPLE** (re-entry) Direction 58 3938	**37**	4 wks
8 Jan 72	**FAMILY AFFAIR** Epic EPC 7632	**15**	8 wks
15 Apr 72	**RUNNIN' AWAY** Epic EPC 7810	**17**	8 wks

SLY FOX US, male vocal/instrumental duo — 16 wks

31 May 86	● **LET'S GO ALL THE WAY** Capitol CL 403	**3**	16 wks

SLY and ROBBIE *Jamaica, male vocal/instrumental duo* **15 wks**

4 Apr 87		BOOPS (HERE TO GO) *Fourth & Broadway BRW 61*		12	11 wks
25 Jul 87		FIRE *Fourth & Broadway BRW 71*		60	4 wks

SMALL ADS *UK, male vocal/instrumental group* **3 wks**

18 Apr 81	SMALL ADS *Bronze BRO 115*		63	3 wks

SMALL FACES *UK, male vocal/instrumental group* **137 wks**

2 Sep 65		WHATCHA GONNA DO ABOUT IT? *Decca F 12208*		14	12 wks
10 Feb 66	●	SHA LA LA LA LEE *Decca F 12317*		3	11 wks
12 May 66	●	HEY GIRL *Decca F 12393*		10	9 wks
11 Aug 66	★	ALL OR NOTHING *Decca F 12470*		1	12 wks
17 Nov 66	●	MY MIND'S EYE *Decca F 12500*		4	11 wks
9 Mar 67		I CAN'T MAKE IT *Decca F 12565*		26	7 wks
8 Jun 67		HERE COME THE NICE *Immediate IM 050*		12	10 wks
9 Aug 67	●	ITCHYCOO PARK *Immediate IM 057*		3	14 wks
6 Dec 67	●	TIN SOLDIER *Immediate IM 062*		9	12 wks
17 Apr 68	●	LAZY SUNDAY *Immediate IM 064*		2	11 wks
10 Jul 68		UNIVERSAL *Immediate IM 069*		16	11 wks
19 Mar 69		AFTERGLOW OF YOUR LOVE *Immediate IM 077*		36	1 wk
13 Dec 75	●	ITCHYCOO PARK (re-issue) *Immediate IMS 102*		9	11 wks
20 Mar 76		LAZY SUNDAY (re-issue) *Immediate IMS 106*		39	5 wks

See also Faces.

'Fast' Eddie SMITH – *See DJ 'Fast' EDDIE; Kenny Jammin" JASON and 'Fast' Eddie SMITH*

Hurricane SMITH *UK, male vocalist* **35 wks**

12 Jun 71	●	DON'T LET IT DIE *Columbia DB 8785*		2	12 wks
29 Apr 72	●	OH BABE WHAT WOULD YOU SAY? *Columbia DB 8878*		4	16 wks
2 Sep 72		WHO WAS IT *Columbia DB 8916*		23	7 wks

Jimmy SMITH *US, male instrumentalist - organ* **3 wks**

28 Apr 66	GOT MY MOJO WORKING *Verve VS 536*		48	2 wks
19 May 66	GOT MY MOJO WORKING (re-entry) *Verve VS 536*		48	1 wk

Keely SMITH *US, female vocalist* **10 wks**

18 Mar 65	YOU'RE BREAKIN' MY HEART *Reprise R 20346*		14	10 wks

Mandy SMITH *UK, female vocalist* **2 wks**

20 May 89	DON'T YOU WANT ME BABY *PWL PWL 37*		59	2 wks

Muriel SMITH *UK, female vocalist* **17 wks**

15 May 53	●	HOLD ME THRILL ME KISS ME *Philips PB 122*		3	17 wks

O. C. SMITH *US, male vocalist* **23 wks**

29 May 68	●	SON OF HICKORY HOLLER'S TRAMP *CBS 3343*		2	15 wks
26 Mar 77		TOGETHER *Caribou CRB 4910*		25	8 wks

Patti SMITH GROUP
US, female vocalist, male instrumental backing group **16 wks**

29 Apr 78	●	BECAUSE THE NIGHT *Arista 181*		5	12 wks
19 Aug 78		PRIVILEGE (SET ME FREE) *Arista 197*		72	1 wk

2 Jun 79	FREDERICK *Arista 264*		63	3 wks

Rex SMITH and Rachel SWEET
US, male/female vocal duo **7 wks**

22 Aug 81	EVERLASTING LOVE *CBS A 1405*		35	7 wks

See also Rachel Sweet.

Richard Jon SMITH *South Africa, male vocalist* **2 wks**

16 Jul 83	SHE'S THE MASTER OF THE GAME *Jive JIVE 38*		63	2 wks

Whistling Jack SMITH *UK, male whistler* **12 wks**

2 Mar 67	●	I WAS KAISER BILL'S BATMAN *Deram DM 112*		5	12 wks

SMITHS *UK, male vocal/instrumental group* **92 wks**

12 Nov 83		THIS CHARMING MAN *Rough Trade RT 136*		25	12 wks
28 Jan 84		WHAT DIFFERENCE DOES IT MAKE *Rough Trade RT 146*		12	9 wks
2 Jun 84	●	HEAVEN KNOWS I'M MISERABLE NOW *Rough Trade RT 156*		10	8 wks
1 Sep 84		WILLIAM, IT WAS REALLY NOTHING *Rough Trade RT 166*		17	6 wks
9 Feb 85		HOW SOON IS NOW? *Rough Trade RT 176*		24	6 wks
30 Mar 85		SHAKESPEARE'S SISTER *Rough Trade RT 181*		26	4 wks
13 Jul 85		THAT JOKE ISN'T FUNNY ANYMORE *Rough Trade RT 186*		49	3 wks
5 Oct 85		THE BOY WITH THE THORN IN HIS SIDE *Rough Trade RT 191*		23	5 wks
31 May 86		BIG MOUTH STRIKES AGAIN *Rough Trade RT 192*		26	4 wks
2 Aug 86		PANIC *Rough Trade RT 193*		11	8 wks
1 Nov 86		ASK *Rough Trade RT 194*		14	5 wks
7 Feb 87		SHOPLIFTERS OF THE WORLD UNITE *Rough Trade RT 195*		12	4 wks
25 Apr 87	●	SHEILA TAKE A BOW *Rough Trade RT 196*		10	5 wks
22 Aug 87		GIRLFRIEND IN A COMA *Rough Trade RT 197*		13	5 wks
14 Nov 87		I STARTED SOMETHING I COULDN'T FINISH *Rough Trade RT 198*		23	4 wks
19 Dec 87		LAST NIGHT I DREAMT THAT SOMEBODY LOVED ME *Rough Trade RT 200*		30	4 wks

SMOKE *UK, male vocal/instrumental group* **3 wks**

9 Mar 67	MY FRIEND JACK *Columbia DB 8115*		45	3 wks

SMOKIE *UK, male vocal/instrumental group* **106 wks**

19 Jul 75	●	IF YOU THINK YOU KNOW HOW TO LOVE ME *RAK 206*		3	9 wks
4 Oct 75	●	DON'T PLAY YOUR ROCK 'N ROLL TO ME *RAK 217*		8	7 wks
31 Jan 76		SOMETHING'S BEEN MAKING ME BLUE *RAK 227*		17	8 wks
25 Sep 76		I'LL MEET YOU AT MIDNIGHT *RAK 241*		11	9 wks
4 Dec 76	●	LIVING NEXT DOOR TO ALICE *RAK 244*		5	11 wks
19 Mar 77		LAY BACK IN THE ARMS OF SOMEONE *RAK 251*		12	9 wks
16 Jul 77	●	IT'S YOUR LIFE *RAK 260*		5	9 wks
15 Oct 77	●	NEEDLES AND PINS *RAK 263*		10	9 wks
28 Jan 78		FOR A FEW DOLLARS MORE *RAK 267*		17	6 wks
20 May 78	●	OH CAROL *RAK 276*		5	13 wks
23 Sep 78		MEXICAN GIRL *RAK 283*		19	9 wks
19 Apr 80		TAKE GOOD CARE OF MY BABY *RAK 309*		34	7 wks

Group were spelt Smokey for first two hits.

Joe SMOOTH *US, male vocalist* **4 wks**

4 Feb 89	PROMISED LAND *DJ International DJIN 6*		56	4 wks

SMURFS – *See Father ABRAHAM and the SMURFS*

SMURPS – *See Father ABRAPHART and the SMURPS*

SNAP *US, male/female rap/vocal duo* — **38 wks**

24 Mar 90	★	**THE POWER** *Arista 113133*	**1**	15 wks
16 Jun 90	●	**OOOPS UP** *Arista 113296*	**5**	12 wks
22 Sep 90	●	**CULT OF SNAP** *Arista 113596*	**8**	7 wks
8 Dec 90	●	**MARY HAD A LITTLE BOY** *Arista 113831*	**8†**	4 wks

SNIFF 'N' THE TEARS
UK, male vocal/instrumental group — **5 wks**

23 Jun 79	**DRIVER'S SEAT** *Chiswick CHIS 105*	**42**	5 wks

Phoebe SNOW *US, female vocalist* — **7 wks**

6 Jan 79	**EVERY NIGHT** *CBS 6842*	**37**	7 wks

SNOWMAN – *See Peter AUTY*

SNOWMEN *UK, male vocal/instrumental group* — **12 wks**

12 Dec 81	**HOKEY COKEY** *Stiff ODB 1*	**18**	8 wks
18 Dec 82	**XMAS PARTY** *Solid STOP 006*	**44**	4 wks

SO *UK, male vocal/instrumental group* — **3 wks**

13 Feb 88	**ARE YOU SURE** *Parlophone R 6173*	**62**	3 wks

Gino SOCCIO *Canada, male instrumentalist - keyboards* — **5 wks**

28 Apr 79	**DANCER** *Warner Bros. K 17357*	**46**	5 wks

SOEUR SOUIRE – *See SINGING NUN*

SOFT CELL *UK, male vocal/instrumental duo* — **96 wks**

1 Aug 81	★	**TAINTED LOVE** *Some Bizzare BZS 2*	**1**	16 wks
14 Nov 81	●	**BED SITTER** *Some Bizzare BZS 6*	**4**	12 wks
9 Jan 82		**TAINTED LOVE (re-entry)** *Some Bizzare BZS 2*	**43**	10 wks
6 Feb 82	●	**SAY HELLO WAVE GOODBYE** *Some Bizzare BZS 7*	**3**	9 wks
29 May 82		**TORCH** *Some Bizzare BZS 9*	**2**	9 wks
24 Jul 82		**TAINTED LOVE (2nd re-entry)** *Some Bizzare BZS 2*	**50**	4 wks
21 Aug 82	●	**WHAT** *Some Bizzare BZS 11*	**3**	8 wks
4 Dec 82		**WHERE THE HEART IS** *Some Bizzare BZS 16*	**21**	7 wks
5 Mar 83		**NUMBERS/ BARRIERS** *Some Bizzare BZS 17*	**25**	4 wks
24 Sep 83		**SOUL INSIDE** *Some Bizzare BZS 20*	**16**	5 wks
25 Feb 84		**DOWN IN THE SUBWAY** *Some Bizzare BZS 22*	**24**	6 wks
9 Feb 85		**TAINTED LOVE (3rd re-entry)** *Some Bizzare BZS 2*	**43**	6 wks

SOHO *UK, male/female vocal/instrumental group* — **1 wk**

5 May 90	**HIPPY CHICK** *Savage 7SAV 106*	**67**	1 wk

Sal SOLO *UK, male vocalist* — **13 wks**

15 Dec 84	**SAN DAMIANO (HEART AND SOUL)** *MCA MCA 930*	**15**	10 wks
6 Apr 85	**MUSIC AND YOU** *MCA MCA 946*	**52**	3 wks

Music and You credits the London Community Gospel Choir.

Belouis SOME *UK, male vocalist* — **26 wks**

27 Apr 85	**IMAGINATION** *Parlophone R 6097*	**50**	7 wks
18 Jan 86	**IMAGINATION (re-issue)** *Parlophone R 1986*	**17**	10 wks
12 Apr 86	**SOME PEOPLE** *Parlophone R 6130*	**33**	7 wks
16 May 87	**LET IT BE WITH YOU** *Parlophone R 6154*	**53**	2 wks

Jimmy SOMERVILLE *UK, male vocalist* — **32 wks**

11 Nov 89		**COMMENT TE DIRE ADIEU** *London LON 241*	**14**	9 wks
13 Jan 90	●	**YOU MAKE ME FEEL (MIGHTY REAL)** *London LON 249*	**5**	8 wks
17 Mar 90		**READ MY LIPS (ENOUGH IS ENOUGH)** *London LON 254*	**26**	6 wks
3 Nov 90	●	**TO LOVE SOMEBODY** *London LON 281*	**8†**	9 wks

First hit features June Miles-Kingston - UK, female vocalist.

SONIA *UK, female vocalist* — **43 wks**

24 Jun 89	★	**YOU'LL NEVER STOP ME LOVING YOU** *Chrysalis CHS 3385*	**1**	13 wks
7 Oct 89		**CAN'T FORGET YOU** *Chrysalis CHS 3419*	**17**	6 wks
9 Dec 89	●	**LISTEN TO YOUR HEART** *Chrysalis CHS 3465*	**10**	10 wks
7 Apr 90		**COUNTING EVERY MINUTE** *Chrysalis CHS 3492*	**16**	7 wks
25 Aug 90		**END OF THE WORLD** *Chrysalis/PWL CHS 357*	**18**	7 wks

See also Big Fun and Sonia.

SONNY *US, male vocalist* — **11 wks**

19 Aug 65	●	**LAUGH AT ME** *Atlantic AT 4038*	**9**	11 wks

See also Sonny and Cher.

SONNY and CHER *US, male/female vocal duo* — **77 wks**

12 Aug 65	★	**I GOT YOU BABE** *Atlantic AT 4035*	**1**	12 wks
16 Sep 65		**BABY DON'T GO** *Reprise R 20309*	**11**	9 wks
21 Oct 65		**BUT YOU'RE MINE** *Atlantic AT 4047*	**17**	8 wks
17 Feb 66		**WHAT NOW MY LOVE** *Atlantic AT 4069*	**13**	11 wks
30 Jun 66		**HAVE I STAYED TOO LONG** *Atlantic 584 018*	**42**	3 wks
8 Sep 66	●	**LITTLE MAN** *Atlantic 584 040*	**4**	10 wks
17 Nov 66		**LIVING FOR YOU** *Atlantic 584 057*	**44**	4 wks
2 Feb 67		**THE BEAT GOES ON** *Atlantic 584 078*	**29**	8 wks
15 Jan 72	●	**ALL I EVER NEED IS YOU** *MCA MU 1145*	**8**	12 wks

See also Sonny; Cher.

SORROWS *UK, male vocal/instrumental group* — **8 wks**

16 Sep 65	**TAKE A HEART** *Piccadilly 7N 35260*	**21**	8 wks

S.O.S. BAND *US, male/female vocal/instrumental group* — **46 wks**

19 Jul 80	**TAKE YOUR TIME (DO IT RIGHT) PART 1** *Tabu TBU 8564*	**51**	4 wks
26 Feb 83	**GROOVIN' (THAT'S WHAT WE'RE DOIN')** *Tabu TBU A3120*	**72**	1 wk
7 Apr 84	**JUST BE GOOD TO ME** *Tabu A 3626*	**13**	11 wks
4 Aug 84	**JUST THE WAY YOU LIKE IT** *Tabu A 4621*	**32**	7 wks
13 Oct 84	**WEEKEND GIRL** *Tabu A 4785*	**51**	5 wks
29 Mar 86	**THE FINEST** *Tabu A 6997*	**17**	10 wks
5 Jul 86	**BORROWED LOVE** *Tabu A 7241*	**50**	5 wks
2 May 87	**NO LIES** *Tabu 650444 7*	**64**	3 wks

David SOUL *US, male vocalist* — **56 wks**

18 Dec 76	★	**DON'T GIVE UP ON US** *Private Stock PVT 84*	**1**	16 wks
26 Mar 77	●	**GOING IN WITH MY EYES OPEN** *Private Stock PVT 99*	**2**	8 wks
27 Aug 77	★	**SILVER LADY** *Private Stock PVT 115*	**1**	14 wks

Left: SIMON AND GARFUNKEL appear to be anticipating by two decades the Dustin Hoffman-Tom Cruise walk in *Rain Man*.

Far Left: Things went off beam for the SMITHS in 1988.

Left: SNAP powered their way to number one with their first hit.

Sylvester Stewart, later the leader of SLY AND THE FAMILY STONE, was a San Francisco disc jockey in his early twenties.

17 Dec 77	● LET'S HAVE A QUIET NIGHT IN *Private Stock PVT 130*.....	8	9 wks
27 May 78	IT SURE BRINGS OUT THE LOVE IN YOUR EYES		
	Private Stock PVT 137	12	9 wks

Jimmy SOUL *US, male vocalist*   **2 wks**

11 Jul 63	IF YOU WANNA BE HAPPY *Stateside SS 178*..............	39	2 wks

SOUL BROTHERS *UK, male vocal/instrumental group*   **3 wks**

22 Apr 65	I KEEP RINGING MY BABY *Decca F 12116*	42	3 wks

SOUL CITY SYMPHONY – *See Van McCOY*

SOUL SONIC FORCE – *See Afrika BAMBAATAA and SOUL SONIC FORCE*

SOUL II SOUL *UK, male producer, Jazzie B – keyboards*   **56 wks**

21 May 88	FAIRPLAY *10 TEN 228*.........................	63	3 wks
17 Sep 88	FEEL FREE *10 TEN 236*	64	2 wks
18 Mar 89	● KEEP ON MOVING *10 TEN 263*	5	12 wks
10 Jun 89	★ BACK TO LIFE (HOWEVER DO YOU WANT ME)		
	10 TEN 265	1	14 wks
9 Dec 89	● GET A LIFE *10 TEN 284*	3	13 wks
5 May 90	● A DREAM'S A DREAM *10 TEN 300*	6	6 wks
24 Nov 90	MISSING YOU *10 TEN 345*...................	22†	6 wks

Fairplay features Rose Windross. Feel Free features Do'reen. Both are UK, female vocalists. Keep On Moving and Back To Life feature Caron Wheeler. Missing You features Kym Mazelle. See also Caron Wheeler; Kym Mazelle.

SOUND 9418 *Jonathan King again*   **3 wks**

7 Feb 76	IN THE MOOD *UK 121*	46	3 wks

See also Jonathan King.

SOUNDS INCORPORATED   **11 wks**
UK, male instrumental group

23 Apr 64	THE SPARTANS *Columbia DB 7239*	30	6 wks
30 Jul 64	SPANISH HARLEM *Columbia DB 7321*..................	35	5 wks

SOUNDS NICE *UK, male instrumental group*   **11 wks**

6 Sep 69	LOVE AT FIRST SIGHT (JE T'AIME ... MOI NON		
	PLUS) *Parlophone R 5797*	18	11 wks

Has credit: Tim Mycroft on organ.

SOUNDS ORCHESTRAL *UK, orchestra*   **18 wks**

3 Dec 64	● CAST YOUR FATE TO THE WIND *Piccadilly 7N 35206*......	5	16 wks
8 Jul 65	MOONGLOW *Piccadilly 7N 35248*	43	2 wks

SOUP DRAGONS *UK, male vocal/instrumental group*   **20 wks**

20 Jun 87	CAN'T TAKE NO MORE *Raw TV RTV 3*	65	1 wk
5 Sep 87	SOFT AS YOUR FACE *Raw TV RTV 4*	66	2 wks
14 Jul 90	● I'M FREE *Raw TV RTV 9*.	5	12 wks
20 Oct 90	MOTHER UNIVERSE *Raw TV BLR 30*	26	5 wks

I'm Free features Junior Reid - UK, male rapper. See also Coldcut.

Joe SOUTH *US, male vocalist*   **11 wks**

5 Mar 69	● GAMES PEOPLE PLAY *Capitol CL 15579*.................	6	11 wks

Jeri SOUTHERN *US, female vocalist*   **3 wks**

21 Jun 57	FIRE DOWN BELOW *Brunswick 05665*	22	3 wks

SOUTHLANDERS *UK, male vocal group*   **10 wks**

22 Nov 57	ALONE *Decca F 10946*..	17	10 wks

SOVEREIGN COLLECTION *UK, orchestra*   **6 wks**

3 Apr 71	MOZART 40 *Capitol CL 15676*...............................	27	6 wks

Red SOVINE *US, male vocalist*   **8 wks**

13 Jun 81	● TEDDY BEAR *Starday SD 142*....................	4	8 wks

Bob B SOXX and the BLUE JEANS   **2 wks**
US, male/female vocal group

31 Jan 63	ZIP-A-DEE-DOO-DAH *London HLU 9646*	45	2 wks

SPACE *France, male instrumental group*   **12 wks**

13 Aug 77	● MAGIC FLY *Pye International 7N 25746*.........................	2	12 wks

SPACE MONKEY *US, male vocal group*   **4 wks**

8 Oct 83	CAN'T STOP RUNNING *Innervision A 3742*..................	53	4 wks

SPAGNA *Italy, female vocalist*   **23 wks**

25 Jul 87	● CALL ME *CBS 650279 7*............................	2	12 wks
17 Oct 87	EASY LADY *CBS 651169 7*.........................	62	3 wks
20 Aug 88	EVERY GIRL AND BOY *CBS SPAG 1*.....................	23	8 wks

SPANDAU BALLET *UK, male vocal/instrumental group*   **159 wks**

15 Nov 80	● TO CUT A LONG STORY SHORT		
	Reformation CHS 2473	5	11 wks
24 Jan 81	THE FREEZE *Reformation CHS 2486*	17	8 wks
4 Apr 81	● MUSCLEBOUND/ GLOW *Reformation CHS 2509*	10	10 wks
18 Jul 81	● CHANT NO.1 (I DON'T NEED THIS PRESSURE ON)		
	Reformation CHS 2528	3	10 wks
14 Nov 81	PAINT ME DOWN *Chrysalis CHS 2560*....................	30	5 wks
30 Jan 82	SHE LOVED LIKE DIAMOND *Chrysalis CHS 2585*	49	4 wks
10 Apr 82	● INSTINCTION *Chrysalis CHS 2602*	10	11 wks
2 Oct 82	● LIFELINE *Chrysalis CHS 2642*	7	9 wks
12 Feb 83	COMMUNICATION *Reformation CHS 2662*	12	10 wks
23 Apr 83	★ TRUE *Reformation SPAN 1*..........................	1	12 wks
13 Aug 83	● GOLD *Reformation SPAN 2*	2	9 wks
9 Jun 84	● ONLY WHEN YOU LEAVE *Reformation SPAN 3*.	3	9 wks
18 Aug 84	ONLY WHEN YOU LEAVE (re-entry)		
	Reformation SPAN 3..........................	74	1 wk
25 Aug 84	● I'LL FLY FOR YOU *Reformation SPAN 4*	9	9 wks
20 Oct 84	HIGHLY STRUNG *Reformation SPAN 5*	15	5 wks
8 Dec 84	ROUND AND ROUND *Reformation SPAN 6*	18	8 wks
26 Jul 86	FIGHT FOR OURSELVES *Reformation A 7264*.............	15	7 wks
8 Nov 86	● THROUGH THE BARRICADES *Reformation SPANS 1*	6	10 wks
14 Feb 87	HOW MANY LIES *Reformation SPANS 2*..................	34	4 wks
3 Sep 88	RAW *CBS SPANS 3*.........................	47	3 wks
26 Aug 89	BE FREE WITH YOUR LOVE *CBS SPANS 4*...............	42	4 wks

SPARKS US/UK, male vocal/instrumental group — 70 wks

4 May 74	● THIS TOWN AIN'T BIG ENOUGH FOR BOTH OF US *Island WIP 6193*	2	10 wks
20 Jul 74	● AMATEUR HOUR *Island WIP 6203*	7	9 wks
19 Oct 74	NEVER TURN YOUR BACK ON MOTHER EARTH *Island WIP 6211*	13	7 wks
18 Jan 75	SOMETHING FOR THE GIRL WITH EVERYTHING *Island WIP 6221*	17	7 wks
19 Jul 75	GET IN THE SWING *Island WIP 6236*	27	7 wks
4 Oct 75	LOOKS LOOKS LOOKS *Island WIP 6249*	26	4 wks
21 Apr 79	THE NUMBER ONE SONG IN HEAVEN *Virgin VS 244*	14	12 wks
21 Jul 79	● BEAT THE CLOCK *Virgin VS 270*	10	9 wks
27 Oct 79	TRYOUTS FOR THE HUMAN RACE *Virgin VS 289*	45	5 wks

SPEAR OF DESTINY UK, male vocal/instrumental group — 43 wks

21 May 83	THE WHEEL *Epic A 3372*	59	5 wks
21 Jan 84	PRISONER OF LOVE *CBS A 4068*	59	3 wks
14 Apr 84	LIBERATOR *Epic A 4310*	67	2 wks
15 Jun 85	ALL MY LOVE (ASK NOTHING) *Epic A 6333*	61	3 wks
10 Aug 85	COME BACK *Epic 6445*	55	3 wks
7 Feb 87	STRANGERS IN OUR TOWN *10 TEN 148*	49	4 wks
4 Apr 87	NEVER TAKE ME ALIVE *10 TEN 162*	14	11 wks
25 Jul 87	WAS THAT YOU *10 TEN 173*	55	4 wks
3 Oct 87	THE TRAVELLER *10 TEN 189*	44	3 wks
24 Sep 88	SO IN LOVE WITH YOU *Virgin VS 1123*	36	5 wks

Billie Jo SPEARS US, female vocalist — 40 wks

12 Jul 75	● BLANKET ON THE GROUND *United Artists UP 35805*	6	13 wks
17 Jul 76	● WHAT I'VE GOT IN MIND *United Artists UP 36118*	4	13 wks
11 Dec 76	SING ME AN OLD FASHIONED SONG *United Artists UP 36179*	34	9 wks
21 Jul 79	I WILL SURVIVE *United Artists UP 601*	47	5 wks

SPECIALS UK, male vocal/instrumental group — 95 wks

28 Jul 79	● GANGSTERS *2 Tone TT 1*	6	12 wks
27 Oct 79	● A MESSAGE TO YOU RUDY/ NITE CLUB *2 Tone CHS TT 5*	10	14 wks
26 Jan 80	★ THE SPECIAL A.K.A. LIVE! (EP) *2 Tone CHS TT 7*	1	10 wks
24 May 80	● RAT RACE/ RUDE BOYS OUTA JAIL *2 Tone CHS TT 11*	5	9 wks
20 Sep 80	● STEREOTYPE/ INTERNATIONAL JET SET *2 Tone CHS TT 13*	6	8 wks
13 Dec 80	● DO NOTHING/ MAGGIE'S FARM *2 Tone CHS TT 16*	4	11 wks
20 Jun 81	★ GHOST TOWN *2 Tone CHS TT 17*	1	14 wks
3 Sep 83	RACIST FRIEND *2 Tone CBS TT 25*	60	3 wks
17 Mar 84	● NELSON MANDELA *2 Tone TT 26*	9	10 wks
8 Sep 84	WHAT I LIKE MOST ABOUT YOU IS YOUR GIRLFRIEND *2 Tone TT 27*	51	4 wks

Gangsters credited to Specials A.K.A. Second hit billed as Specials (featuring Rico +). Tracks on The Special A.K.A. Live!: Too Much Too Young/Guns Of Navarone/Long Shot Kick De Bucket/ Liquidator/Skinhead Moonstomp. Maggie's Farm only listed with Do Nothing from 10 Jan 81. Group were male/female for last three hits.

Chris SPEDDING UK, male vocalist/instrumentalist - guitar — 8 wks

| 23 Aug 75 | MOTOR BIKING *RAK 210* | 14 | 8 wks |

Johnny SPENCE UK, orchestra — 15 wks

| 1 Mar 62 | THEME FROM DR. KILDARE *Parlophone R 4872* | 15 | 15 wks |

Don SPENCER UK, male vocalist — 12 wks

| 21 Mar 63 | FIREBALL *HMV POP 1087* | 32 | 11 wks |
| 13 Jun 63 | FIREBALL (re-entry) *HMV POP 1087* | 49 | 1 wk |

SPIDER UK, male vocal/instrumental group — 5 wks

| 5 Mar 83 | WHY D'YA LIE TO ME *RCA 313* | 65 | 2 wks |
| 10 Mar 84 | HERE WE GO ROCK 'N' ROLL *A &M AM 180* | 57 | 3 wks |

SPINNERS – *See DETROIT SPINNERS*

SPIRITUAL COWBOYS – *See David A. STEWART*

SPIRITUALIZED UK, male vocal/instrumental group — 1 wk

| 30 Jun 90 | ANYWAY YOU WANT ME/ STEP INTO THE BREEZE *Dedicated ZB 43783* | 75 | 1 wk |

SPITTING IMAGE UK, male/female puppets — 18 wks

10 May 86	★ THE CHICKEN SONG *Virgin SPIT 1*	1	10 wks
26 Jul 86	THE CHICKEN SONG (re-entry) *Virgin SPIT 1*	67	1 wk
6 Dec 86	SANTA CLAUS IS ON THE DOLE/ FIRST ATHEIST TABERNACLE CHOIR *Virgin VS 921*	22	7 wks

SPLINTER UK, male vocal/instrumental duo — 10 wks

| 2 Nov 74 | COSTAFINE TOWN *Dark Horse AMS 7135* | 17 | 10 wks |

SPLIT ENZ New Zealand/UK, male vocal/instrumental group — 15 wks

| 16 Aug 80 | I GOT YOU *A &M AMS 7546* | 12 | 11 wks |
| 23 May 81 | HISTORY NEVER REPEATS *A &M AMS 8128* | 63 | 4 wks |

SPLODGENESSABOUNDS
UK, male vocal/instrumental group — 17 wks

14 Jun 80	● SIMON TEMPLAR/ TWO PINTS OF LAGER AND A PACKET OF CRISPS PLEASE *Deram BUM 1*	7	8 wks
6 Sep 80	TWO LITTLE BOYS/ HORSE *Deram ROLF 1*	26	7 wks
13 Jun 81	COWPUNK MEDLUM *Deram BUM 3*	69	2 wks

SPOTNICKS Sweden, male instrumental group — 37 wks

14 Jun 62	ORANGE BLOSSOM SPECIAL *Oriole CB 1724*	29	10 wks
6 Sep 62	ROCKET MAN *Oriole CB 1755*	38	9 wks
31 Jan 63	HAVA NAGILA *Oriole CB 1790*	13	12 wks
25 Apr 63	JUST LISTEN TO MY HEART *Oriole CB 1818*	36	6 wks

Dusty SPRINGFIELD UK, female vocalist — 197 wks

21 Nov 63	● I ONLY WANT TO BE WITH YOU *Philips BF 1292*	4	18 wks
20 Feb 64	STAY AWHILE *Philips BF 1313*	13	10 wks
2 Jul 64	● I JUST DON'T KNOW WHAT TO DO WITH MYSELF *Philips BF 1348*	3	12 wks
22 Oct 64	● LOSING YOU *Philips BF 1369*	9	13 wks
18 Feb 65	YOUR HURTIN' KIND OF LOVE *Philips BF 1396*	37	4 wks
1 Jul 65	● IN THE MIDDLE OF NOWHERE *Philips BF 1418*	8	10 wks
16 Sep 65	● SOME OF YOUR LOVIN' *Philips BF 1430*	8	12 wks
27 Jan 66	LITTLE BY LITTLE *Philips BF 1466*	17	9 wks
31 Mar 66	★ YOU DON'T HAVE TO SAY YOU LOVE ME *Philips BF 1482*	1	13 wks
7 Jul 66	● GOING BACK *Philips BF 1502*	10	10 wks
15 Sep 66	● ALL I SEE IS YOU *Philips BF 1510*	9	12 wks

SOUL II SOUL stop moving long enough to line up for a bow.

SONIA was the top female British solo star of the Stock Aitken Waterman stable.

Far Left: JOE SOUTH wrote 'Rose Garden'. Nobody promised him one, and in this photo he didn't get one.

It's all spangles for SPAGNA.

Date	Title	Pos	Wks
23 Feb 67	I'LL TRY ANYTHING *Philips BF 1553*	13	9 wks
25 May 67	GIVE ME TIME *Philips BF 1577*	24	6 wks
10 Jul 68 ●	I CLOSE MY EYES AND COUNT TO TEN *Philips BF 1682*	4	12 wks
4 Dec 68 ●	SON OF A PREACHER MAN *Philips BF 1730*	9	9 wks
20 Sep 69	AM I THE SAME GIRL *Philips BF 1811*	43	3 wks
18 Oct 69	AM I THE SAME GIRL (re-entry) *Philips BF 1811*	46	1 wk
19 Sep 70	HOW CAN I BE SURE *Philips 6006 045*	36	4 wks
20 Oct 79	BABY BLUE *Mercury DUSTY 4*	61	5 wks
25 Feb 89	NOTHING HAS BEEN PROVED *Parlophone R 6207*	16	7 wks
2 Dec 89	IN PRIVATE *Parlophone R 6234*	14	10 wks
26 May 90	REPUTATION *Parlophone R 6253*	38	6 wks
24 Nov 90	ARRESTED BY YOU *Parlophone R 6266*	70	2 wks

See also Springfields; Pet Shop Boys and Dusty Springfield.

Rick SPRINGFIELD *Australia, male vocalist* — 13 wks

Date	Title	Pos	Wks
14 Jan 84	HUMAN TOUCH *RCA RICK 1*	23	7 wks
24 Mar 84	JESSIE'S GIRL *RCA RICK 2*	43	6 wks

SPRINGFIELDS *UK, male/female vocal/instrumental group* — 66 wks

Date	Title	Pos	Wks
31 Aug 61	BREAKAWAY *Philips BF 1168*	31	8 wks
16 Nov 61	BAMBINO *Philips BF 1178*	16	11 wks
13 Dec 62 ●	ISLAND OF DREAMS *Philips 326557 BF*	5	26 wks
28 Mar 63 ●	SAY I WON'T BE THERE *Philips 326577 BF*	5	15 wks
25 Jul 63	COME ON HOME *Philips BF 1263*	31	6 wks

See also Dusty Springfield.

Bruce SPRINGSTEEN *US, male vocalist* — 102 wks

Date	Title	Pos	Wks
22 Nov 80	HUNGRY HEART *CBS 9309*	44	4 wks
13 Jun 81	THE RIVER *CBS A 1179*	35	6 wks
26 May 84	DANCING IN THE DARK *CBS A 4436*	28	7 wks
6 Oct 84	COVER ME *CBS 4662*	38	5 wks
12 Jan 85 ●	DANCING IN THE DARK (re-entry) *CBS A 4436*	4	16 wks
23 Mar 85	COVER ME (re-entry) *CBS 4662*	16	4 wks
15 Jun 85	I'M ON FIRE/ BORN IN THE USA *CBS A 6342*	5	12 wks
3 Aug 85	GLORY DAYS *CBS A 6375*	17	6 wks
14 Dec 85 ●	SANTA CLAUS IS COMIN' TO TOWN/ MY HOMETOWN *CBS A 6773*	9	5 wks
29 Nov 86	WAR *CBS 650193 7*	18	7 wks
7 Feb 87	FIRE *CBS 650381 7*	54	2 wks
23 May 87	BORN TO RUN *CBS BRUCE 2*	16	4 wks
3 Oct 87	BRILLIANT DISGUISE *CBS 651141 7*	20	5 wks
12 Dec 87	TUNNEL OF LOVE *CBS 651295 7*	45	4 wks
18 Jun 88	TOUGHER THAN THE REST *CBS BRUCE 3*	13	8 wks
24 Sep 88	SPARE PARTS *CBS BRUCE 4*	32	3 wks

SPRINGWATER — 12 wks

UK, male instrumentalist, Phil Cordell under a false group name

Date	Title	Pos	Wks
23 Oct 71 ●	I WILL RETURN *Polydor 2058 141*	5	12 wks

SPYRO GYRA *US, male instrumental group* — 10 wks

Date	Title	Pos	Wks
21 Jul 79	MORNING DANCE *Infinity INF 111*	17	10 wks

SQUADRONAIRES – *See Joan REGAN*

SQUEEZE *UK, male vocal/instrumental group* — 108 wks

Date	Title	Pos	Wks
8 Apr 78	TAKE ME I'M YOURS *A &M AMS 7335*	19	9 wks
10 Jun 78	BANG BANG *A &M AMS 7360*	49	5 wks
18 Nov 78	GOODBYE GIRL *A &M AMS 7398*	63	2 wks
24 Mar 79 ●	COOL FOR CATS *A &M AMS 7426*	2	11 wks
2 Jun 79 ●	UP THE JUNCTION *A &M AMS 7444*	2	11 wks
8 Sep 79	SLAP AND TICKLE *A &M AMS 7466*	24	8 wks
1 Mar 80	ANOTHER NAIL IN MY HEART *A &M AMS 7507*	17	9 wks
10 May 80	PULLING MUSSELS (FROM THE SHELL) *A &M AMS 7523*	44	6 wks
16 May 81	IS THAT LOVE *A &M AMS 8129*	35	8 wks
25 Jul 81	TEMPTED *A &M AMS 8147*	41	5 wks
10 Oct 81 ●	LABELLED WITH LOVE *A &M AMS 8166*	4	10 wks
24 Apr 82	BLACK COFFEE IN BED *A &M AMS 8219*	51	4 wks
23 Oct 82	ANNIE GET YOUR GUN *A &M AMS 8259*	43	4 wks
15 Jun 85	LAST TIME FOREVER *A &M AM 255*	45	5 wks
8 Aug 87	HOURGLASS *A &M AM 400*	16	10 wks
17 Oct 87	TRUST ME TO OPEN MY MOUTH *A &M AM 412*	72	1 wk

Billy SQUIER *US, male vocalist* — 3 wks

Date	Title	Pos	Wks
3 Oct 81	THE STROKE *Capitol CL 214*	52	3 wks

Dorothy SQUIRES *UK, female vocalist* — 46 wks

Date	Title	Pos	Wks
5 Jun 53	I'M WALKING BEHIND YOU *Polygon P 1068*	12	1 wk
20 Sep 69	FOR ONCE IN MY LIFE *President PT 267*	24	10 wks
20 Dec 69	FOR ONCE IN MY LIFE (re-entry) *President PT 267*	48	1 wk
21 Feb 70	TILL *President PT 281*	25	10 wks
9 May 70	TILL (re-entry) *President PT 281*	48	1 wk
8 Aug 70	MY WAY *President PT 305*	25	5 wks
19 Sep 70	MY WAY (re-entry) *President PT 305*	34	8 wks
28 Nov 70	MY WAY (2nd re-entry) *President PT 305*	25	10 wks

See also Dorothy Squires and Russ Conway.

Dorothy SQUIRES and Russ CONWAY — 10 wks

UK, female vocalist, male instrumentalist - piano

Date	Title	Pos	Wks
24 Aug 61	SAY IT WITH FLOWERS *Columbia DB 4665*	23	10 wks

See also Dorothy Squires; Russ Conway.

Jim STAFFORD *US, male vocalist* — 16 wks

Date	Title	Pos	Wks
27 Apr 74	SPIDERS AND SNAKES *MGM 2006 374*	14	8 wks
6 Jul 74	MY GIRL BILL *MGM 2006 423*	20	8 wks

Jo STAFFORD *US, female vocalist* — 28 wks

Date	Title	Pos	Wks
14 Nov 52 ★	YOU BELONG TO ME *Columbia DB 3152*	1	19 wks
19 Dec 52	JAMBALAYA *Columbia DB 3169*	11	2 wks
7 May 54 ●	MAKE LOVE TO ME *Philips PB 233*	8	1 wk
9 Dec 55	SUDDENLY THERE'S A VALLEY *Philips PB 509*	12	5 wks
3 Feb 56	SUDDENLY THERE'S A VALLEY (re-entry) *Philips PB 509*	19	1 wk

Terry STAFFORD *US, male vocalist* — 9 wks

Date	Title	Pos	Wks
7 May 64	SUSPICION *London HLU 9871*	31	9 wks

STAIFFI and his MUSTAFAS — 1 wk

France, male vocal/instrumental group

Date	Title	Pos	Wks
28 Jul 60	MUSTAFA *Pye International 7N 25057*	43	1 wk

Frank STALLONE *US, male vocalist* — 2 wks

Date	Title	Pos	Wks
22 Oct 83	FAR FROM OVER *RSO 95*	68	2 wks

STAMFORD BRIDGE *UK, male vocal group* — 1 wk

Date	Title	Pos	Wks
16 May 70	CHELSEA *Penny Farthing PEN 715*	47	1 wk

SMOKEY ROBINSON (right) AND THE MIRACLES had the first Tamla number one on the US Rhythm and Blues charts, 'Shop Around'. It took the top spot in 1961, six years before Robinson was granted top billing.

JIMMY SOMERVILLE is the only artist to have a chart hit with one of George Bush's campaign phrases ('Read My Lips').

A TOP TEN SMASH!

Percy Sledge

It Tears Me Up

Atlantic 2358

Produced by Marlin Greene & Quin Ivy

ATLANTIC

Far Left: Top Ten on the US R&B charts, yes, but PERCY SLEDGE missed in the UK with his successor to 'When A Man Loves A Woman' and 'Warm And Tender Love'.

Her greatest American success came with her own song 'Poetry Man', but in Britain PHOEBE SNOW scored with a Paul McCartney number.

Lisa STANSFIELD UK, female vocalst   **32 wks**

12 Aug 89	THIS IS THE RIGHT TIME *Arista 112512*	13	8 wks
28 Oct 89 ★	ALL AROUND THE WORLD *Arista 112693*	1	14 wks
10 Feb 90 ●	LIVE TOGETHER *Arista 112914*	10	6 wks
12 May 90	WHAT DID I DO TO YOU (EP) *Arista 113168*	25	4 wks

Tracks on What Did I Do To You *EP:* What Did I Do To You, My Apple Heart, Lay Me Down, Something's Happenin. *See also Coldcut.*

STAPLE SINGERS US, male/female vocal group   **14 wks**

10 Jun 72	I'LL TAKE YOU THERE *Stax 2025 110*	30	8 wks
8 Jun 74	IF YOU'RE READY (COME GO WITH ME) *Stax 2025 224*	34	6 wks

Cyril STAPLETON UK, orchestra   **27 wks**

27 May 55	ELEPHANT TANGO *Decca F 10488*	20	2 wks
1 Jul 55	ELEPHANT TANGO (re-entry) *Decca F 10488*	20	1 wk
22 Jul 55	ELEPHANT TANGO (2nd re-entry) *Decca F 10488*	19	1 wk
23 Sep 55 ●	BLUE STAR *Decca F 10559*	2	12 wks
6 Apr 56	THE ITALIAN THEME *Decca F 10703*	18	2 wks
1 Jun 56	THE HAPPY WHISTLER *Decca F 10735*	22	4 wks
19 Jul 57	FORGOTTEN DREAMS *Decca F 10912*	27	5 wks

STARDUST Sweden, male/female vocal/instrumental group   **3 wks**

8 Oct 77	ARIANA *Satril SAT 120*	42	3 wks

Alvin STARDUST UK, male vocalist   **119 wks**

3 Nov 73 ●	MY COO-CA-CHOO *Magnet MAG 1*	2	21 wks
16 Feb 74 ★	JEALOUS MIND *Magnet MAG 5*	1	11 wks
4 May 74 ●	RED DRESS *Magnet MAG 8*	7	8 wks
31 Aug 74 ●	YOU YOU YOU *Magnet MAG 13*	6	10 wks
30 Nov 74	TELL ME WHY *Magnet MAG 19*	16	8 wks
1 Feb 75	GOOD LOVE CAN NEVER DIE *Magnet MAG 21*	11	9 wks
12 Jul 75	SWEET CHEATIN' RITA *Magnet MAG 32*	37	4 wks
5 Sep 81 ●	PRETEND *Stiff BUY 124*	4	10 wks
21 Nov 81	A WONDERFUL TIME UP THERE *Stiff BUY 132*	56	8 wks
5 May 84 ●	I FEEL LIKE BUDDY HOLLY *Chrysalis CHS 2784*	7	11 wks
27 Oct 84 ●	I WON'T RUN AWAY *Chrysalis CHS 2829*	7	13 wks
15 Dec 84	SO NEAR TO CHRISTMAS *Chrysalis CHS 2835*	29	4 wks
23 Mar 85	GOT A LITTLE HEARTACHE *Chrysalis CHS 2856*	55	2 wks

Alvin started his career as Shane Fenton. See also Shane Fenton and the Fentones.

STARGARD US, female vocal group   **14 wks**

28 Jan 78	THEME FROM 'WHICH WAY IS UP' *MCA 346*	19	7 wks
15 Apr 78	LOVE IS SO EASY *MCA 354*	45	1 wk
9 Sep 78	WHAT YOU WAITING FOR *MCA 382*	39	6 wks

STARGAZERS UK, male/female vocal/instrumental group   **53 wks**

13 Feb 53	BROKEN WINGS *Decca F 10047*	11	1 wk
27 Feb 53 ★	BROKEN WINGS (re-entry) *Decca F 10047*	1	11 wks
19 Feb 54 ★	I SEE THE MOON *Decca F 10213*	1	15 wks
9 Apr 54	HAPPY WANDERER *Decca F 10259*	12	1 wk
4 Mar 55	SOMEBODY *Decca F 10437*	20	1 wk
3 Jun 55	CRAZY OTTO RAG *Decca F 10523*	18	3 wks
9 Sep 55 ●	CLOSE THE DOOR *Decca F 10594*	6	9 wks
11 Nov 55 ●	TWENTY TINY FINGERS *Decca F 10626*	4	11 wks
22 Jun 56	HOT DIGGITY *Decca F 10731*	28	1 wk

STARGAZERS UK, male vocal/instrumental group   **3 wks**

6 Feb 82	GROOVE BABY GROOVE (EP) *Epic EPC A 1924*	56	3 wks

Tracks on Groove Baby Groove *EP:* Groove Baby Groove/Jump Around/La Rock 'N' Roll (Quelques Uns A La Lune)/Red Light Green Light.

STARJETS UK, male vocal/instrumental group   **5 wks**

8 Sep 79	WAR STORIES *Epic EPC 7770*	51	5 wks

STARLAND VOCAL BAND   **10 wks**
US, male/female vocal group

7 Aug 76	AFTERNOON DELIGHT *RCA 2716*	18	10 wks

STARLIGHT Italy, male instrumental/production group   **11 wks**

10 Aug 89 ●	NUMERO UNO *Citybeat CBE 742*	9	11 wks

STARLITERS – *See Joey DEE and the STARLITERS*

Edwin STARR US, male vocalist   **68 wks**

12 May 66	STOP HER ON SIGHT (SOS) *Polydor BM 56 702*	35	8 wks
18 Aug 66	SOS/ HEADLINE NEWS *Polydor 56753*	39	3 wks
11 Dec 68	STOP HER ON SIGHT (SOS)/ HEADLINE NEWS (re-issues) *Polydor 56 753*	11	11 wks
13 Sep 69	25 MILES *Tamla Motown TMG 672*	36	6 wks
24 Sep 70 ●	WAR *Tamla Motown TMG 754*	3	12 wks
20 Feb 71	STOP THE WAR NOW *Tamla Motown TMG 764*	33	1 wk
27 Jan 79 ●	CONTACT *20th Century BTC 2396*	6	12 wks
26 May 79 ●	H.A.P.P.Y. RADIO *RCA TC 2408*	9	11 wks
1 Jun 85	IT AIN'T FAIR *Hippodrome HIP 101*	56	4 wks

Headline News not listed with SOS from 22 Jan 69 to 19 Feb 69.

Freddie STARR UK, male vocalist   **14 wks**

23 Feb 74 ●	IT'S YOU *Tiffany 6121 501*	9	10 wks
20 Dec 75	WHITE CHRISTMAS *Thunderbird THE 102*	41	4 wks

Kay STARR US, female vocalist   **58 wks**

5 Dec 52 ★	COMES A-LONG A-LOVE *Capitol CL 13808*	1	16 wks
24 Apr 53 ●	SIDE BY SIDE *Capitol CL 13871*	7	4 wks
19 Mar 54 ●	CHANGING PARTNERS *Capitol CL 14050*	4	14 wks
15 Oct 54	AM I A TOY OR A TREASURE *Capitol CL 14151*	17	3 wks
12 Nov 54	AM I A TOY OR A TREASURE (re-entry) *Capitol CL 14151*	20	1 wk
17 Feb 56 ★	ROCK AND ROLL WALTZ *HMV POP 168*	1	20 wks

Ringo STARR UK, male vocalist   **55 wks**

17 Apr 71 ●	IT DON'T COME EASY *Apple R 5898*	4	11 wks
1 Apr 72 ●	BACK OFF BOOGALOO *Apple R 5944*	2	10 wks
27 Oct 73 ●	PHOTOGRAPH *Apple R 5992*	8	13 wks
23 Feb 74 ●	YOU'RE SIXTEEN *Apple R 5995*	4	10 wks
30 Nov 74	ONLY YOU *Apple R 6000*	28	11 wks

STARSHIP US, female/male vocal/instrumental group   **32 wks**

16 Nov 85	WE BUILT THIS CITY *RCA PB 49929*	12	12 wks
8 Feb 86	SARA *RCA FB 49893*	66	3 wks
11 Apr 87 ★	NOTHING'S GONNA STOP US NOW *Grunt FB 49757*	1	17 wks

See also Jefferson Starship.

STARSHIP TROOPERS – *See Sarah BRIGHTMAN*

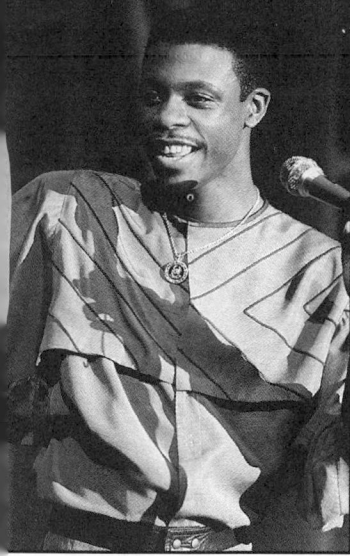

Above: KEITH SWEAT enjoyed a chart pun on his surname.

The star of the SPENCER DAVIS GROUP turned out not be Spencer Davis (top left) but Steve Winwood (bottom right).

FRANK STALLONE is shown with a real monster hit at an art gallery in Santa Monica.

STARSOUND
Holland, producer Jaap Eggermont with male/female session singers   **37 wks**

18 Apr 81	● STARS ON 45 *CBS 1102*	2	14 wks
4 Jul 81	● STARS ON 45 VOL.2 *CBS A 1407*	2	10 wks
19 Sep 81	STARS ON 45 VOL.3 *CBS A 1521*	17	6 wks
27 Feb 82	STARS ON STEVIE *CBS A 2041*	14	7 wks

STARTRAX *UK, male/female session group*   **8 wks**

1 Aug 81	STARTRAX CLUB DISCO *Picksy KSY 1001*	18	8 wks

STARTURN ON 45 (PINTS) *UK, male vocal group*   **9 wks**

24 Oct 81	STARTURN ON 45 (PINTS) *V Tone V TONE 003*	45	4 wks
30 Apr 88	PUMP UP THE BITTER *Pacific DRINK 1*	12	5 wks

STARVATION
Multi-national, male/female vocal/instrumental charity assembly   **6 wks**

9 Mar 85	STARVATION/ TAM-TAM POUR L'ETHIOPE *Zarjazz JAZZ 3*	33	6 wks

STATLER BROTHERS *US, male vocal group*   **4 wks**

24 Feb 66	FLOWERS ON THE WALL *CBS 201976*	38	4 wks

Candi STATON *US, female vocalist*   **47 wks**

29 May 76	● YOUNG HEARTS RUN FREE *Warner Bros. K 16730*	2	13 wks
18 Sep 76	DESTINY *Warner Bros. K 16806*	41	3 wks
23 Jul 77	● NIGHTS ON BROADWAY *Warner Bros. K 16972*	6	12 wks
3 Jun 78	HONEST I DO LOVE YOU *Warner Bros. K 17164*	48	5 wks
24 Apr 82	SUSPICIOUS MINDS *Sugarhill SH 112*	31	9 wks
31 May 86	YOUNG HEARTS RUN FREE (re-mix) *Warner Bros. W 8680*	47	5 wks

STATUS IV *US, male vocal group*   **3 wks**

9 Jul 83	YOU AIN'T REALLY DOWN *TMT TMT 4*	56	3 wks

STATUS QUO *UK, male vocal/instrumental group*   **377 wks**

24 Jan 68	● PICTURES OF MATCHSTICK MEN *Pye 7N 17449*	7	12 wks
21 Aug 68	● ICE IN THE SUN *Pye 7N 17581*	8	12 wks
28 May 69	ARE YOU GROWING TIRED OF MY LOVE *Pye 7N 17728*	46	2 wks
18 Jun 69	ARE YOU GROWING TIRED OF MY LOVE (re-entry) *Pye 7N 17728*	50	1 wk
2 May 70	DOWN THE DUSTPIPE *Pye 7N 17907*	12	17 wks
7 Nov 70	IN MY CHAIR *Pye 7N 17998*	21	14 wks
13 Jan 73	● PAPER PLANE *Pye 7N 45229*	8	11 wks
14 Apr 73	MEAN GIRL *Pye 7N 45229*	20	11 wks
8 Sep 73	● CAROLINE *Vertigo 6059 085*	5	13 wks
4 May 74	● BREAK THE RULES *Vertigo 6059 101*	8	8 wks
7 Dec 74	★ DOWN DOWN *Vertigo 6059 114*	1	11 wks
17 May 75	● ROLL OVER LAY DOWN *Vertigo QUO 13*	9	8 wks
14 Feb 76	● RAIN *Vertigo 6059 133*	7	7 wks
10 Jul 76	MYSTERY SONG *Vertigo 6059 146*	11	9 wks
11 Dec 76	● WILD SIDE OF LIFE *Vertigo 6059 153*	9	12 wks
8 Oct 77	● ROCKIN' ALL OVER THE WORLD *Vertigo 6059 184*	3	16 wks
2 Sep 78	AGAIN AND AGAIN *Vertigo QUO 1*	13	9 wks
25 Nov 78	ACCIDENT PRONE *Vertigo QUO 2*	36	8 wks
22 Sep 79	● WHATEVER YOU WANT *Vertigo 6059 242*	4	9 wks
24 Nov 79	LIVING ON AN ISLAND *Vertigo 6059 248*	16	10 wks
11 Oct 80	● WHAT YOU'RE PROPOSING *Vertigo QUO 3*	2	11 wks
6 Dec 80	LIES / DON'T DRIVE MY CAR *Vertigo QUO 4*	11	10 wks

28 Feb 81	● SOMETHING 'BOUT YOU BABY I LIKE	9	7 wks
28 Nov 81	● ROCK 'N' ROLL *Vertigo QUO 6*	8	11 wks
27 Mar 82	● DEAR JOHN *Vertigo QUO 7*	10	8 wks
12 Jun 82	SHE DON'T FOOL ME *Vertigo QUO 8*	36	5 wks
30 Oct 82	CAROLINE (LIVE AT THE N.E.C.) *Vertigo QUO 10*	13	7 wks
10 Sep 83	● OL' RAG BLUES *Vertigo QUO 11*	9	8 wks
5 Nov 83	A MESS OF THE BLUES *Vertigo QUO 12*	15	6 wks
10 Dec 83	● MARGUERITA TIME *Vertigo QUO 14*	3	11 wks
19 May 84	GOING DOWN TOWN TONIGHT *Vertigo QUO 15*	20	6 wks
27 Oct 84	● THE WANDERER *Vertigo QUO 16*	7	11 wks
17 May 86	● ROLLIN' HOME *Vertigo QUO 18*	9	6 wks
26 Jul 86	RED SKY *Vertigo QUO 19*	19	8 wks
4 Oct 86	● IN THE ARMY NOW *Vertigo QUO 20*	2	14 wks
6 Dec 86	DREAMIN' *Vertigo QUO 21*	15	8 wks
26 Mar 88	AIN'T COMPLAINING *Vertigo QUO 22*	19	6 wks
21 May 88	WHO GETS THE LOVE *Vertigo QUO 23*	34	4 wks
20 Aug 88	RUNNING ALL OVER THE WORLD *Vertigo QUAID 1*	17	6 wks
3 Dec 88	● BURNING BRIDGES (ON AND OFF AND ON AGAIN) *Vertigo QUO 25*	5	10 wks
28 Oct 89	NOT AT ALL *Vertigo QUO 26*	50	2 wks
29 Sep 90	● THE ANNIVERSARY WALTZ - PART 1 *Vertigo QUO 28*	2	9 wks
15 Dec 90	THE ANNIVERSARY WALTZ - PART 2 *Vertigo QUO 29*	16†	3 wks

Don't Drive My Car listed from 20 Dec 80 only. Running All Over The World is a re-recorded version of Rockin' All Over The World, with a slightly changed lyric, released to promote the Race Against Time of 28 Aug 88.

STEALER'S WHEEL *UK, male vocal/instrumental group*   **22 wks**

26 May 73	● STUCK IN THE MIDDLE WITH YOU *A & M AMS 7036*	8	10 wks
1 Sep 73	EVERYTHING'L TURN OUT FINE *A & M AMS 7079*	33	6 wks
26 Jan 74	STAR *A & M AMS 7094*	25	6 wks

STEAM *US, male vocal/instrumental group*   **14 wks**

31 Jan 70	● NA NA HEY HEY KISS HIM GOODBYE *Fontana TF 1058*	9	14 wks

Anthony STEEL and the RADIO REVELLERS *UK, male vocalist/male instrumental group*   **6 wks**

10 Sep 54	WEST OF ZANZIBAR *Polygon P 1114*	11	6 wks

STEEL PULSE *UK, male vocal/instrumental group*   **12 wks**

1 Apr 78	KU KLUX KLAN *Island WIP 6428*	41	4 wks
8 Jul 78	PRODIGAL SON *Island WIP 6449*	35	6 wks
23 Jun 79	SOUND SYSTEM *Island WIP 6490*	71	2 wks

Tommy STEELE *UK, male vocalist*   **145 wks**

26 Oct 56	ROCK WITH THE CAVEMAN *Decca F 10795*	13	4 wks
30 Nov 56	ROCK WITH THE CAVEMAN (re-entry) *Decca F 10795*	23	1 wk
14 Dec 56	★ SINGING THE BLUES *Decca F 10819*	1	13 wks
15 Feb 57	KNEE DEEP IN THE BLUES *Decca F 10849*	15	9 wks
19 Apr 57	SINGING THE BLUES (re-entry) *Decca F 10819*	24	1 wk
3 May 57	BUTTERFINGERS *Decca F 10877*	25	1 wk
17 May 57	● BUTTERFINGERS (re-entry) *Decca F 10877*	8	17 wks
17 May 57	SINGING THE BLUES (2nd re-entry) *Decca F 10849*	29	1 wk
16 Aug 57	● WATER WATER/ HANDFUL OF SONGS *Decca F 10923*	5	16 wks
30 Aug 57	SHIRALEE *Decca F 10896*	11	4 wks
22 Nov 57	HEY YOU *Decca F 10941*	28	1 wk
13 Dec 57	WATER WATER/ HANDFUL OF SONGS (re-entry) *Decca F 10923*	28	1 wk
7 Mar 58	NAIROBI *Decca F 10991*	3	11 wks
25 Apr 58	HAPPY GUITAR *Decca F 10976*	20	5 wks
18 Jul 58	THE ONLY MAN ON THE ISLAND *Decca F 11041*	16	8 wks

14 Nov 58 ●	COME ON LET'S GO *Decca F 11072*	**10**	13 wks
14 Aug 59	TALLAHASSEE LASSIE *Decca F 11152*	**16**	4 wks
28 Aug 59	GIVE GIVE GIVE *Decca F 11152*	**28**	2 wks
25 Sep 59	TALLAHASSEE LASSIE (re-entry) *Decca F 11152*	**25**	1 wk
4 Dec 59 ●	LITTLE WHITE BULL *Decca F 11177*	**6**	12 wks
10 Mar 60	LITTLE WHITE BULL (re-entry) *Decca F 11177*	**30**	5 wks
23 Jun 60 ●	WHAT A MOUTH *Decca F 11245*	**5**	11 wks
29 Dec 60	MUST BE SANTA *Decca F 11299*	**40**	1 wk
17 Aug 61	WRITING ON THE WALL *Decca F 11372*	**30**	5 wks

Handful Of Songs listed *together with* Water Water *from week of 23 Aug 57. See also Various Artists - All Star Hit Parade No.2.*

STEELEYE SPAN   18 wks
UK, male/female vocal/instrumental group

8 Dec 73	GAUDETE *Chrysalis CHS 2007*	**14**	9 wks
15 Nov 75 ●	ALL AROUND MY HAT *Chrysalis CHS 2078*	**5**	9 wks

STEELY DAN *US, male vocal/instrumental group*   21 wks

30 Aug 75	DO IT AGAIN *ABC 4075*	**39**	4 wks
11 Dec 76	HAITIAN DIVORCE *ABC 4152*	**17**	9 wks
29 Jul 78	FM (NO STATIC AT ALL) *MCA 374*	**49**	4 wks
2 Sep 78	FM (NO STATIC AT ALL) (re-entry) *MCA 374*	**75**	1 wk
10 Mar 79	RIKKI DON'T LOSE THAT NUMBER *ABC 4241*	**58**	3 wks

Jim STEINMAN *US, male vocalist*   9 wks

4 Jul 81	ROCK 'N' ROLL DREAMS COME THROUGH *Epic EPC A 1236*	**52**	7 wks
23 Jun 84	TONIGHT IS WHAT IT MEANS TO BE YOUNG *MCA MCA 889*	**67**	2 wks

First hit features vocal by Rory Dodd. Second hit has credit: 'Jim Steinman and Fire Inc'.

STEINSKI and MASS MEDIA   2 wks
US, male producer and rapper

31 Jan 87	WE'LL BE RIGHT BACK *Fourth & Broadway BRW 59*	**63**	2 wks

Mike STEIPHENSON – *See BURUNDI STEIPHENSON BLACK*

Doreen STEPHENS – *See Billy COTTON and his BAND*

Martin STEPHENSON and the DAINTEES   2 wks
UK, male vocal/instrumental group

8 Nov 86	BOAT TO BOLIVIA *Kitchenware SL 27*	**70**	2 wks

See also Daintees

STEPPENWOLF *US/Canada, male vocal/instrumental group*   9 wks

11 Jun 69	BORN TO BE WILD *Stateside SS 8017*	**30**	7 wks
9 Aug 69	BORN TO BE WILD (re-entry) *Stateside SS 8017*	**50**	2 wks

STEPZ – *See QUARTZ featuring STEPZ*

STEREO MCs *UK, male rap group*   1 wk

29 Sep 90	ELEVATE MY MIND *Fourth & Broadway BRW 186*	**74**	1 wk

STETASONIC *US, male rap group*   2 wks

24 Sep 88	TALKIN' ALL THAT JAZZ *Breakout USA 640*	**73**	2 wks

STEVE and EYDIE *US, male/female vocal duo*   13 wks

22 Aug 63 ●	I WANT TO STAY HERE *CBS AAG 163*	**3**	13 wks

See also Steve Lawrence; Eydie Gormé.

April STEVENS – *See Nino TEMPO and April STEVENS*

Cat STEVENS *UK, male vocalist*   96 wks

20 Oct 66	I LOVE MY DOG *Deram DM 102*	**28**	7 wks
12 Jan 67 ●	MATTHEW AND SON *Deram DM 110*	**2**	10 wks
30 Mar 67 ●	I'M GONNA GET ME A GUN *Deram DM 118*	**6**	10 wks
2 Aug 67	A BAD NIGHT *Deram DM 140*	**20**	8 wks
20 Dec 67	KITTY *Deram DM 156*	**47**	1 wk
27 Jun 70 ●	LADY D'ARBANVILLE *Island WIP 6086*	**8**	13 wks
28 Aug 71	MOON SHADOW *Island WIP 6092*	**22**	11 wks
1 Jan 72 ●	MORNING HAS BROKEN *Island WIP 6121*	**9**	13 wks
9 Dec 72	CAN'T KEEP IT IN *Island WIP 6152*	**13**	12 wks
24 Aug 74	ANOTHER SATURDAY NIGHT *Island WIP 6206*	**19**	8 wks
2 Jul 77	(REMEMBER THE DAYS OF THE) OLD SCHOOL YARD *Island WIP 6387*	**44**	3 wks

Connie STEVENS *US, female vocalist*   12 wks

5 May 60 ●	SIXTEEN REASONS *Warner Bros. WB 3*	**9**	11 wks
4 Aug 60	SIXTEEN REASONS (re-entry) *Warner Bros. WB 3*	**45**	1 wk

See also Edward Byrnes and Connie Stevens.

Ray STEVENS *US, male vocalist*   64 wks

16 May 70 ●	EVERYTHING IS BEAUTIFUL *CBS 4953*	**6**	16 wks
13 Mar 71 ●	BRIDGET THE MIDGET (THE QUEEN OF THE BLUES) *CBS 7070*	**2**	14 wks
25 Mar 72	TURN YOUR RADIO ON *CBS 7634*	**33**	4 wks
25 May 74 ★	THE STREAK *Janus 6146 201*	**1**	12 wks
21 Jun 75 ●	MISTY *Janus 6146 204*	**2**	10 wks
27 Sep 75	INDIAN LOVE CALL *Janus 6146 205*	**34**	4 wks
5 Mar 77	IN THE MOOD *Warner Bros. K 16875*	**31**	4 wks

In The Mood *features Ray Stevens not as a conventional vocalist, but as a group of chickens. In the US, he billed himself on this record as Henhouse Five Plus Too.*

Ricky STEVENS *UK, male vocalist*   7 wks

14 Dec 61	I CRIED FOR YOU *Columbia DB 4739*	**34**	7 wks

Shakin' STEVENS *UK, male vocalist*   259 wks

16 Feb 80	HOT DOG *Epic EPC 8090*	**24**	9 wks
16 Aug 80	MARIE MARIE *Epic EPC 8725*	**19**	10 wks
28 Feb 81 ★	THIS OLE HOUSE *Epic EPC 9555*	**1**	17 wks
2 May 81 ●	YOU DRIVE ME CRAZY *Epic A1165*	**2**	12 wks
25 Jul 81 ★	GREEN DOOR *Epic A1354*	**1**	12 wks
10 Oct 81	IT'S RAINING *Epic A1643*	**10**	9 wks
16 Jan 82 ★	OH JULIE *Epic EPC A1742*	**1**	10 wks
24 Apr 82 ●	SHIRLEY *Epic EPC A2087*	**6**	6 wks
21 Aug 82	GIVE ME YOUR HEART TONIGHT *Epic EPC A2656*	**11**	10 wks
16 Oct 82	I'LL BE SATISFIED *Epic EPC A2846*	**10**	8 wks
11 Dec 82 ●	THE SHAKIN' STEVENS EP *Epic SHAKY 1*	**2**	7 wks
23 Jul 83	IT'S LATE *Epic A 3565*	**11**	7 wks
5 Nov 83 ●	CRY JUST A LITTLE BIT *Epic A 3774*	**3**	12 wks
24 Mar 84 ●	A LOVE WORTH WAITING FOR *Epic A 4291*	**2**	10 wks
15 Sep 84 ●	A LETTER TO YOU *Epic A 4677*	**10**	8 wks
24 Nov 84 ●	TEARDROPS *Epic A 4882*	**5**	9 wks
2 Mar 85	BREAKING UP MY HEART *Epic A 6072*	**14**	7 wks
12 Oct 85	LIPSTICK POWDER AND PAINT *Epic A 6610*	**11**	9 wks
7 Dec 85 ★	MERRY CHRISTMAS EVERYONE *Epic A 6769*	**1**	8 wks
8 Feb 86	TURNING AWAY *Epic A 6819*	**15**	7 wks
1 Nov 86	BECAUSE I LOVE YOU *Epic SHAKY 2*	**14**	10 wks

20 Dec 86	MERRY CHRISTMAS EVERYONE (re-entry)		
	Epic A 6769	58	3 wks
27 Jun 87	A LITTLE BOOGIE WOOGIE (IN THE BACK OF MY		
	MIND) *Epic SHAKY 3*.	12	10 wks
19 Sep 87	COME SEE ABOUT ME *Epic SHAKY 4*.	24	6 wks
28 Nov 87 ●	WHAT DO YOU WANT TO MAKE THOSE EYES AT		
	ME FOR *Epic SHAKY 5*	5	8 wks
23 Jul 88	FEEL THE NEED IN ME *Epic SHAKY 6*.	26	5 wks
15 Oct 88	HOW MANY TEARS CAN YOU HIDE *Epic SHAKY 7*	47	4 wks
10 Dec 88	TRUE LOVE *Epic SHAKY 8*	23	6 wks
18 Feb 89	JEZEBEL *Epic SHAKY 9*	58	2 wks
13 May 89	LOVE ATTACK *Epic SHAKY 10*	28	4 wks
24 Feb 90	I MIGHT *Epic SHAKY 11*.	18	6 wks
12 May 90	YES I DO *Epic SHAKY 12*	60	2 wks
18 Aug 90	PINK CHAMPAGNE *Epic SHAKY 13*	59	2 wks
13 Oct 90	MY CUTIE CUTIE *Epic SHAKY 14*.	75	1 wk
15 Dec 90	THE BEST CHRISTMAS OF THEM ALL		
	Epic SHAKY 15.	19†	3 wks

Tracks on The Shakin' Stevens EP: Blue Christmas/Que Sera Sera/Josephine/Lawdy Miss Clawdy.
See also Shaky and Bonnie.

STEVENSON'S ROCKET   **5 wks**
UK, male vocal/instrumental group

29 Nov 75	ALRIGHT BABY *Magnet MAG 47*	37	2 wks
20 Dec 75	ALRIGHT BABY (re-entry) *Magnet MAG 47*	45	3 wks

Al STEWART *UK, male vocalist*   **6 wks**

29 Jan 77	YEAR OF THE CAT *RCA 2771*	31	6 wks

Amii STEWART *US, female vocalist*   **53 wks**

7 Apr 79 ●	KNOCK ON WOOD *Atlantic/Hansa K 11214*	6	12 wks
16 Jun 79 ●	LIGHT MY FIRE/ 137 DISCO HEAVEN (MEDLEY)		
	Atlantic/Hansa K 11278	5	11 wks
3 Nov 79	JEALOUSY *Atlantic/Hansa K 11386*	58	3 wks
19 Jan 80	PARADISE BIRD/ THE LETTER *Atlantic/Hansa K 11424*.....	39	4 wks
29 Dec 84	FRIENDS *RCA 471*	12	11 wks
17 Aug 85 ●	KNOCK ON WOOD/ LIGHT MY FIRE (re-mixes)		
	Sedition EDIT 3303	7	12 wks

See also Amii Stewart and Johnny Bristol; Amii Stewart and Deon Estus.

Amii STEWART and Johnny BRISTOL   **5 wks**
US, female/male vocal duo

19 Jul 80	MY GUY - MY GIRL (MEDLEY) *Atlantic/Hansa K 11550*.......	39	5 wks

See also Amii Stewart; Johnny Bristol.

Amii STEWART and Deon ESTUS   **3 wks**
US, female/male vocal duo

25 Jan 86	MY GUY - MY GIRL *Sedition Edit 3310*	63	3 wks

See also Amii Stewart.

Andy STEWART *UK, male vocalist*   **67 wks**

15 Dec 60	DONALD WHERE'S YOUR TROOSERS		
	Top Rank JAR 427	37	1 wk
12 Jan 61	A SCOTTISH SOLDIER *Top Rank JAR 512*	19	38 wks
1 Jun 61	THE BATTLE'S O'ER *Top Rank JAR 565*.	28	13 wks
12 Oct 61	A SCOTTISH SOLDIER (re-entry) *Top Rank JAR 512*	43	2 wks
12 Aug 65	DR. FINLAY *HMV POP 1454*	50	1 wk
26 Aug 65	DR. FINLAY (re-entry) *HMV POP 1454*	43	4 wks
9 Dec 89 ●	DONALD WHERE'S YOUR TROOSERS (re-issue)		
	Stone SON 2353	4	8 wks

Billy STEWART *US, male vocalist*   **2 wks**

8 Sep 66	SUMMERTIME *Chess CRS 8040*	39	2 wks

Dave STEWART *UK, male instrumentalist - keyboards*   **10 wks**

14 Mar 81	WHAT BECOMES OF THE BROKEN HEARTED?		
	Stiff BROKEN 1.	13	10 wks

Guest vocals: Colin Blunstone. See also Colin Blunstone; Neil MacArthur; Dave Stewart with Barbara Gaskin.

Dave STEWART with Barbara GASKIN   **20 wks**
UK, male instrumentalist - keyboards, with female vocalist

19 Sep 81 ★	IT'S MY PARTY *Broken BROKEN 2*	1	13 wks
13 Aug 83	BUSY DOING NOTHING *Broken BROKEN 5*	49	4 wks
14 Jun 86	THE LOCOMOTION *Broken BROKEN 8*.	70	3 wks

See also Dave Stewart.

David A. STEWART   **14 wks**
UK, male vocalist/instrumentalist - guitar

24 Feb 90 ●	LILY WAS HERE *RCA ZB 43045*	6	12 wks
18 Aug 90	JACK TALKING *RCA PB 43907*	69	2 wks

Lily Was Here is credited to David A. Stewart featuring Candy Dulfer, Jack Talking to Dave Stewart and the Spiritual Cowboys. See also Candy Dulfer.

Jermaine STEWART *US, male vocalist*   **42 wks**

9 Aug 86 ●	WE DON'T HAVE TO... *10 TEN 96*	2	14 wks
1 Nov 86	JODY *10 TEN 143*	50	4 wks
16 Jan 88 ●	SAY IT AGAIN *10 TEN 188*	7	12 wks
2 Apr 88	GET LUCKY *Siren SRN 82*	13	9 wks
24 Sep 88	DON'T TALK DIRTY TO ME *Siren SRN 86*	61	3 wks

John STEWART *US, male vocalist*   **6 wks**

30 Jun 79	GOLD *RSO 35*	43	6 wks

Rod STEWART *UK, male vocalist*   **346 wks**

4 Sep 71	REASON TO BELIEVE *Mercury 6052 097*	19	2 wks
18 Sep 71 ★	MAGGIE MAY *Mercury 6052 097*.	1	19 wks
12 Aug 72 ★	YOU WEAR IT WELL *Mercury 6052 171*	1	12 wks
18 Nov 72 ●	ANGEL / WHAT MADE MILWAUKEE FAMOUS (HAS		
	MADE A LOSER OUT OF ME) *Mercury 6052 198*	4	11 wks
8 Sep 73 ●	OH NO NOT MY BABY *Mercury 6052 371*	6	9 wks
5 Oct 74 ●	FAREWELL/ BRING IT ON HOME TO ME/ YOU		
	SEND ME *Mercury 6167 033*.	7	7 wks
16 Aug 75 ★	SAILING *Warner Bros. K 16600*	1	11 wks
15 Nov 75 ●	THIS OLD HEART OF MINE *Riva 1*.	4	9 wks
5 Jun 76 ●	TONIGHT'S THE NIGHT *Riva 3*	5	9 wks
21 Aug 76 ●	THE KILLING OF GEORGIE *Riva 4*	2	10 wks
4 Sep 76 ●	SAILING (re-entry) *Warner Bros. K 16600*	3	20 wks
20 Nov 76	GET BACK *Riva 6*	11	9 wks
4 Dec 76	MAGGIE MAY (re-entry) *Mercury 6160 006*.	31	7 wks
23 Apr 77 ★	I DON'T WANT TO TALK ABOUT IT/ FIRST CUT IS		
	THE DEEPEST *Riva 7*.	1	13 wks
15 Oct 77 ●	YOU'RE IN MY HEART *Riva 11*	3	10 wks
28 Jan 78 ●	HOTLEGS/ I WAS ONLY JOKING *Riva 10*	5	8 wks
27 May 78 ●	OLE OLA (MUHLER BRASILEIRA) *Riva 15*	4	6 wks
18 Nov 78 ★	DA YA THINK I'M SEXY? *Riva 17*.	1	13 wks
3 Feb 79	AIN'T LOVE A BITCH *Riva 18*.	11	8 wks
5 May 79	BLONDES (HAVE MORE FUN) *Riva 19*	63	3 wks
31 May 80	IF LOVING YOU IS WRONG (I DON'T WANT TO BE		
	RIGHT) *Riva 23*	23	9 wks
8 Nov 80	PASSION *Riva 26*	17	10 wks
20 Dec 80	MY GIRL *Riva 28*.	32	7 wks

Above: STING, spreads a little happiness during his Police days.

'All Around the World' by LISA STANSFIELD and her songwriting partners Ian Devaney and Andy Morris won the Ivor Novello Award for Best Popular Song.

Top Left: ROD STEWART topped the UK and US singles and album charts simultaneously in October 1971 with 'Maggie May' and *Every Picture Tells A Story*.

THE SUGARCUBES were the hottest act from Iceland.

17 Oct 81	● TONIGHT I'M YOURS (DON'T HURT ME) Riva 33	8	13 wks
12 Dec 81	YOUNG TURKS Riva 34	11	9 wks
27 Feb 82	HOW LONG Riva 35	41	4 wks
4 Jun 83	★ BABY JANE Warner Bros. W 9608	1	14 wks
27 Aug 83	● WHAT AM I GONNA DO Warner Bros. W 9564	3	8 wks
10 Dec 83	SWEET SURRENDER Warner Bros. W 9440	23	9 wks
26 May 84	INFATUATION Warner Bros. W 9256	27	7 wks
28 Jul 84	SOME GUYS HAVE ALL THE LUCK Warner Bros. W 9204	15	10 wks
24 May 86	LOVE TOUCH Warner Bros. W 8668	27	5 wks
5 Jul 86	LOVE TOUCH (re-entry) Warner Bros. W 8668	69	3 wks
12 Jul 86	● EVERY BEAT OF MY HEART Warner Bros. W 8625	2	9 wks
20 Sep 86	ANOTHER HEARTACHE Warner Bros. W 8631	54	2 wks
28 Mar 87	SAILING (2nd re-entry) Warner Bros. K 16600	41	3 wks
28 May 88	LOST IN YOU Warner Bros. W 7927	21	6 wks
13 Aug 88	FOREVER YOUNG Warner Bros. W 7796	57	3 wks
6 May 89	MY HEART CAN'T TELL YOU NO Warner Bros. W 7729	49	4 wks
11 Nov 89	THIS OLD HEART OF MINE Warner Bros. W 2686	51	3 wks
13 Jan 90	● DOWNTOWN TRAIN Warner Bros. W 2647	10	12 wks

Ole Ola *features the Scottish World Cup Football Squad. The sleeve of* This Old Heart Of Mine *credits Ronald Isley. See also Faces; Rod Stewart and Tina Turner; Jeff Beck and Rod Stewart; Python Lee Jackson.*

Rod STEWART and Tina TURNER
UK/US, male/female vocalists   **6 wks**

24 Nov 90	● IT TAKES TWO Warner Bros. ROD 1	5†	6 wks

See also Rod Stewart; Tina Turner.

STIFF LITTLE FINGERS
UK, male vocal/instrumental group   **39 wks**

29 Sep 79	STRAW DOGS Chrysalis CHS 2368	44	4 wks
16 Feb 80	AT THE EDGE Chrysalis CHS 2406	15	9 wks
24 May 80	NOBODY'S HERO/ TIN SOLDIERS Chrysalis CHS 2424	36	5 wks
2 Aug 80	BACK TO FRONT Chrysalis CHS 2447	49	4 wks
28 Mar 81	JUST FADE AWAY Chrysalis CHS 2510	47	6 wks
30 May 81	SILVER LINING Chrysalis CHS 2517	68	3 wks
23 Jan 82	LISTEN (EP) Chrysalis CHS 2580	33	6 wks
18 Sep 82	BITS OF KIDS Chrysalis CHS 2637	73	2 wks

Tracks on Listen *EP: That's When Your Blood Bumps/Two Guitars Clash/Listen/Sad-Eyed People.*

Stephen STILLS US, male vocalist   **4 wks**

13 Mar 71	LOVE THE ONE YOU'RE WITH Atlantic 2091 046	37	4 wks

See also Crosby, Stills and Nash; Crosby Stills Nash and Young.

STING UK, male vocalist   **55 wks**

14 Aug 82	SPREAD A LITTLE HAPPINESS A &M AMS 8217	16	8 wks
8 Jun 85	IF YOU LOVE SOMEBODY SET THEM FREE A &M AM 258	26	7 wks
24 Aug 85	LOVE IS THE SEVENTH WAVE A &M AM 272	41	5 wks
19 Oct 85	FORTRESS AROUND YOUR HEART A &M AM 286	49	3 wks
7 Dec 85	RUSSIANS A &M AM 292	12	11 wks
15 Feb 86	MOON OVER BOURBON STREET A &M AM 305	44	4 wks
1 Mar 86	RUSSIANS (re-entry) A &M AM 292	71	1 wk
7 Nov 87	WE'LL BE TOGETHER A &M AM 410	41	4 wks
20 Feb 88	ENGLISHMAN IN NEW YORK A &M AM 431	51	3 wks
9 Apr 88	FRAGILE A &M AM 439	70	2 wks
11 Aug 90	AN ENGLISHMAN IN NEW YORK (re-mix) A &M AM 580	15	7 wks

STINGERS – See B. BUMBLE and the STINGERS

Catherine STOCK UK, female vocalist   **6 wks**

18 Oct 86	TO HAVE AND TO HOLD Sierra FED 29	17	6 wks

STOCK AITKEN WATERMAN UK, male producers   **27 wks**

25 Jul 87	ROADBLOCK Breakout USA 611	13	9 wks
24 Oct 87	● MR. SLEAZE London NANA 14	3	10 wks
12 Dec 87	PACKJAMMED (WITH THE PARTY POSSE) Breakout USA 620	41	6 wks
3 Dec 88	SS PAPARAZZI PWL PWL 22	68	2 wks

The listed flip side of Mr. Sleaze was Love In The First Degree by Bananarama. See also Bananarama; England Football Team; 14-18; Christians, Holly Johnson, Paul McCartney, Gerry Marsden and Stock Aitken Waterman.

Rhet STOLLER UK, male instrumentalist – guitar   **8 wks**

12 Jan 61	CHARIOT Decca F 11302	26	8 wks

Morris STOLOFF US, orchestra   **11 wks**

1 Jun 56	● MOONGLOW/ THEME FROM PICNIC Brunswick 05553	7	11 wks

R & J STONE UK/US, male/female vocal duo   **9 wks**

10 Jan 76	● WE DO IT RCA 2616	5	9 wks

STONE ROSES UK, male vocal/instrumental group   **47 wks**

29 Jul 89	SHE BANGS THE DRUMS Silvertone ORE 6	36	3 wks
25 Nov 89	● WHAT THE WORLD IS WAITING FOR/ FOOL'S GOLD Silvertone ORE 13	8	14 wks
6 Jan 90	SALLY CINNAMON Revolver REV 36	75	1 wk
20 Jan 90	SALLY CINNAMON (re-entry) Revolver REV 36	46	4 wks
3 Mar 90	● ELEPHANT STONE Silvertone ORE 1	8	6 wks
17 Mar 90	MADE OF STONE Silvertone ORE 2	20	4 wks
31 Mar 90	SHE BANGS THE DRUMS (re-entry) Silvertone ORE 6	34	3 wks
14 Jul 90	● ONE LOVE Silvertone ORE 17	4	7 wks
15 Sep 90	WHAT THE WORLD IS WAITING FOR/ FOOL'S GOLD (re-entry) Silvertone ORE 13	22	5 wks

STONEBRIDGE McGUINNESS   **2 wks**
UK, male vocal/instrumental duo

14 Jul 79	OO-EEH BABY RCA PB 5163	54	2 wks

STONEFREE UK, male vocalist   **1 wk**

23 May 87	CAN'T SAY GOODBYE Ensign ENY 607	73	1 wk

STOP THE VIOLENCE   **1 wk**
US, male/female rap charity ensemble

18 Feb 89	SELF DESTRUCTION Jive BDPST 1	75	1 wk

STORM UK, male/female vocal/instrumental group   **10 wks**

17 Nov 79	IT'S MY HOUSE Scope SC 10	36	10 wks

Danny STORM UK, male vocalist   **4 wks**

12 Apr 62	HONEST I DO Piccadilly 7N 35025	42	4 wks

Rebecca STORM *UK, female vocalist* **13 wks**

13 Jul 85	**THE SHOW (THEME FROM 'CONNIE')**			
	Towerbell TVP 3	**22**	13 wks	

STORYVILLE JAZZ BAND – *See Bob WALLIS and his STORYVILLE JAZZ BAND*

Nick STRAKER BAND **15 wks**
UK, male vocal/instrumental group

2 Aug 80	**A WALK IN THE PARK** *CBS 8525*	**20**	12 wks
15 Nov 80	**LEAVING ON THE MIDNIGHT TRAIN** *CBS 9088*	**61**	3 wks

Peter STRAKER and the HANDS OF DR. TELENY **4 wks**
UK, male vocalist and male vocal/instrumental group

19 Feb 72	**THE SPIRIT IS WILLING** *RCA 2163*	**40**	4 wks

STRANGE BEHAVIOUR – *See Jane KENNAWAY and STRANGE BEHAVIOUR*

STRANGLERS *UK, male vocal/instrumental group* **185 wks**

19 Feb 77	**(GET A) GRIP (ON YOURSELF)**		
	United Artists UP 36211	**44**	4 wks
21 May 77	● **PEACHES / GO BUDDY GO** *United Artists UP 36248*	**8**	14 wks
30 Jul 77	● **SOMETHING BETTER CHANGE/ STRAIGHTEN OUT** *United Artists UP 36277*	**9**	8 wks
24 Sep 77	● **NO MORE HEROES** *United Artists UP 36300*	**8**	9 wks
4 Feb 78	**FIVE MINUTES** *United Artists UP 36350*	**11**	9 wks
6 May 78	**NICE 'N SLEAZY** *United Artists UP 36379*	**18**	8 wks
12 Aug 78	**WALK ON BY** *United Artists UP 36429*	**21**	8 wks
18 Aug 79	**DUCHESS** *United Artists BP 308*	**14**	9 wks
20 Oct 79	**NUCLEAR DEVICE (THE WIZARD OF AUS)** *United Artists BP 318*	**36**	4 wks
1 Dec 79	**DON'T BRING HARRY** (EP) *United Artists STR 1*	**41**	3 wks
22 Mar 80	**BEAR CAGE** *United Artists BP 344*	**36**	5 wks
7 Jun 80	**WHO WANTS THE WORLD** *United Artists BPX 355*	**39**	4 wks
31 Jan 81	**THROWN AWAY** *Liberty BP 383*	**42**	4 wks
14 Nov 81	**LET ME INTRODUCE YOU TO THE FAMILY** *United Artists BP 405*	**42**	3 wks
9 Jan 82	● **GOLDEN BROWN** *Liberty BP 407*	**2**	12 wks
24 Apr 82	**LA FOLIE** *Liberty BP 410*	**47**	3 wks
24 Jul 82	● **STRANGE LITTLE GIRL** *Liberty BP 412*	**7**	9 wks
8 Jan 83	● **EUROPEAN FEMALE** *Epic EPC A 2893*	**9**	6 wks
26 Feb 83	**MIDNIGHT SUMMER DREAM** *Epic EPC A 3167*	**35**	4 wks
6 Aug 83	**PARADISE** *Epic A 3387*	**48**	3 wks
6 Oct 84	**SKIN DEEP** *Epic A 4738*	**15**	7 wks
1 Dec 84	**NO MERCY** *Epic A 4921*	**37**	7 wks
16 Feb 85	**LET ME DOWN EASY** *Epic A 6045*	**48**	4 wks
23 Aug 86	**NICE IN NICE** *Epic 650057*	**30**	5 wks
18 Oct 86	**ALWAYS THE SUN** *Epic SOLAR 1*	**30**	5 wks
13 Dec 86	**BIG IN AMERICA** *Epic HUGE 1.*	**48**	6 wks
7 Mar 87	**SHAKIN' LIKE A LEAF** *Epic SHEIK 1.*	**58**	4 wks
9 Jan 88	● **ALL DAY AND ALL OF THE NIGHT** *Epic VICE 1*	**7**	7 wks
28 Jan 89	**GRIP '89 (GET A) GRIP (ON YOURSELF)** (re-mix) *EMI EM 84.*	**33**	3 wks
17 Feb 90	**96 TEARS** *Epic TEARS 1*	**17**	6 wks
21 Apr 90	**SWEET SMELL OF SUCCESS** *Epic TEARS 2*	**65**	2 wks

Go Buddy Go *credited with* Peaches *from 11 Jun 77.* Straighten Out *credited with* Something Better Change *from 13 Aug 77. Tracks on* Don't Bring Harry *EP:* Don't Bring Harry/Wired/Crabs (Live)/In The Shadows (Live).

STRAWBERRY SWITCHBLADE **26 wks**
UK, female vocal duo

17 Nov 84	● **SINCE YESTERDAY** *Korova KOW 38*	**5**	17 wks
23 Mar 85	**LET HER GO** *Korova KOW 39.*	**59**	5 wks
21 Sep 85	**JOLENE** *Korova KOW 42*	**53**	4 wks

STRAWBS *UK, male vocal/instrumental group* **27 wks**

28 Oct 72	**LAY DOWN** *A & M AMS 7035.*	**12**	13 wks
27 Jan 73	● **PART OF THE UNION** *A & M AMS 7047*	**2**	11 wks
6 Oct 73	**SHINE ON SILVER SUN** *A & M AMS 7082.*	**34**	3 wks

STRAY CATS *US, male vocal/instrumental group* **43 wks**

29 Nov 80	● **RUNAWAY BOYS** *Arista SCAT 1*	**9**	10 wks
7 Feb 81	● **ROCK THIS TOWN** *Arista SCAT 2.*	**9**	8 wks
25 Apr 81	**STRAY CAT STRUT** *Arista SCAT 3*	**11**	10 wks
7 Nov 81	**YOU DON'T BELIEVE ME** *Arista SCAT 4*	**57**	3 wks
6 Aug 83	**(SHE'S) SEXY AND 17** *Arista SCAT 6*	**29**	9 wks
4 Mar 89	**BRING IT BACK AGAIN** *EMI USA MT 62.*	**64**	3 wks

See also Dave Edmunds and Stray Cats.

STREETBAND *UK, male vocal/instrumental group* **6 wks**

4 Nov 78	**TOAST/ HOLD ON** *Logo GO 325*	**18**	6 wks

Barbra STREISAND *US, female vocalist* **74 wks**

20 Jan 66	**SECOND HAND ROSE** *CBS 202025*	**14**	13 wks
30 Jan 71	**STONEY END** *CBS 5321*	**46**	1 wk
13 Feb 71	**STONEY END** (re-entry) *CBS 5321*	**27**	10 wks
30 Mar 74	**THE WAY WE WERE** *CBS 1915.*	**31**	6 wks
9 Apr 77	● **LOVE THEME FROM A STAR IS BORN (EVERGREEN)** *CBS 4855*	**3**	19 wks
4 Oct 80	★ **WOMAN IN LOVE** *CBS 8966*	**1**	16 wks
30 Jan 82	**COMIN' IN AND OUT OF YOUR LIFE** *CBS A 1789*	**66**	3 wks
20 Mar 82	**MEMORY** *CBS A 1903.*	**34**	6 wks

See also Barbra Streisand and Barry Gibb; Barbra and Neil; Donna Summer and Barbra Streisand; Barbra Streisand and Don Johnson.

Barbra STREISAND and Barry GIBB **10 wks**
US/UK, female/male vocal duo

6 Dec 80	**GUILTY** *CBS 9315.*	**34**	10 wks

See also Barbra Streisand.

Barbra STREISAND and Don JOHNSON **7 wks**
US, female/male vocal duo

5 Nov 88	**TILL I LOVED YOU (LOVE THEME FROM 'GOYA')** *CBS BARB 2.*	**16**	7 wks

See also Barbra Streisand; Don Johnson.

STRESS *UK, male vocal/instrumental group* **1 wk**

13 Oct 90	**BEAUTIFUL PEOPLE** *Eternal YZ 495.*	**74**	1 wk

STRETCH *UK, male vocal/instrumental group* **9 wks**

8 Nov 75	**WHY DID YOU DO IT** *Anchor ANC 1021*	**16**	9 wks

STRIKERS *US, male vocal/instrumental group* **5 wks**

6 Jun 81	**BODY MUSIC** *Epic EPC A 1290.*	**45**	5 wks

STRING-A-LONGS *US, male instrumental group* **16 wks**

23 Feb 61	● **WHEELS** *London HLU 9278.*	**8**	16 wks

STRINGS OF LOVE
Italy, male/female vocal/instrumental group **2 wks**

3 Mar 90	NOTHING HAS BEEN PROVED *Breakout USA 688*	59	2 wks

Joe STRUMMER *UK, male vocalist* **1 wk**

2 Aug 86	LOVE KILLS *CBS A 7244*	69	1 wk

Chad STUART and Jeremy CLYDE **7 wks**
UK, male vocal duo

28 Nov 63	YESTERDAY'S GONE *Ember EMB S 180*	37	7 wks

STUMP *UK, male vocal/instrumental group* **1 wk**

13 Aug 88	CHARLTON HESTON *Ensign ENY 614*	72	1 wk

STUTZ BEARCATS and the Denis KING **6 wks**
ORCHESTRA *UK, male/female vocal group with orchestra*

24 Apr 82	THE SONG THAT I SING (THEME FROM 'WE'LL MEET AGAIN') *Multi-Media Tapes MMT 6*	36	6 wks

See also King Brothers.

STYLE COUNCIL *UK, male vocal instrumental duo* **103 wks**

19 Mar 83	● SPEAK LIKE A CHILD *Polydor TSC 1*	4	8 wks
28 May 83	MONEY GO ROUND (PART 1) *Polydor TSC 2*	11	6 wks
13 Aug 83	● LONG HOT SUMMER *Polydor TSC 3*	3	9 wks
20 Aug 83	MONEY GO ROUND (PART 1) (re-entry) *Polydor TSC 2*	74	1 wk
19 Nov 83	SOLID BOND IN YOUR HEART *Polydor TSC 4*	11	8 wks
18 Feb 84	● MY EVER CHANGING MOODS *Polydor TSC 5*	5	7 wks
26 May 84	● GROOVIN' (YOU'RE THE BEST THING/ BIG BOSS GROOVE) *Polydor TSC 6*	5	8 wks
13 Oct 84	● SHOUT TO THE TOP *Polydor TSC 7*	7	8 wks
11 May 85	● WALLS COME TUMBLING DOWN! *Polydor TSC 8*	6	7 wks
6 Jul 85	COME TO MILTON KEYNES *Polydor TSC 9*	23	5 wks
28 Sep 85	THE LODGERS *Polydor TSC 10*	13	6 wks
5 Apr 86	HAVE YOU EVER HAD IT BLUE *Polydor CINE 1*	14	6 wks
17 Jan 87	● IT DIDN'T MATTER *Polydor TSC 12*	9	5 wks
14 Mar 87	WAITING *Polydor TSC 13*	52	3 wks
31 Oct 87	WANTED *Polydor TSC 14*	20	4 wks
28 May 88	LIFE AT A TOP PEOPLE'S HEALTH FARM *Polydor TSC 15*	28	3 wks
23 Jul 88	HOW SHE THREW IT ALL AWAY (EP) *Polydor TSC 16*	41	2 wks
18 Feb 89	PROMISED LAND *Polydor TSC 17*	29	5 wks
27 May 89	LONG HOT SUMMER 89 (re-mix) *Polydor LHS 1*	48	2 wks

Tracks on EP: How She Threw It All Away/Love The First Time/Long Hot Summer/I Do Like To Be B-Side The A-Side. The version of Long Hot Summer on the EP is a re-recording of their third hit.

STYLISTICS *US, male vocal group* **143 wks**

24 Jun 72	BETCHA BY GOLLY WOW *Avco 6105 011*	13	12 wks
4 Nov 72	● I'M STONE IN LOVE WITH YOU *Avco 6105 015*	9	10 wks
17 Mar 73	BREAK UP TO MAKE UP *Avco 6105 020*	34	5 wks
30 Jun 73	PEEK-A-BOO *Avco 6105 023*	35	6 wks
19 Jan 74	● ROCKIN' ROLL BABY *Avco 6105 026*	6	9 wks
13 Jul 74	● YOU MAKE ME FEEL BRAND NEW *Avco 6105 028*	2	14 wks
19 Oct 74	● LET'S PUT IT ALL TOGETHER *Avco 6105 032*	9	9 wks
25 Jan 75	STAR ON A TV SHOW *Avco 6105 035*	12	8 wks
10 May 75	● SING BABY SING *Avco 6105 036*	3	10 wks
26 Jul 75	★ CAN'T GIVE YOU ANYTHING (BUT MY LOVE) *Avco 6105 039*	1	11 wks
15 Nov 75	● NA NA IS THE SADDEST WORD *Avco 6105 041*	5	10 wks
14 Feb 76	● FUNKY WEEKEND *Avco 6105 044*	10	7 wks
24 Apr 76	● CAN'T HELP FALLING IN LOVE *Avco 6105 050*	4	7 wks
7 Aug 76	● 16 BARS *H & L 6105 059*	7	9 wks
27 Nov 76	YOU'LL NEVER GET TO HEAVEN (EP) *H & L STYL 001*	24	9 wks
26 Mar 77	7000 DOLLARS AND YOU *H & L 6105 073*	24	7 wks

Tracks on You'll Never Get To Heaven EP: You'll Never Get To Heaven/Country Living/You Are Beautiful/The Miracle.

STYX *US, male vocal/instrumental group* **18 wks**

5 Jan 80	● BABE *A & M AMS 7489*	6	10 wks
24 Jan 81	THE BEST OF TIMES *A & M AMS 8102*	42	5 wks
18 Jun 83	DON'T LET IT END *A & M AM 120*	56	3 wks

SUENO LATINO featuring Carolina **5 wks**
DAMAS *Italy, male production duo and female vocalist*

23 Sep 89	SUENO LATINO *BCM BCM 323*	47	5 wks

SUGAR CANE *US, male/female vocal group* **5 wks**

30 Sep 78	MONTEGO BAY *Ariola Hansa AHA 524*	54	5 wks

SUGARCUBES *Iceland, male/female vocal/instrumental group* **15 wks**

14 Nov 87	BIRTHDAY *One Little Indian TP 7*	65	3 wks
30 Jan 88	COLD SWEAT *One Little Indian 7TP 9*	56	4 wks
16 Apr 88	DEUS *One Little Indian 7TP 10*	51	3 wks
3 Sep 88	BIRTHDAY *One Little Indian 7TP 11*	65	3 wks
16 Sep 89	REGINA *One Little Indian 26TP7*	55	2 wks

7TP 11 is a re-recording of their first hit.

SUGARHILL GANG *US, male rap group* **16 wks**

1 Dec 79	● RAPPER'S DELIGHT *Sugarhill SHL 101*	3	11 wks
11 Sep 82	THE LOVER IN YOU *Sugarhill SH 116*	54	3 wks
25 Nov 89	RAPPER'S DELIGHT (re-mix) *Sugarhill SHRD 0007*	58	2 wks

See also Calibre Cuts

Donna SUMMER *US, female vocalist* **266 wks**

17 Jan 76	● LOVE TO LOVE YOU BABY *GTO GT 17*	4	9 wks
29 May 76	COULD IT BE MAGIC *GTO GT 60*	40	7 wks
25 Dec 76	WINTER MELODY *GTO GT 76*	27	6 wks
9 Jul 77	★ I FEEL LOVE *GTO GT 100*	1	11 wks
20 Aug 77	● DEEP DOWN INSIDE (THEME FROM 'THE DEEP') *Casablanca CAN 111*	5	10 wks
24 Sep 77	I REMEMBER YESTERDAY *GTO GT 107*	14	7 wks
3 Dec 77	● LOVE'S UNKIND *GTO GT 113*	3	13 wks
10 Dec 77	● I LOVE YOU *Casablanca CAN 114*	10	9 wks
25 Feb 78	RUMOUR HAS IT *Casablanca CAN 122*	19	8 wks
22 Apr 78	BACK IN LOVE AGAIN *GTO GT 117*	29	7 wks
10 Jun 78	LAST DANCE *Casablanca TGIF 2*	70	1 wk
24 Jun 78	LAST DANCE (re-entry) *Casablanca TGIF 2*	51	8 wks
14 Oct 78	● MACARTHUR PARK *Casablanca CAN 131*	5	10 wks
17 Feb 79	HEAVEN KNOWS *Casablanca CAN 141*	34	8 wks
12 May 79	HOT STUFF *Casablanca CAN 151*	11	10 wks
7 Jul 79	BAD GIRLS *Casablanca CAN 155*	14	10 wks
1 Sep 79	DIM ALL THE LIGHTS *Casablanca CAN 162*	29	9 wks
16 Feb 80	ON THE RADIO *Casablanca NB 2236*	32	6 wks
21 Jun 80	SUNSET PEOPLE *Casablanca CAN 198*	46	5 wks
27 Sep 80	THE WANDERER *Warner Bros./Geffen K 79810*	48	6 wks
17 Jan 81	COLD LOVE *Geffen K 79183*	44	3 wks
10 Jul 82	LOVE IS IN CONTROL (FINGER ON THE TRIGGER) *Warner Bros. K 79302*	18	11 wks
6 Nov 82	STATE OF INDEPENDENCE *Warner Bros. K 79344*	14	11 wks
4 Dec 82	I FEEL LOVE (re-mix) *Casablanca FEEL 7*	21	10 wks
5 Mar 83	THE WOMAN IN ME *Warner Bros. W 9983*	62	2 wks
18 Jun 83	SHE WORKS HARD FOR THE MONEY *Mercury DONNA 1*	25	8 wks

24 Sep 83	UNCONDITIONAL LOVE *Mercury DONNA 2* **14**	12 wks
21 Jan 84	STOP LOOK AND LISTEN *Mercury DONNA 3* **57**	2 wks
24 Oct 87	DINNER WITH GERSHWIN *Warner Bros. U 8237* **13**	11 wks
23 Jan 88	ALL SYSTEMS GO *WEA U 8122* **54**	3 wks
25 Feb 89 ●	THIS TIME I KNOW IT'S FOR REAL	
	Warner Bros. U 7780 .... **3**	14 wks
27 May 89 ●	I DON'T WANNA GET HURT *Warner Bros. U 7567*......... **7**	9 wks
26 Aug 89	LOVE'S ABOUT TO CHANGE MY HEART	
	Warner Bros. U 7494 .... **20**	6 wks
25 Nov 89	WHEN LOVE TAKES OVER YOU *WEA U 7361* **72**	1 wk
17 Nov 90	STATE OF INDEPENDENCE (re-issue)	
	Warner Bros. U 2857 .... **45**	3 wks

Unconditional Love features the additional vocals of Musical Youth. See also Musical Youth; Donna Summer and Barbra Streisand.

Donna SUMMER and Barbra STREISAND   13 wks
US, female vocal duo

3 Nov 79 ●	NO MORE TEARS (ENOUGH IS ENOUGH)	
	Casablanca CAN 174 and CBS 8000 .... **3**	13 wks

See also Donna Summer; Barbra Streisand. This hit was released simultaneously on two different labels, 7 inch single on Casablanca and 12 inch single on CBS.

SUNDANCE – *See DJ 'Fast' EDDIE*

SUNDAYS *UK, male/female vocal/instrumental group*   5 wks

11 Feb 89	CAN'T BE SURE *Rough Trade RT 218* **45**	5 wks

SUNDRAGON *UK, male vocal/instrumental duo*   1 wk

21 Feb 68	GREEN TAMBOURINE *MGM 1380*.................... **50**	1 wk

SUNFIRE *US, male vocal/instrumental group*   11 wks

12 Mar 83	YOUNG, FREE AND SINGLE *Warner Bros. W 9897* **20**	11 wks

SUNNY *UK, female vocalist*   10 wks

30 Mar 74 ●	DOCTOR'S ORDERS *CBS 2068* **7**	10 wks

SUNSHINE BAND – *See KC and the SUNSHINE BAND*

SUPERTRAMP *UK/US, male vocal/instrumental group*   52 wks

15 Feb 75	DREAMER *A & M AMS 7132* **13**	10 wks
25 Jun 77	GIVE A LITTLE BIT *A & M AMS 7293* **29**	7 wks
31 Mar 79 ●	THE LOGICAL SONG *A & M AMS 7427* **7**	11 wks
30 Jun 79	BREAKFAST IN AMERICA *A & M AMS 7451* **9**	10 wks
27 Oct 79	GOODBYE STRANGER *A & M AMS 7481* **57**	3 wks
30 Oct 82	IT'S RAINING AGAIN *A & M AMS 8255* **26**	11 wks

It's Raining Again is 'featuring vocals by Roger Hodgson'.

SUPREMES *US, female vocal group*   259 wks

3 Sep 64 ●	WHERE DID OUR LOVE GO *Stateside SS 327*................ **3**	14 wks
22 Oct 64 ★	BABY LOVE *Stateside SS 350* **1**	15 wks
21 Jan 65	COME SEE ABOUT ME *Stateside SS 376* **27**	6 wks
25 Mar 65 ●	STOP IN THE NAME OF LOVE	
	Tamla Motown TMG 501 .... **7**	12 wks
10 Jun 65	BACK IN MY ARMS AGAIN *Tamla Motown TMG 516*....... **40**	5 wks
9 Dec 65	I HEAR A SYMPHONY *Tamla Motown TMG 543* **50**	1 wk
23 Dec 65	I HEAR A SYMPHONY (re-entry)	
	Tamla Motown TMG 543............................. **39**	4 wks
8 Sep 66 ●	YOU CAN'T HURRY LOVE *Tamla Motown TMG 575* **3**	12 wks
1 Dec 66 ●	YOU KEEP ME HANGIN' ON *Tamla Motown TMG 585* **8**	10 wks

2 Mar 67	LOVE IS HERE AND NOW YOU'RE GONE	
	Tamla Motown TMG 597............................. **17**	10 wks
11 May 67 ●	THE HAPPENING *Tamla Motown TMG 607* **6**	12 wks
30 Aug 67 ●	REFLECTIONS *Tamla Motown TMG 616* **5**	14 wks
29 Nov 67	IN AND OUT OF LOVE *Tamla Motown TMG 632* **13**	13 wks
10 Apr 68	FOREVER CAME TODAY *Tamla Motown TMG 650* **28**	8 wks
3 Jul 68	SOME THINGS YOU NEVER GET USED TO	
	Tamla Motown TMG 662 .... **34**	6 wks
20 Nov 68	LOVE CHILD *Tamla Motown TMG 677*.............. **15**	14 wks
23 Apr 69	I'M LIVING IN SHAME *Tamla Motown TMG 695* **14**	9 wks
2 Jul 69	I'M LIVING IN SHAME (re-entry)	
	Tamla Motown TMG 695............................. **50**	1 wk
16 Jul 69	NO MATTER WHAT SIGN YOU ARE	
	Tamla Motown TMG 704............................. **37**	7 wks
13 Dec 69	SOMEDAY WE'LL BE TOGETHER	
	Tamla Motown TMG 721............................. **13**	13 wks
2 May 70 ●	UP THE LADDER TO THE ROOF	
	Tamla Motown TMG 735.............................. **6**	15 wks
16 Jan 71 ●	STONED LOVE *Tamla Motown TMG 760* **3**	13 wks
21 Aug 71 ●	NATHAN JONES *Tamla Motown TMG 782* **5**	11 wks
4 Mar 72 ●	FLOY JOY *Tamla Motown TMG 804*.................... **9**	10 wks
15 Jul 72 ●	AUTOMATICALLY SUNSHINE	
	Tamla Motown TMG 821............................. **10**	9 wks
21 Apr 73	BAD WEATHER *Tamla Motown TMG 847* **37**	4 wks
24 Aug 74	BABY LOVE (re-issue) *Tamla Motown TMG 915* **12**	10 wks
18 Feb 89	STOP! IN THE NAME OF LOVE (re-issue)	
	Motown ZB 41963 .... **62**	1 wk

Diana Ross is lead singer on all the hits up to and including Someday We'll Be Together *and on the re-issues. From* Reflections *up to and including* Someday We'll Be Together, *and on the re-issue of* Baby Love *and* Stop! In The Name Of Love, *the group is billed as Diana Ross and the Supremes. See also Diana Ross; Supremes and the Four Tops; Diana Ross and the Supremes and the Temptations.*

SUPREMES and the FOUR TOPS   20 wks
US, female and male vocal groups

26 Jun 71	RIVER DEEP MOUNTAIN HIGH	
	Tamla Motown TMG 777.............................. **11**	10 wks
20 Nov 71	YOU GOTTA HAVE LOVE IN YOUR HEART	
	Tamla Motown TMG 793............................. **25**	10 wks

See also Supremes; Four Tops.

Al B SURE! *US, male vocalist*   10 wks

16 Apr 88	NITE AND DAY *Uptown W 8192*.................... **44**	5 wks
30 Jul 88	OFF ON YOUR OWN (GIRL) *Uptown W 7870* **70**	2 wks
10 Jun 89	IF I'M NOT YOUR LOVER *Warner Bros. W 2908*............. **54**	3 wks

See also Quincy Jones.

SURFACE *US, male vocal/instrumental duo*   12 wks

23 Jul 83	FALLING IN LOVE *Salsoul SAL 104*........................ **67**	3 wks
23 Jun 84	WHEN YOUR 'EX' WANTS YOU BACK	
	Salsoul SAL 106 .... **52**	4 wks
28 Feb 87	HAPPY *CBS 650393 7*.............................. **56**	5 wks

SURFACE NOISE *UK, male instrumental group*   11 wks

31 May 80	THE SCRATCH *WEA K 18291* **26**	8 wks
30 Aug 80	DANCIN' ON A WIRE *Groove GP102* **59**	3 wks

SURFARIS *US, male instrumental group*   14 wks

25 Jul 63 ●	WIPE OUT *London HLD 9751* **5**	14 wks

SURPRISE SISTERS *UK, female vocal group*   3 wks

13 Mar 76	LA BOOGA ROOGA *Good Earth GD 1* **38**	3 wks

SURVIVOR US, male vocal/instrumental group — 26 wks

| 31 Jul | 82 | ★ EYE OF THE TIGER *Scotti Brothers SCT A 2411* | 1 | 15 wks |
| 1 Feb | 86 | ● BURNING HEART *Scotti Brothers A 6708* | 5 | 11 wks |

SUTHERLAND BROTHERS
UK, male vocal/instrumental duo — 20 wks

3 Apr	76	● ARMS OF MARY *CBS 4001*	5	12 wks
20 Nov	76	SECRETS *CBS 4668*	35	4 wks
2 Jun	79	EASY COME EASY GO *CBS 7121*	50	4 wks

First two hits credited to Sutherland Brothers and Quiver.

Pat SUZUKI US, female vocalist — 1 wk

| 14 Apr | 60 | I ENJOY BEING A GIRL *RCA 1171* | 49 | 1 wk |

Billy SWAN US, male vocalist — 13 wks

| 14 Dec | 74 | ● I CAN HELP *Monument MNT 2752* | 6 | 9 wks |
| 24 May | 75 | DON'T BE CRUEL *Monument MNT 3244* | 42 | 4 wks |

SWAN LAKE US, male vocalist/multi-instrumentalist — 4 wks

| 17 Sep | 88 | IN THE NAME OF LOVE *Champion CHAMP 86* | 53 | 4 wks |

SWANS WAY UK, male/female vocal/instrumental group — 12 wks

| 4 Feb | 84 | SOUL TRAIN *Exit EXT 3* | 20 | 7 wks |
| 26 May | 84 | ILLUMINATIONS *Balgier PH 5* | 57 | 5 wks |

Patrick SWAYZE featuring Wendy FRASER
US, male/female vocal duo — 11 wks

| 26 Mar | 88 | SHE'S LIKE THE WIND *RCA PB 49565* | 17 | 11 wks |

Keith SWEAT US, male vocalist — 13 wks

| 20 Feb | 88 | I WANT HER *Vintertainment EKR 68* | 26 | 10 wks |
| 14 May | 88 | SOMETHING JUST AIN'T RIGHT *Vintertainment EKR 72* | 55 | 3 wks |

SWEET UK, male vocal/instrumental group — 159 wks

13 Mar	71	FUNNY FUNNY *RCA 2051*	13	14 wks
12 Jun	71	● CO-CO *RCA 2087*	2	15 wks
16 Oct	71	ALEXANDER GRAHAM BELL *RCA 2121*	33	5 wks
5 Feb	72	POPPA JOE *RCA 2164*	11	12 wks
10 Jun	72	● LITTLE WILLY *RCA 2225*	4	14 wks
9 Sep	72	● WIG-WAM BAM *RCA 2260*	4	13 wks
13 Jan	73	★ BLOCKBUSTER *RCA 2305*	1	15 wks
5 May	73	● HELL RAISER *RCA 2357*	2	11 wks
22 Sep	73	● BALLROOM BLITZ *RCA 2403*	2	9 wks
19 Jan	74	● TEENAGE RAMPAGE *RCA LPBO 5004*	2	8 wks
13 Jul	74	● THE SIX TEENS *RCA LPBO 5037*	9	7 wks
9 Nov	74	● TURN IT DOWN *RCA 2480*	41	2 wks
15 Mar	75	● FOX ON THE RUN *RCA 2524*	2	10 wks
12 Jul	75	ACTION *RCA 2578*	15	6 wks
24 Jan	76	LIES IN YOUR EYES *RCA 2641*	35	4 wks
28 Jan	78	● LOVE IS LIKE OXYGEN *Polydor POSP 1*	9	9 wks
26 Jan	85	IT'S IT'S THE SWEET MIX *Anagram ANA 28*	45	5 wks

It's It's The Sweet Mix is a medley of the following songs: Blockbuster/Fox On The Run/Teenage Rampage/Hell Raiser/Ballroom Blitz.

Rachel SWEET US, female vocalist — 8 wks

| 9 Dec | 78 | B-A-B-Y *Stiff BUY 39* | 35 | 8 wks |

See also Rex Smith and Rachel Sweet.

SWEET DREAMS UK, male/female vocal duo — 12 wks

| 20 Jul | 74 | ● HONEY HONEY *Bradley's BRAD 7408* | 10 | 12 wks |

SWEET DREAMS UK, male/female vocal group — 7 wks

| 9 Apr | 83 | I'M NEVER GIVING UP *Ariola ARO 333* | 21 | 7 wks |

SWEET PEOPLE France, male vocal/instrumental group — 10 wks

| 4 Oct | 80 | ● ET LES OISEAUX CHANTAIENT (AND THE BIRDS WERE SINGING) *Polydor POSP 179* | 4 | 8 wks |
| 29 Aug | 87 | ET LES OISEAUX CHANTAIENT (AND THE BIRDS WERE SINGING) (re-entry) *Polydor POSP 179* | 73 | 2 wks |

SWEET SENSATION UK, male vocal group — 17 wks

| 14 Sep | 74 | ★ SAD SWEET DREAMER *Pye 7N 45385* | 1 | 10 wks |
| 18 Jan | 75 | PURELY BY COINCIDENCE *Pye 7N 45421* | 11 | 7 wks |

SWEET TEE US, female rapper — 6 wks

| 16 Jan | 88 | IT'S LIKE THAT Y'ALL/I GOT DA FEELIN' *Cooltempo COOL 160* | 31 | 6 wks |

SWIMMING WITH SHARKS
Germany, female vocal duo — 3 wks

| 7 May | 88 | CARELESS LOVE *WEA YZ 173* | 63 | 3 wks |

SWING OUT SISTER
UK, male/female vocal/instrumental group — 45 wks

25 Oct	86	● BREAKOUT *Mercury SWING 2*	4	14 wks
10 Jan	87	● SURRENDER *Mercury SWING 3*	7	8 wks
18 Apr	87	TWILIGHT WORLD *Mercury SWING 4*	32	6 wks
11 Jul	87	FOOLED BY A SMILE *Mercury SWING 5*	43	4 wks
8 Apr	89	YOU ON MY MIND *Fontana SWING 6*	28	9 wks
8 Jul	89	WHERE IN THE WORLD *Fontana SWING 7*	47	4 wks

SWINGING BLUE JEANS
UK, male vocal/instrumental group — 57 wks

20 Jun	63	IT'S TOO LATE NOW *HMV POP 1170*	30	6 wks
8 Aug	63	IT'S TOO LATE NOW (re-entry) *HMV POP 1170*	46	3 wks
12 Dec	63	● HIPPY HIPPY SHAKE *HMV POP 1242*	2	17 wks
19 Mar	64	GOOD GOLLY MISS MOLLY *HMV POP 1273*	11	10 wks
4 Jun	64	● YOU'RE NO GOOD *HMV POP 1304*	3	13 wks
20 Jan	66	DON'T MAKE ME OVER *HMV POP 1501*	31	8 wks

SWITCH US, male vocal/instrumental group — 5 wks

| 10 Nov | 84 | KEEPING SECRETS *Total Experience RCA XE 502* | 41 | 5 wks |

SYBIL US, female vocalist — 35 wks

1 Nov 86		FALLING IN LOVE *Champion CHAMP 22*	68	3 wks
25 Apr 87		LET YOURSELF GO *Champion CHAMP 42*	32	6 wks
29 Aug 87		MY LOVE IS GUARANTEED *Champion CHAMP 55*	42	5 wks
22 Jul 89		DON'T MAKE ME OVER *Champion CHAMP 213*	59	5 wks
14 Oct 89		DON'T MAKE ME OVER (re-entry) *Champion CHAMP 213*	19	6 wks
27 Jan 90	●	WALK ON BY *PWL PWL 48*	6	9 wks
21 Apr 90		CRAZY FOR YOU *PWL PWL 53*	71	1 wk

SYLVESTER US, male vocalist — 37 wks

19 Aug 78	●	YOU MAKE ME FEEL (MIGHTY REAL) *Fantasy FTC 160*	8	15 wks
18 Nov 78		DANCE (DISCO HEAT) *Fantasy FTC 163*	29	12 wks
31 Mar 79		I (WHO HAVE NOTHING) *Fantasy FTC 171*	46	5 wks
7 Jul 79		STARS *Fantasy FTC 177*	47	3 wks
3 Sep 83		BAND OF GOLD *London LON 33*	67	2 wks

See also Sylvester with Patrick Cowley.

SYLVESTER with Patrick COWLEY — 8 wks
US, male vocal/instrumental duo

11 Sep 82	DO YA WANNA FUNK *London LON 13*	32	8 wks

See also Sylvester.

SYLVIA US, female vocalist — 11 wks

23 Jun 73	PILLOW TALK *London HL 10415*	14	11 wks

SYLVIA Sweden, female vocalist — 33 wks

10 Aug 74	●	Y VIVA ESPANA *Sonet SON 2037*	4	19 wks
4 Jan 75		Y VIVA ESPANA (re-entry) *Sonet SON 2037*	35	9 wks
26 Apr 75		HASTA LA VISTA *Sonet SON 2055*	38	5 wks

David SYLVIAN UK, male vocalist — 15 wks

2 Jun 84	RED GUITAR *Virgin VS 633*	17	5 wks
18 Aug 84	THE INK IN THE WELL *Virgin VS 700*	36	3 wks
3 Nov 84	PULLING PUNCHES *Virgin VS 717*	56	2 wks
14 Dec 85	WORDS WITH THE SHAMAN *Virgin VS 835*	72	1 wk
9 Aug 86	TAKING THE VEIL *Virgin VS 815*	53	3 wks
10 Oct 87	LET THE HAPPINESS IN *Virgin VS 1001*	66	1 wk

See also Sylvian Sakamoto; Mick Karn featuring David Sylvian.

SYLVIAN SAKAMOTO — 12 wks
UK/Japan, male vocal/instrumental duo

7 Aug 82	BAMBOO HOUSES/ BAMBOO MUSIC *Virgin VS 510*	30	4 wks
2 Jul 83	FORBIDDEN COLOURS *Virgin VS 601*	16	8 wks

Second hit credited to the fuller act names of David Sylvian and Riuichi Sakamoto. See also David Sylvian.

SYMARIP UK, male vocal/instrumental group — 3 wks

2 Feb 80	SKINHEAD MOONSTOMP *Trojan TRO 9062*	54	3 wks

SYMBOLS UK, male vocal/instrumental group — 15 wks

2 Aug 67	BYE BYE BABY *President PT 144*	44	3 wks
3 Jan 68	BEST PART OF BREAKING UP *President PT 173*	25	12 wks

SYREETA US, female vocalist — 15 wks

21 Sep 74	SPINNIN' AND SPINNIN' *Tamla Motown TMG 912*	49	3 wks
1 Feb 75	YOUR KISS IS SWEET *Tamla Motown TMG 933*	12	8 wks
12 Jul 75	HARMOUR LOVE *Tamla Motown TMG 954*	32	4 wks

See also Billy Preston and Syreeta.

SYSTEM US, male vocal/instrumental duo — 2 wks

9 Jun 84	I WANNA MAKE YOU FEEL GOOD *Polydor POSP 685*	73	2 wks

T

TACK HEAD US, male rapper — 3 wks

30 Jun 90	DANGEROUS SEX *SBK SBK 7014*	48	3 wks

TAFFY UK, female vocalist — 14 wks

10 Jan 87	●	I LOVE MY RADIO (MY DEE JAY'S RADIO) *Transglobal TYPE 1*	6	10 wks
18 Jul 87		STEP BY STEP *Transglobal TYPE 5*	59	4 wks

TALK TALK UK, male vocal/instrumental group — 73 wks

24 Apr 82	TALK TALK *EMI 5284*	52	4 wks
24 Jul 82	TODAY *EMI 5314*	14	13 wks
13 Nov 82	TALK TALK (re-mix) *EMI 5352*	23	10 wks
19 Mar 83	MY FOOLISH FRIEND *EMI 5373*	57	3 wks
14 Jan 84	IT'S MY LIFE *EMI 5443*	46	5 wks
7 Apr 84	SUCH A SHAME *EMI 5433*	49	6 wks
11 Aug 84	DUM DUM GIRL *EMI 5480*	74	1 wk
18 Jan 86	LIFE'S WHAT YOU MAKE IT *EMI EMI 5540*	16	9 wks
15 Mar 86	LIVING IN ANOTHER WORLD *EMI EMI 5551*	48	4 wks
17 May 86	GIVE IT UP *Parlophone R 6131*	59	3 wks
19 May 90	IT'S MY LIFE (re-issue) *Parlophone R 6254*	13	9 wks
1 Sep 90	LIFE'S WHAT YOU MAKE IT (re-issue) *Parlophone R 6264*	23	6 wks

TALKING HEADS — 51 wks
US/UK, male/female vocal/instrumental group

7 Feb 81		ONCE IN A LIFETIME *Sire SIR 4048*	14	10 wks
9 May 81		HOUSES IN MOTION *Sire SIR 4050*	50	3 wks
21 Jan 84		THIS MUST BE THE PLACE *Sire W 9451*	51	3 wks
3 Nov 84		SLIPPERY PEOPLE *EMI 5504*	68	2 wks
12 Oct 85	●	ROAD TO NOWHERE *EMI EMI 5530*	6	16 wks
8 Feb 86		AND SHE WAS *EMI EMI 5543*	17	8 wks
6 Sep 86		WILD WILD LIFE *EMI EMI 5567*	43	4 wks
16 May 87		RADIO HEAD *EMI EM 1*	52	2 wks
13 Aug 88		BLIND *EMI EM 68*	59	3 wks

TAMS US, male vocal group — 31 wks

14 Feb 70		BE YOUNG BE FOOLISH BE HAPPY *Stateside SS 2123*	32	7 wks
31 Jul 71	★	HEY GIRL DON'T BOTHER ME *Probe PRO 532*	1	17 wks
21 Nov 87		THERE AIN'T NOTHING LIKE SHAGGIN' *Virgin VS 1029*	21	7 wks

Norma TANEGA US, female vocalist — 8 wks

7 Apr 66	WALKING MY CAT NAMED DOG *Stateside SS 496*	22	8 wks

Above: Randy Traywick recorded under his own name and as Randy Ray before finding country music superstardom as RANDY TRAVIS.

STONE ROSES led the Madchester movement into the Top Ten.

TALK TALK echoed back with remixes.

The Children of TANSLEY SCHOOL
UK, children's choir   **4 wks**

| 28 Mar 81 | MY MUM IS ONE IN A MILLION *EMI 5151* | 27 | 4 wks |

Jimmy TARBUCK *UK, male vocalist*   **2 wks**

| 16 Nov 85 | AGAIN *Safari SAFE 68* | 74 | 1 wk |
| 30 Nov 85 | AGAIN (re-entry) *Safari SAFE 68* | 68 | 1 wk |

TARRIERS *US, male vocal/instrumental group*   **5 wks**

| 1 Mar 57 | BANANA BOAT SONG *Columbia DB 3891* | 15 | 5 wks |

A TASTE OF HONEY *US, female vocal duo*   **19 wks**

| 17 Jun 78 ● | BOOGIE OOGIE OOGIE *Capitol CL 15988* | 3 | 16 wks |
| 18 May 85 | BOOGIE OOGIE OOGIE (re-mix) *Capitol CL 357* | 59 | 3 wks |

TAVARES *US, male vocal group*   **77 wks**

10 Jul 76 ●	HEAVEN MUST BE MISSING AN ANGEL		
	Capitol CL 15876	4	11 wks
9 Oct 76 ●	DON'T TAKE AWAY THE MUSIC *Capitol CL 15886*	4	10 wks
5 Feb 77	MIGHTY POWER OF LOVE *Capitol CL 15905*	25	6 wks
9 Apr 77 ●	WHODUNIT *Capitol CL 15914*	5	10 wks
2 Jul 77	ONE STEP AWAY *Capitol CL 15930*	16	7 wks
18 Mar 78	THE GHOST OF LOVE *Capitol CL 15968*	29	6 wks
6 May 78 ●	MORE THAN A WOMAN *Capitol CL 15977*	7	11 wks
12 Aug 78	SLOW TRAIN TO PARADISE *Capitol CL 15996*	62	3 wks
22 Feb 86	HEAVEN MUST BE MISSING AN ANGEL (re-issue)		
	Capitol TAV 1.	12	9 wks
3 May 86	IT ONLY TAKES A MINUTE *Capitol TAV 2*	46	4 wks

TAXMAN – *See KICKING BACK with TAXMAN*

Andy TAYLOR *UK, male vocalist*   **2 wks**

| 20 Oct 90 | LOLA *A & M AM 596.* | 60 | 2 wks |

Felice TAYLOR *US, female vocalist*   **13 wks**

| 25 Oct 67 | I FEEL LOVE COMIN' ON *President PT 155* | 11 | 13 wks |

James TAYLOR *US, male vocalist*   **18 wks**

| 21 Nov 70 | FIRE AND RAIN *Warner Bros. WB 6104* | 42 | 3 wks |
| 28 Aug 71 ● | YOU'VE GOT A FRIEND *Warner Bros. WB 16085* | 4 | 15 wks |

See also Carly Simon and James Taylor.

John TAYLOR *UK, male vocalist*   **4 wks**

| 15 Mar 86 | I DO WHAT I DO...THEME FOR 9 ½ WEEKS | | |
| | *Parlophone R 6125* | 42 | 4 wks |

Johnnie TAYLOR *US, male vocalist*   **7 wks**

| 24 Apr 76 | DISCO LADY *CBS 4044* | 25 | 7 wks |

R. Dean TAYLOR *US, male vocalist*   **48 wks**

19 Jun 68	GOTTA SEE JANE *Tamla Motown TMG 656*	17	12 wks
3 Apr 71 ●	INDIANA WANTS ME *Tamla Motown TMG 763*	2	15 wks
11 May 74 ●	THERE'S A GHOST IN MY HOUSE		
	Tamla Motown TMG 896.	3	12 wks
31 Aug 74	WINDOW SHOPPING *Polydor 2058 502.*	36	5 wks
21 Sep 74	GOTTA SEE JANE (re-issue) *Tamla Motown TMG 918*	41	4 wks

Roger TAYLOR *UK, male vocalist*   **6 wks**

| 18 Apr 81 | FUTURE MANAGEMENT *EMI 5157* | 49 | 4 wks |
| 16 Jun 84 | MAN ON FIRE *EMI 5478* | 66 | 2 wks |

T-CONNECTION *US, male vocal/instrumental group*   **27 wks**

18 Jun 77	DO WHAT YOU WANNA DO *TK XC 9109.*	11	8 wks
14 Jan 78	ON FIRE *TK TKR 6006*	16	5 wks
10 Jun 78	LET YOURSELF GO *TK TKR 6024*	52	3 wks
24 Feb 79	AT MIDNIGHT *TK TKR 7517.*	53	5 wks
5 May 79	SATURDAY NIGHT *TK TKR 7536*	41	6 wks

T-COY *UK, male vocalist*   **2 wks**

| 20 Jan 90 | CARINO 90 *de Construction PT 43372* | 64 | 2 wks |

Carino 90 was one track from The Further Adventures Of North EP. The other tracks were Dream 17 by Annette, The Way I Feel by Frequency 9 and Stop This Thing by Dynasty Of Two featuring Rowetta. See also Annette, Frequency 9; Dynasty Of Two featuring Rowetta.

TEACH-IN *Holland, male/female vocal/instrumental group* **7 wks**

| 12 Apr 75 | DING-A-DONG *Polydor 2058 570* | 13 | 7 wks |

TEAM *UK, male vocal/instrumental group*   **5 wks**

| 1 Jun 85 | WICKI WACKY HOUSE PARTY *EMI 5519* | 55 | 5 wks |

TEARDROP EXPLODES
UK, male vocal/instrumental group   **50 wks**

27 Sep 80	WHEN I DREAM *Mercury TEAR 1*	47	6 wks
31 Jan 81 ●	REWARD *Vertigo TEAR 2*	6	13 wks
2 May 81	TREASON (IT'S JUST A STORY) *Mercury TEAR 3*	18	8 wks
29 Aug 81	PASSIONATE FRIEND *Zoo TEAR 5*	25	10 wks
21 Nov 81	COLOURS FLY AWAY *Mercury TEAR 6*	54	3 wks
19 Jun 82	TINY CHILDREN *Mercury TEAR 7.*	44	7 wks
19 Mar 83	YOU DISAPPEAR FROM VIEW *Mercury TEAR 8*	41	3 wks

TEARS – *See SNIFF 'N' THE TEARS*

TEARS FOR FEARS *UK, male vocal/instrumental duo*   **127 wks**

2 Oct 82 ●	MAD WORLD *Mercury IDEA 3*	3	16 wks
5 Feb 83 ●	CHANGE *Mercury IDEA 4.*	4	9 wks
30 Apr 83 ●	PALE SHELTER *Mercury IDEA 5.*	5	8 wks
3 Dec 83	THE WAY YOU ARE *Mercury IDEA 6*	24	8 wks
18 Aug 84	MOTHER'S TALK *Mercury IDEA 7*	14	8 wks
1 Dec 84 ●	SHOUT *Mercury IDEA 8.*	4	16 wks
30 Mar 85 ●	EVERYBODY WANTS TO RULE THE WORLD		
	Mercury IDEA 9.	2	14 wks
22 Jun 85	HEAD OVER HEELS *Mercury IDEA 10*	12	9 wks
31 Aug 85	SUFFER THE CHILDREN *Mercury IDEA 1*	52	4 wks
7 Sep 85	PALE SHELTER (re-issue) *Mercury IDEA 2*	73	2 wks
12 Oct 85	I BELIEVE (A SOULFUL RE-RECORDING)		
	Mercury IDEA 11.	23	4 wks
22 Feb 86	EVERYBODY WANTS TO RULE THE		
	WORLD (re-entry) *Mercury IDEA 9.*	73	1 wk
31 May 86 ●	EVERYBODY WANTS TO RUN THE WORLD		
	Mercury RACE 1.	5	6 wks
19 Jul 86	EVERYBODY WANTS TO RUN THE		
	WORLD (re-entry) *Mercury RACE 1.*	73	1 wk
2 Sep 89 ●	SOWING THE SEEDS OF LOVE *Fontana IDEA 12*	5	9 wks

18 Nov 89	**WOMAN IN CHAINS** *Fontana IDEA 13*	**26**	8 wks
3 Mar 90	**ADVICE FOR THE YOUNG AT HEART**		
	Fontana IDEA 14	**36**	4 wks

Mercury RACE 1 was a slightly changed version of Mercury IDEA 9, released to promote the Race Against Time of 15 May 1986. Woman In Chains features Oleta Adams, although uncredited. See also Oleta Adams.

TECHNO TWINS *UK, male/female vocal duo*   **2 wks**

16 Jan 82	**FALLING IN LOVE AGAIN** *PRT 7P 224*	**75**	1 wk
30 Jan 82	**FALLING IN LOVE AGAIN (re-entry)** *PRT 7P 224*	**70**	1 wk

TECHNOTRONIC *Belgium, male producer*   **52 wks**

2 Sep 89	● **PUMP UP THE JAM** *Swanyard SYR 4*	**2**	15 wks
3 Feb 90	● **GET UP (BEFORE THE NIGHT IS OVER)**		
	Swanyard SYR 8	**2**	10 wks
7 Apr 90	**THIS BEAT IS TECHNOTRONIC** *Swanyard SYR 9*	**14**	7 wks
14 Jul 90	● **ROCKIN' OVER THE BEAT** *Swanyard SYR 14*	**9**	9 wks
6 Oct 90	● **MEGAMIX** *Swanyard SYR 19*	**6**	8 wks
15 Dec 90	**TURN IT UP** *Swanyard SYD 9*	**42†**	3 wks

Pump Up The Jam features Felly - Zaire, female vocalist. Get Up Before The Night Is Over features Ya Kid K. Turn It Up features Melissa - UK, female vocalist and Einstein - UK, male vocalist. See also Hi Tek featuring Ya Kid K.

TEDDY BEARS *US, male/female vocal group*   **17 wks**

19 Dec 58	● **TO KNOW HIM IS TO LOVE HIM** *London HL 8733*	**2**	16 wks
14 Apr 79	**TO KNOW HIM IS TO LOVE HIM (re-issue)**		
	Lightning LIG 9015	**66**	1 wk

To Know Him Is To Love Him re-issue was coupled with Endless Sleep by Jody Reynolds as a double A-side. See also Jody Reynolds.

TEENAGERS – *See Frankie LYMON and the TEENAGERS*

TEICHER – *See FERRANTE and TEICHER*

TELEVISION *US, male vocal/instrumental group*   **10 wks**

16 Apr 77	**MARQUEE MOON** *Elektra K 12252*	**30**	4 wks
30 Jul 77	**PROVE IT** *Elektra K 12262*	**25**	4 wks
22 Apr 78	**FOXHOLE** *Elektra K 12287*	**36**	2 wks

TELEX *Belgium, male vocal/instrumental duo*   **7 wks**

21 Jul 79	**ROCK AROUND THE CLOCK** *Sire SIR 4020*	**34**	7 wks

Sylvia TELLA – *See BLOW MONKEYS*

TEMPERANCE SEVEN   **45 wks**
UK, male vocal/instrumental band

30 Mar 61	★ **YOU'RE DRIVING ME CRAZY** *Parlophone R 4757*	**1**	16 wks
15 Jun 61	● **PASADENA** *Parlophone R 4781*	**4**	17 wks
28 Sep 61	**HARD HEARTED HANNAH/ CHILI BOM BOM**		
	Parlophone R 4823	**28**	4 wks
7 Dec 61	**CHARLESTON** *Parlophone R 4851*	**22**	8 wks

Chili Bom Bom only listed with Hard Hearted Hannah for the weeks of 12 and 19 Oct 61.

Nino TEMPO and April STEVENS   **19 wks**
US, male/female vocal duo

7 Nov 63	**DEEP PURPLE** *London HLK 9782*	**17**	11 wks
16 Jan 64	**WHISPERING** *London HLK 9829*	**20**	8 wks

TEMPTATIONS *US, male vocal group*   **165 wks**

18 Mar 65	**MY GIRL** *Stateside SS 378*......................	**43**	1 wk
1 Apr 65	**IT'S GROWING** *Tamla Motown TMG 504*	**49**	1 wk
15 Apr 65	**IT'S GROWING (re-entry)** *Tamla Motown TMG 504*	**45**	1 wk
14 Jul 66	**AIN'T TOO PROUD TO BEG** *Tamla Motown TMG 565*	**21**	11 wks
6 Oct 66	**BEAUTY IS ONLY SKIN DEEP**		
	Tamla Motown TMG 578	**18**	10 wks
15 Dec 66	**(I KNOW) I'M LOSING YOU** *Tamla Motown TMG 587*......	**19**	9 wks
6 Sep 67	**YOU'RE MY EVERYTHING** *Tamla Motown TMG 620*........	**26**	15 wks
6 Mar 68	**I WISH IT WOULD RAIN** *Tamla Motown TMG 641*..........	**45**	1 wk
12 Jun 68	**I COULD NEVER LOVE ANOTHER**		
	Tamla Motown TMG 658	**47**	1 wk
5 Mar 69	● **GET READY** *Tamla Motown TMG 688*	**10**	9 wks
23 Aug 69	**CLOUD NINE** *Tamla Motown TMG 707*	**15**	10 wks
17 Jan 70	**I CAN'T GET NEXT TO YOU** *Tamla Motown TMG 722*	**13**	9 wks
13 Jun 70	**PSYCHEDELIC SHACK** *Tamla Motown TMG 741*	**33**	7 wks
19 Sep 70	● **BALL OF CONFUSION** *Tamla Motown TMG 749*	**7**	12 wks
19 Dec 70	**BALL OF CONFUSION (re-entry)**		
	Tamla Motown TMG 749	**48**	3 wks
22 May 71	● **JUST MY IMAGINATION (RUNNING AWAY WITH**		
	ME) *Tamla Motown TMG 773*	**8**	16 wks
5 Feb 72	**SUPERSTAR (REMEMBER HOW YOU GOT WHERE**		
	YOU ARE) *Tamla Motown TMG 800*	**32**	5 wks
15 Apr 72	**TAKE A LOOK AROUND** *Tamla Motown TMG 808*	**13**	10 wks
13 Jan 73	**PAPA WAS A ROLLIN' STONE**		
	Tamla Motown TMG 839	**14**	8 wks
29 Sep 73	**LAW OF THE LAND** *Tamla Motown TMG 866*	**41**	4 wks
12 Jun 82	**STANDING ON THE TOP (PART 1)**		
	Motown TMG 1263	**53**	3 wks
17 Nov 84	**TREAT HER LIKE A LADY** *Motown TMG 1365*............	**12**	10 wks
15 Aug 87	**PAPA WAS A ROLLIN' STONE (re-mix)**		
	Motown ZB 41431	**31**	6 wks
6 Feb 88	**LOOK WHAT YOU STARTED** *Motown ZB 41733*	**63**	2 wks
21 Oct 89	**ALL I WANT FROM YOU** *Motown ZB 43233*	**71**	1 wk

Standing On The Top is 'featuring Rick James'. See Diana Ross and the Supremes and the Temptations; Rick James; Teena Marie; Bruce Willis.

10 C. C. *UK, male vocal/instrumental group*   **131 wks**

23 Sep 72	● **DONNA** *UK 6*	**2**	13 wks
19 May 73	★ **RUBBER BULLETS** *UK 36*.......................	**1**	15 wks
25 Aug 73	● **THE DEAN AND I** *UK 48*........................	**10**	8 wks
15 Jun 74	● **WALL STREET SHUFFLE** *UK 69*	**10**	10 wks
14 Sep 74	**SILLY LOVE** *UK 77*	**24**	7 wks
5 Apr 75	● **LIFE IS A MINESTRONE** *Mercury 6008 010*..................	**7**	8 wks
31 May 75	★ **I'M NOT IN LOVE** *Mercury 6008 014*....................	**1**	11 wks
29 Nov 75	● **ART FOR ART'S SAKE** *Mercury 6008 017*	**5**	10 wks
20 Mar 76	● **I'M MANDY FLY ME** *Mercury 6008 019*	**6**	9 wks
11 Dec 76	● **THINGS WE DO FOR LOVE** *Mercury 6008 022*...........	**6**	11 wks
16 Apr 77	● **GOOD MORNING JUDGE** *Mercury 6008 025*.................	**5**	12 wks
12 Aug 78	★ **DREADLOCK HOLIDAY** *Mercury 6008 035*...............	**1**	13 wks
7 Aug 82	**RUN AWAY** *Mercury MER 113*	**50**	4 wks

From Things We Do For Love 10 C.C. were a male vocal/instrumental duo.

TEN CITY *US, male vocal/instrumental group*   **17 wks**

21 Jan 89	● **THAT'S THE WAY LOVE IS** *Atlantic A 8963*..................	**8**	10 wks
8 Apr 89	**DEVOTION** *Atlantic A 8916*......................	**29**	4 wks
22 Jul 89	**WHERE DO WE GO** *Atlantic A 8864*	**60**	1 wk
27 Oct 90	**WHATEVER MAKES YOU HAPPY** *Atlantic A 7819*	**60**	2 wks

TEN POLE TUDOR *UK, male vocal/instrumental group*   **26 wks**

25 Apr 81	● **SWORDS OF A THOUSAND MEN** *Stiff BUY 109*...........	**6**	12 wks
1 Aug 81	**WUNDERBAR** *Stiff BUY 120*......................	**16**	9 wks
14 Nov 81	**THROWING MY BABY OUT WITH THE**		
	BATHWATER *Stiff BUY 129*	**49**	5 wks

See also Sex Pistols.

TEN YEARS AFTER UK, male vocal/instrumental group — 18 wks

6 Jun 70 ●	LOVE LIKE A MAN Deram DM 299	10	18 wks

TENNESSEE THREE – See Johnny CASH

TENNILLE – See CAPTAIN and TENNILLE

Tammi TERRELL – See Marvin GAYE and Tammi TERRELL

Helen TERRY UK, female vocalist — 6 wks

12 May 84	LOVE LIES LOST Virgin VS 678	34	6 wks

Todd TERRY PROJECT US, male producer — 3 wks

12 Nov 88	WEEKEND Sleeping Bag SBUK 1T	56	3 wks

Tony TERRY US, male vocalist — 6 wks

27 Feb 88	LOVEY DOVEY Epic TONY 2	44	6 wks

Joe TEX US, male vocalist — 11 wks

23 Apr 77 ●	AIN'T GONNA BUMP NO MORE (WITH NO BIG FAT WOMAN) Epic EPC 5035	2	11 wks

TEXAS UK, male/female vocal/instrumental group — 20 wks

4 Feb 89 ●	I DON'T WANT A LOVER Mercury TEX 1	8	11 wks
6 May 89	THRILL HAS GONE Mercury TEX 2	60	3 wks
5 Aug 89	EVERYDAY NOW Mercury TEX 3	44	5 wks
2 Dec 89	PRAYER FOR YOU Mercury TEX 4	73	1 wk

THAT PETROL EMOTION
UK, male vocal/instrumental group — 16 wks

11 Apr 87	BIG DECISION Polydor TPE 1	43	7 wks
11 Jul 87	DANCE Polydor TPE 2	64	2 wks
17 Oct 87	GENIUS MOVE Virgin VS 1002	65	2 wks
31 Mar 90	ABANDON Virgin VS 1242	73	1 wk
1 Sep 90	HEY VENUS Virgin VS 1290	49	4 wks

The THE UK, male vocalist/multi-instrumentalist. Matt Johnson — 35 wks

4 Dec 82	UNCERTAIN SMILE Epic EPC A 2787	68	3 wks
17 Sep 83	THIS IS THE DAY Epic A 3710	71	3 wks
9 Aug 86	HEARTLAND Some Bizzare TRUTH 2	29	10 wks
25 Oct 86	INFECTED Some Bizzare TRUTH 3	48	5 wks
24 Jan 87	SLOW TRAIN TO DAWN Some Bizzare TENSE 1	64	2 wks
23 May 87	SWEET BIRD OF TRUTH Epic TENSE 2	55	2 wks
1 Apr 89	THE BEAT(EN) GENERATION Epic EMU 8	18	5 wks
22 Jul 89	GRAVITATE TO ME Epic EMU 9	63	3 wks
7 Oct 89	ARMAGEDDON DAYS ARE HERE Epic EMU 10	70	2 wks

THEATRE OF HATE UK, male vocal/instrumental group — 9 wks

23 Jan 82	DO YOU BELIEVE IN THE WESTWORLD Burning Rome BRR 2	40	7 wks
29 May 82	THE HOP Burning Rome BRR 3	70	2 wks

THEM UK, male vocal/instrumental group — 21 wks

7 Jan 65 ●	BABY PLEASE DON'T GO Decca F 12018	10	9 wks
25 Mar 65 ●	HERE COMES THE NIGHT Decca F 12094	2	12 wks

THEN JERICO UK, male vocal/instrumental group — 36 wks

31 Jan 87	LET HER FALL London LON 97	65	3 wks
25 Jul 87	THE MOTIVE (LIVING WITHOUT YOU) London LON 145	18	12 wks
24 Oct 87	MUSCLE DEEP London LON 156	48	4 wks
28 Jan 89	BIG AREA London LON 204	13	7 wks
8 Apr 89	WHAT DOES IT TAKE London LON 223	33	4 wks
12 Aug 89	SUGAR BOX London LON 235	22	6 wks

THEY MIGHT BE GIANTS — 13 wks
US, male vocal/instrumental duo

3 Mar 90 ●	BIRDHOUSE IN YOUR SOUL Elektra EKR 104	6	11 wks
2 Jun 90	ISTANBUL (NOT CONSTANTINOPLE) Elektra EKR 110	61	2 wks

THIN LIZZY Ireland, male vocal/instrumental group — 124 wks

20 Jan 73 ●	WHISKY IN THE JAR Decca F 13355	6	12 wks
29 May 76 ●	THE BOYS ARE BACK IN TOWN Vertigo 6059 139	8	10 wks
14 Aug 76	JAILBREAK Vertigo 6059 150	31	4 wks
15 Jan 77	DON'T BELIEVE A WORD Vertigo 6059 177	12	7 wks
13 Aug 77	DANCIN' IN THE MOONLIGHT (IT'S CAUGHT ME IN THE SPOTLIGHT) Vertigo 6059 177	14	8 wks
13 May 78	ROSALIE - COWGIRLS' SONG (MEDLEY) Vertigo LIZZY 2	20	13 wks
3 Mar 79 ●	WAITING FOR AN ALIBI Vertigo LIZZY 003	9	8 wks
16 Jun 79	DO ANYTHING YOU WANT TO Vertigo LIZZY 004	14	9 wks
20 Oct 79	SARAH Vertigo LIZZY 5	24	13 wks
24 May 80	CHINATOWN Vertigo LIZZY 6	21	9 wks
27 Sep 80 ●	KILLER ON THE LOOSE Vertigo LIZZY 7	10	7 wks
2 May 81	KILLERS LIVE (EP) Vertigo LIZZY 8	19	7 wks
8 Aug 81	TROUBLE BOYS Vertigo LIZZY 9	53	4 wks
6 Mar 82	HOLLYWOOD (DOWN ON YOUR LUCK) Vertigo LIZZY 10	53	3 wks
12 Feb 83	COLD SWEAT Vertigo LIZZY 11	27	5 wks
7 May 83	THUNDER AND LIGHTNING Vertigo LIZZY 12	39	2 wks
6 Aug 83	THE SUN GOES DOWN Vertigo LIZZY 13	52	3 wks

Tracks on Killers Live EP: Bad Reputation/Are You Ready/Dear Miss Lonely Hearts.

3RD BASS US, male rap group — 3 wks

10 Feb 90	THE GAS FACE Def Jam 655627 0	71	1 wk
7 Apr 90	BROOKLYN-QUEENS Def Jam 655830 7	61	2 wks

THIRD WORLD Jamaica, male vocal/instrumental group — 53 wks

23 Sep 78 ●	NOW THAT WE'VE FOUND LOVE Island WIP 6457	10	9 wks
6 Jan 79	COOL MEDITATION Island WIP 6469	17	10 wks
16 Jun 79	TALK TO ME Island WIP 6496	56	5 wks
6 Jun 81 ●	DANCING ON THE FLOOR (HOOKED ON LOVE) CBS A 1214	10	15 wks
17 Apr 82	TRY JAH LOVE CBS A 2063	47	6 wks
9 Mar 85	NOW THAT WE'VE FOUND LOVE Island IS 219	22	8 wks

THIS ISLAND EARTH — 5 wks
UK, male/female vocal/instrumental group

5 Jan 85	SEE THAT GLOW Magnet MAG 266	47	5 wks

THIS MORTAL COIL
UK, male/female vocal/instrumental group   **3 wks**

22 Oct 83	SONG TO THE SIREN *4AD AD 310*	66	2 wks
12 Nov 83	SONG TO THE SIREN (re-entry) *4AD AD 310*	75	1 wk

THIS WAY UP *UK, male vocal/instrumental duo*   **2 wks**

22 Aug 87	TELL ME WHY *Virgin VS 954*	72	2 wks

THIS YEAR'S BLONDE
UK, male/female vocal/instrumental group   **8 wks**

10 Oct 81	PLATINUM POP *Creole CR 19*	46	5 wks
14 Nov 87	WHO'S THAT MIX *Debut DEBT 3034*	62	3 wks

B. J. THOMAS *US, male vocalist*   **4 wks**

21 Feb 70	RAINDROPS KEEP FALLING ON MY HEAD *Wand WN1*	38	3 wks
2 May 70	RAINDROPS KEEP FALLING ON MY HEAD (re-entry) *Wand WN1*	49	1 wk

Carla THOMAS – *See Otis REDDING and Carla THOMAS*

Evelyn THOMAS *US, female vocalist*   **29 wks**

24 Jan 76	WEAK SPOT *20th Century BTC 1014*	26	7 wks
17 Apr 76	DOOMSDAY *20th Century BTC 1017*	41	1 wk
1 May 76	DOOMSDAY (re-entry) *20th Century BTC 1017*	45	1 wk
21 Apr 84 ●	HIGH ENERGY *Record Shack SOHO 18*	5	17 wks
25 Aug 84	MASQUERADE *Record Shack SOHO 25*	60	3 wks

Jamo THOMAS *US, male vocalist*   **2 wks**

26 Feb 69	I SPY FOR THE FBI *Polydor 56755*	48	1 wk
12 Mar 69	I SPY FOR THE FBI (re-entry) *Polydor 56755*	44	1 wk

Lillo THOMAS *US, male vocalist*   **10 wks**

27 Apr 85	SETTLE DOWN *Capitol CL 356*	66	2 wks
21 Mar 87	SEXY GIRL *Capitol CL 445*	23	5 wks
30 May 87	I'M IN LOVE *Capitol CL 450*	54	3 wks

Mickey THOMAS – *See Elvin BISHOP*

Nicky THOMAS *Jamaica, male vocalist*   **14 wks**

13 Jun 70 ●	LOVE OF THE COMMON PEOPLE *Trojan TR 7750*	9	14 wks

Rufus THOMAS *US, male vocalist*   **12 wks**

11 Apr 70	DO THE FUNKY CHICKEN *Stax 144*	18	12 wks

Tasha THOMAS *US, female vocalist*   **3 wks**

20 Jan 79	SHOOT ME (WITH YOUR LOVE) *Atlantic LV 4*	59	3 wks

Timmy THOMAS *US, male vocalist*   **13 wks**

14 Feb 73	WHY CAN'T WE LIVE TOGETHER *Mojo 2027 012*	12	11 wks
14 Jul 90	WHY CAN'T WE LIVE TOGETHER (re-mix) *TK TKR 1*	54	2 wks

See also Nicole with Timmy Thomas.

THOMAS and TAYLOR *US, male/female vocal duo*   **5 wks**

17 May 86	YOU CAN'T BLAME LOVE *Cooltempo COOL 123*	53	5 wks

Carroll THOMPSON – *See MOVEMENT 98 featuring Carroll THOMPSON;*
Courtney PINE featuring Carroll THOMPSON

Chris THOMPSON *UK, male vocalist*   **5 wks**

27 Oct 79	IF YOU REMEMBER ME *Planet K 12389*	42	5 wks

Sue THOMPSON *US, female vocalist*   **9 wks**

2 Nov 61	SAD MOVIES *Polydor NH 66967*	46	1 wk
16 Nov 61	SAD MOVIES (re-entry) *Polydor NH 66967*	48	1 wk
21 Jan 65	PAPER TIGER *Hickory 1284*	50	1 wk
11 Feb 65	PAPER TIGER (re-entry) *Hickory 1284*	30	6 wks

THOMPSON TWINS *UK/New*
Zealand, male/female vocal/instrumental group   **102 wks**

6 Nov 82	LIES *Arista ARIST 486*	67	3 wks
29 Jan 83 ●	LOVE ON YOUR SIDE *Arista ARIST 504*	9	12 wks
16 Apr 83 ●	WE ARE DETECTIVE *Arista ARIST 526*	7	9 wks
16 Jul 83	WATCHING *Arista TWINS 1*	33	6 wks
19 Nov 83 ●	HOLD ME NOW *Arista TWINS 2*	4	15 wks
4 Feb 84 ●	DOCTOR DOCTOR *Arista TWINS 3*	3	10 wks
31 Mar 84 ●	YOU TAKE ME UP *Arista TWINS 4*	2	9 wks
7 Jul 84	SISTER OF MERCY *Arista TWINS 5*	11	8 wks
8 Sep 84	SISTER OF MERCY (re-entry) *Arista TWINS 5*	66	1 wk
8 Dec 84	LAY YOUR HANDS ON ME *Arista TWINS 6*	13	9 wks
31 Aug 85	DON'T MESS WITH DOCTOR DREAM *Arista TWINS 9*	15	6 wks
19 Oct 85	KING FOR A DAY *Arista TWINS 7*	22	6 wks
7 Dec 85	REVOLUTION *Arista TWINS 10*	56	3 wks
4 Jan 86	REVOLUTION (re-entry) *Arista TWINS 10*	75	1 wk
11 Apr 87	GET THAT LOVE (re-entry) *Arista TWINS 12*	66	1 wk
15 Oct 88	IN THE NAME OF LOVE '88 *Arista 111808*	46	3 wks

David THORNE *US, male vocalist*   **8 wks**

24 Jan 63	ALLEY CAT SONG *Stateside SS 141*	21	8 wks

Ken THORNE *UK, orchestra*   **15 wks**

18 Jul 63 ●	THEME FROM THE FILM 'THE LEGION'S LAST PATROL' *HMV POP 1176*	4	15 wks

THRASHING DOVES *UK, male vocal/instrumental group*   **3 wks**

24 Jan 87	BEAUTIFUL IMBALANCE *A &M TDOVE 1*	50	3 wks

THREE DEGREES *US, female vocal group*   **102 wks**

13 Apr 74	YEAR OF DECISION *Philadelphia International PIR 2073*	13	10 wks
13 Jul 74 ★	WHEN WILL I SEE YOU AGAIN *Philadelphia International PIR 2155*	1	16 wks
2 Nov 74	GET YOUR LOVE BACK *Philadelphia International PIR 2737*	34	4 wks

12 Apr 75 ●	**TAKE GOOD CARE OF YOURSELF** *Philadelphia International PIR 3177*	**9**	9 wks
5 Jul 75	**LONG LOST LOVER** *Philadelphia International PIR 3352*	**40**	4 wks
1 May 76	**TOAST OF LOVE** *Epic EPC 4215*	**36**	4 wks
7 Oct 78	**GIVIN' UP GIVIN' IN** *Ariola ARO 130*	**12**	10 wks
13 Jan 79 ●	**WOMAN IN LOVE** *Ariola ARO 141*	**3**	11 wks
24 Mar 79	**THE RUNNER** *Ariola ARO 154*	**10**	10 wks
23 Jun 79	**THE GOLDEN LADY** *Ariola ARO 170*	**56**	3 wks
29 Sep 79	**JUMP THE GUN** *Ariola ARO 183*	**48**	5 wks
24 Nov 79 ●	**MY SIMPLE HEART** *Ariola ARO 202*	**9**	11 wks
5 Oct 85	**THE HEAVEN I NEED** *Supreme SUPE 102*	**42**	5 wks

See also MFSB.

THREE DOG NIGHT *US, male vocal/instrumental group*   **23 wks**

8 Aug 70 ●	**MAMA TOLD ME NOT TO COME** *Stateside SS 8052*	**3**	14 wks
29 May 71	**JOY TO THE WORLD** *Probe PRO 523*	**24**	9 wks

THREE GOOD REASONS   **3 wks**
UK, male vocal/instrumental group

10 Mar 66	**NOWHERE MAN** *Mercury MF 899*	**47**	3 wks

THREE KAYES *UK, female vocal group*   **5 wks**

25 May 56	**IVORY TOWER** *HMV POP 209*	**20**	5 wks

The Three Kayes became The Kaye Sisters. See also Kaye Sisters; Frankie Vaughan and the Kaye Sisters.

THREE TONS OF JOY – *See Johnny OTIS SHOW*

THS - THE HORN SECTION   **3 wks**
US, male/female vocal/instrumental group

18 Aug 84	**LADY SHINE (SHINE ON)** *Fourth & Broadway BRW 10*	**54**	3 wks

Harry THUMANN   **6 wks**
Germany, male instrumentalist - keyboards

21 Feb 81	**UNDERWATER** *Decca F 13901*	**41**	6 wks

THUNDER *UK/US, male vocal/instrumental group*   **14 wks**

17 Feb 90	**DIRTY LOVE** *EMI EM 126*	**32**	4 wks
12 May 90	**BACKSTREET SYMPHONY** *EMI EM 137*	**25**	4 wks
14 Jul 90	**GIMME SOME LOVIN'** *EMI EM 148*	**36**	3 wks
29 Sep 90	**SHE'S SO FINE** *EMI EM 158*	**34**	3 wks

THUNDERBIRDS – *See Chris FARLOWE*

THUNDERCLAP NEWMAN   **13 wks**
UK, male vocal/instrumental group

11 Jun 69 ★	**SOMETHING IN THE AIR** *Track 604-031*	**1**	12 wks
27 Jun 70	**ACCIDENTS** *Track 2094 001*	**46**	1 wk

THUNDERTHIGHS *UK, female vocal group*   **5 wks**

22 Jun 74	**CENTRAL PARK ARREST** *Philips 6006 386*	**30**	5 wks

Bobby THURSTON *US, male vocalist*   **10 wks**

29 Mar 80 ●	**CHECK OUT THE GROOVE** *Epic EPC 8348*	**10**	10 wks

TICH – *See Dave DEE, DOZY, BEAKY, MICK and TICH*

TIFFANY *US, female vocalist*   **45 wks**

16 Jan 87 ★	**I THINK WE'RE ALONE NOW** *MCA MCA 1211*	**1**	13 wks
19 Mar 88 ●	**COULD'VE BEEN** *MCA TIFF 2*	**4**	9 wks
4 Jun 88	**I SAW HIM STANDING THERE** *MCA TIFF 3*	**8**	7 wks
6 Aug 88	**FEELINGS OF FOREVER** *MCA TIFF 4*	**52**	2 wks
12 Nov 88	**RADIO ROMANCE** *MCA TIFF 5*	**13**	11 wks
11 Feb 89	**ALL THIS TIME** *MCA TIFF 6*	**47**	3 wks

TIGERTAILZ *US, male vocal/instrumental group*   **1 wk**

24 Jun 89	**LOVE BOMB BABY** *Music For Nations KUT 132*	**75**	1 wk

TIGHT FIT *UK, male/female vocal group*   **49 wks**

18 Jul 81 ●	**BACK TO THE SIXTIES** *Jive JIVE 002*	**4**	11 wks
26 Sep 81	**BACK TO THE SIXTIES PART 2** *Jive JIVE 005*	**33**	5 wks
23 Jan 82 ★	**THE LION SLEEPS TONIGHT** *Jive JIVE 9*	**1**	15 wks
1 May 82 ●	**FANTASY ISLAND** *Jive JIVE 13*	**5**	12 wks
31 Jul 82	**SECRET HEART** *Jive JIVE 20*	**41**	6 wks

TIJUANA BRASS – *See Herb ALPERT and the TIJUANA BRASS*

TIK and TOK *UK, male vocal duo*   **2 wks**

8 Oct 83	**COOL RUNNING** *Survival SUR 016*	**69**	2 wks

Tanita TIKARAM *UK, female vocalist*   **26 wks**

30 Jul 88 ●	**GOOD TRADITION** *WEA YZ 196*	**10**	10 wks
22 Oct 88	**TWIST IN MY SOBRIETY** *WEA YZ 321*	**22**	8 wks
14 Jan 89	**CATHEDRAL SONG** *WEA YZ 331*	**48**	3 wks
18 Mar 89	**WORLD OUTSIDE YOUR WINDOW** *WEA YZ 363*	**58**	2 wks
13 Jan 90	**WE ALMOST GOT IT TOGETHER** *WEA YZ 443*	**52**	3 wks

TILBROOK – *See DIFFORD and TILBROOK*

Johnny TILLOTSON *US, male vocalist*   **50 wks**

1 Dec 60 ★	**POETRY IN MOTION** *London HLA 9231*	**1**	15 wks
2 Feb 61	**JIMMY'S GIRL** *London HLA 9275*	**50**	1 wk
16 Feb 61	**JIMMY'S GIRL (re-entry)** *London HLA 9275*	**43**	1 wk
12 Jul 62	**IT KEEPS RIGHT ON A HURTIN'** *London HLA 9550*	**31**	10 wks
4 Oct 62	**SEND ME THE PILLOW YOU DREAM ON** *London HLA 9598*	**21**	10 wks
27 Dec 62	**I CAN'T HELP IT** *London HLA 9642*	**42**	1 wk
10 Jan 63	**I CAN'T HELP IT (re-entry)** *London HLA 9642*	**47**	1 wk
24 Jan 63	**I CAN'T HELP IT (2nd re-entry)** *London HLA 9642*	**41**	4 wks
9 May 63	**OUT OF MY MIND** *London HLA 9695*	**34**	5 wks
14 Apr 79	**POETRY IN MOTION/ PRINCESS PRINCESS (re-issue)** *Lightning LIG 9016*	**67**	2 wks

TIMBUK 3 *US, male/female vocal/instrumental duo*   **7 wks**

31 Jan 87	**FUTURE'S SO BRIGHT I GOTTA WEAR SHADES** *IRS IRM 126*	**21**	7 wks

TIME UK *UK, male vocal/instrumental group*   **3 wks**

8 Oct 83	**THE CABARET** *Red Bus/Aroadia TIM 123*	**63**	3 wks

Right: By the time he achieved his overdue British breakthrough JOE TEX had converted to Islam and changed his name to Joseph Hazziez.

Far Right: So these were the mysterious creatures who built Stonehenge --- Gary Glitter and the TIMELORDS.

Bottom Right: Bob Hope had his first hit record in 1939. Fifty years later his television show featured TIFFANY, who had her first hit in 1987.

During his first period of solo success FRANKIE VALLI sported a Vandyke.

Below: Shown in September 1982, the month of the release of their first hit, are TEARS FOR FEARS' Curt Smith (left) and Roland Orzabal.

TIME ZONE UK/US, male vocal/instrumental duo — 9 wks

19 Jan 85	**WORLD DESTRUCTION** *Virgin VS 743*	44	9 wks

World Destruction features John Lydon and Afrika Bambaataa. See also Afrika Bambaataa and James Brown; Afrika Bambaataa and the Soul Sonic Force; Afrika Bambaataa with UB40 and Family.

TIMEBOX UK, male vocal/instrumental group — 4 wks

24 Jul 68	**BEGGIN'** *Deram DM 194*	38	4 wks

TIMELORDS UK, male/female vocal group — 9 wks

4 Jun 88	★ **DOCTORIN' THE TARDIS** *KLF KLF 003*	1	9 wks

TIMEX SOCIAL CLUB US, male vocal/instrumental group — 9 wks

13 Sep 86	**RUMORS** *Cooltempo COOL 133*	13	9 wks

TIN MACHINE US/UK, male vocal/instrumental group — 4 wks

1 Jul 89	**UNDER THE GOD** *EMI-USA MT 68*	51	2 wks
9 Sep 89	**TIN MACHINE/ MAGGIE'S FARM (LIVE)** *EMI-USA MT 73*	48	2 wks

TINGO TANGO UK, male instrumental group — 2 wks

21 Jul 90	**IT IS JAZZ** *Champion CHAMP 250*	68	2 wks

TINY TIM US, male vocalist — 1 wk

5 Feb 69	**GREAT BALLS OF FIRE** *Reprise RS 20802*	45	1 wk

TITANIC Norway/UK, male instrumental group — 12 wks

25 Sep 71	● **SULTANA** *CBS 5365*	5	12 wks

TITIYO Sweden, female vocalist — 4 wks

3 Mar 90	**AFTER THE RAIN** *Arista 112722*	60	3 wks
6 Oct 90	**FLOWERS** *Arista 113212*	71	1 wk

Cara TIVEY – *See Billy BRAGG*

Art and Dotty TODD US, male/female vocal duo — 7 wks

13 Feb 53	● **BROKEN WINGS** *HMV B 10399*	6	7 wks

TOGETHER UK, male vocal/instrumental group — 8 wks

4 Aug 90	**HARDCORE UPROAR** *FFRR F 143*	12	8 wks

TOK – *See TIK and TOK*

TOKENS US, male vocal group — 12 wks

21 Dec 61	**THE LION SLEEPS TONIGHT** *RCA 1263*	11	12 wks

TOL and TOL Holland, male vocal/instrumental duo — 2 wks

14 Apr 90	**ELENI** *Dover ROJ 5*	73	2 wks

TOM TOM CLUB US, female/male vocal/instrumental group — 20 wks

20 Jun 81	● **WORDY RAPPINGHOOD** *Island WIP 6694*	7	9 wks
10 Oct 81	**GENIUS OF LOVE** *Island WIP 6735*	65	2 wks
7 Aug 82	**UNDER THE BOARDWALK** *Island WIP 6762*	22	9 wks

Satoshi TOMIIE – *See Frankie KNUCKLES*

TONGUE 'N' CHEEK UK, male/female vocal/instrumental group — 22 wks

27 Feb 88	**NOBODY (CAN LOVE ME)** *Criminal BUS 6*	59	6 wks
25 Nov 89	**ENCORE** *Syncopate SY 33*	41	4 wks
14 Apr 90	**TOMORROW** *Syncopate SY 34*	20	7 wks
4 Aug 90	**NOBODY** *Syncopate SY 37*	37	5 wks

Act billed as Tongue In Cheek on first hit.

TONIGHT UK, male vocal/instrumental group — 10 wks

28 Jan 78	**DRUMMER MAN** *Target TDS 1*	14	8 wks
20 May 78	**MONEY THAT'S YOUR PROBLEM** *Target TDS 2*	66	2 wks

TONY! TONI! TONÉ! US, male vocal group — 5 wk

30 Jun 90	**OAKLAND STROKE** *Wing WING 7*	50	5 wks

TOO TOUGH TEE – *See DYNAMIX featuring TOO TOUGH TEE*

TOP LINERS – *See Rocky SHARPE and the REPLAYS*

TOPOL Israel, male vocalist — 20 wks

20 Apr 67	● **IF I WERE A RICH MAN** *CBS 202651*	9	20 wks

Mel TORME US, male vocalist — 32 wks

27 Apr 56	**MOUNTAIN GREENERY** *Vogue/Coral Q 72150*	15	11 wks
27 Jul 56	● **MOUNTAIN GREENERY (re-entry)** *Vogue/Coral Q 72150*	4	13 wks
3 Jan 63	**COMING HOME BABY** *London HLK 9643*	13	8 wks

TORNADOS UK, male instrumental group — 59 wks

30 Aug 62	★ **TELSTAR** *Decca F 11494*	1	25 wks
10 Jan 63	● **GLOBETROTTER** *Decca F 11562*	5	11 wks
21 Mar 63	**ROBOT** *Decca F 11606*	17	12 wks
6 Jun 63	**THE ICE CREAM MAN** *Decca F 11662*	18	9 wks
10 Oct 63	**DRAGONFLY** *Decca F 11745*	41	2 wks

Mitchell TOROK US, male vocalist — 19 wks

28 Sep 56	● **WHEN MEXICO GAVE UP THE RUMBA** *Brunswick 05586*	6	17 wks
11 Jan 57	**RED LIGHT GREEN LIGHT** *Brunswick 05626*	29	1 wk
1 Feb 57	**WHEN MEXICO GAVE UP THE RUMBA (re-entry)** *Brunswick 05586*	30	1 wk

Peter TOSH *Jamaica, male vocalist*   **12 wks**

21 Oct 78	(YOU GOTTA WALK) DON'T LOOK BACK		
	Rolling Stones 2859	43	7 wks
2 Apr 83	JOHNNY B. GOODE *EMI RIC 115*	48	5 wks

TOTAL CONTRAST *UK, male vocal/instrumental duo*   **22 wks**

3 Aug 85	TAKES A LITTLE TIME *London LON 71*	17	10 wks
19 Oct 85	HIT AND RUN *London LON 76*	41	5 wks
1 Mar 86	THE RIVER *London LON 83*	44	3 wks
10 May 86	WHAT YOU GONNA DO ABOUT IT *London LON 95*	63	4 wks

TOTO *US, male vocal/instrumental group*   **34 wks**

10 Feb 79	HOLD THE LINE *CBS 6784*	14	11 wks
5 Feb 83	● AFRICA *CBS A 2510*	3	10 wks
9 Apr 83	ROSANNA *CBS A 2079*	12	8 wks
18 Jun 83	I WON'T HOLD YOU BACK *CBS A 3392*	37	5 wks

TOTO COELO *UK, female vocal group*   **14 wks**

7 Aug 82	● I EAT CANNIBALS PART 1 *Radialchoice TIC 10*	8	10 wks
13 Nov 82	DRACULA'S TANGO/ MUCHO MACHO		
	Radialchoice TIC 11	54	4 wks

TOTTENHAM HOTSPUR F.A. CUP FINAL SQUAD *UK, male football team vocalists*   **20 wks**

9 May 81	● OSSIE'S DREAM (SPURS ARE ON THEIR WAY TO WEMBLEY) *Rockney SHELF 1*	5	8 wks
1 May 82	TOTTENHAM TOTTENHAM *Rockney SHELF 2*	19	7 wks
9 May 87	HOT SHOT TOTTENHAM! *Rainbow RBR 16*	18	5 wks

First two hits feature the uncredited vocal and instrumental talents of Chas and Dave. See Chas and Dave.

TOUCH OF SOUL   **3 wks**
UK, male/female vocal/instrumental group

19 May 90	WE GOT THE LOVE *Cooltempo COOL 204*	46	3 wks

TOURISTS *UK, male/female vocal/instrumental group*   **40 wks**

9 Jun 79	BLIND AMONG THE FLOWERS *Logo GO 350*	52	5 wks
8 Sep 79	THE LONELIEST MAN IN THE WORLD		
	Logo GO 360	32	7 wks
10 Nov 79	● I ONLY WANT TO BE WITH YOU *Logo GO 370*	4	14 wks
9 Feb 80	● SO GOOD TO BE BACK HOME AGAIN *Logo TOUR 1*	8	9 wks
18 Oct 80	DON'T SAY I TOLD YOU SO *RCA TOUR 2*	40	5 wks

Carol Lynn TOWNES *US, female vocalist*   **7 wks**

4 Aug 84	99 ½ *Polydor POSP 693*	47	4 wks
19 Jan 85	BELIEVE IN THE BEAT *Polydor POSP 720*	56	3 wks

Pete TOWNSHEND *UK, male vocalist*   **17 wks**

5 Apr 80	ROUGH BOYS *Atco K 11460*	39	6 wks
21 Jun 80	LET MY LOVE OPEN YOUR DOOR *Atco K 11486*	46	6 wks
21 Aug 82	UNIFORMS (CORPS D'ESPRIT) *Atco K 11751*	48	5 wks

TOY DOLLS *UK, male vocal/instrumental group*   **12 wks**

1 Dec 84	● NELLIE THE ELEPHANT *Volume VOL 11*	4	12 wks

TOYAH *UK, female vocalist*   **87 wks**

14 Feb 81	● FOUR FROM TOYAH (EP) *Safari TOY 1*	4	14 wks
16 May 81	● I WANT TO BE FREE *Safari SAFE 34*	8	11 wks
3 Oct 81	● THUNDER IN THE MOUNTAINS *Safari SAFE 38*	4	9 wks
28 Nov 81	FOUR MORE FROM TOYAH (EP) *Safari TOY 2*	14	9 wks
22 May 82	BRAVE NEW WORLD *Safari SAFE 45*	21	8 wks
17 Jul 82	IEYA *Safari SAFE 28*	48	5 wks
9 Apr 83	BE LOUD BE PROUD (BE HEARD) *Safari SAFE 52*	30	7 wks
24 Sep 83	REBEL RUN *Safari SAFE 56*	24	5 wks
19 Nov 83	THE VOW *Safari SAFE 58*	50	5 wks
27 Apr 85	DON'T FALL IN LOVE (I SAID) *Portrait A 6160*	22	6 wks
29 Jun 85	SOUL PASSING THROUGH SOUL *Portrait A 6359*	57	3 wks
25 Apr 87	ECHO BEACH *EG EGO 31*	54	5 wks

Tracks on Four From Toyah EP: It's A Mystery/Revelations/War Boys/Angels And Demons.
Tracks on Four More From Toyah EP: Good Morning Universe/Urban Tribesman/In The Fairground/The Furious Futures.

TOYS *US, female vocal group*   **17 wks**

4 Nov 65	● A LOVER'S CONCERTO *Stateside SS 460*	5	13 wks
27 Jan 66	ATTACK *Stateside SS 483*	36	4 wks

T'PAU *UK, male/female vocal/instrumental group*   **68 wks**

8 Aug 87	● HEART AND SOUL *Siren SRN 41*	4	13 wks
24 Oct 87	★ CHINA IN YOUR HAND *Siren SRN 64*	1	15 wks
30 Jan 88	● VALENTINE *Siren SRN 69*	9	8 wks
2 Apr 88	SEX TALK (LIVE) *Siren SRN 80*	23	7 wks
25 Jun 88	I WILL BE WITH YOU *Siren SRN 87*	14	6 wks
1 Oct 88	SECRET GARDEN *Siren SRN 93*	18	7 wks
7 Jan 89	ROAD TO OUR DREAM *Siren SRN 100*	42	6 wks
25 Mar 89	ONLY THE LONELY *Siren SRN 107*	28	6 wks

TRACIE *UK, female vocalist*   **24 wks**

26 Mar 83	● THE HOUSE THAT JACK BUILT *Respond KOB 701*	9	8 wks
16 Jul 83	GIVE IT SOME EMOTION *Respond KOB 704*	24	9 wks
14 Apr 84	SOUL'S ON FIRE *Respond KOB 708*	73	2 wks
9 Jun 84	(I LOVE YOU) WHEN YOU SLEEP *Respond KOB 710*	59	3 wks
17 Aug 85	I CAN'T LEAVE YOU ALONE *Respond SBS 1*	60	2 wks

Last hit credited to Tracie Young.

TRACY – *See MASSIVO featuring TRACY*

TRAFFIC *UK, male vocal/instrumental group*   **40 wks**

1 Jun 67	● PAPER SUN *Island WIP 6002*	5	10 wks
6 Sep 67	● HOLE IN MY SHOE *Island WIP 6017*	2	14 wks
29 Nov 67	● HERE WE GO ROUND THE MULBERRY BUSH		
	Island WIP 6025	8	12 wks
6 Mar 68	NO FACE, NO NAME, NO NUMBER *Island WIP 6030*	40	4 wks

TRAMAINE *US, female vocalist*   **2 wks**

5 Oct 85	FALL DOWN (SPIRIT OF LOVE) *A &M AM 281*	60	2 wks

TRAMMPS *US, male vocal group*   **50 wks**

23 Nov 74	ZING WENT THE STRINGS OF MY HEART		
	Buddah BDS 405	29	10 wks
1 Feb 75	SIXTY MINUTE MAN *Buddah BDS 415*	40	4 wks
11 Oct 75	● HOLD BACK THE NIGHT *Buddah BDS 437*	5	8 wks
13 Mar 76	THAT'S WHERE THE HAPPY PEOPLE GO		
	Atlantic K 10703	35	8 wks
24 Jul 76	SOUL SEARCHIN' TIME *Atlantic K 10797*	42	3 wks
14 May 77	DISCO INFERNO *Atlantic K 10914*	16	7 wks
24 Jun 78	DISCO INFERNO (re-issue) *Atlantic K 11135*	47	10 wks

TRANSVISION VAMP
UK, male/female vocal/instrumantal group   **52 wks**

16 Apr 88		TELL THAT GIRL TO SHUT UP *MCA TVV 2*	45	3 wks
25 Jun 88	●	I WANT YOUR LOVE *MCA TVV 3*	5	13 wks
17 Sep 88		REVOLUTION BABY *MCA TVV 4*	30	5 wks
19 Nov 88		SISTER MOON *MCA TVV 5*	41	5 wks
1 Apr 89	●	BABY I DON'T CARE *MCA TVV 6*	3	11 wks
10 Jun 89		THE ONLY ONE *MCA TVV 7*	15	6 wks
5 Aug 89		LANDSLIDE OF LOVE *MCA TVV 8*	14	5 wks
4 Nov 89		BORN TO BE SOLD *MCA TVV 9*	22	4 wks

TRANS-X *Canada, female/male vocal/instrumental group*   **9 wks**

13 Jul 85	●	LIVING ON VIDEO *Boiling Point POSP 650*	9	9 wks

TRASH *UK, male vocal/instrumental group*   **3 wks**

25 Oct 69	GOLDEN SLUMBERS/ CARRY THAT WEIGHT *Apple 17*	35	3 wks

TRAVELING WILBURYS
UK/US, male vocal/instrumental group   **19 wks**

29 Oct 88	HANDLE WITH CARE *Wilbury W 7732*	21	13 wks
11 Mar 89	END OF THE LINE *Wilbury W 7637*	52	4 wks
30 Jun 90	NOBODY'S CHILD *Wilbury W 9773*	44	2 wks

Randy TRAVIS *US, male vocalist*   **6 wks**

21 May 88	FOREVER AND EVER, AMEN *Warner Bros. W 8384*	55	6 wks

John TRAVOLTA *US, male vocalist*   **24 wks**

7 Oct 78	●	SANDY *Polydor POSP 6*	2	15 wks
2 Dec 78		GREASED LIGHTNIN' *Polydor POSP 14*	11	9 wks

See also John Travolta and Olivia Newton-John.

John TRAVOLTA and Olivia NEWTON-JOHN *US/UK, male/female vocal duo*   **47 wks**

20 May 78	★	YOU'RE THE ONE THAT I WANT *RSO 006*	1	26 wks
16 Sep 78	★	SUMMER NIGHTS *RSO 18*	1	19 wks
22 Dec 90	●	THE GREASE MEGAMIX *Polydor PO 114*	5†	2 wks

See also John Travolta; Olivia Newton-John.

TREMELOES *UK, male vocal/instrumental group*   **131 wks**

2 Feb 67	●	HERE COMES MY BABY *CBS 202519*	4	11 wks
27 Apr 67	★	SILENCE IS GOLDEN *CBS 2723*	1	15 wks
2 Aug 67	●	EVEN THE BAD TIMES ARE GOOD *CBS 2930*	4	13 wks
8 Nov 67		BE MINE *CBS 3043*	39	2 wks
17 Jan 68	●	SUDDENLY YOU LOVE ME *CBS 3234*	6	11 wks
8 May 68		HELULE HELULE *CBS 2889*	14	9 wks
18 Sep 68	●	MY LITTLE LADY *CBS 3480*	6	12 wks
11 Dec 68		I SHALL BE RELEASED *CBS 3873*	29	5 wks
19 Mar 69		HELLO WORLD *CBS 4065*	14	8 wks
1 Nov 69	●	(CALL ME) NUMBER ONE *CBS 4582*	2	14 wks
21 Mar 70		BY THE WAY *CBS 4815*	35	6 wks
12 Sep 70	●	ME AND MY LIFE *CBS 5139*	4	18 wks
10 Jul 71		HELLO BUDDY *CBS 7294*	32	7 wks

See also Brian Poole and the Tremeloes.

Jackie TRENT *UK, female vocalist*   **17 wks**

22 Apr 65	★	WHERE ARE YOU NOW (MY LOVE) *Pye 7N 15776*	1	11 wks
1 Jul 65		WHEN THE SUMMERTIME IS OVER *Pye 7N 15865*	39	2 wks
2 Apr 69		I'LL BE THERE *Pye 7N 17693*	38	4 wks

T. REX *UK, male vocal/instrumental group*   **227 wks**

8 May 68		DEBORA *Regal Zonophone RZ 3008*	34	7 wks
4 Sep 68		ONE INCH ROCK *Regal Zonophone RZ 3011*	28	7 wks
9 Aug 69		KING OF THE RUMBLING SPIRES *Regal Zonophone RZ 3022*	44	1 wk
24 Oct 70	●	RIDE A WHITE SWAN *Fly BUG 1*	2	20 wks
27 Feb 71	★	HOT LOVE *Fly BUG 6*	1	17 wks
10 Jul 71	★	GET IT ON *Fly BUG 10*	1	13 wks
13 Nov 71	●	JEEPSTER *Fly BUG 16*	2	15 wks
29 Jan 72	★	TELEGRAM SAM *T. Rex 101*	1	12 wks
1 Apr 72	●	DEBORA/ ONE INCH ROCK (re-entry) *Magnifly Echo 102*	7	10 wks
13 May 72	★	METAL GURU *EMI MARC 1*	1	14 wks
16 Sep 72	●	CHILDREN OF THE REVOLUTION *EMI MARC 2*	2	10 wks
9 Dec 72	●	SOLID GOLD EASY ACTION *EMI MARC 3*	2	11 wks
10 Mar 73	●	20TH CENTURY BOY *EMI MARC 4*	3	9 wks
16 Jun 73	●	THE GROOVER *EMI MARC 5*	4	9 wks
24 Nov 73		TRUCK ON (TYKE) *EMI MARC 6*	12	11 wks
9 Feb 74		TEENAGE DREAM *EMI MARC 7*	13	9 wks
13 Jul 74		LIGHT OF LOVE *EMI MARC 8*	22	5 wks
16 Nov 74		ZIP GUN BOOGIE *EMI MARC 9*	41	3 wks
12 Jul 75		NEW YORK CITY *EMI MARC 10*	15	8 wks
11 Oct 75		DREAMY LADY *EMI MARC 11*	30	5 wks
6 Mar 76		LONDON BOYS *EMI MARC 13*	40	3 wks
19 Jun 76		I LOVE TO BOOGIE *EMI MARC 14*	13	9 wks
2 Oct 76		LASER LOVE *EMI MARC 15*	41	4 wks
2 Apr 77		THE SOUL OF MY SUIT *EMI MARC 16*	42	3 wks
9 May 81		RETURN OF THE ELECTRIC WARRIOR (EP) *Ram MBSF 001*	50	4 wks
19 Sep 81		YOU SCARE ME TO DEATH *Cherry Red CHERRY 29*	51	4 wks
27 Mar 82		TELEGRAM SAM (re-entry) *T. Rex 101*	69	2 wks
18 May 85		MEGAREX *Marc On Wax TANX 1*	72	2 wks
9 May 87		GET IT ON (re-mix) *Marc On Wax MARC 10*	54	4 wks

Regal Zonophone and Magnifly hits bill the group as Tyrannosaurus Rex. Teenage Dream is by Marc Bolan and T. Rex. Dreamy Lady is by T. Rex Disco Party. Both hits from 1981 just bill Marc Bolan. Megarex is a medley of extracts from the following T.Rex hits: Truck On (Tyke)/The Groover/Telegram Sam/Shock Rock/Metal Guru/20th Century Boy/Children Of The Revolution/Hot Love. Tracks on EP: Sing Me A Song/Endless Sleep/The Lilac Hand Of Menihol Dan.

TRIBAL HOUSE *US, male vocal/instrumental group*   **2 wks**

3 Feb 90	MOTHERLAND-A-FRI-CA *Cooltempo COOL 198*	57	2 wks

Tony TRIBE *Jamaica, male vocalist*   **2 wks**

16 Jul 69	RED RED WINE *Downtown DT 419*	50	1 wk
9 Aug 69	RED RED WINE (re-entry) *Downtown DT 419*	46	1 wk

A TRIBE CALLED QUEST *US, male rap group*   **3 wks**

18 Aug 90	BONITA APPLEBUM *Jive JIVE 256*	47	3 wks

TRIBE OF TOFFS *UK, male vocal/instrumental group*   **5 wks**

24 Dec 88	JOHN KETTLEY (IS A WEATHERMAN) *Completely Different DAFT 1*	21	5 wks

TRICKY DISCO *UK, male vocal/instrumental group*   **8 wks**

28 Jul 90	TRICKY DISCO *Warp WAP 7*	14	8 wks

TRIFFIDS *New Zealand, male vocal/instrumental group*   **1 wk**

6 Feb 88	**A TRICK OF THE LIGHT** *Island IS 350*.....................	**73**	1 wk

TRINIDAD OIL COMPANY   **5 wks**
Trinidad, male/female vocal/instrumental group

21 May 77	**THE CALENDAR SONG** *Harvest HAR 5122*	**34**	5 wks

TRINITY – *See Julie DRISCOLL, Brian AUGER and the TRINITY*

TRIO *Germany, male vocal/instrumental group*   **10 wks**

3 Jul 82	● **DA DA DA** *Mobile Suit Corporation CORP 5*......................	**2**	10 wks

TRISTRAM – *See NEW VAUDEVILLE BAND*

TRIUMPH *Canada, male vocal/instrumental group*   **2 wks**

22 Nov 80	**I LIVE FOR THE WEEKEND** *RCA 13*	**59**	2 wks

TROGGS *UK, male vocal/instrumental group*   **85 wks**

5 May 66	● **WILD THING** *Fontana TF 689*........................	**2**	12 wks
14 Jul 66	★ **WITH A GIRL LIKE YOU** *Fontana TF 717*	**1**	12 wks
29 Sep 66	● **I CAN'T CONTROL MYSELF** *Page One POF 001*	**2**	14 wks
15 Dec 66	● **ANY WAY THAT YOU WANT ME** *Page One POF 010*	**8**	10 wks
16 Feb 67	**GIVE IT TO ME** *Page One POF 015*	**12**	10 wks
1 Jun 67	**NIGHT OF THE LONG GRASS** *Page One POF 022*.........	**17**	6 wks
26 Jul 67	**HI HI HAZEL** *Page One POF 030*.....................	**42**	3 wks
18 Oct 67	● **LOVE IS ALL AROUND** *Page One POF 040*..................	**5**	14 wks
28 Feb 68	**LITTLE GIRL** *Page One POF 056*.....................	**37**	4 wks

TROUBADOURS DU ROI BAUDOUIN   **11 wks**
Zaire, male/female vocal group

19 Mar 69	**SANCTUS (MISSA LUBA)** *Philips BF 1732*	**28**	6 wks
7 May 69	**SANCTUS (MISSA LUBA) (re-entry)** *Philips BF 1732*	**37**	5 wks

TROUBLE FUNK *US, male vocal/instrumental group*   **3 wks**

27 Jun 87	**WOMAN OF PRINCIPLE** *Fourth & Broadway BRW 70*.........	**65**	3 wks

Doris TROY *US, female vocalist*   **12 wks**

19 Nov 64	**WHATCHA GONNA DO ABOUT IT** *Atlantic AT 4011*......	**37**	7 wks
21 Jan 65	**WHATCHA GONNA DO ABOUT IT (re-entry)** *Atlantic AT 4011*	**38**	5 wks

TRUCKIN' CO. – *See Garnet MIMMS and TRUCKIN' CO.*

Andrea TRUE CONNECTION   **16 wks**
US, female vocalist, male instrumental backing group

17 Apr 76	● **MORE MORE MORE** *Buddah BDS 442*	**5**	10 wks
4 Mar 78	**WHAT'S YOUR NAME WHAT'S YOUR NUMBER** *Buddah BDS 467*..................	**34**	6 wks

TRUSSEL *US, male vocal/instrumental group*   **4 wks**

8 Mar 80	**LOVE INJECTION** *Elektra K 12412*	**43**	4 wks

TRUTH *UK, male vocal duo*   **6 wks**

3 Feb 66	**GIRL** *Pye 7N 17035*	**27**	6 wks

TRUTH *UK, male vocal/instrumental group*   **16 wks**

11 Jun 83	**CONFUSION (HITS US EVERY TIME)** *Formation TRUTH 1*.........................	**22**	7 wks
27 Aug 83	**A STEP IN THE RIGHT DIRECTION** *Formation TRUTH 2*.........................	**32**	7 wks
4 Feb 84	**NO STONE UNTURNED** *Formation TRUTH 3*..............	**66**	2 wks

TUBES *US, male vocal/instrumental group*   **18 wks**

19 Nov 77	**WHITE PUNKS ON DOPE** *A & M AMS 7323*	**28**	4 wks
28 Apr 79	**PRIME TIME** *A & M AMS 7423*	**34**	10 wks
12 Sep 81	**DON'T WANT TO WAIT ANYMORE** *Capitol CL 208*......	**60**	4 wks

TUBEWAY ARMY – *See Gary NUMAN*

Junior TUCKER *UK, male vocalist*   **2 wks**

2 Jun 90	**DON'T TEST** *10 TEN 299*	**54**	2 wks

Louise TUCKER *Holland, female vocalist*   **5 wks**

9 Apr 83	**MIDNIGHT BLUE** *Ariola ARO 289*	**59**	5 wks

Tommy TUCKER *US, male vocalist*   **10 wks**

26 Mar 64	**HI-HEEL SNEAKERS** *Pye 7N 25238*.........................	**23**	10 wks

TURNER – *See SKIPWORTH and TURNER*

Claramae TURNER – *See VARIOUS ARTISTS (Carousel Soundtrack)*

Ike and Tina TURNER   **44 wks**
US, male instrumentalist - guitar, and female vocalist

9 Jun 66	● **RIVER DEEP MOUNTAIN HIGH** *London HL 10046*	**3**	13 wks
28 Jul 66	**TELL HER I'M NOT HOME** *Warner Bros. WB 5753*	**48**	1 wk
27 Oct 66	**A LOVE LIKE YOURS** *London HL 10083*	**16**	10 wks
12 Feb 69	**RIVER DEEP MOUNTAIN HIGH** *London HLU 10242* ...	**33**	7 wks
8 Sep 73	● **NUTBUSH CITY LIMITS** *United Artists UP 35582*	**4**	13 wks

See also Tina Turner.

Ruby TURNER *UK, female vocalist*   **27 wks**

25 Jan 86	**IF YOU'RE READY (COME GO WITH ME)** *Jive JIVE 109*.................................	**30**	7 wks
29 Mar 86	**I'M IN LOVE** *Jive JIVE 118*.................................	**61**	4 wks
13 Sep 86	**BYE BABY** *Jive JIVE 126*.................................	**52**	3 wks
14 Mar 87	**I'D RATHER GO BLIND** *Jive RTS 1*.......................	**24**	8 wks
16 May 87	**I'M IN LOVE** *Jive RTS 2*.............................	**57**	2 wks
13 Jan 90	**IT'S GONNA BE ALRIGHT** *Jive RTS 7*...................	**57**	3 wks

Jive JIVE 109 features Jonathan Butler - South Africa, male instrumentalist - guitar.

Sammy TURNER *US, male vocalist*   **2 wks**

13 Nov 59	**ALWAYS** *London HLX 8963*	**26**	2 wks

Above: U2 are shown in January 1980, little realizing the world fame they would earn in the new decade.

Top Right: TINA TURNER toasts the Eighties, her best decade.

In the late Eighties things were looking up at and for TRANSVISION VAMP.

Tina TURNER US, female vocalist — 127 wks

Date	Title	Pos	Wks
19 Nov 83 ●	LET'S STAY TOGETHER Capitol CL 316	6	13 wks
25 Feb 84	HELP Capitol CL 325	40	6 wks
16 Jun 84 ●	WHAT'S LOVE GOT TO DO WITH IT Capitol CL 334	3	16 wks
15 Sep 84	BETTER BE GOOD TO ME Capitol CL 338	45	5 wks
17 Nov 84	PRIVATE DANCER Capitol CL 343	26	9 wks
2 Mar 85	I CAN'T STAND THE RAIN Capitol CL 352	57	3 wks
20 Jul 85 ●	WE DON'T NEED ANOTHER HERO (THUNDERDOME) Capitol CL 364	3	12 wks
12 Oct 85	ONE OF THE LIVING Capitol CL 376	55	2 wks
23 Aug 86	TYPICAL MALE Capitol CL 419	33	6 wks
8 Nov 86	TWO PEOPLE Capitol CL 430	43	4 wks
14 Mar 87	WHAT YOU GET IS WHAT YOU SEE Capitol CL 439	30	7 wks
13 Jun 87	BREAK EVERY RULE Capitol CL 452	43	3 wks
19 Mar 88	ADDICTED TO LOVE (LIVE) Capitol CL 484	71	2 wks
2 Sep 89 ●	THE BEST Capitol CL 543	5	12 wks
18 Nov 89 ●	I DON'T WANNA LOSE YOU Capitol CL 553	8	11 wks
17 Feb 90	STEAMY WINDOWS Capitol CL 560	13	6 wks
11 Aug 90	LOOK ME IN THE HEART Capitol CL 584	31	6 wks
13 Oct 90	BE TENDER WITH ME BABY Capitol CL 593	28	4 wks

See also Ike and Tina Turner; Bryan Adams and Tina Turner; Eric Clapton and Tina Turner; Rod Stewart and Tina Turner.

TURNTABLE ORCHESTRA — 4 wks
US, male vocal/instrumental duo

Date	Title	Pos	Wks
21 Jan 89	YOU'RE GONNA MISS ME Republic LIC 012	52	4 wks

TURTLES US, male vocal/instrumental group — 39 wks

Date	Title	Pos	Wks
23 Mar 67	HAPPY TOGETHER London HL 10115	12	12 wks
15 Jun 67 ●	SHE'D RATHER BE WITH ME London HLU 10135	4	15 wks
30 Oct 68 ●	ELENORE London HL 10223	7	12 wks

TUXEDOS – See Bobby ANGELO and the TUXEDOS

TWEETS UK, male instrumental group — 34 wks

Date	Title	Pos	Wks
12 Sep 81 ●	THE BIRDIE SONG (BIRDIE DANCE) PRT 7P 219	2	23 wks
5 Dec 81	LET'S ALL SING LIKE THE BIRDIES SING PRT 7P 226	44	6 wks
18 Dec 82	THE BIRDIE SONG (BIRDIE DANCE) (re-entry) PRT 7P 219	46	5 wks

TWENTY 4 SEVEN featuring CAPTAIN HOLLYWOOD — 16 wks
US/Holland/Germany/Italy, male/female vocal/instrumental group

Date	Title	Pos	Wks
22 Sep 90 ●	I CAN'T STAND IT BCM BCMR 395	7	10 wks
24 Nov 90	ARE YOU DREAMING BCM BCM 07504	17†	6 wks

TWICE AS MUCH UK, male vocal duo — 9 wks

Date	Title	Pos	Wks
16 Jun 66	SITTIN' ON A FENCE Immediate IM 033	25	9 wks

TWIGGY UK, female vocalist — 10 wks

Date	Title	Pos	Wks
14 Aug 76	HERE I GO AGAIN Mercury 6007 100	17	10 wks

TWIN HYPE US, male rap duo — 2 wks

Date	Title	Pos	Wks
15 Jul 89	DO IT TO THE CROWD Profile PROF 255	65	2 wks

TWINKLE UK, female vocalist — 20 wks

Date	Title	Pos	Wks
26 Nov 64 ●	TERRY Decca F 12013	4	15 wks
25 Feb 65	GOLDEN LIGHTS Decca F 12076	21	5 wks

TWISTED SISTER US, male vocal/instrumental group — 28 wks

Date	Title	Pos	Wks
26 Mar 83	I AM (I'M ME) Atlantic A 9854	18	9 wks
28 May 83	THE KIDS ARE BACK Atlantic A 9827	32	6 wks
20 Aug 83	YOU CAN'T STOP ROCK 'N' ROLL Atlantic A 9792	43	4 wks
2 Jun 84	WE'RE NOT GONNA TAKE IT Atlantic A 9657	58	4 wks
18 Jan 86	LEADER OF THE PACK Atlantic A 9478	47	3 wks

Conway TWITTY US, male vocalist — 36 wks

Date	Title	Pos	Wks
14 Nov 58 ★	IT'S ONLY MAKE BELIEVE MGM 992	1	15 wks
27 Mar 59	STORY OF MY LOVE MGM 1003	30	1 wks
21 Aug 59 ●	MONA LISA MGM 1029	5	14 wks
21 Jul 60	IS A BLUE BIRD BLUE MGM 1082	43	3 wks
23 Feb 61	C'EST SI BON MGM 1118	40	3 wks

2 FOR JOY UK, male vocal/instrumental duo — 1 wk

Date	Title	Pos	Wks
1 Dec 90	IN A STATE Mercury MER 333	61	1 wk

2 IN A ROOM US, male producer — 1 wk

Date	Title	Pos	Wks
18 Nov 89	SOMEBODY IN THE HOUSE SAY YEAH! Big Life BLR 12	66	1 wk

TWO MAN SOUND — 7 wks
Belgium, male vocal/instrumental group

Date	Title	Pos	Wks
20 Jan 79	QUE TAL AMERICA Miracle M 1	46	7 wks

See also Calibre Cuts.

TWO MEN, A DRUM MACHINE AND A TRUMPET UK, male instrumental duo — 8 wks

Date	Title	Pos	Wks
9 Jan 88	I'M TIRED OF GETTING PUSHED AROUND London LON 141	18	8 wks

See also Wee Papa Girl Rappers.

TWO NATIONS UK, male vocal/instrumental group — 1 wk

Date	Title	Pos	Wks
20 Jun 87	THAT'S THE WAY IT FEELS 10 TEN 168	74	1 wk

TWO PEOPLE UK, male vocal/instrumental group — 2 wks

Date	Title	Pos	Wks
31 Jan 87	HEAVEN Polydor POSP 844	63	2 wks

TYGERS OF PAN TANG — 15 wks
UK, male vocal/instrumental group

Date	Title	Pos	Wks
14 Feb 81	HELLBOUND MCA 672	48	3 wks
27 Mar 82	LOVE POTION NO. 9 MCA 769	45	6 wks
10 Jul 82	RENDEZVOUS MCA 777	49	4 wks
11 Sep 82	PARIS BY AIR MCA 790	63	2 wks

Bonnie TYLER *UK, female vocalist*   **68 wks**

30 Oct 76	● LOST IN FRANCE *RCA 2734*	9	10 wks
19 Mar 77	MORE THAN A LOVER *RCA PB 5008*	27	6 wks
3 Dec 77	● IT'S A HEARTACHE *RCA PB 5057*	4	12 wks
30 Jun 79	MARRIED MEN *RCA PB 5164.*	35	6 wks
19 Feb 83	★ TOTAL ECLIPSE OF THE HEART *CBS TYLER 1*	1	12 wks
7 May 83	FASTER THAN THE SPEED OF NIGHT *CBS A 3338*	43	4 wks
25 Jun 83	HAVE YOU EVER SEEN THE RAIN *CBS A 3517.*	47	3 wks
31 Aug 85	● HOLDING OUT FOR A HERO *CBS A 4251.*	2	13 wks
14 Dec 85	LOVING YOU'S A DIRTY JOB BUT SOMEBODY'S GOTTA DO IT *CBS A 6662*	73	2 wks

Loving You's A Dirty Job... *credits guest vocalist Todd Rundgren. See also Todd Rundgren; Shaky and Bonnie.*

TYMES *US, male vocal group*   **41 wks**

25 Jul 63	SO MUCH IN LOVE *Cameo Parkway P 871*	21	8 wks
15 Jan 69	PEOPLE *Direction 58 3903*	16	10 wks
21 Sep 74	YOU LITTLE TRUST MAKER *RCA 2456*	18	9 wks
21 Dec 74	★ MS GRACE *RCA 2493*	1	11 wks
17 Jan 76	GOD'S GONNA PUNISH YOU *RCA 2626.*	41	3 wks

TYPICALLY TROPICAL   **11 wks**
UK, male vocal/instrumental duo

5 Jul 75	★ BARBADOS *Gull GULS 14.*	1	11 wks

TYREE *US, male producer*   **10 wks**

25 Feb 89	TURN UP THE BASS *FFRR FFR 24*	12	7 wks
6 May 89	HARDCORE HIP HOUSE *DJ International DJIN 11*	70	2 wks
2 Dec 89	MOVE YOUR BODY *CBS 655470 7*	72	1 wk

Turn Up The Bass *features Kool Rock Steady - US, male rapper.* Move Your Body *features J.M.D. - US, male rapper.*

Judie TZUKE *UK, female vocalist*   **10 wks**

14 Jul 79	STAY WITH ME TILL DAWN *Rocket XPRES 17*	16	10 wks

UB40 *UK, male vocal/instrumental group*   **240 wks**

8 Mar 80	● KING/ FOOD FOR THOUGHT *Graduate GRAD 6*	4	13 wks
14 Jun 80	● MY WAY OF THINKING/ I THINK IT'S GOING TO RAIN *Graduate GRAD 8*	6	10 wks
1 Nov 80	● THE EARTH DIES SCREAMING/ DREAM A LIE *Graduate GRAD 10*	10	12 wks
23 May 81	DON'T LET IT PASS YOU BY/ DON'T SLOW DOWN *Dep International DEP 1*	16	9 wks
8 Aug 81	● ONE IN TEN *Dep International DEP 2.*	7	10 wks
13 Feb 82	I WON'T CLOSE MY EYES *Dep International DEP 3*	32	6 wks
15 May 82	LOVE IS ALL IS ALRIGHT *Dep International DEP 4*	29	7 wks
28 Aug 82	SO HERE I AM *Dep International DEP 5.*	25	9 wks
5 Feb 83	I'VE GOT MINE *Dep International 7 DEP 6*	45	4 wks
20 Aug 83	★ RED RED WINE *Dep International 7 DEP 7*	1	14 wks
15 Oct 83	● PLEASE DON'T MAKE ME CRY *Dep International 7 DEP 8*	10	8 wks
10 Dec 83	MANY RIVERS TO CROSS *Dep International 7 DEP 9*	16	8 wks
17 Mar 84	CHERRY OH BABY *Dep International DEP 10.*	12	8 wks
22 Sep 84	IF IT HAPPENS AGAIN *Dep International DEP 11*	9	8 wks
1 Dec 84	RIDDLE ME *Dep International DEP 15.*	59	2 wks
3 Aug 85	★ I GOT YOU BABE *DEP International DEP 20*	1	13 wks
26 Oct 85	● DON'T BREAK MY HEART *DEP International DEP 22*	3	13 wks
12 Jul 86	● SING OUR OWN SONG *DEP International DEP 23*	5	9 wks
27 Sep 86	ALL I WANT TO DO *DEP International DEP 24*	41	4 wks
17 Jan 87	RAT IN MI KITCHEN *DEP International DEP 25*	12	7 wks
9 May 87	WATCHDOGS *DEP International DEP 26.*	39	4 wks
10 Oct 87	MAYBE TOMORROW *DEP International DEP 27.*	14	8 wks
18 Jun 88	● BREAKFAST IN BED *DEP International DEP 29.*	6	11 wks
20 Aug 88	WHERE DID I GO WRONG *DEP International DEP 30*	26	6 wks
17 Jun 89	I WOULD DO FOR YOU *DEP International DEP 32.*	45	4 wks
18 Nov 89	● HOMELY GIRL *DEP International DEP 33.*	6	10 wks
27 Jan 90	HERE I AM (COME AND TAKE ME) *DEP International DEP 34.*	46	3 wks
31 Mar 90	● KINGSTON TOWN *DEP International DEP 35.*	4	12 wks
28 Jul 90	WEAR YOU TO THE BALL *DEP International DEP 36*	35	6 wks
1 Dec 90	IMPOSSIBLE LOVE *DEP International DEP 37.*	47	2 wks

I Got You Babe *and* Breakfast in Bed *feature guest vocalist Chrissie Hynde - US, female vocalist. See also Afrika Bambaataa and Family with UB40; Robert Palmer and UB40.*

UFO *UK, male vocal/instrumental group*   **31 wks**

5 Aug 78	ONLY YOU CAN ROCK ME *Chrysalis CHS 2241*	50	4 wks
27 Jan 79	DOCTOR DOCTOR *Chrysalis CHS 2287.*	35	6 wks
31 Mar 79	SHOOT SHOOT *Chrysalis CHS 2318.*	48	5 wks
12 Jan 80	YOUNG BLOOD *Chrysalis CHS 2399.*	36	5 wks
17 Jan 81	LONELY HEART *Chrysalis CHS 2482.*	41	5 wks
30 Jan 82	LET IT RAIN *Chrysalis CHS 2576.*	62	3 wks
19 Mar 83	WHEN IT'S TIME TO ROCK *Chrysalis CHS 2672.*	70	3 wks

U. K. *UK, male vocal/instrumental group*   **2 wks**

30 Jun 79	NOTHING TO LOSE *Polydor POSP 55*	67	2 wks

U.K. PLAYERS *UK, male vocal/instrumental group*   **3 wks**

14 May 83	LOVE'S GONNA GET YOU *RCA 326*	52	3 wks

U.K. SUBS *UK, male vocal/instrumental group*   **39 wks**

23 Jun 79	STRANGLEHOLD *Gem GEMS 5*	26	8 wks
8 Sep 79	TOMORROW'S GIRLS *Gem GEMS 10*	28	6 wks
1 Dec 79	SHE'S NOT THERE/ KICKS (EP) *Gem GEMS 14*	36	7 wks
8 Mar 80	WARHEAD *Gem GEMS 23*	30	4 wks
17 May 80	TEENAGE *Gem GEMS 30.*	32	5 wks
25 Oct 80	PARTY IN PARIS *Gem GEMS 42.*	37	4 wks
18 Apr 81	KEEP ON RUNNIN' (TILL YOU BURN) *Gem GEMS 45*	41	5 wks

Tracks on EP: *She's Not There/Kicks/Victim/The Same Thing.*

Tracey ULLMAN *UK, female vocalist*   **49 wks**

19 Mar 83	● BREAKAWAY *Stiff BUY 168*	4	11 wks
24 Sep 83	● THEY DON'T KNOW *Stiff BUY 180*	2	11 wks
3 Dec 83	● MOVE OVER DARLING *Stiff BUY 195*	8	9 wks
3 Mar 84	MY GUY *Stiff BUY 197*	23	6 wks
28 Jul 84	SUNGLASSES *Stiff BUY 205*	18	9 wks
27 Oct 84	HELPLESS *Stiff BUY 211*	61	3 wks

ULTRAVOX *UK/Canada, male vocal/instrumental group*   **138 wks**

5 Jul 80	SLEEPWALK *Chrysalis CHS 2441*	29	11 wks
18 Oct 80	PASSING STRANGERS *Chrysalis CHS 2457*	57	4 wks
17 Jan 81	● VIENNA *Chrysalis CHS 2481.*	2	14 wks
28 Mar 81	SLOW MOTION *Island WIP 6691*	33	4 wks
6 Jun 81	● ALL STOOD STILL *Chrysalis CHS 2522.*	8	10 wks
22 Aug 81	THE THIN WALL *Chrysalis CHS 2540.*	14	8 wks
7 Nov 81	THE VOICE *Chrysalis CHS 2559.*	16	12 wks
25 Sep 82	REAP THE WILD WIND *Chrysalis CHS 2639.*	12	9 wks
27 Nov 82	HYMN *Chrysalis CHS 2657.*	11	11 wks
19 Mar 83	VISIONS IN BLUE *Chrysalis CHS 2676.*	15	6 wks
4 Jun 83	WE CAME TO DANCE *Chrysalis VOX 1.*	18	7 wks
11 Feb 84	ONE SMALL DAY *Chrysalis VOX 2.*	27	6 wks
19 May 84	● DANCING WITH TEARS IN MY EYES *Chrysalis UV 1*	3	10 wks

7 Jul 84	**LAMENT** *Chrysalis UV 2*............................	**22**	6 wks
4 Aug 84	**DANCING WITH TEARS IN MY EYES (re-entry)**		
	Chrysalis UV 1	**74**	1 wk
25 Aug 84	**LAMENT (re-entry)** *Chrysalis UV 2*..............	**73**	1 wk
20 Oct 84	**LOVE'S GREAT ADVENTURE** *Chrysalis UV 3*...	**12**	9 wks
27 Sep 86	**SAME OLD STORY** *Chrysalis UV 4*..............	**31**	4 wks
22 Nov 86	**ALL FALL DOWN** *Chrysalis UV 5*...............	**30**	5 wks

Piero UMILIANI *Italy, orchestra and chorus*   **8 wks**

30 Apr 77	● **MAH NA MAH NA** *EMI International INT 530*	**8**	8 wks

UNDERTAKERS *UK, male vocal/instrumental group*   **1 wk**

9 Apr 64	**JUST A LITTLE BIT** *Pye 7N 15607*................	**49**	1 wk

UNDERTONES *UK, male vocal/instrumental group*   **67 wks**

21 Oct 78	**TEENAGE KICKS** *Sire SIR 4007*	**31**	6 wks
3 Feb 79	**GET OVER YOU** *Sire SIR 4010*	**57**	4 wks
28 Apr 79	**JIMMY JIMMY** *Sire SIR 4015*	**16**	10 wks
21 Jul 79	**HERE COMES THE SUMMER** *Sire SIR 4022*	**34**	6 wks
20 Oct 79	**YOU'VE GOT MY NUMBER (WHY DON'T YOU USE**		
	IT?) *Sire SIR 4024*	**32**	6 wks
5 Apr 80	● **MY PERFECT COUSIN** *Sire SIR 4038*	**9**	10 wks
5 Jul 80	**WEDNESDAY WEEK** *Sire SIR 4042*	**11**	9 wks
2 May 81	**IT'S GOING TO HAPPEN!** *Ardeck AROS 8.*	**18**	9 wks
25 Jul 81	**JULIE OCEAN** *Ardeck ARDS 9*	**41**	5 wks
9 Jul 83	**TEENAGE KICKS (re-issue)** *Ardeck ARDS 1*	**60**	2 wks

UNDISPUTED TRUTH   **4 wks**
US, male/female vocal/instrumental group

22 Jan 77	**YOU + ME = LOVE** *Warner Bros. K 16804*	**43**	4 wks

UNION GAP – *See Gary PUCKETT and the UNION GAP*

UNIQUE *US, male/female vocal/instrumental group*   **7 wks**

10 Sep 83	**WHAT I GOT IS WHAT YOU NEED** *Prelude A 3707*	**27**	7 wks

UNIQUE 3 *UK, male rap/scratch group*   **11 wks**

4 Nov 89	**THE THEME** *10 TEN 285*	**61**	3 wks
14 Apr 90	**MUSICAL MELODY/ WEIGHT FOR THE BASS**		
	10 TEN 298	**29**	5 wks
10 Nov 90	**RHYTHM TAKES CONTROL** *10 TEN 327*..........	**41**	3 wks

UNIT FOUR PLUS TWO   **29 wks**
UK, male vocal/instrumental group

13 Feb 64	**GREEN FIELDS** *Decca F 11821*...................	**48**	2 wks
25 Feb 65	★ **CONCRETE AND CLAY** *Decca F 12071*	**1**	15 wks
13 May 65	**YOU'VE NEVER BEEN IN LOVE LIKE THIS BEFORE**		
	Decca F 12144.	**14**	11 wks
17 Mar 66	**BABY NEVER SAY GOODBYE** *Decca F 12333*........	**49**	1 wk

UNITED KINGDOM SYMPHONY   **4 wks**
ORCHESTRA *UK, orchestra*

27 Jul 85	**SHADES (THEME FROM THE CROWN PAINT**		
	TELEVISION COMMERCIAL)		
	Food For Thought YUM 108.	**68**	4 wks

UNITONE – *See Laurel AITKEN and the UNITONE*

UNTOUCHABLES *US, male vocal/instrumental group*   **16 wks**

6 Apr 85	**FREE YOURSELF** *Stiff BUY 221*	**26**	11 wks
27 Jul 85	**I SPY FOR THE FBI** *Stiff BUY 227*	**59**	5 wks

Phil UPCHURCH COMBO   **2 wks**
US, male instrumental group, Phil Upchurch bass guitar

5 May 66	**YOU CAN'T SIT DOWN** *Sue WI 4005*	**39**	2 wks

UPSETTERS *Jamaica, male instrumental group*   **15 wks**

4 Oct 69	● **RETURN OF DJANGO/ DOLLAR IN THE TEETH**		
	Upsetter US 301	**5**	15 wks

URBAN ALL STARS   **2 wks**
UK, male/female vocal/instrumental group

27 Aug 88	**IT BEGAN IN AFRICA** *Urban URB 23*	**64**	2 wks

Midge URE *UK, male vocalist*   **44 wks**

12 Jun 82	● **NO REGRETS** *Chrysalis CHS 2618*	**9**	10 wks
14 Sep 85	★ **IF I WAS** *Chrysalis URE 1*....................	**1**	11 wks
16 Nov 85	**THAT CERTAIN SMILE** *Chrysalis URE 2*........	**28**	4 wks
8 Feb 86	**WASTELANDS** *Chrysalis URE 3*.................	**46**	3 wks
7 Jun 86	**CALL OF THE WILD** *Chrysalis URE 4*...........	**27**	8 wks
20 Aug 88	**ANSWERS TO NOTHING** *Chrysalis URE 5*........	**49**	4 wks
19 Nov 88	**DEAR GOD** *Chrysalis URE 6*...................	**55**	4 wks

See also Midge Ure and Mick Karn.

Midge URE and Mick KARN   **4 wks**
UK, male vocal/instrumental duo

9 Jul 83	**AFTER A FASHION** *Musicfest FEST 1*	**39**	4 wks

See also Midge Ure; Mick Karn featuring David Sylvian.

USA FOR AFRICA *US, male/female vocal group*   **9 wks**

13 Apr 85	★ **WE ARE THE WORLD** *CBS USAID 1*	**1**	9 wks

Bob Geldof also sang on this record. See also Bob Geldof.

U2 *Ireland, male vocal/instrumental group*   **103 wks**

8 Aug 81	**FIRE** *Island WIP 6679*	**35**	6 wks
17 Oct 81	**GLORIA** *Island WIP 6733*......................	**55**	4 wks
3 Apr 82	**A CELEBRATION** *Island WIP 6770*	**47**	4 wks
22 Jan 83	● **NEW YEARS DAY** *Island UWIP 6848*	**10**	8 wks
2 Apr 83	**TWO HEARTS BEAT AS ONE** *Island IS 109*	**18**	5 wks
15 Sep 84	● **PRIDE (IN THE NAME OF LOVE)** *Island IS 202* ..	**3**	11 wks
4 May 85	● **THE UNFORGETTABLE FIRE** *Island IS 220.*	**6**	6 wks
28 Mar 87	● **WITH OR WITHOUT YOU** *Island IS 319*	**4**	11 wks
6 Jun 87	● **I STILL HAVEN'T FOUND WHAT I'M LOOKING FOR**		
	Island IS 328	**6**	11 wks
12 Sep 87	● **WHERE THE STREETS HAVE NO NAME** *Island IS 340*	**4**	6 wks
26 Dec 87	**IN GOD'S COUNTRY** (IMPORT) *Island 7-99385*	**48**	4 wks
1 Oct 88	★ **DESIRE** *Island IS 400*	**1**	8 wks
17 Dec 88	● **ANGEL OF HARLEM** *Island IS 402*	**9**	6 wks
15 Apr 89	● **WHEN LOVE COMES TO TOWN** *Island IS 411*	**6**	7 wks
24 Jun 89	● **ALL I WANT IS YOU** *Island IS 422*	**4**	6 wks

When Love Comes To Town features B.B. King - US, male vocalist/instrumentalist - guitar.

The 1971 hit by THE
VELVELETTES had been an
American R&B charter in
1966.

Her brother's eatery inspired
the two-time hit by
SUZANNE VEGA, once in
the original *a capella* version
and once in the DNA remix.

Far Right: LUTHER
VANDROSS emotes at
New York's Radio City
Music Hall.

V – *See ADVENTURES OF STEVIE V*

VAGABONDS – *See Jimmy JAMES and the VAGABONDS*

Ricky VALANCE *UK, male vocalist*   **16 wks**

25 Aug 60	★ TELL LAURA I LOVE HER *Columbia DB 4493*	**1**	16 wks

Ritchie VALENS *US, male vocalist*   **5 wks**

6 Mar 59	DONNA *London HL 8803*	**29**	1 wk
1 Aug 87	LA BAMBA *RCA PB 41435*	**49**	4 wks

Caterina VALENTE *France, female vocalist*   **14 wks**

19 Aug 55	● THE BREEZE AND I *Polydor BM 6002*	**5**	14 wks

Dickie VALENTINE *UK, male vocalist*   **92 wks**

20 Feb 53	BROKEN WINGS *Decca F 9954*	**12**	1 wk
13 Mar 53	● ALL THE TIME AND EVERYWHERE *Decca F 10038*	**9**	3 wks
5 Jun 53	● IN A GOLDEN COACH *Decca F 10098*	**7**	1 wk
5 Nov 54	ENDLESS *Decca F 10346*	**19**	1 wk
17 Dec 54	★ FINGER OF SUSPICION *Decca F 10394*	**1**	15 wks
17 Dec 54	● MR. SANDMAN *Decca F 10415*	**5**	12 wks
18 Feb 55	● A BLOSSOM FELL *Decca F 10430*	**9**	9 wks
29 Apr 55	A BLOSSOM FELL (re-entry) *Decca F 10430*	**18**	1 wk
3 Jun 55	● I WONDER *Decca F 10493*	**4**	15 wks
25 Nov 55	★ CHRISTMAS ALPHABET *Decca F 10628*	**1**	7 wks
16 Dec 55	OLD PIANNA RAG *Decca F 10645*	**15**	5 wks
7 Dec 56	● CHRISTMAS ISLAND *Decca F 10798*	**8**	5 wks
27 Dec 57	SNOWBOUND FOR CHRISTMAS *Decca F 10950*	**28**	1 wk
13 Mar 59	VENUS *Pye Nixa 7N 15192*	**28**	1 wk
3 Apr 59	VENUS (re-entry) *Pye Nixa 7N 15192*	**25**	1 wk
17 Apr 59	VENUS (2nd re-entry) *Pye Nixa 7N 15192*	**20**	4 wks
22 May 59	VENUS (3rd re-entry) *Pye Nixa 7N 15192*	**25**	1 wk
19 Jun 59	VENUS (4th re-entry) *Pye Nixa 7N 15192*	**28**	1 wk
23 Oct 59	ONE MORE SUNRISE (MORGEN) *Pye 7N 15221*	**14**	8 wks

See also Various Artists - All Star Hit Parade.

VALENTINE BROTHERS *US, male vocal duo*   **1 wk**

23 Apr 83	MONEY'S TOO TIGHT (TO MENTION) *Energy NRG 1*	**73**	1 wk

Joe VALINO *US, male vocalist*   **2 wks**

18 Jan 57	GARDEN OF EDEN *HMV POP 283*	**23**	2 wks

Frankie VALLI *US, male vocalist*   **50 wks**

12 Dec 70	YOU'RE READY NOW *Philips 320226*	**11**	13 wks
1 Feb 75	● MY EYES ADORED YOU *Private Stock PVT 1*	**5**	11 wks
21 Jun 75	SWEARIN' TO GOD *Private Stock PVT 21*	**31**	5 wks
17 Apr 76	FALLEN ANGEL *Private Stock PVT 51*	**11**	7 wks
26 Aug 78	● GREASE *RSO 012*	**3**	14 wks

See also Four Seasons.

David VAN DAY *UK, male vocalist*   **3 wks**

14 May 83	YOUNG AMERICANS TALKING *WEA DAY 1*	**43**	3 wks

George VAN DUSEN *UK, male vocalist*   **4 wks**

17 Dec 88	IT'S PARTY TIME AGAIN *Bri-Tone 7BT 001*	**43**	4 wks

Leroy VAN DYKE *US, male vocalist*   **20 wks**

4 Jan 62	● WALK ON BY *Mercury AMT 1166*	**5**	17 wks
26 Apr 62	BIG MAN IN A BIG HOUSE *Mercury AMT 1173*	**34**	3 wks

VAN HALEN *US/Holland, male vocal/instrumental group*   **42 wks**

28 Jun 80	RUNNIN' WITH THE DEVIL *Warner Bros. HM 10*	**52**	3 wks
4 Feb 84	● JUMP *Warner Bros. W 9384*	**7**	13 wks
19 May 84	PANAMA *Warner Bros. W 9273*	**61**	2 wks
5 Apr 86	● WHY CAN'T THIS BE LOVE *Warner Bros. W 8740*	**8**	14 wks
12 Jul 86	DREAMS *Warner Bros. W 8642*	**62**	2 wks
6 Aug 88	WHEN IT'S LOVE *Warner Bros. W 7816*	**28**	7 wks
1 Apr 89	FEELS SO GOOD *Warner Bros. W 7565*	**63**	1 wk

VAN TWIST   **2 wks**

Zaire/Belgium, male/female vocal/instrumental group

16 Feb 85	SHAFT *Polydor POSP 729*	**57**	2 wks

VANDELLAS – *See Martha REEVES and the VANDELLAS*

Luther VANDROSS *US, male vocalist*   **71 wks**

19 Feb 83	NEVER TOO MUCH *Epic EPC A 3101*	**44**	6 wks
26 Jul 86	GIVE ME THE REASON *Epic A 7288*	**60**	3 wks
21 Feb 87	GIVE ME THE REASON (re-issue) *Epic 650216 7*	**71**	2 wks
28 Mar 87	SEE ME *Epic LUTH 1*	**60**	4 wks
11 Jul 87	I REALLY DIDN'T MEAN IT *Epic LUTH 3*	**16**	10 wks
5 Sep 87	STOP TO LOVE *Epic LUTH 2*	**24**	7 wks
7 Nov 87	SO AMAZING *Epic LUTH 4*	**33**	6 wks
23 Jan 88	GIVE ME THE REASON (2nd re-issue) *Epic LUTH 5*	**26**	6 wks
16 Apr 88	I GAVE IT UP (WHEN I FELL IN LOVE) *Epic LUTH 6*	**28**	5 wks
9 Jul 88	THERE'S NOTHING BETTER THAN LOVE *Epic LUTH 7*	**72**	1 wk
8 Oct 88	ANY LOVE *Epic LUTH 8*	**31**	4 wks
4 Feb 89	SHE WON'T TALK TO ME *Epic LUTH 9*	**34**	4 wks
22 Apr 89	COME BACK *Epic LUTH 10*	**53**	3 wks
28 Oct 89	NEVER TOO MUCH (re-mix) *Epic LUTH 12*	**13**	7 wks
6 Jan 90	HERE AND NOW *Epic LUTH 13*	**43**	3 wks

There's Nothing Better Than Love has credit 'duet with Gregory Hines'. See also Change.

VANGELIS *Greece, male instrumentalist - keyboards*   **23 wks**

9 May 81	CHARIOTS OF FIRE - TITLES *Polydor POSP 246*	**12**	10 wks
11 Jul 81	HEAVEN AND HELL, THIRD MOVEMENT (THEME FROM THE BBC-TV SERIES, THE COSMOS) *BBC 1*	**48**	6 wks
24 Apr 82	CHARIOTS OF FIRE - TITLES (re-entry) *Polydor POSP 246*	**41**	7 wks

See also Jon and Vangelis.

VANILLA FUDGE *US, male vocal/instrumental group*   **11 wks**

9 Aug 67	YOU KEEP ME HANGIN' ON *Atlantic 584 123*	**18**	11 wks

VANILLA ICE US, male rapper   **6 wks**

24 Nov 90	★ ICE ICE BABY SBK SBK 18	1†	6 wks

VANITY FARE UK, male vocal/instrumental group   **34 wks**

28 Aug 68	I LIVE FOR THE SUN Page One POF 075	20	9 wks
23 Jul 69	● EARLY IN THE MORNING Page One POF 142	8	12 wks
27 Dec 69	HITCHIN' A RIDE Page One POF 158	16	13 wks

Randy VANWARMER US, male vocalist   **11 wks**

4 Aug 79	● JUST WHEN I NEEDED YOU MOST Bearsville WIP 6516	8	11 wks

VAPORS UK, male vocal/instrumental group   **23 wks**

9 Feb 80	● TURNING JAPANESE United Artists BP 334	3	13 wks
5 Jul 80	NEWS AT TEN United Artists BP 345	44	4 wks
11 Jul 81	JIMMIE JONES Liberty BP 401	44	6 wks

VARDIS UK, male vocal/instrumental group   **4 wks**

27 Sep 80	LET'S GO Logo VAR 1	59	4 wks

VARIOUS ARTISTS   **25 wks**

15 Jun 56	CAROUSEL - ORIGINAL SOUNDTRACK (LP) Capitol LCT 6105	27	1 wk
29 Jun 56	● ALL STAR HIT PARADE Decca F 10752	2	9 wks
6 Jul 56	CAROUSEL - ORIGINAL SOUNDTRACK (LP) (re-entry) Capitol LCT 6105	26	1 wk
26 Jul 57	ALL STAR HIT PARADE NO. 2 Decca F 10915	15	7 wks
3 Mar 90	● THE BRITS 1990 RCA PB 43565	2	7 wks

All Star Hit Parade on Decca F 10752 featured the following artists with the following songs: Winifred Atwell - Theme From The Threepenny Opera; Dave King - No Other Love; Joan Regan - My September Love; Lita Roza - A Tear Fell; Dickie Valentine - Out Of Town; David Whitfield - It's Almost Tomorrow. See also the separate hit lists of each of these artists. Tracks and artists on Carousel are as follows: Carousel Waltz - Orchestra conducted by Alfred Newman; You're A Queer One Julie Jordan - Barbara Ruick and Shirley Jones; Mister Snow - Barbara Ruick; If I Loved You - Shirley Jones and Gordon MacRae;June Is Busting Out All Over - Claramae Turner; Soliloquy - Gordon MacRae; Blow High Blow Low - Cameron Mitchell; When The Children Are Asleep - Robert Rounseville and Barbara Ruick; This Was A Real Nice Clambake - Barbara Ruick, Claramae Turner, Robert Rounseville and Cameron Mitchell; Stonecutters Cut It On Stone (There's Nothing So Bad For A Woman) - Cameron Mitchell; What's The Use Of Wonderin' - Shirley Jones; You'll Never Walk Alone - Claramae Turner; If I Loved You - Gordon MacRae; You'll Never Walk Alone - Shirley Jones. The cast are American and the sex of each performer should be obvious. See also Partridge Family starring Shirley Jones. All Star Hit Parade 2 featured the following artists with the following songs: Johnston Brothers - Around The World; Billy Cotton - Puttin' On The Style; Jimmy Young - When I Fall In Love; Max Bygraves - A White Sport Coat; Beverley Sisters - Freight Train; Tommy Steele - Butterfly. The Brits 1990 is a montage of the following tracks: Street Tuff - Double Trouble and the Rebel MC; Voodoo Ray - A Guy Called Gerald; Theme From S Express - S Express; Hey DJ I Can't Dance To That Music You're Playing - Beatmasters; Eve Of The War - Jeff Wayne; Pacific State - 808 State; We Call Acieed - D Mob and Got To Keep On - Cookie Crew. See also the separate hit lists of each of these artists.

Frankie VAUGHAN UK, male vocalist   **212 wks**

29 Jan 54	ISTANBUL HMV B 10599	11	1 wk
28 Jan 55	HAPPY DAYS AND LONELY NIGHTS HMV B 10783	12	1 wk
22 Apr 55	TWEEDLE DEE Philips PB 423	17	1 wk
2 Dec 55	SEVENTEEN Philips PB 511	18	3 wks
3 Feb 56	MY BOY FLAT TOP Philips PB 544	20	2 wks
9 Nov 56	GREEN DOOR Philips PB 640	2	15 wks
11 Jan 57	★ GARDEN OF EDEN Philips PB 660	1	13 wks
4 Oct 57	● MAN ON FIRE / WANDERIN' EYES Philips PB 729	6	12 wks
20 Dec 57	● KISSES SWEETER THAN WINE Philips PB 775	8	11 wks

7 Mar 58	CAN'T GET ALONG WITHOUT YOU/ WE'RE NOT ALONE Philips PB 793	11	6 wks
9 May 58	● KEWPIE DOLL Philips PB 825	10	12 wks
1 Aug 58	WONDERFUL THINGS Philips PB 834	22	3 wks
12 Sep 58	WONDERFUL THINGS (re-entry) Philips PB 834	27	3 wks
10 Oct 58	AM I WASTING MY TIME ON YOU Philips PB 865	25	2 wks
9 Jan 59	AM I WASTING MY TIME ON YOU (re-entry) Philips PB 865	27	2 wks
30 Jan 59	THAT'S MY DOLL Philips PB 895	28	2 wks
24 Jul 59	● THE HEART OF A MAN Philips PB 930	5	14 wks
18 Sep 59	WALKIN' TALL Philips PB 931	28	1 wk
2 Oct 59	WALKIN' TALL (re-entry) Philips PB 931	29	1 wk
29 Jan 60	WHAT MORE DO YOU WANT Philips PB 985	25	2 wks
22 Sep 60	KOOKIE LITTLE PARADISE Philips PB 1054	31	5 wks
27 Oct 60	MILORD Philips PB 1066	34	6 wks
9 Nov 61	★ TOWER OF STRENGTH Philips PB 1195	1	13 wks
1 Feb 62	DON'T STOP TWIST Philips PB 1219	22	7 wks
27 Sep 62	HERCULES Philips 326542 BF	42	4 wks
24 Jan 63	● LOOP-DE-LOOP Philips 326566 BF	5	12 wks
20 Jun 63	HEY MAMA Philips BF 1254	21	9 wks
4 Jun 64	HELLO DOLLY Philips BF 1339	18	11 wks
11 Mar 65	SOMEONE MUST HAVE HURT YOU A LOT Philips BF 1394	46	1 wk
23 Aug 67	● THERE MUST BE A WAY Columbia DB 8248	7	21 wks
15 Nov 67	SO TIRED Columbia DB 8298	21	9 wks
28 Feb 68	NEVERTHELESS Columbia DB 8354	29	5 wks

See also Frankie Vaughan and the Kaye Sisters.

Frankie VAUGHAN and the KAYE SISTERS   **20 wks**
UK, male vocalist and female vocal group

1 Nov 57	● GOTTA HAVE SOMETHING IN THE BANK FRANK Philips PB 751	8	11 wks
1 May 59	● COME SOFTLY TO ME Philips PB 913	9	9 wks

See also Frankie Vaughan; Kaye Sisters; Three Kayes.

Malcolm VAUGHAN UK, male vocalist   **106 wks**

1 Jul 55	● EVERY DAY OF MY LIFE HMV B 10874	5	16 wks
27 Jan 56	WITH YOUR LOVE HMV POP 130	20	1 wk
10 Feb 56	WITH YOUR LOVE (re-entry) HMV POP 130	18	1 wk
2 Mar 56	WITH YOUR LOVE (2nd re-entry) HMV POP 130	20	1 wk
26 Oct 56	ST. THERESE OF THE ROSES HMV POP 250	27	1 wk
16 Nov 56	● ST. THERESE OF THE ROSES (re-entry) HMV POP 250	3	19 wks
12 Apr 57	THE WORLD IS MINE HMV POP 303	30	1 wk
3 May 57	THE WORLD IS MINE (re-entry) HMV POP 303	29	2 wks
10 May 57	CHAPEL OF THE ROSES HMV POP 325	13	8 wks
31 May 57	THE WORLD IS MINE (2nd re-entry) HMV POP 303	26	1 wk
29 Nov 57	● MY SPECIAL ANGEL HMV POP 419	3	14 wks
21 Mar 58	TO BE LOVED HMV POP 459	14	12 wks
17 Oct 58	● MORE THAN EVER (COME PRIMA) HMV POP 538	5	14 wks
27 Feb 59	WAIT FOR ME/ WILLINGLY HMV POP 590	28	1 wk
13 Mar 59	WAIT FOR ME (re-entry) HMV POP 590	13	14 wks

Norman VAUGHAN UK, male vocalist   **5 wks**

17 May 62	SWINGING IN THE RAIN Pye 7N 15438	34	5 wks

Sarah VAUGHAN US, female vocalist   **17 wks**

11 Sep 59	● BROKEN HEARTED MELODY Mercury AMT 1057	7	13 wks
29 Dec 60	LET'S/ SERENATA Columbia DB 4542	37	3 wks
2 Feb 61	LET'S/ SERENATA (re-entry) Columbia DB 4542	47	1 wk

See also Billy Eckstine and Sarah Vaughan.

Billy VAUGHN US, orchestra and chorus   **8 wks**

27 Jan 56	SHIFTING WHISPERING SANDS London HLD 8205	20	1 wk
23 Mar 56	THEME FROM THE 'THREEPENNY OPERA' London HLD 8238	12	7 wks

Bobby VEE US, male vocalist · 134 wks

19 Jan 61	● RUBBER BALL London HLG 9255	4	11 wks
13 Apr 61	● MORE THAN I CAN SAY London HLG 9316	4	16 wks
3 Aug 61	● HOW MANY TEARS London HLG 9389	10	13 wks
26 Oct 61	● TAKE GOOD CARE OF MY BABY London HLG 9438	3	16 wks
21 Dec 61	● RUN TO HIM London HLG 9470	6	15 wks
8 Mar 62	PLEASE DON'T ASK ABOUT BARBARA		
	Liberty LIB 55419	29	9 wks
7 Jun 62	● SHARING YOU Liberty LIB 55451	10	13 wks
27 Sep 62	A FOREVER KIND OF LOVE Liberty LIB 10046	13	19 wks
7 Feb 63	● THE NIGHT HAS A THOUSAND EYES		
	Liberty LIB 10069	3	12 wks
20 Jun 63	BOBBY TOMORROW Liberty LIB 55530	21	10 wks

Suzanne VEGA US, female vocalist · 33 wks

18 Jan 86	SMALL BLUE THING A & M AM 294	65	3 wks
22 Mar 86	MARLENE ON THE WALL A & M AM 309	21	9 wks
7 Jun 86	LEFT OF CENTER A & M AM 320	32	9 wks
23 May 87	LUKA A & M VEGA 1	23	8 wks
18 Jul 87	TOM'S DINER A & M VEGA 2	58	3 wks
19 May 90	BOOK OF DREAMS A & M AM 559	66	1 wk

AM 320 features Joe Jackson on piano. See also Joe Jackson; DNA.

Tata VEGA US, female vocalist · 4 wks

26 May 79	GET IT UP FOR LOVE/ I JUST KEEP THINKING		
	ABOUT YOU BABY Motown TMG 1140	52	4 wks

Rosie VELA US, female vocalist · 7 wks

17 Jan 87	MAGIC SMILE A & M AM 369	27	7 wks

VELVELETTES US, female vocal group · 7 wks

31 Jul 71	THESE THINGS WILL KEEP ME LOVING YOU		
	Tamla Motown TMG 780	34	7 wks

VELVETS US, male vocal group · 2 wks

11 May 61	THAT LUCKY OLD SUN London HLU 9328	46	1 wk
17 Aug 61	TONIGHT (COULD BE THE NIGHT)		
	London HLU 9372	50	1 wk

VENTURES US, male instrumental group · 31 wks

8 Sep 60	● WALK DON'T RUN Top Rank JAR 417	8	13 wks
1 Dec 60	● PERFIDIA London HLG 9232	4	13 wks
9 Mar 61	RAM-BUNK-SHUSH London HLG 9292	45	1 wk
11 May 61	LULLABY OF THE LEAVES London HLG 9344	43	4 wks

Al VERLAINE – *See PING PING and Al VERLAINE*

VERNONS GIRLS UK, female vocal group · 31 wks

17 May 62	LOVER PLEASE Decca F 11450	16	9 wks
23 Aug 62	LOVER PLEASE/ YOU KNOW WHAT I		
	MEAN (re-entry) Decca F 11450	39	7 wks
6 Sep 62	LOCO-MOTION Decca F 11495	47	1 wk
18 Oct 62	YOU KNOW WHAT I MEAN (2nd re-entry)		
	Decca F 11450	37	3 wks
15 Nov 62	YOU KNOW WHAT I MEAN (3rd re-entry)		
	Decca F 11450	50	1 wk
3 Jan 63	FUNNY ALL OVER Decca F 11549	31	8 wks
18 Apr 63	DO THE BIRD Decca F 11629	50	1 wk
2 May 63	DO THE BIRD (re-entry) Decca F 11629	44	1 wk

You Know What I Mean was not coupled with Lover Please on the chart of 23 Aug 62, but both sides of this record were listed for the following 6 weeks.

VIBRATIONS – *See Tony JACKSON and the VIBRATIONS*

VIBRATORS UK, male vocal/instrumental group · 8 wks

18 Mar 78	AUTOMATIC LOVER Epic EPC 6137	35	5 wks
17 Jun 78	JUDY SAYS (KNOCK YOU IN THE HEAD)		
	Epic EPC 6393	70	3 wks

VICE SQUAD UK, male/female vocal/instrumental group · 1 wk

13 Feb 82	OUT OF REACH Zonophone Z 26	68	1 wk

VICIOUS PINK UK, male/female vocal/instrumental duo · 4 wks

15 Sep 84	CCCAN'T YOU SEE Parlophone R 6074	67	4 wks

Mike VICKERS – *See Kenny EVERETT and Mike VICKERS*

Maria VIDAL US, female vocalist · 13 wks

24 Aug 85	BODY ROCK EMI America EA 189	11	13 wks

VIDEO KIDS Holland, male/female vocal duo · 1 wk

5 Oct 85	WOODPECKERS FROM SPACE Epic A 6504	72	1 wk

VIDEO SYMPHONIC UK, orchestra · 3 wks

24 Oct 81	THE FLAME TREES OF THIKA EMI EMI 5222	42	3 wks

VIENNA PHILHARMONIC ORCHESTRA · 14 wks
Austria, orchestra

18 Dec 71	THEME FROM 'THE ONEDIN LINE' Decca F 13259	15	14 wks

VIEW FROM THE HILL · 6 wks
UK, male/female vocal/instrumental group

19 Jul 86	NO CONVERSATION EMI EMI 5565	58	3 wks
21 Feb 87	I'M NO REBEL EMI EM 5580	59	3 wks

VIKKI UK, female vocalist · 3 wks

4 May 85	LOVE IS... PRT 7P 326	49	3 wks

VILLAGE PEOPLE US, male vocal/instrumental group · 54 wks

3 Dec 77	SAN FRANCISCO (YOU'VE GOT ME)		
	DJM DJS 10817	45	5 wks
25 Nov 78	★ Y.M.C.A. Mercury 6007 192	1	16 wks
17 Mar 79	● IN THE NAVY Mercury 6007 209	2	9 wks
16 Jun 79	GO WEST Mercury 6007 221	15	8 wks
9 Aug 80	CAN'T STOP THE MUSIC Mercury MER 16	11	11 wks
9 Feb 85	SEX OVER THE PHONE Record Shack SOHO 34	59	5 wks

Gene VINCENT US, male vocalist | 51 wks

13 Jul 56	**BE BOP A LULA** Capitol CL 14599	30	2 wks
24 Aug 56	**BE BOP A LULA** (re-entry) Capitol CL 14599	16	3 wks
28 Sep 56	**BE BOP A LULA** (2nd re-entry) Capitol CL 14599	23	2 wks
12 Oct 56	**RACE WITH THE DEVIL** Capitol CL 14628	28	1 wk
19 Oct 56	**BLUE JEAN BOP** Capitol CL 14637	16	5 wks
8 Jan 60	**WILD CAT** Capitol CL 15099	21	3 wks
10 Mar 60	**MY HEART** Capitol CL 15115	16	6 wks
10 Mar 60	**WILD CAT** (re-entry) Capitol CL 15099	39	3 wks
28 Apr 60	**MY HEART** (re-entry) Capitol CL 15115	47	1 wk
19 May 60	**MY HEART** (2nd re-entry) Capitol CL 15115	36	1 wk
16 Jun 60	**PISTOL PACKIN' MAMA** Capitol CL 15136	15	9 wks
1 Jun 61	**SHE SHE LITTLE SHEILA** Capitol CL 15202	22	10 wks
17 Aug 61	**SHE SHE LITTLE SHEILA** (re-entry) Capitol CL 15202	44	1 wk
31 Aug 61	**I'M GOING HOME** Capitol CL 15215	36	4 wks

VINDALOO SUMMER SPECIAL | 3 wks
UK, male/female vocal/instrumental group

| 19 Jul 86 | **ROCKIN' WITH RITA (HEAD TO TOE)** Vindaloo UGH 13 | 56 | 3 wks |

This single was a collaboration between three acts: We've Got A Fuzzbox And We're Gonna Use It/Ted Chippington/The Nightingales. See also We've Got A Fuzzbox And We're Gonna Use It.

Bobby VINTON US, male vocalist | 29 wks

2 Aug 62	**ROSES ARE RED** Columbia DB 4878	15	8 wks
19 Dec 63	**THERE I'VE SAID IT AGAIN** Columbia DB 7179	34	10 wks
29 Sep 90 ●	**BLUE VELVET** Epic 6505240	2	10 wks
17 Nov 90	**ROSES ARE RED (MY LOVE)** (re-issue) Epic 6564677	71	1 wk

VIOLINSKI UK, male instrumental group | 9 wks

| 17 Feb 79 | **CLOG DANCE** Jet 136 | 17 | 9 wks |

VIPERS SKIFFLE GROUP | 18 wks
UK, male vocal/instrumental group

25 Jan 57 ●	**DON'T YOU ROCK ME DADDY-O** Parlophone R 4261	10	9 wks
22 Mar 57 ●	**CUMBERLAND GAP** Parlophone R 4289	10	6 wks
31 May 57	**STREAMLINE TRAIN** Parlophone R 4308	23	3 wks

V.I.P's UK, male vocal/instrumental group | 4 wks

| 6 Sep 80 | **THE QUARTER MOON** Gem GEMS 39 | 55 | 4 wks |

VISAGE UK, male vocal/instrumental group | 54 wks

20 Dec 80 ●	**FADE TO GREY** Polydor POSP 194	8	15 wks
14 Mar 81	**MIND OF A TOY** Polydor POSP 236	13	8 wks
11 Jul 81	**VISAGE** Polydor POSP 293	21	7 wks
13 Mar 82	**DAMNED DON'T CRY** Polydor POSP 390	11	8 wks
26 Jun 82	**NIGHT TRAIN** Polydor POSP 441	12	10 wks
13 Nov 82	**PLEASURE BOYS** Polydor POSP 523	44	3 wks
1 Sep 84	**LOVE GLOVE** Polydor POSP 697	54	3 wks

VISCOUNTS UK, male vocal group | 18 wks

| 13 Oct 60 | **SHORT'NIN' BREAD** Pye 7N 15287 | 16 | 8 wks |
| 14 Sep 61 | **WHO PUT THE BOMP** Pye 7N 15379 | 21 | 10 wks |

VISION UK, male vocal/instrumental group | 1 wk

| 9 Jul 83 | **LOVE DANCE** MVM MVM 2886 | 74 | 1 wk |

VIXEN US, female vocal/instrumental group | 19 wks

3 Sep 88	**EDGE OF A BROKEN HEART** Manhattan MT 48	51	4 wks
4 Mar 89	**CRYIN'** EMI Manhattan MT 60	27	4 wks
3 Jun 89	**LOVE MADE ME** EMI-USA MT 66	36	4 wks
2 Sep 89	**EDGE OF A BROKEN HEART** (re-entry) EMI-USA MT 48	59	2 wks
28 Jul 90	**HOW MUCH LOVE** EMI-USA MT 87	35	3 wks
20 Oct 90	**LOVE IS A KILLER** EMI-USA MT 91	41	2 wks

VOGGUE Canada, female vocal duo | 6 wks

| 18 Jul 81 | **DANCIN' THE NIGHT AWAY** Mercury MER 76 | 39 | 6 wks |

VOICE OF THE BEEHIVE | 29 wks
US/UK, male/female vocal/instrumental group

14 Nov 87	**I SAY NOTHING** London LON 151	45	5 wks
5 Mar 88	**I WALK THE EARTH** London LON 169	42	4 wks
14 May 88	**DON'T CALL ME BABY** London LON 175	15	10 wks
23 Jul 88	**I SAY NOTHING** (re-issue) London LON 190	22	6 wks
22 Oct 88	**I WALK THE EARTH** (re-issue) London LON 206	46	4 wks

Sterling VOID UK, male vocalist | 3 wks

| 4 Feb 89 | **RUNAWAY GIRL/ IT'S ALRIGHT** FFRR FFR 21 | 53 | 3 wks |

VOYAGE UK/France, disco aggregation | 27 wks

17 Jun 78	**FROM EAST TO WEST/ SCOTS MACHINE** GTO GT 224	13	13 wks
25 Nov 78	**SOUVENIRS** GTO GT 241	56	7 wks
24 Mar 79	**LET'S FLY AWAY** GTO GT 245	38	7 wks

Scots Machine *credited from 24 Jun 78 until end of record's chart run.*

VOYAGER UK, male vocal/instrumental group | 8 wks

| 26 May 79 | **HALFWAY HOTEL** Mountain VOY 001 | 33 | 8 wks |

Adam WADE US, male vocalist | 6 wks

| 8 Jun 61 | **TAKE GOOD CARE OF HER** HMV POP 843 | 38 | 1 wk |
| 22 Jun 61 | **TAKE GOOD CARE OF HER** (re-entry) HMV POP 843 | 38 | 5 wks |

WAH! – *See MIGHTY WAH*

Donnie WAHLBERG – *See SEIKO and Donnie WAHLBERG*

WAIKIKIS Belgium, male instrumental group | 2 wks

| 11 Mar 65 | **HAWAII TATTOO** Pye International 7N 25286 | 41 | 2 wks |

WAILERS – *See Bob MARLEY and the WAILERS*

John WAITE UK, male vocalist | 11 wks

| 29 Sep 84 ● | **MISSING YOU** EMI America EA 182 | 9 | 11 wks |

WAITRESSES UK, female vocal group   **4 wks**

18 Dec 82	**CHRISTMAS WRAPPING** Ze/Island WIP 6821	**45**	4 wks

Johnny WAKELIN UK, male vocalist   **20 wks**

18 Jan 75	● **BLACK SUPERMAN (MUHAMMAD ALI)** *Pye 7N 45420*	**7**	10 wks
24 Jul 76	● **IN ZAIRE** *Pye 7N 45595.*	**4**	10 wks

Black Superman *by Johnny Wakelin and the Kinshasa Band.*

WAKEMAN – *See ANDERSON BRUFORD WAKEMAN HOWE*

Narada Michael WALDEN – *See NARADA*

Gary WALKER US, male vocalist   **12 wks**

24 Feb 66	**YOU DON'T LOVE ME** CBS 202036	**26**	6 wks
26 May 66	**TWINKIE LEE** CBS 202081	**26**	6 wks

See also Walker Brothers.

John WALKER US, male vocalist   **6 wks**

5 Jul 67	**ANNABELLA** Philips BF 1593	**48**	1 wk
19 Jul 67	**ANNABELLA (re-entry)** Philips BF 1593	**24**	5 wks

See also Walker Brothers.

Junior WALKER and the ALL-STARS   **59 wks**
US, male instrumental/vocal group,
Junior Walker vocalist/instrumentalist – tenor sax

18 Aug 66	**HOW SWEET IT IS** Tamla Motown TMG 571	**22**	10 wks
2 Apr 69	**(I'M A) ROAD RUNNER** Tamla Motown TMG 691............	**12**	12 wks
18 Oct 69	**WHAT DOES IT TAKE (TO WIN YOUR LOVE)** Tamla Motown TMG 712.	**13**	12 wks
26 Aug 72	**WALK IN THE NIGHT** Tamla Motown TMG 824	**16**	11 wks
27 Jan 73	**TAKE ME GIRL I'M READY** Tamla Motown TMG 840.	**16**	9 wks
30 Jun 73	**WAY BACK HOME** Tamla Motown TMG 857	**35**	5 wks

Scott WALKER US, male vocalist   **30 wks**

6 Dec 67	**JACKIE** Philips BF 1628..................................	**22**	9 wks
1 May 68	● **JOANNA** Philips BF 1662	**7**	11 wks
11 Jun 69	**LIGHTS OF CINCINATTI** Philips BF 1793	**13**	10 wks

See also Walker Brothers.

WALKER BROTHERS US, male vocal group   **93 wks**

29 Apr 65	**LOVE HER** Philips BF 1409	**20**	13 wks
19 Aug 65	★ **MAKE IT EASY ON YOURSELF** Philips BF 1428	**1**	14 wks
2 Dec 65	● **MY SHIP IS COMING IN** Philips BF 1454	**3**	12 wks
3 Mar 66	★ **THE SUN AIN'T GONNA SHINE ANYMORE** Philips BF 1473	**1**	11 wks
14 Jul 66	**(BABY) YOU DON'T HAVE TO TELL ME** Philips BF 1497	**13**	8 wks
22 Sep 66	**ANOTHER TEAR FALLS** Philips BF 1514	**12**	8 wks
15 Dec 66	**DEADLIER THAN THE MALE** Philips BF 1537	**34**	6 wks
9 Feb 67	**STAY WITH ME BABY** Philips BF 1548	**26**	6 wks
18 May 67	**WALKING IN THE RAIN** Philips BF 1576	**26**	6 wks
17 Jan 76	● **NO REGRETS** GTO GT 42	**7**	9 wks

See also Gary Walker; John Walker; Scott Walker.

WALL OF VOODOO US, male vocal/instrumental group   **3 wks**

19 Mar 83	**MEXICAN RADIO** Illegal ILS 36	**64**	3 wks

Jerry WALLACE US, male vocalist   **1 wk**

23 Jun 60	**YOU'RE SINGING OUR LOVE SONG TO SOMEBODY ELSE** London HLH 9110...	**46**	1 wk

Bob WALLIS and his STORYVILLE JAZZ BAND   **7 wks**
UK, male jazz band, Bob Wallis vocalist/instrumentalist – trumpet

6 Jul 61	**I'M SHY MARY ELLEN I'M SHY** Pye Jazz 7NJ 2043	**44**	2 wks
4 Jan 62	**COME ALONG PLEASE** Pye Jazz 7NJ 2048...................	**33**	5 wks

Joe WALSH US, male vocalist   **15 wks**

16 Jul 77	**ROCKY MOUNTAIN WAY** (EP) ABC ABE 12002	**39**	4 wks
8 Jul 78	**LIFE'S BEEN GOOD** Asylum K 13129........................	**14**	11 wks

Tracks on Rocky Mountain Way *EP: Rocky Mountain Way/Turn To Stone/Meadows/Walk Away.*

Maureen WALSH – *See Maureen*

Sheila WALSH and Cliff RICHARD   **2 wks**
UK, female/male vocal duo

4 Jun 83	**DRIFTING** DJM SHEIL 1..	**64**	2 wks

See also Cliff Richard.

Steve WALSH UK, male vocalist   **18 wks**

18 Jul 87	**I FOUND LOVIN'** A1 A1 299	**74**	1 wk
29 Aug 87	● **I FOUND LOVIN' (re-entry)** A1 A1 299	**9**	12 wks
12 Dec 87	**LET'S GET TOGETHER TONITE** A1 A1 303...............	**74**	1 wk
30 Jul 88	**AIN'T NO STOPPING US NOW (PARTY FOR THE WORLD)** A1 A1 304	**44**	4 wks

Trevor WALTERS UK, male vocalist   **22 wks**

24 Oct 81	**LOVE ME TONIGHT** Magnet MAG 198......................	**27**	8 wks
21 Jul 84	● **STUCK ON YOU** Sanity IS 002	**9**	12 wks
1 Dec 84	**NEVER LET HER SLIP AWAY** Polydor POSP 716............	**73**	2 wks

WANG CHUNG UK, male vocal/instrumental group   **12 wks**

28 Jan 84	**DANCE HALL DAYS** Geffen A 3837............................	**21**	12 wks

Dexter WANSELL US, male instrumentalist – keyboards   **3 wks**

20 May 78	**ALL NIGHT LONG** Philadelphia International PIR 6255	**59**	3 wks

WAR US/Denmark, male vocal/instrumental group   **32 wks**

24 Jan 76	**LOW RIDER** Island WIP 6267....................................	**12**	7 wks
26 Jun 76	**ME AND BABY BROTHER** Island WIP 6303	**21**	7 wks
14 Jan 78	**GALAXY** MCA 339	**14**	7 wks
15 Apr 78	**HEY SENORITA** MCA 359	**40**	2 wks
10 Apr 82	**YOU GOT THE POWER** RCA 201.............................	**58**	4 wks
6 Apr 85	**GROOVIN'** Bluebird BR 16....................................	**43**	5 wks

Anita WARD US, female vocalist   **11 wks**

2 Jun 79	★ **RING MY BELL** TK TKR 7543.................................	**1**	11 wks

Billy WARD US, male vocalist　　　　　　　　13 wks

13 Sep 57	STARDUST London HLU 8465	13	11 wks
29 Nov 57	DEEP PURPLE London HLU 8502	30	1 wk
3 Jan 58	STARDUST (re-entry) London HLU 8465	26	1 wk

Clifford T. WARD UK, male vocalist　　　　　　　　16 wks

| 30 Jun 73 | ● GAYE Charisma CB 205 | 8 | 11 wks |
| 26 Jan 74 | SCULLERY Charisma CB 221 | 37 | 5 wks |

Michael WARD UK, male vocalist　　　　　　　　13 wks

| 29 Sep 73 | LET THERE BE PEACE ON EARTH (LET IT BEGIN WITH ME) Philips 6006 340 | 15 | 10 wks |
| 15 Dec 73 | LET THERE BE PEACE ON EARTH (LET IT BEGIN WITH ME) (re-entry) Philips 6006 340 | 50 | 3 wks |

WARD BROTHERS UK, male vocal/instrumental group　　8 wks

| 10 Jan 87 | CROSS THAT BRIDGE Siren SIREN 37 | 32 | 8 wks |

WARM SOUNDS UK, male vocal duo　　　　　　　　6 wks

| 4 May 67 | BIRDS AND BEES Deram DM 120 | 27 | 6 wks |

Toni WARNE UK, female vocalist　　　　　　　　4 wks

| 25 Apr 87 | BEN Mute CHEW 110 | 50 | 4 wks |

Jennifer WARNES US, female vocalist　　　　　　1 wk

| 25 Jul 87 | FIRST WE TAKE MANHATTAN Cypress PB 49709 | 74 | 1 wk |

See also Joe Cocker and Jennifer Warnes; Bill Medley and Jennifer Warnes.

WARRANT US, male vocal/instrumental group　　2 wks

| 17 Nov 90 | CHERRY PIE CBS 6562587 | 59 | 2 wks |

Dionne WARWICK US, female vocalist　　　　　83 wks

13 Feb 64	ANYONE WHO HAD A HEART Pye International 7N 25234	42	3 wks
16 Apr 64	● WALK ON BY Pye International 7N 25241	9	14 wks
30 Jul 64	YOU'LL NEVER GET TO HEAVEN Pye International 7N 25256	20	8 wks
8 Oct 64	REACH OUT FOR ME Pye International 7N 25265	23	7 wks
1 Apr 65	YOU CAN HAVE HIM Pye International 7N 25290	37	5 wks
13 Mar 68	VALLEY OF THE DOLLS Pye International 7N 25445	28	8 wks
15 May 68	● DO YOU KNOW THE WAY TO SAN JOSÉ Pye International 7N 25457	8	10 wks
23 Oct 82	● HEARTBREAKER Arista ARIST 496	2	13 wks
11 Dec 82	● ALL THE LOVE IN THE WORLD Arista ARIST 507	10	10 wks
26 Feb 83	YOURS Arista ARIST 518	66	2 wks
28 May 83	I'LL NEVER LOVE THIS WAY AGAIN Arista ARIST 530	62	3 wks

See also Dionne Warwick and Friends; Dionne Warwick and Jeffrey Osborne; Dionne Warwicke and the Detroit Spinners.

Dionne WARWICK and FRIENDS　　　　　　9 wks
US, female vocalist and US/UK, male/female vocal/instrumental group

| 9 Nov 85 | THAT'S WHAT FRIENDS ARE FOR Arista ARIST 638 | 16 | 9 wks |

See also Dionne Warwick, her friends Elton John, Stevie Wonder and Gladys Knight, and their associated acts.

Dionne WARWICK and Jeffrey OSBORNE　　3 wks
US, female/male vocal duo

| 15 Aug 87 | LOVE POWER Arista RIS 27 | 63 | 3 wks |

See also Dionne Warwick; Jeffrey Osborne.

Dionne WARWICKE and the DETROIT SPINNERS　6 wks
US, female vocalist, male vocal group

| 19 Oct 74 | THEN CAME YOU Atlantic K 10495 | 29 | 6 wks |

For this hit Dionne Warwick made a small alteration to her surname. See also Dionne Warwick; Detroit Spinners.

WAS (NOT WAS) US, male vocal/instrumental duo　　46 wks

3 Mar 84	OUT COME THE FREAKS Ze/Geffen A 4178	41	5 wks
18 Jul 87	SPY IN THE HOUSE OF LOVE Fontana WAS 2	51	7 wks
3 Oct 87	● WALK THE DINOSAUR Fontana WAS 3	10	10 wks
6 Feb 88	SPY IN THE HOUSE OF LOVE (re-entry) Fontana WAS 2	21	8 wks
7 May 88	OUT COME THE FREAKS (AGAIN) Fontana WAS 4	44	3 wks
16 Jul 88	ANYTHING CAN HAPPEN Fontana WAS 5	67	3 wks
26 May 90	PAPA WAS A ROLLING STONE Fontana WAS 7	12	7 wks
11 Aug 90	HOW THE HEART BEHAVES Fontana WAS 8	53	3 wks

Fontana WAS 4 was a re-recorded version of their first hit.

Dinah WASHINGTON US, female vocalist　　　　4 wks

| 30 Nov 61 | SEPTEMBER IN THE RAIN Mercury AMT 1162 | 35 | 3 wks |
| 18 Jan 62 | SEPTEMBER IN THE RAIN (re-entry) Mercury AMT 1162 | 49 | 1 wk |

Geno WASHINGTON and the RAM JAM BAND　20 wks
UK, male vocalist, male instrumental backing group

19 May 66	WATER Piccadilly 7N 35312	39	8 wks
21 Jul 66	HI HI HAZEL Piccadilly 7N 35329	45	3 wks
25 Aug 66	HI HI HAZEL (re-entry) Piccadilly 7N 35329	48	1 wk
6 Oct 66	QUE SERA SERA Piccadilly 7N 35346	43	3 wks
2 Feb 67	MICHAEL Piccadilly 7N 35359	39	5 wks

Grover WASHINGTON Jr.　　　　　　　　7 wks
US, male instrumentalist - saxophone

| 16 May 81 | JUST THE TWO OF US Elektra K 12514 | 34 | 7 wks |

Although uncredited, Bill Withers vocalises on Just The Two Of Us. See also Bill Withers.

W.A.S.P. US, male vocal/instrumental group　　　　31 wks

31 May 86	WILD CHILD Capitol CL 388	71	2 wks
11 Oct 86	95 - NASTY Capitol CL 432	70	1 wk
29 Aug 87	SCREAM UNTIL YOU LIKE IT Capitol CL 458	32	5 wks
31 Oct 87	I DON'T NEED NO DOCTOR (LIVE) Capitol CL 469	31	5 wks
20 Feb 88	LIVE ANIMAL (F**K LIKE A BEAST) Music For Nations KUT 109	61	3 wks
4 Mar 89	MEAN MAN Capitol CL 521	21	5 wks
27 May 89	THE REAL ME Capitol CL 534	23	5 wks
9 Sep 89	FOREVER FREE Capitol CL 546	25	5 wks

WATERBOYS UK, male vocal/instrumental group — 17 wks

2 Nov 85	**THE WHOLE OF THE MOON** Ensign ENY 520	26	7 wks
14 Jan 89	**FISHERMAN'S BLUES** Ensign ENY 621	32	6 wks
1 Jul 89	**AND A BANG ON THE EAR** Ensign ENY 624	51	4 wks

WATERFRONT UK, male vocal/instrumental duo — 19 wks

15 Apr 89	**BROKEN ARROW** Polydor WON 3	63	2 wks
27 May 89	**CRY** Polydor WON 1	17	13 wks
9 Sep 89	**NATURE OF LOVE** Polydor WON 2	63	4 wks

Dennis WATERMAN and George COLE — 5 wks
UK, male vocal duo

17 Dec 83	**WHAT ARE WE GONNA GET 'ER INDOORS** EMI MIN 101	21	5 wks

See also Dennis Waterman with the Dennis Waterman Band.

Dennis WATERMAN with the DENNIS WATERMAN BAND UK, male vocal/instrumental group — 12 wks

25 Oct 80	● **I COULD BE SO GOOD FOR YOU** EMI 5009	3	12 wks

See also Dennis Waterman and George Cole.

Muddy WATERS US, male vocalist/instrumentalist - guitar — 6 wks

16 Jul 88	**MANNISH BOY** Epic MUD 1	51	6 wks

Roger WATERS UK, male vocalist/instrumentalist — 5 wks

30 May 87	**RADIO WAVES** Harvest EM 6	74	1 wk
26 Dec 87	**THE TIDE IS TURNING (AFTER LIVE AID)** Harvest EM 37	54	4 wks

Jody WATLEY US, female vocalist — 29 wks

9 May 87	**LOOKING FOR A NEW LOVE** MCA MCA 1107	13	11 wks
17 Oct 87	**DON'T YOU WANT ME** MCA MCA 1198	55	3 wks
8 Apr 89	**REAL LOVE** MCA MCA 1324	31	7 wks
12 Aug 89	**FRIENDS** MCA MCA 1352	21	6 wks
10 Feb 90	**EVERYTHING** MCA MCA 1395	74	2 wks

Friends is with Eric B. and Rakim. See also Eric B. and Rakim.

James WATSON – See Paul PHOENIX

Johnny 'Guitar' WATSON — 8 wks
US, male vocalist, instrumentalist - guitar

28 Aug 76	**I NEED IT** DJM DJS 10694	35	5 wks
23 Apr 77	**A REAL MOTHER FOR YA** DJM DJT 10762	44	3 wks

WAVELENGTH UK, male vocal group — 12 wks

10 Jul 82	**HURRY HOME** Ariola ARO 281	17	12 wks

WAX US/UK, male vocal/instrumental duo — 16 wks

12 Apr 86	**RIGHT BETWEEN THE EYES** RCA PB 40509	60	5 wks
1 Aug 87	**BRIDGE TO YOUR HEART** RCA PB 41405	12	11 wks

A WAY OF LIFE US, male/female vocal/instrumental group — 3 wks

21 Apr 90	**TRIPPIN' ON YOUR LOVE** Eternal YZ 464	55	3 wks

WAY OF THE WEST UK, male vocal/instrumental group — 5 wks

25 Apr 81	**DON'T SAY THAT'S JUST FOR WHITE BOYS** Mercury MER 66	54	5 wks

Jeff WAYNE US, orchestra — 3 wks

10 Jul 82	**MATADOR** CBS A 2493	57	3 wks

See also Jeff Wayne's War Of The Worlds.

Jeff WAYNE'S WAR OF THE WORLDS — 18 wks
US/UK, male/female vocal/instrumental cast

9 Sep 78	**EVE OF THE WAR** CBS 6496	36	8 wks
25 Nov 89	● **THE EVE OF THE WAR (re-mix)** CBS 6551267	3	10 wks

The listing of the re-mix mentions Ben Liebrand, the re-mix engineer. See also Jeff Wayne; Ben Liebrand; Various Artists - The Brits 1990.

WE THE PEOPLE OF THE BAND – See ME AND YOU

WEATHER GIRLS US, female vocal duo — 14 wks

27 Aug 83	**IT'S RAINING MEN** CBS A 2924	73	3 wks
3 Mar 84	● **IT'S RAINING MEN (re-entry)** CBS A 2924	2	11 wks

WEATHER PROPHETS — 2 wks
UK, male vocal/instrumental group

28 Mar 87	**SHE COMES FROM THE RAIN** Elevation ACID 1	62	2 wks

WEATHERMEN — 9 wks
UK, male vocalist, Jonathan King under a false name

16 Jan 71	**IT'S THE SAME OLD SONG** B and C CB 139	19	9 wks

See also Jonathan King.

Marti WEBB UK, female vocalist — 42 wks

9 Feb 80	● **TAKE THAT LOOK OFF YOUR FACE** Polydor POSP 100	3	12 wks
19 Apr 80	**TELL ME ON A SUNDAY** Polydor POSP 111	67	2 wks
20 Sep 80	**YOUR EARS SHOULD BE BURNING NOW** Polydor POSP 166	61	4 wks
8 Jun 85	● **BEN** Starblend STAR 6	5	11 wks
20 Sep 86	**ALWAYS THERE** BBC RESL 190	13	12 wks
6 Jun 87	**I CAN'T LET GO** Rainbow RBR 12	65	1 wk

Always There features the Simon May Orchestra. See also Simon May Orchestra.

Joan WEBER US, female vocalist — 1 wk

18 Feb 55	**LET ME GO LOVER** Philips PB 389	16	1 wk

Max WEBSTER Canada, male vocal/instrumental group — 3 wks

19 May 79	**PARADISE SKIES** Capitol CL 16079	43	3 wks

JODY WATLEY successfully looked for a new career after Shalamar split.

WENDY AND LISA departed Prince's Revolution with a successful partnership of their own.

Below: The narrative style of BARRY WHITE inspired the talking introduction of Lisa Stansfield's 'All Around the World'.

WEDDING PRESENT
UK, male vocal/instrumental group   **14 wks**

5 Mar 88	NOBODY'S TWISTING YOUR ARM *Reception REC 009*	46	2 wks
1 Oct 88	WHY ARE YOU BEING SO REASONABLE NOW *Reception REC 011*	42	2 wks
7 Oct 89	KENNEDY *RCA PB 43117*	33	3 wks
17 Feb 90	BRASSNECK *RCA PB 43403*	24	3 wks
29 Sep 90	3 SONGS (EP) *RCA PB 44021*	25	4 wks

Tracks on 3 Songs EP: Corduroy/Crawl/Make Me Smile (Come Up And See Me).

Fred WEDLOCK *UK, male vocalist*   **10 wks**

31 Jan 81 ●	OLDEST SWINGER IN TOWN *Rocket XPRES 46*	6	10 wks

WEE PAPA GIRL RAPPERS *UK, female vocal duo*   **27 wks**

12 Mar 88	FAITH *Jive JIVE 164*	60	4 wks
25 Jun 88	HEAT IT UP *Jive JIVE 174*	21	9 wks
1 Oct 88 ●	WEE RULE *Jive JIVE 185*	6	9 wks
24 Dec 88	SOULMATE *Jive JIVE 193*	45	4 wks
25 Mar 89	BLOW THE HOUSE DOWN *Jive JIVE 197*	65	1 wk

Heat It Up features Two Men And A Drum Machine. See also Two Men, A Drum Machine And A Trumpet.

Bert WEEDON *UK, male instrumentalist - guitar*   **38 wks**

15 May 59 ●	GUITAR BOOGIE SHUFFLE *Top Rank JAR 117*	10	9 wks
20 Nov 59	NASHVILLE BOOGIE *Top Rank JAR 221*	29	2 wks
10 Mar 60	BIG BEAT BOOGIE *Top Rank JAR 300*	37	3 wks
7 Apr 60	BIG BEAT BOOGIE (re-entry) *Top Rank JAR 300*	49	1 wk
9 Jun 60	TWELFTH STREET RAG *Top Rank JAR 360*	47	2 wks
28 Jul 60	APACHE *Top Rank JAR 415*	44	1 wk
11 Aug 60	APACHE (re-entry) *Top Rank JAR 415*	24	3 wks
27 Oct 60	SORRY ROBBIE *Top Rank JAR 517*	28	11 wks
2 Feb 61	GINCHY *Top Rank JAR 537*	35	5 wks
4 May 61	MR. GUITAR *Top Rank JAR 559*	47	1 wk

WEEKEND   **5 wks**
Multi-national, male/female vocal/instrumental group

14 Dec 85	CHRISTMAS MEDLEY/ AULD LANG SYNE *Lifestyle XY 1*	47	5 wks

Frank WEIR *UK, orchestra*   **4 wks**

15 Sep 60	CARIBBEAN HONEYMOON *Oriole CB 1559*	42	4 wks

Eric WEISSBERG – *See 'DELIVERANCE' SOUNDTRACK*

Brandi WELLS *US, female vocalist*   **1 wk**

20 Feb 82	WATCH OUT *Virgin VS 479*	74	1 wk

Houston WELLS *UK, male vocalist*   **10 wks**

1 Aug 63	ONLY THE HEARTACHES *Parlophone R 5031*	22	10 wks

Mary WELLS *US, female vocalist*   **24 wks**

21 May 64 ●	MY GUY *Stateside SS 288*	5	14 wks
8 Jul 72	MY GUY (re-issue) *Tamla Motown TMG 820*	14	10 wks

See also Marvin Gaye and Mary Wells.

Terri WELLS *US, female vocalist*   **9 wks**

2 Jul 83	YOU MAKE IT HEAVEN *Phillyworld PWS 111*	53	2 wks
5 May 84	I'LL BE AROUND *Phillyworld LON 48*	17	7 wks

Alex WELSH *UK, male instrumentalist - trumpet*   **4 wks**

10 Aug 61	TANSY *Columbia DB 4686*	45	4 wks

WENDY and LISA *US, female vocal duo*   **31 wks**

5 Sep 87	WATERFALL *Virgin VS 999*	66	4 wks
16 Jan 88	SIDE SHOW *Virgin VS 1012*	49	5 wks
18 Feb 89	ARE YOU MY BABY *Virgin VS 1156*	70	3 wks
29 Apr 89	LOLLY LOLLY *Virgin VS 1175*	64	3 wks
8 Jul 89	SATISFACTION *Virgin VS 1194*	27	8 wks
18 Nov 89	WATERFALL (re-mix) *Virgin VS 1223*	69	2 wks
30 Jun 90	STRUNG OUT *Virgin VS 1272*	44	5 wks
10 Nov 90	RAINBOW LAKE *Virgin VS 1280*	70	1 wk

Dodie WEST *UK, female vocalist*   **4 wks**

14 Jan 65	GOING OUT OF MY HEAD *Decca F 12046*	39	4 wks

Keith WEST *UK, male vocalist*   **18 wks**

9 Aug 67 ●	EXCERPT FROM A TEENAGE OPERA *Parlophone R 5623*	2	15 wks
22 Nov 67	SAM *Parlophone R 5651*	38	3 wks

WEST HAM UNITED CUP SQUAD   **2 wks**
UK, male football team vocalists

10 May 75	I'M FOREVER BLOWING BUBBLES *Pye 7N 45470*	31	2 wks

WEST STREET MOB *US, male vocal group*   **3 wks**

8 Oct 83	BREAK DANCIN'-ELECTRIC BOOGIE *Sugarhill SH 128*	71	1 wk
22 Oct 83	BREAK DANCIN'-ELECTRIC BOOGIE (re-entry) *Sugarhill SH 128*	64	2 wks

Kim WESTON – *See Marvin GAYE and Kim WESTON*

WESTWORLD *UK/US, male/female vocal/instrumental group*   **23 wks**

21 Feb 87	SONIC BOOM BOY *RCA BOOM 1*	11	7 wks
2 May 87	BA-NA-NA-BAM-BOO *RCA BOOM 2*	37	5 wks
25 Jul 87	WHERE THE ACTION IS *RCA BOOM 3*	54	4 wks
17 Oct 87	SILVERMAC *RCA BOOM 4*	42	5 wks
15 Oct 88	EVERYTHING GOOD IS BAD *RCA PB 42243*	72	2 wks

WET WET WET *UK, male vocal/instrumental group*   **80 wks**

11 Apr 87 ●	WISHING I WAS LUCKY *Precious JEWEL 3*	6	14 wks
25 Jul 87 ●	SWEET LITTLE MYSTERY *Precious JEWEL 4*	5	12 wks
5 Dec 87 ●	ANGEL EYES (HOME AND AWAY) *Precious JEWEL 6*	5	12 wks
19 Mar 88	TEMPTATION *Precious JEWEL 7*	12	8 wks
14 May 88 ★	WITH A LITTLE HELP FROM MY FRIENDS *Childline CHILD 1*	1	11 wks
30 Sep 89 ●	SWEET SURRENDER *Precious JEWEL 9*	6	8 wks
9 Dec 89	BROKE AWAY *Precious JEWEL 10*	19	7 wks
10 Mar 90	HOLD BACK THE RIVER *Precious JEWEL 11*	31	4 wks
11 Aug 90	STAY WITH ME HEARTACHE/ I FEEL FINE *Precious JEWEL 13*	30	4 wks

The listed A-side with With A Little Help From My Friends was She's Leaving Home by Billy Bragg with Cara Tivey. See also Billy Bragg.

VOICE OF THE BEEHIVE gave ex-Madness members Dan Woodgate (second from left) and Mark Bedford (far right) further chart success.

Bottom Right: The best-known songs of TONY JOE WHITE, 'Rainy Night in Georgia' and 'Polk Salad Annie', were hits for other artists.

Right: JANE WIEDLIN left the Go-Gos in a rush.

Below: After having four number ones as WHAM!, Andrew Ridgeley and George Michael wonder what to do with the rest of their lives.

WE'VE GOT A FUZZBOX AND WE'RE GONNA USE IT *UK, female vocal/instrumental group*   **39 wks**

Date	Title	Pos	Wks
26 Apr 86	**XX SEX/ RULES AND REGULATIONS** *Vindaloo UGH 11*	41	7 wks
15 Nov 86	**LOVE IS THE SLUG** *Vindaloo UGH 14*	31	4 wks
7 Feb 87	**WHAT'S THE POINT** *Vindaloo YZ 101*	51	2 wks
25 Feb 89	**INTERNATIONAL RESCUE** *WEA YZ 347*	11	10 wks
20 May 89	**PINK SUNSHINE** *WEA YZ 401*	14	10 wks
5 Aug 89	**SELF!** *WEA YZ 408*	24	6 wks

See also Vindaloo Summer Special.

WHALERS – *See Hal PAGE and the WHALERS*

WHAM! *UK, male vocal duo*   **137 wks**

Date	Title	Pos	Wks
16 Oct 82	● **YOUNG GUNS (GO FOR IT)** *Innervision IVL A2766*	3	17 wks
15 Jan 83	● **WHAM RAP** *Innervision IVL A2442*	8	11 wks
14 May 83	● **BAD BOYS** *Innervision A 3143*	2	14 wks
30 Jul 83	● **CLUB TROPICANA** *Innervision A 3613*	4	11 wks
3 Dec 83	**CLUB FANTASTIC MEGAMIX** *Innervision A 3586*	15	8 wks
26 May 84	★ **WAKE ME UP BEFORE YOU GO GO** *Epic A 4440*	1	16 wks
13 Oct 84	★ **FREEDOM** *Epic A 4743*	1	14 wks
15 Dec 84	● **LAST CHRISTMAS/ EVERYTHING SHE WANTS** *Epic A 4949*	2	13 wks
23 Nov 85	★ **I'M YOUR MAN** *Epic A 6716*	1	12 wks
14 Dec 85	● **LAST CHRISTMAS (re-issue)** *Epic WHAM 1*	6	7 wks
21 Jun 86	★ **THE EDGE OF HEAVEN/ WHERE DID YOUR HEART GO** *Epic FIN 1*	1	10 wks
20 Dec 86	**LAST CHRISTMAS (2nd re-issue)** *Epic 650269 7*	45	4 wks

Where Did Your Heart Go only listed from 2 August.

WHATNAUTS – *See MOMENTS and WHATNAUTS*

Caron WHEELER *UK, female vocalist*   **10 wks**

Date	Title	Pos	Wks
8 Sep 90	**LIVIN' IN THE LIGHT** *RCA PB 43939*	14	6 wks
10 Nov 90	**UK BLAK** *RCA PB 43719*	40	4 wks

See also Soul II Soul.

WHEN IN ROME *UK, male vocal/instrumental group*   **3 wks**

Date	Title	Pos	Wks
28 Jan 89	**THE PROMISE** *10 TEN 244*	58	3 wks

Nancy WHISKEY – *See Charles McDEVITT SKIFFLE GROUP featuring Nancy WHISKEY*

WHISPERS *US, male vocal group*   **52 wks**

Date	Title	Pos	Wks
2 Feb 80	● **AND THE BEAT GOES ON** *Solar SO 1*	2	12 wks
10 May 80	**LADY** *Solar SO 4*	55	3 wks
12 Jul 80	**MY GIRL** *Solar SO 6*	26	6 wks
14 Mar 81	● **IT'S A LOVE THING** *Solar SO 16*	9	11 wks
13 Jun 81	**I CAN MAKE IT BETTER** *Solar SO 19*	44	5 wks
19 Jan 85	**CONTAGIOUS** *MCA 937*	56	3 wks
28 Mar 87	**AND THE BEAT GOES ON (re-issue)** *Solar MCA 1126*	45	4 wks
23 May 87	**ROCK STEADY** *Solar MCA 1152*	38	6 wks
15 Aug 87	**SPECIAL F/X** *Solar MCA 1178*	69	2 wks

WHISTLE *US, male rap group*   **8 wks**

Date	Title	Pos	Wks
1 Mar 86	● **(NOTHIN' SERIOUS) JUST BUGGIN'** *Champion CHAMP 12*	7	8 wks

Barry WHITE *US, male vocalist*   **126 wks**

Date	Title	Pos	Wks
9 Jun 73	**I'M GONNA LOVE YOU JUST A LITTLE BIT MORE BABY** *Pye International 7N 25610*	23	7 wks
26 Jan 74	**NEVER NEVER GONNA GIVE YA UP** *Pye International 7N 25633*	14	11 wks
17 Aug 74	● **CAN'T GET ENOUGH OF YOUR LOVE BABE** *Pye International 7N 25661*	8	12 wks
2 Nov 74	★ **YOU'RE THE FIRST THE LAST MY EVERYTHING** *20th Century BTC 2133*	1	14 wks
8 Mar 75	● **WHAT AM I GONNA DO WITH YOU** *20th Century BTC 2177*	5	8 wks
24 May 75	**I'LL DO ANYTHING YOU WANT ME TO** *20th Century BTC 2208*	20	6 wks
27 Dec 75	● **LET THE MUSIC PLAY** *20th Century BTC 2265*	9	8 wks
6 Mar 76	● **YOU SEE THE TROUBLE WITH ME** *20th Century BTC 2277*	2	10 wks
21 Aug 76	**BABY WE BETTER TRY AND GET IT TOGETHER** *20th Century BTC 2298*	15	7 wks
13 Nov 76	**DON'T MAKE ME WAIT TOO LONG** *20th Century BTC 2309*	17	8 wks
5 Mar 77	**I'M QUALIFIED TO SATISFY** *20th Century BTC 2328*	37	5 wks
15 Oct 77	**IT'S ECSTASY WHEN YOU LAY DOWN NEXT TO ME** *20th Century BTC 2350*	40	3 wks
16 Dec 78	**JUST THE WAY YOU ARE** *20th Century BTC 2380*	12	12 wks
24 Mar 79	**SHA LA LA MEANS I LOVE YOU** *20th Century BTC 1041*	55	6 wks
7 Nov 87	**SHO' YOU RIGHT** *Breakout USA 614*	14	7 wks
16 Jan 88	**NEVER NEVER GONNA GIVE YOU UP (re-mix)** *Club JAB 59*	63	2 wks

See also Quincy Jones.

Chris WHITE *UK, male vocalist*   **4 wks**

Date	Title	Pos	Wks
20 Mar 76	**SPANISH WINE** *Charisma CB 272*	37	4 wks

Karyn WHITE *US, female vocalist*   **30 wks**

Date	Title	Pos	Wks
5 Nov 88	**THE WAY YOU LOVE ME** *Warner Bros. W 7773*	42	5 wks
18 Feb 89	**SECRET RENDEZVOUS** *warner Bros W 7562*	52	3 wks
10 Jun 89	**SUPERWOMAN** *Warner Bros. W 2920*	11	13 wks
9 Sep 89	**SECRET RENDEZVOUS (re-issue)** *Warner Bros. W 2855*	22	9 wks

Snowy WHITE *UK, male vocalist/instrumentalist – guitar*   **12 wks**

Date	Title	Pos	Wks
24 Dec 83	● **BIRD OF PARADISE** *Towerbell TOW 42*	6	10 wks
28 Dec 85	**FOR YOU** *R4 FOR 3*	65	1 wk
18 Jan 86	**FOR YOU (re-entry)** *R4 FOR 3*	72	1 wk

Tam WHITE *UK, male vocalist*   **4 wks**

Date	Title	Pos	Wks
15 Mar 75	**WHAT IN THE WORLD'S COME OVER YOU** *RAK 193*	36	4 wks

Tony Joe WHITE *US, male vocalist*   **10 wks**

Date	Title	Pos	Wks
6 Jun 70	**GROUPIE GIRL** *Monument MON 1043*	22	10 wks

WHITE and TORCH *UK, male vocal/instrumental duo*   **4 wks**

Date	Title	Pos	Wks
2 Oct 82	**PARADE** *Chrysalis CHS 2641*	54	4 wks

WHITE PLAINS *UK, male vocal group*   **56 wks**

Date	Title	Pos	Wks
7 Feb 70	● **MY BABY LOVES LOVIN'** *Deram DM 280*	9	11 wks
18 Apr 70	**I'VE GOT YOU ON MY MIND** *Deram DM 291*	17	11 wks
24 Oct 70	● **JULIE DO YA LOVE ME** *Deram DM 315*	8	14 wks
12 Jun 71	**WHEN YOU ARE A KING** *Deram DM 333*	13	11 wks

17 Feb 73		STEP INTO A DREAM *Deram DM 371*	21	9 wks

WHITEHEAD – *See McFADDEN and WHITEHEAD*

WHITESNAKE *UK, male vocal/instrumental group* — **107 wks**

24 Jun 78		SNAKE BITE (EP) *EMI International INEP 751*	61	3 wks
10 Nov 79		LONG WAY FROM HOME *United Artists BP 324*	55	2 wks
26 Apr 80		FOOL FOR YOUR LOVING *United Artists BP 352*	13	9 wks
12 Jul 80		READY AN' WILLING (SWEET SATISFACTION) *United Artists BP 363*	43	4 wks
22 Nov 80		AIN'T NO LOVE IN THE HEART OF THE CITY *Sunburst/Liberty BP 381*	51	4 wks
11 Apr 81		DON'T BREAK MY HEART AGAIN *Liberty BP 395*	17	9 wks
6 Jun 81		WOULD I LIE TO YOU *Liberty BP 399*	37	6 wks
6 Nov 82		HERE I GO AGAIN/ BLOODY LUXURY *Liberty BP 416*	34	10 wks
13 Aug 83		GUILTY OF LOVE *Liberty BP 420*	31	5 wks
14 Jan 84		GIVE ME MORE TIME *Liberty BP 422*	29	4 wks
28 Apr 84		STANDING IN THE SHADOW *Liberty BP 423*	62	2 wks
9 Feb 85		LOVE AIN'T NO STRANGER *Liberty BP 424*	44	4 wks
28 Mar 87		STILL OF THE NIGHT *EMI EMI 5606*	16	8 wks
6 Jun 87	●	IS THIS LOVE *EMI EM 123*	9	11 wks
31 Oct 87	●	HERE I GO AGAIN (re-mix) *EMI EM 35*	9	11 wks
6 Feb 88		GIVE ME ALL YOUR LOVE *EMI EM 23*	18	6 wks
2 Dec 89		FOOL FOR YOUR LOVING *EMI EM 123*	43	2 wks
10 Mar 90		THE DEEPER THE LOVE *EMI EM 128*	35	3 wks
25 Aug 90		NOW YOU'RE GONE *EMI EM 150*	31	4 wks

Tracks on Snake Bite *EP: Bloody Mary/Steal Away/Ain't No Love In The Heart Of The City/Come On. This EP and* Long Way From Home *were credited to David Coverdale's Whitesnake. EM 123 is a re-recording of their third hit.*

David WHITFIELD *UK, male vocalist* — **181 wks**

2 Oct 53	●	BRIDGE OF SIGHS *Decca F 10129*	9	1 wk
16 Oct 53	★	ANSWER ME *Decca F 10192*	1	13 wks
11 Dec 53		RAGS TO RICHES *Decca F 10207*	12	1 wk
8 Jan 54		RAGS TO RICHES (re-entry) *Decca F 10207*	3	10 wks
29 Jan 54		ANSWER ME (re-entry) *Decca F 10192*	12	1 wk
19 Feb 54	●	THE BOOK *Decca F 10242*	5	12 wks
28 May 54		THE BOOK (re-entry) *Decca F 10242*	10	3 wks
18 Jun 54	★	CARA MIA *Decca F 10327*	1	25 wks
12 Nov 54	●	SANTO NATALE *Decca F 10399*	2	10 wks
11 Feb 55	●	BEYOND THE STARS *Decca F 10458*	8	9 wks
27 May 55		MAMA *Decca F 10515*	20	1 wk
24 Jun 55		MAMA (re-entry) *Decca F 10515*	19	2 wks
8 Jul 55	●	EV'RYWHERE *Decca F 10515*	3	20 wks
29 Jul 55		MAMA (2nd re-entry) *Decca F 10515*	12	8 wks
25 Nov 55	●	WHEN YOU LOSE THE ONE YOU LOVE *Decca F 10627*	7	11 wks
2 Mar 56		MY SEPTEMBER LOVE *Decca F 10690*	19	2 wks
23 Mar 56		MY SEPTEMBER LOVE (re-entry) *Decca F 10690*	18	1 wk
6 Apr 56	●	MY SEPTEMBER LOVE (2nd re-entry) *Decca F 10690*	3	20 wks
24 Aug 56		MY SON JOHN *Decca F 10769*	22	4 wks
31 Aug 56		MY UNFINISHED SYMPHONY *Decca F 10769*	29	1 wk
7 Sep 56		MY SEPTEMBER LOVE (3rd re-entry) *Decca F 10690*	25	1 wk
25 Jan 57	●	ADORATION WALTZ *Decca F 10833*	9	11 wks
5 Apr 57		I'LL FIND YOU *Decca F 10864*	28	2 wks
7 Jun 57		I'LL FIND YOU (re-entry) *Decca F 10864*	27	2 wks
14 Feb 58		CRY MY HEART *Decca F 10978*	22	3 wks
16 May 58		ON THE STREET WHERE YOU LIVE *Decca F 11018*	16	14 wks
8 Aug 58		THE RIGHT TO LOVE *Decca F 11039*	30	1 wk
24 Nov 60		I BELIEVE *Decca F 11289*	49	1 wk

Cara Mia was billed as 'with chorus and Mantovani and his Orchestra'. See also Various Artists - All-Star Hit Parade; Mantovani.

Slim WHITMAN *US, male vocalist* — **75 wks**

15 Jul 55	★	ROSE MARIE *London HL 8061*	1	19 wks
29 Jul 55	●	INDIAN LOVE CALL *London L 1149*	7	12 wks
23 Sep 55		CHINA DOLL *London L 1149*	15	2 wks
9 Mar 56		TUMBLING TUMBLEWEEDS *London HLU 8230*	19	2 wks
13 Apr 56		I'M A FOOL *London HLU 8252*	16	3 wks
11 May 56		I'M A FOOL (re-entry) *London HLU 8252*	29	1 wk

---

22 Jun 56		SERENADE *London HLU 8287*	24	3 wks
27 Jul 56	●	SERENADE (re-entry) *London HLU 8287*	8	12 wks
12 Apr 57	●	I'LL TAKE YOU HOME AGAIN KATHLEEN *London HLP 8403*	7	13 wks
5 Oct 74		HAPPY ANNIVERSARY *United Artists UP 35728*	14	10 wks

---

Roger WHITTAKER *Kenya, male vocalist* — **75 wks**

8 Nov 69		DURHAM TOWN (THE LEAVIN') *Columbia DB 8613*	12	18 wks
11 Apr 70	●	I DON'T BELIEVE IN IF ANYMORE *Columbia DB 8664*	8	18 wks
10 Oct 70		NEW WORLD IN THE MORNING *Columbia DB 8718*	17	14 wks
3 Apr 71		WHY *Columbia DB 8752*	47	1 wk
2 Oct 71		MAMMY BLUE *Columbia DB 8822*	31	10 wks
26 Jul 75	●	THE LAST FAREWELL *EMI 2294*	2	14 wks

See also Roger Whittaker and Des O'Connor.

Roger WHITTAKER and Des O'CONNOR — **10 wks**
Kenya/UK, male vocal duo

8 Nov 86	●	THE SKYE BOAT SONG *Tembo TML 119*	10	10 wks

See also Roger Whittaker; Des O'Connor.

WHO *UK, male vocal/instrumental group* — **245 wks**

18 Feb 65	●	I CAN'T EXPLAIN *Brunswick 05926*	8	13 wks
27 May 65	●	ANYWAY ANYHOW ANYWHERE *Brunswick 05935*	10	12 wks
4 Nov 65	●	MY GENERATION *Brunswick 05944*	2	13 wks
10 Mar 66	●	SUBSTITUTE *Reaction 591 001*	5	13 wks
24 Mar 66		A LEGAL MATTER *Brunswick 05956*	32	6 wks
1 Sep 66		I'M A BOY *Reaction 591 004*	2	13 wks
1 Sep 66		THE KIDS ARE ALRIGHT *Brunswick 05965*	41	2 wks
22 Sep 66		THE KIDS ARE ALRIGHT (re-entry) *Brunswick 05965*	48	1 wk
15 Dec 66	●	HAPPY JACK *Reaction 591 010*	3	11 wks
27 Apr 67	●	PICTURES OF LILY *Track 604 002*	4	10 wks
26 Jul 67		THE LAST TIME/ UNDER MY THUMB *Track 604 006*	44	3 wks
18 Oct 67	●	I CAN SEE FOR MILES *Track 604 011*	10	12 wks
19 Jun 68		DOGS *Track 604 023*	25	5 wks
23 Oct 68		MAGIC BUS *Track 604 024*	26	6 wks
19 Mar 69	●	PINBALL WIZARD *Track 604 027*	4	13 wks
4 Apr 70		THE SEEKER *Track 604 036*	19	11 wks
8 Aug 70		SUMMERTIME BLUES *Track 2094 002*	38	4 wks
10 Jul 71	●	WON'T GET FOOLED AGAIN *Track 2094 009*	9	12 wks
23 Oct 71		LET'S SEE ACTION *Track 2094 012*	16	12 wks
24 Jun 72	●	JOIN TOGETHER *Track 2094 102*	9	9 wks
13 Jan 73		RELAY *Track 2094 106*	21	5 wks
13 Oct 73		5:15 *Track 2094 115*	20	6 wks
24 Jan 76	●	SQUEEZE BOX *Polydor 2121 275*	10	9 wks
30 Oct 76	●	SUBSTITUTE (re-issue) *Polydor 2058 803*	7	7 wks
22 Jul 78		WHO ARE YOU *Polydor WHO 1*	18	12 wks
28 Apr 79		LONG LIVE ROCK *Polydor WHO 2.*	48	5 wks
7 Mar 81	●	YOU BETTER YOU BET *Polydor WHO 004*	9	8 wks
9 May 81		DON'T LET GO THE COAT *Polydor WHO 005*	47	4 wks
2 Oct 82		ATHENA *Polydor WHO 6*	40	4 wks
26 Nov 83		READY STEADY WHO (EP) *Polydor WHO 7*	58	2 wks
20 Feb 88		MY GENERATION (re-issue) *Polydor POSP 907*	68	2 wks

See also High Numbers. Tracks on EP: Disguises/Circles/Batman/Bucket 'T'/Barbara Ann.

WHODINI *US, male rap/scratch duo* — **10 wks**

25 Dec 82		MAGIC'S WAND *Jive JIVE 28*	47	6 wks
17 Mar 84		MAGIC'S WAND (THE WHODINI ELECTRIC EP) (re-issue) *Jive JIVE 61*	63	4 wks

Tracks on EP: (re-issue) Jive Magic Wand/Nasty Lady/Rap Machine/The Haunted House of Rock.

Jane WIEDLIN *US, female vocalist* — **14 wks**

6 Aug 88		RUSH HOUR *Manhattan MT 36*	12	11 wks
29 Oct 88		INSIDE A DREAM *Manhattan MT 55*	64	3 wks

WIGAN'S CHOSEN FEW
US, instrumental track plus UK crowd vocal **11 wks**

18 Jan 75	● FOOTSEE *Pye Disco Demand DDS 111*	**9**	11 wks

WIGAN'S OVATION *UK, male vocal/instrumental group* **19 wks**

15 Mar 75	SKIING IN THE SNOW *Spark SRL 1122*	**12**	10 wks
28 Jun 75	PER-SO-NAL-LY *Spark SRL 1129*	**38**	6 wks
29 Nov 75	SUPER LOVE *Spark SRL 1133*	**41**	3 wks

Jack WILD *UK, male vocalist* **2 wks**

2 May 70	SOME BEAUTIFUL *Capitol CL 15635*	**46**	2 wks

WILD CHERRY *US, male vocal/instrumental group* **11 wks**

9 Oct 76	● PLAY THAT FUNKY MUSIC *Epic EPC 4593*	**7**	11 wks

WILD PAIR – *See Paula ABDUL*

WILD WEEKEND *UK, male vocal/instrumental group* **2 wks**

29 Apr 89	BREAKIN' UP *Parlophone R 6204*	**74**	1 wk
5 May 90	WHO'S AFRAID OF THE BIG BAD LOVE *Parlophone R 6249*	**70**	1 wk

Eugene WILDE *US, male vocalist* **15 wks**

13 Oct 84	GOTTA GET YOU HOME TONIGHT *Fourth & Broadway BRW 15*	**18**	9 wks
2 Feb 85	PERSONALITY *Fourth & Broadway BRW 18*	**34**	6 wks

Personality was coupled with Let Her Feel It *by Simplicious. See also Simplicious.*

Kim WILDE *UK, female vocalist* **152 wks**

21 Feb 81	● KIDS IN AMERICA *RAK 327*	**2**	13 wks
9 May 81	● CHEQUERED LOVE *RAK 330*	**4**	9 wks
1 Aug 81	WATER ON GLASS/ BOYS *RAK 334*	**11**	8 wks
14 Nov 81	CAMBODIA *RAK 336*	**12**	12 wks
17 Apr 82	VIEW FROM A BRIDGE *RAK 342*	**16**	7 wks
16 Oct 82	CHILD COME AWAY *RAK 352*	**43**	4 wks
30 Jul 83	LOVE BLONDE *RAK 360*	**23**	8 wks
12 Nov 83	DANCING IN THE DARK *RAK 365*	**67**	2 wks
13 Oct 84	THE SECOND TIME *MCA KIM 1*	**29**	6 wks
8 Dec 84	THE TOUCH *MCA KIM 2*	**56**	3 wks
27 Apr 85	RAGE TO LOVE *MCA KIM 3*	**19**	8 wks
25 Oct 86	● YOU KEEP ME HANGIN' ON *MCA KIM 4*	**2**	14 wks
8 Aug 87	SAY YOU REALLY WANT ME *MCA KIM 6*	**29**	5 wks
14 May 88	HEY MISTER HEARTACHE *MCA KIM 7*	**31**	5 wks
16 Jul 88	● YOU CAME *MCA KIM 8*	**3**	11 wks
1 Oct 88	● NEVER TRUST A STRANGER *MCA KIM 9*	**7**	9 wks
3 Dec 88	● FOUR LETTER WORD *MCA KIM 10*	**6**	12 wks
4 Mar 89	LOVE IN THE NATURAL WAY *MCA KIM 11*	**32**	6 wks
14 Apr 90	IT'S HERE *MCA KIM 12*	**42**	4 wks
16 Jun 90	TIME *MCA KIM 13*	**71**	3 wks
15 Dec 90	I CAN'T SAY GOODBYE *MCA KIM 14*	**51**	3 wks

See also Kim Wilde and Junior; Mel and Kim.

Kim WILDE and JUNIOR *UK, female/male vocal duo* **11 wks**

4 Apr 87	● ANOTHER STEP CLOSER TO YOU *MCA KIM 5*	**6**	11 wks

See also Kim Wilde; Junior.

Marty WILDE *UK, male vocalist* **117 wks**

11 Jul 58	● ENDLESS SLEEP *Philips PB 835*	**4**	14 wks
6 Mar 59	● DONNA *Philips PB 902*	**3**	16 wks
5 Jun 59	● A TEENAGER IN LOVE *Philips PB 926*	**2**	17 wks
3 Jul 59	DONNA (re-entry) *Philips PB 902*	**25**	2 wks
25 Sep 59	● SEA OF LOVE *Philips PB 959*	**3**	12 wks
11 Dec 59	● BAD BOY *Philips PB 972*	**7**	8 wks
10 Mar 60	JOHNNY ROCCO *Philips PB 1002*	**30**	4 wks
19 May 60	THE FIGHT *Philips PB 1022*	**47**	1 wk
22 Dec 60	LITTLE GIRL *Philips PB 1078*	**16**	9 wks
26 Jan 61	● RUBBER BALL *Philips PB 1101*	**9**	9 wks
27 Jul 61	HIDE AND SEEK *Philips PB 1161*	**47**	2 wks
9 Nov 61	TOMORROW'S CLOWN *Philips PB 1191*	**33**	5 wks
24 May 62	JEZEBEL *Philips PB 1240*	**19**	11 wks
25 Oct 62	EVER SINCE YOU SAID GOODBYE *Philips 326546 BF*	**31**	7 wks

Matthew WILDER *US, male vocalist* **11 wks**

21 Jan 84	● BREAK MY STRIDE *Epic A 3908*	**4**	11 wks

Sue WILKINSON *UK, female vocalist* **8 wks**

2 Aug 80	YOU GOTTA BE A HUSTLER IF YOU WANNA GET ON *Cheapskate CHEAP 2*	**25**	8 wks

WILL TO POWER *US, male/female vocal/instrumental duo* **11 wks**

7 Jan 89	● BABY I LOVE YOUR WAY - FREEBIRD *Epic 653094 7*	**6**	9 wks
22 Dec 90	I'M NOT IN LOVE *Epic 6565377*	**50†**	2 wks

Alyson WILLIAMS *US, female vocalist* **28 wks**

4 Mar 89	SLEEP TALK *Def Jam 654656 7*	**17**	9 wks
6 May 89	MY LOVE IS SO RAW *Def Jam 654898 7*	**34**	5 wks
19 Aug 89	● I NEED YOUR LOVIN' *Def Jam 655143 7*	**8**	11 wks
18 Nov 89	I SECOND THAT EMOTION *Def Jam 655456 7*	**44**	3 wks

My Love Is So Raw features Nikki D - US, female vocalist.

Andy WILLIAMS *US, male vocalist* **228 wks**

19 Apr 57	★ BUTTERFLY *London HLA 8399*	**1**	15 wks
21 Jun 57	I LIKE YOUR KIND OF LOVE *London HLA 8437*	**16**	10 wks
30 Aug 57	BUTTERFLY (re-entry) *London HLA 8399*	**29**	1 wk
14 Jun 62	STRANGER ON THE SHORE *CBS AAG 103*	**30**	10 wks
21 Mar 63	● CAN'T GET USED TO LOSING YOU *CBS AAG 138*	**2**	18 wks
27 Feb 64	A FOOL NEVER LEARNS *CBS AAG 182*	**40**	4 wks
16 Sep 65	● ALMOST THERE *CBS 201813*	**2**	17 wks
24 Feb 66	MAY EACH DAY *CBS 202042*	**19**	8 wks
22 Sep 66	IN THE ARMS OF LOVE *CBS 202300*	**33**	7 wks
4 May 67	MUSIC TO WATCH GIRLS BY *CBS 2675*	**33**	6 wks
2 Aug 67	MORE AND MORE *CBS 2886*	**45**	1 wk
13 Mar 68	● CAN'T TAKE MY EYES OFF YOU *CBS 3298*	**5**	18 wks
7 May 69	HAPPY HEART *CBS 4062*	**47**	1 wk
21 May 69	HAPPY HEART (re-entry) *CBS 4062*	**19**	9 wks
14 Mar 70	● CAN'T HELP FALLING IN LOVE *CBS 4818*	**3**	17 wks
1 Aug 70	IT'S SO EASY *CBS 5113*	**13**	13 wks
7 Nov 70	IT'S SO EASY (re-entry) *CBS 5113*	**49**	1 wk
21 Nov 70	● HOME LOVIN' MAN *CBS 5267*	**7**	12 wks
20 Mar 71	● (WHERE DO I BEGIN) LOVE STORY *CBS 7020*	**4**	17 wks
24 Jul 71	(WHERE DO I BEGIN) LOVE STORY (re-entry) *CBS 7020*	**49**	1 wk
5 Aug 72	LOVE THEME FROM THE GODFATHER *CBS 8166*	**50**	1 wk
2 Sep 72	LOVE THEME FROM THE GODFATHER (re-entry) *CBS 8166*	**44**	3 wks
30 Sep 72	LOVE THEME FROM THE GODFATHER (2nd re-entry) *CBS 8166*	**42**	5 wks
8 Dec 73	● SOLITAIRE *CBS 1824*	**4**	18 wks
18 May 74	GETTING OVER YOU *CBS 2181*	**35**	5 wks
31 May 75	YOU LAY SO EASY ON MY MIND *CBS 3167*	**32**	5 wks
6 Mar 76	THE OTHER SIDE OF ME *CBS 3903*	**42**	3 wks

Andy and David WILLIAMS US, male vocal duo — 5 wks

24 Mar 73	I DON'T KNOW WHY MCA MUS 1183	37	5 wks

Do not see Andy Williams. This Andy is the nephew of the other Andy.

Billy WILLIAMS US, male vocalist — 9 wks

2 Aug 57	I'M GONNA SIT RIGHT DOWN AND WRITE MYSELF A LETTER Vogue Coral Q 72266	22	8 wks
18 Oct 57	I'M GONNA SIT RIGHT DOWN AND WRITE MYSELF A LETTER (re-entry) Vogue Coral Q 72266	28	1 wk

Danny WILLIAMS UK, male vocalist — 74 wks

25 May 61	WE WILL NEVER BE AS YOUNG AS THIS AGAIN HMV POP 839	44	3 wks
6 Jul 61	THE MIRACLE OF YOU HMV POP 885	41	8 wks
2 Nov 61	★ MOON RIVER HMV POP 932	1	19 wks
18 Jan 62	JEANNIE HMV POP 968	14	14 wks
12 Apr 62	● WONDERFUL WORLD OF THE YOUNG HMV POP 1002	8	13 wks
5 Jul 62	TEARS HMV POP 1035	22	7 wks
28 Feb 63	MY OWN TRUE LOVE HMV POP 1112	45	3 wks
30 Jul 77	DANCIN' EASY Ensign ENY 3	30	7 wks

Deniece WILLIAMS US, female vocalist — 39 wks

2 Apr 77	★ FREE CBS 4978	1	10 wks
30 Jul 77	● THAT'S WHAT FRIENDS ARE FOR CBS 5432	8	11 wks
12 Nov 77	BABY BABY MY LOVE'S ALL FOR YOU CBS 5779	32	5 wks
5 May 84	● LET'S HEAR IT FOR THE BOY CBS A 4319	2	12 wks
4 Aug 84	LET'S HEAR IT FOR THE BOY (re-entry) CBS A 4319	75	1 wk

See also Johnny Mathis and Deniece Williams.

Diana WILLIAMS US, female vocalist — 3 wks

25 Jul 81	TEDDY BEAR'S LAST RIDE Capitol CL 207	54	3 wks

Don WILLIAMS US, male vocalist — 16 wks

19 Jun 76	I RECALL A GYPSY WOMAN ABC 4098	13	10 wks
23 Oct 76	YOU'RE MY BEST FRIEND ABC 4144	35	6 wks

Freedom WILLIAMS – See C & C MUSIC FACTORY featuring Freedom WILLIAMS

Iris WILLIAMS UK, female vocalist — 8 wks

27 Oct 79	HE WAS BEAUTIFUL (CAVATINA) (THE THEME FROM THE DEER HUNTER) Columbia DB 9070	18	8 wks

John WILLIAMS UK, male instrumentalist – guitar — 11 wks

19 May 79	CAVATINA Cube BUG 80	13	11 wks

John WILLIAMS US, orchestra leader with US, orchestra — 10 wks

18 Dec 82	THEME FROM 'E.T.' (THE EXTRA-TERRESTRIAL) MCA 800	17	10 wks

Kenny WILLIAMS US, male vocalist — 7 wks

19 Nov 77	(YOU'RE) FABULOUS BABE Decca FR 13731	35	7 wks

Larry WILLIAMS US, male vocalist — 18 wks

20 Sep 57	SHORT FAT FANNY London HLN 8472	21	8 wks
17 Jan 58	BONY MORONIE London HLU 8532	11	10 wks

Lenny WILLIAMS US, male vocalist — 7 wks

5 Nov 77	SHOO DOO FU FU OOH ABC 4194	38	4 wks
16 Sep 78	YOU GOT ME BURNING ABC 4228	67	3 wks

Mark WILLIAMS – See Karen BADDINGTON and Mark WILLIAMS

Mason WILLIAMS US, male instrumentalist - guitar — 13 wks

28 Aug 68	● CLASSICAL GAS Warner Bros. WB 7190	9	13 wks

Maurice WILLIAMS and the ZODIACS
US, male vocal group — 9 wks

5 Jan 61	STAY Top Rank JAR 526	14	9 wks

Vanessa WILLIAMS US, female vocalist — 6 wks

20 Aug 88	THE RIGHT STUFF Wing WING 3	71	1 wk
25 Mar 89	DREAMIN' Wing WING 4	74	2 wks
19 Aug 89	THE RIGHT STUFF (re-mix) Wing WINR 3	62	3 wks

Vesta WILLIAMS US, female vocalist — 13 wks

20 Dec 86	ONCE BITTEN TWICE SHY A & M AM 362	14	13 wks

Wendell WILLIAMS – See CRIMINAL ELEMENT ORCHESTRA and Wendell WILLIAMS

WILLING SINNERS – See Marc ALMOND

Bruce WILLIS US, male vocalist — 30 wks

7 Mar 87	● RESPECT YOURSELF Motown ZB 41117	7	10 wks
30 May 87	● UNDER THE BOARDWALK Motown ZB 41349	2	15 wks
12 Sep 87	SECRET AGENT MAN - JAMES BOND IS BACK Motown ZB 41437	43	4 wks
23 Jan 88	COMIN' RIGHT UP Motown ZB 41453	73	1 wk

Under The Boardwalk credits the Temptations on background vocals. See also the Temptations.

Chill WILLS – See LAUREL and HARDY with the AVALON BOYS

Viola WILLS US, female vocalist — 16 wks

6 Oct 79	● GONNA GET ALONG WITHOUT YOU NOW Ariola/Hansa AHA 546	8	10 wks
15 Mar 86	BOTH SIDES NOW/ DARE TO DREAM Streetwave KHAN 66	35	6 wks

Al WILSON US, male vocalist — 5 wks

23 Aug 75	THE SNAKE Bell 1436	41	5 wks

Dooley WILSON US, male vocalist — 9 wks

3 Dec 77	AS TIME GOES BY United Artists UP 36331	15	9 wks

Disc has credit 'with the voices of Humphrey Bogart and Ingrid Bergman'.

WILSON PHILLIPS, daughters of Brian Wilson of the Beach Boys and John and Michelle Phillips of the Mamas and Papas, were the first act to achieve two American number ones in the Nineties.

Bottom Left: EDGAR WINTER had a monster hit in 1973.

Below: Karl Wallinger, former Waterboy, is the leader of WORLD PARTY.

Jackie WILSON US, male vocalist — 97 wks

15 Nov 57 ●	**REET PETITE** Coral Q 72290	6	14 wks
14 Mar 58	**TO BE LOVED** Coral Q 72306	27	1 wk
28 Mar 58	**TO BE LOVED (re-entry)** Coral Q 72306	23	6 wks
16 May 58	**TO BE LOVED (2nd re-entry)** Coral Q 72306	23	1 wk
15 Sep 60	**ALL MY LOVE** Coral Q 72407	33	6 wks
3 Nov 60	**ALL MY LOVE (re-entry)** Coral Q 72407	47	1 wk
22 Dec 60	**ALONE AT LAST** Coral Q 72412	50	1 wk
14 May 69	**(YOUR LOVE KEEPS LIFTING ME) HIGHER AND HIGHER** MCA BAG 2	11	11 wks
29 Jul 72 ●	**I GET THE SWEETEST FEELING** MCA MU 1160	9	13 wks
3 May 75	**I GET THE SWEETEST FEELING/ HIGHER AND HIGHER (re-issues)** Brunswick BR 18	25	8 wks
29 Nov 86 ★	**REET PETITE (re-issue)** SMP SKM 3	1	17 wks
28 Feb 87 ●	**I GET THE SWEETEST FEELING (2nd re-issue)** SMP SKM 1	3	11 wks
4 Jul 87	**HIGHER AND HIGHER (2nd re-issue)** SMP SKM 10	15	7 wks

Higher and Higher was not listed together with I Get The Sweetest Feeling on Brunswick until 17 May 75.

Mari WILSON UK, female vocalist — 34 wks

6 Mar 82	**BEAT THE BEAT** Compact PINK 2	59	3 wks
8 May 82	**BABY IT'S TRUE** Compact PINK 3	42	6 wks
11 Sep 82 ●	**JUST WHAT I ALWAYS WANTED** Compact PINK 4	8	10 wks
13 Nov 82	**(BEWARE) BOYFRIEND** Compact PINK 5	51	4 wks
19 Mar 83	**CRY ME A RIVER** Compact PINK 6	27	7 wks
11 Jun 83	**WONDERFUL** Compact PINK 7	47	4 wks

Meri WILSON US, female vocalist — 10 wks

27 Aug 77 ●	**TELEPHONE MAN** Pye International 7N 25747	6	10 wks

Mike 'Hitman' WILSON US, male vocalist — 1 wk

22 Sep 90	**ANOTHER SLEEPLESS NIGHT** Arista 113506	74	1 wk

Precious WILSON – See ERUPTION

WILSON PHILLIPS US, female vocal group — 20 wks

26 May 90 ●	**HOLD ON** SBK SBK 6	6	12 wks
18 Aug 90	**RELEASE ME** SBK SBK 11	36	5 wks
10 Nov 90	**IMPULSIVE** SBK SBK 16	42	3 wks

Chris WILTSHIRE – See CLASS ACTION featuring Chris WILTSHIRE

WIN UK, male vocal/instrumental group — 3 wks

4 Apr 87	**SUPER POPOID GROOVE** Swamplands LON 128	63	3 wks

WINANS US, male vocal group — 1 wk

30 Nov 85	**LET MY PEOPLE GO (PART 1)** Qwest W 8874	71	1 wk

WINCHESTER CATHEDRAL CHOIR – See Sarah BRIGHTMAN and Paul MILES-KINGSTON

WINDJAMMER US, male vocal/instrumental group — 12 wks

30 Jun 84	**TOSSING AND TURNING** MCA MCA 897	18	12 wks

Rose WINDROSS – See SOUL II SOUL

WING AND A PRAYER FIFE AND DRUM CORPS US, male/female vocal/instrumental group — 7 wks

24 Jan 76	**BABY FACE** Atlantic K 10705	12	7 wks

Pete WINGFIELD UK, male vocalist — 7 wks

28 Jun 75 ●	**EIGHTEEN WITH A BULLET** Island WIP 6231	7	7 wks

WINGS – See Paul McCARTNEY

Edgar WINTER GROUP US, male instrumental group — 9 wks

26 May 73	**FRANKENSTEIN** Epic EPC 1440	18	9 wks

Ruby WINTERS US, female vocalist — 35 wks

5 Nov 77 ●	**I WILL** Creole CR 141	4	13 wks
29 Apr 78	**COME TO ME** Creole CR 153	11	12 wks
26 Aug 78	**I WON'T MENTION IT AGAIN** Creole CR 160	45	5 wks
16 Jun 79	**BABY LAY DOWN** Creole CR 171	43	5 wks

Steve WINWOOD UK, male vocalist — 33 wks

17 Jan 81	**WHILE YOU SEE A CHANCE** Island WIP 6655	45	5 wks
9 Oct 82	**VALERIE** Island WIP 6818	51	4 wks
28 Jun 86	**HIGHER LOVE** Island IS 288	13	9 wks
13 Sep 86	**FREEDOM OVERSPILL** Island IS 294	69	1 wk
24 Jan 87	**BACK IN THE HIGH LIFE AGAIN** Island IS 303	53	2 wks
19 Sep 87	**VALERIE (re-issue)** Island IS 336	19	8 wks
11 Jun 88	**ROLL WITH IT** Virgin VS 1085	53	4 wks

WIRE UK, male vocal/instrumental group — 4 wks

27 Jan 79	**OUTDOOR MINER** Harvest HAR 5172	51	3 wks
13 May 89	**EARDRUM BUZZ** Mute MUTE 87	68	1 wk

Norman WISDOM UK, male vocalist — 20 wks

19 Feb 54 ●	**DON'T LAUGH AT ME** Columbia DB 3133	3	15 wks
15 Mar 57	**WISDOM OF A FOOL** Columbia DB 3903	13	5 wks

Bill WITHERS US, male vocalist — 29 wks

12 Aug 72	**LEAN ON ME** A & M AMS 7004	18	9 wks
14 Jan 78 ●	**LOVELY DAY** CBS 5773	7	8 wks
25 May 85	**OH YEAH!** CBS A 6154	60	3 wks
10 Sep 88 ●	**LOVELY DAY (re-mix)** CBS 653001 7	4	9 wks

See also Grover Washington Jr.

WIZZARD UK, male vocal/instrumental group — 77 wks

9 Dec 72 ●	**BALL PARK INCIDENT** Harvest HAR 5062	6	12 wks
21 Apr 73 ★	**SEE MY BABY JIVE** Harvest HAR 5070	1	17 wks
1 Sep 73 ★	**ANGEL FINGERS** Harvest HAR 5076	1	10 wks
8 Dec 73 ●	**I WISH IT COULD BE CHRISTMAS EVERYDAY** Harvest HAR 5079	4	9 wks
27 Apr 74	**ROCK 'N' ROLL WINTER** Warner Bros. K 16357	6	7 wks
10 Aug 74	**THIS IS THE STORY OF MY LOVE (BABY)** Warner Bros. K 16434	34	4 wks
21 Dec 74 ●	**ARE YOU READY TO ROCK** Warner Bros. K 16497	8	10 wks
19 Dec 81	**I WISH IT COULD BE CHRISTMAS EVERYDAY (re-issue)** Harvest HAR 5173	41	4 wks
15 Dec 84	**I WISH IT COULD BE CHRISTMAS EVERYDAY (re-entry of re-issue)** Harvest HAR 5173	23	4 wks

I Wish It Could Be Christmas Everyday features vocal backing by the Suedettes plus the Stockland Green Bilateral School First Year Choir with additional noises by Miss Snob and Class 3C.

Terry WOGAN *Ireland, male vocalist*   **5 wks**

7 Jan 78	FLORAL DANCE *Philips 6006 592*	21	5 wks

Bobby WOMACK *US, male vocalist*   **7 wks**

16 Jun 84	TELL ME WHY *Motown TMG 1339*	60	3 wks
5 Oct 85	I WISH HE DIDN'T TRUST ME SO MUCH *MCA MCA 994*	64	2 wks
7 Nov 87	LIVING IN A BOX *MCA MCA 1210*	70	2 wks

See also Wilton Felder; Living In A Box.

WOMACK and WOMACK *US, male/female vocal duo*   **48 wks**

28 Apr 84	LOVE WARS *Elektra E 9799*	14	10 wks
30 Jun 84	BABY I'M SCARED OF YOU *Elektra E 9733*	72	2 wks
6 Dec 86	SOUL LOVE - SOUL MAN *Manhattan MT 16*	58	6 wks
6 Aug 88	● TEARDROPS *Fourth & Broadway BRW 101*	3	17 wks
12 Nov 88	LIFE'S JUST A BALLGAME *Fourth & Broadway BRW 116*	32	5 wks
25 Feb 89	CELEBRATE THE WORLD *Fourth & Broadway BRW 125*	19	8 wks

WOMBLES   **87 wks**
UK, Mike Batt, male vocalist, arranger and producer under group name

26 Jan 74	● THE WOMBLING SONG *CBS 1794*	4	23 wks
6 Apr 74	● REMEMBER YOU'RE A WOMBLE *CBS 2241*	3	16 wks
22 Jun 74	● BANANA ROCK *CBS 2465*	9	13 wks
12 Oct 74	MINUETTO ALLEGRETTO *CBS 2710*	16	9 wks
7 Dec 74	● WOMBLING MERRY CHRISTMAS *CBS 2842*	2	8 wks
10 May 75	WOMBLING WHITE TIE AND TAILS *CBS 3266*	22	7 wks
9 Aug 75	SUPER WOMBLE *CBS 3480*	20	6 wks
13 Dec 75	LET'S WOMBLE TO THE PARTY TONIGHT *CBS 3794*	34	5 wks

See also Mike Batt.

Stevie WONDER *US, male vocalist - multi-instrumentalist*   **364 wks**

3 Feb 66	UPTIGHT *Tamla Motown TMG 545*	14	10 wks
18 Aug 66	BLOWIN' IN THE WIND *Tamla Motown TMG 570*	36	5 wks
5 Jan 67	A PLACE IN THE SUN *Tamla Motown TMG 588*	20	5 wks
26 Jul 67	● I WAS MADE TO LOVE HER *Tamla Motown TMG 613*	5	15 wks
25 Oct 67	I'M WONDERING *Tamla Motown TMG 626*	22	8 wks
8 May 68	SHOO BE DOO BE DOO DA DAY *Tamla Motown TMG 653*	46	4 wks
18 Dec 68	● FOR ONCE IN MY LIFE *Tamla Motown TMG 679*	3	13 wks
19 Mar 69	I DON'T KNOW WHY *Tamla Motown TMG 690*	14	10 wks
9 Jul 69	I DON'T KNOW WHY (re-entry) *Tamla Motown TMG 690*	43	1 wk
16 Jul 69	● MY CHERIE AMOUR *Tamla Motown TMG 690*	4	15 wks
15 Nov 69	● YESTER-ME YESTER-YOU YESTERDAY *Tamla Motown TMG 717*	2	13 wks
28 Mar 70	● NEVER HAD A DREAM COME TRUE *Tamla Motown TMG 731*	6	12 wks
18 Jul 70	SIGNED SEALED DELIVERED I'M YOURS *Tamla Motown TMG 744*	15	9 wks
26 Sep 70	SIGNED SEALED DELIVERED I'M YOURS (re-entry) *Tamla Motown TMG 744*	49	1 wk
21 Nov 70	HEAVEN HELP US ALL *Tamla Motown TMG 757*	29	11 wks
15 May 71	WE CAN WORK IT OUT *Tamla Motown TMG 772*	27	7 wks
22 Jan 72	IF YOU REALLY LOVE ME *Tamla Motown TMG 798*	20	7 wks
3 Feb 73	SUPERSTITION *Tamla Motown TMG 841*	11	9 wks
19 May 73	● YOU ARE THE SUNSHINE OF MY LIFE *Tamla Motown TMG 852*	7	11 wks
13 Oct 73	HIGHER GROUND *Tamla Motown TMG 869*	29	5 wks
12 Jan 74	LIVING FOR THE CITY *Tamla Motown TMG 881*	15	9 wks
13 Apr 74	● HE'S MISSTRA KNOW IT ALL *Tamla Motown TMG 892*	10	9 wks

19 Oct 74	YOU HAVEN'T DONE NOTHIN' *Tamla Motown TMG 921*	30	5 wks
11 Jan 75	BOOGIE ON REGGAE WOMAN *Tamla Motown TMG 928*	12	8 wks
18 Dec 76	● I WISH *Tamla Motown TMG 1054*	5	10 wks
9 Apr 77	● SIR DUKE *Motown TMG 1068*	2	9 wks
10 Sep 77	ANOTHER STAR *Motown TMG 1083*	29	5 wks
24 Nov 79	SEND ONE YOUR LOVE *Motown TMG 1149*	52	3 wks
26 Jan 80	BLACK ORCHID *Motown TMG 1173*	63	3 wks
29 Mar 80	OUTSIDE MY WINDOW *Motown TMG 1179*	52	4 wks
13 Sep 80	● MASTERBLASTER (JAMMIN') *Motown TMG 1204*	2	10 wks
27 Dec 80	● I AIN'T GONNA STAND FOR IT *Motown TMG 1215*	10	10 wks
7 Mar 81	● LATELY *Motown TMG 1226*	3	13 wks
25 Jul 81	● HAPPY BIRTHDAY *Motown TMG 1235*	2	11 wks
23 Jan 82	THAT GIRL *Motown TMG 1254*	39	6 wks
5 Jun 82	● DO I DO *Motown TMG 1269*	10	7 wks
25 Sep 82	RIBBON IN THE SKY *Motown TMG 1280*	45	4 wks
25 Aug 84	★ I JUST CALLED TO SAY I LOVE YOU *Motown TMG 1349*	1	24 wks
1 Dec 84	LOVE LIGHT IN FLIGHT *Motown TMG 1364*	44	5 wks
29 Dec 84	DON'T DRIVE DRUNK *Motown TMG 1372*	71	1 wk
12 Jan 85	DON'T DRIVE DRUNK (re-entry) *Motown TMG 1372*	62	2 wks
7 Sep 85	● PART-TIME LOVER *Motown ZB 40351*	3	12 wks
23 Nov 85	GO HOME *Motown ZB 40501*	67	2 wks
28 Dec 85	I JUST CALLED TO SAY I LOVE YOU (re-entry) *Motown TMG 1349*	64	2 wks
8 Mar 86	OVERJOYED *Motown ZB 40567*	17	8 wks
17 Jan 87	STRANGER ON THE SHORE OF LOVE *Motown WOND 2*	55	3 wks
31 Oct 87	SKELETONS *Motown ZB 41439*	59	3 wks
20 May 89	FREE *Motown ZB 42855*	50	5 wks

See also Diana Ross, Marvin Gaye, Smokey Robinson and Stevie Wonder; Paul McCartney with Stevie Wonder; Dionne Warwick and Friends; Stevie Wonder and Michael Jackson; Julio Inglesias; Jackson Five. You Haven't Done Nothin' has credit : Doo Doo Wopsssss by the Jackson Five.

Stevie WONDER and Michael JACKSON   **4 wks**
US, male vocal duo

28 May 88	GET IT *Motown ZB 41883*	37	4 wks

See also Stevie Wonder; Michael Jackson.

WONDER DOGS *UK, canine vocal group*   **7 wks**

21 Aug 82	RUFF MIX *Flip FLIP 001*	31	7 wks

WONDER STUFF *UK, male vocal/instrumental group*   **24 wks**

30 Apr 88	GIVE GIVE GIVE ME MORE MORE MORE *Polydor GONE 3*	72	2 wks
16 Jul 88	A WISH AWAY *Polydor GONE 4*	43	5 wks
24 Sep 88	IT'S YER MONEY I'M AFTER BABY *Polydor GONE 5*	40	3 wks
11 Mar 89	WHO WANTS TO BE THE DISCO KING *Far Out GONE 6*	28	3 wks
23 Sep 89	DON'T LET ME DOWN GENTLY *Polydor GONE 7*	19	4 wks
11 Nov 89	GOLDEN GREEN/ GET TOGETHER *Polydor GONE 8*	33	3 wks
12 May 90	CIRCLESQUARE *Polydor GONE 10*	20	4 wks

WONDRESS – *See MANTRONIX*

Brenton WOOD *US, male vocalist*   **14 wks**

27 Dec 67	● GIMME LITTLE SIGN *Liberty LBF 15021*	8	14 wks

Roy WOOD *UK, male vocalist/multi-instrumentalist*   **35 wks**

11 Aug 73	DEAR ELAINE *Harvest HAR 5074*	18	8 wks

1 Dec 73	● FOREVER *Harvest HAR 5078*	8	13 wks
15 Jun 74	GOING DOWN THE ROAD *Harvest HAR 5083*	13	7 wks
31 May 75	OH WHAT A SHAME *Jet 754*	13	7 wks

See also Doctor and the Medics.

WOODENTOPS *UK, male vocal/instrumental group*   **1 wk**

11 Oct 86	EVERYDAY LIVING *Rough Trade RT 178*	72	1 wk

Edward WOODWARD *UK, male vocalist*   **2 wks**

16 Jan 71	THE WAY YOU LOOK TONIGHT *DJM DJS 232*	50	1 wk
30 Jan 71	THE WAY YOU LOOK TONIGHT (re-entry) *DJM DJS 232*	42	1 wk

Sheb WOOLEY *US, male vocalist*   **8 wks**

20 Jun 58	PURPLE PEOPLE EATER *MGM 981*	12	8 wks

WORKING WEEK
UK, male/female vocal/instrumental group   **2 wks**

9 Jun 84	VENCEREMOS - WE WILL WIN *Virgin VS 684*	64	2 wks

WORLD OF TWIST *UK, male vocal/instrumental group*   **3 wks**

24 Nov 90	THE STORM *Circa YR 55*	42	3 wks

WORLD PARTY *Ireland/UK, male vocal/instrumental group*   **14 wks**

14 Feb 87	SHIP OF FOOLS *Ensign ENY 606*	42	6 wks
16 Jun 90	MESSAGE IN THE BOX *Ensign ENY 631*	39	6 wks
15 Sep 90	WAY DOWN NOW *Ensign ENY 634*	66	2 wks

WORLD PREMIERE *US, male vocal instrumental group*   **4 wks**

28 Jan 84	SHARE THE NIGHT *Epic A 4133*	64	4 wks

WORLD'S FAMOUS SUPREME TEAM SHOW *US, male vocal group*   **6 wks**

25 Feb 84	HEY DJ *Charisma/Virgin TEAM 1*	52	5 wks
8 Dec 90	OPERA HOUSE *Virgin VS 1273*	75	1 wk

Act billed as World's Famous Supreme Team on first hit. See also Malcolm McLaren

WRECKS-N-EFFECT *US, male vocalist*   **7 wks**

13 Jan 90	JUICY *Motown ZB 43295*	29	7 wks

Betty WRIGHT *US, female vocalist*   **23 wks**

25 Jan 75	SHOORAH SHOORAH *RCA 2491*	27	7 wks
19 Apr 75	WHERE IS THE LOVE *RCA 2548*	25	7 wks
8 Feb 86	PAIN *Cooltempo COOL 117*	42	6 wks
9 Sep 89	KEEP LOVE NEW *Sure Delight SD 11*	71	3 wks

Ruby WRIGHT *UK, female vocalist*   **15 wks**

16 Apr 54	● BIMBO *Parlophone R 3816*	7	4 wks
21 May 54	BIMBO (re-entry) *Parlophone R 3816*	12	1 wk

22 May 59	THREE STARS *Parlophone R 4556*	19	10 wks

Three Stars is narrated by Dick Pike - UK, male vocalist.

Steve WRIGHT *UK, male vocalist*   **10 wks**

27 Nov 82	I'M ALRIGHT *RCA 296*	40	6 wks
15 Oct 83	GET SOME THERAPY *RCA RCA 362*	75	1 wk
1 Dec 84	THE GAY CAVALIEROS (THE STORY SO FAR) *MCA 925*	61	3 wks

First hit credited to Young Steve and the Afternoon Boys - UK, male vocal/instrumental group. Second hit credited to Steve Wright and the Sisters of Soul - UK, female vocalists.

WURZELS *UK, male vocal/instrumental group*   **27 wks**

15 May 76	★ COMBINE HARVESTER (BRAND NEW KEY) *EMI 2450*	1	13 wks
11 Sep 76	● I AM A CIDER DRINKER (PALOMA BLANCA) *EMI 2520.*	3	9 wks
25 Jun 77	FARMER BILL'S COWMAN (I WAS KAISER BILL'S BATMAN) *EMI 2637*	32	5 wks

See also Adge Cutler and the Wurzels.

Robert WYATT *UK, male vocalist*   **11 wks**

28 Sep 74	I'M A BELIEVER *Virgin VS 114*	29	5 wks
7 May 83	SHIPBUILDING *Rough Trade RT 115*	35	6 wks

Michael WYCOFF *US, male vocalist*   **2 wks**

23 Jul 83	(DO YOU REALLY LOVE ME) TELL ME LOVE *RCA 348*	60	2 wks

Pete WYLIE *UK, male vocalist*   **13 wks**

3 May 86	SINFUL *Eternal MDM 7*	13	10 wks
13 Sep 86	DIAMOND GIRL *Eternal MDM 12*	57	3 wks

Bill WYMAN *UK, male vocalist*   **13 wks**

25 Jul 81	(SI SI) JE SUIS UN ROCK STAR *A &M AMS 8144*	14	9 wks
20 Mar 82	A NEW FASHION *A &M AMS 8209*	37	4 wks

Jane WYMAN – *See Bing CROSBY and Jane WYMAN*

Tammy WYNETTE *US, female vocalist*   **23 wks**

26 Apr 75	★ STAND BY YOUR MAN *Epic EPC 7137*	1	12 wks
28 Jun 75	D. I. V. O. R. C. E. *Epic EPC 3361*	12	7 wks
12 Jun 76	I DON'T WANNA PLAY HOUSE *Epic EPC 4091*	37	4 wks

Mark WYNTER *UK, male vocalist*   **80 wks**

25 Aug 60	IMAGE OF A GIRL *Decca F 11263*	11	10 wks
10 Nov 60	KICKING UP THE LEAVES *Decca F 11279*	24	10 wks
9 Mar 61	DREAM GIRL *Decca F 11323*	27	5 wks
8 Jun 61	EXCLUSIVELY YOURS *Decca F 11354*	32	7 wks
4 Oct 62	● VENUS IN BLUE JEANS *Pye 7N 15466*	4	15 wks
13 Dec 62	● GO AWAY LITTLE GIRL *Pye 7N 15492*	6	11 wks
6 Jun 63	SHY GIRL *Pye 7N 15525*	28	6 wks
14 Nov 63	IT'S ALMOST TOMORROW *Pye 7N 15577*	12	12 wks
9 Apr 64	ONLY YOU *Pye 7N 15626*	38	4 wks

Sleeping bag, ZZ TOP, not
punch bag . . .

YAZZ proudly displays
evidence of her first chart
appearance.

Malcolm X *US, male orator*   **4 wks**

| 7 Apr 84 | **NO SELL OUT** *Tommy Boy IS 165* | **60** | 4 wks |

Hit features credit: 'Music by Keith Le Blanc'.

Miss X *UK, female vocalist*   **6 wks**

| 1 Aug 63 | **CHRISTINE** *Ember S 175* | **37** | 6 wks |

Miss X was Joyce Blair.

XAVIER *US, male vocal/instrumental group*   **3 wks**

| 20 Mar 82 | **WORK THAT SUCKER TO DEATH** *Liberty UP 651* | **53** | 3 wks |

XPANSIONS *UK, male producer – Ritchie Malone*   **5 wks**

| 6 Oct 90 | **ELEVATION** *Optimism 113683* | **49** | 5 wks |

X-RAY SPEX *UK, male/female vocal/instrumental group*   **32 wks**

29 Apr 78	**THE DAY THE WORLD TURNED DAY-GLO**		
	EMI International INT 553	**23**	7 wks
22 Jul 78	**IDENTITY** *EMI International INT 563*	**24**	10 wks
4 Nov 78	**GERM FREE ADOLESCENCE**		
	EMI International INT 573	**19**	11 wks
21 Apr 79	**HIGHLY INFLAMMABLE** *EMI International INT 583*	**45**	4 wks

XTC *UK, male vocal/instrumental group*   **64 wks**

12 May 79	**LIFE BEGINS AT THE HOP** *Virgin VS 259*	**54**	4 wks
22 Sep 79	**MAKING PLANS FOR NIGEL** *Virgin VS 282*	**17**	11 wks
6 Sep 80	**GENERALS AND MAJORS/ DON'T LOSE YOUR**		
	TEMPER *Virgin VS 365*	**32**	8 wks
18 Oct 80	**TOWERS OF LONDON** *Virgin VS 372*	**31**	5 wks
24 Jan 81	**SGT ROCK (IS GOING TO HELP ME)** *Virgin VS 384*	**16**	9 wks
23 Jan 82	● **SENSES WORKING OVERTIME** *Virgin VS 462*	**10**	9 wks
27 Mar 82	**BALL AND CHAIN** *Virgin VS 482*	**58**	4 wks
15 Oct 83	**LOVE ON A FARMBOY'S WAGES** *Virgin VS 613*	**50**	4 wks
29 Sep 84	**ALL YOU PRETTY GIRLS** *Virgin VS 709*	**55**	5 wks
28 Jan 89	**MAYOR OF SIMPLETON** *Virgin VS 1158*	**46**	5 wks

Y & T *US, male vocal/instrumental group*   **4 wks**

| 13 Aug 83 | **MEAN STREAK** *A & M AM 135* | **41** | 4 wks |

YA KID K – *See HI-TEK featuring YA KID K; TECHNOTRONIC*

YAN – *See YIN and YAN*

Weird Al YANKOVIC *US, male vocalist*   **7 wks**

| 7 Apr 84 | **EAT IT** *Scotti Bros./Epic A 4257* | **36** | 7 wks |

YARBROUGH and PEOPLES   **20 wks**
US, male/female vocal/instrumental duo

27 Dec 80	● **DON'T STOP THE MUSIC** *Mercury MER 53*	**7**	12 wks
5 May 84	**DON'T WASTE YOUR TIME** *Total Experience XE 501*	**60**	3 wks
11 Jan 86	**GUILTY** *Total Experience FB 49905*	**53**	3 wks
5 Jul 86	**I WOULDN'T LIE** *Total Experience FB 49841*	**61**	2 wks

YARDBIRDS *UK, male vocal/instrumental group*   **62 wks**

12 Nov 64	**GOOD MORNING LITTLE SCHOOLGIRL**		
	Columbia DB 7391	**44**	4 wks
18 Mar 65	● **FOR YOUR LOVE** *Columbia DB 7499*	**3**	12 wks
17 Jun 65	● **HEART FULL OF SOUL** *Columbia DB 7594*	**2**	13 wks
14 Oct 65	● **EVIL HEARTED YOU/ STILL I'M SAD**		
	Columbia DB 7706	**3**	10 wks
3 Mar 66	● **SHAPES OF THINGS** *Columbia DB 7848*	**3**	9 wks
2 Jun 66	● **OVER UNDER SIDEWAYS DOWN** *Columbia DB 7928*	**10**	9 wks
27 Oct 66	**HAPPENINGS TEN YEARS TIME AGO**		
	Columbia DB 8024	**43**	5 wks

YAZOO *UK, female/male vocal/instrumental duo*   **49 wks**

17 Apr 82	● **ONLY YOU** *Mute MUTE 020*	**2**	14 wks
17 Jul 82	● **DON'T GO** *Mute YAZ 001*	**3**	11 wks
20 Nov 82	**THE OTHER SIDE OF LOVE** *Mute YAZ 002*	**13**	9 wks
21 May 83	● **NOBODY'S DIARY** *Mute YAZ 003*	**3**	11 wks
8 Dec 90	**SITUATION** *Mute YAZ 4*	**14†**	4 wks

YAZZ *UK, female vocalist*   **46 wks**

23 Jul 88	★ **THE ONLY WAY IS UP** *Big Life BLR 4*	**1**	15 wks
7 Jan 89	● **STAND UP FOR YOUR LOVE RIGHTS** *Big Life BLR 5*	**2**	12 wks
4 Feb 89	● **FINE TIME** *Big Life BLR 6*	**9**	8 wks
29 Apr 89	**WHERE HAS ALL THE LOVE GONE** *Big Life BLR 8*	**16**	6 wks
23 Jun 90	**TREAT ME GOOD** *Big Life BLR 24*	**20**	5 wks

YELL! *UK, male vocal duo*   **8 wks**

| 20 Jan 90 | ● **INSTANT REPLAY** *Fanfare FAN 22* | **10** | 8 wks |

YELLO *Switzerland, male vocal/instrumental duo*   **36 wks**

25 Jun 83	**I LOVE YOU** *Stiff BUY 176*	**41**	4 wks
26 Nov 83	**LOST AGAIN** *Stiff BUY 191*	**73**	1 wk
9 Aug 86	**GOLDRUSH** *Mercury MER 218*	**54**	3 wks
22 Aug 87	**THE RHYTHM DIVINE** *Mercury MER 253*	**54**	2 wks
27 Aug 88	● **THE RACE** *Mercury YELLO 1*	**7**	11 wks
17 Dec 88	**TIED UP** *Mercury YELLO 2*	**60**	5 wks
25 Mar 89	**OF COURSE I'M LYING** *Mercury YELLO 3*	**23**	8 wks
22 Jul 89	**BLAZING SADDLES** *Mercury YELLO 4*	**47**	2 wks

The Rhythm Divine features Shirley Bassey. See also Shirley Bassey.

YELLOW DOG *US/UK, male vocal/instrumental group*   **13 wks**

| 4 Feb 78 | ● **JUST ONE MORE NIGHT** *Virgin VS 195* | **8** | 9 wks |
| 22 Jul 78 | **WAIT UNTIL MIDNIGHT** *Virgin VS 217* | **54** | 4 wks |

YELLOW MAGIC ORCHESTRA   11 wks
Japan, male instrumental group

14 Jun 80	**COMPUTER GAME (THEME FROM THE INVADERS)** *A & M AMS 7502*...	**17**	11 wks

YELLOWCOATS – *See Paul SHANE and the YELLOWCOATS*

YES *UK/Canada, male vocal/instrumental group*   31 wks

17 Sep 77	● **WONDEROUS STORIES** *Atlantic K 10999*	**7**	9 wks
26 Nov 77	**GOING FOR THE ONE** *Atlantic K 11047*...................	**24**	4 wks
9 Sep 78	**DON'T KILL THE WHALE** *Atlantic K 11184*...............	**36**	4 wks
12 Nov 83	**OWNER OF A LONELY HEART** *Atco B 9817*.............	**28**	9 wks
31 Mar 84	**LEAVE IT** *Atco B 9787*......................................	**56**	4 wks
3 Oct 87	**LOVE WILL FIND A WAY** *Atco A 9449*.....................	**73**	1 wk

YIN and YAN *UK, male vocal duo*   5 wks

29 Mar 75	**IF** *EMI 2282*..	**25**	5 wks

Faron YOUNG *US, male vocalist*   23 wks

15 Jul 72	● **IT'S FOUR IN THE MORNING** *Mercury 6052 140*	**3**	23 wks

Jimmy YOUNG *UK, male vocalist*   88 wks

9 Jan 53	**FAITH CAN MOVE MOUNTAINS** *Decca F 9986*	**11**	1 wk
21 Aug 53	● **ETERNALLY** *Decca F 10130*	**8**	9 wks
6 May 55	★ **UNCHAINED MELODY** *Decca F 10502*....................	**1**	19 wks
16 Sep 55	★ **THE MAN FROM LARAMIE** *Decca F 10597*	**1**	12 wks
23 Dec 55	**SOMEONE ON YOUR MIND** *Decca F 10640*	**13**	5 wks
16 Mar 56	● **CHAIN GANG** *Decca F 10694*	**9**	6 wks
8 Jun 56	**WAYWARD WIND** *Decca F 10736*	**27**	1 wk
22 Jun 56	**RICH MAN POOR MAN** *Decca F 10736*.....................	**25**	1 wk
28 Sep 56	● **MORE** *Decca F 10774*	**4**	17 wks
3 May 57	**ROUND AND ROUND** *Decca F 10875*	**30**	1 wk
10 Oct 63	**MISS YOU** *Columbia DB 7119*...............................	**15**	13 wks
26 Mar 64	**UNCHAINED MELODY** *Columbia DB 7234*	**43**	3 wks

The versions of Unchained Melody on Decca and on Columbia are different recordings of the same song. See also Various Artists - All Star Hit Parade No.2

John Paul YOUNG *Australia, male vocalist*   13 wks

29 Apr 78	● **LOVE IS IN THE AIR** *Ariola ARO 117*	**5**	13 wks

Karen YOUNG *UK, female vocalist*   21 wks

6 Sep 69	● **NOBODY'S CHILD** *Major Minor MM 625*	**6**	21 wks

Karen YOUNG *US, female vocalist*   8 wks

19 Aug 78	**HOT SHOT** *Atlantic K 11180*....................................	**34**	7 wks
24 Feb 79	**HOT SHOT (re-issue)** *Atlantic LV 8*...........................	**75**	1 wk

Leon YOUNG STRING CHORALE – *See Mr Acker BILK*

Neil YOUNG *Canada, male vocalist*   15 wks

11 Mar 72	● **HEART OF GOLD** *Reprise K 14140*	**10**	11 wks
6 Jan 79	**FOUR STRONG WINDS** *Reprise K 14493*	**57**	4 wks

Paul YOUNG *UK, male vocalist*   98 wks

18 Jun 83	★ **WHEREVER I LAY MY HAT (THAT'S MY HOME)** *CBS A 3371*	**1**	15 wks
10 Sep 83	● **COME BACK AND STAY** *CBS A 3636*	**4**	9 wks
19 Nov 83	● **LOVE OF THE COMMON PEOPLE** *CBS A 3585*...........	**2**	13 wks
13 Oct 84	● **I'M GONNA TEAR YOUR PLAYHOUSE DOWN** *CBS A 4786*	**9**	7 wks
8 Dec 84	● **EVERYTHING MUST CHANGE** *CBS A 4972*	**9**	11 wks
9 Mar 85	● **EVERY TIME YOU GO AWAY** *CBS A 6300*..................	**4**	11 wks
22 Jun 85	**TOMB OF MEMORIES** *CBS A 6321*	**16**	7 wks
17 Aug 85	**TOMB OF MEMORIES (re-entry)** *CBS A 6321*	**74**	1 wk
4 Oct 86	**WONDERLAND** *CBS YOUNG 1*	**24**	5 wks
29 Nov 86	**SOME PEOPLE** *CBS YOUNG 2*................................	**56**	3 wks
7 Feb 87	**WHY DOES A MAN HAVE TO BE STRONG** *CBS YOUNG 3*	**63**	2 wks
12 May 90	**SOFTLY WHISPERING I LOVE YOU** *Epic YOUNG 4*	**21**	6 wks
7 Jul 90	**OH GIRL** *CBS YOUNG 5*	**25**	6 wks
6 Oct 90	**HEAVEN CAN WAIT** *CBS YOUNG 6*	**71**	2 wks

Retta YOUNG *US, female vocalist*   7 wks

24 May 75	**SENDING OUT AN S. O. S.** *All Platinum 6146 305*...........	**28**	7 wks

Tracie YOUNG – *See TRACIE*

YOUNG and COMPANY   12 wks
US, male/female vocal/instrumental group

1 Nov 80	**I LIKE (WHAT YOU'RE DOING TO ME)** *Excalibur EXC 501*	**20**	12 wks

YOUNG AND MOODY BAND   4 wks
UK, male vocal/instrumental group

10 Oct 81	**DON'T DO THAT** *Bronze BRO 130*	**63**	4 wks

YOUNG DISCIPLES *UK, male vocal/instrumental group*   1 wk

13 Oct 90	**GET YOURSELF TOGETHER** *Talkin' Loud TLK 2*	**68**	1 wk

YOUNG IDEA *UK, male vocal duo*   6 wks

29 Jun 67	● **WITH A LITTLE HELP FROM MY FRIENDS** *Columbia DB 8205*...	**10**	6 wks

YOUNG M.C. *US, male rapper*   5 wks

15 Jul 89	**BUST A MOVE** *Delicious Vinyl BRW 137*........................	**73**	2 wks
17 Feb 90	**PRINCIPAL'S OFFICE** *Delicious Vinyl BRW 161*..............	**54**	3 wks

YOUNG RASCALS *US, male vocal/instrumental group*   17 wks

25 May 67	● **GROOVIN'** *Atlantic 584 111*	**8**	13 wks
16 Aug 67	**A GIRL LIKE YOU** *Atlantic 584 128*	**37**	4 wks

Sydney YOUNGBLOOD *US, male vocalist*   27 wks

26 Aug 89	● **IF ONLY I COULD** *Circa YR 34*................................	**3**	14 wks
9 Dec 89	**SIT AND WAIT** *Circa YR 40*....................................	**16**	8 wks
31 Mar 90	**I'D RATHER GO BLIND** *Circa YR 43*...........................	**44**	5 wks

Z

Helmut ZACHARIAS *Germany, orchestra*   **11 wks**

29 Oct 64 ● TOKYO MELODY *Polydor YNH 52341*.......................... **9** 11 wks

Pia ZADORA – *See Jermaine JACKSON and Pia ZADORA; PIA*

Michael ZAGER BAND   **12 wks**
US, male/female vocal/instrumental group

1 Apr 78 ● LET'S ALL CHANT *Private Stock PVT 143*...................... **8** 12 wks

ZAGER and EVANS *US, male vocal duo*   **13 wks**

9 Aug 69 ★ IN THE YEAR 2525 (EXORDIUM AND TERMINUS)
         RCA 1860 .... **1** 13 wks

Georghe ZAMFIR *Romania, male instrumentalist - pipes*   **9 wks**

21 Aug 76 ● (LIGHT OF EXPERIENCE) DOINA DE JALE
         Epic EPC 4310.. **4** 9 wks

Tommy ZANG *US, male vocalist*   **1 wk**

16 Feb 61   HEY GOOD LOOKING *Polydor NH 66957*.................... **45** 1 wk

ZAPP *US, male/female vocal/instrumental group*   **6 wks**

25 Jan 86   IT DOESN'T REALLY MATTER *Warner Bros. W 8879*....... **57** 3 wks
24 May 86   COMPUTER LOVE (PART 1) *Warner Bros. W 8805* .... **64** 3 wks

Lena ZAVARONI *UK, female vocalist*   **14 wks**

9 Feb 74 ● MA HE'S MAKING EYES AT ME *Philips 6006 367* .... **10** 11 wks
1 Jun 74   PERSONALITY *Philips 6006 391* .... **33** 3 wks

ZEPHYRS *UK, male vocal/instrumental group*   **1 wk**

18 Mar 65   SHE'S LOST YOU *Columbia DB 7481*......................... **48** 1 wk

ZIGZAG JIVE FLUTES – *See ELIAS and his ZIGZAG JIVE FLUTES*

ZODIACS – *See Maurice WILLIAMS and the ZODIACS*

ZOE *UK, female vocalist*   **5 wks**

10 Nov 90   SUNSHINE ON A RAINY DAY *M&G MAGS 6*.............. **53** 5 wks

ZOMBIES *UK, male vocal/instrumental group*   **16 wks**

13 Aug 64   SHE'S NOT THERE *Decca F 11940* .... **12** 11 wks
11 Feb 65   TELL HER NO *Decca F 12072* .... **42** 5 wks

ZZ TOP *US, male vocal/instrumental group*   **72 wks**

3 Sep 83   GIMME ALL YOUR LOVIN' *Warner Bros. W 9693* .... **61** 3 wks
26 Nov 83   SHARP DRESSED MAN *Warner Bros. W 9576*................ **53** 3 wks
31 Mar 84   TV DINNERS *Warner Bros. W 9334* .... **67** 3 wks
6 Oct 84 ● GIMME ALL YOUR LOVIN' (re-entry)
         Warner Bros. W 9693 .... **10** 15 wks
15 Dec 84   SHARP DRESSED MAN (re-entry) *Warner Bros. W 9576*..... **22** 10 wks
23 Feb 85   LEGS *Warner Bros. W 9272*.................................... **16** 7 wks
13 Jul 85   SUMMER HOLIDAY (EP) *Warner Bros. W 8946* .... **51** 5 wks
19 Oct 85   SLEEPING BAG *Warner Bros. W 2001* .... **27** 5 wks
15 Feb 86   STAGES *Warner Bros. W 2002* .... **43** 3 wks
19 Apr 86   ROUGH BOY *Warner Bros. W 2009* .... **23** 4 wks
4 Oct 86   VELCRO FLY *Warner Bros. W 8650* .... **54** 3 wks
21 Jul 90   DOUBLEBACK *Warner Bros. W 9812*......................... **29** 6 wks

Tracks on EP: Tush/Got Me Under Pressure/Beer Drinkers and Hell Raisers/I'm Bad, I'm Nationwide.

2

BRITISH HIT SINGLES

ALPHABETICALLY BY TITLE

Different songs/tunes with the same title (e.g. 'Absolute Beginners' which has been a hit title for both David Bowie and Jam) are indicated by [A], [B] etc. Where there is no letter in brackets after the title, all hit recordings are of just one song. Individual titles of songs or tunes on EP, LP, medley or megamix singles which made the chart are not included here, with the obvious exception of titles that are actually part of the overall title of the hit in question.

The recording act named alongside each song title is not necessarily exactly the same act that is billed on the record, but is the act under whose name all the information

about the title can be found in Part One. So, for example 'Happy Xmas (War Is Over)' is credited here to John Lennon, but if you look up John Lennon in Part One, you will discover the actual credit for that hit was 'John and Yoko, the Plastic Ono Band with the Harlem Community Choir'.

The year of chart entry column contains the year in which each disc made its very first appearance on the chart. Subsequent appearances are only listed here if they signify a period of success totally separate from the disc's first impact. So, for example, 'Unchained Melody' by the Righteous Brothers is listed as having been a hit in 65 and 90, but Cliff Richard's original version of 'Living Doll', which re-entered the charts for one brief week in 1960 after topping the charts in 1959, is shown only as a hit in 1959.

MADONNA the all-time female chart champ – Madonna was in Vogue more than ever in 1990

340

345

351

3

FACTS AND FEATS

How many Consecutive Top Ten Hits has Kylie Minogue had? Who leaped from number 33 to number one in one week? Has Lonnie Donegan spent more weeks on the chart than Jason Donovan? Who is the oldest person ever to top the charts? Has a woman had a more successful chart career than Madonna? Who takes over from Elton John at the top of the list of those acts who have come so near yet stayed so far – Most Top Ten Hits Without A Number One Single? What chart record is jointly held by Grand Prix, Michael Lovesmith and the Paris Angels among others? What was so great about Vanilla Ice's first week on the charts? Who is the most successful chart star of all time?

The answers to all these questions and many many more are here in the fully revised and updated Facts And Feats section.

ELTON JOHN thanks Britain for the first solo number one of his historic career, 'Sacrifice'/'Healing Hands'

MOST WEEKS ON CHART

This table lists the 220 recording acts that have spent 100 weeks or more on the British singles charts from 14 November 1952 up to and including the chart for 29 December 1990. It is of course possible for an act to be credited with two chart weeks in the same week if that act has two or more records on the chart at once, a feat that New Kids On The Block achieved quite often in 1990. Double sided hits, EPs and double singles only count as one hit each week, as do the handful of albums which have hit the singles chart over the years.

Wks

ELVIS PRESLEY 1141
CLIFF RICHARD 998
(+ 16 with Sarah Brightman, 11 with Young Ones, 9 with Phil Everly, 8 with Elton John, 7 with Olivia Newton-John, 6 with Van Morrison, 2 with Sheila Walsh)
BEATLES 432
(+ 1 with Tony Sheridan)
FRANK SINATRA 401
(+ 18 with Nancy Sinatra, 9 with Sammy Davis Jr)
ELTON JOHN 392
(+ 14 with Kiki Dee, 9 with Dionne Warwick and Friends, 8 with Cliff Richard, 5 with Millie Jackson, 4 with John Lennon, 3 with Aretha Franklin, 3 with Jennifer Rush)
STATUS QUO 377
DAVID BOWIE 366
(+ 12 with Mick Jagger, 11 with Queen, 8 with Bing Crosby, 7 with Pat Metheny)
STEVIE WONDER 364
(+ 11 with Julio Iglesias, 10 with Paul McCartney, 9 with Dionne Warwick and Friends, 5 with Diana Ross, Smokey Robinson and Marvin Gaye, 4 with Michael Jackson)
SHADOWS 359
(+ 404 backing Cliff Richard)
ROD STEWART 346
(+ 46 with Faces, 6 with Jeff Beck, 6 with Tina Turner)
PAUL McCARTNEY/WINGS 345
(+ 25 with Michael Jackson, 10 with Stevie Wonder, 7 with Christians, Holly Johnson, Paul McCartney, Gerry Marsden and Stock Aitken Waterman)
EVERLY BROTHERS 337
(Phil Everly 6 more solo, 9 with Cliff Richard)
ROLLING STONES 334
TOM JONES 330
(+ 6 with Art Of Noise)
ROY ORBISON 324
JIM REEVES 322

LONNIE DONEGAN 321
HOLLIES 316
SHIRLEY BASSEY 313
(+ 2 with Yello)
DIANA ROSS 310
(+ 197 as a Supreme, 27 with Supremes and Temptations, 20 with Marvin Gaye, 12 with Lionel Richie, 8 with Julio Iglesias, 5 with Marvin Gaye, Smokey Robinson and Stevie Wonder, 4 with Michael Jackson)
FOUR TOPS 298
(+ 20 with Supremes)
PAT BOONE 296
QUEEN 295
(+ 11 with David Bowie)
PERRY COMO 294
BEE GEES 288
MADONNA 285
BILLY FURY 281
MICHAEL JACKSON 272
(+ 235 as a Jackson, 25 with Paul McCartney, 4 with Diana Ross, 4 with Stevie Wonder)
SLADE 271
HOT CHOCOLATE 267
DONNA SUMMER 266
(+ 13 with Barbra Streisand)
BEACH BOYS 263
(+ 12 with Fat Boys)
SHAKIN' STEVENS 259
(+ 9 with Bonnie Tyler)

SUPREMES 259
(+ 27 with Temptations, 20 with Four Tops)
FRANKIE LAINE 253
(+ 16 with Jimmy Boyd, 8 with Doris Day, 4 with Johnnie Ray)
ADAM FAITH 251
ABBA 247
PETULA CLARK 247
WHO 245
(+ 4 as High Numbers)
ELECTRIC LIGHT ORCHESTRA ... 243
(+ 11 with Olivia Newton-John)
CONNIE FRANCIS 241
UB40 240
(+ 8 with Afrika Bambaataa and Family, 9 with Robert Palmer)
MADNESS 237
ENGELBERT HUMPERDINCK 235
JACKSON FIVE/JACKSONS 235
(113 as Jackson Five, 122 as Jacksons)
NAT 'KING' COLE 233
KEN DODD 233
ANDY WILLIAMS 228
T. REX 227
(includes 8 billed as Marc Bolan)
FLEETWOOD MAC 223
KINKS 213
FRANKIE VAUGHAN 212
(+ 20 with Kaye Sisters)
HERMAN'S HERMITS 211

Status Quo

The Cure

10 C.C. **131**
TREMELOES **131**
(+ 90 with Brian Poole)
MARMALADE **130**
ANTHONY NEWLEY **129**
DOLLAR................................. **128**
RONNIE HILTON **128**
JONATHAN KING **128**
(67 as Jonathan King and 61 more under pseudonyms: Sakkarin (14), Shag (13), One Hundred Ton And A Feather (9), Weathermen (9), Bubblerock (5), Father Abraphart And The Smurps (4), 53rd And 3rd (4) and Sound 9418 (3))
BARRY MANILOW **128**
SEARCHERS............................ **128**
MATT MONRO **127**
TEARS FOR FEARS **127**
TINA TURNER **127**
(+ 44 with Ike And Tina Turner, 6 with Bryan Adams, 3 with Eric Clapton, 6 with Rod Stewart)
BARRY WHITE....................... **126**
CURE **125**
KARL DENVER....................... **124**
(+ 3 with Happy Mondays)
LIONEL RICHIE...................... **124**
(+ 12 with Diana Ross)
THIN LIZZY **124**
RAY CHARLES **123**
(+ 7 with Quincy Jones)
DORIS DAY............................. **122**
(+ 16 with Johnnie Ray, 8 with Frankie Laine)
BOOMTOWN RATS **121**
COMMODORES **121**
BILLY JOEL **121**
BOB MARLEY
AND THE WAILERS............... **121**
SEEKERS **120**
ERASURE **119**
BRYAN FERRY **119**
IRON MAIDEN **119**
HELEN SHAPIRO **119**
ALVIN STARDUST **119**
(+ 28 as Shane Fenton)
CLASH **118**
A-HA **117**
WINIFRED ATWELL **117**
(+ 9 as one of the artists on All Star Hit Parade)
DARTS.................................... **117**
FRANKIE GOES TO
HOLLYWOOD **117**
MARTY WILDE....................... **117**
DONNY OSMOND **116**
(+91 as an Osmond, 37 with Marie Osmond)
PET SHOP BOYS.................... **116**
(+ 9 with Dusty Springfield)
JOHNNY MATHIS **115**
(+ 20 with Deneice Williams, 2 with Gladys Knight)

GERRY AND THE PACEMAKERS... **114**
(Gerry Marsden +7 with Christians, Holly Johnson, Paul McCartney, Gerry Marsden and Stock Aitken Waterman)
MOODY BLUES **114**
SUZI QUATRO **114**
(+ 8 with Chris Norman)
REAL THING.......................... **114**
BAY CITY ROLLERS.............. **113**
WHITNEY HOUSTON **113**
(+ 5 with Teddy Pendergrass, 5 with Aretha Franklin)
CRAIG DOUGLAS **112**
EARTH WIND AND FIRE **112**
(+ 13 with Emotions)
AC/DC **111**
BAD MANNERS **111**
ALMA COGAN **110**
MOVE **110**
RUBY MURRAY **110**
PRETENDERS **110**
ROSE ROYCE **110**
DAVID CASSIDY **109**
(+ 53 with Partridge Family)
DAWN **109**
(Tony Orlando + 11 solo)
FATS DOMINO **109**
GLORIA ESTEFAN/MIAMI SOUND
   MACHINE **108**
ISLEY BROTHERS.................. **108**
LITTLE RICHARD................... **108**
KYLIE MINOGUE **108**
(+ 14 with Jason Donovan)
OTIS REDDING **108**
(+ 16 with Carla Thomas)
SQUEEZE **108**
NEIL DIAMOND **107**
(+ 12 with Barbra Streisand)
DIRE STRAITS **107**
DES O'CONNOR **107**
(+ 10 with Roger Whittaker)
WHITESNAKE **107**
HERB ALPERT **106**
JOHNNY NASH **106**
JIMMY RUFFIN **106**
SMOKIE **106**
MALCOLM VAUGHAN **106**
ANIMALS................................ **105**
(+ 29 backing Eric Burdon)
GEORGIE FAME **105**
(+ 10 with Alan Price)
EDDIE FISHER **105**
IMAGINATION **105**
THOMPSON TWINS **104**
CULTURE CLUB **103**
STYLE COUNCIL..................... **103**
U2.. **103**
KC AND THE SUNSHINE BAND ... **102**
BRUCE SPRINGSTEEN **102**
THREE DEGREES............................ **102**
(+ 9 with MFSB)

MARVIN GAYE....................... **101**
(+ 61 with Tammi Terrell, 20 with Diana Ross, 11 with Kim Weston, 5 with Diana Ross, Stevie Wonder and Smokey Robinson, 1 with Mary Wells)
MONKEES................................ **101**
HOWARD JONES **100**

31 other solo artists have chalked up over 100 chart weeks on their own and in partnership with other acts, and they are:

CHER **188**
(94 solo, 77 with Sonny And Cher, 17 uncredited with Meat Loaf)
ERIC CLAPTON **174**
(66 solo, 59 with Cream, 21 as Derek And The Dominoes, 16 as a Yardbird, 9 with Delaney And Bonnie And Friends and 3 with Tina Turner)
MARC ALMOND **169**
(58 solo, 96 with Soft Cell, 3 with Marc And The Mambas and 12 with Bronski Beat)
TERRY HALL **167**
(1 solo, 78 with Specials, 50 with Funboy Three, 20 with Bananarama, 18 with Colourfield)
ALAN PRICE........................... **166**
(78 solo, 78 as an Animal, 10 with Fame And Price Together)
EDDY GRANT **163**
(94 solo, 69 as an Equal)
PAUL SIMON.......................... **163**
(83 solo, 80 with Simon And Garfunkel)
JIMMY SOMERVILLE **154**
(32 solo, 76 with Communards, 34 with Bronski Beat and 12 with Bronski Beat and Marc Almond)
JOHN LYDON **150**
(9 as featured vocalist in Time Zone, 80 with Sex Pistols, 2 with Ex Pistols, 59 as leader of Public Image Ltd.)
MIDGE URE **145**
(44 solo, 4 with Mick Karn, 54 as part of Visage, 18 as part of Slik, 5 as a Rich Kid and 20 as a leader of Band Aid. This does not include his 138 weeks with Ultravox listed above)
STEVE WINWOOD.................. **144**
(33 solo, 71 with Spencer Davis Group, 40 with Traffic)
ALISON MOYET **131**
(82 solo, 49 with Yazoo)
BILLY IDOL **130**
(99 solo, 31 with Generation X)
FEARGAL SHARKEY............... **127**
(50 solo, 67 with Undertones, 10 with Assembly)
MORRISSEY............................ **123**
(31 solo, 92 with Smiths)
SCOTT WALKER **123**
(30 solo, 93 with Walker Brothers)

ART GARFUNKEL **117**
(37 solo, 80 with Simon And Garfunkel)
SMOKEY ROBINSON **116**
(29 solo, 71 with Miracles, 11 with Four Tops, 5 with Diana Ross, Marvin Gaye and Stevie Wonder)
BARBRA STREISAND..................... **116**
(74 solo, 13 with Donna Summer, 12 with Barbra and Neil, 10 with Barry Gibb, 7 with Don Johnson)
CHUBBY CHECKER **112**
(97 solo, 4 with Bobby Rydell, 11 with Fat Boys)
SHEENA EASTON............................ **112**
(91 solo, 14 with Prince, 7 with Kenny Rogers)
ROBERT PALMER **110**
(89 solo, 16 with Power Station, 9 with UB40)
DAVID SYLVIAN............................. **110**
(15 solo, 81 with Japan, 12 with Sylvian Sakamoto and 2 with Mick Karn)
KENNY ROGERS **109**
(87 solo, 15 with Dolly Parton and 7 with Sheena Easton)
DAVE EDMUNDS **107**
(87 solo, 14 with Love Sculpture, 6 with Stray Cats)
GARY WALKER................................ **105**
(12 solo, 93 as a Walker Brother)
DAVID GRANT **104**
(38 solo, 45 with Linx, 21 with Jaki Graham)
JANET JACKSON **103**
(96 solo, 7 with Herb Alpert)
DICKIE VALENTINE **101**
(92 solo, 9 with All Star Hit Parade)
DIONNE WARWICK........................ **101**
(83 solo, 9 with Friends, 6 with Detroit Spinners and 3 with Jeffrey Osborne)
DONOVAN **100**
(90 solo, 9 with Jeff Beck Group, 1 with Singing Corner Meets Donovan)

It is no easy task to list in the correct order the individuals who have spent the most weeks on the chart in all formats, whether as a solo act, part of a group or as a back-up or partner for another act. However, the 18 people who have spent more than 400 weeks on the charts, whether alone or as fully paid up members of other acts, are:

ELVIS PRESLEY 1141, CLIFF RICHARD 1057, PAUL McCARTNEY 858, HANK B. MARVIN 798, BRUCE WELCH 763, JOHN LENNON 617, DIANA ROSS 592, MICHAEL JACKSON 549, GEORGE HARRISON 534, RINGO STARR 487, BRIAN BENNETT 460, ELTON JOHN 438, JET HARRIS 437, DAVID BOWIE 429, FRANK SINATRA 428, ROD STEWART 416, STEVIE WONDER 412.

MOST WEEKS ON CHART 1989

BOBBY BROWN	52
GLORIA ESTEFAN	42
LONDON BOYS	38
JASON DONOVAN (+ 10 with Kylie Minogue)	36
JIVE BUNNY AND THE MASTERMIXERS (+ 2 with Bruno Brookes and Liz Kershaw)	34
MADONNA	33
MILLI VANILLI	32
GUNS N' ROSES	31
KYLIE MINOGUE (+ 10 with Jason Donovan)	31
FINE YOUNG CANNIBALS	30
SOUL II SOUL	30
DONNA SUMMER	30

NOTE: ADEVA clocked up 27 weeks solo, and 8 more with Paul Simpson, a total of 35. HOLLY JOHNSON was on the charts for 28 weeks as a soloist and 7 more with Christians, Paul McCartney, Gerry Marsden and Stock Aitken Waterman, also a total of 35 weeks.

In 1989, Bobby Brown became the first American male vocalist to top our annual chart rankings since Elvis Presley in 1977. The only act to remain from 1988's top ten acts was Kylie Minogue, although two other ladies, Madonna and Donna Summer, were celebrating their fourth year on this particular list. For Madonna, back after a quiet year in 1988, it was the first time she has featured in this list without topping it. Donna Summer was enjoying her best chart year for ten years, since her years of glory from 1977 to 1979. Milli Vanilli became the first to feature in the top ten chart acts of the year without actually performing on any of their records.

MOST WEEKS ON CHART 1990

NEW KIDS ON THE BLOCK (Donnie Wahlberg 5 more weeks with Seiko)	56
SNAP	38
STONE ROSES	38
TECHNOTRONIC	37
ADAMSKI	34

MADONNA	33
JASON DONOVAN	31
PHIL COLLINS	30
ROXETTE	30
JANET JACKSON	29

NOTE: UB40 were on the charts for 26 weeks, and another 9 weeks with Robert Palmer. LINDY LAYTON clocked up 23 weeks as vocalist with Beats International and another 7 with Janet Kay, a total of 30 weeks.

New Kids' victory was the clearest since Madonna's 39 week margin over Bruce Springsteen in 1985. They became only the third American group to win the British singles chart title, after Bill Haley and his Comets, who established the chart record annual total of 110 weeks in 1956, and Chic, who shared the 1979 title with a mere 43 weeks. Nobody except Madonna and Jason Donovan survived as top acts from 1989 - Kylie was in 11th place. For Madonna it was her fifth year in the past six among the chart greats. Janet Jackson was enjoying her second year among the elite, the first since her chart debut year of 1986, but for Phil Collins, surprisingly, it was his first.

MOST WEEKS ON CHART IN EACH YEAR

1952	Vera Lynn	10
1953	Frankie Laine	66
1954	Frankie Laine	67
1955	Ruby Murray	80
1956	Bill Haley and his Comets	110
1957	Elvis Presley	108
1958	Elvis Presley	70
1959	Russ Conway	79
1960	Cliff Richard	78
1961	Elvis Presley	88
1962	Mr. Acker Bilk	71
1963	Beatles	67
	Cliff Richard	67
1964	Jim Reeves	73
1965	Seekers	51
1966	Dave Dee, Dozy, Beaky, Mick and Tich	50
1967	Engelbert Humperdinck	97
1968	Tom Jones	58
1969	Fleetwood Mac	52
	Frank Sinatra	52
1970	Elvis Presley	59
1971	Elvis Presley	66
1972	T. Rex	58
1973	David Bowie	55

1974	Wombles	65
1975	Mud	45
1976	Rod Stewart	48
1977	Elvis Presley	51
1978	Boney M	54
1979	Abba	43
	Blondie	43
	Chic	43
1980	Madness	46
1981	Adam and the Ants	91
1982	Soft Cell	49
1983	Jam	55
1984	Frankie Goes To Hollywood	68
1985	Madonna	84
1986	Madonna	59
1987	Madonna	41
1988	Kylie Minogue	50
1989	Bobby Brown	52
1990	New Kids On The Block	56

Elvis Presley has been chart champion six times, over a span of 21 years. 1986 was the first year since the King's chart debut in 1956 in which he did not hit the British singles chart at all.

Two other acts, Frankie Laine and Cliff Richard (once shared) have been chart champions twice, and Madonna has been chart supremo in three - consecutive - years, a feat that not even Elvis has achieved.

Vera Lynn has scored the fewest chart weeks in total of any year's champion - only 46 in her entire chart career. The other chart champions who have not scored a total of 100 weeks are Bobby Brown (70

weeks), Chic (87 weeks), Wombles (87 weeks), Soft Cell (96 weeks) and 1990's winner New Kids On The Block, who have so far clocked up only 68 weeks of chart action in total. Madonna's 41 weeks in 1987 was the fewest weeks needed to take the title in a complete year. Russ Conway (1959) and Mr. Acker Bilk (1962) are the only instrumentalists to have been chart champions, and Acker Bilk barely qualifies: 11 of his 71 chart weeks in 1962 were with vocal/instrumental hits.

110	Bill Haley and his Comets	1956
108	Elvis Presley	1957
97	Engelbert Humperdinck	1967
91	Adam and the Ants	1981
88	Elvis Presley	1961
84	Pat Boone	1957
84	Madonna	1985
80	Ruby Murray	1955
79	Russ Conway	1959
78	Cliff Richard	1960
77	Adam Faith	1960
73	Jim Reeves	1964
72	Beatles	1964
71	Mr. Acker Bilk	1962
70	Bachelors	1964
70	Chubby Checker	1962
70	Elvis Presley	1958

Mud

MOST HITS

Double-sided hits, double singles, EPs and albums only count as one hit each time. Re-issues and re-entries do not count as new hits, nor do re-mixes if the same vocal track is used. We follow the philosophy that if the named act on the label has not gone into the studio to make a new record, then there is no new hit. Re-recordings of the same song by the same act do count as two hits.

A record is a hit if it makes the charts, even if for only one week at number 75.

ELVIS PRESLEY **109**
CLIFF RICHARD **99**
(+ 1 with Olivia Newton-John, 1 with Phil Everly, 1 with Sheila Walsh, 1 with Young Ones, 1 with Elton John, 1 with Van Morrison and 1 with Sarah Brightman)
ELTON JOHN **49**
(+ 1 with Kiki Dee, 1 with Millie Jackson, 1 with John Lennon, 1 with Cliff Richard, 1 with Aretha Franklin and 1 with Jennifer Rush)
DAVID BOWIE **44**
(+ 2 as part of Tin Machine, 1 with Queen, 1 with Bing Crosby, 1 with Pat Metheny and 1 with Mick Jagger)
STEVIE WONDER **43**
(+ 1 with Paul McCartney, 1 with Diana Ross, Marvin Gaye and Smokey Robinson, 1 with Michael Jackson and 1 with Julio Iglesias)
STATUS QUO **42**
DIANA ROSS **41**
(+ 18 with Supremes, 2 with Supremes and Temptations, 2 with Marvin Gaye, 1 with Michael Jackson, 1 with Marvin Gaye, Smokey Robinson and Stevie Wonder, 1 with Lionel Richie and 1 with Julio Iglesias)
PAUL McCARTNEY/WINGS **41**
(21 Wings, 20 McCartney. McCartney + 2 with Michael Jackson, 1 with Stevie Wonder and 1 with Christians, Holly Johnson, Gerry Marsden and Stock Aitken Waterman)
ROLLING STONES **36**
ROD STEWART **36**
(+ 5 with Faces, 1 with Jeff Beck, 1 with Tina Turner)
QUEEN **35**
(+ 1 with David Bowie)
SHAKIN' STEVENS **34**
(+ 1 with Shaky and Bonnie)
FRANK SINATRA **33**
(+ 1 with Sammy Davis Jr. and 1 with Nancy Sinatra)
SLADE **33**

DONNA SUMMER 33
(+ 1 with Barbra Streisand)
SHADOWS 31
(+ 30 with Cliff Richard)
LONNIE DONEGAN 30
HOT CHOCOLATE 30
ROY ORBISON 30
STRANGLERS 30
UB40 30
(+ 1 with Afrika Bambaataa and Family, 1
with Robert Palmer)
BEE GEES 29
EVERLY BROTHERS 29
(Phil Everly + 1 with Cliff Richard)
BILLY FURY 29
HOLLIES 29
TOM JONES 29
(+ 1 with Art Of Noise)
FRANKIE VAUGHAN 29
(+ 2 with Kaye Sisters)
BEACH BOYS 28
(+ 1 with Fat Boys)
BEATLES 28
(+ 1 with Tony Sheridan)
NAT 'KING' COLE 28
MICHAEL JACKSON 28
(+ 2 with Paul McCartney, 1 with Diana
Ross, 1 with Stevie Wonder and 26 as a
Jackson)
WHO 28
(+ 1 as High Numbers)
PETULA CLARK 27
ELECTRIC LIGHT ORCHESTRA 27
(+ 1 with Olivia Newton-John)
FOUR TOPS 27
(+ 2 with Supremes)
SHIRLEY BASSEY 26
PAT BOONE 26
ELVIS COSTELLO 26
(+ 2 as the Imposter)
DEPECHE MODE 26
JACKSON FIVE/JACKSONS 26
(11 as Jackson Five, 15 as Jacksons)
PRINCE 26
JIM REEVES 26
T. REX 26
(includes 2 credited to Marc Bolan)
ABBA 25
MADONNA 25
GARY NUMAN 25
(+ 3 with Sharpe and Numan, 2 with Radio
Heart)
DAVID ESSEX 24
ADAM FAITH 24
FLEETWOOD MAC 24
FRANKIE LAINE 24
(+ 1 with Jimmy Boyd, 1 with Doris Day and
1 with Johnnie Ray)
MADNESS 24
SIOUXSIE AND THE BANSHEES 24
(Siouxsie and Budgie + 3 as the Creatures)

SUPREMES 24
(+ 3 with Temptations, 2 with Four Tops)
PERRY COMO 23
EURYTHMICS 23
CONNIE FRANCIS 23
LEVEL 42 23
SHOWADDYWADDY 23
DAVE CLARK FIVE 22
DURAN DURAN 22
IRON MAIDEN 22
KINKS 22
GLADYS KNIGHT AND THE PIPS ... 22
(Gladys Knight + 1 with Johnny Mathis)
BRENDA LEE 22
DUSTY SPRINGFIELD 22
(+ 5 as a Springfield, 1 with Pet Shop Boys)
TEMPTATIONS 22
(+ 3 with Supremes)
DUANE EDDY 21
(+ 1 with Art Of Noise)
FIVE STAR 21
KOOL AND THE GANG 21
GENE PITNEY 21
(+ 1 with Marc Almond)
KIM WILDE 21
(+ 1 with Junior, 1 with Mel Smith (Mel and
Kim))
ANDY WILLIAMS 21
AC/DC 20
ADAM AND THE ANTS/ADAM
ANT 20
BUCKS FIZZ 20
FATS DOMINO 20
GENESIS 20
HERMAN'S HERMITS 20
ORCHESTRAL MANOEUVRES
IN THE DARK 20
CHRIS REA 20
SIMPLE MINDS 20
SPANDAU BALLET 20

Other acts that have clocked up 20 hits
under more than one name are:

MIDGE URE 36
(7 solo, 17 with Ultravox, 7 with Visage, 2 as
part of Slik, 1 as a Rich Kid, 1 with Mick Karn
plus 1 as a leader of Band Aid)
BRYAN FERRY 33
(17 solo, 16 with Roxy Music)
LIONEL RICHIE 28
(13 solo, 13 with the Commodores, 1 with
Diana Ross and 1 as a leader of USA For Africa)
MARC ALMOND 25
(14 solo, 9 with Soft Cell, 1 with Marc &
Mambas and 1 with Bronski Beat)
STING 25
(9 solo, 16 with Police)
ARETHA FRANKLIN 24
(19 solo, 1 with George Benson, 1 with
Eurythmics, 1 with George Michael, 1 with
Elton John, 1 with Whitney Houston)

DONNY OSMOND 24
(10 solo, 10 as an Osmond, 4 as half of Donny
& Marie)
TINA TURNER 24
(18 solo, 4 with Ike Turner, 1 with Rod Stewart
and 1 with Eric Clapton)
ERIC CLAPTON 23
(11 solo, 7 with Cream, 2 with the Yardbirds, 1
as Derek & Dominoes, 1 with Delaney &
Bonnie & Friends and 1 with Tina Turner)
MORRISSEY 23
(7 solo, 16 as a Smith)
CHER 22
(12 solo, 9 with Sonny and Cher, 1 uncredited
with Meat Loaf)
MARVIN GAYE 22
(11 solo and 11 with various partners)
BUDDY HOLLY 22
(18 solo, 4 as a Cricket)
MANFRED MANN 22
(17 as Manfred Mann, 5 as Manfred Mann's
Earth Band)
GEORGE MICHAEL 22
(10 solo, 10 with Wham!, 1 with Aretha
Franklin and 1 with Boogie Box High)
FRANKIE VALLI 22
(5 solo, 17 with Four Seasons)
JODY WATLEY 22
(5 solo, 17 with Shalamar)
BANANARAMA 21
(18 as a trio, 2 with Funboy Three, 1 with La
Na Nee Nee Noo Noo)
PHIL LYNOTT 21
(3 solo, 17 with Thin Lizzy, 1 with Gary
Moore)
NEW ORDER 21
(18 as New Order, 1 as part of
Englandneworder, and 2 as Joy Division, more
or less)
OLIVIA NEWTON-JOHN 21
(16 solo, 3 with John Travolta, 1 with
Electric Light Orchestra and 1 with Cliff
Richard)
DAVID SYLVIAN 21
(6 solo, 12 with Japan, 2 with Sylvian
Sakamoto, 1 with Mick Karn)
TREMELOES 21
(13 as a group, plus 8 backing Brian Poole)
GEORGE BENSON 20
(19 solo, 1 with Aretha Franklin)
KATE BUSH 20
(19 solo, 1 with Peter Gabriel)
PHIL COLLINS 20
(18 solo, 1 with Marilyn Martin, 1 with Philip
Bailey and 20 more with Genesis)
RUSS CONWAY 20
(19 solo, 1 with Dorothy Squires)
STEVE WINWOOD 20
(6 solo, 10 with the Spencer Davis Group and 4
with Traffic)

MOST TOP TEN HITS

The same rules apply as for the MOST HITS list, except that a disc must have made the Top Ten for at least one week to qualify.

56 CLIFF RICHARD (+ 1 with Phil Everly, 1 with Young Ones and 1 with Sarah Brightman)
55 ELVIS PRESLEY
25 BEATLES
24 MADONNA
22 STATUS QUO
21 ROLLING STONES
20 MICHAEL JACKSON (+ 11 as a Jackson, 2 with Paul McCartney)
20 PAUL McCARTNEY/WINGS (Wings 12, McCartney 8. McCartney + 2 with Michael Jackson, 1 with Stevie Wonder and 1 with Christians, Holly Johnson, Gerry Marsden and Stock Aitken Waterman)
19 ABBA
19 DAVID BOWIE (+ 1 with Queen, 1 with Bing Crosby and 1 with Mick Jagger)
19 ROD STEWART (+ 3 with Faces, 1 with Tina Turner, 1 with Python Lee Jackson)
17 LONNIE DONEGAN
17 HOLLIES
17 ELTON JOHN (+ 1 with Kiki Dee)
17 FRANKIE LAINE (+ 1 with Jimmy Boyd and 1 with Doris Day)
17 QUEEN (+ 1 with David Bowie)
16 SHADOWS (+ 25 backing Cliff Richard)
16 SLADE
16 STEVIE WONDER (+ 1 with Paul McCartney and 1 with Julio Iglesias)
15 BEE GEES
15 MADNESS
14 ELECTRIC LIGHT ORCHESTRA (+ 1 with Olivia Newton-John)
14 TOM JONES (+ 1 with Art Of Noise)
14 SHAKIN' STEVENS (+ 1 with Bonnie Tyler)
13 NAT 'KING' COLE
13 EVERLY BROTHERS (Phil Everly + 1 with Cliff Richard)
13 KINKS
13 MANFRED MANN (+ 3 as Manfred Mann's Earth Band)
13 DIANA ROSS (+ 7 with Supremes, 1 with Supremes and Temptations, 1 with Marvin Gaye and 1 with Lionel Richie)
13 UB40 (+ 1 with Robert Palmer)
13 WHO
12 SHIRLEY BASSEY

12 BEACH BOYS (+ 1 with Fat Boys)
12 DURAN DURAN
12 GARY GLITTER
12 HOT CHOCOLATE
12 GUY MITCHELL
12 SUPREMES (+ 1 with Temptations)
11 WINIFRED ATWELL (+ 1 as part of All Star Hit Parade)
11 CILLA BLACK
11 PAT BOONE
11 PETULA CLARK
11 ADAM FAITH
11 FOUR TOPS
11 BILLY FURY
11 JACKSON FIVE/JACKSONS (6 as Jackson Five, 5 as Jacksons)
11 MUD
11 ROY ORBISON
11 T. REX
11 10 C.C. (+ 1 as Hotlegs, more or less)
11 DAVID WHITFIELD (+ 1 as part of All Star Hit Parade)
10 ADAM AND THE ANTS/ ADAM ANT
10 BAY CITY ROLLERS
10 BLONDIE
10 DAVID ESSEX
10 CONNIE FRANCIS
10 HERMAN'S HERMITS
10 KYLIE MINOGUE (+ 1 with Jason Donovan)
10 PET SHOP BOYS (+ 1 with Dusty Springfield)
10 GENE PITNEY (+ 1 with Marc Almond)
10 POLICE
10 ROXY MUSIC

10 LEO SAYER
10 SHOWADDYWADDY
10 FRANK SINATRA (+ 1 with Nancy Sinatra)
10 SPANDAU BALLET
10 DUSTY SPRINGFIELD (+ 2 with Springfields and 1 with Pet Shop Boys)
10 STYLISTICS
10 SWEET
10 U2

Also strongly represented on Top Ten hits are:

17 GEORGE MICHAEL (6 solo, 9 as part of Wham!, 1 with Aretha Franklin and 1 as part of Boogie Box High)
15 PHIL COLLINS (8 solo, 5 as part of Genesis, 1 with Marilyn Martin and 1 with Philip Bailey)
13 DONNY OSMOND (6 solo, 5 as one of the Osmonds and 2 with Marie Osmond)
13 DAVE STEWART (1 with Candy Dulfer, 8 as part of the Eurythmics, 2 as a Tourist and 1 as a Eurythmic with Aretha Franklin)
11 LIONEL RICHIE (6 solo, 4 as a Commodore and 1 with Diana Ross)
11 FRANKIE VAUGHAN (9 solo and 2 with the Kaye Sisters)
10 BANANARAMA (8 as a group, 1 with Funboy Three and 1 with La Na Nee Nee Noo Noo)
10 JOHNNIE RAY (9 solo and 1 with Doris Day)
10 DORIS DAY (7 solo, 2 with Frankie Laine and 1 with Johnnie Ray)

Cliff Richard

374

26 CLIFF RICHARD *(with the Shadows for 11 consecutive)*
24 BEATLES *(first 24 releases)*
23 MADONNA
23 ELVIS PRESLEY *(first 23 RCA releases)*
19 ROLLING STONES
18 ABBA
12 FRANKIE LAINE
12 SHADOWS *(first 12 hits)*
12 SLADE
11 GARY GLITTER *(first 11 hits)*
11 GUY MITCHELL *(first 11 hits)*
11 T. REX
10 BAY CITY ROLLERS *(first 10 hits)*
10 DURAN DURAN
10 KYLIE MINOGUE *(first 10 hits)*
10 DAVID WHITFIELD

At the start of Elvis Presley's run of 23 consecutive Top Ten Hits, three old HMV releases appeared on the chart, one of which, *Paralysed*, reached the Top Ten. Three EPs by Elvis also hit the charts without reaching the Top Ten during the five and a half years in which every Elvis single hit the Top Ten, with 20 of the 23 reaching the top three.

Holiday by Madonna reappeared in the Top Ten during her run of 23 Top Ten hits with consecutive releases. As it was first a Top Ten hit before the release of *Lucky Star*, her only single to fail to hit the upper reaches, it does not count as one of her consecutive Top Ten hits. All except one of Madonna's 23 consecutive were top five hits. Kylie Minogue also hit the Top Ten in duet with Jason Donovan during her run of ten consecutive Top Ten hits.

Between May 1959 and December 1963, the Shadows released 30 singles, either solo or backing Cliff Richard, all of which hit the Top Ten.

The Rolling Stones' run of 19 consecutive Top Ten hits began on 12 March 1964, with *Not Fade Away*, and finished on 21 July 1978 when *Miss You/Far Away Eyes* dropped out of the Top Ten. This is the longest time span for a run of Top Ten hits with consecutive releases, none of which was a re-mix or re-issue.

New Model Army

AC/DC have had 20 hits to the end of 1990, without ever hitting the Top Ten. Their highest chart placing to date was *Heatseeker* which peaked at number 12 for two weeks from 23 January 1988. **The Clash** charted 19 times to the end of 1990. They reached their highest ever chart placing of number 11 with *London Calling* in 1980.

The Alarm have racked up 15 hits, of which the highest placed was their first, *68 Guns*, which peaked at number 17. **Saxon** also have 15 hits, with a highest placing of 12 for *And The Bands Played On* in 1981. **Luther Vandross** has now had 12 hits and a re-mix without ever climbing higher than number 13, which was achieved by the *Never Too Much* re-mix. **Killing Joke** have had 11 chart hits, only one of which made even the Top Forty. This was *Love Like Blood*, which reached number 16 in 1985. The **Cult** and the **Mission** have both had 11 chart hits, both with a top placing of 11. **Judas Priest** have entered the charts 11 times, twice reaching number 12. None of **Lloyd Cole**'s 11 chart hits has climbed higher than number 17. **New Model Army** have also hit the charts eleven times, but they have never even got as far as the Top Twenty. Their biggest hit was their first, *No Rest*, which reached number 28 during a five week chart run. Despite scoring eleven hits, they have spent only 28 weeks on the charts in total. **Chris Rea**'s 18th hit was his first, and to date only, Top Ten hit. **Fats Domino** had 18 consecutive hits after his only Top Ten hit, hitting the Top Twenty seven more times but never quite breaking back into the Top Ten. **Elvis Costello** has charted 15 times since his last Top Ten hit at the end of 1981, without ever reaching the Top Twenty. He has had two more hits in that time under the name **The Imposter**, neither of which was a Top Ten hit, although *Pills And Soap* made it to number 16. Since **Gary Numan**'s last Top Ten appearance in June 82, he has hit the chart – but with considerably less force – 15 times solo (excluding the re-mix of *Cars*), 3 times with Bill Sharpe and twice with Radio Heart, his highest position being 17 for *Change Your Mind*.

LONGEST GAP BETWEEN CHART HITS

25 acts have waited patiently for over 15 years between hits as follows:

EARTHA KITT	28 years 170 days	(16 Jun 55 to 3 Dec 83)
RITCHIE VALENS	28 years 142 days	(12 Mar 59 to 1 Aug 87)
PATSY CLINE	27 years 340 days	(2 Jan 63 to 8 Dec 90)
BOBBY VINTON	26 years 215 days	(27 Feb 64 to 29 Sep 90)
GLENN MILLER	21 years 312 days	(18 Mar 54 to 24 Jan 76)
GARY 'U.S.' BONDS	19 years 223 days	(18 Oct 61 to 30 May 81)
ROY ORBISON	19 years 19 days	(26 Dec 69 to 14 Jan 89)
NINA SIMONE	18 years 262 days	(11 Feb 69 to 31 Oct 87)
WILSON PICKETT	18 years 255 days	(11 Mar 69 to 21 Nov 87)
PAUL EVANS	18 years 254 days	(6 Apr 60 to 16 Dec 78)
KENNY LYNCH	18 years 16 days	(4 Aug 65 to 20 Aug 83)
BING CROSBY	17 years 338 days	(5 Sep 57 to 9 Aug 75)
WILLIAM BELL	17 years 284 days	(16 Jul 68 to 26 Apr 86)
MONKEES	17 years 109 days	(1 Jul 69 to 18 Oct 86)
JOE COCKER	17 years 92 days	(14 Aug 70 to 14 Nov 87)
SLIM WHITMAN	17 years 86 days	(11 Jul 57 to 5 Oct 74)
MIKE BERRY	17 years 73 days	(22 May 63 to 2 Aug 80)
DOROTHY SQUIRES	16 years 101 days	(11 Jun 53 to 20 Sep 69)
EVERLY BROTHERS	16 years 96 days	(18 Jun 68 to 22 Sep 84)
BORIS GARDINER	16 years 87 days	(1 May 70 to 26 Jul 86)
DEE CLARK	16 years 3 days	(8 Oct 59 to 11 Oct 75)
TAMS	15 years 360 days	(26 Nov 71 to 21 Nov 87)
BILLY FURY	15 years 349 days	(21 Sep 66 to 4 Sep 82)
MAX BYGRAVES	15 years 325 days	(18 Jan 74 to 9 Dec 89)
JOHNNY TILLOTSON	15 years 306 days	(12 Jun 63 to 14 Apr 79)

This table shows which acts had to wait for the longest time between chart hits. The definition of a 'hit' is the same as in other lists in this section, i.e. re-issues and re-entries do not count as new hits. For that reason the Righteous Brothers, for example, do not feature in this list. The gap is calculated between the last day of one chart run and the first day of the chart run of the next hit.

Roy Orbison

William Bell hit the charts with Judy Clay in late 1968 and early 1969. **Dorothy Squires** had a hit with Russ Conway in 1961. In 1983 both **Phil Everly** and **Joe Cocker** had Top Ten hits, with Cliff Richard and Jennifer Warnes respectively. **Roy Orbison** charted as a member of the Traveling Wilburys in 1988. **Glenn Miller** and **Johnny Tillotson**'s reappearances were both as a result of a re-issue of a hit, coupled with tracks that had not previously hit the chart, thus counting the re-issue as a new hit.

After 25 years and 329 days off the chart, **Karl Denver** reappeared in June 1990 with Happy Mondays. **Donovan** made his comeback with Singing Corner on 1 December 1990, 21 years and 307 days since his final solo chart hit, and 21 years and 83 days since his duet with Jeff Beck lapsed into chart oblivion. **Ray Charles** charted as vocalist with Quincy Jones 21 years and 261 days after his final solo hit dropped off the chart. For **P.P. Arnold** there was a chart hiatus of exactly 20 years between her last solo hit and her appearance on the Beatmasters hit, *Burn It Up* in 1988. **Crosby, Stills and Nash** spent 19 years and 269 days in the chart wilderness before Crosby Stills Nash and Young had their first UK chart hit in January 1989. There was a gap of 15 years 304 days between **Des O'Connor**'s last solo appearance and his re-emergence late in 1986 in partnership with Roger Whittaker.

34 other acts have been off the chart for over 10 years between hits. They are, in order of time off the chart:

Sandie SHAW	(14 yrs 315 days)
Trini LOPEZ	(14/223)
Danny WILLIAMS	(14/132)
Dionne WARWICK	(14/92)
Mick JAGGER	(14/60)
Robin GIBB	(13/349)
CHER	(13/271)
Mr. Acker BILK	(13/167)
DION	(13/27)
CHAIRMEN OF THE BOARD	(13/20)
LITTLE RICHARD	(12/345)
Murray HEAD	(12/280)
Donny OSMOND	(12/253)
Marianne FAITHFULL	(12/247)
EXCITERS	(12/219)
Billy PRESTON	(12/105)
Duncan BROWNE	(12/84)
PINK FLOYD	(12/79)
Paul ANKA	(12/37)
Tony OSBORNE	(11/339)
Henry MANCINI	(11/314)

Johnny MATHIS		(11/290)
ENGLAND WORLD CUP SQUAD		(11/232)
Duane EDDY		(11/185)
Millie JACKSON		(11/107)
Robert JOHN		(11/61)
Gene CHANDLER		(10/216)
Dobie GRAY		(10/166)
Linda RONSTADT		(10/158)
Betty WRIGHT		(10/146)
CHAKACHAS		(10/130)
BOOKER T & THE M.G.'s		(10/80)
Wayne GIBSON		(10/68)
Charlie DRAKE		(10/12)

Dionne Warwick, Mick Jagger, Robin Gibb, Billy Preston, Donny Osmond and **Linda Ronstadt** all appeared on the charts as part of groups during their solo absences. Linda Ronstadt's comeback hit was "with Aaron Neville". **Gene Pitney** missed 14 years and 39 days of chart action before hitting again with Marc Almond in 1989. **Shirley Bassey** had been absent from the chart for 14 years 33 days when she reappeared with Yello. **Al Green**'s chart duet with Annie Lennox came 13 years 215 days after his last hit fell off the chart. **Timmy Thomas** disappeared from the charts for 12 years 231 days between his last solo hit and his duet with Nicole. **Lindisfarne** spent 12 years and 7 days out of chart sight before coming back with Gazza on 10 November 1990. **Pete Waterman** hit the charts as 14-18 11 years 239 days before he became one third of Stock Aitken Waterman and hit the charts again. **Scott Fitzgerald**'s solo chart debut came 10 years 44 days after his hit duet with Yvonne Keely. **Roger Whittaker** had a gap of 11 years 9 days between his last solo chart appearance and his hit with Des O'Connor.

Duane Eddy not only had a gap of 11 years 185 days between solo chart hits, he then had to wait a further 10 years 310 days after his last solo hit before re-emerging with Art Of Noise and a re-make of his first Top Ten hit, *Peter Gunn Theme*. **Roy Wood**'s name was out of the chart for 11 years and 127 days before his comeback with Dr. and the Medics, although he had a re-issued hit as leader of Wizzard in the interim.

There was a gap of 11 years 59 days between **Shane Fenton**'s final day on the charts and **Alvin Stardust**'s first appearance.

LEAST SUCCESSFUL CHART ACT

Since 13 May 1978, when the Top 75 was first published, 23 acts have clocked up a chart career consisting of only one week at number 75. Eleven acts have added their names to this list in the past two years, by far the most rapid growth of almost complete failure since the charts began.

Anthony Hopkins

ADICTS	Bad Boy	14 May 83
ANGELWITCH	Sweet Danger	7 Jun 80
JOHNNY CLEGG and SAVUKA	Scatterlings Of Africa	16 May 87
DAYTON	The Sound Of Music	10 Dec 83
DEJA	Serious	29 Aug 87
THULI DUMAKUDE	The Funeral	2 Jan 88
GEORGE FENTON and JONAS GWANGWA	Cry Freedom	2 Jan 88
FISH and TONY BANKS	Short Cut To Somewhere	18 Oct 86
FIVE THIRTY	Abstain	4 Aug 90
GRAND PRIX	Keep On Believing	27 Feb 82
TERRY HALL	Missing	11 Nov 89
ANTHONY HOPKINS	Distant Star	27 Dec 87
LIVING COLOUR★	Type	27 Oct 90
MICHAEL LOVESMITH	Ain't Nothing Like It	5 Oct 85
MELISSA MANCHESTER and AL JARREAU	The Music Of Goodbye	5 Apr 86
MC DUKE	I'm Riffin' (English Rasta)	11 Mar 89
PARIS ANGELS	Scope	3 Nov 90
PRETTY BOY FLOYD	Rock And Roll (Is Gonna Set The Night On Fire)	10 Mar 90
CHERYL PEPSII RILEY	Thanks For My Child	28 Jan 89
SEDUCTION	Heartbeat	21 Apr 90
SPIRITUALIZED	Anyway That You Want Me/ Step Into The Breeze	30 Jun 90
STOP THE VIOLENCE	Self Destruction	18 Feb 89
TIGERTAILZ★	Love Bomb Baby	24 Jun 89

★ Hit again in 1991.

Al Jarreau has had several solo successes. **Fish and Tony Banks** are of course members of two other very successful chart acts, Fish with Marillion and Tony Banks with Genesis. Fish has also had solo chart success since leaving Marillion in 1989. **Johnny Clegg** and **Terry Hall** have been more successful as members of groups - Clegg with Juluka and Hall with Specials, Funboy Three and Colourfield. **Deja** consists of Starlena Young and Curt Jones, who had other hits as members of both Aurra and Slave. **Stop The Violence** is a charity ensemble consisting of several chart acts.

Adicts and **Grand Prix** have also hit the album charts, with marginally more success. **Thuli Dumakude**'s hit was the flip side of

the **George Fenton and Jonas Gwangwa** record, both tracks from the soundtrack of the film, 'Cry Freedom'.

From 10 March 1960 to 6 May 1978, when only a Top 50 was published, 11 acts managed a chart career that consisted of only 1 week at number 50. They were **Angels, Chaquito, Jimmy Clanton, Cookies, Marvin Gaye and Mary Wells, Tim Hardin, Tony Hatch, Moontrekkers, Hal Page and the Whalers, Keith Relf** and **Sundragon**.

The **Ruthless Rap Assassins** are the only act to the end of 1990 whose chart career has consisted of two singles, both of which peaked at number 75 for one week.

ANOTHER ROCK 'N' ROLL CHRISTMAS

Christmas is the season when more records are sold than at any other time of year, so it is also the time when record companies and record stars try their hardest to come up with big hits. In the 39 Christmasses since the charts began in 1952, there have been 396 records which have hit the Christmas Top Ten (the extra six records all appeared in the first ever Christmas Top Ten, which was actually a Top 16 thanks to the odd fact that there were two records placed third, three at number six, two at number eight and three at number ten), but of these 396 records, only 55 were about Christmas. 31 were novelty songs, from *Never Do A Tango With An Eskimo* to *Donald Where's Your Troosers*, and 36 were instrumentals. The rest were just hit singles.

The acts who have featured in the Top Ten at least four times in Christmas week are:

Winifred Atwell

	No. 1s	Other Top 10	Other Top 20	Total	
Elvis Presley	1	3	11	15	
Cliff Richard	3	9	2	14	.... + 1 with Van Morrison
Status Quo	-	3	5	8	
Beatles	4	2	1	7	
Winifred Atwell	1	4	2	7	
Madonna	-	5	1	6	
Tom Jones	1	3	1	5	
Slade	1	3	1	5	.... 'Merry Xmas Everybody' hit the Top 20 twice
Abba	-	4	-	4	
Petula Clark	-	4	-	4	
John Lennon	-	4	-	4	.... 'Happy Xmas (War Is Over)' hit the Top 10 twice

The **Beatles** topped the Christmas charts three years in a row, and four years out of five, in 1963, 1964, 1965 and 1967. In 1963 and 1967 they also held the number two spot in the charts in Christmas week, a chart domination at Christmas that has never been equalled. They never made a record about Christmas. Only the Beatles and **Cliff Richard** have had more than one Christmas number one.

At Christmas time, instrumental hits seem to do better than at any other time of year. Roughly one in eleven of the Top Ten hits at Christmas have been instrumentals. **Winifred Atwell** is the only act to feature in five consecutive Christmas Top Tens, from 1953 to 1957 inclusive, and all her hits were instrumentals.

Apart from Winifred Atwell, the only act to feature in the Christmas Top Ten four years in a row is **Cliff Richard** (from 1962 to 1965). Three consecutive years with a Christmas Top Ten hit has been achieved by **Abba** (1979 to 1981), the **Beatles** (1963 to 1965), **Frankie Laine** (1953 to 1955), **Madness** (1980 to 1982), **Madonna** (1984 to 1986), **Cliff Richard** again (1958 to 1960), **Slade** (1971 to 1973) and **Dickie Valentine** (1954 to 1956). **Cliff Richard** also featured at number one in three consecutive Christmasses, 1988 to 1990, but in 1989 it was as one of the featured vocalists on **Band Aid II**'s single, *Do They Know It's Christmas*.

Winifred Atwell, Frankie Laine (1952 to 1956), **Gene Pitney** (1963 to 1967) and **Elvis Presley** (1960 to 1964) are the only acts to have racked up five consecutive Top Twenty hits in Christmas week. Four consecutive Christmas Top Twenty hits have been achieved by **Tom Jones, Madness, Madonna, Cliff Richard** and **T. Rex.** Three consecutive Christmas Top Twenty hits have been enjoyed by **Abba, Beatles, Blondie, Pat Boone, Bill Haley, Kinks, Mud, Des O'Connor, Police, Cliff Richard** (twice), **Slade, Status Quo, Dickie Valentine, Malcolm Vaughan** and **David Whitfield.**

From **Winifred Atwell** and the **Big Ben Banjo Band** up to **Jive Bunny** and **John Travolta and Olivia Newton-John,** medley records have always done well at Christmas. So have comedy records, even though the comedy is usually nothing to do with Christmas. **Chuck Berry**'s *My Ding-A-*

Ling and **Benny Hill**'s *Ernie* are just two examples of comic hits which were Christmas smashes without being seasonal. Some comedy hits are seasonal, and are medleys as well, like the **Barron Knights'** series of Christmas Top Twenty hits over a 15 year period, or **Chris Hill**'s *Renta Santa* and *Bionic Santa* in 1975 and 1976.

Four records have appeared twice in the Yuletide Top Ten, and 15 other songs have hit the Christmas Top Ten in more than one recording. The four records which have succeeded twice are:

- *Do They Know It's Christmas?* by **Band Aid** (no. 1 in 1984, no. 3 in 1985)
- *Happy Xmas (War Is Over)* by **John and Yoko, the Plastic Ono Band with the Harlem Community Choir** (no. 4 in 1972 and again in 1980)
- *Last Christmas* by **Wham!** (no. 2 in 1984, no. 6 in 1985)
- *Reet Petite* by **Jackie Wilson** (no. 10 in 1957, no. 1 in 1987)

Happy Xmas (War Is Over) has spent more weeks on the chart than any other Christmas record, a total of 31 weeks to the end of 1990. **Slade**'s *Merry Xmas Everybody* has totalled 29 weeks in its original version and a further 2 weeks in a different version by Slade and the Reading Choir.

The other titles which have been a Top Ten hit twice in Christmas week are:

- **Answer Me** (by Frankie Laine and David Whitfield, both in 1953)
- **Because You're Mine** (by Nat 'King' Cole and Mario Lanza, 1952)
- **Do They Know It's Christmas?** (by Band Aid in 1984 and 1985, by Band Aid II in 1989. Both versions hit number one)
- **I Only Want To Be With You** (by Dusty Springfield in 1963 and by the Tourists in 1979)
- **I Saw Mommy Kissing Santa Claus** (by the Beverley Sisters and Jimmy Boyd, 1953)
- **It's Only Make Believe** (by Conway Twitty in 1958 and Glen Campbell in 1970)
- **Mary's Boy Child** (by Harry Belafonte in 1957 and Boney M in 1978, both number one hits)
- **My Prayer** (by the Platters in 1956 and by Gerry Monroe in 1970)
- **Rockin' Around The Christmas Tree** (by Brenda Lee in 1962 and Mel and Kim in 1987)

- **Silent Night** (by Bing Crosby in 1952 and by Bros in 1988)
- **Swedish Rhapsody** (by Mantovani and Ray Martin, both in 1953)
- **Tom Dooley** (by Lonnie Donegan and the Kingston Trio, both in 1958)
- **What Do You Want To Make Those Eyes At Me For?** (by Emile Ford in 1959 and Shakin' Stevens in 1987)
- **When I Fall In Love** (by Rick Astley and Nat 'King' Cole, both in 1987)
- **White Christmas** (by Mantovani in 1952 and by Bing Crosby in 1977)

White Christmas has been a chart hit in eight different versions. The 1987 Christmas Top Ten consisted of only four songs which had not been a chart hit before, and six old songs revived.

Of all the songs which have been a hit at Christmas, the least seasonal must be *April Love* by **Pat Boone**, which was at number 13 in Christmas week 1957. Other unseasonal offerings include *Happy Birthday Sweet Sixteen*, which was at number 10 for **Neil Sedaka** in 1961, *Sun Arise*, by **Rolf Harris**, which was the number seven hit in Christmas week 1962, *Sunshine Superman*, which **Donovan** took to number four at Christmas 1966, and *Money Money Money*, **Abba**'s Yuletide thought for 1976. In 1977, both **Donna Summer** and **Ruby Winters** had Top Ten hits at Christmas.

Only three of **Elvis Presley**'s 15 Christmas Top Twenty hits, and three of **Cliff Richard**'s 14, are about Christmas. Elvis never hit the Top Ten in Christmas week with a Christmas song, although his 1957 hit *Santa Bring My Baby Back To Me* had already dropped to 20 from its peak position of number seven when December 25th rolled around. Cliff never hit the charts with a Christmas song until 1982, when his *Little Town* peaked at number 11 in Christmas week.

The **Goons'** *I'm Walking Backwards For Christmas* was a Top Ten hit in the summer of 1956.

Slade

Elvis

For the first time since 1955, two years have gone by without the name of **Elvis Presley** appearing in the singles charts. This has given **Cliff Richard** an opportunity to move a little closer to the all-time leader, and at the rate at which he has closed in on Elvis over 1989 and 1990, he will take over as British chart history's most successful act sometime in 1997.

Elvis and Cliff are so far ahead of the rest that it is difficult to imagine them being overtaken. Cliff also racked up more chart weeks in 1989 and 1990 than any other act in the Top Twenty. We have to go down to 26th spot, now occupied by the fastest climber, **Madonna**, to find a more successful chart act than Cliff Richard in 1989 and 1990. The race for third place is still close, though, with **Elton John** moving up from 6th to 5th, and **Status Quo** up from 9th to 6th. The biggest climb in the Top Twenty is by **Roy Orbison**, whose final chart fling has raised him from 19th to 15th place. **Tom Jones**, despite a little chart success, makes the biggest fall, from 11th to 14th. However, the list is basically very static, with no new acts breaking into the Top Twenty, and only **Rod Stewart**

replacing the **Everly Brothers** in the all-time Top Ten.

Shirley Bassey retains her title as the most successful female chart act of all time, but only narrowly. **Diana Ross** is now within three weeks of catching her. **Madonna** is

also only 28 weeks off the pace, a total that Miss Ciccone passed in both 1989 and 1990. By 1992, Shirley Bassey will probably be only number three among the ladies, relinquishing a title she has held since overtaking Connie Francis in the early 1960s.

Act/Country	Chart Span	Wks	Hits	Top 10 Hits	No. 1s	Ave Wks/Hit	% of Top 10 Hits
ELVIS PRESLEY USA	56-88	1141	109	55	17	10.5	50.5%
CLIFF RICHARD UK	58-90	998	99	56	12	10.1	56.6%
BEATLES UK	62-89	432	28	25	17	15.4	89.3%
FRANK SINATRA USA	54-86	401	33	10	2	12.2	30.3%
ELTON JOHN UK	71-90	392	49	17	1	8.0	34.7%
STATUS QUO UK	68-90	377	42	22	1	9.0	52.4%
DAVID BOWIE UK	69-89	366	44	19	3	8.3	43.2%
STEVIE WONDER USA	66-89	364	43	16	1	8.5	37.2%
SHADOWS UK	60-81	359	31	16	5	11.6	51.6%
ROD STEWART UK	71-90	346	36	19	6	9.6	52.8%
PAUL McCARTNEY UK	71-90	345	41	20	2	8.4	48.8%
EVERLY BROTHERS USA	57-84	337	29	13	4	11.6	44.8%
ROLLING STONES UK	63-90	334	36	21	8	9.3	58.3%
TOM JONES UK	65-89	330	29	14	2	11.4	48.3%
ROY ORBISON USA	60-89	324	30	11	3	10.8	36.7%
JIM REEVES USA	60-72	322	26	6	1	12.4	23.1%
LONNIE DONEGAN UK	56-62	321	30	17	3	10.7	56.7%
HOLLIES UK	63-88	316	29	17	2	10.9	58.6%
SHIRLEY BASSEY UK	57-73	313	26	12	2	12.0	46.2%
DIANA ROSS USA	70-90	310	41	13	2	7.6	31.7%

THE NUMBER ONE HITS

Date disc hit the top	Title/Artist/Label	Number of weeks at No. 1

· 1 9 5 2 ·

(Top Twelve – *N.M.E* Chart)

14 Nov	HERE IN MY HEART Al Martino (Capitol)	9

· 1 9 5 3 ·

16 Jan	YOU BELONG TO ME Jo Stafford (Columbia)	1
23 Jan	COMES A-LONG A-LOVE Kay Starr (Capitol)......	1
30 Jan	OUTSIDE OF HEAVEN Eddie Fisher (HMV)........	1
6 Feb	DON'T LET THE STARS GET IN YOUR EYES Perry Como (HMV)	5
13 Mar	SHE WEARS RED FEATHERS Guy Mitchell (Columbia)	4
10 Apr	BROKEN WINGS Stargazers (Decca)	1
17 Apr	(HOW MUCH IS) THAT DOGGIE IN THE WINDOW Lita Roza (Decca)	1
24 Apr	I BELIEVE Frankie Laine (Philips)	9
26 Jun	I'M WALKING BEHIND YOU Eddie Fisher (HMV)	1
3 Jul	I BELIEVE Frankie Laine (Philips)	6
14 Aug	MOULIN ROUGE Mantovani (Decca)	1
21 Aug	I BELIEVE Frankie Laine (Philips)	3
11 Sep	LOOK AT THAT GIRL Guy Mitchell (Philips)	6
23 Oct	HEY JOE Frankie Laine (Philips)	2
6 Nov	ANSWER ME David Whitfield (Decca)	1
13 Nov	ANSWER ME Frankie Laine (Philips)	8
	(ANSWER ME by David Whitfield returned to number one for one week to share the top spot with Frankie Laine's version on 11 Dec 1953)	

· 1 9 5 4 ·

8 Jan	OH MEIN PAPA Eddie Calvert (Columbia)	9
12 Mar	I SEE THE MOON Stargazers (Decca)	5
16 Apr	SECRET LOVE Doris Day (Philips)	1
23 Apr	I SEE THE MOON Stargazers (Decca)	1
30 Apr	SUCH A NIGHT Johnnie Ray (Philips)	1
7 May	SECRET LOVE Doris Day (Philips)	8
2 Jul	CARA MIA David Whitfield with chorus and Mantovani and his orchestra (Decca)	10
10 Sep	LITTLE THINGS MEAN A LOT Kitty Kallen (Brunswick)	1
17 Sep	THREE COINS IN THE FOUNTAIN Frank Sinatra (Capitol)	3

Top Twenty began 1 Oct 1954.

8 Oct	HOLD MY HAND Don Cornell (Vogue)	4
5 Nov	MY SON MY SON Vera Lynn (Decca)	2
19 Nov	HOLD MY HAND Don Cornell (Vogue)	1
26 Nov	THIS OLE HOUSE Rosemary Clooney (Philips)	1
3 Dec	LET'S HAVE ANOTHER PARTY Winifred Atwell (Philips)	5

· 1 9 5 5 ·

7 Jan	FINGER OF SUSPICION Dickie Valentine (Decca)	1
14 Jan	MAMBO ITALIANO Rosemary Clooney (Philips)	1
21 Jan	FINGER OF SUSPICION Dickie Valentine (Decca)	2
4 Feb	MAMBO ITALIANO Rosemary Clooney (Philips)	2
18 Feb	SOFTLY SOFTLY Ruby Murray (Columbia)	3
11 Mar	GIVE ME YOUR WORD Tennessee Ernie Ford (Capitol)	7
29 Apr	CHERRY PINK AND APPLE BLOSSOM WHITE Perez Prado (HMV)	2
13 May	STRANGER IN PARADISE Tony Bennett (Philips)	2
27 May	CHERRY PINK AND APPLE BLOSSOM WHITE Eddie Calvert (Columbia)	4
24 Jun	UNCHAINED MELODY Jimmy Young (Decca) ..	3
15 Jul	DREAMBOAT Alma Cogan (HMV)	2
29 Jul	ROSE MARIE Slim Whitman (London)	11
14 Oct	THE MAN FROM LARAMIE Jimmy Young (Decca)	4
11 Nov	HERNANDO'S HIDEAWAY Johnston Brothers (Decca)	2
25 Nov	ROCK AROUND THE CLOCK Bill Haley and his Comets (Brunswick)	3
16 Dec	THE CHRISTMAS ALPHABET Dickie Valentine (Decca)	3

On 30 Dec 1955 the chart was extended to 25 records for one week only.

· 1 9 5 6 ·

6 Jan	ROCK AROUND THE CLOCK Bill Haley and his Comets (Brunswick)	2
20 Jan	SIXTEEN TONS Tennessee Ernie Ford (Capitol) ...	4
17 Feb	MEMORIES ARE MADE OF THIS Dean Martin (Capitol)	4
16 Mar	IT'S ALMOST TOMORROW Dreamweavers (Brunswick)	2
30 Mar	ROCK AND ROLL WALTZ Kay Starr (HMV)	1
6 Apr	IT'S ALMOST TOMORROW Dreamweavers (Brunswick)	1

Top Thirty began 13 Apr 1956.

13 Apr	POOR PEOPLE OF PARIS Winifred Atwell (Decca)	3

4	May	NO OTHER LOVE Ronnie Hilton (HMV)	6
15	Jun	I'LL BE HOME Pat Boone (London)	5
20	Jul	WHY DO FOOLS FALL IN LOVE Teenagers featuring Frankie Lymon (Columbia)	3
10	Aug	WHATEVER WILL BE WILL BE Doris Day (Philips)	6
21	Sep	LAY DOWN YOUR ARMS Anne Shelton (Philips)	4
19	Oct	A WOMAN IN LOVE Frankie Laine (Philips)	4
16	Nov	JUST WALKIN' IN THE RAIN Johnnie Ray (Philips)	7

· 1 9 5 7 ·

4	Jan	SINGING THE BLUES Guy Mitchell (Philips)	1
11	Jan	SINGING THE BLUES Tommy Steele (Decca)	1
18	Jan	SINGING THE BLUES Guy Mitchell (Philips)	1
25	Jan	GARDEN OF EDEN Frankie Vaughan (Philips) ..... (SINGING THE BLUES by Guy Mitchell returned to number one for one week to share the top spot with GARDEN OF EDEN by Frankie Vaughan on 1 Feb 1957)	4
22	Feb	YOUNG LOVE Tab Hunter (London)	7
12	Apr	CUMBERLAND GAP Lonnie Donegan (Pye Nixa)	5
17	May	ROCK-A-BILLY Guy Mitchell (Philips)	1
24	May	BUTTERFLY Andy Williams (London)	2
7	Jun	YES TONIGHT JOSEPHINE Johnnie Ray (Philips)	3
28	Jun	GAMBLIN' MAN/PUTTING ON THE STYLE Lonnie Donegan (Pye Nixa)	2
12	Jul	ALL SHOOK UP Elvis Presley (HMV)	7
30	Aug	DIANA Paul Anka (Columbia)	9
1	Nov	THAT'LL BE THE DAY Crickets (Vogue-Coral) ...	3
22	Nov	MARY'S BOY CHILD Harry Belafonte (RCA)	7

· 1 9 5 8 ·

10	Jan	GREAT BALLS OF FIRE Jerry Lee Lewis (London)	2
24	Jan	JAILHOUSE ROCK Elvis Presley (RCA)	3
14	Feb	THE STORY OF MY LIFE Michael Holliday (Columbia)	2
28	Feb	MAGIC MOMENTS Perry Como (RCA)	8
25	Apr	WHOLE LOTTA WOMAN Marvin Rainwater (MGM)	3
16	May	WHO'S SORRY NOW Connie Francis (MGM) ...	6
27	Jun	ON THE STREET WHERE YOU LIVE Vic Damone (Philips) (On 4 Jul 1958 ON THE STREET WHERE YOU LIVE by Vic Damone and ALL I HAVE TO DO IS DREAM/CLAUDETTE by the Everly Brothers shared the top spot)	2
4	Jul	ALL I HAVE TO DO IS DREAM/CLAUDETTE Everly Brothers (London)	7
22	Aug	WHEN Kalin Twins (Brunswick)	5
26	Sep	CAROLINA MOON/STUPID CUPID Connie Francis (MGM)	6

7	Nov	IT'S ALL IN THE GAME Tommy Edwards (MGM)	3
28	Nov	HOOTS MON Lord Rockingham's XI (Decca)	3
19	Dec	IT'S ONLY MAKE BELIEVE Conway Twitty (MGM)	5

· 1 9 5 9 ·

23	Jan	THE DAY THE RAINS CAME Jane Morgan (London)	1
30	Jan	ONE NIGHT/I GOT STUNG Elvis Presley (RCA)	3
20	Feb	AS I LOVE YOU Shirley Bassey (Philips)	4
20	Mar	SMOKE GETS IN YOUR EYES Platters (Mercury)	1
27	Mar	SIDE SADDLE Russ Conway (Columbia)	4
24	Apr	IT DOESN'T MATTER ANYMORE Buddy Holly (Coral)	3
15	May	A FOOL SUCH AS I/I NEED YOUR LOVE TONIGHT Elvis Presley (RCA)	5
19	Jun	ROULETTE Russ Conway (Columbia)	2
3	Jul	DREAM LOVER Bobby Darin (London)	4
31	Jul	LIVING DOLL Cliff Richard and the Drifters (Columbia)	6
11	Sep	ONLY SIXTEEN Craig Douglas (Top Rank)	4
9	Oct	HERE COMES SUMMER Jerry Keller (London)	1
16	Oct	MACK THE KNIFE Bobby Darin (London)	2
30	Oct	TRAVELLIN' LIGHT Cliff Richard and the Shadows (Columbia)	5
4	Dec	WHAT DO YOU WANT Adam Faith (Parlophone) .... (On 18 Dec 1959 WHAT DO YOU WANT by Adam Faith and WHAT DO YOU WANT TO MAKE THOSE EYES AT ME FOR by Emile Ford and the Checkmates shared the top spot)	3
18	Dec	WHAT DO YOU WANT TO MAKE THOSE EYES AT ME FOR Emile Ford and the Checkmates	6

· 1 9 6 0 ·

| 29 | Jan | STARRY EYED Michael Holliday (Columbia) .... | 1 |
| 5 | Feb | WHY Anthony Newley (Decca) .... | 4 |

Record Retailer, now *Music and Video Week*, **began publication of a Top Fifty on 10 Mar 1960. From this point on their charts are used. The final** *New Musical Express* **chart used is that of 26 Feb 1960, as the chart published in** *Record Retailer* **on 10 Mar 1960 was dated 5 Mar and clearly corresponded with the** *NME* **chart of 4 Mar 1960.**

10	Mar	POOR ME Adam Faith (Parlophone)	1
17	Mar	RUNNING BEAR Johnny Preston (Mercury)	2
31	Mar	MY OLD MAN'S A DUSTMAN Lonnie Donegan (Pye)	4
28	Apr	DO YOU MIND Anthony Newley (Decca)	1
5	May	CATHY'S CLOWN Everly Brothers (Warner Brothers)	7

23 Jun	THREE STEPS TO HEAVEN Eddie Cochran (London)	2
7 Jul	GOOD TIMIN' Jimmy Jones (MGM)	3
28 Jul	PLEASE DON'T TEASE Cliff Richard and the Shadows (Columbia)	2
4 Aug	SHAKIN' ALL OVER Johnny Kidd and the Pirates (HMV)	1
11 Aug	PLEASE DON'T TEASE Cliff Richard and the Shadows (Columbia)	5
25 Aug	APACHE Shadows (Columbia)	5
29 Sep	TELL LAURA I LOVE HER Ricky Valance (Columbia)	3
20 Oct	ONLY THE LONELY Roy Orbison (London)	2
3 Nov	IT'S NOW OR NEVER Elvis Presley (RCA)	8
29 Dec	I LOVE YOU Cliff Richard and the Shadows (Columbia)	2

· 1 9 6 1 ·

12 Jan	POETRY IN MOTION Johnny Tillotson (London)	2
26 Jan	ARE YOU LONESOME TONIGHT Elvis Presley (RCA)	4
23 Feb	SAILOR Petula Clark (Pye)	1
2 Mar	WALK RIGHT BACK/EBONY EYES Everly Brothers (Warner Brothers)	3
23 Mar	WOODEN HEART Elvis Presley (RCA)	6
4 May	BLUE MOON Marcels (Pye International)	2
18 May	ON THE REBOUND Floyd Cramer (RCA)	1
25 May	YOU'RE DRIVING ME CRAZY Temperance Seven (Parlophone)	1
1 Jun	SURRENDER Elvis Presley (RCA)	4
29 Jun	RUNAWAY Del Shannon (London)	3
20 Jul	TEMPTATION Everly Brothers (Warner Brothers)	2
3 Aug	WELL I ASK YOU Eden Kane (Decca)	1
10 Aug	YOU DON'T KNOW Helen Shapiro (Columbia)	3
31 Aug	JOHNNY REMEMBER ME John Leyton (Top Rank)	3
21 Sep	REACH FOR THE STARS/CLIMB EV'RY MOUNTAIN Shirley Bassey (Columbia)	1
28 Sep	JOHNNY REMEMBER ME John Leyton (Top Rank)	1
5 Oct	KON-TIKI Shadows (Columbia)	1
12 Oct	MICHAEL Highwaymen (HMV)	1
19 Oct	WALKIN' BACK TO HAPPINESS Helen Shapiro (Columbia)	3
9 Nov	LITTLE SISTER/HIS LATEST FLAME Elvis Presley (RCA)	4
7 Dec	TOWER OF STRENGTH Frankie Vaughan (Philips)	3
28 Dec	MOON RIVER Danny Williams (HMV)	2

· 1 9 6 2 ·

11 Jan	THE YOUNG ONES Cliff Richard and the Shadows (Columbia)	6

22 Feb	ROCK-A-HULA BABY/CAN'T HELP FALLING IN LOVE Elvis Presley (RCA)	4
22 Mar	WONDERFUL LAND Shadows (Columbia)	8
17 May	NUT ROCKER B. Bumble and the Stingers (Top Rank)	1
24 May	GOOD LUCK CHARM Elvis Presley (RCA)	5
28 Jun	COME OUTSIDE Mike Sarne with Wendy Richard (Parlophone)	2
12 Jul	I CAN'T STOP LOVING YOU Ray Charles (HMV)	2
26 Jul	I REMEMBER YOU Frank Ifield (Columbia)	7
13 Sep	SHE'S NOT YOU Elvis Presley (RCA)	3
4 Oct	TELSTAR Tornados (Decca)	5
8 Nov	LOVESICK BLUES Frank Ifield (Columbia)	5
13 Dec	RETURN TO SENDER Elvis Presley (RCA)	3

· 1 9 6 3 ·

3 Jan	THE NEXT TIME/BACHELOR BOY Cliff Richard and the Shadows (Columbia)	3
24 Jan	DANCE ON Shadows (Columbia)	1
31 Jan	DIAMONDS Jet Harris and Tony Meehan (Decca)	3
21 Feb	WAYWARD WIND Frank Ifield (Columbia)	3
14 Mar	SUMMER HOLIDAY Cliff Richard and the Shadows (Columbia)	2
28 Mar	FOOT TAPPER Shadows (Columbia)	1
4 Apr	SUMMER HOLIDAY Cliff Richard and the Shadows (Columbia)	1
11 Apr	HOW DO YOU DO IT Gerry and the Pacemakers (Columbia)	3
2 May	FROM ME TO YOU Beatles (Parlophone)	7
20 Jun	I LIKE IT Gerry and the Pacemakers (Columbia)	4
18 Jul	CONFESSIN' Frank Ifield (Columbia)	2
1 Aug	(YOU'RE THE) DEVIL IN DISGUISE Elvis Presley (RCA)	1
8 Aug	SWEETS FOR MY SWEET Searchers (Pye)	2
22 Aug	BAD TO ME Billy J. Kramer and the Dakotas (Parlophone)	3
12 Sep	SHE LOVES YOU Beatles (Parlophone)	4
10 Oct	DO YOU LOVE ME Brian Poole and the Tremeloes (Decca)	3
31 Oct	YOU'LL NEVER WALK ALONE Gerry and the Pacemakers (Columbia)	4
28 Nov	SHE LOVES YOU Beatles (Parlophone)	2
12 Dec	I WANT TO HOLD YOUR HAND Beatles (Parlophone)	5

· 1 9 6 4 ·

16 Jan	GLAD ALL OVER Dave Clark Five (Columbia)	2
30 Jan	NEEDLES AND PINS Searchers (Pye)	3
20 Feb	DIANE Bachelors (Decca)	1
27 Feb	ANYONE WHO HAD A HEART Cilla Black (Parlophone)	3
19 Mar	LITTLE CHILDREN Billy J. Kramer and the Dakotas (Parlophone)	2
2 Apr	CAN'T BUY ME LOVE Beatles (Parlophone)	3

23 Apr WORLD WITHOUT LOVE
Peter and Gordon (Columbia) 2

7 May DON'T THROW YOUR LOVE AWAY
Searchers (Pye) 2

21 May JULIET Four Pennies (Philips) 1
28 May YOU'RE MY WORLD Cilla Black (Parlophone) ... 4
25 Jun IT'S OVER Roy Orbison (London) 2
9 Jul HOUSE OF THE RISING SUN
Animals (Columbia) 1

16 Jul IT'S ALL OVER NOW Rolling Stones (Decca) 1
23 Jul A HARD DAY'S NIGHT Beatles (Parlophone) 3
13 Aug DO WAH DIDDY DIDDY
Manfred Mann (HMV) 2

27 Aug HAVE I THE RIGHT Honeycombs (Pye) 2
10 Sep YOU REALLY GOT ME Kinks (Pye) 2
24 Sep I'M INTO SOMETHING GOOD
Hermans's Hermits (Columbia) 2

8 Oct OH PRETTY WOMAN Roy Orbison (London) 2
22 Oct (THERE'S) ALWAYS SOMETHING THERE
TO REMIND ME Sandie Shaw (Pye) 3

12 Nov OH PRETTY WOMAN Roy Orbison (London) 1
19 Nov BABY LOVE Supremes (Stateside) 2
3 Dec LITTLE RED ROOSTER Rolling Stones (Decca) ... 1
10 Dec I FEEL FINE Beatles (Parlophone) 5

· 1 9 6 5 ·

14 Jan YEH YEH
Georgie Fame with the Blue Flames (Columbia) 2

28 Jan GO NOW Moody Blues (Decca) 1
4 Feb YOU'VE LOST THAT LOVIN' FEELIN'
Righteous Brothers (London) 2

18 Feb TIRED OF WAITING FOR YOU Kinks (Pye) 1
25 Feb I'LL NEVER FIND ANOTHER YOU
Seekers (Columbia) 2

11 Mar IT'S NOT UNUSUAL Tom Jones (Decca) 1
18 Mar THE LAST TIME Rolling Stones (Decca) 3
8 Apr CONCRETE AND CLAY
Unit Four Plus Two (Decca) 1

15 Apr THE MINUTE YOU'RE GONE
Cliff Richard (Columbia) 1

22 Apr TICKET TO RIDE Beatles (Parlophone) 3
13 May KING OF THE ROAD Roger Miller (Philips) 1
20 May WHERE ARE YOU NOW (MY LOVE)
Jackie Trent (Pye) 1

27 May LONG LIVE LOVE Sandie Shaw (Pye) 3
17 Jun CRYING IN THE CHAPEL Elvis Presley (RCA) .. 1
24 Jun I'M ALIVE Hollies (Parlophone) 1
1 Jul CRYING IN THE CHAPEL Elvis Presley (RCA) .. 1
8 Jul I'M ALIVE Hollies (Parlophone) 2
22 Jul MR. TAMBOURINE MAN Byrds (CBS) 2
5 Aug HELP! Beatles (Parlophone) 3
26 Aug I GOT YOU BABE Sonny and Cher (Atlantic) 2
9 Sep (I CAN'T GET NO) SATISFACTION
Rolling Stones (Decca) 2

23 Sep MAKE IT EASY ON YOURSELF
Walker Brothers (Philips) 1

30 Sep TEARS Ken Dodd (Columbia) 5
4 Nov GET OFF OF MY CLOUD
Rolling Stones (Decca) 3

25 Nov THE CARNIVAL IS OVER Seekers (Columbia) 3
16 Dec DAY TRIPPER/WE CAN WORK IT OUT
Beatles (Parlophone) 5

· 1 9 6 6 ·

20 Jan KEEP ON RUNNING
Spencer Davis Group (Fontana) 1

27 Jan MICHELLE Overlanders (Pye) 3
17 Feb THESE BOOTS ARE MADE FOR WALKIN'
Nancy Sinatra (Reprise) 4

17 Mar THE SUN AIN'T GONNA SHINE ANYMORE
Walker Brothers (Philips) 4

14 Apr SOMEBODY HELP ME
Spencer Davis Group (Fontana) 2

28 Apr YOU DON'T HAVE TO SAY YOU LOVE ME
Dusty Springfield (Philips) 1

5 May PRETTY FLAMINGO Manfred Mann (HMV) 3
26 May PAINT IT, BLACK Rolling Stones (Decca) 1
2 Jun STRANGERS IN THE NIGHT
Frank Sinatra (Reprise) 3

23 Jun PAPERBACK WRITER Beatles (Parlophone) 2
7 Jul SUNNY AFTERNOON Kinks (Pye) 2
21 Jul GET AWAY
Georgie Fame with the Blue Flames (Columbia) 1

28 Jul OUT OF TIME
Chris Farlowe and the Thunderbirds (Immediate) 1

4 Aug WITH A GIRL LIKE YOU Troggs (Fontana) 2
18 Aug YELLOW SUBMARINE/ELEANOR RIGBY
Beatles (Parlophone) 4

15 Sep ALL OR NOTHING Small Faces (Decca) 1
22 Sep DISTANT DRUMS Jim Reeves (RCA) 5
27 Oct REACH OUT I'LL BE THERE
Four Tops (Tamla Motown) 3

17 Nov GOOD VIBRATIONS Beach Boys (Capitol) 2
1 Dec GREEN GREEN GRASS OF HOME
Tom Jones (Decca) 7

· 1 9 6 7 ·

19 Jan I'M A BELIEVER Monkees (RCA) 4
16 Feb THIS IS MY SONG Petula Clark (Pye) 2
2 Mar RELEASE ME Engelbert Humperdinck (Decca) 6
13 Apr SOMETHIN' STUPID
Nancy Sinatra and Frank Sinatra (Reprise) 2

27 Apr PUPPET ON A STRING Sandie Shaw (Pye) 3
18 May SILENCE IS GOLDEN Tremeloes (CBS) 3
8 Jun A WHITER SHADE OF PALE
Procol Harum (Deram) 6

19 Jul ALL YOU NEED IS LOVE Beatles (Parlophone) ... 3
9 Aug SAN FRANCISCO (BE SURE TO WEAR SOME
FLOWERS IN YOUR HAIR)
Scott McKenzie (CBS) 4

6 Sep THE LAST WALTZ
Engelbert Humperdinck (Decca) 5

11 Oct MASSACHUSETTS Bee Gees (Polydor) 4
8 Nov BABY NOW THAT I'VE FOUND YOU
Foundations (Pye) 2

22 Nov	LET THE HEARTACHES BEGIN		
	Long John Baldry (Pye)	2
6 Dec	HELLO GOODBYE Beatles (Parlophone)	7

· 1 9 6 8 ·

24 Jan	THE BALLAD OF BONNIE AND CLYDE	
	Georgie Fame (CBS)	1
31 Jan	EVERLASTING LOVE Love Affair (CBS)	2
14 Feb	MIGHTY QUINN Manfred Mann (Fontana)	2
28 Feb	CINDERELLA ROCKEFELLA	
	Esther and Abi Ofarim (Philips)	3
20 Mar	THE LEGEND OF XANADU	
	Dave Dee, Dozy, Beaky, Mick and Tich (Fontana)	1
27 Mar	LADY MADONNA Beatles (Parlophone)	2
10 Apr	CONGRATULATIONS	
	Cliff Richard (Columbia)	2
24 Apr	WHAT A WONDERFUL WORLD/CABARET	
	Louis Armstrong (HMV)	4
22 May	YOUNG GIRL	
	Union Gap featuring Gary Puckett (CBS)	4
19 Jun	JUMPIN' JACK FLASH Rolling Stones (Decca)	2
3 Jul	BABY COME BACK Equals (President)	3
24 Jul	I PRETEND Des O'Connor (Columbia)	1
31 Jul	MONY MONY	
	Tommy James and the Shondells (Major Minor)	2
14 Aug	FIRE Crazy World of Arthur Brown (Track)	1
21 Aug	MONY MONY	
	Tommy James and the Shondells (Major Minor)	1
28 Aug	DO IT AGAIN Beach Boys (Capitol)	1
4 Sep	I'VE GOTTA GET A MESSAGE TO YOU	
	Bee Gees (Polydor)	1
11 Sep	HEY JUDE Beatles (Apple)	2
25 Sep	THOSE WERE THE DAYS	
	Mary Hopkin (Apple)	6
6 Nov	WITH A LITTLE HELP FROM MY FRIENDS	
	Joe Cocker (Regal-Zonophone)	1
13 Nov	THE GOOD THE BAD AND THE UGLY	
	Hugo Montenegro and his Orchestra	
	and Chorus (RCA)	4
11 Dec	LILY THE PINK Scaffold (Parlophone)	3

· 1 9 6 9 ·

1 Jan	OB-LA-DI OB-LA-DA Marmalade (CBS)	1
8 Jan	LILY THE PINK Scaffold (Parlophone)	1
15 Jan	OB-LA-DI OB-LA-DA Marmalade (CBS)	2
29 Jan	ALBATROSS Fleetwood Mac (Blue Horizon)	1
5 Feb	BLACKBERRY WAY	
	Move (Regal-Zonophone)	1
12 Feb	(IF PARADISE IS) HALF AS NICE	
	Amen Corner (Immediate)	2
26 Feb	WHERE DO YOU GO TO MY LOVELY	
	Peter Sarstedt (United Artists)	4
26 Mar	I HEARD IT THROUGH THE GRAPEVINE	
	Marvin Gaye (Tamla Motown)	3
16 Apr	THE ISRAELITES	
	Desmond Dekker and the Aces (Pyramid)	1

23 Apr	GET BACK Beatles (Apple)	6
4 Jun	DIZZY Tommy Roe (Stateside)	1
11 Jun	THE BALLAD OF JOHN AND YOKO	
	Beatles (Apple)	3
2 Jul	SOMETHING IN THE AIR	
	Thunderclap Newman (Track)	3
23 Jul	HONKY TONK WOMEN	
	Rolling Stones (Decca)	5
30 Aug	IN THE YEAR 2525 (EXORDIUM AND	
	TERMINUS) Zager and Evans (RCA)	3
20 Sep	BAD MOON RISING	
	Creedence Clearwater Revival (Liberty)	3
11 Oct	JE T'AIME...MOI NON PLUS	
	Jane Birkin and Serge Gainsbourg (Major Minor)	1
18 Oct	I'LL NEVER FALL IN LOVE AGAIN	
	Bobbie Gentry (Capitol)	1
25 Oct	SUGAR SUGAR Archies (RCA)	8
20 Dec	TWO LITTLE BOYS Rolf Harris (Columbia)	6

· 1 9 7 0 ·

31 Jan	LOVE GROWS (WHERE MY ROSEMARY GOES)	
	Edison Lighthouse (Bell)	5
7 Mar	WAND'RIN' STAR Lee Marvin (Paramount)	3
28 Mar	BRIDGE OVER TROUBLED WATER	
	Simon and Garfunkel (CBS)	3
18 Apr	ALL KINDS OF EVERYTHING Dana (Rex)	2
2 May	SPIRIT IN THE SKY	
	Norman Greenbaum (Reprise)	2
16 May	BACK HOME England World Cup Squad (Pye)	3
6 Jun	YELLOW RIVER Christie (CBS)	1
13 Jun	IN THE SUMMERTIME Mungo Jerry (Dawn)	7
1 Aug	THE WONDER OF YOU Elvis Presley (RCA)	6
12 Sep	TEARS OF A CLOWN Smokey Robinson	
	and the Miracles (Tamla Motown)	1
19 Sep	BAND OF GOLD Freda Payne (Invictus)	6
31 Oct	WOODSTOCK	
	Matthews' Southern Comfort (Uni)	3
21 Nov	VOODOO CHILE	
	Jimi Hendrix Experience (Track)	1
28 Nov	I HEAR YOU KNOCKIN'	
	Dave Edmunds (MAM)	6

· 1 9 7 1 ·

9 Jan	GRANDAD Clive Dunn (Columbia)	3
30 Jan	MY SWEET LORD George Harrison (Apple)	5
6 Mar	BABY JUMP Mungo Jerry (Dawn)	2
20 Mar	HOT LOVE T. Rex (Fly)	6
1 May	DOUBLE BARREL	
	Dave and Ansil Collins (Technique)	2
15 May	KNOCK THREE TIMES Dawn (Bell)	5
19 Jun	CHIRPY CHIRPY CHEEP CHEEP	
	Middle Of The Road (RCA)	5
24 Jul	GET IT ON T. Rex (Fly)	4
21 Aug	I'M STILL WAITING	
	Diana Ross (Tamla Motown)	4

18 Sep HEY GIRL DON'T BOTHER ME
Tams (Probe) 3

9 Oct MAGGIE MAY Rod Stewart (Mercury) 5

13 Nov COZ I LUV YOU Slade (Polydor) 4

11 Dec ERNIE (THE FASTEST MILKMAN IN THE WEST)
Benny Hill (Columbia) 4

· 1 9 7 2 ·

8 Jan I'D LIKE TO TEACH THE WORLD TO SING
New Seekers (Polydor) 4

5 Feb TELEGRAM SAM T. Rex (T. Rex) 2

19 Feb SON OF MY FATHER Chicory Tip (CBS) 3

11 Mar WITHOUT YOU Nilsson (RCA) 5

15 Apr AMAZING GRACE
Pipes and Drums and Military Band of the
Royal Scots Dragoon Guards (RCA) 5

20 May METAL GURU T. Rex (EMI) 4

17 Jun VINCENT Don McLean (United Artists) 2

1 Jul TAKE ME BAK 'OME Slade (Polydor) 1

8 Jul PUPPY LOVE Donny Osmond (MGM) 5

12 Aug SCHOOL'S OUT
Alice Cooper (Warner Brothers) 3

2 Sep YOU WEAR IT WELL Rod Stewart (Mercury) 1

9 Sep MAMA WEER ALL CRAZEE NOW
Slade (Polydor) 3

30 Sep HOW CAN I BE SURE David Cassidy (Bell) 2

14 Oct MOULDY OLD DOUGH
Lieutenant Pigeon (Decca) 4

11 Nov CLAIR Gilbert O'Sullivan (MAM) 2

25 Nov MY DING-A-LING Chuck Berry (Chess) 4

23 Dec LONG HAIRED LOVER FROM LIVERPOOL
Little Jimmy Osmond (MGM) 5

· 1 9 7 3 ·

27 Jan BLOCKBUSTER Sweet (RCA) 5

3 Mar CUM ON FEEL THE NOIZE
Slade (Polydor) 4

31 Mar THE TWELFTH OF NEVER
Donny Osmond (MGM) 1

7 Apr GET DOWN Gilbert O'Sullivan (MAM) 2

21 Apr TIE A YELLOW RIBBON ROUND THE
OLD OAK TREE
Dawn featuring Tony Orlando (Bell) 4

19 May SEE MY BABY JIVE Wizzard (Harvest) 4

16 Jun CAN THE CAN Suzi Quatro (RAK) 1

23 Jun RUBBER BULLETS 10 C.C. (UK) 1

20 Jun SKWEEZE ME PLEEZE ME Slade (Polydor) 3

21 Jul WELCOME HOME Peters and Lee (Philips) 1

28 Jul I'M THE LEADER OF THE GANG (I AM)
Gary Glitter (Bell) 4

25 Aug YOUNG LOVE Donny Osmond (MGM) 4

22 Sep ANGEL FINGERS Wizzard (Harvest) 1

29 Sep EYE LEVEL Simon Park Orchestra (Columbia) 4

27 Oct DAYDREAMER/THE PUPPY SONG
David Cassidy (Bell) 3

17 Nov I LOVE YOU LOVE ME LOVE
Gary Glitter (Bell) 4

15 Dec MERRY XMAS EVERYBODY
Slade (Polydor) 5

· 1 9 7 4 ·

19 Jan YOU WON'T FIND ANOTHER FOOL LIKE ME
New Seekers (Polydor) 1

26 Jan TIGER FEET Mud (RAK) 4

23 Feb DEVIL GATE DRIVE Suzi Quatro (RAK) 2

9 Mar JEALOUS MIND Alvin Stardust (Magnet) 1

16 Mar BILLY DON'T BE A HERO
Paper Lace (Bus Stop) 3

6 Apr SEASONS IN THE SUN Terry Jacks (Bell) 4

4 May WATERLOO Abba (Epic) 2

18 May SUGAR BABY LOVE Rubettes (Polydor) 4

15 Jun THE STREAK Ray Stevens (Janus) 1

22 Jun ALWAYS YOURS Gary Glitter (Bell) 1

29 Jun SHE Charles Aznavour (Barclay) 4

27 Jul ROCK YOUR BABY
George McCrae (Jayboy) 3

17 Aug WHEN WILL I SEE YOU AGAIN
Three Degrees (Philadelphia International) 2

31 Aug LOVE ME FOR A REASON
Osmonds (MGM) 3

21 Sep KUNG FU FIGHTING Carl Douglas (Pye) 3

12 Oct ANNIE'S SONG John Denver (RCA) 1

19 Oct SAD SWEET DREAMER
Sweet Sensation (Pye) 1

26 Oct EVERYTHING I OWN Ken Boothe (Trojan) 3

16 Nov GONNA MAKE YOU A STAR
David Essex (CBS) 3

7 Dec YOU'RE THE FIRST THE LAST MY
EVERYTHING Barry White (20th Century) 2

21 Dec LONELY THIS CHRISTMAS Mud (RAK) 4

· 1 9 7 5 ·

18 Jan DOWN DOWN Status Quo (Vertigo) 1

25 Jan MS. GRACE Tymes (RCA) 1

1 Feb JANUARY Pilot (EMI) 3

22 Feb MAKE ME SMILE (COME UP AND SEE ME)
Steve Harley and Cockney Rebel (EMI) 2

8 Mar IF Telly Savalas (MCA) 2

22 Mar BYE BYE BABY Bay City Rollers (Bell) 6

3 May OH BOY Mud (RAK) 2

17 May STAND BY YOUR MAN
Tammy Wynette (Epic) 3

7 Jun WHISPERING GRASS
Windsor Davies and Don Estelle (EMI) 3

28 Jun I'M NOT IN LOVE 10 C.C. (Mercury) 2

12 Jul TEARS ON MY PILLOW Johnny Nash (CBS) 1

19 Jul GIVE A LITTLE LOVE Bay City Rollers (Bell) 3

9 Aug BARBADOS Typically Tropical (Gull) 1

16 Aug I CAN'T GIVE YOU ANYTHING
(BUT MY LOVE) Stylistics (Avco) 3

6	Sep	SAILING Rod Stewart (Warner Brothers)	4
4	Oct	HOLD ME CLOSE David Essex (CBS)	3
25	Oct	I ONLY HAVE EYES FOR YOU	
		Art Garfunkel (CBS)	2
8	Nov	SPACE ODDITY David Bowie (RCA)	2
22	Nov	D.I.V.O.R.C.E. Billy Connolly (Polydor)	1
29	Nov	BOHEMIAN RHAPSODY Queen (EMI)	9

· 1 9 7 6 ·

31	Jan	MAMMA MIA Abba (Epic)	2
14	Feb	FOREVER AND EVER Slik (Bell)	1
21	Feb	DECEMBER '63 (OH WHAT A NIGHT)	
		Four Seasons (Warner Brothers)	2
6	Mar	I LOVE TO LOVE (BUT MY BABY LOVES	
		TO DANCE) Tina Charles (CBS)	3
27	Mar	SAVE YOUR KISSES FOR ME	
		Brotherhood Of Man (Pye)	6
8	May	FERNANDO Abba (Epic)	4
5	Jun	NO CHARGE J.J. Barrie (Power Exchange)	1
12	Jun	COMBINE HARVESTER (BRAND NEW KEY)	
		Wurzels (EMI)	2
26	Jun	YOU TO ME ARE EVERYTHING	
		Real Thing (Pye International)	3
17	Jul	THE ROUSSOS PHENOMENON (EP)	
		Demis Roussos (Philips)	1
24	Jul	DON'T GO BREAKING MY HEART	
		Elton John and Kiki Dee (Rocket)	6
4	Sep	DANCING QUEEN Abba (Epic)	6
16	Oct	MISSISSIPPI Pussycat (Sonet)	4
13	Nov	IF YOU LEAVE ME NOW Chicago (CBS)	3
4	Dec	UNDER THE MOON OF LOVE	
		Showaddywaddy (Bell)	3
25	Dec	WHEN A CHILD IS BORN (SOLEADO)	
		Johnny Mathis (CBS)	3

· 1 9 7 7 ·

15	Jan	DON'T GIVE UP ON US	
		David Soul (Private Stock)	4
12	Feb	DON'T CRY FOR ME ARGENTINA	
		Julie Covington (MCA)	1
19	Feb	WHEN I NEED YOU Leo Sayer (Chrysalis)	3
12	Mar	CHANSON D'AMOUR	
		Manhattan Transfer (Atlantic)	3
2	Apr	KNOWING ME KNOWING YOU Abba (Epic)	5
7	May	FREE Deniece Williams (CBS)	2
21	May	I DON'T WANT TO TALK ABOUT IT/	
		FIRST CUT IS THE DEEPEST	
		Rod Stewart (Riva)	4
18	Jun	LUCILLE Kenny Rogers (United Artists)	1
25	Jun	SHOW YOU THE WAY TO GO	
		Jacksons (Epic)	1
2	Jul	SO YOU WIN AGAIN Hot Chocolate (RAK)	3
23	Jul	I FEEL LOVE Donna Summer (GTO)	4
20	Aug	ANGELO Brotherhood Of Man (Pye)	1
27	Aug	FLOAT ON Floaters (ABC)	1

3	Sep	WAY DOWN Elvis Presley (RCA)	5
8	Oct	SILVER LADY David Soul (Private Stock)	3
29	Oct	YES SIR I CAN BOOGIE Baccara (RCA)	1
5	Nov	NAME OF THE GAME Abba (Epic)	4
3	Dec	MULL OF KINTYRE/GIRLS' SCHOOL	
		Wings (Capitol)	9

· 1 9 7 8 ·

4	Feb	UP TOWN TOP RANKING	
		Althia and Donna (Lightning)	1
11	Feb	FIGARO Brotherhood Of Man (Pye)	1
18	Feb	TAKE A CHANCE ON ME Abba (Epic)	3
11	Mar	WUTHERING HEIGHTS Kate Bush (EMI)	4
8	Apr	MATCHSTALK MEN AND MATCHSTALK	
		CATS AND DOGS Brian and Michael (Pye)	3
29	Apr	NIGHT FEVER Bee Gees (RSO)	2

Top 75 began 6 May 1978.

13	May	RIVERS OF BABYLON	
		Boney M (Atlantic/Hansa)	5
17	Jun	YOU'RE THE ONE THAT I WANT	
		John Travolta and Olivia Newton-John (RSO)	9
19	Aug	THREE TIMES A LADY	
		Commodores (Motown)	5
23	Sep	DREADLOCK HOLIDAY 10 C.C. (Mercury)	1
30	Sep	SUMMER NIGHTS	
		John Travolta and Olivia Newton-John (RSO)	7
18	Nov	RAT TRAP Boomtown Rats (Ensign)	2
2	Dec	DA YA THINK I'M SEXY	
		Rod Stewart (Riva)	1
9	Dec	MARY'S BOY CHILD – OH MY LORD	
		Boney M (Atlantic/Hansa)	4

· 1 9 7 9 ·

6	Jan	Y.M.C.A. Village People (Mercury)	3
27	Jan	HIT ME WITH YOUR RHYTHM STICK	
		Ian and the Blockheads (Stiff)	1
3	Feb	HEART OF GLASS Blondie (Chrysalis)	4
3	Mar	TRAGEDY Bee Gees (RSO)	2
17	Mar	I WILL SURVIVE Gloria Gaynor (Polydor)	4
14	Apr	BRIGHT EYES Art Garfunkel (CBS)	6
26	May	SUNDAY GIRL Blondie (Chrysalis)	3
16	Jun	RING MY BELL Anita Ward (TK)	2
30	Jun	ARE 'FRIENDS' ELECTRIC	
		Tubeway Army (Beggars Banquet)	4
28	Jul	I DON'T LIKE MONDAYS	
		Boomtown Rats (Ensign)	4
25	Aug	WE DON'T TALK ANYMORE	
		Cliff Richard (EMI)	4
22	Sep	CARS Gary Numan (Beggars Banquet)	1
29	Sep	MESSAGE IN A BOTTLE Police (A&M)	3
20	Oct	VIDEO KILLED THE RADIO STAR	
		Buggles (Island)	1
27	Oct	ONE DAY AT A TIME Lena Martell (Pye)	3
17	Nov	WHEN YOU'RE IN LOVE WITH A	
		BEAUTIFUL WOMAN Dr. Hook (Capitol)	3
8	Dec	WALKING ON THE MOON Police (A&M)	1

15 Dec ANOTHER BRICK IN THE WALL (PART II)
Pink Floyd (Harvest) 5

· 1 9 8 0 ·

19 Jan BRASS IN POCKET Pretenders (Real) 2
2 Feb THE SPECIAL A.K.A. LIVE! (EP)
Specials (2 Tone) 2
16 Feb COWARD OF THE COUNTY
Kenny Rogers (United Artists) 2
1 Mar ATOMIC Blondie (Chrysalis) 2
15 Mar TOGETHER WE ARE BEAUTIFUL
Fern Kinney (WEA) 1
22 Mar GOING UNDERGROUND/DREAMS OF
CHILDREN Jam (Polydor) 3
12 Apr WORKING MY WAY BACK TO YOU
Detroit Spinners (Atlantic) 2
26 Apr CALL ME Blondie (Chrysalis) 1
3 May GENO
Dexy's Midnight Runners (Parlophone) 2
17 May WHAT'S ANOTHER YEAR
Johnny Logan (Epic) 2
31 May THEME FROM M*A*S*H
(SUICIDE IS PAINLESS) Mash (CBS) 3
21 Jun CRYING Don McLean (EMI) 3
12 Jul XANADU Olivia Newton-John and
Electric Light Orchestra (Jet) 2
26 Jul USE IT UP AND WEAR IT OUT
Odyssey (RCA) 2
9 Aug THE WINNER TAKES IT ALL Abba (Epic) 2
23 Aug ASHES TO ASHES David Bowie (RCA) 2
6 Sep START Jam (Polydor) 1
13 Sep FEELS LIKE I'M IN LOVE
Kelly Marie (Calibre) 2
27 Sep DON'T STAND SO CLOSE TO ME
Police (A&M) 4
25 Oct WOMAN IN LOVE Barbra Streisand (CBS) 3
15 Nov THE TIDE IS HIGH Blondie (Chrysalis) 2
29 Nov SUPER TROUPER Abba (Epic) 3
20 Dec (JUST LIKE) STARTING OVER
John Lennon (Geffen) 1
27 Dec THERE'S NO ONE QUITE LIKE GRANDMA
St Winifred's School Choir (MFP) 2

· 1 9 8 1 ·

10 Jan IMAGINE John Lennon (Parlophone) 4
7 Feb WOMAN John Lennon (Geffen) 2
21 Feb SHADDAP YOU FACE
Joe Dolce Music Theatre(Epic) 3
14 Mar JEALOUS GUY Roxy Music (EG) 2
28 Mar THIS OLE HOUSE Shakin' Stevens (Epic) 3
18 Apr MAKING YOUR MIND UP Bucks Fizz (RCA) ... 3
9 May STAND AND DELIVER
Adam and the Ants (CBS) 5
13 Jun BEING WITH YOU
Smokey Robinson (Motown) 2

27 Jun ONE DAY IN YOUR LIFE
Michael Jackson (Motown) 2
11 Jul GHOST TOWN Specials (2 Tone) 3
1 Aug GREEN DOOR Shakin' Stevens (Epic) 4
29 Aug JAPANESE BOY Aneka (Hansa/Ariola) 1
5 Sep TAINTED LOVE Soft Cell (Some Bizzare) 2
19 Sep PRINCE CHARMING
Adam and the Ants (CBS) 4
17 Oct IT'S MY PARTY
Dave Stewart with Barbara Gaskin (Broken) 4
14 Nov EVERY LITTLE THING SHE DOES IS MAGIC
Police (A&M) 1
21 Nov UNDER PRESSURE
Queen and David Bowie (EMI) 2
5 Dec BEGIN THE BEGUINE (VOLVER A EMPEZAR)
Julio Iglesias (CBS) 1
12 Dec DON'T YOU WANT ME
Human League (Virgin) 5

· 1 9 8 2 ·

16 Jan THE LAND OF MAKE BELIEVE
Bucks Fizz (RCA) 2
30 Jan OH JULIE Shakin' Stevens (Epic) 1
6 Feb THE MODEL/COMPUTER LOVE
Kraftwerk (EMI) 1
13 Feb A TOWN CALLED MALICE/PRECIOUS
Jam (Polydor) 3
6 Mar THE LION SLEEPS TONIGHT Tight Fit (Jive) 3
27 Mar SEVEN TEARS Goombay Dance Band (Epic) 3
17 Apr MY CAMERA NEVER LIES Bucks Fizz (RCA) ... 1
24 Apr EBONY AND IVORY
Paul McCartney with Stevie Wonder
(Parlophone) 3
15 May A LITTLE PEACE Nicole (CBS) 2
29 May HOUSE OF FUN Madness (Stiff) 2
12 Jun GOODY TWO SHOES Adam Ant (CBS) 2
26 Jun I'VE NEVER BEEN TO ME
Charlene (Motown) 1
3 Jul HAPPY TALK Captain Sensible (A&M) 2
17 Jul FAME Irene Cara (RSO) 3
7 Aug COME ON EILEEN
Dexy's Midnight Runners and the Emerald Express
(Mercury) 4
4 Sep EYE OF THE TIGER Survivor (Scotti Brothers) 4
2 Oct PASS THE DUTCHIE Musical Youth (MCA) 3
23 Oct DO YOU REALLY WANT TO HURT ME
Culture Club (Virgin) 3
13 Nov I DON'T WANNA DANCE Eddy Grant (Ice) 3
4 Dec BEAT SURRENDER Jam (Polydor) 2
18 Dec SAVE YOUR LOVE
Renee and Renato (Hollywood) 4

· 1 9 8 3 ·

15 Jan YOU CAN'T HURRY LOVE
Phil Collins (Virgin) 2
29 Jan DOWN UNDER Men At Work (Epic) 3

Date	Title	Weeks
19 Feb	TOO SHY Kajagoogoo (EMI)	2
5 Mar	BILLIE JEAN Michael Jackson (Epic)	1
12 Mar	TOTAL ECLIPSE OF THE HEART Bonnie Tyler (CBS)	2
26 Mar	IS THERE SOMETHING I SHOULD KNOW Duran Duran (EMI)	2
9 Apr	LET'S DANCE David Bowie (EMI America)	3
30 Apr	TRUE Spandau Ballet (Reformation)	4
28 May	CANDY GIRL New Edition (London)	1
4 Jun	EVERY BREATH YOU TAKE Police (A&M)	4
2 Jul	BABY JANE Rod Stewart (Warner Bros)	3
23 Jul	WHEREVER I LAY MY HAT (THAT'S MY HOME) Paul Young (CBS)	3
13 Aug	GIVE IT UP KC And The Sunshine Band (Epic)	3
3 Sep	RED RED WINE UB40 (DEP International)	3
24 Sep	KARMA CHAMELEON Culture Club (Virgin)	6
5 Nov	UPTOWN GIRL Billy Joel (CBS)	5
10 Dec	ONLY YOU Flying Pickets (10)	5

· 1 9 8 4 ·

Date	Title	Weeks
14 Jan	PIPES OF PEACE Paul McCartney (Parlophone)	2
28 Jan	RELAX Frankie Goes To Hollywood (ZTT)	5
3 Mar	99 RED BALLOONS Nena (Epic)	3
24 Mar	HELLO Lionel Richie (Motown)	6
5 May	THE REFLEX Duran Duran (EMI)	4
2 Jun	WAKE ME UP BEFORE YOU GO GO Wham! (Epic)	2
16 Jun	TWO TRIBES Frankie Goes To Hollywood (ZTT)	9
18 Aug	CARELESS WHISPER George Michael (Epic)	3
8 Sep	I JUST CALLED TO SAY I LOVE YOU Stevie Wonder (Motown)	6
20 Oct	FREEDOM Wham! (Epic)	3
10 Nov	I FEEL FOR YOU Chaka Khan (Warner Bros)	3
1 Dec	I SHOULD HAVE KNOWN BETTER Jim Diamond (A&M)	1
8 Dec	THE POWER OF LOVE Frankie Goes To Hollywood (ZTT)	1
15 Dec	DO THEY KNOW IT'S CHRISTMAS Band Aid (Mercury)	5

· 1 9 8 5 ·

Date	Title	Weeks
19 Jan	I WANT TO KNOW WHAT LOVE IS Foreigner (Atlantic)	3
9 Feb	I KNOW HIM SO WELL Elaine Paige and Barbara Dickson (RCA)	4
9 Mar	YOU SPIN ME ROUND (LIKE A RECORD) Dead Or Alive (Epic)	2
23 Mar	EASY LOVER Philip Bailey (duet with Phil Collins) (CBS)	4
20 Apr	WE ARE THE WORLD USA For Africa (CBS)	2
4 May	MOVE CLOSER Phyllis Nelson (Carrere)	1
11 May	19 Paul Hardcastle (Chrysalis)	5
15 Jun	YOU'LL NEVER WALK ALONE The Crowd (Spartan)	2

Date	Title	Weeks
29 Jun	FRANKIE Sister Sledge (Atlantic)	4
27 Jul	THERE MUST BE AN ANGEL (PLAYING WITH MY HEART) Eurythmics (RCA)	1
3 Aug	INTO THE GROOVE Madonna (Sire)	4
31 Aug	I GOT YOU BABE UB40, guest vocals Chrissie Hynde (DEP International)	1
7 Sep	DANCING IN THE STREET David Bowie and Mick Jagger (EMI America)	4
5 Oct	IF I WAS Midge Ure (Chrysalis)	1
12 Oct	THE POWER OF LOVE Jennifer Rush (CBS)	5
16 Nov	A GOOD HEART Feargal Sharkey (Virgin)	2
30 Nov	I'M YOUR MAN Wham! (Epic)	2
14 Dec	SAVING ALL MY LOVE FOR YOU Whitney Houston (Arista)	2
28 Dec	MERRY CHRISTMAS EVERYONE Shakin' Stevens (Epic)	2

· 1 9 8 6 ·

Date	Title	Weeks
11 Jan	WEST END GIRLS Pet Shop Boys (Parlophone)	2
25 Jan	THE SUN ALWAYS SHINES ON TV A-ha (Warner Bros)	2
8 Feb	WHEN THE GOING GETS TOUGH, THE TOUGH GET GOING Billy Ocean (Jive)	4
8 Mar	CHAIN REACTION Diana Ross (Capitol)	3
29 Mar	LIVING DOLL Cliff Richard and The Young Ones (WEA)	3
19 Apr	A DIFFERENT CORNER George Michael (Epic)	3
10 May	ROCK ME AMADEUS Falco (A&M)	1
17 May	THE CHICKEN SONG Spitting Image (Virgin)	3
7 Jun	SPIRIT IN THE SKY Dr. and The Medics (IRS)	3
28 Jun	THE EDGE OF HEAVEN Wham! (Epic)	2
12 Jul	PAPA DON'T PREACH Madonna (Sire)	3
2 Aug	LADY IN RED Chris de Burgh (A&M)	3
23 Aug	I WANT TO WAKE UP WITH YOU Boris Gardiner (Revue)	3
13 Sep	DON'T LEAVE ME THIS WAY Communards (London)	4
11 Oct	TRUE BLUE Madonna (Sire)	1
18 Oct	EVERY LOSER WINS Nick Berry (BBC)	3
8 Nov	TAKE MY BREATH AWAY Berlin (CBS)	4
6 Dec	THE FINAL COUNTDOWN Europe (Epic)	2
20 Dec	CARAVAN OF LOVE Housemartins (Go! Discs)	1
27 Dec	REET PETITE Jackie Wilson (SMP)	4

· 1 9 8 7 ·

Date	Title	Weeks
24 Jan	JACK YOUR BODY Steve 'Silk' Hurley (DJ International)	2
7 Feb	I KNEW YOU WERE WAITING (FOR ME) Aretha Franklin and George Michael (Epic)	2
21 Feb	STAND BY ME Ben E. King (Atlantic)	3
14 Mar	EVERYTHING I OWN Boy George (Virgin)	2

28 Mar	RESPECTABLE Mel and Kim (Supreme)		1
4 Apr	LET IT BE Ferry Aid (Sun)		3
25 Apr	LA ISLA BONITA Madonna (Sire)		2
9 May	NOTHING'S GONNA STOP US NOW		
	Starship (Grunt)		4
6 Jun	I WANNA DANCE WITH SOMEBODY		
	(WHO LOVES ME)		
	Whitney Houston (Arista)		2
20 Jun	STAR TREKKIN' Firm (Bark)		2
4 Jul	IT'S A SIN Pet Shop Boys (Parlophone)		3
25 Jul	WHO'S THAT GIRL Madonna (Sire)		1
1 Aug	LA BAMBA Los Lobos (Slash)		2
15 Aug	I JUST CAN'T STOP LOVING YOU		
	Michael Jackson with Siedah Garrett (Epic)		2
29 Aug	NEVER GONNA GIVE YOU UP		
	Rick Astley (RCA)		5
3 Oct	PUMP UP THE VOLUME		
	M/A/R/R/S (4AD)		2
17 Oct	YOU WIN AGAIN		
	Bee Gees (Warner Bros)		4
14 Nov	CHINA IN YOU HAND T'Pau (Siren)		5
19 Dec	ALWAYS ON MY MIND		
	Pet Shop Boys (Parlophone)		4

· 1 9 8 8 ·

16 Jan	HEAVEN IS A PLACE ON EARTH		
	Belinda Carlisle (Virgin)		2
30 Jan	I THINK WE'RE ALONE NOW		
	Tiffany (MCA)		3
20 Feb	I SHOULD BE SO LUCKY		
	Kylie Minogue (PWL)		5
26 Mar	DON'T TURN AROUND		
	Aswad (Mango)		2
9 Apr	HEART Pet Shop Boys (Parlophone)		3
30 Apr	THEME FROM S EXPRESS		
	S Express (Rhythm King)		2
14 May	PERFECT Fairground Attraction (RCA)		1
21 May	WITH A LITTLE HELP FROM MY FRIENDS/		
	SHE'S LEAVING HOME Wet Wet Wet/		
	Billy Bragg and Cara Tivey (Childline)		4
18 Jun	DOCTORIN' THE TARDIS		
	Timelords (KLF)		1
25 Jun	I OWE YOU NOTHING Bros (CBS)		2
9 Jul	NOTHING'S GONNA CHANGE MY		
	LOVE FOR YOU Glenn Medeiros (London)		4
6 Aug	THE ONLY WAY IS UP		
	Yazz and the Plastic Population (Big Life)		5
10 Sep	A GROOVY KIND OF LOVE		
	Phil Collins (Virgin)		2
24 Sep	HE AIN'T HEAVY, HE'S MY BROTHER		
	Hollies (EMI)		2
8 Oct	DESIRE U2 (Island)		1
15 Oct	ONE MOMENT IN TIME		
	Whitney Houston (Arista)		2
29 Oct	ORINOCO FLOW Enya (WEA)		3
19 Nov	FIRST TIME Robin Beck (Mercury)		3
10 Dec	MISTLETOE AND WINE		
	Cliff Richard (EMI)		4

· 1 9 8 9 ·

7 Jan	ESPECIALLY FOR YOU		
	Kylie Minogue and Jason Donovan (PWL)		3
28 Jan	SOMETHING'S GOTTEN HOLD OF MY HEART		
	Marc Almond with Gene Pitney (Parlophone)		4
25 Feb	BELFAST CHILD Simple Minds (Virgin)		2
11 Mar	TOO MANY BROKEN HEARTS		
	Jason Donovan (PWL)		2
25 Mar	LIKE A PRAYER Madonna (Sire)		3
15 Apr	ETERNAL FLAME Bangles (CBS)		4
13 May	HAND ON YOUR HEART Kylie Minogue (PWL)		1
20 May	FERRY CROSS THE MERSEY		
	Christians, Holly Johnson, Paul McCartney		
	Gerry Marsden and Stock Aitken Waterman (PWL)		3
10 Jun	SEALED WITH A KISS Jason Donovan (PWL)		2
24 Jun	BACK TO LIFE (HOWEVER DO YOU WANT ME)		
	Soul II Soul featuring Caron Wheeler (10)		4
22 Jul	YOU'LL NEVER STOP ME LOVING YOU		
	Sonia (Chrysalis)		2
5 Aug	SWING THE MOOD Jive Bunny and the		
	Mastermixers (Music Factory Dance)		5
9 Sep	RIDE ON TIME Black Box (deConstruction)		6
21 Oct	THAT'S WHAT I LIKE Jive Bunny and the		
	Mastermixers (Music Factory Dance)		3
11 Nov	ALL AROUND THE WORLD		
	Lisa Stansfield (Arista)		2
25 Nov	YOU GOT IT (THE RIGHT STUFF)		
	New Kids On The Block (CBS)		3
16 Dec	LET'S PARTY Jive Bunny and the		
	Mastermixers (Music Factory Dance)		1
23 Dec	DO THEY KNOW IT'S CHRISTMAS?		
	Band Aid II (PWL/Polydor)		3

· 1 9 9 0 ·

13 Jan	HANGIN' TOUGH New Kids On The Block (CBS)		2
27 Jan	TEARS ON MY PILLOW Kylie Minogue (PWL)		1
3 Feb	NOTHING COMPARES 2 U		
	Sinead O'Connor (Ensign)		4
3 Mar	DUB BE GOOD TO ME		
	Beats International (Go Beat)		4
31 Mar	THE POWER Snap (Arista)		2
14 Apr	VOGUE Madonna (Sire)		4
12 May	KILLER Adamski (MCA)		4
9 Jun	WORLD IN MOTION...		
	Englandneworder (Factory)		2
23 Jun	SACRIFICE/HEALING HANDS		
	Elton John (Rocket)		5
28 Jul	TURTLE POWER Partners In Kryme (SBK)		4
25 Aug	ITSY BITSY TEENY WEENY YELLOW POLKA		
	DOT BIKINI Bombalurina (Carpet)		3
15 Sep	THE JOKER Steve Miller Band (Capitol)		2
29 Sep	SHOW ME HEAVEN Maria McKee (Epic)		4
27 Oct	A LITTLE TIME The Beautiful South (Go! Discs)		1
3 Nov	UNCHAINED MELODY		
	Righteous Brothers (Verve)		4
1 Dec	ICE ICE BABY Vanilla Ice (SBK)		4
29 Dec	SAVIOUR'S DAY Cliff Richard (EMI)		1

17 BEATLES
17 ELVIS PRESLEY
12 CLIFF RICHARD
   (+ 1 with Young Ones)
9 ABBA
8 ROLLING STONES
7 MADONNA
6 SLADE
6 ROD STEWART
5 BEE GEES
5 BLONDIE
5 POLICE
5 SHADOWS *(+ 7 with Cliff Richard)*
4 EVERLY BROTHERS
4 FRANK IFIELD
4 JAM
4 FRANKIE LAINE
4 GUY MITCHELL
4 PET SHOP BOYS
4 SHAKIN' STEVENS
4 T. REX
4 WHAM!
3 ADAM AND THE ANTS/
   ADAM ANT
3 DAVID BOWIE
   (+ 1 with Queen and 1 with Mick Jagger)
3 BROTHERHOOD OF MAN
3 BUCKS FIZZ
3 LONNIE DONEGAN
3 GEORGIE FAME
3 FRANKIE GOES TO HOLLYWOOD
   (Holly Johnson 1 more with Christians, Gerry Marsden, Paul McCartney and Stock Aitken Waterman)
3 GERRY AND THE PACEMAKERS
   (Gerry Marsden 1 more with Christians, Holly Johnson, Paul McCartney and Stock Aitken Waterman)
3 GARY GLITTER
3 WHITNEY HOUSTON
3 MICHAEL JACKSON
   (+ 1 with Jacksons)
3 JIVE BUNNY AND THE
   MASTERMIXERS
3 KINKS
3 JOHN LENNON
3 MANFRED MANN
3 KYLIE MINOGUE
   (+ 1 with Jason Donovan)
3 MUD
3 ROY ORBISON
3 DONNY OSMOND
   (+ 1 with Osmonds)
3 JOHNNIE RAY

3 SANDIE SHAW
3 SEARCHERS
3 10 C.C.

Apart from those listed above, **Phil Collins** has hit the top twice as a soloist, and once more with Philip Bailey. **Jason Donovan** has two solo number ones to his credit, and another in tandem with Kylie Minogue. **Art Garfunkel** has had two solo number ones, and one more with Simon and Garfunkel. **George Michael** has topped the charts twice as a soloist and once with Aretha Franklin, apart from his four chart-toppers with Wham! **Diana Ross** has had two solo number ones and one more with the Supremes, not forgetting her contribution to USA For Africa's success. **Frank Sinatra** has had two solo number one hits, and one in duet with his daughter Nancy.

Boy George has headed the charts twice as lead singer with Culture Club, and once more as a soloist. **Paul McCartney** has topped the charts once as a soloist, once with Stevie Wonder, once as leader of Wings and once with the Christians, Gerry Marsden, Holly Johnson and Stock Aitken Waterman, not to mention his 17 as a Beatle, and his contributions to Band Aid, Ferry Aid and the Crowd. **Midge Ure** first topped the charts as a member of Slik, and went on to co-write, produce and perform with Band Aid, before finally topping the charts as a soloist in 1985.

Olivia Newton-John has had two number ones with John Travolta and one more with Electric Light Orchestra.

By Artist

73 ELVIS PRESLEY
69 BEATLES
   (Paul McCartney 9 more with Wings, 3 more with Stevie Wonder, 3 more with Christians, Holly Johnson, Gerry Marsden and Stock Aitken Waterman and 2 more solo, total 86 weeks. John Lennon 7 more solo, total 76 weeks. George Harrison 5 more solo, total 74 weeks)
40 CLIFF RICHARD
   (+ 3 more with Young Ones)
32 FRANKIE LAINE *(1 week top equal)*
31 ABBA

20 SLADE
19 EVERLY BROTHERS
   (1 week top equal)
18 MADONNA
18 ROLLING STONES
   (Mick Jagger 4 more with David Bowie, total 22 weeks)
18 ROD STEWART
17 FRANK IFIELD
16 SHADOWS
   (+ 28 weeks backing Cliff Richard, total 44 weeks. Hank Marvin 3 more weeks with Cliff and the Young Ones, total 47 weeks)
16 T. REX
16 JOHN TRAVOLTA AND
   OLIVIA NEWTON-JOHN
   (Olivia Newton-John 2 more weeks with Electric Light Orchestra, total 18 weeks)
15 DORIS DAY
15 FRANKIE GOES TO HOLLYWOOD
   (Holly Johnson 3 more weeks with Christians, Gerry Marsden, Paul McCartney and Stock Aitken Waterman, total 18 weeks)
14 GUY MITCHELL *(1 week top equal)*
13 EDDIE CALVERT
13 PERRY COMO
13 BEE GEES
13 POLICE
12 BLONDIE
12 CONNIE FRANCIS
12 PET SHOP BOYS
12 DAVID WHITFIELD *(1 week top equal)*
11 ADAM AND THE ANTS/
   ADAM ANT
11 LONNIE DONEGAN
11 TENNESSEE ERNIE FORD
11 GERRY AND THE PACEMAKERS
   (Gerry Marsden 3 more weeks with Christians, Holly Johnson, Paul McCartney and Stock Aitken Waterman and 2 more weeks as lead vocalist with Crowd, total 16 weeks)
11 ENGELBERT HUMPERDINCK
11 JOHNNIE RAY
11 SLIM WHITMAN
10 MUD
10 DONNY OSMOND
   (+ 3 weeks with Osmonds, total 13 weeks)
10 SHAKIN' STEVENS

George Michael has topped the chart for 17 weeks: 6 solo, 9 with Wham! and 2 with Aretha Franklin, not to mention his contribution to the Band Aid disc. **Queen** have been number one for 9 weeks, plus 2 weeks with **David Bowie**. Bowie has been on top by himself for 7 weeks, plus 4 more with Mick Jagger and 2 with Queen, total 13 weeks. **Art Garfunkel** has been number one for 8 weeks, plus 5 weeks with Simon and Garfunkel. **Mantovani** has been number one for 1 week, plus ten more backing David Whitfield. **Lionel Richie** has had 6 weeks at number one, plus 5 more as one of the Commodores. **Boy George** has also been at the top for 11 weeks, 2 solo and 9 with Culture Club. **Kylie Minogue**'s three solo chart toppers have occupied the number one slot for 7 weeks, and she has a further 3 weeks at the top in duet with Jason Donovan, a total of 10 weeks.

MOST WEEKS AT NUMBER ONE

By an artist in one calendar year

27	FRANKIE LAINE *(1 wk top equal)*	1953
18	ELVIS PRESLEY	1961
16	BEATLES	1963
16	JOHN TRAVOLTA & OLIVIA NEWTON-JOHN	1978
15	ELVIS PRESLEY	1962
15	FRANKIE GOES TO HOLLYWOOD	1984
12	CONNIE FRANCIS	1958
12	FRANK IFIELD	1962
12	BEATLES	1964
12	ABBA	1976

MOST WEEKS AT NUMBER ONE

By one disc, in total

18	I BELIEVE – Frankie Laine	1953
11	ROSE MARIE – Slim Whitman	1955
10	CARA MIA – David Whitfield	1954
9	HERE IN MY HEART – Al Martino	1952-3
9	OH MEIN PAPA – Eddie Calvert	1954
9	SECRET LOVE – Doris Day	1954
9	DIANA – Paul Anka	1957
9	BOHEMIAN RHAPSODY – Queen	1975-6
9	MULL OF KINTYRE/GIRLS' SCHOOL – Wings	1977-8
9	YOU'RE THE ONE THAT I WANT – John Travolta and Olivia Newton-John	1978
9	TWO TRIBES – Frankie Goes To Hollywood	1984

Frankie Laine

MOST WEEKS AT NUMBER ONE

By one disc – consecutive weeks

11	ROSE MARIE – Slim Whitman	1955
10	CARA MIA – David Whitfield	1954
9	HERE IN MY HEART – Al Martino	1952-3
9	I BELIEVE – Frankie Laine	1953
9	OH MEIN PAPA – Eddie Calvert	1954
9	DIANA – Paul Anka	1957
9	BOHEMIAN RHAPSODY – Queen	1975-6
9	MULL OF KINTYRE/GIRLS' SCHOOL – Wings	1977-8
9	YOU'RE THE ONE THAT I WANT – John Travolta and Olivia Newton-John	1978
9	TWO TRIBES – Frankie Goes To Hollywood	1984
8	ANSWER ME – Frankie Laine *(1 week top equal)*	1953-4
8	SECRET LOVE – Doris Day	1954
8	MAGIC MOMENTS – Perry Como	1958
8	IT'S NOW OR NEVER – Elvis Presley	1960
8	WONDERFUL LAND – Shadows	1962
8	SUGAR SUGAR – Archies	1969

Between Stevie Wonder's *I Just Called To Say I Love You* in 1984, and the 1989 Black Box number one, *Ride On Time,* there were 93 chart-toppers, none of which lasted for more than 5 weeks at the peak of the charts.

MOST WEEKS AT NUMBER ONE

By one song

18 weeks	I BELIEVE	
	one version	
11 weeks	MARY'S BOY CHILD	
	two versions	
11 weeks	ROSE MARIE	
	one version	
11 weeks	YOUNG LOVE	
	two versions	
10 weeks	ANSWER ME	
	two versions	

11 in a row:
BEATLES (from *FROM ME TO YOU* through to *YELLOW SUBMARINE/ ELEANOR RIGBY*, 1963 to 1966)
6 in a row:
BEATLES (from *ALL YOU NEED IS LOVE* through to *THE BALLAD OF JOHN AND YOKO*, 1967 to 1969)
5 in a row:
ELVIS PRESLEY (from *LITTLE SISTER/HIS LATEST FLAME* through to *RETURN TO SENDER*, 1961 to 1962)
5 in a row:
ROLLING STONES (from *IT'S ALL OVER NOW* through to *GET OFF OF MY CLOUD*, 1964 to 1965)
4 in a row:
ELVIS PRESLEY (from *IT'S NOW OR NEVER* through to *SURRENDER*, 1960 to 1961) The first number one hat-trick.
4 in a row:
T. REX (from *HOT LOVE* through to *METAL GURU*, 1971 to 1972)
3 in a row:
FRANK IFIELD (*I REMEMBER YOU, LOVESICK BLUES* and *WAYWARD WIND*, 1962 to 1963) The first hat-trick by a British artist.
3 in a row:
GERRY AND THE PACEMAKERS (*HOW DO YOU DO IT, I LIKE IT* and *YOU'LL NEVER WALK ALONE*, 1963)
3 in a row:
ABBA (*MAMMA MIA, FERNANDO* and *DANCING QUEEN*, 1975 to 1976)
3 in a row:
ABBA (*KNOWING ME KNOWING YOU, THE NAME OF THE GAME* and *TAKE A CHANCE ON ME*, 1977 to 1978)
3 in a row:
POLICE (*MESSAGE IN A BOTTLE, WALKING ON THE MOON* and *DON'T STAND SO CLOSE TO ME*, 1979 to 1980)
3 in a row:
BLONDIE (*ATOMIC, CALL ME* and *THE TIDE IS HIGH*, 1980)
3 in a row:
JOHN LENNON (*IMAGINE, (JUST LIKE) STARTING OVER* and *WOMAN*, 1980). Both the fastest and slowest hat-trick depending on whether it started when IMAGINE first entered the chart in November 1975, or when (JUST LIKE)

STARTING OVER came in late in 1980.
3 in a row:
FRANKIE GOES TO HOLLYWOOD (*RELAX!, TWO TRIBES* and *THE POWER OF LOVE*, 1984)
3 in a row:
JIVE BUNNY AND THE MASTER-MIXERS (*SWING THE MOOD, THAT'S WHAT I LIKE* and *LET'S PARTY*, 1989).

Jive Bunny

Successive releases for the purpose of this table are successive official single releases. The Beatles' two runs of number ones were each interrupted by irregular releases. An old single with Tony Sheridan reached number 29 in the midst of their 11 number ones, and their double EP *Magical Mystery Tour* made number two while *Hello Goodbye* was becoming the second of their six chart toppers on the trot. An album track, *Jeepster*, and an old recording, *Debora/One Inch Rock* were released during T. Rex's run of number ones while the group were changing labels. An EP by Elvis, *Follow That Dream*, pottered about the lower reaches of the charts during Elvis' run of five consecutive number ones. During Police's hat trick, one single on another label, one old single re-issued and a six-pack of singles hit the chart in an attempt to distract the compilers of this table. John Lennon's *Imagine* was the first of the three singles of his hat-trick (his last single for five years) but the second of the three to reach the top. During his hat-trick, a flood of old Lennon hits swarmed back on to the chart.

The third hit of the hat-tricks by both Police and Jive Bunny and the Mastermixers came on to the chart at number one.

Only 15 acts in the 38 year history of the chart have hit the top with each of their first two chart hits.

EDDIE CALVERT *Oh Mein Papa; Cherry Pink and Apple Blossom White* 1954, 55
ADAM FAITH *What Do You Want; Poor Me* 1959, 60
TENNESSEE ERNIE FORD *Give Me Your Word; Sixteen Tons* 1955, 56
FRANKIE GOES TO HOLLYWOOD *Relax!; Two Tribes* 1984
ART GARFUNKEL *I Only Have Eyes For You; Bright Eyes* 1975, 79
GERRY AND THE PACEMAKERS *How Do You Do It; I Like It* 1963
JIVE BUNNY AND THE MASTER-MIXERS *Swing The Mood; That's What I Like* 1989
GEORGE MICHAEL *Careless Whisper; A Different Corner* 1984, 86
MUNGO JERRY *In The Summertime; Baby Jump* 1970, 71
GARY NUMAN/TUBEWAY ARMY *Are 'Friends' Electric?; Cars* 1979
NEW KIDS ON THE BLOCK *You Got It (The Right Stuff); Hangin' Tough* 1989, 90
RIGHTEOUS BROTHERS *You've Lost That Lovin' Feelin'; Unchained Melody* 1965, 90
STARGAZERS *Broken Wings; I See The Moon* 1953, 54
ROD STEWART *Maggie May; You Wear It Well* 1971, 72
JOHN TRAVOLTA AND OLIVIA NEWTON-JOHN *You're The One That I Want; Summer Nights* 1978

Of these acts only Frankie Goes To Hollywood, Gerry and the Pacemakers, Jive Bunny, George Michael, Mungo Jerry, New Kids On The Block and John Travolta and Olivia Newton-John hit the top with their first 2 *releases*. For the New Kids On The Block, it took a re-issue to push one of their hits to the top.

Band Aid and Band Aid II both hit number one with their only releases - the African famine relief singles, *Do They Know It's Christmas*.

FIRST THREE HITS AT NUMBER ONE

Three acts have now achieved the feat of taking their first three hits to number one. They are **Gerry and the Pacemakers** in 1963, **Frankie Goes To Hollywood** in 1984 and **Jive Bunny and the Master-mixers** in 1989. All three are British, and all three are male vocal/instrumental outfits, although this loose description barely fits the production team behind Jive Bunny.

Gerry and the Pacemakers and Frankie Goes To Hollywood both came from Liverpool, both chose as their third single a pseudo-religious song (*You'll Never Walk Alone* and *The Power Of Love* respectively), and both took their fourth release to number two. Jive Bunny's fourth single peaked at number four. Gerry Marsden and Holly Johnson, the lead singers of Gerry and the Pacemakers and Frankie Goes To Hollywood subsequently combined with fellow Liverpudlians the Christians and Paul McCartney to create, along with ace producers Stock Aitken Waterman, yet another number one, *Ferry 'Cross The Mersey*.

LAST HIT AT NUMBER ONE

Chart history shows that once an act has scored its first number one, it is far more likely to hit the top again than to have no more hits at all. Disappearing without trace chartwise after a number one hit is fairly rare, and apart from the one-hit wonders, listed separately, only ten acts have failed to follow up a number one. They are:

CHARLES AZNAVOUR
FIRM
ROLF HARRIS
BENNY HILL
JAM
TOMMY JAMES AND THE
** SHONDELLS**
STEVE MILLER BAND
KAY STARR
STARSHIP
WHAM!

Rolf Harris emerged from his fallow chart period by participating in the Crowd's *You'll Never Walk Alone*. Both halves of Wham! have charted separately since the duo broke up, as have all three members of Jam since their demise. Paul Weller led Style Council to many hits, Bruce Foxton had three solo hits and Rick Buckler's Time UK nudged the charts once. Kay Starr uniquely holds the unlikely record of hitting number one with both her first and last British hit singles.

Cliff Richard had not, at the time of going to press, released a follow-up to *Saviour's Day*, but we assume that by the time you read this book he will have charted again.

THE ONE HIT WONDERS

Qualification: one number one hit, and nothing else – ever. 34 immortal acts now make up the list.

Year	Act
1954	KITTY KALLEN Little Things Mean A Lot
1956	DREAMWEAVERS It's Almost Tomorrow
1958	KALIN TWINS When
1959	JERRY KELLER Here Comes Summer
1960	RICKY VALANCE Tell Laura I Love Her
1962	B. BUMBLE AND THE STINGERS Nut Rocker
1966	OVERLANDERS Michelle
1968	CRAZY WORLD OF ARTHUR BROWN Fire
1969	ZAGER AND EVANS In The Year 2525
1969	JANE BIRKIN AND SERGE GAINSBOURG Je T'Aime... Moi Non Plus
1969	ARCHIES Sugar Sugar
1970	LEE MARVIN Wand'rin' Star
1970	NORMAN GREENBAUM Spirit In The Sky
1970	MATTHEWS' SOUTHERN COMFORT Woodstock
1971	CLIVE DUNN Grandad
1973	SIMON PARK ORCHESTRA Eye Level
1975	TYPICALLY TROPICAL Barbados
1976	J. J. BARRIE No Charge
1977	FLOATERS Float On

Partners in Kryme

Year	Act
1978	ALTHIA AND DONNA Up Town Top Ranking
1978	BRIAN AND MICHAEL Matchstalk Men And Matchstalk Cats And Dogs
1979	ANITA WARD Ring My Bell
1979	LENA MARTELL One Day At A Time
1980	FERN KINNEY Together We Are Beautiful
1980	MASH Theme From M★A★S★H
1980	ST WINIFRED'S SCHOOL CHOIR There's No One Quite Like Grandma
1981	JOE DOLCE MUSIC THEATRE Shaddap You Face
1982	CHARLENE I've Never Been To Me
1985	PHYLLIS NELSON Move Closer
1986	NICK BERRY Every Loser Wins
1987	M/A/R/R/S Pump Up The Volume
1988	ROBIN BECK First Time
1990	PARTNERS IN KRYME Turtle Power
1990	★VANILLA ICE Ice Ice Baby

Apart from these acts, 21 other one hit wonders exist, made up of acts who have had hits in other guises, as follows:

Year	Act
1967	NANCY SINATRA AND FRANK SINATRA Somethin' Stupid *(both have had solo number one hits)*
1974	JOHN DENVER Annie's Song *(has also hit with Placido Domingo)*
1976	ELTON JOHN AND KIKI DEE Don't Go Breaking My Heart *(both have had solo hits)*
1980	OLIVIA NEWTON-JOHN AND ELECTRIC LIGHT ORCHESTRA Xanadu *(both have had solo hits)*
1981	QUEEN AND DAVID BOWIE Under Pressure *(both have had solo number one hits)*

1982	PAUL McCARTNEY WITH STEVIE WONDER Ebony And Ivory *(both have had solo number one hits)*

1982 PAUL McCARTNEY WITH
STEVIE WONDER
Ebony And Ivory
(both have had solo number one hits)

1984 BAND AID
Do They Know It's Christmas
(a conglomeration of hitmakers)

1985 ELAINE PAIGE AND BARBARA
DICKSON I Know Him So Well
(both have had solo hits)

1985 USA FOR AFRICA
We Are The World
(another conglomeration of hitmakers)

1985 CROWD You'll Never Walk Alone
(and another conglomeration)

1985 DAVID BOWIE AND MICK JAGGER
Dancing In The Street
(both have had solo hits)

1986 CLIFF RICHARD AND THE
YOUNG ONES WITH HANK
MARVIN Living Doll
*(Cliff and the Young Ones
(a.k.a. Bad News) have both
had solo hits, as has Hank Marvin)*

1987 STEVE 'SILK' HURLEY
Jack Your Body
(Steve is one half of the duo J.M. Silk)

1987 ARETHA FRANKLIN AND
GEORGE MICHAEL
I Knew You Were Waiting For Me
(both have had solo hits)

1987 FERRY AID Let It Be
(yet another conglomeration)

1988 TIMELORDS
Doctorin' The Tardis
(subsequently hit as The KLF)

1989 KYLIE MINOGUE AND JASON
DONOVAN   Especially For You
(both have had solo number one hits)

1989 CHRISTIANS, HOLLY
JOHNSON, PAUL McCARTNEY,
GERRY MARSDEN AND
STOCK AITKEN WATERMAN
Ferry 'Cross The Mersey
*(charity disc for the Hillsborough
Disaster Fund)*

1989 BAND AID II
Do They Know It's Christmas?
*(the first case of two one-hit wonders reaching
the top with the same song. Only Keren
Woodward and Sarah Dallin of
Bananarama appeared on both discs)*

1990 ENGLANDNEWORDER
World In Motion...
*(a combination of New Order and
the England World Cup Squad)*

1990 *MARIA McKEE Show Me Heaven
*(Maria was lead vocalist with
Lone Justice, who hit in 1987)*

* *Both Vanilla Ice and Maria McKee had further hits in 1991.*

GAP BETWEEN NUMBER ONE HITS

Of all the acts that have enjoyed two or more number one hits, only seven acts have suffered through a gap of more than seven years between number ones, although two of them have, incredibly, done so twice. The Beatles crammed all of their 17 chart toppers into a period of 6 years and 54 days.

25 years 259 days	**RIGHTEOUS BROTHERS**	(17 Feb 65 to 3 Nov 90)
23 years 65 days	**HOLLIES**	(21 Jul 65 to 24 Sep 88)
14 years 172 days	**DIANA ROSS**	(17 Sep 71 to 8 Mar 86)
11 years 238 days	**FRANK SINATRA**	(7 Oct 54 to 2 Jun 66)
11 years 124 days	**CLIFF RICHARD**	(23 Apr 68 to 25 Aug 79)
9 years 231 days	**BEE GEES**	(10 Sep 68 to 29 Apr 78)
9 years 80 days	**CLIFF RICHARD**	(21 Sep 79 to 10 Dec 88)
8 years 215 days	**BEE GEES**	(16 Mar 79 to 17 Oct 87)
7 years 357 days	**DON McLEAN**	(30 Jun 72 to 21 Jun 80)

During Cliff's second hiatus, he took the top slot in March 1986 in association with the Young Ones.

Three of the nine 'comeback' chart toppers were written by Barry, Maurice and Robin Gibb, the two Bee Gees hits and Diana Ross' *Chain Reaction*.

There was a gap of 21 years 200 days between 27 November 1963, the last day that **Gerry and the Pacemakers'** *You'll Never Walk Alone* was at number one, and 15 June 1985, when the same song, with Gerry Marsden again on lead vocals, hit number one, this time in the version by the **Crowd**.

20 years and 4 days after *Back Home* by the **England World Cup Squad** dropped from number one, *World In Motion...* by **Englandneworder** knocked Adamski off the top. None of the artistes who appeared on the England World Cup Squad disc in 1970 survived the selectors' axe to be still playing for England on the football field and in the recording studio in 1990.

16 years and 9 days elapsed between the last day of the final **Rolling Stones** number one, and **Mick Jagger's** reappearance at the top with David Bowie.

There was a gap of 14 years and 113 days between **Eddy Grant's** last day at number one as one of the **Equals** and his first day on top as a soloist.

Elton John's first solo number one hit, *Sacrifice/Healing Hands,* happened 13 years 293 days after he and Kiki Dee dropped from number one with *Don't Go Breaking My Heart.*

Tears Of A Clown by **Smokey Robinson and the Miracles** dropped from number one 10 years and 268 days before **Smokey Robinson**'s solo hit *Being With You* reached the summit.

Righteous Brothers

LONGEST SPAN OF NUMBER ONE HITS

Only five acts have scored number one hits over a period of more than twenty years. They are:

31 years 153 days	**CLIFF RICHARD**	(1959 to 1990)
25 years 286 days	**RIGHTEOUS BROTHERS**	(1965 to 1990)
23 years 105 days	**HOLLIES**	(1965 to 1988)
20 years 87 days	**ELVIS PRESLEY**	(1957 to 1977)
20 years 34 days	**BEE GEES**	(1967 to 1987)

Diana Ross first hit number one as lead singer for the Supremes in 1964 and dropped off the top for the final time as a soloist in 1986, over 21 years later.

Cliff Richard is the only act to have number one hits in *five* decades. In the 1950s he hit number one twice, in the 1960s seven times, in the 1970s once, in the 1980s once solo and once more with the Young Ones and Hank Marvin, and so far once in the 1990s. This record is unlikely ever to be equalled.

The only acts, apart from Cliff Richard, to have hit number one in three different decades are **Elvis Presley** (50s, 60s and 70s)

Bee Gees

and the **Bee Gees** (60s, 70s and 80s). Eight other acts (**Abba, Blondie, David Bowie, Don McLean, Police, Kenny Rogers, Diana Ross** and **Rod Stewart**) hit the top in the 70s and 80s, and so have a chance in the 90s to equal Cliff, Elvis and the Gibb brothers. Nine acts topped the charts in both the 50s and the 60s (**Shirley Bassey, Lonnie Donegan, Everly Brothers, Adam Faith, Michael Holliday, Elvis Presley, Cliff Richard, Frank Sinatra** and **Frankie Vaughan**), but only three managed chart-toppers in the 60s and 70s – Elvis, Cliff and the Bee Gees. The **Hollies** hit the top in the 60s and 80s, and the **Righteous Brothers** hit number one in

the 60s and 90s. So far, only **Madonna, Kylie Minogue** and **New Kids On The Block** have duplicated Cliff's feat of hitting number one in the 80s and 90s.

Cliff Richard's first week at the top came after 45 weeks on lower rungs. His final week at number one was his 998th solo week on the chart, a span of 953 chart weeks. **Elvis Presley**'s first week at number one came after he had already clocked up 103 weeks on the British charts. His final week at number one 20 years later was his 1034th of chart action, a span of a mere 931 chart weeks. No other act comes anywhere near these two in chart longevity.

STRAIGHT IN AT NUMBER ONE

23 records, to the end of 1990, have hit the charts at number one. They are:

14 Nov 52	HERE IN MY HEART	Al Martino
24 Jan 58	JAILHOUSE ROCK	Elvis Presley
3 Nov 60	IT'S NOW OR NEVER	Elvis Presley
11 Jan 62	THE YOUNG ONES	Cliff Richard
23 Apr 69	GET BACK	Beatles
3 Mar 73	CUM ON FEEL THE NOIZE	Slade
30 Jun 73	SKWEEZE ME PLEEZE ME	Slade
17 Nov 73	I LOVE YOU LOVE ME LOVE	Gary Glitter
15 Dec 73	MERRY XMAS EVERYBODY	Slade
22 Mar 80	GOING UNDERGROUND/DREAMS OF CHILDREN	Jam
27 Sep 80	DON'T STAND SO CLOSE TO ME	Police
9 May 81	STAND AND DELIVER	Adam and the Ants
13 Feb 82	A TOWN CALLED MALICE/PRECIOUS	Jam
4 Dec 82	BEAT SURRENDER	Jam
26 Mar 83	IS THERE SOMETHING I SHOULD KNOW?	Duran Duran
16 Jun 84	TWO TRIBES	Frankie Goes To Hollywood
15 Dec 84	DO THEY KNOW IT'S CHRISTMAS?	Band Aid
7 Sep 85	DANCING IN THE STREET	David Bowie and Mick Jagger
4 Apr 87	LET IT BE	Ferry Aid
20 May 89	FERRY 'CROSS THE MERSEY	Christians, Holly Johnson, Paul McCartney, Gerry Marsden and Stock Aitken Waterman
10 Jun 89	SEALED WITH A KISS	Jason Donovan
16 Dec 89	LET'S PARTY	Jive Bunny and the Mastermixers
23 Dec 89	DO THEY KNOW IT'S CHRISTMAS?	Band Aid II

Slade remain the only act to enter the chart at number one with consecutive releases. **Gary Glitter**'s *I Love You Love Me Love* and **Slade**'s *Merry Xmas Everybody* were consecutive number ones, as were *Ferry 'Cross The Mersey* and *Sealed With A Kiss* in May and June 1989. In December 1989 for the first time ever, new hits crashed in at

number one in consecutive weeks. Both **Police** and **Jive Bunny & the Mastermixers** completed a hat-trick of number ones by going straight to the top. *Do They Know It's Christmas* is, of course, the only song to have gone straight to number one in two different versions. Five of the last seven hits on this list were charity discs.

BIGGEST JUMP TO NUMBER ONE

There have been 31 records, apart from those that came on to the chart at number one which are listed separately, which have jumped from outside the Top 10 straight to the top spot.

Glenn Medeiros (above) Abba (right)

The biggest jump within the chart is a leap of 62 places from 66 to 4 on 11 Oct 86 by **Nick Berry**'s *Every Loser Wins*. Two other number one hits have climbed over 50 places in one week on their way to the top – the **Firm**'s *Star Trekkin'* which leapt from 74 to 13 to 1, a leap of 61 places followed by a leap of 12 places, and the **Flying Pickets**' *Only You*, which jumped 51 places on 3 Dec 83. The lowest initial entry by a record that went on to hit the top is 74 by *Star Trekkin'*, on 6 Jun 87, beating the previous record-holder, **Charlene**'s *I've Never Been To Me* by one place. Charlene entered the chart at number 73 on 15 May 82.

33 to 1	HAPPY TALK Captain Sensible	3 Jul 82
27 to 1	SURRENDER Elvis Presley	27 May 61
26 to 1	PASS THE DUTCHIE Musical Youth	2 Oct 82
22 to 1	GREEN DOOR Shakin' Stevens	1 Aug 81
21 to 1	HEY JUDE Beatles	11 Sep 68
21 to 1	(JUST LIKE) STARTING OVER John Lennon	20 Dec 80
19 to 1	ARE YOU LONESOME TONIGHT? Elvis Presley	21 Jan 61
19 to 1	(IF PARADISE IS) HALF AS NICE Amen Corner	12 Feb 69
19 to 1	LOVE ME FOR A REASON Osmonds	31 Aug 74
19 to 1	STAND BY ME Ben E. King	21 Feb 87
17 to 1	GET OFF OF MY CLOUD Rolling Stones	4 Nov 65
16 to 1	I HEAR YOU KNOCKIN' Dave Edmunds	28 Nov 70
16 to 1	CHIRPY CHIRPY CHEEP CHEEP Middle Of The Road	19 Jun 71
16 to 1	YOUNG LOVE Donny Osmond	25 Aug 73
16 to 1	DANCING QUEEN Abba	4 Sep 76
15 to 1	I DON'T LIKE MONDAYS Boomtown Rats	28 Jul 79
15 to 1	THE SPECIAL A.K.A. LIVE! EP Specials	2 Feb 80
14 to 1	EYE LEVEL Simon Park Orchestra	29 Sep 73
13 to 1	IN THE SUMMERTIME Mungo Jerry	13 Jun 70
13 to 1	STAR TREKKIN' Firm	20 Jun 87
12 to 1	LOVE GROWS (WHERE MY ROSEMARY GOES) Edison Lighthouse	31 Jan 70
12 to 1	THE POWER Snap	31 Mar 90
11 to 1	(THERE'S) ALWAYS SOMETHING THERE TO REMIND ME Sandie Shaw	22 Oct 64
11 to 1	TICKET TO RIDE Beatles	22 Apr 65
11 to 1	MICHELLE Overlanders	27 Jan 66
11 to 1	LADY MADONNA Beatles	20 Mar 68
11 to 1	SUGAR SUGAR Archies	25 Oct 69
11 to 1	SHE Charles Aznavour	29 Jun 74
11 to 1	SUMMER NIGHTS John Travolta and Olivia Newton-John	30 Sep 78
11 to 1	THE CHICKEN SONG Spitting Image	17 May 86
11 to 1	NOTHING'S GONNA CHANGE MY LOVE FOR YOU Glenn Medeiros	9 Jul 88

BIGGEST FALLS FROM NUMBER ONE

WHEN I'M 64

Only 22 records have fallen out of the top five directly from the very top, as follows:

1 to 12	MARY'S BOY CHILD Harry Belafonte	10 Jan 58
1 to 10	ONLY YOU Flying Pickets	14 Jan 84
1 to 9	YOU'RE DRIVING ME CRAZY Temperance Seven	1 Jun 61
1 to 9	THESE BOOTS ARE MADE FOR WALKIN' Nancy Sinatra	17 Mar 66
1 to 8	HELLO GOODBYE Beatles	24 Jan 68
1 to 8	LONELY THIS CHRISTMAS Mud	18 Jan 75
1 to 7	WAYWARD WIND Frank Ifield	14 Mar 63
1 to 7	YOUNG LOVE Donny Osmond	22 Sep 73
1 to 7	KNOWING ME KNOWING YOU Abba	7 May 77
1 to 6	HERE IN MY HEART Al Martino	16 Jan 53
1 to 6	ROCK AROUND THE CLOCK Bill Haley and his Comets	20 Jan 56
1 to 6	CATHY'S CLOWN Everly Brothers	23 Jun 60
1 to 6	SUMMER HOLIDAY Cliff Richard and the Shadows	11 Apr 63
1 to 6	SUGAR BABY LOVE Rubettes	15 Jun 74
1 to 6	YOU TO ME ARE EVERYTHING Real Thing	17 Jul 76
1 to 6	BRIGHT EYES Art Garfunkel	26 May 79
1 to 6	THERE'S NO ONE QUITE LIKE GRANDMA St Winifred's School Choir	10 Jan 81
1 to 6	IT'S MY PARTY Dave Stewart with Barbara Gaskin	14 Nov 81
1 to 6	LET'S DANCE David Bowie	30 Apr 83
1 to 6	YOU SPIN ME ROUND (LIKE A RECORD) Dead Or Alive	23 Mar 85
1 to 6	A DIFFERENT CORNER George Michael	10 May 86
1 to 6	BELFAST CHILD Simple Minds	11 Mar 89

At the end of 1988, three consecutive chart toppers dropped from number one to number five. They were *Orinoco Flow* by **Enya** on 19 November, *First Time* by **Robin Beck** on 10 December, and *Mistletoe And Wine* by **Cliff Richard** on 7 January 1989.

Recently, several hits have had spectacular tumbles down the chart. **Band Aid II** fell from 1 to 4 to 32 to 66 and then off the chart at the beginning of 1990, while **Jive Bunny**'s third chart topper, *Let's Party,* fell from 4 to 19 to 50 and then out at exactly the same time. Band Aid II's tumble of 28 places out of the Top Ten is the biggest fall from the Top Ten ever recorded. **Iron Maiden**'s *Holy Smoke* came on to the chart at number 3 on 22 Sep 1990, and then fell to number 5 to 23 to 62 and out. Since the chart became a Top 50 in 1960, no Top Ten hit has spent as few as just four weeks

Morrissey

on the chart. **Morrissey**'s seventh hit, *Piccadilly Palare,* had a record-breaking chart career, entering at number 18 on 20 October 1990, slipping to number 39 seven days later and disappearing completely the next week. A mere two weeks' chart life for a Top Twenty hit had only previously been achieved in the days when there was only a Top Thirty published.

On 8 December 1990, there were six artistes in the Top Ten who were at least 50 years old. They were Bill Medley and Bobby Hatfield of the **Righteous Brothers**, at number 2; **Patrick Macnee and Honor Blackman** at number 5; **Cliff Richard** at number 6 and **Tina Turner** in partnership with Rod Stewart at number 7. There have never been so many golden oldies so highly placed in the charts, although at the end of 1988, Petula Clark and at least three of the Four Tops were over 50 when they had Top Ten hits at the same time as Cliff Richard, who was then a mere 48 years old.

Patrick Macnee & Honor Blackman

Very few acts have been actively recording hits beyond their fiftieth birthdays. **Cliff Richard**, the **Four Tops** and **Tina Turner** are among a very select band of artistes who have hit the Top Ten with records made after they clocked up their half century. Others who went on recording hits years after most have given up include **Frank Sinatra** (whose *New York New York* gave him a Top Ten hit at the age of 70, although it first hit the charts when he was a mere 64 years old), **Perry Como,** who was 61 when *For The Good Times* reached number seven in 1973, **James Brown**, who was 57 when he climbed to number 5 in 1986, **Roy Orbison**, whose posthumous Top Ten hit was recorded when he was 52, and **Roger Whittaker**, who was 50 when his duet with Des O'Connor reached number 10 at the end of 1986. In the days before Bill Haley and Elvis Presley changed the chart rules, people like **Ted Heath, Billy Cotton, Gracie Fields** and **Bing Crosby** all had Top Ten hits in their fifties. Posthumous hits for **Jackie Wilson, Red Sovine, Nat 'King' Cole** and **Laurel and Hardy** were all successful well over 50 years after their birth, but it would not really be fair to include them in the list of elderly hitmakers. Re-releases have given not only the Righteous Brothers but also **Andy Stewart, Bobby Vinton** and **Nina Simone** and many others big hits beyond their fiftieth birthday, but these hits were all recorded when the performers were much younger.

The oldest soloists to hit number one with a new recording, listed by their age on their final day at number one, are:

67 years 316 days .... **Louis Armstrong**
15 May 1968
51 years 53 days .... **Telly Savalas**
15 Mar 1975
50 years 186 days .... **Frank Sinatra**
16 Jun 1966
50 years 77 days .... **Cliff Richard**
29 Dec 1990
50 years 59 days .... **Charles Aznavour**
20 Jul 1974
49 years 14 days .... **Clive Dunn**
23 Jan 1971
47 years 272 days .... **Mantovani**
14 Aug 1953
46 years 59 days .... **Chuck Berry**
16 Dec 1972
46 years 31 days .... **Lee Marvin**
21 Mar 1970
45 years 335 days .... **Perry Como**
18 Apr 1958

Frank Sinatra was 51 years 129 days old on the final day that his duet with his daughter Nancy was at number one in 1967. **Mantovani** was 48 years and 292 days old when David Whitfield's *Cara Mia*, with chorus and Mantovani and his orchestra, fell

Louis Armstrong

from the top on 3 Sep 54. **Gene Pitney** was 48 years and 1 day old at number one with Marc Almond in 1989.

Note that every name on this list is male. The senior woman to top the charts is still **Winifred Atwell**, who was celebrating her 42nd birthday on the day when *The Poor People Of Paris* finished its run at the top on 3 May 1956. **Diana Ross** was only four days younger when *Chain Reaction* slipped down the chart. **Petula Clark** was just over 55 years old when her remixed *Downtown 88* hit the Top Ten, and **Honor Blackman** was 64 when *Kinky Boots* took her and Patrick Macnee to number 5 in December 1990. However the oldest lady to be involved in a newly-recorded number one hit is **Grace Slick**, lead vocalist for Starship, who was 47 years and 232 days old when they led the pack with *Nothing's Gonna Stop Us Now* in 1987.

Several re-released singles have climbed to number one. For example, **Jackie Wilson** was born 53 years and 8 days before his *Reet Petite* fell from number one; Bobby Hatfield and Bill Medley of the **Righteous Brothers** were both just over 50 when their career revived late in 1990; **Ben E. King** was 48 years and 165 days old when *Stand By Me* finished its spell at the top of the charts; and **Steve Miller** was 46 years and 352 days old when *The Joker* slipped to number 2 in September 1990.

Several group members have been past fifty when they were part of a big hit. **USA For Africa** included Ray Charles, Harry Belafonte and Quincy Jones among others. The **Crowd** included Rolf Harris, Bernie Winters, Kenny Lynch and Bruce Forsyth. Only six acts have so far been involved in three or more Top Ten hits after their fiftieth birthdays. They are:

Frank Sinatra   (b. 12 Dec 15)
4 Top Ten hits, and one with Nancy Sinatra.
Louis Armstrong   (b. 4 Jul 00)
4 solo Top Ten hits, two when over 60.
Ted Heath   (b. 30 Mar 02)
4 Top Ten hits with his orchestra.
Perry Como   (b. 18 May 12)
3 solo Top Ten hits, two when over 60.
Bing Crosby   (b. 2 May 03)
2 solo Top Ten hits, and one with Grace Kelly. Two more posthumously, one solo and one with David Bowie.
Tina Turner   (b. 26 Nov 38)
2 solo Top Ten hits, and one with Rod Stewart.

Little Jimmy Osmond

Only five soloists have topped the charts below the age of seventeen. They are:

9 years 245 days ... **Little Jimmy Osmond**
17 December 1972
13 years 288 days .... **Frankie Lymon**
14 July 1956
14 years 205 days .... **Donny Osmond**
2 July 1972
14 years 310 days .... **Helen Shapiro**
4 August 1961
16 years 25 days .... **Paul Anka**
24 August 1957

Three very young groups have also hit the number one spot, the **St. Winifred's School Choir, Musical Youth** and **New Edition**. The St. Winifred's Choir certainly included some girls younger than 9 years 245 days. The youngest member of Musical Youth was 11 years old when they hit the top. New Edition, now better known as Ralph Tresvant, Bobby Brown and Bell Biv Devoe, were all aged under 16 when *Candy Girl* reached number one. The youngest member, Bobby Brown was 14 years and 112 days old and the oldest, Ricky Bell, was 15 years and 252 days old.

Donny Osmond and **Cliff Richard** are the only acts to achieve three number one hits before the age of 20, while Donny managed a fourth as part of the Osmonds. **Hank Marvin** and **Bruce Welch** of the Shadows hit the top twice before their 20th birthdays, as well as backing Cliff on his first four chart-toppers. Their total of 22 weeks at number one before their 20th birthdays is a chart record.

SLOWEST NUMBER ONE

Steve Miller

If an artist is ever going to have a number one hit, it usually happens within a year or two of that artist's first hit. About half of all the acts who have hit the very top did so with their first chart hit. The full list of the 16 acts whose first number one came more than ten years after their chart debut is:

29 years 42 days	JACKIE WILSON	(15 Nov 57 to 27 Dec 86)
26 years 19 days	BEN E. KING	(2 Feb 61 to 21 Feb 87)
19 years 151 days	ELTON JOHN	(23 Jan 71 to 23 Jun 90)
18 years 218 days	STEVIE WONDER	(3 Feb 66 to 8 Sep 84)
18 years 216 days	JOHNNY MATHIS	(23 May 58 to 25 Dec 76)
16 years 218 days	BORIS GARDINER	(17 Jan 70 to 23 Aug 86)
15 years 157 days	CHUCK BERRY	(21 Jun 57 to 25 Nov 72)
15 years 127 days	LOUIS ARMSTRONG	(19 Dec 52 to 24 Apr 68)
14 years 279 days	BARBRA STREISAND	(20 Jan 66 to 25 Oct 80)
13 years 327 days	STEVE MILLER BAND	(23 Oct 76 to 15 Sep 90)
13 years 140 days	FOUR SEASONS	(4 Oct 62 to 21 Feb 76)
12 years 321 days	PAUL McCARTNEY	(27 Feb 71 to 14 Jan 84)
12 years 260 days	PINK FLOYD	(30 Mar 67 to 15 Dec 79)
11 years 164 days	JOHN LENNON	(9 Jul 69 to 20 Dec 80)
10 years 298 days	BENNY HILL	(16 Feb 61 to 11 Dec 71)
10 years 8 days	SISTER SLEDGE	(21 Jun 75 to 29 Jun 85)

(Iron Maiden added themselves to this list in the first chart of 1991, hitting number one 10 years and 314 days after their chart debut.)

Of these acts, **Elton John, Stevie Wonder, Paul McCartney** and **John Lennon** had featured on number ones before their solo successes. John Lennon is the only act on this list to achieve more than one number one. His first number one was the first of a hat-trick. Stevie Wonder's first week at number one was his 301st of chart action, but Elton John's was his 371st week on the chart, the longest wait in chart terms for a number one. It was a re-issue of his 45th and 46th hits, the most hits ever achieved by any act before their first number one.

Before **Louis Armstrong** became the first act to take more than ten years to hit the top, in 1968, the slowest ascent of the charts was by **Petula Clark**, who took 6 years 257 days from her chart debut on 11 June 1954 until she first topped the charts on 23 February 1961.

Gene Pitney has never had a solo number one, but there was a gap of 27 years and 311 days from his first week on the charts on 23 March 1961 until he topped the charts with Marc Almond on 28 January 1989.

Eleven recordings have taken longer than 200 days to hit the top after their first appearance on the chart:

29 years 42 days	REET PETITE Jackie Wilson	(15 Nov 57 to 27 Dec 86)
25 years 244 days	STAND BY ME Ben E. King	(22 Jun 61 to 21 Feb 87)
25 years 83 days	UNCHAINED MELODY Righteous Brothers	(12 Aug 65 to 3 Nov 90)
18 years 356 days	HE AIN'T HEAVY, HE'S MY BROTHER Hollies	(4 Oct 69 to 24 Sep 88)
6 years 63 days	SPACE ODDITY David Bowie	(6 Sep 69 to 8 Nov 75)
5 years 70 days	IMAGINE John Lennon	(1 Nov 75 to 10 Jan 81)
322 days	ROCK AROUND THE CLOCK Bill Haley and his Comets	(7 Jan 55 to 25 Nov 55)
308 days	EYE LEVEL Simon Park Orchestra	(25 Nov 72 to 29 Sep 73)
301 days	HEALING HANDS Elton John	(26 Aug 89 to 23 Jun 90)
231 days	SACRIFICE Elton John	(4 Nov 89 to 23 Jun 90)
210 days	THE MODEL/COMPUTER LOVE Kraftwerk	(11 Jul 81 to 6 Feb 82)

All these tracks dropped off the charts between their original chart entry and their chart-topping reappearances. The slowest climb to number one by any record that stayed on the chart all the time is 16 weeks (112 days) by **THE POWER OF LOVE** by **Jennifer Rush**, from 29 Jun 85 to 12 Oct 85. The previous record of 14 weeks (98 days) had been set only seven months earlier by **Dead Or Alive's YOU SPIN ME ROUND (LIKE A RECORD)**, which took from 1 Dec 84 to 9 Mar 85 to climb to number one.

FASTEST NUMBER ONE

At the other end of the scale from Jackie Wilson, these are the acts who moved from chart debut to the number one slot in the shortest time, starting with Al Martino's entry in the very first chart:

0 days AL MARTINO (14 Nov 52)

7 days EDISON LIGHTHOUSE
        (24 to 31 Jan 70)
7 days MUNGO JERRY
        (6 to 13 Jun 70)
7 days DAVE EDMUNDS
        (21 to 28 Nov 70)
7 days NICOLE (8 to 15 May 82)
7 days MUSICAL YOUTH
        (25 Sep to 3 Oct 82)
7 days SPITTING IMAGE
        (10 to 17 May 86)
7 days SNAP (24 to 31 Mar 90)
7 days PARTNERS IN KRYME
        (21 to 28 Jul 90)
7 days VANILLA ICE
        (24 Nov to 1 Dec 90)

Other first-time chart acts who had already been in the charts under some other name, have also had rapid climbs to the top:

0 days BAND AID (1984)
0 days DAVID BOWIE AND
        MICK JAGGER (1985)
0 days FERRY AID (1987)
0 days CHRISTIANS,
        HOLLY JOHNSON,
        PAUL McCARTNEY,
        GERRY MARSDEN AND
        STOCK AITKEN
        WATERMAN (1989)
0 days BAND AID II (1989)

7 days GEORGE HARRISON (1971)
7 days QUEEN AND DAVID BOWIE
        (1981)
7 days CAPTAIN SENSIBLE (1982)
7 days USA FOR AFRICA (1985)
7 days CLIFF RICHARD AND
        THE YOUNG ONES (1986)
7 days ARETHA FRANKLIN AND
        GEORGE MICHAEL (1987)
7 days BOY GEORGE (1987)
7 days ENGLANDNEWORDER
        (1990)

Vanilla Ice made his chart debut at number three, the highest position achieved by a totally new chart act since the first week of the charts 38 years earlier. Apart from the top five acts in the first chart of all (Al Martino, Jo Stafford, Nat 'King' Cole, Bing Crosby and Guy Mitchell) the only acts to have spent their first week of chart action in the Top Five are:

2 Jul 54	KITTY KALLEN Little Things Mean A Lot	5
14 Jul 84	NEIL Hole In My Shoe	5
20 Feb 88	BOMB THE BASS Beat Dis	5
21 Jul 90	PARTNERS IN KRYME Turtle Power	4
24 Nov 90	VANILLA ICE Ice Ice Baby	3

There have been eight records by combinations of previous chart acts which have also crashed straight into the top five. They are the five charity discs which hit number one on their first week, listed above, and:

22 Mar 86	CLIFF RICHARD AND THE YOUNG ONES featuring HANK MARVIN Living Doll	4
10 Dec 88	KYLIE MINOGUE AND JASON DONOVAN Especially For You	2
2 Jun 90	ENGLANDNEWORDER World In Motion...	2

Since the chart became a Top 50 in 1960, only four other new acts have spent their first week of chart action in the Top Ten. They are the **Cars** in 1978 (number 10 first week), **Nicole** in 1982 (number 8 first week), **Style Council** in 1983 (number 6 first week) and **Sigue Sigue Sputnik** in 1986 (number 7 first week). Style Council was led by ex-Jam hitmaker Paul Weller. Three ex-members of chart bands have hit the lower half of the Top Ten in their first week of solo action (**George Harrison, Boy George** and **Morrissey**) as have four combinations of chart acts (**Queen and David Bowie, USA For Africa, Pet Shop Boys and Dusty Springfield** and **Various – Brits 1990**).

Vanilla Ice

MOST WEEKS ON CHART WITHOUT A NUMBER ONE HIT

23 of the 102 acts that have been on the charts for 150 weeks or more have never had a number one hit. They are:

	Wks
BILLY FURY	281
WHO	245
ELECTRIC LIGHT ORCHESTRA	243
(who hit number one with Olivia Newton-John)	
NAT 'KING' COLE	230
BRENDA LEE	210
KOOL AND THE GANG	201
GENE PITNEY	200
(who hit number one with Marc Almond)	
NEIL SEDAKA	190
DEPECHE MODE	189
PRINCE	189
DUANE EDDY	187
STRANGLERS	185
DRIFTERS	176
GLADYS KNIGHT AND THE PIPS	176
MR. ACKER BILK	171
CARPENTERS	168
TEMPTATIONS	165
BANANARAMA	161
LEVEL 42	161
ELVIS COSTELLO	158
DEAN MARTIN	154
ORCHESTRAL MANOEUVRES IN THE DARK	153
KIM WILDE	152

Depeche Mode

MOST TOP TEN HITS WITHOUT A NUMBER ONE

Now that Elton John has finally hit the number one spot, there are very few acts that have hit the Top Ten ten times without enjoying even one brief week on their own at the very top.

14 ELECTRIC LIGHT ORCHESTRA
(who topped the charts in 1980 with Olivia Newton-John)
13 NAT 'KING' COLE
(who has spent nine weeks at number 2)
13 WHO
(who had two number 2 hits)
11 BILLY FURY
(who had only one number 2 hit, the aptly titled 'Jealousy')
10 GENE PITNEY
(who topped the charts with Marc Almond in 1989)

Vince Clarke has been half of two bands who between them have had 12 Top Ten hits without a chart-topper. **Yazoo** had three Top Ten hits, and **Erasure** have so far had nine.

The **Stranglers**, with 30 hits, have had more hits than any act never to top the charts, but only seven of those hits reached the Top Ten.

MOST 'UNSUCCESSFUL' NUMBER TWOS

There has now been a total of 512 records which have reached number two but failed to make that all-important final climb to the very top. The 500th number two was **STEP BY STEP** by **New Kids On The Block**, which came straight on to the chart at number two on 16 June 1990, but failed to climb any higher. Over the past two years, more records have stopped at number two than have hit the very top, an indication that the number one single very often outsells all the other records on the chart by a considerable distance. Being number one is becoming more and more important.

The acts whose chart climb has most often peaked at number two are:

10 CLIFF RICHARD
9 ELVIS PRESLEY
6 MADONNA
5 TOM JONES
5 PAUL McCARTNEY/WINGS
(+1 with Michael Jackson)
5 KYLIE MINOGUE
5 QUEEN
5 SWEET

4 BEATLES, PAT BOONE, DAVID BOWIE, BROS, EVERLY BROTHERS, GARY GLITTER, HOLLIES, DEAN MARTIN, LEO SAYER, SHOWADDYWADDY, SLADE, T. REX, STEVIE WONDER

3 NAT 'KING' COLE, PHIL COLLINS, DARTS, DURAN DURAN, KINKS, FRANKIE LAINE, GUY MITCHELL, STATUS QUO, SHAKIN' STEVENS

The Beach Boys have had two number twos of their own and one with the Fat Boys.

The acts who got so near and yet so far are:

NAT 'KING' COLE .... 9 wks
FRANK CHACKSFIELD .... 8 wks
DRIFTERS .... 7 wks
FATHER ABRAHAM AND THE
SMURFS .... 6 wks
ALLISONS .... 6 wks
BRIGHOUSE AND RASTRICK
BAND .... 6 wks
FREE .... 5 wks
OBERNKIRCHEN CHILDREN'S
CHOIR .... 5 wks
SIMPLY RED .... 5 wks

The most consecutive weeks at number two is six, a record jointly held by *The Smurf Song* and *The Floral Dance*.
Only one record has reached number two on two totally separate occasions. *Honey* by Bobby Goldsboro reached number two on 29 May 1968 for one week. It returned to number two as a re-issue on 26 April 1975, almost seven years later. Fleetwood Mac's *Albatross*, a number one hit when originally released, climbed to number two as a re-issue.

MOST CONSECUTIVE NUMBER TWOS

Four hat-tricks have been performed:

TOM JONES
I'll Never Fall In Love Again, I'm Coming Home, Delilah .... 1967 to 1968
SWEET
Hell Raiser, Ballroom Blitz, Teenage Rampage .... 1973 to 1974
DARTS
Come Back My Love, Boy From New York City, It's Raining 1978
(Darts never had a number one hit)
KYLIE MINOGUE
Got To Be Certain, The Loco-Motion, Je Ne Sais Pas Pourquoi 1988

Cliff Richard, who has never managed a hat-trick of number ones, and who has stopped more often at number two than any other act, has also achieved the unique

Sam Brown with her parents Joe and Vicki

distinction of a hat-trick of number three hits. The three singles were *Theme For A Dream, A Girl Like You* and *When The Girl In Your Arms Is The Girl In Your Heart.* An imported single, *Gee Whiz It's You,* which was never officially released by EMI in Britain, peaked at number four during this odd run.
Electric Light Orchestra achieved three consecutive number six hits in 1978, and **Craig Douglas** peaked at number nine with four consecutive hits, although these were not consecutive single releases. **Adeva**, in 1989, achieved the bizarre distinction of peaking at number 17 with each of her first three hits. No other hat-tricks of any size of hit have been achieved, although **Cinderella** came close, beginning their chart career with hits peaking at 54, 55 and 55.
Elvis Presley and **Lonnie Donegan** are the only people to have had hits peaking at every position from 1 to 10. Elvis has had hits peaking at every chart position from 1 to 19, but has never had a record which stopped at number 20. None of Cliff Richard's 56 Top Ten hits has peaked at number five.

WE ARE FAMILY

The charts are now almost 40 years old, and dynasties of hitmakers are beginning to emerge. It is, however, proving difficult for chartbusters to hand down their skills from one generation to the next.

The Crowd included **Zac Starkey**, son of **Ringo Starr**. Zac and Ringo thus became the first father and son ever to have topped the charts, separately or together. **John Lennon** and **Julian Lennon** are the nearest yet to a father and son topping the charts as soloists. Julian Lennon's biggest hit so far reached number six.

Frank Sinatra and **Nancy Sinatra** became the first instance of a father and daughter topping the charts, and they have achieved this feat both separately and together. Father/daughter combinations are by far the most successful family connections, with **Nat 'King' Cole** and **Natalie Cole** both reaching number two as did **Marty Wilde** and **Kim Wilde**.

The Woodwards, Hilda and Rob, both of **Lieutenant Pigeon**, are the only instance of a mother and son reaching number one. **Marion Ryan**, with a number five hit, and son **Barry Ryan** with a number two hit are the closest to a mother and son separately climbing to the very top.

No mother and daughter have yet both hit the very top of the British singles chart. The closest instance of this is by **Vicki Brown**, who sang on J. J. Barrie's one hit wonder chart-topper *No Charge*, and her daughter **Sam Brown**, whose highest chart placing to date is number four. Dad **Joe Brown** also enjoyed three Top Ten hits, one reaching number two.

MOST WEEKS ON CHART

BY RECORDING

Total weeks on chart, regardless of the number of re-issues or re-entries. This list shows which recording has appeared on the singles charts for the most weeks. Re-recordings of the same song by the same artist do not count but re-mixes of the same track do.

Wks.	Chart Runs		
122	9	MY WAY	Frank Sinatra
67	8	AMAZING GRACE	Judy Collins
57	8	ROCK AROUND THE CLOCK*	Bill Haley and his Comets
56	1	RELEASE ME*	Engelbert Humperdinck
55	1	STRANGER ON THE SHORE	Mr Acker Bilk
52	2	RELAX!*	Frankie Goes To Hollywood
49	4	BLUE MONDAY	New Order
47	2	I LOVE YOU BECAUSE	Jim Reeves
44	5	LET'S TWIST AGAIN	Chubby Checker
43	4	WHITE LINES (DON'T DON'T DO IT)	Grandmaster Flash and Melle Mel
41	5	DECK OF CARDS	Wink Martindale
40	1	RIVERS OF BABYLON/BROWN GIRL IN THE RING*	Boney M
40	2	TIE A YELLOW RIBBON ROUND THE OLD OAK TREE*	Dawn
40	2	A SCOTTISH SOLDIER	Andy Stewart
39	3	HE'LL HAVE TO GO	Jim Reeves
38	2	SOMEWHERE MY LOVE	Mike Sammes Singers
36	1	I BELIEVE*	Frankie Laine
36	1	I PRETEND*	Des O'Connor
36	2	THE POWER OF LOVE*	Jennifer Rush
36	3	SHE LOVES YOU*	Beatles
36	4	TAINTED LOVE*	Soft Cell
35	2	AND I LOVE YOU SO	Perry Como
35	2	ALBATROSS*	Fleetwood Mac
35	2	HOUND DOG	Elvis Presley
35	4	ALL RIGHT NOW	Free
35	4	LEADER OF THE PACK	Shangri-Las
34	1	CHIRPY CHIRPY CHEEP CHEEP*	Middle Of The Road
34	2	WHAT A WONDERFUL WORLD*	Louis Armstrong
34	3	HEARTBREAK HOTEL	Elvis Presley
34	3	JE T'AIME...MOI NON PLUS*	Jane Birkin and Serge Gainsbourg
34	3	NIGHTS IN WHITE SATIN	Moody Blues
34	3	SAILING*	Rod Stewart
32	2	LET'S DANCE	Chris Montez
32	3	I GET THE SWEETEST FEELING	Jackie Wilson
31	1	GHOSTBUSTERS	Ray Parker Jr
31	2	REET PETITE*	Jackie Wilson
31	5	HAPPY CHRISTMAS (WAR IS OVER)	John Lennon
30	1	AS LONG AS HE NEEDS ME	Shirley Bassey
30	1	AGADOO	Black Lace
30	1	SIDE SADDLE*	Russ Conway
30	1	THEME FROM 'A SUMMER PLACE'	Percy Faith
30	1	JUST LOVING YOU	Anita Harris
30	2	PARANOID	Black Sabbath
30	2	TRUE LOVE	Bing Crosby and Grace Kelly
30	2	BREAKING UP IS HARD TO DO	Neil Sedaka
30	2	OH CAROL	Neil Sedaka
30	2	YOUNG GIRL*	Union Gap featuring Gary Puckett
30	3	TAKE MY BREATH AWAY*	Berlin

Only 19 of the 48 records that have spent 30 or more weeks on the chart have reached number one (marked by an asterisk *). Five of the records, those by **Wink Martindale, Mike Sammes Singers, Jane Birkin and Serge Gainsbourg, Percy Faith** and **Bing Crosby and Grace Kelly**, were the only hits by those artists.

MOST CONSECUTIVE WEEKS ON CHART

56 RELEASE ME
   Engelbert Humperdinck
55 STRANGER ON THE SHORE
   Mr Acker Bilk
48 RELAX!
   Frankie Goes To Hollywood
42 MY WAY Frank Sinatra
40 RIVERS OF BABYLON/BROWN
   GIRL IN THE RING Boney M
39 TIE A YELLOW RIBBON ROUND
   THE OLD OAK TREE Dawn
39 I LOVE YOU BECAUSE
   Jim Reeves
38 WHITE LINES (DON'T DON'T
   DO IT) Grandmaster Flash and Melle Mel
38 A SCOTTISH SOLDIER
   Andy Stewart
36 I BELIEVE Frankie Laine
36 I PRETEND
   Des O'Connor
34 CHIRPY CHIRPY CHEEP CHEEP
   Middle Of The Road
32 THE POWER OF LOVE
   Jennifer Rush
32 AMAZING GRACE
   Judy Collins
31 SHE LOVES YOU Beatles
31 AND I LOVE YOU SO
   Perry Como
31 GHOSTBUSTERS
   Ray Parker Jr
30 AS LONG AS HE NEEDS ME
   Shirley Bassey
30 AGADOO Black Lace
30 SIDE SADDLE Russ Conway
30 THEME FROM 'A SUMMER
   PLACE' Percy Faith
30 JUST LOVING YOU Anita Harris

Engelbert Humperdinck

FEWEST WEEKS ON CHART BY A NUMBER ONE

At the other end of the record books, these are the 14 records which spent the fewest weeks on the charts, and yet still climbed to the very peak of the lists.

6	wks	LET'S PARTY	Jive Bunny and the Mastermixers
6	wks	DO THEY KNOW IT'S CHRISTMAS?	Band Aid II
7	wks	CHRISTMAS ALPHABET	Dickie Valentine
7	wks	LET IT BE	Ferry Aid
7	wks	FERRY 'CROSS THE MERSEY	Christians, Holly Johnson, Paul McCartney, Gerry Marsden and Stock Aitken Waterman
8	wks	HEY JOE	Frankie Laine
8	wks	LET'S HAVE ANOTHER PARTY	Winifred Atwell
8	wks	LADY MADONNA	Beatles
8	wks	MARY'S BOY CHILD – OH MY LORD	Boney M
8	wks	WHAT'S ANOTHER YEAR	Johnny Logan
8	wks	MY CAMERA NEVER LIES	Bucks Fizz
8	wks	HAPPY TALK	Captain Sensible
8	wks	DESIRE	U2
8	wks	TEARS ON MY PILLOW	Kylie Minogue

MOST WEEKS ON CHART BY A SONG IN ALL ITS RECORDED VERSIONS

This list shows the most successful *songs* chartwise from 1952 to 1990. Only complete recordings of the song count – parts of songs in medley discs are not included.

Weeks	Chart Versions
163 MY WAY	4, all vocal
94 AMAZING GRACE	2, 1 vocal, 1 instrumental
75 UNCHAINED MELODY	7, 6 vocal, 1 instrumental
70 ROCK AROUND THE CLOCK	3, all vocal
65 STRANGER ON THE SHORE	2, 1 vocal, 1 instrumental
62 THEME FROM 'THE THREEPENNY OPERA'/MACK THE KNIFE	6, all vocal
62 ONLY YOU	5, all vocal
58 JE T'AIME...MOI NON PLUS/ LOVE AT FIRST SIGHT	4, 3 vocal, 1 instrumental
56 DECK OF CARDS	2, both vocal
56 RELEASE ME	1, vocal
54 I BELIEVE	3, all vocal
52 CAN'T HELP FALLING IN LOVE	4, all vocal
52 RELAX!	1, vocal
51 IT'S ONLY MAKE BELIEVE	4, all vocal
50 LET'S TWIST AGAIN	2, both vocal
50 WHEN I FALL IN LOVE	3, all vocal

Conway Twitty

It's Only Make Believe, written by Conway Twitty and Jack Nance, and *Unchained Melody*, written by Alex North and Hy Zaret, are the only songs in British chart history to have been Top Ten hits in 4 different versions.

White Christmas, written by Irving Berlin, has been a hit in 8 different versions – by Pat Boone, Max Bygraves, Bing Crosby, Darts, Jim Davidson, Keith Harris and Orville, Mantovani and Freddie Starr. *Unchained Melody* has been a hit in seven different versions.

Stranger in Paradise (written by Robert Wright and George Forrest, based on a theme by Aleksandr Borodin) and *Theme From 'The Threepenny Opera' (Mack The Knife)* (written by Kurt Weill and Bertholt Brecht, English lyrics by Marc Blitzstein) have hit the charts in 6 versions each. A further instrumental version of the *Theme From 'The Threepenny Opera'*, by Winifred Atwell, hit the chart as one track on the *All Star Hit Parade* in 1956.

The most commonly used title for a hit single is *Tonight*. There have been ten different hit songs called *Tonight*, by Shirley Bassey, Boomtown Rats, David Bowie, Zaine Griff, Steve Harvey, Kool And The Gang, Modettes, Move, New Kids On The Block and the Rubettes. The biggest hit version was by Kool And The Gang, who took it to number 2. New Kids On The Block are the only other act to take this title into the Top Ten, climbing to number 3 in 1990.

Fourteen songs have been taken to number one in two different versions, as follows :

ANSWER ME
David Whitfield 6 Nov 53 for 1 wk and
11 Dec 53 for 1 wk
Frankie Laine 13 Nov 53 for 8 wks
(on 11 Dec 53, these two versions were placed top equal)

CHERRY PINK AND APPLE BLOSSOM WHITE
Perez Prado 29 Apr 55 for 2 wks
Eddie Calvert 27 May 55 for 4 wks

DO THEY KNOW IT'S CHRISTMAS
Band Aid 15 Dec 84 for 5 wks
Band Aid II 23 Dec 89 for 3 wks

EVERYTHING I OWN
Ken Boothe 26 Oct 74 for 3 wks
Boy George 14 Mar 87 for 2 wks

I GOT YOU BABE
Sonny and Cher 26 Aug 65 for 2 wks
UB40 with Chrissie Hynde 31 Aug 85
for 1 wk

LIVING DOLL
Cliff Richard and the Drifters 31 Jul 59
for 6 wks
Cliff Richard and the Young Ones 29 Mar 86
for 3 wks

MARY'S BOY CHILD
Harry Belafonte 22 Nov 57 for 7 wks
Boney M 9 Dec 78 for 4 wks

SINGING THE BLUES
Guy Mitchell 4 Jan 57 for 1 wk, 18 Jan 57
for 1 wk and 1 Feb 57 for 1 wk
Tommy Steele 11 Jan 57 for 1 wk

SPIRIT IN THE SKY
Norman Greenbaum 2 May 70 for 2 wks
Doctor and the Medics 7 Jun 86 for 3 wks

THIS OLE HOUSE
Rosemary Clooney 26 Nov 54 for 1 wk
Shakin' Stevens 28 Nov 81 for 3 wks

UNCHAINED MELODY
Jimmy Young 24 Jun 55 for 3 wks
Righteous Brothers 3 Nov 90 for 4 wks

WITH A LITTLE HELP FROM MY FRIENDS
Joe Cocker 6 Nov 68 for 1 wk
Wet Wet Wet 21 May 88 for 4 wks

YOU'LL NEVER WALK ALONE
Gerry and the Pacemakers 31 Oct 63 for 4 wks
Crowd 15 Jun 85 for 2 wks

YOUNG LOVE
Tab Hunter 22 Feb 57 for 7 wks
Donny Osmond 25 Aug 73 for 4 wks

Three titles have been used twice for different songs at number one – **FOREVER AND EVER** (Slik and Demis Roussos, both 1976), **TEARS ON MY PILLOW** (Johnny Nash in 1975 and Kylie Minogue in 1990), and **WOMAN IN LOVE** (Frankie Laine in 1956 and Barbra Streisand in 1980).

Vanilla Ice's **ICE ICE BABY**, a 1990 number one, sampled heavily from Queen and David Bowie's 1981 number one, **UNDER PRESSURE**. Jive Bunny's three number ones were mixes featuring brief extracts of several chart-toppers.

The ten longest titled songs to hit the top are listed below. The shortest title for a number one is IF (2 letters).

45 letters SAN FRANCISCO (BE SURE TO WEAR SOME FLOWERS IN YOUR HAIR) (Scott McKenzie, 1967)

39 letters ITSY BITSY TEENY WEENY YELLOW POLKA DOT BIKINI (Bombalurina, 1990)

37 letters MATCHSTALK MEN AND MATCHSTALK CATS AND DOGS (Brian and Michael, 1978)

37 letters WHEN THE GOING GETS TOUGH THE TOUGH GET GOING (Billy Ocean, 1986)

36 letters (THERE'S) ALWAYS SOMETHING THERE TO REMIND ME (Sandie Shaw, 1964)

Whitney Houston

36 letters THERE MUST BE AN ANGEL (PLAYING WITH MY HEART) (Eurythmics, 1985)

35 letters WHAT DO YOU WANT TO MAKE THOSE EYES AT ME FOR? (Emile Ford and the Checkmates, 1959)

34 letters TIE A YELLOW RIBBON ROUND THE OLD OAK TREE (Dawn featuring Tony Orlando, 1973)

34 letters WHEN YOU'RE IN LOVE WITH A BEAUTIFUL WOMAN (Dr. Hook, 1979)

33 letters I WANNA DANCE WITH SOMEBODY (WHO LOVES ME) (Whitney Houston, 1987)

The longest title to be used for a hit single is the 12 word, 73 letter long CALLING OCCUPANTS OF INTERPLANETARY CRAFT (THE RECOGNISED ANTHEM OF WORLD CONTACT DAY), the Klaatu song which gave the Carpenters a number 9 hit in 1977. The longest title containing no brackets is the 60 letter 1981 hit from the Freshies, I'M IN LOVE WITH THE GIRL ON A CERTAIN MAN-CHESTER MEGASTORE CHECKOUT DESK. The Bellamy Brothers' IF I SAID YOU HAD A BEAUTIFUL BODY WOULD YOU HOLD IT AGAINST ME contains more words in its title (14) than any other British hit single.

THE GUINNESS BOOK OF BRITISH HIT SINGLES COMES TO LIFE

The Golden Oldies Club of Great Britain and Old Gold Records Ltd are delighted to offer you over 3000 hits on 7 inch singles and other formats.

Now you can buy thousands of the classic Golden Oldies of yesterday that span the pages of our historical archive - to build or rebuild your record collection.

For full details of this exciting service and a FREE Golden Oldies catalogue - photocopy and complete the coupon:

Please send me your FREE catalogue of Golden Oldies, as mentioned in the
Guinness Book of British Hit Singles.

Please write clearly in block capitals.

Surname .... (Mr/ Mrs/ Miss) ....

First name ....

Address ....

....

Post Code ....

Send to: Golden Oldies, PO Box 1479, London, NW9 6JU

THE AUTHORS

JONATHAN RICE travelled all over Britain in 1990, researching his latest book on cricket, *The Pavilion Book Of Pavilions*, which has just been published. He has also spent some time since the previous edition of *British Hit Singles* building up his collection of books on Japan, watching Fulham FC go from bad to worse, and winning his first golf trophy, an award for the highest scoring round of the day in a competition at Sunningdale. 1990 proved to be a bumper year for his tomato crop, so much that he has a cupboard full of tomato chutney and a freezer full of tomato soup. Next year he will grow something totally inedible, like rhubarb.

TIM RICE has been an enthusiastic, indeed, fanatical collector of singles since 1957. 'Singing The Blues' by Tommy Steele and 'Garden Of Eden' by Frankie Vaughan were two of the earliest hits in his record library, both on 78 rpm discs. His first 45 rpm purchase was 'That'll Be The Day' by the Crickets. His collection now includes cylinder recordings from the turn of the century and, inevitably, cassette and CD singles from more recent times. He still prefers to buy every Top 75 hit on vinyl as records are for looking at as well as listening to. He writes lyrics and broadcasts.

PAUL GAMBACCINI, co-author of this book and *British Hit Albums*, is one of the two directors of Top Ten Comics, one of the three authors of the forthcoming *TV Hits*, one of several regulars on TV-am, one of many broadcasters heard on national radio, and just a part of the Regents Park Zoo Crew Softball team. For Paul Gambaccini, it takes at least two.